PROVERBS 10–31

YALE

VOLUME 18B

THE ANCHOR YALE BIBLE is a project of international and interfaith scope in which Protestant, Catholic, and Jewish scholars from many countries contribute individual volumes. The project is not sponsored by any ecclesiastical organization and is not intended to reflect any particular theological doctrine.

THE ANCHOR YALE BIBLE is committed to producing commentaries in the tradition established half a century ago by the founders of the series, William Foxwell Albright and David Noel Freedman. It aims to present the best contemporary scholarship in a way that is accessible not only to scholars but also to the educated nonspecialist. Its approach is grounded in exact translation of the ancient languages and an appreciation of the historical and cultural context in which the biblical books were written, supplemented by insights from modern methods, such as sociological and literary criticism.

John J. Collins
GENERAL EDITOR

THE ANCHOR YALE BIBLE

PROVERBS 10–31

◆

A New Translation
with Introduction and Commentary

BY

MICHAEL V. FOX

THE ANCHOR YALE BIBLE

Yale University Press
New Haven & London

Set in Electra type by DIX.

Printed in the United States of America by Vail-Ballou Press, Binghamton, N.Y.

LIBRARY OF CONGRESS CATALOGING-IN-PUBLICATION DATA

Bible. O.T. Proverbs X–XXXI. English. Fox. 2009.
Proverbs 10–31 : a new translation with introduction and commentary / by Michael V. Fox.
p. cm. — (The Anchor Yale Bible ; v. 18B)
Includes bibliographical references and indexes.
ISBN 978-0-300-14209-9 (alk. paper)
1. Bible. O.T. Proverbs X–XXXI—Commentaries.
I. Fox, Michael V., 1940– . II. Title.
BS1463.F69 2009
223'.707—dc22 2009010835

A catalogue record for this book is available from the British Library.

This paper meets the requirements of ANSI/NISO Z39.48-1992 (Permanence of Paper).

10 9 8 7 6 5 4 3 2 1

CONTENTS

TRANSLATION AND COMMENTARY

ESSAYS

TEXTUAL NOTES

ACKNOWLEDGMENTS

I have been aided greatly in the preparation of this manuscript by the assiduous and alert proofreading and copyediting of Suzanna Leigh Smith, Wendy Widder, and especially my assistant Emmylou Grosser. Others who read part or all of the manuscript and provided helpful comments are David A. Teeter (in matters of textual criticism), Robert Holmstedt (in matters of linguistics and agriculture), Jason Micheli, and Kent Reynolds (who also composed the indexes). I once again acknowledge the care and acumen that my editor, David Noel Freedman, of blessed memory, devoted to my commentary. Some of his ideas are cited as "DNF."

Work on this book was aided at various stages by the American Council of Learned Societies, the George Mosse Foundation Exchange Professorship, the Graduate School of the University of Wisconsin, and the Jay C. and Ruth Halls-Bascom professorship fund. Much of the work on this volume was completed at the Hebrew Union College, Jerusalem. I am grateful to the College and its dean, Dr. Michael Marmur, for granting me special access to its facilities and making my year in Jerusalem very pleasant and productive.

Some of my prior publications are incorporated in this volume in modified form:

"The Rhetoric of Disjointed Proverbs," *JSOT* 29 (*2004c*): 165–77 (in the Introduction to Vol. II).

"LXX-Proverbs as a Text-Critical Resource," *Textus* 22 (*2005a*): 95–128 (in the Textual Critical Notes).

"The Epistemology of the Book of Proverbs." *JBL* 126 (*2007a*): 669–84.

"Ethics and Wisdom in the Book of Proverbs." *HS* 48 (*2007b*): 75–88.

"Concepts of Wisdom in the Book of Proverbs," *Birkat Shalom: Studies . . . Presented to Shalom M. Paul*, ed. C. Cohen et al. (Winona Lake, Ind.: Eisenbaums, 2008, 381–98).

My reflections on "Author and Speaker, Listener and Reader," and "Speaking and Writing" in Vol. I, 73–75 were subsequently refined and developed in "Wisdom Performance and the Self-Presentation of Wisdom Literature," *Reading from Right to Left: Essays on the Hebrew Bible in Honour of David J. A. Clines*, ed. J. Cheryl Exum and H. G. M. Williamson (JSOTSup 480; Sheffield: Sheffield Academic Press, *2003b*, 153–72).

ABBREVIATIONS AND SIGLA

◆

Abbreviations

abs.	absolute
AEL	*Ancient Egyptian Literature*, Lichtheim 1973–80
ÄHG	*Ägyptische Hymnen und Gebete*, Assmann 1975
Ant	Antinoe Papyrus (prophetologion; 3rd c. C.E.), Roberts 1950, Zuntz 1956
APV	Aramaisms per verse
Aq	Aquila
AS	*Ägyptologische Studien*, Firchow 1955
AW	*Altägyptische Weisheit*, Brunner 1988a
AYB	Anchor Yale Bible
AYBD	*Anchor Bible Dictionary*, ed. D. N. Freedman *1992*
b.	Babylonian Talmud
BA	*La Bible d'Alexandrie*: *Les Proverbes*, ed. d'Hamonville *2000*
Baum.	A. Baumgartner 1890: *Etude Critique*
BDB	Brown, Driver, and Briggs, *Hebrew and English Lexicon of the Old Testament*
BH	Biblical Hebrew, including the language of Ben Sira
BHS	Biblia Hebraica Stuttgartensia
BTM	*Before the Muses*, B. Foster 1993
BWL	*Babylonian Wisdom Literature*, Lambert 1960
CAT	*Cuneiform Alphabetic Texts*, ed. Dietrich, Loretz, and Sanmartín, *1995* (= KTU, 2nd edition)
CATSS	Computer Assisted Tools for Septuagint Studies: Hebrew-Greek Parallel Aligned Database
CBH	Classical Biblical Hebrew (preexilic)
CG	Cairo Geniza Biblical MSS (cited from the BHS apparatus)
cj.	conjecture (emendation)
cl.	clause
CLEM	*Late-Egyptian Miscellanies*, Caminos 1954 (translation and commentary of LEM)
CML	*Canaanite Myths and Legends*, Gibson 1978
COHL	*Catalogue des ostraca hiératiques littéraires de Deir el Médineh*, Posener 1938ff.
coll.	collective
Comment	reference to the exegesis in the body of the Commentary
const.	construct
CSP	Cook 1997: *The Septuagint of Proverbs*
CTA	*Corpus des tablettes en cunéiformes alphabétiques*, Herdner 1963
D	D-stem, Piel (Aram. Pael)
DCH	*Dictionary of Classical Hebrew*, Clines 1993ff.

dittog.	dittography (loss of one of two identical letters or words that are in sequence)
DNF	David Noel Freedman, editorial communication
Dp	D passive stem, Pual
Dr	D reduplicated stem, Polel
DSS	Dead Sea Scrolls
Dt	Dt-stem, Hitpael (Aram. ʾEtpaal)
Esdr	Esdras
ET	English translation
FAL	*Fragen an die altägyptische Literatur,* ed. Assmann et al., 1977
fem.	feminine
FS	Festschrift
G	G-stem, Qal
GBH	*A Grammar of Biblical Hebrew,* Joüon and Muraoka 1991
GELS	*A Greek-English Lexicon of the Septuagint,* Lust et al. 1992ff.
Gk	Greek
GKC	Gesenius and Kautsch and Cowley, *Gesenius' Hebrew Grammar,* 1910
Gp	G passive stem
H	H-stem, Hiphil
HAHL	*Handbook of Ancient Hebrew Letters,* Pardee 1982
HALAT	*Hebräisches und Aramäisches Lexikon,* Baumgartner and Stamm 1967ff.
HALOT	*Hebrew and Aramaic Lexicon of the Old Testament,* Koehler and Baumgartner and Stamm 1994ff. (translation of HALAT)
haplog.	haplography (loss of one of two identical letters or words that are in sequence)
HB	Hebrew Bible (including Aramaic portions)
HO	*Hieratic Ostraca,* Černý and Gardiner 1957
Hp	H passive stem, Hophal
HPBM	Hieratic Papyri in the British Museum
IBHS	*Introduction to Biblical Hebrew Syntax,* Waltke and O'Connor 1990
impf.	imperfect
impv.	imperative
inf.	infinitive
IW	*Israelite Wisdom,* ed. J. Gammie et al. 1978
Jäg.	*Observationes in Proverbium,* Jäger 1788
Jdt	Judith
JPSV	Jewish Publication Society Version, 1965 ff.
juss.	jussive
K	ketiv (see Vol. I, xviii)
KAI	*Kanaanäische und Aramäische Inschriften,* Donner and Röllig 1962
KÄT	Kleine Ägyptische Texte (series)
Kenn.	Kennicott 1776–80: *Vetus Testamentum hebraicum cum variis lectionibus*
KJV	King James Version
K-R	Kenn. + J. B. De Rossi, *Variae Lectiones VT,* I–IV, 1784
KTU	*Die keilalphabetischen Texte aus Ugarit,* ed. Dietrich, Loretz, and Sanmartín
LÄ	*Lexikon der Ägyptologie,* ed. W. Helck et al. 1972ff.
LAE	*Letters from Ancient Egypt,* Wente 1990
Lag.	*Anmerkungen zur griechischen Übersetzung der Proverbien,* de Lagarde 1863
LBH^{1}	Late Biblical Hebrew, first phase (mid-sixth to mid-fifth century)

LBH^2	Late Biblical Hebrew, second phase (mid-fifth to approx. second centuries)
LEM	*Late Egyptian Miscellanies*, Gardiner 1937
Les.	*Ägyptische Lesestücke*, K. Sethe 1959
LEWL	*Late Egyptian Wisdom Literature*, Lichtheim 1983
l(l).	line(s)
LRL	*Late Ramesside Letters*, Wente 1967
LSF	*Die Lese- und Schreibfehler im AT*, Friedrich Delitzsch 1920
LSJ	Liddell-Scott-Jones, *Greek-English Lexicon*
LXX	Septuagint (manuscript sigla according to the Göttingen system)
m.	Mishna
masc.	masculine
mg.	marginal reading
Mid.	Midrash
MK	Middle Kingdom (Egypt)
m.l.	mater lectionis
MS(S)	manuscript(s)
MT	Masoretic text (edition used: BHS)
N	N-stem, Niphal
NIV	New International Version
NK	New Kingdom (Egypt)
NRSV	New Revised Standard Version
O.	ostracon
OBM	Ostracon of the British Museum
Oc	Occidental: the reading of the Palestinian Masoretes
ODAE	*Oxford Encyclopedia of Ancient Egypt*, ed. D. Redford, 2001
ODeM	Ostracon from Deir el-Medineh (see Posener 1938ff., FIFAO series)
OG	Old Greek, the (reconstructed) original Septuagintal text
OHDM	*Ostraca hiératiques littéraires de Deir el Médineh*, see Posener 1938ff.
OL	Old Latin (Vetus Latina) translation
om.	omit(s)
Oc	Occidentalis: the reading of the Palestinian Masoretes
Or	Orientalis: the reading of the Babylonian Masoretes
Pap.	papyrus
pass.	passive
per.	person
pf.	perfect
pl.	plural
^{pl}	*syamē*, the plural marker in Syriac words
PN	personal name
poss.	possessive
Prot.	*Protagorus*
ptcp.	participle
Qimḥis	Qimḥi family: Riyqam, Ramaq, and Radaq; see Talmage 1990
RA	*Reallexikon der Assyriologie*, ed. Ebeling et al., 1932ff.
rco.	recto
ref.	reference in[240]

[240] Used in citing an idea from an unavailable secondary source; for example, "Capellus ref. Baumgartner" means citing Capellus, according to a reference in Baumgartner.

rel.	relative (grammatical)
RH	Rabbinic (Mishnaic) Hebrew
SAIW	*Studies in Ancient Israelite Wisdom*, Crenshaw 1976
SAK	*Studien zur altägyptischen Kultur*
SAL	*Studien zu altägyptischen Lebenslehren*, ed. Hornung and Keel 1979
sfx.	suffix
sg.	singular
SIANE	*The Sage in Israel and the Ancient Near East*, ed. Gammie and Perdue 1990
sim.	similarly
Sir	Ben Sira (Ecclesiasticus)[241]
SPOA	*Les Sagesses du Proche-orient ancien*, 1963. See "Sagesses" in the Bibliography.
SWA	*Seeking Out the Wisdom of the Ancients*, ed. Troxel, Friebel, and Magary 2005
Sym	Symmachus
Syr	Syriac: the Peshitta translation (Leiden edition)
SyrH	Syro-Hexapla
TAD	*Textbook of Aramaic Documents*, Porten and Yardeni 1993.
TCN	Text-Critical Notes in this commentary (in cross-references)
TDOT	*Theological Dictionary of the Old Testament*, Botterweck and Ringgren 1974ff.
Tg	Targum, the Aramaic translation (for other MSS see Healey 1991: 3–4)
Tg^L	*Hagiographa Chaldaice*, Lagarde 1873
Tg^Z	Zamora text of Tg Prov (= San Bernardo 116–Z-40); Díez Merino 1984
Theod	Theodotion
var(s).	variant(s)
vso.	verso
Vul	The Vulgate (Jerome's Latin translation)
WAI	*Wisdom in Ancient Israel*, ed. Day, Gordon, and Williamson 1995
y.	Talmud Yerushalmi

For other standard abbreviations, see the *SBL Handbook of Style*, ed. P. H. Alexander et al. (Peabody, Mass.: Hendrickson, 1999). Standard abbreviations for Egyptian texts can be found, together with bibliography, in Raymond Faulkner, *A Concise Dictionary of Middle Egyptian* (Oxford: Griffith Inst., 1964) xiii–xvi, and Leonard Lesko, ed., *A Dictionary of Late Egyptian* (Berkeley, Calif.: BC Scribe, 1982–90), xiii–xix.

Sigla

*	hypothetical or reconstructed form. In the Bibliography, this indicates a work referenced by name of author only.
=	equals; that is, the same as or *virtually* the same as

[241] References to Ben Sira indicate manuscript only when there are differences significant to the matter under discussion. For problems of chapter numbering see Vol. I, 24, n. 34. For abbreviations of the manuscripts and discussion of textual witnesses see Skehan and Di Lella, *Ben Sira*, pp. 52–59. The Hebrew text of P. Beentjes 1997 is used in this volume.

≠	not equal to, substantively different from
≈	similar to
//	parallel to
< >	a later addition
{ }	not in MT; supplied
$^{\alpha\beta, \gamma, \delta}$	Superscripted Greek letters mark line (stich) divisions *within the* LXX. See "Verse Numbering in the Septuagint" in Vol. I, 362–63.

CORRECTIONS AND DEVELOPMENTS

◆

The following notes include corrections of typographical errors in Volume I as well as some revisions, mostly marginal, in my own interpretations of chapters 1–9.

Page/line	Change to (→) **Correction in boldface.**
xv, Ant (Antinoe)	8th c. → **3rd c.** C.E.
5	VIa 30:1–14 → **VIa 30:1–9** and VIb 30:15–33 → **VIb 30:10–33** (See the introduction to Prov 30:1–9.) **Omit** "the Massa[ite]" (This is now treated as a common noun meaning "pronouncement"; see the Comment on 30:1b.)
18–19	With regard to the transmission of Amenemope, I offer a modified view in "Translation and Transmission," after the Commentary on 22:17–24:22.
23, after Shube'awilum	Add: **Babylonian "Counsels of Wisdom" (BTM 328–31). Admonitions in personal and ethical matters. Text BWL pp. 27–29.**
23, Ahiqar	6th c. → **7th c.** B.C.E. (See "Ahiqar and Proverbs," after the Commentary on 22:17–24:22. This also has an augmented list of parallels, replacing Vol. I, 23, n. 32.)
25	Under "Later Works Affiliated with Wisdom Literature," add: **"Wisdom Psalms": These are biblical psalms heavily influenced by Wisdom literature. The minimal scope of the Wisdom Psalm genre has been demarcated by means of linguistic criteria by Hurvitz 1991, who identifies Psalms 19:8–15; 34; 37; 111–112; and 119 as Wisdom Psalms. (Ps 111 is Wisdom only if it is paired with Ps 112.) To Hurvitz's list I would add Ps 1 because of its schematic wicked-righteous contrast, its praise of study, its proverbial ending, and its contrasting of the two "ways," which is an important topos in Proverbs. Ps 127 is loosely affiliated with Wisdom Literature by its ideas. Other psalms (esp. Pss 49; 72; and 138) are associated with critical (speculative) wisdom like Job. Wisdom psalms can share in the characteristics of other genres as well, and other psalms can use motifs favored by Wisdom. Possibly the Wisdom Psalms were used in the Temple, but there is no good indication of a distinct social setting. Crenshaw *2000* is skeptical about the category, but it is a useful way of grouping certain psalms with related features."**
34, line 3	Prov 21:30. This is now translated differently; see the Comment.
39, line 4	"who can be a *peti*" → "who can be **an innocent**"

96, line 16	1:29–33 → 1:20–33
112, line 15	"To *know* what God does means to *do* it." → "To *know* what God **wants** means to *do* it."
129, line 26	For a new interpretation of 11:5a, see the Comment.
137, line 21	**Delete** "*of Shuruppak*"
154	Here I say that Lecture III lacks a Conclusion. Now it seems to me that the quatrain in 3:11–12 has the generalizing, summary force of a Conclusion, because it explains that to trust and honor God (vv 5–10) requires accepting the ultimate goodness of the difficulties he sends (vv 11–12). Lecture V alone does not have a Conclusion that stands apart from the Lesson (3:27–32). Form critical practice does not, however, require that all criterial elements for a genre be present in a particular exemplar.
208, line 29	"In Proverbs, arguments against infidelity do not adduce the harm it causes the cheated wife." This is true, with the subtle exception of 23:28; see the Comment.
220, on 6:13	*ʿōṣeh* need not be emended to *ʿōṣēm* in 16:30; see the Comment.
224, line 2	In 14:25, *yāpiaḥ* is probably a verb; see the Comment on that verse.
264, on 8:24	The translation "sources" presumes the emendation to ***nibkê*** (MT *nikbaddê*); see the Comment. This should be added to the apparatus in Vol. I, 265.
316, line 14	9:7–11 → 9:7–**10**
355, line 6	"he rational" → "**the** rational"
360, line 23	"Plene-lene" → "Plene-**defective**"
363, line 36	**Delete** "be"
363, line 39	"before" → "**after**"
364, line 1	"but it does explain" → "but it does **not** explain"
364, line 4	"copyist, Cook believes" → "copyist, **as** Cook believes"
364, line 13	"Or a copyist, etc." → "**Or a copyist may have skipped over a major block, which was then restored at the wrong place.**"
372, on 1:32	Add: "**4QProv^{a} reads *mwškt* (Ulrich *2000*: 182), which Ulrich translates 'cords,' or 'narrowmindedness.' A graphic error for *mšwbt* seems more likely.**" (See the introduction to the Textual Notes, Vol. II.)
375, on 2:18	Theodotion actually reads ***tōn gigantōn***. Deut 2:10 → Deut 2:**11**
379, on 3:15	3^{α}, 3^{β}, 3^{γ} → **15^{α}, 15^{β}, 15^{γ}**
393, line 22, on Tg	*dḥṣdʾ* → ***dḥsdʾ***
393, line 40	"lene" → "**defectively**"
413, line 33	"(for *šm*) LXX" → "(for ***šmʿ***) = LXX"
413, lines 34, 41	"that which is above the sky" → "**the clouds above**"
415, in 8:32–34, line 5:	→ "The OG thus read 32a, 34a, **32b**, 34b, 35, 36." Add: 32b.
427–74	Bibliography: Several errors in the Bibliography in Vol. I are corrected in the combined bibliography in Vol. II, which should now be consulted for all entries. It should be noted that "ZÄS" (*Zeitschrift für Ägyptische Sprache und Altertumskunde*) several times appears as "ZAW" in Vol. I.

MISCELLANEA

◆

Pagination: This is the second volume of my Anchor Yale Bible Proverbs commentary and should be read in tandem with Volume I (*Proverbs 1–9* [New York: Doubleday, 2000; reprint, New Haven: Yale University Press]). Volume II continues the pagination and note numbering of Volume I.

Small Type: The commentary is intended as a resource for different kinds of reading and study. The exegesis proper requires no knowledge of Hebrew and can be read without reference to the more technical investigations. These matters of more specialized interest, in particular, analysis of philological problems and discussions of scholarly theories and interpretations, are discussed in embedded notes, the type of which is smaller than that of the text proper.

Typography: Capitalization and boldface: When discussing sound patterns, the stressed syllable of a Hebrew word is capitalized. Assonance or consonance is indicated by boldface. Ground metaphors (see Vol. I, 128) are capitalized.

Internal References: The body of the Commentary of both volumes is cited as "Comment," and the Textual Notes in both volumes are cited as "Textual Notes," in spite of the misleading header in Vol. I, 367–423.

Citations: Works appearing only in Vol. II are distinguished by italicization of dates; for example, "Nel *1998*: 115."

Verse-Segments: The designation of verse-segments in Proverbs (10:1a, 10:1b, etc.) is according to the physical verse-lines in my translation. For other books, the conventional designations, based on the Masoretic accents (e.g., Jer 15:1aβ), are used. In the case of Proverbs, with its unmistakable verse structure, these designations are almost always the same.

Ahiqar References: For the present volume, I use the definitive edition of Porten and Yardeni (TAD). References are by the numbering in Lindenberger (1983), as in Vol. I, with Porten and Yardeni's numbering in brackets; e.g., (100a–102 [1.1.84–86]).

Translation: In a few cases, the translations of verses in Prov 1–9 are cited differently from Vol. I. Translations from the Egyptian may vary slightly as well. Usually the difference is for the sake of bringing out a particular nuance relevant to the current discussion.

Unless otherwise noted, all translations are my own, except for Sumerian, Akkadian, Demotic Egyptian, and Attic Greek, which are taken from the cited sources. For classical Greek sources, the translations are cited in the Bibliography by the names of the ancient authors. Though the Egyptian translations are my own, I also give page references to Lichtheim's translation (AEL), so that the reader can locate the passages in context.

Joining Lines in Couplets: In Hebrew, parallel lines are typically linked by the versatile conjunction *waw*, which usually means "and" but is sometimes better rendered "but" or "while" or even left untranslated. These are not separate "meanings" of *waw*, but different ways of rendering its conjunctive force to fit the context. I generally use "while" in antithetical couplets because the relation between the lines is not really adversative. In 10:4, for example, the second line ("and the hand of the diligent brings wealth") is not contrary to the first ("The hand of the deceitful causes poverty") but states a concomitant and equivalent fact. The second line is the obverse of the first, the flip side of the coin. In fact, "and" would be a correct translation in such cases—line A is true *and* line B is true—but this often is clumsy because it seems to coordinate the lines too closely.[242]

"Man": This usage is currently perceived, and often repudiated, as male-oriented and as giving women a secondary status. But because this is an accurate reflection of the biblical authors' perspective, the present commentary maintains this usage when translating and paraphrasing the ancient authors' thoughts. Though the sages of Proverbs were quite aware of women's wisdom and would undoubtedly agree that most of their own advice was applicable to women, they were oriented to males, addressing them and concerned for males' experience, feelings, and benefits—even when praising women, as in 31:10–31. Recently, many translators and scholars have tried to neuter this perspective, by translating, for example, "One wise person went up against a city of warriors" (21:22), as the NRSV does. This practice—if meant as a representation of the original and not an updating and recentering of its message—is unfaithful to the mind-set of the authors and their audiences.

Recent Commentaries Used: In this volume, the commentaries regularly consulted include the following:

Richard J. Clifford, *Proverbs* (OTL), 1999.
Roland E. Murphy, *Proverbs* (WBC), 1998.
Raymond Van Leeuwen, *Proverbs* (NIB), 1997.
Bruce K. Waltke, *The Book of Proverbs, Chapters 1–15* (NICOT), *2004* (used for chapters 10–15).

Some of the older commentaries listed in Vol. I, 13 are cited less regularly, because their insights are often incorporated into the more recent ones.

The manuscript of this volume went first to the publisher in the spring of 2007. Works that came to my attention subsequently are included in the bibliography but could not be adequately addressed in this book. Particularly noteworthy are K. Dell *2006* (reviewed by me in Fox *2007c*), T. Forti *2008*, T. J. Sandoval *2006* (see my Comment on 10:4), and R. Tavares *2007* (see the excursus in the introduction to chapters 28–29).

Units of Proverbs: The major divisions of the book are as follows:

Part	*Verses*	*Heading or Contents*
I	1:1–9:18	"The proverbs of Solomon the son of David, king of Israel" (1:1)
II	10:1–22:16	"Proverbs of Solomon" (10:1a)
IIa	10:1–15:33	

[242] R. Steiner (*2000*) analyzes the uses of conjunctive *waw* and argues that often it is semantically empty, but when it is meaningful, it has only one meaning, definable in terms of the truth table, as "*p we q* is true whenever *p* is true and *q* is true" (p. 267). Conjunctive *waw* in itself is not truly adversative or contrastive (p. 260), nor does it strictly speaking mean "while," because the circumstantial function is signaled, if at all, by other syntactic factors. This means that there is no great difference between a couplet joined by *waw* and one in which the couplets are joined asyndetically. The *waw* just gives a sense of greater binding.

IIb	16:1–22:16	
III	22:17–24:22	"Words of the wise" (22:17a)
IIIa	22:17–23:11	The Amenemope Collection
IIIb	23:12–24:22	Words of the Wise, Continued
IV	24:23–34	"These too are of the wise" (24:23a)
V	25:1–29:27	"These too are proverbs of Solomon, which the men of Hezekiah king of Judah transcribed" (25:1)
Va	25:1–26:28	
Vb	27:1–29:27	
VI	30:1–31:31	Four Appendices
VIa	30:1–9	The Words of Agur
VIb	30:10–33	Epigrams and Aphorisms
VIc	31:1–9	The Teaching of Lemuel's Mother
VId	31:10–31	The Woman of Strength

I have changed my view on the boundary between Parts VIa and VIb (see the Commentary). I also subdivide some units without implying that they were once separate collections.

I often refer to the "Lectures" and "Interludes" of Prov 1–9, presuming my discussion in Vol. I, 322–30. The following are the interlaced components of Prov 1–9:

Prologue: 1:1–7
Lectures:
- I. 1:8–19
- II. 2:1–22
- III. 3:1–12
- IV. 3:21–35
- V. 4:1–9
- VI. 4:10–19
- VII. 4:20–27
- VIII. 5:1–23
- IX. 6:20–35
- X. 7:1–27

Interludes:
- A. 1:20–33
- B. 3:13–20
- C. 6:1–19
- D. 8:1–36
- E. 9:1–6 + 11, 13–18

INTRODUCTION

I. Reading Proverbs as a Collection

◆

A. "A SWEET DISORDER"

A different kind of literary composition begins in Prov 10. Chapters 1–9 are composed of long poetic units—the Lectures and the Interludes.[243] Chapters 10–29 (Parts II–V) consist largely of independent proverbs, almost all of them couplets. A significant compositional issue facing the reader is whether these proverbs are organized into larger structures. My view is that for the most part they are not. There are, to be sure, numerous pairs of proverbs and quite a few proverbs clustered about a shared topic, and there are a few epigrams in which several verses form a poetic unit.[244] But there are no overall designs determining the placement of the sayings. Chapters 30–31 are again quite different. They hold four appendices (Parts VIa–VId), each a relatively long, cohesive poem.

In his introduction to 10:31, Hame'iri says that, unlike the first part of the book (chapters 1–9), "the second part [beginning in chapter 10] does not proceed sequentially in sections, but is composed of separate verses, which have no connection or combination [*hitqaššᵉrut wᵉharkabah*] with each other, except for proximity. Each verse has its own topic, except for a few cases where the verses interconnect."[245] In the course of his commentary on these chapters, Hame'iri identifies numerous cases of "connection or combination" among the verses, which form clusters. (See below, I.B.2. "Clusters.") Along the same lines, Franz Delitzsch (1873), in his introduction to 10:1–22, says:

> The succession of proverbs here is nevertheless not one that is purely accidental or without thought; it is more than a happy accident when three of the same character stand together; the compiler has connected together proverb with proverb according to certain common characteristics (Bertheau). And yet more than that: the mass separates itself into groups, not merely succeeding one another, but because a certain connection of ideas connects together a number of proverbs, in such a way that the succession is broken, and a new point of departure is arrived at (Hitzig). There is no comprehensive plan, such as Oetinger in his summary view of its contents supposes; the progressive unfolding follows no systematic scheme, but continuously wells forth. (1873: 208)

---

[243] See Vol. I, 44–47, 322–30.

[244] Prov 23:26–28; 23:29–35; 24:30–34; and 27:23–27. These are similar in scope and form to the epigrams in Interlude C.

[245] My translation. A longer passage, in which Hame'iri describes different relations between lines of a couplet, is translated and analyzed by Perry *1993a*: 73–75.

I share the view of these two commentators, in principle if not in particulars. Consequently, I try to respect the individuality of each proverb by interpreting it alone as well as considering the new meanings created by context. In cases in which several proverbs have particularly strong cohesion, I translate them together. When the proverbs are less closely related, I translate each one separately and comment on their relationships as I proceed. The distinction is meant for ease of exposition and is subjective.

B. GROUPING PROVERBS

Though most of the proverbs seem placed at random, one proverb often does connect to the next, forming significant groupings of varying scope.

1. Pairs

T. Hildebrandt (1988b) defines the minimal unit beyond the verse or couplet as the "proverbial pair." A proverb pair must be distinct from contiguous verses and bear its own message. The two couplets should be linked by similarities of form as well as content. Hildebrandt also finds triads (e.g., Prov 23:26–28; 24:10–12) and some longer units. The pairings, he stresses, are not accidental but reveal the theological goals and literary sensitivities of the editors (p. 209). In Prov 10–29, Hildebrandt counts sixty-two examples, or 21 percent of the verses (ibid.).

The notion of "proverbial pair" seems right to me in principle. An example is Prov 25:16–17:

(16) If you find honey, eat just enough,
lest you become satiated with it and vomit it up.
(17) Go but rarely to your neighbor's house,
lest he become satiated with you and hate you.

Each couplet makes sense separately. The first warns against excess in any pleasure. When the two verses are juxtaposed, they interact. The second narrows the focus of the first to a particular excess, and the first provides the second with a vivid and memorable image.

It is quite feasible for a compiler to record (or for an author to compose) one proverb, then add another to amplify or give nuance to its teaching. I find a fair number of proverb pairs, though fewer than Hildebrandt. Whether I join the verses in the translation or address them separately depends on the degree of cohesion I see between them.

2. Clusters

In my view, the most important principle of grouping in Prov 10–29 is *thematic clustering.* Thematic clusters are groups of at least two sayings that speak on the same topic or share catchwords. Each proverb in the cluster can function independently. The minimal cluster is the proverb pair. Some clusters are proverb strings, in which each saying prepares the way for the next, and whose sequence is therefore relevant to the larger meaning.[246]

Attempts to identify proverb-clusters go back to Ramaq, in the twelfth century C.E., with precedents in Saʿadia and Riyqam. Ramaq frequently describes two or three verses, sometimes more, as "adhering" (*dᵉbeqim*) and interprets them as a thematic unit. Ramaq strongly influenced Hameʾiri, in the next century, who groups proverbs even more extensively. Though some of the groupings proposed by Ramaq and Hameʾiri are persuasive, others are forced and involve extraneous assumptions.

Many of Ramaq's clusters are thematically cohesive and would be accepted by most readers. For example, Prov 15:1 ("A soft reply turns away wrath, while an irritating word provokes anger") and 15:2 ("The tongue of the wise adorns knowledge, while the mouth of dolts pours out folly") are linked by the theme of speech. In other proposed groupings the linkage is feasible but not strong. For example, Ramaq joins 14:31 ("He who oppresses the poor insults his maker, while he who is kind to the needy honors him") to v 32 ("The wicked man will be shoved down in his wickedness, while the righteous man trusts in his innocence"). His reasoning is that "the wicked man will be shoved down and fall into the evil that he planned to do to the poor." This makes sense, but threats such as 14:32 are so common that it is hard to know if it is meant to comment on the preceding verse or is a general warning relevant to this and all other admonitions.

An example of a forced grouping is Ramaq's treatment of Prov 15:27–29. He calls these verses "adhering" on the grounds that v 27 speaks of unjust gain, v 28 refers to judges (whether righteous or wicked) speaking in judgment, and v 29 states the consequences of their deeds, namely, that God will be far from wicked (judges) but will hear the prayer of righteous ones. Hameʾiri accepts this grouping and summarizes its implications thus: "These verses are an admonition to judges and magistrates to try with all their strength to avoid issuing a flawed judgment." But Hameʾiri is imposing the common denominator of *judgment* on the contiguous proverbs.

K. Heim (*2001*) divides the entirety of 10:1–22:16 into "clusters" ranging in scope from two to thirteen verses. These clusters, he argues, were composed to create a context for the understanding of the individual sayings and to convey a special message of their own. Heim's main indicators of cluster-delimitation are not boundary markers but *linking* devices. Most important are repetitions of any sort, insofar as these are made significant contextually (p. 107).

The need for a totalizing approach like Heim's (one shared by many of the "Affirmers" he surveys in chapter 3) is unclear. Why must all the proverbs be in clusters—or pairs, or strings? An editor could do several sorts of things, sometimes writing down independent proverbs, at other times following up on one proverb by adding a couple more on the same topic. This could happen by intention or unconscious association. Some genuine, functional clusters will appear, but phantom ones will as well, because—as Heim says in criticizing Scoralick 1995—"the number of subjects in Prov 10:1–22:16 is restricted. Repetitions of concepts and vocabulary are unavoidable" (*2001*: 57). In my view, many of the segments that Heim brackets strain plausibility; see my review in Fox *2003a*.

S. Weeks (*1994*: 20–40) undertakes a "nearest-neighbor analysis," tabulating links between adjacent sayings: thematic, verbal, and literal (same initial letters or letter-sequences). He finds that over 58 percent of the sayings in 10:1–22:16 have some sort of link to their neighbors. Verbal/literal links predominate, with thematic links common only in chapters 10–14. The distribution of links and forms supports the view that 10:1–22:16 and 25:1–29:37 each contain two major subcollections. However, the statistical significance of 58 percent is hard to gauge, given the multiplicity of items—letters, words, themes—whose co-occurrence is counted. Experimenting with Weeks's methods on

[246] S. Weeks identifies "thematic chains" as an editorial principle but is skeptical about their significance in "bringing out the proper meaning" of the individual proverbs (*1994*: 38). In my view, the chaining *belongs to* their "proper," if not original, meaning.

several batches of verses taken from different parts of the book and randomly scrambled, I found nearest-neighbor linkages in 36–60 percent of the verses in each batch. A more liberal use of "theme" would have yielded much higher percentages, while an elimination of "literal" links would have reduced them. Weeks also concludes that thematic considerations were not of major importance to the editors (p. 37). This is probably true overall, but when thematic clusters do occur, they are relevant to interpretation.

The process that best explains the groupings is associative thinking. This also accounts for most of the phenomena sometimes thought to indicate editorial designs: alliteration, wordplay, catchwords, and repetitions of words, roots, and phrases.[247] When one thought gives rise to another or one word evokes a related one, the result is an associative sequence. An "editor" (or "compiler") writes down one proverb he knows, and this makes him think of another on the same theme, and since it is on the same theme, it is likely to use similar wording. This process is prominent in the series of righteousness-wickedness antitheses in Prov 10:1–15:33, in the string of sayings on divine control in 16:1–9, and in the reflections on kingship in 16:10–15.

An example of an associative sequence is Prov 19:11–14. The importance of patience (v 11) calls to mind the king's wrath (v 12), which is the opposite of patience and a dangerous form of irritation. This leads into a proverb on an irritable wife (v 13), which in turn evokes a proverb on a virtuous one (v 14), which balances the negative picture. This train of thought is explained in the Comment.

A clue to editorial practice is the way a series of sayings may momentarily digress from the topic. For example, Prov 26:1–12 is a long sequence of proverbs on the fool, with the exception of v 2. As I picture the process, v 1—"Like snow in summer and a downpour in harvest, so honor is not suitable to a dolt"—called to the editor's mind the identically structured but not apropos v 2, "As a sparrow for wandering and a swallow for flying, so a gratuitous curse will not alight." Then his thoughts returned to the theme of the fool in v 3: "A whip for a horse and a bridle for an ass, and a rod for the back of dolts." Another example of digression is the presence of a proverb on hasty speech (29:20) between two sayings recommending strict discipline of slaves (29:19, 21). A similar case is 10:15; see the Comment. The interposition of such digressions shows that the editor was often gathering (i.e., recalling or composing) proverbs on a theme, with association of word or motif—and not some grand design—causing a digression.

Sometimes a digression may be the doing of a later scribe. The most likely cause for such an insertion is moralizing. This seems to be the case in Prov 19:5—"A lying witness will not go unpunished, and he who testifies deceitfully will not escape"—which interrupts a somewhat cynical series of proverbs on the effect of wealth on friendship in vv 4, 6, 7. But most digressions cannot be explained as later moralizing additions.

[247] On the importance of lexical cohesion, Berlin observes that "if word X is used in connection with idea A and then with idea B, the two ideas are in some way equated, or drawn together into a unified field of vision" (1989: 39).

3. *Larger Structures?*

For some scholars, discovery of structures organizing the sayings seems to be something of a moral imperative. Hildebrandt (1988b: 207) dismisses scholars who do not recognize larger structures as "willy-nilly advocates," which certainly sounds like something one should avoid being. Whybray discards McKane's view of the lack of organization in the proverb collections on the grounds that it "amounts to no more than an admission that modern scholars have so far not been able satisfactorily to discover what such a 'context,' whether literary or theological, might be" (1990: 65). Whybray presumes that there must be intentional patterns, whether "contexts" or "structures." If we start with this assumption, the Rorschach principle guarantees that we will see such patterns or define them into existence. But there is no reason to expect well-structured forms of organization. There are other forms of literary artistry.

Much scholarly energy has recently been invested in the search for complex structures in various units even and the book as a whole. The structures are not just thematic groupings. They are intricate designs, with connections among their parts created and indicated by the recurrence of themes, catchwords, or roots. Some of these proposals are discussed in the relevant sections of Commentary.[248] To my mind, the proposals are not persuasive.

It is far-fetched to imagine editors compiling proverbs according to grand and detailed designs. It is implausible that an editor would write down all the proverbs on little bits of papyrus or parchment and move them around until they fit into tidy, well-organized groupings and larger, well-designed structures, with certain repeated words and phrases—which were already present in the original sayings—being located in exactly the right places. It is even more implausible that the editor did all this in his head. And what would have been the purpose of such designs? Rhetorical effect is an unlikely motivation, seeing that very few commentators—who have studied the book far more intently than most readers—have uncovered the same patterns.

There is, in any case, no literary motive for elaborate designs. A proverb is like a jewel, and the book of Proverbs is like a heap of jewels. Indeed, it is a heap of different *kinds* of jewels. Is it really such a loss if they are not all laid out in pretty, symmetric designs or divided into neat little piles? The heap itself has the lushness of profusion and the charm of a "sweet disorder in the dress."

There have been numerous attempts to discover the key to proverbial structures in Proverbs. R. Van Leeuwen's influential 1988 study of Prov 25–27 is discussed in the introduction to Part V in the Commentary. A. Meinhold's and B. Waltke's commentaries propose proverb structures throughout the book. R. Scoralick (1995) assigns special importance to catchwords that bind successive proverbs. She divides Prov 10:1–15:32 into five segments: I. 10:1–11:7; II. 11:8–12:13; III. 12:14–13:13; IV. 13:14–14:27; V. 14:28–15:32. Her list of catchwords (pp. 127–29) is reproduced in Murphy's commentary (pp. 65–67). Heim (*2001*: 51–59) surveys and criticizes her work. A major problem is that she simply ignores repetitions that run contrary to her segmentation.

P. Skehan provides a grand organizational schema encompassing the entire book. Skehan be-

[248] See especially Prov 25:2–27; 27:23–29:27; 30:1–30; and 31:1–31.

lieves that there was "A Single Editor for the Whole Book of Proverbs" (as he titles his *1971a* article, which should be read in conjunction with Skehan *1971b*). He argues for this on the grounds that the entire book of Proverbs was laid out in three series of fifteen columns to form the design of a house—"Wisdom's house"—though there are no examples of pictorial layouts of texts on scrolls that early. This design is supposedly supported by gematria, or numerology. Prov 10:1–22:16 comprises 375 one-line proverbs, the numerical value of the letters of Solomon's name (*šlmh*). Skehan counts "proverb-lines," an undefined concept that can apparently refer to couplets, tristichs, or even quatrains (e.g., 24:33–34; *1971b*: 44), even though each line is supposed to fit in the same space. He finds 140 lines in 25:1–29:27 (*1971b*: 44), which is the gematria of Hezekiah—when MT's *ḥzqyh* is emended to *yḥzqyh*. The total number of lines in the book is 930 (as reckoned in Skehan *1971b*: 44, but not in *1971a*: 25). This is the gematria of Solomon + David + and Israel, mentioned in 1:1. Skehan has other arguments as well, but much of his procedure is ad hoc and self-serving, such as combining 4:1–9 + 3:13–24 + 3:35 into one 22-verse "column" and 5:1–19 + 6:22 + 5:20 into another; displacing several major blocks of material to fit his schema; moving 30:15–33 to precede chapters 25–29, as in the Greek, but not following the Greek placement in other regards; and numerous other assertions. In any case, a large number of numerological correspondences are always possible and some will inevitably arise through chance.

Valuable surveys and critiques of structural theories are provided by K. Heim (*2001*: 7–19; 27–66) and S. Weeks (*1994*: 20–40).

C. RELIGIOUS PROVERBS AND CONTEXTUAL INTERPLAY

Sayings in a collection tend to be read in the light of others in their vicinity. One type of saying that has particular significance for nearby verses is the religious proverb. Its function is to assert Yahweh's control of human fate and his demands for ethical behavior. These proverbs provide a counterweight to the pragmatism and eudaimonism of the secular proverbs, which emphasize the practical benefits of sensible behavior and the power of human wisdom in shaping people's fate. I use the label "secular" not to describe the author's worldview but, as R. B. Y. Scott puts it, the "plain fact" that many proverbs "neither express nor necessarily imply religious belief" (1972: 147). The proverb, "The teaching of a wise man is a fount of life" (13:14a), is secular; the variant, "The fear of the Lord is a fount of life" (14:27a), is religious.

According to the theory of W. McKane (1970: 10–22), the "Yahweh" proverbs were inserted into the monarchic-period collections in Prov 10–29 by a pietistic postexilic redactor. The flaw with McKane's chronological distinctions is that both religious and secular maxims are found throughout ancient Near Eastern Wisdom Literature, and there is no reason to suppose that the first Israelite compilers were restricted to the secular. It is significant that the maxims in Prov 22:19, which promises to inculcate trust in Yahweh, and 22:22–23, which is an admonition to the same effect reinforced by the warning that Yahweh protects the poor, belong to the unit that is dependent on Amenemope and thus has an ancient, non-Yahwistic, source. Moreover, in the passage in Amenemope on which Prov 22:22–23 is dependent, Amenemope adduces the power of Thoth in the same way that Prov 22:23 does the power of Yahweh; see the Comment. These verses can hardly be assigned to a later redaction. The "Yahwistic" saying in Prov 15:6 also has its origins in Amenemope.

The value of McKane's distinction is to call our attention to the effect of the "Yahweh" proverbs on the sayings in their vicinity—and beyond. An example of contextual interplay is in the cluster in Prov 10:1–6, which says that hard work pays off while laziness brings poverty (vv 4–5) but also insists that Yahweh "will not let a righteous man starve, but he rebuffs the desire of evildoers" (v 3), and, further, that blessings come by righteousness (v 6a). Religious proverbs affect the perception of sayings close by, but they also influence the reading of the collections and the book as a whole. Prov 10:22—"The Lord's blessing is what makes one rich, and striving adds nothing more thereto"—is a cautionary note pertinent to all the book's exhortations to work hard. The fact that many religious proverbs do *not* interact with their immediate contexts suggests that they are not interpolated polemics against an "old" wisdom but part of the natural effort of the compilers to provide a balanced selection of counsels and principles.

McKane (1970: 11–21) separates all proverbs into three groups. Class A proverbs belong to the "old wisdom," which is "concerned with the education of the individual for a successful and harmonious life" (p. 11). Class B proverbs, of unspecified dating, have the community rather than the individual in focus (ibid.). Class C proverbs belong to a postexilic Yahwistic redaction. These are identified by the presence of "God-language" and vocabulary expressing "a moralism which derives from Yahwistic piety" (ibid.). R. Scott (1972) identifies seven types of proverbs, three of which he considers religious and later than the others. Both McKane's and Scott's classifications are reasonable typologies, but they say nothing about dating or authorship. Scott's arguments for later dating (characteristic ideas and vocabulary, the addition of a religious dimension, topics and thoughts found only in the Yahweh sayings, vocabulary peculiar to these sentences, and the use of "fear of Yahweh" as a conventional term for piety; 1972: 162–63) are simply further descriptors of the *type* of proverb and indicate nothing about authorship or dating.

D. Römheld (1989: 117–84) comes to a conclusion similar to McKane's by a different route. He maintains that the editor of Prov 22:17–23:11, even while borrowing extensively from Amenemope, ignored the personal piety prominent in that work. Hence those proverbs that express this religious stance are later—exilic or postexilic. This theory is discussed in "Foreign Background," after the Commentary on 22:17–24:22.

Whybray (1979, passim, and 1994: 76–78; 86–89 and passim) emphasizes the contextual roles of "Yahweh proverbs," especially in the case of paired couplets (e.g., 10:3–4, 27–28, 29–30; 11:19–20; 15:16–17; 18:10–11). These generally emphasize Yahweh's role in determining a man's fate. Whybray recognizes that at least some of the Yahweh proverbs could have preexisted the collection. In fact, I would add, the desire to convey a religious message may even have been the motivation for the decision to include the popular, secular saying in the first place.

For further arguments against the theory of a Yahwistic reinterpretation, see S. Weeks (*1994*: 57–73), F. M. Wilson (1987: 328–31), and particularly K. Dell (*2006*: 90–124). Dell argues that the frequent proverbs that mention Yahweh or allude to his activity are well integrated into their contexts and are no later than the secular ones.

II. Reading a Proverb

◆

A. Oral Performance

Many of the sayings in the book of Proverbs, it is reasonable to assume, were composed orally and meant for actual use in daily life, or "performance." The notion of proverb performance is important to paremiology, the study of proverbial literature throughout the world. It was introduced into Bible studies by C. Fontaine, in her *Traditional Sayings in the Old Testament* (1982).[249] In every new use, Fontaine says, a proverb must meet a particular need, and this imbues it with ever-fresh "performance-meaning." A proverb receives its full meaning only in application, when it is spoken to a particular end. "What good is a proverb that no one quotes?" Fontaine asks (*2002*: 157).

Fontaine (1982: 72–170) studies the way proverbs perform in interactions described in biblical narratives, since these presumably reflect the use of folk sayings in ancient Israel. Though she includes some sayings from the book of Proverbs in her study, she does not deal with the barriers to applying her methodology to a collection of this sort.

The dimension of proverb performance is absent in a collection. The editors have, by the very nature of their task, detached the sayings from actual use and assembled them (along with new coinages) in readiness for deployment in a limitless variety of new contexts.[250] The most a reader can do with regard to performance potential is imagine some of the ways a proverb *could* be used: how it might influence people, what goals it could serve, how it could be slanted in different directions depending on the wishes of the user.

A proverb has a fairly stable semantic core that is communicated to most readers, otherwise the proverb could not be used in new interactions. Contrary to the oft-quoted and refuted dictum of W. Mieder (*1974*: 892), a proverb in a collection is not dead, but it is alive only as a potential. A proverb is like a coin, which has a "meaning" within its particular currency system and can be situated in relation to other coins in that system and translated into other currencies. Also like a coin, a proverb has a finite range of potential applications—a coin can buy some things but not everything. The coin gains its "performance-meaning" only when it is spent on something, when it is *used* in a particular situation to attain a certain goal. So too a proverb.

---

[249] In later works (*2002* and *2004*), Fontaine concentrates on women's use of proverbs.

[250] We can, however, speak of the performance setting of the collections and the book as a whole. For Proverbs, this setting (probably fictitious, but based on the traditions of the genre) is father-to-son instruction. This is discussed in this Commentary in Vol. I, 80–83, 92–93 and (in a more developed analysis) in my article "Wisdom and the Self-Presentation of Wisdom Literature" (*2003b*). I examine the participants, media, and function of Wisdom texts in their literary setting. These observations, however, tell us little about the employment of the individual sayings in actuality.

Fontaine's studies pertain particularly to oral use of proverbs. Whether any of these sayings were originally oral cannot be determined. None are quoted in biblical narratives. It seems likely that, as O. Eissfeldt (1913: 45–52) proposed, Proverbs holds many originally monostichic (one-line) folk sayings that were later expanded by addition of a parallel line. In biblical narratives, proverbs are sometimes identified as *mᵉšalim* or marked by a phrase such as "therefore they say." Such sayings are almost always single lines; for example: "Is Saul too among the prophets?" (1 Sam 10:12bβ); "Wickedness issues from the wicked" (1 Sam 24:14aβ); and "Like Nimrod, a mighty hunter before Yahweh" (Gen 10:9b). Longer proverbs, such as "The fathers have eaten sour grapes and the sons' teeth stand on edge" (Ezek 18:2), are compound sentences but not parallelistic. This suggests that folk sayings in Proverbs are to be found in individual lines, probably the first in a couplet. Perhaps the following were originally one-line folk proverbs:

The fear of the Lord is the beginning of knowledge. (1:7a)
The memory of the righteous is for a blessing. (10:7a)
When the arrogant come then insult comes (too). (11:2a)
A gracious woman holds honor. (11:16a)
Pride comes before a fall. (16:18a)
Even a fool who keeps silent is reckoned wise. (17:28a)
He who digs a pit will fall in it. (26:27a)
Let a stranger praise you, and not your own mouth. (27:2a)

I have observed that when Israelis quote the book of Proverbs in oral discourse, as they often do, what they cite is almost always a single line of the couplet. (I have heard the above lines used, always by themselves.) This reinforces the supposition that what is most natural to oral discourse is the one-line saying. But there are no objective criteria for identifying which sayings in Proverbs are oral folk proverbs.[251]

---

[251] C. Westermann (1990; ET 1995) and F. Golka (1983; 1986; 1993: 4–53) hold that the book of Proverbs is composed primarily of oral folk sayings; see my discussion in Vol. I, 6-12.

To my remarks on Vol. I, 9–10 about the dichotomy between folk and royal (literary) settings, I would like to add an instructive example of the interplay between the two settings. The valuable study of proverb performance in Akan rhetoric by Kwesi Yankah (1989: 82-86) used as informants Akan "chief's spokesmen," officials who were the chief's confidants, spokesmen, and advisors, and who were considered repositories of traditional wisdom. (Compare the office of the "king's men"; Vol. I, 10.) The primary Akan informant was the *okyeame* "chief's spokesman" Antwi Boasiako, who, it turns out, was something of a paremiologist himself, having published a book of Asante sayings (Yankah 1989: 85). Again note the similarity to Hezekiah's men. This does not show that the Asante proverbs are *not* folk proverbs, but that folk proverbs could be introduced into the royal court and *become* court proverbs, which could then be disseminated as part of the national literature and quoted by future readers. The threads of traditions, oral and written, folk and courtly, are inextricably tangled, and proverb performance is by no means confined to "folk" environments.

B. SOUND PATTERNS

Phonetic patterns are essential to poetry, and the poetry of proverbial literature is no exception. These patterns are especially relevant to the oral use of proverbs. A proverb has only about three seconds to work its effect, or at least to make itself memorable, and it must make maximal use of aesthetic and rhetorical resources to do so. Of the various commentaries on the book of Proverbs, Clifford's gives the most attention to the rhetorical force of sound effects and quotes in transliteration many proverbs with sound-play. The present commentary will do the same, but less extensively.

The Study of Sound Patterns. G. Boström (*1928*) is credited with being the first to investigate paronomasia in Proverbs, by which he means all repetitions of sounds or phonetic groups. His interest is in editorial composition, not aesthetics or rhetoric. He regards paronomasia as the organizing principle of the collections and explains it as an aid to memorization. J. Krispenz (1989) also uses paronomasia—understood very broadly—as a criterion for identifying groupings in 10:1–22:16.

Berlin (*1985*: 103–26) treats the phonological aspect of parallelism in biblical poetry in general. She defines "sound pair" very broadly, namely, as "*the repetition in parallel words or lines of the same or similar consonants in any order within close proximity*" (p. 104, italics in original). She is concerned with sound pairs in parallel lines (e.g., ***b*ʾ*zny ksyl* // *ybwz lśkl*** in Prov 23:9[252]), not within a line.

T. McCreesh (*1991*) examines a variety of phenomena: assonance (repetition of vowels), consonance (repetition of consonants), alliteration (combinations of these two), sound patterns that link components of a proverb, correlation (reinforcement of key words by certain kinds of echo), tagging patterns (punctuation of syntax or thought by sounds), and word (or root) repetition.

Prov 15:12 is an example of the way McCreesh describes phonetic phenomena:

A	***lō*ʾ *ye*ʾ*ĕhab lēṣ hôḵēaḥ lô*,**	The impudent man does not like being rebuked.
B	**ʾ*el ḥăḵāmîm lō*ʾ *yēlēḵ***	He will not go to the wise.

The sounds /lo/ and /le/ alternate: *lō*ʾ . . . *lē* . . . *lô* . . . ʾ*el* . . . *lō*ʾ . . . *ēlē*. McCreesh thinks that this pattern draws attention to the attitudes of the *impudent man* (*lēṣ*) toward the wise, *to* (ʾ*el*) whom he will not *go* (*yēlēḵ*). Each line has its own sound pattern, the first based on /l/ and /h/, the second on /l/ and /k/. Each line begins and ends with a word that starts with the same sound: /lo/ in the first and /el/ in the second. The first two verbal phrases in each have the same pattern in /lō'/-/ye/, while *hôḵēaḥ lô* and ʾ*el ḥăḵāmîm* share the consonants /k/-/ḥ/-/l/, with the sequence reversed chiastically. The chiasm relates *ḥăḵāmîm* to the first line and *hôḵēaḥ lô* to the second.

McCreesh exaggerates the phonetic relationships here and elsewhere. That is, he gives significance to some accidental phenomena, describes some of the same features in different ways, and assumes that any repetition is significant. If all of this really affected the listener, the impression would be a clutter of signals that would cancel each other out. Considerations of psycholinguistics should also be brought to bear on such analyses. As Z. Zevit says, "The fact of the presence of a given pattern is not necessarily an indication of the pattern's relevance" (*1990*: 393). Zevit also cautions that we should not confuse letters with sounds. Still, McCreesh demonstrates that a variety of phonetic patterns is important to a proverb's working.

The problem of defining "similarity" of sounds has not yet been addressed. The similarities relevant to sound effects are not necessarily the same as the features by which sounds are grouped by linguists. Poetic relevance is determined by the language in question. Moreover, all descriptions of phonetic effects in the biblical text are subject to considerable uncertainty. The phonetic observa-

---

[252] I have added boldface here, as often in this volume, to mark the repeated consonants and, sometimes, vowels.

tions proposed at various places in the present commentary are subject to the same caveat. We do not know, for example, if the ancient audience would have heard phonetic similarities that seem relevant in transliteration, such as a rhyme between *segol* and *ṣeré* (any more than the vowels of the words "get" and "raid" are felt to rhyme in English), or if it would have associated /s/, /ś/, /z/, /ṣ/, and /š/ just because they are all sibilants, or /t/ and /d/ because they are dentals, as McCreesh (e.g., pp. 112–13) and others who describe Hebrew poetics often assume.

C. PROVERB PERMUTATIONS

1. *Templates*

With great frequency, couplets, lines, or components of lines recur elsewhere in the book in the same or similar form. In the Commentary, cross-references are marked by = for identical or virtually identical components, in which the differences have no semantic weight, and ≈ when the related lines or couplets do differ semantically, but in minor ways that do not obscure the fundamental equivalence of the related components.

D. Snell has catalogued and diagrammed the recurring components in painstaking detail in his study of doublets called "Twice-Told Proverbs" (*1993*: 35–59; reviewed in Fox *1995a*). It is, however, somewhat misleading to call the phenomenon "repetition," as he does, because there is usually some variation in the doublet lines or couplets. Cases of recurring couplets with no variation or nonsignificant variation are infrequent: 9:4 = 9:16 (this, however, is really a refrain in a single poem); 14:12 = 16:25; 18:8 = 26:22; 20:16 = 27:13; 21:9 = 25:24; 22:3 = 27:12. More often there is recurrence with variation.

Recurrence with variation is far more frequent in the book of Proverbs than in any other Wisdom text, with the exception of Qohelet. (Qohelet is different because it is spoken by a single voice, and the repeated phrases are a refrain and always serve the context.) Snell (pp. 10–14; 70–73) weighs various hypotheses as to the reason for this phenomenon but does not come to a conclusion.

These hypotheses, together with my objections in parentheses, are as follows:

(1) "Literary cleavage." Proverbs or clichés were taken into separate collections, and they became "repetitions" when the collections were joined. (This is often true, but this hypothesis cannot explain the numerous "repetitions" *within* collections.)

(2) Numerology. The compiler repeats a proverb in order to give the collection a specific number of proverbs. (But numerology is problematic, see the critique of Skehan, in "Designs," above. In any case, numerology would not explain why the collector chose repetition to fill out his number rather than inserting a new proverb.)

(3) Emphasis. To repeat an idea is presumably emphatic. (This would not explain repetition at a distance or in different collections, nor would it account for variations between instances of repetition.) C. Yoder (*2005*, at 169) explains two features—repetition and contradiction (or incongruity)—as a didactic strategy to reinforce the lesson. (It is indeed likely that the editors repeated certain ideas in order to drive them home, though that would not account for the variation. It makes sense to explore the didactic *intent* of repetition, as Yoder does, before assigning repeated phrases obscure structuring functions.)

(4) Oral formulaic composition. (But the "repetitions" are not fixed, conventionalized epithets or phrases of the kind associated with oral poetry, and they are too scattered and variegated to aid in

memorization. In some cases, moreover, we can be certain that written transmission was at work, as in 22:28a and 23:10a, which has its antecedents in Amenemope.)

To these explanations may be added the following:

(5) A structuring device, serving primarily to frame material; thus Scoralick 1995: 145 and passim. (This hypothesis is relevant only sporadically and requires ignoring other types of grouping and other possible borders. It has been effectively critiqued by K. Heim *2001*: 52–59.)

(6) Combination of monostichic sayings with new lines, to form couplets. Eissfeldt (1913: 47–48) identified this as a major device for proverb production. (Contrary to Eissfeldt, we cannot assume that the monostich sayings were "folk proverbs," though this may sometimes be true; see Hermisson 1968: 47–52.)

Though not unproblematic, this last hypothesis, that new couplets were created by adding a new line to an old one, is worth exploring further. An author could start with the statement, "A smelter for silver and a furnace for gold" (17:3a; 27:21a) and produce two new proverbs by adding two different lines: "and the tester of hearts is the Lord" in 17:3 and "and a man (is tested) by the mouth of him who praises him" in 27:21. The process could account for a number of partial-doublets; for example:

From the fruit of his mouth, a man will be sated with good things,
and the recompense of a man's hands will return to him. (12:14)

From the fruit of his mouth a man will eat good things,
and the gullet of the treacherous, lawlessness. (13:2)

A man's belly will be sated by the fruits of his mouth;
he will be sated by the produce of his lips. (18:20)

Proverbs 12:14a; 13:2a; and 18:20a are close variants and can be said to provide a way to produce for new proverbs. To it are paired three very different lines, and three different couplets result, all with the same premise. Proverbs 18:20b has a particular contextual function because it is followed (in v 21) by the theme of the produce of speech, which is no less than life and death.

Still, this process accounts only for the reuse of lines. It is only part of a broader process, in which not only lines but also parts of lines, or clichés, or syntactic patterns, recur. The overall process is best described as *proverb permutation*, the constant transformation of proverbs based on templates implicit in other proverbs. A template is a a recurrent pattern of syntax or wording that serves as a mold for constructing new couplets. What makes a feature a template is its reuse. In the following examples, the components that constitute the template are in italics.

The pattern *Better* A *than* A′ is a template by which new proverbs could be easily produced. It can be expanded to *Better* A *with B than A′ with B′*. A more specific template is produced when some of the details are supplied. The template *Better to dwell in/on* [situation] X *than with* [situation] Y generates the following couplets: "*Better to dwell on* the corner of a roof *than with* a contentious woman in a house with other people" (Prov 21:9 and 25:24) and "*Better to dwell in* a desert land, *than with* a contentious and angry woman" (21:19). We cannot usually determine which form came first, so to call one proverb a "variant" or "permutation" of another should not be understood as giving chronological priority to one, but only as describing the relation between variant forms. The variants are more precisely conceived as having been generated by the same underlying template. An excursus on the "better than" proverbs follows the Comment on 15:17.

A template can be a syntactic pattern. An example is the repetition of a word in the subject and the predicate, as in "*He who loves* discipline *loves* knowledge" (Prov 12:1a) ≈ "*He who loves* an offense *loves* strife" (17:19a) and—using the same template but with a different verb—"*He who has found* a wife *has found* something good" (18:22a; cf. the same template in 19:16a; 21:23; and elsewhere). A template can be expanded by the repetition of a word, as when "step" in 16:9b is the mold for "a man's steps" in 20:24a. (S. Yonah 2005 defines the phenomenon of expanded repetition.) This is relevant to template formation only when the doublets are clearly similar in distinctive ways. It is also possible that the template was the longer phrase that was condensed in the generated proverb. Numerous examples of these and other templates can be found in Snell's collation, though his categories, which are largely defined by the number of similar components shared by the repetitions, are too mechanical to give a good sense of the incessant and variegated churning of sayings generated by the underlying proverb templates. In Essay 8, "Coherence Theory," I explore the implications of template use for Wisdom epistemology.

2. *Old and New*

Proverb templates provide a useful (and easy) way to produce proverbs. (Better to use a template that is shopworn but has the ring of authority than to make up a pattern that is clever but obscure. Sometimes.) I would go further and say that proverb templates are intrinsically relevant to Wisdom Literature because they allow for a creative dialectic between the old and the new. An author can ground his innovations in the wisdom and language of the past, holding one part of a proverb stable while modifying another.

I do not claim that every case of proverb doublets reflects an investment of thought and talent. Some are stamped out mechanically. (In my view, this is the case with many of the righteous-wicked antitheses in chapters 10–15.) Still, a template can be more than a cookie-cutter. It can be used creatively, to shape proverbs that introduce new ideas and express old ones in new ways.

If it is just good sense that "*you should make war by strategy*" (Prov 24:6a ≈ 20:18b)—and who would deny it?—then a sage could use this commonplace to commend thoughtful discussion by adding "and victory comes through many counselors" (24:6b ≈ 20:18a). Then, by judicious positioning of the couplet, he could use it to give priority to wisdom itself, as when it is placed after 24:5: "Stronger a wise man than a mighty one, and a man of knowledge than one great in power."

The sentence "*Showing partiality in judgment is not good*" (Prov 24:23b ≈ 28:21a) is put to various uses. In 24:23b, it is left as a monostich and defines the topic of the next verse: "He who says to the guilty, 'You are innocent'—peoples will curse him and nations revile him." This monostich puts v 24 into a judicial context, which is unambiguous in the Hebrew; see the Comment. In 28:21, this same line is matched with a concession: "but a man may transgress for a piece of bread." To be sure, the proverb concedes, it is not good to show partiality in judgment, but a judge must recognize exigencies. The line "*Showing partiality in judgment is not good*" thus provides a stable template that can be put to very different uses.

The line "*The deceitful witness will perish*" (*ʿed k^{e}zabim yoʾbed*) (Prov 21:28a) serves as a template. In 19:9, it is expanded by words inserted in the middle to produce "A lying *witness* will not go unpunished, and he who testifies *deceitfully will perish*." This is a conventional synonymous couplet that merely repeats the same idea in the B-line. In 21:28, however, the template is matched with a more interesting line to read, "*The deceitful witness will perish*, but the man who listens will speak victoriously." The new combination suggests that, in litigation, listening carefully is the opposite of testifying falsely. We are to see litigation not only as a clash between opposing claims, but as an occasion of interaction between individual personalities. This topic is explored in the next verse as well; see the Comment on 21:28–29.

A template can account for series of variants. In the following case, the template is almost an entire couplet. But when it is complemented, two very different proverbs are formed:

> *He who works his land will be sated with bread,*
> *while he who pursues trifles* lacks sense. (12:11)

and

> *He who works his land will be sated with bread,*
> *while he who pursues trifles* will be sated with poverty. (28:19)

Though the differences between these proverbs might seem trivial, more is going on than mechanical rearrangement of proverb parts. The first proverb is slightly disjointed, for "lacks sense" is not antithetical to "sated with bread." The result is a richer proverb, in which each line completes the other to teach that he who works his land has good sense, and the senseless man will starve. The second proverb has a tighter antithesis, but by repeating "will be sated" adds a facetious note: The trifler too will be "sated"—but with poverty, not bread. But that's not all. The permutation in 28:19b, by introducing the notion of satiation by poverty, prepares the way for the next verse: "The faithful man has many blessings, but he who hastens to get rich will not go unpunished." Verse 20a extends v 19a's promise of good fortune for the diligent man to another virtuous type, the faithful man. Verse 20b extends v 19b's threat against the frivolous man to his opposite, the compulsive worker. "He who works his land" is, we learn, not the same as "he who hastens to get rich" (v 20b).

Three interrelated templates generate a number of comparison proverbs in Prov 25–26; see the introduction to Part V, before chapter 25. Another important template is the *toʿebah*-series, used twenty-seven times. This is a way of describing behaviors in terms of the disgust they provoke in Yahweh and, occasionally, others; see the Comment on 3:32.

Proverb permutation continues beyond the book of Proverbs. Ben Sira borrows Prov 28:20b—itself used to fill out the template in that verse—as the basis for a new proverb and appends it to a line on a different topic: "My son, why should you increase your busy-ness [or: "anxiety" (*ʿśqk*); MS A]. *He who hastens to gain increase will not go unpunished*" (Sir 11:10ab). Ben Sira is using a slight variant of Prov 28:20b to reinforce a warning against *ʿeśeq*, which means both "busy-ness" and "anxiety." (The ambiguity is deliberate.) In this way, Ben Sira subtly and incisively defines the punishment for avid pursuit of wealth, which is left vague in Prov 28:20b, as psychological.

Sometimes we can trace proverb permutation from Proverbs backwards. Proverbs 22:24–25 derives from a sentence in Amenemope §9, which has its own permutation in Amenemope §12. Both Amenemope passages are reformulations of Anii 18.7–8. These and other examples of proverb permutation are discussed in the Comments on Part IIIa.

Proverb variations, whether consisting in the substitution of an entire line or in the modification of words and phrases, are typically ascribed to an editor. The distinction between author and editor in Prov 10–29 is fuzzy, since we do not know to what extent the creative hand was writing down existing sayings or composing new ones. Still, there is no reason to class proverb permutation as an editorial activity, since it goes on constantly, not only in Proverbs but in proverb creation everywhere, and mostly not by editors. Ben Sira would not be called an "editor" of sayings from Proverbs, nor is Amenemope an editor of Anii. Benjamin Franklin was certainly an editor of proverbs, and his proverbs were reused in literature, rhetoric, and everyday speech, usually in contexts that could not be called editorial creations. He was also an author, sometimes ascribing his own coinages to a fictional sage, "Poor Richard."

Sometimes in Prov 10–29, as noted in some of the previous examples, the variant produced by a template serves the context of its collection. It must also be granted that often, and perhaps usually, there is no good contextual explanation for a particular variant. But even without a particular contextual function, the fresh ideas or nuances expressed by the permutations are a sufficient rationale for the process.

3. *Paremiology and Permutations*

The process of proverb permutation has been extensively studied by scholars of proverbs, called paremiologists. The eminent paremiologist Wolfgang Mieder traced and catalogued the evolution of numerous examples. (Rich resources for this process are Mieder, Kingsbury, and Harder 1992 and Mieder 1993.)

An interesting case of proverb permutation is "Early to bed, early to rise, makes a man healthy wealthy and wise," studied by Mieder 1993: 98–134. It can be traced back at least as far as 1496, but it was apparently known earlier as a medieval Latin adage. Benjamin Franklin, most famously, cited it in 1735. Thereafter, it was widely assumed that Franklin *wrote* it. It was reused, rephrased, and parodied countless times. Recently, its association with Franklin has faded for many people, and, Mieder says, "[T]he proverb is once again becoming a piece of true folk wisdom attached to no individual person" (ibid., p. 127).

The process of proverb permutation is of ongoing interest, and not only for Bible scholars. An instructive example appeared in the *New York Times*, in the Arts Section on May 10, 2005, and the Letters to the Editor section on May 15, 2005, in a debate about who authored John F. Kennedy's famous aphorism, "Ask not what your country can do for you; ask what you can do for your country." Was it Kennedy or Ted Sorensen, his speechwriter (who denies authorship)?

Kennedy undoubtedly heard the slogan of his prep school that declared that what is important is "not what Choate does for you, but what you can do for Choate." But one correspondent observed an affinity of topic to what Kahlil Gibran wrote in 1925: "Are you a politician asking what your country can do for you or a zealous one asking what you can do for your country?" Another identified the source of the maxim as King George VI, who broadcast on D-Day, "We shall not ask that God may do our will, but that we may be enabled to do the will of God." Still another noted a more distant source in Calvin Coolidge's autobiography, "The only hope of perfecting human relationship is in accordance with the law of service under which men are not so solicitous about what they shall get as they are about what they shall give." More readers chimed in with more of the same.

The discussion (which could be extended well beyond this group of letters—consider the innumerable times that people have reused Kennedy's sentence, giving it a spin of their own) illustrates, first, that the entity that is passed about and evolves is not a proverb and not even specific words, but rather a proverb template, in this case: *Ask not how* X *can benefit you; ask rather how you can benefit* X. Second, there are some proverb templates that, in a sense, *no one* composed. These were shaped over the course of time by many people. The origins of a great many proverbs are not recoverable, so that it is impossible to determine where the template originated and perhaps even pointless to insist on "origin." The templates are just there, available for redeployment, citation, and reshaping. Third, the distinctions between folk and elite, or oral and literary, quickly break down. Many people learned of Kennedy's dictum by hearing it on television, others read it in the newspaper. (The advent of television did not change matters fundamentally. In the ancient world, adages were a staple of public rhetoric; see Aristotle, *Rhetoric* 2.21.) We do not know where Kennedy (or Sorensen) picked up the template: certainly, in part, from Choate (oral), but also perhaps from Kahlil Gibran (written) or King George VI (perhaps heard on the radio, perhaps read—but does it matter?). Fourth, despite one correspondent's claim that he doesn't particularly care who invented Kennedy's phrase, the vigorous debate showed that many people *do* care. This was also the case with the editors of Proverbs who ascribed authorship to Solomon rather than to some obscure scribes or officials in the royal court.[253]

D. PARALLELISM

Parallelism is the earmark of Hebrew poetry. In the 1980s, a number of scholars redescribed and clarified the nature and workings of biblical parallelism. Some of their conclusions have direct implications for exegesis. Most important, the semantic relationships between the lines in a parallelistic couplet are many and variegated, even when the parallelism is synonymous. Usually the B-line supplements the second or defines it more narrowly.

J. Kugel's *The Idea of Biblical Poetry* (1981) established that the second line in a couplet does not merely restate or echo the first line but in some way goes beyond it, typically having an emphatic "seconding" effect: "A is so, and what's more, *B*" (pp. 1–58, passim). R. Alter's *The Art of Biblical Poetry* (1985) speaks of "the characteristic movement of meaning" from one line (verset, in his terminology) to another (p. 19). This movement can take many forms: intensification, focusing, specification, concretization, and dramatization (p. 19), as well as sequentiality and consequentiality (p. 35). There may sometimes be a movement from specific to general, or from figurative to literal (p. 22). His subtle chapter on Proverbs, "The Poetry of Wit" (1985: 163–84), is cited in my Comments on a number of proverbs. Alter's ideas on the literary workings of proverbial parallelism, along with those of J. G. Williams (1980), are summarized in Vol. I, 15–16 of this Commentary. A. Berlin's *The Dynamics of Biblical Parallelism* (1985) examined parallelism in linguistic categories, for "parallelism activates all the levels of language" (p. 26)—grammatical, lexical and semantic, and phonological. Parallelism imposes similarity on contiguity. "Parallelism sets up relationships of equivalence or opposition" (p. 135), while linguistic modifications from line to line create a multiplicity of changing relationships between the two lines. Basically, the A-line is read retrospectively in the light of the B-line, which typically disambiguates it and imbues it with new meaning (pp. 97, 99, and passim).

The dynamics of parallelism, as described in these three mutually reinforcing works, is crucial in individual proverbial couplets, where much must be done in little space. "[W]ithin the confines of the one-line poem nice effects and sometimes suggestive complications are achieved through the smallest verbal movements" (Alter 1985: 175). The authors of the sayings in the book of Proverbs have chosen to cast almost all of the sayings as parallelistic couplets.

Parallelism frames an idea in the first line so that it may be modified and commented on in the second. Unlike the monostich, the couplet allows for a short, compressed dialectic between an idea and its restatement. It embodies the intellectual process called wisdom, for it involves thinking about an idea as well as simply stating it.

There is not always a movement between lines. Many parallelistic couplets are static. Alter cites Prov 19:5 as an example: "A false witness will not get off, /

[253] I can't help noticing the analogy between Ted Sorensen and the circles to which I ascribe the creation of the book of Proverbs (see Vol. I, 10–11). Sorensen was an educated man of letters who served the head of state as administrator, advisor, legal counsel, and diplomat.

a lying testifier will not escape" (1985: 22, his translation). Since dynamism is a typical feature of parallelism, static parallelism is probably deliberate, not simply the result of lazy writing. Static proverbs may have their own value. They may suggest the equilibrium of retributive justice. The immobility of such proverbs has a certain sturdiness, appropriate for teaching immutable principles to the young. A reader may justifiably feel that such maxims are rather dull, but that is true of much in education.

E. DISJOINTED PROVERBS[254]

It is now a given in Bible studies that the lines of a parallel are rarely if ever exactly parallel in meaning, and that we have to be alert to the subtleties of their relationships. One type of relationship, often ignored, is violation of parallelism: Not only do the lines say something different, they don't quite work together—at first.

Sometimes violation of parallelism is simply a literary inelegance, but there are cases when it ultimately enriches the meaning. An example of the latter is Prov 28:7:

> The perceptive son keeps the teaching,
> while he who consorts with gluttons shames his father.

The clause "keeps the teaching" is not the antithesis of "shames his father." I call this type of couplet "disjointed" because the two lines do not seem well joined. It is as if the author approaches a neat parallelism, but does not arrive. Another example is 13:5:

> The righteous man hates a deceitful word,
> while the wicked man will be ashamed and disgraced.

The subjects of the sentences, "righteous" and "wicked," are a conventional antithetical pair, but the predicates, "hates a deceitful word" and "will be ashamed and disgraced," are not congruent. The first line mentions a moral stance, the second the consequence of an unnamed offense.

Disjointed parallelism leaves a gap between the lines and invites the reader to fill it. When the missing component is mentally supplied, the couplet gains cohesiveness and a tighter linkage. I do not refer to the well-known phenomenon of syntactic gapping, which requires us to supply from one line a constituent missing in the syntax of the other. The "gapping" relevant to the present study is semantic. It may be called *rhetorical*, since what is elided is an entire premise or conclusion. Such gaps do not necessarily disturb the syntax of the clause, nor can they be filled simply by supplying a grammatical constituent directly from a parallel line. Most

[254] This discussion of disjointed proverbs is based on Fox *2004c*, which offers a more extensive examination of examples.

often, rhetorical gaps are to be filled by taking an idea from one line into the other or by reversing the valence (positive or negative) of a term of the parallel line.

Saʿadia recognized the phenomenon and described its workings in his comment on Prov 28:7, "The perceptive son keeps the teaching, while he who consorts with gluttons shames his father":

> [Solomon] made the antitheses dissimilar in order to imply two further oppositions in the passage. "He who keeps the teaching" [in effect] glorifies his father, inasmuch as he is the opposite of "he who shames his father," while "he who consorts with gluttons" is a foolish son inasmuch as he is the opposite of the "perceptive son." And in this fashion you can clarify all cases of two dissimilar antitheses.

Lines can gap a premise (the principle or a fact on which a conclusion is based) or a conclusion (the consequence of a behavior defined in the premise or a rule drawn from it). Following are a few examples to illustrate the mechanics and function of disjointed proverbs. Others are discussed in the Comments; see especially 10:12, 13, 14; 12:11, 20; 13:5, 17, 19; 14:17, 25; 15:5, 6, 20; 26:2; 27:6; 28:25; and 29:3.

> He who builds his stores in the summer is an astute son;
> he who drowses off at harvest is a disgraceful son. (10:5)

"Astute" (*maśkil*) is not the proper antonym of "disgraceful" (*mebiš*). But if "stupid" had been the parallel to "astute," the couplet would have been rather inert, for the second line would have merely been the negative image of the first. The effect of the slight asymmetry is to make the two lines complement each other. By clamping "disgraceful" to "astute," the couplet reminds the reader that a lazy son shames his parents, while a diligent one makes them proud.

> Better a little with the fear of the Lord,
> than a great storehouse with turmoil in it. (15:16)

"Fear of the Lord" is not the antithesis of "turmoil." The LXX sensed this and tried to straighten the parallelism by rephrasing *umᵉhumah bo* as "with lack of fear." But this does not solve the problem, because there are *two* gaps between the lines: the consequence of the fear of God and the cause of turmoil. The thought in full is as follows:

> Better a little with the fear of the Lord,
> *when the heart is peaceful,*
> than a great storehouse with turmoil in it,
> *which is brought on by the lack of fear of the Lord.*

"Peaceful" (or the like) and "lack of fear of the Lord" are supplied by reversing "with turmoil" and "fear of the Lord," respectively.

In this case, we know exactly how one of the gaps was created because we can compare the source-text, two adjacent couplets in Amenemope:

(9.5) Better is poverty in the hand of the god,
(6) than wealth in the storehouse.
(7) Better is (simple) bread when the heart is pleasant,
(8) than wealth with vexation.[255] (from §6 [cf. AEL 2.151–52])

"To be in the hand of the god" here means to trust in God and his providence. It is a near equivalent of "the fear of the Lord." The author of Prov 15:16 collapsed Amenemope's four lines into a couplet. He elided "Better is bread," allowing this to be present in silhouette in MT's "a little," which corresponds to Amenemope's "poverty." He also omitted "when the heart is pleasant," allowing this to be suggested by reversal of the phrase "with turmoil in it" (Prov 15:16b). (Both components of Amenemope 9.7 are incorporated more exactly in Prov 17:1a: "Better a dry piece of bread with tranquility in it.")

A comparison of Prov 15:16 with the very similar 16:8 gives insight into the enhancement of meaning potential in gapping. Proverbs 16:8 reads: "Better a little with righteousness than great produce without justice." Whereas 15:16 contrasts an ethical virtue (fear of Yahweh) with a circumstance harmful to the possessor, and in so doing implies a reason for its own assertion, 16:8 contrasts an ethical virtue (righteousness) with an ethical failing (lack of justice). The latter is neatly symmetrical, but also rather predictable and flat, and it suggests no rationale for the assertion. Proverbs 15:16 does provide a reason, but only implicitly—literally between the lines. The contrast between these two formulations reveals the rhetorical edge of gapped proverbs and shows how they can pack more into two lines than the lines themselves contain.

The mouth of the righteous man produces wisdom,
but the perverse tongue is cut off. (10:31)

Standing in antithesis to *yanub* "produces," which implies producing fruit, the verb *tikkaret* "be cut off" is suggestive of a branch being lopped off. The images are complementary, yet the lines still seem mismatched. The first line speaks of a virtue—producing wisdom—while its antithesis speaks of a punishment—being cut off. Gapped are one conclusion ("c")—the reward of wisdom—and one premise ("p")—the folly of perverse speech. They are to be supplied thus:

(p^1) The mouth of the righteous man produces wisdom,
  (c^1) *and wisdom preserves wholeness;*[256]
  (p^2) *but the perverse tongue produces folly;*
(c^2) (*consequently*) the perverse tongue is cut off.

[255] Egyptian *šnn* can be translated "vexation" or "conflict."

[256] "Preserves wholeness" is approximately the opposite of being "cut off." What is being supplied is a notion, not a particular phrase. Still, in cases where a word is a component of a common an-

Conclusion c^1, the consequence of premise p^1, is reached retrogradely by taking the converse of consequence c^2, while premise p^2 is supplied by taking the converse of p^1. Only when reaching c^2 does the reader realize that this must be done. The retrograde gapping is feasible because the entirety of the couplet is read in a moment and is comprehended as a unit. The B-line is immediately available to supply what is missing in the A-line.

The effort of gap-filling should encourage the reader to recognize how the shallow man's arrogance causes strife—not, say, by inducing him to insult others. That is true, but not the point here. Here the cause of strife is his unwarranted self-reliance. Rather than conferring with others, he blunders ahead and does whatever he wishes, and this inevitably provokes conflict—or so the proverb suggests. If we deduce that taking counsel is the opposite of arrogance, then we still might wonder *why* it is wise to take counsel. It is not self-evident that this is so; perhaps it is wiser to keep one's own counsel (a behavior recommended in 10:14, 19a; 14:33; 17:27, 28, etc.). The answer, derived from the parallel line, is that conferring with others preserves peace.

Disjointed proverbs are a type of enthymeme. The enthymeme is crucial in rhetoric, though scholars describe it in different ways. The Aristotelian enthymeme is usually understood as an "incomplete" syllogism with "suppressed" premises or conclusions. Though this may not be an adequate formulation of Aristotle's concept (in fact, he apparently was not fully consistent in his view of the enthymeme), there is agreement that the enthymeme is an argument with gaps. This classical concept of enthymeme must be supplemented by L. Bitzer's important insight that it is the *listener* who fills in the gaps (1959, passim). The rhetor builds on premises that the audience *would* supply in its responses if this were dialectic, and he simultaneously elides them. In other words, the rhetorical enthymeme implies a latent dialogue between rhetor and audience. Consequently, Bitzer says, "Owing to the skill of the speaker, *the audience itself helps construct the proofs by which it is persuaded*" (1959: 408; italics in original).

The expectation of seeing the lines of a didactic, parallelistic couplet "clicking dutifully into place," as Alter puts it (1985: 164), is likely to prod the reader into trying to make them do so. I suggest that when the reader senses an awkwardness or deficiency in proverbs of the type described, that sense is an intimation of the sort of "question" that Bitzer is speaking of. This is a question that we might ask of the proverb's author if we could, but that we are now required to ask *and answer* for ourselves.

The gap-filling may take place unconsciously, as happens with syntactic gapping. Or, in a study setting (school or home), the semantic gap might serve to en-

---

tonymic word-pair, such as *rašaʿ // ṣaddiq* and *ḥakam // kᵉsil*, it is likely that precisely that antonym would occur to the reader by virtue of the association.

Berlin (1985: 96–99) shows how each line in a parallelistic couplet can disambiguate the other. In particular, the second line focuses the interpretation of the first. This is a way of overcoming the ambiguity inherent in terseness. The phenomenon I am describing is a form of this process. Disambiguation in this case comes through filling gaps in one line by reversal of a semantic component in the other.

courage the pupil to interpret a proverb by forcing him to think about the relation between the lines. Perhaps these proverbs are examples of riddles, which, according to Proverbs' Prologue (1:6), the book will help us understand. In any case, by actively supplying the missing assumptions and conclusions, the reader participates in the reasoning process, and by unpacking the argument, he helps teach himself. He is then more likely to interpret, amplify, and extend the message. If read carefully, then, the gapped proverbs not only transmit packets of truths, they *train* the reader in a mode of thinking: identifying behaviors and associating them with their consequences. In other words, they train the reader to think like a sage.

III. The Dating and Social Setting of the Proverb Collections

◆

A. The Growth of the Book of Proverbs

My view of the book's development is as follows: The four older collections in chapters 10–29 (Parts II–V) were composed and edited during the monarchy, probably in the eighth to seventh centuries B.C.E. No distinctions of date or setting can be drawn among these four collections. Next, the Lectures in Prov 1–9 were prefixed as a hermeneutical introduction to the older collections. Then the Interludes were inserted among them at various times; see Vol. I, 322–29. Subsequently, the four units in chapters 30–31 were appended, probably sequentially, to the end of the book. The dating of the composition of these appendices is very uncertain. See the Commentary on those units. In the book of Proverbs as it has reached us, Prov 1–9 is introductory to the proverb collections and seeks to refine and redefine the concept of wisdom in them.

My reasons for regarding chapters 1–9 later than chapters 10–29 are as follows:

(1) Chapters 1–9 function as an introduction, above all by defining wisdom and giving it theological content. Whereas the authors of Prov 10–29 praise and teach wisdom, the authors of chapters 1–9 (especially Lecture II) reflect *about* it in a more analytical way and seek to define its status. W. Zimmerli observes that chapters 1–9 were placed at the start of the book "as a canon for the understanding of the other collections" (1933: 189). As R. Van Leeuwen says, chapters 1–9

> introduce readers to the book's worldview, to its fundamental framework of meaning. The seemingly random and scattered events of life, so richly described in the tiny sayings of chaps. 10–29, are here given an interpretive context. Chapters 1–9 provide a moral map of the world, a portrait of the "universe" as made by God and with wisdom (3:10–20; chap. 8). (1997: 31)

(2) Interlude C is a pastiche of verses and phrases from the proverb collections. It draws together proverbs and phrases from chapters 10–29 in a way that shows awareness of those chapters as a written collection; see Vol. I, 225–27.

(3) Interlude D (Prov 8) especially is dependent on Prov 10–29. It introduces what follows and seeks to explain what wisdom really is; see Vol. I, 357–59. Lady Wisdom's call for attention is a grand exordium that in fact demands attention to the wise words to follow, as if they are in some sense *her* words; see Vol. I, 289, 292.

The eighth–seventh centuries were a time of growth in the Judean royal administration and a concomitant expansion in literacy, as evidenced in epigraphic remains (Jamieson-Drake 1991: 48–106; Carr 2005: 164–67). The fall of the Northern Kingdom in 722 B.C.E. may have provided the impetus to record, reshape, preserve, and, in effect, "canonize" the wisdom of the people and the royal court.

B. THE SOCIAL SETTING OF PROVERBS 10–29

The most securely locatable and datable proverbs are the "royal proverbs," the sayings that deal with the king and his court. ("Court" should be understood broadly as the elite circle of men who served the royal and state interests and whose status and duties might bring them into direct contact with the king.[257]) Since it is unlikely that other social groups would compose, transmit, and insert royal proverbs, these proverbs help us identify the court as the locus of the editorial activity that shaped the collections.

The royal proverbs are clearly grounded in the monarchy, probably in Jerusalem, given the editorial associations with Solomon and Hezekiah's court (Prov 1:1; 25:1); see Vol. I, 10–11. The evidence for this is not merely the mention of the king, but, more significantly, the *perspective* of the authors and implied audience. Altogether, there are twenty-four royal proverbs in chapters 10–29.[258] To these may be added the proverbs that speak about and to royal counselors (11:14; 15:22; 20:18; 24:6). The royal proverbs help date the collections, for they indicate that the men of the court inserted and composed proverbs reflecting their own perspective.

Some of the royal proverbs are most relevant as an admonition to a king or prince;[259] for example, "A king who judges the poor faithfully—his throne will be established forever" (29:14; see also 28:15–16a). The presence of proverbs applicable to the king himself suggests that princes were educated along with other scions of the elite, as in Egypt. Some proverbs are pertinent only to men who might actually find themselves working in the royal court; for example, "Do not exalt yourself before the king, and do not stand in the place of the great. For better that he say, 'Come up here,' than that he degrade you before a nobleman whom your eyes have seen" (25:6–7). The possibility of proximity to the king is a real one, and it is viewed as desirable and beneficial. The reader is assumed to be a young man eager for service in the presence of the king (22:29), perhaps *too* eager (25:6).

---

[257] This is not to say that the courtiers bore the title *ḥăkamim* "wise men." The term is used generally for persons who have natural or acquired talents and knowledge, not for a specific class. See Whybray 1974, passim, and 1990: 134.

[258] Prov 14:28, 35; 16:10, 12, 13, 14, 15; 19:12; 20:2, 8, 26, 28; 21:1; 22:11, 29; 24:21; 25:2, 3, 5, 6; 28:15 (*mošel*); 29:2 (*mošel*), 4, 14. A *mošel* is not necessarily a king (see the Comment on 23:1), but a *mošel* over a *people* probably is (28:15; 29:2).

The oracle of Agur in Prov 30:1–9 is ascribed to a king, but its teaching is not royal in character. The teaching of Lemuel's mother, Prov 31:1–10, is directed to a king and is a royal instruction, whose advice is directly pertinent only to a king or prince. The unit is not, however, associated with the Israelite or Judean monarchy and does not help us date the book. The mention of kings and governors in Prov 8:15 refers generally to all rulers of the earth and is likewise not indicative of a particular setting of composition.

[259] Some scholars have described Prov 28–29 as an instruction to a prince; see the excursus introducing Prov 28–29.

A teaching such as "The king favors an astute servant, while his wrath is directed toward the disappointing one" (14:35) is of little use to anyone but servants of the king. These are men who could be expected to come into contact with the king and even to be involved in making plans for war (11:14; 20:18; 24:6), an activity for royal counselors and military officials that was impossible between the exile and the Hasmonean dynasty.

It is hard to imagine anyone other than royal counselors showing such enthusiasm for royal counselors as to declare, "There is victory in a multitude of counselors" (11:14b; cf. 24:6b; 15:22). The attribution to Hezekiah's men in 25:1, accurate or not, shows that the royal court was the expected locus for proverb collection and transmission. This is not to say that all the proverbs and their monostichic components originated there. Nor does it mean that *wisdom* was located in court circles, but rather that proverbial literature such as we have in chapters 10–29 was cultivated, collected, and redacted there.

In these chapters, Proverbs promulgates a royalist ideology. The king provides—or at least *should* provide—social stability, justice, and peace (16:12), and not merely for the purpose of enforcing his control and exacting taxes. The throne as such is assumed to be inherently just, unless contaminated by the "dross" of unworthy servants (25:4–5; cf. Ps 101). In a similar vein Prov 16:13 says, "Kings favor righteous lips, and they love the word of the upright."[260]

There are analogous writings in Egyptian Wisdom Literature, in particular the "Loyalist Teaching" and "A Man to His Son," which demand loyalty to the king and verbosely exalt his virtues and powers.[261] The Israelite instructions are more subdued in this regard but likewise promote the socialization of young men into the scribal culture around the royal administration.[262]

This argument for a monarchical dating must, however, address a problem, namely, that the Hellenistic Wisdom books of Qohelet and Ben Sira also speak about kings. Why, then, assume that royal sayings in Proverbs come from the time of the Israelite monarchy? The reason is, first, that the Hellenistic authors have a very different attitude toward kingship, and, second, that their statements are not really meant as practical advice to courtiers.

Comparison with the royal sayings in Qohelet and Ben Sira helps delineate Proverbs' attitude. For the later books, the monarchy is merely a source of danger. It is best to keep one's distance from the king (Sir 7:4–6), or at least to get out of the way quickly when he is irritated (Qoh 10:2–4). The king's absolute authority is not a source of encouragement to these authors, as it is in Proverbs, but only a reason

[260] In discussing wisdom and kingship in the religion of Israel, G. E. Bryce (1979: 189–210) goes so far as to call Wisdom "propagandistic literature, exalting the king and seeking to strengthen the kingdom by encouraging the loyalty of its officials" (p. 204). This is indeed one aspect of Proverbs, but it does not accurately characterize the book as a whole.

[261] There are deep differences between Proverbs and the royalist instructions; most important was the Egyptian belief in the king's divinity. For a comparison of the views of kingship in Egyptian and Israelite Wisdom, see Blumenthal 2003: 1–36.

[262] On the socialization of the elite by means of written instruction, see D. Carr 2005: 31, 55, 67–68, and passim.

for fear and submission (Qoh 8:4). In Proverbs, the king is to be feared (16:14; 20:2), but he is also respected, even held in awe. As in Qohelet, the king in Proverbs may flash forth sudden anger, and, as in Qohelet, his anger is like God's (24:21–22). The difference is that Proverbs, unlike Qohelet, is confident of God's justice.

Neither Qohelet nor Ben Sira would come up with wide-eyed praise such as Prov 16:12, "Kings loathe the doing of evil, for the throne is established by righteousness," or 20:8, "A king sits on the throne of judgment and scatters all evil with his eyes," or 16:15, "In the light of the king's face there is life, and his favor is like the cloud of the spring rain" (so try to please him!). Such adulation is closer to Egyptian royalist instructions than to postexilic Jewish Wisdom. It is not that Judean kings were individually worthy of this esteem, but a Judean, and especially a courtier, could look upon the national dynasty with pride and patriotism. Proverbs projects a royalist ideology from up close. Royalist ideology does not deny the possibility of a bad king. Prov 28:15–16 describes the grim effects of oppressive rulers (not called "kings"). But the king as an ideal and kingship in itself is inherently righteous and glorious.[263]

Qohelet and Ben Sira view kingship from the perspective of subjects in an enormous empire, not as subjects of an indigenous monarchy, and their attitude is closer to the one later expressed by Rabban Gamaliel—"Be wary of the (civil) authorities, for they do not bring a man near except for their own needs, and they seem to be friendly when it is to their benefit, but they do not aid a man when he is in distress" (*'Abot* 2:3).

Qohelet's advice in 8:2–4 does seem to assume the possibility of immediate contact with the king, and this would have been feasible for a few important Jews in Ptolemaic times on special missions. Examples are the Tobiads Joseph (chief tax farmer of Syria and Phoenicia) and his son Hyrcanus, who (according to a story reported by Josephus in *Antiquities* 12.166–224) went to meet the Ptolemaic king in Alexandria. But this kind of contact must have been extremely rare and brief, whereas Proverbs pictures a group of courtiers working in the king's presence. Moreover, Qohelet's advice in 8:2–4, warning the reader to get away from an angry king (v 3), is a way of reminding the reader that humans stand insecurely before God like one who stands before an irritable and unpredictable human autocrat. The following verses, vv 5–8, speak of man's frailty and ignorance generally. Indeed, "king" here may allude to God. When Qohelet warns against cursing the king and the nobility (10:20), his real message is broader: Don't even *think* ill of the king and the powerful, let alone speak ill of them, for the power of the state, like the power of God, is far-reaching and harsh. In the book of Qohelet, kingship—including Qohelet's own Solomon-like status—is a fictional device (see Fox 1999: 153–55).

One passage in Ben Sira does seem to speak to men aspiring to become royal officials:

(4) Do not ask rulership (*memšelet*) from God
or a place of honor from the king.
(5) Do not assert your righteousness [possibly, "show yourself right"] before the king,
or flaunt your wisdom before the king.

[263] Hausmann (1995: 142) suggests that the proverbs critical of (some) kings avoid the word "king" in favor of "ruler" or "prince" to avoid tainting the *institution* of kingship. There are, however, too few examples of such proverbs to prove this. She also thinks that it may have been too dangerous to mention the king directly. However, no king would see *himself* in the image of a vicious beast or oppressive ruler.

(6) Do not seek to be a high official,
if you do not have (the power) to put a stop to arrogance. (7:4–6; MS A)

The "place of honor" could be a local office, namely, *memšelet*, "rulership," the position of a *mošel*. The latter term refers to a wide range of officials (see the Comment on Prov 23:1). The Greek of Sir 7:6 translates *mošel* as *kritē* "judge," and the subsequent verses describe a man active in the law courts and the city assembly. Before 175 B.C.E., high-placed Jews might seek preferments from—though not necessarily *in*—the imperial court (Hengel 1974: 134). Ben Sira warns the reader *not* to seek such a position. In any case, to seek an appointment from the king does not imply a direct appeal to the king or assume immediate contact with royalty, for many royal preferments would be allocated by subordinates.

Since the royal proverbs are scattered throughout chapters 10–29, except for a couple of thematic clusters, it seems unlikely that they were preserved separately through the years of destruction, exile, and return, and only later recorded in a collection. No one then would have been interested in ways to maintain the king's favor and the importance of royal counselors. Moreover, the royal proverbs are indistinguishable in style and language from the other sayings in Prov 10–29. My conclusion is that the royal proverbs are integral to the proverb collections and are therefore indicative of the date of the collections.

It should be emphasized that not all of the proverbs in Prov 10–29 necessarily came from the date and setting previously described. Most of the proverbs could have come from a great array of social locations. The Egyptian analogy would indicate that the court was only one locale of Wisdom authorship, and there is no reason to think it was the sole one in Israel. Moreover, some proverbs may have been inserted later than the monarchy.

Editing in the Persian Period? H. Washington (1994b: 161 and passim) holds that Proverbs was assembled and edited in the Persian period. A Persian dating for the editing of the book as a whole cannot be excluded; nor can a Hellenistic dating. However, nothing in the substance of the teachings reflects the social circumstances of the Persian period. There is no hint of inner-communal conflicts such as we read about in Ezra-Nehemiah. The poor are defined only by their poverty, not by their caste or genealogical affiliations. There is no hint of struggles such as would arise between the returnees and the "people of the land." There is no suggestion of competing claims to landed property except in the individual exploitation of the weak. Nothing is suggestive of a "civic-temple community," as Washington understands Yehud to have been. The Temple and sacrificial cult exist, unproblematically, but play a small role. The sovereign is a king, not a governor or a distant emperor, and the polity is an *ʾereṣ* "land," not a *mᵉdînāh* "province." There is no concern for intermarriage or mixing with gentiles, unless one assumes that the warning against *zārôt* "strange women" in Prov 22:14 is concerned with intermarriage and not just fornication. (Fornication is clearly in view in Prov 1–9; see Vol. I, 134–41.) The only kin unit mentioned is the immediate family—father, mother, son—not the large paternal estates, which Washington considers the basic social unit in this period. In other words, the distinctive features of the Achaemenid background that Washington himself describes *are absent or contradicted* in Prov 10–29.

C. LINGUISTIC INDICATORS OF DATING IN PROVERBS 10–29

The linguistic features of proverb collections are tricky indicators of dating because a particular proverb may be older or younger than the collection. Nevertheless, the language of Prov 10–29 supports a preexilic dating for the collections as a whole, without ruling out the possibility of later additions. There are a number of lexical usages distinctive of preexilic, Classical Biblical Hebrew (CBH). There are also a number of Aramaisms in these chapters that would accord well with a dating in the late-eighth and seventh centuries B.C.E., when Aramaic was known among the Jerusalem elite.

Classical Biblical Hebrew Features in Proverbs 10–29. As far as I can tell, there are no distinctively LBH features in Prov 10–29. There are some distinctively CBH features. CBH locutions are uncertain evidence for early dating because most continue beyond the exile, and even those that fade away can be revived at any time. Still, certain features combine to give Prov 10–29 a CBH profile, associating it typologically with preexilic literature. The following listing draws on several sources, in particular A. Bendavid *1967*: 60–80; R. Polzin 1976: 28–69; 123–53; Hurvitz *1972*: passim; and R. Bergey *1983*: 90–167, as well as some others cited below. These studies are mainly concerned with identifying LBH features, but in the process they note the CBH equivalents as well.

(1) Preference for the verbal suffix (84x) over *'et* + suffix (0x). LBH usage strongly favors *'et* + suffix.

(2) The asseverative *'ak*, meaning "indeed," occurring five times in these chapters (Prov 11:23; 14:23; 17:11; 21:5 [2x]). This use of *'ak* disappears in LBH.

(3) The imperatival use of the infinitive absolute, with four definite occurrences (Prov 12:7; 13:20 ketiv; 25:4, 5). Of the forty-eight instances in BH that Zohari includes in his list of infinitive absolutes (*1990*: 95–97), only Zech 6:10 is clearly postexilic, and his language, like that of the other late sixth-century prophets, is basically CBH.

(4) The gerundival use of the infinitive absolute—as subject (Prov 15:22; 17:12; 24:23; 25:27; 28:21), as direct object of a verb (15:12), as a nominal predicate (25:2), and as the head of a bound construction (21:16). Zohari (*1990*: 111–13) lists seventy-eight occurrences of the gerundival use of the inf. abs in BH. There are eight occurrences in Prov 10–29. Occurrences in postexilic texts are rare: Qoh 10:10; Neh 8:8; and possibly 1 Chr 15:22 (*yāsōr*; but see BHS). (In 1 Chr 21:12, read *nskh* for *nispeh*; cf. LXX, Vul.) Other possibly postexilic occurrences are in Job (9:18; 13:3; 15:3; 25:2), whose dating is a matter of dispute.

(5) The order of the pair *kesep w^ezāhāb* "silver and gold" (Prov 17:3; 22:1; 27:21; the words are not a pair in 25:11). The order "gold and silver" is preferred in LBH. (See Hurvitz *1972*: 248–51.)

(6) Use of the earlier member of lexical contrast pairs. Among the CBH/LBH lexical contrast pairs that I am aware of (based on the above-mentioned sources), Proverbs uses the earlier member exclusively or overwhelmingly. (The older members did not fall out of use.) In Esther, for example, Bergey (*1983*: 90–167) identifies thirty-six contrast pairs. Eleven of these have one member in Prov 10–29, and this is always the CBH member, with three exceptions: (1) *bihēl* "hurry" (rather than *mihhēr*); (2) *he'ĕdāh* "remove" (rather than *hēsîr*), and (3) *qibbēl* "receive" (rather than *lāqaḥ*). In exceptions (2) and (3), the CBH usage still predominates. Importantly, the three exceptions are Aramaisms.

Aramaisms. The identification of Aramaisms is often problematic. In my view, the following locutions are likely Aramaisms, because they are standard usages in Aramaic and there were earlier native Hebrew synonyms: *'zl* "depart" (Prov 20:14); *'kp* "force" (16:26); *'lp* "learn" (22:25); *bhl* Dp "hurry" (earlier: "terrify") (20:21; cj. 13:11); *bḥr* "assay," "test" (10:20); *bqr* D "examine" (20:25; meaning uncertain) ; *b'l* + abstract noun, meaning "possessor of a certain quality" (18:9; 22:24; 23:2; 24:8) (CBH: *'îš*); *ḥōsen* "strength" (15:6); *ḥsd* "disgrace" (verb and noun: 25:10; 14:34); *môtār* "advantage" (14:23;

21:5); *millāh* "word" (23:9); *ʿdh* H "remove" (25:20); *qbl* D "receive" (19:20); *qōšṭ* "truth" (22:21); *rab* "many" before the modified noun (19:21); *rēaʿ* "thought" (20:30, revocalized); *śakkîn* "knife" (23:2).

Hurvitz has suggested that the presence of Aramaisms in Wisdom Literature may be due to the international connections of that genre and its authors (1968: 236). I would add that some Aramaisms may reflect more specifically the influence of the Aramaic Ahiqar and—possibly—an Aramaic translation of Amenemope. See the introduction to Prov 22:17–24:22 and "Translation and Transmission" (A.4) in "Foreign Background" after the Comments there.

In the course of the eighth century, Aramaic became the lingua franca of the Near East, and the elite in Jerusalem knew it by the turn of the seventh century. The three Jerusalemites who, according to 2 Kgs 18:26–27, ask the Babylonian officer to speak Aramaic are officials of the royal court. They distinguish themselves from *ha'am*, the ordinary people, who are presumed not to know that language. A seventh-century courtly setting would account for the Aramaisms in Proverbs as well as for the evidence of the influence of Aramaic Wisdom Literature, on which see "Ahiqar and Proverbs" in "Foreign Background" after the Comments on 22:17–24:22.

I will proceed with the assumption that the collections in Prov 10–29 were shaped in the Jerusalem court, mainly in the seventh century, possibly starting in the eighth. It is worthwhile asking how the proverbs in general, and not just the royal proverbs, reflect and serve that setting. This can be answered most clearly about the proverbs that promote the royalist ideology, but it is relevant to understanding the social world of other proverbs as well. I have argued that this world is not that of smallholding farmers or the agrarian village (Vol. I, 9–12 and 1996b), but rather the life of the entire land—village, city, and court—*as seen from the perspective* of the well-to-do classes and their learned employees. In fact, it is likely the latter who are constructing the world as it exists in Proverbs. The royalist ideology is as much *for* the king as *by* the king. The authors are not imposing an elitist ideology so much as instructing the elite on what they themselves *should* be. They teach the wealthy and powerful how to validate their wealth and power. They speak also to a class somewhat lower on the socioeconomic ladder, not "simple farmers" but men who own land or run businesses that would call for diligence and enterprise, who might take or offer loan guarantees, who might send others as messengers; men who if they are not yet rich may be striving, even overstriving, for wealth. These same teachings can easily be applied to others as well—the craftsman, the housewife, the small farmer, even the slave, but they are not written in the first instance with them in mind.

Excursus: K. Kitchen's Typology of Wisdom Literature. Kitchen (1977–78) provides a typology of ancient Near Eastern Wisdom that, he believes, proves a dating of Prov 1–24 (which he calls "Solomon I," as if it were a single collection) in the early tenth century B.C.E. Waltke (2005: 31–36) bases his argument for Solomonic authorship on Kitchen's arguments and his own conviction that "[n]o attribution of authorship within the Old Testament has been proved spurious" (p. 35). I will discuss Kitchen's dating because it is the only scholarly argument for a Solomonic dating since von Rad's (1956), which is no longer influential.

Kitchen claims that certain features of Prov 1–24 are transitional between the second and first millennia:

(1) brief subtitles;
(2) use of direct address in prologues in "hearkening" contexts;
(3) exhortative content of prologue;

(4) two or three-sectioned main texts;
(5) dominance of parallelistic couplets, including "organic" usage of units (p. 98).

According to Kitchen, the length of the "prologue" (consisting of 1:7–9:18, by his reckoning) is a first-millennium feature (ibid.). A "transitional" dating supports Solomonic authorship, because "the named author . . . should be regarded as the real author or compiler in default of evidence to the contrary" (p. 95). (Critical scholars would not accept such "default" arguments, which naturally default to the biblical assumptions.)

Kitchen (p. 73) distinguishes on structural grounds "Type A" collections, which have a formal title + main text (e.g., Prov 25–29 = "Solomon II") from "Type B" collections, with a formal title + prologue + main text (e.g., Prov 1–24 = "Solomon I"). He asserts that "Solomon I" is a single, cohesive unit, with Prov 1:1–6 as its title and 1:7–9:18 as its prologue. But one could as well class Prov 1–9 (without 10–24) as Type B (with 1:2–7 its prologue). The headings in 10:1 and 24:23 could just as well begin Type A collections. (Kitchen does not recognize 22:17 as a heading.) Bracketing chapters 1–24 as a single unit ("Solomon I") requires classifying 10:1 and 24:23 as subtitles rather than as titles, but doing so assumes that Prov 1–24 *is* a single unit. Kitchen (p. 80) believes that these short subtitles find their best analogues in the second millennium B.C.E. In fact, however, no other work, early or late, has a subtitle that simply repeats the identification of the author, as 10:1a does, or that identifies a different one, as 24:23 does, in the *middle* of the "main text." (Ptahhotep's long subtitle [ll. 42–50] resumes the initial introduction *prior* to the instruction proper. Shuruppak's long subtitles [ll. 78–85; 147–56] are at the *beginnings* of the second and third sessions of instruction.)

Crucial to Kitchen's typology is the way he defines Prov 1–9 as the prologue to 10–24 alone. Proverbs' "prologue," as Kitchen defines it, is scarcely comparable to the other long prologues that he lists, such as the twenty-four-stich "prologue" of Amennakhte, which is all that exists of the instruction and may have been its entirety, or the narrative settings of Anchsheshonq (ca. eighty written lines) and Ahiqar (at least seventy-eight lines). In any case, Prov 1:7–9:18 is *not* intermediate in length between the second- and third-millennium prologues, but, with 249 verses, is much longer than any of Kitchen's designated prologues.

Kitchen's definitions and categories are tendentious and his argumentation circular. The similarities he notes, when valid, show only that Proverbs belonged to an ancient tradition of Wisdom Literature. And even if we were to accept Kitchen's typology, there is no reason to suppose that the older features could have survived into the early tenth century but no later. In fact, to some degree they demonstrably did so, as shown by the case of Ben Sira, ca. 180 B.C.E., which Kitchen entirely ignores.

The third-century B.C.E. book of Ben Sira has certain features that Kitchen's typology would assign to the third and second millennia: (1) A "medium" length prologue (1:1–30). (2) A titular exclamation (39:12–15). (3) Brief "formal subtitles" (at 31[34]:12 MS B and 30:1 Gk). (4) A "two/three sectioned main text" (I. 1:1–43:33; II. 44:1–50:21; III. 50:22–51:30, according to Skehan and Di Lella 1987: 4–5). (4) A "predominance of poetic and allied parallelism" (a second-millennium feature, according to Kitchen, p. 90). By Kitchen's criteria, Sira too would be transitional to the first millennium, if not earlier!

Translation and Commentary

PART II: PROVERBS 10:1–22:16

◆

"PROVERBS OF SOLOMON"

The title "Proverbs of Solomon" in 10:1a signals the start of a new collection. Though no title indicates the start of a new collection within Part II, the proverbs in 10:1–15:33 differ in character from those in 16:1–22:16, and two subsections, here numbered IIa and IIb, are commonly distinguished. Part IIa has a much higher density of antithetical sayings and places more emphasis on the antithesis between the righteous and the wicked. Most of the proverbs are formulaic assertions of the rewards of virtues and the penalties of vices. Part IIb has a greater variety of topics and gives more prominence to kingship. These distinctions are not evidence that the subsections were once separate collections.

The exact boundary between Parts IIa and IIb is uncertain. Whybray (1994: 89) identifies 15:33 as a pivot verse, for it looks back to sayings about education and the fear of the Lord and forward to a group of Yahweh sayings. Or we might conclude the unit with 15:20, which brackets the subcollection together with 10:1. The present Commentary begins IIb at 16:1, because it begins a thematic cluster of sayings on God's power. Snell (1993: 6) finds three sections in Part II: 10:1–14:25; 14:26–16:15; and 16:16–22:16. However, there is no indication that these ever existed as separate collections. A single collector simply may have varied his choice of topics and proverb-types as he proceeded. The main point is that there need be no sharp boundaries between subsections of a collection. Components of one theme can carry over into a new unit, and pivotal proverbs can look in both directions.

PART IIA: PROVERBS 10:1–15:33

Fourteen of the thirty-two proverbs in chapter 10 are chiastic (A-B-B′-A′), as in the following example. (The examples here are translated mechanically. Chiasm cannot regularly be reflected in translation, because English is more rigid than Hebrew in the location of subject and predicate.)

[A] *m^{e}qor ḥayyim* [B] *pi ṣaddiq*	(predicate-subject)
[B′] *upi r^{e}šaʿim* [A′] *y^{e}kasseh ḥamas* (10:11)	(subject-predicate)
[A] A fount of life [B] is the mouth of the righteous,	(predicate-subject)
[B′] but the mouth of the wicked [A′] covers up lawlessness.	(subject-predicate)

Other proverbs are coordinate (A-B-A′-B′); for example:

[A] *p^{eʿ}ullat ṣaddiq* [B] *l^{e}ḥayyim,*	(subject-predicate)
[A′] *t^{e}buʾat rašaʿ* [B′] *l^{e}ḥaṭṭaʾt* (10:16)	(subject-predicate)
[A] The wage of the righteous man [B] (leads) to life;	(subject-predicate)
[A′] the produce of the wicked [B′] (leads) to sin.	(subject-predicate)

The proverbs of Part IIa often have a very mechanical feel, as if they were being quickly produced from stock topoi and standard antithetical pairs. But variety was not necessarily the author's goal. Most of the sayings are straightforward, sturdy statements of principle. McKane's description of chapter 11 can be applied to most of Part IIa:

> On the whole, these aphorisms are marked by plainness of expression and explicitness of reference, rather than by any desire to exploit the possibilities of language. Although there are figures of speech in 11:3, 5, 22, 21b, 29a, and 30, there are no 'proverbs.' These sentences are elegantly expressed, definitive statements, but they do not employ imagery whose interpretation is left open and to whose representative potential no limits are set. (p. 427)

Most of these proverbs are different formulations of a single principle, the core axiom of the book of Proverbs: It is wise to be righteous and foolish to be wicked. Part IIa says little about the *actions* of the righteous and wicked; rather, most of its proverbs speak in abstractions and deal with the *consequences* of being righteous or wicked (Skladny 1962: 8). Part IIb (16:1–22:16) describes the actions of these types with greater specificity. In contrast, foreign Wisdom authors, with the notable exception of Amenemope, place far less emphasis on describing righteousness and wickedness, and even he does not structure his teachings on this antithesis. The form of antithetical righteous/wicked sayings is distinctively Israelite (Hermisson 1968: 74; Steiert 1990: 85–92), but the underlying ideology is not.

10:1a Proverbs of Solomon

As I trace the book's evolution, a book of proverbs once began here, before chapters 1–9 were prefixed as an introduction. (See Essay 1 in Vol. I, 322–30, and "Dating" in the Introduction to Vol. II ([III.A].) The LXX omits the title in 10:1. By eliminating or obscuring this and other headings (except in 25:1), the translator avoids the implication that anything in the book was written by anyone besides Solomon.

10:1bc A wise son makes his father rejoice,
while a stupid son is his mother's misery.

This proverb nicely introduces Part II. It suggests that the entire collection is to be read as parental instruction (Murphy, p. 72), though many of the proverbs were probably not first composed for that purpose. As Sa'adia observes, both statements in v 1bc apply to both parents. A wise son makes his parents rejoice while a stupid one gives them both grief. Hame'iri explains this kind of complementation as a basic principle (of what we call parallelism) and applies it frequently in his commentary. Similar statements are made in 13:1; 15:20; 17:21; 23:24–25; 28:7; and 29:17. Prov 10:1bc ≈ 15:20. Verses 1–6 form a cluster; see the Comment on v 6.

Westermann (1990: 38–40 [ET 26–28]) considers sayings such as 10:1bc to be exhortations by schoolteachers to their wards, instructing them to please their parents (who are, after all, paying the tuition). But there is no reason to suppose that schoolteachers would urge this virtue more than others—such as fathers—would. As Saʿadia says, this saying has two purposes: to encourage parents to educate their children, and to admonish children to learn wisdom so as to please their parents.

The present proverb (like 23:15 and 27:11a) assumes that the son *wants* to make his parents happy and that his effect on them motivates him to seek wisdom.

stupid son [*ben kᵉsil*]: I usually translate *kᵉsil* as "dolt," as in Vol. I, except in the phrase *ben kᵉsil* (10:1; 17:25; 19:13), where "stupid son" seems more appropriate. In fact, "stupid" is a good rendering of *kᵉsil* because "stupid" refers not to a simple lack of intelligence but to a smug intellectual laziness, a *refusal* to think of the consequences of one's deeds.

10:2 Treasures of wickedness will not avail,
but righteousness saves from death.

The "treasures of wickedness" are riches gained by wicked means (Riyqam). They will not help their possessor in the circumstance described in v 2b and defined again in 11:4a, namely, the day when death threatens.

"Righteousness saves from death" does not promise a "spiritual, eternal life," contrary to Waltke. (Interestingly, the traditional Jewish commentators consistently explained the "death" in question as a natural, precipitate death. Hameʾiri sees an allusion to salvation from "eternal death," but only as a "hidden meaning.") Comparison with 11:4 shows that "death" in 10:2b is equivalent to the "day of wrath" in 11:4a, which is any day when God's anger flares up and he sends widespread (and rather indiscriminate) disaster. Such events are a fact of life: famine, earthquakes, wars, storms, and the like. Ezekiel lists some in 14:13–21. Similarly, Prov 1:27 speaks of the day when disaster comes like a storm. Prov 10:2a and 11:4a assert that the wicked will not be able to buy protection or to bribe their way out of danger. Hence one should not trust in wealth (11:28a). Prov 11:6 declares the same principle.

To be sure, it is a simple fact of life that wealth provides a measure of protection, while poverty leaves one vulnerable to danger (10:15). As 13:8a acknowledges, "The ransom of a man's life is his wealth." But counterbalancing these realities, the sages believe, is the force of justice. Its working is not always evident in the short run, but its certainty is asserted as a point of faith.

10:3 The Lord will not let a righteous man starve,
but he rebuffs the desire[a] of evildoers.

---

[a] *ḥayyat-* (MT *hawwat*).

a righteous man: Lit., "a righteous man's appetite [*nepeš*]" or ". . . soul." *Nepeš* (on which see the Comment on 3:22) means "soul" in the sense of the complex of emotions and thoughts that constitute an individual personality but not in the theological sense of an immortal soul. It frequently designates the appetite and other desires. The hunger in question in this verse is first of all for food but may allude to other needs as well.

In Psalm 37, a Wisdom psalm, the teacher professes the same tenet as the present proverb: "I was young and now am old, but I have never seen a righteous man abandoned, or his descendants begging bread" (v 25). Since the psalmist is well aware that the wicked can prosper (v 7), it is unlikely that he was so naïve or obtuse as to think that the righteous *never* hunger. Rather, the psalmist and the sage are insisting that satisfaction will ultimately come to those worthy of it, before it is too late. Prov 13:25 makes the same point.

Possibly, *hawwat* is equivalent to *ʾawwat*, as, uniquely, in Mic 7:3. More likely, we should emend to *ḥayyat*, "desire," "appetite," "life." See the Textual Notes. Hebrew *ḥayyāh* parallels *nepeš* several times (Job 33:18, 22, 28; Ps 78:50; etc.) and is its near-synonym. In Job 33:20 (// *nepeš*) and 38:39, *ḥayyāh* means "appetite," whereas *hawwāh* never clearly has that meaning. (In Mic 7:3, *hawwāh* could as well mean "deceits.") See the Comment on 11:6.

10:4 The hand of the deceitful causes[a] poverty,[b]
while the hand of the diligent brings wealth.

[a] *ʿōśāh* (MT *ʿōśeh*). [b] *rēʾš* (MT *rāʾš*).

deceitful [*rᵉmiyyah*]: Lit., "deceit," an abstract-for-concrete metonymy, as the parallel with "diligent" (men) shows. The word functions in this way also in 12:24, 27 and 19:15. In Prov 26:28 and Ps 120:3, "deceptive tongue" is unquestionably a *man* of deceitful tongue.

The word *rᵉmiyyah* "deceit" implies "laziness" as well. (In fact, there is a homophonous root *r-m-h* meaning "be slack," "neglectful"; see HALOT 1239b; Klopfenstein *1964*: 313.) I usually translate *rᵉmiyyah* as "deceitful," but the notion of slackness is activated by the parallelism in 10:4; 12:24; and 19:15, and that aspect of the word is primary in 12:24, 27. Deceit and laziness are affiliated in Proverbs' value-system, because the sages tended to conflate intellectual qualities with moral ones. Indeed, Prov 15:19 sets the lazy man (there called "sluggard") in antithesis to the upright. The lazy man is sneaky and deceitful insofar as he is trying to gain labor's fruits without investing the requisite effort.

The present verse states a principle, not an absolute rule. The sages were aware that the deceitful could be rich, at least temporarily, and that the diligent may fail to prosper. Whybray (1990: 60–74) and Murphy (1998: 260–64) emphasize that Proverbs holds a variety of views on wealth and poverty, some of them in tension.

T. Sandoval (*2006*) argues for a basic coherence underlying the proverbs on wealth and poverty. This discourse comprises three subdiscourses, each with its own goals and rhetoric: (1) the "wisdom's virtues discourse," which is not directly concerned with wealth and poverty but rather uses these conditions to inculcate wisdom and its virtues; (2) the "discourse of social justice," which offers observations of the social world and implicitly criticizes social injustices by describing them. In all cases, the metaphorical language and the inclusion of folk proverbs indicate that proverbs implying cause and effect—expressions of the much discussed "deed-consequence nexus" (Vol. I, 91–92)—are not to be interpreted as literal or absolute statements. The book's educational rhetoric "employs the language of wealth and poverty as motivational symbols in meshalim that should be understood more figuratively. . . . Though sometimes employing an act-consequence rhetoric and implicitly promising well being or hardship to the hearer, neither sort of saying, moreover, ought to be reduced to a flat, literat or quasiempirical description of the world of objects. (p. 68, and passim).

Still, there is some inconsistency, due in part to different opinions but mainly to the different purposes of the various sayings. When the sages have moral qualities in view, they teach that virtues—righteousness, wisdom, and diligence—pay off in material benefits, while vices lead to penury. When they are considering wealth and poverty, they do not want to imply that these are invariably a reward or punishment. They seek to inculcate both humility about one's own wealth and compassion for others' poverty.

The LXX adds: "An educated son will be wise, and will use the fool as a servant."

MT's *rā'š 'ōśeh kap-r^e^miyyāh*, lit. "A poor man makes a deceitful hand," does not make good sense. We should vocalize *rā'š 'ōśāh kap-r^e^miyyāh*, lit. "The deceitful hand makes (its possessor) into a poor man," or (better) vocalize *rē'š* "poverty" (thus LXX) and translate as above. The ptcp. is emended to fem. to agree with *kap*. The MT apparently intends it to be read as the predicate of *rā'š*.

The word *ḥārûṣ*, prominent in Proverbs, is invariably translated "diligent," but its exact sense is not certain, and it may alternatively mean "honest." The first meaning is supported by the antithesis with "sluggard" in Prov 13:4 and the distinction between the *ḥārûṣ* and *'āṣ*, "everyone who hastens," in 21:5. The second meaning, "honest" (advocated by Riyqam and Hame'iri [in his first explanation]), is based on the antithesis with *r^e^miyyāh* in 10:4; 12:24, 27, if that is understood as "deceit." BDB translates "sharp" (hence) "diligent," since a blade can be *ḥārûṣ* "sharp" (Isa 41:15; Amos 1:3). There is, however, no inherent semantic relationship between literal sharpness and diligence.

10:5 He who builds his stores in the summer is an astute son;
he who drowses off at harvest is a disgraceful son.

Like 10:1, this proverb is not concerned with the consequences of diligence and laziness for the possessor of these qualities but rather with their effect on one's parents. This is emphasized by the repetition of "son."

Continuing the theme of diligence, this proverb says that during the late-summer harvest (the *qaṣir*), the sensible, prudent son puts food in storage, while the disgraceful one falls asleep. More generally, storing up food in summer is a metaphor for all preparations made in their proper time (Riyqam).

astute [*maśkil*]: The root-meaning of *maśkil* (from *ś-k-l*) is "see" (e.g., Gen 3:6; Prov 21:12), hence "discern," "be astute" or "prudent"; see "Words for Wisdom" §8, I, 36–37. The same verb can mean "successful" (e.g., Deut 29:8; 1 Sam 18:5; Prov 17:8), and it is often difficult to determine which sense is intended.

drowses off [*nirdam*]: *R-d-m* refers to untimely sleep or stupefaction, not to normal sleep at night.

disgraceful: The Hebrew word *mebiš* ("disgraceful" or "disappointing") designates a type of person in Proverbs (10:5; 12:4; 14:35; 17:2; 19:26; in 29:15 it functions as a verb). The root *b-w-š* (G- and H-stems) refers to shame and disgrace, but often indicates the frustration of hopes and expectations as well (e.g., Jer 51:17; Joel 1:11, 12, 17). The participle *mebiš* is always used of a person in a subordinate relation to another: a son to his parents (10:5; 19:26; 29:15), a wife to her husband (12:4), a slave (or royal retainer) to the king (14:35), and a slave to his master (17:2). A *mebiš* causes disappointment to one who had reason to expect better. By using *mebiš* instead of the more specific *ʿaṣel* "lazy," the proverb implies that a lazy son disappoints his parents while a diligent one makes them proud.

10:6 Blessings for the head of the righteous man!
But the mouth of the wicked covers up lawlessness.

Verse 6a modulates the preceding praise of diligence: It is not hard work alone, but also—and more essentially—righteousness that brings blessings. "Blessings" may be the God-given bounty itself, as in Gen 49:26, "blessings . . . will be for the head of Joseph" (Ramaq). (That these are material blessings is shown by v 25.) Alternatively, the blessings may be *words* of praise heaped on the righteous man. In Prov 11:26, "blessing for the head of—" is the antithesis of *cursing*, a form of speech.

In its current position, 10:6b returns to the theme of the "deceitful" of 10:4. Still, the A-line is a poor parallel to the B-line, and it is possible that the latter was erroneously copied from v 11b, where it fits the context better. The sentence in v 6b and in v 11b can be read in two ways:

(1) "Lawlessness covers the mouth of the wicked" (JPSV; cf. Delitzsch)—as if lawlessness were filth smeared on their faces. This itself may be read in two ways: (a) The wicked speak wickedly—a character flaw antithetical to the virtue of righteousness in v 6 and especially v 11, which refers to righteous speech. (b) "The lawlessness that the evildoer commits covers and destroys him" (Riyqam). Though the second interpretation tightens the antithesis between 10:6b and 6a, *kissah* "covers" is not used this way elsewhere. Also, the parallelism with "the mouth of the righteous" in 10:11a indicates that "mouth" is the subject in v 11b and thus in v 6b as well.

(2) "The mouth of the wicked covers up lawlessness." In other words, they speak in such a way as to obscure their *own* crimes, for "to be successful, self-serving speech must be veiled" (Waltke). To be sure, the idea of concealing one's offenses or transgressions does not provide a neat antithesis to 10:6a or 10:11a, but this is what "covering up" means elsewhere in Proverbs, as well as in Ps 32:5 and Job 31:33; see the Comments on 10:11, 12, 18. Sayings dealing with "covering up" different things are 10:6 ("lawlessness"); 10:11 ("lawlessness"); 10:12 ("offenses"); 10:18 ("hatred"); 11:13 ("a matter"); 12:16 ("an insult"); 12:23 ("knowledge"); 17:9 ("an offense"); 26:26 ("his hatred"); 27:5 ("love," using *m^{e}sutteret* "hidden"); and 28:13 ("his offenses").

Verses 1–6 form a cluster. Usually this cluster is delimited as vv 1–5 (e.g., Plöger; Whybray 1994: 94; Heim *2001*: 111–13), because the similar vv 1 and 5 are thought to bracket the intermediate verses. They do have this effect, but then v 6 caps off the bracketed group by summarizing the preceding verses, which speak of blessings. ("Blessings" resonates also in v 7, but the boundaries between units are not impermeable.) Two themes, diligence and God's blessing (and their opposites), are interwoven in vv 1–6, so as to suggest that Yahweh is the ultimate source of material blessings. When read in the light of the subsequent verses, the "wise son" and the "stupid son" of v 1 are to be understood retrospectively as diligent and lazy. In the light of vv 3 and 6, the positive and negative results mentioned in vv 2, 4, and 6 are understood as coming from God.

10:7 The memory of the righteous is for a blessing,
while the name of evildoers will rot.

"Memory" (*zeker*) and "name" (*šem*) are virtually synonymous; both can mean name (cf. Exod 3:15; Hos 12:6) and remembrance (e.g., Isa 26:14; Ps 111:4).

the name of evildoers will rot: Everyone's *corpse* rots, but in the case of the evildoer, even the intangible and potentially enduring name putrefies. "Rot" may connote that his name will stink and be offensive, or that it will decompose and disappear, or both. Not only will people not use his name in blessing, they may even use it in curses and insults, as when we call a traitor a quisling.

The blessing and rotting in Prov 10:7 have two aspects. First, they refer to the way one is remembered, for good or ill. As a saying quoted in the Egyptian tomb autobiography of Menhuhotep says, "The good character of a man is truly valuable for him more than a thousand gifts" (l. 15). To support this assertion, the inscription cites the saying, "A man's goodness is his memorial, while an evil person is forgotten." This is in part quoting Ptahhotep, who said, "Kindness is a man's memorial" (l. 487) and "A good character will be for a memorial" (l. 494 [cf. AEL 1.72]).

Second, the blessing and rotting happen even *before* death. The prosperity that the righteous will enjoy makes them a standard of comparison in blessing others. Jacob blesses his grandsons by citing the comparison others will use in pronouncing blessings of their own: "And he blessed them on that day and said, 'By you Israel will bless, saying, "May God make you as Ephraim and Manasseh" ' " (Gen 48:20). The exact opposite of this blessing is the curse that Jeremiah throws in the faces of his two prophetic opponents. Their fates will be so terrible that "there shall be derived from them a curse, for use by the entire Judean exile in Babylon, as follows: 'May God make you as Zedekiah and as Ahab, whom the king of Babylon roasted in fire' " (Jer 29:22).

10:8 The wise of heart takes in precepts,
while one foolish of lips will be cast aside.

Speech is the predominant theme in 10:8–32, appearing in vv 8b, 10b, 13a, 14b, 18, 19, 20a, 21a, 31, and 32. Verse 8b = v 10b. The present verse says that it is wise—smart—to absorb (the teacher's) commands but self-destructive to blather.

One who is "wise of heart" has the ability to gain wisdom, though he may not yet be fully wise. People who are "wise of heart" in Exod 28:3 are those whom God filled with the "spirit of wisdom"—that is, the faculty of wisdom. Thus endowed, they can *then* receive the substance of wisdom, the knowledge and skills themselves (Exod 31:6).

The two lines of this proverb are not parallel but complement each other. The reward consequent on absorbing wisdom is implicitly the opposite of the fool's downfall. There is an antithesis between absorbing wisdom ("takes in precepts") and emission of folly ("foolish of lips"). Instead of listening, as the truly intelligent person does, the fool babbles and spews out his folly, which makes any learning impossible. As Prov 12:23b puts it, "The heart of dolts cries out, folly!" Qohelet says, "The fool starts out speaking folly and ends up speaking evil inanity. And it is the fool who speaks at length" (10:13–14a). Ptahhotep draws a similar contrast between the wise son who listens and the foolish son who does not. The values of the latter are distorted; consequently, "distortion of speech is his bread" (ll. 575–82; quoted in Vol. I, 118).

cast aside [*yillabeṭ*]: Possibly "be destroyed" or "go astray."

The verb in vv 8b and 10b, *yillābēṭ*, is commonly glossed "will be ruined." The Arabic cognate *labaṭ* means "to throw down to the ground," hence "be thrown down" (Saʿadia). But it is difficult to know exactly the nature of the misfortune. The contexts of this verb in Prov 10:8, 10, and Hos 4:14 do not allow us to be more precise. All the occurrences in RH refer to being buffeted about or expelled in some way, not to being destroyed. *Gen. Rab.* 52.5 applies Prov 10:8b to Lot, playing on different senses of *yillābēṭ*. Rather than refusing to commit incest, Lot *yillābēṭ*—perhaps "went back and forth" or "shilly-shallied." "What did he bring upon himself? That he would *yillābēṭ*. (That is,) he brought on himself *libṭê libbûṭîm* the rejections [wanderings?] of outcasts." This punishment is supposedly manifest in the fact that descendants of an Ammonite or Moabite cannot come into the congregation of the Lord (Deut 23:4). Other occurrences indicate that the core meaning of *l-b-t* is "dislodge," "force one to move," and not just "to trouble"; cf. Mekilta Beshallaḥ, Amaleq, §2.5; Sifré Num. §84; and Yal. Num. §729, where it may mean "were troubled" or "forced to wander," but definitely does not mean "were ruined." Possibly the verb in Prov 10:8b refers to a character flaw, such as "be irresolute." In 1QHoda 4.7, *lbṭ* indicates a failing rather than a punishment: "Speakers of deceit led them astray, and they *lbṭ* without understanding [*ylbṭw bl' bynh*]"; sim. 2.19. In Prov 10:8, either "go astray" (in sin) or "be cast aside" (in punishment) seems possible.

10:9 He who goes in innocence goes in confidence,
while he who makes his ways crooked will be found out.

Though the devious man seeks to conceal his nature, his duplicity will be exposed and he will pay the price. This saying pictures behavior in terms of the MANY PATHS metaphor (discussed in Vol. I, 128–31). There are many ways to traverse the landscape of life. It is best to stride straight ahead, simply and confidently, in accordance with the precept, "Make level the path you travel, and you'll walk steady wherever you go" (4:26). Then you will not stumble (3:23) but will live in confidence, unafraid (1:33). "In confidence" (*beṭaḥ*) refers to both inner confidence and safety from external danger.

Toy, BHS, and others would sharpen the antithesis by emending MT's *yiwwādēaʿ* "be found out" to *yērôaʿ* "suffer," as in 11:15 and 13:20. This is a possible reading, but since the disgrace of discovery would be an adequate threat, the change is not necessary. The verb *nôdaʿ* means "be recognized for what one is" in Sir 12:8 and Jer 28:9.

10:10 He who winks his eye causes grief,
and the one with foolish lips will be cast aside.

winks [*qrṣ*]: Squinting or winking the eye was thought to reveal hostility, but not of a candid sort. It is one of the ticks and gesticulations that betray the scoundrel; see 6:13 and 16:30. Squinting is also a symptom or gesture of scheming (see Sir 27:22). The scoundrel "crafts trouble, constantly foments strife" (Prov 6:14) and "causes grief" (10:10a). Such a man is sly and secretive (10:18). Far better to rebuke someone frankly and honestly. The Holiness Code makes this a religious obligation: "You shall not hate your brother in your heart. (Rather,) you should most definitely reprove your fellow and not bear sin for him" (Lev 19:17).

grief [*ʿaṣṣebet*]: Or "irritation."
cast aside: See the Comment on 10:8.

The MT is maintained in the above translation because it is meaningful, but it is also somewhat awkward and flat. Though the couplet has parts of the body in each line, there is a certain asymmetry. Verse 10a describes how one undesirable type of person affects others, while v 10b speaks of the punishment awaiting a different unworthy type. It is hard to relate the lines or even to explain them as a disjointed proverb. The following alternative, found in the LXX and Syriac, is preferable (though whether it is the original or an improvement on it is hard to determine):

He who winks his eye causes grief,
while he who reproves openly makes peace.

The underlying Hebrew of v 10b was, approximately, *whmwkyḥ yʿśh šlwm*. This balances v 10a nicely. MT's v 10b was very likely a vertical dittography from v 8b.

10:11 The mouth of the righteous is a fount of life,
while the mouth of the wicked covers up lawlessness.

fount of life: A life-preserving power, conferred in this case, as in Prov 13:14; 14:27; 16:22; and Ps 36:10, on those who listen to wise and virtuous speech (Ramaq). The present proverb, like Prov 10:10 and 10:12, speaks about the effect one has on others.

As a sequel to v 10b—if read according to the LXX—v 11a refers more specifically to the wise man's life-giving chastisements (compare "disciplinary reproof is the way to life" in 6:23b; cf. 10:17; 15:10, 31). In harsh contrast to this is the wicked man, who conceals ugly truths, probably about his own behavior, and this concealment (as is implicit in the antithesis to "fount of life") leads to death. MT Prov 10:11b = 10:6b.

10:12 Hatred stirs up conflict,
while love covers up all offenses.

"Hatred" and "love" may be metonymic for the hateful man and the loving man (Ramaq). Juxtaposed with v 11b, v 12 is a nice paradox. Though covering up lawlessness is wrong when the misdeeds are one's own (Prov 10:11b; 28:13; see Job 31:33), covering up offenses against oneself—in the sense of concealing one's anger and passing over offenses in silence, or at least downplaying them—is the way of life (Prov 12:16; 17:9; 19:11). (Ahiqar uses the expression "cover" in a similar way when he admonishes the reader, "Do not cover the word of a king. Let it be a healing for your [hea]rt (or flesh)" (100a [1.1.84]). That is, do not ignore his word. Even if we do not condone another's offense, we need not rake it up and put it on display (10:12), though in private, we should remonstrate with a friend—"Better open rebuke than hidden love" (27:5).

The consequence of covering up offenses, elided in 10:12b, can be deduced from the first line: Covering up consequences lays to rest conflicts like those that will flare up even among friends if one takes all slights to heart and holds grudges.

10:13 On the lips of the discerning man wisdom is found—
and a rod for the back of the senseless.

The B-line is usually translated as a separate statement contrasting with the A-line; for example, "but a rod is for the back of one who lacks sense" (NRSV). A rod, though, does not stand in contrast with wisdom. It is, rather, the form wisdom takes when delivered to the fool, and it is an instrument of *musar* "discipline" (Prov 22:15; 23:13). The lines are not adversative but complementary. The "rod" is an additional thing that is "found" on the lips of the wise and—as the parallel shows—is to be construed metaphorically, as a form of speech. Although it is the part of love to cover up offenses (10:12b), the wise know how to chastise effectively (v 13). Their wisdom, when directed at fools, comes in the form of stinging rebukes—a tongue-lashing. (Compare the idiom, "He will smite the earth with the rod of his lips" [Isa 11:4bα].) The speech of fools too can be a rod (14:3), but it is one that causes pain wrongly. Prov 10:13b ≈ 19:29b; 26:3b.

10:14 Wise men store up knowledge,
and the mouth of the fool, imminent ruin.

The wise absorb knowledge and retain it (Prov 2:1; 7:1); see the Comment on 2:1. (Hebrew *ṣapan* means to "store up" rather than "to conceal"; compare "My heart stored up your word" [Ps 119:11; cf. Job 23:12b]; thus Ramaq.) This is not only a statement but, as Saʿadia notes, an implicit exhortation: A wise man should preserve and guard his wisdom no less zealously than a rich man does his wealth.

Foolish speech harms the speaker (thus too 10:8b). Prov 13:3 and 18:7 (both using *mᵉḥittah* "disaster," "ruination," as here) show that the ruin in view is what the fool suffers rather than what he brings upon others.

The parallelism is asymmetrical, because what the subject stores in each line is of a different type: in v 14a, a virtue, in v 14b, self-inflicted harm. The gapped assumption is that knowledge brings its possessor the opposite of ruination. The "mouth of the fool" in v 14b links up with "the lips of the discerning" in v 13a and together their theme is the harm that speech brings on the fool.

10:15 The rich man's wealth is his fortified city;
the poverty of the poor is their ruin.

This proverb, which interrupts a series of sayings on the righteous/wise and their opposites, was probably evoked by the word *mᵉḥittah* "ruin" in v 14. A *mᵉḥittah* is not the cause or process of ruination but rather the outcome, namely, the rubble left behind. *Mᵉḥittah* can refer to the ruins that a fortress *becomes*, as in "You breached all his walls; you made his fortresses into a *mᵉḥittah*" (Ps 89:41; cf. Prov 10:29). Therefore, the background image in v 15b is of a destitute man living exposed to danger in the ruins of a defeated city. Prov 10:15a ≈ 18:11a.

To explain why a proverb would assert the value of material wealth, Shadal construes v 15a as referring to the rich man's thoughts, namely, his *delusion* that his wealth is his fortress (see 11:4). But the disaster of penury in the B-line is no illusion, and the A-line too should be read as a statement of fact. (Prov 18:11b, however, may speak of a delusive fortress.) Waltke observes that half of the ten occurrences of *hon* "wealth" speak of its value and half warn against trust in it.

This proverb bluntly notes the advantage of wealth (as in 13:8a; 14:20b; 19:4a; 22:7a) and the misery of the poor (as in 14:20a; 15:15a 19:4b, 7). Ben Sira (6:10–12; 13:21–23) offers similar observations, supplemented by cautionary and moralizing remarks. Such proverbs are not merely indifferent remarks on the obvious. When read in the context of a book that inculcates charity toward the poor and insists on God's concern for their well-being (e.g., Prov 14:21, 31; 19:17; 22:22–23; 23:10–11; 28:27; and frequently in Wisdom Literature), this verse underscores the misery of the poor and their need for special consideration. The juxtaposition of 14:20 and 21 makes this clear; similarly in 22:7–9.

H. Washington (1994b: 196–202) shows how contextual clues qualify ethically neutral or problematic sayings and emphasize concern for the poor (cf. Hermisson 1968:182 and Van Leeuwen 1992: 31–33). This is commonly achieved by the addition of ethically evaluative sayings to an (ostensively) neutral observation. The corrective statements may be in proximity to the neutral ones, but not necessarily adjacent. In fact, Washington grants, they may be anywhere in the collection. If so, the interpretive context is the collection (and later the book), and, perhaps, the Wisdom tradition in its entirety. In other words, the people composing and reading such sayings were assumed to be aware that the poor need compassion and charity.

10:16 The wage of the righteous man leads to life;
the produce of the wicked to sin.

leads to, etc.: Lit., "are to life" . . . "to sin." In this disjointed proverb (see pp. 494 ff.), there is an asymmetry between "life"—a reward—and "sin"—a moral fault. When the conceptual gaps in each line are supplied from the other, the proverb says that the wage of the righteous man is conducive to (righteousness and hence to) life and the product of the wicked is conducive to sin (and hence to death).

wage: *Pᵉʿullah* means both "work" and "wage." The latter is a better parallel to *tᵉbuʾah*, "product" or "income." Some understand *ḥaṭṭaʾt* ("sin") to mean "lack," a sense the word supposedly has in 21:4 and Job 14:16 (e.g., Radaq, Clifford). However, nowhere (and certainly not in Job 14:16) does the translation "lack" fit the context better than "sin."

10:17 He who obeys an admonition is a path to life,
while he who ignores reproof leads (others) astray.

This proverb speaks not about the consequences of moral virtues and flaws for their possessors but about the influence of two types of person on others, either by example or by precept. Like breeds like. The person who pays heed to admonitions *is* a path to life, a model for others to follow, while the one who refuses moral correction leads others into a wasteland. Rashi says that the implicit object of "leads astray" is double, "himself and others" (thus too Waltke). But the causative verb *matʿeh* excludes a reflexive notion.

admonition: Or "instruction," "discipline." *Musar* means a rebuke or admonition with a corrective message; see Vol. I, 34–35. The "path to life" (*ʾoraḥ lᵉḥayyim* and variants) is the ethical behavior taught by Wisdom Literature and is an important concept in Egyptian texts as well; see Vol. I, 128–31.

ignores [*ʿozeb*]: Rather than "abandons," the usual translation. Since a fool is unlikely to have embraced reproof, he can better be said to "ignore" it rather than to "abandon" it. See also 27:10.

10:18 Deceitful lips cover up hatred,
while the slanderer is a dolt.

Returning to the theme of wise and foolish speech (10:6b, 10b, 11, and 13a, vv 18–21 teach the ethics of speech (Prov 10:18a ≈ 10:11b). The practical lesson of 10:18a is that you should avoid consorting with devious people, for beneath the veneer of friendly and flattering words they actually despise you (16:23–28). Of an enemy it is said, "He who covers his hatred by deceit—his evil will be exposed in public" (26:26) and "The flatteries of his mouth are smooth, but his heart was set on war" (Ps 55:22a). Prov 27:6 too recognizes that outward demeanor can be deceptive. A friend may wound you, whereas an enemy may bestow kisses in profusion. Jeremiah describes a deceitful man thus: "His [lit. "their"] tongue is a sharpened arrow; he speaks deceit with his mouth. Each one speaks peace to the other, but places an ambush within him" (9:7), that is, he plans an ambush in his heart. On false friendship and honest chastisement, see the Comment on 10:10.

Slander—as opposed to a private reprimand—is just stupid and self-defeating. By calling the fool in question a *kᵉsil* ("dolt"), the proverb emphasizes that it is stupid to go around prattling about others' faults, even without any malicious intent. Malice would have been indicated more precisely had *'ĕwil* or *leṣ* been used for "fool" (see Vol. I, 40–42). On the theme of "covering up," see the references at 10:6.

Deceitful lips [*śiptey šaqer*]: "Deceitful lips," parallel to (lit.) "He who brings forth slander" (*moṣi' dibbah*), is a synecdoche for "a man of deceitful lips" and hence can govern a masculine singular verb, as here. The sentence can also be translated: "He who conceals his hatred has lying lips" (NIV). Waltke construes the verse as enjambed and translates: "As for the one who conceals hatred with lying lips and who publishes an injurious report, he is a fool."

Klopfenstein (*1964*: 321) distinguishes *šeqer* from *kāzāb*, the other common term for lies and deceits. *Šeqer* (used here) refers to the treatment of others and implies perfidy and trickery, the opposite of loyalty. It points to the pragmatic aspect of deceit. *Kāzāb* refers to the truth-value of speech and means untrue, counterfactual. It is unclear if Klopfenstein's distinction is strictly maintained, but it is supported by the antitheses in 11:18; 12:17; 12:22; 14:5. Note that in 14:5, *kᵉzābîm* are what the *ʿēd šeqer* ("lying witness") speaks. *Šeqer* is his moral quality, while his words are *kᵉzābîm*. In 31:30, "comeliness" (i.e., a lovely appearance) is called *šeqer*. Good looks are not contrary to truth, but they are deceptive in their ephemerality.

10:19 In a multitude of words offense will not be absent,
while he who restrains his lips is astute.

Not only is slander stupid (10:18), but any excess of speech will ultimately be harmful (v 19), for the tongue is always on the verge of stumbling and the more one prattles on, the greater the danger of a fall (cf. Hame'iri). A fool characteristically blurts out whatever pops into his head (29:11a). Qohelet is caustic about the folly of garrulousness: "For a dream comes with much busyness, and the fool's voice with much talk" (5:2; cf. 5:6); and "(If) there are many words, they only increase absurdity, and what is the advantage for man?" (6:11). *Pirqey 'Abot* warns, "Whoever increases words brings sin" (1:17). The "Loyalist Instruction" expresses a similar suspicion of loquaciousness: "The man of many words has deceit in his heart" (§12.10). See also Prov 13:3; 21:23; and Sir 20:8.

offense [*pešaʿ*]: *Pešaʿ* originally referred to crimes against persons and property (thus in Prov 28:21, using the verb). In Wisdom Literature, however, it usually signifies affronts to other people, offenses that issue in personal conflicts rather than judicial punishment (10:12; 12:13; 17:9, 19; 19:11; 29:22). (In Prov 28:13, 21 [verb], however, *pešaʿ* refers to transgressions against law and order.

astute: The *maśkil*—the "astute" or "prudent" one—knows how to husband his speech. This recalls the ideal type in Egyptian Wisdom, the *gr* or *gr m'ʿt*. This is usually translated the "silent" or "truly silent" man, but *gr* more precisely means to be reposed and reserved, to be able to hold in one's words until the right time.

Egyptian texts often advise reticence and avoidance of garrulousness. Simply put, "Do not speak words in excess" (Pap. Beatty IV 4.7).

**10:20 The tongue of the righteous man is choice silver;
the heart of the wicked is but a trifle.**

Like fine silver, the words of the righteous are precious and attractive. Since thoughts are internal speech and a preliminary to verbal speech, "heart" can be parallel to "tongue." Hebrew *nibḥar* may mean "choice" or "refined," that is, devoid of impurities (cf. LXX *pepyrōmenos* "purged"). (Bühlmann *1976*: 38–41 discusses the connotations of this metaphor.)

a trifle: People who fancy themselves clever might be stung by the thought that their mind is worth a trifle more than by hearing that it is dangerous and evil.

**10:21 The lips of the righteous man shepherd many,
while fools die because of senselessness.**

This couplet is disjointed, with the effects of the speech of the righteous on others loosely paralleling the consequence of folly to the fools themselves. The link between the lines is the implicit premise that fools in their senselessness refuse to be shepherded and to "graze" on the wisdom of the righteous. Thus they wander mindlessly onto the paths of death.

shepherd [*yirʿu*]: The root *r-ʿ-h*, together with some homophonous roots, has five meanings: (1) "to shepherd," and metaphorically, "to guide"; (2) "to graze"; (3) "to associate with" (a by-form of *r-ʿ-ʿ*); (4) "to desire" (an Aramaism); and (5) "to honor."[264] Here the verb refers to the shepherd's activity, but there is a certain surprise in the A-line, because when "lips" are the subject, we would expect *rʿh* to be intransitive, meaning "graze" or "feed."

The righteous man in view in this verse is a person in authority who does his duty in caring for and nurturing the people through his wisdom and teaching (Van Leeuwen, see Sir 37:22–23; cf. Sir 24:33). Compare Jer 3:15b, *wᵉraʿu ʾetkem deʿah wᵉhaśkeyl*, "And [the new shepherds] shall pasture you in knowledge and insight." Hebrew *rabbim* can mean either "many" or "great (people)," hence "honored" (Hameʾiri).

**10:22 The Lord's blessing is what makes one rich,
and striving adds nothing more thereto.**

This proverb first of all reminds the successful man that his prosperity comes from God rather than his own efforts and talents; thus Hameʾiri, comparing Deut 8:11–18, esp. v 12; cf. Ps 127:1–2. Second, the proverb teaches that human efforts

---

[264] This less-known usage appears in Sir 38:1, where *rʿh* is translated by Greek *tima* "honor." Rabbinic citations of Sir 38:1 rephrase the verb as *kabbēd* "honor." See Segal 1958: 149. Just possibly, a double entendre with this sense is at work in Prov 10:21 and 15:14.

have a limited effect. Work is good and necessary, but *overwork*—strenuous and strained exertions—is wasted effort. The distinction between the former—called "diligence"—and the latter—called "hastening"—is clear in Prov 21:5: "The plans of the diligent surely lead to a surplus, but everyone who hastens is surely headed for want."

thereto: Lit., "with it," namely, God's blessing. Striving can give a man no more than God's blessing provides.

Several sayings in Proverbs praise industry and condemn sloth; see esp. 10:4–5. The present proverb warns against the opposite extreme, namely *ʿeṣeb* "striving," excessive efforts. Prov 14:23a is more sanguine about the value of hard work: "In all striving [*ʿeṣeb*] there is profit." The disagreement is a matter of perspective. Prov 14:23a considers prosperity from the standpoint of human effort, while 10:22a focuses on God's contribution to good fortune. The proverb does not dispute the value of work but only the value of excessive striving, using *ʿeṣeb*, a word with dark connotations of irritation (cf. Prov 15:1) and pain (cf. Gen 3:16).

The proverb does not intend that a man should sit idle, waiting for good fortune to come to him. When one works diligently but reasonably, God carries the efforts to fruition. The way God grants prosperity is by blessing the work of one's hands (e.g., Deut 2:7; 15:10; 28:2; Job 1:10), not by simply bestowing wealth. Ptahhotep expresses this divine-human collaboration nicely, explaining why one should respect a man who has recently become rich:

(181) Property does not come of itself.
(182) It is (the gods') decree for the one they love.
(183) As for abundance—he gathered it for himself.[265]
(184) It is the God who made him capable,[266]
(185) and he guards him while he sleeps. (cf. AEL 1.66)

In contrast, excessive effort is a form of hubris, as if one were presuming to push beyond the blessing that God would grant. Such striving is thus not only imprudent and useless, it is also impious, and he who does this is a sinner (Prov 19:2). His guilt is indelible: "The faithful man has many blessings, but he who hastens to get rich will not go unpunished" (28:20). Scrambling for wealth causes instability: "An inheritance gained in a rush at first—its outcome will not be blessed" (20:21). The suspicion of overwork and excessive striving is expressed in Prov 13:11 (as emended); 19:2; 20:21; 21:5; 23:4; and 28:20, 22. Psalm 127 says the same:

If the Lord does not build a house,
in vain do its builders toil at it.
If the Lord does not watch a city,

[265] Or: "As for his abundance—it was gathered for him of itself." The reference is to the newly rich man.

[266] Or: "rich" (*iqr*). The sentence is ambiguous as to whether the god has made this man rich or given him the capability to become rich without excessive effort. The word *iqr* usually refers to personal excellence or status in Ptahhotep.

uselessly does the watchman keep watch.
You are wasting your time, you who rise early and go to rest late,
and eat the bread of strain,
for he gives sleep to his beloved. (vv 1–2)

Man must build houses and guard cities, but God must be working behind the scenes to bring the effort to completion. God gives "sleep" to his beloved by supplying their needs without excess toil. (Compare the use of this concept in Qoh 2:23–25.) Still, man must do his share in building and guarding, rather than simply waiting for God to do the job.

A "blessing," when bestowed by God, is not a verbal benediction, but rather a favorable attitude toward the recipient along with the benefits (also called "blessings") that flow from this relationship. These benefits come without the need for specific divine interventions. They include fertility, wealth, peace, victory, and more; see C. Mitchell, 1987: 165 and passim.

For Ptahhotep, overwork is tantamount to scheming for wealth: "Live, then, in contentment," he urges. "What [the gods] give comes by itself" (ll. 117–18). Ptahhotep is not counseling inertia; throughout his work he urges an active engagement in the tasks of life. Rather, like Prov 10:22, he believes that certain activities are naturally productive, without excessive effort, just as a tree naturally bears fruit unless other factors inhibit its vitality. In contrast, work that involves scheming, dishonesty, or overexertion violates the simple and natural rhythm of life and manifests distrust of divine goodness.

Amenemope believes that overwork goes against the grain of the divine order and is therefore self-defeating: "If (a man) exerts himself in seeking success, in just a moment he ruins it [or "himself"]" (§18; 20.1–2 [cf. AEL 2.158]; also §21, 22.17–18). Amenemope discourses on this at length in §7 (quoted in the Comment on 23:4–5).

Qohelet teaches that there are two ways to go wrong in labor: by sitting immobile and destroying oneself (4:5) and by toiling obsessively (4:6–8). Both are folly. A man should go about his business in *naḥat*, "inner repose" (4:6). But Qohelet advises this because he has little faith in the efficacy of human efforts in any regard, whereas Proverbs bases its advice on faith in God's beneficence.

Both overwork and laziness offend the proper balance of the world. This offense is close to hubris, both for the sluggard, who smugly assumes that he can fill his needs without investment, and for the one who works excessively, who assumes that he can force a way beyond the natural limits God has set on human achievement. The right measure means harmony with the right order, and this harmony is the key to success. In fact, it *is* success.

adds [*yôsip*]: *Hôsîp* is frequently used without a dir. obj. The implied dir. obj. must be extracted from context, as in Deut 4:2 (anything); Qoh 3:14 (anything); Ezra 10:10 (guilt); and Ps 71:14 (blessings).

ʿimmāh: The preposition *ʿim* does not elsewhere mean "to" (and thus does not allow for the translation "add to it," for which *ʿal* would be required). Here *ʿim* means "in addition to." It points to a further (potential) source of wealth. That is, striving is not an additional source of wealth alongside God's blessing.

The Hebrew of Prov 10:22b allows for the translation, "and he [the Lord] adds no sorrow with it" (NRSV; thus Syr, Tg, McKane; sim. Vul) This would mean that when God blesses a man he does not also make him suffer or work harder. This thought, however, is banal, for a blessing naturally would not include a component of misery.

10:23 Committing vice is like an amusement to a dolt,
but wisdom (is thus) to the man of good sense.

The fool's values, like those of the evildoer, are deviant (on the latter, see Vol. I, 117–18). The dolt (*kᵉsil*), silly-headed and mentally slothful, gives no thought to the consequences of his deeds. He even treats sexual vice as an amusement. (The noun *śᵉḥoq*, lit., "laughter," means "amusement" or "merriment" in, for example, Qoh 2:2 and 10:19.)

Committing vice [*ʿăśot zimmah*]: Lit., "doing vice" or "doing scheming." *Zimmah* usually refers to sexual offenses. Sometimes it means "scheme" (Isa 32:7 [pl.]; Ps 119:150) or "thoughts" (e.g., Job 17:11 [pl.]; Prov 21:27; 24:9), but neither would make much sense here, especially since a *kᵉsil* is unlikely to be capable of the thought or energy necessary for scheming. Misdeeds called *zimmah* include taking bribes (Ps 26:10), lying (Sir 51:5), and murder (Hos 6:9). But it usually refers to commissions of lewdness or fornication (Judg 20:6; Jer 13:27; Ezek 16:27, 43, 58; Job 31:11; etc.; and consistently in Rabbinic Hebrew). To "do" or "commit" (*ʿśh*) *zimmāh* (as here) means to commit an illicit sexual act (Judg 20:6; Ezek 16:43; 22:9; sim. Ezek 23:48).

The proverb is a ratio: Just as lewd behavior is an amusement to a fool, so is wisdom to the perceptive. The latter too have fun, but theirs comes from the delights of wisdom. (See the remarks in Vol. I, 294.) Prov 21:15 similarly describes the opposing values of the antithetical types: "Doing justice is a pleasure [*śimḥah*] to the righteous man but a ruin to evildoers"; sim. 15:21.

10:24 What the wicked man dreads—that will come upon him,
but (the Lord) will grant what the righteous desire.

Reward and punishment not only fit the crime, they fit the criminal. Whatever danger the wicked most fear will strike them. Lady Wisdom warns fools of the hour "when your worst fear arrives like a storm" (1:27a)—and the fears of the wicked are keen and incessant. Ben Sira says that anxiety afflicts the wicked seven times worse than others, and this itself is retribution (40:8). The Wisdom of Solomon explores at length the ways that the wicked are punished by their own anxieties (17:2–16).

yittēn ["he grants"]: The implicit referent of "he" is Yahweh, who was mentioned as a source of blessing in Prov 10:22a. Ehrlich suggests that the antecedent is the aforementioned wicked man, who will be forced to give the good man what he wants. This notion is possible as an expression of the "futility curse," for example, Job 31:8; Deut 28:30–31; Amos 5:11; and Mic 6:15. (Futility curses are discussed by D. Hillers *1964*: 28–29.) Nevertheless, while the evildoer may *lose* what he owns, he does not exactly *give* it to the righteous, for "give" implies volition. Others vocalize the verb Gp *yuttān* "shall be granted." Though the subject is plural, the Gp seems to be indeclinable (see Lev 11:38; Num 26:54; 32:5; 2 Sam 21:6 qeré; 1 Kgs 2:21). Still, the MT can be maintained on the grounds that the granter of rewards to the righteous is self-evidently Yahweh. The same ellipsis appears in Prov 13:21.

10:25 When the gale has passed, the wicked man is no more,
while the righteous man is an enduring foundation.

This gale hits everyone, not just the wicked. Thus it represents whatever crisis or disaster befalls a society, not a punishment for a particular sin. The righteous hold firm, while the wicked are swept away. (Compare the parable in Matt 7:24–27.) The wicked are not securely based or deeply rooted (Ps 1:4; see the Comment on 2:21–22). They walk on through the dark on broken ground, and they stumble (Prov 4:19). They are blown away like chaff before the wind, while the righteous are secure and spared death on the "day of wrath" (11:4). The righteous will inherit the earth (2:21; Ps 37:29), meaning that they will remain alive when the others are eliminated (see the Comment on 2:21). Righteousness is a persistent and steady investment in prosperity. Wickedness, in contrast, is a sudden snatching at immediate desires. Its successes can only be ephemeral.

The themes of 10:24–25—punishment by the object of one's fears (10:24a) and the storm that blows away the wicked (10:25a)—are conjoined also in Lady Wisdom's contemptuous threat to fools, which is probably derived from the present passage: "(I will) mock when your worst fear arrives, when your worst fear arrives like a storm [*šo'ah*], and your downfall comes nigh like a gale [*supah*]" (1:26b–27a).

an enduring foundation [*y*ᵉ*sod ʿolam*]: *ʿolam* refers to the indefinite future and can usually be translated "forever," but sometimes it refers to a lifetime, the entirety of the period relevant to context. An *ʿebed ʿolam* (Deut 15:17) is a "permanent slave," a "slave for life" (HALOT 798a). Samuel will live in the sanctuary *ʿad ʿolam* "permanently" (1 Sam 1:22). The righteous man, the present verse says, will be like a firm building foundation that endures when the storm has blown all else away.

10:26 Like vinegar to the teeth and smoke to the eyes,
so is the sluggard to his senders.

An unreliable messenger is infuriating to his employer. ("Sluggard" is *ʿaṣel*, translated "loafer" in 6:9.) Hence, it is foolish to employ one and dangerous to be one!

A messenger is anyone sent on a task on behalf of another; see the Comment on 22:21. Messengers were indispensable until modern times, for communication at a distance required delegating others to travel and represent one's interests. Much depended on their honesty, diligence, and accuracy.

A messenger may be an envoy or a representative. As well as repeating a message, he (and occasionally she—see S. A. Meier *1991*: 545–47 and 2 Sam 17:17) may have to offer explanations and elaborations or enter into negotiations on his employer's behalf. (We may think of the leeway allowed Abraham's servant in

Gen 24.) A messenger may also be delegated to transport money and receive payments. For a comprehensive discussion of the role of messenger in the ancient Near East, see Meier 1988. A careless or dawdling messenger could cause his patron severe losses, and this proverb warns both the messenger and the employer of this danger.

Proverbs on messengers are 10:26; 13:17; 22:21; 25:13; and 26:6. Proverbs warning against laziness and the lazy are 6:7–10; 10:26; 13:4; 15:19; 19:15, 24; 20:4; 21:25; 22:13; 24:30–34; and 26:13–16.

10:27 The fear of the Lord increases one's days,
while the years of the wicked are cut short.

Verse 27 describes the objective consequences of virtue and vice, v 28 their subjective impact.

The fear of God means having a conscience; see Vol. I, 69–71. This is the foundation of both wisdom and righteousness (1:7; 2:5; 9:10). By keeping a person from transgression, the fear of God saves him from the premature death awaiting the sinner.

increases . . . cut short: Two ways of conceiving of a lifespan are found in the Bible. One way is to think of a normal lifespan that can be increased or reduced. This is about seventy years (Ps 90:10). A person who dies then is said to die "in his time," while one who dies prematurely may be said to perish "not in his time" (see the usage in Qoh 7:17 and Job 22:16). The righteous will live their full lifespan, as God promises in Exod 23:26b: "I will fulfill the number of your days." Another way of viewing a lifespan is to believe that people are allotted a certain number of years (at birth or perhaps later), but their behavior can increase or decrease that number. When Hezekiah was about to die, he prayed and God answered, "I will add fifteen years to your life" (2 Kgs 20:6). In a discussion in *Qohelet Rabba* (III.2 §3), Rabbi Akiva affirms the first concept, while the other rabbis assert the second. Prov 10:27 assumes the second concept, as the expression "increases days" (or "adds days") shows.

10:28 The expectation of the righteous is joy,
while the hope of the wicked will perish.

"The expectation of the righteous is joy" means that they can justifiably expect to receive joy. (Compare similar sentences in 11:23a, 23b; Job 11:20b; and Sir 7:17.) In contrast, the wicked man's hopes will come to naught. This restates the idea of Prov 10:24. Other proverbs on the "hope" of the righteous and wicked are 11:7, 23; 23:18; and 24:14. A rare meaning of *śimḥah* "joy" is "shines"; hence "the expectation of the righteous shines." There may be a deliberate play here on the two senses.

joy [*šimḥāh*]: Tur-Sinai (p. 35) points *śmḥh* as a verb: *śām*ᵉ*ḥāh* (perf.) or *ś*ᵉ*mēḥāh* (stative ptcp./adj.), from a hypothetical root *ś-m-ḥ* "to rise"; hence: "The hope of the righteous rises up." The existence of such a root is doubtful, and in any case "hope rises up" is no clearer. G. R. Driver similarly translates "springs up," which he understands to mean that hope springs eternal in the human breast (1951: 179). But the proverb is contrasting what *happens* to the hopes of the two types of people, not what they feel. More persuasive is the recovery of a homonymous root *ś-m-ḥ* "shine"; see the Comment on 13:9.

10:29 The way of the Lord is a stronghold for the innocent,
but a ruin for those who commit iniquity.

There are two ways to grammatically construe this proverb:

(1) Taking *derek YHWH* "the way of the Lord" as the subject and translating "The way of the Lord is a stronghold for the innocent" (as above). Thus understood, v 29a is structured like 18:10a: *migdal ʿoz šem YHWH*, "The name of the Lord is a fortified tower." (The Hebrew has "fortified tower" in initial position.)

"The way of the Lord" is the behavior God demands of humans (Deut 28:9; etc.). To "go" in it or "keep" it means to obey his commands; see esp. Gen 18:19; Deut 8:6; 11:22, 28; and 26:17. (These phrases are characteristically Deuteronomic; see Weinfeld 1972: 333.) The Lord's "way" is equivalent to his *mišpaṭ* "law" (Jer 5:4–5). God's "way" has a double effect. It protects the righteous and ruins the wicked insofar as their behavior brings them weal or woe. A didactic coda to the book of Hosea says: "For the ways of the Lord are straight. The righteous will walk in them, but transgressors will stumble in them" (14:10b). In Prov 21:15, a similar duality refers to the ways different types of people *perceive* justice; see the Comment.

MT structures the verse as translated above. MT points *ltm* as *lattōm* "for the innocence" and joins *derek* to *YHWH* as an accentual unit. MT's *tōm* "innocence" is an abstract-for-concrete figure for "innocent person" (Radaq), as in 13:6. To the same effect, many commentators revocalize this as *tām* "innocent (man)." The latter is in line with the use of *māʿôz l*-X elsewhere, in which X is a type of person; for example, *māʿôz laddāl*, "a stronghold for the poor" (Isa 25:4; sim. Ps 31:3; Joel 4:16).

(2) Taking *ltm-derek* as a bound phrase, lit. "for the one innocent of way"; hence: "Yahweh is a fortress to the man whose conduct is blameless" (McKane). The image of Yahweh as a fortress is found in Ps 27:1; 37:39; and 46:2. The phrase *tom derek* occurs in Prov 13:6a, which says that *righteousness* protects "him whose way is innocent" [lit. "innocence"]."

ltm drk: This construction is paralleled by the phrase *tōm dᵉrākeykā*, "the innocence of your ways" (Job 4:6); cf. *tᵉmîmê dārek*, lit. "the (people) innocent of way" (Prov 11:20; Ps 119:1). This reading requires repointing *lattōm* as *lᵉtam* or *lᵉtom* (*qameṣ qaṭan*), as in Prov 13:6, and overriding the Masoretic accents. This is possible, but the subject seems awkwardly delayed. We would expect *māʿôz YHWH lᵉtom-derek*, "Yahweh is a fortress to the one innocent of way" (Delitzsch).

10:30 The righteous man will never totter,
while the wicked will not abide in the earth.

This proverb states the consequence of the preceding verse (Ibn Kaspi) and is the equivalent of 10:25. This is a variant of the theme "The upright will abide in the earth, but the wicked shall be cut off from the earth," discussed in the Comment on 2:21–22. This theme means that the righteous will live (long), while the wicked will die (prematurely). This is the main message of Ps 37.

10:31 The mouth of the righteous man produces wisdom,
while the perverse tongue is cut off.

The righteous man's mouth yields wise speech as its fruit. (Verbs from *n-w-b* imply producing fruit; see Zech 9:17; Ps 92:15 [cf. 14], and compare the noun *t^e^nubah* "produce," Deut 32:13; Judg 9:11; etc.) Wise speech is valuable both to the righteous man himself and to those who hear him. The metaphor of fruit of the mouth appears in Prov 12:14; 13:2; and 18:20; cf. Isa 57:19. In the present verse, wisdom is, unusually, a by-product of righteousness rather than its source. See "Disjointed Proverbs" in the Introduction to Vol. II (II.E).

The wicked, in contrast, will be rendered dumb. The mutilation of the organ of speech is the object of a curse in Ps 12:4, "May the Lord cut off [*yakret*] all flattering lips, the tongue that speaks big things." Ahiqar raises a similar warning in similar terms: *y'pk 'l pm 'pk' wynsḥ lšn*[*h*], "God will twist the twisted man's mouth and tear out his tongue" (156 [1.1.156], discussed in Greenfield *1971*). Aramaic *'pk'* "twisted man" (or "twister") is cognate to Hebrew *tahpukot* "distortion" or "perversity," used in Prov 10:31b and 32b, also in connection with "mouth"; see the Comment on 2:12.

In certain Mesopotamian law codes, mutilation of the tongue was the sanction for breaking an agreement (Greenfield *1971*: 54–55). Though Proverbs does not threaten legal sanctions, the notion of judicial punishment may be in the background.

A submerged metaphor of TREES is suggested in both lines. The evildoer's tongue will be *cut off* as a branch might be. This is the opposite of the fate of the healthy tree, which will produce fruit. Other passages using the TREE (or FOLIAGE) metaphor to contrast the fates of two types of people are Prov 11:28b; Jer 17:8; Ps 1:3; 92:13–15; and Amenemope §4 (AEL 2.151–52).

10:32 The lips of the righteous express[a] favor,
and the mouth of the wicked—perversities.

---

[a] *yabbîʿûn* (MT *yēdᵉʿûn*).

This proverb on the organs of speech echoes the previous verse's "mouth" and "perversities." As Clifford observes, *raṣon*, "favor" or "good will," always designates acceptance granted by a higher authority. Hence 10:32a refers to the way a righteous man treats subordinates.

express: The MT reads "*know* favor" in v 32a.

express [*yabbîʿûn*]: The MT has *yēdᵉʿûn*, whose expected meaning is "know," from *y-d-ʿ*. But since lips cannot be said to "know" things, other interpretations have been proposed. M. Scott emends to *yʿrwn* from (*ʿ-r-h* "pour out"). A few MSS have *yrʿwn* "shepherd," "guide" (influenced by 10:21), but this is not an appropriate verb for the dir. obj. *rāṣôn* "(good) will." It is best to emend *ydʿwn* to *ybʿwn* "pour out," "express" (Toy, BHS, and others); compare 15:2, 28. This assumes only a *b/d* confusion, which is feasible in the early square script, and a later m.l. *yod*.

11:1 The Lord loathes deceitful scales,
while he favors an undiminished weight.

The stability of commerce depends on reliable weights and measures, and God demands them (20:10, 23). Indeed, it was he who set the standards (16:11). Nevertheless, they can easily be falsified. By nicking off a bit of the balance stone used in measuring grain, a merchant could inflate the payment he was receiving, and by using a heavier stone when measuring the silver paid, he could make the payment seem less than it was really worth. False weights are prohibited in Lev 19:36 and Deut 25:15. Amos condemns merchants who plan to "reduce the ephah and increase the shekel-weight and make deceitful scales" (8:5). See also Mic 6:11 (which uses vocabulary similar to this proverb) and compare the insistence on honest measures in Amenemope:

(17.18) Do not dislocate the hand-balance or falsify the *qd*-measure (of weight),
(19) or diminish the fractions of the bushel [*dbḥ*].[267]
(20) Do not desire a bushel from (another man's) field,
(21) nor neglect those of the treasury.
(22) The Ape (Thoth) sits next to the scale,
(18.1) with his heart (as) the plumb-bob.
(2) What god is as great as Thoth,
(3) he who invented these things [i.e., the measures], to make them?
(from §16; cf. AEL 2.156–57)

The topic continues in Amenemope §17. See also the Comments on 16:11 and 20:10.

loathes, favors: On the concept of "loathing" or "abomination" (*toʿebah*), see the Comment on 3:32. Its opposite is *raṣon* "favor," that is, what one favors or finds pleasing.

The image in this maxim can be read as a metaphor and its application extended in various directions. Honest measures are a symbol of God's standards in all regards. He demands honesty of humans, and he himself gives just recompense. God demands that rulers and judges make their decisions only on the basis of firm and clear testimony, not merely plausible arguments and analogies (Hame'iri).

---

[267] The *dbḥ* was a measure of volume associated particularly with sacred offerings. Honest weights were essential for cult and taxation (l. 21) as well as commerce.

11:2 When the arrogant come then insult comes (too), while wisdom is with the modest.

Literally, "Arrogance came and insult came . . . ," in the narrative past tense (*wayyiqtol*). The first line rhymes and has an internal rhythm, with two stresses balanced by two stresses: ***BA' zadON wayyaBO' qalON.*** The line has the ring of a popular adage.

R. Alter speaks of "narrative vignettes in which some minimally etched plot enacts the consequences of a moral principle" (1985: 169). He explains that "[t]he predominant use of narrative development is to articulate the perception of orderly process: certain actions, whether because of our psychological constitution or because of the system of retributive morality God has built into reality, will inevitably lead to certain consequences, as surely as second verse follows first" (p. 162). Such proverbs encapsulate truths by narrating little anecdotes (see J. A. Cook 2005: 130–31). Clifford (commenting on this verse) calls them "mini-narratives."

the arrogant [*zadon*]: Lit., "arrogance." In view of the parallel with "the modest" (plural), *zadon* is probably an abstract-for-concrete metonymy referring to the arrogant *person*. To the same effect, several medieval commentators, including Ramaq, Radaq, and Hame'iri, explain *zadon* as elliptical for *'iš zadon*, "arrogant man." This interpretation is supported by Prov 22:10a, which is the obverse of the present saying: "Banish the impudent and conflict will depart." Construed thus, the proverb warns against associating with the arrogant, for when they come, they bring along their contempt for others—as an uninvited guest, as it were. The modest, in contrast, bring with them wisdom for the benefit of all.

Alternatively, *zadon* can refer to the *attitude* of arrogance, condemning it in terms similar to 15:25; 16:18; and 29:23. Arrogance brings with it insult, both for other people and for the arrogant themselves. They may think themselves wise and clever, but ignominy awaits them. It is the modest who possess real wisdom, and (as the contrast with the A-line indicates) they will enjoy the very blessing they do not demand: honor.

then insult comes (too) [*wayyābō' qālōn*]: The *wayyiqtōl* form in BH overwhelmingly represents a past-tense action or event in a temporal sequence or (more rarely) a pluperfect tense (called "epexegetical" in IBHS §33.2.2a). The grammars traditionally allow for a "gnomic" or "gnomic aorist" *wayyiqtōl* expressing a general truth, a concept borrowed from Greek grammar. Many of the examples of "gnomic" *wayyiqtōl*, most of which come from Proverbs, are ambiguous. Those cited in IBHS §33.3.1b ##12–14 are ambiguous: Isa 40:24 can mean, "No sooner does he blow on them *than they have withered* [*wayyibāšû*]"; Job 7:9 can mean, "No sooner does a cloud waste away *than it has gone* [*wayyēlak*]; and Prov 11:2 can be translated as above. After a *qātal*, the *wayyiqtōl* implies immediate succession. There do seem to be cases with present tense indication (GBH §118p, q, r), though the pointing in such cases is sometimes suspect. The nature of the (possibly) gnomic *wayyiqtōl* has yet to be properly examined, but rather than blending *wayyiqtōl* into the other verb forms, I have tried to preserve something of its narrative and past-tense implications, so as to allow recognition of little anecdotes, as discussed above.

11:3 The innocence of the upright guides them,
while the corruption of the treacherous destroys them.

Verses 3–11 are built on the contrasting fates of the righteous and the unrighteous.

corruption [*selep*]: Words from the root *s-l-p* imply distortion and twisting of words and deeds. They can refer to a flaw in words, deeds, or character (Exod 23:8; Deut 16:19; Job 12:19; Prov 11:3; 19:3). In 21:12 and 22:12, *s-l-p* refers to undermining or ruin. In the present verse *selep* clearly means moral crookedness, because its consequence is destruction.

11:4 Wealth will not avail in the day of wrath,
while righteousness saves from death.

This is equivalent to 10:2; see the Comment there. The day of wrath is not a single Judgment Day; it is any catastrophe that threatens everyone. Only righteousness, not wealth, can extricate one from this danger. Ezekiel puts it explicitly: "Their silver and gold will not be able to save them in the day of the Lord's wrath" (7:19a). The next sentence shows in what way wealth *might* but *will not* save the wealthy: "Their appetite they will not satisfy and their stomachs they will not fill" (7:19b). Prov 11:4, as Van Leeuwen notes, draws on the prophetic concept of the "day of the Lord," when Yahweh will judge and punish the nations (Isa 13:9, 13; Ezek 7:19; Zeph 1:15, 18), though in Proverbs the end of an individual life is in view.

11:5 The innocent man's righteousness makes his way straight,
while the wicked man falls in his wickedness.

This verse continues the theme of the fates of righteous and wicked people. A straight way can signify honesty in behavior (e.g., Prov 4:11; 21:2; Jer 31:9) or success and security in life—"smooth-going," we might say (e.g., Prov 3:6; Ezr 8:21). The point of Prov 11:5a is not (contrary to the Comment in Vol. I, 129) that righteousness makes one honest (that would be a tautology), but that it makes one's life secure and relatively easy (thus Ehrlich).

falls in his wickedness [*b^eriš^cato yippol*]: This can mean "*because* of his wickedness" or "*into* his wickedness," the latter picturing wickedness as a pit into which the evildoer stumbles (as in "He who digs a pit will fall in it," 26:27a). We may picture the wicked man's path as full of holes into which he may stumble (thus Ramaq). Kselman (*2000*: 546) hears a pun, with *b^eriš^cato* "in his wickedness" suggesting *b^erišto* "in his net." The association with "net" is reinforced by the words "will fall" (v 5b) and "be trapped" (v 6b), which occur elsewhere in association with snaring, for example, Ps 35:7–8.

11:6 The righteousness of the upright will save them,
while the treacherous will be trapped by deceit[a].

[a] *ûb^ehawwātām* (MT *ûb^ehawwat*).

This reformulates the preceding two proverbs as well as 10:2. The word for evil, *hawwah*, is usually translated "disaster," but, judging from v 5, here it refers to the evildoer's own behavior rather than a disaster.

The principle of 11:6b, reiterated throughout the book, is nicely encapsulated in 5:22: "The evildoer's iniquities will trap him; in the cords of his sin he'll be seized" (see the Comment there).

by deceit: That is, by their own deceit.

MT's *ûbᵉhawwat bōgᵉdîm yillākēdû* (v 6b) must be translated, "and in the deceit of the treacherous they [namely, the "honest"] will be trapped," which is an impossible notion in Proverbs and flatly contradicts v 6a. We should emend to *ûbᵉhawwātām* "in their deceit/disaster" (haplog. with the similar-looking *bet* of *bgdym*) or possibly revocalize *ûbᵉhawwōt* "in deceits/disasters." (Hame'iri, without actually emending, says that the MT is equivalent to one of these readings. The strong disjunctive *rᵉbiaʿ mugraš* on *wbhwt* separates it from the next word, in defiance of the construct state of *ûbᵉhawwat*.) "In their deceit" is a better parallel to *ṣidqat yᵉšārîm*.

hawwāh: The lexicons differ on how many lexemes with this spelling there are and how to group their senses. These include (1) "Disaster" (19:13; Job 6:2 qeré; 30:13) (thus LXX) or "evil" (thus Syr). (2) "Desire"; but see the Comment on 10:3. (3) "Word" (Job 6:30?), cognate to Ugaritic *hwt* and Akkadian *awātu*. Kselman (2002: 545–46) sees a deliberate ambiguity: The treacherous will be ensnared by both their greedy desire and their malicious words. (4) "Deceit." Nowhere do behaviors called *hawwôt* seem to be violent deeds or robbery. Though the deceit may be verbalized (Ps 38:13; Prov 17:4; Job 6:30), it is not necessarily so. In Ps 5:10 and 55:12, for example, *hawwôt* are malicious thoughts.

11:7 When the wicked man dies, hope perishes,
and the expectation of strength perishes.

Prov 10:28b uses similar wording to declare that the hopes of the wicked will come to naught, but the present verse refers particularly to the loss of hope at death. "Hope" here is not the wicked man's feeling of hope, which inevitably disappears when one dies, but rather the object of hope, the thing hoped for.

The object of hope is more closely defined in the parallel line as "the expectation of strength" (*toḥelet ʾonim*). Like other words for strength, *ʾon* (or *ʾonim*) can refer specifically to wealth (Hos 12:9), which is how McKane and Murphy understand it here. The word can also connote sexual virility (e.g., Gen 49:3; Deut 21:17; Ps 78:51 [pl.]), hence progeny. Rashi glosses it here as "sons." This makes sense, because no other form of strength—certainly not wealth—may reasonably be expected to continue beyond death. The threat implied in this proverb, then, is the loss of family continuity and the sort of permanence that such continuity was thought to provide beyond death. The repetition of the word *ʾbd* "perish" underscores the certainty of the grim event.

The text in v 7a seems overloaded, with five words against the three in v 7b. The word *ʾādām* is unnecessary; the repetition of the verb *ʾbd* "perish" seems awkward to some; and the synonymous parallelism is unusual in this unit. Clifford deletes *rāšāʿ* and surmises that the original was "when a man dies, hope is lost," and that *rāšāʿ* was added later by a pious scribe. (The absence of this word from two medieval MSS is poor evidence for an original reading, even if it happens to coincide with the original.) But it is unlikely that the editor of Part IIa (whose orthodox piety is evident in the numerous "righteousness"-proverbs and proverbs about Yahweh) would include a deliberately pessimistic, skeptical proverb such as results from Clifford's emendation. BHS produces a new proverb: "When the righteous dies, hope is not lost, but the hope of fools is lost." Most likely, *'ādām* should be deleted (thus following Gemser and others). This does not affect the translation.

11:8 The righteous man is extricated from trouble,
and the wicked comes into his place.

The theme of vv 4–6—the escape of the righteous and the ensnarement of the wicked—is resumed, but now the theme is broadened from fatal dangers to trouble generally. This idea is formulated also in Prov 21:18. The present proverb concedes that the righteous man can, temporarily, find himself in danger. The traditional commentators often adduce Haman (Esth 7:10; 9:24–25) as a satisfying instance of this doctrine. The three words in the A-line are linked by the alliteration of the sibilant /ṣ/: *ṣaddiq miṣṣarah neḥĕlāṣ*.

This proverb is an anecdote illustrating an expected sequence of events, a "narrative in a nutshell" (Van Leeuwen). We should paraphrase, "No sooner had the righteous man been extricated from trouble, than the wicked came into his place." See the Comment on 11:2.

11:9 By (his) mouth the impious man harms his fellow,
but the righteous are extricated by knowledge.

The theme of the "extrication" (*ḥ-l-ṣ*) of the righteous (vv 4–6, 8) continues. The B-line, rather than being an antithetical restatement of the A-line, limits its scope by mitigating the danger implied. To be sure, it concedes, the impious man harms others by his words; yet the righteous can save themselves from this danger. Given the book's reiteration of the dangers presented by the wicked, it was important to remind the reader that these dangers are avoidable. This happens, for example, in 2:12, 16; 14:3; and 20:22.

The proverb does not say that God intervenes to deliver the righteous miraculously but that they are protected by "knowledge" (*da'at*), which is to say, their wisdom. The proverb assumes that the righteous, being wise, have the mental resources to get *themselves* out of trouble; see Vol. I, 102.

11:10 When it goes well with the righteous, the city rejoices,
and when the wicked perish, there is jubilation.

The community rejoices when the righteous flourish and the wicked die—events spoken of in vv 4–9; cf. 29:2. This idea provides another motive for moral behavior: the feelings of one's peers. Though the wicked man may imagine that he has comrades (1:11–14), he is really a lonely figure, deprived of fellowship and sympathy.

**11:11 By the blessing of the upright, a city is exalted,
but it is ruined by the mouth of the wicked.**

As placed, this proverb gives the reason for the preceding (Ibn Kaspi [MS B]). Syntactically identical with v 10a, v 11a might mean that when the upright *receive* good fortune ("blessings"), their city is consequently exalted and prospers with them. Riyqam thinks of civic benefactions: "When (the upright) are rich, the poor will grow richer. (For the upright) will build the walls of the city and erect its doors from their wealth." Radaq says that all the inhabitants of the city will be blessed for the sake of the righteous. (This principle is presumed in Gen 18:22–33. It is rejected, at least for a wicked land, in Ezek 14:12–20.) Radaq's is a valid first reading and perhaps the original meaning of the line, if it was once a monostichic saying. But the B-line, which is syntactically parallel to the A-line (with the elision of the subject), speaks of the destructive power of the *speech* of the wicked. Thus on second reading the A-line means that the righteous are able to pronounce effective blessing on their town.

The two kinds of speech work their effect differently. The righteous invoke a blessing, a wish or prayer for prosperity, and it comes to pass. The wicked slander, deceive, and abuse others, and this engenders conflict, uncertainty, and oppression all around them.

**11:12 The senseless man insults his fellow,
while the man of good sense keeps silent.**

This saying continues the theme of injurious speech and comments on a particular type: insult. The man of good sense is not always silent. The type of speech he avoids is defined by the parallel "insults his fellow." In a circumstance in which one person might hold another in contempt, the fool lets his scorn spill out, while the sensible person, who may have the same feelings, holds his peace. The contempt envisioned may even be justifiable, since otherwise the sensible man would not feel this way to start with. As an example of enduring insults in silence, Saʿadia cites the example of David's restraint before Shimei's curses (2 Sam 16:10–12), but he stipulates that when the affronts concern matters of religion, one must respond, as David did to Goliath (1 Sam 17:42–45).

**11:13 The slanderer reveals secrets,
while the man of loyal spirit covers up a matter.**

A further maxim in praise of silence; see the discussion of "covering up" in the Comments on 10:6, 11, 18, and esp. 10:12b ("love covers up all offenses"). The present verse teaches that a loyal friend covers up another's *dabar* ("matter," "word"), which is defined by the parallel as a secret. Revealing secrets, even of actual offenses, is tantamount to slander, which Lev 19:16 forbids. Prov 11:13a ≈ 20:19a.

11:14 Without strategy a people will fall,
while there is victory in a multitude of counselors.

Kings and their counselors should conduct war by *taḥbulot* "strategy" (20:18; 24:6). Comparison with 24:6a ("For you should make war by strategy") suggests that "fall" (*yippol*) in 11:14a alludes to defeat in battle. *Taḥbulot*—"strategy" or "guidance" (see Vol. I, 37)—is one of the talents that the Prologue promises the students of Proverbs (1:5). "People" (*ʿam*) can refer specifically to the army (Riyqam; cf. Judg 20:10; 1 Sam 14:17; 2 Sam 10:10; 2 Kgs 13:7). The author of this proverb, which expresses such esteem for the value of royal advisors (similarly 15:22; 20:28; 24:6), presumably belonged to their ranks.

victory [*t*ᵉ*šuʿah*]: The verb *hošiaʿ* and the cognate nouns *t*ᵉ*šuʿah* and *y*ᵉ*šuʿah* (usually translated "save," "salvation") almost always refer to giving someone victory in a struggle. (Ps 36:7, in which a struggle is not in view, is one of the rare exceptions.) *T*ᵉ*šuʿah* can also designate the condition that arises from this success. It does not mean just to extricate from trouble. (Thus the verb for saving someone from drowning would be *hiṣṣil*, not *hošiaʿ*.) God or his representative is almost always the subject. (See further TDOT 6.441–63).

11:15 "He shall be severely[a] harmed, because he has given surety for a stranger!"
But he who hates agreements will feel secure.

---

[a] *rōaʿ* (MT *raʿ*).

Avoid becoming entangled in commercial obligations. The A-line quotes what someone, perhaps a judge, exclaims about the man who gave surety for a stranger. The device of quotation makes the reader a spectator to a little scene, whose meaning is clarified in the B-line. Prov 20:16 does the same: " 'Take his garment, because he has given surety for a stranger! And seize it, because (he has given surety) for aliens.' " The quotation dramatically evokes the straits the guarantor would find himself in. With regard to the practice of giving surety, see Vol. I, 214–16 and the Comments on 6:1–5.

agreements [*toq*ᵉʿ*im*]: Lit., "clasping [of hands]," alluding to surety contracts of the sort mentioned in the A-line.

severely harmed: The MT pointing *raʿ* ("bad man" = LXX) calls for the translation, "The bad man shall be harmed." But the harm in this case comes not to men who are bad so much as imprudent. Hence vocalize *rōaʿ*, inf. abs.

will feel secure [*boteaḥ*]: Or, "is confident." The verb *bataḥ* does not mean to "*be* safe" (as implied by NRSV's paraphrase, "but there is safety in refusing to do so"), but instead designates an attitude—"trust (in)"—or (as here) a feeling—"feel confidence." Clear examples of the latter nuance are Isa 12:2; Prov 28:1; Job 6:20; and 11:18. The reward promised in Prov 11:15b is a psychological one. One who avoids giving surety will enjoy a sense of security and confidence. He need not fear the creditor.

11:16 A gracious woman holds honor,
and diligent men[a] hold wealth.

[a] *weḥārûṣîm* (MT *weʿārîṣîm*).

gracious: The primary meaning of *ḥen* is "attraction"; see the Comment on 3:4. Attraction takes many forms, one of them physical beauty. (A garland [1:9] or a stone [17:8] can have *ḥen* just by virtue of its appearance, and *ḥen* can be coupled with *yopi* "beauty" in describing ephemeral attractions [31:30].) But a more significant aspect of *ḥen* is the favor and good regard, divine and human, which wisdom and piety evoke (3:4). A woman who possesses this deeper grace will have honor (31:30).

holds: Hebrew *tamak* connotes laying hold of something and grasping it tightly. The same phrase is used in 29:23b, "he whose spirit is humble will hold honor." The verb in both 11:16a and 11:16b implies that not only do the two types gain their respective rewards, they *keep* them.

Lady Wisdom possesses "wealth and honor" (8:18), and she holds them together in her left hand (3:16). "Honor" and "wealth" are a prominent combination-pair; for example, 1 Kgs 3:13; Qoh 6:2; Esth 1:4. They always appear in the order "wealth"/"honor," (13×) except here and in Esth 5:11.

The crux of the verse lies in v 16b. MT reads, "and violent [or "powerful"] men [w*eʿariṣim*] hold wealth." This seems to promise wealth to the violent, which is something no sage would do. To be sure, an *ʿariṣ* can prosper (Ps 37:35), but only momentarily (Ps 37:36), and this proverb does not make the latter stipulation. Various options are available, none of them entirely satisfactory:

(1) Reading the verse as an observation of fact: A gracious woman holds fast to honor, while brutal men hold fast to wealth. However, there would be no reason for the first statement to be limited to women, since the verse is contrasting kinds of behavior (holding fast to honor, holding fast to wealth), not types of woman. Moreover, the comparison would not put the gracious woman in a good light. It would imply that she is greedy for honor, which is not a quality of graciousness.

(2) Understanding *ḥen* as physical attraction, without regard to inner grace. When said of a woman, *ḥen* usually means "beauty" (31:30; Nah 3:4; and esp. Sir 9:8; noted by Van Leeuwen), and *kabod* can mean "wealth" as well as "honor." The proverb is then a shrewd (and cynical) observation that women can use beauty to get wealth, and men can use violence. But while the sages recognized that the unworthy *can* get rich (Prov 10:2; 11:4; 15:16; 21:6), they would not baldly state that they do receive this reward. Nor would they affirm that beauty, apart from intellectual and spiritual gifts, necessarily brings wealth, especially when this is called *kabod*, which would mean honorable wealth.

(3) Emending *ʿryṣym* "brutal" to *ḥrwṣym* "diligent." The verse then promises the expected rewards: honor for gracious women, wealth for diligent men. The

specific reward for diligence in males is wealth; for women it is honor, not wealth, because women are not usually considered to be possessors of property. (What they earn accrues to their husbands.) The LXX has *andreioi* ("vigorous," "virtuous") here, probably representing *ḥrwṣym*, though the LXX translator or a Hebrew scribe might be translating by using a word that refers to a virtue in order to improve the moral tone. Still, this reading makes the best sense, and MT's *ʿariṣim* is not meaningful.

11:17 A kind man rewards himself,
while the cruel one troubles his flesh.

The kind man creates his own reward (lit. "requites himself"), whereas the cruel man hurts "his (own) flesh" (*šeʾero*)—that is, himself, his very being. "Flesh" can also signify a blood relative, and the B-line can mean that the cruel man afflicts (*ʿoker*) his family. Supporting the equivalence of "flesh" and "family" is the idiom *ʿoker beyto*, "troubles his house"—that is, his family—in 11:29 and 15:27. The double meaning is likely intended: the cruel man causes distress to his family *and* himself.

troubles: The verb *ʿkr* means to cause emotional discomfort or to harm morale. It refers to the exacerbation of emotional distress in Ps 39:3. "Harm morale" seems to be its sense in Josh 6:18; 7:25; and 1 Sam 14:29. The variety of glosses proposed by the lexicons (including "bring disaster," "throw into confusion, ruin," "make taboo"; see HALOT) is excessive. In Josh 6:18, it is not the verb *ʿkr* that indicates making others taboo or banned, but rather the verb *ḥrm* "ban," as well as the narrated events. Jephthah's daughter has (accidentally) caused him emotional devastation (Judg 11:35), not made him taboo. Ahab and Elijah accuse each other of having harmed the public morale (1 Kgs 18:17–18). Ehrlich says that *ʿkr* is used only of trouble caused by someone expected to be friendly, but (given the last-mentioned verse) it is unclear if this belongs to the word's denotation.

11:18 The wicked man produces a deceitful wage,
while he who sows righteousness has a reliable reward.
19 So does righteousness go to life,
and he who pursues evil (goes) to death.

The first couplet of this quatrain says that what the wicked man gains by deceit deceives *him*, because it is unsatisfying and transitory. The image of sowing righteousness (as in Hos 10:12) suggests that performance of righteous deeds is an investment in the future—a secure one, at that.

The second couplet, v 19, means, lit., "So righteousness (is) to life, and he who pursues evil (is) to his death." The verse starts with an adverb of ratio, *ken* ("so," "in this way"), as in Prov 1:19; 6:29; 24:14; 26:19; and 30:20. Since *ken* cannot be deleted (the line would be too short), its presence shows v 19 was written by the editor to elaborate on v 18. The chiastic ratio that resulted magnifies the importance of the (true) "reward" and (deceitful) "wages" of v 18: they are no less than life and death. This is the thought of 10:16 as well.

righteousness: The parallel suggests that this is a metonymy for "righteous man."

kēn "so," "thus": LXX and Syr have *bn* "son" = Heb *bēn*. A "son of righteousness" would mean "a righteous man," similar to *ben ʿawlāh* "son of iniquity" = "an iniquitous man" (Ps 89:23). However, *ben ṣᵉdāqāh* would be unique. Other emendations are *tōkēn* (Ehrlich, claiming it means "equivalent to") and *tikkōn* "firm," "established" (Murphy and Clifford). These do not improve the sense. The verses that start with *kēn*, cited above, indicate that this is a deliberate linking device, a way of making one proverb interpret the preceding.

he who pursues evil—(goes) to death [*ûmᵉraddēp rāʿāh lᵉmôtô*]: This construction, with *l* + noun as the predicate of a nominal clause indicating goal or consequence, appears in 17:21 and Job 27:14.

11:20 The Lord loathes the crooked of heart,
while he favors those whose way is innocent.

The book of Proverbs, like Egyptian Wisdom, often measures actions and qualities against the standard of what God hates and loves. Conformity to this standard is motivated not only by expectation of reward and punishment, but also by love of God and the desire to please him. On the concept of "loathing" (*toʿebah*), see the Comment on 3:32.

11:21 Hand to hand: the evil man will not go unpunished,
while the descendants of the righteous will escape.

Hand to hand: This idiom (also in 16:5) underscores an asseveration, as if to say "You can be certain" or "You have my word for it." The idiom probably reflects the custom of clasping hands to seal an agreement, as in 11:15. The intensity of the asseveration here, as in 11:19, suggests that the author is insisting on an outcome that visible reality would often contradict. The assertion is based not on observation but on beliefs about God's nature (Van Leeuwen).

not go unpunished [*loʾ yinnaqeh*]: Lit., "not be cleansed" or "not be held innocent." This phrase probably originates as a legal usage (compare Exod 21:19, 28; Num 5:31), where it means to avoid judicial punishment; sim. Jer 30:11; 46:25) (S. Yonah 2008). In Wisdom Literature, the usage is broadened to include any sort of punishment (Prov 6:29; 11:21; 16:5; 17:5; 19:5, 9; 28:20; cf. Sir 9:17; 11:1). Even if the evildoer avoids detection or judicial punishment, and even if retribution is delayed, guilt will cling to him and, some time in the future, God will make him pay for his sins. Sins that are said to be indelible include crimes of commission (e.g., Prov 6:29; 19:5, 9; Exod 20:7; Jer 25:29) and repugnant attitudes, such as arrogance (Prov 16:5), malicious pleasure in another's suffering (17:5), and greed (28:20).

will escape: The danger from which the descendants (lit. "seed") of the righteous will "escape" is a general disaster of the sort envisioned in 10:2; 11:4, 6. (*Nimlaṭ* always means escape from a danger, stated or implicit, and not merely "be safe" [contrary to JPSV].)

11:22 A gold ring in a pig's snout:
a beautiful woman lacking good sense.

Two images, each with three components, are juxtaposed. The second one is to be seen in the (lurid) light of the first. There are two ways of parsing the relationship between the metaphor (v 22a) and the referent (v 22b):

(1) a pig with a gold ring in his nose = a woman lacking discretion

By this interpretation, a certain reality is equated with an image, and there is no further breakdown of components. It is as if the proverb read, "A pig with a gold ring in its snout [is like] a beautiful woman lacking good sense." This is the way the proverb is usually read, and, though it is plausible, it does run contrary to the structure of the comparison.

(2)	ring	=	a woman
	golden	=	beautiful
	location in pig's nose	=	lack of discretion
	pig	=	husband

As the images line up, the pig is within the component "in a pig's nose" and is not to be equated with the woman. The pig has an second function. If the ring is the woman, he is the one wearing it, just as in Prov 12:4a, which describes the desirable circumstance, "The woman of strength is her husband's diadem."[268] If, however, one's wife is empty-headed, he may think he has a trophy-bride, but he is really strutting about with a preposterous creature. He makes himself preposterous and piggish.

K. Heim (2008) reviews the interpretation of this verse and presents a detailed argument for the following metaphorical equations (translating according to RSV): (1) a ring = a woman; (2) golden = beautiful; (3) "in the snout of" = "who has turned"; and (4) pig = "from discretion." The ground metaphor is WIFE = (HUSBAND'S) ADORNMMENT. Hence the pig also represents the husband of an indiscrete wife, who leads him by the nose. I tend to agree with this analysis, except that "in the snout of" does not represent "who has turned," that is, lacks. Rather, lack of discretion must first be identified with location in a *pig's* nose, because location in the nose does not by itself have a negative implication. Then a second function of "pig" in the verse is to call to mind the husband who has chosen an indiscrete woman.

The proverb not only admonishes women to be prudent but also warns young men to choose a wife who has good sense (thus Whybray 1995 ad loc.; Clifford; Heim, ibid.). Heim (ibid.) observes that the book of Proverbs often warns young men against women with vices (e.g., 12:4b; 14:1b; 19:13; 21:9; 21:19; 22:14; 25:24; 27:15–16; 31:3). The present proverb warns men "not to make fools of themselves by marrying a socially inept woman simply because of her good looks" (ibid.). This observation is in fact true by both of the above interpretations. Whether the foolish woman is identified with the pig (interpretation 1) or the ring (interpretation 2), the saying warns men not to take such a wife.

---

[268] Likewise grandchildren adorn grandfathers and fathers adorn sons; see Prov 17:6 and the Comment on 12:4.

By neither of the two interpretations does the proverb denigrate beauty. In the Bible, beauty is sometimes thought to be a mark of God's favor (1 Sam 16:12, 18), but unless matched by an inner moral grace, it is useless. Rather than moralizing about the frailty of beauty or the disgrace of folly, this proverb uses ridicule to lance vanity. It shows the beautiful fool to be grotesque (whether she is identified with a pig or a ring in a pig's nose). This feature at once ridicules women who flaunt their looks and men who boast of their wives' glamour.

As Kugel nicely notes, the conjoining of the woman's beauty and the folly does not make them equals: "On the contrary, the woman's physical beauty ends up being submerged and overwhelmed by something much bigger, a dirty, sloppy, wallowing: it becomes a small detail, an insignificant little glint of gold quite lost in or dwarfed by her piggish behavior" (1997: 13).

The sound effects in this saying (described by McCreesh 1991: 108–109) are striking: *NEzem zaHAB* ***b**ᵉ***ʾAP** *ḥăZIR, ʾiššAH yaPAH wᵉSARat ṭaʿam*. The "gold ring"—*NEzem zaHAB*—is joined to the "nose of the pig"—***b**ᵉ***ʾAP** *ḥăZIR*—*by the /z/ and the labials /b/ and /p/. In the second line, the repeated /a/ sound has the effect of an internal rhyme.*

lacking good sense [*sārat ṭāʿam*]: The Hebrew phrase might seem to mean, lit., "who has departed from good sense" (sim., Waltke, Heim), but this meaning would require the preposition *min* "from." The phrase is actually a construction of the sort described by Muraoka 1977. The genitive *taʿam* is semantically the subject of the const. ptcp. *sārat*, in spite of the gender agreement between the ptcp. and *ʾiššāh*. In other words, the woman's *good sense* has departed. The phrasing suggests passivity and loss.

11:23 The righteous desire what is good.
What the wicked can hope for is wrath.

Literally, "The desire of the righteous is but good [noun]." The hope of the wicked is wrath." The righteous desire nothing but the good, whereas the wicked desire and "hope" for God's wrath. The statement is paradoxical and facetious, for the wicked do not really hope for this. It is *as if* they did, because the evil things for which they lust will inevitably bring wrath upon them. For examples of facetious uses of words see Prov 7:21; 12:12; 15:10; 18:17; and especially the use of *musar* in 16:22.

what is good [*ṭôb*]: Lit., "good"; in other words, goodness is what they desire. The proverb does not say that the desire of the righteous *is* good. (If *ṭôb* were an adjective, it would be feminine.).

11:24 There is one who scatters yet gets more,
and one who saves out of honesty yet ends up in need.

Does this proverb (1) affirm the principle of retribution or (2) contradict it?

(1) Some understand v 24a as assuring reward to one who gives charity to the poor (thus *Midrash Proverbs* and most of the traditional commentators). This verse, Riyqam says, is "joined to" v 23, by which he means that it is elaborated in

v 24. He explains that the "good" that a righteous man desires (v 23a) must be "to scatter his coins in fulfillment of a commandment." This understanding is reinforced by vv 25–27, which speak of right and wrong ways of treating others.

Riyqam's interpretation may be correct with respect to the function of v 24a in the context of vv 25–26, in which v 25 echoes v 24a and v 26 points back (vaguely) to v 24b. By this interpretation, however, v 24b is out of place, for v 26 speaks of an unworthy "holding back." Ramaq construes v 24b as referring to "one who withholds [*ḥosek*] his wealth from doing the honest thing," but this is forced.

(2) If, however, v 24 is read by itself—as almost all the couplets in Part II can be—it does not directly moralize, but rather states a paradox: A man's personal economy does not always receive the results it deserves. The B-line clearly points to a paradox, for saving money "out of honesty" (*miyyošer*) must be a virtue, not a fault, such as "anti-social miserliness" (McKane), which would warrant deprivation. Thus also the A-line presumably describes a puzzling event rather than a fitting outcome. Moreover, the introductory *yeš*, "there is," shows that the sentence states an anomaly, not an expected scenario.

Nevertheless, v 24, even when read by itself, does imply a lesson, namely, that we should not automatically admire the man who gets rich or despise one who ends up needy because they may have reached their condition through no virtue or fault of their own. (See Ptahhotep ll. 181–82, quoted in the Comment on 10:22.) Such cases are anomalies and serve as a warning against overconfidence in one's own industry and acuity.

This kind of paradoxical statement becomes prominent in Hellenistic Egyptian and Jewish Wisdom (see Lichtheim 1983: 138–50). Phibis (Pap. Insinger 7.13–19) says:

> (13) There is one who lives on little so as to save, yet he becomes poor.
> (14) There is one who does not know, yet the fate gives (him) wealth.
> (15) It is not the wise man who saves who finds a surplus.
> (16) Nor is it the one who spends who becomes poor.
> (17) The god gives a wealth of supplies wihout an income.
> (18) He also gives poverty in the purse without spending.
> (19) The fate and the [fortune] that come, it is the god who sends them.
> (AEL 3.191)

Similarly, Anksheshonq asserts: "There is one who saves and does not profit. All are in the hand of the fate and the god" (26.7–8; trans. AEL 3.179). The similarity between these Ptolemaic period statements and Prov 11:24 is striking. (Compare particularly v 24a with Insinger 7.16 and v 24b with Insinger 7.13 and Anksheshonq 26.7). Rather than assuming direct influence, we should conclude that this paradox was a Wisdom topos that reached the three books. The purpose of such paradoxes is to exalt "God's all-embracing power, a power that surpassed man's understanding and limited his foresight" (Lichtheim 1983: 149–50). The same message underlies the paradoxes in Prov 11:24; 22:16; and, perhaps, 13:7. This idea is found earlier, notably in Amenemope §25 (quoted in the Comment on Prov 14:31) and in a statement by Anii on the vagaries of fate (21.5–10; AEL 2.142). Paradoxes of this sort show that the authors of Wisdom Literature did not assume a rigid deed-consequence nexus or assume that reward and punishment worked in a mechanical and invariable fashion (see G. Freuling *2004*: 107).[269]

there is [*yeš*]: This is used to introduce a paradox or anomaly in Prov 11:24; 13:7, 23; Qoh 2:21; 7:15; 8:14; Sir 4:21 (2x); 6:9, 10; 10:30 (2x); 11:11, 12; and elsewhere. It is the primary structuring device in the Hellenistic Egyptian book of Phibis, whose main point is that God's control of fate is absolute and can override the logic of reward and punishment; see "God's omnipotence and omniscience" in the Commentary on 16:1–9.

one who scatters yet gets more [*w^e nosap ʿod*]: Lit., "one who scatters and it is added more." The passive *nosap* suggests that this man's aggrandizement is not necessarily due to his own efforts. Somehow wealth just comes to him.

and one who saves . . . : Lit., "and one who saves from honesty but to neediness [*l^e maḥsor*]." He husbands his resources, doing so honestly and not hoarding in greed, yet he ends up needy.

11:25 A generous person will be sated[a];
he who gives drink—his own thirst will be slaked.

[a] *yirwe'* (MT *yôre'*).

Literally, "A soul of blessing shall be made fat, and he who slakes (sc., others' thirst)—he too will be slaked." A "soul of blessing" (*nepeš b^e rakah*) is a person who *bestows* blessings on others. (Thus the Vulgate: *anima quae benedicit* "a soul that blesses.") "Blessing" here means material gifts, as in Gen 33:11; Josh 15:19; 1 Sam 25:27; and 2 Kgs 5:15; see the Comment on 10:22. In conjunction with v 24, this verse reinterprets v 24a (in spite of 24b) by identifying the one who "scatters" as one who is generous to others.

be sated: Lit., "be fattened," that is, having one's throat moistened with rich foods (13:4). This is a metaphor for prosperity (28:25).

MT's *ywr'* at the end of the verse should be emend to *yirwe'* (= *yirweh*) "be slaked," to fit the subject *marweh* "he who gives drink." The Masoretes point it *yôre'* (= *yôreh*) "teach," calling for the translation: "He who slakes (others') thirst (for wisdom)—he too teaches" (cf. Riyqam). But the teaching (*yôreh*) cannot be said to be *additional* ("too") to slaking others' thirst for wisdom, since to do that is itself to teach. The anomalous spelling *ywr'* is confirmed by the Masorah but normalized to *ywrh* in many MSS and cited thus by Riyqam and Ramaq.

[269] Freuling's persuasive study of the concept of the "deed-consequence nexus," first formulated by K. Koch (1952) (discussed in Vol. I, 91-92) shows that the "deed-consequence nexus" cannot be understood as mechanical and inevitable. Rather, the kind of connection that Proverbs implies is an orderly, recurrent, and experienced phenomenon, not an absolute principle dogmatically stated. Freuling stresses the pedagogical function of the deed-consequence nexus in helping the pupil orient himself in life (see esp. *2004*: 107). The connection between deed and consequence can be formulated either with or without a reflection of Yahweh's role. The efficacy of Yahweh and the dynamics of human deeds are not conceived of as alternatives. Both aspects converge, neither excluding the other (p. 105).

11:26 He who withholds grain—the nation will curse him,
while there will be blessing for the head of a distributor.

The theme of disbursement continues from vv 24a, 25. A *mašbir* "distributor" is a major distributor of grain, either a rich landholder or, more likely, a government official who effectively controls the region's food distribution. Examples of *mašbirim* are Joseph (Gen 42:6), Sihon (Deut 2:28), and the greedy rich men in Amos (8:5, 6). A *mašbir* is not a small farmer. Such a man, working just to feed his family, could not affect the market on his own or even afford to withhold his products for long. Moreover, the withholder of grain in this proverb is cursed by the *le'om*, which always refers to a nation as a whole, not just one's neighbors or townspeople.

11:27 One who pursues the good seeks good will,
but as for him who pursues evil—it will come upon him.

This verse summarizes vv 24a, 25–26. To "pursue" or "seek" (*šḥr*) the good, that is to say, the welfare of others, is tantamount to seeking (*bqš*)—and attaining—their goodwill toward oneself. But he who pursues the harm of others will suffer it himself.

11:28 He who trusts in his wealth—he will fall,
while the righteous will flourish like foliage.

The "fall" in the A-line, when read in the light of the B-line, is evocative of a tree falling. On this image, see the Comment on 10:31. The folly of trusting in the saving power of wealth is the message of 10:2 and 11:4.

11:29 He who troubles his house will inherit the wind,
and the fool will be slave to the wise of heart.

One who causes his family distress, perhaps by wasting the familial holdings, ends up with nothing of value; see 11:17b. On *ʿkr* "trouble," "distress," see the Comment on 11:17.

Who is this troubler, father or son? The reference to "his house" suggests that the troublemaker is the father, the master of the household. However, the expectation of an inheritance is something a son, not the father, would have. Riyqam identifies the troublemaker as a son, relating this proverb to 17:2: "An astute slave will rule over a disappointing son and divide an inheritance among brothers." This interpretation gives the two lines of 11:29 greater coherence. The issue here, Riyqam explains, is inheritance among brothers and how it is cultivated. The son who "troubles his house" is one of the brothers seeking an inheritance (11:29a ≈ 17:2b). He will end up with nothing, like a slave, and be subject to an intelligent slave (11:29b ≈ 17:2a). But both readings are relevant, for whoever causes the distress will suffer the consequences. On the status of a household *ʿebed* "slave," see the Comment on 17:2.

**11:30 The fruit of the righteous is a tree of life,
and the wise man captivates souls.**

The A-line praises the benefits the righteous person confers on others. This line is an elliptical comparison equivalent to "The fruit of the righteous is (like the fruit of) the tree of life." The "fruit" is probably the product of speech; see 12:14a and 13:2a. The tree of life confers life and health; see the Comment on 3:18.

The B-line can be interpreted variously. In the above rendering, "captivate" translates *loqeaḥ*, lit. "takes," from *l-q-ḥ*. Through his words, the wise man "takes" souls, and (unlike the adulteress's murderous "taking" of souls in 6:25) this captivation brings them life. The choice of *laqaḥ* gives a twist to the saying. "Take souls" usually means to kill, but when the wise man "takes souls," he preserves them.

Ramaq (followed by Snell 1983) defines *lqḥ* as "teach," deriving this sense from the noun *leqaḥ* "lesson," "teaching," and comparing Prov 4:2. However, the verb *laqaḥ* never means "teach." Nevertheless, *laqaḥ* may in context connote teaching, because a lesson is supposed to attract and "take" the listener; see the Comment on 1:5.

captivates souls [*wᵉlôqēaḥ nᵉpāšôt*]: This phrase may be interpreted in several ways.

(1) The locution *lqḥ nepeš* usually means to kill someone (Prov 1:19; Ezek 33:6; Jon 4:3). This sense fits the present proverb only if we emend *ḥkm* "wise" to *ḥms* "violence," "lawlessness," based on LXX's "transgressor" (Ehrlich, Toy, McKane, Murphy, and many), and translate, "Violence takes lives"—in other words, kills.

(2) "Take" can also mean "extricate," "save," as in Ps 49:16: "God will surely save my soul [*napšî*] from the underworld, for he will take me," that is, take me out of the danger. ("My soul," *napšî*, means "me" or "my life.") Prov 11:30b then reinforces 11:30a: The wise man bestows life by "taking" people away from danger through his teachings (thus Riyqam, using other examples). This is supported by numerous promises of "life" to those who embrace wisdom, as in 8:35a, where Lady Wisdom says, "For he who finds me finds life." The problem with this interpretation is that there is no indication of the danger *from which* the souls are extricated.

(3) Irwin (1984) says that the metaphor of fruit continues into the second line, and "taking" in connection with fruit means "pick," "gather," as in Gen 3:6, 22; 40:9–11. The line then means that the wise "take lives" in the sense of saving them, an ironic usage. But if the metaphor of v 30a is implied in 30b, then the "taking" would be removal *from* the tree of life, which gives the opposite of the message that Irwin sees here.

(4) "Take" can mean "capture," "captivate" (1 Sam 2:16; 5:1; Job 40:24). Using a different verb, *ṣ-w-d* "hunt," "trap," Prov 6:26b says, "a married woman hunts for [or "traps"] a precious life [*nepeš*]," meaning that she seduces and entraps her victim. Prov 6:26b restates the seductress's aim, namely, to "take you in with her glances" (6:25b). This suggests a partial synonymy of "taking" and "trapping" souls. We may thus understand 11:30b to mean that the wise man captivates souls in a positive way—wins their hearts, we might say—either through his gracious behavior or through his teaching.

**11:31 Since the righteous man receives what he deserves on the earth,
how much the more so do the wicked man and the sinner!**

"On the earth" (*ba'areṣ*) means in the land of the living, as in Ps 119:19, "I am a sojourner on the earth," and Ps 119:87, "They nearly wiped me off the earth." Just retribution, whether reward or punishment, will take place in this life (Ramaq), though it may tarry. Everything awaits its proper time (Hame'iri). The *a fortiori* argument assumes that the punishment of the wicked is more urgent, hence even more certain, than the rewarding of the righteous. Waltke sees here an affirmation of postmortem retribution. On earth, the righteous will receive "remedial punishment," whereas the wicked, in contrast, will be punished after death. But the proverb's *a fortiori* reasoning shows that the wicked will undergo the *same kind* of repayment as the righteous, though with even greater certainty. Both will receive their just due *on earth*.

This insistence on retribution in this life has something of a polemic tone. This may be a response to the belief, growing during the Hellenistic period, that rectification of wrongs may have to wait until the afterlife. Qohelet was aware of the idea of an afterlife in heaven, but he rejects the possibility as unknowable (3:21), and hence must worry about whether justice really is assured on earth. Ben Sira believes that just retribution in this life is a certainty, even if it must wait till the day of death (11:26).

The particle *hēn* introduces shared knowledge, a premise that is believed to be secure and obvious. Thus it can introduce the protasis in an *a fortiori* argument (Garr *2004*, esp. 332).

12:1 He who loves discipline loves knowledge,
while he who hates reproof is an ignoramus.

discipline: *Musar* connotes chastisement or correction (see Vol. I, 34–35). One may not yet be fully wise or knowledgeable, and some of his actions may call for correction, but he can still love discipline. Then his great virtue lies in his attitude: He has the humility to appreciate the value of reproof and thus can progress toward wisdom. He who resents chastisement is a *baʿar*, an "ignoramous," brutish and unthinking.

It is unclear why Murphy feels that "[t]he love/hate relationship [in this verse] is without the emotional impact these words carry with us; it is a question of firm choice, of either/or, cf. 1:22; 9:8" (p. 89). On the contrary, throughout the book the authors seek to inculcate strong and polarized feelings toward right and wrong behaviors. The intensity of these feelings is best captured in the calls to embrace and cherish wisdom (3:13–18; 4:6; 7:3–4; etc.), as well as in Interlude D (esp. 8:30–35), whose glow of eros Murphy himself has described (see Vol. I, 294–95). The intensity has a sharp edge in Lady Wisdom's diatribe in Interlude A (1:20–33). Essay 3, "Wisdom in the Lectures" (Vol. I, 347–51), examines how the Lectures seek to shape attitudes and desires.

12:2 The good man will receive favor from the Lord,
but he will condemn the scheming man.

he will condemn [*yaršiaʿ*]: Who is "he"? There are three possibilities: (1) "The good man," who will condemn the schemer in judgment. But that makes a poor contrast with the A-line. (2) "The man of *mᵉzimmot* ("schemes")—understood in a positive sense; thus Saʿadia. In other words, the shrewd man will win his arguments. For this sense of *hiršiaʿ* Saʿadia compares 1 Sam 14:47, but the text there is doubtful and, if correct, does not support the meaning required. (3) God. This is most likely, since the proverb focuses on God's actions, not man's.

The verb *hiršiaʿ* "condemn" usually means to convict or declare someone guilty. God, in his ongoing judgment of all humans, will condemn the schemer. If the two lines are read in close conjunction, the first one implies that when the good man faces judgment, God will show him favor and judge him with mercy.

scheming: *Mᵉzimmot* "schemes" are usually viewed with suspicion in Proverbs 10–29 and considered tricky and illicit (12:2; 14:17; 24:8). It is not so much the type of thinking itself that troubles the sages—the very similar *ʿormah* "shrewdness" is commended—but rather the fact that *mᵉzimmot* are not open and public. *Mᵉzimmah* and related words basically mean hidden thoughts (see Vol. I, 34). The authors of Prov 1–9, however, insist on the inherent moral worth of all effective intellectual powers and assign even *mᵉzimmah* to wisdom (1:4; 2:11; 3:21; 5:2; 8:12). Prov 12:2a ≈ 8:35b; 18:22b.

12:3 No one is established by wickedness,
but the root of the righteous does not totter.

The righteous man is pictured as a tree firmly rooted in the ground. See the Comment on 10:31. The verb *mwṭ* "totter," "collapse," is properly predicated of something that can totter and fall, such as a mountain, a statue, legs, or a person. This does not seem to be the most appropriate word for describing the destruction of a tree's roots, which grasp and enter the earth and have little vertical rise. It seems that the author of this insipid maxim probably had righteous *people* in mind when choosing this verb. He may have been influenced by statements in which the righteous man is said not to "totter" (*mwṭ*), such as Prov 10:30; Ps 15:5; 62:3, 7, 9; Pss 112:6; and 125:1. (But contrast Prov 25:26.)

Van Leeuwen says that the fact that the righteous man is said to be "established on righteousness" shows a democratization of the principle of divine and human kingship, according to which it is the throne that is established (*k-w-n*) on righteousness (Prov 16:12; 25:4–5). But this verb is predicated of many things, including "man" (Ps 140:12), and the promise of being "established" has no inherent connection to kingship.

12:4 The woman of strength is her husband's diadem,
while the disgraceful one is like a rot in his bones.

It is not a wife's beauty that reflects honor (or prestige) on her husband but her *ḥayil*—strength of mind and character. If one takes a wife who lacks this, he will suffer pain and shame to the core of his being.

The woman of strength [*ʾešet ḥayil*]: The Woman of Strength is lauded expansively in Prov 31:10–31. Hebrew *ḥayil* basically means "strength." This may come in the form of physical strength (e.g., Qoh 10:10), wealth (e.g., Ezek 28:5), or martial power (e.g., 2 Sam 11:16, esp. in the phrase *ʾiš ḥayil* "man of power," and variants), hence an army or military "force" (e.g., Exod 14:4). The phrase *ʾiš ḥayil* is used of a warrior (e.g., Judg 3:29), a possessor of practical competencies (e.g., Gen 47:6), and a man of strong moral character (e.g., Exod 18:21, 25; 1 Kgs 1:42). The woman of *ḥayil* in Prov 31:10–31 is praised for a variety of strengths: vigor, practical skills, kindness, wisdom, and piety. Ruth is recognized as a "woman of *ḥayil*" for the strength of character she exhibits in her steadfast loyalty to her mother-in-law (Ruth 3:11).

In this saying and in Prov 31:10–31, women are valued for the benefit they bring their husbands. To praise benefits is to speak of their value to *oneself*; hence the verse speaks from the man's perspective. This orientation is natural in a book that addresses males and exhorts them to cherish the right qualities in women. To call a woman her husband's diadem is not to trivialize her as a mere ornament. To be sure, an actual diadem is beautiful and expensive, and as a metaphor it can signify any object of pride. For a base person, a "diadem of pride" is phony and trivial (Isa 28:1–4). But a diadem usually signifies genuine, warranted dignity. Among the things called diadems are the benefits of wisdom (Prov 4:9), wisdom herself (Sir 6:31), the gray hair of age (Prov 16:31), and grandchildren and fathers (Prov 17:6). Zion is a diadem to God (Isa 62:3), and God himself is one to the remnant of Israel (Isa 28:5). "Diadem" is an emblem of honor and is parallel to *kabod* "honor" in Job 19:9.

The virtuous wife is her husband's diadem insofar as she brings him honor and perhaps a measure of protection (see the Comment on 4:9). Moreover, there is evidence, albeit slight, to suggest that bridegrooms customarily wore diadems at their weddings (Cant 3:11 and, from a later period, *B. Soṭah. 49a*). If that is so, to call a wife her husband's diadem evokes a visible practice, one associated specifically with marriage.

The contrary type is the *m^ebišah*, the "disgraceful" or "disappointing" woman. (See the Comment on 10:5.) In Prov 10:5; 14:35; and 17:2, her male counterpart, the *mebiš*, is the antithesis of the *maśkil*, the intelligent and insightful man. In 10:5, the *ben maśkil*, the "astute son," is said to build up his stores in the summer, displaying a combination of diligence and prudence. These three examples suggest that what is disgraceful about the masculine *mebiš*, and probably the female *m^ebišah* as well, is negligence and indolence. (In 19:26, the meaning of *mebiš* is hard to specify.) By contrast, the abilities of the "woman of strength" include diligence and astuteness, like the woman extolled in Prov 31:10–31.

The two types of women differ also in the visibility of their effects. The good wife evokes in her husband a pride that he displays openly, while the disgraceful wife causes hers a grief that gnaws at him from within, like a wasting disease. The chiastic shape of this verse, Alter notes (1985: 174), sharpens the contrast. "The woman of strength" and "the disgraceful woman" are at the beginning and end of the couplet. They frame the words "diadem" and "rot," which are conjoined in its middle.

12:5 The plans of the righteous are just;
the stratagems of the wicked are deceitful.

just, deceitful: Lit., "justice" [*mišpaṭ*], "deceit" (*mirmah*). (On this type of predication see the Comment on 3:17 and cf. GBH §154e.) The word *taḥbulot* "stratagems," contrary to McKane, does not bear a negative connotation. It is used positively in 1:5; 11:14; 20:18; and 24:6. The negative connotation in the present verse comes from the conjunction with "the wicked."

This maxim seems tautologous, but it is less so if read as an implicit exhortation to make one's own plans fair and honest, so as to place oneself among the righteous and avoid the wicked and their fate.

12:6 The words of the wicked are a murderous ambush,
but the mouth of the upright will save them.

Words can kill and preserve. "The words of the wicked" may be deceitful schemes, such as are mentioned in 12:5b, or they may be slanders. Against them stands the speech of the upright—powerful because it is honest.

The scenario of a "murderous ambush" (lit., "an ambush of blood") is developed in Prov 1:8–19 (see v 11). There the focus is on the danger to the naïve youth who joins the schemers, whereas here it is on the peril facing their victim. The righteous will not only escape the temptation, they will evade the danger to their own persons. Several proverbs insist on this; see 10:2b; 11:6a, 8a, 9b; 12:21; and 12:26 (as emended). On the deliverance of the righteous, see the Comment on 11:9. In the present verse, the ambush is metaphorical and the attack verbal.

Delitzsch and McKane identify the referent of "them" in v 6b not as the upright but as others whom the righteous save from the schemes of the wicked. But no victims other than "the upright" are available as an antecedent. The point is that the righteous have the verbal powers to save *themselves*.

12:7 Overturn the wicked and they are no more,
but the house of the righteous will stand.

At the first disaster, the wicked disappear (lit., "and they are not"), whereas the righteous—and their families ("house")—endure. This proverb is equivalent to 10:25, especially the first line: "When the gale has passed, the wicked man is no more, while the righteous man is the foundation of the earth." Similarly Ps 37:10, 11.

Overturn [*hāpôk*]: The inf. abs. here functions as an imperative. It is a rhetorical imperative, that is, not an actual command to do something, but a way of evoking a little scenario and inviting the reader into it. Examples are Isa 43:8 ("Bring forth the blind people with eyes") and Isa 6:10 (God's command to Isaiah to make the people's minds stupid). Further examples are Prov 20:16; Cant 2:6; 8:4; and probably Prov 27:10b.

12:8 A man is praised according to his good sense,
while he who is perverse of heart becomes an object of scorn.

An intellectual quality, *śekel* "good sense" (sometimes translated "insight" or "intelligence"), is counterpoised to a moral quality, perversity of heart. (Hebrew *naʿăweh* "perverse" is from the root *ʿ-w-h*, "twist" or "bend.") This antithesis is in line with Proverbs' intellectualist ethic, which assumes that intelligence is morally good (see Essay 6, "Ethics"). One's wisdom or malevolence will eventually come to light, bringing the praise or scorn one deserves (Clifford). Thus the praise one receives is an index of character (≈ 27:21b).

12:9 Better a lowly man who has produce[a]
than one who glorifies himself and lacks bread.

[a] *waʿăbûr lô* (MT *w*[e]*ʿebed lô*).

Praise—especially when self-conferred—loses its sheen when coupled with poverty. As a sequel to a proverb that promises social esteem as a reward for good sense, this one slightly restricts the value of public perceptions. Sometimes lowliness is better than prestige.

lowly [*niqleh*]: This does not mean being poor, but rather to being held in low esteem. (In Isa 3:5 it is the opposite of *nikbad* "honored"; see the related uses in Deut 25:3; 1 Sam 18:23; and Isa 16:14.) This is a complex "better than" formula, on which see the excursus after 15:17.

one who glorifies himself [*mitkabbed*]: The contrary of the lowly man is the smug *self*-glorifier, the boaster. *Hitkabbed* has this sense in Sir 3:10; 10:26, 27 (restored); and 10:31 (MS A, interlinear). The saying makes the self-glorifying man (*mitkabbed*, reflexive), rather than the truly honored man (*nikbad*, passive), the opposite of the lowly man. This opposition weakens the force of the maxim somewhat, because little good can be said of self-glorification even when one is not poor. The author may have recoiled from giving the lowly man any advantage over a truly honored one.

The MT of Prov 12:9a reads, "Better a lowly man who has a slave" (*w*[e]*ʿebed lo*). The MT compares a man who has a slave to one who lacks bread. It is, however, unclear why owning a slave would be singled out for special importance. Moreover, the "better than" comparison is weakened by matching something of relatively high cost (owning a slave) with something that costs less and is almost universally possessed (bread). It would be like saying, better a lowly man who owns a car than a self-important man who is starving. Most *anything* is better than *that*.

This translation assumes a consonantal emendation of *wʿbd* "and a slave" to the very similar *wʿbr* "and (agricultural) produce," to be vocalized *waʿăbûr*; thus Tur-Sinai 1947: 102. The latter is a synonym of *t*[e]*buʾah* "produce" (Josh 5:11, 12). *ʿăbur* is written *ʿbr* in Arad 31.10, a form that could easily be corrupted to *ʿbd*. Thus read, the proverb advocates working one's land, similarly to Prov 12:11; 27:23–27; and 28:19.

Ben Sira uses Prov 12:9 as the starting point for a long reflection on the nature of honor and disgrace (Sir 10:19–11:6). He teaches that one who respects himself when he is poor will be even more honored if he becomes rich, and one who holds himself in low esteem when he is rich will be despised even more so if he becomes poor. This is an interesting exposition of Prov 12:9 but does not reflect its original intention.

w^{e}*ʿebed lô*: LXX, Syr, and Vul construe *wʿbd lw* as *w*^{e}*ʿōbēd lô* and translate "and serves himself" or "and works for himself." By this reading, the verse gives preference to a lowly man who works for his own benefit. Ben Sira seems to have understood it thus. He recasts the proverb as *ṭwb ʿwbd wywtr hwn m*[*mt*]*kbd* [*wḥ*]*s*[*r*] *m<zw>n* "Better he who works and increases wealth than one who glorifies himself but lacks food" (10:27 MS A, corrected from the Gk and Syr). Without revocalizing, Riyqam understands the MT to praise the lowly man who is a servant to *himself*, that is to say, he does his own work; sim. Malbim. The reflexive notion would, however, require a clearer marker, such as *l*^{e}*napšô*, and even so the idea expressed would not be antithetical to "lacking bread." Also, as Ehrlich notes, *ʿābad* + *l-* means to serve God or a political superior but not to work as another's employee. Ehrlich understands *niqleh w*^{e}*ʿebed lô* to mean one who lowers himself to be his own slave, which is also syntactically doubtful. Tur-Sinai's minor emendation makes the best sense.

12:10 The righteous man understands what his beast desires, while the "mercies" of the wicked are cruel.

In only a few places in the Bible is humanitarian concern shown toward animals: One must not muzzle an ox when threshing (Deut 25:4). When taking eggs from a nest, one must not seize "the mother together with the children" (Deut 22:6). A sacrificial animal must be left with its mother for seven days after birth (Exod 22:29; Lev 22:27). One must not sacrifice an animal and its offspring on the same day (Lev 22:28). One must not seethe a kid in its mother's milk (Exod 23:19b = 34:26b = Deut 14:21b; see Haran *1985*). The motives for these injunctions are not transparent, but humanitarian feelings are certainly reflected in some of them. These concerns may be motivated less by sympathy for the animals' suffering (for they will still suffer) than by a sense of decency, a desire to respect the proper order. Solicitude for one's livestock also has a practical aspect, since it is just good husbandry to keep them well-fed; see Prov 27:23–27.

what his beast desires [*nepeš*]: Lit., "his animal's appetite." *Nepeš* is commonly translated "soul" elsewhere, and "soul," if understood as the complex of desires and feelings, is appropriate in this verse too. The phrase "to know/understand the *nepeš* of" implies empathy, as in Exod 23:9: "You shall not oppress the sojourner—and you know the soul of the sojourner, for you were sojourners in the land of Egypt." The present proverb may be read narrowly—knowing the appetite, what the livestock need to eat—or broadly—knowing their "soul," what they feel and what they require for their well-being. In either case, to "know" a *nepeš* is to care about it.

Saʿadia understands Prov 12:10a as the figure later called meiosis: the righteous man cares for everyone, *even* his animals. But there is no indication of this emphasis, such as would be given by adding the adverb *ʾap* "even" or putting "his animal's appetite" before the verb.

The "mercies" of the wicked [*pl.*] *are cruel*: This is a strange way of saying that the wicked are cruel or that they lack mercy. "Mercy" is, by definition, the opposite of cruelty. This line is an oxymoron that expresses sarcasm: What is reckoned as "mercy" on the part of the wicked, or what they themselves might claim as generosity (such as a few handfuls of grain tossed to their oxen) is scarcely better than cruelty.

The proverb does not exactly say that it is righteous to care for one's animals and wicked to fail to do so. It rather portrays and evaluates the two types of farmer. The righteous one, good by nature, naturally cares for helpless creatures. The wicked one, even when not doing something specifically wicked, is mean.

cruel [*ʾakzārî*]: Formally singular, *ʾakzārî* may be indeclinable. It is predicated of a plural subj. here and in Jer 50:42. A plural or collective sense would be appropriate in Prov 5:9 as well.

12:11 He who works his land will be sated with bread,
while he who pursues trifles lacks sense.

The preceding mention of animal husbandry evoked this thought about working the land. It does not necessarily praise the physical labor of farming. Amenemope also commends agriculture (§6 [AEL 2.152]), and though his son and other intended readers may have held land, they were educated scribes and officials and certainly did not labor with their own hands. (Amenemope was, among other things, an overseer of fields.) Nor is the purpose of Prov 12:11 to exalt agricultural labors above other sorts. That would be expressed by "works *the* land." Farming was the primary means of livelihood in ancient Israel and, as such, working one's land can stand for all honest work. Praise of farming as such is found in Sir 7:15 (Greek).

The couplet juxtaposes images of fullness and emptiness: The worker is rewarded with satiety, while they who pursue trifles—lit., "empty things"—are mindless. The second line appears to be a literary expansion of a folk proverb in the first.

This proverb has a near-doublet in Prov 28:19, "He who works his land will be sated with bread, while he who pursues trifles will be sated with poverty." The form in 28:19 has tighter parallelism. The disjointed parallelism in the present proverb—having enough food versus lacking sense—tells us to complete each line from the other: He who works his land has good sense and will have plenty of food, while he who fritters his time away is empty-headed and will starve.

The LXX adds: "He who takes pleasure in diversions of wine will leave behind disgrace [as a legacy] for his own fortresses." See the Textual Note for an explanation of this awkward couplet.

**12:12 The wicked man covets a snare for the wicked,
but the root of the righteous is secure[a].**

---

[a] *'êtān* (MT *yittēn*).

Many commentators despair of making sense of this verse. It is, however, meaningful. What the wicked man desires—another man's wealth, for example, or another's wife—are deadly traps for himself. He does not *really* covet a snare, but the object of his desire is tantamount to being just that. Compare the similarly facetious 11:23b, "What the wicked can hope for is wrath," and the Comment on that verse. The greedy man expects gratification, but this is a deadly illusion. The Strange Woman (Prov 7) epitomizes such illusions. The fool impulsively and stupidly hurries to her "like an ox going to slaughter, like a stag bounding to bonds, like a bird rushing to a trap" (7:22 + 23b).

a snare for the wicked [*m*[e]*ṣod ra'im*]: Lit., "a snare of the wicked [pl.]." The point of this line is that what the wicked man desires will ensnare him. Compare 5:22: "(The evildoer's) iniquities will trap him, in the cords of his sin he'll be seized." Clifford translates: "A wicked person desires the catch of evil people" (sim. JPSV, NRSV, and many commentators, based on Ugaritic *mṣd* "catch," "game"). But the notion that one evildoer desires what another evildoer has trapped is unrelated to the B-line and is too intricate and narrow to be its parallel. The danger implied by this interpretation would be of concern only to evildoers, whose plunder is coveted by other criminals. Moreover, elsewhere in Biblical Hebrew (Job 19:6, Qoh 7:26) *maṣod* means the snare itself, not what is ensnared.

The first line has evoked some unusually strained emendations, including BHS's alternatives, *yiššāmēd y*[e]*sôd rā'îm* "the foundation of evildoers will be destroyed" and, obscurely, *ḥōmed* [actually *ḥōmer*!] *rō'ēš m*[e]*ṣûdat rā'îm* "the fortress of evildoers is shaking clay" (thus Hitzig). For other radical rewritings, see McKane.

but the root of the righteous is secure: The MT has "but the root of the righteous he will give [*ytn*]." This might mean that God gives them a firm rooting, but the syntax is strained. Clifford explains "gives" as short for "gives fruit," but this ellipsis is unique. A minor emendation from *ytn* "give" to *'ytn* "firm, enduring" (Toy) makes good sense and fits the parallelism. By this emendation, 12:12b is a rephrasing of 12:3b, with "secure" equivalent to "not totter."

"Root" is a metaphor for a hold on life, including family, home, and property. A good rooting is a stable and secure foundation in life; compare the metaphorical connotations of "root" in 12:3; Am 2:9; Job 8:17; and 14:8.

MT's *yittēn* "will give" is difficult. Hitzig, McKane, and others associate *ytn* with Arabic *watana* "to abide, be permanent" (more precisely: "to flow constantly"), and Tg's *ntqyym* "will endure" interprets *ytn* in this way. But there is no evidence for the verbal use of this root in Hebrew. An emendation to *'ytn* (Toy, etc.) is preferable.

12:13 In the transgression of the lips there is an evil snare,
but the righteous man escapes the trouble.

The metaphor SIN-AS-A-TRAP continues from v 12. The scenario can be viewed in two ways. First, a man who transgresses verbally—by schemes or seductions—is setting a trap in which he himself will be caught. The similar proverb in 18:7 describes how a fool traps himself; see also the "pit" topos in 26:27, etc. Second, a man lays a snare for others, and this is a real danger, but the righteous can evade it by refusing to listen to temptations. This is the message of 11:9 and 29:6.

The LXX adds, "He who gives gentle looks will (himself) receive mercy, but he who meets (men) in the gates [for litigation] will afflict souls."

12:14 From the fruit of his mouth, a man will be sated with good things,
and the recompense of a man's hands will return to him.

This verse continues the theme of the effects of speech, now turning to the beneficial ones. The verse epitomizes the "deed-consequence nexus" (see Vol. I, 91–92). Every action, whether in word or deed, "returns" to harm or benefit the doer. Prov 12:14a ≈ 13:2a; 18:20a.

From the fruit of his mouth [*mippᵉrî pî ʾîš*]: Lit., "from the fruit of a man's mouth." Shupak (*1984–1985*: 481–83) suggests that the idiom *pᵉrî pî-* "the fruit of the mouth of," found also in 13:2 and 18:20, derives from the frequent Egyptian idiom *prt n/m r*ʾ, lit. "what comes forth from the mouth." The Egyptian verb *pri* "go forth" could have been confused with Hebrew *pᵉrî* "fruit" (thus Shupak), or the Hebrew could be a bilingual pun.

Reading with the ketiv *yšwb* ("will return"), the proverb indicates that this recompense will happen naturally, without the need for direct divine intervention. Reading with the qeré *yšyb* ("bring back"), the sentence assigns God a more direct role and is to be translated: "and the recompense of a man's hands he [i.e., God] will bring back upon him." (Thus read 12:14b ≈ 19:17b; 24:12b.) Either reading is possible, for "God's mysterious hand is present in the processes of the world God has made (Pss 7:11–16; 9:15–16)" (Van Leeuwen).

The LXX witnesses to a variant proverb in 12:14b: "and the recompense of a man's lips will return to him." Compare how a very similar line in 18:20a is paralleled by "and will be sated with the produce of lips" in 18:20b. In the LXX, all of 12:14 pertains to speech. Both MT and LXX are meaningful and neither need be corrected to the other.

12:15 The fool's way is right in his own eyes,
while the wise man listens to counsel.

The fool imagines that whatever he does is right; thus he can never take rebuke or advice and change his ways. Doing so requires the humility to recognize that one's behavior ("way") may be flawed, and one who has this is, by definition, not a fool. Other verses that speak of a man's way being right in his own eyes are 14:12; 16:2; 21:2; 28:11; and 30:12. Prov 12:15a ≈ 16:2a; 21:2a.

way: Typical behavior.

12:16 The fool makes his anger known[a] at once,
while the shrewd man covers up an insult.

[a] *yôdîaʿ* (MT *yiwwādaʿ*).

Verses 16–19, and perhaps the entirety of 12:15–23, are about speech. They advocate restraint, honesty, and gentleness. Verse 16 teaches that the smart man swallows his pride and conceals an insult he has suffered. This is conducive to peace and thereby shows him to be "shrewd" (*ʿarum*; see Vol. I, 35–36), because avoidance of conflicts is also the counsel of self-interest. Forbearance before insult is urged in 10:12b; 17:9; and 19:11.

The MT vocalizes the verb in v 16a as passive, *yiwwādaʿ* (N-stem): "The fool—on that very day his anger shall be known." The LXX translates the verb as active, vocalizing *yôdîaʿ* (H-stem), "make known." The latter, followed here, produces a tighter parallel to v 16b, with both lines describing how one chooses to deal with his anger.

at once [*bayyôm*]: Lit., "in the day" = "in that very day," as in Neh 3:34.

12:17 The faithful witness speaks the truth,
and the lying witness—deceit.

This sentence seems true by definition. The verse is less banal if we construe it as explaining how judges can determine the verity of a witness's words, namely, whether the latter *ordinarily* speaks truth or falsehood.

Maxims on the vital importance of honest testimony are found in Prov 6:12; 12:17; 14:5, 25; 19:5, 9, 28; 21:28; 24:28; 25:18; and elsewhere in Wisdom Literature. Though some of the warnings are stereotyped and self-evident, the principle is of immense importance and worthy of iteration. The judicial system is viable only if people can, on the whole, be relied on to produce honest testimony. This is the realm of Wisdom Literature: matters of conscience and character that are usually beyond the realm of legal sanctions.

witness: Etymologically, *yapiaḥ* means "one who breathes out." On this problematic word, which should perhaps be pointed *y^epîaḥ* here, see the Comment on 6:19 but also the Comment on 14:25.

truth: Hebrew *ʾĕmunah*, usually translated "faith," "loyalty," also means "truth." It is often paired with its synonym *ʾĕmet* "truth," which too means "faith," "loyalty." The antonym of "faithful witness" is *yapiaḥ k^ezabim*, "a witness of deceit" or "one who breathes out deceit" (in testimony); see 6:19; 14:5, 25; 19:5, 9.

**12:18 There is one whose speech is like a sword's stabs,
but the tongue of the wise is a balm.**

Gentle, calming speech is effective. Sharp speech, however, is not exactly repudiated. It may have its purposes. Proverbs often commends the use of reproof, and Lady Wisdom's castigation of fools slashes like a sword (1:23–32). Yahweh's servant boasts of this power in Isa 49:2; cf. Isa 11:4; Jer 5:14; et al. Wisdom Literature knows that speech can hurt or heal; see Prov 15:4; 16:24; 25:15; Qoh 10:12–13; Ahiqar 105b-106a (1.1.89–90, quoted in the Comment on 25:15).

There is one whose speech, etc.: Lit., "There is one who speaks [*boṭeh*] like stabs of a sword"—an elliptical comparison, omitting "words" after "speaks."

bôṭeh (Oc) and *bôṭēʾ* (Or; see Baer *1880*: 58): Both forms of this word, *bṭh* and *bṭʾ* continue in RH. The verb seems to connote impetuosity in Lev 5:4 and Ps 106:33 (Murphy: "talks on and on"; Clifford: "rash speech"), but this nuance may be dependent on context. In Sir 5:13 ("Honor and disgrace are in the power of a speaker [*bwṭʾ*], and a man's tongue is his downfall"), *bwṭʾ* itself just means "speak," for the speech in question can bring honor as well as disgrace. In the present verse, since only some speakers are dangerous, *bôṭeh*/*bôṭēʾ* probably is a broad, neutral term for speaking.

balm: The word *marpeʾ* "medicine," "balm," plays on the roots *r-p-ʾ* "heal" and *r-p-h* "soft" (Tur-Sinai p. 47). Qohelet (10:4) says that *marpeʾ* can soothe an angry official.

**12:19 Honest lips will be established forever,
while the deceitful tongue is for but a moment.**

For the organs of speech to endure or pass away means that what they say is proved true or false. Only the truth endures and can be effective. Alternatively, the "lips" and "tongue" can stand for those who speak (Van Leeuwen).

for but a moment: Some treat *ʾargîʿāh* as a verb in the H-stem and translate "make a twinkling" (BDB) or "as long as I grant rest" (HALOT), but this is far-fetched. The parallel line requires understanding *ʾargîʿāh* as a by-form of *regaʿ* "moment" with a prosthetic *ʾaleph* (Saʿadia). For the syntax, compare Job 20:5, "The joy of the impious is for a moment [*ʿădê rāgaʿ*]." In Jer 49:19 (= 50:44) as well, *ʾargîaʿ* seems to be equivalent to *regaʿ* because a verb (which might mean "I shall grant rest") does not fit that context.

**12:20 Deceit is in the hearts of those who devise evil,
while those who plan peace have joy.**

In Prov 6:14, "devising evil" (*ḥoreš raʿ*) is associated with provoking strife: "With perversity in his heart, [the worthless man] crafts trouble [*ḥoreš raʿ*], constantly foments strife." On the opposite side is he who devises ways to bring about harmony among people.

There is an imbalance in the antithesis between "deceit" and "joy." (McKane translates *mirmah* as "self-deceit," but the word never has that meaning, nor does that sense provide a better antithesis.) This is a cue to read the verse as a disjointed proverb (see the Introduction to Vol. II [II.E]) and supplement each line from the other. Deceitful schemers are *unhappy*, while those who plan peace are *honest* (and not only peaceable). Construed in this way, the verse is more interesting and less obvious.

12:21 No trouble shall befall the righteous man,
but the wicked are filled with evil.

The righteous are protected against *ʾawen* "trouble." This does not promise blanket immunity to all misfortune (Prov 24:16 and 25:26 concede that the righteous can suffer temporary setbacks). Rather, it asserts that the righteous will not succumb to evil plans and deeds. Hebrew *ʾawen* always refers to wickedness (e.g., 6:12; 10:29; 17:4) or (less frequently) to its consequences (e.g., 22:8; Job 21:19; Ps 41:7). The wicked have no such protection. They are filled with evil (*raʿ*), which endangers others but also harms the evildoer, as if they have devoured evil like a poison. (See the image in 1:31; 14:14).

12:22 The Lord loathes deceitful lips,
while he favors those who act faithfully.

This returns to the theme of vv 15–19, the ethics of speech. Amenemope makes the same observation as this verse in very similar terms: "God hates him who speaks deceit. His great abomination is duplicity"[270] (§10 [14.2–3] [cf. AEL 2.154]).

loathes: See the Comment on 3:32.

12:23 The shrewd man covers up knowledge,
while the heart of dolts cries out folly.

It is shrewd and prudent (*ʿarum*) to be modest about one's knowledge and not put it on display. The fool blurts out what he thinks is wisdom and immediately exposes his folly (Riyqam); similarly 13:16. On the question of "covering up," see 10:12 and the references there. This verse echoes 12:16. Heim (*2001*: 152–57) regards the entirety of 12:13–23 as a proverb-cluster whose topic is speech.

knowledge: That is, what he knows. According to Clifford, this refers to specific things known rather than to knowledge in general. But "knowledge" in Proverbs is synonymous with wisdom. It means the breadth of knowledge relevant to effective and ethical behavior. It does not refer to a specific item of knowledge, such as a bit of gossip or an embarrassing secret.

the heart of dolts: The fact that it is their *heart* that cries out folly suggests that their mind exposes their stupidity even when they would rather hide it. Compare

[270] "Duplicity" is, lit., "strife in the belly"—the deceitful man has two conflicting thoughts in his mind. One of them he holds within, the other he speaks aloud. Similarly: "Do not speak to a man deceitfully—the abomination of the god" (§10, 13.15 [≈ AEL 2.155]); see also §13 (AEL ibid.).

Qoh 10:3, "And even when the fool walks in the road his heart is absent, and it says to everyone, 'He is a fool!' "

12:24 The hand of the diligent will rule,
while the slack will be put to forced labor.

Draft labor, the corvée (*mas*), was a form of taxation. David is said to have instituted it (2 Sam 20:24). Solomon used the practice extensively, putting the original inhabitants of the land to work in his building projects (1 Kgs 9:15, 21), and is said to have taken 30,000 men of Israel to work in Lebanon one month out of three (1 Kgs 5:27–28). Such impositions (even if the numbers were exaggerated) provoked resentment among the northern tribes (1 Kgs 12:4). Jews were taken for the corvée during the Seleucid period, as implied in 1 Macc 10:34–35. See further AYBD 6.339.

Why would lazy and deceitful men be put to the corvée more than worthier ones? The most likely way for a district to have met its draft would be to require each clan or village to supply a certain number of workers. The entire male population could hardly be taken. Clan local leaders and local administrators would naturally send those they considered the least valuable.

On *r^e^miyyah* "slack(ness)" or "deceit," see the Comment on 10:4. Similar phrases are used in 10:4, which promises wealth to the industrious. Compare 17:2, "An astute slave will rule over a disappointing son."

12:25 Worry in a man's heart brings him low[a],
while a good word cheers him up[b].

[a] *yašḥenhû* (MT *yašḥennāh*). [b] *y^e^śamm^e^ḥenhû* (MT *y^e^śamm^e^ḥennāh*).

The verse emphasizes the importance of good cheer. The message lies in the B-line: A good word can cheer up even the depressed. The two lines are linked by the consonance (/š/, /ś/, /ḥ/, /h/) and assonance (/a/, /e/) in the words *ʾîš yašḥenhû* and *y^e^śamm^e^ḥenhû*.

The MT of the A-line is grammatically impossible, but the gist comes through. This translation is based on two conjectural emendations. Sayings on good cheer are Prov 15:13a, 30; 17:22a. Sayings on sadness are 15:13b; 17:22b; 18:14.

There are severe grammatical incongruences in the MT of this verse. The masc. verb *yašḥennāh* is the predicate of the fem. *d^e^ʾāgāh* "worry." The gender of the verb may be conforming to the masc. *ʾîš* (for the phenomenon see GBH §149a). More problematic are the suffixes of *yašḥennāh* (*š-ḥ-h*) and *y^e^śamm^e^hennāh* (*ś-m-ḥ*), which are fem., although the antecedent, *leb ʾîš*, is masc. It seems necessary to emend the problematic words to *yšḥnhw* and *yśmḥnhw*, assuming two haplographies. (BHS treats *-nh* as a defective writing of *-enhû*, but the orthography would be unique.)

B. Yoma 75a records two readings of Prov 12:25a: If one has worry in his heart, (1) he should *tell it* (*y^e^śîḥennāh*, from *ś-y-ḥ*) to others or (2) he should *remove it* (implicitly pointing *yaśśîḥennāh*, as if from *n-s-ḥ* H "remove"). JPSV is close to (2): "If there is anxiety in a man's mind let him quash it (*yašḥennāh*, from *š-ḥ-ḥ* H), and turn it into joy with a good word." But the elliptical conditional presumed in this interpretation is unnatural for BH, and neither *š-ḥ-h* (= *š-ḥ-ḥ*) H ("cause to bow down") nor *ś-m-ḥ* D ("make happy") provide the meanings required for JPSV's translation.

12:26 The righteous man is released[a] from misfortune[b],
while the way of the wicked leads them astray.

[a] *yuttar* (MT *yātēr*). [b] *mērāʿāh* (MT *mērēʿēhû*).

The MT of v 26a is incomprehensible and requires emendation. The above changes are conjectural but involve only vocalization. The emended sentence says that the righteous man is released (*yuttar*) from trouble. This is a variant of 11:6a and 11:8a, the latter reading, "The righteous man is extricated [*neḥĕlaṣ*] from trouble [*ṣarah*]." (The verb *ḥlṣ* "extricate," lit. "untie, release" [e.g., Deut 25:9, 10] is a close synonym of *hittir* [from *n-t-r*], lit., "untie, undo.")

In contrast, the "way of the wicked"—that is, their character and typical behavior—leads them astray, into disaster. This is the opposite of Prov 11:5a, "The innocent man's righteousness makes his way straight."

MT's obscure *yātēr mērēʿēhû ṣaddîq* is sometimes vocalized *yātûr mirʿēhû ṣaddîq* ("The righteous man seeks out his pasture") on the basis of Job 39:8a (Hitzig, Delitzsch, and Clifford, among others), but that statement is no less true of the wicked. M. Scott (p. 41) emends to *yᵉtad* "(tent)-peg," that is, an anchoring. BHS suggests *yāsur mērāʿāh* "turns away from evil," but *samek-taw* confusions are unlikely. Also, the second line would then imply that the wicked *can* lead the righteous astray, whereas in Proverbs, the righteous cannot go wrong.

The emendations proposed above—*yuttar* and *mērāʿāh*—follow Emerton 1964. The first word is vocalized as the Hp of *n-t-r*. The H-stem *hittîr* means "loosen," "release" (as from a cord, hence, metaphorically, from bondage), as in Isa 58:6; Ps 105:20; 146:7; and often in RH.

12:27 The slacker will not roast his game,
but the wealth of the honorable man is pure gold.

Though generally considered obscure, the first line makes good sense. "Roast his game" is a natural metaphor for enjoying one's spoils. Although the deceitful slacker may cheat and "hunt" others, he will not be allowed to enjoy his gains (thus Riyqam and Hame'iri, among other medievals). "Hunting" and "trapping" are metaphors for the evildoer's schemes and enticements; for example, 6:26; Mic 7:2; Lam 3:52; Ps 124:7; 142:4.

slacker [*rᵉmiyyah*]: Or "deceiver," lit., "slackness," "deceit. On the ambiguity of *rᵉmiyyah*, see the Comment on 10:4. The masculine-singular verb shows that *rᵉmiyyah* (grammatically feminine-singular) is an abstract-for-concrete metonymy.

The second line is loosely related to the first. The point seems to be to contrast the illusory character of the slacker's gains with the high value of the man of honor's achievements.

In v 27b, *wᵉhôn ʾādām yāqār ḥārûṣ*, some transpose *yāqār* and *ḥārûṣ* and translate "but the wealth of the diligent man [*ḥārûṣ*] is precious" (thus Murphy), but this does not improve the sense.

Hebrew *yāqār* usually means "precious." It mostly modifies an item of value, though in Prov 6:26 it is said of a *nepeš*, "person" or "life." As an Aramaism (or a rabbinic usage), it can mean "honorable" (*y^eqār* = "honor," e.g., Esth 1:20; 6:6, 7, 11). This nuance gives a better antithesis to "deceitful man."

12:28 In the path of righteousness there is life,
while the way of [wickedness[a]] leads to[b] death.

---

[a] Conjecture; original uncertain (MT *n^etîbāh*). [b] *'el* (MT *'al*).

The MT of v 28b can be translated, lit., "and the way of a path not [*'al*] death." But this makes little sense. The phrase *derek n^etibah*, "way of a [or "its"] path," is meaningless, but no satisfactory emendation has been suggested. The parallel between "life" and "death" suggests that this proverb, like almost all of the others in this unit, is antithetical, not synonymous. An antithesis to "righteousness" is required. I supply "wickedness" for the general sense, without knowing which Hebrew word was used.

In the latter part of the line, the Masoretic vocalization of *'al* "not" rather than *'el* "to" was traditionally assumed to affirm immortality, as if the verse meant: "the way of its [righteousness's] path is non-death" (Delitzsch; Dahood 1960; Waltke: "immortality"). The syntax, however, is impossible. In any case, "not death" would not necessarily imply living forever but only avoiding a premature death. Waltke objects that *ḥayyim* cannot be "merely" temporal life, but temporal life is no small thing.

Emendations proposed for MT's *n^etîbāh* "path" include *m^ešûbāh* "waywardness" (BHS) and *tô'ēbāh* "abomination" (Murphy). The last word, however, is not used by itself to designate evil. See further the Textual Notes. MT's *n^etîbāh* "path" looks like it is a doublet of *derek* and accidentally displaced another word.

to death: *'el* for MT's *'al* "not." Those who want to maintain the notion of immortality in this text adduce a Ugaritic phrase in CAT 1.17.VI.27: *bl mwt* "not dying" // *ḥym* "life" (Dahood 1960; Waltke). But in Hebrew, the particle *'al* negates only imperatives and jussives, not nouns. When it is directly attached to a noun, a jussive notion or imperative notion is implied by context, as in 2 Sam 1:21, "(Let there be) no dew, (let there be) no rain, upon you"; sim. Prov 8:10; 17:12; 27:2; Ps 83:2. We should point *'el* "to" with the versions; see the Textual Notes. For the syntax, compare Prov 11:19a.

13:1 A wise son—a father's discipline,
while an impudent one does not heed a rebuke.

A son's wisdom "is" paternal discipline, in the sense of witnessing to it, because the former arises from the latter. Naḥmias accurately paraphrases: "When you see a wise son, you may be certain that his father has disciplined him, and when you see an impudent one, you may be certain that he never heard a rebuke in his father's house." Naḥmias adduces the example of David's failure to rebuke his sons (1 Kgs 1:6). Still (the B-line cautions), discipline (*musar*) is not in itself sufficient. The *leṣ*, by nature impudent and scornful (see Vol. I, 42), will not pay heed to paternal rebukes and is impervious to the benefits of discipline. This idea is developed in Prov 9:7–9; see the Comment there.

ben ḥakam musar 'ab: Lit., "A wise son a father's discipline" or "A wise son is a father's discipline." The syntax of the clause is the usual form of nominal predication in Hebrew: "X Y" means "X is Y." But this sentence is different, for a son cannot actually *be* discipline, nor does "discipline" imply an adjectival idea that could qualify "son."[271] The sentence is an example of blunt juxtaposition, in which two nouns are set side-by-side without an obvious or usual semantic connection, leaving the reader to tease out the connection. The literal translation, "A wise son—a father's discipline," reflects the feel of the Hebrew. The connection in this case is a form of implication: "X (is) Y" means "X implies Y" or "Y is the cause of X." Other examples of blunt juxtaposition are 13:18a; 14:8; 14:30b; 15:15b; and 19:11a.

Blunt juxtapositions such as 13:1a could be termed "stroboscopic," as J. G. Williams defines it: "a juxtaposition of images which are . . . projected stroboscopically: they are seen quickly side by side, then they are shut off" (1980: 41; and see Vol. I, 15). Williams, however, would apply this to all nominal predications in Proverbs, although these are of the sort usual in Hebrew (X Y = X is Y). Murphy calls the syntax of 13:1a juxtaposition, but he does not distinguish it from the usual type of predication in Proverbs. The relationship between the two substantives is usually more transparent, expressing identity, classification, or quality. In blunt juxtaposition, the predication is not comfortably translated by "is." Nevertheless, the construction is syntactically regular.

Other proposals for 13:1a include emending *'b* to *'ōhēb* "loves" (BHS); deriving *'b* from *'wb*, supposedly an Aramaizing form of *'hb* "love" (G. R. Driver 1932a: 144); emending to *mᵉyussār 'āb* "is disciplined by [his] father" (G. R. Driver 1940: 174; McKane); supplying the notion of "obeys" (cf. Syr, Gk, Tg). The traditional Jewish commentators commonly supply the verb *mqbl* "receives."

13:2 From the fruit of his mouth a man will eat good things,
and the gullet of the treacherous, lawlessness.

Good speech is like a fruit (cf. 12:14; 18:20, 21), a source of nourishment for those who hear it. One "eats" what he produces and, if he speaks goodness, he will enjoy it himself. In contrast, treacherous men "eat" lawlessness. (The verb in v 2a applies in 2b.) Lawlessness is both their food and their poison. See Prov 4:17; 19:28; and the excursus on "The Wicked Man," Vol. I, 117–18. Prov 13:2a ≈ 12:14a ≈ 18:21b.

From . . . things: Lit., "From the fruit of a man's mouth he eats good (things)."

and the gullet [nepeš] of the treacherous, lawlessness: That is, eats lawlessness. The two lines of 13:2 are linked by the two functional synonyms "mouth" and "gullet" and the antonyms "good(ness)" and "lawlessness." Still, the lines are poorly related because the mouth is the source of the fruit in the A-line while the gullet is the consumer of lawlessness in the B-line.

13:3 He who watches his mouth guards his life.
He who opens wide his lips—disaster is his.

This couplet is linked to the preceding by the words *peh* ("mouth") and *nepeš* ("gullet"/"appetite"/"life"), and also the theme of speech. Wisdom often advises

[271] Nor can the verb "not heed" (*lo' šamaʿ*) be implicit in the first line because retrograde gapping is possible only if the gapped verb is in final position. Thus C. Miller 2005: 43–45.

caution in speech. Together the lines suggest an image of guarding a gate. A prudent man guards his mouth as one would a gate and thereby protects his *nepeš*—his gullet, his emotions, his life (see the Comment on 3:22). A fool opens his mouth wide, allowing disaster to go forth and also, less obviously, to enter. We learn this from the metaphor of "eating" in the preceding verse and the image of guarding one's *nepeš* "life," "gullet," in the A-line. Since *nepeš* means both "life" and "gullet," this proverb incorporates three images from the area of the mouth and neck.

opens wide [*pośeq*]: *Pśq* is not the usual verb for opening either gates or lips; that would be *ptḥ* "open." *Pśq* appears elsewhere only in Ezek 16:25 (D-stem), where it is used of a woman spreading her legs wide to paramours. Possibly *pśq* means "gape wide" and has harsh or crude connotations.

Intertwined sound patterns make this proverb striking: ***noṢER PI(Y)W šoMER napŠO, poŚEQ śᵉpaTA(Y)W mᵉḥitTAH LO.*** Note the rhyming of *noṢER-šoMER* ("watches" and "guards") and *napŠO-LO* as well as the alliteration in ***noṣer*** and ***napšo***, *šomer* and *napšo*, and (chiastically) ***pośeq*** *and* ***śᵉpata(y)w***.

On the importance of guarding speech, see the Comment on 4:23 and compare 21:23, a variant of this proverb. Prov 13:3a ≈ 16:17b.

13:4 It hungers but has nothing: the appetite of the sluggard;
but the appetite of the diligent will be sated.

From the mouth as the organ of speech (13:3), the thought turns to the mouth as the organ of consumption. The first line is, literally, "the soul [*nepeš*] of the sluggard desires and (there is) nothing." "Sated" (*dšn*) is, literally, "made fat," that is, moistened with rich food. The promise of this verse is restated in 13:25; sim. 6:11; 10:4; 20:4; 21:5, 25.

The delay of the identification of the subject until the end of the clause, after the predicate, gives 13:4a the feel of a riddle. What hungers but has nothing? The appetite of the sluggard.

napšô: It is unnecessary to emend to *nepeš* (Ehrlich). This is a case of an anticipatory suffix with the adjoined noun in apposition, as in Ezek 10:3, *bᵉbōʾô hāʾîš*; sim. Jer 52:20; Ezek 42:14; and several times in the Gezer calendar. For the phenomenon see GBH §146e.

13:5 The righteous man hates a deceitful word,
while the wicked man will be ashamed and disgraced.

This proverb returns to the theme of speech (13:3) and describes the speakers. One line in this antithetical couplet speaks of an emotion—hatred of a deceitful word, the other of a consequence—being ashamed and disgraced. Each line is to be complemented by the other. The thought in full is that the righteous man hates a deceitful word *and will gain honor*, while the wicked one *loves a deceitful word* and will be ashamed—and *stink*. The verb *yabʾiš* "be ashamed" is a pun on the roots *b-w-š* "be ashamed" and *b-ʾ-š* "stink."

The first verb in 5b, *yabʾîš*, is probably a by-form of *yābîš*, from *b-w-š* "be ashamed." The verbs *yābîš* and *yaḥpîr* can be ingressive ("become ashamed and disgraced") or causal ("cause shame and disgrace," i.e., to others). The verb, as written here, can also be from *b-ʾ-š* and mean "stink" or "cause a bad odor" (preferred by Waltke). McKane understands this as idiomatic for scandal mongering.

13:6 Righteousness will guard him whose way is innocent,
while wickedness will ruin the sinner.

"Innocent" and "sinner" are literally "innocence" (*tom*) and "sin" (*ḥaṭṭaʾt*). Both are abstract-for-concrete metonymies, such as are often used of moral qualities in Proverbs. ("Wickedness will ruin sin" makes little sense.) The wording of the B-line allows us to construe "sin" as the subject and translate, "Sin ruins the wicked," but since the expected antithesis of "righteousness" is "wickedness," the latter word rather than "sin" is probably the subject. Righteousness and wickedness are here personified as agents that hold sway over one's existence; compare 11:4–6 (Van Leeuwen, Murphy). Other personifications in Parts I–VI are 13:21; 16:14; 18:6; and 20:1; see Vol. I, 352–56.

13:7 There is one who pretends to be rich and has nothing,
and one who pretends to be poor and has great wealth.

This remark on human character derides phonies and indirectly warns the reader against pretense and pretension (thus Hameʾiri, who notes that the Dt stem can indicate pretense). The verse may be alternatively read as a paradox: "There is one who grows rich and (nevertheless) has nothing, and there is one who becomes poor and (nevertheless) has great wealth." The alternative reading is equivalent to 11:24, "There is one who scatters yet gets more, and one who saves out of honesty yet ends up in need."

The "great wealth" may consist in nonmaterial values, such as fellowship with God or satisfaction in one's lot (Murphy). An older interpretation, construing the verbs as "becomes rich" and "becomes poor," reads the proverb as a contrast between the man who grows rich dishonestly but then loses everything and the one who grows poor by giving all to charity (thus, e.g., Riyqam). But there is no indication of a moral distinction between the two types.

13:8 The ransom of a man's life is his wealth,
but the poor man does not heed a rebuke.

The first line points to an unfair reality: People can sometimes—contrary to 11:4—buy their way out of trouble. "Ransom" (*koper*) is a payment to an aggrieved person or family to compensate for their loss or shame and to deflect their vengeance. A ransom is not inherently illegitimate. Prov 6:35 assumes that one might well try this tactic, though in the case of adultery it will not work. Delitzsch thinks of ransom paid to buy off robbers, but *koper* does not elsewhere refer to that kind of ransom. (Probably *pidyon* would be used; cf. Ps 49:9.)

The second line seems both irrelevant and untrue. To find a connection, scenarios have been imagined. Radaq, for example, explains that there is a rich man who must give all his wealth to save his life and there is a poor man who lives his life in ease and never *hears* a rebuke. But it is unclear why the poor man would have a life of ease, and, moreover, in Proverbs, *šmʿ* "hear," "heed," is used only of *intentional* hearing or listening (contrast Qoh 7:21). Note how an insolent person does not *šmʿ* a rebuke (Prov 13:1b). Plöger reads the saying as an ironic statement to the effect that while a rich man can buy his way out of danger, a poor man can only play dumb ("does not hear") because he has nothing to offer. But *geʿarah* means "rebuke," not "threat." The phrase "does not heed a rebuke" seems to have been mistakenly copied from the end of 13:1b. Waltke explains that since a rich man can save himself by paying a ransom, he will pay heed to a rebuke, but since a poor man cannot pay up, he has no motivation to accept chastisement, and will ignore a threatening rebuke. This is too convoluted to be persuasive. Moreover, there is no reason for the rich man to heed a rebuke if the ransom (or bribe) were effective, and the poor man would have all the more reason to show humility. Anyway, in no circumstances would accepting a "rebuke" help avert a death penalty. This line has not been satisfactorily explained.

13:9 The light of the righteous will shine,
while the lamp of the wicked will go out.

"Light" and "lamp" are metaphors for life itself but also for the quality of life (e.g., Job 18:5–6, which uses the same language). Darkness connotes misery (e.g., Job 18:6, 19:8) and premature death (e.g., Job 18:18; Qoh 6:4), both of which are relevant here. (On this imagery, see TDOT 1.160; 5.254–56). The lamp may also allude to one's progeny; see the Comment on 20:20. Prov 13:9b = 24:20b.

will shine [*yiśmaḥ*]: The root *ś-m-ḥ* has a double sense, "rejoice" (its usual meaning) and "shine" (an archaic but attested usage; see Greenfield 1959: 147). Both senses may be present here in a way that suggests fusion of light and joy. Saʿadia glosses *śmḥ* as "to flower," "grow" (related to *ṣ-m-ḥ*) in his *Agron*, while in his commentary to Proverbs he assigns it the related sense of "increase"; but neither usage is well established.

The LXX adds, "Deceitful souls wander in sins, but the righteous have compassion and show mercy."

13:10 A shallow man[a] causes strife by arrogance,
while wisdom is with those who take counsel.

[a] *rēq* (MT *raq*).

The smart thing to do is to listen to others' ideas, not to stick pigheadedly to one's own notions. There are two mismatches in this couplet. First, arrogance and taking counsel are not direct contraries; second, wisdom is not the antithesis of causing strife. Each line provides a component gapped in the other. Line A receives from line B the premise that a shallow man *does not take counsel*. This is the missing connector between arrogance and conflict. The shallow man is too puffed up with self-importance to look to others for wise counsel. Facing a difficult situation, he rushes in and ignites conflict. Taking counsel makes one pause and assess a tense situation more judiciously. The wise speak with each other rationally and reasonably, without arrogance (Riyqam). This is a disjointed proverb, on which see the Introduction to Vol. II (II.E).

shallow [*req*]: Lit., "empty." *Reqim* are rootless, unstable men. They are attracted to agitators and get involved in conflicts (Judg 9:4; 11:3; 2 Chr 13:7), and they are a byword for lewdness and lack of dignity (2 Sam 6:20).

rēq: The MT reads "Only [*raq*] by arrogance does he cause strife." This lacks an overt subject, and the "only" is a pointless limitation on the applicability of the statement because other flaws besides arrogance can cause conflict. We should vocalize *rēq*, which is sometimes written *rq* (2 Sam 6:20; Prov 28:19; 2 Chr 13:7).

take counsel [*noʿaṣim*]: A variant of this line, Prov 11:2, has *ṣᵉnûʿîm* "modest." The two variants envision the same type of persons: those who have the humility to confer with others.

13:11 Wealth got in a rush[a] will dwindle,
but he who gathers carefully gains increase.

[a] *mᵉbōhāl* (MT *mēhebel*).

It is self-defeating to try to get rich in a hurry. This is a teaching of Prov 10:22; 20:21; 28:20, and 22. The wealth that endures—called *ʿateq* in 8:18—is the sort earned in wisdom.

got in a rush: Read *mᵉbōhāl*, following LXX's *epispoudazomenē*, lit. "hastened"; cf. 20:21, qeré. (See the Textual Notes.) MT's consonantal *mhbl*, "from less than a vapor," arose by a simple metathesis of *mbhl* "hurried," "got in a rush." Plöger suggests that wealth gained too quickly raises the suspicion that it was gained illegally. (Thus the ancient versions add the notion of illegality; see the Textual Notes.)

The MT reads "Wealth will decrease to less than a vapor [*mhbl*]." Wealth (*hon*)—meaning movable assets—is an unstable form of property and may disappear, unlike (it is implied) the more durable and renewable profits of agriculture and animal husbandry (recommended in 27:23–27).

Both the MT and LXX forms of this verse are meaningful, but the primacy of the MT's reading is doubtful, because the book does not elsewhere disparage *hon* "wealth" in itself. The traditional interpreters usually explain *hon mehebel* as wealth gathered *by* (*me-*) vapor, understanding vapor to signify deceit, based on the connotations it has in several places; see Zech 10:2; Jer 16:19; Prov 21:6; etc. (Riyqam, Radaq, et al.).

gathers carefully [*qobeṣ ʿal yad*]: Lit., "gathers by/on hand." This idiom is not precisely paralleled elsewhere. The phrase *ʿal yad-* often means "near" (e.g., Exod 2:5; Num 2:17; 2 Sam 15:2) or "into the control/possession of" (e.g., 1 Sam 17:22;

2 Kgs 12:16; Ezr 1:8), but in these cases the phrase is dependent on a noun or possessive pronoun, such as "by his hand." Riyqam explains the phrase to mean "by his own hand," that is, one's own work, in contrast to dishonest gains, but the possessive "his" would be needed for the contrast. In the present verse, the contrast with "got in a rush" suggests that "by hand" means "gradually," "item by item" (Malbim, Toy, Murphy).

13:12 A drawn-out hope sickens the heart,
but a desire fulfilled is a tree of life.

This proverb states an obvious fact of psychology, but it also implies advice not to trifle with people's hopes. As 3:28 admonishes, "Don't say to your fellow, 'Go away and come back, and tomorrow I'll give it to you,' when you have it all along." Prov 18:14 similarly recognizes the psychosomatic effects of feelings. The tree of life represents a source of health and vitality (3:18; 11:30; 13:12; 15:4). If "gathers by hand" in 13:11 does indeed mean to work patiently, 13:12 can be read as a cautionary remark that things must not move *too* slowly or discouragement will set in (Van Leeuwen).

13:13 He who despises a word will be harmed,
while he who fears a precept will be well[a].

---

[a] *yišlām* (MT *y*[e]*šullām*).

Verses 13–14 emphasize the importance of heeding the teachings of wisdom. "Word" (in parallel with "precept") refers to a wise counsel. To fear a precept is to respect and obey it. The implication is that a precept or command (*miṣwah*) holds a power that will punish those who violate it; sim. Qoh 8:5a. Prov 19:16, especially as emended below, says much the same thing.

LXX adds: "For the deceitful son, there shall be nothing good, but affairs will be successful for a wise servant, and his way will prosper." This is an expansion of v 13.

will be harmed [*yēḥābel lô*]: Though *ḥ-b-l* in the sense of "harm," "destroy" usually appears in the D or Dp stem, the G means, approximately, "act corruptly" in Neh 1:7 and Job 34:31. The N-stem + *lô* is an impersonal construction (cf. GBH §128b) meaning, lit., "it will be harmed to him." Deriving the verb from the homonym *ḥ-b-l* "take in pledge," hence, lit., "it is taken in pledge for him" does not provide good sense.

will be well: The verb in 13b should be vocalized as a G-stem, *yišlām* ("be well"), rather than a Dp ("be recompensed") as in MT; thus Ehrlich.

13:14 The teaching of a wise man is a fount of life
for avoiding deadly snares.

Prov 13:14 is identical to 14:27, except that the latter has "the fear of the Lord" instead of "the teaching of a wise man." The teachings of wisdom (like the fear of

God) are like a conscience that accompanies the one who absorbs them and protects him by warning him away from temptations, which can get one entangled in crimes (11:6b). Compare the rewards for obedience promised in Prov 3:1–2, 21–23; 4:22; and elsewhere.

The metaphors of this single-sentence couplet seem rather stereotyped and do not work well together, but the proverb gains a striking tonality by a series of /m/ sounds: *torat ḥakam **m**ᵉqor ḥayyi**m**, lasur **mimm**oqᵉšey **m**awet.*

lāsûr: Lit., "to turn away from." As in 1:2–6, the infinitive dependent on a noun expresses purpose; see Vol. I, 58. The *lamed* is replaced by *lᵉmaʿan* ("so as to") in the equivalent phrase in 15:24.

13:15 Good sense bestows favor,
but the way of the treacherous is their destruction[a].

[a] *ʾêdām* (MT *ʾêtān*).

This verse complements the preceding: The teaching of the wise (v 14a), which is to say, the good sense (v 15a) it conveys, makes others look on the wise with favor and affection, and it is a source of life for them and their listeners. The way of the wicked leads in the opposite direction, to disgrace and death.

their destruction: MT's *ʾytn*, "unchanging" or "stable," is difficult. Ramaq says that the way of the wicked is "strong," that is, enduring or stubborn, "and the intelligent man cannot deflect them from the path of treachery by his intelligence." Hame'iri compares 22:6, which speaks of a person not turning aside from his accustomed "way." Still, when applied to "way," *ʾeytan* would most naturally connote safety and durability. It is best emended to *ʾydm* "their calamity," "destruction."

enduring, unchanging [*ʾêtān*]: "This is usually a desirable attribute connoting firmness and security. Though it does have a negative connotation in Job 33:19, where it refers to a persistent illness, that sense is not appropriate here because a "way," unlike an illness, is not inherently bad. Ehrlich emends to *ʾî ḥēn*, "not favor," but this produces a banal and static parallelism. G. R. Driver (1951: 181) emends to *ʾî ʾêtān* "not lasting." Most emend *ʾytn* to *ʾydm* "their destruction" (BHS et al.). DNF suggests that the error was aural. In any case, this emendation makes the best sense.

13:16 Every shrewd man acts thoughtfully,
while the dolt spews out[a] folly.

[a] *yaprîš* (MT *yiprōś*).

Whoever wants to be shrewd or cunning (*ʿarum*) will act *bᵉdaʿat* "thoughtfully" (lit., "in knowledge" or "in thought"), not on impulse. The fool does not pause to think but just blurts out his thoughts, as is observed in similar language in 12:23 and 15:2. Of the forty-nine sayings on the *kᵉsil,* twelve deal with the folly of his speech: 10:18; 12:23; 13:16; 14:7; 15:2; 18:2, 6, 7; 19:1; 26:7, 9; 29:11.

spews out [*yaprîš*]: MT's *yiprōś* "spreads out" makes little sense here. Attempts to stretch the meaning of *prś*, such as by translating "displays" (Clifford) or supplying "net" as dir. obj. (Riyqam) are forced.

We should vocalize *yaprîš* "spew," "spit," used of a viper spitting venom in 23:32. The near-duplicate in 15:2b has *yabbîaʿ* "pours out," a metaphor for speaking similar to "spewing."

13:17 A wicked messenger will fall into evil,
but a trustworthy envoy brings healing.

An unreliable messenger harms himself (13:17a) as well as his sender. The missing link between the lines is that the bad messenger gets into trouble along the way and never completes his mission. An envoy's professional value requires moral character. Prov 17:20 says that one who speaks deceit "will fall into evil" (*yippol bᵉraʿah*), using the same expression as here. On the importance of messengers in the ancient world, see 10:26.

envoy [*ṣîr*]: This word is used here and in 25:13. Judging from its uses elsewhere (Isa 18:2; 57:9; Jer 49:14; Obad 1; Ps 49:15 [?]), a *ṣîr* went on distant missions. A *malāʾk* "messenger" is anyone sent on a mission, near or far.

13:18 Poverty and disgrace: he who casts off discipline.
But he who heeds a rebuke will be honored.

Poverty and disgrace [*reš wᵉqalon*]: The two abstract nouns are in blunt juxtaposition with "he who casts off discipline." On blunt juxtaposition, see the Comment on 13:1.

Rejection of discipline is tantamount to insult and poverty, as cause to effect. We can paraphrase: "He who rejects discipline is sure to become impoverished and disgraced." The path to honor requires swallowing one's pride. Ehrlich observes that *yᵉkubbad* means both "be honored" and "receive a rich reward" and is the antithesis of both "poverty" and "disgrace."

13:19 A desire fulfilled is sweet to the soul.
What dolts loathe is turning away from evil.

The lines of the couplet at first seem unrelated. Indeed, McKane treats them as separate proverbs. Commentators have tried to connect the lines in various ways. Radaq, following a common medieval explanation (based on an incorrect understanding of Dan 8:27) glosses *nihyah* (translated here as "fulfilled") as "be broken." In other words, a desire to sin that is "broken" or suppressed is sweet to the soul, whereas fools hate avoiding sin. Riyqam finds coherence by identifying the fulfilled desire as "the desire of the righteous," which, when fulfilled, ". . .[272] is sweet to the pure soul," and, he goes on to say, "The end of the verse shows this." He infers that the A-line is speaking about the righteous by contrast with the B-line. Though the proverb is too broadly stated to allow restriction to *righteous* desire, as Riyqam would have it, the technique of reversing one line to fill out the meaning of the verse is correct. Riyqam recognizes here what I call a "disjointed

[272] There is a small lacuna in the manuscript, but the gist is clear.

proverb"; see the Introduction to Vol. II (II.E). By reversing the A-line we learn that fools *desire* bad things. It is a given that a fulfilled desire is sweet. This is why fools are loath to turn away from their evil cravings. (*Ta'ăwah* "desire" often refers to illegitimate lusts and cravings; e.g., Num 11:4; Ps 10:3; 112:10.)

13:20 He who goes with the wise becomes wise,
but he who consorts with dolts will be harmed.

People are shaped by the company they choose. This message is iterated in, for example, Prov 14:7; 22:25; and 26:4. The second line plays on two distinct words with similar sounds: ***roʿeh*** *"consorts" and yeroaʿ* "be harmed." This translation follows the qeré *hōlēk* and *yeḥkām*. If we read with the ketiv, *hlwk* and *wḥkm*, the sentence is in the imperative: "Go with the wise and become wise." The qeré and the ketiv represent variant proverbs.

13:21 Evil will pursue sinners,
while (the Lord) will repay the righteous with good.

Evildoers will have no repose, being ever pursued by evil (i.e., misfortune) as if it were a demon. (The D-stem of *r-d-p* seems to connote persistent and repeated pursuit rather than a one-time chase, e.g., 15:9; 28:19.)

The first line suggests a vague personification of evil as a pursuer (compare Sir 27:10). The positive counterpart is "Surely goodness and mercy shall pursue me," in Ps 23:6 (Van Leeuwen).

The second line can be construed in three ways: (1) "Goodness [or "good"] will recompense the righteous." In this case, "goodness" is the source of reward instead of the reward itself, while *raʿah* ("evil," "misfortune") in v 21a is the punishment. (2) "But the righteous are repaid with good," that is, prosperity (thus Clifford, emending to the passive *yᵉšullam* as in 11:31 and 13:13). (3) "He will repay the righteous with good," as above, with God as the implied subject. Prov 10:24b has a similar ellipsis.

13:22 A good man will pass on an inheritance to his sons' sons,
while the wealth of the sinner is stored away for the righteous man.

Reward and punishment extend to the second and third generations. The good man has a durable inheritance to pass on. The sinner's wealth is also durable and "stored away"—but for the ultimate benefit of the righteous, not the sinner's own children (Plöger). JPSV makes the second line motivate the first: "A good man has what to bequeath to his grandchildren, for the wealth of sinners is stored up for the righteous."

Amenemope teaches a similar lesson. If a man encroaches on the fields of others, "His property will be taken from his children, and his belongings will be given to another" (§6; 8.7–8 [cf. AEL 2.152]). The same belief is expressed in Job 27:13–17 (where the speaker is probably Zophar). Prov 28:8 asserts a similar sort of recompense but suggests that the forfeiture will occur in the individual's lifetime; sim. Job 27:17.

13:23 The great man[a] devours[b] the tillage of the poor,
and some people are swept away without justice.

[a] *rab* (MT *rob-*). [b] *'ōkēl* (MT *'okel*).

The verse states a raw injustice. The sages of Proverbs were quite aware that life can be unfair, at least temporarily. Clear examples are 10:15; 14:20; 18:23; 22:7a; and esp. 30:14, which speaks of rapacious men whose teeth are swords and knives "to devour [*'kl*] the poor from off the earth, and the indigent from among men." Observations of anomalies or injustices imply a duty to prevent them (24:11–12).

The translation proposed here rests on minor revocalizations, though some ancient interpreters, even without actually revocalizing, construe the verse similarly. The Targum (MS[Z]) translates, "The great man [*rb'*] devours the land of the poor one, and there is a man who is swept away for lack of justice." This understanding underlies R. Simeon bar Yochai's comment on this verse: "In this world the rich consume the poor" (*Mid. Prov.* ad loc.).

The MT of v 23a reads: "Poor men's tillage is an abundance of food." This is usually understood to mean that the poor man's plot of land produces as much as the rich man's. "Nature does not discriminate against the poor. Their problem is rather a lack of justice, which puts their harvest at risk" (Clifford; sim. Waltke). The difficulty with this interpretation is that people who have an abundance of food cannot be called poor.

and some people [*wᵉyeš*]: Lit., "and there are." Though *yeš* can mean "property," "substance," in this verse its usual sense, "there is/are," is preferable, since *nispeh* "swept away" is elsewhere used of people, not property.

The alliteration of /r/, the sibilants /š/ and /s/, and the bilabials /b/ and /p/ is striking: ***RAB*** *'oKEL* ***NIR*** *ra'ŠIM, wᵉ****YEŠ*** *nis****PEH*** ***b****ᵉLO' miš****PAṬ****.*

Hebrew *rab* often means "chief" or "commander" in compound titles, such as *rab bêtô* "chief of his palace" (Esth 1:8); see HALOT 1173a. It can also be used absolutely, a usage clear in Job 32:9 (*rabbîm* // *zᵉqēnîm* "elders"); Isa 53:12 (*rabbîm* // *ʿăṣûmîm* "mighty"). Especially relevant is Job 35:9, in which the *zᵉrôaʿ rabbîm* "the arm of the mighty" is a tool of oppression. *Rab* in the sg. is used absolutely in RH to mean "master" (e.g., *b. Gitt.* 23b; see Jastrow, *Dictionary*, 1438b). In various dialects of Aramaic, *rab* means "noble" (e.g., Sefire I A 39, 40; II B 3, C 15–16 [pl., distinguished from *ʿm* "(common) people"]).

MT's *rā'šîm* = *rāšîm* "poor" (e.g., 2 Sam 12:1, 4). Some derive the word from *rō'š* and translate "heads," "eminent people" (thus Plöger, who translates, "Viel Nahrung bringt der Neubruch der Vornehmen"). But *rā'šîm* "heads" would mean chiefs or commanders and not be a synonym for the wealthy.

13:24 He who spares the rod hates his son,
while he who loves him disciplines him zealously.

Here is a paradox: a harshness prompted by love, a lenience motivated by hatred. Though the lax father does not really *hate* his son, his laxity will have disastrous consequences (19:18b) and is thus tantamount to hatred. The vital importance of discipline is underscored in 23:13–14. The present proverb assumes, as Waltke says, that "the home is the basic social unit for transmitting values (cf. Exod. 20:12)." On corporal discipline see also 19:25, 29; 20:30 (?); 22:15; 23:13–14; 26:3; 29:15.

Exodus Rabba §1 identifies the hatred not as the cause of paternal negligence but as its result: "As for whoever withholds punishment from his son, (his son) will develop a bad character, and (his father) will hate him."

Ancient Wisdom commended child beating with some zeal. For a similar maxim in Ahiqar, see the Comment on 23:13–14. Ben Sira, who dilates on this principle with vehemence (30:1–13), restates the present verse as "He who loves his son persists [*endelechēsei*] in beating him" (Sir 30:1). And further, "Smash his loins when he is still young. Bow his head down when he is young, and split his loins when he is small" (30:12b–13). Proverbs does not go that far. Still, a "rod" (*šebeṭ*) is not a flexible switch but a rigid staff that can even be used as a weapon (2 Sam 23:21).

The couplet's concision, rhythm, and pungency get lost in translation. Two attempts to reflect its force are "Who spares the rod, hates his son;/who loves him, seeks to reprove" (Alter 1985: 166) and "Spare the rod and spurn the child;/respect him by spanking early" (Salisbury 1994: 455). The English proverb based on Prov 18:24a catches the rhythm of the Hebrew: "Spare the rod and spoil the child." The A-line has four words, the B-line three. The couplet abounds in sibilants, and the first line has a complex internal rhyme—/ô/-/ē/-/ô/—/ô/-/ē/-/ô/: (a) *ḥoŚEK šibṬO śoNE' b^eNO*, (b) *$w^{e'}$ohăBO šiḥăRO muSAR*.

zealously: Lit., " early." This may mean to discipline the child from an early age or to do so persistently (cf. Ben Sira's "persist," *endelechēsei*). The former is close to the word's etymological sense.

zealously [*šiḥărô*]: This is actually a verb in the Hebrew. In BH it means "to seek"—hence, perhaps, "to seek him out for a beating" (HALOT). But in RH, as a denominative from *šaḥar* "dawn," the verb *šiḥar* also means "do something early," hence persistently and diligently. Ramaq: "will discipline him every dawn."

13:25 The righteous man eats till his appetite is sated,
while the belly of the wicked is empty.

Here (as also, e.g., in 10:3; 11:25; 21:6; and Ps 37:25), abundance and indigence are reward and punishment for moral virtue and vice respectively rather than being natural outcomes of industry and sloth (as they are, e.g., in Prov 6:11; 10:4; 20:4; 21:5, 25).

Other interpretations are possible: The righteous man eats just enough to satisfy his appetite (understanding *l^eśobaʿ napšo* as "for the satisfaction of his appetite" or "himself"). Or, the righteous man is satisfied by whatever he eats, whereas the wicked man's belly is always empty, in the sense that he is always greedy for more (thus the Qimḥis). But the righteous/wicked antithesis argues against this, because control of one's appetite belongs to prudence, not ethics.

14:1 Wisdom[a b] builds her house,
while folly tears hers down with her own hands.

---

[a] *ḥokmôt* (MT *ḥakmôt*). [b]Omit *nāšîm*.

Wisdom [*ḥokmot*]: MT has *ḥakmot našim*, lit., "the wise ones (fem.) of women"; compare the construction in Judg 5:29 (*ḥakmot śaroteyha*, "the wisest of her princes"). But the verb "builds" is singular, whereas "women" is plural. The word *našim* "women" overloads the line and is probably a gloss added by someone who assumed that *ḥkmwt* was plural. Despite its appearance, *ḥokmot* (as in 1:20 and 9:1) is a singular (see the Comment on 1:20). Its literal meaning is "wisdom," but it serves as an abstract-for-concrete metonymy meaning "wise woman."

builds: She gives birth to children and raises a family (Ruth 4:11) and takes care of her household and its economy.

house: That is, her household, her family and its economy (compare 24:3–4; 31:15, 21, 27). This is not the physical structure, for even a foolish woman would not (and probably could not) tear down her house by herself. Radaq says that the wise woman "manages her household honestly and properly and does not squander money, while the foolish woman does the opposite and thus ruins her house, that is to say, brings her husband to poverty." This is indeed what is meant by the woman's "house" both here and in 31:10–31, and her husband's prosperity is in view in both places. The present proverb reminds young men that their material well-being will benefit from the choice of a wise wife.

folly [*'iwwelet*]: "Folly" is also a metonymy for "foolish woman." It is unlikely that "wisdom" and "folly" in this verse are either abstractions or personifications of abstract wisdom and folly, as they are in Interludes A, D, and E. The older collections have little interest in wisdom (or folly) in the abstract. It is likely, however, that the personifications in the Interludes were in part inspired by this verse. "Wisdom has built her house" in 9:1a is probably a quotation of 14:1a. The author of Interlude E reapplied the line, making Wisdom's house a building, as in the case of Folly's in 9:14, whereas in Prov 14:1, *bayit* is a household.

tears hers down: Lit., "tears it down."

with her hands: That is, "by herself" (Riyqam). She needs no assistance in her self-destruction.

14:2 He who walks in his rectitude fears the Lord,
while he whose ways are twisted despises him.

One's conduct is inseparable from his attitude toward God, and the former reveals the latter. In each line it is debatable which noun phrase is the subject and which the predicate. We could translate, "He who fears the Lord walks in his rectitude, while he who despises him is twisted of ways." The translation used above has the advantage of making a less obvious point. While it can be taken for granted that the God-fearer is honest in behavior, it is not self-evident that the honest man fears God or that the dishonest one holds him in contempt. The proverb observes that one's behavior is indicative of true piety or blasphemy. The dishonest man, whatever his outward piety, actually despises God.

his rectitude [*bᵉyošro*]: This is not rectitude in the abstract, but the virtue of rectitude as realized in a person's actions. It is *his* honesty. This specificity is indicated by the possessive pronoun "his" in "his rectitude" and "his ways." (*Yošer* has a possessive suffix elsewhere only in Job 33:23.)

fears the Lord: Lit., "is a fearer of the Lord."

14:3 In the mouth of the fool is a rod of pride,
but the lips of the wise will guard them[a].

---

[a] *tišmᵉrûm* (MT *tišmûrēm*).

The *ʾĕwil*, sly and malevolent, can bruise others by his haughty, contemptuous words, but the wise man can defend himself by his own verbal powers. The wise man's response may be sharp, gentle, admonitory, or even humble (thus Murphy), as the moment requires. Indeed, his speech can have the force of a rod (10:13). A number of proverbs state that the wise can escape dangers presented by fools and evildoers; see the Comment on 11:9.

MT's *tišmûrēm* could be an anomalous 3 fem. sg. verb + 3 masc. pl. suffix. In *yišpûṭû* (Exod 18:26) and *taʿăbûrî* (Ruth 2:8) the *û* represents an unreduced long *ô* in the penultimate syllable, as is common in Qumran Hebrew. However, in the present verse, a fem. pl. verb is required, and MT's *tšmwrm* is probably a metathesis for *tšmrwm* (*tišmᵉrûm*), a rare but regular impf. 3 fem. pl. + 3 masc. sg. suffix.

14:4 In the absence of oxen, the stall is bare,
while by the bull's strength there is much produce.

This proverb is full of puns based on Hebrew *bar*, which can mean "bare," "clean," or "grain." (1) A stall without oxen may be *clean*—of dung—but it is also *bare*—of fodder. What is productive is not always neat. (2) With *bar* = "grain" in mind, the first line can mean, "Where there are no oxen, (there is) a stall of *grain*." This too is double-pronged: (a) One may have grain in the stall if there are no oxen to eat it. But (b) that is a false economy, because then the stall is *empty*. An abundant harvest requires investment in draught animals. Animal husbandry is commended in 27:23–27.

Labials /b/ and /p/ control the flow of this proverb: ***b**ᵉʾeyn ʾăla**p**im ʾe**b**us **b**ar, wᵉra**b** tᵉ**b**uʾot **b**ᵉkoaḥ šor.* The chiastic couplet is nicely bracketed by the first and last phrases, which are syntactically identical: *bᵉʾeyn ʾălapim*, "in the absence of oxen," and *bᵉkoaḥ šor*, "in/by the strength of the ox."

A minor emendation that simplifies the proverb is *bʾwn* "by the strength of" for the negative *bʾyn* (Tur-Sinai p. 98). This provides a precise parallel to *bkwḥ* in v 4b. Ibn Kaspi equates *bʾyn* lexically with *bʾwn*, but an emendation would in fact be required.

14:5 A trustworthy witness does not deceive,
while a lying witness breathes out deceits.

This sentence is not a tautology. It observes that both honesty and deceit are indivisible qualities: A trustworthy witness does not deceive in any way, while a false one lies with every breath. A witness's dependability requires meticulous veracity. A reliable one is the kind of person who does not deceive even in ordinary matters, while a lying witness is the kind of person who is always "breathing out" lies. (Similarly Hame'iri, who, however, takes *yapiaḥ kᵉzabim* as the subject of "is a lying witness.") "Trustworthy" (*'ĕmunim*) means loyal and dependable, in deed as well as in speech (13:17; 20:6).

Prov 14:5b = 6:19a (where the line functions as a single noun-clause). Similar proverbs are 14:25; 19:5, 9; 21:28a.

14:6 The insolent man seeks wisdom but cannot find it,
while knowledge comes easy to the sensible one.

When an insolent, cynical *leṣ* is in need of wisdom, perhaps in the form of the shrewdness needed to get out of a fix, he cannot find it within him (Riyqam). See the Comment on 1:28–30. The sensible or perceptive man (a *nabon*) has it ready at hand.

Another interpretation: Even if an insolent man wishes to acquire wisdom, he fails. This reading is favored by 17:16, which says that an insolent man might try to *buy* wisdom. In this case, the *ḥokmah* in view is probably learning, which even an arrogant man might desire for its prestige and utility. Such wisdom is available only to one with the right attitude and disposition, sometimes called *ḥakam leb*, lit. "wise of heart" (see Vol. I, 33). In contrast, adding to one's knowledge is easy for the sensible *nabon* (see 1:5) who (according to 16:21) is also called *ḥakam leb*.

14:7 Go before a dolt,
and you will not know knowledgeable lips.

If you choose to be around stupid people, you won't hear wise words.

before: The assumption that *minneged l-* means "away from" (because *min* usually means "from") causes confusion. Clifford calls this "one of the most difficult sayings in the book" and translates, "Go away from the face of a fool! You will not encounter wise lips" (sim. Murphy). This, however, produces two unrelated lines. In fact, the phrase does not mean "away from," but rather "opposite," "facing." To go *minneged l-* someone may mean to come to confront him or oppose him, in which case you'll hear stupid insults (9:7); thus Ringgren and Heim *2001*: 174. Or it may mean to come to meet him and converse with him, in which case you will hear inanities and acquire no wisdom (13:20b).

Minneged l- does not show movement away from but means "opposite," "in front of," as is clear in Judg 20:34, in which the ambush squad comes *opposite* Gibeah, not away from it. *Minneged l-* is equivalent to *neged*, in line with a series of compound prepositions that show location rather than movement away: *mittaḥat l-* "under" (e.g., Gen 1:7); *mēʿal l-* "over" (e.g., Gen 1:7); *miqqedem l-* "east of" (e.g., Gen 12:8), etc. Saʿadia aptly compares Ps 39:2, "I will keep a muzzle to my mouth, as long as the wicked are in my presence [*lᵉnegdi*]" (NRSV).

knowledgeable lips: Lit., "lips of knowledge," a metonymy for knowledgeable, wise words.

14:8 The shrewd man's wisdom consists in considering his way, while the folly of dolts is deceit.

The wisdom of the truly shrewd lies not so much in cleverness and tactical talents as in self-awareness. He is able to assess his own behavior and realize where it leads. The point is that if one wants to be clever, he will think before acting.

The shrewd man's wisdom . . . : The line reads literally "The shrewd man's wisdom (is) considering his way." For this construction see on the Comment on 13:1.

considering [*habin*]: The verb *b-y-n* H means "perceive" or "consider" as well as "understand." Prov 21:29b (qeré) says that "the *upright* understands [*ybyn*] where he is going," lit., "his way," though there "his way" may be his opponent's.

is deceit: that is, it is deceitful. Since the A-line alludes to wisdom's benefit to its possessor, the B-line presumably speaks of folly's harms to *its* possessor. Hence the deceit in question is self-delusion.

hābîn: Several times there is confusion between two similar-looking words, the H of *k-w-n* "prepare" and the H of *b-y-n* "understand." In the present verse, if *hbyn* is emended to *tkyn* "makes firm" (Ehrlich) or *hkyn* (*hākîn*; inf. abs., as in Jer 10:23), 14:8a means "The cunning man's wisdom makes his way secure." For one's way or steps to be "firm" or "secure" (*k-w-n*) means either that he walks faithfully in the right path (e.g., 21:29 ketiv; Ps 119:5; 2 Chr 27:6) or that he enjoys security in life (e.g., Prov 4:26; 16:9; Ps 37:23; Jer 10:23). Emendation to the root *k-w-n* creates a tighter antithesis: The cunning man makes his way firm, that is, walks securely in the right path, which is the opposite of the *path* of deceit. One can compare the ketiv of Prov 21:29. Emending to *hākîn* in the present verse makes sense, but it has no support in the versions and is not necessary. The same uncertainty arises in 20:24, but there it seems best to emend to *yākîn*.

14:9 In the tents of the impudent there is guilt,[a] but among the upright there is favor.

[a] *bᵉʾohŏlê lēṣîm ʾāšām* (MT *ʾĕwilîm yālîṣ ʾāšām*).

The first line in the MT is meaningless. A literal translation might be "fools scorns [*sic*] guilt" (*ʾašam*, which may also mean "a guilt offering" and "reparation offering"; see AYBD 5.880). The translation proposed here is very uncertain and based on a conjectural emendation, which, however, relies in part on the LXX. As emended, it expresses an idea reinforced in v 11. The B-line in the MT reads "while favor is among the upright." Good will predominates among good people.

The usual translation of 14:9a is "Fools mock at the guilt offering" (NRSV; sim. Clifford, Murphy). There is noncoordination between the plural "fools" and the singular "scorns." But noncoordination of number happens often enough that it is not a severe problem. More problematic is the fact that scorning a particular type of cultic offering is an unlikely failing, especially since fools (*'ĕwîlîm*) are likely to calculate that a guilt offering is an easy way to appease God. Nor does it help to translate "fools scorn guilt," when they are more likely to embrace it. (Hebrew *'āšām* can refer to the state of being guilty of a wrongdoing but not to the *feeling* of guilt.) Some take "guilt" as the subject: A fool's guilt will mock him and testify against him (Saʿadia); sim. Delitzsch, understanding *'ašam* as "guilt offering." But the notion of the guilt or a guilt offering doing the mocking is far-fetched, and the presumed use of *yālîṣ* is without parallel.

The emendation used above is the best recourse, though it is rather radical for a conjectural emendation. It agrees with the LXX, except for a prefixed *b-*; see the Textual Notes. Other proposals: Fools "mock guilt" in the sense of exposing others' faults to ridicule, while the upright conceal them (Riyqam). "Reparations mediate between fools, // Between the upright, good will" (JPSV). But this is assigning the verb *yālîṣ* and the noun *'āšām* unique senses. An *'āšām* is never a "reparation" given to humans.

14:10 The heart knows its own bitterness,
and no one else shares in its happiness.

No one knows how others really feel, and no one can truly communicate his own feelings. This expression of isolation is unique in Proverbs; contrast 20:5. To recognize that more is going on in the heart than meets the eye is to respect another's individuality and complexity. Van Leeuwen sees here a message of the "self-reflective singleness of the heart in all circumstances" and a recognition of the limits of human community. "Bitterness" and "happiness" he takes as a merism meaning the span of human emotions.

shares [*yitʿarab*]: Or, "associates with" (20:19) or "mingles with" (Ezra 9:2). Not knowing and not associating connote isolation and lack of social contact.

14:11 The house of the wicked will be destroyed,
while the tent of the righteous will flourish.

"Flourish" [*yapriaḥ*] is, lit., "bloom" or "blossom." The notion of a house "blossoming" shows that house and tent stand for the families that live in them. "Blossom" is used metaphorically of the prosperity of the righteous in 11:28; Pss 72:7; 92:13–14.

It is not clear if a distinction is intended between house and tent. If it is, the latter suggests impermanence, and the saying observes that a house can, paradoxically, be less secure than a tent, if the tent's inhabitants are righteous (Malbim). Alternatively, the "house" of the wicked can be imagined as a mansion, in contrast to the modest "tent" of the righteous poor (Ehrlich).

14:12 There is a way that is straight before a man
but that turns out to be the way to death.

People sometimes delude themselves about what course of behavior is beneficial. Fools especially do this (Prov 12:14a), but the potential for self-deception is universal, for "A man's every way is straight in his eyes" (21:2a). But this delusion is not inevitable; it is embraced over one's better judgment, as is implied in 21:2b: "but the Lord examines hearts." There is something in the heart that God can perceive that differs from what people imagine. In their *eyes*, on the superficial level of vision and desire, a certain way may seem straight, but deep in their hearts they are aware of their guilt, and God recognizes this. The two kinds of seeing are contrasted in 1 Sam 16:7bβ: "For a man sees by the eyes"—and thus perceives only the surface—"whereas the Lord sees into the heart." On the complexities of inner-duality, see the Comment on 16:2.

"Straight" (*yašar*) in this verse (as in Prov 12:15 and 21:2) does not mean "honest," as if the "way" in question were a behavior that seems honest but is not. The moral order is not opaque or delusive. What seems honest *is* honest. Rather, "straight" in 14:12 means flat and smooth; see the Comment on 12:15. The delusion has to do with what at first seems *pleasant* but ultimately is not. A striking example is the talk of a seductress that seems delectable—and may be so at first—but quickly turns odious (5:5). Prov 14:12 = 16:25; 14:12a ≈ 21:2a; 16:2a.

turns out to be [*we'aḥăritahh*] . . . : Lit., "but its end is the ways [*sic*] of death," that is, it ultimately leads to death.

14:13 Even in merriment a heart may hurt,
and the outcome of pleasure[a] is sadness.

[a] *we'aḥărît haśśimḥāh* (MT *we'aḥărîtahh śimḥāh*).

This continues the theme of the unexpected end or outcome (*'aḥărit*). Pleasure may be a deceptive path.

The A-line says either that merrymaking (*śeḥoq*) may be a disguise for melancholy (compare 14:10b), or that "there is no merrymaking (or laughter) without a tinge of sadness" (Riyqam). The B-line means that pleasure may issue in misery. (This idea is found in the LXX of 27:9.) The first line observes the ambiguous and alloyed quality of pleasure during the experience, the second speaks of its paradoxical outcome (Clifford). Qohelet observes a similar paradox: "Better irritation than merriment [*śeḥoq*], for the heart is improved [lit. "becomes good"] by a scowl [lit. "badness of face"]" (7:3).

The verb in 14:13a seems to be modal, "*may* hurt" (rather than "does hurt"), since the sentence does not seem to be universally true (thus Murphy). Even in amusement or laughter the heart may hurt, and pleasure (or happiness) ensues in sadness. Still, v 13b is phrased like an indicative statement, not a statement of possibility, and it is hard to determine whether the verse states a possibility or a fact.

merriment, pleasure [*śimḥah, śeḥoq*]: *Śeḥoq* means "laughter" (e.g., Qoh 3:4; 7:3, 6), but also "merriment" and "amusement" (e.g., Qoh 7:6 and 10:19). *Śimḥah* may mean "happiness" (e.g., Isa 30:29; Pss 21:7; 126:3) or "pleasure"—both the emotion and the material means of pleasure (e.g., Prov 21:17; Isa 22:13; Qoh 2:1, 2, 10b). The cognate verbs have corresponding ranges of meanings. (These terms are discussed in Fox 1999: 113–18.)

**14:14 The man of devious heart will be sated from his ways,
and the good man (will be sated) from his deeds[a].**

[a] *ûmimmaʿălᵉālyw* (MT *ûmēʿālāyw*).

A person's own deeds come back to reward or punish him; indeed, they fill him up, with good things or bad, as he deserves and in just measure; see Vol. I, 91–92. The sages were quite aware of unfair turns of fortune, but they expected ultimate rectification.

The man of devious heart is the one whose natural tendencies divert him from the right path.

devious heart [*sûg lēb*]: Here *sûg* is a G pass. ptcp. (compare the use of the N in Ps 44:19), lit., "turned aside of heart," that is, one whose heart is turned aside from the right path. Compare the syntax of *šᵉbûrê lēb* (Ps 147:3), "those broken of heart." Ehrlich interprets *sûg lēb* as "Hartherzigen," one whose heart is fenced about (cf. *sûgāh* in Cant 7:3) and inaccessible to requests. The *ʾîš ṭôb* is, by contrast, the good-hearted man (Ehrlich). The only other occurrence of *ʾîš ṭôb*, 2 Sam 18:27, seems to refer to a man of good will rather than to a righteous person.

from his deeds: The MT's *wmʿlyw* "and from upon him" is clearly an error (haplog.) for *wmmʿlyw* "and from his ways." Compare *dᵉrākāyw* "his ways" // *maʿălālāyw* "his deeds" in Jer 17:10.

**14:15 The callow man believes everything,
while the shrewd one watches his step.**

The purpose of this apparent tautology is to caution the reader not to believe everything he hears (lest he be gullible) and to urge him to watch his step (so that he may be among the cunning). Verse 15a restates v 8a.

callow man [*peti*]: Or "boy." The *peti* is gullible and simple (Vol. I, 42–43). Though he is intellectually the opposite of the devious man (v 14a), he too gets in trouble.

watches his step [*yabin laʾăšuro*]: He is cautious in all that he does.

yābîn: Possibly "understands." But the translation "observe," "watch" (a sense particularly associated with the G-stem; e.g., Deut 32:7; Ps 5:2; 50:22) seems more appropriate here, as in 23:1.

**14:16 The wise man fears and turns away from trouble,
while the dolt confidently butts in.**

It is wise to avoid trouble (*raʿ*), that is, quarrels. (*Raʿah* "trouble," "evil," clearly means quarreling in 22:3.) Prov 26:17 too warns against meddling in others' conflicts. Parallels from other Wisdom books are cited in the Comment on 22:3. The present proverb continues the prudential advice, with 14:16a restating v 15b.

fears: He is cautious. "Fear" here is not fear of God (as claimed by Ramaq, Radaq, and some moderns). Compare the caution exhibited by the shrewd man in 22:3.

confidently butts in: Lit., "butts in and trusts," a hendiadys. The lazy-minded, overconfident *kᵉsil* (see I, 41), blithely sticks his nose into some quarrel or disturbance that he comes upon and (as 22:3b and 26:17 tell us) is harmed.

mitʿabbēr usually means "be angered" (Deut 3:26; Ps 78:59, 52; 89:39). In Prov 20:2, it means "become the target of anger" or the like; see the Comment. This last sense could work here, though it does not provide a contrast to "turns away." Context requires "interferes." We might emend to *mtʿrb* "interfere" (the support of the versions is uncertain; see the Textual Note), but since *mtʿbr* means "interfere" in 26:17 as well, it is likely that the two verbs became confused, because their meanings, "interfere" and "anger," are related as cause and effect.

The second line can alternatively be construed as "while the dolt butts in and falls" (Hameʾiri; sim. HALOT 120b). Hebrew *boteaḥ* "falls" is a rare homonym of "trusts," occurring clearly only in Jer 12:5. Both senses are relevant in a pun (as in Jer 12:5): The dolt is *confident* in his own powers and *falls* into trouble.

14:17 The short-tempered man commits folly,
and the scheming man is hated.

The themes of anger (implied by the "trouble" in v 16) and folly (the dolt's behavior) continue. As in v 16, the first line of the couplet picks up the theme of the second line of the previous one and adds a new theme. This couplet is not antithetical, though it speaks of opposite types—the short-tempered man who acts on impulse (on whom see 14:29) and the schemer whose thinking is guarded and paced. Combining the two lines, we may say that both the hothead and the schemer commit folly and are hated.

14:18 The callow inherit folly,
while the shrewd are crowned with knowledge.

Shrewdness is rewarded by knowledge. A crown or diadem is a reward and an object of just pride (12:4; 14:24; 16:31; 17:6). This proverb does not aim primarily at persuading the reader to strive for shrewdness, for this is by definition a pragmatic faculty, and no one wants to be dumb. Rather, it indirectly encourages the reader to seek knowledge, that is, wisdom. If spoken to a pupil, it urges him to study harder. Since knowledge is worn proudly by smart, clever people, you should work to gain it for yourself. Shrewdness or cunning (*ʿormah*), being an aspect of wisdom, has become a virtue in its own right.

callow: The naïve *pᵉtaʾim* are not inherently corrupt, but they are in constant danger of sliding into corruption (1:32). That they "inherit" folly (*ʾiwwelet*) means that they come to possess it (*naḥal* = "gain possession" in, for example, Prov 3:35; 28:10; Sir 10:11). It may well become their portion in life.

inherit [*nāḥălû*]: McKane (following Driver 1951: 18) emends to *neḥĕlû* "be adorned," supposedly an N-stem denominative from *ḥălî* "necklace." Hence, "Untutored youths are adorned with folly." He reasons that untutored youths do not *inherit* folly; they are already foolish. But this misses the point, for although the young *petî* may be foolish in some ways, he is not yet a morally degenerate *ʾĕwîl*.

14:19 Evil men bow before good ones,
and the wicked (bow) at the gates of the righteous.

This continues the theme of the prestige that comes with wisdom (v 18b) by describing the reverse side. The wicked eventually will be subordinate to the righteous, figuratively bowing at their gates. This may mean that they will bow like supplicants (Hame'iri) or servants (LXX), or that they will be defeated in legal dispute. The use of *šaʿar* "gate" supports the latter. When used of a physical gate, *šaʿar* is a gateway in a major wall. Only the city or a palace or at least a large compound would have a *šaʿar*. Hence the proverb pictures the gateway of the city rather than the gate of a fence about a house. Different kinds of humiliation are possible at the city gate, but defeat in a legal conflict is the most likely. Hame'iri (second interpretation) says that the gate is the "place of the meeting of the wise" (= judges). The humiliation of the wicked in the gate is in view also in Prov 24:7: "Wisdom is beyond the fool's [*ʾĕwil*] reach: In the gate he cannot open his mouth."

In what way can city gates be the "gates of the righteous"? The answer is that a city is characterized by the overall quality of its dwellers. In Gen 18:32; Ezek 9:1–6; and Ezek 14:12–21, for example, certain cities are deemed wicked even if there are a few righteous people in them. Conversely, a city can be righteous even if it has criminals in it, if these are justly punished (Isa 1:21). In the gates of a city of righteous people, justice is done and the wicked are humbled.

14:20 A poor man is hated even by his fellow,
while the friends of the rich are many.

Some proverbs state the disadvantages of poverty and the advantages of wealth without expressly providing a value judgment (see the Comment on 10:15). Though originally they may have been meant as sardonic quips, as many folk proverbs are, in the context of the collected proverbs they serve to evoke the reader's sensitivity to the burdens of poverty. The next verse makes this clear. Prov 14:20 is rephrased in 19:4. See also Qoh 9:16.

fellow [*reaʿ*]: Or "neighbor." A *reaʿ* is another person (other than a kin) in one's sphere of interaction; see the Comment on 3:28. Here it is defined by the parallel as an intimate associate. But why would the poor irritate their neighbors or associates? Radaq suggests that the poor importune their neighbors for help more boldly, even arrogantly, than they do strangers. (Among Jews, we might add, mendicants have traditionally felt entitled to alms and demanded them rather brashly.) In contrast, the rich are loved for lending to others.

Ben Sira expands the idea into an acidic epigram:

(19) As wild-asses of the desert are food for the lion;
so are the poor fodder for the rich.
(20) The proud loathe humility,
and the rich loathe the poor.

(21) When the rich man totters he is supported by a friend,[273]
but when a poor man totters, he is thrust from evil to evil.
(22) When a rich man speaks, his helpers are many,
and his ugly words are prettified.[274]
When the poor speaks they say, "Come, come, speak up!"
yet though he is talking sense, they will not give him a chance.[275]
(23) When a rich man speaks all give heed,
and his intelligence is extolled to the clouds.
A poor man speaks and—"Who is this?" they say,
and if he stumbles, they give him a shove. (13:19–23)

14:21 He who despises his fellow sins,
while he who is kind to the poor—how fortunate is he!

Those who show contempt for the poor (v 20) are guilty of sin (v 21a), while those who are kind rather than contemptuous will enjoy good fortune (v 21b). When the two verses are read in conjunction, Radaq's interpretation of v 20, which identifies the popular rich man as a generous lender, becomes persuasive. Being gracious to the poor means giving them alms or loans, and this is the opposite of showing contempt (v 20a).

14:22 Surely the devisers of evil will go astray,
while the devisers of good are kindness and fidelity itself.

go astray: Hebrew *taʿah* means to wander and get lost. It can imply going astray morally (e.g., Isa 47:15; Ezek 14:11) or to stagger around stupidly and helplessly (Isa 21:4; 28:7; Job 38:41). Read according to the latter sense, the proverb is somewhat less banal. The asymmetrical opposition between "kindness and fidelity" (good behavior) and "go astray" (bad consequence) indicates that the former virtues protect one from getting lost.

kindness and fidelity (itself): For the construction, see the Comment on 3:17.

14:23 In all striving there is profit,
but mere talk just leads to neediness.

Hard work pays off, while mere words bring no profit. See the Comment on 10:22, which uses similar terms to caution against *over*work.

mere talk [*dᵉbar śᵉpatayim*]: Lit., "a word of the lips." The meaning of this idiom is clear in 2 Kgs 18:20.

---

[273] Reading *nsmk mrʿ*, with Segal 1958.

[274] See ibid.

[275] Thus Skehan and Di Lella 1987; but the text of v 22cd is corrupt.

**14:24 The diadem of the wise is their wealth;
the garland[a] of dolts is folly.**

[a] *liwyat* (MT *ʾiwwelet*).

The first line can be read two ways: (1) The diadem of the wise is their wisdom (cf. 4:9; Sir 6:31), and *this* is their true wealth. Perles (1895: 82) calls it their "geistiger Reichtum," their "spiritual wealth." (2) The monetary wealth of the wise is a diadem for them, a legitimate source of pride. Wisdom brings prosperity, so wealth may be worn with pride. As Lady Wisdom says, "Wealth and honor are with me, enduring riches and righteousness" (Prov 8:18). Qohelet states, "To be in the shelter of wisdom is to be in the shelter of silver" (7:12a); in other words, wisdom brings wealth among its benefits. The purpose of such promises is not to flatter the affluent but to enhance the attractiveness of wisdom. Wisdom itself is a "splendid diadem" and a source of protection (Prov 4:9). Other "diadems" in Proverbs are the excellent wife (12:4), gray hair (16:31), and grandchildren (17:6); and in Ben Sira, wisdom (6:31) and sons (50:12).

their wealth [*ʿšrm*]: The LXX had *ʿrm* or *ʿrmh* "cunning" in its Hebrew text; see the Textual Notes. Both readings are meaningful.

the garland . . . : MT has "the folly of dolts is folly [*ʾiwwelet*]," which is pointless. The emendation of *ʾwlt* "folly" to *lwyt* "garland" (Ehrlich) is conjectural but fits perfectly. In 4:9, *liwyat* "garland" is parallel to *ʿăṭeret* "diadem." As in Isa 28:1, "diadem" is used facetiously. What fools tout as their pride and joy—in this context, their wealth—is merely foolish and makes them look silly.

**14:25 A faithful witness saves lives,
while a deceiver breathes out lies.**

Similar vocabulary is used in Prov 6:19; 12:17; 14:5; and 19:5. The second line is less of a truism if we mentally supply "and kills" by reversing "saves lives"; see the Introduction to Vol. II (II.E).

yāpiaḥ: Contrary to the Comment on 6:19, *yāpîaḥ* is probably a verb here, not a noun, since it is parallel to a verb in the A-line. But there is constant ambiguity in the use of this word.

mirmāh "deceiver": Lit., "deceit," an abstract-for-concrete metaphor (Murphy). *Mirmāh* clearly means "deceiver" in Ps 109:2. Note that in the doublet in Prov 14:5, *ʿēd šāqer* "lying witness" fills the same slot as *mirmāh* does here.

**14:26 In the fear of Yahweh there is a mighty stronghold,
and for his sons there will be a shelter.**

This proverb compresses a train of thought: The fear of the Lord provides a stronghold for the possessor of this virtue. On the day of danger, such a one does not enter the (figurative) fortress alone, but brings his children with him. The fortress metaphor allows the proverb to promise that the God-fearer's children are also protected, though in reality this is a non sequitur.

stronghold [*mibṭaḥ*]: This derives from *b-ṭ-ḥ* "trust" or "confidence" and means "something one can trust in." The proverb brings together the concepts of fear and trust, which are apparent contraries, to teach that the fear of God is a source of confidence. Jeremiah brings out the meaning of *mibṭaḥ*: "Blessed is the man who trusts in the Lord, and whose *mibṭaḥ* is the Lord" (17:7; see vv 5–8).

his sons: That is, the God-fearer's.

14:27 The fear of the Lord is a fount of life,
for avoiding deadly snares.

This proverb restates the principle of the previous one, the life-giving and protecting power of piety. It seems that the editor wished to continue the theme of fear of the Lord and employed 13:14 to do so, by substituting "fear of the Lord" for "the instruction of a wise man." Elsewhere it says that the fount of life is with God (Ps 36:10) and *is* God (Jer 2:13; 17:13). On the well as religious metaphor, see Fishbane 1992.

14:28 A king's majesty lies in a multitude of people,
while a governor's[a] disaster lies in a lack of a nation.

[a] *rôzēn* (MT *rāzôn*).

A large population redounds to the glory of its ruler, for it attests to his success in securing peace (or victory) and prosperity. The practical message to a man in authority is that he should enhance the growth of his people for his own sake.

The two lines make a combined statement about a "king" or "governor." *Rozen*, which means "governor" or the like, always refers to a foreign ruler; see Prov 8:15. The Instruction to Merikare says: "Powerful is the king who possesses an entourage. Noble is he who is rich in officials" (XVcd). The present proverb applies this principle to all the ruler's subjects.

The word *ʿam* "people" can refer to a king's army and servants (as in Judg 20:10; 2 Kgs 13:7; 18:26). Riyqam and Radaq assign it this meaning here. But the parallel term *lᵉʾom* "nation," "people," shows that it here means the whole populace. A "people" (*ʿam*) is a populace or nation united by presumed genealogical relationship. It is unclear what precisely *lᵉʾom* refers to. It is usually used of foreign nations and is almost always parallel to other terms for "people"—*goy* or *ʿam*.

governor [*rôzēn*]: The MT has *rāzôn*, which elsewhere means "starvation." If this is the sense the Masoretes intended, the line would presumably mean: "and the lack of a nation (lies) in the disaster of starvation." Possibly, however, the Masoretes thought that *rāzôn* was a variant of *rôzen* (thus Riyqam, comparing the adj. formation *qāṭôl*). But "governor" is consistently vocalized *rôzen* elsewhere.

14:29 The patient man has much good sense,
while the short-tempered one gains folly.

An intelligent, learned person may seem to be wise and consider himself so, but if he is impatient and irritable he will soon prove to be a fool. The sage gives correction, to be sure, but he must do so patiently and calmly. Wisdom Literature esteems patience because it reflects trust in the working of the moral order (Waltke). The impatient man is not inherently a fool, certainly not necessarily an *ʾĕwil*, but his rashness puts him in danger of sliding into folly (see 14:17).

gains [*mērîm*] : The word is difficult and textually uncertain; see the Comment on 3:35. Here it apparently means "gain," "acquire." In 3:35, *mērîm* parallels *yinḥālû* "inherit." In 14:18 it is said that the callow "inherits" (*n-ḥ-l*) "folly" (*ʾiwwelet*, as here). These equivalences suggest that *mērîm*, like *nḥl* "inherit," means to come into a possession that is expected but not currently held. (HALOT 1205a lists "to cream off, select" among the word's meanings.)

The idiom *ʾerek ʾappayim* "patient," lit., "long of nostrils," plays on *qᵉṣar ruaḥ* "short-tempered," lit., "short of spirit/breath" (Clifford).

14:30 A gentle heart is the life of the body,
while jealousy is a rot in the bones.

On the psychosomatic benefits of a gentle and cheerful heart and spirit, see 17:22 and 18:14.

gentle heart [*leb marpeʾ*]: Lit., "heart of healing" or "heart of balm," that is, a heart that gives health to its body (Ibn Kaspi, MS A). The word *marpeʾ* plays on the root *r-p-h* "soft," as in 12:18 (Ibn Kaspi, MS B). "Life" means "health" (Ramaq); compare the uses of the cognate verb *ḥ-y-h* "live," "make healthy" in Num 21:8–9; Josh 5:8; Isa 38:9; etc. On "blunt juxtaposition," see the Comment on 13:1.

lēb marpēʾ: In form, as spelled, the second word derives from *r-p-ʾ* "heal," hence: "a heart of healing" = a healthy mind. In sound, this is indistinguishable from *marpeh*, "gentle," from *r-p-h* "soft," "slack." (*Marpēʾ* = "gentle" also in Qoh 10:4). Certainly both senses are at play here, as in 15:4.

body [*bᵉśārîm*]: Lit., "fleshes," the pl. of *bāśār*. Riyqam, observing that the pl. *bᵉśārîm* occurs only here, suggests that the author invented the pl. for the sake of the parallelism (the "joining," as he calls it) with *ʿăṣāmôt* "bones." But sg.//pl. parallelism is not problematic. The pl. of this word may designate the multiplicity of soft organs in the body.

14:31 He who oppresses the poor insults his maker,
while he who is kind to the needy honors him.

One should not suppose that poverty is a mark of divine displeasure and that the contempt the poor suffer mirrors God's own feelings. The epithet "his maker" reminds us that God is the craftsman, and mistreatment of his handiwork insults him. If God created someone poor or afflicted, he did so for a reason. Amenemope says

(24.8) Do not laugh at a blind man,
(9) or mock a dwarf.
(10) Do not harm the interests of a cripple,

(11) nor mock a man who is in the hand of the god,[276]
(12) nor be angry when he offends.
(13) As for man, he is clay and straw,
(14) The god is his builder.
(15) He throws down and builds (anew) up every day.[277]
(16) He makes a thousand people poor as he wishes,
(17) and he makes a thousand into overseers,
(18) when he is in his hour of life.[278]
(19) How happy is he who reaches the (eternal) West,
(20) when he is safe in the hand of the god.

(§25, complete [cf. AEL 2.160])

Disabilities such as insanity (being "in the hand of the god") do not prove God's disfavor, for he treats people in accordance with his mysterious will. Prov 14:31a ≈ 17:5a; 14:31b ≈ 19:17a.

14:32 The wicked man will be shoved down in his wickedness,
while the righteous man trusts in his innocence.[a]

[a] *b^{e}tummô* (MT *b^{e}môtô*).

trusts in his innocence [*b^{e}tummo*]: Thus the LXX and Syriac. Most modern commentators follow this reading, emending *bmtw* ("in his death") to *btmw* ("in his innocence), a small change in the Hebrew. When faced with danger, the righteous man trusts in (*ḥsh b-*) his innocence for protection, rather than in his own cunning (28:26) or wealth (11:28). Prov 11:6 puts it in very similar terms: "The righteousness of the upright will save them, while the treacherous will be trapped by deceit." The verb *ḥsh* refers to seeking shelter or taking refuge, and not primarily to *feeling* trust. Therefore, the implication of the present verse is that when disaster (*raʿah* = "trouble") befalls the wicked—which might be a "time of trouble" for everyone around (see the Comment on 10:2)—the upright can *take refuge* and

[276] That is, an insane person, who is under god's special protection. More broadly, the idiom may refer to any ill person and thus include the blind man, cripple, and dwarf (Shirun-Grumach 1972: 159).

In spite of the impression of monotheism that the phrase "the god" gives, it does not designate a single, omnipotent deity. It refers to whatever god is relevant to a particular situation. "In the act of worship, whether it be in prayer, hymn of praise, or ethical attachment and obligation, the Egyptians single out one god, who for them at that moment signifies everything; the limited yet colossal might and greatness of god is concentrated in and focused on the deity who is addressed, beside whom all other gods vanish into insignificance and may even be deliberately devalued" (Hornung 1982: 236 and elsewhere). The effect, however, is a sort of practical monotheism.

[277] The image of building does not refer to God's shaping a person at birth as a potter shapes a vessel (contrary to Brunner AW 482). In Pap. Beatty IV 1.13b–2.1, the image clearly refers to giving a man a prosperous life: "If you are rich (2.1) and power has come to you, your god having built you up." In Amenemope 2.15, "building" and "throwing down" (or "tearing down") do not mean to give life and take it away, but to make one prosperous and powerful, or wretched and weak.

[278] That is, when the sun god is "alive" and active, during the daytime.

seek shelter in their innocence. This is also the message of 10:2b and 11:4b: When disaster strikes, "righteousness saves from death."

The MT of 14:32 reads "trusts in his death" (*bmwtw*, vocalized *b^e^môtô*). This seems to imply that the righteous man has trust and confidence for his future life when he dies. This would presuppose a belief in an afterlife not attested in the Bible before Daniel 12 (ca. 170 B.C.E.) or in Israelite Wisdom Literature before the Wisdom of Solomon (first century B.C.E.–first century C.E.).

MT's *bmwtw* is unlikely to have been the original reading, because its syntax is unnatural. The verb *ḥsh* governs the preposition *b* + the source of hope and is not used absolutely, in the sense of "have faith." Once in existence, however, the variant would reasonably, and without excessive forcing, have been construed as an allusion to the afterlife, as has indeed been done consistently by traditional commentators and modern apologists.

Possibly the change to *bmwtw* "in/at his death" was intended to promote hope in a compensatory afterlife. A. Geiger (*1857*: 175) explained MT's reading as a theologically motivated modification implying "auf die Belohnung, die ihm in der erneuten Welt werden wird" ("in the reward he will have in the renewed world"). The purpose, according to Geiger, was to bring the proverb into accord with Pharisaic doctrine. It is, however, unlikely that the sense of the word can be expanded that far. But a temporal sense—"in his death" = "at the time of his death"—would loosely convey that idea, and is still advocated by Waltke. Geiger reasonably compares MT's variant here to the Masoretic vocalization of Qoh 3:21, which, in a rather forced manner, seeks to deflect doubt about the afterlife. Still, the use of vocalization to make a doctrinally difficult text acceptable is a less radical move than a change in consonants in a doctrinally unexceptionable verse. It is probable that MT's reading arose accidentally, from a *t/m* metathesis and the subsequent addition of the *mater lexionis waw*.

Some prefer the MT, but without seeing in it implications of immortality. B. Vawter (*1972*: 167) translates "and the just man rejoices in his [the wicked man's] death." But *ḥsh b-* is always followed by a *source* of hope and protection, whether real (such as Yahweh, in most occurrences) or putative (such as the shadow of Egypt, in Isa 30:2). It is not followed by an event, whether good or bad. In other words, *ḥsh* means "rely on" or "seek refuge in," not "expect" or "rejoice in."

14:33 Wisdom rests in the heart of the sensible man,
but in the midst of dolts it makes itself known.

Wisdom rests, peacefully and naturally, in the heart of the *nabon*, the astute and sensible man. He need not display it at all times, and he has the good sense to know when to keep his own counsel. After all, "The heart of the righteous man reflects before responding" (15:28a). But when the wise man is among fools, his wisdom will make itself known, either because he will be forced to chastise them (and sensible rebukes are "wisdom") or because his wisdom will be immediately manifest by contrast with such company.

it makes itself known [*tiwwadeaʿ*]: There is ambiguity as to just what "it" refers to. At first, it seems to be *wisdom* as such, but the notion of wisdom being known among fools is puzzling, for isn't it a *stranger* to their company? Delitzsch explains v 33b to mean that fools waste what little wisdom they have by babbling it out (thus 15:2, 28). Similarly, Clifford says that while wisdom has its natural habitat in the wise person's heart, it is not at home among fools and must speak out and reveal itself. But Proverbs does not ascribe even a little wisdom to fools, and, in any case, to make one's wisdom known is not to waste it. Murphy would read v 33b as a rhetorical question: "but among fools can it come to be known?" But nothing signals the switch from the indicative in the first line. It is also a measure of desperation to simply add a "not," as do LXX, Theodotion, and Aquila. The Targum too "corrects" the line, rendering it "*stupidity* makes itself known." In fact, as Ehrlich sees, the subject of "makes itself known" is the *sensible man's* wisdom. His wisdom becomes known in the form of a rebuke or is highlighted by contrast with his surroundings.

14:34 Righteousness exalts a nation,
while sin is the disgrace of peoples.

The true glory of a nation lies in its righteousness rather than its wealth or power; see 14:28. The word meaning "disgrace"—*ḥesed* (only in Lev 20:17 and Sir 41:22 [M])—is a rare homonym of the very common *ḥesed*, "kindness." One may read the first two words of the B-line, *ḥesed le'ummim*, as "the kindness of peoples" and expect a positive evaluation. Then the surprising *ḥaṭṭa't* "sin" requires a revision of the first word. This double-take adds spice to an otherwise predictable moralism.

Van Leeuwen (1988: 58, n. 3) prefers to gloss *ḥesed* here as "guilt," "condemnation"; sim. Waltke. But this is an Aramaism whose meaning in various dialects is consistently "shame," "revilement," and this sense fits in its occurrences in Biblical Hebrew as well.

14:35 The king favors an astute servant,
while his wrath is directed toward the disappointing one.

his wrath [*'ebrato*] . . . : Lit., "his wrath is the disappointing one." Ehrlich says that the proverb declares not a fact but a norm, that is, what a king *should* do. (Compare 16:12a as an example of an indicative sentence implying a desideratum or rule.) But the B-line shows that the proverb does not state a desideratum, and it would be superfluous to say that such a disappointing servant (a *mebiš*; see the Comment on 10:5) *should* anger a king when he would inevitably have this effect anyway. Rather, the proverb is a warning to courtiers and scribes who work in the royal administration, who are called the king's "servants" (e.g., in 1 Kgs 1:47; 10:5; 2 Kgs 22:12). The *'ebed* of a king could be an actual slave or a freeborn man.

This translation takes *'ebrato* ("his wrath") as a metonymy for the *object* of wrath. Also possible is Hame'iri's suggestion that the *l-* ("toward") of *le'ebed* is elided in v 35b, hence: "while his wrath will be *toward* the disappointing one." The resulting translation is much the same, but, in terms of syntax, the verb *tihyeh* in v 35b probably prevents the forward-gapping of the preposition.

is directed toward: Lit., "is toward."

The advice implied by this rather obvious observation is: Don't irritate the king! It provides no particular guidance in this regard, but the warning may aim to keep the men of the court on their toes, to remind them to be dexterous in their work (cf. Prov 22:29). The earmark of the *maśkil* ("astute man") is his prudence (see I, 36–37), and this is prudential advice. The attitude that the king should maintain toward his servants is delineated in Ps 101; see the introduction to Prov 16:10–15.

Ramaq (unlike many modern commentators who are influenced by the chapter divisions[279]) notices that this proverb is associated with Prov 15:1 by the theme of *anger*. The soft reply is spoken by the discerning servant and the irritating word by the disappointing, shameful one. This association may be secondary, but it is reasonable in view of the advice about assuaging the wrath of a ruler in 16:14; 19:12; 20:2; and Qoh 10:4. Hame'iri reads 14:35–15:2 as a unit instructing kings to appoint servants who are intelligent and well-spoken.

15:1 A soft reply turns away wrath,
while an irritating word provokes anger.

This verse pivots between the themes of the king's anger (Prov 14:35) and effective speech (15:2, 4, and 7). Qohelet associates the two themes explicitly: "If the ruler grows angry at you, do not leave your place, for the ability to soothe anger [*marpe'*] can set aside great offenses" (10:4). On the power of gentle speech see Prov 25:15. There are many warnings against strife; see "Strife" in the index.

Egyptian wisdom inculcates the virtue of gentle speech, emphasizing especially its importance for avoiding conflict with the "heated man" or the "hot-mouthed" man. Ptahhotep (ll. 60–83 [AEL 1.63–64]) teaches how to deal with an angry man, whether he is your superior, equal, or inferior. In all cases, the right tactic is silence. This will both expose your opponent's unworthiness and establish your own reputation for honorable character.

Anii counsels a similar approach when answering an irritable supervisor:

Do not answer back to an angry superior.
Let him get it out of his system.[280]
Say what is sweet when he says what is bitter:
This is a remedy that calms his heart. (22.7–8 [cf. AEL 2.143])

Amenemope teaches:

(5.10) Do not join quarrel with the hot mouthed man,
(11) nor assail him by words.
(12) Give in[281] to an opponent, bow before an offender.

* * *

[279] Most modern commentaries are organized by chapters, which gives the impression that these are meaningful compositional units. But chapter divisions were introduced only in the thirteenth century C.E. by Stephen Langton, archbishop of Canterbury, and they have little significance in Proverbs.

[280] Lit., "Cause that an 'in the outside' be done for him."

[281] Egyptian *wsf*, lit., "Be slack."

(17) The god will know how to answer him.

(from §3 [cf. AEL 2.150])

Amenemope is urging a quiet, composed response as an attitude of piety. This attitude requires not absence of resentment so much as reliance on God to punish the hothead appropriately, as Amenemope describes in §4 (6.1–12): The heated man will end up like a tree chopped up for lumber.

Proverbs, like the foregoing works, advises a soft response for tactical reasons, motivating it by appeal to its psychological and social benefit: Such behavior appeases anger, while an irate reaction inflames it.

15:2 The tongue of the wise adorns knowledge,
while the mouth of dolts pours out folly.

The wise do not merely speak the truth bluntly; they give it elegant form. The sages do not identify form with content. The knowledge, the substance of wisdom, is already there, and the wise man employs rhetorical skills in conveying it. Fools just vomit up their nonsense. Verses 1 and 2 form a proverbial pair, bound together by related theme and identical syntax (Hildebrandt 1988b: 217). Prov 15:2b ≈ 15:14b; see also 10:32.

Fine speech is an essential ingredient of wisdom and is strongly promoted in Wisdom texts, some of which see eloquence as their primary offering. Ptahhotep's book is titled *The Sayings of Fine Speech*, and it promises "to instruct the ignorant in wisdom and in the rules of fine speech" (ll. 47–48 [cf. AEL 1.63]). Much of what Ptahhotep offers is indeed guidance in how to speak effectively in various situations. Anii promises verbal powers as a reward for studying the writings (20.4–5 [AEL 2.140]).

adorns knowledge [*teyṭib daʿat*]: Lit., "makes knowledge good," that is, ornaments it, phrases it gracefully. Riyqam explains *teyṭib* as "adorn"; sim. Ehrlich (*schmücken*); cf. 2 Kgs 9:30. Ramaq glosses it *ttqn* "prepares," comparing *b*ᵉ*heyṭibo* "when he prepares" in Exod 30:7. Alternatively, we might translate, "improves knowledge." The wise man receives knowledge from others and makes it even better when he speaks it.

15:3 The eyes of the Lord are everywhere,
observing the wicked and the good.

God sees everything; therefore (it is implied), be careful what you do. See 15:11.

15:4 The tongue's balm is a tree of life,
while any distortion in it breaks the spirit.

The theme of fine and gentle speech continues from vv 1–2. The expected opposite of the "tongue's balm" is speech that is harsh, insulting, depressing, or irritating. Instead, the contrary in v 4b is verbal dishonesty. Dishonest speech, this proverb suggests, is sickening—literally.

tongue's balm [*marpe' lašon*]: Gentle, restorative speech. *Marpe'* is a noun meaning "cure" (Prov 6:15) or "balm of healing" (4:22; 12:18; Jer 14:19), such as a medicinal balm (Jer 33:6). *Marpe'*, from *r-p-'* "heal" is easily confused with—or plays on—the root *r-p-h* "soft"; see Jer 8:15 (*marpeh*). On the balm of pleasant speech, see the Comment on 15:1.

tree of life: See 3:18.

distortion: Hebrew *selep* means anything twisted or dishonest.

breaks the spirit: Lit., "is a break in the spirit." This means despondency and emotional pain, as in Isa 65:14, where "a break of the spirit" parallels "pain of the heart"; cf. Jer 30:15.

15:5 A fool despises his father's discipline,
while he who accepts reproof becomes shrewd.

We are to deduce from the B-line the consequence unstated in the A-line, namely, remaining stupid. In other words, the fool despises his father's discipline *and becomes dull-witted*, while he who *is wise* accepts reproof and becomes smart. The fool—in this case, the wicked *'ĕwil*—very likely fancies himself *ʿarum* "shrewd," "cunning," so the proverb targets the very quality he prides himself on.

Discipline and *reproof* [*musar* and *tokaḥat*] are ethical corrections, not chidings for clumsy or ineffectual behavior in practical matters. Nevertheless, they make a person *shrewd* because wisdom's purview includes *ʿormah* "shrewdness," "cunning" (Prov 8:12). The point of this proverb becomes dulled when *ʿormah* is translated "prudent" (KJV, NRSV, and many), for it is obvious that accepting reproof enhances prudence. The reward that this proverb holds out for receptivity to rebuke is less expected: It makes a man smart and clever, helping him maneuver his way through life to his best advantage. A desire for this faculty might pique a young man's interest. Prov 15:32 has a similar message.

15:6 In the house[a] of the righteous there is much wealth,
but the produce[b] of the wicked is troubled.

[a] *b^{e}bêt* (MT *bêt*). [b] *ût^{e}bû'at* (MT *ûbitbû'at*).

The antithesis to *much* wealth would be *small* produce. Instead, the proverb says that the produce of the wicked is *troubled*. The asymmetry of this disjointed proverb asserts by implication that though the wealth of the wicked might well be great, it is contaminated by disquiet. Perhaps there is contention over its distribution, or perhaps its owner frets about losing it or being punished for the way he attained it (thus in 10:24a). Symmetry is restored when the reader reverses "is troubled" and infers that the produce of the righteous is *not* troubled. The serenity surrounding his possessions is itself great wealth. Similar proverbs are 16:8 and especially 15:16. On *ʿkr* "trouble," see the Comment on 11:17.

MT's *bêt* "house of" should probably be read *b*ᵉ*bêt* "in the house of" (haplog.), in spite of the adverbial uses of *bêt* such as in Ruth 1:9; 2 Kgs 11:3; and 12:11. The preposition seems to be necessary at the start of a sentence (as in Prov 1:21; 8:2, 20; 15:3, and very often). The preposition must be omitted from *ûbitbû'at*, lit., "and in the produce," where it is impossible. See the Textual Notes.

15:7 The lips of the wise disperse knowledge, not so the heart of dolts.

When the wise speak, they scatter knowledge about like seeds. Fools do not.

not so [*lo' ken*]: The word *ken* can also be an adjective meaning "honest" or (less likely) "steadfast" (cf. LXX *asphaleis* "firm"), hence: "The hearts of the fools are not steadfast" (Clifford). This, however, leaves the B-line unrelated to the A-line. Another option is suggested by Hame'iri: "but the hearts of fools (scatter) *dishonesty*."

Hame'iri glosses *lō' kēn* as *dbrym lw' knym* "dishonest words," explaining the phrase as a case of "stating the affirmative by means of the negation." He compares (alongside some less relevant verses) Ezek 18:18, *wa'ăšer lō' ṭôb 'āśāh* "and he did what is not-good." And indeed, the negative particle *lō'* can negate nouns, similar to English "un-" or "dis-"; for example, *b*ᵉ*lō' 'ēl* "by a non-god" (// "by their vanities") (Deut 32:21); *lō' 'îš* "a non-man" and *lō' 'ādām* "a non-person"—both genitives and thus substantival (Isa 31:8); and notably *lō' kēn 'ănaḥnû 'ōśîm hayyôm hazzeh*, "We are doing what is 'unright' today" (2 Kgs 7:9). For further examples see GKC §152*a* n. 1 (which, however, mixes substantival and attributive uses).

15:8 The Lord loathes the sacrifice of the wicked, while he favors the prayer of the upright.

We should combine the lines (Riyqam) and paraphrase, "The Lord loathes the sacrifice and prayer of the wicked, while he favors the sacrifice and prayer of the upright." Sacrifice and prayer serve as a single concept here, embracing the range of cultic activity, public and individual. This means that the proverb does not contrast sacrifice and prayer but only the moral quality of the actors. Far from denigrating cult, this proverb holds it in esteem. The exalted rites of sacrifice and prayer are efficacious only for the upright, for only they can achieve the communion with God that cultic acts were meant to facilitate (Perdue 1977: 156–58). There is nothing in this and similar sayings that even a priest could dispute. According to the Holiness Code (Lev 17–26), of undeniably priestly origin, evildoers will be excluded from the cultic community (Lev 20, esp. v 6); see Perdue 1977: 160–61.

Perdue's 1977 study of wisdom and cult undermined the once-dominant idea that Wisdom Literature ignores—or opposes—cultic practices. Though some Wisdom texts reject certain behaviors and assumptions associated with the cult, the basic stance toward cult is affirmative. Still, it should be noted that Proverbs gives less attention to cult than do the Egyptian texts and is less specific in its demands, except for 3:9.

In addition to the texts that Perdue examines, another Egyptian text that affirms cultic activity is Pap. Beatty IV (vso. 4.10–5.10; AW 227–28). This anonymous instruction enjoins regular worship and sacrifice, respect for the gods' property, cultic purity, proper comportment at festival processions, maintenance of silence in the temple, and attention to the priests (probably meaning donation of benefices). An interesting counsel is, "Make offerings to [God] with a loving heart, that he may give you food of his own gift. As a man loves him who acts on his behalf, so does this god" (4.11). This advice combines a cultic duty with a love for God *and* hope for reward. These concerns are not contradictory.

The principle of Prov 15:8a is expressed also in 21:27a; sim. 15:29a; 28:9b; Isa 1:11–15; Jer 7:22–23; Sir 7:9; and elsewhere. The second line has parallels in Prov 15:29b and 28:9b. The basic principle is stated in 21:3. The Instruction to Merikare says, "More acceptable is the loaf of bread[282] of the honest of heart than the ox of an evildoer" (XLIVgh [cf. AEL 1.106]). This is no criticism of cult, because the teacher immediately proceeds to say, "Act for God that he may act likewise for you, with offerings that make the altar rich and with an inscription: It makes your name known. A god is aware of him who acts on his behalf" (XLVa–d).

The Lord loathes [*toʿăbat YHWH*]: See the Comment on 3:32. Though the terms *toʿebah* ("loathing" or "abomination") and *raṣon* ("favor") may be used in any context, they have special intensity in the realm of cult and purity. Particularly in the Priestly Code and Deuteronomy, violations of basic moral and ritual purity are called "abominations" (e.g., Lev 18:22, 29; Deut 7:25, 26; 14:3; and often), while cultic acts properly performed rouse God's "favor" (Exod 28:38; Lev 1:3; 19:5; and often).

15:9 The Lord loathes the way of the wicked,
but the pursuer of righteousness he loves.

This standard-issue proverb is paired with v 8 (Hildebrandt 1988b: 212–13), continuing the theme of God's "loathing" (*toʿebah*) and favor, here stated in the broadest terms.

15:10 Harsh discipline for him who abandons the way:
He who hates reproof shall die.

The second line defines the "discipline" threatened in the first. "Discipline" (*musar*) and "reproof" (*tokaḥat*) are near-synonyms. He who hates verbal reproof (*tokaḥat*) will face a *musar* of a far worse kind—death. He will die because he will step off the right path, the way of life, and wander into deadly territory, with no hope of correction to save him.

Musar, "discipline" or "education," does not mean punishment except when intended to educate. Death cannot be said to discipline or educate someone, for then no change is possible. Here the term is used facetiously or in deliberate exaggeration (see the Comment on 11:23): It is a severe correction indeed that awaits the reprobate!

Only here is the right path called simply *ʾoraḥ* "way" with no further specifica-

---

[282] This is a nice pun on Egyptian *bit*, which means both "loaf of bread" and "character."

tion. This is *the* way (though the definite article is not used)—the safe and natural path through the broken and booby-trapped landscape of life; see Vol. I, 129. It is defined as the right way by its antithesis with hating reproof, for loving reproof *is* wisdom (Prov 12:1), and it leads to life (4:13; 10:17).

15:11 Sheol and Abaddon are before the Lord:
All the more so human hearts!

If God can see into the dark and distant recesses of the underworld, called both Sheol and Abaddon ("destruction"), how much more does his omniscience reach the much shallower and more accessible depths of the human heart. Thus one must fear God—actually be afraid of him—for he is watching *you*, everywhere, always (see Vol. I, 69–71).

In the Bible, as M. Carasik (*2000*) has shown, God is not usually presumed to know what humans are thinking. He deduces thoughts from behavior. When God "tests" the heart (as in Prov 17:3; 2 Chr 32:31), he does so by creating a dilemma in which the person must prove his loyalty by the choice he makes. In the present verse, however, and a very few others, it is assumed that God can directly perceive thoughts. Though the reader of this proverb might not have disputed God's omniscience, he would not have regarded it as self-evident.

15:12 The impudent man does not like being rebuked.
He will not go to the wise.

One should go to the wise for instruction, even if it means bearing the unpleasantness of honest criticism. (Where the MT has "to [*ʾel*]," the LXX has "with [*ʾet*]"; cf. MT 13:20a and 22:24ab.) To go *with* the wise is to associate with them regularly; to go *to* them means to approach them for instruction; cf. Prov 6:6.

The sounds of *hokeaḥ* "rebuke" are echoed in *ḥăkamim* "wise," helping to tighten the association between the rebukes and wise, both of which the scoffer rejects. Salisbury (1994: 45) offers an extended analysis of the rhetoric of this verse.

15:13 A happy heart brightens the face,
while by the heart's sadness the spirit grows ill.

Verses 13–17 are threaded together by the keywords *leb* "heart" and *ṭob* "good" (translated "better" in comparisons). With the exception of v 14, they define the conditions for good cheer and describe its benefits. Prov 15:13b ≈ 17:22b; 18:14.

"Brightens the face" is lit. "makes the face good," that is, cheerful. Although it is true that v 13a describes an external effect while v 13b remains interior (Murphy), the look on one's face is symptomatic of one's spirit and thus may be a metonymy for it. The heart is the locus of both cheer and melancholy, as well as thoughts and ideas. Though "heart" (*leb*) and "spirit" (*ruaḥ*) are both organs of emotions, the second line distinguishes between the two, as if the state of the latter were caused by the condition of the former.

Unless this proverb is a static statement of psychosomatic facts, it implies that one should *choose* good cheer and avoid sadness. It is assumed that one's moods are in his control. One indicator of this notion is the use of verbs for "rejoice" in the imperative; for example, Prov 5:18; Deut 33:18; Judg 9:19; Joel 2:21. Various proverbs affirm the power of a cheerful spirit. Prov 17:22 (≈ 15:13) describes the salubrious *physical* effect of good cheer (sim. Sir 13:25–26). Qohelet paradoxically reverses Prov 15:13 when he says, "Better is anger than laughter, because by a sad face [lit., "badness of face"] the heart is improved" (7:3), or "Irritation is better than merriment, for the heart is cheered by a scowl."

15:14 The heart of the astute man seeks knowledge,
while the mouth of dolts feeds on folly.

The astute, sensible man (the *nabon*) seeks his own sustenance and finds it in knowledge, while fools graze on folly. When read together with this verse, the cheerful heart in vv 13 and 15 is redefined as the mind that desires wisdom.

seeks . . . feeds. The words *biqqeš* ("seek") and *raʿah* ("feed," "graze," "shepherd"/"pursue") are near synonyms; see Ps 34:15, and compare Zeph 2:3 with Deut 16:20. The verb *rʿh* here can be translated "pursues" as well as "feeds," and both senses are in play.

mouth [*wpy*]: Thus the qeré, supported by the doublet in 15:2b.

The verb *raʿah* denotes both what the shepherd does—pursuing his sheep and feeding them—and what the sheep do—feeding or grazing. *Raʿah* is equivalent to *radap* "pursue" in Hos 12:2. Aramaic speakers might hear a pun on the Aramaic verb *r*^{e}*ʿah* "desire" (noted by Hameʾiri). The interplay among the meanings of *r-ʿ-h* is discussed in the Comment on 10:21. *Raʿah* can be a transitive verb, and in Prov 10:21, the wise are said to "shepherd" other people, but that sense would not work well here, where the direct object is "folly."

This folly is called *ʾiwwelet*, the most pernicious sort. Thickheaded dolts (*k*^{e}*silim*) are not necessarily *ʾĕwilim* at the outset, but their smugness and indifference make them susceptible to the insidious attractions of *ʾiwwelet*. The background image is sheep-like fools "grazing" on folly. Prov 15:14a ≈ 18:15a; 15:14b ≈ 15:2b, the latter referring to the fool's speech.

15:15 All the days of the poor man are bad,
but he whose heart is cheerful (has) an ongoing feast.

To be sure, the days of a poor man are (objectively) wretched, but if he has inner happiness, he enjoys, as it were, an unending feast. This observation is reaffirmed in the next verse. This reverses the expected notion—that feasting brings cheerfulness. With regard to observations on the harsh realities of poverty, see the Comment on 10:15.

The second line says, literally, "(He who is) good of heart—an ongoing feast." (On blunt juxtaposition see the Comment on 13:1.) This may be elliptical for "but all the days of him whose heart is cheerful are an ongoing feast." "Bad" and "good" here mean unpleasant and pleasant.

whose heart is cheerful: The phrase *ṭwb leb*, lit. "goodness of heart" (in various formations), means good cheer. This feeling may be a sense of satisfaction and well-being (Deut 28:47; Isa 65:14; 1 Kgs 8:66 = 2 Chr 7:10; Esth 5:9). It may also be the gaiety or cheerfulness attendant on merrymaking, sometimes with a degree of inebriation (explicitly in 1 Sam 25:36; 2 Sam 13:28; probably also in Judg 16:25 and Esth 1:10). Contrary to Clifford, a "good heart" does not mean "an instructed mind."

**15:16 Better a little with the fear of the Lord,
than a great storehouse with turmoil in it.**

Material wealth is good, but other things are more important. Piety compensates for its lack, and turmoil cancels its value. As Ehrlich observes, *ṭob* ("good"/"better") is not here a moral quality, but a "purely physical one." In other words, "good" means pleasurable. This verse reinforces the preceding one, and read together they identify the cheerful man (lit., "the one good of heart") as the pious, serene person rather than, say, the one who indulges in actual feasting all the time.

turmoil [*m*^{e}*humah*]: *M*^{e}*humah* (from *h-w-m* = *h-m-m*) commonly refers to the anarchy and strife consequent upon a breakdown in order, such as follows a military rout (e.g., 1 Sam 5:9; Isa 22:5; Zech 14:13), when "each man's sword is against his fellow" (1 Sam 14:20). The "turmoil" in the great storehouse, then, is agitation and conflict, as when brothers wrangle over their shares of an inheritance. Quarreling is described in similar terms in Prov 15:17b and in 17:1b.

The present verse does not praise poverty or (as McKane thinks) identify it with Yahwistic piety. (See "Religious Proverbs" in the Introduction to Vol. II [I.C]). On the contrary, it assumes that, all things being equal, more wealth is better than less. But fear of the Lord is so good, and turmoil so bad, as to outweigh wealth for better or worse. Similar ideas are expressed using the "better than" template in Prov 15:17; 16:8; 17:1; Ps 37:16; and Sir 30:14. On the "better than" template, see the excursus after 15:17.

This verse is a disjointed proverb with two premises gapped. The thought in full is: "Better a little in the fear of Yahweh (*when the heart is peaceful*) than a great storehouse with turmoil in it (*which is brought on by the lack of fear of Yahweh*). When set in antithesis, fear of Yahweh and turmoil are shown to be opposites. This example of the disjointed proverb is particularly instructive because the parallels in Amenemope show us how it was formed. The process is discussed in "Disjointed Proverbs" in the Introduction to Vol. II (II.E).

It should be noted that the proverbs in the complex template can be overdetermined. After all, "Better a little with the fear of the Lord, than a great storehouse" without fear of the Lord, whether or not turmoil is in it. But the author seeks to teach additionally that turmoil is bad and arises for lack of fear of God.

15:17 Better are provisions of greens where there is love
than a fattened ox where there is hatred.

Meat was a luxury, usually eaten as part of a sacrifice offered on feast days. Greens or herbs were ordinary fare. This verse reformulates the preceding one and is structured like it.

provisions: Though always translated "meal" (JPSV) or "dinner" (KJV, NRSV), *ʾăruḥah* actually means "provisions" (HALOT). This is clear in its other occurrences, where it refers to ongoing royal provisioning of retainers (2 Kgs 25:30; Jer 40:5; 52:34). (In LXX 2 Kgs 25:30 *ʾăruḥah* is translated *hestiatoria* "allowance of food.") This definition sharpens the comparison: It is better to have cheap green vegetables even for one's *regular* provisions, if love is present, than to have a regular rich fare of meat, if the atmosphere is spoiled by hostility.

fattened ox: Lit., "an ox of a stall"; that is, one that is raised in a stall and fattened rather than being set loose to graze for itself.

Prov 15:16 and 17 are based on Amenemope 9.5–8:

(5) Better is poverty in the hand of the god,
(6) than wealth in the storehouse.
(7) Better are (mere) loaves of bread when the heart is pleasant,
(8) than wealth with vexation. (from §6 [cf. AEL 2.152])[283]

The priority given to love in 15:17a recalls another passage from Amenemope.

(16.11) Better to be praised when loved by people
(12) than to have wealth in the storehouse.
(13) Better is bread when the heart is pleasant,
(14) than wealth with vexation. (from §13 [cf. AEL 2.156])

Parallels to Amenemope's better-than maxims also appear in Prov 15:16; 16:8; and 17:1.

Proverbs	*Amenemope*
15:16a ≈ 16:8a	9.5
15:16b ≈ 16:8b	9.6
17:1a	9.7
15:16b ≈ 15:17b	9.8
15:17a	16.11
15:16b	16.12
17:1a	16.13
15:16b ≈ 15:17b	16.14

More distant variations of this formula are Prov 16:19; 19:1; and 28:6. It is significant that Prov 15:16a, 16b, 17a; and 17:1a have their closest parallels in Amen-

[283] Amenemope chapter 6 is quoted in full in the Comment on 22:11.

emope, not in other Hebrew proverbs. As well as being the source of Prov 22:17–24:22, Amenemope influenced the formation of proverbs in other collections.

EXCURSUS. THE "BETTER THAN" PROVERBS

Prov 15:16 is shaped to a pattern I will call the "complex 'better than' template." Its underlying structure is A + B > A′ + B′, which is realized as "Better (A) a little with (B) the fear of the Lord, than (A′) a great storehouse with (B′) turmoil in it." The point is that B is so good that it outweighs something everyone desires, *even when* combined with something less desirable. The logic requires that A be less desirable than A′, and B much more desirable than B′. The order of the components can vary, as in the chiastic 28:6: "Better (A) a poor man (B) who goes in his innocence than (B′) a man of crooked ways (A′) who is rich"; likewise 19:1. Sometimes two terms are collapsed into a single phrase, as in 17:1: "Better (A) a dry piece of bread with (B) tranquillity in it, than (B′) a house full of contentious (A′) sacrifices."[284] Another example is 27:5: "Better (B) open (A) rebuke than (B′) hidden (A′) love." The template can have three terms, as in 16:19: "Better (B) to be humble of spirit and (A) to be with the lowly than (A′) to divide booty with the proud." We could complete the thought by adding, "and (B′) to be proud oneself." Examples of the complex template are Prov 12:9; 15:16, 17; 16:8, 19, 32a, 32b; 17:1; 19:1; 21:9, 19; 25:24; 27:5; 28:6; Qoh 4:13; Sir 10:27; 20:31 (= 41:15).

There is also a simple template with two parts: "Better (A) to dwell in a desert land than (B′) with a contentious and angry woman" (21:19) (bad and worse), or "Better (B) a patient man than (A′) a mighty one" (16:32a) (very good and less good). Examples are Prov 3:14a, 14b; 8:11a, 19a, 19b; 16:16ab, 32a, 32b; 19:22b; 25:7; 27:10c; Ps 37:16; 118:8, 9; Qoh 4:9, 13; 6:9; 7:1ab, 2a, 3a, 5, 8ab; 9:16a, 18a; Sir 42:14a, 14b (Some verses fuse two simple comparisons and are counted as two examples; 8:19a + 19b: "Better my fruit than finest gold, [better] my yield than choice silver." Sometimes "better" is elided in the second line.) The simplicity of this kind of proverb can be deceptive. It is actually structured on a more complex paradigm; see below. The "better than" template can be varied by a different adjective or modifier, such as *nibḥar* "preferable," as in 16:16b and 22:1a (counted above as being semantically equivalent to *ṭob*). Sometimes two "better than" proverbs are joined in a couplet to reinforce each other, as in 22:1: "A name is preferable to great wealth, and good favor to silver and gold."

This description of the logic of the "better than" proverbs is in accord with the structuralist analysis of proverbs proposed by T. A. Perry (*1993a*: 40–44 and elsewhere). Perry describes a four-part structure that underlies the "better than" proverbs (and, in his view, many others). His analysis helps uncover the matrices of values that make proverbs meaningful. Particularly important is his observation that the quadripartite paradigm reveals a wisdom that does not merely "encapsulate" experience, but also "evaluates experience and the *methods* of encapsulating it. Wisdom is thus analytic as opposed to simply assertive" (p. 95).

[284] The LXX unpacks this template to its full form; see the Textual Note on 17:1.

The following application of Perry's method is my own, as is the choice of examples, and it employs the notation used in the preceding paragraphs.

According to Perry, the "better than" proverbs are the quintessential wisdom sayings because they are assertions of relative value or "valuational propositions" (p. 24). The point of wisdom sayings is to compare values, and in particular to relativize worldly values. In the following analysis of Prov 15:16, "+" and "–" mark positive and negative values (in the speaker's implied value system) and the numbering ranks the scenarios from best to worst.

1. (A′) a great storehouse and (B) fear of the Lord (+/+)
2. (A′) a great storehouse and (B′) turmoil (+/–)
3. (A) sparse food and (B) and fear of the Lord (–/+)
4. (A) sparse food and (B′) turmoil (–/–)

(It is clear that fear of the Lord and turmoil are taken as antithetical values, as described in the Comment, and this is an embedded assumption with its own message.) The weighting of the components in such calculations expresses a culture's values (Perry, pp. 42–43).

Especially helpful is Perry's insight that components of the full schema are often partly concealed. In the simple or two-part "better than" proverbs, which Perry calls "proverbs of simple preference" (p. 44), two components or "scenarios" are concealed but relevant to the full understanding of the sentence. For an example (not used by Perry), consider Prov 16:32a: "Better (B) the patient man than (A′) the mighty one." On the surface, this does not make good sense, because it compares incomparables—an internal disposition with an unrelated practical and physical power—and creates a false dichotomy. But on a deeper level, a different comparison is at work. The proverb is built on the following quadripartite schema:

1. (A′) mighty and (B) patient (+/+)
2. (A) weak and (B) patient (–/+)
3. (A′) mighty (B′) impatient (+/–)
4. (A) weak and (B′) impatient (–/–)

The statement in full would be: "Better (A) a weak man who is (B) patient than (A′) a mighty man who is (B′) impatient." In the actual proverb, all components except for B > A′ are elided, but they are essential to the communication; they are like the back and side walls of a house that are not seen from the front but still must be there. Scenarios 1 and 4 are so easily evaluated that it would be banal to state them, but they frame the grid that makes A > A′ significant. The better-than evaluation that is really being expressed by the proverb is that scenario 2 is better than scenario 3. The negotiation of values—the locus of *wisdom*—is in the center of the grid. The "better than" sayings with elision of components are instances of what I call "disjointed proverbs"; see the Introduction to Vol. II (II.E).

15:18 The heated man provokes strife,
while the patient one quiets conflicts.

The theme of strife continues. Verse 18a ≈ 29:22a; compare 26:20.

Egyptian Wisdom often speaks about the danger of conflict and how to avoid it. Some parallels are quoted in the Comment on 15:1. Bryce (1979: 69) associates the phrasing of Prov 15:18 with Egyptian usages; sim. Shupak *2005*: 213. The warning against the ill-tempered man in Prov 22:24–25 is based on Amenemope; see the Comment there.

This verse has an Egyptian background and shows affiliations with Amenemope. Egyptian texts typically contrast the "hot man," who provokes strife, with the "silent" one, who is quiet and composed. This same contrast appears in the present verse, where "the heated man" is the opposite of the patient man who *quiets* (*yašqiṭ*) conflicts. The metaphor ANGER = HEAT in 15:18a is used in 22:24–25, of definite Egyptian background. (The equation is explicit in 26:20–21.) The verb *šqṭ* "to be quiet" (here in the causative: "to make quiet") refers to the quelling of strife only in this verse. This word was likely influenced by Egyptian *gr*, which means "silent" in the sense of quiet and reposed. The association of three sequential proverbs, 15:16–18, with Amenemope strengthens the case for the dependency of this cluster on Egyptian wisdom (Bryce 1979: 69).

15:19 The sluggard's path is like a hedge of thorns,
while the way of the upright is smoothed down.

Idleness corrupts. An idle man will resort to phony excuses to avoid work (22:13; 26:13) and is thus contrasted with the upright and honest (Bronzick *2001*: 171–72). More fundamentally, the sluggard is trying to have his needs satisfied without investing the requisite work, as others do, and this too is dishonest; see the Comment on 10:4.

Walking through a hedge of thorns would be slow and painful. A hedge can be pictured as blocking someone's path, as in Prov 22:5, "Thorns and snares are in the path of the crooked man," and the image of the unfortunate man in Job 3:23. (A person's "path" or "way" can be anywhere he is walking, not necessarily a cleared roadway.) The loafer might think he is taking the easy path through life, but, the sages insist, his behavior will inevitably cause him misery.

Another interpretation: The path of the sluggard is literally overgrown and blocked by thorns and bramble because he neglects to clear it; cf. 24:31ab (Van Leeuwen).

Another interpretation: The sluggard *imagines* his way to be impassable (Hameʾiri), or uses this as a pretext for inaction, one as implausible as "There is a young lion in the streets" in 26:13; sim. 22:13 (Riyqam; Murphy). Conversely, the upright *see* their way as smooth (Hameʾiri). It is doubtful, however, that a person's "way" could refer to the tasks before him. Also, 15:19b describes the actual, not imagined, quality of a "way."

The LXX translates Hebrew *yšrym* "upright" as *andreiōn* "vigorous" or "diligent." It seems that the LXX had *ḥrwṣym* "diligent" in its Hebrew text, and some would emend to this (Toy, McKane, et al.). But both forms are valid as variant proverbs. MT's "the upright" is the less expected and probably earlier variant. It is in line with the equations that Proverbs sometimes draws between laziness and dishonesty and between diligence and honesty. Compare the antithesis between "deceit(ful)" (*rᵉmiyyah*) and "diligent" (*ḥăruṣim*) in 10:4 and elsewhere, which is discussed in the Comment on 10:4.

15:20 The wise son makes his father rejoice,
while the dolt despises his mother.

The first line speaks of a son's *effect*, the second of his *behavior*. The expected antithesis occurs in 10:1bc: "makes his father rejoice" // "is his mother's misery." In the present proverb, there are gaps between the lines, which are to be supplied by contrast with each other:

> A wise son (honors his father) and makes him rejoice,
> while a dolt despises his mother (and makes her miserable.)

On the phenomenon, see "Disjointed Proverbs" in the Introduction to Vol. II (II.E). Both lines apply to both parents (Saʿadia). See the Comment on 10:1bc, of which this verse is a variant.

Hameʾiri associates 15:20 with the preceding one on the sluggard, "for the wise son is his opposite." There is also clustering insofar as vv 20, 21, and 23 define types of *śimḥah* "happiness." This word covers a range of positive feelings, from ephemeral pleasure (Qoh 2:10, etc.; Prov 21:17), including the trivial externals of merrymaking (Isa 22:13a; Ps 137:3), to deep and lasting joy (e.g., Isa 30:29; Pss 21:7; 122:1; 126:3). See Fox *1999*: 113–15.

15:21 Folly is pleasure to the mindless,
while the sensible man walks straight.

The mindless man—lit., "one who lacks a heart"—is not so much malicious as devoid of values to guide his moral choices. In his shortsightedness, he even thinks that folly is pleasurable. Prov 10:23 makes a similar observation about the dolt. The opposite is 21:15a, "Doing justice is a joy to a righteous man."

folly: This is *ʾiwwlet*, folly of the most pernicious sort; see Vol. I, 117–18. Even this is fun in the eyes of the mindless.

The second line, read in the light of the first, describes not only behavior but a predilection: Walking straight is what the what the sensible man *likes* to do. That is where he finds his pleasure.

15:22 Plans are thwarted by lack of counsel,
while by a multitude of advisors they succeed.

This saying shows an appreciation of collaborative wisdom, as in Prov 11:14; 20:18; and 24:6.

15:23 A man gets pleasure from his mouth's response,
and a word in its time—how good it is!

If (as is the case) people enjoy just having their say, how much the more so do they savor it when their response is timely.

his mouth's response: "His mouth's" is not redundant. It is a way of indicating one's *own* mouth, whereas "response" alone could mean anyone's.

a word in its time: A remark that meets the needs of the particular situation is deeply satisfying to both speaker and listener. Hebrew *ʿet* here is "time," defined by a set of events and their configurations. The Catalogue of Times in Qoh 3:1–9 uses *ʿet* in this way. Qohelet teaches that every *type* of event and deed has an *ʿet*, a set of circumstances (whether recurrent or unique) in which it is appropriate; see Fox *1999*: 194–208. Likewise, a "word"—an utterance or type of utterance (praise, e.g., or a rebuke)—lies in readiness, as it were, for use. It is not effective or elegant in itself but only when it comes forth at *its* time.

LXX has a different proverb here: "The thoughts of an intelligent man are ways of life, so that by inclining away from Hades, he might be preserved." See the Textual Note.

15:24 The way of life is upward for the astute man,
that he may turn away from Sheol below.

The adverb "upward" here implies success, not difficulty. The "way of life" is not elsewhere pictured as sloping upward, but is said to do so here to contrast with the way to the netherworld. Saʿadia and some other medievals understood the verse as asserting immortality for the righteous. Interpreting the verse this way, McKane deletes "upward" and "downward" (or "below") as later additions asserting belief in immortality. It is true that these words are not reflected in the LXX, but "upward," at least, is essential to the syntax of the Hebrew in the first line, and without "below," the second line is abrupt and too short. But immortality is not implied. "Upward" is merely the opposite of "downward" and describes the continuation of mortal life (Toy). To die is to go downward; see 2:18 and 7:27.

The phrase "for the astute man" is redundant because the "way of life" is the path *to* life, and everyone who goes on it is astute (*maśkil*). See "Paths through Life," Vol. I, 128–31.

15:25 The Lord will rip away the house of the arrogant
and secure the boundary of the widow.

The lines in this couplet are sequential and suggestive of an anecdote. We may picture an arrogant landowner trying to encroach on the property of a widow—a deed forbidden in Prov 22:28 and 23:10. God, we are assured, will ultimately ruin that man's holdings while preserving the widow's. The widow is the epitome of the lowly and helpless (Hame'iri) and is thus the antithesis of the wealthy and arrogant.

Radaq says that some interpreters read this proverb as a prayer. When Solomon foresaw the pride of Esau (equated with the kingdom of Edom, in turn equated with Rome) alongside the degradation of Israel in exile, he prayed that God might overthrow Esau and establish the borders of Widow Israel. Others, Radaq reports, read it as a prayer that the oppressors of widows and orphans be humbled and their victims saved. These readings regard the proverb as a statement of faith or hope rather than an observation of present events.

rip away: Judging from Deut 28:63; Ps 52:7; Ezra 6:11 (Aramaic), and Sir 10:17;

48:15, *nsḥ* means to rip something *away* from something else. (In the Deuteronomy and Sira passages, it refers to Israel's being removed from the land of its inheritance.) The image in this proverb is not so much of God smashing the oppressor's house as of seizing it and removing it violently from the landowner's property—the opposite of what happens to the widow.

the boundary of the widow: "Boundary" is equivalent to territory or property. Women could not ordinarily hold property in ancient Israel. When no sons were available to inherit property, daughters, according to Num 27:1–11, could inherit the ancestral holdings. Also, widows could gain control of their husband's property (Ruth 4:3, 9; 2 Kgs 8:3, 6; Jdt 8:7), at least to hold it in trust during their sons' minority. The latter case is envisaged here.

Women in that situation had a precarious legal status in ancient Israel because only males had direct access to the courts. Men were ethically bound to defend the widow's rights (e.g., Deut 27:19; Isa 1:17, 23), but widows had no direct recourse to the courts. This proverb expresses the belief that God will ultimately, somehow, protect the widow and orphan and rectify wrongs done them; thus too Prov 23:11; Deut 10:18; 27:19; Ps 68:6, and elsewhere).

15:26 The Lord loathes the plans of the evil man,
but pleasant words are pure.

This proverb teaches that not only are pleasant, friendly words agreeable and sweet (thus Prov 16:24), they are *pure* (15:26b) and hence are acceptable to God (implied by reversal of v 26a). In this context, "pleasant words" (*'imrey no'am*) are friendly ones, the opposite of hostile plans. (*No'am* parallels *šalom* "peace" in Prov 3:17.)

Ehrlich understands the proverb as hinting, cautiously, that pleasant words, even when not strictly true, are "pure" in God's eyes, even though they are less than what he really desires. (That would be called *rᵉṣono* "his desire," meaning what pleases him, which is the usual antithesis of *to'ebah* "[object of] loathing," here translated "loathes.") One is, after all, encouraged to "cover up" offenses against oneself (see the Comment on 10:12). Purity in its cultic sense is not a high moral quality but, as in the case of "pure" animals, merely the lack of taint, ritual or moral. Ehrlich's interpretation seems possible but may be more intricate than the wording justifies. Moreover, with respect to deeds, "pure" does signify high moral virtue.

15:27 He who grasps ill-gotten gain troubles his house,
while he who hates gifts will live.

With illicit wealth comes unease and friction. As Prov 15:6 says, "the produce of the wicked is troubled," using *'kr*, the same verb as here; and see the Comment on 11:17.

troubles his house: In antithesis with "will live," this clause takes on implications of effects beyond the psychological. The LXX's "destroys himself" may correctly paraphrase the clause.

hates gifts: Taking gifts—that is, bribes—is an instance of grasping ill-gotten gain. This couplet is the equivalent of Prov 1:19: "This is what happens to everyone who grasps ill-gotten gain: It robs him who holds it of life"; see the Comment there. Gifts and bribes are not always unacceptable; see 17:8; 18:16; 19:6; and 21:14. In fact, only the present proverb seems concerned with their moral effects.

15:28 The heart of the righteous man reflects before responding,
while the mouth of the wicked pours out evils.

Thoughtfulness in one's responses is not just a prudential or a social asset. It is an ethical virtue, one characteristic of the righteous. Conversely, according to this proverb, the wicked man is garrulous and his words are evil. This is not self-evidently so, since the evildoer may hold his plans within him (Prov 6:14a; 12:20) and even conceal his hostility (10:18; 26:26). Nevertheless, Proverbs asserts, the speech that people "pour forth" exposes their real character, whether wicked (15:28), dolts (15:2), or wise (1:23; 18:4).

reflects before responding [*yehgeh laʿănōt*]: Lit., "reflects to answer." *Laʿănôt* is an infinitive of purpose. In other words, the righteous man reflects (beforehand) *in order* to answer (properly).

15:29 The Lord is far from the wicked,
but he hears the prayer of the righteous.

For God to be far from the wicked means that he ignores their prayers. (The opposite, God's being near someone, means that he hears his prayers; see Ps 145:18.) The prayers of the wicked are loathsome (Prov 15:8).

Verses 29–33 form a proverb string, with vv 29–32 sharing the theme of *hearing*. Verse 31 speaks about hearing *reproof*, and vv 32–33 continue the topic of reproof, using the word *musar* "discipline."

15:30 The sight[a] of the eyes makes the heart glad;
a good report fattens the bones.

[a] *marʾēh* (MT *mᵉʾôr*).

The sight of the eyes (reading *mrʾh ʿynym* or *mrʾh hʿynym*, with the LXX): This refers to (1) something that is present to a person in actuality and (2) a desirable sight. Qoh 6:9 contrasts *marʾeh ʿeynayim* ("what the eyes see") with *hălok nepeš* ("the wandering of desire"; lit., "the going of the soul"), meaning a yearning for what one does not possess, a fata morgana. In 11:9, Qohelet urges the young: "Go in the ways of your heart and in the sight of your eyes [*marʾey ʿeyneyka*]" (discussed in Fox 1999: 246).

The MT of v 30a reads, "The *light* [*ma'or*] of the eyes makes the heart glad." This means something like "Joy makes the heart glad" or "Vitality makes the heart glad." (Compare the idiom with *'or* "light" in 1 Sam 14:27, 29; Ps 13:4; Prov 29:13, and elsewhere.) This is possible but still awkward and tautologous. The "light of the eyes" cannot refer to one's own eyes because that would be the *effect* of the glad heart, not (unlike the good report in the parallel line) its cause. Delitzsch (like most commentators) explains MT's phrase as referring to the bright eyes of *others*, that is, their smiles and favor, which gladden us. However, "light of the eyes" is not used in this way. "Sight" is a better parallel to "report" (*r-'-h* "see" // *š-m-ʿ* "hear" in Ps 66:18; Job 13:1; Cant 2:14, and elsewhere).

fattens the bones: Makes them moist and juicy, considered a feature of good health; see the Comment on 3:8.

15:31 The ear that listens to the reproof of life
dwells among the wise.

the ear: The ear represents, *pars pro toto*, its possessor. The ear that is receptive to criticism "dwells," or is typically found, among the wise. If one wants to join their number, with the prestige and benefits that they enjoy, he must first take criticism to heart. This restates Prov 15:12. The wording of the proverb suggests that it is "as if the ear were a welcomed guest in an accommodating household" (Brown 2002: 159).

the reproof of life: The reproof that leads to and preserves life (Prov 6:23; 10:17).

15:32 He who casts off discipline despises himself,
while he who hears reproof acquires a mind.

This restates v 31. "Despises himself" (*mo'es napšo*) can be translated "despises his life" (*nepeš*). One who "acquires a mind" (lit., "heart") is the antithesis of him who despises himself because the former, it is assumed, has the wisdom that will bring him benefits.

"Despises" (*mo'es*) denotes repudiation and contempt. Though one may rebuff criticism out of a false sense of pride, he is actually holding himself in contempt, even if he does not realize it. "Despises himself" can be read in two ways, which are not mutually exclusive. It can mean that his rejection of discipline is *tantamount* to self-hatred, because it will bring him ruin. (See the Comment on 6:32 and the phrase "hates himself" in 29:24).) And, more subtly, it can be a psychological insight: The ill-disciplined, uncontrollable person is on some level unhappy with himself and unconsciously self-destructive. This is clearly true of many children with behavioral difficulties.

15:33 What wisdom teaches is the fear of the Lord,
and before honor comes humility.

Just as the fear of God is the prerequisite of wisdom (as Prov 1:7 and 9:10 declare), so is humility the prerequisite of (true) honor. What may appear to be contrary qualities, humility and honor, are paired as cause and effect. Comparison with 18:12 shows that "before" in v 33b indicates both temporal and causal priority. The humility to accept correction enables one to grow in wisdom and thus to attain honor.

According to Van Leeuwen, the editor composed this verse as a conclusion to the collection in Prov 10:1–15:33, deriving its vocabulary from the book's motto in 1:7 and asserting the fundamental principle of fear of God. However, the importance of the fear of God is also stressed in places where it does not mark the end of a unit (9:10; 14:27; 22:4; 23:17). The present verse may serve equally well to introduce 16:1–9, which speaks of God's omniscience and omnipotence, to which the only acceptable responses are fear and its near equivalent, humility.

What wisdom teaches [*musar ḥokmah*]: Lit., "wisdom's instruction." This is the instruction wisdom *gives*, just as *musar ʾab* "the father's teaching" (Prov 4:1; 15:5) is the instruction a father gives. Wisdom teaches that fear of the Lord is the right and prudent attitude. Sir 1:25–27 elaborates on this verse. Related proverbs are discussed in the Comment on 1:7. Prov 15:33b = 18:12b. For *mwsr* (*musar*), "discipline," Perles (1895: 60) reads *mwsd* "foundation," but the MT makes good sense.

W. R. Domeris (1996: 96) observes that placing humility above honor (sim. 22:4; 29:23) contradicts the stereotype of the honor-based value system that many scholars believe to be characteristic of ancient Mediterranean societies. Domeris (pp. 99–100) argues that the honor-shame system in Proverbs has a much broader basis than the sexual and familial-based honor system that supposedly characterizes the widely studied modern Mediterranean village culture. Proverbs does place honor high on its scale of values but subordinates it to wisdom and defines honor largely in terms of personal and social virtues.

PART IIB: PROVERBS 16:1–22:16

Starting approximately at 16:1, equivalent rather than antithetical parallelism becomes the predominant form of the couplet. The beginning of chapter 16 holds two groups of proverbs. Verses 1–9 speak about Yahweh, verses 10–15 about the king. The collocation of these themes associates the king's powers with God's (Plöger; Whybray 1994: 88–89). Verses 16–24 also form a loose unit, whose teachings stress individual virtues: honesty, wisdom, humility, fine speech. There thus seems to be a movement from God, to the king, to ordinary people. Another thematic cluster is 16:27–30, which describes types of scoundrels. For the most part, the remainder of the 16:25–22:16 comprises independent clusters with no extended thematic clustering.

16:1 The dispositions of the heart belong to a man,
but the answer of the tongue is from the Lord.

2 **The ways of a man are all pure in his own eyes,**
but the Lord examines spirits.

3 **Entrust your deeds to the Lord,**
and your plans will succeed.

4 **The Lord made everything for its purpose[a]—**
even the evildoer for the evil day.

5 **The Lord loathes every haughty-hearted man;**
hand to hand, he will not go unpunished.

6 **Through kindness and constancy, iniquity will receive atonement,**
but by the fear of the Lord evil is avoided.

7 **When the Lord favors a man's ways,**
even his enemies make peace with him.

8 **Better a little with righteousness**
than great produce without justice.

9 **A man's heart plans his way,**
but it is the Lord who makes his step secure.

---

[a] *lᵉmaʿănēhû* (MT *lammaʿănēhû*).

God's Omnipotence and Omniscience. Prov 16:1–9 is a thematic cluster, whose individual verses are self-contained proverbs. Verse 8 is extraneous and perhaps added later. The unit teaches that God controls human deeds and that this principle must direct one's faith and action.

It is an axiom of Wisdom Literature that human wisdom has its limits both in human frailties and in God's sometimes mysterious will. This is discussed by von Rad 1970: 131–48 (ET 97–110). We should not, however, exaggerate the humility behind this belief. The sages still assume that many human frailties, such as self-deception, can be mastered by the discipline of wisdom, and that the principles governing God's favor and dislike are well known. One must not rely on his *own* understanding (Prov 3:5) because an individual's wisdom can be deluded and inadequate. But wisdom as such cannot be defective because it *includes* reliance on God. (Note the antithesis between "he who trusts in his own heart" and "he who goes in wisdom" in 28:26.) While no one can fathom the divine wisdom or control God's will by the exercise of his own wisdom and virtue, one *can* conform to God's standards. Although this conformity does not guarantee the success of any particular undertaking (thus 20:24), it does help secure ultimate well-being. Indeed, when God favors a man, he may protect him from his own plans and give him blessings beyond his expectations (see von Rad 1970: 135, 143 [ET 100, 106]). The form and timing of success remain in question but its certainty does not.

The conviction that humans are ignorant of the ways of the gods was probably universal, but it was accompanied by a variety of attitudes. In the Babylonian *Ludlul Bel Nemeqi*, for example, a righteous sufferer complains about man's inability to fathom the will of the gods:

> What seems good to one's self could be an offense to god,
> What in one's own heart seems abominable
> could be good to one's god!
> Who could learn the reasoning of the gods in heaven?
> Who could grasp the intentions of the gods of the depths?
> Where might human beings have learned the way of a god?
> (2.33–38; trans. BTM 314–15)

This is spoken in bitterness by a man who is baffled about the reason for his suffering. He is, however, finally released from his illness, and the tone of the book, taken as a whole, is actually one of confidence. Proverbs shares this confidence. Humans may not fully understand God's will, but they can rely on his goodness and wisdom. Indeed, enough of God's will is known to enable humans to make their way through life quite well.

The bewildering constraints on human control of the future are the main point in the Hellenistic Egyptian book of Phibis (Pap. Insinger). Every chapter gives advice but then restricts its validity by a paradox. The nineteenth instruction, for example—titled "The teaching of making your speech calm"—commends quiet, calm speech and condemns the folly of noisiness. But it concludes with a paradox:

> There is the evil man who is calm like a crocodile in water.
> There is the fool who is calm like heavy lead.
> He is not a restless fool who is gripped by unrest.
> It is the god who gives calm and unrest through his commands.
> The fate and the fortune that come, it is the god who sends them.
> (23.15–19; trans. AEL 3.204)

In other words, people can shape their behavior for better or worse and can expect appropriate consequences. Nevertheless, it is God who determines fates, and he is free to violate these expectations. Therefore, we cannot judge others by their appearances or circumstances.

Other sayings that affirm the limits of human wisdom, in contrast to the boundlessness of God's powers, are Prov 3:5; 19:21; 20:24; 21:30–31; 27:1; and 28:26.

16:1. *The dispositions of the heart* [*maʿarkey leb*]: These are thoughts that one arranges (*ʿrk*) before speaking (Hameʾiri). Though one can (and should!) craft his thoughts carefully before speaking, it doesn't always work. The "answer of the tongue," what a person actually says, is not necessarily what he intended to say, for better or worse. One may blunder in unexpected ways. For Job, the fact that God "removes speech from reliable men" (12:20) is further evidence of his arbitrary exercise of his powers. None of this means, however, that the utterance is entirely outside human influence or even that "Human beings are totally dependent on [God]," as Murphy says. People are ultimately dependent on God, but not totally. In the end, however, God determines what actually will be said.

This sense of a mysterious disjunction between thought and utterance seems alien to the confident tenor of most of Proverbs, but a similar note of uncertainty is heard elsewhere in the book. Prov 20:24 says, "A man's steps are from the Lord, and a human—how can he understand where he is going [lit., "his way"]?"; sim. 16:9. Hence one should not rely on his own understanding (3:5).

Ahiqar too believes that the right words are ultimately a gift of the gods:

If a lowly man becomes great,
his words will soar up above him,
for the opening of his mouth exalts the gods.
And if he is beloved of the gods,
they will put in his mouth something good to say. (114–15 [1.1.162])[285]

The gods can, by the same token, deny a man an effective utterance. The speaker in the Sumerian composition, "A Man and His God," complains to his personal deity for *failing* to answer those who insult him:

The wrongdoer says shaming things to me,
but you, my god, do not answer them back,
you take away my wits! (Kramer 1955: 174)

The frustration of failing to find the right words at the right time is a well-known experience. Yiddish has a term for words that occur to you a moment too late, just as you're leaving the building: *treppworter*, "stairway words."

16:2. This proverb extends the principle of v 1, namely, that human understanding is limited, even with respect to one's own behavior. In this case, the limitation is not inevitable. It is a willed ignorance, and God will perceive it. Prov 16:2 ≈ 21:2 (with "pure" for "straight" and "spirits" for "hearts"); and 16:2b ≈ 24:12b.

Though formulated as a generality, the A-line does not mean that all people are inevitably self-righteous. Proverbs nowhere displays such a jaundiced view of humanity. (In 30:12, being pure in one's own eyes is a mark of a particularly pernicious generation, not a universal trait.) Rather, the present proverb acknowledges the human penchant for self-justification and rationalizing one's own behavior. The belief that one's ways are righteous is superficial. See the Comment on 14:12. Deeper within lies the spirit and the heart, and God sees into them (Prov 15:11), even when a man can not or will not do so himself (1 Sam 16:7b).

What might God see there? Not merely that a person has behaved rightly or wrongly, for God would only need to observe *actions* ("ways") to know this. Not merely a person's thoughts, for the proverb contrasts a man's spirit with his *thinking* that his ways are pure. What God examines is human sincerity in its depths, even beneath a person's delusive opinions of himself.

[285] Other renderings are possible. Lindenberger (1983: 101) translates: "If a young man utters great words, they will soar above him, when his utterance exalts the gods. If he is beloved of the gods, they will give him something worthwhile to say." The gist is the same as in my translation.

A person who thinks that his behavior is righteous may realize, deep down, that it is not. He may even deny that knowledge to himself. God, however, will ferret out this hypocrisy and hold the hypocrite fully responsible for his misdeeds, knowing that they were done not in innocent error but willfully. One cannot hide from God and *must* not hide from himself.

This proverb reveals a subtle concept of human psychology, recognizing different levels of the self. These are not neatly identified and labeled, but there is an awareness that different and sometimes contradictory thoughts can be held by one person.

The proverb distinguishes between the eyes and the heart, these being the organs of superficial notions and deeper awareness, respectively. Of all the sages of Wisdom Literature, Qohelet has the most complex relationship with his heart. He distinguishes his heart from his self, the "I" in his narration. Qohelet speaks to his heart, tests it, "goes about" in it, and can even write, "I and my heart" (Qoh 7:25); see Fox 1999: 78. Elsewhere, an idiom for insincerity is "a heart and a heart," that is, double-mindedness (Ps 12:3; 1 Chr 12:34; cf. James 1:7; 4:8). Another usage, *leb šalem*, "a complete heart," "wholeheartedness" (Isa 38:3; 1 Chr 28:9; 29:9), describes the heart's desirable state and implies the possibility of a divided or incomplete, hence insincere, mind. Prov 16:2 recognizes a type of duplicity of which the subject is not fully conscious but for which he is still responsible.

The Socratic ethic, as interpreted by Hannah Arendt in *The Life of the Mind* (1978), recognizes the two-in-one nature of the human mind and insists on the inner harmony of the mind as the prerequisite of ethical behavior. Socrates says, "It would be better for me that my lyre or a chorus I directed should be out of tune and loud with discord, and that multitudes of men should disagree with me than that I, *being one*, should be out of harmony with myself and contradict me" (*Gorgias* 482c, 484cd; trans. Arendt 1978: 181).

The experience of the thinking ego is a "soundless dialogue *eme emautō*—between me and myself" (Arendt, p. 185). Conscience is a by-product of this inner dialogue. "A person who does not know that silent intercourse (in which we examine what we say and what we do) will not mind contradicting himself, and this means he will never be either able or willing to account for what he says or does; nor will he mind committing any crime, since he can count on its being forgotten the next moment" (Arendt, p. 191). The present proverb recognizes the duality of the human mind and the need for harmony within it, a harmony that is God's criterion for human honesty.

The LXX substitutes a less subtle proverb: "All the works of the humble are visible to God, but the wicked perish in the evil day."

16:3. *Entrust* [*gol*]: Lit., "roll to," hence "turn over to." This does not mean merely planning and then hoping for the best. It means to make one's plans congruent with God's will. An addition to Sir 7:17 in MS A shows this: "Do not hurry to say 'Disaster!' Rely on [*gl 'l*] God and desire his way." Prov 16:3 has a near-duplicate in Ps 37:5: "Turn your way over to the Lord. Trust in him and he will act"; sim. Ps 22:9a.

succeed [*yikkonu*]: Lit., "be firm," "secure."

This advice is grounded in the principles of the preceding two proverbs: humans are limited and God is in control. Given the frail and fragmented character of human faculties, one cannot simply rely on his own abilities, but must turn his deeds over to the Lord. He will bring one's plans to fulfillment. The present proverb teaches *how* to accomplish one's plans: by God's help. This is a pragmatic piety, and the trust is an active means to success, not a passive resignation to one's fate.

The practical course of behavior implied by this and similar proverbs is that once one has done his work and applied his wisdom to his affairs, he should not fret or strain to accomplish further goals. That is called "hasten(ing) to get rich" (28:20). "Hastening" is itself suspicious behavior (19:2). We should leave the outcome to God and trust that the results will be appropriate.

This principle is the kernel of a poem in Lecture III; note esp. Prov 3:5–6:

(3:5) Trust in the Lord with all your heart,
and rely not on your own understanding.
(6) In all that you do, hold him in mind,
and *he* will keep your path smooth.
(7) Do not reckon yourself wise,
but fear the Lord and shun evil.

Amenemope offers much the same advice:

(19.11) Do not lie down while fearing for the morrow.
(12) When the day dawns, what is the morrow like?
(13) Man is ignorant of what the morrow is like.
(14) God is in his success,
(15) while man is in his failure.[286]
(16) Different are the things that men say
(17) from what God does. (§18 [cf. AEL 2.157])

This is not a counsel of despair or an assertion of human helplessness. Humans decide the direction they go. Success lies not in pushing toward achievement but rather in choosing one's course and opening oneself to God's guidance. See Shirun-Grumach 1972: 126–28 on this passage. Even Ptahhotep, who offers vigorous practical advice in personal and professional matters, realizes this, stating hyperbolically:

(115) Never have men's plans come to pass;
(116) what comes to pass is what God commands.
(117) So live in contentment,
(118) because what (the gods) give comes of itself.

[286] God is the source of a man's success, whereas failure is man's own doing.

16:4. *for its purpose* [*lᵉmaʿănehu*]: Hebrew *maʿăneh* means "purpose" only here and perhaps in Sir 43:14 (*lmʿnw*) and 26 (*lmʿnhw*).

The anomalous *lammaʿănēhû* must be vocalized *lᵉmaʿănēhû*. Though *maʿăneh* elsewhere means "answer" (noun), attempts to make this meaning fit here are forced. McKane jumps from "answer" to the unattested notion of "counterpart." Rather, the word is best related to the preposition *lᵉmaʿan*, "for the sake of," which indicates purpose. Sir 43:14 is particularly relevant: "For its [possibly "his"] own purpose [*lmʿnw*] he created the storehouse [sc., of punishments; cf. Sir 14:26 and 39:30b], and let clouds fly forth like birds." A marginal reading to 43:26 has *lmʿnhw* for *lmʿnw*. This idea is reformulated in 39:30b (MS B) as: "All these were created for their need [*lṣwrkm*]." "Their need" is a near-synonym of "purpose."

God made everything for its purpose or, we might say, its time, the time when there is a need (in God's plans) for it. Ben Sira develops this idea by admonishing: "One should not say, 'This—why is this?' For everything was created for its need" (39:30b, MS B).[287] Later he rephrases this idea: "Do not say, 'This is worse than that,' for everything dominates in its own time [*ky hkl bʿtw ygbr*]" (39:34).[288] (That is, one possibility "dominates" over other potentialities in the sense of moving from latency to reality.) One should not say that hail or wild beasts are evil, for God has a purpose for them too. When the need arises (namely, at a time of judgment [Sir 39:29; see Ezek 14:21; Job 21:30[289]]), he will deploy them to fulfill this purpose. Even the disasters and ills that afflict mankind "were created for their purposes [*lṣwrkm*, lit., "for their needs"], and they are kept in his storehouse for the time [*ʿet*] when they will be mustered" (Sir 39:30b[290]). That time is the day of visitation, which Job 38:23 calls "the time of trouble [*ʿet ṣar*], the day of battle and war [*yom qᵉrab umilḥamah*]." Like Sir 39:30 and 34, Prov 16:4 insists that God's will governs all events.

We would expect a proverb to say, as Ben Sira's does, that God made the evil day for the punishment of the wicked. Prov 16:4 turns things around and says that God makes the evil *man* so that the "evil day" will have someone to punish. This is a put-down. Rather than implying that the evildoer is so important that God created and stored away cosmic powers to deal with him when the need arises, the present proverb says that the evildoer (as a *type*) was created just to give God's grim judgments something to do, to keep them busy, as it were.

This verse reveals the idea of world order relevant to Proverbs as well as to earlier Wisdom. It is not a mechanistic grid laid down at creation that constrains the course of events independently of God's will (see Fox 1995), but rather a harmonious moral ecology in which everything is, ideally, integrated and serves its proper role, at least in the long run. Everything that violates that harmony will be neu-

---

[287] The textual evidence is varied. This is from MS B, with *nbḥrw* corrected to *nbḥr* "is chosen," on the basis of Greek *ektistai* "was created." The proper place of this couplet is at v 34, where a variant occurs. The variants explore different ways of formulating essentially the same idea.

[288] In MS B this is v 21.

[289] Job 21:30 should be translated, "For the evildoer is held in reserve for the day of disaster, for the day when wrath is led forth."

[290] Reading Sir 39:30bβ with MS B mg.: *whmh bʾ[ṣ]rw lʿt ypqdw*. The *ʾwṣr* is God's storehouse of punishments, on which see Sir 39:17; 43:14; cf. Job 38:22; Jer 10:13.

tralized by a corrective force. God is the guarantor of justice because he created those forces, and he need not impose his will directly in every event.

16:5. *hand to hand*: That is, assuredly; see the Comment on 11:21a, of which this is a doublet. Saʿadia, Riyqam, Hameʾiri, and some others gloss the phrase as "immediately" (like *miyyad*), but this proverb teaches the certainty of punishment, not its proximity.

not go unpunished [*loʾ yinnaqeh*]: Lit., "not be cleansed" or "not be considered clean." To my Comment on 6:29, I would add that this idiom implies that even if the wrongdoer is not apprehended or punished in a judicial forum, he will still be held guilty by God and face chastisement of some sort. (See Shadal on Deut 5:11.)

16:6. To be sure, one can find forgiveness through faithful kindness, but it is best to avoid the offense altogether. This is made possible by the fear of God (cf. 3:7), which is a conscience founded on a sense of God's presence and attention (see Vol. I, 69–71). Prov 16:6b ≈ 3:7b.

Whose kindness enables atonement—the sinner's or God's? It might seem that the sinner's kindness toward others brings him forgiveness by compensating for his iniquity. This would seem to be supported by the parallelism with "fear of the Lord," which is a human virtue. Elsewhere, however, it is God's kindness alone that makes atonement possible (Pss 103:3–4, 10–11; 106:43–45; etc.). In Prov 3:3a, as in Gen 24:27, Ps 40:11, and elsewhere, the phrase "kindness and constancy" designates a quality of God. Moreover, to *give atonement* (*k-p-r*) for an *ʿawon* "iniquity" is something God does, not man (except for a priest performing an atonement ritual). Finally, the phraseology in 16:5b–6a recalls, and probably directly draws on, the proclamation of Yahweh's attributes in Exod 34:6–7: "The Lord, the Lord, a merciful and compassionate God, patient and great in *kindness and constancy*, who preserves *kindness* to thousands (of generations), forgiving *iniquity* and offense and sin. But he will not let (the guilty) go *unpunished*, as he visits the *iniquity* of the fathers upon the sons and upon the sons' sons even unto the third and fourth (generations)." (A different word for "forgiving" is used here, but the sense is the same.) If this is correct, then "the fear of the Lord" in Prov 16:6b, a human virtue, is syntactically but not semantically parallel to "kindness and constancy," a divine attribute.

evil is avoided [*sûr mērāʿ*]: Lit., "is the avoidance [inf. cst.] of evil."

16:7. When God favors someone, he shields and rescues him from the hostility of others. God may even prevent the dangers from ever arising. He does this by granting the favored person a sheltering sphere of harmony that includes even his enemies and brings them into amity with him.

16:8. See the Comment on the very similar passage, 15:16–17, where the "better than" formula is discussed, and also the discussion of disjointed proverbs in the Introduction to Vol. II (II.E). In the present verse, the antithesis is symmetrical—an ethical virtue versus an ethical vice—but also rather predictable and flat, and it provides no underlying rationale for the assertion. The contrast between the variant formulations demonstrates the rhetorical edge of disjointed proverbs and shows how they can radiate more meaning from the intersection of the two lines than the lines themselves contain.

A predecessor of 16:8 is found in Merikare: "More acceptable is the character of the honest man than the ox of the evildoer," or, understood with a different determinative: "More acceptable is the *loaf*" (XLIVg; cf. AEL 1.106)—"loaf" = *bit*, punning on "loaf" and "character." Prov 16:8 derives from Amenemope 9.5–6, quoted in the Comment on 15:17.

with righteousness [*biṣdāqāh*]: This could mean (gathered) *by means of* righteousness (Ramaq, Clifford, etc.). But in view of the fact that *bᵉyirʾat YHWH* is paralleled by *ûmᵉhûmāh bô* ("with turmoil in it") in 15:16, the *b*- in the "better than" comparisons probably indicates concomitance. Likewise, *bᵉlōʾ* in "without justice" indicates the ongoing condition of the produce rather than the means of acquisition.

16:9. Humans can plan for the future but cannot secure it. Despite the sages' esteem for the powers of the human mind and their confidence in the value of planning (see, e.g., Prov 8:14; 11:14; 15:22; 24:6), they were quite aware of the limits of wisdom's scope; see the Comment on 16:3. Like 16:3, this proverb neither asserts fatalism nor impugns the efficacy of the human mind. Planning, when done for the right purposes, is still effective, but ultimately God's intention is what determines success. Prov 19:21 says the same.

This verse is a counterweight to the overconfident Prov 4:26: "Make level the path you travel, and you'll walk steady wherever you go [lit., "and all your ways will be established (*yikkonu*)"]." Prov 16:9 does not dispute this idea but cautions that one cannot manage alone.

A belief in God's role in enabling success should instill both humility and a sense of security. Jeremiah cites a proverb similar to the present one: "I know, O Lord, that a man's path is not his own, and that a man is not able to make his step secure [*hakin ʾet ṣaʿădo*] when he walks" (10:23). When planning does pay off, one should recognize that success is finally God's gift (Deut 8:18; Hameʾiri).

but: Or "and." This verse can be read as an affirmation, not a denigration, of intellectual effort, even while ascribing the decisive role to God. A man's heart *should* plan where he is going, and *then* God will give the plans to fruition (thus Naḥmias, based on Hameʾiri). Commenting on Prov 16:20, Hameʾiri adduces 16:9 to show that human planning and trust in God are complementary.

makes . . . secure [*yakin*]: The usual translation is "directs his steps" (RSV) or the like. This places the emphasis on divine determinism of the outcome of planning. Although this idea would not be out of place in Proverbs (e.g., 20:24), the verb *yakin* means "to make firm," hence to secure success. The proverb speaks of reward, not predetermination.

The verb *yākîn* (*k-w-n* H) means "to establish" or "make firm," with the passive in N. For one's steps to be made firm (*k-w-n*) means that one walks securely and safely, hence attains his goal (Prov 4:26; 12:3, 19; 16:3, 12; 20:18; 21:29 [ketiv]; Ps 119:133). With "way" or "step," *k-w-n* means "make (or be) firm," "secure," as in Jer 10:23 and Prov 4:26.

16:10 There is divination on the king's lips.
In judgment no one can defy what he says.
11 A just balance and scales are the Lord's.
All the weights of the purse are his work.
12 Kings loathe the doing of evil,
for the throne is established by righteousness.
13 Kings favor righteous lips,
and they love the word[a] of the upright.
14 The wrath of kings is a deadly messenger,
but a wise man can assuage it.
15 In the light of the king's face there is life,
and his favor is like the cloud of the spring rain.

---

[a] *dᵉbar-* (MT *dōbēr*).

The Royal Ideal. This cluster of proverbs describes the king's powers and responsibilities. (Verse 11 is commonly considered extraneous, but see the Comment.) The book of Proverbs, like Wisdom Literature generally, adulates kings and rulers *ex officio*, but it does not assume that individual rulers are inevitably righteous (see 28:15).[291] Sayings that declare the king's powers and righteousness hold up an ideal for the rulers to emulate. They also teach the people, both commoners and courtiers, the importance of maintaining the king's favor through righteous behavior. Proverbs expressing admiration—sometimes adulation—for the king are 14:28, 35; 16:10, 12, 13, 15; 19:12; 20:2, 8; 21:1; 24:21; 25:2, 3; and 30:31b.[292] Proverbs instructing the king in his duties, or his servants in theirs toward him, are 22:11; 24:21; 25:4–5, 6–7; 29:4, 14; and 31:2–9. Similar statements about the king are found in Ahiqar 100a–108 [1.1.84] (= §§18–26; §22 seems extraneous). Adulation of the king is the substance of most of the Egyptian "Loyalist Instruction," but most Egyptian Wisdom books give relatively little attention to kingship, despite the centrality of the king in Egyptian religion.

Psalm 101 is quite similar to Prov 16:10–15 (and other royalist proverbs), except that it is spoken by a king in the first person. The speaker addresses an audience in the singular, perhaps speaking to his son, and says, "I will teach (you) in the way of innocence. When will you [sg.] come to me?" (Ps 101:2aα). (In other words: When will you be worthy to be king? When you do as I do, as described in the following statements.) The king declares that he hates dishonest people, slanderers, and the haughty, while favoring the faithful and honest. Only the latter will be among his intimates and allowed to serve him. Such statements are not a boast but a declaration of intention. Likewise, Psalm 72 articulates the royal ideal. The king receives

---

[291] This was occasionally true even in Egypt, even though the king there was considered a god. For example, Pap. Ramesseum II.4.1 says, "If a king behaves foolishly, God corrects his faults like a teacher." Merikare's royal father confesses serious failings (AEL 1.105).

[292] G. E. Bryce (1979: 189–210) emphasizes that the royalist ideology in Proverbs derives from a sacral context, which assigned to the king a semi-divine status; see esp. Ps 2:7 and 45:6–7.

righteous judgments from God whereby to judge the people in equity (vv 1–2). This psalm can be read as a description or as a hope. Like the royal maxims in Proverbs, it addresses men whose occupation might bring them close enough to the source of power to be either warmed by favor or scorched by anger. These are men who will serve the king and "dwell" in his house, that is, serve in the palace (Ps 101:6–7). On the social setting of Prov 10–29, the royal court, see "Social Setting" in the Introduction to Vol. II (III.B).

16:10. *divination* [*qesem*]: This is not to be taken literally. *Qesem* is elsewhere used only of divination judged illicit and usually practiced by foreigners. Moreover, we have no indication that Israelite kings actually used divination in judicial decisions. Rather, this awed (or sycophantic) aphorism insists that the king's judgment is as true *as if it were* an oracle from God ascertained by mantic means. (Compare the adulation in 2 Sam 14:17, 20.)

defy what he says: Lit., "transgress against his mouth."

When directed to the king's subjects, this proverb glorifies the king's wisdom and enjoins obedience to his dictates (sim. Qoh 8:2). When directed to the king, the proverb enjoins him to take care in judgment, because his word holds great power.

16:11. God is the ultimate source of standards, and any distortion in their accuracy offends him directly (Prov 20:10, 23). Amenemope, speaking of the obligation to maintain honest measures, says, "What god is as great as Thoth, he who invented these things [the measures], to make them?" (§16; 18.2–3 [cf. AEL 2.156–57]).

Read in the context of the cluster of royal proverbs, Prov 16:11 alludes to the king's duty to oversee weights and measures. Ezekiel sets out in detail this responsibility of the future prince (45:9–14). See the Comment on 11:1.

In context, just measures may also be a metaphor for the royal administration of justice generally. According to Ehrlich, the unique phrase "scales of justice [*mo'zᵉney mišpaṭ*]" (rather than "scales of righteousness [*ṣedeq*]") points to this signification.

By itself, the first line can mean that God is a righteous judge, assessing human works by true measures (Radaq; Hame'iri). The second line narrows the focus to actual weights and measures.

16:12. This is a statement of obligation, not fact: Kings *must* loathe evil—which is not to say that they all do. Not even kings would make that claim. It is ambiguous as to whose evil deeds kings (should) loathe, their own or others. If the former, then the verse is directed to kings and informs them what they should avoid. If the latter (which a comparison with 16:13 and 25:5 supports), it is directed to the people as a warning against doing evil, because kings will enforce justice for the sake of their own thrones. The proverb may face both ways at once.

Kings loathe: Lit., "the abomination [*to'ăbat-*] of kings," that is, the loathing they feel. In the frequent phrase *to'ăbat*-X, X is always the one who feels the loathing, not the one who causes it (contrary to Delitzsch and Toy).

The partial-doublet in 25:5 says, "Remove the wicked from before the king, and his throne will be established in righteousness"; sim. 20:28 and 29:14. The royal speaker of Ps 101 declares, "The crooked heart shall be removed from my presence. I shall not know evil" (v 4). The establishment of a just and righteous society was the primary responsibility of the king throughout the ancient Near East; see Weinfeld 1995: 45–56.

16:13. When directed to a king, this proverb states that kings, in principle, love honesty. This is what *he* should do. The king who speaks in Ps 101 and models in himself the ideal of kingship, declares, "In my house there shall not dwell one who commits deceit and speaks lies. He shall not remain before my eyes" (v 7). When directed at men in the royal service, the proverb tells them that the way to the king's favor is honesty. It is not meant for the edification of commoners, because the king was not considered a sort of omniscient deity who knows what his individual subjects are saying throughout the realm.

they love: Lit., "he loves." Shifts in number happen frequently in Hebrew and were presumably not felt to be awkward.

the word of the upright: MT is apparently to be translated "the speaker of upright things" (thus Ramaq), but the phrase is difficult in the Hebrew and calls for a minor emendation, as indicated above.

The problem with MT's *dōbēr yᵉšārîm* is that *yᵉšārîm* does not elsewhere have an abstract sense, which would require *mêšārîm*. It is the plural of *yāšār* and means "upright people." Hence vocalize *dᵉbar* "word of" (LXX, Syr).

16:14. Rulers are unpredictable and can blow up for all sorts of reasons. A courtier should not imagine that he can exploit the king's anger for his own purposes, by directing it, say, at a rival. Once the king's anger is ignited, it can flare out of control like a wildfire and scorch everyone around, except for the wise.

Read one way, the proverb extols the efficacy of wisdom—that is, wise speech—as having the power to calm even an irate ruler. Read another way—with "will" for "can"—it advises *assuaging* anger as the wise thing to do.

Read in conjunction with 16:13, the present verse reinforces the practical importance of honesty, which (it is claimed) is what wins the king's favor and deflects his wrath. Verse 14b does not quite serve this purpose, probably because the couplet was originally independent before being placed in its present setting.

a deadly messenger: Lit., "messengers of death." This is translated as singular for the benefit of the English but the plural is meaningful: The king's wrath sends out many deadly messengers in all directions.

These messengers may be royal servants sent on a deadly mission. Prov 17:11 ("A rebel seeks only evil, and a cruel messenger will be sent against him") speaks of this practice. An example is Solomon sending Benaiah to kill Joab (1 Kgs 2:29). Since Hebrew *mal'ak* means both "messenger" and "angel," the proverb may alternatively be comparing the king's wrath to a band of destructive angels. Angels can be sent on a mission of deadly retribution, as in Ezek 9:1–8, where God dispatches a band of seven "destroyers." The plural shows that the present proverb is not referring to the Angel of Death, who was in any case not a biblical figure.

Other proverbs on the king's wrath are Prov 19:12; 20:2; and 24:21–22. (Prov 28:15 worries about the wrath of a *wicked* king.) Qohelet advises, "If the ruler grows angry at you, do not leave your place, for the ability to soothe anger can set aside great offenses" (10:4). Ben Sira rephrases the present verse and says: "The man who pleases the great atones for wrongdoing" (Sir 20:28b). (For "atones" he uses *kpr*, the verb translated "assuage" here.)

Ahiqar too warns against provoking the king:

> Do not cover [= ignore] the word of a king.
> Let it be a healing for your heart.[293]
> The king's word is soft,
> but it is sharper and stronger than a double-bladed sword.
> Here before you is a serious matter:
> Do not stand opposed to the king.
> His anger is swifter than lightning.
> So be wary!
> Do not let him show it [= his anger] against your words,
> lest you depart before your time. (100a–102 [1.1.84–86])

Ahiqar goes on to describe the king's command as a fire *and* a delight. Man can no more strive with a king than logs with fire. But the king's tongue is gentle as well as powerful (103–108 [1.1.87–88]).

16:15. "Light of the face" signifies graciousness and friendliness. It is used of God (e.g., Pss 4:7; 44:4; 89:16) and man (Qoh 8:1b; Sir 7:24a [MS A]; 13:26a [MS A]; 32:11a). The visual expression of the "light" or brightness is a smile.

the cloud [*ʿab*] *of the spring rain*: A cloud is a harbinger of the spring rain in March or April and the blessing it brings. This is the last precipitation until the fall and is crucial to the cereal harvest.

There is a certain paradox in identifying the king's favor with both light and the grayness of a rainy day. An *ʿab* is a dense rain cloud that produces darkness (Ps 18:12). For Qohelet (12:2), it suggests darkness and gloom (see also the image in 2 Sam 23:4). Prov 16:15b ≈ 19:12b.

Ahiqar expresses similar awe and veneration for the king:

> A king is as beautiful to look at as the sun,
> and his majesty is glorious
> to them who tread the earth in peace. (108 [1.1.92])

Perhaps the authors of praises of kingship like this and Prov 16:10–15 hoped that their enthusings would reach the king's eyes or ears.

---

[293] Or "flesh." Most of the word is lost.

16:16 How much better to gain wisdom than fine gold!
And gaining understanding is preferable to silver.

"Gaining" or "acquiring" (*qnh*) wisdom and understanding is the theme of Prov 4:5, 7. For the gold/silver comparison, see the Comment on 8:10. Since 16:16 does not say, "wisdom is better than fine gold, etc.," "gaining" should be understood more precisely as the process of acquiring wisdom, in other words, studying and learning it (compare 2:4 and see the Comment on 4:7). The effort of learning, not only its product, is a joy; see Vol. I, 294 and the Comment on 8:31.

is preferable: The second line may continue the exclamation of the first, with *mah* ("how much more!") gapped. We could translate, "and how much more preferable to silver is gaining understanding."

16:17 The high road of the upright is the avoidance of evil.
He who watches his way guards his life.

A high road (*m^esillah*) is a roadway that is raised or banked on the sides so as to keep pedestrians out of the mud and on a smooth path. The avoidance of evil is such a road. "Evil" also means "misfortune"; hence the saying also—and at the same time—means that walking on this path keeps one away from misfortunes, while to leave it is to step into the muck and pits of misery. The high road (literally and metaphorically) is both easy and safe.

Prov 16:17b ≈ 13:3a; 16:17b ≈ 19:16a. Where the doublet in Prov 13:3a has "mouth," 16:17b has "way," in accordance with the PATH metaphor in the A-line. The B-line has assonance and internal rhyme: *šoMER napŠO noṢER darKO.*

his life [*napšo*]: Or, "himself."

16:18 Pride comes before a fall,
and before stumbling—haughtiness of spirit.

Arrogance blinds a man to his limitations and deafens him to reproofs. It precedes a calamity as cause does effect (Prov 29:23). It leads one to do evil or stupid things, which bring on humiliation and disaster. "Fall" (*šeber*) is literally "break" or "disaster." Prov 16:18a ≈ 18:12a.

16:19 Better to be humble of spirit and to be with the lowly
than to divide booty with the proud.

Since pride leads to a fall (v 18), it is better to be humble even than to divide the spoils of victory, an occasion that epitomizes joy in Isaiah 9:2. In fact, it is better to be humble, even if this means being among the poor and lowly, than to divide spoil, even if one is among the proud. If we press the logic of this proverb, we must note that it assumes that being with the lowly is less desirable than dividing booty, though both are outweighed by the greater value of humility, and that being "with the proud" enhances the value (at least in terms of prestige) of the division of booty. The structure of this "better than" saying is discussed in the excursus after 15:17.

šᵉpal rûaḥ: Lit., "lowliness of spirit." This is probably an inf. cst., as in Qoh 12:4, parallel to *ḥallēq* (Toy). Possibly, however, it is a stative ptcp. (as in Prov 29:23) and the clause means "better is he who is humble of spirit, etc." (Yonah Gerundi and, implicitly, the other medievals).

16:20 He who is astute in a matter will gain a benefit,
and he who trusts in the Lord—how fortunate is he!

This verse may be read two ways. (1) The astute man and the one who trusts in God are equivalent and have the same reward, namely, good fortune. (2) The second type is superior to the first (though both virtues may reside in the same person). According to the latter reading, there is a heightening in the B-line: The man who is perceptive in a particular instance will receive a benefit, a particular reward, whereas he who trusts in the Lord has a deep virtue of character and the resulting benefit is a fortunate life as a whole. Sometimes Proverbs places trust in Yahweh (and the virtually synonymous "fear of Yahweh") on a higher rung than ordinary intellectual powers, or at least recognizes the former as the highest form of wisdom (1:7; 2:5–6; 9:10); see 3:5 and Vol. I, 154–55.

a matter [*dabar*]: Or "thing." Possibly this has the shading of an ordinary, practical affair.

gain a benefit [*yimṣaʾ ṭob*]: Lit., "find good," that is, something good. The idiom "finding good" occurs only in Prov 16:20; 17:20; 18:22; and 19:8.

how fortunate . . . ! [*ʾašrayw*]: This is a macarism, a form discussed in Vol. I, 161.

16:21 The wise of heart is called astute,
and he whose speech is pleasing increases instruction.

Verses 21–24 concern effective speech and teaching. He who is "wise of heart" has the inclination and desire to learn. He will succeed and become astute and perspicacious (*nabon*). He who is skilled in speech will increase instruction (*leqaḥ*) among others. There may be a distinction between the persons mentioned, the first being a man who (in Sira's words) is "wise for himself" and the latter he who is also "wise for others" (Sir 37:22–23). The latter is the more admirable (Hameʾiri). See also Sir 24:34 and the Comment on Prov 9:12.

wise of heart [*ḥăkam leb*]: This is the predisposition for wisdom (see Vol. I, 109). Though not necessarily fully learned, one who has this predisposition and develops it will come to be called *nabon*, "astute" or "sensible."

he whose speech is pleasing [*meteq šᵉpatayim*]: Lit., "sweet of lips."

instruction: *Leqaḥ* is instruction or teaching eloquently expressed; see the Comment on Prov 1:5. Here, since the *leqaḥ* is conveyed by "sweet lips," it refers primarily to effective teaching.

meteq šᵉpātayim: Tur-Sinai (1947: 26–27) offers an unusual interpretation: It is good when an astute man happens to meet (*yqrʾ* = *yqrh*) another man who is wise of heart, for in this way he will receive counsel (*meteq*) from the wise man and enhance his own learning and wisdom. Tur-Sinai says that here and in 27:9, *meteq* means "counsel"; compare *namtîq sôd* "we held (sweet?) counsel" in Ps 55:15. He derives the word from *m-t-q* "suck," as in Aramaic, a usage found in Job 21:33 and 24:20. Even if this is not the primary meaning of *meteq śᵉpātayim*, it may be present here as an overtone or pun.

16:22 Discretion is a fount of life for its possessor,
while the "education" of fools is folly.

Discretion [*śekel*]: Or "perceptiveness." This is the ability to understand practical matters and interpersonal relations and to make beneficial decisions; see Vol. I, 36. Discretion is a fount of life to its possessor but also, as the second line indicates, to others. Similarly, the teaching of a wise man (13:14) and the mouth of the righteous (10:11) are founts of life to their listeners. The two lines of the couplet are poorly related and do not even work as a disjointed proverb.

the "education" of fools [*musar ʾĕwilim*]: This is the "education" or "discipline" that fools impart to others. Fools teach folly. *Musar* here is meant facetiously: "education" in scare quotes, as it were, just like the Strange Woman's "instruction" [*leqaḥ*] in Prov 7:21. (See the Comment on 11:23.) Fools teach folly not only in formal instruction but also in the bad examples they set; see 22:24–25. Some commentators explain this to mean that what fools *gain* from education is folly, so it is foolish to try to educate them (Naḥmias, comparing 9:7; sim. McKane, Murphy). But although the attempt to educate fools may be futile, it is hardly pernicious and would not be called *ʾiwwelet*—folly of the worst sort.

16:23 The wise man's heart instructs his mouth,
and it enhances instruction on his lips.

It is wise—smart, prudent, shrewd—to think before speaking. The wise man lets his thoughts guide his mouth and doesn't blabber or ejaculate mindlessly (Prov 10:19). His teaching, unlike the sort described in the previous verse, is thus wise and effective. On *leqaḥ* "instruction," see 16:22 and the Comment on 1:5.

16:24 Pleasant words are honeycomb—
sweet to the taste and healing to the bones.

Gentle and eloquent words are pleasant and salutary (Naḥmias). In conjunction with v 23, this refers in particular to words of instruction. On the balm of pleasant speech, see Anii 22.7–8 (AEL 2.143), quoted in the Comment on 15:1.

taste [*nepeš*]: *Nepeš* is usually translated "soul" or "appetite." Physically the *nepeš* is the gullet, or perhaps the entire eating and breathing apparatus. Honey was thought to have medicinal properties (see Fox 1985b: 33; ODAE 1.174). A bit of honey can make a famished man's eyes "light up" (1 Sam 14:27, 29).

16:25 There is a way that is straight before a man,
but which turns out to be the way to death.

This verse is an exact doublet of 14:12; see the Comment there. Hame'iri suggests that the proverb was placed here to pair it with v 24. There are two kinds of sweetness: the sweetness of wisdom, which provides healing, and the sweetness of folly, which is deceptive and turns out to be foul and even poisonous. As 20:17 says, "The bread of deceit is sweet to a man, but later it fills his mouth with gravel." Thus too 9:17–18.

turns out to be [*w*ᵉ'*aḥăritahh*]: Lit., "its end" or "outcome"; the same word is used in 14:13.

16:26 The appetite of the toiler toils for him,
because his mouth forces it on him.

The toiler is driven to his labors by a harsh taskmaster—his own appetite, his *nepeš*. The proverb assumes that man is not by nature inclined to toil but does so only by compulsion (Ehrlich). The proverb thus has sympathetic overtones, for it appreciates just how urgent are the demands of the basic requirements for survival.

Qohelet says something similar: "All a man's toil is for his mouth, but the appetite is never filled" (6:7). For Qohelet, this pertains not only to hunger but to the entire range of desires that nag at a man and are never assuaged by actual possessions.

J. G. Williams (1980: 52) uses Prov 16:26 to demonstrate how proverbs are open to multiple interpretations. Is this proverb concerned with the human need for incentives, the reader may ask, or with the struggle of the toiler, or with the great capacity of the human *nepeš*? Or is "mouth" a metaphor both for both "appetite" and "speech"? Aphorisms gain their power in part by inviting such questions without providing closure. They can radiate meaning in many directions at once.

16:27 The worthless man mines evil,
and on his lips there is a scorching fire.
28 The perverse man foments strife,
and the slanderer separates friends.
29 The lawless man entices his fellow
and leads him in a path not good.
30 He squints his eyes to plan perversities,
winces his lips, while planning evil.

Scoundrels. Verses 27–30 form a cohesive epigram that describes three types of scoundrels: the worthless man (v 27), the perverse man (v 28), and the lawless man (vv 29–30). This passage is the main source for 6:12–19. Compare the similar epigrams in chapter 6 and see Vol. I, 222, 224–27.

16:27. *mines* [*koreh*]: Or "digs." The scoundrel, or "man of *b*ᵉ*liyya*ʿ*al*" (see the Comment on 6:12), digs for evil like a miner does ore. Clifford suggests that the line may be elliptical for "digs an evil pit" for others to fall into (cf. 26:27a), but this does not match the metaphor in the B-line.

The evil that is "mined" may be a scheme, a slander, or an insult. The scoundrel digs for this, perhaps, in his heart, and when he brings it to his lips, his mouth is like a blast furnace that sears all who come near. Consequently, he foments strife (6:14). Digging is a metaphor for eager searching in Job 3:21, and here too it suggests the schemer's eagerness and intensity in contriving his plots.

16:28. The perverse man, of whom the slanderer (*nirgan*) is an instance, spreads hostility all about him. He creates enmity not only toward himself, but also among others, breaking up friendships by calumnies and insinuations.

16:29. Men as well as women can seduce, and seduction is not only sexual. Men can lure others into crime, as described in Prov 1:10–16. Prov 1:10 and 15 recall the phraseology of 16:29a and 29b, respectively. More is said about the hypocritical friend in 26:23–28.

not good [*lo' ṭob*]: Being "not good" is worse than it sounds. Remarking on 20:23, Hame'iri observes that Scripture often refers to bad qualities by negating the good; for example: "and who has not done good within his people" (Ezek 18:18) and "punishing the righteous man is not good" (Prov 17:26). This trope is called litotes. Other examples are 19:2; 24:23; 28:21 (all with "not good"); and 30:11.

16:30. Visible symptoms belie the hearty and amiable words the sneaky man uses to entangle others in his schemes. See the Comment on 6:13.

squints: Squinted or squinched eyes were considered a sign of malevolent thoughts; see the Comments on 6:13 and 10:10.

ʿōṣeh "squints": Contrary to my Comment on 6:13, this need not be emended to *ʿōṣēm*. There are etymological grounds for recognizing a lexeme *ʿṣh* "to press," "squeeze"; see HALOT 866a. This verb probably appears in Ps 32:8, where we should read *'eʿĕṣeh ʿāleykā ʿênî* (BHS), "I will squint my eye against you," whereupon follows a quotation of chastisement.

Jenni (1999: 107–9) construes *ʿōṣeh* as the subject and *laḥšōb* as the predicate, indicating "epistemic modality," meaning that it indicates a degree of probability. Hence: "He who squeezes his eyes shut is *likely to* plan perversities." Thus too G. R. Driver 1951: 196; but see the Comment on 19:8. My translation construes the sentence as a continued description of the lawless man (compare the use of the participles in 6:12b, 13a, 13b) and takes *laḥšōb* as an inf. of purpose dependent on *ʿōṣeh*.

while planning evil [*killah raʿah*]: Lit., "he completes evil." His squinted eyes show that he is scheming and resolving to do evil. The intransitive equivalent of this phrase is *kalᵉtah haraʿah meʿimmo*, "the evil is determined by him," that is, he has definitively decided to bring it to pass (1 Sam 20:7, 9; sim. Esth 7:7; cf. 1 Sam 25:17).

G. Bryce (1975) argues that Proverbs includes a genre of sayings based on omen wisdom, as known from Babylonian texts. These are moral teachings in omen form, which adduce physiological and moral behavior to formulate teachings. Examples of wisdom omens (quoted from Bryce 1975: 24–33) include the following:

If he (a man) shuts his eyes, he will speak falsehood. [Compare Prov 16:30a.]
If he looks at the ground when he speaks, he will speak treachery.

If he points his finger at his father and his mother, the curse of (his) father and (his) mother will seize him. [Compare Prov 6:13c.]
If a man's way of looking is straight, his deity will always be with him for his good; he will live in truth. [Compare Prov 4:25.]

Bryce is unconvincing when he argues that the proverbs *are* omen wisdom. He downplays the differences in form and translates some verses tendentiously. Also, the parallels do not justify his hypothesis that the proverbs in question belonged to an esoteric priestly tradition. Nevertheless, the similarities, especially with regard to squinting, suggest that the two types of texts are based on widespread notions of body language and symptomatic gestures.

16:31 Gray hair is a splendid diadem.
It is found on the way of righteousness.

Old age is (or should be) a source of pride, for it is gained by a righteous life. On diadem as a metaphor see the Comments on 1:9; 4:9; and 12:4. Prov 16:31a ≈ 20:29b (with "glory" instead of "diadem").

16:32 Better the patient man than the mighty one,
and he who controls his temper than he who captures a city.

The virtue and power of patience are praised also in 14:29; 15:18; 19:11; 25:15, 28. Control of anger is advocated frequently in all the branches of Wisdom Literature. Rabbi Ben Zoma recast this proverb as "Who is mighty? He who conquers his desire" (*'Abot* 4:1). The logic of 16:32a (and other "better than" proverbs) is examined in the excursus after 15:17.

16:33 The lot is cast into the bosom,
and whatever it decides is from the Lord.

This saying affirms the value of casting lots by observing that (as was universally assumed) the practice discovers God's will. Throughout the Bible, lot-casting was valued as a way of resolving conflicts; see 18:18. But the real purpose of the present proverb is less to advise the use of lotteries than to emphasize God's control of events and the need to trust in his judgment (Hame'iri).
whatever it decides: Lit., "all its judgment."

17:1 Better a dry piece of bread and tranquility with it,
than a house full of contentious sacrifices.

The value of animal sacrifices (which the comparison itself assumes) is nullified by contention. (See the Comment on 15:8.) Sacrifices can be "contentious" insofar as the participants are squabbling over their distribution. Sacrificial meals were an occasion for fellowship, intended to enhance harmony among the participants and between them and God. The presence of conflict would be the opposite of what was intended (Perdue 1977: 159–60).

Still, the proverb may not really be making a statement about the sacrificial cult, but simply using "sacrifices" to refer to the meat, and, *pars pro toto*, the meal in which it is eaten. That is what is in view in 15:17. Before Deuteronomy (12:15), and probably until the destruction of the Temple, animal slaughter was typically, perhaps universally, in the form of sacrifice. Even afterwards, meat was expensive, and the typical occasion for eating it would be in conjunction with a sacrificial offering. The "house full of sacrifices," then, is equivalent to a luxurious repast (thus Plöger); see the Comment on 7:14. Moreover, the sentence in Amenemope on which this is based (see below) has "wealth" where the MT has "sacrifices," indicating that the original proverb, at least, was not concerned with the sacral status of the valuable item being spoiled by contention. The structure of "better than" sayings is discussed in the excursus after 15:17; compare Ps 37:16 and Sir 30:14.

and tranquility with it [*w^{e}šalwah bahh*]: That is, with (or in) the bread, which is a synecdoche for the meal.

This verse is based on Amenemope:

(9.7) Better is (simple) bread when the heart is pleasant,
(8) than wealth with vexation. (from §6 [cf. AEL 2.152])

**17:2 An astute slave will rule over a disappointing son
and divide an inheritance among brothers.**

The author of Prov 19:10 found it unseemly for a slave to rule over princes. The author of 30:22 felt that the very earth would shudder under a slave who became king. Such things they believed ludicrous and inappropriate. The author of 17:2 does not fundamentally disagree. He is using the situation of a slave entering into an inheritance as an extreme case: Astuteness (*śkl*), an aspect of wisdom, is such a powerful force that it can overcome even extreme disadvantages.

It is unlikely that this proverb seeks to inspire diligence in slaves by letting them hope to inherit as a family member. That eventuality would be too far-fetched. To be sure, it was possible for a slave to be manumitted and adopted (AYBD 1.78). Mesopotamian practice allowed for this possibility (AYBD 6.61), and it is presupposed in Gen 15:2–3. A genealogy in Chronicles (1 Chr 2:34–35) includes a slave (a foreigner, no less) whose presence in the family line indicates that he was adopted. Possibly this practice is behind the promise of the present verse. In the above-mentioned cases, however, there were no sons in the family.

Even if the scenario of 17:2a were possible on rare occasions, it would have been very unlikely, and its implausibility is relevant. The point of the proverb lies in the second line. The proverb warns sons against shirking their duties, lest they lose out *even* to a household slave (cf. Murphy). A slave holding power is undesirable and is a special threat to those who may become subject to him.

slave: Hebrew *ʿebed* (pl. *ʿăbadim*) has no exact English equivalent. It can refer to anyone who is subordinate to someone else; see TDOT 10.387–92. The king's servants, including high ministers, were his *ʿăbadim* (Prov 14:35). A household *ʿebed*, however, was almost certainly a slave, another person's property—his "money," as Exod 21:21 puts it. The *ʿăbadim* in Prov 29:21 and 30:10 are clearly bondsmen. An *ʿebed* is to be distinguished from a *śakir* "hireling," a man employed for a daily wage.

disappointing son [*ben mebiš*]: The particular failing in view may be negligence in tending to the family's land (its "inheritance") and business (Radaq). The use of *mebiš* in 10:5 (where too it stands in opposition to *maśkil*) supports this identification of the failing in question; see Comment there.

Taking a cue from this verse, Ben Sira says, "As for an intelligent slave—nobles [or "free men"] shall serve him" (10:25c [MS B] = Gk v 25a).

17:3 A smelter for silver and a furnace for gold—
and the tester of hearts is the Lord.

God "tests" the heart as a furnace assays and purifies metallic ore by heating it until the pure silver or gold melts away from the dross and can be collected. Since God is the tester, the analogy here (but not in Prov 27:21) connotes more than examination of thoughts. As in Isa 48:10, the smelting also implies a hard trial, which will both prove the sufferer's loyalty and purify him in the process. Prov 17:3a = 27:21a.

17:4 An evildoer pays attention to iniquitous lips,
a liar listens[a] to a deceitful tongue.

[a] *māzîn* (MT *mēzîn*).

Liars and evildoers not only speak deceits, they pay attention to them. (The verb *hiqšib* means to listen with attention, not just to hear something.) They do not merely prevaricate tactically. Falsehood stains their character to the core and makes them susceptible to *others'* lies, even eager for them.

liar [*šeqer*]: Lit., "lie," "deceit." This is an abstract-for-concrete trope, of which there are a great many in Proverbs, and it need not be emended to *šaqqār* or *mᵉšaqqēr* "liar" (BHS, HALOT). This trope tightens the identification of the person with the abstract quality. In this case the liar is, we might say, "deceit itself." The same happens with *rᵉmiyyah* "deceit" = "deceiver"; see the Comment on 10:4.

listen [*māzîn*]: MT's *mēzîn* is a mistake, pointing *mzyn* as if from *z-w-n* H and apparently intending "nourishes," "cares for." The parallelism favors *māzîn*, a contracted form of *maʾăzîn* (which appears secondarily in two MSS). On such contractions see GKC 68*i*.

17:5 He who mocks the poor insults his maker.
He who takes joy in (another's) disaster will not go unpunished.

God cares not only about visible offenses (v 5a) but about unspoken attitudes as well (v 5b). The first line goes beyond the condemnation of *oppression* of the poor in Prov 14:31 and censures even verbal abuse. Amenemope similarly forbids mocking the handicapped because God is man's "builder" (§25; quoted in the Comment on 14:31). The second line extends the principle from poverty to all suffering: One must not treat others' misfortunes with contempt.

To insult the poor man is to disparage his maker by implying that his handiwork is slipshod (Radaq). It is, moreover, grossly arrogant to do so, for it presumes knowledge unavailable to mortals. We cannot know whether the impoverished man caused his own troubles or whether God brought them on him for unfathomable reasons. Ben Sira reminds us of the latter possibility in a similar context, "Wondrous are the works of the Lord; hidden from humans his deeds" (Sir 11:4b). Similar teachings about God as creator of the lowly are Prov 19:17; 22:2; and Sir 11:4–6. Adducing God's creatorship of man as a motivation for ethics has direct parallels in Egyptian Wisdom, especially in Amenemope; see the Comment on 14:31, and also L. Boström 1990: 154. Prov 17:5a ≈ 14:31a; see the Comment on the latter.

Another interpretation is possible: Mocking the poor insults God by insinuating that the poor man brought his poverty on himself by his folly. This in turn implies that one's own good fortune is his own doing. But poverty and wealth are from *God's* hand, as it says in 1 Sam 2:7; Deut 8:17–18; and elsewhere (Hame'iri; Naḥmias).

Both interpretations presume that God is responsible for poverty and that he may bring it about for unknown reasons, and not only as punishment. Contrary to a certain scholarly stereotype, the sages did not blame the poor for their poverty or sufferers for their suffering; see Vol. I, 91–92 and the Comment on 3:12.

takes joy in (another's) disaster: Lit., "rejoices in disaster." Plöger explains this as referring to the poor man's disaster, but the sentence in the B-line seems to be a broadening of the principle of the A-line to include all misfortunes.

Schadenfreude, feelings of glee at another's misery, is malicious in all ways (Prov 24:17). While it may not harm the sufferer, it insults God. It is presumptuous to suppose that one knows why God has caused misfortune. Moreover, this glee makes God collude, as it were, in one's own spiteful wishes. It is as if one imagines himself joining God in sneering at their mutual enemies.

'êd "disaster": BHS and others emend to *lᵉ'ōbēd*, "the one perishing," based on LXX *apollymenǭ* "at him who is perishing." To be sure, Prov 31:6–7 speaks of an *'ōbēd* possessing *rîš* "poverty." But the notion of taking joy in a *person* who is perishing is peculiar, and it is not clearly malicious, as context requires.

17:6 The diadem of the aged is sons of sons,
and the splendor of sons is their fathers.

The aged can glory in their grandchildren as in a "diadem," for they are considered a token of a well-earned long life and righteousness (Prov 16:31). Moreover (and less obviously), children can take pride in their parents and ancestors. ("Fathers" can mean both parents together and include ancestors.) They can share in the honor their parents radiate. Many traditional commentators, such as Riyqam, Ramaq, and Radaq, emphasize that the first line is true only when the sons are wise and righteous. Saʿadia sees an implicit exhortation: The first line encourages people to beget and educate sons, the second exhorts sons to behave in such a way that their parents can take pride in them.

diadem, splendor: See the Comment on 12:4. The phrase *ʿăṭeret tipʾeret*, "diadem of splendor," appears in Isa 62:3; Ezek 16:12; 23:42; and Prov 4:9. Here the terms are distributed between the lines of the couplet.

sons: The sages would probably include daughters in the message of this saying. Though *banim* is masculine and refers primarily to sons, it does not exclude daughters. It includes a female explicitly in 1 Chr 5:29, but more often it includes daughters incidentally, by virtue of context, as in Gen 3:16; 21:7; and Exod 21:5. Still, the primary source of paternal pride in a patriarchal society is sons, and they are in focus here.

The LXX adds: "To the faithful person belongs the entire world of possessions, but to the unfaithful one, not a penny."

17:7 Excessive speech is not fitting for a scoundrel;
how much the less so false speech for a noble!

A person of high social station has a special duty to avoid dishonesty. The wrongness of false speech, as well as the inappropriateness of excessive talk, is expressed in aesthetic terms: *loʾ naʾwah*, "unfitting" or "uncomely." Wisdom Literature fuses the right with the beautiful (Bryce 1979: 151). Honesty is elegant. Other things called unsuitable to a fool are honor (26:1) and pleasure (19:10). The way this attitude fits into Proverbs' idea of knowledge is discussed in Essay 8 (II), "Coherence Theory."

Excessive: Hebrew *yeter* can mean "remainder" (inapplicable here) or "surplus," hence "much" or "too much" (Dan 8:9; Isa 56:12; Ps 31:24). Translations implying a rhetorical quality, such as "fine speech" (NRSV, Clifford) or "lofty words" (JPSV) are unwarranted. Waldman (1976: 143–45) suggests that *śᵉpat yeter* means arrogant, overbearing speech, with the additional connotation of falseness, like Akkadian *atirtu*. (According to CAD, *ša atrāti* means "one who exaggerates," "one who lies.") This is possible, and it is not necessarily a separate meaning, because a person who exaggerates necessarily distorts the truth. But the uses of *yeter* elsewhere suggest that the speech condemned here is excessive in quantity rather than hyperbolic. According to the B-line, false speech is improper in anyone, but *especially* in a noble, who should display a probity befitting his station. Hence the A-line should mention a type of speech that is always improper, but especially so for a contemptible man, and *excessive* fits that slot. Even in a basically decent person, garrulousness can cause offense; see the Comment on 10:19. It is worse when a *scoundrel* talks too much, for he speaks bad things.

scoundrel [*nabal*]: A *nabal* is a species of fool, base and worthless and an object of scorn. He is never merely stupid, but, like the *ʾĕwil*, morally deficient.

W. Roth (1960) argues that the basic meaning of *n-b-l* is "outcast." In Job 30:8, *nabal* is paired with *b^{e}ney b^{e}li šem* "no-names," who are obscure, socially marginal people. This is implied also in 2 Sam 3:33. Still, "outcast" is not an adequate rendering. The *nabal* is not merely a member of the lower class. According to Prov 30:21–23, the earth shudders when a *nabal* is sated with bread, and no one, certainly not the sages of Proverbs, would object to a poor person having food. In fact, a *nabal* may be rich, like Nabal the Carmelite (1 Sam 25:2–3), who is a *nabal*, at least in his wife's eyes (v 25). Isaiah complains that people are calling the *nabal* a *nadib*, a "noble" (32:5), meaning that he has high social and economic status. The *nabal* is someone tainted by personal baseness. Social disgust and rejection are always implicit in the use of *nabal* and cognate forms. Even if the *nabal* is not always a social outcast, he is, or should be, a pariah.

excessive [*yeter*]: Toy, BHS, and others emend *yeter* to *yōšer* "honest." This is unhelpful because "honest speech" *would* befit anyone, including the *nābāl*, who in any case would not speak honestly. Plöger emends to (an ungrammatical) *yāqār* or (better) *y^{e}qār* (an Aramaism meaning "honor"), hence "vortreffliche Lippe" ("excellent lip"). Neither emendation is necessary, nor is either supported by LXX's *pista* "trustworthy"; see the Textual Notes.

17:8 A bribe is a beautiful jewel in its possessor's eyes:
Wherever he turns he succeeds.

Bribes are useful, or at least thought so. In Proverbs' view, and in the ancient view generally, gifts are illicit only when used to wrong ends (17:23). Their efficacy is recognized in 18:16; 19:6; and 21:14; see the Comment on 18:16. An addition in the LXX recognizes the dangers of bribes to their recipients; see the Textual Note on 22:9a. The word *šoḥad* almost always means "bribe" and connotes corruption, but it has a neutral connotation in Prov 21:14; 1 Kgs 15:19; and 2 Kgs 16:8.

beautiful jewel [*'eben ḥen*]: Lit., "stone of favor" or "attractive stone." Most commentators understand this to be not merely a jewel but a stone with magical properties (Ehrlich, Toy, etc.).

Who is the bribe's "possessor," its *b$^{e\text{c}}$alim* (sg.)? He may be the recipient (Hame'iri, comparing Prov 1:19). If so, the gift is compared to an amulet that excites the favor of the recipient (thus Ehrlich). This construal, however, leaves the second line obscure. The subject of "succeeds" would have to be the recipient, but what would *his* success matter? A bribe is supposed to advance its *giver's* interests.

Alternatively, the "possessor" may be the giver (thus Toy, McKane, Clifford, McKane, and most commentators). Then the problem is the function of the phrase "in his eyes" because it makes the statement in the A-line sound like a matter of perspective, not fact. If that is the case, then the B-line must also state the briber's thoughts, namely, that he *expects* to succeed. Sa'adia thinks this is a case of man deeming something to be right while God knows the contrary, as in Prov 14:12. If so, the proverb is a psychological observation, but one left without comment or even implication of evaluation. Is the briber *wrong* in his expectation? Most proverbs about bribes assume their efficacy (18:16; 19:6; 21:14). Even Prov

15:27, which is leery of their moral effects, does not deny their efficacy. Perhaps the value of the bribe is stated as a matter of fact, without "its possessor's eyes" implying that the gift is valuable *only* in its possessor's eyes.

17:9 He who seeks love covers up an offense,
while he who repeats a matter alienates a friend.

A man who wants others' affection will "cover up"—overlook—offenses against himself. See the Comment on 10:6 and contrast 28:13.

covers up: That is, *should* cover up.

repeats a matter: Most commentators understand this to be verbal recounting of the incident by the offended party; this is the opposite of "covering up" (JPSV: "harps on a matter"). By this interpretation, the "matter" (*dabar*) is the offensive incident. Prov 11:13 offers the same advice.

Ehrlich says that *šanah* in the G-stem means to repeat an *action* (which is introduced by *b*-), as in Prov 26:11 and Rabbinic Hebrew (e.g., *b. Qidd*. 40a). "He who repeats a matter" is, then, the offender. Though the offended person (the "friend" in the B-line) may be gracious enough to bury the incident, if the offender repeats his deed, alienation is inevitable. However, Sir 42:1, which is based on this proverb, uses *šnwt dbr* to mean repeating what one hears, and in Sir 44:15 the verb means to retell.

17:10 A rebuke comes down harder on a perceptive person
than a hundred blows on a dolt.

comes down harder: It is felt more acutely, because he has the sensitivity to be ashamed. Such a one (a boy is probably in mind) takes correction from verbal reproofs and does not need beatings (Prov 19:25).

tēḥat: This is a G-stem impf. of *n-ḥ-t*, "descend." It here refers to the force with which the rebuke or blow is *felt*. Naḥmias glosses, "descends on and resides within," comparing the use of the N-stem in Ps 38:3. But the G of *n-ḥ-t* does not connote penetration, and even the verse adduced speaks of arrows "falling on," not necessarily penetrating. The LXX reads the word as *tāḥēt* "shatter," from *ḥ-t-t*. The first parsing is more likely, since a rebuke should not *shatter* its recipient, or even "terrify" him, as a derivation from the latter root would imply.

a perceptive person: A *mebin* is someone who is *able* to comprehend (see Vol. I, 30). He is perceptive and intelligent, but not necessarily flawless. (Observe that in Prov 17:24, wisdom is close to the *mebin* but not necessarily "in" him.) The present proverb presumes that the "rebuke" is justified. If one is rebuked, that does not mean that he is a fool, so long as he responds quickly and properly. The dolt, thickheaded and smug, would not do so.

than a hundred blows on a dolt: Lit., "than smiting a dolt a hundred times."

17:11 A rebel truly seeks evil,
and a cruel messenger will be sent against him.

Whatever public benefits the rebel or factionalist may promise, however benevolent the motives he protests, he is really up to no good. His fate recalls Prov 16:14a, "The wrath of kings is a deadly messenger." The king will project his wrath in the form of a "messenger"—perhaps a contingent of soldiers, or simply official assassins—against the rebels.

rebel [*m^{e}ri*]: Lit., "rebellion."

Alternatively, the A-line can be translated: "An evil person [*ra*ʿ] seeks only rebellion [*m^{e}ri*]." The basic idea is the same, but the first reading is preferable because, as Delitzsch observes, "seeks evil" is a more likely locution than "seeks rebellion."

The "messenger" (*mala'k*) sent against the rebel may be human or angelic. LXX has the latter. Some would have it both ways. Saʿadia says that if a man rebels against a king, a human messenger is sent to punish him. (Kings send messengers to arrest or kill men considered seditious in 1 Sam 19:14–15 and 2 Kgs 6:32.) If he rebels against God's word, punitive angels are dispatched (Ps 78:49; Ezek 9:2; etc.). It is possible that the punishment is executed by angels, because God himself, as this socially conservative book sees it, defends the political order, if it is just. Murphy thinks that the ambiguity is deliberate, to make the threat more ominous.

Some connect this verse with the preceding: An intelligent man gets off with a rebuke; a fool gets beaten; but the rebel is put to death (thus, basically, Radaq and Yonah Gerundi, who understand the messenger as angelic).

17:12 Better to come upon a bear bereft of her young
than a dolt in his folly!

Stupid people (*k^{e}silim*) cause harm to everyone in their vicinity. Avoid them! (14:7). A she-bear bereft of her young is the epitome of anger and ferocity (2 Sam 17:8; Hos 13:8). Plöger says that the analogy lies in the fool's aggressiveness. A *k^{e}sil*, however, is not inherently aggressive; he is more of a blunderer who does not think of consequences. This fact may even give the comparison more of a bite. The *k^{e}sil*, blithely obtuse and oafish, even without investing energy in deliberate aggression, can be as destructive as one of the most ferocious, powerful, and implacable of creatures. The *k^{e}sil*, after all, speaks provocative words (18:6), blunders into quarrels (14:16), and devours others' belongings (21:20). He easily slides into evildoing (10:23; 13:19). Thus he harms his friends (13:20) and ruins any mission on which he is sent (26:6).

The proverb literally says: "Let a bereft bear come upon a man and let not a dolt in his folly (come upon a man)." The bear and the fool are the active parties in the comparison, but this is difficult to translate.

pāgôš dōb šakkûl b^{e}'îš . . . : This verse is always translated along the lines of the NRSV: "Better to meet a she-bear robbed of its cubs than to confront a fool immersed in folly." But this does not account for *b^{e}'îš* "upon a man," which implies that the bear is the active party, the one "coming upon" a man. If the bear is active in the analogy, we would expect the dangerous party in the comparison, the dolt, to be the active one in the parallel. Loewenstamm (1987: 222) emends to *bᵉyēʾûšô* "in its desperation." Emendation is not necessary if the inf. abs. is understood to function as a jussive, as shown by the use of *ʾal* to negate it in the B-line (where the verb is gapped).

17:13 He who returns evil for good—
evil will not depart from his house.

One who is so ungrateful as to harm a benefactor will himself suffer harm more severe than what he caused. He will suffer unremittingly, and his family with him. The B-line states the punishment starkly, without allusion to a causal mechanism. The retribution is a *curse*, a punitive power outside the natural causation of the deed-consequence nexus (Vol. I, 91–92). The curse will ensconce itself in the miscreant's house and stay there, radiating misery, for "the Lord's curse is in the house of the wicked" (3:33a; see the Comment).

17:14 Starting strife is (like) releasing water,
so before a quarrel breaks out, leave off!

The first line says, literally, "Releasing water—the start of a quarrel." Provoking a quarrel is like opening a sluice. The flow starts in a trickle but quickly surges out of control (Clifford; thus most commentators). Alternatively: The start of a quarrel is like a small seepage of water from a dam, which becomes a torrent (McKane).

releasing water [*poṭer mayim*]: This phrase is similar to Akkadian *nagbē puṭṭuru* "(he) opened springs," which is parallel to "brought rain" (CAD N: 109b; see HALOT 925a). This parallel supports the first interpretation, since the verb same verb, *pṭr*, is used of opening a reservoir of water rather than of letting water trickle out.

The LXX has Greek *logois* "words," which renders *mlym* "words," where the MT has the similar-looking *mym* "water." Using *mlym*, but translating differently from the rather confused rendering in the LXX, the verse reads, "Releasing words starts a quarrel, so before a quarrel breaks out, leave off!" The teaching that uncontrolled speech provokes conflict is familiar in Wisdom Literature; see, for example, Prov 10:19 and 17:27. The phrase *yapṭiru bᵉśapah* "let loose (words of scorn) with the lip" in Ps 22:8 supports the connection of *pṭr* with speech (though that verse uses the H-stem rather than the G). Both the LXX and MT readings are viable and can stand as variant proverbs.

releasing [*pôṭēr*]: This is best parsed as an abstract *qôṭēl*, like those mentioned by Kedar-Kopfstein 1977: 165–66, 169. Alternatively, the sentence can be read as a blunt juxtaposition (see the Comment on 13:1); hence, "He who releases water—the start of strife."

breaks out: The exact meaning of *hitgallaʿ* is uncertain. The uses in 18:1 and 20:3 allow for the meaning "break forth" (in anger). Usages in Rabbinic Hebrew suggest that the root means "open" or "lay bare." In the D-stem it refers to attacking in an argument; see Jastrow, *Dictionary*, p. 250.

leave off! [*nᵉṭôš*]: The imperative at the end of the sentence is awkward, but a similar construction is found in Qoh 5:6.

**17:15 He who exonerates the guilty and he who condemns the innocent—
the Lord loathes them both.**

This fundamental rule of judicial decisions is meant for judges. It seems to be based on Deut 25:1: "If there is conflict between men and they approach for judgment, then they [the judges] shall judge them. And they shall exonerate the innocent and condemn the guilty [*w^{e}hiṣdiqu ʾet haṣṣaddiq w^{e}hiršiʿu ʾet harašaʿ*]." The last sentence uses almost the same words as this proverb. Hence the above translation of Prov 17:15a uses judicial terms. Alternatively, one might render the line in broader moral terms: "He who justifies the wicked [*maṣdiq rašaʿ*] and he who condemns the righteous [*maršiaʿ ṣaddiq*], etc." Then the proverb refers to whoever lies about someone's character, even outside court.

By either interpretation, duality is important: Not only is the injustice to the innocent (an obvious wrong) loathsome to God, but also the failure to punish the guilty, even though the latter is the lesser judicial offense (Naḥmias) and might even seem merciful (Ehrlich).

This verse has a strong parallel in a Sumerian proverb from the Old Babylonian period:

The one who perverts justice,
the one who loves an unjust verdict,
He is an abomination to Utu.[294] (trans. G. D. Young *1972*: 132)

R. Yaron (*1985*) argues that this and some other "abomination" proverbs are tristichs: "He who acquits the guilty / and he who condemns the innocent— / the Lord loathes them both." But the criteria for the division are unclear, and the first two stichs, each with two words, would be unusually short for lines in Proverbs.

**17:16 What's the point of a payment in a dolt's hand
to buy wisdom, when he lacks a mind?**

Even a dunce may desire wisdom, at least some sorts of it, for he might covet the respect and benefits that he sees the wise enjoying. But he would want it fast and easy. What kind of wisdom might he desire? If it were sagacity, prudence, and moral acumen that he sought, he would not be a *k^{e}sil*, a dolt, but at worst a *peti*, a simple or callow person—and a *peti* of the best sort. A dolt would desire wisdom in the form of cunning, but he could not expect to buy that. In any case, he probably thinks himself cunning already, for the earmark of the *k^{e}sil* is smugness. The fool in this saying is probably seeking to acquire erudition, not so much for the sake of the learning itself as for its trappings: prestige and profits.

The evidence of the fool's eagerness for "wisdom" is said to be that he is willing to pay for it. But he does not have the intellectual aptitude ("mind," lit., "heart") to attain it. Ramaq says that what the dolt lacks is true *desire* for wisdom. But in

[294] Shamash, the sun god, overseer of justice.

Proverbs, lack of "heart" (as in the idiom *ḥăsar leb*, lit., "lacking a heart") means low intelligence.

The "payment" the dolt brings may be school tuition (McKane), but not necessarily so. That wisdom could be purchased somewhere is the fool's notion, and it might be just silly. Job 28:15–19 says that wisdom cannot be bought—not because it is so expensive, but because no valuables can be compared to it. Wisdom belongs to a different category of value and hence cannot be acquired in this fashion.

17:17 A friend loves at all times,
and a brother is born for sorrow.

Some commentators see a contrast between the two lines: Whereas friends are always friendly (at least for socializing; see 18:24) a brother, can be counted on even in crisis (Van Leeuwen). This interpretation is supported by Prov 18:24 and 27:10c, which presume that a brother, all things being equal, is more reliable than a friend. Others take the two lines as synonymous, equating friend and brother in loyalty (Toy, Clifford). The proverb is more cogent by the second reading, for if a friend loves at all times, this would include, not exclude, times of trouble. A friend and a brother love—or *should* love—at all times, even difficult ones.

17:18 A senseless man shakes hands,
giving surety to his acquaintance.

The situation envisioned in this proverb is the subject of the epigram in 6:1–5. A loan guarantor shakes (lit., "strikes" or "clasps") the lender's hand to seal an agreement to provide surety *on behalf of* a third party, the borrower. The lender is the guarantor's *reaʿ* ("neighbor," "acquaintance"; see the Comment on 3:28). The borrower is a "stranger" (6:1b; 20:16a), who may go away and leave the guarantor stuck with the debt. That is why the guarantor is called "senseless." See the Comment on 6:1 and the discussion of loan guarantees in Vol. I, 214–16.

According to Van Leeuwen, verses 17 and 18 form a proverb-pair sharing the word *reaʿ* "friend," "neighbor." *Reaʿ* is an ambiguous term, which can refer both to a true friend and a greedy neighbor. The first is trustworthy, the second not, and one must know what sort he is dealing with. But the neighbor in v 18 is not the borrower, nor is he greedy. Probably the only connection between the two proverbs is the shared word. Possibly, however, v 18 is meant to narrow the scope of v 17: One need not, and should not, help others in *every* way.

17:19 He who loves an offense loves strife,
and he who makes his door high seeks a fall.

"He who loves an offense" may be a person who likes to harp on offenses done to himself (Clifford). Or he may "love to offend" and have a propensity for insulting others. Either way, he may love conflict consciously, but, even if not, his proclivity to offend is *tantamount* to loving strife. Compare the nature of the statements in

12:12 and 13:24 and see the Comment on 11:27a, a line which is the mirror image of 17:19a. The combination of the two lines of this verse suggests that love of strife is equivalent to seeking one's own fall, but the actions described are different.

makes his door high [*magbiah pitḥo*]: On the literal level, this means to build a large, ostentatious house that draws envy. In an epilogue to the instruction of Shube'awilum, the son praises his father's accomplishments thus: "My father, you have built a house. You have made the gate high. Sixty ells is the breadth of the storeroom—what have you taken with you?" (Dietrich 1993: 61). This phrase may more generally indicate any grandiose, showy action.

Petaḥ "door" refers specifically to the opening of the doorway. Thus, making one's "opening [*petaḥ*] high" may at the same time be a sarcastic idiom for shooting one's mouth off, or, we would say, "opening his trap." The parallel line about giving offense supports this. *Petaḥ* "opening" is likely a slang term for mouth. It does not have this meaning elsewhere, but the phrase "open [*ptḥ*] the mouth" means to begin speaking (Ps 39:10; Job 3:1; etc.). Also compare 1 Sam 2:3, in which "high" refers to arrogant speech (similarly Riyqam, Ramaq; cf. Ehrlich).

fall [*šeber*]: Lit., "break." This is the consequence of pride according to Prov 16:18 and 18:12, a fact supporting the above interpretation of making one's door high.

NRSV translates 17:19b as "One who builds a high threshold invites broken bones"—perhaps the result of a fall. But the message of the verse by that phrasing is obscure. Also, to "make the door high" means raising the lintel rather than the sill.

17:20 He whose heart is crooked will not attain good,
and he who is perverse of tongue will fall into evil.

attain good: Lit., "find good," that is, good fortune.

perverse of tongue [*nehpak bilšono*]: Lit., "turned-over in his tongue" or "perverse in his tongue." He speaks *tahpukot* "distortions" or "perversities" (Prov 2:12).

17:21 He who begets a dolt gets grief,
and the father of a scoundrel knows no joy.

scoundrel [*nabal*]: See the Comment on 17:7.

There would be little point in this verse if it were directed to fathers, for they have no control over whether they beget a fool. Rather, it is directed to boys who are not yet incurably corrupt, urging them to avoid folly so as not to cause their fathers misery. This verse is very similar to 10:1 (see the Comment); 13:1; and 15:20. There is no reason to assume, as Delitzsch does, that verses with this theme head a section.

He who begets [*yōlēd*] . . . : Lit., "He who begets a fool: it is (only) for grief for him [*lᵉtûgāh lô*]." See the Comment on 11:19.

17:22 A cheerful heart improves the body,
and an ill spirit dries up the bones.

On the psychosomatic effects of cheer and gloom, see the Comment on 15:13; cf. also 12:25. Prov 17:22 ≈ 15:13.

body [*gehah*]: The meaning of this noun (used only here) is uncertain. Other possibilities are "face" and "health."

gēhāh: Explanations include the following: (1) "Face." Thus Naḥmias, comparing *yêṭib pānîm* in 15:13; sim. Tur-Sinai p. 44. (There is, however, no connection with Arabic *jihat* "face," which derives from *w-j-h*, as noted by Hitzig.) (2) "Age." Thus Sym *hēlikian*, Vul *aetatem*. (3) "Healing" or "health." Thus Radaq (*Sefer Hashorashim*) and almost all lexicons and translations. This rendering is based on the supposed use of *yghh* (point *yagheh*?) in Hos 5:13bb (// *rp'*, but in a different construction) and Sir 43:18 MS B (mg. *yhgh*). Both verses are textually suspect and difficult, so the rendering remains uncertain. (4) "Body." Thus Syr and Tg *gwyh* "body." Heb *ghh* is perhaps a by-form of *gēwāh* "back," "body." Compare cases in which a medial *waw* appears in a by-form of a medial-weak root, though these examples have an *'aleph*: *nāweh* (fem. sg. *nāwāh*, e.g., Jer 6:2; H: Exod 15:2)/*nā'weh* (e.g., Prov 19:10)/ *nā'eh* ("lovely"; *gēwāh*/*gē'eh* "pride" (Jer 13:17); and possibly *rē'ah*/*rwh* "saturate" (Job 10:15; Isa 53:11). This gloss fits the context.

dries up the bones: Dry bones were considered a cause and indicator of bad health; see the Comment on 3:8. The image (probably intended literally) is suggestive of the pains and creakiness of arthritis.

17:23 The wicked man takes a bribe from the bosom
to pervert the ways of justice.

What is wrong in this deed, as Clifford observes, is not the practice of gift-giving itself (see 17:8) but its abuse. The corrupt man does not merely give gratuities to officials to expedite a legitimate petition or to reward a favor (a practice that seems to have been very widely accepted as a perquisite of office until very recent times). Rather, he gives a gift for corrupt purposes. This practice is condemned in Exod 23:8 and Deut 16:19; and see also the Textual Note on LXX 22:9a. Psalm 15:5aβ says that the righteous man "does not take a bribe against the innocent." The first line crackles and hisses with alliteration: *ŠOḥad meḤEQ raŠA' yiqQAḤ*.

The MT has *meḥeq . . . yiqqaḥ* "takes . . . from the bosom." This means that the briber takes the gift from his own bosom, that is, from the opening on the front of his garment. (Hame'iri may be right that this movement connotes stealth.) The LXX has "in the bosom," representing Hebrew *bḥyq*, "in [or "into"] the bosom" (as in Prov 21:14), implying that the subject of "takes" is the recipient, who tucks the gift away in his garment. Either is possible.

17:24 Wisdom is before the face of the perceptive man,
while the eyes of the dolt are in the ends of the earth.

The "perceptive man," the *mebin*, may not yet possess *ḥokmah* "wisdom," at least not to the extent of his potential. But a fuller wisdom is near at hand, because he is receptive to it. As Radaq correctly paraphrases: "Wisdom stands before the perceptive man." Wisdom's truths are not hidden, but not everybody is willing to perceive them, to take them to themselves and realize their significance.

perceptive man [*mebin*]: The verb *hebin* (participle *mebin*), usually translated "understand," here retains something of its root sense, "perceive." "Perceive," "discern," is clearly the sense of the verb in Prov 7:7; 23:1; 24:12; and 29:19. (In these cases, the word may be in the G-stem, but the form is the same as the H-stem, and it is unlikely that the ancient reader or writer would have distinguished them.) Wisdom is nearby, and the *mebin* is able to perceive it.

ends of the earth: Lit., "end of the earth"—a metaphor for intellectual distance. A fool may search the world for wisdom, but he will not find it, because he does not realize its proximity. He will not find wisdom in foreign or esoteric learning. One might object that a dolt would not look for wisdom at all (McKane), but he is said to do so in 17:16. He presumably wants wisdom's benefits and prestige. More precisely, the point of this and similar proverbs is not to describe fools but to condemn and ridicule those guilty of the actions described. It is especially caustic to call the very men who would pride themselves on their erudition *k*ᵉ*silim*, which connotes torpor and dullness.

Job 28 says that wisdom is not to be found in the far reaches and depths of the earth. Rather, it is close at hand and obvious to whoever is open to it. God defined wisdom for mankind at the beginning at creation, making it part of the shared human heritage: "Behold the fear of the Lord is wisdom, and the avoidance of evil, understanding" (Job 28:28). Deut 30:11–14 says the same of God's instruction (*torah*) to Israel.

Some see the issue in this proverb as one of focus and concentration. The perceptive man keeps his attention on wisdom (Gemser) or on the teacher (McKane), whereas the fool is distracted and impervious to learning. This is possible, but it is not favored by the phrase *'et p*ᵉ*ney* "before the face," which never implies willed focus, but simply proximity. For example, when Jacob camps *'et p*ᵉ*ney* Shechem (Gen 33:18), the phrase only implies his proximity to the place. Willed focus might be expressed as *śam panayw/libbo 'el* "sets his face/heart toward."

17:25 A stupid son is an irritation to his father
and an embitterment for his mother.

See the Comment on 10:1bc.

17:26 Also, punishing the righteous man is not good—
smiting noble people for honesty.

This couplet speaks of a single offense: punishing a righteous man of noble character for his honesty. To tell judges not to inflict punishment upon the innocent, as this proverb is invariably understood to do, would be exceptionally banal. The insipidity is reduced if we understand "honesty" as candid, blunt speech (*yošer*, as in Job 6:25; 33:3). "Smiting" may be metaphor for harming or insulting. "Noble" (*nadib*) can refer not only to a member of the nobility but also to a person of upright, generous character, as in Prov 17:7 and Isa 32:8. "(It) is not good" may be understood as a pragmatic evaluation, meaning not beneficial, harmful. Then the message is that it helps no one to harm or insult people of good character for their candid speech. Prov 18:5 has the same structure and message.

Also [*gam*]: The function of this particle is unclear here. According to Delitzsch, it applies to *laṣṣaddiq* "the righteous man"; hence, punishing the righteous man (in addition to the guilty) is not good (see Prov 17:15). Ehrlich says that *gam* introduces an argument from minor to major ("all the more so"), but it is doubtful that this is ever its function. Naḥmias explains it to mean *even*: It goes without saying that killing a righteous man is wrong, but *even* punishing (or fining) him is not good. However, the first proposition is absent from the proverb.

not good: That is, "bad"; see the Comment on 16:29.

17:27 The knowledgeable man restrains his words,
and the sensible man is calm.

One should be reserved in speech generally (see the Comment on 10:19), but this proverb teaches us in particular to control what we say when provoked. This is the message of Prov 15:1, 18; and 14:29 (17:27b ≈ 14:29a). Speech is the theme of most of the proverbs in 17:27–18:8, overtly or implicitly.

calm: Lit., "cool of spirit [*qar ruaḥ*]." "Cool of spirit" (the ketiv), rather than "precious of spirit" (*y*[e]*qar ruaḥ*, the qeré), is certainly the correct reading. The variant in 14:29 has *'erek 'appayim*, "patient" or "long-suffering," instead of "cool of spirit." The latter phrase recalls the Egyptian idiom "the cool man," whose opposite is the "hot man," on whom see the Comment on 15:1.

17:28 Even a fool who keeps silent is reckoned wise;
he who keeps his lips closed—astute.

If *even* a fool (*'ĕwil*) who keeps his mouth shut does not expose his folly (compare Job 13:5), how much the more so of ordinary people. The type of fool known as a *k*[e]*sil* pours out words (Prov 15:2; 18:2; 29:11; Qoh 10:12–14[295]), but a clever *'ĕwil* might be able to hold his thoughts secret.

When read in conjunction with Prov 17:28, v 27 reinforces the importance of being sparing in words. And v 28, when read in conjunction with v 27, reinforces the value of a cool temper.

18:1 The misfit seeks pretexts[a];
he attacks all competence.

---

[a] *l*[e]*tō'ănāh* (MT *l*[e]*ta'ăwāh*).

---

[295] Qohelet calls the fool *k*[e]*sil* in 10:12 and *sakal* in 10:14, showing the synonymity of the terms. The *sakal* in Qohelet has the features of the *k*[e]*sil* in Proverbs.

The misfit seeks pretexts for quarreling, and he lashes out at *tušiyyah* "competence," meaning either competent people or counsels and strategies characterized by this quality, as in Job 5:12 and 26:3. Restraint in speech is the theme of Prov 17:27–18:3.

misfit [*niprad*]: Lit., "one who is separated" or (reflexively) "one who separates himself, sets himself apart." The word is used only here, and its exact meaning is uncertain (McKane: "alienated man"; Clifford: "misfit"; JPSV: "He who isolates himself"; Radaq: "separated from God"). The verb in the causative (H) form (*maprid*) is used of alienating a friend in 17:9. Here (in the passive/reflexive N-stem) it means one who deliberately sets himself apart from the community (Naḥmias, second interpretation). The present proverb emphasizes the fool's isolation and incompatibility. Conversely, the ability to get along with people is, throughout the book, a sign and reward of wisdom.

seeks pretexts [*lᵉto'ănah*; lit. sg.]: The MT has "seeks desire" (*lᵉta'ăwah*), which is generally understood to refer to *his* desire, what the misfit desires. He "goes his own way" (Murphy) or "seeks to go after his desire and does not keep himself from sin" (Radaq). But the suffix "his" would seem necessary for that sense. There is, moreover, no particular relation between a misfit and desire, whereas such a person would indeed seek pretexts for quarrels. The reading *to'ănah* "pretexts," supported by LXX *prophaseis* "pretexts," differs from the MT only in the very similar letter *nun* in place of *waw*.

he attacks all competence [*bᵉkol tušiyyah yitgallaʿ*]: The verb *hitgallaʿ* appears in Prov 17:14 and 20:3 in the context of quarrels and seems to mean "break forth in anger" or the like. (See the Comment on 17:14.)

18:2 The dolt does not desire good sense,
but only to reveal his heart.

Continuing the theme of reserve in speech, this proverb contrasts the disclosure of one's thoughts with *tᵉbunah* "good sense." (It is not always a mistake to reveal one's thoughts, but the fool should certainly keep *his* hidden. In this context, the thoughts that should be hidden are angry ones, which the fool is unable to repress (Prov 12:16).

to reveal his heart [*bᵉhitgallot libbo*]: Lit., "in his heart's revealing itself." The reflexive verb suggests that the fool's self-exposure isn't even a deliberate choice. His heart bares itself, his mouth blurts out his folly, and he is rather pleased with the results, because "revealing his heart" is what he enjoys doing. Prov 12:23b too speaks of the fool's self-disclosure: "The heart of dolts cries out folly"; sim. Qoh 10:3.

18:3 When the wicked man enters, contempt enters too,
and with insult (comes) reproach.

Contempt and insult may here be the feelings directed at the wicked man, or they may be his disdain toward others. The latter is supported by Prov 22:10, which advises banishing the insolent scoffer (*leṣ*) so as to eliminate conflict and insult (*qalon*). This proverb looks like a reworking and expansion of 11:2.

wicked man [*rāšāʿ*]: Toy, McKane, and others vocalize this as *rešaʿ* "wickedness" to make a better parallel with *qālôn* "insult." In fact, the parallelism is sequential. The MT vocalization suggests that insult accompanies the wicked man when he enters a room.

18:4 The words of a man's mouth are deep waters,
a flowing stream, a fount of wisdom.

Words are like deep, fresh water, for they can hold and convey wisdom, a source of refreshment and vitality. Words are compared first to two types of water sources, then to a source of wisdom. The third comparison is compounded of a metaphor ("fount") and a literal referent ("wisdom"). By merging the metaphorical and the literal, the third comparison interprets the first two. Prov 18:4a ≈ 20:5a.

Where the MT has *ḥokmah* "wisdom," the LXX has *zōēs* "life." Elsewhere waters are used as a figure of *life*, as in Prov 10:11a: "The mouth of the righteous is a fount of life [*mᵉqor ḥayyim*]"; sim. 13:14 and 14:27. The MT and the LXX are variant proverbs and neither need be adjusted to the other.

deep waters, a flowing stream: That is, a great supply of fresh water. "Deep waters" are waters in a well, as indicated by the verb *dlh* "draw up" in Prov 20:5: "The counsel in a man's heart is deep waters, and a sensible man will draw it up." There, *ʿeṣah* "counsel" is called deep waters. This parallel suggests that the "words" (*dibrey-*, from *dabar*) praised in the present saying are implicitly of the same sort—wise counsel. *Dabar* and *ʿeṣah* are paired in Judg 20:7 and are parallel in Isa 8:10 and 44:26. In a well, "deep" waters are great in quantity, hence offer much life-giving refreshment. The image also suggests coolness and purity (Ramaq). It is less likely to allude to profundity and erudition, for those qualities are not suggested by the flowing stream. It does not mean that the words are hidden or enigmatic, for this is not necessarily a virtue, especially in words of counsel. A "flowing stream" is a river with its own springs that is thus perpetual, not seasonal.

18:5 It is not good to be partial to the guilty,
to subvert the innocent in judgment.

This proverb is less of a banality if "not good" (*loʾ ṭob*) is meant in a pragmatic rather than an ethical sense. Showing partiality to the guilty is not *useful*; it is downright deleterious (Ehrlich; see the Comment on 16:29). Read with this nuance, the verse expresses a belief in the inexorable victory of justice: Even if a judge favors the guilty, in the long run it will not do that person, or anyone else, any good. This proverb is structured exactly like 17:26 and carries much the same message. As in that verse, the second line is introduced by an infinitive of circumstance defining "to be partial."

Hebrew *rašaʿ* and *ṣaddiq* mean "wicked" and "righteous," but in a judicial context they refer more specifically to the guilty and the innocent.

18:6 The lips of the dolt come into strife,
and his mouth calls for blows.

Verses 6–8 continue the theme of speech from v 4. Verse 5 also is relevant, since it refers to a verbal crime. The present verse can be read in two ways: (1) By his provocative words, the dolt gets into quarrels and virtually cries out to be beaten. (2) When he calls you to him, he is in effect summoning *you* to a beating, because you will get into trouble with him.

The organs of speech are personified, as the mouth and tongue are in Ps 73:9. Compare the way that the fool's heart proclaims his folly in Prov 12:23b and Qoh 10:3.

come [*yaboʾu*]: Equally valid, and rather more vivid, is LXX's vocalization *yābîʾû* "bring": "The lips of the dolt bring into conflict." The elided object could be the dolt himself or others. The ambiguity is productive: the fool's lips bring him and others to strife. The LXX provides a better parallel to the B-line, which describes something that an organ of speech does *to* people (whether to the fool or to others).

18:7 The dolt's mouth is his ruination,
and his lips are his mortal snare.

The fool causes his own destruction; see the Comment on 1:19.

his mortal snare: Lit., "the snare of his life [*napšo*]." Or "his own snare," that is, he snares himself.

18:8 The words of the slanderer are like delicacies,
and they descend to the chambers of the belly.

Complaints are like delicious morsels that are eagerly swallowed and held deep within. The belly is where thoughts are stored; see the Comment on 22:18. The notion is Egyptian in origin; see Shupak *1984–1985*: 478–81. The "belly" (*beṭen*) includes the entire abdominal region with its visceral organs, and not just the stomach, though in these proverbs the stomach is most relevant. The "chambers" of the belly (mentioned in Prov 20:27, 30) are its innermost parts. Here they are imagined as storage chambers. Ramaq explains that the belly is equivalent to the heart. Prov 18:8 = 26:22.

slanderer [*nirgan*]: "Slanderer" or "gossiper" fits this context as well as 16:28; 26:20; and Sir 11:31a ("The slanderer turns good into evil"). The verb seems to mean more broadly "complain" or "say bad things about"; see Deut 1:27 (where the words of *rogᵉnim* "complainers" are quoted) and Ps 106:25. Radaq attaches both senses, "slanderer" and "complainer," to the word. In the present verse, the "complaint" may be hostile words toward another person, that is, "slander," but it might designate more broadly a grievance that infects others, like the griping in Deut 1:27.

delicacies [*mitlahămim*]: The meaning of this word (appearing elsewhere only in the doublet, 26:22) is taken from context. The Arabic cognate *lahima* (I and

VIII) means "to devour greedily" (HALOT 521a), and perhaps the image this line gives is of someone wolfing down gossip like food. In conjunction with 18:6 and 7, which also speak about misuse of the mouth, this verse indicates a further way in which "the dolt's mouth is his ruination" (v 7a). But that is not the main point in the proverb itself, because the focus, as the B-line shows, is not on the slanderer's mouth but on the listener's. It is he who devours gossip, and he too is a fool.

18:9 He who is slack in his work—
he too is brother to a vandal.

The lazy and negligent man not only fails to contribute to the work, he impairs and harms it. He is the "brother" of a habitual vandal, that is, of the same sort.

too [*gam*]: Since there is no sentence-additive function pertinent here, the adverb *gam* modifies the following item *mitrappeh* "he who is slack." In other words, he too, *among others* (such as the sort mentioned in Prov 28:24), is like a vandal.

vandal [*baʿal mašḥît*]: *Mašḥît*, though in appearance an active ptcp., can be an abstract noun meaning "destruction," for example, Ezek 9:6; 21:36; and Dan 10:8. Or the phrase *baʿal mašḥît* can be a construct of coordinates, like *baʿal qôrēʾ* (Torah reader) in RH or *rōbeh qaššāt* (lit., "shooter-bowman") in Gen 21:20 (Hurvitz 1986: 12). Either way, *baʿal mašḥît* means "destroyer" or "vandal," and the use of *baʿal* implies a permanent attribute.

18:10 The name of the Lord is a fortified tower,
into which the righteous can run and be safe.

The name of the Yahweh is a *migdal ʿoz*, "tower of strength," "fortified tower" (Ps 61:4), into which the righteous can flee for safety. Divine names were considered powerful throughout the ancient Near East. The Bible invests great power and mystery in the name of Yahweh. Fleeing to Yahweh's *name* for safety probably means calling upon him in prayer. Alternatively, Yahweh's name may stand for Yahweh himself, perhaps as a hypostasis, as in Ps 54:3a, "O God, help me by your name." However, the concepts of answering prayer and giving salvation are closely identified, as in Ps 20:2: "May Yahweh answer you in the day of trouble; may the name of the God of Jacob give you safety," using the same verb for "give safety"—*śgb*—as here.

be safe [*wᵉniśgab*]: Lit., "be raised up," "elevated," that is, out of danger; sim. Prov 29:25b. Being placed high on a rock or fortress gives safety (Pss 27:5b; 59:2).

18:11 A rich man's wealth is his fortified city
and like a lofty wall—in his imagination.

Wealth is power: who could doubt it! Like the name of the Lord (v 10), wealth is a strong city (*qiryat ʿuzzo* ≈ *migdal ʿoz* "fortified tower" in v 10a) and a high wall (*niśgabah* ≈ *niśgab* "be elevated," "be safe," in v 10b). But, unlike the security of God's name, the protection that wealth provides lies largely in the possessor's estimation. After all, "a rich man is wise in his own eyes" (28:11a).

The first line repeats 10:15a, but the second steps away from its unqualified praise of wealth and cautions that the protection it affords is in the rich man's mind. It might fail to save him in crisis. His belief in money's protective power is not necessarily delusive, for wealth might often a source of security, though not a reliable one.

One would expect the second line to end with a term parallel to "a rich man's wealth." Instead we get a prepositional phrase in another semantic category: "in his imagination." This violation of expectations provokes an ironic reconsideration of the power of wealth.

in his imagination [*bemaśkîtô*]: The exact meaning of *maśkît* is not certain. In Lev 26:1; Num 33:52; Ezek 8:12; and Prov 25:11, it refers to various kinds of graphic and glyptic images. Ps 73:7b speaks of making (read ʿbdw, cf. Syr) *maśkiyyôt lēbāb*, "images of the heart" or "devisings of the heart." From here it is a small step to "devisings" or "imaginings." The rich man mentally pictures his wealth as a fortress city with a high wall. Ramaq and Radaq derive *maśkîtô* from *ś-k-k* "cover" and explain it as a hiding place for treasures, but this does not fit the syntax well.

18:12 Before a man falls his heart grows haughty,
but humility precedes honor.

Verses 10–12 are a proverb-cluster (Ramaq) whose theme is the sense of security, whether justified or illusory. Overconfidence in one's powers begets arrogance, which leads to disaster. Temporal priority implies causality; see the Comment on 15:33. Prov 18:12a ≈ 16:18a; 18:12b = 15:33b. Warnings against arrogance appear also in 11:2; 16:5; 17:19b; and 29:23.

18:13 As for him who replies before listening—
this is folly for him, and disgrace!

Interrupting another person makes one look like a disgraceful fool. It is wise to listen and think before responding. See the Comments on 10:19; 15:28; and 17:7, and compare Qoh 5:2, 6.

Reusing this verse, Ben Sira cautions, "My son, do not reply before you listen, and do not speak in the middle of (another's) speech" (11:8). *'Abot* 5:7 says: "The wise man . . . does not interrupt his companion's words."

18:14 A man's spirit can sustain him in sickness,
but an ill spirit—who can bear it?

Disease of the body is bearable; disease of the spirit is not. The "spirit" (*ruaḥ*) is the totality of a person's psychology and emotions. In the first line, the spirit is the instrument of support, but it is an insupportable burden in the second. The spirit can help one endure physical maladies, but it becomes unbearable when it is "ill"—depressed and anxious—for then there is no other "spirit" that can support the weight. On the severity of an "ill spirit" (*ruaḥ n^{e}ke'ah*) see Prov 17:22b; cf. 12:25a.

**18:15 The heart of the astute man gets knowledge,
and the ear of the wise seeks knowledge.**

The lines are equivalent and together express the observation that the heart and ear of the astute, wise man bring him knowledge and wisdom. A wise man does not merely have knowledge, he seeks it constantly. Prov 18:15a ≈ 15:14a.

"Gets" (*qnh*) here refers not to the state of possessing something but to the process of acquiring it, meaning in this case absorbing the teachings (see the Comment on 4:7). We might translate, "goes about acquiring knowledge." "Listening" is used frequently of attending to instruction.

**18:16 A man's gift[a] clears his way
and leads him before the great.**

[a] *mattan* (MT *mattān*).

The background image is of a group of officials, who are bunched sycophantically around their superior, parting to let someone through who has oiled his way with a gift. This proverb is directed to men who have hopes of working their way up in the royal administration. In the higher echelons reside the "great" (*g*[e]*dolim*), meaning the rich and powerful, who can provide patronage.

clears his way [*yarḥib lo*]: Lit., "makes wide for him," "gives him room."

Whether a gift (or a bribe) is legitimate depends on its purpose; see the Comment on 17:8. Prov 21:14 also commends bribes intended to influence people. Prov 15:27b is more suspicious of the practice, but there the parallel line indicates that the gifts in question are illicit, seeking "ill-gotten gain."

Gifts and payoffs to officials were an accepted practice in public life until very recently. Anii advises the cultivation of local officials (referring to one with police powers) and says, "Befriend the constable of your city quarter. . . . Give him food, if you have it in your house. Do not neglect his requests!" (from 22.10–13 [cf. AEL 2.143]).

The tenor of this proverb changes somewhat when read in conjunction with the next verse, which warns against judicial partiality. The fact that a gift can get the ear of the powerful is a reason for caution when assessing the giver's requests and complaints.

mattān [absolute]: Vocalize *mattan* (construct), hence "a man's gift." Apparently the MT intends, "(By) a gift a man clears his way."

**18:17 The first (to speak) in his lawsuit is "right,"
until the other person comes and sees through him.**

Lit., "The first one is right [*ṣaddiq*] in his conflict. But his fellow will come and examine him." The context seems to be judicial, but the language allows for application to verbal disputes of all sorts. "Right" here must mean "seems right," or is used facetiously.

This proverb is not a cynical observation but a warning to hear both sides to the dispute before reaching a decision. When only one side has been presented, there is a tendency to believe it (Radaq). In a similar vein, *ʾAbot* 1:8 instructs judges to consider both parties guilty—that is, to be suspicious of both—during the arguments. The validity of the proverb is not limited to law courts, but applies to the first hearing of any argument.

sees through him [*waḥăqaro*]: By the usual translation—"and examines him" or the like, the verse just describes court procedure without presenting an alternative to the first party's seeming to be right. It is better to take *ḥaqar* as resultative, indicating the consequence of examination: to "see through" someone or "get to the ground of a matter" (Ehrlich). *Ḥaqar* is used similarly in Prov 28:11; Ps 44:22; Job 28:3, 27; and probably Job 32:11.

18:18 The lot stops quarrels
and separates litigants.

Continuing the theme of conflict, this verse commends the use of lots in resolving disputes. Lots were used particularly in the division of property and wealth. "Separates" (*yaprid*) means to separate the two disputants by ending the conflict. While the preceding verse speaks of decision-making by the human mind, this one endorses a device that entrusts the decision to God; see the Comment on 16:33.

litigants [*ʿăṣumim*]: This word usually means "powerful," but in this context its primary meaning is "litigants" (Saʿadia; thus G. R. Driver 1951: 183). This may be a double entendre meaning "powerful litigants."

Derivatives from *ʿ-ṣ-m* "be powerful" can refer to conflict ("strong words" or the like). In Isa 41:21, *ʿăṣumôt* means, approximately, "arguments" (Saʿadia), parallel to *rîb* "conflict," "claim." RH *hitʿaṣṣēm* means "to quarrel stubbornly" or the like, as in *b. Sanh.* 31b, *šnym šntʿṣmw bdyn*, which Jastrow (*Dictionary*, p. 1103a) translates, "if both parties to a law-suit are stubborn." Syr *ʿṣam* has been adduced as a cognate (Driver 1951: 183), but the antiquity of the usage is unclear.

18:19 An offended brother is like[a] a fortified city,
and quarrels are like the bar of a palace.

[a] *keqiryat* (MT *miqqiryat*).

The MT is obscure. It has something to do with quarrels, continuing the theme from vv 17–18 (and using *midyanim* "quarrels," as in v 18). The MT can be mechanically (but uncertainly) translated: "A brother who is offended [*nipšaʿ*] from ["more than"?] a fortified city, and strife is like the bar of a palace." A fortified city is elsewhere a symbol of security and salvation. It is not clear that *nipšaʿ* can mean "offended against" or the like, though most commentators assume it can. No satisfactory emendations have been proposed. Possibly the verse means that a man who has been offended by his brother "shuts him out," excluding him emotionally as if by an iron bar.

Ramaq interprets: "The lot separates powerful quarrelers (v 18), even if a brother is more offensive than a fortified city which transgresses against its king." Delitzsch translates: "A brother toward whom it has been acted perfidiously resists more than a strong tower; and contentions are like the bar of a palace." He explains that "strifes and lawsuits between those who had been friends form as insurmountable a hindrance to their reconciliation, are as difficult to be raised, as the great bars at the gate of a castle." Clifford explains: "A brother offended is more unyielding than a fortified city; such quarrels are more daunting than castle gates." But there is no justification for adding "resists" or "unyielding" or "daunting," and the hapax *nipšaʿ* (passive) is an unlikely formation from the intransitive G *p-š-ʿ* "offend." Delitzsch's literal translation, "against whom it has been acted perfidiously," shows the problem rather than solving it.

The LXX reads: "A brother helped [*boēthoumenos*] by a brother is like a fortified and lofty city, and is as strong as a well-founded palace." "Helped" reflects Hebrew *nwšʿ*, which would actually mean "saved." This is still obscure, and the second line is garbled. However, the comparative *kqryt* "like a city" fits the comparison and is supported by the parallelism. See the Textual Note.

On the frequent ketiv-qeré variant *mdwnym-midyānîm*, see the Textual Note.

**18:20 A man's belly will be sated by the fruits of his mouth;
he will be sated by the produce of his lips.**

When one speaks wise, honest, and friendly things he is rewarded in unspecified ways. Alternatively, one who speaks well will enjoy the satisfaction inherent in eloquent and wise speech; see Prov 15:23. Conversely, one who speaks folly and evil will drink the poison he himself spews forth. The imagery is something of a surprise. Not only do *others* enjoy the nourishment of a wise man's words (10:11, 21), but he himself does as well (13:2a; see next verse). Prov 18:20a ≈ 12:14a.

**18:21 Life and death are held by the tongue,
and those who love it will eat its fruit.**

Speech has the power to give and preserve life and well-being and to bring death and destruction, both to the speaker (12:6b, 13a; 13:2a, 3; 18:7) and to others (10:11a; 11:9a; 12:6a, 13a, 18). Radaq says that slander kills three people: its speaker, its listener, and its victim. Paired with 18:20, however, v 21 concerns particularly its impact on the speaker.

are held by the tongue: Lit., "are in the hand of the tongue." J. G. Williams (1980: 47) sees this as an allusion to Lady Wisdom: "The tongue is like a woman who offers fruit to her friends." See the image in 8:19.

those who love it [fem.]: Namely, the tongue. Those who cherish fine speech and hold it in respect will (as the preceding verse says) enjoy its fruit.

Delitzsch wonders if the (fem.) antecedent of "it" refers to wisdom, which is the usual object of love in Proverbs, but that word is not available in the context. Since one does not actually love the tongue, Clifford identifies the antecedent of "it" (fem. sg.) as "life" (masc. pl.) *or* "death" (masc. sg.) and translates "those who choose one shall eat its fruit." But though it is true that a fem. sg. pronoun can have a vague plurality as its antecedent, it cannot have a disjunctive antecedent (either-or), especially when neither of the antecedents agrees grammatically with the pronoun.

**18:22 He who has found a wife has found something good
and received favor from the Lord.**

The best things come not from an inheritance (Prov 19:14) but from God (2:6; 8:35), among them a wife. Finding a wife is evidence of divine favor. But human deserts are necessary before God will activate the blessing. As Clifford observes, the human and divine work together in achieving a blessing.

Prov 18:22a reads, lit., "He found a woman, he found good," a capsule anecdote (see the Comment on 11:2). Aware that not *every* wife is a blessing (consider 7:1–27; 21:9, 19; 30:20; etc.), some versions and rabbinic quotations supply the modifier "good" in v 22a (LXX, Syr, Vul, Tg, *b. Ber.* 8a, *b. Yeb.* 63b, *Mid. Shoḥer Tov* 151ab). In a similar vein, Prov 19:14 speaks of the special blessing of an *intelligent* wife. The present proverb, however, celebrates the value of a wife as such, without excluding the possibility of exceptions. Prov 18:22b = 8:35b ≈ 12:2a.

The LXX adds: "He who expels a good wife expels happiness, but he who retains an adulteress is foolish and wicked." See the Textual Note.

**18:23 The poor man speaks entreaties,
and the rich one answers with harsh words.**

This is "a description of a reality that [Solomon] found in the world" (Saʿadia). By itself, the proverb is a sad or sour remark on the way the rich treat the poor, similar to Sir 13:1–13. Read in the context of the book of Proverbs, it implies criticism of rich men who act thus, for they are abusing God's own handiwork; see 14:31; 17:5; 22:2; and 10:15 (and the Comment there). Even read thus, the verse is not a social critique; the social structure as such is not being condemned. It is an ethical critique, with an implied admonition to avoid such contemptible behavior.

Whybray (1990: 22) observes that the rich are not portrayed sympathetically in Prov 10:1–22:16 and 25:1–29:27. They may have many "friends" (14:20), but they act harshly (18:23), lord it over the poor (22:7a), and are convinced of their own cleverness (28:11).

harsh words [*ʿazzot*]: Lit., "strong (things)," connoting obstinacy or insolence. In construction and probably sense as well, "answer *ʿazzot*" resembles the phrase "speak *qašot* ["hard things"]," which describes the way Joseph at first treats his brothers (Gen 42:30) (Ramaq).

**18:24 There are companions for socializing with,
and (then) there is a friend who cleaves closer than a brother.**

A true friend is contrasted with a less constant companion, the sort one spends time with socially but cannot expect more of. Though the latter is not necessarily "superficial" or "untrustworthy" (Toy), he is not as close and reliable as the true friend, here designated *ʾoheb*, lit. "one who loves." The words *ʾoheb* "friend" and *reaʿ* "companion" or "friend" do not in themselves distinguish the degree of fidelity. An *ʾoheb* may be opportunistic (Prov 14:20), and a *reaʿ* may "love at all times"

(17:17).The implication of higher fidelity comes from the distinction between "socializing" and "cleaving closer than a brother."

Other proverbs have different things to say about friendship. Prov 17:17 apparently equates the constancy of a friend (*rea*ʿ) and that of a brother, but see the Comment. Prov 27:10 recognizes that a neighbor (*šaken*) may prove more loyal, or at least more useful, than a brother, though the latter is still the standard of steadfastness. Prov 19:4, 6, and 7 express a more jaundiced view of friendship; see the Comment on 19:7. Influenced by the present verse, Ben Sira offers a disquisition on different kinds of friends, faithful and faithless (Sir 6:7–17), which includes the observation: "There is a friend [*'whb*] who is a table companion, but he won't be found in time of trouble" (v 9).

socializing with [*l*ᵉ*hitro*ʿ*ea*ʿ]: There is strong paronomasia between *re*ʿ*im* "companions" and *l*ᵉ*hitro*ʿ*ea*ʿ "to socialize with."

cleaves [*dabeq*]: This connotes committing oneself unreservedly to another person (e.g., Gen 2:24; Deut 10:20; Ruth 1:14).

There are: MT has *'yš* (*'îš*), which usually means "man." But a Masoretic note (*sebir*) indicates that this word is to be understood as *yēš* "there are." The same *sebir* occurs with *'š* (*'iš*) in 2 Sam 14:19 and Mic 6:10, and *'yš* = "there is" in Mur 24 C:7. The word in this verse should probably be written *'š*, as in the other two places. This is a lexical variant of *yēš*, corresponding more closely to Ugaritic *i*ṯ and Aramaic *'yt*. In rephrasing this verse, Sir 6:9 uses *yš*.

There are several ways to parse the verb *l*ᵉ*hitrō*ʿ*ēa*ʿ. It can be derived from *r*-ʿ-ʿ "be bad," or the homonymic *r*-ʿ-ʿ "be broken" (the latter an Aramaism cognate to Hebrew *r*-*ṣ*-*ṣ*). Or it can be regarded as a by-form of *r*-ʿ-*h* "be a friend," "socialize with." There are other possibilities as well. This ambiguity, as well as the misunderstanding of *'yš* as "man," has produced quite a variety of translations of v 24a, such as "A man of many companions may come to ruin" (NIV); "A man of many friends cometh off a loser" (Delitzsch); and "There are companions who are likely to break each other in pieces" (McKane, alternative). Tur-Sinai derives the verb from *r*-*w*-ʿ "to shout" and explains it as "to sing," "to shout," hence (and this is a jump) "to party with." None of these translations accords well with the Hebrew or forms a good parallel to the B-line. The verb is best understood as a *hitpōlēl* from *r*-ʿ-ʿ (or *r*-*w*-ʿ), a by-form of *r*-ʿ-*h* "be a friend," whose Dt is used in this way in Prov 22:24. Given the intermingling (and interplay) of the roots *r*-ʿ-*h*, *r*-ʿ-ʿ, and *r*-*w*-ʿ, there is no need to emend to *l*ᵉ*hitrā*ʿ*ōt* (Toy) to produce this meaning. In the present verse, the inf. is a gerundive, lit., "socializing," though an inf. of purpose also captures the idea: "(a friend) to socialize with," the notion of "with" being implied by the reciprocal Dt. Explaining this verb as "to socialize with" provides the best sense, for it is parallel to (and distinct from) *dābēq* "cleave to." Jenni (1999: 113) considers the construction to indicate epistemic modality, but see the Comment on 19:8.

19:1 Better a poor man who walks in his innocence
than a man of crooked lips who is rich[a].

---

[a] ʿ*āšîr* (MT *k*ᵉ*sîl*).

As emended (following the doublet in 28:6), this proverb says that although wealth is good, its value is canceled if its owner is dishonest. On the "better than" formula, see the excursus after the Comment on 15:17.

This verse is one of many that recognize that wealth and poverty do not always go to those who most deserve them. This is not a "paradox," as Murphy (at 28:6) calls it, but rather what he calls a "faith statement," for it asserts that justice is at work even when invisible. The reasons why an innocent poor man is better than a dishonest rich one are not stated here, but other proverbs give them: The innocent man lives in confidence, the wicked one in anxiety (28:1). The innocent man is delivered from disaster, and the wicked one takes his place (11:8). The innocent man is remembered after death, while the wicked one sinks into oblivion (10:7). The list goes on and on. All the benefits ascribed to righteousness easily outweigh the benefits of wealth.

The MT has "Better a poor man who walks in his innocence than a man of crooked lips who is a dolt." This is overkill, for an innocent poor man is better than either a mendacious man *or* a fool, and combining the two only weakens the force of the contrast. In a "better than" proverb like this, the second line should mention a quality that, other things being equal, is more desirable than indigence; see the excursus after the Comment on 15:17. Riyqam and Radaq gloss over the problem by explaining that the fool in question is a rich one, probably deducing this from the antithesis. But this is no more justified than Riyqam's supposition that the poor man in 19:4 and 7 is a fool, which he deduces from the way he is treated. Though it is possible that the present proverb is simply vapid, there is evidence that some manuscripts read *ʿašir* "rich" in place of *k^e^sil* "dolt" (see the Textual Note). A scribe accustomed to the frequent condemnations of fools might have accidentally replaced *ʿašir* with *k^e^sil*.

a man of crooked lips: Lit., "one who makes his lips crooked," the active verb suggesting a willful perversion. This verse is a variant of 10:9 and 28:6, both of which use the more expected *mʿqš drkyw/drkym*, "one who makes (his) ways crooked."

19:2 Without knowledge, desire is not good,
and he who hurries with his feet sins.

Desires ungoverned by good sense propel one to rush in pursuit of their fulfillment. The point of the second line is not so much to condemn haste as to describe a danger: The frenetic pursuit of wealth is likely to lead to sin. The purpose of the hurrying is not stated, but the A-line indicates that it is to fulfill a desire. Although hurrying is not in itself wrong, it is indicative of straining too hard to get what one wants, and this in turn is symptomatic of overconfidence in one's own powers. Compare 10:22; 21:5; 28:20, and 22; and see the Comment on 10:22. The problem of control over one's destiny is discussed in the introduction to 16:1–9.

Saʿadia connects the two lines by observing that one who is always scurrying about in mundane pursuits is diverted from the pursuit of knowledge (and thus, it is implied, comes to sin). The juxtaposition does indeed associate hurrying about and lacking knowledge; that is, running about mindlessly.

desire: The *nepeš* (translated "soul" among other ways) is the seat or organ of desire and thus represents desire. This "soul" is neither good nor bad in itself. When it is uncontrolled by *daʿat* "knowledge" (a synonym of *ḥokmah*), it is "not good"—a litotes meaning *bad*; see the Comment on 16:29.

hurries with his feet: Or "scurries about." This phrase (like "everyone who hastens" in 21:5) means much the same as *ʾaṣ lᵉhaʿăšir* "hastens to get rich" in 28:20.

lōʾ ṭôb: The lack of agreement between the masc. *lōʾ ṭôb* "not good" and the consistently fem. *nepeš* is surprising, especially since the words are conjoined. Possibly *ṭôb* is a noun, hence *lōʾ ṭôb* = "a not-good thing."

19:3 A man's folly corrupts his way,
but his heart rages against the Lord.

Folly corrupts a man's behavior and he suffers the consequences; then he blames God. Just what does he blame God for? Undoubtedly for the unhappy results of his own failings. But also, more subtly, for his corruption itself. The latter is closer to the proverb's wording, which suggests an immediate connection between the man's corruption and his raging. Ben Sira expounds on the idea of this verse in Sir 15:11–20 and says, "Do not say 'My offense is from God,' for what he hates he did not make. Do not say, 'He made me stumble,' for he has no need for lawless men. Evil and abomination the Lord hates, and he does not let it befall those who fear him" (vv 11–13). "I couldn't help it" and "That's just the way I am" and "Society made me what I am" are common ways of evading responsibility for one's failings, and blaming God is another excuse of this sort.

The man in question is the *ʾĕwil*, the perverse, deliberately wicked fool, and the "corruption" of his way is moral debasement, not mere brutishness.

19:4 Wealth adds many friends,
but the poor man is separated from his fellows.

This proverb is cynical about the quality of human friendship. It is not primarily critical of the rich. In a sense, they are the victims of their wealth, for they can never be sure of their friends' sincerity. Rather, the proverb jabs at people generally, or at least those who fit the description of fraudulent friendship. Toward the rich, they are sycophantic (see v 6), and the wealthy are deluded if they think otherwise. It is not them they like, but their wealth, for (as the wording shows) this is what has gained their friendship (Malbim). Toward the poor, people are contemptuous, and if a friend becomes poor, they turn away in scorn. Through no fault of his own, the poor man is "separated" (*niprad*), treated as an outcast. The same verb is used of the self-segregating "misfit" in 18:1.

The second line, as Naḥmias says, "describes the practice of this world, and it is an evil practice." But beyond its cynicism, the proverb implies a demand to be sensitive to the lowly and their isolation; see the Comment on 10:15. The same idea is expressed in 14:20; see the Comment there.

his fellows [*reʿehu*]: Traditionally, "his neighbor"; on *reaʿ* see the Comments on 3:28 and 6:1.

19:5 A lying witness will not go unpunished,
and he who testifies deceitfully will not escape.

This stock warning has a near-doublet in 19:9. With regard to testimony, see the Comment on 12:17.

19:6 Many make entreaties to the noble,
and everyone is a friend[a] to the gift-giver.

[a] *w^e^kullōh rēa^c^* (MT *w^e^kol hārēa^c^*).

This saying, like v 4, is sarcastic about friendship that is contaminated by money. Its didactic value lies in putting people on guard against the bogus friend.

make entreaties to [*y^e^ḥallu p^e^ney*]: Or "curry favor with" (Murphy); lit., "beseech the face of." The idiom is always used of seeking the favor of superiors, usually God, and connotes subordination or servility.

noble: Like "noble" in English, Hebrew *nadib* can mean generous as well as noble in status. Naḥmias combines the connotations: This particular *nadib* in this saying is a rich man who voluntarily gives (*hammitnaddeb latet*) to those who ask. Similarly Radaq calls him "a ruler who is generous and good." The connotation of generosity is elicited by the parallelism with *ʾiš mattan*, lit. "man of gifts."

The proverb is strangely ambiguous. The *nadib* and the gift-giver might be truly generous men. If so, the proverb promises that generosity will be rewarded with popularity (thus Radaq). But perhaps, like 17:8; 18:16; and 21:14, it alludes to and *commends* liberality of the sort that greases the axles of interpersonal relations. By itself, 19:6 could offer a hard-nosed practical tip of this sort, but in its current location it is tempered by the proximity of the jaundiced view of purchased friendship in v 4.

MT's *w^e^kol hārēa^c^* (lit., "and every friend") requires the rendering "and every friend (makes entreaties) to the gift-giver," which does not make good sense. Dividing the words differently, we should read *w^e^kullōh rēa^c^* "and everyone is a friend to the gift-giver" (Tur-Sinai p. 63). For examples of the usage and orthography, see Jer 8:10; 15:10.

19:7 All the poor man's brothers hate him.
How much the more so do his friends distance themselves from him!
* * *[a]

[a] An unintelligible fragment.

As a neutral observation, this verse would be pointless (and untrue). It is, instead, a picture of relationships gone awry. As Saʿadia says, "This too [like v 6] is what people choose to do out of stupidity, and it describes them as they are."[296]

[296] Qohelet's indignant observations about the injustices and absurdities of life thus have precedents in the Wisdom tradition and do not show him to be "radical" or even "skeptical," as he is often called. See Fox 1999: 59–63.

The saying reinforces vv 4 and 6 in exposing the fraudulent underside of human associations. It also tempers the warmth of 18:24 and esp. 17:17: "A friend loves at all times, and a brother is born for sorrow." That is the way things *should* be and sometimes are. The present proverb exposes a seamier reality, and both are valid.

The first line speaks about "all" a poor man's brothers. That this is hyperbole is shown by the way the first line is intensified *a fortiori* in the second, for, strictly speaking, there cannot really be a degree beyond "all." The saying was not meant to state a universal reality, as if true fraternity and friendship were impossible. It is, rather, a burst of indignation that should remind the reader of what true friendship is.

hate: It is unclear why Murphy thinks that "hate" here "has no emotional overtones; it simply indicates the choice that is opposed to another." "Hate" (*śnʾ*) encompasses a variety of feelings—enmity, disgust, contempt, repudiation, and more—and any or all of them can factor into the feelings people have toward the poor. The proverb is speaking about real hatred, which makes prejudice against the poor all the more foul.

Following the couplet is a meaningless group of four words, *mrdp ʾmrym lʾ* [qeré *lô*] *hmh*, which might be translated mechanically as "He who pursues words to him are they" (or "He who pursues words not they," with the ketiv). This looks like the mangled fragment of a lost couplet.

The LXX has two additional couplets after 19:7: "Good understanding will come near those who know it, and a sensible man will find it. He who does much evil fully accomplishes evil, and he who gives provocation by words will not be saved." See the Textual Note.

19:8 He who acquires a mind loves himself,
and he who keeps good sense will surely find good fortune.

acquires a mind [*leb*]: Lit., "gets a heart," as in 15:32. The "heart" is the mind, the faculty of intellect. Still, a "heart" is not inborn but attained (8:5; 15:32). See the Comment on 2:2.

loves himself [*napšo*]: This is meant positively: He cares about his well-being. The line can also be translated "loves his life."

keeps good sense: That is, holds it in himself, preserves it.

find good fortune [*limṣoʾ ṭob*]: Lit., "find good," as in 16:20, etc.

limṣōʾ ṭôb. According to G. R. Driver (1951: 196), *l* + infinitive, when predicated of a noun, means "is likely to." He compares 16:30; 18:24; 19:27; and 30:14, not all of which are germane. This sense does not fit the present verse, because the sages would not promise mere likelihood of reward. Jenni (1999: 113) identifies the nuance here as necessary inference, calling it "epistemic modality" and translating: "Wer Einsicht bewahrt, muss Gutes finden" (He who guards insight, must find good) (1999: 114). It is better to describe this construction as implying certitude. Syntactically it resembles the construction substantive + *l* + noun in Jer 43:11, *ʾăšer lammāwet lammāwet* "Whoever is to death will (go) to death" (plus two similar phrases). In other words, whoever is headed to death, or is destined for death, will go there. The notion of fate or certain result is conveyed by the *lamed* of directionality; cf. Jer 15:2, where the phrase is preceded by the verb *yṣʾ* "go forth."

19:9 A lying witness will not go unpunished,
and he who testifies deceitfully will perish.

Prov 19:9 ≈ 19:5; 19:9b ≈ 21:28a. See the Comment on 12:17.

19:10 Luxury is unsuitable for a dolt.
How much the more so for a slave to rule over princes!

Luxury or pleasure (*taʿănug*), like all good things, should be earned and deserved. When a fool comes into wealth and can indulge himself, it is an affront to those who achieve such things through the application of intelligence and effort—or who never do acquire them. How much the worse when a slave receives powers that properly belong to the free and well-born.

The sages had a conservative view of society. While demanding fair and compassionate treatment of the lower classes, they assumed that the structure of society as they knew it was fundamentally the right one. Hence they were shocked by the notion of a slave becoming king (or playing the king; see Prov 30:21–22). They viewed such anomalies as comparable to—and worse than—cases of *unmerited* rewards, because slaves *by nature* do not merit power. To be sure, an intelligent slave can profit from his acumen and industry, and to the author of 17:2, at least, this seemed right. But even he did not consider it natural for a slave to hold power, and that verse is really a warning to sons; see the Comment there.

The authors of 19:10 and 30:21–22 probably had prejudices similar to those held by Radaq, who likewise lived in a slave-owning society. He explains that the fool does not know how to behave when he has luxuries—he gets arrogant and insults others and so on. Likewise a slave who comes to power is ignorant of how to behave among princes—he honors other slaves rather than the nobility while humbling good people. Hame'iri too believes that a slave in power will "bring low the great and raise up the lowly," and (unlike the author of 1 Sam 2:7) he finds this intolerable.

Various ancient authors felt the same. Qohelet says, "There is an evil I have seen under the sun, an error that proceeds from a magnate: a fool is appointed to great heights while rich men sit in lowly places. I saw slaves (riding) on horses and princes walking on the ground like slaves" (Qoh 10:5–7). Like Prov 19:10, Qohelet lumps slaves and fools in the category of the unworthy, at least when it comes to wielding power. Dislocations of the social order seemed somehow ridiculous and distasteful. This is also the attitude of the Egyptian "prophetic laments" of Neferti (AEL 1.139–45), Khakheppere-sonb (AEL 1.145–49), and Ipuwer (AEL 1.149–63). Ipuwer, for example, bemoans the fact that "Poor men have become men of wealth. He who could not afford sandals owns riches" (AEL 1.151).

These complaints belong to a widely used "world-turned-upside-down" theme, in which the social order is violated, with the high brought low and the low raised to wealth and power; see Van Leeuwen 1986b. It is not, however, accurate to say that 19:10 has an "anti-revolutionary thrust" (Van Leeuwen 1997: 179). The notion of social revolution was foreign to the ancient Near East, and when there were armed bands of disaffected and marginalized men, they were just out for loot and, occasionally, power. What this proverb envisions is the case of a slave gaining power for himself, rather than a shift in class structure.

It is interesting that a slave attaining power over princes was enough of a possibility to warrant comment. Most likely, the proverb pictures a situation in which a king appointed his slaves to oversee some of his affairs. (This would be a way for a king to keep tighter control of sensitive matters.) Such an appointment would give the slave authority over high officials and nobles, who would feel it as an insult. (A situation of this sort is what Qohelet has in mind in 10:5–6.)

In spite of this hostility toward allowing a slave authority, Ben Sira can say, "As for an intelligent slave—nobles shall serve him" (10:25c [MS B]).

19:11 A man's insight makes him patient,
and overlooking an offense is his splendor.

Hame'iri makes an important distinction between the two lines (sim. Malbim). "Being patient" (*he'ĕrîk 'ap*) means to restrain one's anger until the outcome of a matter is known, at which time retribution may be appropriate. This virtue is called *śekel* ("discretion," "perceptiveness," or the like), which is an instrumental faculty (see Vol. I, 36). The greater virtue, praised in the B-line, is "overlooking" or (lit.) "passing by" an offense (*'ăbor 'al peša'*), which means granting complete forgiveness. The proverb calls such behavior "splendor" (*tip'eret*) because it is "a very lofty virtue" (Hame'iri). The second line thus raises the level of virtue.

makes him patient: Lit., "is his patience." The subject is the cause of the predicate. On blunt juxtapositions, see the Comment on 13:1.

overlooking an offense: That is, an offense against himself (Radaq). See the Comments on 10:12 and 17:9. On *peša'* "offense" see the Comment on 10:19.

makes him patient [*he'ĕrîk 'appô*] and *overlooking an offense* [*'ăbōr 'al*]: Two verses establish the distinction Hame'iri draws. Exod 34:6–7 says that Yahweh is *'erek 'appayim*—he holds off the punishment while waiting for repentance. Nevertheless, the passage goes on to say, *naqqēh lō' yᵉnaqqēh* "he will not hold one guiltless," that is, he will not ultimately overlook sin and let it go without retribution. Micah says, "Who is a God like you, forgiving sin and overlooking [*'ōbēr 'al*] offenses for the remnant of his inheritance? He does not hold on to his anger forever, because he takes pleasure in kindness" (7:18). In other words, God *is* angry but he will, in his kindness, "pass over" the nation's sins and let go of his anger. But this does not cancel all retribution; punishment has already occurred.

he'ĕrîk: Though often emended to the usual inf. form, *ha'ărîk* (Toy, BHS, etc.), it is likely, as Riyqam and other medievals recognized, that the Masoretes intended *he'ĕrîk* as an inf. cst., a rare form like the *hiqtîl infinitives* in Num 21:35; Deut 7:24, etc. (GBH §54*c* cites examples but not the present one. The frequency of this form makes GBH's skepticism about the phenomenon unwarranted.)

19:12 Like a lion's growl is the king's wrath,
while his favor is like dew on the grass.

Hame'iri tightens the connection between the lines of this saying: In this context, the king's "favor" (*raṣon*) refers to the good that will result from propitiating him and not to his approval in general. (Qohelet too speaks about propitiating an angry ruler; 10:4.) Prov 16:14; 20:2; and 24:21–22 also warn of the king's wrath (sim. Qoh 8:2–4), and 16:15 speaks of the pleasure of receiving his favor. (Prov 28:15 concerns the dangers of a *wicked* ruler.)

A lion's growl portends disaster. The verb *naham* means "growl" rather than "roar" (which would be *ša'ag*) and is used of quieter sounds like groaning (Prov 5:11; Ezek 24:23; Isa 5:30 [first occurrence; the second refers to the ordinary murmur of the sea, not a storm]). Thus the king need merely "growl" to be menacing; he need not "roar" in fury. The dew is refreshing and a source of blessing. Moreover (as Hame'iri observes), it is dependable and constant, for it collects even when the rains end.

When read after v 11, v 12 not only puts courtiers on guard but also encourages a king to be patient and forgiving, however righteous and leonine he may feel his wrath to be. Prov 19:12a ≈ 20:2a; v 12b ≈ 16:15b.

19:13 A stupid son is his father's ruin,
and a woman's bickering is an irksome dripping.

Two things that can cause a man misery are a foolish son and a cantankerous wife. We would expect to see the first observation paired by a description of the effect on the mother. By complementing it instead with a complaint about the irritating wife, the theme becomes the dysfunctional home, described in terms of things that may afflict a man as father and husband. On ruinous sons see also Prov 10:1; 17:21, 25; 26. On quarrelsome wives see also 21:9, 19; 25:24; and 27:15.

The proverb evaluates relationships from the perspective of a husband and father, which is basically the perspective of the entire book. It does not disparage all women any more than it condemns all sons. It should be noted that *hawwot* "ruin" (an abstract pl.) is even worse than being annoyed or driven out of the house

bickering [*midyan(im)*]: Usually translated "contentions."

an irksome dripping [*delep ṭored*]: Or, "a dripping that drives one out." "Dripping" (*delep*) is not just a dreary drizzle but a leak that seeps through the roof (Riyqam, Ehrlich). It is extremely annoying and even drives her husband out of his house (Ramaq, Ehrlich).

ṭōrēd: Hebrew *ṭrd* (only here and 27:15 in BH), like its Aramaic cognate (Dan 4:22, 29, 30; 5:21) and its RH sense, means "banish," "drive away." In Sir 51:19 (11QPs[a] 21.16), *ṭrdty npšy* (for *ṭrty npšy*; see J. A. Sanders 1967: 75) can mean "I bothered myself," in other words, drove myself to work zealously for wisdom. In Sir 32[35]:9, *lṭrd* seems to mean "to annoy" (Segal), a sense it also has in RH and which would fit the present verse as well. This sense too is connected to the notion of driving away.

19:14 A house and wealth are an inheritance from fathers,
but an astute wife comes from the Lord.

This proverb counterbalances the comment on the querulous wife. Like Prov 18:22, it treasures marriage. An intelligent wife is more precious than material wealth. And since it is assumed that God would not bestow such a gift at random, she is presumably a reward for a man's merits and is therefore a source of pride, as in 12:4. The verse thus encourages a young man to be virtuous, so as to gain such a precious reward.

Malbim sees a causal connection between the two lines: A man may transmit his wealth to future generations *if* God gives him an intelligent wife. Such a wife will manage his property well, for a wise woman "builds her house, while folly tears hers down with her own hands" (Prov 14:1).

Verses 11–14 proceed in associative sequence: The importance of patience (v 11) calls to mind the royal wrath, which is a dangerous form of *impatience* (v 12), and this makes one think of an irritable (and impatient) wife (v 13), and this evokes a proverb on a virtuous one (v 14).

19:15 Sloth brings on a stupor,
and the deceitful man will starve.

brings on a stupor [*tappil tardemah*]: Lit., "makes a stupor fall." A stupor or deep sleep (*tardemah*) is usually said to "fall" on someone (e. g., Gen 2:21; 15:12), as if it descends with overwhelming force. This phrase suggests that not only does sloth make a man drowsy, it even knocks him out, as it were, and renders him useless.

deceitful man [*nepeš r^e^miyyah*]: The secondary meaning of *r^e^miyyah*, namely, "slacker," is elicited here by the parallelism. Deceit and laziness are mutually implicated; see the Comment on 10:4 and the references there. While it is natural to say that sleepiness causes indolence, the causality here is reversed. Once one chooses to be lazy, his lethargy is like a physical ailment that dulls him and throws him into a stupor.

19:16 He who guards a precept guards his life,
while he who despises[a] a word[b] will die.

---

[a] *ûbôzēh* (MT *bôzēh*). [b] *dābār* (MT *d^e^rākayw*).

Obedience to the teachings of wisdom secures life. Prov 19:16a ≈ 16:17b.

guards [*šomer*]: The verb *šmr* is usually translated "keeps."

a precept [*miṣwah*]: Or "command." As elsewhere in Proverbs, the precept is the sage's instruction not God's; see the Comment on 1:8.

despises a word: The MT has "despises his ways [*drkyw*]," which is obscure. A man would not die because he had contempt for his own ways (a feeling that might be well-deserved!). A reference to God's ways would be apropos, but God is not mentioned in context, and "ways" is not specific enough to allude to him without further clues.

We should read *dbr* for MT's *drkyw* "his ways" (Toy, Ehrlich, BHS). Thus emended, this proverb is the equivalent of 13:13 and uses similar wording: "He who despises a word will be harmed, while he who fears a precept will be well." The "word" here, parallel to "precept" (*miṣwah*), refers to counsel; see the Comment on 18:4.

ûbôzēh: The conjunction, witnessed by the versions, was lost by haplog. The antithesis is awkward without it.

dābār: The first three letters of MT's *drkw* are an easy graphic distortion of *dbr*, while the *waw* arose by dittog., and the *yod* was later added as an m.l. (Ramaq's text had *drkw*.) This emendation is simpler than Emerton's proposal that the original was *drk yhwh* "the way of Yahweh," which was abbreviated to *drk yw*, then joined to the preceding word (1969: 206–209). It is in any case very uncertain that abbreviation took place within the Masoretic tradition. However, it is possible that the MT intends God as the unstated antecedent of "his ways."

will die [*yāmût*, qeré]: The ketiv is *ywmt* (*yûmat*), "be killed," "be put to death." Since Proverbs does not speak about judicial execution, this would mean being put to death (prematurely) by God. The qeré *yāmût* "will die," read by LXX and Syr, is the expected form (5:23; 10:21; 15:10; 23:13) and implies a premature demise, without pointing directly to an agent.

19:17 He who is kind to the lowly lends to the Lord,
and he will pay him the recompense of his hands.

The poor are under God's special protection. They are his wards, like the widow and orphan who have no human protector (Ps 68:6). One who helps the poor is helping God, and gifts to them are loans to God.

he will pay him: Recompense is certain, because God himself will repay the "debt." The repayment may be in the form of material benefits, but it may also consist of God's love, to match the charity the lender has shown (cf. Malbim). On the duty of charitable giving and lending, see Prov 14:21, 31; 21:13, 26b; 22:9, and on God's care for the lowly see the Comments on 14:31 and 17:5a. Deut 15:7–11 prescribes charitable loans as a moral obligation. Sir 29:8–13 develops the idea of lending to the poor as both an obligation of charity and a good investment.

the recompense of his hands: That is, what he deserves. This principle appears in Prov 12:14b; 24:12b.

19:18 Discipline your son, for there is hope,
and do not desire to kill him.

Be diligent in punishing your son for his faults, even if he is recalcitrant, because there is always hope he will improve. (Translating "while there is hope" [Toy, NRSV, and many others] is contrary to the syntax.) If you neglect his discipline, it is as if you are killing him, for he will fall into bad ways and the results of your neglect will be deadly (Saʿadia). Parental responsibility is put in starkest terms. Failure as a moral teacher is tantamount to negligent homicide and incurs mortal guilt.

and do not desire [*'al tiśśa' napšeka*]: Lit., "and do not lift up your soul" (to his killing). The phrase connotes yearning and expectation; see, for example, Deut 24:15; Pss 25:1 (// *bṭḥ* "trust"); 143:8. If you fail to discipline your son, it is as if you actively *desired* to kill him.

to kill him [*wᵉ'el hămito*]: Lit., "and to his killing." Some understand this as a warning not to beat one's son to death (Murphy, Plöger) or to get so enraged that you *want* to kill him. But to express that notion, the B-line should warn about the intensity of the beating, not the father's emotions.

Ahiqar says, "If I beat you, my son, you will not die. But if I leave you to your heart [you will not live]" (82 [1.1.177]). This is the point of Prov 13:24 and, more clearly, 23:14, "If you smite him with a rod, you will save his life from Sheol." If you do not desire your son's death, you will punish his wrongdoings, so that he not continue on the deadly path of folly.

hămîtô: Baumgartner (following Jäger) would vocalize *hemyātô* "his moaning" (see Isa 14:11): "and do not pay attention to his moaning" (when he is being beaten). Ralbag and Naḥmias [in the first of two alternatives he offers] explain the MT thus without revocalizing. However, "lift up your soul" does not mean to pay attention. Gemser emends to *ḥēmōt* "wrath"; hence: "do not get carried away to wrath." But the parallel in Ahiqar supports the MT.

19:19 The hot-tempered man bears (his) punishment,
for if you save him, you will have to do so again.

People with nasty tempers are always getting themselves into trouble and paying the price. This verse tempers the optimism of the preceding one. The second line implies the advice, "Don't waste your time on him." But the threatened consequences of "saving" or "extricating" such a one are not very severe, and it is likely that the verse has a further message: A foul temper gets a man in trouble repeatedly. We could paraphrase, "The hot-tempered man will always be getting into trouble, no matter how often someone gets him off the hook." This in turn implies a warning not to be quick to anger.

hot-tempered [*geᵉdol ḥemah*]: Lit., "great of wrath." ("Man" is not in the original.) By itself, this refers to any angry man. But placed next to v 18, which insists that a son can be disciplined into good behavior, the hot-tempered person would be a son whose angry temperament makes him uneducable and who should be abandoned to the punishments he will bring on himself (Ramaq). The age of this person is not indicated, but being "great of wrath" does not sound like one of the flaws that Proverbs typically ascribes to youngsters, who are usually thought to be naïve, gullible, inattentive, and stubborn.

Since the mention of "saving" in v 19b seems to echo "not killing" in v 18b, some scholars have tried to explain v 19 in the light of the preceding. Ehrlich says that v 19 continues the advice about child-rearing. The A-line is a parenthetical warning to the father not to punish excessively, while the B-line urges him to "save" the son (by chastising him) constantly.

19:20 Hear counsel and receive discipline,
that you may become wise in the future.

This abrupt second-person exhortation (which resembles the exordia of Prov 1–9) suggests that the editor conceives of this collection as an instruction aimed at a boy or young man. There is no indication, however, that this begins a new collection or major unit. The presence of the characteristic components of the instruction form outside of Part I is discussed in Vol. I, 46.

in the future [*bᵉʾaḥăriteka*]: Lit., "in your end" or "later time." This does not mean at the end of life or even the latter part of one's life, as in Job 8:7 (*pace* Delitzsch), because one needs wisdom long before that, and those who "hear counsel and receive discipline" will gain wisdom much sooner. Murphy says it refers to the end of the training. But, so far as we know, there was no formal period of "training," and if there were, its conclusion would not be called "your end." Rather, *ʾaḥărit* means a later time, the future. In Prov 29:21, it means the future after childhood. Some other verses where *ʾaḥărit* means "future" are 5:4; 23:18; 24:14, 20; 25:8; Gen 49:1; Num 23:10; and Isa 46:10. (HALOT assigns this meaning to a number of verses, but not all are pertinent.) It probably means "posterity" in Prov 23:18 and 24:20, where the LXX translates it *egkona* "offspring." (See Talmon 2003: 801.) In Sir 11:28, *ʾaḥărit* is translated *teknoi* "children."

19:21 Many designs are in a man's heart,
but it is Lord's plan that comes to pass.

This counsels humility, not fatalism. Human plans *may* succeed, especially if they are formed in reliance on God (Prov 16:3), but the outcome depends on God's will. However many plans a man may devise, they may be overridden by a single decision of God. See the introduction to 16:1–9 and the Comment on 16:9. The proverb in fact assumes that human plans are generally effective, unless impeded by folly, immorality, or God's will. It also assumes that, all things being equal, more planning is better than less. See 11:14; 15:22; 24:6.

rabbôt maḥăšābôt: This is probably an Aramaism and usually, but not necessarily, LBH, as in Neh 9:28; 1 Chr 28:5; Sir 11:5 (the preceding are mid-fifth c. or later); Ps 89:51 (clearly exilic), but also Jer 16:16 (on the border of the exile). The same structure appears in Prov 7:26 and 31:29 (*rabbôt bānôt*). In the Commentary on 7:26, I treated *rabbîm ḥălālîm* as predicative (lit., "many are the victims that she has cast down"). This is certainly a possible translation, but most other examples of this construction are not amenable to that construal. Also, the expected predicative form would have a definite subject: *rabbîm haḥălālîm*.

19:22 A man's kindness is his fruit,[a]
and better a poor man than a deceitful man.

[a] *tᵉbûʾat* (MT *taʾăwat*).

Even a poor man has a "fruit," a benefit he can provide to others, namely, his kindness. This itself is a form of largesse. Because he has this benefit to offer, a poor man (if he is honest) is better off than a (rich one, if he is) deceitful. (The words in parentheses are implied by reversal.) The two lines are not well related, and the sentiment of the B-line is rather trite. Perhaps the A-line was once an independent saying.

is his fruit: Lit., "His kindness [*ḥasdo*] is the produce [*tᵉbûʾat*] of a man." When *tᵉbuʾah* has a possessive pronoun, it often signifies the benefit that the possessor provides to *others*. For example, in Prov 8:19, *tᵉbuʾati* "my fruit" means the benefits that Wisdom brings her disciples; the "produce of his lips" in 18:20b is the benefit a wise man's speech gives to others and that he then enjoys himself; the "produce of the land" (Lev 23:39, etc.) is what the land provides to its inhabitants; and so on.

The MT has *ta'ăwat* "desire." The only unforced translation of this is "A man's desire is his kindness," which does not make much sense. The above translation is based on the LXX, whose *karpos* "fruit" reflects Heb *tbw't*, lit., "produce."

MT *ta'ăwat 'ādām ḥasdô*: There are several ways of understanding the first line.

(1) "A man's desire is his kindness." This takes *ḥesed* in its usual sense, "kindness" (others translate "loyalty"; but see the Comment on 3:3a). Sa'adia says that the desire of a man is to *receive* kindness (thus too Lowe 1980, who examines this verse at length). But this sense does not fit the syntax well, and the insight the verse provides by this interpretation is trivial. *Of course* a man desires to be shown kindness.

(2) "What is desired of a person is his fidelity" (Clifford). But this violates the Hebrew. "Man" here can only be the semantic subject, the party doing the desiring, as is always the case in construct phrases with *ta'ăwat*, for example, 10:24; 11:23; 21:25. Also, *ta'ăwāh* is always a sensory or sensual hunger or an intense yearning. "Hunger" (such as for food, sex, or basic needs) is usually a good translation of *ta'ăwāh*. It is not a cooler, reflective *desideratum*.

(3) "A man's desire *should be* [to show] kindness" (Ramaq, Radaq, Hame'iri). This assigns the line a modal nuance, but modality is not implied, and may be excluded, by the nominal predication.

(4) Read *ḥesed* for *ḥasdô* (dittog.; cf. LXX), hence: "Kindness is a man's desire"; in other words, a man desires kindness toward himself. Again, *ta'ăwāh* does not seem like the right word to convey this kind of desire, and, like proposal (1), the statement is trivial.

(5) "A man's desire is his disgrace," taking *ḥesed* in its Aramaic sense, as in Prov 14:34 and Lev 20:17 (Kaspi; Murphy; JPS 1917; NEB). This presumes that *ta'ăwāh* "desire" means "greed" or "lust," but, by itself, a *ta'ăwāh* can be legitimate (e. g., Prov 10:24; 11:23; Isa 26:8; Ps 38:10; see further Lowe 1980: 26).

(6) Emending *ta'ăwat* to *tᵉbû'at-* (based on LXX *karpos* "fruit"), as advocated here. Gemser and McKane, among others, use this emendation. But McKane's "productivity" is too abstract and not in accord with the meaning of *tᵉbû'āh* elsewhere, and Gemser's "Gewinn" ("profit") assumes that the benefit in question is what the kind man *receives*, but see above.

better [*ṭob*] *a poor man*: It is better to *be* a poor man. When *ṭob* ("good," "better") is predicated of a person in the "better than" sayings, it means "better off" (for oneself) rather than "more beneficial" (to others).

19:23 The fear of the Lord (leads) to life,
and he (who fears the Lord) will dwell content, unafflicted by evil.

(leads) to life [*lᵉḥayyim*]: Lit., "is to life." For the phrasing and the idea, see 10:16. The subject of the second line is implicit in the first. Prov 19:23a ≈ 14:27a.

content [*śabea'*]: Or, "sated"; that is, he has all he desires. He will lack for nothing, in accordance with 13:25a: "The righteous man eats till his appetite is sated" (Radaq, Naḥmias). Alternatively, or additionally, he will know spiritual contentment regardless of what he owns (Riyqam).

19:24 The sluggard hides his hand in the bowl,
and he won't even bring it back to his mouth.

Lethargy is ludicrous. The sluggard is so greedy that he doesn't just take a piece of food, he buries his hand deep in the bowl. But then he is too lazy to bring his hand back to his mouth! Although a sluggard would not really hesitate to eat, the silly scenario ridicules him for his self-destructive sloth. Qohelet makes a similar jibe with a very different image: "The fool locks his hands together and eats his flesh" (4:5). Prov 19:24 ≈ 26:15. On the relation between these variants, see the Comment on the latter.

The image in the first line is easily extended to negligence in all matters. Many opportunities for profit present themselves, but the sluggard refuses to make the slightest effort to take advantage of them. Saʿadia interprets the verse this way and adds that in matters of religion the opportunities in question are prayer and study. For Riyqam, the image represents the failure to complete one task in a series of actions, such as plowing before sowing and sowing before harvesting, and so on. Then the initial investment goes to waste.

19:25 Strike a scoffer and the callow will gain shrewdness,
but rebuke an astute person and he will gain knowledge.

A simple, callow youngster (a *peti*) may take a warning from seeing the *leṣ*, the impudent scoffer, beaten. Even if he doesn't exactly become wise, he will at least gain enough cunning (*ʿormah*) to steer clear of beatings himself. (The *leṣ* himself is probably hopeless, see Prov 9:7–8; 13:1b; and 15:12.) But an intelligent, discerning person, a *nabon*, can learn from verbal chastisement, for "A rebuke comes down harder on a perceptive person than a hundred blows on a dolt" (17:10). Indeed, the sensible man can gain not only the instrumental faculty of cunning or shrewdness (*ʿormah*), but also *daʿat*, knowledge itself, which is equivalent to *ḥokmah* and includes intellectual and ethical discernment on a deeper level. This teaching is rephrased in Prov 21:11. The purpose of the proverb is not so much to recommend corporal punishment as to urge the reader to respond wisely to verbal chastisement: Be smart and learn from rebukes or you'll get thrashed like a simpleton.

scoffer, callow [sg.], *astute person*: Though the wording of the proverb does not indicate the age of the persons in question, the proverb clearly speaks about education of boys, because striking an adult scoffer could get one a bloody nose in return (Prov 30:33).

he will gain knowledge [*yabin daʿat*]: Lit., "understand knowledge." For this type of locution, see the Comment on 8:5. Some commentators (e. g., Ehrlich, Plöger) identify the subject of "gain knowledge" as the callow youth, but the scene this interpretation presupposes, in which a simpleton observes and learns from a rebuke aimed at the intelligent person, is peculiar and assumes a greater level of acumen than the simpleton could muster.

19:26 He who robs his father and drives away his mother
is a shameful and disgraceful son.

This couplet can be read two ways. If the subject of "robs" is "son" in v 26b, we would translate "A shameful and disgraceful son robs his father and drives away his mother." This means that a son who is generally disgraceful humiliates his parents so much that it is as if he robbed them and chased them away. If the subject comes in v 26a (as translated above), the verse means that a son who misappropriates the property of his elderly parents and drives them out of the ancestral home is shameful and disgraceful. The latter understanding is supported by Prov 28:24: "He who robs his father and mother and says 'No wrong was done!'—he is a companion to a vandal." See also 20:21.

his, his: Added in translation.

19:27 Cease, my son, to listen to instruction,
to stray from words of knowledge!

This translation is literal, and the Hebrew allows no real alternatives, but it makes no sense. The first line exhorts the son *not* to listen to instruction; the second, more understandably, (to cease) straying from it. Both infinitives are dependent on "cease," and there is no relevant distinction between "instruction" (*musar*) and "words of knowledge."

Almost all commentators understand the first line as ironic or a sort of rhetorical challenge, as if to say: "I *dare* you to cease to listen to my instruction!" Examples of perverse and ironic demands of this sort are found in Amos 4:4 ("Go to Beth El and sin!") and Ezek 20:39 ("Go, each one of you, and worship his idols!"); similarly Jer 44:25. In these cases, however, the context clearly shows the demands to be facetious. Seeing irony in the present proverb would be credible if a threat followed, but the B-line is not a threat or a painful consequence of the A-line; it is its exact opposite. Also problematic in this proposal is the fact that the second line tells the son to cease from *straying*. Could the irony in the first clause abruptly turn into sincerity in the second, when the second is dependent on the same verb as the first? The two commands just do not work together.

There is very likely a textual error here. Instead of *lšmʿ* "to listen," the text probably had a word implying repudiation, such as *lśnʾ* "to hate" (Toy; cf. 5:12) or *lprʿ* "to spurn," "to throw off" (compare Prov 8:33; 13:18; and 15:32). A scribe might have looked at *lprʿ mwsr* and carelessly written the familiar *lšmʿ mwsr* "to listen to instruction." But the graphic similarity in either case is slight.

Scholars have resorted to various expediencies to deal with this problem, but they all override the MT no less than a major emendation would.

(1) There are some variants indicated by the LXX (see the Textual Note), but they do not solve the problem.

(2) Rashi would have us mentally switch the infinitival clauses, and NRSV follows him, translating: "Cease straying, my child, from the words of knowledge, in order that you may hear instruction." But the syntax does not allow this switch.

(3) Saʿadia says that the *musar* in question is "*musar* in name only." It is an "instruction" (in scare quotes, as it were) whose message is to stray from words of knowledge. But *musar* is never used of

illegitimate teachings (though *leqaḥ* "teaching" is used facetiously in Prov 7:21), and it does not elsewhere have a dependent infinitive defining its content.

(4) Clifford and Murphy understand the irony not in the word *musar* but in the demand itself. They translate, "My son, stop attending to correction; start straying from wise words." But "start" is in no way implied.

(5) Plöger says that the imperative combines irony and threat. He translates, "Lass ab, mein Sohn, auf Zurechtweisung zu hören—zum Abirren von Worten der Erkenntnis (führt es)." ("Cease, my son, to hear correction—[it leads] to straying from words of knowledge.") The subject of "it leads" is supposedly the *renunciation* of hearing. But this supposition is entirely ad hoc and supplies too much.

(6) Delizsch paraphrases, "Cease from hearing instruction if you will use it only to depart from words of knowledge." This construes "to stray" as a complement of the first infinitive, "to hear" ("to hear so as to stray"). But a foolish or naïve son would refuse to listen to start with, so there would be no reason for him to listen *so as* to stray. Besides, the construction proposed is awkward and violates the parallelism.

19:28 A corrupt witness mocks justice,
and the mouth of the wicked swallows iniquity.

corrupt witness [*ʿed bᵉliyyaʿal*]: A dishonest witness not only perjures himself in a particular litigation, he also shows contempt for justice itself, the process and the principle.

swallows [*yᵉballaʿ*]: Some emend to *yabbiaʿ* "spouts" because a verb indicating the *output* of the mouth seems required as a parallel to the verb of speaking in the first line (Toy, BHS, etc.). But the second line actually explains the cause of the first malfeasance: The scoundrel "ingests" evil (Delitzsch, Clifford, etc.). The metaphor of swallowing iniquity appears in Prov 4:17; 13:2; and Job 15:16. One who would mock justice must be permeated with evil, and the metaphor of digestion conveys this. See "The Wicked Man," in Vol. I, 117–18.

The alliteration in ***bᵉliyyaʿal and yᵉballaʿ*** ("corrupt" and "swallows") is striking. The consonants /b/, /l/, /y/, and /ʿ/ are repeated, and the dominant vowel in both words is /a/. (This consideration also supports MT's *yᵉballaʿ*.) The complex interplay of sound-patterns in this verse is analyzed by McCreesh 1991: 79–81.

19:29 Rods[a] are readied for the impudent,
and blows for the back of dolts.

[a] *šᵉbāṭîm* (MT *šᵉpāṭîm*).

The impudent and stupid will be beaten—a warning popular among the sages (Prov 19:25; 22:15; 26:3; 29:15); and see the Comment on 13:24.

rods [*šᵉbaṭim*]: That is, beatings. The MT has *šᵉpaṭim* "judgments." Alter justifies this reading on poetic grounds: It is a generalization applied or concretized in the second line (1985: 173). But *šᵉpaṭim*, as Delitzsch points out, is used only of divine judgments, never of penalties inflicted by a human court of justice. Delitzsch in fact believes that divine affliction is meant. Elsewhere, however, stupid people (*kᵉsilim*) face mundane chastisements, usually beatings. God's attitudes or actions toward the stupid are never mentioned. The LXX has *mastiges* "blows," which sometimes translates *šᵉbaṭim* "rods" (see the Textual Note). The only difference between the two Hebrew words is in the letters *bet* and *peh*, which are very similar in early Jewish scripts. MT's "judgments" may have been induced by the mention of *mišpaṭ* "justice" in the preceding verse. Verse 29b has near-doublets in Prov 10:13b and 26:3b, which in turn support the appropriateness of reading *šᵉbaṭim* "rods." The parallelism of this couplet, like many others, has no intensification but rather static balance. The impudent and the stupid are treated alike.

20:1 Wine is a mocker and beer is rowdy,
and no one who goes astray in them will become wise.

Wine and beer are together personified as the kind of person they make the drinker become: impudent (*leṣ*) and rowdy (*homeh*). To the same effect, Ramaq and some other medievals explain "wine" and "beer" as equivalent to "a man of wine" and "a man of beer," that is, winebibbers and beer guzzlers.

rowdy [*homeh*]: Noisy, boisterous and unsettled. This is used of the Strange Woman in 7:11 and of Lady Folly in 9:13. It can also be translated as a noun, "rowdy man."

goes astray [*šgh*]: This verb means to err and get lost. In Isa 27:8 it describes what happens to a drunk. It is also used of becoming intoxicated by a woman's love in Prov 5:19; see the Comment. It does not usually refer to malicious sins.

in them [*bo*]: Lit., "in it." In the second line, wine and beer are treated as a single figure.

To warn someone that he will not become wise assumes that he desires wisdom. The implied listener is thus not presumed to be debauched or degenerate. Nevertheless, he too may overindulge in hard drink. Other warnings against drunkenness are Prov 21:17; 23:21; and 23:29–35, and see the Comment on the latter.

20:2 The king is as fearsome as a lion's growl;
the man who provokes his anger harms himself.

To provoke the king is self-destructive. Prov 20:2a ≈ 19:12a. Saʿadia says that this verse is more intense than 19:12. That verse pointed out the danger of the king's anger, while this one says that he is fearsome even when *not* angry. It is all the more perilous, then, to provoke him! Like a lion's growl, the king's aura of dread is not in itself harmful; it is a warning.

the king is as fearsome . . . : Lit., "A growl like a lion's is a king's fearsomeness."

harms himself [*ḥoṭeʾ napšo*]: Lit., "offends against himself"; cf. Hab 2:10, and see the Comment on 8:36.

the king's fearsomeness [*ʾêmat melek*]: *ʾêmāh* usually means the emotion of being afraid or in awe, but sometimes it refers to things that *cause* terror (Jer 50:38; Pss 55:5; 88:16). It is unnecessary to emend to *ḥămat* "wrath" (Ehrlich, BHS, Clifford).

the man who provokes his anger [*mitʿabbᵉrô*]: The verb *hitʿabbēr* usually means to *become* angry

(Deut 3:26; etc.). In Prov 14:16 and 26:17, it seems to be conflated with *hitʿārēb* "butt in." The Dt-stem has a reflexive sense here, more precisely, "one who brings anger upon himself" (HALOT 781a) or "makes himself an object of anger." Thus too in Sir 16:8 (*hmtʿbrym*; Gk *ebdeluxato*); also Prov 24:21, as emended.

20:3 It is to a man's honor to avoid conflict,
while every fool has tantrums.

Conflicts often revolve on questions of "honor," which is to say, pride, but the true honor belongs to him who steps away from disputes.

avoid [*šebet*]: This does not mean "cease" or "desist" (JPSV), which would have the unlikely implication that the wise man is already in the conflict. That sense would require the verb to be vocalized as an infinitive, *šābōt*, from *š-b-t* "cease." MT's *šebet* derives from *y-š-b* "sit," hence "sit away from," "have nothing to do with" (Ehrlich).

while every fool has tantrums [*yitgallaʿ*]: In other words, whoever has tantrums is a fool (*ʾěwil*). The precise meaning of *hitgallaʿ* is uncertain. It is used elsewhere of outbreaks of anger; see the Comment on 17:14.

20:4 After the rainy season the sluggard does not plow.
Then in the harvest he inquires and there is nothing.

At the end of the *ḥorep*, the cold and wet season (October through March), the ground is soft and ready for plowing and planting cereal crops. If a man is slack in plowing then, he will have nothing at harvest time. More generally, one must act at the right time in all matters to prepare for the future (thus Saʿadia, who includes preparations for the next life).

Like Prov 19:24, this proverb ridicules the sluggard. He is stupid enough to come around asking where the crops were, as if they could grow without the ground being prepared.

20:5 The counsel in a man's heart is deep waters,
and a sensible man will draw it up.

Counsel (*ʿeṣah*), that is, any careful, deliberate thinking (see Vol. I, 32), is a deep well full of refreshing, life-giving water. A discerning, competent man will draw on others' counsel and enjoy their wisdom.

The metaphor does not illustrate *difficulty*, because it is no more difficult to draw up water from a deep well than from a shallow one. (On the contrary, the shallower the waters the farther the bucket must be pulled up. The bucket in any case goes just beneath the surface.) Counsel is called "deep" not because it is secret or necessarily profound, but because, like water in a deep well, it is fresh and abundant; see the Comment on 18:4. Isa 29:15, which does refer to secrecy, is not comparable, because "Those who go deep [*hammaʿămiqim*] from the Lord to conceal a plan" are metaphorically *putting* the plan deep, whereas here the counsel is compared to waters which *are* deep. Prov 20:5a ≈ 18:4a.

No special skill or erudition is needed to avail oneself of others' wisdom, but only the *tᵉbunah*—"good sense" or "competency"—to pay attention to another's advice, whether it concerns wise behavior generally or the execution of a specific project, as in Prov 20:18.

This proverb is usually thought to say that "[a] man's real thought . . . is hard to fathom, but may be discovered by one who knows how to sound the mind" (Toy). In fact, no secrecy is suggested or difficulty implied. The proverb just praises the value of listening to counsel, much like Prov 12:15b, "the wise man listens to counsel."

Prov 20:5a has the same image as the proverb in Amenemope 23.19–20: "A great man in his office is like a well full of water" (from §23 [cf. AEL 2.160]). This means that a high official has his deep plans about whom to favor, and one must accept them without trying to fathom them. The full passage is discussed in the Comment on 23:3.

20:6 Many a one is called[a] a kind[b] man,
but a trustworthy man, who can find?

---

[a] *yiqqārēʾ* (MT *yiqrāʾ*). [b] *ḥesed* (MT *ḥasdô*).

True fidelity is all the more precious for being so rare. Prov 18:24 similarly contrasts different kinds of friendship.

a kind man [*ʾiš ḥesed*]: Though "loyal man" fits the parallelism (Clifford: "Many are called loyal"), *ḥesed* means "kindness" (see the Comment on 3:3a) and *ʾiš ḥesed* is the opposite of a cruel man in Prov 11:17. Malbim's distinction between *ḥesed* and *ʾĕmunim* "trustworthy" is on the mark: "*Ḥesed* is what is done not because of obligation or promise but only voluntarily, whereas *ʾĕmunah* is what is done out of obligation or promise." It would be logical, he observes, for one who does *ḥesed* also to do *ʾĕmunim*, but in reality people are more inclined to do the former because that is what brings praise and admiration.

The MT of v 6a reads, lit., "Many men call a man his kindness," which is obscure. Riyqam understands it to mean: "Most people proclaim each one [*ʾiš*] the kindness he has done" (sim. Naḥmias, Murphy), but the sense this attributes to the phrase *yiqraʾ ḥasdo* is doubtful. These emendations, which are very minor (revocalization and omitting a *waw* as a dittography), produce a meaningful text and better parallelism; see the Textual Note. The resulting phrase, *ʾiš ḥesed*, lit., "the man of kindness," appears elsewhere (Prov 11:17; Isa 57:1).

20:7 The righteous man goes about in his innocence.
Happy are his children after him!

A man's children reap the rewards of his righteousness; sim. Prov 13:22. The mechanism of blessing is left vague. Radaq says that the father's wealth will endure and his sons will share in the honor his honesty earned him. Or they will learn his virtues and enjoy their reward (Hameʾiri). Direct divine blessing, such as is promised in Exod 34:7, is another source of reward. The medievals emphasize that the reward is passed on only if the children are themselves righteous.

goes about [*mithallek*]: The Dt-stem indicates that this is his regular and constant course of life.

20:8 A king sits on the throne of judgment
and scatters all evil with his eyes.

The king sitting in judgment is so powerful that he can disperse evil with but a glance. The proverb is an expression of awe, even sycophancy, toward the king. At the same time, the proverb instructs the king in what he *should* do, if he wants to fit this flattering image of a monarch. See the introduction to 16:10–15 and the references to related proverbs there. The doublet in Prov 20:26 modifies this one by stipulating that it is a *wise* king who does this. This condition is implicit here as well, for if a king is banishing evil he must be righteous.

The phrase *kol raʿ* may mean "every evil *person*" (Ramaq; Radaq; Ehrlich). This interpretation is supported by Prov 20:26, which has *m*^{e}*zareh r*^{e}*šaʿim* "scatters the wicked." It is, however, uncertain that *zrh* "scatters" would be used of expelling an individual from a group. Still, "scatters all evil" is equivalent to expelling evildoers.

with his eyes: By his "penetrating, fear-inspiring" glance (Delitzsch). Alternatively, "in his wisdom he looks on the faces of men, and when he sees among them a wicked one, he expels him and removes him from his presence" (Radaq).

This saying may apply to royal duties beyond forensic judgment. The king's throne is called the Throne of Judgment whether or not he is sitting in judgment, and the expulsion of evil and evildoers from his retinue is always his duty. He does not allow evil men to stand before him in judgment (Saʿadia) *or* in his service (Ramaq). In Ps 101 (on which see the introduction to Prov 16:10–15), the king declares how he will not allow evildoers to serve him: "I will not set a worthless thing before my eyes. The crooked heart [= the crooked of heart] shall be removed from my presence; I shall not know evil" (vv 3–4). And "there shall not dwell within my house one who commits deceit. He who speaks lies will not stand before my eyes" (v 7). In a like vein, Prov 25:5 says, "Remove the wicked from before the king, and his throne will be established in righteousness."

20:9 Who can say, "I have made my heart pure,
I am cleansed from my sins."

No human is entirely innocent. This verity is stated in 1 Kgs 8:46; Ps 143:2; Job 4:17–19; and Qoh 7:20. This is not to say that humanity is inherently and indelibly stained by sinfulness, but rather that the task of moral purification is never complete. Even so, humans can attain a state of *tom*—"innocence" or "wholeness" (Prov 13:6; 19:1; 28:6; 20:7).

**20:10 Disparate stones and disparate measures:
the Lord loathes them both.**

Literally, "a stone and a stone, an ephah and an ephah." In other words, you shall not have two different weights or dry measures, a large one for when you buy, a small one for when you sell. An ephah was the most common dry measure, about 13 to 22 liters. The present proverb looks like an expansion of Prov 20:23. Deut 25:13–16 reformulates this saying as

(13) You shall not have in your purse a stone and a stone, a large one and a small one.
(14) You shall not have in your house an ephah and an ephah, a large one and a small one.
(15) You shall have an undiminished and just stone; an undiminished and just ephah.
(16) so that you may live long upon the land that Yahweh your God is giving to you.

This is one of many instances of wisdom influence on Deuteronomy; see Weinfeld 1972: 244–319. The greater expansiveness of the Deuteronomy passage and the interpretative addition "a large one and a small one" indicate that Deuteronomy is the borrower. The phrase "an undiminished weight" is found in Prov 11:1. Variations on this precept appear in a number of places; see the Comment on 11:1.

**20:11 Even by a child's actions it is known
whether his behavior is pure and upright.**

Literally, "A child is known even by his deeds, if his behavior is pure and upright." This is rephrased above because what is actually made known is the quality of the child's behavior. The "actions" (*ma'ălalim*) in question are probably child's play or just childish behavior. What his actions reveal is not so much whether he is virtuous *now*, as what he will be like in the future. "His behavior" (*po'ŏlo*) refers to the overall quality of his comportment.

The proverb is ambiguous, because *hitnakker* can have opposite meanings:

(1) "Feign," "disguise oneself." This is the meaning of *hitnakker* elsewhere (Gen 42:7; 1 Kgs 14:5, 6; Sir 4:17). Clifford translates, "In his actions even a boy can play act, though his deeds be blameless and right." Clifford explains that if a child can fake virtuous actions, an adult can do so even more. But "innocent" and "upright" do not sound like feigned virtues, and a child who was "pretending" to be good by acting good would *be* good.

(2) "Be known," "recognized." (The verb *n-k-r* does not have this sense in the Dt-stem elsewhere, but such a use is feasible as a passive or reflexive of the D-stem, which means "recognize" in Job 21:29 and 34:19.) By this parsing, the proverb means that even an unformed child or youth (*na'ar*) reveals by his actions, even

his play, whether his character, including the way he will behave as an adult, is pure and upright.

Some commentators have noted that the second clause seems to have a "whether . . . or" structure (*ʾim . . . wᵉʾim*), which would lead us to expect an antithesis, such as "whether he is innocent *or* wicked." For this reason Toy emends *yšr* to *rašaʿ* "wicked" and Ehrlich emends *zk* to *zr* "strange." The construction can, however, be explained as a single protasis stated distributively, in other words, as a sort of hendiadys, equivalent to *ʾim zak wᵉyašar poʿŏlo* "if the child is innocent and upright." The synonyms "innocent" and "upright" (*zak* and *yašar*) form a word-pair in Job 8:6, and the behavior of an innocent man is called "upright" in Prov 21:8.

gam ["even" or "also"]: As often, it is unclear just what *gam* qualifies. By its initial position it should apply to "by his deeds" or to the entire clause. The latter would imply that this verse adds something relevant to the preceding, which it does not. Toy says that *gam* qualifies "child," but *gam* always modifies the following word, clause, or sentence. Understanding *maʿălālāyw* as child's play—a connotation the word receives from context—gives the particle a clear functions. "Even" introduces the unexpected case.

20:12 An ear that hears and an eye that sees—
the Lord made them both.

This is the ear that *really* hears and the eye that *really* sees. (The distinction between simple physical sensation and real perceptiveness is drawn in Isa 6:9–10.) True perception is a gift from God. "The Lord made them both" means either that he endows individuals with them or that he created these faculties in the beginning as a potential that people could henceforth adopt for themselves. In view of its divine origin, perspicuity is to be treasured and used properly. The practical lesson is that one should diligently attend to wisdom and observe the word carefully. To fail to do so is folly, for the fool does not know how to see or hear properly (Prov 17:24; 23:9).

The verse may also imply that the ear and eye were created in such a way that it is their nature to hear and see, and if a man uses them other than to perceive the truth, it is because he has deliberately accustomed himself to wickedness (Saʿadia). Another interpretation: If humans can see and hear, how much the more so can God! Ps 94:9 makes this argument *a fortiori*: "Does not he who planted the ear hear? Does not he who formed the eye see?" (Ehrlich, Clifford). The problem is that, unlike Ps 94, this proverb is not about *God's* hearing.

20:13 Do not love sleep lest you become impoverished.
Open your eyes and have your fill of bread.

Excessive sleep is thought to be a manifestation of laziness, which leads to poverty (Prov 6:4, 9, 10; 10:5; 19:15; 24:33).

become impoverished [*tiwwareš*]: This verb (*y-r-š* N-stem) usually means "be dispossessed." That might be its sense here, for the idler may lose his rights to the ancestral property (Murphy). But in Prov 23:21; 30:9; and Gen 45:11, the verb means "be impoverished," with no special reference to inheritance. *Yiwwareš* may be associated or confused with the similar sounding *raš* "be poor."

In conjunction with v 12, this proverb teaches the reader to make full use of the God-given "eye that sees" (thus Ramaq, who reads vv 12–15 as a cluster.)

20:14 "Bad bad!" the buyer says,
but when he goes away, *then he boasts.*

A prospective buyer denigrates wares to lower the price, only to pride himself afterward on his cleverness. Dissembling is common in the marketplace—and in life generally. One can imagine a merchant quoting this proverb to a balky customer. It does not censure the buyer's action explicitly, but it jabs at his hypocrisy. He disparages the merchandise or the price, but he really thinks they are good. The broader message, Saʿadia says, is that "one should call the good good and the bad bad."

According to Saʿadia, the proverb condemns inconsistent people, who praise something one day and belittle it the next out of envy. But it is not just certain people who act this way; everyone should see himself in this picture. At the same time, the proverb puts the reader on guard against petty deceits (Delitzsch).

20:15 There are gold and much rubies,
but knowledgeable lips are a precious ornament.

Wise speech is more valuable than precious metals and stones; thus too in Prov 3:14; 8:10, 19; and 16:16.

precious ornament [*kᵉli yᵉqar*]: A *kᵉli* can be almost any manufactured item, but a "precious *kᵉli*" is probably jewelry. Fine jewelry is more valuable than gold and rubies because it is made of these materials and has the added value of artistry. Besides connoting material value, the metaphor suggests the artistry of fine speech, for it too must be carefully wrought.

Contrary to Toy (who translates, "Store of gold, wealth of corals and precious vessels—all these are wise lips"), the syntax draws a contrast between the two lines. This is clear in the other proverbs with the *yeš* . . . *w-* pattern, namely, 11:24; 12:18; 13:7; 14:12; 16:25.

20:16 "Take his garment, because he has given surety for a stranger!
And seize it, (because he has given surety) for aliens[a]."

[a] *nkrym* (ketiv; qeré *nokriyyāh*).

The man who gives surety for others' loans will end up forfeiting his own property. Like 11:15a, this proverb assumes the voice of an unidentified onlooker to dramatize the dangers of giving loan guarantees. Here it sounds like the judge or the creditor speaking. On the practice of surety and the motives for it, see the discussion in Vol. I, 214–16.

The author wants us to think of the act of providing surety as the immediate cause of the confiscation. That is why he has the judge or debtor say "because he has given surety for a stranger," which is not really natural to the exclamation. The tightness of the causality is reinforced by omitting the intermediate step, the stranger's default on the loan.

The "garment" (*beged*) in question is probably a *śalmah* (or *śimlah*), a large cloak that one could wear in the cold and wrap oneself in at night. The actuality of this procedure and the distress it could cause are illustrated by the seventh century B.C.E. letter from Yavneh Yam. A laborer complains to an official that one Hoshayahu took his garment (*beged*): "[So please return] my garment. If the commander does not consider it his obligation to have [your servant's garment] sent back, [do] it out of pity! You must not remain silent [when your servant is without his garment]" (ll. 12–14; restorations and translation according to Lindenberger *1994*: 97–98).

The importance of the cloak and its use in lending is shown by the fact that the Law requires that when a poor man's garment is given in pledge, it be returned to him each evening (Exod 22:25–26; Deut 24:12–13). *However*—and this fact eludes many commentators—the law applies only to the borrower's garment. As Saʿadia observes, nothing prohibits permanent confiscation of the *guarantor's* property. The guarantor is worse off than the bankrupt borrower! (Malbim). The mention of the garment in the proverb—the very cloak off his back!—emphasizes the severity of the loss.

has given surety [*ʿarab*]: Homophones of the root *ʿ-r-b* appear in vv 16, 17, and 19, each time with a different meaning: "give surety," "be sweet" and "associate with." Van Leeuwen says that "the verbal connection [between vv 16 and 17] suggests that someone can be enticed by a 'sweet deal' but has in fact swallowed a bad deal."

strangers, aliens: These are unfamiliar persons, not necessarily foreigners; see Vol. I, 139–40 and the Comment on 6:1.

for aliens [*nkrym*, ketiv]: The qeré and the doublet in Prov 27:13 have *nokriyyah* "alien [= strange] woman." The latter reading would imply that the man in question borrowed money to pay for sex or that he owes a prostitute her wages. (Judah's pledge to Tamar in Gen 38:17–18 may have inspired this reading.) But judging from the parallelism, the "stranger" in the A-line, who is the borrower, should be matched in the B-line by "aliens," which also refers to the borrower. (Sg./pl. parallelism is frequent and not a problem.) It was perhaps possible for a woman to seek surety for a loan, but it was undoubtedly very unusual, and the proverb requires a typical case, not a marginal one. Also, when *zar* is parallel to *nokri* elsewhere, the genders always match. We should read *nkrym* "alien men" with the ketiv and emend in Prov 27:13.

and seize it [*ḥablēhû*] . . . : The syntax of v 16b is very concise, having only three words in Hebrew: *ûbeʿad nokrîm ḥablēhû*, lit., "and seize-[from]-him [*ḥablēhû*] for [*beʿad*] aliens [*nōkrîm*]." *Ḥbl* means to hold something in pledge for a loan or to confiscate it in default thereof. Gramatically, the suffix of *ḥablēhû* refers to the garment's possessor.

20:17 The bread of deceit is sweet to a man,
but later it fills his mouth with gravel.

Profits gained by deception seem like a special delicacy at first. The swindler feels that he has received more than he invested and thinks himself clever. As Lady Folly says, "Stolen water is sweet, secret food a delight" (Prov 9:17; see the Comment there). But the taste quickly goes bad. It is as if the bread turned into gravel and cracked the eater's teeth and made him gag. "Bread of deceit" is bread gained by deceit, but at the same time it is bread that deceives. Zofar says the same with a different image in Job 20:12–14; sim. Prov 23:3. Prov 16:25 states the principle more broadly: "There is a way that is straight before a man but which turns out to be the way to death."

20:18 Plans succeed by counsel,
so wage war by strategy.

Strategic planning is crucial in war (Prov 11:14—see the Comment there; 24:6). War is an instance of endeavors that require forethought (Plöger). This and similar proverbs indirectly praise the power of planning and taking counsel in all ways, as stated in 15:22, "Plans are thwarted by lack of counsel, while by a multitude of advisors they succeed." Verse 18b ≈ 24:6a.

so wage war: Lit., "and wage war," an imperative.

ʿăśēh: The abrupt switch to the 2nd per. impv. is awkward here, and some (e.g., Ehrlich, Clifford) follow Syr, Tg, and Vul and emend to *tēʿāśeh* "is made." But the 2nd person is confirmed by 24:6, where the ethical dative *lᵉkā* prevents emendation to the passive. And compare the 2nd per. prohibition in 20:19b. We might emend to *taʿăseh* here as in 24:6, without effect on the meaning.

20:19 The slanderer reveals secrets,
so do not associate with a big-mouth.

The one who traffics in slander will reveal *your* secret, so stay away from him. Prov 20:19a ≈ 11:13a.

big-mouth [*poteh śᵉpatayw*]: Lit., "one who makes his lips wide." Such a person is likely to babble about your private matters. This explanation derives *poteh* from *p-t-h* "be/open wide" (HALOT 985a), a rare root appearing in the H-stem in Gen 9:27. But perhaps, as Saʿadia suggests, *poteh* is one who speaks from naivety. This analysis derives the word from the homonymous root meaning "seduce," hence "gullible." Such a person is less pernicious than a slanderer, who is violating the Law (Lev 19:16). Not only should you avoid the slanderer, as the law requires, you should even keep away from a person who is merely garrulous.

Amenemope offers similar advice within a warning against speaking too boldly or freely:

(22.11) Do not pour out your heart[297] to everyone
(12) and (so) diminish the respect in which you are held.
(13) Do not make your words travel about among others,

[297] Lit., "empty your belly."

(14) nor associate with a voluble man.[298]
(15) Better off is the man whose speech remains in his belly
(16) than one who speaks it to (his) harm. (from §21 [cf. AEL 2.159])

**20:20 He who curses his father or his mother—
his lamp will be extinguished in deep darkness.**

This proverb, like the preceding one, condemns a verbal offense. Cursing one's parents—meaning to disparage and insult them—is loathsome; see Prov 30:11. The Law makes it a capital offense (Exod 21:17; Lev 20:9). Even just looking at one's parents contemptuously brings on severe punishment (Prov 30:17). According to Ben Sira (3:16), cursing one's parents is tantamount to blaspheming and provoking God.

his lamp [*nero*]: The lamp (*ner*) is a symbol of life, prosperity, spiritual illumination, and posterity. It seems to represent posterity in Prov 13:9 and 24:20, which use the same image as v 20b. It is likely (but not certain) that *nir* means "lamp" in the frequent phrase *nir lᵉdawid* "a lamp for David," signifying the continuation of his dynasty (1 Kgs 11:36; 15:4; etc.). (The frequent use of lamps in tombs suggests their association with continuation of the family line [TDOT 10.21].) If "lamp" signifies posterity here, the second line implies that one who insults his parents will have his own line of descendants severed. An offense against one's parents would make the extinction of his own line a fitting punishment. Also, the intense "deep darkness" seems to go beyond the ordinary darkness of death.

deep darkness: On the problem of *'yšwn/'šwn*, see the Comment on 7:2.

**20:21 An inheritance gained in a rush at first—
its outcome will not be blessed.**

The sages viewed hastiness with a certain suspicion. It seemed to suggest grasping at more than God allots—more than the natural fruits of one's labors. See the Comment on 10:22.

Unlike the other warnings about haste (Prov 19:2; 21:5; 28:20), this one speaks of gaining a *naḥălah* "inheritance," which is inalienable family property. This proverb is about premature appropriation of the family property (McKane). Prov 19:26 apparently alludes to a transgression of this sort. Prov 20:20 too speaks of an offense within the family.

It is, however, possible that *naḥălah* is used somewhat loosely here, in the sense of property that a man earns and *intends* to transmit to his children as their inheritance (Hame'iri). An estate of this sort, if gathered hastily, will not be "blessed," that is, prosper. Though called a *naḥălah*, his estate won't end up as much of an inheritance after all.

---

[298] Egyptian *pr ib*, lit., "one who goes forth (with respect to) heart" or "one whose heart goes forth." This may also mean "excitable" or "impetuous." These are aspects of a single personality trait, which is similar to *poteh śepatayim*, especially if the translation "big-mouth" is correct. Using *pr ib*, Duachety warns, "Do not speak impetuous words when you sit with a hostile man" (XXXVc).

in a rush [*m*[e]*bohelet*, qeré]: The verb *bhl* "hasten," more than *'wṣ* "hurry" (Prov 19:2; 21:5; 28:20; 29:20; and elsewhere in the Bible), connotes rushing, impetuosity, and confusion (see Qoh 5:1; 7:9). (It sometimes connotes terror, which is not relevant here.) Prov 28:22 applies *b-h-l* (N-stem) to the greedy man. (In 13:11, LXX reflects Hebrew *m*[e]*bōhāl* "done hastily," hence: "Wealth gathered in a rush will dwindle.") Thus *bhl* implies hurrying beyond ordinary hustle and bustle.

m[e]*bōhelet*, qeré: The ketiv *mbḥlt* is a graphic error, though some explain it as "nauseated" or "an object of disgust"; cf. Zech 11:8 (Ramaq). Geiger (*1857*: 270), on the basis of RH *bḥl* "grow early," explains the ketiv *mbḥlt* as "in vollen Wachsthum begriffen sein" ("be in the process of full growth"). The etymology might, in fact, allow for the gloss "precipitous," but the usage is not attested.

will not be blessed: This threat, appearing also in Prov 30:11, sounds rather pale, but it is probably a litotes equivalent to "will be cursed"; see the Comment on 16:29.

20:22 Do not say, "I will repay (evil) with harm."
Wait for the Lord, and he will give you victory.

Seeking revenge shows lack of confidence in God's justice. Not only should you refrain from taking revenge on your enemy, you shouldn't even *intend* ("say") to do so (Sa'adia). You may hope for requital, but you must leave the execution to God; sim. Prov 25:21–22; see the Comment there. Taking vengeance is forbidden in Lev 19:18.

do not say [*'al to'mar*]: Several sayings in Israelite Wisdom employ the formula, "Do not say" followed by an erroneous claim or thought (Prov 24:29; Qoh 7:10; Sir 5:1, 3, 6; 7:9; 11:23–24; 15:11–13; 16:17; *'Abot* 2:4; 4:5). Variants of the formula appear elsewhere in biblical and rabbinic literature; see Rofé *1978*, 105–9. The formula is frequent in Egyptian Wisdom too, but not in Aramaic or Mesopotamian. This is further evidence of the special connection between Israelite and Egyptian Wisdom (Rofé *1978*: 108).

give you victory [*w*[e]*yoša'*]: On the root *y-š-'*, see the Comment on 11:14. Toy, translating "and he will save thee," says that the proverb represents God as saving, not avenging. But the "salvation" here is not the extrication of the pious man from harm, but the defeat of his enemies as well. The idea of repaying evil with harm caries over from the first line to the second.

For Amenemope, eschewing vengeance is a religious duty. When you have been harmed, do not look for a powerful man to take your side (§21), and when you are in a conflict, do not provoke your adversary (§22). Instead, wait silently and confidently:

(22.3) Do not say, "I have found a strong protector.
(4) I will attack my enemy,"
(5) for you do not know the plans of God.
(6) You should not weep for the morrow,

(7) but seat yourself in the arms of God,
(8) and your silence will cast them down.
(from §21; repeated in §22 [cf. AEL 2.158–59])

Since you do not know what God plans, do not fret about the future. Submit to his will, and *this* will defeat your enemies. The submissiveness that Amenemope counsels is tactical. By trusting in God, by not trying to force the progression of events leading to justice, a man enlists God's aid to defeat one's enemies. Similarly, to when a hothead is raging at you, "Withdraw from him, leave him alone. God knows how to answer him" (§3; 5.16–17 [cf. AEL 2.150]).

Anii offers similar advice. He depicts divine vengeance in vehement terms:

Do not rush to attack him who attacks you,
but leave him to the God.
You should report him daily to the God.
Tomorrow is like today.[299]
You will see what God does,
when he tears up him who tears you up. (21.14 [cf. AEL 2.142])

20:23 The Lord loathes disparate weights,
and deceitful scales are not good.

This is a variant of 20:10; see the Comment there. The second line is not a truism if, following Ehrlich, we understand "not good" in a pragmatic sense, meaning "not useful or profitable," hence, as a litotes, "harmful"; see the Comment on 16:29. Prov 20:23a ≈ 11:1a.

disparate weights: Lit., "a stone and a stone."

20:24 A man's steps are from the Lord,
and a human—how can he understand where he is going?

Man cannot fully plan or control the course of his life, for God is ultimately in control, and God's plans are not transparent. This is the message of Prov 16:9, "A man's heart plans [*yᵉḥaššeb*] his way, but it is the Lord who makes his step secure [*yakin*]." The verb *yᵉḥaššeb* is equivalent to *yabin* "understand," used in 20:24b. Likewise Prov 19:21 insists that God's decisions override human designs, and 14:12 (= 16:25) says that a man cannot be certain about the issue of his "way," the course he is on.

Prov 20:24 is phrased as a statement of strong determinism, but it is not a dogma asserting that humans are helpless puppets. This proverb does not stand alone, and the rest of the book assumes that humans are free to choose their basic course of action. The aphorism expresses, instead, a humble awareness of the limitations of human powers and, like 20:22, implicitly counsels trust in God.

[299] In other words, be patient, for justice need not be done immediately.

Even as it warns against arrogant overconfidence, the present saying also encourages optimism, for God may override human plans for the better. As Saʿadia observes, a man may, for example, be planning to go to sea and something prevents him. He feels frustrated, but it may well be that God wished to save him from drowning.

A *man's steps are from the Lord*: That is, God determines where he will step, where he will go.

where he is going: Lit., "his way," the course of his life.

Where the qeré has *ybyn* (*yābîn*) "understand," the ketiv has *ykyn* "determine." With the ketiv, the verse reads: "A man's steps come from the Lord, and a human—how can he determine [*ykyn*] where he is going?" Both variants produce meaningful proverbs. Moreover, a number of texts in Qumran support the ketiv variant, directly or indirectly; see Van Leeuwen *1997b*.

There is frequent confusion between the verbs *hbyn* (imperfect *ybyn*) "understand" and *hkyn* (imperfect *ykyn*) "make firm," "determine." The verbs are graphically almost identical; see the Comment on 14:8. In 20:24, the variant *yākîn* "secure" is supported by the Syriac, while the LXX agrees with MT's *ybyn*. *Ykyn*, in a different form, appears also in Ps 37:23, "From the Lord a man's steps are secured, and he favors his way." ("Secured" is *kônānû*, from the same root as *ykyn*.) Jeremiah cites a proverb like this when he says, "I know, O Lord, that a man's way is not his own, and that a man is not able to walk and make his step secure [*wᵉhākîn ʾet ṣaʿădô*]" (10:23).

A sentence in Ahiqar teaches the same idea: "For it is not in men's power to lift their feet or set them down, apart fro[m the gods]" (122 [1.1.170]). Ahiqar is saying that man cannot act *contrary* to the gods' will, not that the gods predetermine his every action. See the introduction to 16:1–9.

20:25 It is a snare to a man to blurt out "Holy!"
and after making vows to reconsider.

Since the future is unknown (v 24b), a man must be very deliberate in making vows. He cannot know if he will be able to pay them when the time comes. Payment of vows is required in Num 30:3; Deut 23:22–24; and Ps 50:14. Qohelet warns at length against making impetuous vows and delaying in their fulfillment (4:17–5:5), as does Ben Sira (18:22–23).

blurt out [*yālaʿ*]: As pointed, this word is either a G perf. or a shortened H impf. from *l-w-ʿ* or *l-ʿ-ʿ*, with retraction of the accent. The verb appears in Job 6:3 and means "speak rashly" or the like. Translated literally, the MT means "He blurts out 'Holy!'—a snare to a man." The verbal clause is nominalized and serves as the actual subject. Alternatively, one might vocalize as *yālōaʿ* (inf. abs.). Some medievals derive *yālaʿ* from *l-ʿ-ʿ* "swallow," comparing *yᵉʿalʿû* (Job 39:30) and the noun *lōaʿ* "gullet" (Prov 23:2). In that case, the snare consists in *eating* offerings one has dedicated (Riyqam, Ramaq).

"Holy": This is an abbreviated declaration consecrating an item of value to God, whereupon it is owed to the temple. An equivalent one-word vow is quoted in Mark 7:11, "But you say, 'If a man says to his father or mother, "Korban" ' (that

is, 'Offering')." The Mishna records other substitutions for *qorban*: *qonam*, *qonaḥ*, *qonas* (*m. Nedarim* 1:2, 4).

reconsider [*l*ᵉ*baqqer*]: Lit., "to investigate," "scrutinize," that is, to examine your property to secure the means to pay. You should do this *first*. As Ben Sira says, "Before vowing, prepare yourself" (18:23a).

20:26 The wise king scatters the wicked
and rolls a wheel over them.

Whereas Prov 20:8 speaks as if all kings do justice, this verse more cautiously restricts the assertion to *wise* kings. The proverb may refer to forensic judgment or to the banishment of all evildoers—from his court and from his land. Riyqam says, "If he has a wicked official he will send his wrath against him and cast him down and bring him low." Even a righteous king may have employed a corrupt man because, as Riyqam observes, "Perhaps he did not really know him when he promoted him." Such sayings pertain in particular to the court retinue; see the Comment on 20:8.

and rolls a wheel over them: The B-line reiterates and focuses the A-line, explaining how the scattering (winnowing) is carried out. "Rolls" (*wayyašeb*) is, lit., "return," that is, he brings the wheel over them repeatedly. One technique for threshing grain was the wheel-thresher (*ʿopan ʿăgalah*), mentioned in Isa 28:27. Two or more heavy wheels were attached to a frame, which was drawn by animals over the grain to crack the husk (as described by Borowski *1987*: 65). This is a metaphor of punishment and destruction. Saʿadia compares the challenge God issues to Job, "And crush the wicked where they stand" (40:12).

Some think that an actual wheel was used in torture to force confessions (thus Malbim). But there is no evidence for judicial torture in Israel or for the use of the wheel as an instrument for that purpose elsewhere. The Hittite texts that Snell (1989) adduces are completely obscure.

Graetz 1884 emends *ʾôpān* to *ʾônām*, comparing Ps 94:23, *wayyāšeb ʿălêhem ʾet ʾônām*. This would mean "and he returns their iniquity upon them." The sentence as emended makes good sense, but the emendation is rather distant graphically and not supported by the versions.

20:27 The life-breath of man is the lamp of the Lord.
He examines all the chambers of the belly.

Nothing, even hidden thoughts, will escape God's notice. This is both a warning and a comfort (Plöger).

Almost all commentators understand this to mean that God uses the human soul—understood as conscience or wisdom—to illuminate and examine man's hidden thoughts and feelings ("the chambers of the belly"). Thus when a man searches his own heart, God himself is examining him.

This interpretation, however, presents difficulties. "Breath" (*n*ᵉ*šamah*) in the Bible means the literal breath and the life-breath and, by extension, the being it keeps alive. It does not mean "soul" in the sense of "man's moral and intellectual perception, the conscience" (Toy). In Biblical Hebrew and Rabbinic Hebrew, the locus of conscience is the heart, and, according to Ps 77:7b, this is what inspects the *ruaḥ* "spirit." *Nᵉšamah* acquires this sense in Rabbinic Hebrew, but there is no hint of it in the Bible. And even if *nᵉšamah* meant "soul," it is unclear how this could aid *God* in his examination of the "chambers of the belly." In any case, the soul requires scrutiny no less than the "belly," the repository of thoughts.

nᵉšāmāh: Van Leeuwen (1997: 188) cites Dhorme (1967: 378) to the effect that the breath is "not only the principle of life . . . but also the principle of wisdom." Dhorme adduces Job 26:4; 32:8, 18 and compares 20:3, but only the first two are relevant. In Job 26:4, Job chides his friends by saying, "With whom have you spoken words, and whose breath [*nᵉšāmāh*] has come out of you?" That is, have you been speaking with someone else's words? The "breath" carries words and thoughts. The someone else who has *not* spoken through them is God, though Job's friends tend to see themselves as his representatives. Later Elihu says, "Indeed there is a spirit in man, and the breath [*nᵉšāmāh*] of Shaddai gives them understanding" (32:8). But this is *God's* breath, which has special powers (Isa 30:33; Job 4:9; 37:10).

Clifford comes closer to the saying's intention: "Lifebreath is an apt symbol for the divine spark in a human being, for it is powerful, invisible, and disappears at death. The divinely given breath flowing through the inner part of the body ("the chambers of the stomach") functions like a claim. There is no part of a human being that is beyond divine scrutiny."

Human vitality itself reaches the hidden recesses of human thought. But, contrary to Clifford, the purpose of the proverb is not to say something about the power or role of the life-breath. It is, rather, to emphasize how far and deep God's vision penetrates. God sees wherever the breath's vital power reaches—which is to say, everywhere, including the organs of thought. It is he, not the lamp, who searches, contrary to most translations. It is as if humans have a lamp in the chambers of the belly that illuminates its recesses to the divine vision. The image of lamps has the same function in Zeph 1:12a: "On that day I will examine [*ʾăḥappeś*] Jerusalem with lamps [*nerot*]." These lamps are not a metaphor for something else, some particular power that God uses in his inspection. Instead, they are part of the picture of searching, and they emphasize the thoroughness of the search.

nēr: Ehrlich, BHS, and others emend to *nôṣēr* "guards" to make a smoother sentence, but there is no scribal explanation for the loss of the *ṣadé*, nor does "guards" provide a good parallel to "examines." Tur-Sinai (p. 27) explains *nēr* as the ptcp. of *n-y-r*, "plow," "dig a furrow," used in Jer 4:3; sim. Loewenstamm (1987: 223–24), who vocalizes *nār*. This would mean that God "plows," that is, "digs," beneath the surface to investigate man's heart. Loewenstamm adduces *ḥāpar*, which means both "dig" and "investigate," as a semantic parallel. But the image of plowing a furrow, which just breaks up the surface, is not suggestive of the notion of digging deep in an investigation.

20:28 Kindness and fidelity guard the king,
and he supports his throne by kindness.

The royal throne is founded on justice and righteousness, according to Prov 16:12; 25:5; and 29:14. Kindness and fidelity may be imagined as two guards on either side of the throne, which rests on a pedestal of kindness. If the king fails in his ethical duties, he is personally endangered, and his rule will crumble beneath him. Loader (1999: 230) observes that this proverb is the essence of the advice the elderly courtiers give in 1 Kgs 12:7, when they urge the new king Jeroboam to treat the northern tribes in a conciliatory manner.

Clifford says that it is *God's* loyalty and fidelity that guard the king, but the other proverbs about the foundation and security of the throne make it dependent on the *king's* virtues. See the Comment on Prov 16:12.

he: That is, the king.

by kindness [*baḥesed*]: Or, "on kindness." Saʿadia says that "fidelity" (*ʾĕmet*) is to be supplied in the B-line. He compares the omission of "silver" in Dan 5:3 (compare v 2). It does seem true that the absence of "fidelity" in the B-line is just for the sake of quantitative balance and does not indicate a substantive distinction between the two lines.

20:29 The splendor of young men is their strength,
and the grandeur of old men is white hair.

This saying expresses esteem for the endowments of both youth and old age. Even in their frailty, the aged have a power comparable to the widely admired physical strength of young men. The parallelism suggests that the age of the old is in itself a power. "White hair" represents old age, and this is something to take pride in. In the sages' eyes, white hair is evidence of both a successful life and the wisdom of years. Prov 20:29b ≈ 16:31a.

20:30 Severe bruises scour[a] the mind,[b]
and they smite the chambers of the belly.

[a] *timrôq* (MT qeré *tamrûq*; ketiv *tmryq*). [b] *bᵉrēaʿ* (MT *bᵉrāʿ*).

Corporal punishment, so often recommended in Prov 10–29 (see the Comment on 13:24), strikes the surface but also reaches deeper to scour the mind (lit., "heart" and "belly") and to discipline even hidden thoughts (Ehrlich). A similar idea is found in 22:15, "Folly is bound to the heart of a youth, (but) the rod of discipline will remove it from him."

Severe bruises [*ḥăbûrôt peṣaʿ*]: Lit., "bruises of a wound," a construct of synonyms connoting intensity.

scour: The qeré *tamrûq* means "ointment," which does not fit well here. We should read with the consonants of the qeré, but point *timrôq*, from the verb meaning "polish" (Jer 46:4; 2 Chr 4:16) or "scour" (Lev 6:21 [G pass.]; see Milgrom 1991 ad loc.). The fem. sg. verb with the fem. pl. subj. is not a problem; see Prov 20:18. Ehrlich retains *tamrîq*, but the H-stem is unattested. On the basis of Old Aramaic *tmryq*, W. von Soden (1990: 120–21) glosses *tmryq* as "insult," but this does not solve the verse's problems.

the mind [*bᵉrēaʿ*]: MT has *bᵉrāʿ* "in/on evil." The latter reading is possible but awkward, because *mrq* "rubbing," "scouring" has its effect on the surface that is rubbed and not on the material that is scoured out. Ehrlich points *bᵉrēaʿ* and translates "im Innern"—"in the inside" or "inner person." The word means "desire" or "thought" in Ps 139:2, 17. Sim. Gemser, translating "den Willen, "the will."

21:1 The king's heart is like channels of water in the hand of the Lord:
he directs it wherever he wishes.

As the farmer employs irrigation channels to his own ends, so does God make use of the king's mind. The teaching points in two directions. Directed to the king's subjects, it flatters the king by equating his intentions with God's. What the king wants must be what God wants. Directed to the king, it prompts him to make God's will (presumably as taught by the sages and other authorities) his own. The king must, moreover, avoid pride (Deut 17:20), for he is only a tool in God's hands (Hame'iri). The saying also implies that the king's will is not predictable; see Prov 25:3. On the royal ideal, see the introduction to 16:10–15.

is like channels of water: Lit., "is channels of water." Water channels are used in irrigation and thus connote productivity rather than flooding and danger, as a *naḥal* ("river," "wadi") might. When princes and kings rule justly, Isaiah says, they will be a refuge from the elements and "like water channels on parched ground" (32:2).

directs it: Water was diverted from one channel to another by means of hinged wooden hatches, which were pivoted back and forth by a handle.

21:2 A man's every way is straight in his eyes,
but the Lord examines hearts.

Like the preceding proverb, this one declares God's power over the human heart. God sees even subconscious intentions. "Eyes" and "hearts" are the organs of superficial and deep perception, respectively; see the Comment on 14:12. Prov 21:2a ≈ 14:12a; v 2b ≈ 16:2b, the latter using *ruḥot* "spirits" instead of *libbot* "hearts." There is no practical distinction in this case.

Though a man might convince himself that his course of action is best, God can perceive what the heart really thinks and feels. The antithesis between the two lines shows that what God may see in a man's heart is the awareness that the way he has chosen is *not* straight and honest. In other words, in his heart he *knows* he is wrong, but he insists on convincing himself (superficially) of the rightness of his deed. God sees his hypocrisy. On the two levels of knowledge, see the Comment on 16:2 and compare 14:12 and 30:12.

21:3 Doing righteousness and justice
is more valued by the Lord than sacrifice.

The Lord ranks righteousness even above sacrifice. See the Comment on 15:8 and the parallels cited there.

valued: Lit., "chosen."

**21:4 Haughtiness of eyes and arrogance[a] of heart:
the lamp[b] of the wicked is sin.**

[a] *rōḥab* (MT *rᵉḥab-*). [b] *nēr* (MT *nir*).

The wicked employ haughty arrogance as their lamp, to illumine their way and guide them. They use arrogance as the wise use instruction (Prov 6:23; sim. Ps 119:105, "Your word is a lamp to my feet and a light to my path"). But the lamp of the wicked is sin and therefore it is really darkness and casts a black light by which the wicked can only stumble (Prov 4:19). "Lamp" is used facetiously; see the Comment on 11:23.

arrogance of heart [*rōḥab lēb*]: Lit., "breadth of heart." MT's *rḥb lb* can mean either "arrogant"/"arrogance," as in Ps 101:5, or "greed"/"greedy," if it is equivalent to *rᵉḥab nepeš* in Prov 28:25 (thus Saʿadia; but *nepeš* is more specifically associated with appetite than *lēb* is). The notion of arrogance is supported by the conjoined phrase "haughtiness of eyes" in Ps 101:5. By MT's pointing, the line means that the arrogant *man* is a lamp, which is awkward. We should point the word as an abstract, *rōḥab lēb*, lit., "breadth of heart" (see 1 Kgs 5:9), coordinated with *rûm ʿeynayim*, lit., "height of eyes," in Prov 21:4.

lamp [*nēr*]: The MT has *nir* (consonantally *nr*), which some understand to mean "tillage," that is, virgin ground ready for plowing. (This is probably the intention of the Masoretic vocalization.) Delitzsch translates, "and the tillage of the wicked is sin"; sim. McKane, JPSV, and others. This would mean that the way in which the wicked cultivate their lives produces a crop of sin. Delitzsch's argument against "lamp" is that the "lamp of the wicked" (which alludes either to life or prosperity) is said to "go out" (Prov 13:9; 20:20; 24:20), so how can it be a lamp? This is a weak argument because the lamp must shine for a while *before* it goes out, and in any case the metaphor here has a different tenor, namely, guidance. "Tillage" is a less appropriate metaphor because that is what one works *on*, whereas a lamp is something that one uses to get through life *with*.

lamp: This translation takes "lamp" as resuming the proleptic phrases in the first line. "Haughtiness" and "arrogance" *are* the lamp, which is then identified as sin. We should probably vocalize *nēr* with some MT manuscripts. To the same effect, *nr* can be parsed as a (unique) defective writing of *nîr*, which probably means "lamp" when it is a metaphor for the royal lineage (see the Comment on 20:20).

Another interpretation: In 1 Kgs 5:9, *roḥab leb* is Solomon's capacity to hold wisdom. Tur-Sinai (pp. 28–29) applies the phrases in Prov 21:4a to God: He is wise, and his eyes are on high, whence he looks down on humans and "investigates" (*nār*) the wicked and their *ḥaṭṭa't* "sin-offering" (translated above as "sin"). But, contrary to Tur-Sinai, God is not said to be "lofty of eyes," even though he does sit on high and look down (as in Ps 138:6, e.g.). Also, it is unlikely that *n-y-r* can mean "to plow" and connote investigation; see the Comment on 20:27.

**21:5 The plans of the diligent surely lead to a surplus,
but everyone who hastens is surely headed for want.**

Reasonable diligence is profitable, but excessive hurrying and straining to get rich demonstrate greed—a desire for more than one is naturally allotted—and are self-defeating. In practical terms, one who rushes and scurries in pursuit of his goals is likely to make a mess of things, for "he will not be aware of their distortion and disorder" (Hame'iri). On the problem of haste see the Comments on 10:22 and 19:2; compare also 20:21; 23:4; and 28:20.

**21:6 He who gains[a] treasures by a deceitful tongue
is a driven vapor who seeks[b] death.**

[a] *pōʿēl* (MT *pōʿal*). [b] *mᵉbaqqēš* (MT *mᵉbaqšê*).

The man who resorts to deceit is driven by the same lust for wealth as the striver (v 5) but is far worse because he goes from unadvisable to prohibited behavior. Therefore he is buffeted about like a vapor and (though he may not realize it) is seeking death. The conjunction of vv 5 and 6 associates haste with sin, as happens explicitly in Prov 19:2b, "and he who hurries with his feet sins."

"Vapor" [*hebel*] is a frequent metaphor for transience. Humans are compared to a vapor in Pss 39:12 and 144:4. A "driven vapor" is even more ephemeral, like a puff of smoke on a gusty day. The wicked are likened to windblown chaff in Ps 1:4 and to smoke in Ps 68:3.

He who gains [*pōʿēl*]: Lit., "makes." MT has "The making [*pōʿal*] of treasures . . ." But the verbs "gains" and "seeks" are more appropriately predicated of people than actions, and likewise the metaphors in the B-line are *things* and not properly predicated of an action. The proposed change is in pointing only.

a driven vapor who seeks death [*hebel niddāp mᵉbaqqēš* (MT *mᵉbaqšê*) *māwet*]: The MT can be translated (lit.) "a driven vapor who seek (pl.) death" or "a driven vapor, the seekers of death," both of which are awkward. The LXX and several Hebrew MSS (including, it seems, the one Rashi used) read (1) *môqᵉšê* "snares" (a reading suggested by Hitzig, Toy, etc.); cf. 13:14b. But by this reading, "making" is called a "vapor" and "snares of death," which are awkward predications. Or (2) *bimᵉbaqᵉšê*. But the notion of seeking vanity *by* a snare conveys little, and the plural remains problematic. The proposed emendation to the singular *mᵉbaqqēš* is conjectural but minor and solves the verse's problems.

**21:7 The violence of the wicked will drag them away,
because they refuse to do justice.**

The wicked are snared by their own evil; see the Comment on 1:19. The device that catches them and hauls them in is pictured as a fishing net, as implied by the verb *yᵉgorem* "drag away"; see Hab 1:15 (Hame'iri). Ehrlich notes that the root *g-r-r* means, more precisely, to drag *in*, not drag away, from the point of orientation. But, contrary to Ehrlich, this does not mean that violence *attracts* the wicked, but rather that it drags them away from their place and to itself, as a fisherman hauls in his catch.

violence . . . drag away: This metaphor is doubly meaningful because *šod* can mean "violence"—what the wicked do—and "destruction"—what they suffer. It is as if the violence the wicked commit is of a piece with the destruction awaiting them. (Isaiah 13:6 calls the latter *šod miššaday* "destruction from Shaddai.") The *šod* the wicked do pulls them out of the "sea," in which they can live, and toward the *šod* they suffer. The productive ambiguities of the saying are increased by the fact that *ygrm* (if pronounced *y^egûrēm*) can mean "attack" (*g-w-r* II; e.g., Isa 54:15ab; Ps 59:4). The violence the wicked wreak on others will turn on *them* and attack *them*.

21:8 A man's behavior may be tortuous,[a]
(even) while his deeds are pure and upright[b].

---

[a]omit *wāzār*. [b] *w^eyāšār* (MT *yāšār*).

"[U]nfamiliar does not always mean bad," as Clifford phrases the gist of the verse. The proverb should not be read as a contrast between the devious and the upright, he notes, because the words describing the behavior (lit., "way") are ethically neutral. The saying is still strange, because in Proverbs, and usually elsewhere, derivatives of *h-p-k*, such as *hăpakpak* "tortuous," "crooked," connote dishonesty.

wāzār: By pointing the *waw* with a *qameṣ*, the MT makes *'îš wāzār* a linked pair meaning something like "a man-and-a stranger," that is, "a man who is a stranger," rather than two things, a man *and* a stranger. (On the phenomenon see GBH §104d.) The sentence would mean: "A man who is a stranger is tortuous." But this sort of xenophobia has no place in Wisdom Literature. We might, with most commentators, construe *zār* as a second adjective modifying *derek* "way": "The way of a man may be tortuous and strange, though his actions are blameless and proper" (JPSV). This construction requires vocalizing *w^ezār*. Older commentators explained *wāzār* as "sinful," on the basis of a doubtful Arabic etymology, *wzr* "commit sin" (Cappellus, ref. Toy; but see Ehrlich). But the line is overlong and the word is probably a dittograph of the nearly identical *wzk*. MT's *yāšār* requires a *waw*, lost by near-dittography.

21:9 Better to dwell on the corner of a roof
than with a contentious woman in a house with other people.

We can picture a harried husband hounded from his house (see the Comment on 19:13b) and taking refuge on the roof, exposed to the elements. He doesn't even get the whole roof, but just a corner. Yet even this is better than being cooped up inside with a shrew. Prov 21:9 = 25:24 ≈ 21:19.

Tur-Sinai (pp. 10–12) says that the image is of bird sitting on roof of a ruined house in the wasteland. A variant of this proverb, 21:19, has "in a desert land" instead of "on the corner of a roof." In fact, both images come into play: The badgered husband is compared to a man sitting on a roof, who is *like* a bird roosting on a desolate house. There he is isolated (see Ps 102:7–8, esp. 8b: "I lie awake and am like a lone bird on a roof"). He may also be hungry if, following Tur-Sinai, we read Prov 21:9 in the light of the other "better than" proverbs, most of which make neediness the point of comparison (12:9; 15:16–17; 16:8; 17:1).

in a house with other people [*beyt ḥaber*]: This literally reads "and a house of community" or "and a common house," contrasting with the isolation described in the first line.

bêt ḥāber: The meaning is uncertain. There are several possibilities: (1) "Shared house" or "common house," as above (McKane and others). (2) A house with magic in it; cf. Deut 18:11 (Saʿadia). (3) "Alehouse" (Albright 1955: 11–12, comparing Akkadian *bît ḫubūri* "brewery," "alehouse" and Ugaritic *bt ḫbr*, on which see below). (3) "A noisy house" (Clifford, based on Akkadian *ḫabāru* "be noisy" and other cognates). The logic of the "better than" formula calls for a desirable attribute here, which noise is not, but it must be granted that the near-doublet in 21:19 has *kaʿas* "anger," which is also something unpleasant. (4) Emending to *bayit rāḥāb* "wide house" (Toy and Ehrlich).

Keret I (KTU1.14 ii 25) reads: "Let Keret come down from the roof. Let him prepare corn for the city, wheat for *bt ḫbr*." Gibson (CML 84) translates "Beth Khubur." Gordon (UT glossary #924) explains it as either a place-name or a common noun meaning "community." It is interesting that Keret descends from the roof to supply grain to his city.

But what's the good of a saying like this? It could be of little use in choosing a wife, because, in the absence of a long courtship, a young man would be unlikely to know whether his bride is of a contentious sort. Its practical use would be to offer the comfort of cynicism and anonymous camaraderie, to let a man who feels harried see his experience as a common one—that's just the way women are.

Murphy is troubled that sayings about shrewish wives are never balanced by complaints about quarrelsome *husbands*. This imbalance is due to the fact that the compilers were men who saw things from the male standpoint alone. But proverbs are everywhere and everyone's, and women may have had equally sharp sayings of their own about nasty husbands.

Wisdom Literature shows an occasional awareness that it is also the husband's duty to avoid quarreling. Anii instructs his son to appreciate his wife's domestic skills and not to be overbearing. He also says, "If a man desists from strife at home, he will not find its beginning" (22.5–6 [cf. AEL 2.143]). In other words, peace begins at home. Ben Sira shows some disapproval of male irascibility: "Do not be like a lion in your home and tremulous [impetuous? (*mtpḥz*)] in your work" (4:30, MS C ≈ Gk), or "Do not be like a dog in your home and strange and fearful in your work" (MS A ≈ Syr). The text is difficult, but the gist is: Don't be a bully at home and a coward in public.

21:10 The soul of the wicked man desires what is bad;
he will find no forgiveness in the eyes of others[a].

[a] *bᵉʿênê* (MT *bᵉʿênāyw*).

The wicked man's desires are perverse (see Vol. I, 117–18). He *wants* what is bad—bad for others and, though he may not realize it, bad for himself. Others will not forgive him for this, because he harms them willfully and regularly and not just carelessly or occasionally.

in the eyes of others [*bᵉʿeyney reʿehu*]: Lit., "in the eyes of his fellow." The MT has "his neighbor will not be forgiven in his eyes [*bʿynyw*]," but the relationship between the wicked man's appetite for evil and his refusal to forgive or absolve others is tenuous. Hence *bʿynyw* "in his eyes" is emended to *bʿyny* "in the eyes of," following the Syriac. This reading connects the two lines, so that the second line states the consequence of one's own evil desires.

21:11 When a scoffer is punished the callow person will gain wisdom,
and when a wise person is taught he gains knowledge.

A naïve youth can learn from seeing an impudent mocker punished, while one who is wise will gain knowledge directly by listening to instruction. The variant in Prov 19:25 contrasts the effects of a beating and a verbal rebuke. Here, the callow, naïve person (*peti*) learns from observing the scoffer undergoing any kind of punishment. See the Comment on 19:25 and compare 17:10.

person, person: These words are not in the Hebrew. The age is left indefinite, but the education of young boys is probably in mind here as generally in Proverbs. The gender is masculine, but female education is not excluded.

This interpretation takes "a wise person" as the subject of "gains knowledge." It is also possible that the subject is the naïve youth of v 11a (Ehrlich, Murphy). In that case, we should translate v 11b as "and he gains knowledge when a wise man is taught." The simple person can be educated by negative or positive example (Murphy). But it is unlikely that someone alert enough to learn from observing someone else receiving verbal instruction could be called a *peti*. In the first interpretation, he has the compelling example of a punishment to gain his attention.

21:12 The righteous one observes the house of the wicked,
confounding the wicked into evil.

The MT, translated above, apparently means that the righteous person observes the house of the wicked and (verbally) consigns the wicked to catastrophe. This verse is connected mechanically to the preceding one by the repetition of the verb *hiśkil*, here meaning "observe," there meaning "instruct."

The MT, however, presents problems. Who is the *ṣaddiq* "righteous" (or "righteous one")? Most commentators (e.g., Delitzsch, McKane, Murphy, Clifford) agree that the *ṣaddiq* is God, for he alone can "confound the wicked to evil." Yet *ṣaddiq*, without an article or contextual definition, is unlikely to serve as a nominal epithet of God, especially in Proverbs, which only calls God "God" and "Yahweh."

"Righteous" is most naturally understood as any righteous human. But how can a human, however righteous, confound or destroy (*slp*) the wicked? Saʿadia says that the righteous man *overthrows* his adversaries' houses. But it is not the duty of the righteous to punish the wicked, except in a legal context, and *slp* would not designate a judicial penalty. Some commentators frame the event in psychological terms. Radaq explains that the righteous man observes the house of the wicked and *knows* that God (though unmentioned) will overthrow it. Hame'iri assigns to *meśallep* a sort of declarative-estimative force (on which see GBH §52d): The righteous man *declares* or *regards* the wicked to be overthrown.

Ha'meiri is supported by Job 5:3–4, in which Eliphaz says, "I saw the fool take root, and I immediately cursed [*'eqqob*] his habitation. His sons are far from victory [or "salvation" (*yešaʿ*)]—they shall be defeated in the gate with none to save them." Eliphaz was so certain that the house of the wicked, no matter how prosperous, would be devastated, that he burst out with a curse—as if the pronouncement of his malediction were tantamount to the event. It is to be noted that Eliphaz's cursing of the fool's "habitation" refers to his *sons*. This is very likely what is meant by the "house" that the righteous man "confounds" in the present verse.

The LXX and Syriac read *lbwt* "hearts" for MT's *lbyt* "the house," hence: "The Righteous One observes the *hearts* of the wicked man." This reading is open to the objections that *ṣaddiq* by itself is an unlikely epithet of God, and that it is incongruous to speak of the (plural) "hearts" of the (singular) "wicked man." Nevertheless, the proverb in this form basically makes sense and can be supported by v 2, and similar thoughts appear in 15:11; 17:3; 24:12; and esp. Ps 7:10b, "and the righteous God examines hearts and kidneys" (all with *libbot*). In fact the LXX reading may have arisen under the influence of Prov 21:2 and can stand as a variant proverb.

21:13 He who blocks his ear from hearing the cry of the lowly—
he too will call out and will not be answered.

The poor are under God's special protection (Prov 19:17; 22:23; cf. Ps 68:6), and whoever is indifferent to their plea will himself be ignored—perhaps by humans but primarily by God—in his hour of need. Compare Lady Wisdom's stony scorn of fools in 1:28, "Then they'll call me, but I won't answer; they will seek me but find me not." Consequently, "they shall eat of the fruit of their way" (1:31).

21:14 A gift in secret assuages[a] anger,
and a bribe in the bosom—strong wrath.

[a] *yekappēr* (MT *yikpeh*).

Proverbs has mixed attitudes about gifts and bribes. Prov 15:27b expresses suspicion, while 17:8, 18:16, and 19:6 seem to approve of them and even commend their utility, though perhaps with a tinge of cynicism. See the Comments on 15:27 and 18:16. In the present verse the gift is intended to make peace and is acceptable for that reason. Still, the fact that it is slipped into the recipient's garment "in secret" suggests a certain impropriety, as if the giver were trying to gain a special advantage for himself and did not want others to know.

Read in conjunction with the preceding verse, this one gains an additional message: One who refuses another's plea for help, rather than discretely offering charity, will himself be ignored by God. However, he who gives to the poor assuages *God's* anger (Saʿadia). As Prov 16:6 says, "Through kindness and constancy, iniquity will receive atonement" (*yekuppar*, using the verb restored here). It is important that the gift be given in secret to spare the recipient embarrassment (Hame'iri).[300]

y^e^kappēr: Lit., "assuages," "appeases," "atones for." The MT has *yikpeh*, of uncertain meaning. The medievals (sim. Gemser, HALOT 492b) understand the latter to mean "subdue," equivalent to *kpp*, but *kph/kpp* means "to bend down" or "to force upon" and would not express easing someone's anger. In support of the emendation are Prov 6:35 and 16:14, which use forms of *k-p-r* to refer to a payment that (potentially) assuages wrath, and Gen 32:21, in which Jacob says, "I will appease him [lit., "atone (*kpr*) to his face"] by a gift."

21:15 Doing justice is a pleasure to a righteous man,
but a ruin to evildoers.

Not only do the righteous *do* justice, they *enjoy* doing it. Righteousness is a configuration of the soul, a quality of character. Thus too with wisdom; see Vol. I, 347–48.

justice: The word *mišpaṭ*, though conveniently translated "justice," has a much broader range than the English word. It basically means "what is right" (Murphy) and may be used with regard to daily practices, law and legal procedure, and social relations. It can mean the collectivity of laws, judgments, legal decisions, executions of judgment, and claims and customs. See TDOT 9.86–98.

a ruin to evildoers: They *regard* justice as ruinous. This does not mean that justice ruins them, for justice here is the virtue of doing what is right, not the process of punishment. The B-line speaks of an attitude, as does the A-line. Ptahhotep says of the moral pervert, "He sees knowledge as ignorance, benefit as harm" (ll. 577–78; see Vol. I, 117–18). The present proverb is close in structure and thought to Prov 15:21 and esp. 10:23: "Committing vice is like an amusement to a dolt, but wisdom (is thus) to the man of good sense."

Ramaq explains the verse to mean that "The joy of salvation will come to [the righteous] when he does justice, and ruin will come to evildoers"; sim. Clifford. But the parallels in 10:23 and 15:21 show that the proverb speaks about attitudes and inclinations, not rewards and punishments.

Ehrlich insists that the verse is strictly utilitarian, reasoning that "the inner satisfaction that the awareness of a good deed secures is an unknown concept in the OT. The ancient Israelites did what is right because the Law demands it and because thereby one goes through life most securely." Hence he translates, "Dem Gerechten ist eine Freude, wenn ihm nach Recht geschieht, dem Frevler aber ist solches ein Schrecken." ("To the righteous it is a joy when what is just befalls him; to the wicked, however, such a thing is a terror.") (Ehrlich treats the infinitive *ʿăśot*, translated above as an active "doing," as a passive.) Contrary to Ehrlich, this verse shows that the "ancient Israelites"—or, rather, some of them—were also motivated by a desire to do what was right for its own sake. Ehrlich's assumption, once widespread among scholars, is disproved in particular by Ps 19:8–15 (esp. vv 9, 11); Ps 119 (esp. vv 14, 16, 24, 47, 48, 92, 159); and Deuteronomy, with its

[300] Radaq's commentary ends here.

insistence on love of God as a motivation for obeying his Torah (e.g., Deut 6:5; 10:12; 11:1; 30:20).

21:16 A man who strays from the way of insight
will repose in the community of the ghosts.

One who strays from the way of *haśkel*, insight and prudence (as in Prov 1:3), which is the way to life, will inevitably, and prematurely, wander onto the path to death (2:18; 7:27; 14:12; 16:25; cf. 12:28b), there to rest among the dead (2:18; 9:18). On the "ghosts" or Rephaim, see the Comment on 2:18. Ironically, the man who strays from the path of wisdom wanders restlessly in this life only to find "repose" in Sheol (Ehrlich). One is reminded of the "banquet" of ghosts hosted by Lady Folly (9:18).

21:17 He who loves pleasure (becomes) a needy man;
the lover of wine and oil will not grow rich.

pleasure [*śimḥah*]: *Śimḥah* "happiness," "pleasure" here refers to the means of sensual pleasures, namely, feasting and being anointed with fragrant oils. Spending too much money on sybaritic pleasures causes a financial burden.

śimḥāh: Jerome correctly translates this as *epulas* "feasting." A "day of *śimḥāh*" is a feast day (Num 10:10); compare *yôm mišteh wᵉśimḥāh* "a day of feasting and *śimḥāh*" in Esth 9:18. Two rabbinic dicta define the basics of ritual *śimḥāh* bluntly: *ʾyn śmḥh ʾlʾ bbśr*—"*śimḥāh* required meat"—(when the Temple was standing) and *ʾyn śmḥh ʾlʾ byyn*—"*śimḥāh* requires wine"—(in the present age) (*b. Pes.* 109a). In the Bible too *śimḥāh* has a distinct behavioral aspect, which includes eating, drinking, and anointing with oil (G. Anderson 1991: 19–26, 46–47).

21:18 The wicked man is ransom for the righteous one,
and the treacherous man is substituted for the upright.

When God sends a punishment against a community, all are in danger, even the righteous (Ezek 21:8–9). However, this proverb says, the righteous man will escape trouble (see Prov 11:8) because God takes the wicked as his substitute—his ransom, as it were.

A "ransom" (*koper*) is a compensatory payment to buy someone out of trouble; see 6:35. In the present verse, the endangered person is innocent. An example of a *koper* releasing from collective danger an individual who does not personally bear guilt is the "poll tax" levied during a census. Taking a census was thought to endanger the community, though individuals bore no guilt (Exod 30:12, 15–16; Num 31:50). A "ransom" extricated a person from that danger. Likewise, when it is said that God gives Cyrus other nations as a "ransom" for Israel's redemption, this does not imply any guilt on Israel's part (Isa 43:3). The logic of ransom should not be pressed further, as if the wicked are suffering vicariously for the righteous. After all, the wicked must be punished for their own deeds. The ransom metaphor is a vivid way of contrasting their fates, and it may also suggest that the wicked will suffer doubly.

21:19 Better to dwell in a desert land
than with a contentious and angry woman.

This proverb goes further than its variant in 21:9 (= 25:24) because it is even worse to dwell in the desert than on a roof (Saʿadia). The couplet follows a two-part "better than" formula: Better A (something bad) than A′ (something worse). In full, the reasoning is, "Better to dwell in a desert land (without a contentious woman) than (in a decent house) with a contentious woman." The deep structure of such proverbs is discussed in the excursus after 15:17.

mēʾēšet midyānîm wākāʿas: The MT vocalization of *wākāʿas* joins this word closely to *midyānîm*, indicating that the Masoretes understood this phrase as a construct with two genitives defining the woman; lit., "a woman of contention and anger." Compare *miṭṭōt zāhāb wākesep* "couches of gold and silver" in Esth 1:6.

21:20 A delightful treasure dwells[a] in the habitation of the wise,
but a stupid man swallows it up.

---

[a] *yiškôn* (MT *wāšemen*).

This continues the theme of dwelling (*škn*) from v 19. As soon as wealth comes his way, the fool consumes it (Ramaq), just like the pleasure-lover in 21:17. "Swallow up" means to waste by bad management (Saʿadia). It is also possible that the object of "swallows it up" is the wise man's treasure, which goes to waste "if his son is a fool" (thus Riyqam).

treasure [*ʾôṣar*]: This refers to both a storeroom and its contents. These may be anything of value, such as wine and oil, as well as precious items.

The MT reads, "A delightful treasure and oil is in the house of the wise." This is comprehensible, but it is also awkward, listing "oil" alongside "treasure" as if they were equal and commensurate goods.

yiškôn, for MT *wšmn* "and oil." Using the similar looking *yškn* (thus LXX, see the Textual Note), we can translate as above. This provides a tighter antithesis: The delightful treasure is not merely "in" the righteous man's house (thus the MT), it *dwells* there—permanently—whereas in the house of the fool it is quickly consumed. This emendation also provides a sg. antecedent for the suffix of *yᵉballᵉʿennû*.

swallows it up: That is, "he swallows his up," referring to whatever of value is found in a fool's house.

21:21 He who pursues righteousness and kindness
will find life[a] and honor.

---

[a] Omit *ṣᵉdāqāh* "righteousness."

The pursuit of ethical virtues, which benefit others, will reward the pursuer as well. The person praised here does not merely do these things, he actively *pursues* them, for they (and not only their rewards) are what he desires (Prov 11:23a).

Most modern commentators omit the second *ṣᵉdaqah* as a dittography from the A-line. It is absent in the LXX and properly belongs only in the A-line among the virtues, not in the B-line among the rewards. To be sure, as Hame'iri, Naḥmias, and Ehrlich observe, *ṣᵉdaqah* can be a reward, as in Ps 24:5. Ehrlich says that it can mean "Wohlstand, eigentlich die Festigkeit" (" 'prosperity,' properly 'stability' "). But there is no indication of the abrupt shift in meaning in this verse.

**21:22 A wise man went up against the city of warriors
and brought down its strong fortifications.**

Related as an event in the past, this is an illustration of what a wise man can do. Such a man might be a king, but he may also be an advisor or general, for Proverbs is insistent on the power of counsel and strategy (11:14; 20:18; 24:5–6). Wisdom includes practical shrewdness, and it is primarily this that would subdue military might. But by calling the possessor of these practical powers *ḥakam* "wise," the proverb subtly promises the powers to men who gain wisdom in the ethical, religious, and interpersonal domains.

Qohelet too insists that "wisdom is better than might" (9:16a) and "wisdom is better than weapons" (9:18a), though he immediately complains of its vulnerability (9:16b, 18b). He offers an anecdote about a wise man who saved his besieged city (9:13–18), but as is his wont, Qohelet gives the anecdote an unhappy twist: The wise man was forgotten. A story in the David narrative tells of a woman using wisdom to avert the conquest of her city (2 Sam 20:15–22).

In conjunction with the next verse, Prov 21:22 can be applied to the wisdom that conquers and controls one's desires and passions, for "Better the patient man than the mighty one, and he who controls his temper than he who captures a city" (16:32).

**21:23 He who guards his mouth and his tongue
guards himself from troubles.**

One must guard his speech (Prov 10:19; 13:3) and, equivalently, his heart (4:23). This does not mean being secretive, but rather being circumspect and avoiding prolix and impetuous speech, which can be silly, offensive, and provocative. Some foreign parallels are quoted in the Comment on 4:23. The mouth and the tongue are both mentioned to remind us that there is much to be guarded and much diligence is required.

This proverb is alliterative and even rhymes: ***šomer** piw ulᵉšono, **šomer** miṣṣarot napšo*. Together with the alliteration, the couplet's coordinated structure, with *šomer* in the initial position in each line, intimates the close connection of the virtue and its reward. See McCreesh 1991: 104–105.

21:24 The arrogant, insolent man—*leṣ is his name;*
he acts in the rage of arrogance.

This couplet defines the *leṣ* (on whom see Vol. I, 42), so the word is left untranslated. Elsewhere it is translated "impudent man" or "mocker." The primary attribute of the *leṣ* is arrogance. This makes him contemptuous of others and resistant to teaching (9:7–8; 13:1; 15:12) and consequently prone to violence and irrationality. One who "guards his mouth and his tongue" (v 23) avoids such behavior.

While this verse provides a lexical definition of *leṣ*, it is primarily a brief portrayal of a character type, such as we have with other bad types in Prov 2:12–16; 6:12–15 and 16:27–30. Like those passages, the purpose of 21:24 is to identify a type of person one should avoid and an attitude one should beware of in oneself.

the rage of arrogance [*ʿebrat zadon*]: This is a rage induced by arrogance. The one certain meaning of *ʿebrah* (34 occurrences) is "anger" or "outburst of anger." However, some find the mention of anger out of place here. Toy says that *ʿebrah* can also refer to an outburst of pride, and Delitzsch glosses it "superfluity" here (also in 11:23), but the evidence for these usages is slight. The word is paired with two words for pride in Isa 16:6, but it is not clear whether *ʿebrah* is synonymous or represents a different demeanor. Still, "rage" makes sense here, for *ʿebrah* refers to a new aspect of the description of the *leṣ*: his nasty temper. The bloated and hypersensitive ego of the arrogant man gives him a hair-trigger temper. Seeing affronts everywhere, he easily explodes in rage.

21:25 The sluggard's desires kill him,
because his hands refuse to work.

The sluggard may starve to death because he refuses to work for his necessities (13:4; 20:4; 24:34, etc.). "Desire" here is equivalent to unsatisfied hunger, which is what kills him.

21:26 He feels desire constantly,
but the righteous man gives without stinting.

The sluggard has incessant appetites because, paradoxically, he won't work even to meet his needs. The righteous are unstintingly generous.

The only available subject for "feels desire" (*hitʾawweh*) is the sluggard in v 25. Verse 26a is a reasonable continuation of v 25: The lazy man's desires gnaw at him constantly. Verse 26b, however, speaks about something quite different—the generosity of the righteous. Ramaq tries to connect the two verses by explaining that the righteous man will give charity to the starving sluggard, but such solicitude toward the unworthy poor is unparalleled and unlikely. Some supply an indefinite subject in the first line: "one" (Murphy) or "some" (Clifford), but this is ad hoc and does not make good sense, because the statement is true of a specific type of person, not generally. Toy surmises that the A-line may be a corruption of v 25 or a gloss on it, with the B-line added later, an explanation that fails to account for *why* it was added later. Ehrlich believes that "desire" is a metonymy for the pleasure-seeker, but "desire" as an abstract-for-concrete metonymy would mean "desirer"; and the resulting sentence, "The desirer desires constantly," would not make much sense, since everyone is, legitimately, a desirer to some degree; see Prov 11:23a.

This verse is a disjointed proverb (on which see the Introduction to Vol. II [II.E]). Two presuppositions of the book of Proverbs are necessary to bridge the two lines. First, laziness is considered a moral failing; see the Comment on 10:4. Indeed, hunger is a consequence of wickedness (13:25b) as well as laziness. Second, the virtues of the righteous man will keep him financially secure; see, for example, 10:3; 13:25; 15:25; and esp. 10:24b, "The (Lord) will grant what the righteous desire" (using *ta'awah*, as in 21:26a). We can then supplement each line in the present verse from its parallel: The (morally defective) sluggard feels constant desire (i.e., hunger), (and is consequently stingy with what he has), whereas the righteous man (whose virtues keep him solvent; 10:3) has the wherewithal to give to the needy without stinting. Laziness, with its consequent deprivation, further constrains moral behavior, whereas ethical virtue, with its consequent prosperity, facilitates it.

21:27 The sacrifice of the wicked is loathsome.
All the more so when he offers it with some scheme in mind.

God despises sacrifices brought by the wicked (unless, Delitzsch points out, they do so in true repentance. But then they are no longer really wicked). See the Comment on 15:8. It is bad enough if they bring a sacrifice merely in a display of formal piety. It is far worse if they offer it with an ulterior motive, such as buying God's support in a selfish plan. Prov 21:27a ≈ 15:8a.

is loathsome: That is, to God, as in 15:8.

with some scheme in mind [*b^{e}zimmah*]: Lit., "in a scheme." *Zimmah* usually means "misdeed," particularly in sexual matters, but it sometimes means "scheme" or "design," usually bad; see the Comment on 10:23. Here it implies something like an ulterior motive. Or it may mean that the wicked hope to appease God even while intending to sin again (Riyqam).

21:28 The deceitful witness will perish,
but the man who listens will speak victoriously.

The first line expresses a familiar idea (19:5, 9b), but the second line is surprising and not obviously connected to the first, for it is not immediately apparent in what way listening carefully is the opposite of testifying falsely. In fact, however, the first line creates a context for the second: In litigation, he who listens carefully and patiently to a perjurer's testimony will, when he finally speaks up, win his case. The ability to truly hear what is said is held in esteem (20:12), as is the wisdom to listen before speaking (18:13). By this reading, this verse is closely aligned to the next as well.

the man who listens [*ʾîš šomeaʿ*]: The form of the phrase shows that listening is the man's personality trait. He is a person who habitually listens. Someone who merely happened to hear the deceitful witness would be called *haššomeaʿ* "the listener" or "one who hears" (Ehrlich).

victoriously [*laneṣaḥ*]: Lit., "to victory." The word *neṣaḥ* usually means "forever," but it would be neither a virtue nor a reward to speak "forever." (*Neṣaḥ* does not mean "continuously," "without interruption.") In Sir 43:5, 13, the verb *nṣḥ* (probably D-stem) means "to give victory." In Rabbinic Hebrew it means "conquer," "prevail" (in the G- and D-stems). (A related usage may be attested in Lam 3:18 and Job 23:7, but these are ambiguous.) Several ancient translators (Aquila, Theodotion, Symmachus, Vulgate) translate *laneṣaḥ* as "victoriously."

Some other interpretations: Delitzsch thinks that the verse contrasts a man who falsifies testimony with one who listens carefully before testifying so as to avoid false reporting. The latter will speak "continually," meaning either that he will not be silenced in court or that his speech has enduring validity. Driver (1932a: 144–45) argues that *ʾîš šomeaʿ* is the witness and *laneṣaḥ* means "rightly," "truthfully": "The truthful/successful witness shall speak (on)," without being silenced. Emerton (1988: 165–69) vocalizes *yadbîr* and translates, "and he who listens will subdue (or, destroy) (him) completely." That is, he will detect the inconsistencies and weaknesses in the perjurer's claims. (Emerton has a critical survey of a variety of interpretations and emendations.) All these proposals are strained and explain the words in unnatural ways.

21:29 The wicked man puts on a bold face,
but the upright understands where he is going.

The wicked man puts on a bold front to conceal his lie. He literally fixes his facial expression to avoid betraying his deceit. But the honest man can perceive the deception and expose it (see Garrett 1990). This situation resembles the scene in v 28, in which one man prevaricates while the wise man listens and realizes what is happening. Although v 29 has general applicability, in conjunction with v 28 it alludes to a legal conflict.

understands: Reading with the qeré *yābîn*. The ketiv is *ykyn* "prepares," "secures." To say that "the upright man makes his way secure" does not complement the first line well. On *ykyn/ybyn* confusions see the Comment on 14:8.

where he is going [*darko*, qeré]: Lit., "his way." The honest man understands the *evildoer's* way; he knows where he is heading (Riyqam; Garrett 1990). It would also be meaningful to say that the honest man understands or considers his *own* way (as in Prov 14:8), but the first interpretation gives the couplet greater cohesiveness.

21:30 There is no wisdom or understanding
or counsel before the Lord.

Human wisdom counts for naught in God's eyes. Because of this, strategies and armaments will be ineffectual unless God provides victory.

before the Lord [*l^e neged*]: This verse is universally understood among modern scholars to refer to wisdom *hostile* to God (thus too earlier in this commentary, in Vol. I, 34). It is assumed that *l^e neged* means "against," and the verse is translated, "No wisdom, no understanding, no counsel, can avail against the LORD" (NRSV) or the like. By this understanding, the proverb declares the obvious—that no wisdom can defeat Yahweh's will, or, more subtly, that "wisdom consists in the knowledge that there is no 'wisdom' contrary to Yahweh" (Steiert 1990: 169).

L^e neged actually means "before" (spatially) or "opposite." When the context implies hostility (e.g., Dan 10:13), the hostile party is physically "before" the threatened person. *L^e neged* can mean "before" mentally, as in Hab 1:3: "Violence and lawlessness are before me" (cf. Pss 39:2; 50:8; 90:8, etc.). The phrase in the present verse is thus equivalent to "in your sight."

The comments of some medieval commentators assume that *l^e neged* means "before." Sa'adia understood the verse to mean, among other things, that "the Lord does not give wise men and astute men or counselors any special status (*'erek*) in judgment," that is, when they are standing before him in judgment. And also that "the strategy of wise men and astute men and counselors will not be effective before him." Riyqam fuses vv 30 and 31 thus: "Neither wisdom . . . nor the horse . . . can save their owner unless this is the Lord's will." In other words, this wisdom might *not* be contrary to God's will. Of the moderns, Waltke (*2005*: 165) translates *l^e neged* as "before," but he believes that the verb "can stand" is elided; hence the wisdom in question is hostile to God. But in most contexts, *l^e neged* has no such connotation.

When *l^e neged* is understood as "before," the verse still declares the uselessness of any "wisdom" that is hostile to Yahweh and his plans, like Edom and Babylon's, condemned by the prophets (Jer 49:7; Isa 47:10). But, beyond that, it also insists on the frailty of *all* human wisdom, even when moral values are not at issue, such as in the case of the strategy and planning that Proverbs finds worthwhile (11:14; 15:22; 20:18; 24:6; etc.). Just as from God's lofty perspective, humans are like grasshoppers in stature (Isa 40:22), so in his view human wisdom is of little consequence. This verse restates the principle of Prov 20:24: "A man's steps are from the Lord, and a human—how can he understand where he is going?" Still, true wisdom will lead to righteousness and piety, and God does treasure those virtues.

21:31 The horse is ready for the day of battle,
but victory belongs to the Lord.

The couplet shifts dramatically from the moment of tension and expectation before battle to its resolution. This too, as the previous verse teaches, depends not on preparations but on God's will. He alone decides the outcome of war and, by extension, of other enterprises, such as the crafts and commerce (Sa'adia). Neither wisdom (v 30) nor might (v 31) can attain its aims if these are contrary to God's designs. Nevertheless, one should not be passive but should take counsel and make preparations for war (Prov 20:18; 24:6); for, as Sa'adia says, "Sometimes God makes [horses] a cause of victory," that is, a proximate cause. God works his will through natural means and in this way helps those who help themselves; see the introduction to 16:1–9.

The idea that God's will prevails over human wisdom and might is a theme throughout the Bible (e.g., in Isa 8:9–10; 30:15–16; and esp. Isa 31:1–3). In particular, the vulnerability of warhorses (on whose power see Job 39:19–25) is a topos used in other forms. In Isa 31:1–3, Isaiah condemns the Judean officials for buying horses and trusting in them. They think their plan wise, but, Isaiah says, "(God) too is wise [that is, clever] and will bring misfortune" (v 2). A psalmist says, "The king is not given victory by a greatness of might, or a warrior saved by great strength. The horse is useless for victory, nor will it give deliverance by the greatness of its might" (Ps 33:16–17).

22:1 A name is preferable to great wealth,
and good favor to silver and gold.

Both "a name" and "good favor" refer to how one is regarded by others. What makes this kind of regard important is that it is gained through wisdom (Prov 3:4; 13:15a) and is not merely prestige, but true honor. The LXX reads "good name," but goodness is implied in the MT by the parallel line.

The value of a name is declared in Qoh 7:1a, "A name is better than good oil," and Prov 10:7a, "The memory of the righteous is for a blessing, while the name of evildoers will rot." ("Memory" is equivalent to "name"). A good repute (even in poverty) is better than (its absence) even with wealth. On the way that "better than" proverbs imply the premises in parentheses, see the excursus after 15:17. The lower value assigned to wealth in 22:1 leads into the next proverb, which places rich and poor on the same level.

22:2 The rich man and the poor man meet:
the Lord is maker of both.

When rich and poor come together, their differences are accentuated. The sages did not blur these differences (see, e.g., Prov 10:15; 14:20; 18:23; 22:7) and had no expectation that they would, or should, be neutralized. But when rich and poor come into contact they must keep in mind that as *creatures* they are equal, and God cares for them both. Given their unequal social status, however, it is primarily the rich man who must be careful to respect the divine handiwork in the other. The proverb warns the rich not to anger God by offending his creation. Similar teachings are in 14:31 and 17:5a.

Proverbs about the creation of humans aim to defuse social tensions and conflicts (Doll 1985: 29). Like Prov 14:31 and Amenemope §25 (quoted in the Comment on that verse), Prov 22:2 assumes that inequality, social and economic, is a fact of life and in conformity with God's will. Deuteronomy expresses the same attitude: "For the poor will never cease from the land. Therefore I command you: 'You shall open wide your hand to your needy and poor brother in the land' " (Deut 15:11). Prov 22:2 ≈ 29:13; see the Comment there.

meet [*nipgašu*]: In what sense do the rich and the poor "meet"? There is a wide array of possibilities:

(1) The rich man and poor man may meet in an incidental encounter on the street, despite their different spheres of life.

(2) The meeting might occur when the poor man approaches the rich man for help (Rashi; Perdue 1994: 112).

(3) They might meet in the sense of *clashing*, since they are contraries and come from opposite directions.

(4) This clash might be specifically a legal adjudication in the city gate (Doll 1985: 19).

(5) To opposite effect, they may meet or come together in concord, like the "meeting" of personified Loyalty and Kindness in Ps 85:11. In that case, the doublet in Prov 29:13 envisions a reconciliation between the weak and the powerful.

(6) Their *stations* in life could "meet" in the sense of becoming equal, when a rich man grows poor or a poor one rises in station, as may happen, because God "makes poor and makes rich" (1 Sam 2:7a; see Ralbag; Malbim; Tur-Sinai p. 30). In this case, the proverb observes something that happens only rarely.

(7) Rich and poor are found side-by-side in every community (McKane).

(8) The meeting may be life itself, which God has bestowed on all (Murphy). In other words, "meet" may be a way of saying that both are alive.

It is hard to decide among these alternatives, and they are not all mutually exclusive. The meanings ascribed to "meet" in vv 5, 7, and 8 seem too broad for the verb in question. All sorts are in the community and in this "common life," as Murphy explains it, but what is special about the conjunction of the rich and poor? Most likely, the meeting is their occasional contact in everyday life (1), which might also be a moment of conflict or oppression (3, 4); see Prov 29:13. When this happens, the rich and poor—and possibly their judges—must keep in mind that God is watching over them. He cares about all his creations, and, from his lofty perspective, the difference between them is insignificant. The emphasis, however, is on his care for the poor, who need it more. (However, in 29:13, when the oppressor and poor man meet, God is presumably less solicitous of the former.)

Readers have drawn various lessons from this proverb. The rich man should remember that he too might have been created poor and must treat the poor man charitably, while the poor man will accept his station and rest assured that God will help him (Riyqam). Rich and poor will remember that they are both necessary for the survival of the community (Ralbag). The meeting should be a "school of virtue," whereby the rich will learn to avoid pride and the poor to refrain from envy (Delitzsch). The rich will realize that all humans are equally God's creatures and not tools for exploitation (Whybray 1990: 42). In the context of Proverbs' social ethics, the proverb is implicitly teaching concern for the poor and denunciation of economic oppression (L. Boström 1990: 67). The proverb invites and legitimates such extrapolations.

22:3 The shrewd man sees trouble and hides,
while the callow pass and are punished.

It is foolish to stick one's nose into others' quarrels.

trouble [*raʿah*]: Or "evil." This refers to something bad going on, namely, a conflict, rather than a moral evil or crime. A callow person would not be punished for standing up to evil, but rather for getting embroiled in brawls. Prov 22:3 ≈ 27:12.

pass: That is, they come toward the commotion instead of skirting it. Hebrew *ʿabar* usually means "pass by" or "pass through," but it sometimes means to move up to a point without moving beyond it (e.g., Jer 2:10; Amos 6:2; Ps 48:5).

and hides: The qeré is *wᵉnistār*. The ketiv *wystr*, that is, *wayyissātēr*, is a narrative past tense and would call for translating the proverb as a narrative; see the Comment on 11:2.

are punished [*wᵉneʿenašu*]: The original meaning of *ʿnš* is "to impose a fine" (e.g., Exod 21:22; Deut 22:19; Amos 2:8), but its scope broadens to include other punishments, as in Prov 17:26 (a beating) and 19:19; 21:11; 22:3; Sir 9:5 (which speak of situations in which fines would not apply). In Rabbinic Hebrew, *ʿanaš* often means "punish." Punishment is always executed by a third party with legitimate punitive powers. Hence in the present verse, someone outside the dispute, undoubtedly a governmental authority, is imposing a penalty. On the nature of this penalty, see below.

Advice to avoid others' quarrels appears in a number of Wisdom texts. These often warn about the judicial consequences of embroilment. Anii admonishes his son:

(21.16) Do not enter into a crowd
when you find it gathered (17) in front of a fight.[301]
Do not pass in its vicinity,
so that you may stay safe from their wounds
(18) and not be taken to court before the magistrates,
when testimony is taken. (cf. AEL 2.142)

It is dangerous to approach a brawl because one may become embroiled in it, and also because a bystander may be forced to give testimony in legal proceedings, and such testimony, in Egyptian practice, might well be extracted by beatings.

The Babylonian "Counsels of Wisdom" admonishes:

Don't go stand where there's a crowd,[302]
Do not linger where there is a dispute.
They will bring evil upon you in the dispute,
Then you will be made their witness,
They will bring you to bolster a case not your own.
When confronted with a dispute, avoid it, pay no heed.
If it is a dispute with you, put out the flame,

[301] MSS D and G speak explicitly of a fistfight: *ʿḥʾ m* [= *n*] *qnqn*, lit., "a fight of beating."

[302] Lambert (BWL 101) translates, "(31) Do not frequent a law court, (32) Do not loiter where there is a dispute."

A dispute is a wide-open ambush,
a wall of sticks that smothers its opponents. (ll. 31–39; trans. BTM 328)

Here too the danger to the spectator lies in becoming entangled in legal proceedings and being forced to testify. This passage is so close to Anii that both seem to be using an international wisdom topos.

The Arabic Ahiqar is preserving ancient wisdom when it warns,

> O my son! let not a word issue from thy mouth till thou hast taken counsel with thy heart. And stand not betwixt persons quarreling, because from a bad word there comes a quarrel, and from a quarrel there comes war, and from war there comes fighting, and thou wilt be forced to bear witness; but run from thence and rest thyself. (trans. Coneybeare 1913: 137, §54)

In view of this widespread worry about finding oneself compelled to testify in court, we should understand "are punished" (*neʿĕnašu*) in Prov 22:3 as alluding specifically to unpleasantness arising from judicial investigation or trial rather than construing it more vaguely as referring to any sort of harm.

Several other Wisdom texts admonish the reader to shun a fray. "A Man to His Son" warns, "Do not separate two men in their quarrel, for their dispute will turn against him who would adjudicate it" (XVIII.2–3). Anchsheshonq says, "When two brothers quarrel, do not come between them. He who comes between two brothers when they quarrel will be placed between them when they are reconciled" (19.11–12; trans. AEL 3.174). Similar warnings are given in the Syriac Ahiqar (S_2 §55); Sir 11:9; and more. See Lichtheim 1983: 13–18 and the Comment on 26:17. On the paronomasia and alliteration in this verse, see the Comment on 27:12.

22:4 The reward of humility is fear of the Lord,
wealth and honor and life.

Humility is closely bound up with fear of God. "Humility means subjugating oneself to the Lord, so that the believer does what he is commanded, and fear means trepidation, whereby one avoids what he is warned against" (Saʿadia). These attitudes are Wisdom's gifts (Prov 8:18, 35). Fear of the Lord is the first reward of humility.

wealth and honor and life: Fear of God brings further rewards. These rewards sum up the benefits promised the wise throughout the book, and they are the gifts that Lady Wisdom offers her disciples in 8:18 and 35; see the Comments there.

22:5 Thorns and snares are in the path of the crooked man.
He who guards his life will keep far from them.

The life-path of the dishonest is short and miserable; see Vol. I, 128–31. Saʿadia draws a distinction between the two dangers on this path: "Thorns hurt one temporarily, whereas snares kill." These punishments contrast with the life promised to the God-fearing and humble in the preceding verse.

Thorns and snares [*ṣinnim, paḥim*]: The first word may mean "hooks." Prov 15:19 speaks of thorns as impediments on the lazy man's path, using a different word (*ḥedeq*). The literal translation of this phrase is "thorns, snares." This may have a more abrupt sound than "thorns and snares," though the latter is required in translation.

path of the crooked man [*bᵉderek ʿiqqeš*]: This warns both against *being* a crooked man and *following* his path to temptation. The phrase can also be translated "a crooked path," that is, a difficult and dangerous path, which in Proverbs is inevitably the immoral one.

22:6 Train a youth according to his way,
and even when he grows old he will not depart from it.

A child educated to go in the right path will stick to it throughout life. "His way" (*darko*) must refer to the *right* way, the way he ought to go in (McKane; thus *b. Qid* 30a), for that is the only one from which he must never depart. This is *his* way in the sense that it is truly his, the way proper to him, if he is morally educable and educated. Job uses *derek* "way" similarly: "If my steps went aside from the way and my heart followed my eyes . . ." (31:7). Job is asserting that he never strayed from *his* path and entered an evil way.

his way: "Way" is used similarly in Prov 23:19: "Listen, my son, and become wise, and go straight in the way of your heart." The "way of your heart" is the right way only if one has gained wisdom; see the Comment there.

Other identifications include the following:

(1) The child's personal aptitude. He should be taught according to his age and ability (Saʿadia). But what would it mean to stick to these factors when he grows old? And if he is not educated "according to his way," will he then abandon this way when he grows old?

(2) The nature of youth as such, the way the young behave (Delitzsch). But there would be no virtue in not departing from youthful behavior, especially since it tends to be foolish (Prov 22:15).

(3) One's social position, namely, that of a squire, who should be trained according to his future role. (Delitzsch; Hildebrandt 1988a). But *derek* does not mean status and "squire" is an anachronistic translation of *naʿar*.

(4) Whatever the boy wishes. Then the verse is facetious (Ralbag; Shadal). Clifford paraphrases: "Let a boy do what he wants and he'll grow up to be a self-willed adult incapable of change!" But this is not the meaning of "his way" elsewhere.

train [*ḥănōk*]: Elsewhere, this rare verb means "dedicate," "initiate the use of" (Deut 20:5 [2x]; 1 Kgs 8:63 = 2 Chr 7:5). The noun *ḥănukkāh* means "dedication" or "dedicatory celebration" (Num 7:10, 11, etc.). In Prov 22:6, *ḥnk* must mean "train," a sense the D-stem has in RH and that is related to the notion of initiating someone into a position. Abraham's *ḥănîkîm* (Gen 14:14) are usually understood to be "trained men," hence "retainers." These are called *nᵉʿārîm* in Gen 14:24.

youth: In reference to age, *naʿar* can designate anyone from birth (e.g., 1 Sam 4:21) to early maturity (e.g., Gen 37:2; 41:12). MacDonald (*1976*), supported by Hildebrandt (1988a: 10–14), says that *naʿar* designates status, not age. But it clearly refers to a child or adolescent elsewhere in Proverbs, for it is the young who are in their father's tutelage and subject to corporal punishment (22:15; 23:13). "Youth" is the appropriate translation here because childhood is the time for moral training, and it is distinguished from the time "when he grows old."

22:7 The rich man rules over the poor,
and the borrower is slave to the lender.

One should keep out of debt, for as surely as the rich subjugate the poor, so does the lender soon subjugate the borrower. The subjugation may be economic (because of the burden of the debt) or legal (if the debtor defaults and is forced into debt slavery).

The proverb does not assert that the rich *should* rule over the poor, nor does it censure this relationship. It assumes this dominance as a social fact and uses it as a point of comparison. The borrower becomes a "slave" insofar as he is subjecting himself to the lender's goodwill, whims, and control. He may even end up as his actual slave, if forced to sell himself into debt slavery.

The proverb hisses with sibilants (/š/) and flows with liquids (/l/, /r/) and bilabials (/b/, /w/, /m/): *ʿaŠIR **b**^{e}raŠIM yimŠOL, **w**^{e}ʿEbed loWEH l^{e}ʾIŠ **m**alWEH*. For more aural features of this proverbs, see McCreesh *1991*: 66.

22:8 He who sows wickedness will harvest evil,
and the rod of his wrath will fail.

evil [*ʾawen*]: Usually *ʾawen* means iniquitous behavior, but here, as in Prov 12:21, it refers to the consequences of evil, that is, misfortune.

the rod of his wrath: Or "his rod of wrath." His oppression of others will cease to be effective, "whether because of natural death, or because of punitive death at God's hands, or because of the incapacity that overtakes him" (Saʿadia).

In the light of the figure in the A-line, the metaphor in the B-line may have a more specific vehicle. The "rod" in the context of harvesting is the flail used in threshing grain (Clifford). The evil that the wicked man sows will sprout into poisonous grain, and the flail, namely, his wrath, will prove useless in neutralizing the danger he faces. The topos of one reaping the evil he sows is used also in Hos 10:13 and Job 4:8, and its reverse appears in Prov 11:18.

The LXX inserts here: "God will bless a cheerful and gift-giving man, and he will make an end to the vanities of his works." This is a variant of the next verse. See the Textual Note.

22:9 As for the generous man, he will be blessed,
because he has given of his bread to the lowly.

generous man: Lit., "good of eye." His opposite is "bad of eye," the stingy and greedy man (23:6; 28:22). The generous man will be blessed—in deed by God and in word by the poor (Saʿadia, Murphy). He stands in contrast to the man mentioned in 22:7: That one lends money at interest; this one bestows it freely (Malbim).

The LXX inserts a new proverb: "He who gives gifts secures victory and honor. But he takes away the soul of the possessors."

22:10 Banish the impudent and conflict will depart,
and disputes and insult will cease.

The impudent scoffer provokes quarrels; similarly Prov 11:2; 18:3; 30:33.

disputes [*din*]: The word *din* consistently belongs to the legal sphere and means "litigation" or "judgment." Here too it probably refers to legal disputes (thus Ramaq; Naḥmias; and Mezudat David) rather than ordinary squabbling.

22:11 He who loves purity[a] of heart,
whose speech is gracious—
the king is his companion.

[a] *ṭōhar* (MT qeré *ṭᵉhor* [*ṭhr*]; ketiv *ṭhwr*).

The king wants honest, gracious men for his intimates; thus too Prov 16:13. The present saying recalls 22:29, which commends a certain behavior by promising proximity to the king as its reward. Both proverbs are directed to men who frequent the royal court and desire advancement. The royal ideal holds that the king will tolerate only honesty and purity in his presence (Ps 101) and that only "he who goes in the way of the innocent" will be allowed to serve him (Ps 101:6b). See the introduction to Prov 16:10–15.

the king is his companion [*reʿehu melek*]: He will "stand before kings" (22:29). "Companion of the king" is the title of a member of the royal entourage in 1 Kgs 4:5. Perhaps the original reading in this proverb was *rʿh hmlk* (LXX, Syriac) "the king's companion." The relationship is basically the same by either reading.

loves: The LXX adds "the Lord" and translates, "The Lord loves him who is pure of heart." Bühlmann (1976: 59–61) supplies "Yahweh" but translates: "Ein Freund Jahwehs, wer reinen Herzens ist." ("A friend of Yahweh is whosoever is pure of heart"). But the addition overloads the line and is unnecessary.

He who loves purity of heart [*ʾohēb ṭōhar lēb*]: The MT (with *ṭᵉhor*, qeré) reads, "a friend pure of heart . . . his friend is the king." (The ketiv is a plene spelling of the qeré.) But it is awkward to say "a friend . . . is a companion of the king," because there would be no reference point for the first "friend" in the first line (a friend of whom?). Delitzsch parses *ṭᵉhor-* (the qeré) as a construct form of *ṭōhar* "purity" or a "neutral" form of *ṭāhôr*, as if "one who is pure" can mean "purity" (sim. Murphy). There is no evidence for either supposition, but the sense suggested fits the text well. But vocalizing the qeré *ṭhr* as *ṭōhar* (penultimate stress) is less of a conjecture.

whose speech is gracious [*ḥēn śᵉpātāyw*]: Lit., "his lips are grace." This translation construes the phrase as an asyndetic relative clause (sim. Delitzsch; for the phenomenon see GBH §158b). Alternatively, as implied by the accents, the phrase can belong to the predicate: "One who loves purity of heart—gracious are his lips, etc." (cf. Murphy).

G. R. Driver (1951: 186–87) moves *melek* "king" to the start of the verse, hence (in Clifford's translation): "The king is a friend to the pure hearted; one gracious of lips is his companion." This radical emendation is unnecessary if we revocalize *ṭhr* as *ṭōhār*, as suggested above.

22:12 The eyes of the Lord guard knowledge,
while he confounds the words of the treacherous.

God guarantees that wise, virtuous words will prove valid and effective, but he confounds the claims and schemes of the treacherous. God acts as a catalyst in bringing to completion the moral potentials that the speakers themselves plant in their words (see Prov 13:2).

guard knowledge [*naṣᵉru daʿat*]: How do God's eyes "guard knowledge"? To say that a human's *lips* "guard" or "keep" knowledge means that they speak only wisdom (5:2; Mal 2:7), but this does not fit the present context. Ramaq and Hameʾiri understand "knowledge" here as equivalent to "a man [or "men"] of knowledge," that is, an abstract-for-concrete figure (sim. Clifford). But the parallel phrase, "words of the treacherous," indicates that *daʿat* is a metonymy for "*words* of knowledge," as in Prov 22:17c (see the Comment and Textual Note), rather than signifying knowledgeable people or knowledge in the abstract.

As the antithesis of subverting words, which means to undermine their efficacy, guarding words of knowledge means to protect them from failure—"to validate (one's) thoughts and plans" (Ralbag).

confounds [*wayyᵉsallep*] *the words*: God thwarts the claims and schemes of the treacherous. The treacherous are characterized by *selep* "corruption," "distortion" (11:3), and their words will suffer from *selep* in a different sense—"subversion," "undermining." In other words, their schemes fail, or if we take the *wayyiqtol* past-tense indication seriously, they have *already* failed. We might translate, "The eyes of the Lord guard knowledge, *for he has confounded* the words of the treacherous."

This use of *slp dᵉbarim* differs from the sense of the same phrase in Exod 23:8 and Deut 16:19, where a bribe is said to *slp* words, that is, to corrupt them, making them dishonest. But the uses are not unrelated; for whether a man makes his own words untrue by lying or God makes them *prove* untrue by nullifying their effectiveness, the validity of the utterance is being subverted.

22:13 The sluggard says, "There is a lion in the street,
among the plazas I will be murdered!"

The lazy man comes up with the silliest excuses to beg off work. Other droll descriptions of the lazy man in Proverbs are found in 19:24 and 26:13–15. This proverb is a near-doublet of 26:13, except that it has a more explicit pretext: "I will be murdered!" The verse is highly alliterative: ***ʾamar ʿaṣel ʾări baḥuṣ // bᵉtok rᵉḥobot ʾeraṣeaḥ***. The /b/, /r/, /ḥ/, and /ṣ/ sounds are emphasized by repetition. Note also the assonance in the /a/ vowels in the first line and /o/ and /e/ vowels in the second.

22:14 The mouth of strange women is a deep pit.
It is the man cursed by the Lord who falls into it.

Forbidden women (*zarot*, lit., "strangers" [fem.]) work their seduction above all by slippery speech; see the Comment on 2:16. The doublet in Prov 23:27 says that the woman herself is a pit.

A Strange Woman's mouth is a deadly pitfall. One whom God has cursed (or "is angry at") and wishes to kill will fall into it. This man has presumably already sinned. God's curse will make him sin further and then suffer the deadly consequences.

The notion that God may make a person sin as a consequence of prior offenses is not foreign to the Bible. Ezekiel quotes God as saying, "And when a righteous man turns away from his righteousness and does iniquity, I will place a stumbling block before him and he will die" (Ezek 3:20a). To place a stumbling block before someone here means to cause him to stumble into sin (Zimmerli 1979, ad loc.). When someone deserves punishment, God may make sure that he sins even more, so that his punishment becomes inevitable. Thus it was that God "hardened Pharaoh's heart" (Exod 4:21). Sometimes the prior offense is not mentioned, as when God says, "And the prophet who is misled and speaks a word—it is I the Lord who have misled that prophet. And I will stretch out my hand against him and extirpate him from the midst of my people Israel" (Ezek 14:9; cf. vv 4–5). In 2 Sam 24:1, God gets angry at Israel for unspecified reasons and *incites* David to take a census, a deed that brings down God's wrath on the people.

This sort of divine intrusion is not predeterminism. The principle motivating God's actions is retribution. It is as if God had to create the conditions that would fully justify a punishment on the scale he intends to send. In all cases the person who has aroused God's anger can choose not to sin.

strange women [*zarot*]: Not foreigners, but women other than a man's own wife; see Vol. I, 134–41. Elsewhere the singular *zarah* is used. (The doublet, Prov 23:27, has *zonah* "prostitute," but this is probably an error for *zarah*.) Mezudat David identifies the "foreign women" as heresy, and Malbim explains the phrase as alluding to "idolatrous wisdom and philosophy," continuing an allegorical exposition frequently applied to Prov 2:16–22; 5:1–23; 6:20–35; and esp. 7:1–27; see Vol. I, 254–55. Some understand it to mean "the mouth of strange things" (cf. 23:33)—foreign, improper or wicked speech (Hame'iri, Naḥmias) or insults (Sa'adia). But most commentators understand *zarot* as strange women.

In "The Dialogue of Pessimism," a Babylonian book of a cynical cast, a slave gives his master reasons for loving a woman, then supplies reasons to avoid it:

> "Servant, listen to me." "Yes, master, yes." "I will fall in love with a woman." "[So], fall in love, master, fall in love. The man who falls in love with a woman forgets sorrow and care."
>
> "No, servant, I will certainly not fall in love with a woman." "[Do not] fall in love, master, do not fall in love. A woman is a pitfall, a pitfall, a hole, a ditch, a woman is a sharp iron dagger that slashes a man's throat." (BWL 816).

The LXX adds: "There are evil ways before a man, and (yet) he does not like to turn away from them. But it is necessary to turn away from a crooked and evil way." This expands on v 14, understanding *zarot* as "strange things" = "evil ways."

22:15 Folly is bound to the heart of a child.
The rod of discipline will remove it from him.

The folly called *'iwwelet* is the worst sort: perverse and largely immune to reform (Prov 27:22). The present proverb, however, holds out the possibility of removing it, if discipline is applied early. Folly is "bound" to the child's heart in the sense that he is attracted to it, not in the sense that he is intractably foolish. His predilection for folly can be removed by beatings, not words (15:5). Various proverbs teach the value and efficacy of corporal punishment; see the references in the Comment on 13:24.

As translated here, the proverb implies that a child is born with bad inclinations (thus Gen 8:21; Hame'iri compares Ps 51:7a: "I was conceived in sin"). Hence the first task of education is to eliminate them. Left to his own inclinations, a child will go bad, as Prov 29:15 says: "The rod of rebuke gives wisdom, while a youth let loose [*m^{e}šullaḥ*] disgraces his mother."

Van Leeuwen reads this verse as an unmarked conditional: "If folly is bound to the heart of a child, the rod of discipline will remove it from him." Then its point is how to correct a fault in certain children. But it is not clear that the syntax justifies this restriction.

Ramaq connects this verse to the preceding: A man cursed by God will be trapped by a Strange Woman, but a child can still be purged of the tendency to sin.

22:16 There is one who oppresses a poor man yet he ends up giving him more.
There is one who gives to a rich man yet he ends up in need.

The literal translation is, "One who oppresses the lowly to increase for him [or "himself"]; one who gives to a rich man only to neediness" [or "indeed to neediness"]. This elliptical saying is susceptible to different interpretations, primarily because of the ambiguity about who receives the increase in the first line and who is brought to poverty in the second.

Who ends up in need? Clifford thinks it is the donor, who gives presents to the rich man to bribe him or curry favor, but whose tactics fail him and only leave him poorer. In that case, however, the relevant quality of the recipient would be power, not wealth, and the consequence of the gift's failure to have its intended effect would not necessarily be poverty. Rather, it is the rich recipient in the B-line who ends up in need, just as it is the poor man in the A-line who ends up rich. By this interpretation the lines are neatly antithetical and paradoxical. Oppression of the poor man would be expected to make him poorer, and gifts to the rich man would ordinarily enrich him, but sometimes the effect is the opposite. God's plans alone decide. Such paradoxes are discussed in the Comment on 11:24.

The following paraphrase eliminates the ambiguities: Sometimes a person oppresses a poor man yet *he*, the oppressor, ends up giving the poor man even more. And sometimes a person gives to a rich man yet he, the *rich man*, ends up poor.

The above translation follows Tur-Sinai (p. 15) in supplying "there is" and reading the couplet as two paradoxes, much like Prov 11:24: "There is [*yeš*] one who scatters yet gets more, and one who saves out of honesty yet ends up in need." Both 22:16 and 11:24 conclude with the phrase *ʾak lᵉmaḥsor*, lit., "only to neediness," as do 14:23 and 21:5.

oppresses [*ʿošeq*]: In the technical sense, *ʿšq* (used also in Prov 14:31; 28:3, 17) means to deny persons their legal due. *Gzl* "rob" (used in 4:16; 22:22; 28:24) means to take property away from the victim; see Westbrook 1988: 35–38.

The infinitive *lᵉharbôt* indicates result (cf. IBHS §36.2.3d), not purpose. The elliptical form of the sentence—"one who gives to the poor—to increase for him"—allows the predicate to be explained in various ways. To much the same effect one can read the couplet as two statements of likelihood (McKane). According to Jenni *1999*, the construction, nominal subject + *l*-inf., can indicate "epistemic modality"; see the Comment on 19:8. The existence of this construction is uncertain, but the basic sense of the verse is the same.

PART III: PROVERBS 22:17–24:22

◆

"WORDS OF THE WISE": THE THIRTY MAXIMS

Part III comprises two subcollections, IIIa (22:17–23:11) and IIIb (23:12–24:22). It begins with a title (22:17a) and an exordium (22:17bc–21), like the instructions in Part I (see Vol. I, 46), and proceeds with thirty maxims:

(1)	22:17–21	Listen to my wisdom! (Exordium)
(2)	22:22–23	Do not steal from the poor.
(3)	22:24–25	Avoid quarrelsome men.
(4)	22:26–27	Do not give surety.
(5)	22:28	Do not encroach on others' boundaries.
(6)	22:29	Be diligent in your work.
(7)	23:1–3	Control your appetite when dining with your superior.
(8)	23:4–5	Do not strain to get rich.
(9)	23:6–8	Do not dine with a stingy man.
(10)	23:9	Do not speak with a fool.
(11)	23:10–11	Do not encroach on orphans' fields.
(12)	23:12–14	Take discipline and give it.
(13)	23:15–16	Be wise and make your parents happy.
(14)	23:17–18	Do not envy sinners.
(15)	23:19–21	Avoid dissipation.
(16)	23:22–25	Gain wisdom and make your parents happy.
(17)	23:26–28	Avoid the temptress.
(18)	23:29–35	Avoid drunkenness.
(19)	24:1–2	Do not envy the wicked.
(20)	24:3–4	Wisdom is precious.
(21)	24:5–6	Wisdom is powerful.
(22)	24:7	The fool is inarticulate.
(23)	24:8–9	Scheming is loathsome.
(24)	24:10	Negligence means weakness.
(25)	24:11–12	Rescue those in mortal danger.
(26)	24:13–14	Savor wisdom's sweetness.
(27)	24:15–16	Do not rob the righteous.
(28)	24:17–18	Do not gloat.
(29)	24:19–20	Do not envy the wicked.
(30)	24:21–22	Fear God and the king.

The maxims together are comparable to the "Lessons" in Part I (see Vol. I, 45). Part IIIb begins with a call to attention in 23:12. But since similar exhortations appear also in 23:19, 22, and 26, which are too close together to mark new sections, they cannot be considered unequivocal boundary markers. The difference between IIIa and IIIb lies in their history, not their content: Most of the maxims in Part IIIa are adaptations of Amenemope, while those in IIIb have diverse origins, including one strong parallel to Ahiqar and a thematic parallel to Anii.

The entire unit has a high frequency of Aramaisms. This suggests the possibility that Part III drew on international sources by way of Aramaic, a hypothesis to be discussed below, in "Ahiqar and Proverbs," after the Comments on Part IIIb.

V. A. Hurowitz (*2001c*: 157) identifies the following Aramaisms in IIIa: *qōšṭ* (22:21), *te'ĕlap* (22:25), *milleykā* (23:9), and expressions like *ba'al 'āp* (22:24), *ba'al nepeš* (23:2), and *ba'al m^{e}zimmôt* (24:8). (On the idiom *ba'al*-X, see A. Hurvitz 1986.) To these we can add *śakkîn* "knife" (23:2). (V. Hurowitz also mentions some locutions that are less clearly Aramaisms—for example, *ḥzh* "see" used of ordinary vision. He also finds parallels to Akkadian usages, but these are less clear.)

Statistically, Part IIIa has a greater frequency of Aramaisms than any other Part besides VIc (Lemuel), which is ascribed to a foreign queen. This is true also for Part III as a whole. The frequencies of Aramaisms in the different parts of Proverbs are as follows:

Part	*Occurrences per verse (rounded to second decimal place)*	*Part*	*Occurrences per verse (rounded to second decimal place)*
I	.01	V	.06
II	.04	VIa	none
IIIa	.25	VIb	none
IIIb	.02	VIc	.44
III	.18	VId	.04
IV	none	book	.04

The identification of Aramaisms for this count is based on Wagner *1966*:17–121, with some additions and omissions that do not affect the overall proportions. The numbers are too small to allow for firm conclusions, but they add support to the possibility that Amenemope reached Israel in Aramaic form. This, I suggest below in "Amenemope and Proverbs"—"Translation and Transmission," would have been most likely to occur in the eighth–seventh centuries B.C.E.

The material based on Amenemope may have undergone various stages of transformation on its way to its present form in Proverbs. Nevertheless, it is fair to ascribe the basic form of Part III to an individual, an "author-editor," because the decision to organize Part III in thirty maxims could not have evolved in a lengthy process. The number implies awareness of a version of Amenemope that was still in thirty units, or that at least included the end of the book with its mention of "thirty chapters" (27.7). The voice of this author-editor is heard in 22:20, in the rhetorical question, "Have I not written for you thirty (maxims)?" (as emended; see the Comment on 22:20 and "Amenemope and Proverbs" below). The thirty maxims are numbered and given captions in the Commentary.

Since the question of Egyptian background comes to the fore in Part IIIa, I will quote extensively from Egyptian wisdom, and not only Amenemope, to illustrate this unit's treatment of the main themes. This is not to assert that the specific parallels were known to the Israelite sages, except in the case of Amenemope. In the translations below, **boldface** identifies the lines and phrases that are echoed in Proverbs, whether by verbal citation or thematic borrowing. I will usually quote the entirety of the chapters of Amenemope in order to show the original context of the parallel material.

My translations of Amenemope presume some minor and easily recognizable emendations, most of which were proposed already by Lange 1925 and Shirun-Grumach 1972. My translations and philological observations owe much to Lange, Shirun-Grumach, and Römheld 1989. These three works are here cited by name of author.

PART IIIA: PROVERBS 22:17–23:11

THE AMENEMOPE COLLECTION

Title

22:17a [a]Words of the wise.

Maxim 1: Exordium. Listen to my wisdom!

17bc Incline your ear and hear my words,[a]
and direct your heart to my knowledge;
18 for it will be pleasant if you keep them in your belly,
that they may all be secure on your lips.
19 In order that your trust may be in the Lord,
I have taught them to you, even you, today.
20 Have I not written for you thirty[b] (maxims)
in deliberation and knowledge?—
21 to teach you the truest of words,
to give answer[c] to those who send you.

[a–a] *dibrê ḥăkāmîm haṭ ʾozn^{e}kā ûš^{e}maʿ d^{e}bārāy* (MT *haṭ ʾozn^{e}kā ûš^{e}maʿ dibrê ḥăkāmîm*). [b] *š^{e}lōšîm* (MT ketiv *šlšwm*; qeré *šālîšîm*). [c] Omit *ʾĕmet*.

22:17–21. *Exordium*. Verses 17bc–21 form an exordium, with v 17bc as its exhortation and vv 18–21 as an extended motivation praising the teaching's excellence and value.

22:17. *Words of the wise*: The reconstructed title applies to the entirety of 22:17–24:22. The title is apt, because Part III draws on the teachings of a number of sages, at least indirectly, of which Amenemope, Anii, and Ahiqar can be identified. The MT of v 17a reads "Incline your ear and hear the words of the wise." This emendation is based on the LXX; see the Textual Note.

Several considerations support this emendation, first proposed by Gressmann 1924: 274. (1) It provides a title for the unit. (2) The title in 24:23, "These too are of the wise," indicates awareness of a previous ascription of proverbs to "the wise," which is otherwise missing. (3) Other exordia call for attention to the *speaker's* teachings, not the words of other sages, as the MT's formulation does. (4) The first-person possessive pronoun of *d^{e}bārāy* "my words" (instead of *dibrê* "words of") is parallel to "my knowledge." This emendation is accepted by Clifford, Murphy, Plöger, and many others. Even before the appearance of Amenemope alerted scholars to the beginning of a proverb collection here,

Toy (1899) proposed reading *haṭ ʾozn*^{e}*kā ûš*^{e}*maʿ d*^{e}*bārāy* and omitting *ḥăkāmîm* as a "gloss, a marginal title, perhaps originally *lḥkmm*."

my knowledge: That is, my words of knowledge, the wisdom that I impart.

22:18. *in your belly*: In his exordium (quoted in the Comment on 22:21), Amenemope teaches: "**Make (my words) rest in the casket of your belly**" (3.13). Elsewhere he teaches: "Better is the man whose speech remains in his belly than him who speaks it to cause harm" (22.15–16), and "Place the good utterance on your tongue, while the bad is hidden in your belly" (11.10–11). Thoughts are held in the belly prior to utterance. As Anii says:

> The belly—it is wider than a storehouse.
> It is deeper than a deep well.
> It is a field that no one can cross.
> The heart is its doorkeeper. (D 5.2–3[303])

A man has a great many thoughts, not all of them worthy of utterance, and it is the heart, that is, the intellect, that must decide which ones to let out of their "storehouse."[304] This notion of the belly's function, found also in Prov 18:8; 20:27, 30; and 26:22, is Egyptian in origin. The metaphor "casket of the belly" is based on an Egyptian practice, the storage of papyrus rolls in a special kind of box. In Proverbs, this is modified to the more familiar picture of *chambers* (Shupak 1993: 293–97 and 2005: 210). The notion of the belly holding words also appears in Job 15:2 and 32:18–19, but there it is the source of gaseousness rather than the proper locus of thought.

that they may all be secure on your lips: If you store the teachings in your belly, you will utter their wisdom when you speak, both by quoting the teachings and by crafting all your speech in conformity with their principles.

Prov 22:17–18 also draws on Amenemope's exordium (3.9, 10, 11, 13, 16), which is quoted below, after the Comment on Prov 22:21. Note in particular the promise that the teachings will help you control your mouth. When emotions flare, "they will be a mooring post for your tongue" (3.16).

22:19. *In order that your trust may be in the Lord*: This asserts that the purpose of the teachings of Part III is to inculcate trust in God. This is the promise also of the Prologue (1:1–7) and Lecture II (2:1–22), especially 2:5. Yet few of the maxims teach this directly. (Prov 23:4 and 23:17 imply it.) It is an axiom for this author that all wisdom leads to trust in God. When one learns the right modes of behavior and their consequences, in the practical as well as moral realms, one comes to view the world as an orderly, just system and comes to trust its ruler.

In this verse there is extra emphasis on three levels. In the Hebrew, "in Yahweh" (the Lord) is in emphatic position—in italics, as it were. This suggests a contrast: trust in Yahweh rather than in your own independent powers and faculties; see

---

[303] MS D of Anii is not translated in AEL. This text is found in Quack 1994.

[304] Or, in another image, "Let your heart be a great dyke, at whose banks the flood is powerful" (Amennakhte, OBM 5–6).

the Comment on 3:5. Also emphasized are the purpose clause, "In order that your trust may be in the Lord" (v 19a) and the "you" in "I have taught you." We can represent this triple emphasis thus: "The sole reason that—with you specifically in mind—I have taught you these things today is to teach you to place your trust in the Lord alone."

The complement of the infinitive (*bYHWH*) is inverted with the subject of the infinitive (*mibṭaḥekā*) for the sake of focus. The purpose clause itself is also emphasized: Dependent infinitives preceding the main verb (here, *hôdaʿtîkā*) are very rare (other examples are Gen 42:9 and Ps 90:12). Furthermore, the object of the main verb (*-kā*) is underscored by the repetition of an independent pronoun (*ʾāttāh*).

McKane is wrong in asserting that this verse "belongs to a later stage of the history of the Wisdom tradition in Israel and is associated particularly with the theological reorientation of the Instruction" (p. 376; see also the Comment on 3:5). It is gratuitous to assume that the principle of trust in God, so important to Amenemope, was not included in the original composition of Part III but was inserted only later. Although 22:19a is not verbally dependent on Amenemope, it is very much in line with the spirit of his teachings, the only real difference being that it uses the name of Israel's God. The verse also shows that Römheld exaggerates in claiming that Prov 22:17–24:22 lacks "any echo of Egyptian personal piety" (p. 184).

I have taught them to you [*hodaʿtika*]: Lit. "I have made you know (them)." The second object ("them") is implied in the Hebrew. It is supplied from "my words" and "my knowledge" in v 17bc.

even you [*ʾap ʾattah*]: This phrase is very emphatic. The focus on *you*, unlike the stereotypical address to "my son" in most exordia, implies a distinction between the addressee and others. The sudden focus on a particular listener or reader is functional if this unit (Part III) was composed as an instruction addressed first of all to the author's son, and only indirectly to others. This is the way Amenemope sees his audience; see the excursuses on "Author and Speaker, Listener and Reader" and "Speaking and Writing" (Vol. I, 73–75).

Gemser and others emend *ʾp ʾth* to *ʾorḥōtāyw* "his ways" ("I inform you of his [God's] ways"). They assume that this reading is reflected in the LXX, but see the Textual Note on this verse.

22:20. *Have I not written . . . ?*: Verse 20a states that the teaching exists as a written document. The reference to writing down one's own wisdom is unparalleled in Proverbs. Prov 25:1 presumes that Hezekiah's men redacted already existing wisdom. Whether it was already in writing is not indicated. The idea of writing a teaching for one's son and other readers *and* speaking it is fundamental to Egyptian Wisdom Literature's self-presentation; see Vol. I, 73–75 and, more extensively, Fox *2003b*. D. Carr *2005* examines the complex intertwining of writing and orality in the scribal cultures throughout the ancient Near East; in brief: "most cultural usage of written traditions has involved significant elements of both oral performance and cognitive mastery" (p. 288).

Like the phrase "even you" in v 19, the question in v 20a suggests a remark to a specific individual. Ehrlich's conjecture (in his comment on 23:15) that the unit was composed as a "poetischer Lehrbrief" ("a poetic didactic letter") cannot be proved. The genre of didactic letters did exist in Egypt, but their contents were typically quite different, aimed mostly at getting the recipient, a pupil at a scribal school, to work harder.

thirty [*šᵉlošim*]: The MT qeré is *šālîšîm,* which has traditionally been understood to mean "noble things" or "three times" (LXX, Syr, Tg). But *šališim* does not mean either. The ketiv *šlšwm* usually means "the day before yesterday," but that does not make sense here.

šālîšîm: A *šālîš* is a type of military officer, in particular a charioteer (e.g., Exod 14:7; 1 Kgs 9:22) or an adjutant (Ezek 23:15, 23; 2 Chr 8:9). The word bears no special connotations of excellence. Many commentators (such as Hame'iri and Delitzsch) adduce the analogy of *nᵉgîdîm* in Prov 8:6, which they explain as "princely words." But this example itself presupposes that words for noble rank or caste can mean "noble words," and it is circular to adduce it to reinforce the same supposition here. Also, as I argue in the Comment on 8:6, *nᵉgîdîm* probably means "candid things" and has no direct relation to *nāgîd* "prince."

The ketiv *šlšwm* "the day before yesterday" cannot be correct, because the word appears only as part of a fixed idiom, *tᵉmôl šilšôm*, lit., "yesterday (and) the day before yesterday." Toy and BDB hesitantly suggest adding *tᵉmôl*, but even that would not make good sense here. "Have I not written for you formerly?" would imply a contrast between the attempt to instill trust in Yahweh *today* (v 19b) and the intention to teach true words and good answers *in the past*, and this contrast is meaningless.

Adolph Erman, who first identified Prov 22:17–24:22 as a translation of Amenemope, recognized that this word should be vocalized *šᵉlōšîm* and translated "thirty" (1924a: 89).[305] This emendation, currently accepted by most commentators, takes its cue from Amenemope's epilogue:

(27.7) **Look to these thirty chapters:**
(8) they divert,[306] they instruct.
(9) **They are the foremost of all books.**
(10) They make the ignorant wise.
(11) If they are read before an ignoramus—
(12) he is made pure through them.
(13) Be filled with them, put them in your heart,
(14) and you will become a man who can interpret them,
(15) who interprets them as a teacher.[307]
(16) As for the scribe skilled in his office,
(17) he will be found worthy to be a courtier.
(§30, complete [cf. AEL 2.162])

[305] Strikingly, F. Perles proposed this vocalization nearly twenty years earlier, with no knowledge of Amenemope (*1905–1906*: 390). The reason for the emendation seems to have been a matter of Perles's excellent feel for the language, though he tried to associate the number vaguely with the number of chapters in Proverbs.

[306] See "Wisdom is Fun," Vol. I, 294.

[307] The text reads "as a teaching." Add a man-determinative, with Shirun-Grumach.

"Thirty" is a significant number in Egypt because the vizierial court (mentioned in Amenemope §19) had thirty judges, as did the court of deities who judge the dead. Amenemope's "thirty" was taken as a model by the author-editor of Part III, who then composed his own book of thirty sayings. Since *thirty* has no thematic significance in a Hebrew text, the word could easily have become obscured in scribal transmission. In any case, there are not thirty maxims drawn from Amenemope, but thirty in the entirety of Part III. "Thirty" must count shorter units here than Amenemope's "chapters," which are about ten to twenty lines.[308]

Scholars have divided up Part III with somewhat varying results. Although there is no consensus, there are several reasonable ways of dividing Part III into thirty maxims, more or less. Most of the topical groupings in Part III are quite distinct, and there is considerable agreement in identifying most of them. One matter of uncertainty is how to treat the exordium, 22:17–21. Most commentators leave it out of the count, since it is an introduction. But, as Hurowitz (*2001c*: 148) observes, Amenemope himself counts his exordium as chapter one. (This follows his prologue, which states the benefits of the book and its author's titles.) The short exhortations in Prov 23:12, 19, and 26, however, have no independent content and are to be bracketed with the maxims they precede.[309]

Most scholars find approximately thirty units. Some, such as McKane and Römheld, for example, count exactly thirty (excluding 22:17–21).[310] It is interesting that even some commentators who wrote before Erman's discovery subdivided Part III into approximately thirty maxims. Saʿadia's comments on the unit fall into twenty-eight segments, largely identical to the ones proposed below. Delitzsch, writing in 1872, with little discussion of segmentation, divided 22:17–24:22 into thirty-two groups for comment or, excluding the exordium, thirty-one. He separates 24:8 from 24:9, but since he considers v 9 to be "connected" to v 8, he is in effect counting thirty-one units or, without the exordium, thirty. Kautzsch (*1910*) distinguished twenty-eight units typographically.[311]

My proposed segmentation groups verses by shared topic or syntactic connectors. This division is not the only feasible one. We might, for example, take 23:12 as an independent maxim. But even if the details of the count are debatable and one finds twenty-nine or thirty-one maxims, the proximity to thirty (which is the only explanation of *šlyšym* / *šlšwm* that makes good sense) is unlikely to be coincidental. As Bryce observes (1979: 81–87), the precise number could have been blurred by subsequent additions or subtractions. Moreover, there may still be

---

[308] These are the units marked as "§" in my translations of Amenemope.

[309] There are no renewed exhortations to listen in Amenemope, but there is a conditional sentence with a similar function: "If you spend your lifetime with these (words) in your heart, your children will see them" (3.17–18, in §1; repeated in 17.15–16, in §15). ("Them" apparently refers to exemplary deeds.) This is in effect a call to carry out the teaching. In neither occurrence is it an independent chapter.

[310] (**1**) 22:22–23; (**2**) 22:24–25; (**3**) 22:26–27; (**4**) 22:28; (**5**) 22:29; (**6**) 23:1–3; (**7**) 23:4–5; (**8**) 23:6–8; (**9**) 23:9; (**10**) 23:10–11; (**11**) 23:12; (**12**) 23:13–14; (**13**) 23:15–16; (**14**) 23:17–18; (**15**) 23:19–21; (**16**) 23:22–25; (**17**) 23:26–28; (**18**) 23:29–35; (**19**) 24:1–2; (**20**) 24:3–4; (**21**) 24:5–6; (**22**) 24:7; (**23**) 24:8–9; (**24**) 24:10; (**25**) 24:11–12; (**26**) 24:13–14; (**27**) 24:15–16; (**28**) 24:17–18; (**29**) 24:19–20; (**30**) 24:21–22.

[311] Kautzsch treats 24:5–7 and 24:10–12 each as a single maxim.

thirty maxims even if there is no unanimity on their segmentation. For the list of the thirty maxims as I demarcate them, see the introduction to Part IIIa.

in deliberation and knowledge: This may be compared to Amenemope's praise of his teachings in §30, though this feature is shared by other Wisdom books as well.

22:21. *the truest of words* [*qošṭ ʾimrey ʾĕmet*]: Lit., "the truth of words of truth," a superlative.

qōšṭ ʾimrê ʾĕmet: *Qōšṭ* is an Aramaism, the construct form of *qōšeṭ* (Ps 60:6). It should not be deleted as a gloss (contrary to Toy), for Heb *ʾĕmet* would hardly require an Aramaic gloss and in any case a gloss would follow the word it explains. The phrase is a superlative, similar to *ḥakmôt śārôteyhā* "her wisest princesses" (Judg 5:29) and *qômat ʾărāzāyw* "his tallest cedars" (// *mibḥar bᵉrōšāyw* "his choicest cypresses"; Isa 37:24). The phrase *qōšṭ ʾimrê ʾĕmet* has its precise equivalent in *yōšer dibrê ʾĕmet*, "the most honest words of truth," lit., "honesty of words of truth," in Qoh 12:10.

to give answer to those who send you: The qualities of honesty and reliability in messengers and other delegates were crucial to the functioning of commerce and administration in a culture in which much of the communication depended on sending messengers and delegating decisions to envoys; see the Comment on 10:26. A messenger is anyone delegated to bear a message or conduct business on another's behalf.

The messenger topos elsewhere in Proverbs concerns accurate transmission of a message or faithful fulfillment of a mission. Only the present sentence speaks of reporting back to the sender. The impression a messenger would make on his employer depended not only on how well he delivered messages but also on the precision and clarity with which he could report back, for he was generally the employer's only source of information about the undertaking. The unique perspective of this verse is another indicator of derivation from Amenemope. The Egyptian sage promises to teach the reader "**to return an (oral) response to one who says it, to bring back a (written) message to the one who sends it**" (1.5–6).[312] Both Prov 22:17bc–21 and Amenemope's Prologue (quoted in full in Vol. I, 71–72) list this goal alongside ethical aims. Amenemope promises "to guide one in the way of life . . . steering (him) away from evil" (1.7, 10). Proverbs promises "to teach you the truest of words" (22:21a). The art of reply is *not* a topic of instruction in Prov 22:17–23:11; the promise in 22:21b is simply imported from Amenemope.

Other Egyptian sages too give advice about transmitting communications in both directions. Ptahhotep says, "If you become a trusted man, sent by one important man to another, be entirely precise when he sends you. Carry out his mission just as he said it" (ll. 145–47 [cf. AEL 1.65]). Anii enjoins his son to be careful in giving answers, "for you will not be sent (on missions) if you rashly mix up[313] your

[312] The antecedent of *sw* ("it" or "him") in both lines is ambiguous. In both, the pronoun seems to refer to the original communication, which is not mentioned but alluded to by *wšbt* "reply." It is also possible that *sw* "him" in l. 6 refers to the messenger ("to the one who sends him"). The latter understanding is reflected in MT's *lešoleḥeyka* "to those who send you," with the 3rd per. adjusted to 2nd per. to fit the new context (Römheld pp. 69–70). In l. 5, read *r rḫ ḫsf* (Lange).

[313] "Mix up": lit., "take and bring."

words (?). If a man excels in his responses, his tongue will be safe from harm" (15.8–9 [not in AEL]). But Prov 22:21b is closer to Amenemope.

to give answer [*lᵉhašib ʾămarim*]: Lit., "to return words." The MT has, awkwardly, *lᵉhašib ʾămarim ʾĕmet*, lit., "to return words truth." "Truth" should be omitted as an overcautious moralizing gloss. If this is done, the line is even closer to Amenemope's "to return an (oral) response to one who says it" (1.5).

MT's *ʾĕmet* "truth" is clumsy and redundant after "words of truth" in the A-line. It is either a dittography (possibly vertical) with the first *ʾĕmet* (Clifford) or a moralizing gloss intended to make it absolutely clear that only the giving of *true* replies is being taught. Erman excised the word because it is absent in the parallel maxim in Amenemope (1924a: 89), but Proverbs is too distant from Amenemope for the latter to be more than suggestive as textual evidence. DNF says that the final *mem* of *ʾmrym* may be enclitic; hence: "words of truth." Cody says that *ʾĕmet* here means "reliable" (1980: 423, q.v. for a lengthy defense of the MT).

Both Prov 22:17–21 and Amenemope's Prologue promise to teach how to return a proper answer to a sender, and both associate this with ethical goals. Then Amenemope opens the book proper by an exhortation:

(3.9) **Give your ears, that you may hear the things that are said**;
(10) **apply your heart** to interpret them.
(11) Putting them in your heart is **beneficial**,
(12) but (they are) a woe to him that ignores them.
(13) **Make them rest in the casket of your belly**;
(14) lock them up in your heart.
(15) When there is a storm of words,
(16) **they will be a mooring post for your tongue**.
(17) If you spend your life with these (teachings) in your heart,
(18) you will find them a profit.
(4.1) You will find my words a storehouse of life,
(2) and your body will prosper on earth.
(§1, complete [cf. AEL 2.149])

This resembles the exordia elsewhere in Wisdom Literature, especially Prov 1–9, but there are special affinities to Prov 22:17–21. First, the exhortation to retain the teachings in one's belly is not found elsewhere in Wisdom prologues. Second, as Bryce (1979: 101–102) observes, the key phrases in 22:17–18 occur in the same sequence as in Amenemope. The following comparison differs somewhat from Bryce's, and the translation here is more literal than above:

Amenemope col. 3		*Proverbs chap. 22*	
9	**give/set your ears**	17b	**incline your ear**
9	**the things that are said**	17b	**my words**
10	**give/set your heart**	17c	**and set your heart**
11	**beneficial**	18a	**pleasant** (*naʿim*)
13	**make them rest**	18a	**if you keep them**
13	**in** the casket of **your belly**	18a	**in your belly**

Egyptian *ḏdwt* "the things that are said" (3.9) could as well be translated "the words," and Hebrew *tašit* "direct," "set" (22:17c) is an almost exact equivalent of Egyptian *imi*, which means "give" and "set," though the latter is translated above (3.10) as "apply," for stylistic reasons.[314] The author of Prov 22:17–23:11 is not merely picking up a few motifs from a common tradition; he knows a written form of Amenemope and mines it for his own purposes.

At this point, the LXX has a short essay (Prov 24:21–22e) on the importance of fearing the king. It is cited in the Textual Notes before 24:21.

Maxim 2: Do not steal from the poor.

22:22 Do not rob a lowly man because he is lowly,
and do not oppress the poor man at the gate.
23 For the Lord will strive on their behalf,
and will steal away the life of those who steal from them.

Do not rob the poor in legal proceedings ("at the gate"). Even if they lack a human protector, they have God himself to champion their cause and avenge their wrongs (19:17; 22:23; cf. Deut 10:18; 27:19; Ps 68:6).

rob [*tigzol*]: On the difference between *gzl* "rob" and *ʿšq* "oppress," see the Comment on 22:16.

because he is lowly: This could be (1) the reason why one might dare to rob the poor man (for his vulnerability may tempt exploitation): Do not rob a lowly man just because he is poor. Or it could be (2) the reason *not* to rob him (for it is especially evil to rob the lowly): Because a lowly man is lowly, do not rob him. The first reading is less likely because the oppressor's motives are irrelevant to the apodictic admonition. By the second reading, the verse recalls Ptahhotep:

(74) If you meet a contentious man in his moment[315]—
(75) a lowly man, not your equal,
(76) let not your heart rage against him, because he is weak,
(77) Leave him alone, that he may punish himself. (cf. AEL 1.64)

His lowliness is all the more reason not to assault him.

steal away [*qbʿ*]: The verb *qbʿ* is of uncertain derivation and meaning. It occurs four times in Mal 3:8–9, where it means approximately "deprive," "rob," or "cheat." There it is a nonviolent, illicit action, namely, failing to pay God his cultic dues. On the basis of a possible Arabic cognate (*qabaḍa* "squeeze," "oppress"), Cody (1980: 425–26) translates: "and he [Yahweh] will press the life out of those who oppress them."

The retribution threatened in Prov 22:23 goes beyond the principle of talion ("an eye for an eye") by requiting theft of property with deprivation of life. The

[314] Bryce would also include "for your tongue" (3.16) and "on your lips" (22:18b) among the parallels, but these refer to different actions.

[315] "Doing his thing," we might say.

wording of the verse creates the illusion of equity by repeating the verb *qbʿ* "steal": theft for theft, as it were. Saʿadia justifies the surplus punishment on the grounds that "(poor people's) wealth is their sustenance" (sim. Hameʾiri).The poor possess only the necessities, and stealing these puts their lives in peril.

In Amenemope, as in the present unit, a warning against cheating the poor follows immediately upon the exordium:

(4.4) **Beware of robbing the lowly,**
(5) of **oppressing** the weak.
(6) Do not stretch your hand out to attack an elder,
(7) or insult (?)[316] the great.
(8) Do not let yourself be sent on a detrimental errand,
(9) nor envy (?) him who does so.
(10) Do not make an outcry against him who transgresses against you,
(11) nor reply to him yourself.
(12) He who does evil—the riverbank casts him off,
(13) and its floodwaters take him away.
(14) The north wind descends to end his hour (of life),
(15) and it joins with the storm.
(16) The clouds are high, the crocodiles evil.
(17) O heated man, how are you now?
(18) He cries out; his voice goes to heaven,
(19) **but** the Moon **declares his crime**.
(5.1) Steer! Let us ferry the evil man across,[317]
(2) so that we not act like him!
(3) Raise him up, give him your hand;
(4) leave him in the hands of God.
(5) Fill his belly with your own bread,
(6) that he may be sated and ashamed.
(7) Another thing good to God's heart
(8) is to pause before speaking. (§2, complete [cf. AEL 2.150])

The words translated "rob(bing)," "lowly," and "oppressing" (4.4–5) are close equivalents of the Hebrew words translated thus. The Hebrew has expanded these elements by making the noun "lowly" in Amenemope 4.4 into a clause—"because he is lowly"—and adding a motive clause in Prov 22:23. Amenemope goes on to describe how nature itself (which is, for the Egyptians, infused with divinity) rises up to punish the offender (4.12–19), whereas Proverbs has Yahweh directly

[316] The meaning of the idiom "take the mouth" or "take a portion" (*ṯʾy r*), used also in Amenemope 15.13 (quoted in the Comment on 22:24), is uncertain. Lichtheim: "Don't stretch out your hand to touch an old man, nor open your mouth to an elder" (AEL 2.150). Shirun-Grumach (p. 30) translates: "Strecke nicht die Hand aus, dich einem Alten vertraulich zu nähern, und habe keinen Anteil an einem Grossen" ("Do not stretch forth the hand to approach an elder familiarly, nor get involved with a great man").

[317] Rather than letting him drown.

executing the punishment (22:23). In Amenemope, the forensic context is only alluded to: "but the Moon declares his crime" (4.19). The Moon is Thoth, the god of scribes and administration of justice, and the verb translated "declares" (*sʿḥʿ*) means to accuse or convict someone of a crime (noted by Washington 1994b: 186). Amenemope's statement, "but the Moon declares his crime," has its echo in "For Yahweh will strive on their behalf" (22:23), with Israel's deity replacing Thoth. Even beyond that, the editor has transposed Amenemope's admonition into an Israelite context, with the gate as the site of judgment and Yahweh as the protector of the poor.

Maxim 3: Avoid quarrelsome men.

22:24 Do not consort with an ill-tempered man,
and do not go with a hothead,
25 lest you learn his ways
and get yourself snared.

The danger of being an angry man or associating with one is a common topos in both Egyptian Wisdom and Proverbs (15:18; 27:3, 4; 29:22; etc.). Ptahhotep says, "The flame of the hothead [*t’-ib*, lit., "hot-hearted"] sweeps over" (l. 378 [cf. AEL 1.70]). Amenemope warns against this type (who is also called the "hot mouth") in §§3, 4, 10, and 12.

hothead [*’iš ḥemot*]: Lit., "man of heat." This phrase (occurring also in Prov 15:18) is almost an exact equivalent of Egyptian *p’ šmm* "the heated (man)" (see Shupak 1993: 117–18, 129–31; *2005*: 211). Both refer to a chronically angry person.

and get yourself snared: Lit., "and take a snare to yourself" (or "to your life" [*nepeš*]).

This quatrain has a close parallel in Amenemope:

(11.13) **Do not consort with the heated man,**
(14) **or approach him for conversation.**
(15) Preserve your tongue from answering your superior,
(16) and beware of insulting him.
(17) Do not make him cast his words to lasso you,
(18) and do not give free rein to your answer.
(19) Converse with a man who is of your own standing,
(20) but beware of inquiring of him rashly (?).
(from §9 [cf. AEL 2.153])

The chapter goes on to describe at length the miseries that an irate man causes himself and others. Amenemope offers a variant of this advice when he warns against envying a noble's wealth:

(15.13) Do not share a portion **with the heated man**
(14) **or consort with a contentious man.** (from §12 [cf. AEL 2.155])

In §3 (5.10–12), quoted in the Comment on 15:1, Amenemope tells how to deal with a heated man when he is angry. Prov 22:24–25 is closest to Amenemope 11.13–14.

In the two passages cited above (11.13–14 and 15.13–14), Amenemope is apparently reworking a precept from Anii:

(18.7) Keep far from a contentious man,
and do not make him your companion.
Befriend one who is honest and true,
(8) whose actions you have seen. (cf. AEL 2.138)

In both Amenemope §9 and §12, the advice to avoid the hothead is subordinated to a larger issue, namely, the danger of angering one's superior. Proverbs' editor has extracted the warning about consorting with the hothead from this context and given it broad validity.

The reason given in Prov 22:25 for avoiding the hothead is that you will come to resemble him. "Get yourself snared" in v 25b means that you may become enmeshed in his influence and share his fate. (Compare Prov 3:25–26, where to "keep your foot from the snare" means to avoid sharing "the calamity of the wicked, when it comes.") Amenemope employs a similar motivation, but in a different context, namely, a warning against vindictiveness: "Steer! Let us ferry the evil man across, so that we not act like him!" (5.1–2; the chapter is quoted in the Comment on 22:22–23).

In the sages' view, the great danger in malicious types (especially as depicted in Prov 1–9, but elsewhere as well) is not so much that they may harm their intended victims directly, but that they may corrupt those who associate with them. The scenario in Prov 1:10–18 shows this happening. (See further Vol. I, 347–48.) The sages believed that character, in normal people at least, is malleable and susceptible to the influence of example, for the better (as in 13:20a) or worse (as in 13:20b; 14:7; and 26:4). Proverbs for the most part is concerned with keeping the reader on the right path; it seeks to shape a state of soul.

Maxim 4: Do not give surety.

22:26 Do not be among those who shake hands,
among those who guarantee loans,
27 lest—if you don't have the wherewithal to pay—
they take your bedding from beneath you.

Proverbs warns against giving surety in 6:1–5; 11:15; 17:18; and 20:16 (= 27:13); see Vol. I, 214–16. There is nothing comparable in Amenemope. The practice of loan guarantees was not known in Egypt until much later (LÄ 5.182–83; Römheld, p. 38 n. 3).

shake hands: In order to seal an agreement to guarantee someone's loan (Prov 6:1; 11:15; 17:18).

loans [*maššaʾot*]: These are usurious, exploitive loans (TDOT 10.55–59). The brutal consequences of this kind of lending are described in Neh 5:2–11 (using *n-š-ʾ*, from which *maššaʾot* is derived).

they take: Lit. "he take," understood as an indefinite third person (thus in LXX).

bedding [*miškabᵉka*]: One's bedding was commonly the garment or cloak in which he would wrap himself to sleep (20:16; see the Comment there).

lest . . . : Lit.: "If you don't have (the wherewithal) to pay, why should he take your bedding from beneath you?" "Why" (*lāmmāh*) is equivalent to "lest" and its force actually applies to the A-line.

Maxim 5: Do not encroach on another's boundaries.

22:28 Do not encroach on the ancient boundary,
which your ancestors made.

This couplet is based on Amenemope §6, which is quoted in its entirety in the Comment on 23:10–11. Especially relevant is Amenemope's admonition, "**Do not displace the stone on the boundary of the fields** . . . nor encroach on the boundary of the widow" (7.12, 15).

Prov 22:28 has an expanded variant in 23:10–11. It seems that the editor later decided to redo 22:28 with more emphasis on Yahweh's role as protector of the poor (23:11). The two maxims are discussed in the Comment on 23:10–11.

Maxim 6: Be diligent in your work.

22:29 Have you seen a man adept in his work?
He will stand before kings.
He will not stand before the lowly.

The reward promised for professional diligence shows that some proverbs, at least, were directed at young men who were slated to enter officialdom and could hope to land a job in the royal court.

Have you seen a man . . . ?: Prov 26:12 and 29:20 likewise begin with attention-focusing questions asking, "Have you seen . . . ?"

adept [*mahir*]: *Mahir* means "skilled," "adept," "trained," like Syriac *mhiraʾ* (as noted by Shadal on Isa 16:5). (*Mahir* does not mean "speedy," which would be *maher.*) Though this verse does not use the word for scribe, *mahir* itself implies it. Ezra is called "a scribe adept [*mahir*] in the Law of Moses" (Ezr 7:6a). A psalmist calls his own tongue "the pen of an adept scribe [*soper mahir*]" (Ps 45:2b). This refers (metaphorically) to his training and skill in singing the king's praises. Isaiah says that the ideal Davidic king will be a seeker of justice and *mᵉhir ṣedeq* "adept in righteousness" (Isa 16:5b). Even in Isaiah, where *mahir* is not directly connected to the scribal office, the powers in question concern the administration of righteous judgment, to which scribes were also relevant. Ahiqar is a *spr ḥkym wmhyr*, "a wise and adept scribe" (1.1:1). The Egyptian equivalent of *soper mahir* is *sš šsʾ* (= *šsʾ*, *sšsʾ*), used in Amenemope §30 (see below). On these terms see Shupak 1993: 226–27 and also the quotations on I, 77 of this commentary. The phrase "*mahir* in the Law of Moses" (Ezr 7:6a) is equivalent to Egyptian "expert [*sšs*ʾ] in the writings" (Pap. Beatty IV vso. 4.6; Anii 20.4).

stand before [*yityaṣṣeb lipney*]: This idiom implies service only here and in Sir 8:8. Usually it means to position oneself before or to present oneself. The synonymous *ʿmd lipney*, "stand before," often means "serve" (Deut 1:38; Ezek 44:15; etc.; likewise *ʿmd ʾet pᵉney* "stand before" in 1 Kgs 12:6). Here the phrase also indicates the physical position of the successful scribe in the court, which is in the proximity of the king; see the Comment on 25:6–7. Ben Sira says that the wise man will "stand before princes" (8:8).

the lowly [*ḥăšukkim*]: Or "common people" (NRSV); lit., "dark." "Lowly" is more pertinent than the usual "obscure" because it is the social rank of one's employer, rather than the degree of his renown, that is the gauge of one's own status.

Aramaic *ḥšykʾ* translates Hebrew *dl* "lowly" in Tg. Jonathan to Jer 39:10 and Gen 41:19, as noted by Ramaq and Radaq, *Sefer Hašorašim*. Jastrow (*Dictionary*, p. 510a) ascribes *ḥšyk*, *ḥšwk* "poor," etc. to a different root than *ḥ-š-k* "dark." This is unnecessary, because lowly status is an easy metaphorical extension of darkness; cf. English "obscure."

The end of Amenemope's epilogue (quoted in full in the Comment on 22:20) declares:

> **As for the scribe [*sš*] skilled [*šsʾ*[318]] in his office,**
> **he will be found worthy to be a courtier.**
> (from §30; 27.16–17 [cf. AEL 2.162])

Prov 22:29 is clearly borrowed from Amenemope. In fact, the maxim is somewhat out of place in Proverbs. It is a statement in indicative form that promises professional advancement, whereas the neighboring proverbs are ethical admonitions in "do not" form. In Amenemope, this promise is better integrated into the context. Amenemope does not teach professional skills as such, but several of his maxims do give counsel in scribal comportment, such as the prohibitions against writing false assessments (§13), cheating in writing (§16), and altering weights and measures (§17). In his epilogue (§30), Amenemope would have us understand these ethical norms to be *skills* of the scribe and a prerequisite of professional success.

In Prov 22:29a, the editor broadens Amenemope's "scribe" to "man," but, as indicated above, *mahir* itself is a talent associated with scribaldom, and the promise in 22:29 speaks to much the same circles as in Amenemope, namely, young men in the state service, whose highest levels served in the royal court. Egyptian *sš* "scribe" basically means literate man, and scribes were extensively employed throughout the administrations of temple and palace. Probably most officials and bureaucrats could be called *sšw*, though most did not so style themselves, and *sšw* more narrowly refers to scribes who copied, wrote, and read for a living. The Israelite scribe (*soper*) could also reach high office. An example is Shaphan, the chief

[318] The nice alliteration of *sš šsʾ* is lost in the Hebrew (but suggested in the English).

scribe in the Jerusalem court (2 Kgs 22:3; etc.). In Hebrew, the title *soper* refers to a more specialized range of functionaries and is not used as *sš* is in Egypt.

Maxim 7: Control your appetite when dining with your superior.

23:1 When you sit to dine with an official,
look carefully at what is before you,
2 and put a knife to your throat,
if you are a voracious man.
3 Do not desire his delicacies,
for they are deceitful bread.

When dining with a superior, be satisfied with what is placed before you and don't be glancing at others in envy and greed.

23:1. *official* [*mošel*]: Or "ruler." A *mošel* can be a king (Josh 12:2; 1 Kgs 5:1), a vizier or governor (Gen 45:8; Zech 6:13), or an administrator of a lower rank (Isa 28:14; 2 Chr 23:20). Ben Sira regards his reader as reasonably seeking to become a *mošel* (Sir 7:6, translated *kritēs* "judge" by the LXX). The word is used in Prov 6:7; 23:1; 28:15; and 29:12, 26. I translate it "ruler" or "official," depending on the degree of power that seems to be ascribed to him.

look carefully [*bin tabin*] *at what is before you*: This seems like a reminiscence of Ptahhotep l. 123, "but look at what is before you," also in the context of table comportment. It also draws on Amenemope 23.17, "Look at the bowl that is before you"; these passages are discussed below.

at what is before you [*'et 'ăšer lᵉpāneykā*]: As Ehrlich observes, this cannot mean "at him who is before you." (Thus Malbim and Toy. Clifford thinks that there is deliberate ambiguity.) That would be *lipnê mî 'attāh yôšēb*. MT's "what is before you" means "what is put at your disposal [Verfügung]" (Ehrlich).

23:2. *and put a knife to your throat*: A startling metaphor for self-control. Slit your throat, as it were, rather than giving in to hunger.

voracious man [*baʿal nepeš*]: Lit., "a possessor of an appetite." This indicates a regular disposition, not an occasional hunger.[319]

23:3. *deceitful bread* [*leḥem kᵉzabim*]: The official's food is "deceitful" because the pleasure it gives is fleeting, and it may leave a bitter aftertaste. Perhaps your hunger will be viewed as a symptom of greed and a lack of self-control. As Prov 20:17 says of the synonymous *leḥem šeqer*, "The bread of deceit is sweet to a man, but later it fills his mouth with gravel."

The issue in Prov 20:17 and 23:1–3 is not only the importance of controlling one's hunger. In Egyptian formal dining, the host would signal his favor by the amount of food he distributed to each guest. One Mentuwosre boasts in his memorial stone, "I apportioned big cuts of meat to those who sat next to me" (*Les.* 79.12); in other words, he was generous, but distributed food according to rank as assessed by the host, on the basis of careful planning, not whim. Ptahhotep says,

[319] On this usage of *baʿal*, see HALOT 143a (A.6).

(135) As for the great man, when he is at dinner,
(136) his plan is what his Ka[320] commands.
(137) He gives to him whom he favors.
(138) It is the plan of the night.
(139) It is his Ka that stretches forth his hands. (cf. AEL 1.60)

The great man serves out food as his Ka (soul) inclines him, and no one can influence his decision[321]—except for God:

(142) For eating is under the counsel of god.
(143) It is the counsel of the night,[322]
(144) and only the fool complains about it.

Clearly this decision is a matter of importance, one that the official mulls over in advance the night before. Distributing food at dinner is not simply offering someone a bit more to eat, but a display of favor. The Joseph story is aware of this. Joseph—an Egyptian *mošel*!—shows Benjamin favor by assigning him a portion five times as great as his brothers' (Gen 43:34). Seating arrangements too were according to status, as in Gen 43:33.

Comportment at the table is an important theme in Wisdom Literature. We can trace advice in this matter from Kagemeni, one of the earliest Wisdom books, to Ptahhotep, to Amenemope, to Prov 23:1–3. In the following, the words that influenced the later Wisdom book are in boldface, but most important is the similarity in the content of the advice. Kagemeni's father says:

If you are sitting with a group of people,
refuse [lit., "hate"] the bread you love.
Controlling the heart takes but a moment.
Gluttony is base and brings reproach.
(Pap. Prisse 1.3–5 [cf. AEL 1.60])

Kagemeni's father is describing a meal in a group and one's good standing in the group. He also gives advice on what to do when sharing a table with a glutton (1.7–11; quoted in the Comment on 23:8).

Ptahhotep teaches:

(119) **If you are one of those sitting**
(120) **at the table of one greater than you,**
(121) take what he places before you.
(122) Do not stare at what is before him;[323]

---

[320] The *ka* is the appetitive soul, very similar to Hebrew *nepeš*.

[321] This is apparently the meaning of "It is the plan of the night." The official already decided on it the night before.

[322] In Pap. Prisse, the oldest manuscript of Ptahhotep, l. 143 appears before this passage.

[323] Line 122 is in the later MS L_2 only.

(123) **(but) look at what is before you.**
(124) Do not pierce him with many glances.
(125) Offending him is disgusting to the Ka. (cf. AEL 1.65)

Ptahhotep proceeds to instruct the reader to wait till he is spoken to. Later, Amenemope says:

(23.13) **Do not eat food before an official**[324]
(14) while setting (?) your mouth before (him).
(15) If you become sated by that which is chewed **deceitfully** (?),
(16) you will (have to) be content with your spittle (?).
(17) **Look at the bowl that is before you,**
(18) and let that serve your needs.
(19) A great man in his office
(20) is like a well full of water.[325] (§23, complete [cf. AEL 2.160])

Amenemope §23 is the source of Prov 23:1–3. The editor of Part IIIa has joined two noncontiguous lines into a couplet and elaborated them in his own way, but the essence of the advice is the same.

The instructions of Ptahhotep, Amenemope §23, and Prov 23:1–3—unlike Kagemeni—are not warning against simple greed, because that warning would not be limited to the context of meals "before an official." The advice concerns comportment in a dinner with one's superior and co-workers. One must not steal glances at his co-workers' portions in an attempt to see who ranks where in their superior's favors.

Ptahhotep's influence on Proverbs comes mainly by way of Amenemope, who in §23 is citing him. This is shown in detail by Römheld, pp. 61–95. Prov 23:1b is a close rephrasing of Amenemope

---

[324] "Official" is *wr*, which is the same word as *wr* "greater" in Ptahhotep l. 120, though it is written differently.

[325] There are several difficulties in this text. Shirun-Grumach translates ll. 13-14 as: "Iss nicht Brot vor einem Beamten und lass deinen Ausspruch nicht vor ihm" ("Do not eat bread before an official and let your utterance (loose) before him" (p. 148), referring to a verbal offense. The sense of the idiom "set [w'ḥ] your mouth" or (lit.) "make your mouth remain" is unclear, but in the light of the following lines, which describe the right behavior, it must be an indication of greed. Perhaps it means to make your mouth agape.

The sense of *ir s''.k (m) wg'y n 'ḏ'* in ll. 15–16 is obscure, but possibly it is similar to Hebrew *leḥem kᵉzabim*, "food of deceit." Lichtheim translates, "If you are sated, pretend to chew." This presumes that one should give the impression of continuing to eat, but that would suggest greed. (Kagemeni does say that when eating with a glutton, "take what he gives you; do not refuse it" [1.9–10 (cf. AEL 1.60)], but his point is that you should accept your portion even if it is inadequate.) Shirun-Grumach translates "Wenn du dich mit unrechtem Geschwätz sättigst" ("If you sate yourself with wrongful chatter"), but the relevance to context, which concerns greed (for food or status), is tenuous. The literal sense is "If you are sated (with) that which is chewed [*wgy(t)*] falsely."

In the last two lines, which look like an adage, we should omit mi from 23.19 (Shirun-Grumach). The last line is, lit., "he is like the greatness (of) a drawing well [*ẖnmt n itḥ*]." This would be underground water as distinct from a shaduf or wheel well (ibid.). These two lines resemble Prov 18:4 and esp. 20:5; see the Comment on the latter.

23.17. Prov 23:1a, however, is syntactically closer to Ptahhotep ll. 119–20 than to Amenemope 23.13, and it might be thought to come directly from Ptahhotep or another source. Shirun-Grumach (pp. 149–52) assigns it to the "Alte Lehre" (her theory is discussed below, in "Amenemope and Proverbs"—"Connections"). Washington (1994b: 143) believes that Prov 23:1–3 comes directly from Ptahhotep. Since Ptahhotep's maxim was very popular in Egyptian literature, eventually making its way some 3000 years later into the Coptic Apothegmata (Brunner 1961; Brunner-Traut 1979: 201), it is possible that some form of this maxim was known to the editor of Part IIIa and that he reworked Amenemope's maxim under its influence. But the keyword in Prov 23:1a, *mošel* "official," which is the equivalent of Egyptian *wr* "official," shows a special connection to Amenemope. Ptahhotep, for his part, is reworking phrases from two maxims in Kagemeni (AEL 1.59, 60). Kagemeni is not Proverbs' immediate source here.

Maxim 8: Do not strain to get rich.

23:4 Do not strain to get rich.
Leave off your staring!
5 If you but let your eye fly on it, it is no more,
for it will surely make itself wings like an eagle's
and fly off[a] to the sky.

---

[a] *w^{e}ʿāp* (MT qeré *yāʿûp*; ketiv *wʿyp*).

Whereas diligence is praiseworthy and productive, straining for wealth shows an excessive trust in one's own powers. One should, instead, have full confidence that God will ensure an appropriate reward for reasonable efforts. One may gain some wealth by straining, but it is not stable. This quatrain elaborates on the message of 10:22; 19:2b; 21:5b; and esp. 28:20b: "but he who hastens to get rich will not go unpunished." (See the Comment on 10:22.)

23:4. *Leave off your staring* [*mibbinat^{e}ka ḥădal*]: Don't be fixated on wealth! The line is usually understood differently. The word translated "staring"—*binah*—usually means "understanding," "intelligence," or the like. Other commentators explain this line to mean "because of your intelligence [*binah*], cease"; in other words, "be wise enough to desist" (NRSV). Job 39:26 can be compared for a similar use of *mibbinat^{e}ka* (lit., "from your understanding): "Is it because of your intelligence that the hawk flies?" However, *ḥadal mn* elsewhere means "cease from," not "cease because of." Ramaq and Hameʾiri take *binah* in Prov 23:4 to be the intelligence one uses in pursuing wealth; sim. Delitzsch. Then "cease from" means to desist from applying this form of practical intelligence. Naḥmias says that one should desist from *thinking that* cleverness and stratagems are what gain wealth, because wealth is really from God's hand. But this is not a natural construal of "from your intelligence." In any case, while one should not *trust* in his own understanding, he should certainly not *cease* using it, as all these interpretations imply.

Binah here is better understood as the feminine G infinitive of *b-y-n*, which means "look at intently," as in 23:1b. One should not stare at wealth or focus on it obsessively. The noun "wealth" is implied in the verb *l^{e}haʿăšir* "to get rich" and assumed by the word *bo* "in it" in the next verse. This interpretation of 23:4b ties in well with the continuation: Do not fixate on wealth, because no sooner do you look at it than it's gone. Verse 4b, by this interpretation, echoes Amenemope 9.12, "Do not cast your heart outward"—in other words, do not let your heart go about looking for something you desire.

The wealth one gains by overwork is ephemeral. This is essentially the teaching of 20:21, which speaks of an inheritance gained in a rush. Such wealth, unlike property gained properly and reasonably, has no rooting. The reason for this assertion is unstated. Is it because one who grasps for wealth too quickly fails to lay the economic basis for its continuance, or because such behavior is suspect of lack of faith in God's providence?

23:5. *If you but let your eyes fly on it, it is no more*: Lit., "Do you let your eyes fly on it? [*hătāʿîp*, qeré]? Then it is not." This use of a rhetorical sentence is equivalent to a conditional. The ketiv, *htʿwp*, means "If your eyes fly, etc." (Numerical non-agreement is quite frequent with feminine verbs.) "It" refers to wealth, a noun implicit in the verb "to grow rich" in v 4. It is unclear why Toy finds "the flying of the eyes" to be "an impossible expression." It is actually a transparent metaphor for glancing quickly at something. It was created to resonate with *w^{e}ʿap haššamayim* "fly off to the sky."

The image suggests ephemerality, using phraseology similar to that in Job 7:8: "The eye of him who looks at me will not see me. Your eyes are upon me and I am not [*ʿeyneyka bi w^{e}ʾeynenni*]." That is, no sooner do you look at me than I am gone.

it will surely make itself wings [*ʿaśoh yaʿăśeh lo k^{e}napayim*]: This is a description of sprouting wings (Amenemope 10.4–5 supports this) rather than an idiom for flying away.

w^{e}ʿāp: The ketiv is an impossible form, *wʿyp*. It should be corrected to *wʿp* (= *w^{e}ʿāp*), or *wyʿp* (= *w^{e}yāʿûp*), to the same effect. The qeré is *yāʿûp*," which needs a conjunction added to introduce the consequence of making wings.

This sentence is based on Amenemope:

(9.10) **Do not cast your heart after wealth,**
(11) (for) no one is unaware of Shay and Renenet.[326]
(12) **Do not cast your heart outward;**[327]
(13) every man has his hour.[328]
(14) **Do not strain to seek a superfluity,**
(15) so that your own property may be safe.
(16) If riches are brought to you by robbery,
(17) they will not spend the night with you.
(18) When the day dawns, they are no longer in your house.

---

[326] The gods of destiny who determine one's life span. This line means that everyone knows that his "hour" (9.13), his appointed time of death, awaits him.

[327] Do not yearn for what you do not have.

[328] Lit., "every man is in his hour," that is, he is bound to his fate and limited by it.

(19) **Their place is seen, but they are no longer.**[329]
(20) The ground has opened its mouth, leveled them, and swallowed them,
(10.1) and made them sink into the underworld.
(2) They have made a hole as big as they are
(3) and have sunk into the netherworld.
(4) **They have made themselves wings like a goose**
(5) **and have flown to the sky.**
(6) Do not rejoice in wealth from theft,
(7) nor groan at poverty.
(8) If the lead bowman goes (too far) forward,
(9) his troop abandons him.
(10) The boat of the greedy is abandoned in the mud,
(11) while the skiff of the truly silent man (sails) in the breeze.[330]
(12) Pray to the Aten when he rises,
(13) saying, "Give me safety and health,"
(14) and he will give you what you need for living,[331]
(15) while you are safe from fear. (§7, complete [cf. AEL 2.152–53])

Like Prov 23:4–5, Amenemope §7 warns against excessive striving for wealth and declares the ephemerality of riches gained in that fashion. Such striving will tend to slide into wrongdoing. In the context of "straining to seek a superfluity" (9.14), robbery and theft in 9.16 and 10.6 are probably hyperbolic expressions for improper efforts (Shirun-Grumach). The lust for wealth is such a deep defect that it is tantamount to robbery.

The direct dependency of Prov 23:4–5 on Amenemope §7 is clear. From a stanza of twenty-six lines, the Hebrew author has excerpted six, as indicated in boldface, and redeployed them in the same order and with little change. The image of a bird taking wing in Prov 23:5 is not a stereotyped figure for the loss of wealth. The editor learned the image from Amenemope, then sharpened it, changing the goose into the faster eagle. As Bryce has shown (1979: 109), the editor has fused two images from Amenemope, that of wealth descending (into the ground) and that of wealth flying off like a bird. In Proverbs the movements are combined in the image of *flying*: the eye swooping down (like a bird), and wealth flying up like a bird. "With considerable skill the Hebrew poet has integrated the imagery of descent and ascent, using the bird as his focal point" (Bryce 1979: 109). Forti (1996: 55) sees further metaphorical associations, noting a "flash of associations: fluttering eyes and fluttering winds."

Amenemope restates his teaching in §18, which speaks of man's ignorance of

---

[329] Lit., "and they are not [*ḫr bn st*]." This is the exact equivalent of Hebrew *we'eynennu* "and it is no more" (lit., "and it is not") in Prov 23:5a.

[330] A bowman who gets too far ahead of his troop is an image of overbearing ambition. The boat of the greedy man may have gotten stuck in the mud because in his haste he took it out on a becalmed day rather than waiting for a breeze.

[331] Compare Prov 30:8.

the future and the importance of trusting in God's will; see the quotation in the Comment on 16:3. Amenemope also says, "If (a man) exerts himself in seeking success, in just a moment he ruins it [or "himself"]" (§18; 20.1–2 [cf. AEL 2.158]).

Maxim 9: Do not dine with a stingy man.

23:6 Do not eat the bread of the stingy man,
nor desire his delicacies.
23:7 For like one who calculates[a] in his mind, thus is he:
"Eat and drink," he says to you,
but his heart is not with you.
23:8 You eat your morsel, you vomit it up,
and ruin your fine words.

---

[a] *šōʿēr* (MT *šāʿar*).

23:6. *stingy man* [*raʿ ʿayin*]: Lit., "bad of eye" (also in 28:22), the opposite of "good of eye" (22:9), that is, generous; see the Comment on 28:22.

23:7. *calculates* [k^e*šoʿer*] *in his mind* [*napšo*]: While he invites you to eat, he is silently calculating costs and benefits. He is brooding on the cost of every bite you take and wondering if you are worth it. Instead of "his mind," some would translate *napšo* as "his throat," depending on their understanding of *šʿr*, here rendered "calculates."

k^e*mô šʿr* b^e*napšô*: *šʿr/śʿr* (here translated "calculates") can be understood or repointed in several ways:

(1) *Śēʿār* "hair" (thus LXX *trichas*); hence, "for it is like a hair [*śēʿār*] in his throat." This would mean that your eating the miser's food sticks in *his* throat like a swallowed hair (McKane). This translation resembles *šnʿ* "blockage" in Amenemope 14.7, but there is a significant difference. In Amenemope, the blockage is in the throat of the "eater" (who is consuming the metaphorical food, that is, property). In Prov 23:7, if the word does mean "hair," the blockage would be in "his throat," that is, the throat of the man who *provides* the (literal) food.

(2) *Šōʿār* "foul thing," based on the very uncertain analogy of Jer 29:17 (Bryce 1979: 110).

(3) *Šaʿar* "storm" (Gressmann *1924*: 277). This is based on understanding *šnʿ* in Amenemope 14.7 as "storm." This interpretation is open to the same objection as #1: The storm should not be in "his"—the stingy man's—throat but in "your"—the reader's—throat.

(4) *Šāʿar* "calculates" (MT); hence: "For as if he calculated in his mind, thus he [it?] is."

(5) *Šōʿēr* "one who calculates" (Delitzsch). This provides an antecedent for *ken hûʾ* "thus is he" and improves the syntax, though the gist is the same as in the MT. Sim. Sym *eikazōn* "conjecturing."

23:8. *vomit it up . . . fine words*: One would not actually vomit in these circumstances. Rather, vomiting is a farcical image for how one feels in a situation where mutual disgust is barely concealed beneath the surface of social proprieties. The guest is conversing pleasantly, perhaps paying his host compliments (see below) and thanking him, all the while feeling disgust at the host for his stinginess and at himself for eating the begrudged food and acting the hypocrite. His gorge rises and he throws up on the floor, so to speak, messing up the impression his polite words may have made.

Römheld (pp. 30–34) and Clifford think that the underlying offense in Prov 23:6–8 is intruding into a meal uninvited, a crudity supposedly warned against in Anii 21.10–13 (AEL 2.142) and Duachety 9.7–9 (AEL 2.190). (Anii speaks of entering another's home uninvited and Duachety warns against rushing to the table before being summoned.) The fault in Prov 23:6–8, according to this interpretation, lies with the uninvited guest, not the host, who is ill-willed only because of the intrusion. But there is no suggestion in Prov 23:6–8 that the guest has come unbidden, and *raʿ ʿayin* does not mean "unwilling host" (Clifford), but rather a stingy or envious man. Still, Clifford asks good questions about the usual interpretation: "Why would anyone go to a known miser's in the first place?" The answer is that social obligations coupled with professional duties and expectations would impose this ritual on both the guest and the host. "Why does the host say one thing and mean another?" Because he is a hypocrite. Though stingy, he must put on a good face. "Why does the guest vomit up the food?" He doesn't. This is a metaphor for disgust.

The Instruction of Kagemeni gives similar advice:

(1.7) If you are sitting (8) with a glutton,
you should eat (only) when his craving has passed.
If you drink with (9) a drunk,
you should partake (only) when his heart is content.
Do not pounce on the meat (when sitting) next to a greedy man.
(10) Take what he gives you, do not refuse it.
This is the way to soothe.
He who is without reproach in regard to food—
no word (11) will prevail against him. (Pap. Prisse; cf. AEL 1.60)

When you dine with a greedy man (the teacher probably has a superior official in mind), restrain your appetite, for he will begrudge the food you take, even if he puts on a gracious face. The underlying rule is to minimize tension, even with base types. The parallel to Prov 23:6–8 is thematic, not verbal.

Some of the phraseology of Prov 23:6–8 resembles an image in Amenemope that which warns against coveting the poor man's goods:

(14.5) **Do not covet** a poor man's **property**,
(6) **nor hunger for** his bread.
(7) The property of a poor man—it is a blockage[332] in the throat,
(8) **and it makes the gullet vomit**.
(9) As for him who promotes himself by false oaths,
(10) his heart is confounded (?)[333] in his chest,

[332] Or "storm"; hence the suggestion to read *šʿr* in Prov 23:7 as *śaʿar* "storm"; cf. BHS.

[333] Or "turns about" (*sh*ʾ), perhaps indicating dishonest intentions. Lichtheim translates, "His heart is misled by his belly" (AEL 2.155).

(11) because of the hostility.
The profit dwindles,
(12) and the bad harms the good.[334]
(13) You will be harmed before your superior,
(14) **while you are ineffective** (?) **in your replies,**[335]
(15) **your flatteries being rebuffed by curses,**
(16) and your obeisance by blows.
(17) The big mouthful of bread you swallowed, **you vomit it up,**
(18) and are emptied of your good (things? words?).
(19) Be aware that the oppressor (?) of the poor—
(15.1) the rod befalls him.
(2) All his people are fettered in stocks,
(3) and he is led to the overseer[336] of the place of execution.
(4) When you are released from the presence of your superior,[337]
(5) you are (still) hated by your subordinates.
(6) Steer clear of the poor man on the road,
(7) when you see him, stay away from his goods.[338]

(§11, complete [cf. AEL 2.11])

Proverbs borrows from this passage but shifts the issue from social ethics to social comportment. The main resemblance is in the mention of vomiting as a metaphor for revulsion. Also, the mention of "flatteries" in Amenemope 14.15 shows that "your fine words" in Prov 23:8b alludes to the guest's flattery of the host. In Proverbs, the connection between the vomiting and the fine words is not explained. In Amenemope, the connection is clearer: If you exploit the poor, your superior will be angry at you. He will rebuff your compliments and confound your replies until, in despair, you disgorge your food.[339] (Vomiting seems to be a metaphor for emotional distress.)

Ben Sira has a discourse on table etiquette (31[34]:12–21), in which he rewords and conflates Prov 23:1–3 and 6–8. In the following quotation, phrases that recall

---

[334] The evil of the false oaths and/or the hostility the perjurer arouses will diminish the value of whatever wealth he may gain thereby.

[335] Or "reports" (*sḏw*).

[336] Read *iw.f ṯ'y (n) ḥy n nmt*.

[337] After devouring the poor man's goods.

[338] Amenemope 15.6–7 looks like a literary allusion to "The Eloquent Peasant" (AEL 1.169–84), which tells how a peasant was assaulted and robbed of his goods by a minor official while traveling to market. The peasant complains to the official's superior, the high steward. He rails against the injustice at length, in elegantly bitter words, while, unbeknownst to him, his words are being recorded for Pharaoh's aesthetic pleasure. In the end, the high steward confiscates the official's goods and gives them to the peasant.

[339] It is significant that Amenemope motivates his admonition against cheating the poor by threatening social disgrace. The ethic of the elite demands decent treatment of one's inferiors because the preservation of the just order, Ma'at, requires respecting the rights of the poor in their place. He who violates the Ma'at due them will incur the wrath of his superiors. The ethical obligations of Egyptian officialdom toward the lowly receive powerful expression in "The Eloquent Peasant," on which see the preceding footnote.

Proverbs are boldfaced, and the corresponding verses in Prov 23 are cited in brackets. Sometimes synonyms are used for the same concept (e.g., *gadol* "important man" for *mošel* "official").

(31[34]:12a) The teaching of bread and wine together.
(12b) My son, **if you are seated at the table of an important man** [*gadol*], [// 1a]
do not open your throat at him, [// 2]
(12c) Do not say (to yourself), "He has plenty of food!"[340]
(13a) but remember that **the stingy eye** is bad [*rʿh ʿyn rʿh*]. [// 6a]
(13b) God hates **the stingy man**, [// 6a]
and worse than him he did not create.
(13c) That is why (the eye) weeps in every matter,
and tears stream from the face.
(13d) God did not create evil from the eye;
therefore its moisture flees from everyone's face.
(14) To the place that (the stingy man) looks, do not stretch out your hand,
and do not join with him in (taking from) the basket. [// 6b]
(15) Know that your neighbor feels as you do,
and examine all that you hate.[341]
(16) Recline like a man who is chosen,[342]
and be not a glutton, lest you be despised.
(17) Be the first to stop, for the sake of propriety [*musar*],
and do not gulp (your food), lest you be despised.
(MS B, with marginal readings)

The discourse continues for four more verses, arguing for moderation in eating on the grounds of health. Ben Sira plays on the phrase *raʿ ʿayin* "stingy," lit., "bad of eye." He uses phrases and concepts of the Proverbs passages in much the same way that the author of Part III drew on Amenemope: selecting, rephrasing, and expanding his source material to make it serve his own purposes. These techniques are in play in the development of Wisdom Literature from earliest times; see in particular E. Hornung's 1979 study of the reuse of Ptahhotep in the Egyptian tradition.

Maxim 10: Do not speak with a fool.
23:9 Do not speak in the ears of a dolt,
for he will despise the insight of your words.

[340] And therefore imagine that you can take whatever you want.

[341] Be aware of what you hate and avoid doing it to others. In other words, "What is hateful to you, do not unto your neighbor," as Hillel says in *b. Shab.* 31b.

[342] Perhaps: like a man chosen to head the banquet, who must behave with dignity; see Sir 32[35]:1–2 and Vol. I, 305 in this Commentary.

Prov 9:7–8 warns against trying to instruct an impudent person, because he will just hate you for it. (Thus too Sir 22:9–10.) Proverbs, however, often does advocate chastisement of such types. Indeed, Lady Wisdom herself rebukes them (1:22). Wisdom Literature contains different ideas about the value of speaking to fools (see "Who Can Learn?" [Vol. I, 309–17]), and these ideas are even placed side-by-side in Prov 26:4–5.

Though one may have to rebuke a fool, in actuality (this proverb maintains), words won't help. Beatings are what he needs. Putting it another way, if you don't want to be a fool (and get a beating), you must listen to verbal correction; see 17:10; 19:25; and 21:11.

speak in the ears: To make yourself distinctly heard (Delitzsch).

This couplet has no parallel in Amenemope, but Ptahhotep makes much the same point.

(575) As for the fool who cannot listen,
(576) he can do nothing.
(577) He sees knowledge as ignorance,
(578) benefit as harm. (cf. AEL 1.74)

See Vol. I, 118 for more of this text.

Maxim 11: Do not encroach on orphans' fields.

23:10 Do not encroach on the ancient boundary,
nor enter the fields of orphans,
11 for their redeemer is strong.
He will contend with you on their behalf.

Fields were marked by boundary stones. Displacing them for the sake of aggrandizing one's own property was a crime that was hard to prove. The crime was especially heinous when committed against widows (15:25b) and orphans (23:10b), for these were powerless to seek legal redress unless they had an adult male to argue their case in court. This was true even when the orphan was not destitute. Prov 23:10b assumes that the orphan in question has a field as his patrimony, though as a child he cannot protect it. A field untended or unprotected during the owner's minority would be a tempting target for encroachment.

ʿôlām ["ancient"]: The emendation to *ʾalmānāh* for the sake of parallelism (Ehrlich, Toy, BHS, etc.) is graphically dissimilar and unnecessary, though one might adduce the reference to the widow in Amenemope 7.5. Nor should we emend to *ʿûlîm* "infants," "nurslings," with Tur-Sinai (p. 52), following the reading presupposed in *m. Peʾah* 5:6 and possibly *y. Sotah* 4.4. This reading is questionable because infants as such would not be presumed to be legally helpless, since their fathers may be alive. Nor would there be any reason to limit the admonition to the fields of infants, since older minor children would be no less vulnerable. In 22:28, the endangered property is called *gᵉbûl ʿôlām* "ancient boundary." "The fields of orphans" specifies the kind of "ancient boundary" most susceptible to encroachment.

orphans [*y^etomim*]: In biblical terms, an orphan (*yatom*) is a minor who has lost one parent. The loss of a father would have made a child vulnerable to exploitation and unable to seek legal redress on his own.

their redeemer [*go'ălam*]: Orphans and widows are vulnerable but not truly helpless. Lacking a human protector (Job 29:12), they are under God's special protection (Deut 10:18; Ps 68:6). A *go'el* was first of all a kinsman obliged to protect a helpless relation by avenging his murder, buying him out of debt slavery, or acquiring an ancestral plot that had been sold or forfeited. The purpose of the institution of *go'el* is to keep the extended family or clan intact. Since the duties of a *go'el* (at least in early times) included executing blood vengeance, to say that Yahweh is the orphan's *go'el* implies a threat of violent punishment against the encroacher as well an assurance of help for the weak.

contend with you on their behalf [*yarib 'et ribam 'ittak*]: The same idiom is used in 22:23a in warning against cheating the lowly.

Prov 23:10–11 is a variant of 22:28. It repeats the first line of 22:28 and extends it differently, using the wording of 22:23a and ideas from Amenemope §6, quoted here in its entirety:

(7.12) **Do not displace the stone on the boundary of the fields,**
(13) nor move the position of the measuring cord.
(14) Do not be greedy for (even) a cubit of a field,
(15) nor **encroach on the boundary** of the widow.
(16) The trodden furrow[343] shortens the lifetime
(17) of him who cheats in the fields.
(18) Should he ensnare (something) by false oaths,
(19) **he will be caught by the powers** of the Moon.
(8.1) Know that he who does this on earth
(2) is a foe of the weak.[344]
(3) He is an enemy who is cast down in (his) body.
(4) (This crime) takes life from him who does it.
(5) His house is an enemy of the town;
(6) his barns will be demolished,
(7) his property taken away from his children,
(8) and his belongings given to another.
(9) **Beware of encroaching on the boundaries of the fields,**
(10) lest a terror take you away.
(11) One pleases God by the powers of the Lord,
(12) (in) determining the boundaries of the fields.[345]
(13) Desire that your body be well,

---

[343] In another's field; see 8.15.

[344] Adding a man-determinative to Egyptian *qb* = *gbw* "weak."

[345] When a scribe, with the help of the power of the Lord (Thoth), marks out the boundaries of the fields correctly, he pleases God, which is to say, whichever divinity is relevant to the situation.

(14) and beware of the All Lord.[346]
(15) **Do not traverse the furrow of another;**
(16) it is good for you to be kept well by them.
(17) Plow in the fields and you will find what you need
(18) and get food from your own threshing floor.
(19) Better is the bushel that God gives you
(20) than five thousand gained by force.
(9.1) They do not last the day in storehouse or barn;
(2) they make no food for the jar.
(3) Their time in the granary is but a moment;
(4) when day dawns, they sink down.
(5) **Better is poverty in the hand of the god,**
(6) **than wealth in the storehouse.**
(7) **Better is (simple) bread when the heart is pleasant,**
(8) **than wealth with vexation.** (§6, complete [cf. AEL 2.151–52])

Prov 22:28 and 23:10a are based on Amenemope 7.12 and 8.9. More loosely, Prov 23:10b echoes Amenemope 8.15, and Prov 23:11 recasts the warning of divine punishment in Amenemope 7.19 and 8.14. Amenemope 9.5–8 is the source of Prov 15:16 and 17:1; see the Comments there.

Amenemope refers to a specifically Egyptian practice. The fields had to be marked out each year after the Nile floodwaters subsided. The scribes who kept records of the landholdings would mark the boundaries anew with measuring lines. The mention of the cord indicates that the crime envisioned here is that of a scribe aggrandizing his own property, or, more likely, a protector's or briber's, by a dishonest configuration of the fields. Amenemope's chapter 6 excoriates the scribe who falsifies the land-register. This maxim speaks directly to Amenemope's own situation, because he was a scribe "who determines the islands of new land" (1.17), "who fixes the markers on the borders of fields" (1.19), and "who makes the land-register of Egypt" (2.2), and his son would likely inherit those positions (cf. AEL 2.148–49).

In words very similar to Prov 22:28, Deut 19:14 commands: "You shall not encroach on the boundary of your neighbor, which the ancients marked out in the inheritance which you will receive." This command is not necessarily directed at scribal deception, but could refer to anyone surreptitiously moving a neighboring boundary marker. The relationship between Deut 19:14 and the similar sayings in Proverbs, namely, Prov 22:28 and 23:10–11, is hard to determine. Possibly a form of Amenemope was known to the authors of both these texts and used by them independently. Alternatively, Deuteronomy may be quoting from the most ancient parts of Proverbs. The latter is likely because Deuteronomy is familiar with

[346] A virtual conditional: *If* you desire that your body be well (13), *then* beware of the All Lord (14). "All Lord" is an epithet of various gods, especially the sun god and the king.

other parts of the book.[347] Other options can be excluded. Deuteronomy is not the source of Prov 22:28, for the editor of Part IIIa is using Amenemope extensively and would not have resorted to Deuteronomy for a lone proverb. Nor is it likely that the editor inserted a free-floating Hebrew saying that just happened to closely resemble a maxim of Amenemope when he is borrowing so much from that book to start with.

PART IIIB: PROVERBS 23:12–24:22

WORDS OF THE WISE, CONTINUED

The thirty maxims continue, but now without recourse to Amenemope. The sources of most of the maxims are unknown, but 23:13–14 is closely related to Ahiqar and 23:29–35 resembles a passage in Anii. Shupak (2005: 214–15) notes a variety of Egyptian parallels.

Maxim 12: Take discipline and give it.

23:12 Bring your heart to discipline
and your ear to words of knowledge.
13 Do not withhold discipline from a youth,
for if you smite him with a rod he will not die.
14 If you smite him with a rod,
you will save his life from Sheol.

23:12. Like Part IIIa, IIIb opens with a call to attention. Renewed exhortations appear also in 5:7; 8:32–33; and 23:19, 22–25, and 26. The conjunction of two instructions about discipline indicates that wisdom is transmitted by taking it as a child and dispensing it as an adult. The listener, at least fictionally the son of the speaker, is told how to educate *his* son, as in the Ahiqar passage below.

Bring your heart . . . your ear: The idioms "bring your heart" and "(bring) your ear" are unique.

discipline, knowledge: In particular, the words of the present teaching.

23:13–14. Beat your son, the maxim advises, in order to save him from the early death he will probably suffer if allowed to run wild. See the Comment on 13:24.

he will not die: Verse 13b is not reassurance that corporal punishment will not kill the boy (as Saʿadia, Hameʾiri, Delitzsch, and many others read it). Rather, as the restatement in v 14b shows, it means that discipline will prevent your son from going astray into deeds that would put his life in peril (McKane). The latter

[347] Weinfeld 1972: 265–67 argues that Deut 19:14 (cf. 27:17) was influenced "by the school of wisdom" (if not directly by Proverbs). Deuteronomy expands the aphorism in its characteristic manner, adding "in your inheritance which you will inherit in the land that the Lord your God gives you" and replacing "ancient" (*ʿolam*) by "the previous generations" (*riʾšonim*).

interpretation is supported by the very similar teaching in Ahiqar (assuming that Lindenberger's restoration of *l' tḥyh* at the end of l. 82 [1.1.177] is correct):

Do not keep your son from the rod.
If you are not able to save him [from wickedness]
* * *[348]
If I beat you, my son, you will not die.
And if I leave you to your own heart,
[you will not live].[349] (81–82 [1.1.176–77])

To avoid beating one's son is tantamount to leaving him to his own "heart," or inclinations.

The advice is used differently in the two books. Whereas in Proverbs, a father addresses his son and advises him to beat *his* son, Ahiqar first gives this advice, then uses it to convince his (adopted) son that he should appreciate the beatings *he* receives. Other counsels about child raising are Prov 19:18; 22:6; and 29:17. Other verses in Proverbs advocating corporal punishment are 13:24; 19:25, 29; 22:15; 26:3; and 29:15.

Maxim 13: Be wise and make your parents happy.

23:15 My son, if your heart becomes wise,
my heart too will rejoice,
16 and my kidneys will exult
when your lips speak rectitude.

The speaker encourages his son to seek wisdom by appealing to his filial sentiments; see the Comment on 10:1bc.

my heart too [*libbi gam 'ani*]: By the very emphatic additive *gam 'ani* the speaker indicates that both he and his son will rejoice when the son gains wisdom.

kidneys: These were considered an organ of emotion.

Maxim 14: Do not envy sinners.

23:17 Let not your heart envy sinners,
but rather the fear of the Lord every day.
18 For if {you maintain it},[a] there is a future,
and your hope will not be cut off.

[a] + *tišmᵉrennāhh.*

Do not envy sinners their possessions. (The proverb seems to assume that sinners characteristically do prosper.) You should, instead, desire to possess the fear

[348] In a careful examination of the second line, *hn lw l' tkhl thnṣln*[*hy*], Römheld (1989: 46–51) argues that *hn lw l'* can only mean "if not." The extant words are a protasis whose apodosis is lost in the lacuna, which constitutes nearly half of line 82 [176] in the MS. Römheld translates, "Wenn du (ihn) nicht erretten kannst . . ." ("If you cannot save him . . .") (p. 47; ellipsis in the German).

[349] Thus Lindenberger (1983: 49, 51), who restores *l' tḥyh*, "you shall not live," at the end of l. 82.

of God, for its rewards endure, unlike the prosperity of the wicked. Envy of the wicked stems from the failure to realize that they will soon die (Pss 37:2, 9a, 36a, 38; 73:18–20) and thus betrays lack of faith in God's justice. Similar advice appears in Prov 3:31; 24:1–2, 19–20; and Ps 37:1; cf. Ps 73:3.

23:17. *but rather*: That is, "but rather let your heart envy . . ."

the fear of the Lord: This is probably to be understood as equivalent to "those who fear the Lord" (Ehrlich, G. R. Driver [1951: 196]). By this explanation, the parallelism is tighter and the sentence makes better sense, because one envies persons, not things. Strictly speaking, one need not actually envy the God-fearing because what they possess can be possessed by anyone, once he realizes that the fear of God is desirable.

23:18. *For if {you maintain it}*: The MT is missing a word. "Maintain" or something similar is required by context.

kî ʾim {tišmᵉrennāhh}: A verb is required after *kî ʾim*. The MT would have to be translated "for if there is a future" or "for if there is hope," which is not a logical protasis. *Kî ʾim* never means "surely" (contrary to most commentators). We should add *tišmᵉrennāhh* (Gemser, McKane, BHS, and many others) or *tinṣᵉrennāhh*, following LXX's *tērēsēs auta* "keep them" (but using a sg. suffix to refer to "fear of the Lord"). Alternatively, we could omit *ʾim* and translate, "For there is a future" (Toy).

there is a future [*ʾaḥărit*]: That is, hope for a good future *for you* (*// tiqwatᵉka* "your hope"), with special reference to a long life and possibly offspring; see the Comment on 19:20. Prov 23:18 ≈ 24:14bc. (And note that 24:14a repeats the theme of 23:15–16.) In 23:18 "future" is more integrated into context, for a "future" is equivalent to "life," which is the reward for fearing God (10:27; 19:23).

Maxims 15–18. Prov 23:19–35 forms a long, loosely structured instruction warning against debauchery. Verses 19–26 serve as an exordium, with exhortations to listen (vv 19, 22–23, 26) and motivations (vv 24–25). The exordium also introduces the main theme of the instruction, namely, the avoidance of gluttony and drunkenness. These two vices may represent dissolute behavior generally and include sexual wantonness, the theme of vv 26–28. Drunkenness becomes the theme again in vv 29–35.

Maxim 15: Avoid dissipation.

23:19 Listen, my son, and become wise,
and go straight in the way[a] of your heart.
20 Do not be among the winebibbers,
among those who gorge on meat,
21 for he who imbibes and gorges himself will be impoverished,
and sleep will clothe one in rags.

[a] *bᵉderek* (MT *badderek*).

You should desire to go straight, rather than turning aside to profligacy and sloth. These vices reinforce each other to waste a man's money and prevent him from earning more. Drunkenness and gluttony characterize the rebellious son in Deut 21:20 (which uses the same words as here) and seem to stand for dissolute behavior in general.

go straight [*wᵉʾaššer*]: The verb *ʾaššer,* actually "go," "tread" (as in 4:14 [D] and 9:6 [G]), has the connotation of "go straight," by association with *y-š-r* "straight"; thus Isa 1:17. It is also a relevant pun on *ʾaššer* "make happy," "declare happy."

in the way of [*bᵉderek*] *your heart*: The way of one's heart is what he desires to do. It is not inherently the right way, but in this case it is defined as right because the second line is consequent upon the first, in which the son becomes wise. We might translate, "*and then* go straight in the way of your heart." Moreover, the youth is told to "go straight" in it. That makes it the right way. ("His way" [that is, a youth's] is used similarly in Prov 22:6.) One should listen to one's own (instructed) mind rather than to companions and tempters (Clifford).

The MT, which reads *badderek* "in the way" must be translated, "and guide your heart in the way." *ʾšr* means "guide" in Isa 3:12 and 9:15. The problem is that "the way" without further definition is not a metaphor for modes of life in Proverbs. According to one metaphor, there are *two* paths—the path to life and the path to death. According to another metaphor, there are *many* paths—types of behavior in life; see Vol. I, 128–31. But there is not a single path through life, one that could be called *the* way. The MT avoids the expression "the way of your heart" to preclude the impression that one *should* go in the way of his heart, that is, to follow one's desires (Qoh 11:9), which can lead one astray (Isa 57:17).

gorges himself [*zôlēl*]: When *zll* has "meat" as its object (Prov 23:20) or is parallel to *sbʾ* "drink excessively" (Deut 21:20; Prov 23:20, 21; Sir 18:33), it means to be a glutton, but that is not its primary sense. Etymologically, *z-l-l* means "be light," "trivial," and in the G-stem its sense is "be thoughtless," "rash" (HALOT 272a), or the like. In Jer 2:36 and 15:19, it means to "act or be contemptible, worthless," with no relation to gluttony; sim. Lam 1:11. Even when referring to actual gluttony, this particular vice, together with drunkenness, appears to represent other failings, *pars pro toto.* In Deut 21:20, the "gluttonous and drunken son" is guilty of decadence in many ways. LXX translates *zwll* here as "whoremonger" (*pornokopos*), perhaps reflecting an old interpretation of these terms as including dissipation of different sorts.

Maxim 16: Gain wisdom and make your parents happy.

23:22 Listen to your father, who begot you,
and be not contemptuous when your mother grows old.
23 <Get truth and do not sell it:
wisdom and discipline and understanding.>
24 The father of a righteous (son) will greatly rejoice,
and he who begets a wise (son) will rejoice in him.
25 Let your father and mother rejoice,
and she who bore you exult!

This maxim resumes the exhortation. It urges the son to listen to the father's teaching and to gain wisdom, for this will make his father happy. The epigram lays emphasis on the parents' role as teachers (v 22) and their joy in a wise son. On the parents' feelings as a motivation for wisdom and folly, see the Comment on 10:1bc. On the parents' roles in education, see Vol. I, 80–83.

The words "father," "mother" and "beget," "bear (a child)" (Hebrew *yld*) weave together verses 22, 24, and 25 of this epigram: father and *yld* (22a); mother (22b); father (24a); *yld* (24b); father and mother (25a); *yld* (25b). The verb *yiśmaḥ* "rejoice" at the end of v 24 and the start of v 25 links those two verses.

23:22. The two lines of v 22 are complementary and mean: "Listen to your father and mother and be not contemptuous when they grow old." Refusing to listen to one's parents is tantamount to holding them in contempt, an attitude excoriated in 20:20 and 30:17. Ben Sira (3:12–13) elaborates on the present verse: "My son, be strong in the honoring of your father, and do not abandon him all the days of your life. And even if his mind is diminished, give him help, and do not shame him all of his days." The Egyptian O. Petrie 11 (recto 2) similarly says, "Do not mock an old man or an old woman because they are weak, lest (they utter a curse) upon *your* old age."

23:23. This is a variant of Prov 4:5 and 4:7, which exhort the reader to "get [*qᵉneh*] wisdom!" Here *qᵉneh* "get," being the antonym of "sell," has the specific nuance of *buying*. The pattern of *one object + three objects* appears also in 1:3. The objects in 23:23b are in apposition with "truth" and define it as *words* of truth, that is, the teachings of wisdom. (If the B-line were listing three objects *in addition to* "truth," then "truth," the initial word in the Hebrew A-line, would be at the end of the A-line, or at least the Hebrew conjunction *waw* ["and"] would begin the B-line.)

This verse is probably a later addition intended to provide the exhortation in v 22 with a motivation in accordance with the usual structure of exordia (see Vol. I, 415). While v 23 is appropriate to the general context, it is extraneous to the theme and keywords of this otherwise cohesive epigram, vv 22 + 24–25. Verse 24 would follow nicely on v 22. Verse 23 is absent from the LXX, and there is no motivation, ideological or graphic, for an omission by a copyist or translator.

23:24. *righteous (son), wise (son)*: That is, the righteous, wise person. "Son" is not in the Hebrew, but only "righteous" and "wise." These words are nouns in the Hebrew. They can refer to adults and children and do not exclude females.

This translation follows the qeré readings; see the Textual Note.

23:25. *Let . . . rejoice . . . exult*: Become wise and thereby make your parents rejoice, in accordance with v 24. See the connection of wisdom and joy in 23:15–16.[350]

rejoice, exult: The verb in the B-line, *tāgēl*, is a jussive, so the parallel in the A-line, *yiśmaḥ*, is as well. This is reinforced by the verb–subject word order, which, in the absence of a "trigger" that causes frontal positioning, indicates modality (Revell 1989: 14–15; Holmstedt 2002: 134–55).

[350] As Frydrych (2002: 41) observes, the conjunction of vv 24 and 25, which are almost identical in content but differ in syntax, shows that there is no fundamental difference in the force of what he calls a "wisdom sentence" (in the indicative) and an "instruction" (in the imperative or jussive). The former formulation too can be intended to induce action. This is contrary to a distinction drawn by McKane (1970: 3).

Maxim 17: Avoid the temptress.

23:26 Give your heart to me, my son,
and let your eyes keep my ways,
27 for the strange woman[a] is a deep pit,
the alien woman a narrow well.
28 She also lurks like a bandit,
and eliminates traitors among men.

---

[a] *zārāh* (MT *zônāh*).

Prov 23:26–28 warns against the temptress as a deadly danger. This epigram may have inspired the anecdote in Prov 7. There too, the call to attention and the warning against the Strange Woman are fused syntactically.

23:26. *Give your heart to me*: Pay attention to me—not to the Strange Woman. McKane says that this phrase means not just "Give me your undivided attention" but also "Rely absolutely on my advice." Hame'iri recognized that this verse contrasts with the next: "The eye and the heart are the pimps of sin, as is written in the Torah, 'And you shall not go wandering after your heart and after your eyes' " (Num 15:39).

Give your heart (*ntn lēb*): This idiom is used in an unusual if not unique way in this verse, where it means "pay attention." The idiom *ntn lēb* "give heart" can mean to make one intelligent (Deut 29:3; 1 Kgs 3:9), to give one a certain disposition (Ezek 36:26), or to intend something (Qoh 1:13, 17; Dan 10:12; 1 Chr 22:19). It means "pay attention" in Qoh 7:21a, but in a somewhat different sense, namely, "take them to heart," "let them bother you." In Egyptian the idiom *imi ib.k* (or *ḥ'ty.k*) "give your heart" means "pay attention" and frequently appears in school texts (e.g., Hori [recto 3]; further references in Fischer-Elfert 1986: 2). Amenemope says: "Give your heart to interpret them" (3.4). The use of this idiom in Prov 23:26 is an Egyptianism.

keep [*nṣr*] *my ways*: That is, the ways I am teaching you. (Compare the idiom in Ps 119:33 and, with *šmr* "keep," in Prov 2:8, 20; 8:32.) This is according to the qeré *tiṣṣornah*. The ketiv *trṣnh* (= *tirṣeynāh*) is also meaningful: "Let your eyes desire [or "delight in"] my ways" (as opposed to the Strange Woman's). Delitzsch prefers the ketiv on the grounds that it seems more affectionate, but exhortations often speak of *keeping* the commands.

23:27. *the strange woman* [*zarah*]: The term *zarah* "strange" (fem.), like *'iššah zarah* ("strange woman"), implies that she is married. She is "strange" insofar as she belongs to another man (see Vol. I, 139–41).

The MT has *zonah* "prostitute." While *zonah* is possible, the prostitute was less of an object of aversion to the sages than the adulteress was; see Vol. I, 138. We should emend to *zarah*.

zārāh: The B-line line of the present verse has *nokriyyāh* "alien." *Nokri(yyāh)* is always parallel to *zār(āh)* in Proverbs (2:16; 5:20; 7:5; 20:16; 23:27; 27:13), with the exception of 6:24. There it is parallel to *'ēšet rē'ekā*, "another man's wife," which is equivalent to *zārāh/'iššāh zārāh*; see Vol. I, 139–41. The doublet in 22:14 has *zārôt* "strange women." Emending *zwnh* to the graphically similar *zrh* has the support of LXX's *allotrios* "stranger."

pit [*šuḥah*] // *well* [*bᵉʾer*]: A pit or well, as Saʿadia notes, is easy to fall into and hard to get out of. A woman's sexuality is metaphorically a "cistern" (*bor*) and a "well" (*bᵉʾer*). These terms allude to the vagina, for both its shape and its productivity; see the Comment and the Textual Note on 5:15. The sexuality of a man's own wife is regarded as a blessed, productive well and a source of joy (5:15–18), whereas the "well" of another man's wife is a trap. A "pit" (*šuḥah* or *šaḥat*), however, is not a symbol of productive sexuality, because it is dry and barren. It is an epithet of Sheol (e.g., Isa 51:14; Ezek 28:8; Ps 16:10), which is a relevant allusion here (McKane). "The Dialogue of Pessimism," cited in the Comment on 22:14, says that a woman—any woman, and not just a fornicator—is "a pitfall, a pitfall, a hole, a ditch" (BWL 816). Anii says that the female "outsider" "sets a trap" (16.15; see Vol. I, 135).

23:28. *like a bandit* [*ḥetep*]: This word probably designates a criminal who kills or kidnaps. This woman is not only a passive hazard like a cistern or pit; she is an active danger, like a robber lying in ambush. The adulteress is at once the lure and the trap. She is the crime and its punishment. The Strange Woman is described this way in 7:12.

ḥetep: Hurowitz (*2001c*: 159) explains this word on the basis of Akkadian *ḫatăpu* "to kill," "spill blood." He proposes vocalizing *ḥattāp* "killer" or the like, but, to the same effect, the form *ḥetep* could be a metonymy—"killing" for "killer"—or perhaps an "occupational" segolate, like *melek* "king." In Job 9:12, *ḥtp* could mean "kill" or "snatch away," and both senses are possible in the present verse. In Ps 10:9, the related verb *ḥtp* "snatch" is used of trapping a poor man in a net.

and eliminates traitors [*bogᵉdim*] *among men*: The Strange Woman is the cause of the destruction of the men who fall in her trap. They are "traitors" or "betrayers." The use of the term *bogᵉdim* here alludes obliquely to the wrong inflicted on the wives of these men.

The condemnation of male marital infidelity as a betrayal of the wife is a rarity. Condemnation is usually directed at women who have committed adultery or men who have violated other men's marriages, and the wronged party is the cuckolded husband. The root *b-g-d* "betray" implies an existing bond between two parties, a bond that demands fidelity. The wrong done by the adulterers to the Strange Woman's husband is not betrayal as such. The bonds that are violated by the "traitors" must be marriage vows, and the victims must be their own wives.[351] Malachi uses *bgd* in reference to a man's betraying his wife by unwarranted divorce (2:14–15; see the Comment on Prov 2:17).

Adultery in ancient Israel meant sex between one man and another's wife or betrothed. The concern was to protect the integrity of a man's marriage and ensure that his heirs were in fact his own offspring. This proverb's sensitivity to the wife's right to her husband's fidelity shows that a married man, quite apart from the prohibition of adultery, was morally bound to marital fidelity. The enthusiastic praise

[351] In view of this, my assertion that "[i]n Proverbs, arguments against infidelity do not adduce the harm it causes the cheated wife" (Vol. I, 208) should be modified to exclude this verse, in which one word is sufficient to show awareness of this harm.

of the joys of monogamous sexual fidelity in Prov 5:15–20 is aimed at convincing young men to avoid harming *themselves* by being enticed into sex with another man's wife.

eliminates [*tôsip* = *tôsîp*]: The verb *hôsîp* usually means "add," "increase." Most commentators understand this line to mean that the Strange Woman "adds to faithless men" (Murphy), that is, increases their number. This is a tautology. McKane (following G. R. Driver 1951: 196) assigns *bôgᵉdîm* an abstract sense, "treachery." Then "she increases treachery among men" means that she "deceives men again and again." Similarly, Saʿadia glosses *bôgᵉdîm* as "heresy and wickedness." But by these explanations the B-line says nothing about the evil effects of the woman's action. The fact that the Strange Woman (or prostitute, in the MT) turns many men into adulterers would not intimidate a potential adulterer. *Tôsip* (though formally from *y-s-p* H) is here a by-form of *teʾĕsôp*, from *ʾ-s-p* "gather," "take away," hence "destroy," "exterminate"; sim. 1 Sam 15:6 (*y-s-p* H) and Zeph 1:2–3 (*ʾāsēp*, from *s-w-p* H, another by-form of *ʾ-s-p*).

Maxim 18: Avoid drunkenness.

23:29 Who (cries) "Woe!"? Who cries "Alas!"?
Who has quarrels? Who has complaints?
Who has wounds without cause?
Who has bloodshot eyes?
30 Those who tarry late over wine,
who come to inspect mixed wine.
31 Don't look at wine when it glows red,
when it gives its gleam in the cup,
flowing down smoothly.
32 In the end it bites like a serpent,
and spews (venom) like a viper.
33 Your eyes will see strange things,
and your heart speak perversities.
34 And you will be like one who lies (in bed) in the heart of the sea,
or like one who lies in the rigging.
35 "They beat me but I felt no hurt,
battered me but I was unaware.
When will I wake up?
I'll go and look for more."

This epigram mocks the folly of drunkenness and lampoons the drunkard by quoting him the morning after as he longs for more wine even while suffering a hangover. The epigram does not forbid consumption of wine, which was a staple of the ancient diet, but only its excess, as when one drinks deep into the night. Isaiah similarly mocks the dissolute "who arise early in the morning and chase after beer, who stay up late at night, and wine inflames them" (Isa 5:11). Other warnings against drunkenness are Prov 21:17; 23:21; and (for kings) 31:4–5; sim. Qoh 10:17. Ben Sira both warns against excessive drinking (31:30–31, 39–40 [34:25–26, 29–30]) and praises the pleasure that moderate drinking offers (31:32–36 [34:27–28]; 32:7–8 [35:5–6]; 40:18).

After a set of six derisive questions (v 29) and their answer (v 30), the epigram thrusts the reader into the drama by addressing "you"—the pupil/reader and potential drunk—then quoting what *you* will say in the misery of the next morning.

The epigram comprises four segments or strophes: (I) vv 29–30: questions and answer (6 lines); (II) vv 31–32: warning against wine (5 lines); (III) vv 33–34: how the drunkard will feel (4 lines); (IV) v 35: what he will say (4 lines).

23:29. *Who (cries) "Woe!" etc.?*: Lit., "To whom is 'Woe!'? To whom is 'Alas!'?" "Woe" and "alas" are not nouns but interjections spoken by the drunkard the next morning, and they rhyme: *ʾoi! ʾăboi!*

bloodshot eyes [*ḥaklilut ʿeynayim*]: Lit., "darkness of eyes." Though dark eyes can be attractive (as in Gen 49:12, using the same word), the red streaking caused by intoxication is ugly, *not* "sparkling" (contrary to HALOT 313b).

23:30. *to inspect* [*laḥqor*]: Most translations substitute a more predictable term, such as "to drain the cups" (JPSV), "often taste" (Toy, Murphy), or "quaffing" (liquor) (Clifford). But this obscures the facetious tone. The sots come to "inspect" or "investigate" wine, as it were. We can picture them hunched over their cup, staring dully at the object of their "study."

23:31–32. Wine is appealing, not only in its taste, but in its appearance, with its deep red color and sparkling *éclat*, and it glides smoothly down the throat. But it's really poison. "Don't (even) look at wine" is a "clever exaggeration" (Murphy). It's just too tempting.

gleam [*ʿeyno*]: *ʿayin* can mean "gleam," as in Ezek 1:4, 7, 16, 22, but it almost always means "eye." The use of a very common word in a rare sense activates a pun: The wine's shining "eye" stares back at the drinker, who is "inspecting" it. Moreover, in certain lighting conditions, a dark red wine (try a merlot or pinot noir) will reflect back the drinker's own eye. In the end, the drinker's own eyes will be dark and bloodshot red.

flowing down smoothly [*yithallek bᵉmeyšarim*]: *Meyšarim* (whose sense elsewhere in Proverbs is "rectitude") is a quality of fine wine in Cant 7:10: "And your palate is like the best wine—flowing smoothly [*lᵉmeyšarim*] to my beloved." *Hithallek* means "flow," like *hlk* in Cant 7:10 and Qoh 1:7.

In the end [*ʾaḥărîtô*] *it bites*: Lit., "Its end is . . . it will bite." *Aḥărîtô* functions adverbially. Compare the construction in Prov 29:21b; Num 24:20; and probably Qoh 7:8. Sim. Qoh 9:3, with *ʾaḥărāyw*.

23:33. Wine will make you hallucinate and cause your heart to "speak"—that is, imagine—perverse and crazy things. *Tahpukot*, "perversities" or "distortions" (see the Comment on 2:12), are often, as Saʿadia notes, "the opposite of honesty."

23:34. *lies (in bed) in the heart of the sea*: The Hebrew is, lit., "like one who lies in the heart of the sea." This does not mean that he has drowned (contrary to Delitzsch), for a drowned man does not hallucinate—or wake up the next morning. Rather, we are to picture someone (probably a landlubber) lying seasick in a rolling ship.

in the rigging: The second picture is even worse: someone clasping the rigging of a ship and rolling back and forth in a huge, nauseating arc.

rigging [*ḥibbēl*]: The primary meaning of this word is uncertain. As a derivative of *ḥebel* "rope," it probably means "rigging." Even if its primary meaning is "mast" (Hame'iri, Gemser), the reference here is still to the rigging on the mast or possibly the crow's nest.

23:35. *"They beat me . . ."*: The drunkard, waking up with a hangover, groans these words. It is not that he has been in a fight and is "congratulat[ing] himself that he feels no bad effects from the blows" (Toy). He is hardly in a condition to feel good about anything, nor has he really gotten into a brawl. He is saying that though he can't remember getting beaten up, it sure feels that way. As far as he can remember, he "felt no hurt" and "was unaware" of getting thrashed *at that time*. But now he aches all over and his head is splitting open. These are his "wounds without cause" (v 29b).

The drunk is not going to let his beating faze him. He resolves that as soon as he wakes up (maybe it's just a bad dream) he will go out looking for more wine, like, we might say, "a dog returning to his vomit" (26:11). He drank late (v 30a), and will now drink early. Thus it goes, day after dismal day.

Anii too offers a facetious warning against drunkenness:

(17.6) Do not overdo it when drinking beer,
(7) for unlovely (?) is the evil speech that will come forth from your
 mouth,
without your knowing that you spoke it.
You have fallen, (8) your body hurt,
while no one gives you a hand.
Your drinking companions—(9) they stand up and say,
"Away from this drunk!"
(10) (If) someone comes seeking you, to converse with you,
you will be found lying on the ground,
while you are like a (11) little child. (cf. AEL 2.137)

Washington (1994b: 142–43) outlines the following sequence in both Anii 17.6–11 and Prov 23:31–35:

1. Prohibition of drink
2. Description of unpleasant effects:
   a. Perverse speech and confusion
   b. Prostration
   c. Abuse by companions

("Abuse by companions" is absent from Prov 23:31–35, unless one understands the "blows" in v 34 as an actual beating. This is unlikely, since the epigram is describing the evils the drunk brings on *himself*.) There are similarities in theme and sequence of events, but the imagery differs. The similarities may result from the universal facts of what happens to drunks, but they are especially relevant to texts addressing young men. Anii himself is picking up a topos from school letters, in which a father scolds his son for his dissipation, including drunkenness. One such letter says, "Beer makes (you) stop being a man. It makes your soul to wander, and you are like a crooked steering oar in a boat that obeys on neither side" (Pap. Anastasi IV 11.9–11; LEM 47). It is fair to say that the ridicule of inebriation is a topos of scribal tradition taken into the Wisdom tradition. A derivation of Prov 23:29–35 from Anii or another instructional book that used this topos is likely.

Maxim 19: Do not envy the wicked.

24:1 Do not envy evil men,
nor desire to be with them.
2 For their heart meditates destruction,
and their lips speak deceit.

24:1. The admonition not to envy the wicked in their prosperity appears also in Prov 3:31; 23:17a; 24:19; and Ps 37:1; cf. Ps 73:3. Prov 24:1a ≈ 3:31a; 24:19b.

24:2. *destruction* [*šod*], *deceit* [*ʿamal*]: The reason that one should not envy the wicked is implicit in v 2, for "destruction" can point to the affliction the evildoers will *suffer* (compare 21:7), and *ʿamal* too hints at the misery awaiting the schemers. This word, which usually means "toil," can also mean misery and futility (e.g., Job 7:3; Jer 20:18) or deceit and evil (e.g., Isa 10:1; Ps 7:15; Hab 1:13).

The fact that the wicked think and speak evil does not precisely explain why one should not envy them or be "with them." For that, we would expect to hear of the harm they will cause *you*, the addressee. Several reasons can be supplied. The wicked will bring upon themselves a punishment of such force that others in their company will be afflicted by it. The wicked will teach their associates to do evil, for which the latter too will suffer. And the evildoers' propensity to harm others will one day turn against their confrères. Prov 24:1–2 takes it for granted that evildoing *must* bring punishment and that the reader shares this assumption.

Hurowitz *2000a* finds an acrostic in 24:1–22. At most, however, only the first five letters of the alphabet follow in sequence, and even this requires emendation and selective choice of which line is identified as part of the acrostic. Hurowitz finds other letters of the alphabet, but not in sequence at the starts of lines. Though it is not alphabetic, 24:1–22 is clearly demarcated as a unit of 22 verses (couplets or bicola), corresponding to the number of letters in the Hebrew alphabet. D. N. Freedman (*1972a*, passim) observes that Lam 5, which has 22 bicola, is attached to four preceding acrostics, which serve as the cue to recognizing chap. 5 as a non-alphabetic acrostic. In the case of Proverbs, he suggests, the interest in acrostics is cued by the 22–verse chap. 2 and the concluding alphabetic acrostic in chap. 31. Thus, while Prov 24:1–22 is not alphabetic, its 22 verses (like those of Psalms 33, 38, and 103) evoke the alphabetic matrix. The alphabet is imbued with power for its potential to express all words. See D. N. Freedman *1972a*: 367–92.

Maxim 20: Wisdom is precious.

24:3 By wisdom a house is built,
and by good sense it is established;
4 and by knowledge rooms are filled
with all sorts of wealth, precious and pleasant.

Wisdom (practical, and by extension, ethical) is needed in building a house, then in producing wealth to store in it. On the stages of building, see the Comment on 3:20.

This maxim and the next tell us that true prosperity (vv 3–4) and power (vv 5–6) come from wisdom, not from nefarious schemes or exercise of force. This maxim thus reinforces the previous one: "Do not envy evil men, etc." (24:1a).

Maxim 21: Wisdom is powerful.

24:5 Stronger[a] a wise man than a mighty one,[b]
and a man of knowledge than one great[c] in power.
6 For you should make war by strategy,
and victory comes through many counselors.

[a] *gābar* (MT *geber*). [b] *mēʿaz* (MT *baʿôz*). [c] *mēʾammîṣ* (MT *m[e]ʾammeṣ*).

Wisdom is mightier than other powers, whether physical or military. Compare the similar proverbs in 11:14; 15:22; and 20:18; and see the Comment on 11:14. Prov 24:6a ≈ 20:18b and 24:6b ≈ 11:14b.

This maxim does not really intend to give advice on making war, because, directed to officers and strategists, v 6 would be trite and too vague to be useful. Its purpose is to praise the efficacy of ethical wisdom by associating it with the sort of wisdom that wins wars, a faculty whose power is esteemed by all.

The MT of 24:5 reads, "A wise man is in strength, and a man of knowledge increases [lit., "strengthens"] strength." This is meaningful, but the first line is awkward and does not provide a good parallel to the B-line. We should emend as indicated above.

The emended form of v 5 is *gābar ḥākām mēʿaz, w[e]ʾîš daʿat mēʾammîṣ kōaḥ*. The changes, which are in vocalization except for a *bet-mem* change, have some versional support; see the Textual Note. For the sense and construction of the emended text, compare *mēʾărāyôt gābērû* ("they were stronger than lions") in 2 Sam 1:23 and *ʾammîṣ kōaḥ* in Isa 40:26 and Job 9:4. For *ʿaz* as a noun meaning "strong man," compare Ps 59:4, which has the plural.

For [*kî*] . . . : Verse 6 does not directly give the reason for the truth of v 5. Rather, it reinforces it by restating the same principle. Verse 6 is a sort of proof text, and *kî* could be translated, "As it is said." This is related to the "evidential" function of *kî*; see the Comment on 1:32.

Maxim 22: The fool is inarticulate.

24:7 Wisdom is beyond the fool's reach:
In the gate he cannot open his mouth.

The fool (*ʾĕwil*) cannot speak in the city gate, the place of judicial, business, and various public affairs, because he lacks the integrity for effective speech. The wicked *ʾĕwil* (unlike the dull-witted *k[e]sil*) may be glib and clever, but he will not be effective in the public forum, especially the law court. The proverb does not mean that the fool actually does keep silent (see Prov 15:2), but that he cannot speak *effectively*, and at crucial moments he cannot find the right words and thoughts.

Wisdom [*ḥokmot*]: The form *ḥokmot* is plural, lit., "wisdoms." In 1:20 (see the Comment), 9:1, and 14:1 (revocalized), this form is only an apparent plural and actually functions as a singular, "wisdom." Here alone is it a true plural, modified by a plural adjective, *ra'mot* "lofty." This probably indicates a plurality of wise words and ideas.

beyond the . . . reach [*ra'mot*]. Thus Clifford. Lit., "lofty."

rā'môt: This does not mean "corals" (thus Toy, who, however, emends) but rather is equivalent to *rāmôt* "high," "lofty." The *'aleph* is actually an unusual (and late) m.l. for long *ā*. For the phenomenon see GBH §7b. Compare the different spellings for the place name Ramot: *rā'mōt* (Deut 4:43) and *rāmōt* (Josh 21:38). Hurowitz *2000a* emends to *dmwt* (vocalization not given) and translates, "Silence for the fool is wisdom and in the city gate he should not open his mouth." This could be supported by comparison with Prov 17:28, but no such word as *dmwt* "silence" is known. In any case, the form is morphologically unlikely as a derivative of *d-m-m*.

Maxim 23: Scheming is loathsome.

24:8 He who plans to do evil—
he will be called a schemer.
9 Foolish scheming is sin itself,
and people loathe the scoffer.

Both of these proverbs on "scheming" (*mᵉzimmot*, *zimmat*) say that the schemer will be the object of public hostility.

24:8. Like folly, scheming is widely held in contempt.

He who . . . : The A-line is a *casus pendens* construction, a focused indirect object that is resumed by *lô* "to him" in the B-line; cf. 24:24.

schemer [*ba'al mᵉzimmot*]: Lit., "possessor of schemes." The construction indicates one who schemes habitually, an inveterate schemer. In other words, he who plans evil even once will get the reputation of being a chronic conniver.

24:9. Foolish schemes, and not only foolish actions, are sinful.

is sin itself [*ḥaṭṭā't*]: For the construction, see the Comment on 3:17.

people loathe [*wᵉtô'ăbat lᵉ'ādām*]: This is a case of double binding, conflating *wᵉtôēbāh lᵉ'ādām* and *wᵉtô'ăbat 'ādām*.

Maxim 24: Negligence means weakness.

24:10 If you are lax in the day of distress,
your strength will be constrained.

The meaning of the proverb is uncertain, but the present text seems to say that if you fail to exercise your faculties and powers in a difficult time, you will be weakened thereby.

The MT says, literally, "You are lax in the day of distress, your strength (is) constrained." The conditional in the above translation is implicit, as is the future tense. The B-line is a verbless clause, which is not a natural way to formulate an apodosis expressing a consequence. For that we would expect an imperfect, *yeṣar koḥekah* ("your strength will be constrained"). Still, the MT is best explained as a subtle warning that if one neglects to use his faculties and strengths in crisis, they will be diminished by this failure of nerve.

Another possible translation is "[If] you become disheartened in the day of trouble, your strength is small" (Frydrych 2002: 132). In other words, you do not know your real inner strength until it is tested.

This warning against laxity in the "day of distress" is puzzling. The "day of distress" is the time when one pays the price for prior neglect of virtues, not the time when they are neglected (see Prov 1:24–33). Also, the threat of a future lessening of strength seems rather mild to one who has survived the day of trouble in spite of his laxity. Römheld (1989: 41–46) argues that the verse as it stands is incomplete. He fills out the line thus: "If you are lax in the day of *good fortune, in the day of* trouble, your strength will be constrained" (my translation; restored words italicized). This presumes that a copyist's eye skipped from "day" to "day." This is an attractive proposal but is rather distant from the MT and conjectural.

hitrappîtā: The conditional particle *'im* is apparently elided. If the sentence were not conditional, the verse would be a scolding without context: "You have been lax in the day of distress. Your strength is constrained."

The following are some of the proposals for explaining this text: (1) Ramaq fills out the verse thus: "If you are lax in the day of distress" (that comes upon others, then) "your strength will be constrained" (when your own trouble comes). But the parenthetical words are not really implied by the present text. (2) We could add (in accordance with Ramaq's insight) *b^{e}bō' ṣārāteka̅*, "when your trouble comes," to the end of the verse. (3) Gemser adds *b^{e}ṣorkekā*, hence: "your strength will be constrained in your need." This produces nice alliteration—*ṣar kōḥăkā b^{e}ṣorkekā* "your strength will be constrained when you need it"—but it is entirely conjectural. (4) Römheld (see above) reads: *htrpyt (bywm ṭwbh), bywm ṣrh ṣr kḥkh*.

distress, constrained: This is a paronomastic pair in Hebrew: ***ṣarah/ṣar***. The root-meaning of *ṣar* (*ṣ-r-r*) is "be bound," "straitened."

Most commentators join v 10 to vv 11–12 (Saʿadia, Riyqam, Ramaq, Gemser, and Plöger, e.g.). But v 10 is speaking of a different situation, because "the day of distress" is always a time of danger to oneself (in this case, "you," the reader), whereas vv 11–12 speak of danger to others. Also, v 10b already indicates the unfortunate consequence for the reader: *your* strength will be diminished. This does not prepare the way for a demand, such as we have in the following verses, to *use* one's strength on behalf of others.

Römheld observes that warnings against laxity (such as v 10) can stand alone. He cites Egyptian model school letters, which include exhortations such as "Be not lazy, or you will be beaten. . . . Be not slack! Write! Be not contrary" (Pap. Anastasi III 3.10; 4.3; etc. [LEM 3]). But these warnings are not apt comparisons to Prov 24:10, because they concern slackness in one's studies, not in facing crises.

Maxim 25: Rescue those in mortal danger.

24:11 Save those who are being taken away to death,
and those who are tottering on (the brink of) slaughter, do not stint (in helping).
12 For if you say, "We did not know this,"
will not he who examines hearts perceive,
will not the guardian of your soul know,
and repay a man in accordance with his deed?

It is not enough to refrain from committing wrongs; you must actively try to prevent them. If you fail to do this, and you pretend ignorance of what was happening, God will know what you are really thinking and punish your cowardice. The apposite punishment would be that God will ignore *you* in your day of need.

24:11. Almost all commentators (e.g., Delitzsch and Plöger) assume that "those who are being taken away to death" are being led to judicial execution. But in judicial retribution, the question of guilt and innocence is crucial. Verse 11 is not about the wrongly condemned, because their innocence could not go without mention. Nor is the verse about the treatment of the guilty, because execution for capital crimes would raise no objection. On the contrary, it should *not* be resisted, since it is divinely commanded in all law codes (Exod 21:12, 14; Lev 24:17, 21; Deut 19:11–13) and cannot be remitted even by monetary compensation (Num 35:30–31). The notion that one is duty-bound to intervene to prevent capital punishment is grossly anachronistic. Moreover, the phrase "those tottering on (the brink of) slaughter" can describe anyone in mortal peril. For these reasons, the clause "those who are being taken away to death" is best understood as a reference to anyone facing death—at the hand of robbers, perhaps. These are the same people as those who are "tottering on (the brink of) slaughter (v 11b).

Save: This may be done in a number of ways, including "words and bribes" (Riyqam).

slaughter: Or "killing." The word *hereg* is neutral with regard to the legitimacy or legality of the act.

Do not stint [*'im taḥśôk*]: The particle *'im* introduces an adjuration. The variant *'l* (see the Textual Note) is a normalization.

24:12. "*We did not know this* [*zeh*]": Namely, the fact that someone was about to be killed. (Examples of masculine *zeh* used as a neuter, with reference to situations or events, are found in Exod 3:12; Qoh 1:10, 17; and 2:21, 23.) The line might be translated, "We did not know this one [*zeh*]" (LXX; cf. Saʿadia). However, this would imply that God *would* excuse your inaction if the victim really were a stranger.

the guardian [*noṣer*] *of your soul*: That is, God. We might expect a word meaning "watch" or "perceive," but *nṣr* elsewhere means to guard or to observe (as one observes commandments). The point is that God, who protects *you*, cares that you defend others.

This maxim has a striking parallel in Pap. Beatty IV:

(1.13b) If you are rich (2.1) and power has come to you,
your god having built you up,
do not ignore a man you know [*lacuna*].
Release another whom you find (2.2) bound.
Be a protector for the sufferer.
He is called "good" who does not act unknowing.

The Egyptian maxim demands helping a sufferer, not specifically a person slated for execution. Comparing this passage to Prov 24:11–12, Römheld (1989: 89–95) says that Proverbs does not envision a realistic chance to save someone about to be executed, but rather mentions execution as the ultimate instance of the obligation to free those in bondage. Prov 24:11–12, he says, makes an unlimited demand for participation in the fate of one's neighbors. This demand arises not from the innocence of the imperiled man but from natural group solidarity. The problem with Römheld's interpretation is that there *is* no moral demand to save condemned criminals, and execution can hardly represent all bondage.

Maxim 26: Savor wisdom's sweetness.

24:13 Eat honey, my son, because it is good,
and honeycomb (because it is) sweet to your palate.
14 So should you learn wisdom for yourself.
If you find it, there is a future,
and your hope will not be cut off.

One should desire to learn wisdom, for it is as sweet as honey. Then, in addition to gaining wisdom, he will have hope for a future. Gaining wisdom is not just a matter of hard work and harsh discipline. If pursued with love, learning is a joy (see Vol. I, 289, 294). Other things likened to honey are seductive speech (Prov 5:3), pleasant words (Prov 16:24), wisdom (Sir 24:20), and God's words and commands (Pss 19:11; 119:103). Especially interesting is the use of honey to represent both sensual temptation and intellectual pleasure. Since honey was thought to have medicinal value, the image implies health as well as sweetness. Food is a metaphor for absorbing wisdom in Prov 10:21a; 12:14a; Job 12:11; and Sir 24:20; see further Sandelin 1986. On the actual and metaphorical uses of honey in the Bible, see Forti 2006.

learn [*dᵉʿeh*]: Lit., "know!" (impv.), equivalent to *dᵉāh*. The verb *yādaʿ*, which is usually means "know," can also refer to the process of acquiring knowledge, that is, learning. The phrase *y-d-ʿ ḥokmāh* means "to learn wisdom" in Prov 1:2; Qoh 1:17; 8:16; sim. *y-d-ʿ bînāh* (lit., "to know understanding") in Isa 29:24. There is no need to emend to *rᵉʿēh* "see" (Tur-Sinai p. 102) or associate it with a (doubtful) Arabic cognate *dʿw* meaning "seek," "desire" (D. Winton Thomas 1937a: 401).

for yourself [*napšᵉka*]: Or, "for your soul"; on *nepeš* see the Comment on 3:22. It can refer to the "soul" in the sense of a person's complex of emotions and thoughts.

The learning spoken of here is not merely intellectual storage of information (which might be expressed by "learn wisdom") but learning *for your nepeš*—a deep appropriation of wisdom to yourself, making it your own. This is the condition promised in Prov 2:10: "for wisdom will enter your heart, knowledge become delightful to your soul."

there is a future: The "future" can refer to a long life or posterity or both. Verse 14bc is a near-duplicate of 23:18, where the phrase is more closely connected to its context.

Maxim 27: Do not rob the righteous.

24:15 Do not enter[a] [b] the habitation of the righteous—
don't plunder the field of his pasturing!
24:16 Though the righteous man may fall seven times, he will rise,
while the wicked will stumble in evil.

[a] *tābō'* (MT *te'ĕrōb*). [b]Omit *rāšā'* "wicked man."

24:15. This is a warning against encroaching on the property or goods of the righteous. That the "entering" envisioned in v 15a is illegitimate is shown by the parallel line.

The MT reads: "Do not lie in wait [*t'rb*], O wicked man [*raša'*], for the habitation of the righteous man!" This is awkward because one does not "lie in wait" for "habitations" but rather for persons or prey. We should emend *t'rb* to *tb'* ("come," "enter") as indicated by the LXX (see the Textual Note). To enter another's property, when the context refers to an illegitimate act, means to encroach upon it and misappropriate it, as in 23:10b: "nor enter the fields of orphans."

The MT's vocative, "(O) wicked man" [*raša'*]," is a gloss probably inserted by a scribe who was puzzled why it should be illegitimate to "enter" the habitation of the righteous. The puzzlement was unnecessary, however, because the illegitimacy is adequately indicated by the B-line. The gloss overweights the line and introduces a new addressee. The direct address to the wicked is in itself doubtful, because the book does not try to influence their behavior, which is assumed to be hopeless. To be sure, the sluggard is addressed in 6:6, 9, but laziness is not irremediable (6:6–9). Lady Wisdom speaks to various types of fools in 1:22; 8:5; and 9:16, but these verses depict rhetorical situations designed to illustrate how wisdom relates to fools and do not actually attempt to educate them.

Hebrew *bô' l-* can mean "come to *and into*," as in Pss 96:8; 132:7; Esth 6:4, and the verb can be translated "go" when the action is viewed from the perspective of its goal (e.g., Lev 21:11; Ezek 10:2a; Ps 132:7).

24:16. If the righteous man suffers harm—such as an encroachment on his field—he will recover, but wickedness is a dead-end road. A Wisdom Psalm states this principle theologically: "Many are the misfortunes of a righteous man, but the Lord will save him from them all" (Ps 34:20).

Though [*kî*]: Since the thematic connection to the preceding verse is slight, the introductory *kî* should be construed as conditional ("if") or concessive ("though") rather than causal ("because").

seven times: *Even* seven times. This is equivalent to "many" (Saʿadia). The Syriac Ahiqar (version S_2) says: "My son, the wicked falls and does not arise, while the honest man is not shaken, because God is with him" (§21). This is based on the present verse.[352]

Maxim 28: Do not gloat.

24:17 When your enemy falls, do not rejoice,
and when he stumbles, don't let your heart exult,
18 lest the Lord see and be displeased,
and turn his wrath away from him.

God resents it when you gloat at another's suffering (17:5), so much so that he might suspend your enemy's punishment just to deprive you of your smug glee. Since the suffering results from God's wrath, it must be a punishment for an offense, not an accidental misfortune. This teaches that you must not take pleasure in suffering even if it is deserved.

Prov 20:22 warns against seeking revenge or even intending to do so; see the Comment there. The present maxim goes further, condemning an unworthy feeling even when it does not lead to vengeance. Prov 11:10b, in contrast, allows for jubilation at the punishment of the wicked, as do some psalms, for example, Pss 52:8–9; 58:11–12; 59:17; 69:33. Lady Wisdom intends to gloat and savor the moment when the fools who shunned her meet disaster (Prov 1:26).

Why is schadenfreude thought to anger God? Perhaps God resents others enjoying an event in which he himself takes no pleasure. Perhaps schadenfreude is a sign of arrogance, as if the rejoicer were imagining himself taking God's side against his own enemies.

Saʿadia distinguishes two kinds of rejoicing: "Do not rejoice" prohibits expressing joy in words. "Don't let your heart exult" forbids even exultation that is silent, "in your soul." This distinction is not clear for the first clause, but the second one explicitly speaks of inner joy. Proverbs is concerned with the quality of man's deepest and hidden thoughts and feelings, for they are the substance of character and determine deeds as well.

Prov 24:17–18 is connected to the preceding maxim by the mention of *falling* and *stumbling*, but the theme has changed. The editor has arranged—or recalled, or composed—thematically distinct maxims by word-association.

When your enemy falls . . . stumbles: It is impossible to determine if the preposition *b-* of *binpōl* and *bikkāšᵉlô* is temporal (as in the above translation) or (as Ehrlich thinks) marks the oblique complement of rejoicing: Do not rejoice *in* his falling . . . *in* his stumbling.

---

[352] The Syriac MSS date from the twelfth–thirteenth centuries (S_1) and seventeenth century (S_2) and show some biblical influence.

and turn [*wᵉhešib*] *his wrath away from him*: Saʿadia (followed by other traditional commentators) says that we should (mentally) add "to you." In other words, schadenfreude will deflect God's anger from your enemy to *you*. The motive for reading the verse this way is that otherwise the proverb is explaining how to make sure that your enemy receives maximal retribution. This makes the warning against vindictiveness sound vindictive. The sensibility is, however, Saʿadia's, not the author's. The proverb does indeed assume that the reader would naturally and reasonably desire that his enemy continue to suffer God's wrath. What is castigated here is not the wish to see one's enemy suffer but rather the delight in that suffering. At any rate, the desired vengeance is left to God's justice and does not contradict Prov 24:17 (Van Leeuwen).

The two Syriac versions of Ahiqar rephrase this maxim:

My son, be not angry at the good fortune of your enemy,
nor rejoice at his misfortune. (S2 §17)

My son, if you see your enemy fallen,
do not mock him,
lest he should rise up and repay you. (S1 §17)

(In these medieval recensions, close proximity to the biblical wording probably indicates biblical influence. Here the wording resembles the Syriac translation of Prov 24:17–18.) The latter reworking makes refraining from schadenfreude a matter of prudence and removes God from the picture.

Maxim 29: Do not envy the wicked.

24:19 Be not vexed at evildoers
and don't envy the wicked,
20 for there shall be no future for the evil man;
the light of the wicked will go out.

24:19. Envy of evildoers is caused by shortsightedness and lack of faith in God's justice; see the Comment on 23:17. Variants of this admonition appear in 3:31; 23:17a; 24:1; and Ps 37:1.

24:20. *the light of the wicked will go out*: They will die and perhaps leave no posterity. Verse 20 is a stereotyped threat; see Prov 13:9b; 20:20b; and 23:18. It is the converse of 23:18. On *ʾaḥărit* "future," "posterity," see the Comment on 19:20.

Maxim 30: Fear God and the king.

24:21 Fear the Lord, my son, and the king.
Do not anger[a] either of them[b].
22 For suddenly catastrophe will go forth from them;
and who can understand the disaster either can cause?

---

[a] *titʿabbār* (MT *titʿārāb*). [b] *šᵉnêhem* (MT *šônîm*).

God and the king are powerful and can inflict severe damage on those who anger them. The proverb flatters the king by likening him to God in his righteous anger. Verse 21a is a positive formulation of the law in Exod 22:27: "Do not revile God, and do not curse a prince in your people." The phrase "revile [lit., "bless"—a euphemism] God and king" appears in 1 Kgs 21:10 and 13; cf. Isa 8:21. It signifies a double blasphemy.

Other proverbs warning of the king's wrath are Prov 16:14; 19:12; and 20:2. Ahiqar is quoted in an Aesop's fable as saying, "My son, above all fear God and honor the king" (Greek text in Coneybeare et al. 1913: 164). See too the words of Ahiqar on the danger of the king's anger quoted in the Comment on 16:14.

24:21. *Do not anger either of them*: In the MT the B-line reads: "With *šonim* do not mingle [*titʿarab*]." The first problem is *šonim*. The literal meaning of the word is "those who change" (intransitive) or "those who become different" (from others). Proposed solutions based on this sense (see below) do not really agree with the word's use elsewhere or fit the present context. Also difficult is *titʿarab* "mingle." It might make sense to warn against "mingling" with a king, but how could one do so with *God* even if he wished to? Also, if *šonim* refers to a third category of persons (e.g., "those who change"), then *šᵉneyhem*, lit., "the two of them," in v 22b lacks a two-item antecedent.

A very minor emendation of the consonantal text, following the LXX, yields: "Do not anger either of them" (Gemser). This produces a more meaningful text and improves the sense of v 22b; see the Textual Note.

Šônîm is commonly understood to mean "dissidents," "revolutionaries" (Delitzsch), "those of a different view" (Clifford), or the like. But this assigns the G-stem of *š-n-h* a sense it does not have elsewhere and also seems rather anachronistic, as if the proverb were concerned with political dissidents. The biblical term for political rebels is *môrᵉdîm*, and their offense lies not in being different in viewpoint but in the act of insurrection. *Šônîm* could mean "different," but different from *what*? Elsewhere, *šôneh* in this sense is followed by *min* (e.g., Esth 3:8; Sir 42:24 MS B [in Esth 1:7 it means "various"]). Without an explicit comparison, the terms of comparison would be implied by context, namely Yahweh and the king. But *everyone* is different from them.

Others appeal to an Arabic etymology—*saniya* "to become high," "exalted in rank"—and give *šônîm* the unique meaning of "nobility," "men of rank," or the like (D. Winton Thomas 1934: 237; Kopf 1959: 280–82). But this does not fit the context because the pupil being addressed is, ideally, headed for the royal service (Prov 22:29) and will *be* a man of rank. We should emend to *šᵉnêhem*, "both of them" or (negated in translation) "not either."

On *hitʿabbēr* meaning "make oneself the object of anger," see the Comments on 14:16 and 20:2.

24:22. *catastrophe* [*ʾeydam*], *disaster* [*piyd*]: These refer to a single event: the catastrophe/disaster that the king or God causes.

ʾêdām, pîd šᵉnêhem: The Hebrew is, lit., "their catastrophe," "the disaster of both of them. These are subjective genitives (cf. Job 30:12). The catastrophe/disaster belongs to the king and God in the sense that they are its cause.

At this point, the LXX elaborates on the theme of the king, his responsibilities, and his wrath. The LXX epigram begins with 24:21–22 (= MT) and continues with five additional couplets.

21 Fear God, O son, and the king,
and be not disobedient to either of them.
22 For suddenly they [sc. God and king] will punish the wicked,
and who knows the punishments (that will befall) either?
22a A son who keeps a word is free from destruction,
and receiving it, he (has truly) received it.
22b Let no falsehood from the tongue be said to a king,
nor any falsehood proceed from his tongue.
22c For the tongue of a king is a sword and not flesh,
and whoever is delivered (to it) will be shattered.
22d For if his anger is provoked, he consumes men with sinews,
22e and the bones of men he gnaws up.
Like a flame he burns them up,
so that they are inedible (even) by young eagles.

After this, the LXX proceeds with 30:1–14.

THE FOREIGN BACKGROUND OF PROVERBS 22:17–24:22

A. AMENEMOPE AND PROVERBS

1. Connections

By the latter part of the nineteenth century, Bible scholars had become well aware that ancient Israel had been deeply influenced by foreign literatures, laws, and religions—especially Mesopotamian. Foreign Wisdom literature, including Amenemope, had been compared in a general way to the biblical Proverbs. The first to compare Proverbs with Egyptian Wisdom Literature was F. Chabas (*1872*), writing shortly after Pap. Prisse (Ptahhotep) became available, but before Amenemope was known. He noted remarkable parallels between Israelite and Egyptian moral doctrine (as expressed in a variety of documents, not only Wisdom texts) and explained them as analogies, which grew from the "fonds commun d'origine divine" ("the common ground of divine origin") (*1872*: 173).

The Instruction of Amenemope was published by E. A. W. Budge in 1923 but was accessible earlier. It is a perfectly preserved book of thirty numbered chapters, each with its own topic. Its goal is to teach "the way of life," which is the path of honesty, kindness, piety, and humility. Its ideal is the "truly silent man," who is characterized by self-control, serenity, and trust in God. See further Vol. I, 21. Amenemope is, in my view, a book of considerable moral force and literary grace.

In 1924, the Egyptologist Adolf Erman argued that Proverbs 22:17–24:22 was a translation of sayings from the Wisdom of Amenemope (Erman 1924a). The impact of this claim was immediate and deep. Comparative research got under way with great energy and various studies extended the comparison to other Egyptian texts and other biblical books. The most important comparative studies of the first decade after Erman's discovery were H. Gressmann *1924*, 1927 (which approached Amenemope from the biblical perspective); W. O. E. Oesterley *1927a*, *1927b* (which also considered parallels in Deuteronomy and Psalms and noted connections with Ahiqar); P. Humbert 1929 (which compared the Bible to a broad range of Egyptian literature); and J. Fichtner 1933 (which included Babylonian Wisdom in its comparison and sought to show how Israelite-Jewish Wisdom progressively distanced itself from its international foundations). The deep rooting of Israelite Wisdom in the Wisdom of the Ancient Near East was now visible and well recognized.

To explain how Amenemope became known to the Hebrew sages, Erman (1924a: 93) suggested that a Jew living in Egypt in the Saitic or Persian period (late eighth to mid-fourth centuries) translated it into Hebrew or Aramaic, changing Egyptian divinities (usually called simply "the God" in Amenemope) into "Yahweh" and making further modifications to meet the needs of his community. Later collectors, Erman believed, chopped the book up into sayings and sentences with little understanding of what they were doing.

Erman's core thesis has stood the test of time. Several studies contemporary to it, particularly those by Gressmann (*1924*), Erman himself (*1924b*), Humbert (1929), and Fichtner (1933), reinforced the comparison, though sometimes pushing it too far. Subsequent commentaries addressed the parallels, and scholars quickly discovered affiliations between Proverbs and other Egyptian wisdom books (Fichtner 1949; Gressmann *1924*, 1927; Humbert 1929; and others). In recent years, studies by G. Bryce (1979), H. Washington (1994b), D. Römheld (1989), and N. Shupak (*2005*) have confirmed the connection while bringing greater nuance to the comparison.

The parallels between Part IIIa (22:17–23:11) and Amenemope are too numerous and too specific to be reasonably ascribed to anything other than literary dependence, though intermediate states of transmission and transformation are likely. These parallels are discussed in the Comments above and listed in the table on pp. 757–60.

The concentration of parallels in Part IIIa is evidence for a unique connection between it and Amenemope.[353] Out of twenty-four verses in Part IIIa, fifteen have one or more strong parallels in Amenemope, two have thematic but not verbal affinities, and only seven have none. Looking from the other direction, of the 487 lines in Amenemope (excluding the titularies in 1.13–2.7 and the chapter numbers), forty-one have parallels in the forty-two stichoi of Collection IIIa. (Each physical line in Amenemope constitutes a poetic line, equivalent to a stich in biblical poetry.) Other foreign Wisdom texts have parallels in Proverbs, but with nowhere near this frequency or concentration. As for the (non-verbal) thematic parallels noted below, these do not in themselves prove dependence. However, the demonstrable borrowings from Amenemope in numerous sayings show that

[353] For Prov 22:17–23:11, Shupak (*2005*) substantiates direct dependence on Amenemope, while for 23:12–24:22 she sees a looser dependence on Egyptian wisdom generally.

the book was known in Israel, and this increases the likelihood that some of the thematic parallels, too, ultimately derive from Amenemope.

Shared sequence too is a sign of dependence. The Comments have noted some clusters in which Proverbs maintains the sequence of Amenemope: Prov 22:17–18 ≈ Amenemope 3.9–10, 11–16 and Prov 23:5–8 ≈ Amenemope 9.19; 10.4–5.[354] With slight variations, this is true also of Prov 23:1–3 ≈ Amenemope 23.13–17. Especially striking is the way that 9.19 and 10.4–5 are spliced together to form Prov 23:5. See the Comments. In fact, as the next section seeks to show, shared sequence extends through the entire list of parallels, though not in simple linear order.

There have been objections to Erman's theory. J. Ruffle diligently underscores Proverbs' differences from Amenemope and emphasizes the parallels of Part IIIa with other Wisdom texts. But even he concedes that ten sayings are significantly connected to Amenemope, and these, he allows, do show "some sort of relationship closer than coincidence" (1977: 65). Perhaps, he suggests, an Egyptian scribe in the court of Solomon composed some ten sayings based on memories of a text he had heard or used in scribal training. This conjecture comes close to the standard theory of dependency, except that it interposes the unnecessary intermediary of memory in a literate scribal culture.

Some scholars propose that the parallels are no more than similar literary responses to similar situations in similar cultures (Krispenz 1989: 129–31; Whybray 1994: 133). But this does not explain why the Amenemope parallels are so concentrated in a short unit. If the resemblance were merely cultural homology, Part IIIa should show a greater number of affinities to other Wisdom books, since in total quantity they far surpass Amenemope. We would also expect the high density of Amenemope parallels in Part IIIa to be matched in other units of Proverbs, but this does not happen. For strong refutations of Whybray's skepticism, see Emerton *2001* and Shupak *2005*, the latter bringing both Egyptological and Hebrew evidence to bear on the question.

Theories of Amenemope's Origin. As well as examining the Amenemope-Proverbs connection, scholars have looked into Amenemope's own origins. One early proposal was that Amenemope worked from a Hebrew or other Semitic source (Oesterley *1927a*; Kevin *1930*; Drioton 1959). But this theory was based on misunderstandings of the Hebrew and the Egyptian (see R. Williams 1961; Couroyer 1963; Bryce 1979: 39–56). Subsequent studies showed Amenemope itself to be rooted in older Egyptian Wisdom, which it quotes frequently; see Shirun-Grumach 1972 and the above Comments.

Shirun-Grumach argues that Amenemope and Proverbs 22:17–24:22 descend independently from an older book. Taking a cue from A. Alt (*1955*), Shirun-Grumach argued that a common source, which she calls the *Alte Lehre* ("Ancient Teaching"), lay behind both Proverbs *and* Amenemope (1972: 1–6 and passim). The hypothesized *Alte Lehre* would have consisted largely of the maxims in Amenemope that have parallels in Proverbs. Amenemope, according to Shirun-Grumach, elaborated these maxims largely by the addition of material characterized by a spirit of deep piety and the ideal of the *gr mꜣʿ* "the righteous silent man" or "the truly silent man," the humble man who surrenders himself to God. This elaboration would be in line with personal piety, a religious attitude given heightened expression in the Ramesside period; see Vol. I, 154–55.

---

[354] Note that Proverbs is cited by *chapter:verse* (e.g., 23:11), while Amenemope is cited by column. line (e.g., 23.11). The physical lines in the major Amenemope manuscript almost always coincide with poetic lines and are marked in the translations.

Shirun-Grumach's theory assumes that the Hebrew translator stuck close to his Egyptian source (a version of the *Alte Lehre*) and also that the subsequent editor or editors of Part IIIa replicated that translation. The text of Proverbs, however, diverges too greatly from Amenemope to warrant these assumptions. Proverbs 22:17–24:22 is constituted of short maxims (except for 23:29–35), in accordance with common practice in Prov 10–29, whereas Amenemope, like most Egyptian Wisdom books, is composed of longer, well-organized discourses (the thirty "chapters"), each of which has thematic unity. It is unlikely that Amenemope worked from an older Egyptian source whose literary forms were closer to the the practices of Hebrew Wisdom than to the usual Egyptian ones. Moreover, Proverbs (and not only Part IIIa) shows the influence of passages from the beginning, middle, and end of Amenemope (see the tables of parallels below). This shows that more than a small core of the present Egyptian work was available to the Israelite sages. The text of Amenemope used by the editor of Prov 22:17–24:22 was much closer to Amenemope than to the hypothetical *Alte Lehre*.

2. *Editorial Procedure*

A close comparison of Proverbs with Amenemope provides insight into the methods the editor of Part III used in assembling a collection of the "Words of the Wise" from earlier sources.

In assembling the first section of his thirty maxims, Part IIIa, the editor cycled through Amenemope in five passes or "sweeps." In each "sweep" he picked up passages of interest and recast them to compose his own maxims. This procedure is a natural way to use a scroll, for a scroll does not allow for easy skipping about but requires constant unrolling and re-rolling. In the process, he also composed a few verses independently of his source, namely, Prov 22:19 (in maxim 1), 22:25 (in maxim 3), 22:27 (in maxim 4), 23:2 (in maxim 7), 23:7 (in maxim 9), and 23:9 (= maxim 10). All of these non-dependent verses, except for 23:9, are actually integral components of maxims that make use of Amenemope. Hence Part IIIa virtually in its entirety is based on Amenemope.

From the listing in the table on the following pages, we can deduce that the editor of Proverbs Part III proceeded as follows:

(1) To begin the collection, at Prov 22:17bc, he drew on Amenemope's exordium, in §1, 3.9–10, which is virtually the start of the book. Amenemope's prologue proper is in 1.1–12. This is followed by a long titulary, in 1.13–3.7, which would have been meaningless to non-Egyptian readers and unlikely to have been translated. (The lines of the titulary are not included in the following calculations.) Amenemope's chapter 1 (the exordium) begins in 3.8, and this was (I conjecture) adjacent to the prologue in the translation. Then the editor jumped to the end of Amenemope, §30 at 27.7. The editor created his own prologue by combining material from the beginning of the body of Amenemope's instruction and its end.

(2) He returned to Amenemope 1.5 to produce Prov 22:21, then moved forward. At 5.10–11, he composed Prov 22:24, using not only the verses in the sequence but also material from later in the book (11.13–14 and 15.13–14), which would still have been fresh in his mind. After Amenemope 8.9, he jumped to 27.16–17, where the book ends.

(3) He then moved back a few columns, to 23.13 and 23.17, and drew on Amenemope to produce Prov 23:1a, b. Then, one verse later, he went backwards, but

Lines from Amenemope Reworked into Proverbs

Indent and italics: deviation from sequence. Parentheses: thematic, not verbal, dependence. → develops into, is used to form. § chapter number in Amenemope. # maxim number in Proverbs, by my count.* / indicates place in chapter after title, for example, "5–6/45 = fifth and sixth lines out of forty-five in the chapter.

Amenemope			Proverbs	
citation	col. line per BM 10474	chap. number and place in chapter	verse and maxim number	citation
SWEEP I				
Give you ears, that you may hear the things that are said;	3.9	§1 1/12	22:17b #1	Incline your ear and hear my words,†
apply your heart to interpret them.	3.10	§1 2/12	22:17c #1	and direct your heart to my knowledge
They will be a mooring post for your tongue.	(3.16)	§1 8/12	22:18b #1	that they may all be secure on your lips.
Look to these thirty chapters:	27.7	§30 1/11	22:20a #1	Have I not written for you <thirty>
SWEEP II				
to return an (oral) response to one who says it, to bring back a (written) message to the one who sends it.	1.5–6	Prologue 5–6/12	22:21 #1	to teach you the truest of words, to give answer to those who send you.

* There are different ways of numbering the maxims in Collection IIIa, but the overlap among the systems is considerable. Since my concern is the relative placement of the parallels, the exact numbering system is not important. For the unit divisions see the introduction to Prov 22:17–24:22 above.

† As emended; see the Commentary.

(continued)

Amenemope			Proverbs	
citation	col. line per BM 10474	chap. number and place in chapter	verse and maxim number	citation
Beware of robbing the lowly,	4.4	§2 1/24	22:22a #2	Do not rob a lowly man because he is lowly,
of oppressing the weak.	4.5	§2 2/24	22:22b #2	and do not oppress the poor man at the gate.
but the Moon declares his crime.	(4.19)	§2 16/24	22:23 #2	For Yahweh will strive on their behalf, and will steal away the life of those who steal from them.
Do not join quarrel with the hot mouthed man, nor assail him by words.	5.10–11	§3 1–2/10	22:24–25 #3	Do not consort with an ill-tempered man, lest you learn his ways and get yourself snared.
Do not consort with the heated man, or approach him for conversation,	*11.13–14*	§9 1–2/36		
Do not share a portion with the heated man or consort with a contentious man.	*15.13–14*	§12 5–6/10		
Do not displace the stone on the boundary of the fields.	7.12	§6 1/36	22:28 #5	Do not encroach on the ancient boundary, which your ancestors made.
Beware of encroaching on the boundaries of the fields,	8.9	§6 17/36		
As for the scribe skilled in his office,	27.16	§30 10/11	22:29a #6	Have you seen a man adept in his work?

he will be found worthy to be a courtier.	27.17	§30 11/11	22:29bc #6	He will stand before kings. He will not stand before the lowly.
SWEEP III				
Do not eat food before an official,	23.13	§23 1/8	23:1a #7	When you sit to dine with an official,
Look at the bowl that is before you,	23.17	§23 5/8	23:1b #7	look carefully at what is before you,
If you become sated by that which is chewed deceitfully (?),	*23.15*	§23 3/8	23:3 #7	Do not desire his delicacies, for they are deceitful bread.
SWEEP IV				
Do not cast your heart after wealth.	9.10	§7 1/26	23:4 #8	Do not strain to get rich. Leave off your staring!
Do not cast your heart outward.	(9.12)	§7 3/26		
Do not strain to seek a superfluity.	9.14	§7 5/26		
Their [sc. 'ill-got riches'] place is seen, but they are no longer	9.19	§7 10/26	23:5a #8	If you but let your eye fly on it, it is no more,
They have made themselves wings like a goose	10.4	§7 15/26	23:5b #8	for it wil surely make itself wings like an eagle's
and have flown to the sky.	10.5	§7 16/26	23:5c #8	and fly off to the sky.
Do not covet a poor man's property,	14.5	§11 1/22	23:6a #9	Do not eat the bread of the stingy man,

(continued)

Amenemope			Proverbs	
citation	col. line per BM 10474	chap. number and place in chapter	verse and maxim number	citation
nor hunger for his bread	14.6	§11 2/22	23:6b #9	nor desire his delicacies.
and it makes the gullet vomit.	14.8	§11 4/22	23:8a #9	You eat your morsel, you vomit it up,
The big mouthful of bread you swallowed, you vomit it up,	14.17	§11 13/22		
while you are ineffective (?) in your replies,	*14.14*	§11 10/22	23:8b #9	and ruin your fine words.
and are emptied of your good (things? words?).	14.15	§11 11/22		
SWEEP V				
Do not displace the stone on the boundaries of the fields,	7.12	§6 1/36	23:10 #11	Do not encroach on the ancient boundary, nor enter the fields of orphans,
Beware of encroaching on the boundaries of the fields,		17/36		
Do not traverse the furrow of another.	8.15	§6 23/36		
[The encroacher] will be caught by the powers of the Moon.	*(7.19)*	§6 8/36	23:11 #11	for their redeemer is strong. He will contend with you on their behalf.

only two lines, to Amenemope 23.15, which would still be in his range of vision, and wrote Prov 23:3.

(4) He returned to Amenemope 9.10–14 to produce Prov 23:4, then proceeded forward to 14.17. He then moved back only slightly to 14.14–15.

(5) In the final sweep, he returned to Amenemope 7.12, which, together with 8.9 and 8.15, he used to compose Prov 23:10. At the same time, he drew on materials from 8.9 and 8.15. The texts in columns 7 and 8 are close enough to have been visible together in the exposed segment of the scroll. The entire procedure ended in column 8.

Further evidence of the editorial procedure—observed by P. Overland (1996)—is that the editor took material from the opening lines of the chapters of Amenemope with disproportionate frequency of parallels. (According to Overland, he also made special use of chapter endings but I do not see any special emphasis on these components.) This pattern shows an awareness of the structure of the Egyptian book (Overland 1996: 280). The choice of the beginnings of chapters can be explained by the thematic, generalizing nature of the opening couplets. The presence of chapter numbering in the editor's copy of Amenemope would have focused his attention on the beginnings of chapters and would explain his decision to compose a book of "thirty" maxims (22:20).

In 1968, W. Helck briefly proposed that Amenemope influenced Proverbs through the mediary of an abbreviated prompting text of the Egyptian book. This text recorded the first and last lines of chapters and, for longer chapters, the middle couplet (Helck 1968: 26–27). This hypothesis, however, runs counter to the fact that paralleled material is found in a variety of places in the chapters. It is also disproved by the way the Proverbs editor extracts and splices lines from different parts of a chapter. (A good example is Prov 23:4–5, which is a composite of Amenemope 9.10+12+14+19+10.4+5.)

Overland (1996), more convincingly, ascribes the distribution of parallels to editorial procedure. Of the seventeen parallels in his count, nine come from the beginnings or ends of chapters, or both. Sometimes, two consecutive lines in Proverbs have their parallels in the initial and terminal lines of a single chapter in Proverbs—a "telescoping" of a chapter, as it were (p. 280). I count the parallels differently from Overland, but, by any enumeration, relative positions are significant. As the table shows, nine verses in Proverbs draw on the beginnings of chapters in Amenemope: 22:17; 22:20; 22:22; 22:24 (this verse draws on the openings of both §3 and §9); 22:28; 23:1; 23:4; 23:6; and 23:10. However, the significance of the borrowings from the ends of chapter, whether this happens once, as in my reckoning (22:9bc), or twice, as in Overland's (which includes 22:24b//13.9) is statistically minor.

We also learn something about the editor's procedure from the way the Amenemope parallels are concentrated in one subcollection, IIIa (22:17–23:11), then come to an abrupt halt, though Part III, the thirty maxims, continues. The editor was not simply pulling random bits of Amenemope from his memory. If he had been, the parallels would be more evenly distributed in Part III. He was using a *text*, a single scroll. Having finished drawing sayings from Amenemope, he proceeded (in IIIb) to gather sayings from other sources. One of these was Ahiqar (see the Comment on 23:13–14). Another likely source was Anii or a book that cited some of his sayings (see the Comment on 23:29–35). We do not know if there were other sources, but the title itself—"Words of the Wise" (22:17a, as emended)—suggests that a variety of textual or oral traditions was used.

3. *How Much of Amenemope Was Known in Israel?*

There are several cases of Proverbs' dependency on Amenemope outside Part III. These passages (on which see the Commentary) bear strong affinities to Amenemope in wording and structure while lacking equally strong parallels elsewhere in Egyptian (or Mesopotamian) Wisdom:

Proverbs	*Amenemope*	*Proverbs*	*Amenemope*
1:1–6	1.1–12	16:11	18.2–3
11:1	(17.18–19)	17:1	9.7–8
12:22	14.2–3	20:19b	(22.11–16)
15:16	9.5–8	20:22	(22.3–8)
15:17	9.5–8; 16.11–14	25:21–22	5.5–6; 22.3–8
16:8a	9.5	27:1	19.13; (22.5–6); 23.8–9)
16:8b	9.6		

Together with the parallels adduced for Part IIIa, this listing shows that the editors of Proverbs used materials from a number of columns throughout the entire length of Amenemope. (This does not mean that the editors of the various collections used Amenemope directly, but they at least used proverb sources that descended from Amenemope in its entirety.)

Amenemope was used not only as a source for particular proverbs; it provided models for the composition of a variety of passages in Proverbs. Proverbs' prologue (Prov 1:1–7), while differing in significant ways from the wording of Amenemope's, maintains the basic structure of the latter, a structure not shared by the prologues of other Wisdom books; see Vol. I, 72–73, 76–77. The key feature shared by the two prologues is a title with a series of infinitival clauses dependent on it, which express the book's goals; see Vol. I, 72. Another structural model taken from Amenemope is the complex "better than" template ("Better A with B than A′ with B′"; see the excursus after the Comment on 15:17). This was used twelve times in Proverbs (15:16, 17; 16:8, 19, 32a, 32b; 17:1; 19:1; 21:9, 19; 25:24; 28:6), of which only four verses (15:16, 17; 16:8; and 17:1) can be traced directly to Amenemope. This shows that not only did the Israelite sages use passages with the "better than" template, they also used it to compose some of their own. Qohelet (4:13) and Ben Sira (10:27; 20:31 = 41:15) continued to use the template, by now totally out of contact with Amenemope. These examples show that Amenemope's teaching had worked its way deep into Israelite Wisdom and left its impress even on texts that do not use it directly.[355]

[355] A possible example of Amenemope's influence—not necessarily direct—outside of Proverbs is Jer 17:5–8, which describes two types of men—he who trusts in man and he who trusts in Yahweh—using the metaphor of two types of trees, as in Amenemope 6.1–12 (§4). Amenemope, it should be noted, is contrasting the heated man and the "truly silent man," and both these temperaments—agitation versus repose—are expressions of trust in God or the lack thereof, respectively. Psalm 1, which has strong affiliations to the Wisdom Psalms, also compares two types of men to plants.

4. *Translation and Transmission*

Though scholarship has established that Amenemope was translated and transmitted to Israel, we can say little that is definite about how and when this happened. At best we can look for historical circumstances that would facilitate the transmission.

Some have suggested that the background for a translation from Egyptian to a Semitic language later accessible to Hebrew scribes would be the late New Kingdom. The Egyptian empire had come to an end in about 1375 B.C.E., but Egypt exercised influence in Palestine in varying degrees until the middle of the twelfth century. If Amenemope was composed in the early twentieth dynasty (1186–1069 B.C.E.; thus Washington 1994b: 11–24), this would allow for a translation at the tail end of Egyptian imperial influence. I earlier accepted this hypothesis (Vol. I, 18), but now I consider it unlikely. One problem with the hypothesis is that the foreign language Egyptian scribes were learning in Palestine was Akkadian rather than a Canaanite dialect, and Canaanite knowledge of written Egyptian would be extremely restricted, possessed perhaps by a few hostage princes but little more. Also, the basis for such an early dating of Amenemope is shaky.

Some have pointed to Solomon's reign as the likely setting for literary transmission, on the assumption that this was a time of substantive political and cultural contact between Israel and Egypt (von Rad *1956*; Ruffle 1977: 65–66; Shupak 1993: 352–54). This hypothesis is based almost entirely on the biblical narrative (1 Kgs 3:1; 5:1, 10; 10:28–29; 11:17–40), whose reliability, especially for the semi-legendary era of the United Monarchy, cannot be taken for granted. The evidence assembled and sifted by B. Schipper (*1999*) shows this hypothesis to be problematic. Between the end of the Egyptian Empire and the late eighth century B.C.E., Egypt had no notable commercial and political involvement in Israel and Judah. In response to the rise of Assyrian power under Tiglath-Pileser III in the middle of the eighth century B.C.E., and especially in the reign of Hezekiah (715–687 B.C.E.), the Egyptian political presence in Palestine intensified, and commercial and personal contacts increased as well (Schipper *1999*: 285–94 and passim). This engagement continued and expanded during the Saitic period (664–525 B.C.E.). Amenemope was probably composed in the late 20th or 21st dynasties (1188–945 B.C.E.), but it was still being copied as a school text at least as late as the 26th or 27th dynasty (672–359 B.C.E.).[356] Only the period from the end of the eighth century to the exile provided the preconditions for literary transmission, such as between Amenemope and Proverbs (Schipper, p. 293).

It is usually assumed that Amenemope was translated from Egyptian into Hebrew. But it is highly unlikely that an Egyptian scribe would have bothered to

---

[356]The main manuscript of Amenemope, Pap. BM 10474, as well as Tab. Turin 6237 (Posener 1966: 59) and several ostraca, were inscribed in the 26th–27th dynasties. The dating of the other witnesses is less certain. B. Peterson (1966) assigned a fragmentary papyrus, Stockholm MM 18416, to the 21st–26th dynasties. No copies can confidently be dated even to the 20th dynasty (ending in 1069 B.C.E.), though some would date its authorship then on internal (nonlinguistic) grounds. Later, Amenemope is apparently quoted in a Demotic text (H. Brunner 1979: 165–66).

learn Hebrew, a language of trivial importance on the international scene, and it is virtually impossible that a Judean would have learned to read Egyptian, which requires years of schooling in the difficult hieratic cursive.[357] A translation into Aramaic would be much more feasible. Erman himself raised the possibility that Amenemope was translated into Aramaic in Persian period Egypt (525–332 B.C.E.), where the book became known to Jews in Elephantine and from there was transmitted to Judea (1924a: 92). But this would place Part III of Proverbs—and much of the rest of the book, which has drawn on Amenemope in various places—too late to fit the character of the language and the indicators of a monarchical setting of Prov 10–29 (see Vol. I, 10 and "Social Setting" in the Introduction to Vol. II [III.B]). Even within Part III, two maxims (22:29 and 24:21–22) speak to persons in the royal court.

The most likely scenario for the translation and transmission of Amenemope is the early seventh century, and the most likely language for the translation was Aramaic. Some scribes in Egypt knew Aramaic, which was introduced into Egypt starting in the period of Assyrian hegemony (671–660 B.C.E.). An Aramaic translation could easily have been brought to the Levant by scribes in the Neo-Assyrian empire. Bilingual scribes of the Jerusalem court would have introduced it into Israelite Wisdom some time in the seventh century.

Aramaic had emerged as the lingua franca of the Near East during the eighth century. This was an era of considerable international movement and contact. The Assyrians fostered international trading by developing an infrastructure of roads and way-stations (see Kuhrt 1995: 2.356–57). Nahum, written not long after the fall of Nineveh in 612 B.C.E., says that the Assyrian merchants were "more numerous than the stars in heaven" (3:16). Esarhaddon's conquest of Memphis in 671 and Assyrian hegemony in Lower Egypt provided a channel for the transmission of texts between Western Asia and Egypt in both directions. And Jerusalem was in the middle.

The elite in Jerusalem knew Aramaic at least by the end of the eighth century B.C.E., according to 2 Kgs 18:26–27. The conditions were present for the assimilation of Amenemope and Ahiqar into Israelite Wisdom. The case of Ahiqar (see "Ahiqar and Proverbs," below) shows that Wisdom texts in Aramaic could become assimilated to Israelite Wisdom, probably in the seventh century, and that it was feasible for the same to have happened with Amenemope.

As with Ahiqar, Amenemope was (I hypothesize) excerpted, rearranged, and reformulated. It is impossible to know how much of this was carried out by the translator and how much by an editor or a string of revisers, but it is likely that the original translation included some form of the complete Egyptian text. As noted on pages 757–60, there are clear parallels to Amenemope in Proverbs' Prologue and Parts I, II, III, and V. Moreover, these parallels derive from different parts of Amenemope, including its Prologue and final chapter. The diffuseness of the impact shows that much, perhaps all, of Amenemope became a popular

[357] Hieratic numerals were used by Israelite scribes in the seventh–sixth centuries, but there is no evidence for any broader knowledge of Egyptian language and writing.

book of *Hebrew* wisdom, serving as a source of ideas and a model for formal usages.

The editor of Proverbs Part III was doing nothing unusual in appropriating and reshaping material from an older source. Egyptian sages incorporated older Wisdom in their own books. Amenemope himself used earlier texts, including Ptahhotep, Mentuhotep, the Ramesside Prayer to Thoth (AEL 2.114), and especially Anii (see Shirun-Grumach 1972, esp. 35–38). The Kemit, Djedefhar, Amenemhet, the Loyalist Instruction, and Ptahhotep, among others, were cited in later Egyptian texts. (Some of these quotations are gathered in Hornung 1979.) Ptahhotep in particular was popular in later literature; for an example of his influence see the Comment on 23:3. Amenemope himself is quoted in a Demotic text written on a jar (Hornung 1979: 165), and some of his teachings (though not his book) were known even in the early Christian period (AW 235). The citations of Egyptian literature in Egyptian Wisdom are mostly rephrasings, abbreviations, or expansions of the original—just what we see in Proverbs' treatment of Amenemope. Ben Sira treated the book of Proverbs, among other ancient texts, in the same time-honored fashion.[358]

The author of Part III called his book "Words of the Wise" (21:17). He might well have used the title of another Egyptian text, "The Instruction According to Old Writings."

5. *Ideas*

The editor of Part III used Amenemope as a resource and reshaped its material in numerous ways. But does this reshaping reveal any overall plan? Was it driven by an ideological agenda?

Römheld (1989: 117–84) argues that the editor of Prov 22:17–23:11 was blind to the personal piety that is so intense in Amenemope. In the mind-set of personal piety, humans have an individual relationship to a god. (I discuss this in Vol. I, 154–55.) God freely controls human fate, and God (or a god) executes justice with a freedom that denies humans certainty about the outcome of their deeds.

---

[358] The following are examples of Ben Sira's use and reformulation of Proverbs. Verses preserved only in Greek are in parentheses:

Sir	*Prov*	*Sir*	*Prov*
(1:4)	8:22	4:12	8:35
(1:14a)	1:7a	5:8b	11:4a
(1:16–17)	8:18–19	15:5b	24:7b
(2:5)	17:3	6:27b	4:13b
3:13	23:22	40:17	10:30a
3:29	2:2	50:29a	19:23a

For an extensive listing of Hebrew passages in Ben Sira that cite and reuse biblical phraseology, including many verses in Proverbs, see Schechter and Taylor 1899: 12–27. A valuable study of the way that Ben Sira reapplied Proverbs in the areas of theology, social ethics, and formal structure, is provided by Corley 2005. See also Skehan and Di Lella 1987: 41–44.

Part III, in Römheld's view, returned to an earlier worldview, one characteristic of Wisdom in the Middle Kingdom and earlier. In this view, the world is governed by a stable, self-regulating order accessible to human understanding. In this order, reward and punishment flow naturally and inevitably from deeds (the "deed-consequence nexus"; Vol. I, 91–92).[359] According to Römheld (pp. 183–84), when Part III was edited, Israelite Wisdom, following its own pace of development, had not yet matured to the level of personal piety and was not ready to assimilate Amenemope's religious attitudes in their fullness.

Römheld is right that the intensity of Amenemope's piety, humility, and resignation to God's will is more prominent and emphatic than in Proverbs, which is more oriented to practical concerns. But it is hard to know what ideological weight to give to the different emphasis. Since the editor of Part III has used only about 10 percent of the material in Amenemope, the absence or infrequency of certain elements need not have been motivated by ideology.

Significant components of personal piety comparable to Amenemope's remain in Part IIIa and are found throughout Proverbs. The distinctions I draw between New Kingdom personal piety and the religion of Proverbs (see Vol. I, 155) are valid. Still, it is going too far to say that "[p]ersonal piety in the Egyptian form is thus foreign to Proverbs. In fact, it was largely strained out of the sections of Amenemope incorporated in Proverbs" (Vol. I, 155).

Trust in Yahweh is one of the stated goals (22:19a) in the Exordium to Part III, and even if the author-editor does not extensively teach this virtue, he embraces the ideal. Also, 22:22–23 asserts that Yahweh intervenes directly on behalf of the oppressed. In Part IIIb (collected, as Römheld argues, by the same editor as IIIa), there are two expressions of a personal piety. Prov 24:12 speaks of God's knowledge of the individual heart and direct divine retribution. Prov 24:17–18 shows that Yahweh cares about an individual's attitudes and punishes contemptuous ones.

In every major unit of Proverbs except for Parts VIb (30:10–33) and VIc (31:1–9), we find sayings redolent of personal piety. Examples are the praise of humility in 16:5 and 19; the assertion of divine control in 16:9; the demand for trust in God in 16:3; the insistence on God's control of the tongue in 16:1; and the prohibition on desiring revenge in 24:29 (which implicitly calls for reliance on God's justice). Other examples are 3:5, 11–12; 10:22; 12:2; 15:16, 25, 29; 16:18; 18:10; 20:22, 24; 21:30; 22:20–21; 29:25; and 30:8. It is circular to claim, as Römheld does (pp. 185–90), that proverbs of this sort must be later, postexilic additions. (This has affinities to McKane's theory of a Yahwistic redaction, discussed in "Religious Proverbs" [I.C] in the Introduction to Vol. II.) Since personal piety is not alien to Proverbs, there is no reason for the editor of Part III to refuse to incorporate expressions of personal piety in his collection.

There are inevitably differences in tone and emphasis between Part IIIa and its

[359] It should be noted that personal piety was not an invention of the New Kingdom (see Vol. I, 155). Silence and humility are praised in the Middle Kingdom "A Man to his Son": "Righteous is the silent man who bends the shoulder. Effective is the heart of him who does what is said" (I.5–6). And "if you are silent, you will reach your goal and you will give answer in the end" (XV.6).

source-text. Above all, the only deity named is Yahweh, and there is less emphasis on divine intervention (appearing only in 22:23 and the related maxim 23:11). There are also adjustments to a different social context; see the Comment on 23:11. But there is no fundamental shift of belief.

B. AHIQAR AND PROVERBS

The book of Ahiqar was the most popular Wisdom book in the ancient Near East and was actively transmitted and revised even in medieval times. A frame-narrative tells how Ahiqar, the vizier of Esarhaddon, was falsely accused by his adopted son Nadan. During and after these events Ahiqar delivers a series of counsels of practical and religious nature. See further Vol. I, 23.

Ahiqar is the inspiration for several sayings in Proverbs. In the following table of parallels, parentheses indicate where the similarity is thematic but not verbal.

Proverbs	*Ahiqar*
4:23	98 [1.1.191]
8:1–35	(94b–95 [1.1.187–88]) (see Vol. I, 332–33)
10:31	156 [1.1.156]
12:18	105b–106a [1.1.89–90]
16:1	(114–15 [1.1.162])
16:14	(100a-102 [1.1.84–86])
20:24	(122 [1.1.170])
22:3	(Arabic: Coneybeare 1913: 137, §54)
23:13–14	81–82 [1.1.176–77]
25:6–7	194 [1.1.1293]
25:15	106–106 [1.1.89–90]
27:3	111 [1.1.159]
29:19	(83 [1.1.178])
30:32–33	Syriac S_1 8

Prov 23:13–14 and 30:32–33 have the strongest parallels. Some of the above are less clearly instances of dependency, but overall the evidence indicates that the sages of Proverbs knew the book of Ahiqar. Features common to Proverbs and Ahiqar but not Egyptian Wisdom include the following: (1) The personification of wisdom (see Vol. I, 332–33). (2) The address to "my son" (Ahiqar 65–66 [1.1.148]). (Egyptian Wisdom uses "son"; "my son" is also in Babylonian Wisdom.) (3) The graded numerical sequence (Ahiqar 92–93a [1.1.187–88]; see the introduction to Prov 30:10–33). (4) The righteous/wicked antithesis (Ahiqar 167–68 [1.1.103–104]), which is common in Prov 10–15.[360] The similarities are not only with Proverbs. I. Kottsieper (*1996*: 144–53) shows that 2 Kgs 14:9b and Judg 9:8–15 have strong structural affinities with several fables in Ahiqar, which he believes are evidence of a south-Syrian/Palestinian genre.

[360] See the surveys in J. Day *1995a*: 63–64 and B. Estelle *2004* passim.

Further evidence for the knowledge of Ahiqar in Israel is the fact that Ben Sira draws on parts of Ahiqar besides those used in Proverbs. (The book was apparently known to him in a form with affinities to the Syriac versions.) An example of Ahiqar's influence on Ben Sira is Sir 22:15, "Sand and salt and the burden of iron are easier to bear than a foolish man." The burden of sand is a trope found in Prov 27:3 and Job 6:2–3, but the combination of sand and salt appears only in Ben Sira and Ahiqar, the latter stating, "I have carried sand and borne salt, but nothing is more burdensome [lit., "heavier"] than a (foreigner?)" (111 [1.1.159]). Also, Ahiqar is a figure in the Jewish-Hellenistic book of Tobit (S 11:19).

The earliest extant copy of Ahiqar is the fifth-century Elephantine manuscript, but the book itself was written much earlier. Kottsieper's definitive study of the language of the sayings of Ahiqar places it in the late eighth or early seventh centuries. (The frame-narrative is later.) He identifies the dialect of the sayings as south Syrian, that is, situated near Damascus or in the Anti-Lebanon (*1990*: 241–46), in a small-state culture area similar to Israel and Judah.[361] The setting of the events in the reign of Esarhaddon (680–669 B.C.E.) restricts the dating to after the second quarter of the seventh century.[362]

A variety of elements in the frame-narrative are in line with an origin in Esarhaddon's time or shortly thereafter (Greenfield *1995*: 49). A Late Babylonian tablet from Warka mentions an *ummânu*—a sage and high official—in Esarhaddon's court named *a-ba-^{d}NINNU-da-ri* (= Aba-enlil-dari), whom (according to the tablet) "the Arameans call *^{m}a-ḫu-'u-qa-a-ri* [Aḥuqar]" (Lindenberger 1983: 22; Greenfield *1995*: 44). The tablet is from the Seleucid era, but it shows that Ahiqar was ensconced in Babylonian traditions. Moreover, the fact that the tablet can distinguish an Aramaic name from an Akkadian one—one unmentioned in extant sources—suggests a much earlier origin for the idea. The sage Ahiqar may well have been an historical character of known date.

The Aramaic text of Ahiqar known (on this hypothesis) in seventh-century Jerusalem would not have been the same as the Elephantine version. There are other versions of Ahiqar with connections to Proverbs. Two fragments of a Demotic translation of Ahiqar dated to the first century C.E., also from Elephantine (Zauzich *1976*), differ from the known Aramaic version. There are, according to Coneybeare et al. (1913: xxxii), six Syriac recensions. The two published Syriac versions (S_1 and S_2) differ radically from the Aramaic one. The Syriac versions are problematic for comparative purposes because they come to us in late manuscripts (twelfth–seventeenth centuries) and sometimes show biblical influences (see the Comment on 24:17). They are, moreover, agreed to be descendants of an earlier Syriac translation. Still, elements of the extant Syriac versions show signs of considerable antiquity.

The Egyptian author of Anchsheshonq, from the Ptolemaic period and written

[361] For a brief discussion of this issue and a survey of the teachings of Ahiqar, see Kottsieper *2006*.

[362] This is not to say that Ahiqar is actually Assyrian. It lacks Akkadian usages and shows signs of belonging to a basically independent *Aramaic* Wisdom tradition. See Kottsieper *1996*: 128–38.

in Demotic, seems to have known a Demotic version of Ahiqar with close relations to the version known from the Syriac (esp. S1) and Slavonic translations;[363] see Lichtheim 1983: 15–17. Moreover, the narrative in S2, though greatly elaborated, has a parallel in a Demotic fragment of Ahiqar (Zauzich *1976*: 182): the incident when Ahiqar is tricked into going with an army to a valley, giving the king the impression he is trying to subvert him (Coneybeare et al. 1913: 111–12).[364] This shows the antiquity of the version ancestral to the Syriac.

In one case, Proverbs has a close parallel in S1 and Anchsheshonq that is absent from the Elephantine Ahiqar; see the Comment on Prov 30:32–33. I have noted a number of parallels to the Syriac Ahiqar texts in various places in the Commentary on the assumption that they are witnesses—though distant and nonlineal—to the Aramaic text available to the Judean sages. Sometimes, however (24:17–18, e.g.), the Syriac texts may have been influenced by the Bible.

[363] The Slavonic translation is from a non-extant Greek translation, which is on a different branch from the Syriac. Both the Greek and the old Syriac traditions go back to an Aramaic text different from the Elephantine Aramaic manuscript.

[364] Some fragmentary lines have a confession of folly ("Wir waren töricht, wir waren töricht" ["We were foolish, we were foolish"]) and refer to a rebellious army led by "prince Ahiqar" (Zauzich *1976*: 182; see Lindenberger 1983: 310–12 for a translation from the German). These are apparently the words of Sennacherib (as the king in this version is called) as he sees Ahiqar coming toward him with an army. Sennacherib thinks Ahiqar is attempting a rebellion, but in fact he has been tricked by Nadan into undertaking this march. (In the Elephantine version, Nadan simply slanders his uncle to the king.) Only the event itself is parallel; the wording differs considerably. But this is enough to establish the antiquity of the core of the story as preserved (and elaborated) in S_2 and to show that there was more than one Aramaic version known in ancient Egypt—both in Elephantine. The common source of the Demotic and Syriac must have been Aramaic.

PART IV: PROVERBS 24:23–34

◆

MORE WORDS OF THE WISE

24:23a These too are of the wise.

The title of this short collection, like the one restored in 22:17, ascribes the sayings to anonymous sages. The word "too" shows that the editor was aware of 22:17 and regarded this unit as an appendix to the preceding. The themes of Part IV are justice and industriousness. Prov 24:23b–25 is a thematic cluster and 24:30–34 is a well-organized epigram, but no overall organization is apparent.

Meinhold proposes the following structure for Prov 24:23b–34:

(1) behavior in the law court	I: (judge) (23b–25)	IV. witness (28)
(2) speaking and thinking	II. right answer (26)	V. false answer (29)
(3) behavior in work	III. positive (27)	VI. negative (30–34)

This outline is not helpful. The horizontal relationships between items are fuzzy. The issue in v 29 is not speech but rather vengeance, and only Meinhold's choice of label, "speaking and thinking," associates vv 26 and 29. The more significant associations are honest speech and judgment (vv 23b + 24) and honest speech and false testimony (vv 28 + 29). These are noticeable linkages and run contrary to Meinhold's pattern. Verses 27 and 30–34 do share a theme, but it is that theme rather than their place in a symmetrical structure that associates them.

In order to maintain Solomonic authorship, the LXX, Syriac, and the medieval commentators obscure the attribution of authorship to the wise. The LXX renders, "These things I say to you, wise men." Ramaq paraphrases: " 'These things are for the wise,' that is, they are known to the wise, who in this case are the judges." Similarly, according to Hame'iri, Solomon, after having addressed the son and all pupils, speaks to the wise, who are the judges.

A. Luc (2000: 253–54) has revived this interpretation, arguing that *laḥăkāmîm* means "for the wise," like *lammôkîḥîm* "for the rebukers" in v 25. He notes that this title differs syntactically from the others, which are *mišlê* X "proverbs of X" or *dibrê* X "words of X." Contrary to Luc, however, *laḥăkāmîm* is unproblematic; it is a typical use of the *lamed* of authorship, most common in Psalm titles (25:1; 26:1; 27:1; and often). The syntax of 24:25a, moreover, is not comparable, since it is a verbal clause.

24:23b Showing partiality in judgment is not good.
24:24 He who says to the guilty, "You are innocent"—
peoples will curse him and nations revile him.
24:25 But with those who rebuke it shall go well,
upon them shall come a blessing of good.

The three maxims in Prov 24:23b–25 concern the administration of justice. They look like originally independent proverbs, but they now form a thematic cluster and are to be read in light of each other.

24:23b. This is one of the few monostichs in Proverbs; see the Comment on Prov 27:5. Verse 23b ≈ 28:21a, but the latter does not specify a legal context. The principle of v 23b is embodied in the Law, in Deut 1:17 and 16:19.

Showing partiality [*hakker panim*]: Lit., "recognizing a face"; in other words, regarding one party in a legal case favorably rather than viewing both parties as strangers.

not good: "Not good" = "bad" (Hame'iri); see the Comment on 16:29.

24:24. Read in the light of v 23b, v 24 speaks of administration of justice. A judge or ruler who exonerates the guilty will be reviled by all "because he destroys the foundations of justice and righteousness" (Malbim). This verse is a variant of 17:15a. But whereas 17:15b says that God loathes a person who perverts justice, 24:24b says that *nations* do so.

Read in the light of v 25—as the conjunction *waw* ("and" or "but") at the start of v 25 encourages us to do—v 24 speaks about honesty in speech in all spheres of life. It is shameful to tell a wicked person that he is righteous (v 24), rather than condemning his wickedness to his face (v 25).

guilty [*raša*], *innocent* [*ṣaddiq*]: Or: "wicked," "righteous." We can translate, "He who says to the wicked, 'You are righteous' . . ." Read thus, the saying applies to anyone who flatters an evil person by lying about his wickedness.

24:25. Rather than flatter those who are in the wrong (v 24), you should rebuke them to their face. People may at first be annoyed by chastisement, but (it is asserted) they will eventually come to appreciate those who spoke it.

it shall go well [*yinʿam*]: Lit., "it will be pleasant." Chastisement could be expected to provoke hostility and make the critic miserable. The proverb claims that it will ultimately lead to harmony and good feelings. This formulation pictures, at least as an ideal, a harmonious environment in which people generally wish to do the right thing, but may not be fully aware of what it is.

upon them shall come: The fronting of the prepositional phrase strongly suggests a restrictive reading—"a blessing of good shall come *only* upon them" (R. Holmstedt, personal communication).

a blessing of good: People will bless the rebukers by wishing them good fortune. Job describes his better days with a similar idiom: "The blessing of the lost would come upon me" (29:13a).

24:26b He who answers with honest words
26a kisses the lips.

The literal translation is "Kisses the lips—he who answers with honest words." The lines have been reversed in translation for clarity. The MT's word order evokes a certain surprise by delaying the subject, as if to suggest a riddle: Who gives true kisses? One who answers to the point—even if his words are blunt. This verse reinforces v 25. The most genuine sign of affection is telling someone the truth.

honest words: N^{e}*koḥim* "honest" reflects the sounds of *mokiḥim* "rebukers" (v 25).

kisses the lips: This expression does not occur elsewhere, but it must be synonymous with "kiss the mouth," which occurs in Gen 41:40. There Pharaoh tells Joseph, "You will be over my household, and all my people will kiss your mouth." This is meant metaphorically, but the metaphor must be based on an actual practice of kissing the mouth as a token of love and honor.

kisses [*yiššāq*]: J. Cohen (1982: 420–23) translates, "He that gives forthright judgement will silence all hostile lips." Cohen ascribes to *yiššāq* (G) the sense that the H-stem has in RH, "to seal," "bind," and cites this interpretation in *b. Git.* 9a. But "hostile" is not implied in this proverb, and the sense that *nāšaq* has elsewhere, "kiss," is entirely appropriate here, as it is in Gen 41:40, if it is understood metaphorically.

24:27 Prepare your work in the soil,
and ready it in the field.
Afterwards build your house.

First carry out your tasks on the farm and only then work on your own house. Most commentators understand "building a house" as an idiom for taking a wife (Saʿadia, Rashi, Riyqam, and many others) or founding a household (McKane, Murphy, Clifford, and many others). ("Build a house" means "found a household" in Deut 25:9. The other texts that McKane cites are not relevant or at least not clear.) But, as Ehrlich observes, this picture is anachronistic. In ancient Israel (and in patriarchal societies generally), men married young and lived in the father's extended household while working the family holdings. They would receive their own fields only when their father died. "Build your house" here is meant literally. First do your work in the fields, the saying advises, and only then work on constructing your own house. The latter is desirable (we may assume) because it allows a young man to move out of his father's house into his own; nevertheless, planting is most urgent. This advice can be generalized as "first things first."

soil [*ḥuṣ*]: Lit., "outside." This sometimes means "field" or "ground"; see the Comment on 8:26.

24:28 Do not be a gratuitous witness against another person,
nor open your lips wide[a].

[a] *w^{e}hiptîtā* (MT *wahăpittîtā*).

gratuitous witness [*ʿed ḥinnam*]: One who testifies against another person without justification.

nor open your lips wide: Don't blather. In context this alludes to false or, perhaps, incoherent and excessive testimony.

nor open . . . wide [*w^{e}hiptîtā*]: MT's *wahăpittîtā* is an anomalous form. Apparently it is supposed to represent *wa-* + interrogative *hă* + D perf. (from *p-t-h*) and to be understood as "and would you seduce?" (Ramaq). Some medievals regard the form as equivalent to *wahăpittôtā*, from *p-t-t* H "break into bits," and understand it as a metaphor for destroying a person (Ibn Janaḥ, *Perush*; Yehudah Hayyuj, cited by Radaq in *Sefer Hašorašim*). But the H-stem of this verb does not appear. We should emend to *w*^{e}*hiptîtā* (*p-t-h* H). The verb *p-t-h* "make wide" does appear in the H (Gen 9:27), and the G has a similar meaning, as in Prov 20:19, *pōteh ś*^{e}*pātāyw*, lit. "he who makes his lips wide" (collocated with "lips," as here). LXX correctly renders 24:28: *mēde platynou sois cheilesin*, "nor make wide with your lips."

24:29 Do not say, "As he did to me so I will do to him,
I will repay the man according to what he did."

Do not seek revenge. Do not even *intend* it. (See the Comment on 20:22.) Read in juxtaposition with v 28, v 29 means that you should not testify falsely to get revenge. Nor, if someone testifies falsely against you, should you repay him in like manner. The antecedent of "he" is "another person" in v 28. The Syriac shows this understanding by starting v 29 with "and."

Deuteronomy commands: If a witness is found to have lied, "you [pl.] shall to do to him as he schemed to do to his brother" (19:19a; see vv 16–19). According to Ehrlich, Prov 24:29 warns us against this very law. But there is no actual disagreement because the verses have a different orientation. Deuteronomy speaks to the judges or the community, for it is they who carry out or approve the retribution, not the intended victim. The proverb speaks to a victim or one who considers himself wronged. (This is the orientation of Lev 19:18 as well.) Retribution is God's role (Prov 24:12b). He may devolve it on the community and its representatives, but an individual must not seek vengeance on his own behalf (Prov 20:22). Older custom and legislation, however, did expect murder to be avenged by the "blood redeemer," a family member of the victim (Num 35:19–21; Deut 19:11–12). It is unlikely that Proverbs, which presupposes an organized social order under a monarchy, would accept that practice. In any case, homocide is not what the present proverb refers to, as indicated by the fact that the wronged party is still alive.

24:30 I passed by the field of a lazy man,
and by the vineyard of a senseless person,
31 and I saw that it was overgrown with weeds,
the ground was covered with nettles,
and its stone wall was destroyed.
32 And I looked and took note,
I saw and drew a lesson:
33 A bit more sleep, a bit more snoozing,
a bit more lying with folded arms,
34 and penury will come upon you like a vagabond,
and poverty like a man of arms.

Laziness begets poverty. This epigram resembles Prov 6:6–11 in its rhetoric, theme, and conclusion. Both epigrams use an observation (here of the sage, there of the listener) as a prop for the concluding quatrain, which is the same in both epigrams. See the remarks in Vol. I, 216–19. Prov 6:6–8, however, is not anecdotal. The only anecdotes in Proverbs are 7:6–23 and 24:30–32, unless one counts the narration of Wisdom's birth in 8:22–31. Anecdotes are not used in earlier Wisdom, but Qohelet has three: 2:3–10; 4:13–16; 9:13–15.

This epigram has often been thought to embody the empirical methodology commonly ascribed to Wisdom Literature. This issue is discussed in Essay 8 (I), "Empiricism?"

24:30. *field, vineyard*: The speaker may have passed by both of these (they are not synonyms) but, as Haran shows (1972: 243–44), the depiction focuses on the vineyard. In v 31, the poet speaks of a single place, not two. Stone walls were typical of vineyards (see Num 22:24; Isa 5:5; Ps 80:13) and were needed to keep animals from trampling and eating the vines (Isa 5:5). Fields were marked with boundary stones (Prov 22:28; 23:10; etc.). The field is mentioned for the sake of parallelism.

man, *person: These are the same person.*

24:31. *and I saw* [w^{e}hinneh]: Lit., "and behold," marking the speaker's perspective.

24:32. *drew a lesson* [laqaḥti musar]: Lit., "took a lesson." This idiom does not mean to derive logical conclusions from data or premises, but rather to take to heart something already known. *Musar* in this idiom is a corrective lesson, whether by chastisement, punitive discipline, or a strong warning. See "Words for Wisdom" §6 (Vol. I, 34–35) and the Comment on 1:3.

24:33–34. This quatrain is a doublet of 6:10–11; see the Comments there for details. Prov 24:30–34 is the source of the locutions and sayings in 6:6–8; see Vol. I, 227.

The conclusion in Prov 24:33–34 insists that even a bit of sleep (beyond the essential) brings on poverty. This conclusion is hardly justified by the anecdote in vv 31–32, which describes extreme negligence. The author is using the anecdote as a prop for an existing aphorism.

A *bit more*: Lit., "a little."

penury will come upon you: Lit., "your poverty will come."

Prov 6:11a has *kimhallēk*, lit. "like one who walks about," where 24:34a has *mithallēk* "vagabond," which is the archaic form; see the Comment on 6:11.

In the LXX, 30:15–31:9 follow.

Part V: Proverbs 25:1–29:27

The Hezekian Collection

The title of Part V is unusual in giving information about when and where the collection was composed: in the court of Hezekiah, who ruled from about 728 to 699 (or 687) B.C.E. The collection is characterized by a low frequency of sayings mentioning Yahweh[365] and a tendency to group proverbs thematically. This collection (especially chaps. 25–26) is distinguished also in its frequent use of three proverbial forms or templates:

(1) A metaphor in the A-line, with the referent held in abeyance till the B-line: "Apples of gold in engravings of silver: a word spoken in the right way" (Prov 25:11). This gives the proverb the feel of a riddle: What are apples of gold? Words spoken in the right way. This template may constitute a quatrain, with the first couplet holding the metaphor, the second the referent. Examples are 25:4–5, 11, 12, 14, 18, 19, 20bc, 25, 26, 28; 26:3, 6, 7, 9, 17, 20, 21, 23; 27:3, 15, 21; 28:3b, 15. In the remaining 85 percent of the book, this form is found only in 11:22. The metaphor can be in a verbal clause, as in 27:9, 17, and 27:20: "Sheol and Abaddon are not satisfied, and the eyes of man are not satisfied."

(2) A simile in the A-line of a couplet or the first line of a quatrain, with the preposition *k*- "like" in initial position, which is coordinated with *ken* "thus" in the B-line (or second verse): "Like snow in summer and a downpour in harvest, so honor is not suitable to a dolt" (Prov 26:1; also 26:2, 8, 18–19; 27:8, 19). In Proverbs, this occurs elsewhere only in 10:26.

(3) A simile in the A-line without a coordinated *ken* in the B-line: "Like the chill of snow on a harvest day is a reliable envoy to his senders" (Prov 25:13; sim. 26:11). In Proverbs, this occurs outside this collection only in 10:23. The simile formula smoothes the transition between the two lines and does not present a riddle as the first template does.

The special stylistic profile of Part V shows the work of a single editor (or a unified group of editors) who was collecting and composing proverbs according to his own criteria and not merely gathering sayings at random.

Part V is commonly divided into two sections, Va (chaps. 25–26) and Vb (chaps. 27–29), with the heading in 25:1 applying to both. Though the distinction is not sharp, the division is useful. Part Va has several thematic clusters, while Vb is composed of individual maxims, either couplets or quatrains. Part Va uses rich imagery; Vb does not. Va has few antithetical couplets; Vb has several. This does not prove that the sections were ever separate collections, for an editor

[365] In Part V, Yahweh is mentioned 6 times in 138 verses = .043 per verse. In the rest of Proverbs, he is mentioned 81 times in 777 verses = .104 per verse, or 2.4 times as frequently.

can group similar sayings together, whether by intention or by memory association.

It is a matter of debate whether there are larger groups of proverbs organized in complex structures in some or all of these chapters. (One theory holds that chapters 28–29 are a separate collection; see "Chapters 28–29: A 'Royal Instruction'?" before the Comments on Prov 28.) In my view, the maxims of Part V are not organized in large-scale designs, though there are some thematic clusters.

Developing an idea of G. Bryce (1972) and using techniques of structuralism and rhetorical criticism, R. Van Leeuwen (1988: 57–86) seeks to uncover an intricate design in Prov 25:2–27. Van Leeuwen also finds proverb poems in 26:1–12; 26:13–16; 26:17–28; but not in 27:1–22.

The unit is delimited by the inclusio of 25:2b and 27b, the second being translated, "and to seek difficult things is (no) glory" (see the Comment on 25:27). The unit is supposed to form a "proverb poem" with a double theme: (a) social hierarchy, rank, or position (God–king–subjects) and (b) social conflict and its resolution. Its audience is young courtiers. Its main components are as follows:

25:2–5	Introduction
25:6–15	Section I
25:16–20	Section II A
25:21–27	Section II B

Overlapping this division is a threefold chiasm. Van Leeuwen traces various patterns in addition to these, mapping forms (Saying and Admonition) and valence—whether a proverb depicts something that is evaluated as good (+) or bad (–). He finds patterns and exceptions, as well as patterns that account for the exceptions (e.g., ibid., pp. 64–65).

Van Leeuwen's intricate analysis cannot be adequately dealt with here. The validity of this analysis should be tested, first of all, against the reader's perceptions. For me, the structure has no relation to my experience of reading. Even Van Leeuwen's own commentary (1997) does not seem to be much constrained by the proposed design. This design is, in my view, too intricate and too muddied by countervailing factors to be rhetorically effective. In any case, I do not think that an editor could construct such a design by collecting existing proverbs. There would be no way to control the mass of unrelated factors that Van Leeuwen considers relevant to structure-formation. In sum, Prov 25 has some thematic clusters but does not work as a "poem" of any sort.

PART VA: PROVERBS 25:1–26:28

25:1 These too are proverbs of Solomon,
which the men of Hezekiah king of Judah transcribed.

The "too" in this title shows awareness of the previous Solomonic collection, introduced in Prov 10:1. Together with the "too" in 24:23a, this gives the impression of a book growing by stages, starting in chapter 10.

In the wake of the destruction of the northern kingdom in 722 B.C.E., the process of national re-entrenchment in the south would likely have included preservation of older literature in addition to the cultic reforms described in 2 Kgs 18:3–4 and 2 Chr 29–30 (Fishbane 1985: 33; R. B. Y. Scott 1955: 274–79; Plöger ad loc.). Similar movements were under way at roughly the same time in Egypt and Mesopotamia.

The royal administration (including the royal court and the palace and the entire central administration) was a locus of literary activity in both Mesopotamia and Egypt. In Egypt, the palace, closely associated with the temple, sponsored the "House of Life," which was a scriptorium, library, and school. In Assyria, Tiglath-pileser I (1114–1076) established a royal library in Ashur, and Ashurbanipal (668–27) assembled a great library in Nineveh, some forty years after Hezekiah's death in 687. In creating his library, Ashurbanipal had tablets copied, appropriated from private collections, and edited. The colophon of one text is especially revealing: "Palace of Ashurbanipal, King of the world. . . . The wisdom of [the scribal god] Nabu, the signs of writing, as many as have been devised, I wrote on tablets. I arranged (the tablets) in series, I collated (them),[366] and for my royal contemplation and recital I placed them in my palace." (Weitemeyer *1956*: 228)

The "writing," "arranging," and "collation" of texts—presumably carried out by royal scribes, though this particular king was literate—comes close to the idea expressed by *heʿtiqu* "transcribed" in Prov 25:1.

P. Skehan (*1971a*: 17, 23) asserts that Hezekiah was considered a fountainhead of the Wisdom tradition but is mentioned primarily for numerological reasons. M. Carasik (1994) argues that the title is a fictional ascription of a text to a historical personage, such as we have often in Psalms. Carasik finds thematic and linguistic links between the title and 2 Kgs 18–19. One strong link, Carasik believes, is *yôm ṣārāh* "day of trouble" in Prov 25:19 and 2 Kgs 19:3, as well as the theme of trust in that story. The "traitor" in Prov 25:19 could be Rabshakeh. Carasik is not saying that these linkages were originally intended, but that the scribe who added 25:1 *thought* they were. But it is difficult to reconstruct a notion in someone's mind, particularly when it is erroneous, on the basis of such slight hints. In any case, Prov 25:1 does *not* ascribe the authorship to Hezekiah but rather to Solomon, so the associations with Hezekiah in the 2 Kings narrative are irrelevant.

transcribed [*heʿtiqu*]: The exact meaning of the verb is uncertain. "Transcribed" reflects the verb's etymology (*ʿ-t-q* "move") and suggests the gathering of proverbs from a variety of sources, whether written or oral. Rendering the verb as "transcribed" rather than "copied" is supported by the plurality of the subject "men" because a short text like this collection would have been copied by one scribe, not a collectivity.

heʿtîqû: The root *ʿ-t-q* basically means "move" or "change place." In the H-stem, its transitive use means "move from one place to another," "remove" (mountains) (Job 9:5). The intransitive use is similar (Gen 12:8; 26:22). Applying this notion to the present verse allows for a range of activities. "Copy" is a common translation (RSV, et al.), but mere copying was a constant activity for all texts and would not warrant special mention in a title. Also, the verb is plural, whereas, judging from scribal colophons elsewhere, a manuscript would be copied by a single scribe, not several. Saʿadia explains the verb as meaning to inscribe orally transmitted proverbs. This would normally be expressed as *kātab* "write."

Heʿtiqû may mean "assembled" or "collected" (Clifford). Though the expected verb for this is *ʾāsap* "collect," *heʿtiqû* could express this idea by suggesting the transfer of sayings from various texts or from the memory of various people into a collection; thus Ramaq, sim. Vul *transtulerunt* "transcribed."

[366] Akkadian *abrēma*, lit., "looked through carefully."

"Hezekiah's men" were men in the employ of the royal court. Such officials were known also as the "king's servants" (see 1 Kgs 10:8). In the present verse, they are envisioned as creating a new text by gather sayings from old (Solomonic) traditions. A similar process is implied by the title of a New Kingdom Egyptian Wisdom book: "Instruction According to Old Writings" (see Vol. I, 22, n. 31). This implies that sayings were copied from various older books into a new collection.

25:2 It is to God's honor to conceal a matter,
and to the honor of kings to examine a matter.
3 **The heavens for height and the earth for depth,**
and the heart of kings for being unsearchable.
4 **Remove dross from silver,**
and a vessel comes forth for the smith.
5 **Remove the wicked from before the king,**
and his throne will be established in righteousness.
6 **Do not exalt yourself before the king,**
and do not stand in the place of the great.
7 **For better that he say, "Come up here,"**
than that he degrade you before a nobleman
whom your eyes have seen.

Kings and Their Courts. The proverbs in this cluster, like Prov 16:10–15, certainly originated in the court. They speak of kings and their wisdom with awe, even sycophancy. They are most relevant for young men who might work in the royal court as clerks and administrators but are not necessarily of noble rank (v 6).

The main theme throughout vv 2–7 is the king. The section is made up of three quatrains: vv 2 + 3, speaking of concealment and investigation; vv 4 + 5, on the importance of removing wicked courtiers (with v 4 providing a metaphor for v 5); and vv 6 + 7 on the importance of maintaining humility in the royal court. The theme of God's and the king's honor is explicit in v 2, while the issue of the courtiers' honor is implied in vv 6 + 7. Verses 2–7 form a proverb cluster, not a coherent epigram with a single point. It is likely that the three quatrains originated as separate proverbs.

25:2. It redounds to God's glory that he cloaks his creation in mystery, for he thus preserves his own numinous mystery and brings humans to humility. As Deut 29:28a says, "The concealed things belong to the Lord our God." It is to the king's glory to probe difficult matters, whether in affairs of state or in judgment, for this requires and displays his wisdom and perspicuity.

The antithesis between "conceal a matter" and "examine a matter" might give the impression that these are the same "matter" and that the king should be investigating what God has hidden. But esoteric investigation is nowhere a royal duty or prerogative. Solomon's vaunted wisdom (1 Kgs 5:10–14) is not of that sort, though esoteric wisdom was ascribed to him in much later times.

25:3. While the king's honor lies in investigating others, he is himself inscrutable in his loftiness. As the heavens and earth are the epitomes of height and depth and are unfathomable, so is the king's mind unfathomable and mysterious. ("Unsearchable" [*'eyn ḥeqer*] is used elsewhere only of God and the vast creation [Job 5:9; 9:10; Ps 145:3; Isa 40:28; see Van Leeuwen 1988: 75–76].)

In practical terms, the saying implies, you cannot figure out what the king is really after. His pleasantness might conceal anger and his intentions might change from one moment to the next, or he might simply leave you in suspense when you propose or request something of him. God alone controls the king's decisions (Prov 21:1), which makes them all the more enigmatic. The author has put elegantly—and prudently—what was certainly a source of frustration to many royal advisors: their employer's quirky mind and changing whims. The proverb manages to both flatter the king and put novice courtiers and officials on guard against him.

earth: The earth, considered in three dimensions, has great depth, reaching to the underworld. The word *'ereṣ* "earth" can refer to the underworld, as in Jon 2:7 ("earth" = "the pit"); Pss 22:30 (read *yšny* "sleepers" for *dšny* "fat ones"); 71:20; Sir 51:9 (// Sheol); and see TDOT 1.398.

25:4–5. Before a silver vessel can be cast, the ore must be refined by melting it down and removing its impurities. So too must the king remove the human scum that collects around the power and wealth of the royal court in order to allow his reign to rest firmly on righteousness. The comparison to smelting suggests that the purge will be a harsh process. Prov 16:12, 13; 20:8, and 26 have a similar message, as does Ps 101 (see the introduction to Prov 16:10–15). Prov 25:5b ≈ 16:12b.

comes forth for the smith: Van Leeuwen (1986c) notes the puzzling jump from the refining of the metal to the emergence of the finished vessel. In Exod 32:24, Aaron claims that he received gold from the people, and "I threw it in the fire and this calf came out." Isa 54:16 jumps from the creation of the smith, to the blowing on the coals, to the production of a weapon. Van Leeuwen says that "comes forth" is a metallurgical term describing the molten metal effluent that "comes forth" of the smelting process refined and ready for casting (1986c: 113). But the subject of the verb in Prov 25:4b is "a vessel," not the silver effluent, and there is still a gap between the effluent and the appearance of the finished product. This gap is to the point. In Exodus, Aaron is being disingenuous, pretending that the golden calf had somehow appeared on its own. (In Isaiah, the point is somewhat different: God claims that he is the real creator of weaponry and is not describing the sequence of the procedure.) The imagery in this quatrain gives the impression that, once impurities are removed, the silver vessel appears suddenly—"for the smith." So too the security of the throne is imagined as the automatic and immediate result of removing corrupt men from the court.

This is a message for the king himself, for it is he who is to compare himself to a smith and give thought to his duty to forge a just society. It is not directed at royal advisors, for their task is to assist and facilitate, and they are not analogous to the artisan.

25:6–7. Many of the sayings about the king and his court are for the benefit of men who will serve in the king's presence (Prov 22:29) but do not themselves belong to "the great"—the grandees and nobles. Such employees must learn their place; this is the teaching of Sir 7:4 as well. To exalt oneself beyond one's proper station is imprudent and even morally suspect, like pushing too hard to get rich; see the Comment on 10:22. Still, there are legitimate ways to advance one's status, such as gifts (Prov 18:16; 19:6) and skill in one's work (22:29). Ahiqar offers very similar advice when, speaking of "your master" (192 [1.1.191]), he says, "[and let him say], 'Approach me,' and let him not say, 'Go, get away from me' " (194 [1.1.193]). Ben Sira seems to be responding to Prov 26:6–7 when he says, "The wisdom of the lowly man raises his head and seats him among princes" (11:1). In Ben Sira it is wisdom rather than the king that exalts the lowly.

exalt yourself . . . stand in the place: This refers to any type of self-promotion and maneuvering to reach above one's station. But the maxim also warns against actually moving unbidden toward the king to a place above one's rank, perhaps onto the dais where the king and his highest nobles sit. This you can rightfully do only if invited.

than that he degrade you before a nobleman: You will be humiliated if the king demotes you and gives preference to one of the nobility. "Degrade you" or (lit.) "make you low" (*hašpil*^{e}*ka*) means both to humiliate and to send one back to a physically lower place.

whom your eyes have seen: The third line of v 7 is puzzling. On the face of it, it is a relative clause describing a noble, but it is unclear what the clause contributes to the proverb. Perhaps the clause refers to someone you knew already, a colleague who is allowed to advance beyond you. Perhaps it is a fragment of a different proverb.

Proposals about 7c include the following: (1) Join v 7c to v 8a, following the LXX and Vulgate. Murphy translates, "Whatever your eyes see, do not be quick to argue for." However, *lārib* + dir. obj. does not mean to argue for something but to argue *with* someone. Either way the words have no function and do not belong with either verse. (2) Join vv 7c and 8a and translate, "What thine eyes have seen, report not hastily in public" (Toy). This follows Sym, *mē exenegkę̄s eis plēthos tachu* "Do not bring forth to abundance quickly," which vocalizes *'al tōṣē' lārōb mahēr*. Plöger takes from this just the vocalization of *tōṣē'* and translates, "Was deine Augen gesehen haben—geh (damit) nicht eilig zum Prozess, etc." ("Do not go quickly to judgment with what your eyes have seen.") The translation of *rôb* in the sense of "public" is doubtful and the relation to v 8a is tenuous, especially in Plöger's reading.

The Egyptian instructions give similar advice. Ptahhotep says, "If you are in the antechamber, stand and sit according to your rank that was assigned you on the first day. Do not trespass or you will meet with opposition" (ll. 220–22 [cf. AEL 1.67]). Duachety says to his son, whom he is taking to the scribal school at the palace, "If you are walking behind nobles, approach (only) at a distance, (and walk) at the very end!" (XXIVa [cf. AEL 1.190]). Anii teaches, "Go according to the customary way of every day. Proceed according to position. 'Who is there?' people always say.[367] An office receives its due" (19.13–15 [cf. AEL 2.140]). So important is this advice that Anii repeats it: "Keep your eye on your position,

[367] This is a put-down, as if to say, "What is *he* doing here?"

be it low or high. It is not good to push forward. Proceed in accordance with your rank" (21.10–11 [cf. AEL 2.142]). Such counsels are natural to any hierarchical setting.

25:8 Do not go out to quarrel hastily,
for what will you do afterwards,
when your neighbor insults you?
9 Have your quarrel with your neighbor,
but do not reveal another's secret;
10 lest one who hears revile you,
and your bad reputation never end.

Do not be quick to quarrel because that may bring insults. But if you do get into an argument, don't *you* say hurtful things. Even when you are angry with someone, preserve his secrets. For if you violate his confidence, your own reputation will be cheapened. The person to whom you are gossiping will hold you in contempt and subsequently speak badly of *you* (v 10). Gossip spreads like a plague, and the gossiper himself will catch it. Respecting another's privacy is not a favor; it is a moral obligation and must be maintained whether or not relations are warm.

Ben Sira (27:16–21) elaborates on this idea, recognizing that revealing another's secrets is worse than quarreling with him: "He who reveals a secret will lose loyalty, and he will not find a friend close to his soul" (v 16). Furthermore, "A wound can be bound up, and there is mollification for quarrels.[368] But he who reveals secrets destroys hope" (v 21).

The maxim applies to any argument that can lead to bitter words. Many commentators (e.g., Delitzsch, Murphy, Clifford) relate the maxim specifically to lawsuits, but *rib* "quarrel" is not restricted to lawsuits. Moreover, revelation of another's secret would most often occur in personal circumstances, not forensic ones.

25:8. *afterwards* [*beʾaḥăritahh*]: Lit., "in its future." At some point after the quarrel, you might wish to get back at your neighbor by gossiping about *him*. Don't.

lest: MT's *pen mah-* ("lest what") is an awkward construction. The clauses in v 8bc can be explained as an anacoluthon (Delitzsch), a syntactic break in a sentence that leaves one construction unfinished (here, a "lest" clause), then suddenly shifts to a different construction (here, a rhetorical question). We could paraphrase: Do not enter a quarrel hastily, lest you find yourself in a quandary later, when your neighbor insults you. The "lest" clause is thus equivalent to a motive clause. Alternatively, *pn* may be vertical dittog. with the *pn* of v 10, or possibly a near-dittog. with *ky* (Ehrlich, Toy).

25:9. *another's*: That is, your neighbor's.

25:10. *your bad reputation* [*dibbatᵉka*]: Lit., "your slander," that is, the slander against you.

---

[368] Or "insult." The Hebrew of Sira is not extant in other places where the Greek has *loidoria*, but Greek *loidoria* renders Hebrew *ryb* in Prov 20:3 and Exod 17:7, and this is very likely the Hebrew word Ben Sira used.

never end [*lo' tašub*]: Lit., "not return." Once released, gossip, like a bird (to use the metaphor in Prov 26:2 and Qoh 10:20) never comes back.

The LXX adds: "Graciousness and love make one free. Guard them for yourself, lest you become disgraceful. But guard your ways peacefully." This summarizes vv 7–10.

25:11 Apples of gold in engravings of silver:
a word spoken in the right way.
12 A ring of gold and an ornament of fine gold:
a wise man giving a rebuke to a listening ear.

Eloquent words—even when they are reprimands—are like well-crafted jewelry in well-matched settings.

The quatrain holds a complex ratio:

Precious item	*Setting*
Just as	
(A) a word	in the right way
is like	
apples of gold	in engravings of silver
so too	
(B) a wise man giving a rebuke	to a listening ear
is like	
a ring of gold	(in) an ornament of fine gold.

Separately, each couplet praises a word that is spoken when or where it belongs. Combined, they compare degrees of likeness. Since gold is more precious than silver, the virtue extolled in v 12b exceeds the one praised in v 11b. A wise rebuke to a listening ear is even lovelier and more fitting than a word spoken in just the right way. The comparison in v 12 is more surprising than the one in v 11, since one would expect a rebuke to be unwelcome and jarring. It is, after all, intended to shake the listener out of complacency. The metaphor in v 11 says otherwise: A wise rebuke and a listening ear are a match for each other and enhance each other no less than two elegant pieces of jewelry. The image in v 12 further implies that a "listening ear" is adorned, not demeaned, by a rebuke, and also that the listener need not be merely a passive object of chastisement. If he cooperates with the sagacious rebuker, they together make harmony, not discord.

25:11. *Apples of gold*: These are not actual apples and oranges in a silver tray (Delitzsch) but, like the ring and the ornament in v 12, a type of jewelry or decoration. Though jewelry shaped as apples or apricots (as a *tappuaḥ* may actually mean) is not extant, pomegranates are a common artistic motif, and a necklace with golden pomegranates was found in Late Bronze Cyprus (Bühlmann 1976: 49).

engravings: In Num 33:52, *maśkiyyot* are sculpted or engraved images; see also the Comment on 18:11.

in the right way [*ʿal ʾopnāyw*]: I understand this difficult idiom as equivalent to MH *ʾwpn* (*ōpen*) "way." "Its ways" (pointed as a dual) means the ways proper to it, that is, the "right" ways or, in translation, "way." (It is possible, however, that the rabbinic usage derives from this verse and is not independent evidence for this meaning.)

ʾopnāyw is a dual + possessive from **ʾōpen*, a hapax. (The plural would be **ʾŏpānāyw*.) It resembles *ʾôpān* "wheel," and MT's dual may reflect that understanding. The dual *ʾwpnyym* occurs in RH as well (see Jastrow *Dictionary* 31b). One might conjecture that "on its two wheels" is an idiom meaning something like "in the place where it can move most efficiently," hence "in the right/effective place." But it is anachronistic as well as speculative to read this as literary-critical praise of parallelistic couplets, as if it referred to "the compact elegance of expression produced by the balancing halves of a wisdom sentence" (Toy; sim. Plöger). Ben Sira (50:27) calls his own teaching *mwšl ʾwpnym*, but this too is obscure. HALOT (79a) and many commentators explain *ʾōpen* as cognate to Arabic *fann* / *ifānn* "time"; sim. Sym *en kairǭ autou* "in its time." The latter is, however, probably influenced by Prov 15:23b and not independent evidence. Another puzzling dual is *dᵉrākayim* in Prov 28:6 (see the Comment) and 28:18.

25:12. *ring*: Hebrew *nezem* can be a nose-ring or an earring. The latter would fit nicely with the image in the B-line.

an ornament of fine gold: It is not clear if this is attached to the ring or is another piece of jewelry worn at the same time.

a wise man giving a rebuke [*mokiaḥ ḥakam*]: The comparison of a rebuker to a ring is awkward, and a *mokiaḥ* "rebuker" is not equivalent to the subject of v 11b, which is a spoken word. But the next verse too compares a person to a desirable thing.

25:13 Like the chill of snow on a harvest day
is a reliable envoy to his senders:
He refreshes the soul of his masters.

The harvest in question is probably the wheat and barley harvest in May–June (mentioned in Ruth 2:23), when it can be quite hot and when people are working all day in the sun. The arrival of a reliable envoy, or, more precisely, his message, is as refreshing as a bit of a chill would be on such a day. An envoy (*ṣir*) or messenger is anyone sent out to represent another's business; see the Comment on 10:26. Prov 25:13b ≈ 13:17b, "a trustworthy envoy brings healing." Reliability in messengers is often extolled in ancient Near Eastern literature and letters; see S. Meier *1988*: 23–24.

Delitzsch (sim. Toy) says that snow in the time of harvest would be a calamity or at least unwelcome. He believes this is implied in Prov 26:1. Delitzsch explains the snow as a drink cooled by snow, even though transporting snow from the Lebanon to a hot region (thus Delitzsch) would be impossible. McKane explains the snow as "the cold of snow." But they are being too literal minded. Snow during the summer harvest in Israel is a meteorological impossibility. The point of the metaphor is that a reliable messenger is as refreshing as snow during the hot harvest *would* be—and perhaps as rare.

There is strong alliteration of /ṣ/ and /š/: *kᵉṣinnat šeleg bᵉyom qaṣir, ṣir neʾĕman lᵉšolᵉḥayw, wᵉnepeš ʾădonayw yašib*. Note also the assonance and rhyme of *qaṣir ṣir*.

He refreshes [*yašib*] *the soul*: Lit., "brings back the soul [*nepeš*]." By bringing an awaited report, the messenger restores the "soul" of his employer, which had gone forth in concern and hope; compare the idiom in Cant 5:6 (Saʿadia, Ramaq). The line may be a gloss explaining (unnecessarily) just why snow would be desirable (Toy). It continues the assonance of the preceding lines, but glosses need not be devoid of artistry.

25:14 Clouds with wind and no rain:
a man who boasts of a gift that disappoints.

The autumn rains in Israel are preceded by a couple of weeks of growing clouds and humidity. A man who postures as a benefactor but does not follow through on his promises is like clouds and winds at the end of the summer that augur a rain that does not come. The disappointment is keen.

clouds with wind: Not "clouds and wind," as this is almost always understood, for the wind would have no part in portending rain, but rather "clouds *with* wind." The wind disperses the clouds and prevents the rain (Ehrlich). The metaphor can be pressed further: the posturer is full of wind. The words of his mouth are "a mighty wind," to use Bildad's phrase (Job 8:2).

The word for "clouds," *nᵉśiʾim*, has a homonym meaning "princes." This creates a pungent pun, for the line can also mean, "Princes with wind but no rain." There are princes who are full of hot air and never give what they promise. Tur-Sinai (p. 22) further suggests, on the basis of an Arabic usage, that *gešem* "rain" means "generosity." Even without the Arabic analogy, rain, as a source of blessing, can be a metaphor for gifts and beneficences.

a gift that disappoints: Lit., "a deceitful gift," meaning one that never arrives.

25:15 By patience an official can be beguiled,
and a soft tongue breaks a bone.

Gentle, patient speech is so powerful that it can overcome even a hardened, stubborn official. The image in v 15b is jarring and incongruous, meant to drive home the sheer force of soft speech. The stubborn official is not merely persuaded by gentle words; he is broken, defeated. Gentle words can also *heal* the bones (Prov 16:24; cf. 12:18; 15:4). The power of speech can be applied to different ends.

be beguiled [*yᵉputteh*]: The verb can also be translated, more sharply, as "be gulled," that is, made to act like a *peti*, a naïf (McKane).

Qohelet offers similar advice: "If the ruler grows angry at you, do not leave your place, for the ability to soothe anger [*marpeʾ*] can set aside great offenses" (10:4). And, as Prov 12:18b says: "The tongue of the wise is a balm [*marpeʾ*]." Other proverbs that teach the power of quiet, patient speech are 15:4, 18; 16:24.

Ahiqar too uses the topos found in Prov 25:15b: "Soft is the tongue of a king, but it breaks a dragon's ribs. It is like death, which is unseen" (105 [1.1.89–90]). ("Soft" is Aramaic *rkyk*, cognate to Hebrew *rakkah* "soft," used here.) While Ahiqar speaks of the danger in the king's quietly spoken words, the present proverb speaks of the effect of quiet persuasion on one's superiors, which is a more surprising assertion. The two maxims are using the same topos—the paradox of a soft tongue breaking bones—to describe different potentials of speech. Ben Sira too reuses the topos: "A blow from a whip raises welts; a blow of the tongue smashes bones" (28:17).

25:16 If you find honey, eat just enough,
lest you become satiated with it and vomit it up.
17 Go but rarely to your neighbor's house,
lest he become satiated with you and hate you.

Don't overdo good things (v 16), not even friendship (v 17). Just as you should not overindulge on sweets, so you shouldn't overstay your welcome. However pleasant you may be, your neighbor will get fed up (in two senses) and "vomit" you out. Both verses can stand as separate proverbs and very likely were originally independent. In context, v 17 applies v 16 to a particular circumstance. The idea of v 16 is stated also in 25:27a and 27:7a.

Go but rarely: Lit., "make your foot rare."

neighbor [*reʿeh*]: A *reʿeh* is another man, one's fellow, not one necessarily living nearby; see the Comment on 3:28. English "neighbor" has acquired the broader sense of "fellowman" as well.

25:18 A club[a] and a sword and a sharpened arrow:
a man who testifies falsely against his neighbor.

[a] *mappēṣ* (MT *mēpîṣ*).

In Prov 25:18–20, a series of metaphors in the A-lines depict nasty behavior stated in the B-lines. The translation of this and similar verses (see the Introduction to Part V) maintains the Hebrew line order, but the sense might be better represented by reversing it: "A man who testifies falsely against his neighbor is a club and a sword and a sharpened arrow."

club: Most commentators agree that the word should be vocalized *mappēṣ* "club," in line with the other two weapons, rather than MT's *mēpîṣ*, "scattering" or "scatterer."

25:19 A broken tooth and a shaky[a] foot:
a treacherous refuge in a day of trouble.
20a <One who removes a garment on a cold day.>

[a] *môʿādet* (MT *mûʿādet*).

We instinctively rely on our teeth and feet, and, when they fail us, they are not only useless but cause unexpected distress. Thus too is a friend who proves unreliable.

refuge: This can be a *person* who offers refuge and protection; cf. Jer 2:37; Ps 40:5 (Ehrlich).

broken [*rōʿāh*]: The MT's pointing associates the word with *r-ʿ-ʿ* "break," "shatter," perhaps a G perf. or a ptcp. equivalent to *rōʿăʿāh* (GKC §67*s*). The G of this root is intransitive in Isa 8:9.

shaky: Emending to the G ptcp. *môʿādet* (from *m-ʿ-d*) (BHS et al.) is certainly necessary. MT's *mûʿādet* apparently parses the word as *y-ʿ-d* Hp, which would mean something like "appointed," "designated."

One who removes [*maʿădeh*] *a garment on a cold day*: This line looks like a scribal accident. It does not relate to the foregoing or the following, and it does not provide a suitable analogy to the one who sings songs to a sad heart (v 20b). Removing a garment on a cold day is imprudent to the one who does it and does not cause others discomfort.

mʿdh bgd bywm qrh: This line is probably a distorted dittography of the last five words of v 19 (Hitzig and many). Verse 20a is not clearly represented in the LXX, but the matter is complicated; see the Textual Note.

Malbim explains the clause as referring to adorning oneself with a decorative garment, one useless for warmth. He derives *maʿădeh* from *ʿădî* "ornament" (see Isa 64:5). But if there were such a verb, the clause would mean "adorn a garment" and imply nothing about lack of warmth. Hebrew *maʿădeh* is an Aramaism meaning "remove" (HALOT 789a and most).

25:20bc Vinegar on natron:
one who sings songs to a sad heart.

Vinegar makes natron sizzle, as if the acid and base were in conflict or the natron despised the vinegar. Likewise, songs, at least merry ones, are unwanted and irksome to one who is sad. Ben Sira takes it as a given that music is distasteful to a mourner: "Conversation at the wrong time is like song in (a time of) mourning, but a whip and discipline are at all times wisdom" (i.e., wise measures) (22:6a).

Other interpretations are possible: (1) As acid neutralizes a base, so too does music buffer misery, as David's did for Saul (1 Sam 16:23). This seems less likely, because the sizzling created by the two substances is not suggestive of pleasant or soothing music. (2) As vinegar neutralizes natron and make it useless for cleaning clothes, so too does melancholy neutralize the effectiveness of music; cf. Hameʾiri. Thus read, the saying is not a commonplace but rather a rebuttal of the notion (see 1 Sam 16:23) that music heals the heart. (3) Singing irks a saddened soul like vinegar sears a wound (Gemser, Murphy, based on LXX). However, *neter* is natron, that is, sodium carbonate (Jer 2:22), not "wound," and the relationship to Arabic *natratu* "wound" (Driver 1954: 240–42; McKane) is tenuous.

The LXX adds, "As a moth (does) to a garment and a worm to wood, so does a man's suffering harm (his) heart."

25:21 If your enemy hungers,
feed him bread,
and if he is thirsty,
give him water to drink.
22 For you will heap coals on his head,
and the Lord will reward you.

Mercy is the best revenge. If you treat your enemy humanely, you will put him to shame, either pricking his conscience or scorching his pride, and God will reward you. The issue of revenge is discussed in the Comment on 20:22

The importance of requiting good for evil is a Wisdom topos. Schadenfreude angers God (Prov 24:17–18). Other texts counseling decent treatment of one's adversaries are Lev 19:18; Exod 23:4; Phibis ("It is better to bless someone than to do harm to one who has insulted you" [Pap. Insinger 23.6; translation from AEL 3.203]); Romans 12:17–21; and the two quoted below. The sentiment in 25:21–22, however, is not devoid of vindictiveness, for it motivates the humane treatment by promising shame to one's opponent and a reward to oneself.

heap coals on his head: This is a metaphor for causing pain (sim. Prov 6:27–28), in this case, the pain of humiliation. That it also symbolizes contrition (Toy) or "self-accusing repentance" (Delitzsch) is doubtful. The figurative coals do not effect moral change.

S. Morenz (1953) explains this image as an allusion to an Egyptian expiation ceremony, mentioned in a Ptolemaic text (Setne I; AEL 3.136), in which a penitent carried coals on his head. A penitent thief appears before Pharaoh with a forked stick and a lighted brazier on his head. This practice is not, however, attested earlier, and there is no evidence for such a rite in Israel. In any case, the metaphor speaks of heaping coals on another, not on oneself.

Ptahhotep too advises responding graciously to one's opponent in order to let him harm himself.

(74) If you meet a contentious man in his moment[369]—
(75) a lowly man, not your equal,
(76) let not your heart rage against him, because he is weak,
(77) Leave him alone,[370] that he may punish himself. (cf. AEL 1.64)

More broadly, the Babylonian *Counsels of Wisdom* enjoins the following:

(41) Do no evil to the man who disputes with you,
(42) Requite with good the one who does evil to you.
(43) Be fair to your enemy,
(44) Let your mood be cheerful to your opponent.
(45) Be it your ill-wisher, tr[eat him generously].

[369] "Doing his thing," we might say.
[370] Lit., "put him on the ground."

(46) Make up your mind to no evil,
(47) Suc[h is not] acceptable [to the] gods,
(48) Evil [ ] is abhorrent to [ ] Marduk.
(49) Requite with good the one who does evil to you.

(trans. BTM 329)

The above passage uses the typical Wisdom locution of "abhorrent to" (l. 48), equivalent to Hebrew *toʿebah* "loathsome" (see the Comment on 3:32). This passage is very close in spirit to Prov 25:21–22 and to Amenemope (from §2, quoted in full in the Comment on 22:22–23):

(4.10) Do not make an outcry against him who transgresses against you,
(11) nor reply to him yourself.

* * *

(5.1) Steer! Let us ferry the evil man across,[371]
(2) so that we not act like him!
(3) Raise him up, give him your hand;
(4) leave him in the hands of God.
(5) Fill his belly with your own bread,
(6) that he may be sated and ashamed.

Amenemope 5.5–6 is the likely source of Prov 25:22. They share the utilitarian motivation for showing mercy—namely, that it will humble one's enemies—together with the expectation that God will bring the matter to a just conclusion. Prov 25:21–22 has another parallel in Amenemope:

(22.3) Do not say, "I have found a protector (?),
(4) I will attack my enemy."
(5) for you do not know the plans of God.
(6) You should not weep for the morrow,
(7) but seat yourself in the arms of God,
(8) and your silence will cast them down.

(from §21; repeated in §22 [cf. AEL 2.158–59])

25:23 The north wind produces rain,
and a secretive tongue, an angry face.

Just as the north wind brings rain, a gossip or talebearer makes people angry. Although rain is welcome for the crops, it can be unpleasant (Prov 19:13; 28:3b) and evocative of a gloomy countenance.

north wind: It is often noted that the west wind, not the north, brings rain in Israel (1 Kgs 18:44). However, the wind during the rainy season does not neces-

[371] Rather than letting him drown.

sarily come from due west. "North" here is, more precisely, northwest (Toy), but geographical precision is not required in popular sayings. Note that the proverb does not say that *only* the north wind has this effect.

Some scholars see a pun in "north wind" (*rûaḥ ṣāpôn*), which by a slight change of vocalization could be *rûaḥ ṣāpûn* "hidden wind/spirit"; thus van der Ploeg 1953, Clifford, Murphy, and Van Leeuwen (1988: 60). Van Leeuwen translates, "A north [hidden] wind produces a downpour, and a 'hidden' tongue (produces) angry faces." (Van Leeuwen's "hidden" represents different Hebrew words and creates a wordplay not present in the Hebrew.) It would, however, be a case of extreme discordance for *rûaḥ* to be treated as a masc. in the conjoined adjective and as fem. in the next word, *tᵉḥôlēl*. Nevertheless, a pun is possible if we take *ṣāpôn* as an inf. abs. A "wind of hiding" could be a wind or spirit (*ruaḥ* = "temperament") that hides things and operates in stealth.

Morenz (1953: 191) explains the proverb in terms of Egyptian geography, in which fertility comes from the Nile, not from rain. Rain would therefore, according to Morenz, have a negative connotation and could be suitably compared to slander. This interpretation assumes that the proverb was a literal translation of an (unknown) Egyptian saying and that an Israelite reader would be expected to understand the connotations peculiar to Egyptian geography. This is unlikely also because rain does not have particularly negative connotations in Egypt, unless it is torrential.

produces [*tᵉḥolel*]: Lit., "gives birth to." This verb can also mean "make whirl." (A storm is said to "whirl about," using the *hitpolel* of this verb, in Jer 23:19.) The powerful north wind makes rain swirl about during a storm, and a secretive tongue makes faces "stormy" or angry at the talebearer.

secretive tongue [*lᵉšon sater*]: That is, a *person* who whispers gossip and slander; see Ps 101:5.

Tur-Sinai's unique exegetical method is well illustrated by his treatment of this verse. He reads it as a riddle that can be solved by creative rereading of the consonantal text and exploitation of ambiguities. In the following expansion, words that are in the Hebrew text are boldfaced: **Conceal** [*ṣapon*] your **spirit** and anger [*ruaḥ* = "wind," "spirit," "emotion"], and then **you will produce** [*tᵉḥolel*] **a rain** of generosity (from the prince or king). For all that, your **angry face** will betray your real feelings, because it is a "**tongue**" and is liable to reveal what is **secreted** in *your* heart (Tur-Sinai, pp. 29–30; my rephrasing). He compares the likewise enigmatic Prov 27:16. This massive expansion is not as far-fetched in the Hebrew as it seems in English, but it is still strained, especially in the second line.

Still, some of this wordplay actually is at work, and we can paraphrase the secondary meaning as: "Hide your spirit (temper) and you will bring about rain, but by a secretive tongue (you will bring about) angry faces." Hiding one's "spirit" is a good thing and will produce blessing while a secretive *tongue* is a bad thing, for it means gossip and whispering, and it will make people angry.

25:24 Better to dwell on the corner of a roof
than with a contentious woman in a house with other people.

This is a duplicate of 21:9 and discussed there.

25:25 Cold water to a thirsty soul:
good news from a distant land.

Good news from afar (and hence long in coming) is awaited with eagerness and nervousness, and its arrival refreshes the soul. Prov 25:13 says the same thing. "Soul" is *nepeš*, which means both "throat" and the feeling of desire. This verse and the next share the analogy of water.

25:26 A muddied spring and a polluted well:
a righteous man tottering before a wicked one.

The downfall of a righteous person is a scandal that fouls a society's purity. In spite of assertions that the righteous will be protected (e.g., Prov 10:30a, "the righteous man will never totter"; sim. 12:3b), the sages were quite aware the righteous might fall; see the Comment on 14:14. But the "tottering" need not be final, for "though the righteous man may fall seven times, he will rise" (24:16a).

25:27 Eating honey too much is not good,
[a]and being sparing in speech is honorable.[a]

[a–a] *w*^{e}*hōqēr dabbēr m*^{e}*kubbād* (MT *w*^{e}*ḥēqer k*^{e}*bōdām kābôd*).

Don't overdo good things (v 27a), not even speech (v 27b). This saying uses the same analogy as Prov 25:16 and, as emended, has the same logic as 25:16–17.

The literal meaning of v 27b, "and the investigation of their honor is honor," is obscure. This translation uses an emendation based on the LXX.

MT *w*^{e}*ḥēqer k*^{e}*bōdām kābôd*: A number of suggestions have been offered to deal with this difficult sentence, including the following: (1) Emending to *w*^{e}*hōqēr dabbēr m*^{e}*kubbād* (as above). This emendation is based on the consonantal text reflected in the LXX; see the Textual Note. (2) Translating the second line as "but to investigate difficult things [pointing *k*^{e}*bēdîm*] is glorious [*kābôd*]" (Bryce 1979: 141). But the pl. of *kābēd* is not used as a noun, and *kābēd* never means "hard to understand." (In Exod 18:18, it means "difficult to do." In Ezek 3:5–6, the "lip" of the foreign people is figuratively "heavy" and their tongue figuratively "deep," as if they have a speech defect. Compare Moses's "heaviness" of mouth and tongue [Exod 4:10], which has nothing to do with the obscurity of a foreign language.) (3) Understanding *k*^{e}*bēdîm* as "honorable," but carrying the force of *lōʾ* from the first line to the second and translating, "and to seek difficult things is (no) glory" (Van Leeuwen 1986a: 112). This is open to the same criticisms as #2, and the gapping of a negative particle after a new subject is unlikely. (4) Reading *w*^{e}*hōqar k*^{e}*bōdîm* (or *kibbûdîm*) *kābôd* (Tur-Sinai p. 106). This could be translated, "Making honors scarce is honor"; in other words, it is most honorable to show restraint in declaring or distributing honors. But *kābôd* does not have a pl. and *kibbûdîm* (or the sg.), though a possible formation, is unattested. (5) Reading *w*^{e}*hōqēr kābōd m*^{e}*kubbād* (Perles 1922: 20). Perles translates, "und wer Ehre verschmäht (d. h. wer frei von Ehrsucht ist), der ist gerade geehrt" ("and he who spurns honor [that is, who is free from the desire for honor]—it is precisely he who receives honor"). But the inf. *hōqēr* cannot be translated as a ptcp. ("he who . . ."), nor does it mean "spurn." (6) Emending to *w*^{e}*hōqar dibrê kābôd* "so be sparing with eulogizing words" (Frankenberg, BHS). But comparison with other construct phrases with *kābôd* shows that *dibrê kābôd* would mean words that *are* honorable, not words that *give* honor. Further proposals are surveyed by Van Leeuwen 1986a.

25:28 A breached city without a wall:
a man whose spirit lacks restraint.

The praise of control of speech continues. The ability to govern one's temper is compared to a city wall. The temper (*ruaḥ*, lit., "spirit" or "wind") is held within, and, when it is angry, it must be restrained to keep it from bursting forth like a storm. Only a fool releases all his "spirit" (Prov 29:11). A truly strong person keeps it under control (16:32b).

The metaphor is not entirely apropos since a city wall is meant to keep things out, whereas a "restraint" is meant to hold things in. Perhaps the metaphor is also meant to suggest that self-control, like a wall, protects its possessor in addition to restraining him.

26:1 Like snow in summer and a downpour in harvest,
so honor is not suitable to a dolt.
2 As a sparrow for wandering and a swallow for flying,
so a gratuitous curse will not[a] alight.
3 A whip for a horse and a bridle for an ass—
and a rod for the back of dolts.
4 Don't answer a dolt according to his folly,
lest you become just like him.
5 Answer a dolt according to his folly,
lest he be wise in his own eyes.
6 One who cuts off his legs and drinks violence:
he who sends word by means of a dolt.
7 Legs dangle[b] from a cripple,
and a proverb in the mouth of dolts.
8 Like one who binds[c] a stone in a sling,
so is he who gives honor to a dolt.
9 A thorn coming into the hand of a drunk:
a proverb in the mouth of dolt.
10 [d]All the flesh of the fool is greatly wounded,
and the drunkard crosses the sea.[d]
11 Like a dog returning to his vomit,
so is a dolt repeating his folly.
12 Have you seen a man wise in his own eyes?
There is more hope for a dolt than him.

---

[a] *lōʾ* ketiv (*lô* qeré). [b] *dallû* (MT *dalyû*). [c] *k^{e}ṣōrēr* (MT *kiṣrôr*). [d–d] *rab m^{e}ḥōlāl kol b^{e}śār k^{e}sîl, w^{e}šikkōr ʿōbēr yām* (MT *rab m^{e}ḥōlēl kōl, wśōkēr k^{e}sîl w^{e}śōkēr ʿōb^{e}rîm*).

The Dolt. This passage views the fool—the *k^{e}sil*—from the standpoint of suitability. The concept of suitability, expressed by the word *naʾweh* "comely," "fitting" (v 1 and implied in vv 3, 4–5, 7, 8, and 9), means being in harmony with some implicit standard or norm (Van Leeuwen 1988: 99).

Verse 2, which is not about the dolt, is nevertheless identical in structure to v 1 and likewise takes note of an unfitting thing, namely, a baseless curse. Verse 3 turns to the theme of the dolt (or the dolt in his various relations; Van Leeuwen 1988: 90). The grouping is united by mnemonic association and thematic clustering.

Van Leeuwen believes that 26:1–12 is constructed "to force the reader to confront perennial problems which are properly labeled hermeneutic. That is, how are the proverbs to be used and applied in various, even contradictory life settings?" (1988: 99). Other readers seem not to have felt this compulsion, perhaps because only vv 7 and 9 have anything to do with proverb use, and these do not speak of application or interpretation. The concern of the passage as a whole can be called hermeneutic only in a very broad sense: "the universal fact of interpretation of people, proverbs, things, events, situations, and times" (ibid., p. 105). It is unclear what would *not* be hermeneutic discourse by this definition.

26:1. Though snow in summer might be welcomed for its coolness (Prov 25:13), it is still out of place and incongruous. Rain during the summer harvest is incongruous as well, for it can make the crops rot. Moreover, heavy rain during the harvest of grains often prolongs the act of harvesting, particularly if the rain is hard enough to bend the stemmed crops. This makes cutting the crop extremely difficult, time-consuming, and less productive (Robert Holmstedt, personal communication). Other things unsuitable for fools are pleasure (19:10) and excessive speech (17:7).

26:2. *sparrow*: *Ṣippor* means "bird" or, when collocated with another species of bird, "sparrow."

not alight: Lit., "not come." The curse will not come to roost and harm its target. It is assumed that curses are effective, though not mechanically or magically. The sparrow and swallow are mentioned as epitomes of wandering (as in Prov 27:8), though they do have nests. Gapped in the first line is the premise that the sparrow and swallow do not find a place to land, an idea implied by its complementary opposite in the second line (Van Leeuwen 1988: 91).

not alight: This is according to the ketiv, *l'*. The qeré, *lô* "to him," produces a very different sense: ". . . so a gratuitous curse will come (back) *to him*." As migratory birds return to their nests, so do vain curses recoil upon him who made them; thus Riyqam, Rashi, and others. "To him," however, lacks an antecedent. Moreover, "come back" would most naturally be *tāšûb*, not *tābô'* "come." Moreover, Prov 27:8 shows that the bird (or, specifically, the sparrow) exemplifies wandering away from home, as in the ketiv.

26:3. "Beasts" have means of discipline and control that best suit them. The harsh images here lump dolts (*k^{e}silim*), who are brutish and desire-driven, with dumb beasts who (it is assumed) can learn only by pain; sim. 19:29. Prov 26:3b ≈ 10:13b and 19:29b. There is little hope of educating the fool with words (17:10, 16; 23:9, and see the Comment on 13:24). Sayings like this are both advice on how to treat fools and a warning to boys not to be one of them. They are concerned with the education of the young, since they are the only ones who a wise man would try to educate by the application of force.

The formula *X for Y* implies "X is fitting (or "is meant") for Y" (Van Leeuwen 1988: 91). Verses 1–3 thus form a cluster with almost identical structure.

26:4–5. These two verses should be first treated separately, then in combination.

Don't answer a fool . . .: Verse 4 warns against responding to a stupid man in kind—with shouts or insults, for example—lest you come to resemble him. Prov 29:9 too warns against arguing with fools. Verse 4 agrees with the Egyptian counsel: "Good is pleasantness, good is patience. Answer a wise man; chase away a fool" ("A Man to His Son," XIV.3). Ben Sira too instructs the reader to avoid the company or conversation of fools (22:7–8 [9–10], 13). But far more frequent are demands to chastise the fool, verbally or physically.

according to his folly [*kĕʾiwwalto*]: Here the phrase means "with behavior similar to his"—shouting, insults, and the like.

Answer a fool . . .: If you leave the fool unchallenged, he will assume that he has impressed, intimidated, or confounded you, and he will be even more obnoxious than usual.

according to his folly [*kĕʾiwwalto*]: Here the phrase means "with an answer appropriate to his particular folly."

In oral use, each proverb could have stood alone to be used as appropriate—to urge someone to turn away and ignore someone who is acting like a fool or to encourage someone to give a fool the rebuke he deserves. Side-by-side, however, they create a little conundrum that makes us ponder the relationship between the two counsels.

The contradiction is usually resolved by assuming that the proverbs apply to different situations, and various suggestions have been proposed for distinguishing them. For example:

(1) Don't answer back in matters of Torah. Answer back in ordinary affairs. This solution is ascribed to the rabbis in who considered withdrawing Proverbs from circulation because of the contradiction between these two verses until they came to this resolution (*b. Shabbat* 30b).

(2) Don't answer back in mundane affairs—when someone insults you. Answer back in religious matters, when someone attacks you in matters of faith or commandments, "in order that it not seem that he has proof or that his words are true" (Saʿadia).

(3) Don't answer back in situations in which both you and the fool are known to others around you (for people will think you are alike, and may come just to watch the row). Answer back when neither of you is known (*Mid. Prov.*).

(4) Don't answer back when the fool says something the response to which would put you on the same plane as him. Answer back when the fool's utterance claims a status equal to the wise man's (Plöger).

But all these distinctions are arbitrary, and nothing in the verses connects them to particular settings. One might propose that a great many distinctions are possible, and the editor is leaving it to the reader to draw them, for wisdom is relative to the situation. But the advice the combined verses provide by this understanding would not very helpful, since no further guidance is offered as to when one should do what. Along similar lines, Murphy embraces the ambiguity itself. The purpose of the contradiction, he says, is "to educate the reader to the ambiguities of life and to be careful in speech" (p. 203). But the cautionary advice in v 4 seems to be undone by v 5. Nor does anything speak of ambiguity in *life*.

Hoglund 1987b says that 26:4–5 presupposes a "dialogic encounter between the fool and the wise" (p. 175). The sages saw this encounter as a dilemma, and, in fact, Hoglund says, the entirety of 26:1–12 is wrestling with this dilemma. Verse 12, which views being wise in one's own eyes as an incurable ailment, confirms v 5, even while granting the danger signaled in v 4 (ibid., p. 169).

I suggest that while it is true that both proverbs could be used effectively in different situations, when the proverbs are conjoined, the second proverb becomes a cautionary limitation to the first. Yes, it is dangerous to respond to a fool (v 4), but the wise have a duty to speak up (v 5). (Clifford explains the verses similarly.) By virtue of their placement, v 5 responds to v 4 and has the last word. In the end, there may be no choice but to give the fool a tongue-lashing.

26:6. A messenger is the sender's "legs." If one appoints an unfit man to do this job, he cripples himself.

cuts off [*m*ᵉ*qaṣṣeh*] *his legs*: Lit., "cuts off legs." Does this mean to *cut off* one's own feet, that is, harm oneself, or to *wear out* the feet of the many messengers who must be sent to rectify the damage caused by the fool? Rashi supports the latter, but the former is more likely because the proverb calls for a metaphor describing self-inflicted injury, similar to "drinking violence." Saʿadia understands "cuts off legs" to be harm done to a man assigned a task beyond his capacity. This places a humane construction on the proverb, but Proverbs shows no sympathy for fools (*k*ᵉ*silim*), since their flaw is not just limited ability but willful obtuseness.

*m*ᵉ*qaṣṣeh* ["cuts off"]: This is apparently a by-form of the expected *m*ᵉ*qaṣṣēṣ* (cf. Deut 25:12; Judg 1: 6–7; 2 Sam 4:12). The D of *q-ṣ-ṣ* means "cut off" in 2 Sam 4:12, for example. If we maintain the sense that *q-ṣ-h* D has in 2 Kgs 10:32, we could translate "cuts off the ends of his legs," that is, his feet or toes.

26:7. The dolt is a verbal cripple. Proverbs become lame when *he* uses them. To be effective, a proverb must be spoken with skill, in the right time and way (Prov 15:23; 25:11). As Ben Sira says, "A proverb in the mouth of the dolt is spurned, for he does not say it at its time" (20:20).

Legs: Lit., "thighs."

dangle: MT's anomalous *dalyû* is unlikely to be a "composite" of *dāl*ᵉ*yû* (*d-l-h*) and *dallû* (*d-l-l*) (McKane; HALOT 223a), for it lacks the essential gemination of the second root letter, and *d-l-h* actually means "draw up." Semantically, the verb belongs with *d-l-l* "hang down" and should be emended to *dallû*, a case of a simple *waw-yod* near-dittog.

in the mouth [*b*ᵉ*piy*]: "In the mouth of dolts" is not parallel to "from a cripple." Instead, as Emerton observes (1969: 211), the parallelism pertains to each image as a whole, not to their components. The proverb actually likens a *proverb* that is in the mouth of fools to *legs* that dangle from a cripple's body. No comparison is drawn between the fool and the cripple.

26:8. Giving a fool honor (in the form of adulation or high station) just arms him to hurt others, like putting a stone into his sling. The honor he receives becomes a nasty missile, making him even more arrogant and obnoxious.

one who binds [*kᵉṣōrēr*]: The MT's inf. cst. *kiṣrôr* means "like the binding of." But the comparison requires a participle, which is how the LXX construes it, and revocalization is warranted.

binds: Does binding the stone refer to folding it into the leather pouch in preparation for slinging it, or does it mean tying the stone to the sling in a way that would make it impossible to cast (Toy, McKane, Murphy)? The first is an image of a dangerous act, the second of a self-defeating one. The first alternative is preferable. First, *qašar b-* "binds *in*" is suggestive of putting a stone in the pouch, not disabling it by attaching it *to* another thing. Second, there are many other tools that could be more clearly disabled, if that were the tenor of the metaphor. The stone and honor are instruments of harm when given to a sling or a fool.

26:9. A proverb wielded by a fool is not merely useless (v 7), it is downright harmful to others (v 9), like a thorn (or thornbush) brandished by a staggering drunk. A proverb is not simply a packet of truth always valid and virtuous, but a device that can be put to various uses and (as this verse alone concedes) even misused.

coming into the hand [*ʿalah bᵉyad-*]: Lit., "goes up in the hand of (a drunk)." The rabbinic idiom *ʿalah bᵉyad* X means "comes into the possession of X" or (changing the subject) "X comes upon," "gets hold of" (cf. Delitzsch). The phrase *bᵉpiy* "in the mouth of" is syntactically but not semantically parallel to "in the hand of." (The idiom is *ʿalah bᵉyad*, not just *ʿalah*.) As in v 7, the semantic parallelism is between the lines in their entirety, as in the preceding verse.

ʿālāh bᵉyad: Interpretations of this idiom here include the following: (1) As a thorn *pierces* the hand of a drunkard who staggers and falls on the ground, so does a proverb hurt the fool who tries to use it. Perhaps he aims it at others but sticks himself in the process. (Compare the figure of a broken reed piercing the hand of whoever leans on it in 2 Kgs 18:21.) But *ʿalah bᵉ-* does not mean "pierce." (2) "A thorn is (like) a *leaf* [vocalizing *ʿāleh*] in the hand of the fool." Just as he handles a thorn as if it were a harmless leaf, so too is he unaware of the danger of a proverb (Ehrlich). (3) A proverb in the mouth of fools is like "a ring [vocalizing *ḥāḥ*; cf. Exod 35:22] which has come into the possession of a drunkard" (Emerton 1969: 214). The drunk is too stupefied to appreciate the value of a proverb.

proverb [*mašal*]: The kind of proverb that a fool could use to offend others is not the sort preserved in the book of Proverbs, but rather the popular sayings such as recorded elsewhere. Popular sayings can be sneers ("Is Saul too among the prophets?" [1 Sam 10:12]); insults ("From the wicked comes forth wickedness" [1 Sam 24:14]); provocations ("Let not him who girds on his sword boast like him who takes it off" [1 Kgs 20:11]); lame excuses ("The fathers have eaten sour grapes and the children's teeth stand on edge" [Ezek 18:2]); and more. A *mašal* (on which see Vol. I, 54–56) is not necessarily wisdom.

26:10. The MT is clearly corrupt. It would have to be translated "A great man causes [or "wounds"] everything, and he who hires a fool and hires passersby" or "An archer pierces everyone, and he who hires a fool and hires passers-by." The proposed translation is based on an emended text that is not distant from the MT consonantally. See proposal 6, below.

As emended, the verse describes the condition of the drunkard—who is certainly a fool—during his binge and the next morning. "All his flesh"—that is, his whole body—is wracked with pain. Prov 23:29–35 describes this condition vividly. Note in particular vv 34–35: "And you will be like one who lies (in bed) in the heart of the sea, or like one who lies in the rigging. "They beat me, [you will say], but I felt no hurt, battered me but I was unaware. When will I wake up? I'll go and look for more."

Proposed explanations of Prov 26:10 include the following:

(1) Translating "The powerful, aggressive man [*rab*] wounds [*mᵉḥōlēl*] everyone but gives a reward [*śākār*] to fools and transgressors [*ʿōbᵉrîm*]" (based on Ralbag).

(2) Emending to *rab mᵉhôlēl kōl wᵉšikkōr kᵉsîl ʿōbᵉrîm*, "A great one makes a fool of everyone, but a drunkard is a fool (even of) passers-by" (Snell 1991: 353). But *mᵉhôlēl* does not mean "make a fool of" in the sense of treating another as a fool, and *kᵉsîl ʿōbrîm* would not mean "a fool *to* passers-by," which is the translation that Snell's interpretation actually requires.

(3) Translating "An archer wounding all who pass by: one who hires a fool and a drunkard [*šikkōr*]" (Murphy; sim. Gemser, moving *ʿôbᵉrîm* to follow *kōl*). The image, however, would be unrelated to the referent.

(4) Translating "A master can produce anything, but he who hires a dullard is as one who hires transients" (JPSV). This presumes that the hiring of transients was widely considered a dreadful decision. The rendering also leaves the lines unconnected.

(5) Emending to *rab mēḥôl lᵉkullô šᵉkôr kᵉsîl ušᵉkôr ʿăbûrîm*,"More difficult [lit., "greater"] to measure than the sand (of the sea): the drunkenness of the fool and the drunkenness of sots"; Tur-Sinai (p. 67). This requires changing only word division and vocalization. The last word, Tur-Sinai argues, means "drunks," "sots." This verse is then an instance of the principle of the next verse. Tur-Sinai's explanation could be supported by the similar comparison in 27:3: "The weight of stone and the burden of sand: the fool's anger is heavier than either." The reconstructed proverb is built like many others in this unit: a metaphor followed by its referent. To argue that *ʿăbûrîm* can mean "drunks," Tur-Sinai adduces Jer 23:9, "and I was like a drunken man and a man through whom wine had passed [*ʿăbārô*]." There, however, the subject of "passed" is specified as "wine."

(6) Emending to *rb mḥll kl bśr ksyl, wškr ʿbr ym*, "All the flesh of the fool is greatly wounded, and the drunkard crosses the sea." This is tentatively accepted here. The reading is suggested by the Syr; see the Textual Note. The MT would have arisen by a series of graphic errors. *Mᵉhōlēl* means "afflicted," as in Isa 53:5.

26:11. This is a coarse and memorable image of repeated folly. Dogs do lick their vomit, giving the impression that they like it. In like manner, fools seem to enjoy the stupid things they do. Just how repulsive these things are the simile makes clear. In practice, this proverb would likely be used as a rebuke to one who has repeated a stupid action.

The proverb could be applied to all kinds of folly. Saʿadia applies it to the drunkard, who drinks and vomits (Jer 25:27) and goes back for more (Prov 23:35). Van Leeuwen (1988: 97) calls the drunk a subtype of the fool and observes that every time the noun *qiʾ* "vomit" occurs it is associated with *škr* "beer," "drunkenness."

After this verse, the LXX quotes Sir 4:21, "There is a shame that brings on sin, and there is a shame that is honor and grace." The sinful shame is described in Prov 26:11; the honorable shame is the humility alluded to in v 12. See also the discussion in the Textual Note on 26:11a.

26:12. A man who thinks himself wise has no hope of change. Neither is there much hope for dolts, although there may be a bit, since Wisdom does summon them in Prov 8:5, as if they *might* listen. Or perhaps she is just fulfilling her duty to admonish even the hopeless; see the Comment there. Prov 26:12 has the same structure as 22:29ab and 29:20. Prov 26:12 ≈ 29:20. The latter uses the same comparison to warn against hasty speech.

The present proverb seems to distinguish a man who is wise in his own eyes from the *k*^{e}*sil*, the dolt or dullard. There are certain types of fools, in particular the ^{ʾe}*wil* and the *leṣ*, who are not necessarily dull and slow witted. These "clever" fools might well hold the *k*^{e}*sil* in contempt. Yet their self-infatuation bespeaks an even deeper stupidity.

in his own eyes: The expression, "in the eyes of (someone)" refers to "a person's subjective evaluation of things in implicit, paradigmatic opposition to some *other's* evaluation," these being other people or some higher judge of what is right or wise (Van Leeuwen 1988: 104, n. 43). The man condemned in v 12a is thus not a wise man who recognizes his own wisdom, but one who is wise only in his own estimation, not by a higher standard. Being wise in one's own eyes means reliance on oneself rather than God (see Vol. I, 105–106). This contrast is explicit in Prov 16:1–2. In a similar vein, 28:26 condemns "he who trusts in his own heart," who is much the same as the sort reproached here. The fool's way is "right in his own eyes" (12:15). The sluggard is called wise in his own eyes (26:16), as is the rich man (28:11; cf. Isa 5:21).

Given that this wisdom is fraudulent, there is no particular paradox here, as Murphy thinks: "As soon as the wise person can say that he is wise, he turns out to be *worse* than a fool" (p. 201). This is not so, because a truly wise man is by definition, not merely "wise in his own eyes." Nor is this a "dangerous Saying" that turns against the reader: "Even as 'you' look down upon the fool whose self-perception is awry, you yourself may be 'wise in your own eyes' (cf. vv 4b, 5b)" (Van Leeuwen 1988: 105). It is true, however, as Van Leeuwen says, that "It is finally the failure of self-knowledge that defines the fool" (p. 105). This important insight also allows the wise man to respect his achievements without becoming arrogant, for he is aware of the limitations of his wisdom and his virtue.

26:13 The sluggard says, "There is a young lion in the street,
a lion in the plazas."
14 The door turns on its hinge,
and the sluggard on his bed.
15 The sluggard hides his hand in the bowl,
too weary to bring it back to his mouth.
16 The sluggard is wiser in his own eyes
than seven men who can respond intelligently.

The Sluggard. This cluster is well focused on the theme of laziness, though each verse could stand as an independent saying. The first three proverbs ridicule the sluggard in ways similar to Prov 19:24 and 22:13, while the fourth concludes the series with a non-ironic observation. For other proverbs on the sluggard, see the references at 10:26. Within this thematic cluster we see a sequence of actions: The sluggard makes his excuse (v 13), rolls over in bed (v 14), and refuses even to eat (v 15).

26:13. The sluggard offers a lame and ludicrous pretext for avoiding work. This saying is a near-doublet of 22:13, where the reason for the pretext is more explicit: "I will be murdered!" Two different words for lion are used in the Hebrew.

26:14. The couplet sets two statements in parallel and lets us construct a metaphorical relation between them (Alter 1985: 177). The couplet may imply that the sluggard *turns* on his bed. Like a door swinging back and forth, the sluggard turns over in his bed without going anywhere. Or it may mean that he is just a senseless slab of inert matter (ibid.). Or perhaps only the door turns: "The door turns on its hinge, but the sluggard is in his bed." That is, the door opens but the lazy man stays put rather than going out to work. Or it could suggest that *even* a door turns, but not a sluggard. The image is open-ended. It can be read in many ways to the same general effect.

26:15. The sluggard is too lazy too eat. This is a hyperbole showing the epitome of laziness (Riyqam). It also hints at the danger he faces: starvation (Prov 13:4; 20:4; 21:25). This verse differs from its doublet of 19:24 by identifying the sluggard's problem as weariness.

26:16. The surprising insight that the sluggard thinks he is *wise* harks back to vv 5 and 12. Being wise in one's own estimation blocks all hope for improvement.

The lazy man is not merely devoid of energy and motivation, he is also smug and conceited. He fancies himself smart for avoiding work while others go about their daily toils. He just lies in bed preening himself on his cleverness. He supposes himself wiser than "seven" (= several) men who are skilled in giving responses, because he can come up with excuses for avoiding work that he thinks quite witty and even convincing, even though they are transparently preposterous. His own remark in v 13 sounds like a response to someone who is demanding that he get up and go to work, someone like the speaker of Prov 6:6–11, for example.

seven men who can respond intelligently: Sa'adia, though recognizing that "seven" is a thematic number, considers it possible that these are royal advisors, such as the seven advisors of Artaxerxes (Ezr 7:14) and Xerxes (Esth 1:14).

26:17 One who seizes the ears of a passing dog[a]:
he who interferes in a conflict not his own.
18 Like a reckless man shooting deadly darts and arrows,
19 so is the man who cheats his fellow and says,
"Look, I was just joking."
20 When there's no wood, the fire dies out,
and when there's no slanderer, contention is hushed.

---

[a] keleb (MT kāleb).

21 **Charcoal for embers and wood for fire:**
and a contentious man for kindling strife.
22 **The words of the slanderer are like delicacies,**
and they descend to the chambers of the belly.

Prov 26:17–22 is a cluster of sayings that warn against provocations and quarrels.

26:17. Butting into others' quarrels is a good way to get hurt. (See also Prov 14:16; 22:3 = 27:12.). See the parallels quoted at 22:3.

a passing dog [*keleb ʿober*]: The MT divides the sentence after "dog" (which precedes "passing" in the Hebrew). This calls for the translation, "One who seizes the ears of a dog: a passerby who interferes in a conflict not his own." But this division makes the second line much longer (in the Hebrew) than the first. Balance is restored by placing the pause after *ʿober* "passing," and this makes better sense. It is seizing the ears of a passing dog—that is, a strange one—that can get one bitten. (To be sure, there were, so far as we know, no domesticated dogs in ancient Israel, but one who lives near one's house might be less hostile.) Likewise, it is the danger of interfering in *strangers'* quarrels (rather than, say, the squabbling of two family members) that is the object of this particular warning. See the other verses on this topic cited in the Comment on 22:3.

passing, interferes: There is strong paronomasia here: ***ʿōbēr mitʿabbēr.*** On *mitʿabbēr* "interferes" see the Comment on 14:16.

26:18–19. Deception is no laughing matter. A man who cheats others and claims he meant no harm is as bad as a lunatic who shoots arrows about him then ducks responsibility for the damage they cause.

reckless [*mitlahlēahh*]: Various meanings are possible. In Sir 32[35]:14, 15 it means "be reckless," "irresponsible," or possibly "be mad." (In Prov 26:18, NJPS translates "madman.") The root *l-h-h* usually means "exhaust oneself." Syr, *ʾetlahlah* (*ʾetpalpel* of *l-h*) means "be amazed," "confused," which seems close to the sense required here.

deadly darts and arrows: Lit., "darts, arrows, and death." The phrase is a hendiadys meaning "deadly darts and (deadly) arrows."

26:20. Slander fuels strife, whether it is between the slanderer and his victim or between two people whom the slander has incited against each other. On the metaphor anger = HEAT, see the Comment on 15:18.

26:21. A querulous man, like a slanderer, lights the fire of strife. The form of the couplet is the same as 26:2, 3. The metaphor of 26:20 continues.

charcoal [*pḥm*]: Perles (1895: 90) proposes *mpḥ* (*mappuaḥ*) "bellows" (Jer 6:29) as a better analogy to a provocative man. Still, *mpḥ* would then stands alongside wood, a fuel, so the analogy would not be exact in any case.

26:22. Prov 18:8 is repeated here because of its thematic relevance to v 20 particularly but also to vv 17–22 generally. See the Comment on 18:8.

26:23 Adulterated silver glazed on earthenware:
smooth[a] lips and an evil heart.
24 An enemy disguises himself in his speech,
while he sets deceit within him.
25 When he makes his voice pleasant, do not believe him,
for seven abominations are in his heart.
26 He who covers up[b] his hatred by deceit:
his evil will be exposed in public.
27 He who digs a pit will fall in it,
and he who rolls a stone—it will come back on him.
28 A deceptive tongue hates those it afflicts,
and a smooth mouth gives a shove.

---

[a] *ḥălāqîm* (MT *dôlᵉqîm*). [b] *mᵉkasseh* (MT *tikkasseh*).

The Phony Friend. The proverbs in this cluster are closely centered on the theme of feigned friendship. Verses 24–26 describe a single character type. The motif of *covering* in vv 23, 24, and 26 further unites the cluster. It is cohesive enough to be treated as a unit, though the sayings are self-contained (with vv 24–25 forming a single maxim) and probably began as independent sayings.

26:23. A metaphorical introduction to the portrayal of the hypocrite. Adulterated silver (lit., "silver of dross") is not only cheap, it lacks the tensile strength of pure silver. A vessel with such a sheen, though superficially attractive, is more fragile and worth less than it seems. Thus it is with a man who speaks warm words of friendship falsely. Of such a one a psalmist says, "The flatteries of his mouth were smooth, but his heart was (set) on war. His words were softer than oil, but they were (actually) drawn swords" (Ps 55:22). On this sort of person, see the Comment on Prov 2:16.

Adulterated silver [*kesep sîgîm*]: A number of scholars follow Ginsberg (*1945*: 21, n. 45) and Albright (1945) in reading *kᵉsapsîgîm* "like glaze," based on Ugaritic *spsg*. But a good glaze would improve the pottery, whereas the comparison here requires an inferior veneer for the analogy. In any case, Ug *spsg* does not mean glaze; see Dietrich and Loretz *1976*.

smooth lips [*śᵉpātayim ḥălāqîm*]: It is possible that MT's *dôlᵉqîm* "burning" may be intended in an extended sense: burning "with the fire of love" (Hame'iri; Delitzsch). However, burning is not a metaphor for love elsewhere in Proverbs, though (using different terms) it has that function in Cant 8:6b. Van Leeuwen (1988: 111 n. 4) prefers *dôlᵉqîm* on the grounds that, in Prov 16:27, the worthless man is said to have "scorching fire" on his lips. He notes further the congruence of 26:20–23 and 16:27–28. But in 16:27, the fire represents malice and slander, whereas the present verse speaks of a quality that is superficially attractive. We should read *ḥălāqîm* "smooth" with the LXX (*leia*); compare Ps 55:22a. This presupposes only the detachment of the left vertical of the *ḥ* to produce *dw*.

26:24–26. The hypocrite conceals his malice and schemes under a cheap sheen of pleasant words. His deception will end in public exposure. See the Comment on 10:18. It is not clear, however, how one can avoid believing an "enemy" who has successfully concealed his hatred.

covers up: MT has "will be covered."

mᵉkasseh. With MT's *tikkasseh* (Dt), the line means, "Hatred will be covered by deceit." However, this leaves "his evil" in the B-line without an antecedent. The ptcp. *mᵉkasseh* (BHS and many) is supported by the similarly structured descriptions of the worthless man in Prov 6:12–15 and 16:27–30, which are built on series of participles. The LXX and Syr have participles, but this may be *ad sensu*.

deceit [*maššaʾon*]: The particular kind of deceit indicated by *maššaʾon* would include trickery and beguilement, as does *hiššîʾ*, also from *n-š-h*, in Gen 3:13; 2 Kgs 18:29; Jer 4:10; Obad 3, 7; etc. The deception of the hypocritical friend involves enticement and illusion and not just dishonesty. This sort of deception is described in Prov 16:29: "The lawless man entices [*yᵉpatteh*] his fellow, and makes him go in a path not good."

public [*qahal*]: A *qahal* is not necessarily a formal assembly; see the Comment on 5:14.

26:27. *digs a pit*: "Covering hatred" in v 26 calls to mind the act of digging a pitfall and disguising it with branches. The popular "pit" topos reinforces v 26, which teaches that concealment will result in exposure. On the reversal of fortunes known as peripety, see the Comment on 1:19. The "pit" topos is found in various forms also in Pss 7:16; 9:16–17; 35:7–8; 57:7; 141:10; Qoh 10:8–9, and Sir 27:25–27.

The second line refers to a stone so heavy that it must be rolled, as in Gen 29:8, 10. Qohelet warns of the same danger: "He who moves stones may be hurt by them" (10:9a). Two self-inflicted injuries—by the pit and the stone—are conflated in a psalm:

> He digs a hole and excavates it—
> and falls in the pit he dug.
> His wickedness returns upon his own head,
> and his lawlessness comes down on his skull. (Ps 7:16–17)

26:28. The unctuous hypocrite feigns friendship but, as v 26 says, actually hates his victims (compare Prov 29:10) and contrives their downfall. Perhaps he hates them because he assumes they hate him for harming them (Ralbag).

a deceptive tongue: The man of deceptive tongue, as in Ps 120:3.

those it afflicts [*dakkayw*]: Lit., "its oppressed ones," "those oppressed by it." (Ralbag).

yiśnāʾ dakkāyw: Proposals to explain this ambiguous phrase include the following: (1) Deriving *dkyw* from Aramaic *d-k-y* "pure." Thus LXX: "The lying tongue hates truth"; sim. Syr, Tg. (2) Reading *dikkûy* "acquittal," a hypothetical noun from Aram *d-k-y* "be pure"; hence, "A lying tongue hates to see innocence established [lit., "acquittal"], and smooth speech has destructive ends" (McKane); sim. G. R. Driver 1940: 174–75, vocalizing *dikyû*, a hypothetical Aram word meaning "purity." (3) Various emendations, such as *ʾădōnāyw* "his lord" or *bᵉʿālāyw* "his possessor"; hence, "(hates) its possessor" (Gemser) or *yābîʾ šeber* "brings about destruction" (Toy, who is in effect composing a new proverb). But the text makes sense as it stands. (4) Construing *dakkāyw* as a noun in the absolute state from *d-k-h* (a by-form of *d-k-ʾ*, as in Pss 10:10; 38:9), like *ʿānāw* / *ʿānāyw* "humble" (see Num 12:3) from *ʿ-n-h* (Riyqam). (We would have to point *dākāyw*.) This would mean "oppressed person" and the awkward suffix "his" would disappear. (5) *Dakkāyw* = "those it afflicts," "its victims" (see Pss 9:10;

10:18; 74:21; etc.). It is unusual for *dak* (from *d-k-k*) to refer to one harmed by speech rather than by social oppression, but the related root *d-k-h* (whose basic meaning is "to crush") is used of various types of oppression. In Ps 38:9, the psalmist says that he has grown faint and "oppressed" (*nidkêtî*)—we might say "depressed"—and walks in gloom because of his sins. A penitent has a heart that is "broken and afflicted [*nidkeh*]" (Ps 51:19). Van Leeuwen (1988: 112, n. 5) observes that speech can metaphorically crush; cf. Job 19:2.

gives a shove [*midḥeh*]: *Dḥḥh* means "push down"; see esp. Pss 36:13; 118:13; 140:5. Imagine walking along with an apparent friend, unsuspecting of the hostility he harbors, when he suddenly shoves you to the ground.

PART VB: PROVERBS 27:1–29:27

27:1 Do not boast of the morrow,
for you know not what a day may bring forth.

Do not boast (to yourself or others) of future achievements or virtues, or be confident of prosperity, for the future is opaque and beyond human control. Moreover (it is implied) you should not delay in doing what needs to be done today, for you do not know what may happen to prevent it (Hame'iri). Recognizing this message, the LXX adds a variant of Prov 27:1b to 3:28: "for you do not know what the morrow will produce." See the Textual Note there.

To "boast of the morrow" means trusting in one's own powers rather than in God's. Instead, "Entrust your deeds to the Lord, and your plans will succeed" (Prov 16:3; see the Comment). This same lack of trust can engender fear for the future.

Ignorance of the future is a favorite topos in Egyptian literature. Several sages quote a popular saying similar to Prov 27:1 in various permutations. Ptahhotep advises generosity to one's friends because "One does not know what will happen such that he could understand the morrow" (l. 343). The Eloquent Peasant says, "Do not prepare for the morrow before it comes. One does not know what misfortune will come in it" (B 1.183–84). Amenemope says that one should not fret about the future:

(19.11) Do not lie down while fearful for the morrow,
(12) (thinking) "When day dawns, what will the morrow be like?"
(13) Man is ignorant of what the morrow is like.
(from §18 [cf. AEL 2.157])

He comes back to this principle in other contexts. Do not look for a protector against an enemy:

(22.5) Since you do not know the plans of God,
(6) do not weep for the morrow. (from §21 [cf. AEL 2.159])

This exact saying is quoted in Amenemope 23.8–9 (§22 [cf. AEL 2.159]), in an admonition not to provoke one's adversary in an argument.

O. Petrie 11 says, "Do not prepare today for tomorrow before it comes. Yesterday is not like today in God's hands" (recto 1); and "Do not deliberate about the morrow before it comes. It is today until tomorrow comes" (verso 5). In other words, events are in constant flux and all one really has is the present moment. Similar sayings appear in Kagemeni 2.2, Pap. Ramesseum I A 18, and elsewhere.

Such admonitions do not inculcate a helpless passivity in the face of a predetermined fate. The same books offer much advice on how to prepare vigorously for the future. Ptahhotep, for example, uses the saying in l. 343 to reinforce his advice on cultivating friends as a way of preparing for reversals of fortune. Such maxims teach humility but also preparedness for different eventualities. This is also Qohelet's teaching in Qoh 11:1–6.

may bring forth [*yeled*]: Lit., "beget" or "give birth to." The grammatical subject in this verse is masculine, but the image may still be of giving birth. "It is as if the day gives birth to the event" (Ramaq).

27:2 Let a stranger praise you, and not your own mouth,
an alien, and not your own lips.

Modesty is a tactical as well as moral virtue, for others are more likely to speak of a person's virtues and accomplishments if he himself is silent on them, and "He whose spirit is humble will hold honor" (29:23b). A further implication is that one should *act* in such a way that other people, and not only his own mouth, will praise him (Saʿadia).

stranger, alien [*zar, nokri*]: That is, someone else; see Vol. I, 139. This verse clearly shows that these words do not necessarily imply foreignness. If they did, that would leave praise by one's acquaintances—the most valued kind—unmentioned. Praise by foreigners would be of no special value.

27:3 The weight of stone and the burden of sand—
the fool's anger is heavier than either.
4 The cruelty of fury and a torrent of anger—
but who can stand before jealousy?
5 Better open rebuke than hidden love.

This cluster comments on the emotions of anger and love.

27:3. This proverb is concerned with the effect of fool's anger on others. The type of fool here is the *ʾĕwil*, who is known for his nasty temper (Prov 12:16; 29:9). The wise man's anger would be stirred up only when justified, and it would be expressed in a way that made it bearable, indeed *welcome* to the wise (12:1; 17:10; 27:5). In the analogy to the fool's anger in 27:3, it is actually the mass of stone and sand that is relevant here, that is, their weight compared to that of other materials in the same quantity. Job uses a similar comparison to describe the effect of his anger on *himself* (Job 6:2–3).

Ahiqar uses the same images in a different comparison: "I have carried sand and hauled salt, but there is nothing heavier than [de]b[t]" (111 [1.1.159]).[372] Ben Sira expands on the image: "Sand and salt and the burden of iron are easier to bear than a foolish man" (22:15).

27:4. Like the preceding verse, this one describes the unbearable burden of another's intense emotion. This has the same syntax as v 3: noun phrase + noun phrase + clause. The nouns phrases in the A-line are exclamations, suspended proleptically until they receive their significance retroactively from the B-line, namely, the difficulty in standing before them.

The force of rage is hard to withstand, but it does not compare to that of sexual jealousy because the latter includes anger and much else. Jealously embraces the shame of betrayed love, the affront to personal honor, and, in the case of sexual love, the insult to sexual prowess, and more. Their combined force is irresistible, both to their possessor and their target: "For jealousy enrages a man; he'll not relent in the day of vengeance" (Prov 6:34). In cases where the love is not betrayed, the jealousy is directed at anyone who might intrude in the couple's bond. Then the jealousy is infused with the power of love itself and is insuperable:

For love is as strong as death,
jealousy as hard as Sheol.
Its darts are darts of fire—
lightning itself!
Mighty waters cannot extinguish love,
nor rivers wash it away. (Cant 8:6b–7a)

27:5. Openness is to be prized above secretiveness, even when what is revealed is as unpleasant as a rebuke and what is concealed is as pleasant as love. An open rebuke reveals a friend's offenses, but only to *him*, not to others. Note the distinction between slandering and "covering hatred" in 10:18, and see the Comment on 10:12.

The Holiness Code makes it a religious duty to rebuke others for sin: "You shall not hate your brother in your heart. You should reprove your fellow and not bear sin on his behalf. You shall not take vengeance or bear a grudge against your people, but you should love your neighbor as yourself. I am Yahweh" (Lev 19:17–18).

open [*m^egullah*] *rebuke*: Lit., "a revealed rebuke," contrasting with "hidden love." The comparison is at first puzzling. In "better A than B," B should be something whose inherent goodness is increased or at least undiminished by the adjoining adjective. Here we would expect *revealed* love. Moreover, rebuke and love are not mutually exclusive; they can certainly coexist (3:12; 13:24) and are false contraries. The apparent contrast between rebuke and love is really just a prop

[372] Last word is uncertain; restoration according to TAD.

for praising openness over concealment. After all, a sage could hardly say, "Better open hatred than hidden love."

The underlying logic of this proverb is revealed by Perry's (1993) quadripartite schema, explained in the excursus after the Comment on 15:17:

1. love and openness +/+
2. rebuke and openness –/+
3. love and hiddenness +/–
4. rebuke and hiddenness –/–

What is being compared beneath the surface are scenarios 2 and 3, with preference given to 2. Since this evaluation is far from self-evident, the proverb is interesting, if problematic upon further thought.

Monostichs like this verse are rare in Proverbs. Except for headers and citations clauses (e.g., 1:23a), they occur only in 1:23a; 3:3a; 8:13c; 8:31c; 27:10c; 27:5; 27:20a (if correct), and 28:16b.[373] Some of these seem to be later additions. Still, they are the common form of biblical sayings outside the book of Proverbs. The Masoretic verse division usually joins them to other verses.

27:6 Faithful are wounds by a friend,
and profuse the kisses of an enemy.

The theme of the chastisement of love continues. The "wounds" inflicted by a friend affect one's feelings. These wounds are "faithful" or loyal inasmuch as they seek one's welfare. (This is spoken from the viewpoint of the critic.) An enemy, in contrast, may feign friendship, but however effusive his expressions of amity, they mean nothing.

When the friend (lit., "one who loves") is a parent or teacher, the wounds may be literal bruises and welts (20:30). In other cases, the wounds would be verbal (Hame'iri), for hitting an adult would provoke violence.

"Faithful" and "profuse" are not antithetical, though the proverb is antithetical in structure. Neither does the second line by itself tell us what is wrong with an enemy's demonstrations of affection. Each line has a gap to be supplied by the reversal of the other. See "Disjointed Proverbs" in the Introduction to Vol. II (II.E). We can expand the thought thus: Faithful *but few* are the wounds of a friend, while profuse *but treacherous* are the kisses of an enemy.

Naʿtārôt "profuse" is an Aramaism. The root is used in the H-stem in Ezek 35:13 (// *wattagdîlû* // *wᵉhaʿtartem*). There is no need to emend to *naʿăwôt* "deceitful" (Toy) or to posit the sense "turbulent"/ "wanton" (Driver 1940: 175), which is inappropriate anyway, since the false kisses would be smooth, not turbulent. Waldman (1976: 143) finds a semantic parallel in Akkadian *watāru* (from an unrelated root), which can connote exaggeration, hence lies. He suggests that Hebrew *ʿtr* can also imply deceit.

[373] As for other possible monostichs: Prov 3:3a and 8:13c are probably later additions. Prov 4:4a does not stand alone but forms a triplet with 4:3. Prov 5:19a should probably be regarded as a parallelistic couplet with two short lines.

It is true that the enemy's kisses are fraudulent, but this is implied by the parallelism and is not inherent in their profuseness, for a true friend also could kiss profusely. Perles (1922: 82) derives the word from *ʿātār* "smoke" and explains it as "dunstgleich," "trügerisch" ("smoky," "illusory").

by a friend: Lit., "of a friend," that is, inflicted by a friend.
friend, enemy: Lit., "lover," "hater."

27:7 A sated appetite scorns (even) the honeycomb,
but to a hungry appetite, everything bitter is sweet.

Taste, actual and metaphorical, is a matter of perception and is defined by the individual's condition and needs. "Hunger makes the bitter sweet," as Ahiqar puts it (188 [1.1.123]). Moderation is the key to satisfaction. An excess of material pleasures will paradoxically inhibit one's enjoyment, whereas a scarcity makes one derive even greater pleasure from whatever he does have (Malbim). Another implication is that one should avoid overdoing even pleasant things (Prov 25:16, 17) and should accept necessary unpleasantness, such as "the wounds" of a friend's criticism praised in v 6.

appetite [*nepeš*]: Or "person"; see the Comment on 10:3.

scorns [*tābûs*]: Either emend to *tābûz* or parse *tābûs* as a phonetic variant thereof. *Tābûs* would ordinarily mean "treads under foot" (Delitzsch) or "tramples" (Murphy). But satiety causes a loss of interest in food rather than an aggressive and irate detestation for it. *Bûz* means to reject something unappealing in Cant 8:7, which is the sense required here.

27:8 As a bird wandering from its nest,
so is he who wanders from his place.

It is as undesirable and unnatural for a man to wander from home as it is for a bird to wander from his nest (Ralbag), for they are both lonely and vulnerable. Awareness of this should stir sympathy toward the stranger (Saʿadia, Hame'iri). Riyqam explains the point of comparison to be that both bird and wanderer desire to return home. In that case, however, we would expect a reference to returning rather than wandering off.

bird [*ṣippor*]: Translated "sparrow" in Prov 26:2.

wandering [*nodedet*]: This means permanent displacement, not occasional traveling, which may be necessary. (The bird must leave the nest to find food, and people must travel on business and the like.) "Wandering" may signify roaming as a way of life, as nomad or beggar, or removal to a new dwelling place in another community. (Ehrlich prefers the latter, but the verb is ambiguous.)

his place: As well as one's domicile, his "place" could be his given station in life or another metaphorical location. The applications of the image are manifold: a husband wandering from his wife, a youth wandering from his home to a gang, and so on. Malbim understands the place to be the soul's proximity to God, which is its true place. Ben Sira uses the image to describe a man lacking wife and home: "Who would trust an armed band, which skips from city to city? Thus it is with a man who has no nest, who takes his rest wherever nightfall finds him" (36:31–32).

27:9 Oil and incense please the heart,
and the sweet advice of a friend[a] (pleases the heart) more than the soul's counsel.

---

[a] *rēʿeh* (MT *rēʿēhû*).

Sometimes advice given from another person is more persuasive than ideas thought up by oneself. Indeed, advice itself (so claims this book of advice) is sweet to the recipient, perhaps because it shows the adviser's concern. The theme of friendship ties in with the theme of rootedness in one's community in v 8.

sweet advice: The Hebrew has one word, *meteq*, usually translated "sweetness," which is the basic meaning of the root. Using this meaning alone, we would translate, "Oil and incense please the heart, and the sweetness of a friend (pleases the heart) more than the soul's counsel." But the comparison between sweetness and counsel is obscure. Tur-Sinai (p. 26) argues that *meteq* can mean counsel; see the Comment on 16:21. Whatever etymology is assigned here, *meteq* would have connoted both advice and sweetness to the Hebrew speaker.

of a friend: MT has "of his friend," but there is no antecedent for the "his," and the suffix of *reʿehu* cannot be indefinite, "one's. We should emend *rʿhw* "his friend" to *rʿh* "friend," with some support from the LXX; see the Textual Note.

the soul's counsel: This is the counsel and ideas that come from within.

The LXX translates this verse, "By myrrh and wines and incense the heart is pleased, but a soul is torn by misfortunes." For the B-line, the LXX's source-text had *wmtqrʿh mʿṣbt npš*, which is not distant from the MT. This could be read two ways: (1) Although oil and incense may be pleasing, misfortunes can overwhelm pleasures and cause deep grief. (2) Even when enjoying sensual pleasures, one may be inwardly grieving. As Prov 14:13 says, "Even in merriment a heart may hurt, and the outcome of pleasure is sadness." The LXX and MT both make sense and are variant proverbs. Whichever is original, the MT's variant fits its context, which speaks of friendship and its preciousness (27:10, 11).

Other proposals include the following: (1) "Oil and frankincense rejoice the heart; And the sweet discourse of a friend from a counseling of soul" (Delitzsch). That is, a friend's discourse that comes from his soul's deliberation pleases the heart. (This still strains the syntax. It also requires emending to *rʿh*.) (2) Emending to *ûmeteq raʿăwāh mᵉʾammēṣ nāpeš*, "The sweetness of friendship [Aram] strengthens the spirit" (McKane, Plöger). But this is distant from the MT and lacks evidence.

27:10ab Do not ignore your friend or your father's friend,
and go not into your brother's house on the day of your disaster.

When you are in serious trouble, you can turn to a friend—your own or your family's—for he will prove helpful—more so than even a brother might. In other words, "There is a friend who cleaves closer than a brother" (18:24b).

ignore [*taʿăzob*]: Usually *ʿazab* means "leave," "abandon," but if the verb is translated "abandon" here, the first line loses connection to the second. For *ʿzb* = "ignore," compare 1 Kgs 12:8 (Ehrlich); see also Prov 10:17.

your friend or your father's friend: Do not ignore either. Or this could mean, "your friend and your father's friend," that is, a friend who is also a longtime family friend (Ralbag, Ehrlich). In either case, do not overlook such a friend when you are in trouble.

disaster [*ʾed*]: This word signifies calamity or ruin (Prov 1:26, 27; 6:15; 17:5; 24:22), not ordinary difficulties.

The second line is not a warning against excessive reliance on one's brothers. It is a sort of rhetorical imperative (see the Comment on Prov 12:7) that intensifies the first line. Turn to an old friend rather than (always or immediately) to a brother. Malbim understands this as a cynical statement about brotherly love, along the lines of 19:7a: "All the poor man's brothers hate him." But there would be little point in a saying whose purpose was to disparage brotherhood; neither should 19:7 be understood that way; see the Comment there. The purpose of 27:10b is, instead, to encourage us to cherish friendship. Brotherhood is mentioned as a point of comparison. The brother is still the benchmark for fidelity because "A brother is born for sorrow" (17:17b).

27:10c Better a nearby neighbor than a distant brother.

Verse 10c is a separate proverb, distinguished from v 10ab by its form while reinforcing its message. It is a one-line "better than" proverb like 27:5. The present proverb assumes that, all things being equal, a brother is a better source of support than a neighbor, while observing that this advantage is neutralized by distance. This may be either physical distance or "the distance of the heart" (Hame'iri).

27:11 Be wise, my son, and make my heart rejoice,
that I may reply to him who insults me.

When a man is disparaged, he can boast of his son, if his son is intelligent. Hame'iri associates this verse with Ps 127:

(4) Like arrows in the hand of a warrior,
thus are sons of one's youth.
(5) Happy is the man who fills his quiver with them.
He will not be disgraced
when he speaks with (his) enemies in the gate.

When a father of many sons comes into a dispute, he has the confidence that comes from having the backing of a large family. Like the present proverb, the psalm associates sons with defiance of enemies. The setting implied is a disputation between clans in the public forum, which may or may not be a formal lawsuit. Compare Sir 30:2a: "He who educates his son will make his enemies jealous." On the theme of making parents happy, see the Comment on 10:1b.

27:12 The shrewd man, seeing trouble, hides;
callow men, passing, are punished.

This verse is a doublet of Prov 22:3, but with omission of all the *waws* ("and," "while"). The literal translation is "The shrewd man sees trouble, hides. The callow pass, are punished." The staccato syntax gives a sense of quick and inevitable succession. The elimination of the *waws* also makes the paronomasia more dramatic, clustering the /ʿ/ and /r/ sounds in the first line and the /ʿ/ in the second. The first line also has an internal chiastic rhyme, ***ʿar-raʾah-raʿah***:

ʿarUM ***raʾ***AH ***raʿ***AH *nis*TAR
p^{e}*taʾ*IM *ʿab*^{e}RU *neʿĕ*NA*šu*

27:13 "Take his garment, for he has given surety for a stranger!
And seize it, (because he has given surety) for aliens[a]."

[a] *nokrîm* (MT *nokriyyāh*).

This is a doublet of Prov 20:16 and discussed there. The MT here and the qeré in 20:16 have *nokriyyah* "alien" (fem.). This could be another man's wife (see Vol. I, 139–41). The implication of the MT, with *nokriyyah*, is that the man in question has borrowed money to pay for sex or owes a prostitute her wages. Still, an emendation from *nkryh* to *nkrym* "aliens" (masc.) is called for; see the Comment on 20:16. In this case, the "aliens" are *zarim* "strangers," which is to say, men outside one's family.

27:14 He who greets his neighbor in a loud voice
early in the morning—
it will be reckoned to him as a curse.

Excessive cheeriness early in the morning can be grating. This has nothing to do with the greeting being perceived as exaggerated, insincere, or harmful (Murphy; sim. Gemser, McKane); no hypocrisy is implied. Nor does it allude to specific events, such as Balaam's blessing (*Mid. Tanḥ*. Num 23:15) or Saul's early-morning greeting to Samuel (1 Sam 15:12–13; Zer-Kavod 1975: 9–10). It is just that many people are grumpy in the morning, while others are chipper "morning people," and neither type can understand the other.

greets [*m*^{e}*barek*]: A *b*^{e}*rakah*, usually translated "blessing," is not always a prayer for divine blessing ("May the Lord bless you"). It may be a simple greeting with no particular religious implications, as in 2 Kgs 4:29, and even when it does mention

Yahweh, it is often formulaic, with no real religious function; see Mitchell 1987: 106–110.

curse [*q^elalah*]: A *q^elalah* is usually just an insult, not an imprecation that attempts to employ prayer or magic to bring suffering on its object. See Brichto 1963: chap. IV.

27:15 An irksome dripping on a rainy day
and a contentious woman are alike.
16 He who hides her[a] hides the wind,
and he is called,[b] "Right."[c]

[a] *ṣōpnāhh* (MT *ṣōpneyhā*). [b] *ûš^emô* (MT *w^ešemen*). [c] *y^emānî* (MT *y^emînô*).

The theme of annoying things continues from v 14 with a complaint about the contentious woman, using the drizzly-day analogy, as in 19:13b, "and a woman's bickering [lit., "contention"] is an irksome dripping." Prov 27:15 expands 19:13b into a couplet about the quarrelsome woman, who is further described in v 16. Verse 16 is supposed to explain the similarity, but it is quite obscure. Several proverbs have bad things to say about the quarrelsome woman; see 21:9 = 25:24 ≈ 21:19.

27:15. *an irksome dripping* [*delep ṭored*]: Or, "a dripping that drives one out"; see 19:13.

are alike [*ništawah*]: This way of indicating likeness is not used elsewhere. Just possibly, it should be translated as a passive: "An irksome dripping on a rainy day and a contentious woman have been compared." This could allude to the comparison in Prov 19:13, perhaps familiar as a popular saying.

The peculiar *ništāwāh* is either a Nt (common in RH; also Ezek 23:48 [?] and Deut 21:8) or a metathesis for N *nišwātāh* (BHS). The verb is fem. sg. by attraction to the preceding noun.

27:16. The MT has: "Those who hide her hides [*sic*] the wind, and he calls his right hand oil." We should change the plural *ṣopneyha* to the singular *ṣofnahh*, as required by grammar and sense. Another minor emendation that makes the verse somewhat clearer is *šmw* "his name" for *šmn* "oil." The idiom (lit.) "One calls his name" means "he is called" or "named"; cf. Gen 26:33; Num 11:34; Isa 60:18.

The standard translations—"to restrain her is to restrain the wind, or to grasp oil in his right hand" (RSV; NRSV) or "As soon repress her as repress the wind, or declare one's right hand to be oil" (JPSV)—are guesses. Still, since the verse has the makings of a riddle, guesses are in order.

He who hides her . . . : That is, attempts to conceal her. "One can no more hide a quarrelsome wife from one's neighbors than one can hide a storm wind" (Clifford). She is a public embarrassment, the opposite of the Woman of Strength, who brings her husband public honor (12:4; 31:23).

Right [*y^emani*]: That is, the opposite of left. The MT has "his right hand," but the "his" is peculiar in a name or epithet. LXX's *dexios* reflects *ymyny* (close to MT's *ymnw*) or (more correctly) *ymny* "right" (adj.) or "one of the right side." Since "right side" signifies the south (e.g., 1 Kgs 6:8; Ezek 47:1–2), we could translate, "and he will be called 'Southerner.' " This does not exactly solve the problem, but it does allow for a play on *ṣāpan* "hide," which calls to mind *ṣāpôn* "north." "The Southerner" may be the southern wind, the opposite of the north wind which, according to Prov 25:23, produces rain.

hides her [*ṣōpnahh*—MT *ṣôpneyhā*; *ṣāpan*]: Numerical non-agreement of contiguous subject and verb is very awkward and an emendation to sg. is called for. The verb *ṣpn* (discussed in the Comment on 2:7) means "hide away" or "store up." It connotes exclusivity (storing up for the owner and not others) and preservation against external dangers but never (contrary to the Vulgate and many translations) *restraint* of what is held within.

The emendation of *šmn* "oil" to *wšmw* "and his name" is supported by the LXX's *onomati* "by name" and provides an appropriate object for the following verb, "calls" = "is called."

This verse has some intriguing connections with 25:23 ("The north [*ṣapon*] wind [*ruaḥ*] produces rain, and a secretive tongue, an angry face"). The two verses share the motifs of rain (though using different words) and wind (*ruaḥ*), words from the root *ṣpn* ("hide" and "north"), and the motif of anger. But the riddle remains unsolved.

27:17 Iron joins[a] to iron,
and a man joins[b] with the face of his fellow.

[a] *yēḥād* (MT *yāḥad*). [b] *yēḥad* (MT *yaḥad*).

Just as (magnetized) iron is attracted to iron, so is a man attracted to his fellow's face; he is drawn to look into it, for the sake of fellowship and communication (Tur-Sinai, p. 24). Verses 17–19 share the theme of fellowship.

The interpretation of the present verse depends on two ambiguous words, both spelled *yḥd* consonantally. In the MT's vocalization they mean "together," hence, "Iron and iron together, and a man together (with) the face of his fellow." This translation assumes a different vocalization, but the distance in meaning from the MT is not great.

The LXX and many medieval interpreters understood the word to mean "sharpen," from *ḥ-d-d*. Vocalizing *yāḥēd* (BHS), we could translate "Iron sharpens iron, and one man sharpens the face of his neighbor." Based on this, the NRSV and JPSV translate *panim* (lit., "face") as "wits." This is the interpretation implied in *b. Taʿanit* 7a, which reformulates the verse thus: "Just as one piece of iron can sharpen another, so do two wise students sharpen each other in the Halakhah." But there is no evidence that "sharpen the face" means to challenge and sharpen a person's wits.

The syntax is improved by vocalizing *yēḥad* "be joined" for *yaḥad* "together"; see Gen 49:6 and Isa 14:20.

**27:18 He who tends a fig tree will eat its fruit,
and who keeps his master will be honored.**

tends a fig tree: Tending the sycamore fig requires notching every fig to enable it to ripen and is thus the epitome of painstaking labor. Just as one profits from tending to his own possessions, so does he benefit from taking care of his superiors.

keeps his master [*ʾădono*]: Or, "his masters." (The plural form of this word is used also for the singular.) The verb *šmr* "to keep" means "to guard" when the object is a human. The verb can also mean "to tend to." Riyqam identifies "his master" as God, but there is no way in which a man can "keep" God. Ehrlich emends to *ʾdmtw* "his land" (Ehrlich). This does provide a better parallel to "fig tree," but it is not too close graphically, and the present text makes good sense.

will be honored [*yᵉkubbad*]: "Honored" can mean to be richly rewarded, as in Num 22:17.

**27:19 As in water, a face to a face,
so a man's heart to a man.**

As when one looks into water and sees a reflection of his own face, so when one looks at another man's heart—attempting to ascertain how he feels—he sees a reflection of his own heart. He sees love if he feels love, hate if he feels hate. In other words, we project our own feelings onto others. *Midrash Proverbs* on this verse says, "Just as when you put water in a vessel and gaze at it, it seems as though the water has a face in it, *so the heart of man to man* (actually reflects what the seer has in his own heart)" (according to Visotzky 1992: 113); sim. Gemser.

This enigmatic saying is open to various interpretations:

(1) Community of feelings. "Just as water reflects the face, so one human heart reflects another" (NRSV). This does not match the analogy, which calls for the heart one observes to reflect his *own* heart, just as his face reflects his own face.

(2) Insight. The heart is a mirror, and gazing into it (whether one's own heart or another's) gives greater knowledge (Murphy). But the proverb does not mention an increase of knowledge, just seeing a reflection.

(3) Introspection. The heart is a mirror in which a man's true nature is reflected (Plöger). But one's heart *is* his true nature.

(4) Fellowship: Clifford, following the LXX and Syriac in reading *kmw* "like" for *kmym* "like water," translates, "As one's face turns to another, so one's heart turns to another. But "turns" is not implied in the Hebrew, nor is the idea of turning to other people.

(5) Using the same emendation, one might translate, "Like a face to (another) face, so a man's heart to (another) man." This could mean that just as people see each other externally, so they see into others' hearts—though concealment is possible.

(6) Recognition of others' feelings. Naḥmias says: "He who looks in water will see opposite him the image of a face, and if his own is angry, he will find an image of an angry face. . . . So it is with a man's heart. From it he discerns if his friend

hates him or loves him, for hearts are loved only by him who loves them and hated only by him who hates them" (ad loc., second interpretation). By looking into your own heart, you see what *others* feel. This subtle interpretation is possible, but it runs contrary to the structure of the analogy.

27:20 Sheol and Abaddon are not satisfied,
and the eyes of man are not satisfied.

The eye, as the organ of desire (Qoh 2:10; 4:8), is as insatiable as the underworld, which is infinitely ravenous to devour all life. Sheol is the epitome of insatiability in Prov 30:15b–16. Abaddon ("Destruction") is another name for Sheol.

The analogy of death and eyes hints that your eyes are like the underworld in constantly tugging *you* in their direction. In this verse, unlike in Prov 2:18–19; 7:25–27; 9:18, it is one's own self, rather than external seducers, that is the great tempter. The danger lies within. The practical message is: Be wary of your appetites, so that, to use the words of Num 15:39, you do not go "wandering after your heart and after your eyes, which you (tend to) go whoring after."

Abaddon: Ketiv *w'bdh*, qeré *wa'ăbaddô* (*'bdw*). The qeré looks like a graphic error for *wa'ăbaddōn* (final *nun-waw* confusion). The latter is the form the word has elsewhere and which some MSS have here (some as the qeré).

The LXX, continuing the motif of body organs improperly used, adds, "He who stares is disgusting to the Lord, and the uninstructed are intemperate of tongue."

27:21 A smelter for silver and a furnace for gold,
and a man (is tested) by the mouth of him who praises him[a].

[a] *m*ᵉ*hal*ᵉ*lô* (MT *mahălālô*).

As metals are assayed for purity by a smelting furnace, so is a man's character assayed by those who praise him. To see what he is like, consider what sort of person holds him in esteem, for, as Prov 28:4 says, "Those who ignore the teaching praise the wicked man, but those who keep the teaching contend with them." The proverb does not assume that "public opinion is generally right" (as Toy summarizes the idea, which he considers a "half-truth"), but that people praise in others what they esteem in themselves. Ideally, "A man is praised according to his good sense, while he who is perverse of heart becomes an object of scorn" (12:8), but this is not always so. Prov 27:21a = 17:3a. Prov 17:3b ("and the tester of hearts is the Lord") shows that the analogy in 27:21a (and 17:3a) pertains to the testing and revealing of quality rather than to purification.

The MT reads *l*ᵉ*pî mahălālô* "according to his praise." But then the analogy is lost: Silver is not smelted *according to* a smelter, and a man would not be assayed *according to* his praise. Vocalizing *m*ᵉ*hal*ᵉ*lô* or as the plural *m*ᵉ*hal*ᵉ*lāw* (= LXX) allows *l*ᵉ*pî* to mean "by the mouth of," that is, *tested* by the literal mouth of those who praise him. The mouth of praisers is viewed as an instrument, like the smelter and furnace.

The LXX adds, "The heart of the wicked man seeks evils, but the heart of the upright man seeks knowledge." This is placed here to elucidate 27:21: People "seek"—that is, have a liking for—and therefore "praise"—whatever matches their character, for better or worse. The Vulgate and Syriac also have this couplet, and it probably was present in their Hebrew.

27:22 Even if you crush the fool in a mortar
with a pestle amidst the groats
his folly will not leave him.

Grain is crushed by a pestle in a mortar to rid it of its husk. The comparable treatment of fools (and boys generally, since they all have some folly in them) is a beating. But even such harsh means, though much recommended in Proverbs (see the Comment on 13:24), will not be effective with the *ʾĕwil*, whose pernicious folly is willful and ingrained. (To be sure, 22:15 asserts that some folly can be beaten out of a boy.)

with a pestle amidst the groats: Toy excises this phrase as overloading the first line and as inappropriate, since it is the fool alone that is pounded (Toy; BHS). But the verse forms a well-balanced tristich, and the excision blurs the image. The image is of the fool being one kernel immersed in a handful of groats, which are being mashed. Unlike the other "kernels," his husk will not be removed, and he will be useless and discarded. The pounding, then, corresponds to education, not simply punishment. All the boys get "pounded" as part of their education, but this does not really work on the fool.

will not leave [*tāsûr*]: Some commentators prefer *tāsîr* "you will (not) remove," following the LXX (thus Toy), which does tighten the parallelism. But both readings make sense.

27:23 Know well the appearance of your sheep;
give thought to the herds.
24 For wealth is not forever,
nor does a crown endure generation after generation.
25 (When) grass disappears and verdure appears,
and the grasses of the hills are gathered,
26 (there will be) sheep for your clothing
and goats—the price of a field;
27 and enough goat's milk for your food,
the food of your household,
and provisions for your maidservants.

This epigram urges devotion to animal husbandry and praises its special benefits. Wealth and power do not endure (v 24), whereas livestock reproduce and continue "generation after generation." The grass they live on renews itself and provides their needs, and their yield provides *your* needs.

This passage resembles Prov 12:11a (= 28:19a), "He who works his land will be sated with bread," but here it is applied to raising livestock. Also, that verse does not actually favor farming over other occupations (see the comment on 12:11), but the present epigram does promote animal husbandry. Providing food is an ongoing task and requires persistence and diligence, but the resources are renewable and the profit is great. This shows an awareness of an ecosystem, as Clifford calls it. The anecdote of the lazy vintner in Prov 24:30–34 describes what befalls one who fails in his responsibility to one aspect of this ecosystem.

Riyqam interprets Prov 27:23–27 as an instruction to the king. On v 23, he says, "[Solomon] says this to the ruler of a land, comparing him to a shepherd who keeps his sheep." B. Malchow (1985) argues that 27:23–27 is an introduction to chapters 28 and 29, with shepherding as a symbol of kingship. (See "Chapters 28–29: 'A Royal Instruction'?" before chapter 28.) Van Leeuwen too reads this as a royal instruction (1988:131–43). They both compare the teachings of Amenemhet and instruction to Merikare, Egyptian royal instructions that are directed to the prince or young king.[374] Certainly there is nothing implausible about Proverbs' including an instruction to a prince. This would belong to a genre of world literature commonly known as a *Fürstenspiegel*, which has many exemplars in ancient and medieval times. In fact, Deut 17:14–20, which requires the king to read a copy of the Deuteronomic instruction (*torah*) continually so that he may "learn to fear Yahweh his God" (v 19), seems based on a background picture of a king studying an ethical tractate, even though Deuteronomy is not a *Fürstenspiegel* as such.

Still, the royal interpretation hangs too much on too little. Nothing in the epigram alludes to specifically royal duties, such as the maintenance of justice, the righting of wrongs, and care for the weak. And, whereas "shepherd" in royal metaphors and titulary always refers to the king's obligations toward his people, nothing in the present epigram speaks of responsibilities *toward* the livestock, except insofar as they profit the owner. The sole possible allusion to royalty is the mention of "crown" in v 24b, but this same verse weighs against the royal interpretation. According to that reading, the advice of the epigram is directed to a king or crown prince. But no king—and certainly not a Davidide, whose dynasty believed it was permanent (2 Sam 7:12–16)—would want to hear that kingship or dynasty is transitory. To be sure, the passage could be allegorically *applied* to kingship, and the basic message could be addressed to a king, but that is not its primary meaning.

The epigram does have considerable allegorical potential. The LXX, especially at 27:27, reads it as a discourse on the value of the sage's teachings (see the Textual Note). *Midrash Proverbs* identifies the flock as Israel and the audience of the passage as God himself, to whom Israel says, "Master of all worlds, 'You know well the appearance of your flocks'—in this world. 'Give thought to your herds'—in the World to Come." Hame'iri extends the force of the passage to encompass an ethical demand to show mercy to the poor and lowly (called "sheep" and "herds") by giving charity. Naḥmias says that the sheep can represent any merchandise that

[374] The instruction to Merikare claims that it provides "all rules concerning a king" (XLVIIIb).

one should tend to, and further that keeping sheep can allude to taking care of one's children. These applications, however, extend beyond the primary sense of the passage.

Van Leeuwen (1988: 140–41), expanding on Delitzsch and Barucq (ad loc.), argues that the epigram was placed here as a redactional indicator of a unit boundary, as is the case with the poems in 23:29–35; 24:30–34; and 31:10–31. Such poems do give the sense of a coda and the second two do conclude units (31:10–31 inevitably so), but there is no particular reason to think that 23:29–35 does so. Even if the present epigram feels like a coda, there is nothing to distinguish chap. 28 from chap. 27. Perhaps Stephen Langton, who created the chapter divisions in the twelfth–thirteenth centuries C.E., felt that a poem such as 27:23–27 (and 23:29–35 and, for that matter, 26:23–28) was a good place to end a chapter, and this numbering has helped reinforce that impression in subsequent readers.

Van Leeuwen finds lexical and thematic affinities between 27:23–27 and 31:10–31, which he believes "cannot be accidental" (p. 142) and that supposedly show that the two poems have a similar message, namely, that "kings and rulers must carry out their office with wisdom" (ibid.). This requires understanding 31:10–31 as a continuation of Lemuel's mother's advice. The affinities that Van Leeuwen finds are indeed not accidental. They result from the fact that both passages describe the management of a rural estate.

27:23. *Know well* [*yadoaʿ tedaʿ*] *the appearance* [*pᵉney*, lit., "*faces*"] *of your sheep*: Give careful attention to how your flocks look, for this is a cue to their nutritional needs. Malbim senses that the phrasing "know well the faces" rather than just "know well"—implies an immediate knowledge, as if to say, take care of things yourself. Prov 12:10, using the same verb (*ydʿ* "know"), says, "The righteous man knows his animal's appetite." There the concern is humanitarian, but the implication is the same: Be aware of your livestock's needs.

27:24. *crown* [*nezer*]: Sometimes *nezer* is the priestly or royal crown or the dignity associated with it (Pss 89:40; 132:18 [where it is the antonym of *bošet* "shame"]). The word does not itself denote kingship or dynastic rule.

I understand this verse to mean that wealth does not endure, and *not even* do the royal office and its dignity endure in an individual, who will pass away. This can be said to anyone, king or commoner, for it is mentioned by way of comparison. What does endure are animal resources. But perhaps the advice is especially relevant to members of the royal family. As the example of Absalom shows (2 Sam 13:23), a member of the dynasty and court could own estates and herds outside the city. The epigram tells such a one that "in the long run these will serve him better stead than the glittering but ephemeral prizes to be won at court, or through trade, which was mainly in the hands of those active in government" (Whybray 1972: 158–59).

nor does [*wᵉʾim*] . . . : This clause is actually a rhetorical question equivalent to a negative (Hameʾiri); lit. "and is a crown for generation to generation?"

nezer: Some emend to *ʾôṣār* "treasure," cf. Isa 23:18; 33:6; and esp. Jer 20:5 (Toy, Gemser, Plöger) or *ʿōšer* "wealth" (also Plöger), but each reading shares only one letter with *nzr*. Tur-Sinai (p. 103) emends to *nāzîd*, but that means cooked food or pottage, and it would be strange to say that "pottage" will not last forever. Ehrlich reads *nîr* "plowed land," which does not last forever because it becomes depleted. However, it can be renewed by lying fallow.

27:25. Pasturage is a renewable resource. When hay is removed it is replaced by new growth (*deše'*). Moreover, the herbage of the hills (in addition to one's plantings in the fields) can be gathered for fodder. Verse 25 is a temporal clause dependent on vv 26–27 (Rashi, Toy, and many).

27:26–27. Great wealth is not promised, but only what one needs for sustenance—or perhaps especially comfortable sustenance. The needs envisaged are those of an estate.

and goats—the price of a field: Goats can be sold to buy more fields. This clause can also be read, "and the price of a field, goats." In other words, fields can be sold to buy more goats (Naḥmias). The first reading makes for better advice, because fields are a permanent asset and will enable further purchases of livestock.

for your food, the food of your household: These clauses are in apposition: "your food," which is to say, "the food of your household." The latter defines and expands the scope of the first.

household . . . maidservants: That is, *even* your maidservants. The maidservants are mentioned as the least of the servants. An estate owner's responsibility extends even to them. The mistress of the estate whose diligence is praised in 31:10–31 is diligent in supplying the needs of her household and maidservants (31:15).

provisions [*ḥayyim*]: Lit., "life," here meaning food for sustenance (Gemser, p. 14).

EXCURSUS. CHAPTERS 28–29: A "ROYAL INSTRUCTION"?

U. Skladny (1962: 57–58) first suggested that chapters 28–29 (which he considers a separate collection) are addressed to a prince. B. Malchow (1962) accepts this characterization but starts the unit at 27:23–27; see the Comment there. It is true that many of the royal proverbs in 27:23–29:27 are particularly pertinent to a prince or king (28:2, 15–16a; 29:2, 4, 14). However, these proverbs constitute only a small part of the two chapters, and there is no reason to characterize the entirety as a royal instruction. Many of the proverbs in this section (and elsewhere, especially 16:10–15) have messages relevant to kings, but they pertain to others as well. The unit as a whole is not directed specifically to the needs of royalty and, unlike in the Egyptian royal instructions, kings and princes are never addressed.

Malchow (1962) describes chapters 28 and 29 as a "manual," carefully structured and having a "conspicuous unity" (p. 239), with its introduction in 27:23–27. The manual is organized by couplets that mention the "righteous" and the "wicked." The unit proper opens (28:1) and closes (29:27) with couplets using these words. Four interrelated couplets form a symmetrical pattern organizing the unit: 28:12, 28; 29:2, 16.

The unity Malchow sees is certainly not "conspicuous." The relations among the couplets that are supposed to provide the structure are sometimes tenuous, esp. in the cases of 28:12a and 29:2a (which have only "rather similar first lines" [ibid., p. 239]). Likewise tenuous is the connection between 28:28b and 29:16b (both of which "treat the destruction of the wicked" [ibid.]). The structural couplets are unevenly spaced and provide no particular organization. To be sure, most of the verses *could* be relevant to future monarchs (thus the themes of law and justice to the poor "are very apropos for the future sovereign to whom they are addressed" [ibid., p. 240]), but they are also applicable to everyone and found throughout the book. In any case, in these two chapters, only six verses out of fifty-five (28:15; 29:2, 4, 12, 14, 26) mention the king or other ruler.

Wisdom Literature does include instructions to kings and princes. The teachings of Amenemhet, the instruction to Merikare, and the counsel to king Lemuel (Prov 31:1–9) are immediately distinguishable from Prov 25 and 28–29 by being addressed *to* the king or prince and instructing him in royal tactics and duties. Djedefhar is spoken by the prince to his son, but the extant fragment is of a general character. Merikare includes advice arising from particular historical circumstances and is in large part relevant only to a particular king—Merikare. The Babylonian "Advice to a Prince" (BTM 760–62), which is sometimes classified as Wisdom, also describes the king's duties unequivocally, using the omen form (e.g., "If a king does not heed justice, his people will be thrown into chaos, and his land will be devastated. . . . If he does not heed his nobles, his life will be cut short" [BWL 113]). In contrast, Prov 25 and 27–28 speak *about* the king, not to him, and kingship is only one topic among many. Royal instructions are explicitly royal, and their message is not dependent on teasing out this or that pattern supposedly hidden in the woodwork.

Even if these chapters do not constitute a manual for monarchs (or even a discrete collection), Skladny's observation that the proverbs in them are not *about* the ruler but *for* the ruler, does have merit for some verses. Prov 29:4, 12, and 14 teach the importance of the ruler's maintaining righteousness, and 28:15 and 29:2 describe the suffering a wicked ruler inflicts on his land. Prov 29:26, however, speaks to everyone, to remind them that God, and not the ruler, is the real power. In any case, proverbs that can serve to educate the ruler are not exclusive to these chapters. Other examples are Prov 14:28; 16:12, 13; 20:8, 26, 28; and 25:5. Many proverbs have a message for the ruler, but at the same time they tell courtiers what kinds of behavior to embrace or avoid. Some proverbs, such as 28:15, could even have served as a courtier's dig at a nasty potentate. It is fair to say that kings and rulers (the latter including nonroyal officials) were *part* of the audience of some proverb collections and that the editors were men of the court for whom these concerns were of particular relevance; see Vol. I, 6–12, and compare 25:1.

The recent book by R. Tavares (2007) will be at the center of future study of Prov 28–29. Tavares regards 27:23–27 as an introduction to the instruction proper, 28:1–29:27. The two chapters are a distinct and coherent instruction built of four blocks with beginnings and endings marked by shared pivot verses.

The instruction has two simultaneous audiences (often thought, mistakenly, to be mutually exclusive): the king (addressed in sayings of general validity), and every member of the society. This duality is found also in the royal instructions of Amenemhet and Merikare, to which Tavares carefully compares Prov 28–29, noting both similarities and differences. In spite of some significant differences, Prov 28–29 shares with the Egyptian works important components of political ideology and, surprisingly, theology: the belief in God as the omnisicient protector of mankind, especially the poor, the deity before whom all humans are equal. (This comparison should be extended to include both Mesopotamian ideas of kingship and other Egyptian texts.) In Prov 28–29, the humanity of the king is emphasized. He is viewed as a man who must be educated in preparation for his social calling. His father and mother are responsible for this education (on this, see my remarks in Vol. I,

80–83). Tavares believes that at several points the unit alludes to Solomon and implies a critique of his unbridled wealth and social oppressiveness. The instruction belongs to the time of Hezekiah, which saw increased contact with Egypt.

28:1 The wicked flee with no one pursuing,
while the righteous are as confident as a lion.

The wicked live in constant anxiety (Prov 1:26–27). On some level they are aware of their guilt and know that retribution must come, but they do not know its time or form. For a person to "flee with no one pursuing" is a misfortune threatened in curse formulas (Lev 26:17, 36). In contrast, the righteous enjoy a sense of security; see Prov 1:33 and 3:23–26.

The wicked flee . . . : Lit., "They flee and there is no pursuer—the wicked (man)." The unusual delay of the subject, "the wicked," until the end of the verse gives the line the feel of a riddle: "They flee with no one pursuing." Who is that?—"The wicked."

flee, are . . . confident: Strangely, *nāsû* ("flee") is a pl. verb with a sg. subject (*rāšāʿ*), while *yibṭāḥ* (lit. "is confident") is a sg. verb with a pl. subject. Ehrlich suggests that the *waw* on *nāsû* is a dittog., but that leaves *yibṭāḥ* unexplained. Since the subjects represents types of persons rather than individuals, and also not contiguous to their verbs, the lack of agreement apparently was not disturbing.

28:2 For the transgression of a land, its princes are many,
but through an understanding[a] man honesty endures.

[a] Omit *yōdēaʿ*.

"The transgression of a land"—widespread, systemic violations of law—brings on anarchy, both as its natural consequence and as its fitting punishment, and with anarchy comes an oppressive multiplicity of rulers and factions. The multiplicity of rulers can take the form of competing princes (Delitzsch) or frequent changes of rulership (Ehrlich, Clifford). "Its princes" may be chieftains or warlords with effective local power in a time of anarchy, or they may be *claimants* to legitimate rulership. The chaos envisioned in the proverb recalls Hos 8:4, "They set up kings, but not by me. They made princes, whom I knew not." The proverb warns rulers against allowing crime and oppression to infect the land, on pain of losing their own position.

but through an understanding man honesty endures: The MT has, lit., "*but through an understanding knowledgeable man honesty endures* [*ĕbᵉʾādām mēbîn yōdēaʿ kēn yaʾărîk*]." But the line is overloaded. Probably *yōdēaʿ* "knowledgeable" should be deleted as a doublet of *mēbîn* "intelligent," "perceptive." Then the line says that a perceptive man—in this context, a wise ruler—secures honesty and therefore stability.

Interpretations of 28:2b include the following:

(1) "[B]ut with an intelligent ruler there is lasting order" (NRSV). The NRSV is interpreting *kēn* as "order." The word (when it does not mean "thus") is usually an adjective meaning "honest," but in Qoh 8:10; Isa 10:7; 16:6; Jer 48:30; and Prov 15:7, it is a noun meaning "that which is honest," "right." It does not mean "order" (NRSV) or "stability" (JPSV).

(2) By means of a prince who understands and knows honesty and truth and knows the rights of the poor, the well-being of the people will endure (Riyqam).

(3) Because of the transgression of the people of the land, they have many rulers to harm them. Nevertheless, by means of a righteous and understanding man, they will endure (Ramaq). Ramaq construes *ʾereṣ* "land" as *ʿam hāʿāreṣ* "the people of the land." *ʾereṣ* in the sense of "people," "mankind" is supported by, for example, Gen 11:1; Ps 33:8; and Qoh 1:4. In Prov 28:2a, it is undoubtedly the people of a land as a polity, and not the physical territory, that transgresses.

(4) Emending radically on the basis of the LXX to *b^{e}pešaʿ ʿārîṣ rîbîm yēʿôrû, ûb^{e}ʾādām yidʿākûn* (delete *yaʾărîk*) and translating, "Durch das Vergehen eines Gewalttätigen werden Streitigkeiten erweckt aber durch einen einsichtsvollen Menschen verlöschen sie." ("Through the transgression of a violent man, conflicts will be stirred up, but through a discerning man they are extinguished"); (Gemser). Instead of MT's *ydʿ kn* LXX has *katasbesei autas* = *ydʿkwn* (*yidʿākûn*) "they are extinguished," but this lacks an appropriate subject.

(5) "[A]ber durch einen einsichtigen Menschen, der das Recht kennt, besteht es [das Land] dauerhaft" ("but through an insightful man, who knows what is right, the land is enduring") (Plöger). This is probably the closest to the MT, but the syntax is awkward. A problem facing most interpretations is that *yaʾărîk* "endures" is masc., whereas the noun *ʾereṣ* "land" is almost always fem. However, Ezek 21:24, in which *ʾereṣ* is modified by the masc. *ʾeḥād*, makes it just possible that the masc. verb "endures" has "land" as its subject.

28:3 A man who is poor and oppresses the lowly:
a torrential rain without bread.

When a powerful man leeches money off those beneath him, there may be some trickle-down benefit to his assistants. This would be merely "a torrential rain," one that causes damage but at least brings water. It is worse when someone lower down the ladder oppresses others, for then no one benefits. This is a torrential rain "without bread" (cf. Ehrlich).

Some commentators find it puzzling that a poor man could be called an oppressor. Clifford thinks the oppressor is a tax farmer; Murphy believes he is a *nouveau riche.* These persons, however, would not be poor. In fact, not all oppression is class-based. A poor man can be a neighborhood bully and tyrannize others, physically or financially, perhaps at the bidding of a more powerful man. The poor are not flawless. Ben Sira includes among the hateful types of people "a poor man who is arrogant" (25:2).

geber rāš: Emendations that eliminate the poverty of the oppressor include the following: (1) *Geber rōʾš*, supposedly meaning "a man in authority" (McKane; BHS). But *geber* is elsewhere modified by adjectives (like *rāš*), not by nouns in apposition (as *rōʾš*). (2) *G^{e}bîr rāšāʿ* "a wicked lord" (Toy) or *geber rāšāʿ* "wicked man" (Frankenberg). (This is inspired by the LXX's *en asebeiais* "in wickedness" [pl.].) The emendation is unnecessary and produces a banality.

without bread: This may mean that the rain produces no food, or it may be equivalent to "with famine." The benefits of an ideal ruler are described as a productive rain in Ps 72:6–7.

28:4 Those who ignore the teaching praise the wicked man,
but those who keep the teaching contend with them.

The values of those who ignore (or "abandon") the teachings of wisdom are distorted to the point that they will call the wicked just (cf. 17:15). Those who obey the teachings come into dispute with the wicked man despite the fact that others praise him (Sa'adia). Prov 29:27 describes the same alignment of values; sim. Isa 5:20; Mal 2:17.

ignore [*'zb*]: This does not necessarily mean that the men in question are religious apostates who have "abandoned" the Law. The verb *'zb*, which usually means "to leave," "abandon," can mean "to ignore"; see the Comment on 27:10ab.

teaching [*torah*]: *Torah* is used in undetermined form in Prov 6:23; 28:4, 7, 9; and 29:18. It is best understood as wisdom instruction, as is clear in 6:23. Prov 28:7 shows this, for abandoning a *father's* instruction is what would shame the father. The *torah* in the present verse is unlikely to be the divine Law, which in the lack of further context would (at least in Biblical Hebrew) require definition as "the *torah* of the Lord" or "the *torah* of Moses," or at least "*the* Torah," to distinguish it from the human *torah* "teaching" or another instruction from God.[375] An arguable exception is 29:18, but see the Comment.

praise the wicked man: They *in effect* praise the wicked by affirming his way of life.

contend [*yitgaru*]: This verb means to initiate conflict, to provoke or challenge. (Clear examples are Deut 2:9; Dan 11:25; and Jer 50:24.) The word implies that the righteous proactively confront the wicked.

with them: That is, with the wicked man. It is possible that "with them" refers to "those who ignore the teaching," but since "contend with them" is the antithesis of "praise," "with them" probably has its antecedent in "the wicked man" (*raša'*), though that is singular. Numerical agreement is often treated loosely in Proverbs, especially in regard to types of persons (Hame'iri).

28:5 Evil men do not understand what is just,
but those who seek the Lord understand everything.

Verses 4 and 5 emphasize the bond between knowledge and ethics. The wicked do not understand *mišpaṭ* "what is just." Wickedness entails a failure of intellect, whereas he who seeks God—and is therefore righteous—finds wisdom. Verse 5a is equivalent to 1:7b, "Fools despise wisdom and correction." Verse 5b is equivalent to 1:7a, "The fear of the Lord is the beginning of knowledge."

what is just [*mišpaṭ*]: *Mišpaṭ* can mean "justice" or "judgment" or "the right way." The proverb can be applied to right behavior generally or to forensic judgment in particular.

---

[375] A few verses speak of *torah* (undetermined) from God, meaning an instruction from God, usually via the priests, and not specifically the Torah of Moses (Isa 2:3; 42:21; 51:4). This is true even in Deut 33:4, where *torah ṣiwwah lanu mošeh* means "Moses commanded us an instruction," not *the* Torah. In 2 Chr 15:3 and 19:10 *torah* refers to a type of law, not *the* Torah, which would not be distinguished from *miṣwah* "commandment."

everything: This does not mean all there is to know, which would be a ridiculous claim, but all things relevant to *mišpaṭ*.

The scope of *kōl* ("everything," "all") is often defined by what precedes: for example, Gen 9:3 (*kōl* = *kol remeś* "all that swarms"); 2 Sam 12:3 (*kōl* = any of the items mentioned in v 2); Isa 30:5 (*kōl* = all the princes and envoys mentioned in v 4); Gen 6:19 (two of *kōl* = two of "every living thing of all flesh"); and Gen 27:33 (*kōl* = all the game).

28:6 Better a poor man who goes in his innocence
than a man of crooked ways who is rich.

Although wealth is good, its value is nullified if its owner is dishonest. See the Comment on 19:1, which was emended to agree with this verse. On the "better than" formula, see the excursus after the Comment on 15:17.

man of crooked ways: Lit., "one who makes his ways crooked/uneven." "Crooked" means both dishonest and uneven, that is, difficult and dangerous to traverse.

ways [*dᵉrakayim*]: This is a dual, as in Prov 28:18. The reason for the dual is unclear. Malbim (on v 18) says that the two ways are the extremes on either side of the golden mean. But, if so, going in either, and not only making them crooked, would be wrong. Murphy explains this as the doctrine of the "Two Ways," the good and the bad, which the crooked man switches around. This is not quite applicable, since one cannot distort the right way. Possibly, however, this is what the Masoretes had in mind. Delitzsch also sees in the dual the idea of two ways, but explains it to mean that the sinner actually goes in the dishonest way while *pretending* to walk in the right one (Delitzsch).

Ben Sira speaks of two paths, "Woe to (those of) faint hearts and weak hands, and to the sinner who goes on two paths" (2:12). These may be the traditional faith and the Hellenistic culture (Skehan and Di Lella 1987, ad loc.), or the verse may refer to one who goes in the way of the Lord when he prospers but abandons it when trouble comes upon him (Segal 1958, ad loc.). However, the dual cannot be formed freely, but appears with only a few nouns, mostly with items that naturally come in pairs. We should perhaps revocalize as plural, as in the same idiom in Prov 10:9, though that leaves unexplained the MT's dual. Another puzzling dual is *ʾopnāyw* in 25:11.

The Greek of Sir 2:12, *epi duo tribous*, does not indicate whether the Hebrew (not extant) read a dual or *šty drkym*. It is unlikely that Ben Sira saw *drkym* in Prov 28:6b and somehow knew that the original author intended *dᵉrākayim*, and that his translator did the same thing with the word in Sir 2:12. It does show that there existed an idea of "two ways," and that this tradition emerges in the Masoretic pointing in Prov 28:6 and 18.

28:7 The perceptive son keeps the teaching,
while he who consorts with gluttons shames his father.

Gluttony connotes a pursuit of various appetites and dissolute behavior; see the Comment on 23:20.

This is a disjointed proverb, discussed in the Introduction to Vol. II (II.E).

28:8 He who amasses his wealth by interest and usury—
is (actually) gathering it for him who is kind to the lowly.

Biblical law forbids taking interest on loans to a fellow Israelite (Exod 22:24; Lev 25:36; Deut 23:20; Ezek 18:8, 13). Loans to the poor are to be given interest-free, as an act of charity (Deut 15:1–6). No other kind of loans are explicitly permitted, though, in reality, interest-bearing loans are necessary to provide capital for commerce and often for agriculture as well. The law is not concerned with these so much as with usurious loans to the poor (explicitly so in Exod 22:24 and Lev 25:36). Prov 28:8 does not necessarily condemn all taking of interest, but only the excessive use of the practice, the "amassing" or "increasing" of wealth thereby.

As for the proverb's confidence that the results will somehow turn out to be fair and appropriate, Ehrlich's comment is to the point: "Es lässt sich nicht leugnen, dass dieser Spruch nicht auf Erfahrung, sondern lediglich auf frömmen Glauben beruhrt." ("It cannot be denied that this proverb rests not on experience but simply on pious belief.") More debatable is the continuation: "Es gibt aber nicht viele solcher Sprüch in diesem Buche." ("But there are not many such proverbs in this book.")

interest [*nešek*] *and usury* [*tarbît*]: It is often maintained that *nešek* is a fee deducted from the principle of the loan when issued and that *tarbît* is interest subsequently accrued (see HALOT 1787b and the references there). This distinction, which goes back to the twelfth-century commentator Eliezer of Beaugency, rests on presumed etymology (*nešek* = "bite" and *tarbît* [var. *marbît*] = "addition") but is not evident in actual usage; see Tigay 1996: 217, 387 n. 83.

28:9 He who turns a deaf ear to the teaching,
even his prayer is loathsome.

He who refuses to hear the teaching will fall into evil (an idea reinforced by the next verse). This will make his prayer loathsome (sim. Prov 15:8), and God will ignore it (15:29).

He who turns a deaf ear to: Lit., "he who removes his ear from hearing." It is not mere dullness, and certainly not low intelligence, that keeps one from paying attention to the teaching, but a deliberate refusal to do so.

teaching [*torah*]: *Torah* elsewhere in Proverbs is the father's or teacher's instruction. Why, then, does disobedience to it provoke God? McKane believes that this verse is "clear proof" that *torah* has been reinterpreted to refer to Yahweh's demands, but this is not unambiguous. The content of *torah* is open-ended. It may refer to whatever is taught in the book of Proverbs, or in the present collection, or in instructions of this sort; see the Comment on 28:4. These teachings are not exclusively of a practical nature; many are ethical and religious in character. (To be sure, McKane would assign such teachings to a later stratum, but that is circular.)

The present proverb warns us that if we reject instruction of the sort we are reading in this book, we will stray into evil paths and anger God.

28:10 As for him who misleads the upright into a bad path—
he will fall into his own pit,
but the righteous will inherit goodness.

If one leads another into a bad path, the intended victim is in danger of falling into disaster. But the deceiver will himself fall into the pit he dug. This verse mixes two standard topoi: the bad path and the pit (see the Comment on 26:27). The pit (called variously *šᵉḥut* [as here], *šuḥah, šiḥah,* or *šaḥat*) is a pitfall, dug as a trap, as is clear in Ezek 19:4, 8; Pss 7:16; and 9:16. (The words for "pit" may also play on words from *š-ḥ-t* "corrupt," "destroy.") We are to picture a sneaky man laying a trap in a path and leading another onto it, but, as they walk along, the deceiver himself falls in. Prov 22:5 also joins the two topoi: "Thorns and snares are in the path of the crooked man. He who guards his life will keep far from them."

How can the upright be misled into a bad path, when elsewhere it is the callow or naïve who are susceptible to misdirection? Naḥmias says that this can happen because "There are righteous people who are not wise." This is not quite accurate, because the sages of Proverbs would not agree that the righteous can be other than wise. We can imagine a scenario in which a righteous man is enticed to participate in a dishonest project whose corruption he does not realize. Still, righteousness and the attendant wisdom *should* alert one to the dishonesty. Most likely the "path" in this verse is "bad" in the sense of being rough, broken, and dangerous rather than wicked. The "pit" topos basically describes an attempt to harm another person, though it may secondarily be applied to an attempt to induce him to do evil. The sages would concede that wisdom cannot protect the righteous at every step (e.g., Prov 24:16).

The third line in this verse looks like a clumsy addition, or perhaps it was part of a couplet that lost a line. Instead of v 10c, the LXX reads: "The lawless will pass through good things but not enter into them." But it is hard to relate this to MT 10c; see the Textual Notes.

28:11 A rich man is wise in his own eyes,
but a perceptive pauper can see through him.

The rich tend to believe that their success came from their own cleverness (Deut 8:17) and are much taken with themselves, a self-image reinforced by the flattery they are accustomed to receiving. But a perceptive man, even a poor one, can penetrate the pretense of wisdom; sim. Prov 18:17. "Wise in his own eyes" means that he is not truly wise; see the Comment on 26:12 and compare 26:5b, 16a. In a unit directed at the Jerusalem elite, Isaiah condemns "those who are wise in their own eyes and astute in their own sight" (Isa 5:21). The author of Prov 28:11 shares Isaiah's contempt for rich, smug men, even though he himself likely belonged to the circles of officialdom that Isaiah excoriates.

Perceptiveness or understanding (*binah*) may not guarantee prosperity (contrary to some proverbs), but it is not tied to social class, and the poor can at least have *that* power. The sages did not assume that poverty was always the consequence of folly or vice. One implication of this proverb, according to Hame'iri, is that the wisdom of the poor man should not be held in contempt, an offense of which Qohelet complains: "The wisdom of the poor man is despised, and his words are not heard" (Qoh 9:16).

see through him [*yaḥqᵉrennû*]: Thus JPSV, Murphy, and others. The verb *ḥāqar* usually means "investigate," "examine," but a poor man would not have the opportunity to investigate or interrogate a rich one. *Ḥāqar* here must refer to the result: penetration into concealed layers of truth.

28:12 When the righteous exult, great is the splendor,
but when the wicked arise, men are sought.

Four closely related proverbs, 28:12; 28:28; 29:2; and 29:16, describe the contrary effects of the domination by the righteous and wicked on the public welfare and happiness. It might be useful to quote them together, with a slight adjustment in 28:12a to reflect repeated Hebrew words:

(28:12) When the righteous exult, splendor is increased,
but when the wicked arise, men are sought.
(28) When the wicked arise, men hide,
and when they perish, the righteous increase.
(2) When the righteous increase, the people rejoice,
but when the wicked man rules, the people groan.
(16) When the wicked increase, transgression increases,
but the righteous will see their downfall.

These verses use four paired concepts in various arrangements: (1) righteous / wicked; (2) happiness / unhappiness; (3) increasing / being scarce; (4) rising to power / downfall. The cluster illustrates how proverbs can be produced by permutation of the components of older ones. They work so well as a unit that it is surprising that the editor did not put them in a cluster.

Prov 28:12 declares that the happiness of the righteous radiates joy to others (11:10a; 29:2a), presumably because the righteous are widely loved. When the wicked arise (i.e., become dominant), decent people hide themselves, attempting to avoid danger, oppression, and corruption.

men [*'adam*]: Lit., "man" (sg.) or "person." (*'adam* refers to both sexes, though it is usually evident that Proverbs has males in view.) Since most people are still visible when the wicked arise, *'adam* must be elliptical for "worthy man" or "intelligent man," as in Qoh 7:28a. (Qohelet says he found "one *'adam*" among a thousand, meaning that he found one *worthy* man among a thousand—but no such woman.)

are sought [*yᵉḥuppaś*]: "Sought" in vain. They have gone into hiding or are at least keeping their heads down. "Are sought" is equivalent to *yissater* "hide (themselves)" in Prov 28:28. In Ezek 7:26, "seek" implies not finding and is paralleled by "be lost." "Disaster on disaster will come, and rumor follow upon rumor. And they will seek vision from the prophet, and instruction will be lost [or "will have disappeared"] from the priest, and counsel from the elders."

y^e^*ḥuppaś*: Some explain "searched out" to mean searched out for purposes of plunder, as in Ob 6 (Ramaq, Naḥmias). G. R. Driver (1951: 192–93), followed by Emerton (1969: 214), assigns the word the meaning "are brought low," on the basis of a dubious Arabic cognate. Also possible is that the Dp has the same meaning as the Dt, "disguise oneself" (1 Sam 28:8; 1 Kgs 20:38; etc.; thus Malbim). To the same effect, Gemser emends to *yitḥappēś*, which assumes only a *ḥ-t* near-haplography.

28:13 He who covers up his offenses will not prosper,
while he who confesses and leaves off them will receive mercy.

This is the only clear reference to repentance and mercy in Proverbs; indeed, it is almost unique in the entirety of didactic Wisdom. The sages of Proverbs divided the world into the righteous and the wicked, and there is little thought of the first backsliding or the second repenting. Still, there must be a third group, never explicitly mentioned, outside the dichotomy, namely, most of us, to whom the book of Proverbs speaks. The behavior of the righteous is lauded to serve as a model to those who are not fully righteous, and the evil of the wicked is excoriated as a warning to people who are not fully mired in wickedness. The possibility of repentance and mercy is essential lest people think that once they have done wrong there is no more point in trying to do right.

covers up his offenses: Tries to conceal them rather than confessing them. The proverb is ambiguous as to whether the offense is against God or man and to whom the repentance must be made. "Covering up" in Proverbs elsewhere refers to hiding one's feelings and offenses toward other people; see 10:18; 11:13; 17:9; 26:26 and the Comment on 10:6. But in this verse, honesty and contrition toward both God and man are essential. Like Job (31:33), the speaker in Ps 32:5 declares that he has not covered up his transgression, but has confessed it to God.

28:14 Happy is the man who fears continually,
while he who hardens his heart will fall into evil.

fears continually: The righteous man is elsewhere supposed to be confident and unafraid (1:33; 3:23–26; 28:1), and some kinds of fears are dangerous (29:25). What is the praiseworthy kind of fear? It may be fear of punishment (Hame'iri, Naḥmias), or of sin itself (Delitzsch), or of God (Ramaq, though that is expressed by *yr'* elsewhere in Proverbs, not by *pḥd*, as here). Most likely the implied object is *ra'ah* ("misfortune" or "evil"), to be supplied from the B-line. Compare Prov 14:16a, "The wise man fears and turns away from trouble [*ra'*]," where the object of "fears" appears only in the following clause.

will fall into evil: As the antithesis of *'ašrey* "happy," "evil" here is the misfortune of punishment, not the wickedness itself.

28:15 A growling lion and a ravenous bear:
a wicked ruler over a wretched people—
16a a prince devoid of good sense and abounding in oppression.

If the king's growl is menacing even when he is not wicked (19:12; 20:2), how much the more frightful are wicked, foolish, and oppressive rulers. They are like murderous beasts. Since the ruler in this verse is over a "people," he is presumably a king. On *mošel* "ruler," "official," see the Comment on 23:1.

The MT's verse division joins v 16a and v 16b even though they are not directly related and form an awkward couplet. Verse 16a is constructed like v 15b and likewise describes a wicked ruler. Verse 16a should be joined to v 15 to form a triplet. This is different from the usual pattern of aphorism common in Part V—a couplet with a metaphor in the first line explicated in the second—but in any case v 15 differs in having *two* images in the first line. As the verses are arranged here, a roaring lion is identified as "a wicked ruler," and "a ravenous bear" is the metaphor for "a prince devoid of good sense and abounding in oppression."

Commentators try various devices to relate the two lines of v 16. Murphy translates, "A prince lacking in revenues, increases oppressions." This requires emending *tbwnwt* to *tbw'wt* (*tᵉbû'ôt*) (cf. LXX) and *wrb* to *yrb* (*yerebû*) (though the short yiqtol is unlikely here). McKane emends *wrb* to *whrbh* (*wᵉhirbāh*) and translates, "an undiscriminating ruler piles oppression on oppression." Both translations leave the two lines of v 16 still disconnected. Clifford (following Toy) removes *nāgîd* as a mistaken gloss by someone who assumed that the topic of princes is continuing in v 16a; hence, "Who abounds in extortions is lacking in sense." Delitzsch construes v 16a as a vocative: "O prince devoid of understanding and rich in oppression!" But this address would have no function, since the foolish prince is not told to do anything.

ravenous: This rendering of *šôqēq* is based on its likely sense in Isa 29:8 and Ps 107:9. It may also mean "growling." There is a metonymic relation between emotions and the sounds that express them. Hence *š-q-q* can mean both "be hungry, desirous" and "growl" (Greenberg 1996: 340, 344). Less plausible translations are "charging" (Clifford), "about to attack" (HALOT 1647a; cf. Joel 2:9), and "ranging," "roaming about" (Toy; cf. Nah 2:5).

28:16b He who hates ill-gotten gain will live long.

This principle is stated in 1:19: "This is what happens to everyone who grasps ill-gotten gain: It robs him who holds it of life"; see the Comment there.

Riyqam correctly identifies this line as a "short verse" (*miqra' qaṣar*). In other words, it is a monostich, of which Proverbs has only a few; see the Comment on 27:5. Though distinct from the preceding tristich, 28:16b as placed does comment broadly on the oppressive ruler's love of unjust gain.

28:17 A man who oppresses[a] by bloodshed
will flee to a pit.
Let no one hold him!

[a] *'ōšēq* (MT *'āšuq*).

This verse continues the theme of oppression from v 16a. A man who oppresses others murderously ("by bloodshed") will sometime later need to flee and hide, even in a hole if necessary. The pit may at the same time allude to the grave and the underworld (1:12), for that is where the oppressor will ultimately "hide," though he does not realize it yet. He deserves no help (28:17c).

The MT of v 17a reads, "A man who is oppressed [*ʿašuq*] by spilt blood." This seems to mean that he suffers from "the anguish of a guilty conscience" (Delitzsch). But a repentant man would not need threats of additional afflictions. Also, the verb *ʿšq* does not denote self-afflicted distress, emotional or spiritual. Hence we should vocalize *ʿšq* as an active, not a passive participle.

by bloodshed [*bᵉdam napeš*]: Examples of "blood" meaning "bloodshed" are Lev 17:4 (first occurrence); Ezek 5:17; and 14:19.

pit [*bor*]: Holes are hiding places in 1 Sam 14:11 (there called *ḥorim*).

hold [*tmk*] *him*: *Tamak* basically means "grasp" (Prov 3:18; 4:4; 5:5; 5:22). Some understand 28:17c to mean that nobody should assist or "support" this person (Murphy; NRSV). But while *tmk* elsewhere can mean to aid and support (Isa 41:10; Ps 41:13), it does not mean to assist someone in a particular task. Most likely the sentence means that nobody should lay hold of him to prevent his flight to death (Delitzsch, Plöger).

Let no one hold him! [*ʾal yitmᵉkû bô*]: Lit., "Let them not hold him!" The subject of the plural verb is indefinite.

LXX adds two maxims: "Educate (your) son and he will love you and adorn your soul" and "You should not obey a lawless nation."

28:18 He who goes in innocence will be kept safe,
while the man of crooked ways will fall in a pit.[a]

[a] *bᵉšaḥat* (MT *bᵉʾeḥāt*).

As emended, this is a second proverb about the pit awaiting the evildoer. One who goes in crooked, broken paths is likely to step into a pit, actually and metaphorically. The pit (*šaḥat*) is a pitfall; see the Comment on 28:10. V 18 ≈ 10:9.

ways: The MT has the dual, as in 28:6; see the Comment there.

in a pit [*bᵉšaḥat*]: The MT has *bᵉʾeḥat*, lit., "in one." Most of those who maintain this understand it to mean "at once," "immediately" (Delitzsch, etc.), though there is no justification for this. Others understand it to refer to one of the "two ways" indicated by MT's dual (Riyqam, Malbim), though one does not fall into a "way" as if it were a pitfall. We should read *bᵉšaḥat* "in a pit," with the Syriac; see the Textual Note. The "pit" represents the evildoer's punishment, as in 26:27; 28:10; Pss 7:16; 9:16; cf. 57:7.

28:19 He who works his land will be sated with bread,
while he who pursues trifles will be sated with poverty.

The proverb praises industry in work, of which farming is mentioned as the prime example. See the Comment on 12:11, of which this verse is a variant. Neither verse exalts farming above other occupations. Prov 28:19a = 12:11a; 28:19b ≈ 12:11b.

The repetition of "will be sated" is sarcastic. Both types of person will be *sated* with what they seek, but with quite different results. "Trifles" is literally "empty things" (*reqim*). *That* is what will fill the prodigal's belly.

28:20 The faithful man has many blessings,
but he who hastens to get rich will not go unpunished.

If, as the preceding verse says, laziness and frivolity are foolish and self-destructive, so is the opposite extreme, the compulsive pursuit of wealth. It is not only self-destructive, it is a sin, as is implied by the warning that he who does this "will not go unpunished." This is the sin of hubris; see the Comment on 10:22. Its antithesis is faithfulness (28:20a), that is, trusting in God to reward one's efforts in due time and measure (28:25). Verses 19 and 20 seem to speak of very different virtues and flaws. The frivolous man and the compulsive striver seem to be polar opposites. Yet the conjunction of these verses suggests a certain affinity between the two types. They both pursue something to excess, and in the end "getting rich" and "trifles" prove to be not so different after all.

Verse 20b is rephrased in Sir 11:10aβ, "He who hastens to gain increase will not go unpunished."

go unpunished [*yinnaqeh*]: Lit., "be cleansed" or "held innocent"; see the Comments on 6:29 and 16:5. "Not go unpunished" is the opposite of "has many blessings." God is implicitly the punisher, blesser, and object of fidelity.

28:21 Showing partiality is not good,
but a man may transgress for a piece of bread.

Though partiality in judgment is not right (24:23a), a judge should remember that a man may commit a crime just to keep alive (6:30–31) and show him some mercy.

not good: That is, bad; see the Comment on 16:29.

but a man may transgress: If the second line is translated, "*and* a man may transgress," it relates poorly to the first. If it is translated "*but* a man, etc.," it is conceding the reality recognized in Prov 6:30: "People don't despise a thief if he steals to fill his belly when starving."

for a piece of bread: Almost all commentators understand the piece of bread to be a bribe given the judges to buy their favor. But if it is a bribe, it is a trivial one indeed. Hame'iri understands the point to be that a judge must be on guard because he might be influenced by even a small bribe. The low price of corruption has been explained as expressing contempt for the greed that perverts the integrity of the court (Clifford), or as deliberate exaggeration to show how paltry and despicable a bribe can be (Murphy). According to McKane, the small quantity shows that the proverb alludes to the suborning of a witness rather than the judge. (Witnesses presumably cost less.) Still, this would be a paltry bribe, too small to win favor. More to the point is Ehrlich's observation that theft of bread is an example of the kind of issue that judges must deal with, and must do so fairly. I understand the transgressor to be the defendant, and the proverb to be a reminder to the judge to temper justice with mercy, perhaps taking Prov 28:13 to heart.

A judge should recognize mitigating circumstances, such as the desperation that can impel one to minor crimes. This idea tempers the principle of Exod 23:3, "You shall not favor a poor man in his disputation." Similarly Lev 19:15: "You shall not commit iniquity in judgment. You shall not favor a lowly man or exalt a great man. You shall judge your fellow in righteousness." The present proverb, however, is not advising the judge to favor the poor man over someone else, but only to temper his judgment against someone forced into theft. This is quite different from favoring the guilty over the innocent (Prov 18:5; 24:23b).

28:22 The greedy man rushes after wealth,
unaware that penury will come upon him.

This proverb restates the warning of v 20. Wealth hastily amassed will, for unspecified reasons, quickly dwindle (20:21). The avaricious man may use illegitimate means in his pursuits. Or he may arouse jealousy and anger, which will come back to harm him. Or he may build his fortune on fragile schemes and speculations rather than accruing it step-by-step by patient industry. He pursues something he desires, but suddenly his quarry turns on him—and it is a dangerous beast.

greedy [*ra*ʿ *ʿayin*]: Lit., "bad of eye"; see 23:6, where it is translated "stingy." Stinginess is a particular manifestation of greed.

28:23 He who reproves another[a]
will find more favor than a flatterer.

[a] *ʾaḥēr* (MT *ʾaḥăray*).

Frank criticism will ultimately win favor. Prov 15:12 indicates that the wise will love their rebukers, and 27:6 praises honest, harsh words over phony displays of love.

The MT of 28:23a reads, "He who reproves a man after me [*ʾaḥăray*]," which makes no sense. Minimally, a small emendation, of *ʾḥry* to *ʾḥr*, is called for. But by either form the word is superfluous and should perhaps be deleted.

ʾaḥăray ("after me"): Ramaq proposes that Solomon means "after my death," but this does not clarify matters. Riyqam explains *ʾaḥăray* as an (otherwise unknown) adjective, comparing RH formations such as *ʾšmʾy* "guilty" and *zkʾy* "innocent." He also compares *ʾāḥôr* in Isa 42:17. There it is actually an adverb, but the phrase *nāsōgû ʾāḥôr* "retreat backwards" does imply recalcitrance. Delitzsch compares *lᵉʾāḥôr* "backwards" in Jer 7:24. Ehrlich (sim. Malbim) also understands *ʾaḥăray* as an archaic adverbial, hence (in JPSV's translation) "He who reproves a man will in the end find more favor, etc." (sim. Vul). But no such word is known. We should read *ʾḥr* "another," as Syr probably does.

28:24 He who robs his father and mother
and says, "No wrong was done"—
he is companion to a vandal.

He who cheats his parents and denies (to himself and others) that he did anything wrong is no better than someone who causes them physical harm or damage to their property. Such a cheater might rationalize his deed on the pretext that he will eventually inherit their wealth (Hame'iri), or he might convince himself that it is "really" his own (Ramaq). Elderly parents would be vulnerable to domination and exploitation. Prov 19:26 too condemns the son who "robs his father and drives away his mother."

No wrong was done [*'eyn paša'*]: Lit., "there is no transgression." The adulteress's words in Prov 30:20 are similar.

companion: They are two of a kind; compare the construction in Prov 18:9b.

vandal [*'iš mašḥit*]: This can refer to one who harms persons or property.

28:25 The greedy man provokes conflict,
but he who trusts in the Lord will prosper.

Each line fills a gap in the other: The greedy man, because he provokes conflict, *will not prosper*, and the trusting man *does not provoke conflict* and will therefore prosper. See "Disjointed Proverbs" in the Introduction to Vol. II (II.E).

greedy [*r^{e}ḥab nepeš*]: Lit., "wide of appetite" or "voracious maw" (Clifford), that is, insatiable (cf. Isa 5:14; Hab 2:5). Greed is a repudiation of trust in God, for he who trusts in God accepts what God gives and does not crave more. Prov 28:25a ≈ 29:22a.

will prosper [*y^{e}duššan*]: Lit., "will be made fat"; cf. 11:25; 13:4. The fatness refers to being "moistened" with rich food (11:25; 13:4) or to having "fat" or "moist" bones (15:30; Sir 26:13). In Prov 11:25 and 15:30, the metaphor of fatness signifies prosperity and happiness.

28:26 He who trusts in his own heart—he is a dolt;
while he who goes in wisdom—he will escape.

The theme of *trust* continues. There are two opposing types of trust; the first (v 25b) is well-founded, the second (v 26a) deceptive. Trusting one's own heart means not trusting in God. (Hence "Trust in the Lord with all your heart" [3:5a] is the equivalent of "and rely not on your own understanding" [3:5b].) The verse is a disjointed proverb in which semantic balance is to be restored by supplying gapped items from each line: He who trusts in his own mind is a dolt and *will not escape*, whereas he who goes in wisdom *is wise* and will escape (Sa'adia); see the Introduction to Vol. II (II.E).

He who . . . : Both lines foreground the subject and resume it by a pronoun, placing emphasis on the subject as distinct from others: It is he who is a dolt . . . it is he who will escape.

his own heart [*leb*]: That is, his mind. Unlike the English usage, to trust in one's heart does not mean "to follow the untrained suggestions of the mind (passion, selfishness, dishonesty)" (as Toy says), but rather "to rely wholly on one's own mental resources" (as Toy also says). Though "heart" by itself can signify wisdom and good sense, as in Prov 19:8 and 15:32, one's own heart is not the same as wisdom; here it is its *opposite*. A person's intelligence and knowledge are trustworthy only if these conform to the principles and attitudes of wisdom, such as taught in Proverbs. He must assess his thoughts by the standards inculcated in the wisdom of his teachers and the writings. "He who is astute in a matter" (16:20a) is, in Proverbs' view, the same as "he who trusts in the Lord" (16:20b). The relationship between one's own intelligence and trust in God is discussed in the Comment on 3:5.

escape: From whatever disaster comes along. Wisdom promises such protection in Prov 1:33. For the mechanism of wisdom's deliverance, see Vol. I, 103, 105. The fool, it is implied, will not escape; see Prov 1:24–32.

As Toy observes, vv 26a + 25b form a natural couplet, but he is wrong in concluding that vv 26b and 25a "have lost their correspondents," the lines with which they were originally paired. It is very unlikely that an accident produced two new, well-formed couplets such as vv 25 and 26. It is more probable that vv 25b + 26a constituted a couplet that was deliberately split and provided with parallel lines to form two new proverbs.

28:27 He who gives to the poor will not go needy,
while he who turns his eyes aside will be much cursed.

Verse 25 raised two themes: greed (v 25a) and trust (v 25b). Verse 26 elaborated on the second, and v 27b returns to the first. Generosity pays off; stinginess is punished by curses, whether from God (cf. 3:33) or the needy. Ben Sira rephrases this verse and interprets it in the latter fashion when he admonishes: "Do not scorn the requests of the lowly, and do not turn aside from the oppressed of soul, and do not give him a reason to curse you. For an embittered man cries out in the pain of his soul, and his Rock will hear his cry" (4:4–6). Charity is urged in Prov 11:25 (and, by one interpretation, 11:24); 14:21; 19:17; and 22:9.

He who gives . . . : Lit., "He who gives to the poor—there is no lack. And he who hides his eyes—great of curses." This has the "stroboscopic" feel described by J. G. Williams; see the Comment on 13:1.

28:28 When the wicked arise, men hide,
and when they perish, the righteous increase.

The principle of this proverb can be directed to different audiences. It may be "encouragement to the king to appoint the most righteous men as assistants and executors and judges in all his affairs, for through them the state will be established, and (encouragement) not (to appoint) the wicked, because men will hide in fear of them" (Saʿadia). It may also be advice to all, that they *should* hide themselves when the wicked become leaders and counselors (Hameʾiri). Prov 28:28a ≈ 28:12b; 28:28b ≈ 29:2a; cf. 29:16.

arise: Succeed or come to power.

men [*ʾadam*]: Lit., "man," "person." That is to say, "worthy man," as in 28:12. The parallel with "the righteous" supports this (Ramaq). Hameʾiri identifies these men as the righteous, who must hide because, in evil times, righteous and honest deeds must be performed in secret.

they perish: That is, the wicked.

hide // increase: These concepts define each other by contrast. "Hide" means that men make themselves scarce (as in the American idiom) or keep a low profile, so as to escape the attention of the thugs in power. "Increase" means not that the righteous are more numerous than previously (by the subtraction of the numbers of wicked who have perished), but that they are *seen* more; they have a greater public presence. This can only enhance the common welfare, bringing about an era when "great is the splendor" (28:12a).

increase: The verb *rbh* usually means "increase" (in numbers), but occasionally signifies being (or becoming) great in status or power, as in Job 33:12; 1 Kgs 5:10; and Gen 7:17–18. In line with the second sense, Saʿadia and Hameʾiri understand the verb to imply an enhancement of honor. The NRSV translates, "are in authority" (at Prov 29:2). In the three variant proverbs, 28:28; 29:2; and 29:16, both connotations are relevant but one or the other may be more in forcus. In 28:28, the connotation of "increase" is elicited by the parallelism with "hide"; in 29:2, "become great" provides a sharper parallel to "rules"; and in 29:16, either nuance could stand opposite *mappaltam* "their downfall." I translate "increase" everywhere to maintain the cohesiveness of the topos "increase/decrease of the righteous/wicked," described in the Comment on 28:12.

29:1 A man often rebuked, who stiffens his neck,
will suddenly be broken, beyond remedy.

A man who rebuffs criticism may persist in his stubbornness for some time, but punishment will befall him when he least expects it. Suddenness is usually associated with disasters and intensifies their severity; see the Comment on 6:15. The present verse can also be translated as two sentences: "A man often rebuked stiffens his neck. He will be suddenly be broken, beyond remedy."

A *man often rebuked* [*ʾiš tokaḥot*]: Lit., "a man of rebukes." The expected meaning of this phrase is "a man who (habitually) gives rebukes." The problem is that elsewhere in Proverbs, rebukes are enthusiastically recommended as a means of correction, and they would hardly bring punishment on the rebuker. For this reason, all commentators understand *ʾiš tokaḥot* to be a man who is the *object* of rebuke or who deserves to be rebuked. Ramaq says such a man is "one who needs rebukes, and who is continually rebuked."

ʾîš tôḥākôt: The construction "man of X" is usually equivalent to "*baʿal* ("possessor") of X," in which X is an attribute of the man's character or behavior (Prov 22:24; 29:22; and often elsewhere; IBHS §9.5.3b).

Here, however, "man" is the object of the verb implicit in *tôḥākôt*. (IGBH §;9.5.1e calls this construction "an abstract subjective genitive," but does not cite the present verse.) Another example of this construction is *ʾîš ḥermî*, "the man of my ban" (1 Kgs 20:42), which is equivalent to "the man whom I am banning." Another relevant phrase is *ʾîš rîb wᵉʾîš mādôn lᵉkol hāʾāreṣ*, "a man who is the target of quarreling and strife to all the land" (Jer 15:10). Jeremiah sees himself as the victim of strife, not its agent.

29:2 When the righteous increase, the people rejoice,
but when the wicked man rules, the people groan.

The public morale rises and falls with the fortunes of the righteous and wicked. This closely resembles 28:12, 28 and 29:16 in thought and language.

increase [*birbot*]: Increase in public presence and power; see the Comment on 28:28.

Toy emends to *birdōt* "when (the righteous) rule," here and in 29:16. But "increase" itself connotes power and provides a parallel to "rules." Also, *yirbeh* "increases" is used in 29:16, in speaking of the opposite circumstance.

29:3 A man who loves wisdom makes his father rejoice,
but he who consorts with harlots loses money.

He who chases after whores wastes money, squandering it on base pleasures. It might actually be his father's wealth that he is wasting, for the "man" might be a young one, still dependent on his father (Ralbag, Malbim). Alternatively, the lost wealth may be the son's own money. He loses it by squandering it, but also (as suggested by the antithesis) by provoking his father into withholding his inheritance, at least the alienable part.

Lemuel's mother warns her son not to waste his "strength" (= vigor *and* wealth) on women (by which she presumably does not mean his own wife) (Prov 31:3). Ben Sira (9:1–9) warns against sexual dalliance for similar reasons. A later expansion in Ben Sira warns, "Do not consort [*tstyyd*] with a harlot, lest you be caught in her punishment" (9:3b, MS A). Prostitution and resorting to prostitutes were scorned but not prohibited, and condemnation of the practice is rather muted; see Vol. I, 138 and AYBD 5.505–506. Prov 29:3a ≈ 10:1b and 15:20a.

The antithesis between "makes his father rejoice" and "loses money" is asymmetrical and the couplet is disjointed (see the Introduction to Vol. II [II.E]). The lines are to be cemented together by mentally supplying "and makes his father grieve" at the end of the B-line. Further, "consorts with harlots" gives definition to what kind of wisdom is relevant here, namely sexual morality.

29:4 By justice a king gives stability to the land,
while a deceitful[a] man destroys it.

[a] *tarmît* (MT *tᵉrûmôt*).

A just ruler makes a country safe and secure, while a deceitful one undermines it.

gives stability [*yaʿămid*]: Thus RSV; lit., "makes stand," that is, makes the realm stable and long-lasting. (Compare the use of *ʿmd* in Exod 9:16; 1 Kgs 15:4; Qoh 1:4; Isa 66:22; and Ps 19:10.) Malbim compares *ʾAbot* 1:17, "The world stands [*ʿomed*] on three things," one of which is justice (*din*).

deceitful man [*ʾiš tarmit*]: The MT has *ʾiš tᵉrumot*. Almost all commentators (e.g., Saʿadia, Riyqam, Delitzsch) understand MT's *tᵉrumot* as taxes. Ramaq explains the second line as directed against *excessive* taxation (without defining *tᵉrumot* more precisely). Clifford says they are "confiscatory taxes," but nothing in the verse suggests this. *Tᵉrumot*, however, is not used of royal taxation, but only sacral donations to the Temple. These are divinely commanded and could not be the antithesis of "justice," except in the mouth of a modern anticlericalist. Van Leeuwen says that whether *tᵉrumot* are bribes (NIV) or excessive taxes (NRSV), the verse speaks of "the government's misuse of income (perhaps intended for the sanctuary?) in a way that compromises its responsibility to do justice." If *tᵉrumot* did mean secular taxation, no editor in the royal service, such as the redactors of Part V (25:1), would condemn it as destructive of the state. *Trwmwt* is either a variant form of *trmyt* "deceit" (derived from *r-w-m* rather than *r-m-h*) or, more likely, a scribal corruption of *trmyt*.

In parallel with "king," the deceitful man is a deceitful ruler. It is such a one (rather than an ordinary citizen) who could undermine the realm by his corruption.

29:5 A man who flatters his fellow
spreads a net for his feet.

Flattery is a pretense of friendship intended to lower someone's guard and bend him to the flatterer's will. The Comment on 2:16 discusses flattery. Flattery is a snare (2:16; 7:5; 26:28; 28:23). It is, by definition, dishonest. For honest praise, *hll* or *šbḥ* would be used, rather than *maḥăliq*, which literally means "make (one's words) slippery."

net: The image is not of a pitfall but of a net spread on the ground and covered with leaves or a thin layer of dirt. In this context, and parallel to *poreś* "spreads," *maḥăliq* ("who flatters") can be heard as a pun meaning both to flatter and to smooth out the net. In Isa 41:7, the same root, *ḥ-l-q*, refers to smoothing out metal with a hammer.

his feet: This refers, first, to the intended victim's feet and, secondarily, to the flatterer's as well (Saʿadia; Naḥmias). He spreads a net for another but will step into it himself. The proverb warns both parties about the dangers of flattery.

29:6 In the transgression of an evil man there is a snare,
and the righteous will rejoice and be glad.

Concealed within the evil man's transgression lies a snare. He intends it for another, but it traps himself instead. On this kind of punishment, see Prov 1:19;

26:27; and I, 91–92. This verse is linked to the preceding by the motif of *trap*, though different kinds of traps are meant. Prov 29:6 ≈ 12:13.

and the righteous will rejoice and be glad: The righteous man, the intended victim, will escape the snare (12:13b) and rejoice. Ramaq suggests that the righteous will be glad to see the evil man ensnared (thus 11:10). The sequence of events favors Ramaq's explanation, though the gloating would be contrary to 24:17.

29:7 The righteous man knows the rights of the lowly;
the wicked man does not have knowledge.

Righteousness demands that one actively seek to know the rights of the poor. This proverb gives insight into the ethics of Proverbs, in which knowledge is a prerequisite of morality. Doing the right thing requires knowing the right thing, but being able to know this requires the right moral disposition to start with. But the wicked man bears the responsibility for his wickedness, just as the righteous man gains credit for his righteousness. The wicked man's ignorance is willful because he wills what is evil.

the rights of the lowly [*din dallim*]: Hebrew *din* refers to forensic judgment as well as to the legal rights or justice due someone, as in Prov 31:5, "the rights of all the poor"; sim. Jer 22:16; Ps 140:13. It is a near-synonym of the more common *mišpaṭ*, "justice," "rights." (In Prov 22:10 *din* means, irregularly, quarreling in personal relations.)

does not have knowledge [*lo' yabin da'at*]: Lit., "does not understand knowledge"; see the Comment on 2:5. Prov 29:7b is equivalent to 28:5a, "Evil men do not understand what is just." In the present proverb, the knowledge of which the wicked man is ignorant has two meanings. First of all, it is wisdom generally. Second, when read in conjunction with the A-line, it is knowledge specifically of the rights of the poor, or "knowledge of rights and justice [*din umišpaṭ*]" (Radaq). (Compare how "understand everything" in 28:5b is further defined by its parallel term.)

29:8 Impudent men inflame a city,
while the wise assuage anger.

Arrogant, cynical men stir up strife that is here political in nature, as indicated by the mention of the "city." It is wise to soothe public passions rather than exacerbating them.

Impudent men [*'anšey laṣon*]: Isaiah applies this phrase to the "rulers of this people who are in Jerusalem" (28:14), who imagine that their political schemes have given them immunity from the oncoming disaster.

inflame [*yapiḥu*]: See the Comment on 6:19. Conflict is compared to fire in Prov 26:21.

assuage anger: Lit., "turn aside anger." The medieval commentators ask *whose* anger this is. Sa'adia says it is God's, comparing the way Phineas deflected God's wrath from Israel (Num 25:11). Riyqam thinks it is the ire of the king whose realm is disturbed. Probably the source of the wrath is more diffuse, for the factionalism will spark anger on all sides.

29:9 A wise man disputes with a foolish one,
and he is angry and laughs and there is no calm.

Continuing the theme of public disputes, this verse warns that if a wise man gets into an argument with a fool (*ʾĕwil*), presumably to chastise him, the results will be disappointing. The fool will be truculent and derisive, and peace will not ensue. The saying thus warns against arguing with fools, similarly to Prov 26:4. Though the sages often commend the use of reproof, they see little hope that it will work on fools (e.g., 1:23–30; 23:9), especially when these are *ʾĕwilim* (1:7b; 15:5a; 27:22) or *leṣim* (9:7–8; 13:1b; 15:12).

disputes [*nišpaṭ*]: This does not refer to a legal dispute (contrary to Toy and McKane), because then the opponent's anger and attitudes would not be an issue. The verb *nišpaṭ* refers to a private debate, as in 1 Sam 12:7; Jer 2:35; Ezek 17:20; and 20:35–36 (Clifford).

and he is angry: That is, the fool. The behavior in the B-line can only be the fool's, for a wise man would not act that way.

29:10 Men of blood hate the innocent man,
while the upright seek his life.

Murderous men do not just rob and kill the innocent man, they *hate* him, "because he is the opposite of their nature" (Naḥmias). Similar observations are made in Prov 26:28 and 29:27b.

seek his life [*yᵉbaqšu napšo*]: This phrase is very problematic, because elsewhere (29x) it means to seek someone so as to *kill* him (e.g., Exod 4:19; 1 Sam 20:1; Jer 19:7), which is impossible here. Here it must be understood (uniquely) as seeking a life so as to *preserve* it (Saʿadia). It is a "term of affection" (Rashi) and probably a deliberately paradoxical use of the phrase.

Other proposals include the following: (1) The upright will "seek (the innocent man's) life" in the sense of "seeking his blood from (the murder's) hand," that is, they will avenge his death (Ramaq [first interpretation] and Hame'iri [second interpretation]). But that sense would require *bqš dāmô* "seek his blood" (2 Sam 4:11; Ezek 3:18, 20; 33:8). (2) "Men of blood [pl.] hate the innocent man *and* the upright [pl.], and they seek his [sg.] life—so as to destroy it." The awkward shift from pl. to sg. is explained as "particularizing" or "individualizing" (Delitzsch, cf. Riyqam, Malbim). But this is strained and violates the line division. Also, there is no conjunction before "seek." (3) Emend *wyšrym* "and the upright" to *wršʿym* "and the wicked" (BHS). But this is ad hoc and distant from the MT.

29:11 A dolt lets all his emotions out,
while a wise man quiets them down.

Only a fool loses his temper. The ability to control anger is a great and necessary virtue, emphasized especially in Egyptian Wisdom. Amenemope says: "Better off is the man whose speech remains in his belly than one who speaks it to (his) harm" (22.15–16, from §21 [cf. AEL 2.159]); and see the Comments on 15:1, 20:19; and 22:24 and the quotations theres. Prov 29:11 implies the same admonition as 12:16: "The fool makes his anger known at once, while the shrewd man covers up an insult"; sim. 16:32.

his emotions [*ruḥo*]: Or "spirit." The basic meaning of *ruaḥ* is "breath," "wind." The image is of the angry man expelling his breath in a storm of words. It is possible that "all of his spirit" means whatever comes into his mind (Hame'iri), but the B-line suggests that the "spirit" in question is anger or other agitated emotions.

quiets them. That is, his emotions, as when he starts to feel anger. The verb *šbḥ* means "calm (something)" in Pss 89:10 (D, as here) and 65:8 (H).

down [*bᵉʾaḥor*]: Lit., "back." Holding one's emotions back means keeping them in the heart, as Ramaq says, comparing *nasogu ʾaḥor* "retreat back" in Isa 42:17. Other explanations work less well: "in the past" (cf. Saʿadia); "in the end" (Hame'iri); "afterwards," that is, after the fool finishes his ranting (Rashi).

29:12 An official who heeds a lying word—
all his servants are wicked.

This is a warning to the king to be "careful and concerned, even more than the populace, that he not go astray" (Saʿadia). Corruption quickly seeps down and permeates the power hierarchy. If a ruler's minions learn that falsehood is what gets the boss's ear, that's what they will give him. It is the ruler's duty to rid his staff of crooks. See the "The Royal Ideal" before 16:10–15 and also the Comments on 16:13 and 25:5. Prov 29:12a describes the opposite of 16:13a.

The Hebrew of this proverb hisses with sibilants: *mošel maqšib ʿal dᵉbar šaqer, kol mᵉšarᵉtayw rᵉšaʿim.*

29:13 A poor man and an oppressive man meet:
It is the Lord who gives light to the eyes of both.

Throughout Proverbs, the existence of disparities of wealth is taken as a fact of life, neither deplored or condemned. The point of this saying is to remind people—particularly those who have the power to oppress others—that both the poor and their oppressors are God's creations, and it is he who gave them life. From the divine perspective, they are brothers, and their quarrel is all the more hateful. A moral is not drawn explicitly, but the mention of Yahweh's relation to the poor implies an admonition to the potential oppressor: He must remember that his own life is dependent on the poor man's creator (Plöger). Prov 29:13 ≈ 22:2; see the Comment there.

oppressive man [*ʾîš tᵉkākîm*]: See HALOT 1729a, under *tōk*. *Tōk*, the presumed by-form of *tᵉkākîm*, is collocated with *mirmāh* "deceit" in Pss 10:7; 55:12, and with *ḥāmās* "lawlessness," "violence" in Ps 72:14.

gives light to the eyes of both: Not "the Lord is maker of both," as in Prov 22:2, because that could be understood to mean that God makes or creates certain persons to be oppressive. "Gives light to the eyes" means to give life. If the oppressive are alive, that must be by God's grace. He created a world in which evil people are allowed to live; hence he must have a purpose for them.

The doublet in 22:2 reads, "The rich man and the poor man meet: The Lord is maker of both." Whereas the rich man in 22:2 is not necessarily bad and is only being reminded of his duties to the poor, the oppressor in 29:13 is, by definition, transgressing against the poor and their maker. The earlier proverb describes the unquestioned order of society, not an evil. This one depicts a distortion of the right order. In 22:2, the reference to the "rich man" continues the topic of wealth from v 1. In 29:13, the mention of the "oppressive man" prepares the way for the demand of justice for the poor in v 14. The tight antithesis between rich and poor is sacrificed for the sake of context.

29:14 A king who judges the poor faithfully—
his throne will be established forever.

Prov 29:12 spoke of a corrupted ruler; v 13 mentioned the poor and their oppressor; v 14 combines these themes by promising an enduring dynasty to the king who gives justice to the poor.

judges[*špṭ*] *the poor*: "Judges" here does not mean that the king sits in judgment on the poor, deciding their individual cases. In spite of the stories of royal judgment in 2 Sam 14:4–11; and 1 Kgs 3:16–28 (which have special narrative roles), a king would hardly have time for such cases on a regular basis. Rather, he "judges" them by giving them justice, defending their rights and securing their *mišpaṭ*, their due, what is justly theirs (cf. Deut 10:18). This is the meaning of the numerous demands to "judge" the widow and orphan. This includes delivering them from their oppressors (as, e.g., in Isa 1:17; Ps 82:3–4). Throughout the ancient Near East, protecting the rights of the poor was a royal duty and not a matter of charity; see Weinfeld 1995: 45–56.

his throne will be established forever: His dynasty will endure. "It is as if the righteousness of their father preserves them" (Saʿadia). Prov 29:14b ≈ 16:12b; 20:28b; 25:5b.

29:15 The rod of rebuke gives wisdom,
while a youth let loose disgraces his mother.

This verse and v 17 urge discipline of children. The underlying metaphor is of animals. Some are controlled by the shepherd's rod and protected, others are "let loose" (*š-l-ḥ* Dp) to go astray (cf. Job 39:5a [D] and Isa 16:2a [Dp]) (Clifford). Beatings, often advocated in Proverbs (see the Comment on 13:24), are viewed as means of control rather than punishment. Without control, it is believed, a child will go wild and bring shame on his parents.

Noteworthy is the mention of the mother alone as the source of wisdom (sim. 31:1, 26). Her honor is being singled out for concern, and not only insofar as she is an auxiliary of the father. Riyqam suggests that the mother is in focus because the boy "is at home at all times, and the neighbors will come and shout at him, and the mother will be ashamed of his bad upbringing."

rod of rebuke [*šebeṭ w^e^tokaḥat*]: Lit., "rod and rebuke." The singular verb "gives" probably indicates that this is a hendiadys (Toy). Still, grammatical agreement of number in Proverbs is rather flexible, and it is possible that two means of chastisement, physical and verbal, are intended.

29:16 When the wicked increase, transgression increases,
but the righteous will see their downfall.

This saying is a permutation of 28:28 and 29:2a. When the wicked become a greater public presence, the rights and well-being of others will be violated and people will hide in fear (28:28). But, the sages insist, one day the tables will be turned, and the righteous will be present to see the downfall of the wicked and take satisfaction in their own virtue. See the Comment on 28:28.

29:17 Discipline your son and he will bring you comfort
and give delight to your soul.

Just as an undisciplined son shames his parents (29:15), so does a disciplined one bring them joy. He gives them "comfort" or "relief" (*n-w-ḥ*, v 17a) and a feeling of luxuriant pleasure (*maʿădannim*, v 17b).The words suggest the image of a parent taking a deep breath and letting out a sigh of relief and pleasure at a child who has turned out well. See the Comment on 10:1.

delight [*maʿădannim*] *to your soul* [*nepeš*]: Lit., "delicacies to your soul" or "appetite." The saying can be understood as promising both that the well-raised son will supply his parents' needs in their old age and that he will bring them the joy of pride and contentment.

29:18 When there is no vision, the nation is disorderly,
but he who keeps the teaching, how happy he is!

When prophetic vision is absent, the social order is disrupted, but the teachings of wisdom can provide the necessary guidance and bring welfare. Some scholars consider mention of prophecy to be out of place in Wisdom Literature (Driver, Toy, Ehrlich; see below) or at least a sign of lateness (McKane). But a single affirmation of prophecy in Proverbs is no more unlikely than a single endorsement of the temple cult, as we have in 3:9–10. Proverbs has little to say about prophecy and cult because they are not central to the private sphere, about which the book is educating its readers. Nevertheless, there is no reason to imagine that at any stage the "wise man" repudiated either.

When there is no vision [*b*ᵉ*ʾeyn ḥazon*]: This does not refer to a particular historical period, but to any time or situation in which prophetic oracles are not forthcoming *or are not used*. The construction *b*ᵉ*ʾeyn* X can be temporal ("when X is lacking"), as in Prov 8:24, or causal ("because of the lack of X"), as in 5:23; 11:14; and 15:22. Sometimes the phrase is ambiguous, as in 26:20. A saying very similar in structure to the present one is 11:14: "Without strategy a people will fall [*b*ᵉ*ʾeyn taḥbulot yippol ʿam*], while there is victory in a multitude of counselors." This means that strategy must be employed for victory, not that it has gone out of existence or even that strategy is everywhere unavailable. It is another way of saying that one *should* use strategy. The present verse too affirms the importance of prophecy for national success.

A similar phrase is used in 1 Sam 3:1, "And the word of the Lord was rare in those days; vision was not widespread [*ʾeyn ḥazon nipraṣ*]." This means that divine guidance in current decisions and information about the future was temporarily being withheld. Other texts complain about the absence of prophecy (Ps 74:9; Lam 2:9) or threaten that it will be withheld in a future punishment (Amos 8:12; Ezek 7:26). None of these mean that the historical period of prophecy had concluded; and see F. Greenspahn *1989*: 40. Note that in Ezek 7:26 prophecy stands alongside the priest's *torah* and the elders' counsel, *neither of which*, Ezekiel insists, will be available during the disaster to come; sim. Lam 2:9. The issue is the punitive absence of guidance, not the cessation of the vehicle of prophecy.

Toy feels that "*vision* can hardly be genuine" and suggests emending to *taḥbûlāh* "strategy" (though the sg. does not exist and the emendation shares only one letter with the MT). G. R. Driver (*1947a*: 235) glosses *ḥāzôn* as "magistrate." He adduces Akkadian *ḥaziān* "magistrate" and RH *ḥazzān* "superintendent" and notes LXX's *exēgētēs* "guide." Ehrlich emends to *rāzôn* "governor," as in Prov 14:28 (where, however, he emends to *rôzēn*).

is disorderly [*yipparaʿ*]: People are disturbed and out of control. (The verb is used of the Israelites running wild at the incident of the Golden Calf in Exod 32:25ab.) The verb *prʿ* is also used of brushing aside the demands of *musar*, words of discipline (8:33; 15:32; and see the Comment on 1:25). The present proverb values prophetic vision as a source of public *musar*, but allows that in its absence individual teaching can fill the gap.

teaching [*torah*]: *Torah* elsewhere in Proverbs means instruction, usually parental. The present verse is the one place where *torah* might refer to God's instruction, or even the codified Pentateuch. Still, the pairing of *torah* with "vision" does not prove this to be so. Prophecy ("the word" of the prophet) stands alongside the sage's counsel and the priest's instruction (*torah*) in Jer 18:18. Interestingly, Saʿadia identifies *torah* in Prov 29:18 with various prophetic instructions, and Hameʾiri says that *ḥazon* is another name for the Torah in Jer 18:18 and Ezek 7:26, where *torah* refers to *priestly* decisions and pronouncements in cultic matters. (Ezek 7:26 uses *ḥazon*, as here.) *Torah* here is ambiguous. It can mean wisdom instructions or the entire body of traditional teachings.

The present verse can hardly be an "inner-biblical" reflection on the first two sections of the Bible, namely, the Law and the Prophets (a possibility weighed by Van Leeuwen, ad loc.). If it were, that would imply that the prophetic canon could somehow go out of existence.

The present proverb can be understood variously:

(1) A description of a historical reality: Now that the age of prophecy has passed, the nation is susceptible to indecision and anarchy. The remedy lies in the Law—"response to whose demands is the affair of the individual" (McKane; sim. Malbim).

This interpretation assumes that prophecy *did* cease at the dawn of the Second Temple period, but this is a myth. Greenspahn (1989) has shown that, contrary to later rabbinic and Christian theological assertions, prophecy did not end with the biblical prophets. Nor is there any evidence that Jews of the Second Temple period thought it had, though later some rabbis believed that the Holy Spirit had ceased to communicate in that fashion (ibid., pp. 45–49). It is also untrue that response to the Law was only an affair of the individual in Second Temple times. The Law continued to be a national obligation, its fulfillment as necessary for the Jewish people as for the individual.

(2) A concessive: To be sure, prophecy is important for the public order, but *even when* prophecy is unavailable—or is going unheeded—one's own welfare can be secured by keeping the teachings of wisdom. These are a source of reproof and discipline, just like prophetic revelation. This interpretation accords with the use of the verse's phraseology elsewhere; see above on *bᵉʾeyn ḥazon*. Elsewhere, however, Proverbs does not separate the public from the private sphere, even though it is mostly concerned with the latter.

(3) A declaration of the benefits of two sources of knowledge: prophecy and the teachings of the wise, without necessarily distinguishing the public and private spheres. In fact, the subject of "keeps" in v 18b can be *ʿam* ("people" or "nation"): "the people that keeps the teaching [or law]—how happy it is!" Compare the macarisms said of the people (*ʿam*, as here) in Pss 89:16 and 144:15.

The two themes of control of children and control of the nation are interlaced in Prov 29:14–18 in such a way that they comment on each other.

(29:14) The king's responsibility to the poor
(15) Instruction of children (danger of disorder)
(16) Increase of the wicked
(17) Instruction of children
(18) Instruction of nation (danger of disorder)

The pattern is nation, home, nation, home, nation. All need instruction. For the nation, this is in the form of *ḥazon* and *torah*.

29:19 A slave will not take discipline by words (alone),
for if he understands, there will (still) be no response.

The proverb gives advice for managing a household. Since a slave is deprived of material interests of his own, he must, it was presumed, be beaten into submission, like a brute animal or a fool. Slaves were apparently felt to be of a qualitatively lower order; see the Comment on 19:10. This verse continues the theme of obeying the teaching in v 18 by mentioning a case in which a person does not do so (Plöger). Strict treatment of slaves is advised again in 29:21.

None of the biblical law codes place restrictions on beating one's slaves (male or female). If, however, the owner kills a slave, vengeance of an unspecified sort is exacted (Exod 21:20). If the slave survives the beating, no compensation is required, for the slave "is his (master's) money" (Exod 21:21). If the master causes permanent injury, he must pay compensation in the form of manumission (Exod 21:26–27). This set of rules implies that slaves do own the integrity of their own bodies as well as their lives, although they have no rights to their comfort, their well-being, the fruits of their labor, or even their children born in slavery.

take discipline [*yiwwaser*]: *Y-s-r* N means to take discipline (verbal or physical) to heart, to really be convinced (Lev 26:23; Jer 6:8; 31:18; Ps 2:10).

for if he understands: Even though a slave, unlike an animal or fool, *can* understand verbal chastisement, he will not be persuaded by it.

there will (still) be no response [*maʿăneh*]: The slave will sullenly refuse to give a genuine response to the castigation. Such a response would be equivalent to "taking discipline" (to heart). It seems unlikely that many slaves would remain completely mum, refusing even lip service. Plöger says that this line means that the slave will not *carry out* the command because he need not expect punishment. But *maʿăneh* elsewhere is a verbal response. For Murphy, "there is no response" indicates "silent resistance." Clifford, to the contrary, reads the phrase as implying "silent acquiescence" of the slave. This supposedly precludes "the give and take of reproving" and "honest and free dialogue." But this implies a view of education too liberal for ancient Wisdom, in which silent acquiescence was precisely the desired response, in children and certainly in slaves. Hameʾiri derives *maʿăneh* from *ʿ-n-h* "subjugate," "humble," comparing Exod 10:3, "How long will you refuse to subjugate yourself [*leʿanot* N] before me?" But the noun does not elsewhere have this meaning, and the noun pattern is not one appropriate for a reflexive action. Understanding the lack of response to mean surly noncooperation fits the context best.

However the second line is construed, the point of the proverb is that verbal remonstrance will not work on a slave. A beating is necessary. As Ahiqar says:

A blow for the servant,[376]
a rebuke for the slave girl,
and also for all your slaves: discipline. (83 [1.1.178])

[376] "Servant" is Aramaic *ʿlym*, which like Hebrew *naʿar* can mean "youth" or "slave." The other persons mentioned in this saying indicate that the latter is meant.

Ben Sira has similarly harsh advice for the control of slaves (33:25–30a). This is followed by an exhortation to treat them humanely (vv 30b), especially if the owner has only one slave, but the motivation is self-interest: Mistreatment might drive the slave to escape (vv 31–33). Ben Sira tells the reader not to be ashamed of "beating the back of a disloyal [lit., "bad"] servant" (42:5c, Greek). It is interesting that Ben Sira includes this in a list of things that one *might* be ashamed of, as if some people might consider it as not quite the gentlemanly thing to do. The author of Prov 29:19 (unlike Ahiqar and Ben Sira) is rather indirect in the way he recommends the practice, as if he hesitated to come out and bluntly urge the reader to whip his slaves.

29:20 Have you seen a man hasty in his words?
There is more hope for a dolt than him.

A dolt *might* be taught some good sense, or at least a degree of prudence, by means of corporal punishment if nothing else. A quick-tongued man, however, gets himself into trouble at once. This comparison is an exaggeration intended to warn against hasty speech (Murphy). It is not necessarily meant precisely, for stupidity is a condition of the entire character, whereas hasty speech is a particular flaw. This proverb is a close variant of 26:12, which warns against overconfidence in one's own wisdom.

29:21 He who pampers his slave from youth—
he will be a misery afterwards.

This proverb returns to the theme of v 19: discipline of slaves. Several traditional commentators soften the warning by interpreting "slave" as the evil inclination, which usually refers to sexual desire (Rashi), or to one's physical desires generally. One must not pander to such desires during one's youth, lest they become the master and make the intellect their slave (Ralbag; sim. Saʿadia, Hame'iri).

he will be a misery [*manon*]: The subject may be the master, who will be *in* misery, or the slave, who will *cause* misery. Clifford prefers the former because the master is the subject of the A-line, but a switch in subject from line to line occurs in 29:9 and elsewhere. *Manon* is found only here, and its meaning must be guessed from context. Other guesses are "arrogant," "insolent," and "rebellious" (see HALOT 600b) and "heir" (RSV: "He who pampers his servant from childhood, will in the end find him his heir).

mānôn: (1) Ramaq identifies *mānôn* with *nîn* "offspring" (Gen 21:23; Isa 14:22; Job 18:19) and *yinnôn* (qeré) "endure" (?) (Ps 72:17). Barucq emends to *nînô* "his descendant." A spoiled slave will become, as it were, the master's son and control his wealth. But *nîn* is a distant offspring and is always paired with *neked* "grandson." Though a slave might inherit from his master (17:2), he would not in any sense become a distant descendant. (2) Saʿadia (*Ha'egron*) derives *mānôn* from *mnh* "appoint" and explains it as "superintendent," "overseer." (3) Symmachus translates *estai goggysmos* "will be a murmuring" or "object of murmuring." (4) Plöger emends to *mādôn* and translates *Ärger* ("vexation," "anger"). This would mean "There will in the future be anger" (on the part of the slave owner). This fits the context but is not what *mādôn* actually means.

afterwards [*ʾaḥărito*]: See the Comment on 19:20.

29:22 The angry man provokes strife,
and the heated one is full of offenses.

This is an implicit warning against both being a hothead and associating with one. Prov 29:22a ≈ 15:18a; 28:25a. The Comment on 15:18 discusses anger.

is full of offenses [*pešaʿ*]: Lit., "is great of offense" (or "transgression"). He offends others. Contrary to Ehrlich, *pešaʿ* always has an ethical meaning, but it does not always mean crimes.

Rab pāšaʿ is not the direct object of "provokes" (as in the NRSV: "One given to anger stirs up strife, and the hothead causes much transgression"; sim. Clifford, Murphy). This would require *pešaʿ rāb* or *pᵉšāʿîm rabbîm*. Also, the idiom *gērāh pešaʿ* "provoke transgression" is not found elsewhere.

V. A. Hurowitz (*2001a*) sees in 22:22–27 a partial acrostic. Its six couplets begin with five letters in alphabetical order, *ʾaleph, gimel, ḥet, ḥet, reš, taw*. Hurowitz does find a *bet* following the *aleph*, but in the second line of v 22, not in the next couplet. His schema assumes a very liberal notion of acrostic, in which some letters of the sequence can be randomly skipped while others are repeated and others placed at the beginnings *or* ends of couplets *or* lines. Against such hypotheses we should weigh the probability of partial alphabetic sequences appearing by chance in a corpus of 915 verses.

29:23 A man's pride will cast him down,
but he whose spirit is humble will hold honor.

Pride, which offends both God and man, will ultimately ruin and humble the arrogant (16:18; 17:19b; 18:12a), while humility is a source of benefit (16:19) and honor (15:33b; 18:12b; 22:4). Pride is elsewhere said to kindle conflict (11:2a; 17:19a). Hence 29:22 (conflict) and 29:23 (pride) are linked thematically.

will hold honor: This is said of the gracious woman in 11:16.

29:24 He who divides (spoil) with a thief hates himself.
When he hears the curse he will not testify.

He who shares in a thief's takings must (whether or not he realizes it) hate himself, because he is endangering his life. (Compare "despises himself" in 15:32.) He will fail to respond when he hears the curse, the publicly proclaimed *ʾalah*, which adjures anyone aware of the theft to come forward and give evidence under oath.

The *ʾalah* is a conditional curse, a particular use of which is stipulated in Lev 5:1 (words that appear in Prov 29:24 are italicized): "If a person sins (as follows): If he *hears* the proclamation of *the curse*, and he was a witness—having either seen (the crime) or (otherwise) learned (of it)—if he does *not testify*, he will bear his guilt." ("Bearing one's guilt" in the Priestly source indicates that the punishment will be executed by God, not man [Milgrom 1991: 292].) The verbal similarities make it likely that Prov 22:24 is derived from Lev 5:1. *Higgid* ("testify," lit. "tell") means to give evidence only in these two verses.

The way an *'alah* was thought to work is described in Zech 5:3–4, where God sends forth a curse against thieves and perjurers who have gone unpunished. " 'I will bring it [the *'alah*] forth,' declares the Lord of Hosts, 'and it will enter the house of the thief and the house of him who perjures by my name, and it will lodge in his house and obliterate it down to its timber and stones' " (v 4). The scroll with the curse is sent forth like a destroying angel and works its effects without human intervention.

It is not clear that receiving stolen goods was a violation of law. The proverb does not say that this act will result directly in punishment. The danger is indirect: Sharing in the stolen goods will put one into a situation where he is likely to commit a punishable crime in God's sight. The receiver will find it extremely difficult, if not impossible, to denounce the thief, and he will thereby violate the *'alah*. *Midrash Leviticus Rabba* (6.2) pictures a situation where this could happen: "Reuben stole from Simeon and Levi knew of it. (Reuben) said, 'Do not expose me and I will give you a portion.' The next day they entered the synagogue and heard the proclamation by the superintendent declaring, 'Who has stolen from Simeon?' And Levi was standing there. Does not the Torah decree, 'and he was a witness *or* saw *or* knew' " (Lev 5:1)? The phrase "or knew" is understood to show that not only direct witnesses to a crime are required to respond to the adjuration.

Milgrom (1991: 292) says that Wisdom Literature unanimously advises against testifying even *after* one hears the imprecation. He adduces the texts quoted in the Comment on 22:3. The import of those counsels, however, is not that one should avoid testifying when required to do so, but rather that one should avoid getting entangled in a situation where testimony will be required.

29:25 The fear of man sets a snare,
but he who trusts in the Lord will be safe.

Fear of other people endangers the fearful man, as if they were enemies setting a trap to ensnare him. The imagined victim is the fearful man himself, as the antithesis "will be safe" shows. What kind of fear is this? Delitzsch says that it is fear of other men's threats, as a result of which one does wrong and conceals the truth. Toy explains it as fearing the hostility of "untrained men" and regulating one's conduct according to their opinion. The parallel to "trusts in the Lord," however, shows that the "fear of man" is not the fear of particular dangers posed by others, but an attitude toward other humans. It is the exaggeration of human powers, which is the opposite of trust in God. Though "fear" and "trust" are sometimes opposites, here they are two sides of the same attitude. To fear God is to respect his power, and this respect means trusting in his protection. (Prov 14:26 specifically makes confidence consequent on fearing Yahweh.) Conversely, to fear man is to believe in human power, hence to rely on humans and bend to their will rather than to God's.

Jeremiah contrasts the two kinds of trust: "Cursed is the man who trusts in man, and who relies on mortals [lit., "makes flesh his arm"], and whose heart turns away from the Lord. . . . Blessed is the man who trusts in the Lord, and whose stronghold is the Lord" (Jer 17:5, 7; see 5–8). ("Stronghold" is *mibṭaḥo*, lit. "object of trust" or "source of confidence.") A recurrent declaration in the Psalms is, "I trust in God. What can mortals do to me?" (Ps 56:5; variants in Pss 56:12; 118:6). For Second Isaiah, fearing man is tantamount to forgetting God: "I, I am he who comforts you. Who are you that you should be afraid of man, who is mortal, and of humans, who are made like grass, and forget the Lord your maker . . . ?" (Isa 51:12–13aα).

fear of man [*ḥerdat ʾadam*]: A strong word is used for fear, *ḥăradah*, whose root meaning is "to tremble." The parallel phrase, "he who trusts in the Lord," shows that "man" is semantically the object of "fear." "Fear of man," then, is like "fear of God": the fear of another being. Feeling fear is not in itself a snare, because sometimes it is justified and can even help one avoid sin and trouble (Prov 14:16).

The lack of gender agreement between the feminine *ḥerdat-ʾadam* and the masculine *yitten* ("sets" or "gives") led Rashi to construe the masculine *moqeš* "snare" as the subject. According to this we would translate, "The snare [sc., of sin] causes fear of man," that is, makes a man constantly fearful. But the parallelism argues against this, and "snare" by itself does not signify sin.

be safe [*yᵉśuggab*]: Lit., "be elevated," as when one flees to a high fortress (called a *miśgab*). The fortress metaphor is explicit in Prov 18:10.

29:26 Many make entreaties of an official,
but a man's judgment comes from the Lord.

"This is a call to place one's trust in God (who is blessed), for that is the highest of virtues" (Hameʾiri). This verse is a sequel to v 25, which contrasts fear of man with trust in God. People commonly turn to powerful men with requests. Petitioning rulers is not a snare or in any way forbidden, but people should realize that the real decision (one's *mišpaṭ* "judgment") comes from God. This may mean that God puts the decision in the ruler's heart (compare 21:1), so that regardless of the decision the ruler comes up with, the petitioner's fate rests with God. Prov 29:26a ≈ 19:6a.

make entreaties: Lit., "seek the face."

official [*mošel*]: Or "ruler"; see the Comment on 23:1.

a man's judgment [*mišpaṭ*]: That is, the decision *about* him. This may be any decision the ruler makes and not only a judicial verdict. We may equally well translate *mišpaṭ ʾiš* as 'the justice due a man"; see the Comment on 29:14.

29:27 The righteous loathe the iniquitous man,
while the wicked loathe him whose way is straight.

Not only do the righteous and the wicked behave differently, they *feel* differently. Observe that a saintly charity for all is *not* demanded of the righteous. Like

God (in the "abomination" sayings; see the Comment on 3:32) and Lady Wisdom (8:13bc), the righteous naturally feel repugnance for the realm of evil and all in it. Likewise, the wicked hate the upright (thus 29:10; sim. 26:28a). "For men," Naḥmias explains, "it is natural for everyone to hate whoever is the opposite of his nature and to love whoever is of the same nature." This idea is stated also in 28:4. On the twisted values of the wicked, see Vol. I, 117–18.

This proverb is implicitly an admonition, "a general call at the conclusion of [Solomon's] words to keep far from the company of evildoers" (Naḥmias). It is also a way of firming up someone who is striving to become righteous: Not everyone will love you if you are righteous; some people will hate you. But this must not cause discouragement (Saʿadia).

PART VI: PROVERBS 30:1–31:31

◆

FOUR APPENDICES

Four appendices conclude the book:

VIa (30:1–9)	The Words of Agur
VIb (30:10–33)	Epigrams and Aphorisms
VIc (31:1–9)	The Teaching of Lemuel's Mother
VId (31:10–31)	The Woman of Strength

No editorial principle governs the arrangement of these units, except that VIc and VId share the theme of women. The appendices were most likely added to the end of the book sequentially. The growth of a book by appending material to its end is a natural and common process. The exegetical significance of the placement of an appendix varies. Sometimes an appendix may be intended to comment on the earlier material; this is the case with VIa and, to a degree, VId. Sometimes material is added at the end just because that is where space was left on the papyrus or parchment. This seems to be the case with VIb and VIc. Hence the term "editor" is somewhat misleading, insofar as it implies that someone took the entire book in hand and shaped its contents toward a certain goal. At the end of the book, the "editors"—perhaps just a series of scribes who finished copying the manuscript—seem to have simply appended short texts that seemed appropriate. It should be noted that appended material is not necessarily later in origin than the text to which it is added.

There are many examples of textual growth by accretion at the end. Deuteronomy concludes with appendixes (31:24–32:52; 33; 34). Lev 27 is an appendix (the original ending is marked by the postscript in 26:46), as is Num 36 (which qualifies the stipulations of 27:1–11). Jer 52 (which does not mention Jeremiah) was borrowed with minor modifications from 2 Kgs 24:18–25:30 in order to provide historical information about Jeremiah's times. Ben Sira's postscript in 50:27–29, clearly intended as the book's conclusion, is followed by three appendices: a prayer, a hymn, and an autobiographical poem. *Pirqey 'Abot* has a complex internal history, but it is clear that chap. 5, whose material is quite different in character from the gnomes in the first four chapters, was appended later. For several centuries, *'Abot* comprised these five chapters. In the Gaonic period, a separate homiletic tract with its own name, *Qinyan Torah* ("Acquisition of Torah"), was added as chapter 6. This chapter is found in other midrashic compilations.

Even when there is an attempt at canonical fixation, material can be subsequently appended. A medieval example is the Passover Haggadah. The service proper concludes with a formal declaration ("The service of the Passover has ended according to its law, etc."), but then (in some editions) there follow three songs with no inherent connection to Passover.

PART VIA: PROVERBS 30:1–9

THE WORDS OF AGUR

30:1a The words of Agur the son of Yaqeh,
b the pronouncement, the oracle of the man:
c I am weary, God,[a]
d I am weary, God,[a] and have wasted away,[b]
2 for I am the most ignorant of men,
and have not human understanding.
3 I have not learned wisdom
or have knowledge of the Holy One.
4a Who has ascended to the heavens and come down?
b Who has gathered the wind in his lap?
c Who has wrapped the waters in his garment?
d Who has set up all the ends of the earth?
e What is his name and what is the name of his son?—
f For you know.
5 All of God's words are pure;
he is a shield to those who trust in him.
6 Add not to his words,
lest he chastise you and you be proved false.
7 Two things I ask of you;
do not deny me them before I die:
8 Falsehood and deceit keep far from me.
Give me neither poverty nor wealth,
but grant me my apportioned bread,
9 lest I become sated and renounce (you),
and I say, "Who is Yahweh?"
and lest I become poor and steal,
and misuse the name of my God.

[a, a] *lāʾîtî ʾēl* (twice) (MT *lᵉʾîtîʾēl* [twice]). [b] *wāʾēkel* (MT *wᵉʾukāl*).

Agur's Oracle: Scope and Structure. Earlier (Vol. I, 5), I demarcated this unit as 30:1–14, as do a number of commentators. Now, however, I do not believe that there is a significant connection between vv 1–9 and 10–14. Verses 1–9 form a cohesive first-person meditation. Including vv 10–14 in the unit makes Agur's words into a miscellaneous collection. Regardless of the authorship of vv 10–33, vv 1–9 constitute a distinct unit with its own shape and message that must be treated on its own.

The components of vv 1–9 cohere and presuppose one another. Without the preceding confession of frailty and ignorance (vv 1c–3), v 4 would lack context, for that verse extends Agur's own confession (vv 1c–3) to encompass all people. Human deficiency (v 4) means that the source of enlightenment and support is God's word (v 5)—and that alone (v 6). The humility and trust in God voiced in vv 2–6 receive practical expression in vv 7–9. Since God takes care of those who trust him and his word, all one need pray for is a sufficiency. This is crucial, not only for sustenance, but because humans cannot be confident in their own ability to maintain their integrity if faced by excess or privation. This lack of confidence in human powers points back to Agur's opening confession.

The scope of Agur's words has been delineated variously: (1) Verses 1–4. Plöger confines Agur's words to vv 1–4, with 5–6 as an addition. McKane identifies Agur's original (skeptical) teaching as vv 1c–4, to which vv 5–6 were added as a pious corrective, after which vv 7–9 were appended only because of the catchword *kzb* "deceit" in vv 6b and 8a. (2) Verses 1–9. Franklyn (1983) describes vv 1–9 as a unified, symmetrically structured composition. In his commentary, Van Leeuwen (1997: 251) calls vv 1–9 "an editorial, 'anthological' poem," whose original components are vv 1–3, 4, 5–6, and 7–9. Verses 1–3 and 7–9 would, however, have little meaning in isolation, and Van Leeuwen's own exposition gives the unit a degree of cohesiveness that looks authorial rather than secondary. (3) Verses 1–10. Clifford (p. 257) delimits the unit thus, on the grounds that vv 1–5 and 7–9 are logically coherent, and both sections are followed by sentences with similar syntax (negative imperatives followed by *pen* "lest"; vv 6a, 10a); sim. Steinmann *2001*: 59–66 (see below). But these connections do not produce a coherent unit. (4) Verses 1–14. Thus Gemser, Whybray 1994: 148–50, Crenshaw, Plöger, Fox (earlier; Vol. I, 5), Murphy, Sauer 1963: 92 (who regards vv 1–30 as a single collection), and others. In support of this delineation, it has been noted that the LXX places 30:1–14 after 24:22. Commentators who extend the unit through v 14 regard its organization as loose. Crenshaw describes vv 1–14 as a dialogue between a radical skeptic (vv 1c–4) and a conventional believer (vv 5–14), which mixes a variety of genres and viewpoints to produce a deliberate cacophony (1989a: 59–61). (5) Verses 1–33. Saʿadia divides the chapter into an introduction (vv 1–6) and six "topics" (*ʿinyānîm*) of four "sentences" (*dᵉbārîm*) each. Delitzsch treats chap. 30 as a proverb collection. Perdue observes that a major theme running throughout 30:1–33 is "the arrogance or self-exaltation that leads to rejection of divine sovereignty and rebellion against or upsetting of the social order" (1994: 116); note vv 1c–4, 7–10, 13, 17, 21–23, and 29–33. Steinmann (ibid.) believes that vv 11–33 are a coherent unit connected editorially to vv 1–10, intended to be understood as Agur's words. If Agur's "oracle" does indeed extend that far, the collection is composed of at least two unrelated units.

Building in four steps, the author reflects on the theme of knowledge and its implications.

A. vv 1c–3 Agur's ignorance
B. v 4 Human inadequacy
C. vv 5–6 The perfection of God's words
D. vv 7–9 A prayer for honesty and simplicity

This unit progresses by theme and logic: B elaborates on A, C on B, and these culminate in the prayer in D, which draws a practical conclusion from the earlier segments.

This difficult poem has received a multitude of varying and conflicting interpretations, of which only a sampling can be mentioned below. Its message is discussed after the Comments.

30:1a. *Agur the son of Yaqeh*: Agur is otherwise unknown.

ʾāgûr bin yāqeh: The name Agur has parallels in Egyptian Aramaic and Old South Arabic (see HALOT 10b). With a different morphology, the root is used as a god-name in Ugaritic: *ugr* (= *ugāru* but possibly *ʾagāru* "hireling" [Sauer 1963: 96], CAT 1.4.VII.54, VIII.47, etc.). *Yāqeh* (*yāqeʾ* in some MSS) is obscure. The LXX translates the phrase as "Fear my words, son," a loose midrashic paraphrase; see the Textual Notes. The Syriac reads the words as a proper name. Ramaq says that Agur was a sage of Solomon's time whose words Solomon included in his book. The midrash identifies Agur with Solomon, who "gathered [*ʾāgar*] wisdom," and Yaqeh with David, because he "assembled" (*wayyaqhēl*) and united the nation, or with Solomon himself, because he "disgorged" (*hiqîʾ*) wisdom (*Num. Rab.* 10:4 [88a]). Alternatively, Solomon was called Agur because he "gathered his loins" for wisdom and also called Yaqeh because he was "innocent" (*nāqî*) of sin (*Mid. Prov.*). (See the Textual Notes on the LXX and Vul.) Using similar methods, Skehan explains the name as a coded answer to the riddle in v 4e, namely, Jacob-Israel. Agur, he says, means "I am a sojourner" (from *g-w-r*; see Gen 47:9), and *yqh* is an abbreviation for *YHWH qādōš hûʾ*, "Yahweh is holy" (Skehan 1971*b*: 41–43). But Jacob was a sojourner in Egypt, and that would no longer apply to the people of Israel. Neither the abbreviation nor the phrase is known from elsewhere.

30:1b. *the pronouncement* [*hammaśśāʾ*]: The word *maśśāʾ* could be a proper noun, Massa, which is a northern Arabian tribe (Gen 25:14; 1 Chr 1:30; also mentioned in Assyrian sources). In Prov 31:1, Lemuel is called "king of Massa." The translation "Agur . . . the Massaite" requires reading *mmśʾ* "from Massa" or *hmśʾy* "the Massaite," for *hmśʾ* (BHS and many others). (The MT cannot mean "king of Massa" or "king of Massans," contrary to Delitzsch.)

Earlier (Vol. I, 5), I followed the emendation *hmśʾy* in assigning a title to this unit, but I now consider it more likely that *hammaśśāʾ* is a common noun meaning "pronouncement" or "oracle." It is true that the "sons of the East," meaning the Arabians, were renowned for wisdom (1 Kgs 5:10), but Agur does not speak like a foreigner. He is a Yahwist (Prov 30:9) who is concerned for the integrity of divine revelation (vv 5–6).

pronouncement [*hammaśśāʾ*], *oracle* [*nᵉʾum*]: Both words denote oracles or "inspired utterances" (Toy). (The word *maśśāʾ*, from *n-ś-ʾ* "lift up," gains the sense of "speech" because in Hebrew one is said to "lift up" a speech [Num 24:15a].) *Nᵉʾum* and *maśśāʾ* are near-synonyms.

Maśśāʾ and *nᵉʾum* are used of the same oracle in Zech 12:1. The pairing of *maśśāʾ* with *nᵉʾum* shows that the former refers to a type of prophetic utterance, as is always the case except in Sir 9:18. In Jer 23:34–40, *maśśāʾ* clearly means "prophetic oracle." Nᵉʾûm is usually in construct with YHWH and means "the oracle of Yahweh." Exceptions are Balaam's oracles in Num 24:3, 4, 15, 16 and David's last words in 2 Sam 23:1. Balaam's oracles are introduced as *nᵉʾum bilʿām bᵉnô bᵉʿōr* "the oracle of Balaam son of Beor" (Num 24: 3b), sometimes with other appellatives, such as "whose eye is open" (Num 24:15; cf. vv 4, 16).

If there is a distinction, it is that *maśśāʾ* refers to the *event* or *experience* of prophecy. It is something that can be "seen" (Isa 13:1; Hab 1:1; Lam 2:14; sim. Deir ʿAlla I, 1) and that can "occur" (*hāyāh*) (Isa 14:28). In 2 Kgs 9:25 it is used of the prophesied event itself, which had just come to pass. *Nᵉʾum*, which comes from a root meaning "utter," is a citation formula referring to the prophecy's *verbal form*. A notable difference is that *maśśāʾ* can be bound in construct to a place-name, indicating the target of the oracle (e.g., "*maśśāʾ* of [= concerning] Babylon" [Isa 13:1], "*maśśāʾ* of Duma" [Isa 21:11]), but it cannot be bound to a personal name indicating author or prophet. *Nᵉʾum*, in contrast, can be bound to the personal name of the prophet or God (e.g., "*nᵉʾum* of Balaam" [Num 24:3, etc.]; "*nᵉʾum* of Yahweh" [1 Sam 2:30, and elsewhere]) but not to the name of a place or a people.

the oracle of the man [*nᵉʾum haggeber*]: In other words, the oracle of Agur. Other occurrences of *nᵉʾum haggeber* add a relative clause defining "the man," such as "who has been set on high" or "whose eye is open" (see below). This definition is not provided here, even if *l'yty'l* is a proper noun. *Haggeber* "the man" is added as a possessive because *n*ᵉ*'um* does not take suffixes.

The words of Agur the son of Yaqeh, the pronouncement, the oracle of the man: The title of Agur's oracle resembles 2 Sam 23:1, "These are the last words of David, the oracle of David the son of Jesse, the oracle of the man [*n*ᵉ*'um haggeber*] who has been set on high." David proceeds to say that God spoke to him and quotes God in v 3b. God's words there simply praise the just ruler in a way that recalls a sapiential generalization. Similar too is Num 24:15: "And (Balaam) began [lit., "lifted up"] his parable and said, 'The oracle [*n*ᵉ*'um*] of Balaam the son of Beor, and the oracle of the man [*n*ᵉ*'um haggeber*] whose eye is open.' "

Though Agur declares that he is speaking an oracle, the poem is cast as his own words, with none actually ascribed to God. Similarly, while Balaam insists that he speaks only what God told him (Num 24:13), the oracles are mostly formulated as his own words. If anything in Agur's oracle might quote God, it is the questions in Prov 30:4, which Barucq calls "a response of God to the sage" (*1964*, ad loc.). They resemble the rhetorical questions in Yahweh's revelation in Job 38–41, which call on Job to acknowledge God's infinite wisdom and power. The challenge at the end of Prov 30:4, "for you know," would make sense as God's words, as in Job 38:5. Still, there is no indication of change of speaker, and God is clearly being addressed in Prov 30:7–8. The questions and challenge in v 4 could be addressed to the reader. Like God's message to David in 2 Sam 23:3b–4, the revelation in Prov 30:4 communicates no prophecy about the future or any new information, but only a verity known to all. A *n*ᵉ*'um* claims divine origin without necessarily recording God's words.

30:1cd. *I am weary, God, I am weary, God, and have wasted away* [*l'yty 'l l'yty 'l w'kl*]: As emended, this sentence reverberates in the clause "before I die" in v 7b, which is suggestive of approaching death, as in Gen 27:4 and 45:28. (The way to express "as long as I am alive" without implying approaching death is *b*ᵉ*'odi*, as in Ps 104:33; 146:2.) Agur's oracle is his last words. Likewise, David's last words are called a *n*ᵉ*'um* in 2 Sam 23:1a. The psalmist of Ps 73, who also confesses ignorance (v 22), says that his flesh "is wasting away" (v 26, using *klh*, as here in the emended text).

This enigmatic verse has been construed in various ways, none of which requires major consonantal emendations. The translation closest to the Masoretic punctuation and vocalization is, "The words of Agur son of Yaqeh: the pronouncement, oracle of the man to Ithiel; to Ithiel and Ukhal." (The major dichotomy in the Masorah is marked here by the semicolon.) Ithiel and Ukhal are usually understood to be Agur's sons or pupils. (In this case, the *l-* is the preposition "to.") The name Ithiel is known from Neh 11:7; the name Ukhal is otherwise unattested.

Ithiel and Ukhal? There are several problems with reading *'yty'l* (twice) and *'kl* as personal names. (1) The next verse starts with *kî* ("for," "because"), which presumes an earlier sentence, not only a title compounded of nouns. (2) If Ithiel is a name, why is it repeated? (3) If these are personal names, we would expect the addition of "his sons." In other titles that state the audience of a Wisdom instruction, the audience is always identified as "his son" or "his children" and not by name alone. (In Amennakhte and Hori, the audience is identified as the son of a friend.) (4) Nowhere is a *maśśā'* "pronouncement" or *nᵉ'ûm* "oracle" spoken to a named individual.

l'yty 'l l'yty 'l w'kl: Another way these words might be rendered is, "I am weary, God, and I am able" (or ". . . will overcome"). MT's vocalization *wᵉ'ukāl* (*kaph raphah*), derives the word from *y-k-l*. This, however, does not yield a good sense; moreover, the writing of the sg. impf. of this verb without a *waw* would be aberrant. We should redivide MT's *l'yty'l* (twice) as *l'yty 'l* and vocalize *l'yty* and *'kl* as verbs from *l-'-h* and *k-l-h*, respectively (Sauer 1963: 98, ref. H. F. Mühlau 1869). Verse 2 explains this complaint. LXX's *kai pauomai* "and I cease" likewise derives *w'kl* from *k-l-h* "cease"; sim. Aq *kai teleson* "and finish" (impv.). Delitzsch vocalizes *wā'ēkel* (*k-l-h*, G, pausal), and translates, "but I have withdrawn"; but this usage of a very common word is otherwise unknown. R. Scott, followed by McKane, emends and reads the words as Aramaic: *l' 'ty 'lh* (*lā' 'îtay 'ĕlāhh*), "there is no God." McKane understands this as the despairing cry of one whose search for God has failed.

The repeated vocative "O God" is peculiar. Perhaps the second *l'yty'l* should be omitted, as in LXX and Syr; see the Textual Note. This omission is essential if *'yty'l* is to be construed as a name but optional if it is a verb, as preferred here.

30:2–3. Agur professes himself the most ignorant of men, devoid of ordinary human understanding, learned wisdom, and (apparently) knowledge of the Holy One. Agur's humility is often compared with that of the psalmist who says "Knowledge is too wondrous for me, too lofty for me to grasp" (Ps 139:6). Psalm 139 as a whole, esp. vv 7–16, shows that the knowledge the psalmist is disavowing is of a kind that *no one* has: an understanding of how God can be transcendent yet close enough to humans that he can see into the depth of their souls. Agur disavows for himself knowledge that others *do* have (human understanding, wisdom) but that he considers of lesser importance, and also knowledge that is beyond human ken ("knowledge of the Holy One").

Agur's self-humbling in v 2 is not a supplicant's tactic for gaining God's sympathy and help (contrary to Clifford, p. 257). He does not speak as a wretch begging for mercy. Rather, his protestations are a way of glorifying a higher kind of wisdom—the knowledge of God's words (v 5)—and a loftier spiritual stance—a humble fidelity to Yahweh's will (this is the message of vv 6–9). Agur contrasts these virtues with wisdom and "knowledge of the Holy One," a distinction foreign to the rest of the book of Proverbs, especially 2:5–6 and 9:10.

ignorant [*baʿar*]: The root-meaning of *baʿar* is "beast," and it retains that connotation here (see Vol. I, 39). Verse 2a has a double entendre that can be rendered, "I am more beast than man." Agur is animal-like and does not have "human understanding."

of men [*me'iš*]: Lit., "than man," that is, *any* man. Or (also lit.): "from a man"; that is, he is ignorant "in a way that separates him from men and equates him to the beasts" (Toy).

or have knowledge of the Holy One [*wᵉdaʿat qᵉdošim* (pl.) *'edaʿ*]. This too is knowledge that Agur does *not* have. Though there is no negative particle in v 3b, the force of the negative in v 3a is usually understood to apply to v 3b as well. All of the medievals apply the force of the negative to v 3b. Malbim, to the same effect, treats the sentence as a rhetorical question, "Do I have knowledge of the Holy One?," and the Targum simply adds a negative.

Since the negative is not explicit, the clause could also be read as affirmative, hence adversative to the preceding: "but I do have knowledge of the Holy One." This is the interpretation I preferred earlier; see Vol. I, 112, 309. However, it seems unlikely that Agur would lay claim to such knowledge, since in the next verse he insists on human limitations, the first being the inability to ascend to heaven and come down—in other words, reach a divine realm beyond human grasp.

In the Hebrew, the extension of the force of the negative is more strained than in English, because nonsequential Hebrew verbs normally require their own negations. Syntactically, the negative reading of v 3b is feasible because the constituent structures of the two lines are parallel and the negative is in initial position; see C. L. Miller *2005*. Clear examples where this happens are Isa 38:18; Ps 9:19; and esp. Ps 35:19. The gapping of the negative in the second line is not, however, obligatory in such constructions; for example, Ps 59:17 (ibid., 50).

knowledge of the Holy One [*daʿat qᵉdošim* (pl.)]: This phrase, used also in Prov 9:10, is open to various interpretations:

(1) Knowledge of holy matters, that is, sacred mysteries of some sort. Ben Sira—using different wording—includes among the activities of the sage the fact that "he examines [God's] mysteries" (39:7). This too is a form of wisdom, though not the kind taught in Proverbs. It is the kind of wisdom whose attainability is denied in Job 28:1–22 (Saʿadia). Agur does say that it is impossible to attain, only that he himself has not learned it.

(2) Knowledge such as is possessed by the holy ones, that is, the angels (Hameʾiri). Elevated wisdom is ascribed to the angels; cf. 2 Sam 14:17, 20; Dan 8:16; 9:22; 10:14; etc. (The "holy ones" may have originally referred to gods, in polytheistic contexts.) However, it would be trite for any human to disclaim a superhuman level of knowledge.

(3) Knowledge of the Holy One, that is, God. This explanation, advocated by most medievals, is the most probable. *Daʿat qᵉdošim* has equivalents in *daʿat ʾĕlohim* "knowledge of God" (Prov 2:5b) and *daʿat ʿelyon* "knowledge of the Most High" (Num 24:16). It is parallel to "fear of the Lord" in Prov 9:10. *Qᵉdošim* is an epithet of God in Hos 12:1.

Daʿat qᵉdôšîm: Most of the medievals understood the plural as a plural of majesty. IBHS §7.4.3b calls this an "honorific" plural. Alternatively, *qᵉdōšîm* may be a "concretized abstract plural," the category that J. Burnett applies to *ʾĕlōhîm* "God" (*2001*: 21–24). There are numerous abstract plurals in BH and some instances of concretization, such as *ḥămûdôt* "desirable things" (fem. pl.) → "desirableness" → "desirable one" in Dan 9:23 (ibid., p. 23). Burnett's examples, however, are adjectives, so the category is less appropriate for *ʾĕlōhîm* than for *qᵉdōšîm*.

The concept of "knowledge of God" is discussed in conjunction with Prov 2:5 in Vol. I, 111–12. Agur, however, uses it differently from that verse. For Agur, "knowledge of the Holy One" is specialized, esoteric knowledge of God's ways, a knowledge accessible only (at most) to an elect few. Agur can do without it. There seems to be an escalation in the listing of things Agur lacks, moving from (ordinary) "human knowledge" to (learned) "wisdom" to (esoteric) "knowledge of the Holy One." They are all forms of human, non-revealed knowledge, but the latter two require greater erudition. The wisdom Agur disclaims in v 3b is not equivalent to the fear of the Lord (contrary to 9:10), for Agur surely would not disclaim the latter virtue, which is piety itself.

30:4. Four questions (vv 4a, 4b, 4c, 4d) are reprised by a double question (v 4e) and a challenge to respond to them (v 4f). The questions are really the same and have a single response, as the singular "his" ("his name," "his son") in v 4e shows. Three responses to these questions are possible: (1) someone; (2) God; (3) no one.

(1) "Someone may have done these things, but I don't know who." If this is the expected response, the questions are a riddle, together forming a genuine question meant to stump the reader. But this answer can be excluded, since no human could conceivably have done these things. And even if someone had done them, ignorance of his identity would be irrelevant to the human condition.

(2) "God, of course." Murphy considers this answer "obvious." Similar questions in Isa 41:2, 4; 45:21; Job 38:5, 6, 25, 37, 41; and elsewhere require this answer. To be sure, God could be imagined as holding the wind in his garment (or hands; see below) and collecting the waters in his garment (see Job 26:8), and God alone "set up all the ends of the earth." Also, since some narratives report that God descended to earth (Gen 11:5; Exod 19:20; 34:5, etc.), he presumably *ascended* afterwards (as he is said to do in Ps 68:19, for example). Still, the order "ascended"—"come down" is not the natural way to describe God's movements, since his starting point is the heavens. Also, this answer causes difficulties in v 4e, for though we could answer the first question by "Yahweh," who would his son be? Traditional Christian interpreters naturally answered that he is the Christ, and Delitzsch maintains this interpretation, but it is obviously anachronistic. Skehan (*1971b*: 42–43) says that the answers to v 4e are Yahweh and Israel. Franklyn (1983: 247) follows the LXX in vocalizing *bānāyw* "his sons," which he understands as a reference to the angels. But there would be no point in asking who can recall the name of Israel or the angels, as if their glory or identity were relevant here.

(3) "No one, of course." This is the intended response. (The rhetorical question in Qoh 7:24 is also to be answered this way.) The scope of the questions is implicitly confined to humanity, because Agur is speaking about the inadequacy of human wisdom. When Gilgamesh asks "Who can go up to heaven, my friend?" (see below), the question clearly pertains only to mankind, for gods regularly do this. No human has the capability of doing godlike things: traversing the universe, controlling the elements, creating the world. This is a fact known to all, and Agur adduces it to remind the readers of their own ignorance. Humans must always be aware that they are infinitely less powerful and wise than God. Therefore they must rely on him and his word (Prov 30:5–6).

A Mesopotamian proverbial topos, studied by F. Greenspahn (1994) and R. Van Leeuwen (*1997a*), uses similar images to declare the limitations of human powers. Van Leeuwen distinguishes three topoi in Mesopotamian literature that use the heaven/earth motif to emphasize the vast chasm between human and divine powers:

(1) Extension of stature and grasp, especially vertical (from earth to heaven) but also horizontal (the breadth of the earth). This is God's alone. A Sumerian proverb says, "The tallest (man) cannot reach heaven, the wisest man cannot cover the mountains" (ll. 17–18; Alster 1975b: 88). The interlocutor in the "Dialogue of Pessimism" quotes the proverb, "Who is so tall as to reach to heaven? Who is so broad as to encompass the netherworld?" (ll. 83–34; BTM 817).

(2) Cosmic scope of divine investigative knowledge. The goddess Gula praises her "towering husband" who "examines the heights of heaven, who investigates the bottom of the netherworld" (BTM 493).

(3) Ascension to heaven. This topos is based on the mythological motif of a hero's attempted ascent to heaven and descent to the earth or the underworld. Such heroes are the ancient king Etana and the primordial man Adapa. In stories with this motif, the human's attempt to ascend to heaven either proves impossible or has disastrous consequences. Only gods can make the journey easily. For humans, ascent to heaven betrays an attempt to usurp the place of the high god. The principle is stated by Gilgamesh, who uses the very proverb quoted in Prov 30:4a:

> Who can go up to heaven, my friend?
> Only the gods dwell with Shamash forever.
> Mankind can number his days.
> Whatever he may achieve, it is only wind. (III.iv 3–8; Dalley 1989: 144)

The function of this motif is "to reaffirm the great gulf that separates humans from the divine realm and the prerogatives of deity," namely, immortality, superhuman wisdom, and power (Van Leeuwen *1997a*: 121).

In Israelite mythology, only God and the angels (see Gen 28:12) can go to and fro between earth and heaven. For a mortal to presume to do so would be ridiculous and arrogant (Isa 14:13–14), and any such attempt must fail (Isa 14:15; Gen 11:1–9). Deut 30:11–12 says that the Torah provides wisdom without requiring ascent to heaven. Agur says the same but does not call it wisdom. The later Enoch traditions would have answered that Enoch went up to the heavens (esp. 1 Enoch 72–82), but these postdate the present chapter and, in any case, do not offer an answer to the other questions.

In spite of the similarity between these questions and Yahweh's in Job 38, the expected answers have different emphases. Most of the ones in Job 38 call for the answer, "God, of course," as in v 5: "Who fixed its measurements—for you know—and who stretched a line over it?" Other questions elicit awe and humility: "Where were you when I founded the earth?" (v 4a). (Nowhere; I had no part in it.) And "Were the gates of death revealed to you, or did you see the gates of deep darkness?" (v 17). (Of course not.) The rhetorical questions in Job 38 and Prov 30:4 demand recognition of God's power (this is emphasized in Job) and human ignorance (this is emphasized in Agur). None are riddles; see Fox *1981*: 53–61

in his lap [*bᵉḥopnayw*]: That is, in the front of his garment (cf. 6:27); alternatively: "in his hands."

Heb *ḥōpen* usually means the palm of the hand, but can also refer to the lap and to a garment of some sort, probably one that covers the lap. Compare Ugaritic *ḫpn* "garment." Thus Cathcart 1970 and Malul 1997, esp. pp. 361–62.

For you know: When God says "for you know" in Job 38:5, he is demanding that Job admit something he *does* know, namely, that it was God who designed and shaped the physical universe. Here, the same remark reminds the reader that he knows very well that *no one* fits the description. Clifford deletes the remark on the grounds that Agur, not God, is the questioner, and it makes poor sense for Agur to say this. Barucq believes that God *is* the questioner; see the Comment on v 1b. But, in fact, Agur continues to speak, and this challenge does make sense when said to the reader, the "you" addressed in the warning in 30:6.

30:5. Far superior to human wisdom is God's revealed word because it alone is pure in the sense of refined (*ṣᵉrupah*) and devoid of the dross of falsehood. The other sages in Proverbs would not deny this, but, unlike Agur, they make the same claim for wisdom itself (2:7, 11; 4:6; 6:22; etc.).

All of God's words [*kol ʾimrat ʾĕloahh*]: Lit., "the entire utterance of God." Verse 5 is taken from, or at least used in, Ps 18:31aβb (= 2 Sam 22:31b), which has "Yahweh" where the present verse has *ʾĕloahh* "God," a form unique in Proverbs. Variants of this saying appear in Pss 12:7 and 119:140.

30:6. *Add not to his words*: Anything added to God's pure words would be dross. This verse echoes the first part of Deut 4:2a: "You shall not add to the word that I am commanding you nor shall you subtract from it"; sim. Deut 13:1b. Deuteronomy's injunction assumes a revelation of defined scope and wording, namely, the Deuteronomic code (Deut 12–26) or an earlier stage thereof. Agur too must have in mind a defined corpus of revealed instruction, though he does not identify it further. It could be the Pentateuch or an earlier stage in its growth, such as Deuteronomy or the code it contains. Since the injunction is most at home within a written code, where it warns against changing the sacred document in question, it is likely that Agur is borrowing from Deuteronomy rather than the other way around.

Agur is not warning against false prophecies being added to the true ones. "Do not add to them" suggests a fixed corpus of writings rather than a fluctuating visionary tradition or even the Prophets as a canonical division, since that collection cannot be described simply as "God's word." (Nor, contrary to Toy, are the Psalms included in "God's word.") When the "Do not add/subtract" topos is applied to prophecy, it refers to a particular prophetic oracle, not the entirety of approved prophetic traditions. Thus when God tells Jeremiah, "do not subtract even a word" (26:2), he is referring to the message quoted or summarized in vv 4–6. The same is true of the colophon of the Late Babylonian Erra epic, in which the poet claims that he heard the composition from a god in a dream and wrote it down exactly: "[The prophecy] was revealed to him in the night, and when he spoke in the morning, he did not leave out a single line, nor did he add one to it" (5.43–44; trans. Weinfeld 1972: 262; cf. BTM 804).

Similar warnings with the "add/subtract" topos occur in various genres in ancient Near Eastern literature, including treaties (see Weinfeld *1991*: 200) and Wisdom Literature. Ptahhotep says, "Do not take away [*iṯi*] a word or bring [= add] one. Do not put one (word) for another" (ll. 608–609).[377] Duachety says: "If an official sends you on an errand, speak his words just as he has spoken them. Do not take away (from them) or add to them" (XXVIIa–c). The book of Revelation (22:18–19) uses the formula, and Qohelet (3:14aβ) and Ben Sira (18:6a; 42:21b) reapply it to God's immutable works.

lest he chastise you [*yokiaḥ bᵉka*] *and you be proved false* [*nikzabta*]: The penalty for adding to God's words is a divine chastisement of unspecified nature, which will show that the one who did this is deceptive. The chastisement is probably a punishment (as in 2 Sam 7:14; Ps 6:2; 39:12; Prov 3:12; etc.) rather than a verbal rebuke, since the latter would imply some form of revelation to the offender.

tôsp: Ramaq parses this anomalous form (unexplained in the modern grammars) as a conflation of *tôsēp* (from *y-s-p* H) and *tisp* (from *s-p-h* G, which means "add" in Isa 30:1b).

30:7–9. Agur prays to God, who is mentioned in vv 5–6. God is the only possible audience for the imperatives in v 8.

Agur prays for two things: to be kept free of deceit (v 8a) and to receive a sufficiency for daily needs (v 8c), neither more nor less (v 8b). An excess (v 9ab) might fill him with an arrogance that would make him denigrate God, and a deficiency might push him into theft (v 9c). Theft might then eventuate in perjury and profanation of God's name by lying under oath (v 9d). Agur is not primarily concerned with poverty or even the guilt of theft, but with the subsequent insult to God. Thus his two prayers have the same goal: to be kept free from temptation.

The second prayer (v 8bc) is an expression of trust in God, which is the virtue advocated in v 5b. Verse 8c is a restatement of v 8b, not a third request (contrary to Murphy). It is circular simply to add "three" before v 7b, as Sauer 1963 does (p. 101), to adjust the count to the number of requests, and two *is* the accurate count. In any case, v 8 is *not* a graded numerical saying—X//X+1 (on which see the Comment on 30:18)—but simply mentions a number.

Like the rest of Proverbs, and the Hebrew Bible generally, Agur neither idealizes poverty nor condemns wealth as such. The sages recognize that wealth is insufficient for safety and happiness, and it is conducive to arrogance; see the Comment on 10:15. Poverty is deemed a misfortune, though it can be offset by inner peace and righteousness (15:16; 16:8; 17:1). Prov 6:30 recognizes that the pressures of poverty can lead to theft, but this outcome is not inevitable. Agur does not say that wealth and poverty will necessarily result in contempt of God or perjury, but he recognizes hazards in the extremes of temptations that he does not trust his own ability to withstand.

---

[377] Similarly AEL 1.74. Žába (1956: 104) translates differently: "Ne dis pas une fois ceci, une autre fois cela, et ne confonds pas une chose avec l'autre" ("Do not say this one time and that another time, and do not confuse one thing with the other"). The verb *iṯi* (lit., "take away") can imply a disordered movement and confusion (ibid., p. 169). But the use of this verb in Duachety XXVIIc, which is unambiguous and is dependent on Ptahhotep, supports the translation "take away."

30:8. *Falsehood* [*šawʾ*] *and deceit* [*dᵉbar kazab*]: "Falsehood" and "deceit" are synonyms collocated for intensity. Agur is not asking to be protected against the deceit of others but to be prevented from being deceitful himself. He is concerned throughout with the state of his soul rather than with the harm other people may cause him and others.

The two "lest"-clauses in v 9 are formally dependent on the second request (v 8bc), but they also reinforce the first (v 8a) by giving instances of falsehood. The fact that both of the "lest"-clauses pertain to both requests indicates that Agur's double prayer is essentially one: that he not be forced into circumstances that might drive him to dishonesty.

my apportioned bread [*leḥem ḥuqqi*]: Translations such as "the food that I need" (NRSV) or "my daily bread" (JPSV) do not reflect the fact that *ḥ-q-q* (lit., "engrave") means "ordain," "appoint," or "assign." This sense is seen, for example, in Job 23:14, where *ḥuqqi* means "what is appointed for me," that is, my fate. A specific portion of the cereal offering is the priest's *ḥoq* "assigned portion" (Lev 6:11; and often). In Prov 31:15, *ḥoq* refers to the quantity of food the mistress of the house allocates to each member of her household each day; see the Comment there. The implication here is that God designates a certain amount of food for everyone as their proper portion. Individuals may receive more or less than this, for reasons not necessarily dependent on themselves. In a similar fashion, God sets the human life span at about seventy or eighty years (Ps 90:10), but not everybody receives it. Agur's prayer is echoed in Matt 6:11 = Luke 11:3.

30:9. *lest I become sated* . . . : The overconfidence that comes with wealth is condemned in Deut 8:12–14; 31:20; 32:15; Job 21:7–15; and 31:24–28 (with *kḥš* "renounce" in v 28, as here), among other places. In Hos 13:6, God complains, "And as they were pastured, they became sated; and being sated, their hearts grew arrogant. Therefore they forgot me." The Psalm of Solomon 5:16b states bluntly: "If a man has too much, he sins."

"Who is Yahweh?" [*mi YHWH*]: An insinuation that this god is a nobody, an insignificant god, as in Exod 5:2. (YHWH, probably pronounced "Yahweh," is usually translated "the Lord," but it was a personal name in biblical times and is here rendered as such to sharpen the question.) LXX's reading, *my yḥzh* "Who will see (me)" is possibly original (see the Textual Note). The graphic changes from *h* to *ḥ* and *w* to *z* could go in the reverse direction, and the claim that God does not see the sinner is cited in Isa 29:15; Ps 64:6; and Job 22:14.

misuse [*tapaśti*]: Lit., "grasp"; used in reference to perjury only here. The idiom implies taking possession of God's name and misusing it to one's own ends. The danger that involvement in illegal activities will lead to a violation of oath is the concern of Prov 29:24 as well.

By the same semantic development, *t-p-s* (D and Dt) means "desecrate" in Aramaic; see *Tg. Yer I* Deut 23:18 and *Tg. Job* 15:20. Jastrow (*Dictionary* 1166b) parses this use as a by-form of *p-y-s* "break," but the latter does not mean "desecrate" elsewhere.

AGUR'S TEACHING

Agur's oracle is compelling and strange. It is out of place in a Wisdom book. The speaker first declares his own ignorance, not only stating inevitable human limitations but also placing his own wisdom beneath others. This is an unparalleled stance in Wisdom Literature. (In the epilogue to Anii, the son declares his own ignorance, but this is not the author speaking.) Agur also addresses God (v 1c) and, in vv 7–9, offers a prayer. Prayers are virtually unknown in Wisdom Literature. (An exception is Sir 51, which, like Agur's words, is an appendix to a Wisdom book.) In fact, Agur's oracle would not be reckoned as Wisdom if it were not attached to Proverbs. Its closest affinities are with certain psalms, in particular Ps 73, in which religious affirmation is grounded in confession of human frailty and ignorance. Agur is also ideologically affiliated with the exaltation of Torah in Ps 119; see Essay 7 (III.B).

Agur confesses that he lacks wisdom (Prov 30:3a). He does not seem troubled by this lack, though he seems to associate it with his weariness. His attitude to wisdom differs profoundly from what we see elsewhere in Proverbs, whose authors consider wisdom a prime virtue, the lack of which means not just ignorance but folly. To be sure, some sayings condemn reliance on one's *own* wisdom (Prov 3:5; cf. 21:30; 28:26), but this is distinct from the wisdom constantly lauded throughout elsewhere. (See the Comment on 3:5.) Agur does not make this distinction. The wisdom that he manages to live without is not necessarily delusive, but it has secondary importance in his eyes.

What is the wisdom that Agur says he lacks? It is certainly not the wisdom of ethical character, as conceived in the Lectures (see Vol. I, 347–51), for that is virtually the same as fear of the Lord, and Agur would not disclaim that virtue while acclaiming God's word. Nor is it likely that Agur has in mind the practical good sense called wisdom in chapters 10–29. Although such wisdom is indeed "human understanding," it would not be set in contrast with "the word of God." An advocate of God's word, as Agur is, would insist that the latter also is prudential wisdom. (This is implied by Deut 4:6.) Agur is just not thinking of wisdom in terms of the concepts of Wisdom Literature.

The wisdom in which Agur is deficient must be *erudition*. *Ḥokmah* refers to erudition in several places. It is the learning that Daniel acquired in the Babylonian court (Dan 1:4) and the knowledge that Qohelet amassed prior to embarking on his intellectual odyssey (Qoh 1:16).[378] Agur is deficient also in "knowledge of the Holy One" (v 3b). This is probably esoteric knowledge of divine mysteries (see the Comment). Agur does not condemn learning of either sort, but he gives it secondary importance. Agur takes the rhetorical pose of the most ignorant of men in order to exalt a different form of wisdom—the knowledge of God's word—and also to promote the piety that comes from keen consciousness of human deficiencies.

The fact that the wisdom that Agur marginalizes is not the sort taught in Proverbs suggests that the poem was not originally composed as an appendix and is not

[378] See also Jer 8:8 (*ḥăkamim*); 9:22; Sir 14:20; 51:15.

polemical. Quite likely it was appended to Proverbs because an editor believed that a cautionary comment was called for, after Proverbs' incessant glorification of wisdom, and he approved of Agur's exaltation of Torah.

Agur's meditation is close in word and spirit to Ps 73. Frustrated in his attempt to understand the prosperity of the wicked, the psalmist says, "I was ignorant and lacking knowledge. I was a beast with you" (v 22). ("Ignorant" is *baʿar*, a word Agur uses of himself in Prov 30:2a.) Only in the sanctuary did the psalmist receive enlightenment (Ps 73:17), and then he can declare, "But I am continually with you. You grasp my right hand; you guide me by your counsel. And afterwards you will take me [in] honor" (vv 23–24). Like Agur, the psalmist combines confession of ignorance with a profession of faith and exultation in the insight that comes from God alone.

Agur entreats God to shape his life in such a way that he not be inclined toward sin. It is as if he does not trust his willpower alone to steel him against temptation. The other sages of Proverbs are well aware of temptation, but they believe that the character strength that comes from the discipline of the teachings is a safeguard against temptation. Agur would have us turn directly to God for such a safeguard.

The issue that Agur deals with indicates an origin at a time when some saw a certain tension between the claims of human wisdom and divine Torah. This situation would fit the time between Ezra and Ben Sira—the late fifth to the end of the third centuries B.C.E. The history of this tension is traced in Essay 7, "Revelation."

PART VIB: PROVERBS 30:10–33

EPIGRAMS AND APHORISMS

Part VIb is a miscellany of epigrams, similar to Interlude C (6:1–19), with three short aphorisms among them.

Aphorism a	30:10	Denouncing a Slave
Epigram i	30:11–14	The Wicked Generation
Aphorism b	30:15a	The Epitome of Greed
Epigram ii	30:15b–16	Four Greedy Things
Aphorism c	30:17	Contempt for Parents
Epigram iii	30:18–20	Four Wondrous Ways—and One More
Epigram iv	30:21–23	Four Things That Shake the Earth
Epigram v	30:24–28	Four Creatures Small but Wise
Epigram vi	30:29–31	Four Creatures with a Stately Gait
Epigram vii	30:32–33	Churning Up Quarrels

Most of the epigrams take the form of lists. Epigrams ii, iii, iv, and vi are graded numerical sayings, in the form of X // X + 1 ("Three things . . . and four . . .").

Epigrams i and vii are unnumbered lists whose items are grouped by theme and anaphora (each line beginning with the same word). Epigram v is a single-number list with four items.

The graded numerical saying is a prominent template in the Bible and ancient Near Eastern literature; see W. Roth 1965 and M. Haran 1972, esp. I, 253–57. See further the Comment on 6:16, with references. The single-number list is much rarer in the Bible but very common in later Hebrew literature.[379] Early examples are Sir 25:1, 2 and *'Abot* 5:1–15 (every verse but 9); see W. S. Towner's form-critical study (1973).

It is almost always the second number, X + 1, that corresponds to the subsequent listing. Often, however, the actual enumeration is vague or ambiguous, and it seems that the numbers are a way of saying "a couple" or "several." The final item in the series is usually the climax and focal point. When a list is followed by a supernumerary item that oversteps the boundaries of the template (v 20), the additional item is the culmination and main point of the epigram *as it stands now.* In the nonnumerical epigram in Prov 30:11–14, v 14cd stands outside and beyond the syntactical structure of the preceding verses. It is likely that the supernumerary item was added by the editor to give the old epigram a new twist.

W. Roth (1965: 18–21) says that enumeration was an aid to reflection and facilitated the organization of thoughts and observations. He understands Epigrams iii, v, and vi as observations of nature whose purpose is to discover and formulate "an order inherent in the phenomena encountered" (p. 19). He does not believe that the numerical sayings in this chapter express "moral sentiment," though at a later stage moral lessons could be derived from them (p. 21). He describes the lists as "general science" (p. 21).

This label is misleading. The epigrams offer little information or "scientific" insight and are not oriented to intellectual discovery. The ancient Near East was capable of sophisticated science and engineering. Though Israel was on the margins of the great cultures, it could not have been so backward that a list of four "ways," associated merely by the fact of their wondrousness, would have served as science of any sort. Rather, poems such as we have in Part VIb—with the possible exception of Epigram ii—list types of human behavior that provide implicit moral guidance by analogy, as will be explained in the Comments. The numerical template served rhetorical, not scientific, purposes.

The list-epigrams, including the nonnumerical ones, assemble phenomena that at first seem to be quite disparate. The listing organizes the reader's *perceptions* of the phenomena. It frames them in a single category and counts the items to give the impression that they form a set with clear definition and with a header that defines the criteria for inclusion. Bracketing diverse phenomena in this way

---

[379] We should exclude prosaic counting of items in which the numbering is simply factual and has no particular rhetorical function, such as: "The sons of Jacob were twelve, etc." (Gen 35:22–26). In a true numerical saying, the choice of numbers should govern the selection of items and not merely count the items in an existing group. Thus there could be any number of "things too wondrous for me" (Prov 30:18) or "things there are that are excellent of stride" (v 29), whereas there were only two sons of Eli (1 Sam 1:3b), no more or less. This criterion would exclude several of Roth's examples.

induces the reader to look for other shared features beyond the lowest common denominator. (Thus all commentators try to find stronger affinities among the "ways" in Epigram iii besides their being amazing and incomprehensible.) The framing also makes the qualities of each item permeate the reader's perception of the others.

The reader can easily add further phenomena to the set by analogy. A human who is "small" in strength, status, or wealth can succeed by the wisdom of preparing for the future (Epigram v). If a slave becoming king disturbs the right order, as Epigram iv warns, so does a king falling into poverty, and so on. This is categorical thinking, which is well recognized in its pernicious form of group stereotyping but is in fact a necessary means of organizing the unruly mass of data that constantly flood our perceptions.

There are also isolated sayings whose placement seems to be due to word-association (*qll* "curse" in vv 10 and 11; *nešer* "eagle" in vv 17 and 19) and thematic affinity. The theme of greed laces together otherwise independent sayings in vv 11–14, v 15a, vv 15b–16, and perhaps v 17.

For an attempt to find an inclusive structure in 30:11–33, see Steinmann *2001*. He believes that this unit is "a tightly organized and coherent unit" (p. 62) structured by the "intricate use of numbers" (p. 61)—indeed, extremely intricate, as he describes it. He divides the passage into seven subunits organized in a chiasm (A. vv 11–14; B. vv 15–16; C. vv 17–20; D. vv 21–23; C′. vv 24–28; B′. vv 29–31; A′. vv 32–33) and finds other patterns based on threes, fours, and sevens.

Aphorism a. Denouncing a Slave

30:10 Do not denounce a slave to his master,
lest he curse you and you be held guilty.

This couplet stands alone. It has no thematic connection with what precedes or follows, except for the word "curse" here and in v 11.

denounce [*talšen*]: Or "slander" (NRSV, and many others). The verb *hilšin* (in the H-stem here; in the D-related *poʿel* stem in Ps 101:5) means to say bad things about someone behind his back. Here it could mean lying about a slave or truthfully but maliciously divulging some misbehavior. The same verb (*tlšn*) is used to describe Anat's denunciation of Aqhat to El (CAT 1.17.vi.51). The preceding narrative shows that she is complaining, not lying, about his refusal to give her a bow she wants. According to Riyqam and Naḥmias, Prov 30:10 prohibits the betrayal of an escaped slave. This may indeed be the implication of "do not denounce" in the present verse.

The action indicated by *talšen*—whether slander, denunciation, or betrayal—is always wrong, regardless of who does it to whom. This admonition singles out the slave as victim because he is most defenseless. If you denounce him, his only recourse is to curse you for doing so. Apparently, however, this is deemed effective, for you will then be "held guilty" (*ʾšm*), that is, culpable before God, who will hear his cry and hold you responsible. Maltreatment of the orphan and widow, the poor, and others who cannot enforce their rights has the same consequence; see, for example, Exod 22:20–23, 26; Deut 15:9.

Deuteronomy, with a heightened humanitarianism, commands, "You shall not turn over to his master a slave who seeks refuge with you from his master" (23:16). Without denying that a slave is his master's possession, Deuteronomy recognizes the slave's natural and legitimate right to try to escape from slavery. Deuteronomy seems to realize that slavery is not a just institution, at least for fellow Israelites, even if it is a social fact. Prov 30:10 shows a similar sympathy: A slave's master may own him and have the legal right to punish him, but others should not be complicit in the master's enforcement of his power.

An Egyptian ostracon with sapiential content cites the following as a proverb: "Do not slander a man to his master or . . .[380] by your words, when his master is alive."[381] (The "master" can be an owner or a supervisor.)

Epigram i. The Wicked Generation

30:11 A generation that curses its father,
and does not bless its mother.
12 A generation that is pure in its own eyes
and is not cleansed of its filth.
13 A generation of arrogant eyes,
and whose eyelids are haughty.
14 A generation whose teeth are swords,
and its molars knives—
to devour the poor from off the earth,
and the indigent from among men.

Epigram i is a nonnumerical list whose cohesiveness comes from anaphora ("a generation"). On the assumption that the epigrams must all be numerical, G. Sauer adds an introduction to Prov 30:11–14: "Six things there are that the Lord hates, // seven his soul does loathe"; cf. Prov 6:16 (1963: 103). But there is no reason to insist that this epigram must be a numerical proverb, especially since the four generations are really a single group.

Epigram i is a series of complex noun phrases with no expressed predicate. The one-member sentence implies a predication of existence; in other words, "*There is* a generation that . . ." Nothing is said *about* this generation, for the description itself is enough to condemn it.

The epigram describes one generation, not four. It is corrupted by contempt of parents (v 11), self-righteousness (v 12), arrogance (v 13), and rapaciousness (v 14). By grouping these defects, the epigram teaches that one who despises his parents is also self-righteous and malevolent toward others, and so on. No one should, for example, fancy himself a benefactor to society while holding his own parents in contempt. Character is indivisible, and when someone sullies himself by one sin, he joins the society of the wicked and is contaminated by all their vices.

[380] A gap in the text.

[381] ODeM 1209 x+3–4. The non-royal male determinative with the second "master" indicates that the royal determinative in the first occurrence is an error, and that the saying applies to everyone.

By speaking of a "generation" rather than persons, the epigram also recognizes the "collective character" of sin (Van Leeuwen). Prov 6:12–15 lists the characteristics of the good-for-nothing (the man of Belial). Prov 16:27–30 is an epigram about three kinds of scoundrels, who are really one and the same. Much of the book of Proverbs is dedicated to describing evildoers and fools. What is unusual about the present epigram is that it profiles an entire generation. An entire generation (or, by another interpretation, a group within it) becomes infested by evil. We are not told the mechanism of infection. Perhaps it is that the wicked find support among corrupt members of the society, and they in turn make corruption profitable. When that happens, the contamination spreads to families and infects individual attitudes. Oppression of the poor becomes rife, and people's self-righteousness blinds them to the evil of their deeds.

generation [*dor*]: There is a biblical notion that certain generations, such as the generation of the Flood (Gen 6:5, 9), the generation of the tower of Babel (Gen 11:1–9), and the generation of the wandering in the desert (Deut 32:20), were distinguished by a certain failing. There can also be a righteous generation, one that seeks God (Ps 24:6; sim. 112:2, though the meaning of *dor* there is disputed; see below). A "generation" can be everyone alive at a certain time, or a certain age cohort within a particular time-span. English "generation" is used similarly, as when we speak of the generation of the sixties or "Generation X" and assume that they have certain collective attributes. This notion need not mean that everyone in a generation is wicked or righteous, but that the period as a whole is thus characterized. Since generations are not discrete, *dor* is often equivalent to "period." The "generation" described in this epigram is like the ones in which the wicked "arise" or "increase" (Prov 28:12b, 28a; 29:16). By another interpretation, *dor* means "group."

Dôr can also mean "assembly" or a group of some other sort, and recent translations often give it this sense (JPSV: "breed"; NRSV, blandly: "There are those who"; Clifford: "a sort"). NRSV's "There are those who" reduces the collective character of the evil to individual failings. The word means "assembly" or the like a few times in Ugaritic (e.g., CAT 1.15.iii.19) and Phoenician (Karatepe iii 19), with reference to the assembly of the gods. F. Neuberg *1950* assigns this meaning to *dôr* in Pss 14:5; 24:6; 49:20; 73:15; 84:11; 112:2; and Jer 2:31; see also P. Ackroyd *1968*. Some of the suggested passages are ambiguous, but this usage is clear in Ps 14:5, in which the *dôr ṣaddîq* is contrasted with (contemporary) evildoers. Translations like JPSV's and NRSV's are seemingly more logical, but the logic is not necessarily that of the Bible, which recognizes that a generation or age as a whole can be corrupt. Whether *dôr* means "generation" or "group," the epigram describes the depravity of a collectivity, not just individuals.

30:11. *curses*: He who curses his parents incurs the death penalty according to Exod 21:17 and brings a curse on himself according to Deut 27:16; sim. Prov 20:20b. Similar warnings are Prov 23:22 and 30:17. "Curse" (*qll*) means to insult and demean; see Brichto *1963*: chap. IV.

does not bless: This is a litotes meaning "curses"; see the Comment on 16:29.

30:12. *pure in its own eyes*: As Prov 20:9 says, no one can rightly claim to be pure. According to 16:2, to imagine oneself innocent is a universal delusion; see the Comment.

30:13. A *generation of arrogant eyes*: Lit., "A generation—how high its eyes!" "Generation" is a casus pendens. The following clause, surprisingly, is an exclamation: "how high . . . !"

and whose eyelids are haughty: Lit., "whose eyelids are raised." Lacking a true synonym for "eyes," the poet uses a word with approximately the same meaning. The intention is not that their eyes are wide open, but that they look upwards. This connotes arrogance, as in Prov 21:4 and Pss 18:28; 101:5; and 131:1. The notion that raised eyes are a symptom of haughtiness presumes a social practice of keeping one's eyes directed slightly downward as a sign of modesty, rather than walking with them raised and gazing directly at other people. Prov 6:12–13 lists various types of gesticulations and facial expressions that are thought to mark the scoundrel.

30:14. *whose teeth are swords* . . . : The people of this generation are as cruel and rapacious as wild beasts.

to devour the poor . . . : Standing outside the "generation" series, this couplet (v 14cd) is the climax of the listing. The apex of the generation's evils lies in pillaging and destroying the poor.

Aphorism b. The Epitome of Greed
30:15a The leech has two daughters: "Give!" "Give!"

This monostich differs sharply from the didactic couplets and epigrams typical of proverbs and has the character of a folk saying. It would work nicely, say, as a jibe about a woman and her daughters or about any greedy person. It serves here as a pivot verse between two epigrams. By its placement, Prov 30:15a tells us that the rapacious generation that devours the poor (v 14) is no better than a contemptible leech. It further connects this greed to the four insatiable forces in vv 15b–16.

Leeches, belonging to the genus *hirudinea*, have a sucker at each end. Since the word *ʿăluqah* is feminine, this leech is considered the mother. She has two daughters—twins, judging from their identical names and demands. The sentence can simultaneously be read in two ways: They are both named "Give," and they both say "Give!" The image of the leech and her daughters can be used of anyone who leeches off others, and it is a way of ridiculing and chastising a greedy person.

The leech's daughters are as greedy as she is—and that is her fitting punishment. Her daughters nag *her* by whining, as it were, "Gimme!" "Gimme!" Like mother, like daughter. The lesson is: Be careful what you are, because your children will be just like you!

This saying can be extended to other rapacious entities. The Talmud (*b. ʿAbodah Zarah* 17a) says: "What is meant by 'Give, give'? Mar Uqba said: It is the voice of the two daughters who cry from Gehenna calling to this world: 'Give, give!' And who are they? Heresy and the government." These "daughters" of human society call from the underworld because they are as deadly and voracious as Death itself.

leech [*ʿăluqah*]: According to Schneider (1961: 260–61), this is the horse-leech, found in the Mediterranean region. It is especially repulsive because it fixes itself inside the nostrils of animals as they drink in rivers and ponds.

daughters: These are the leech's two suckers. Schneider (ibid.) notes that the branches of a tree are called "daughters" in Gen 49:22 (though this is not certain). He regards the present saying as a riddle whose answer is that the leech's two daughters are its heads (p. 262). The leech, he says (expressing what is in fact an allegorical interpretation), represents the powerful oppressors of the poor, mentioned in Prov 30:14.

Epigram ii. Four Greedy Things

30:15b Three things there are that are insatiable,
four that do not say, "Enough!":
16 Sheol, and barrenness,
the earth, which is not sated with water,
and fire, which does not say, "Enough!"

These are the four great consumers. Sheol consumes people, earth consumes water, fire consumes combustibles, but what does barrenness consume? Not children, for they have escaped its demands by being born, and barrenness cannot be said to desire children the way that the earth "desires" water. Rather, barrenness, personified like the other devourers, craves *non-existence*. Even more hostile than Sheol, barrenness desires to preclude life before it begins.

A practical purpose is not evident in Epigram ii. It does not derive a lesson from these phenomena or use them as analogies to human behavior. Nor do the images rebuke greediness, for, unlike the leech, the items in this listing are not insignificant and disgusting and their desires are not demeaned by association with them. It would, however, be misleading to call the epigram "natural science," for it does not infer new knowledge by examination of natural phenomena or provide information about them beyond the obvious.

It would be more accurate to call this epigram a *meditation*. Taken as illustrations of universal qualities, the listing conveys an unexpected perception of the world. The world, even nature itself, is full of unappeasable desires. All around us and within us are voices nagging (in the words of v 15a) "Give! Give!" This voraciousness is not inherently wicked; it is just the way things are. Indeed, powerful desires are a dynamic force, without which the world would stagnate.

30:15b. *there are* [*hennah*]: See the Comment on Prov 6:16.

Enough! [*hon*]: Lit., "wealth!" The implication of this exclamation is, "This is wealth! I have plenty." The four great "consumers" never feel wealthy. Their "income" is boundless, but they always feel poor.

30:16. *Sheol*: Death's appetite is infinite. Death is an active power and not just a receptacle of the dead. This is vividly concretized in Mesopotamian mythology. In the Neo-Assyrian "Nergal and Ereshkigal," Ereshkigal, queen of the Underworld, is a grim nymphomaniac, desperately copulating with her consort Nergal without any satisfaction or hope of fertility and birth (see BTM 410–28).

barrenness: Barrenness (lit., "the closure of the womb") is treated not as an absence but, like Sheol, as an active force that desires and makes demands.

Some explain "barrenness of womb" as a trope for the barren woman (Clifford), who insatiably craves sexual intercourse (Rashi: *tašmiš*) because of her desperate yearning for children. Ehrlich is able to inform us that childless women have a greater sexual drive than mothers, "who during pregnancy and nursing scarcely experience it at all." With equal expertise, Delitzsch explains that the barren woman, not fearing pregnancy, "invites to her many men, and always burns anew with lust." There is no reason to think that the sexual urge is stronger in childless women than in mothers or, more important, that the author thought it was. But it does seem likely that, like Rashi, the author thought that a barren woman demands more intercourse out of desperation for children. The fact that barrenness itself, rather than "love" or "desire," is the insatiable power supports this explanation. Rachel's insistence that Jacob sleep with her (Gen 30:1, 16) comes to mind. This seems to be the case also in "Nergal and Ereshkigal," for Ereshkigal has never known joy and never will.

earth . . . : No matter how much water is poured on the earth, the ground absorbs it and can always take more. Or: the earth always needs more rain (Murphy).

Aphorism c. Contempt for Parents

30:17 An eye that mocks the father
and disdains obedience[a] to the mother—
the ravens of the creek will gouge it out,
and the young of the eagle will devour it.

[a] *lᵉyiqqᵉhat-* (MT, most MSS *lîqqăhat*).

Showing contempt for one's parents will be punished harshly. The gouging out of the eye matches the crime, for the eye is the organ of greed. That the punishment comes from wild animals suggests that nature itself feels revulsion for such a violation of decency.

eagle: Or "vulture." Hebrew *nešer* includes both eagles and vultures. It is translated "eagle" here to resonate with the same word in v 19, but here the scavenger rather than the predator is in mind.

The raven and vulture are scavengers. We are to picture them as eating the eyeballs of the dead and unburied sinner (Murphy). A proper burial was necessary for a comfortable existence in the underworld, and sons, especially the firstborn, were duty-bound to care for their parents' existence in Sheol.[382] To despise one's

[382] Our knowledge of mortuary practices in ancient Israel is derived largely from what is *prohibited* by the Law (particularly the Deuteronomic) and condemned by prophecy. These practices included offerings to the dead (Deut 26:14; Ps 106:28) and necromancy (Deut 18:11). On the "cult of the dead" in ancient Israel, see Lewis *1989*: esp. 177–81. We cannot know just what assumptions and attitudes the authors of Proverbs held in these matters, but proper burial was universally considered important.

source means to destroy one's future. This is the message of Prov 20:20: "He who curses his father or his mother—his lamp will be extinguished in deep darkness." See the Comment there and on 23:22.

According to Prov 27:20, the eye, as the organ of desire, is insatiable. In Prov 23:20–21, the son is admonished to avoid gluttony. Then follows the exhortation, "Listen to your father, who begot you, and be not contemptuous when your mother grows old" (23:22). This associative cluster—greedy eye, greedy son, offense to parents—could explain the placement of 30:17 after Epigram ii. The editor would have understood this proverb as another example of insatiability, but one that is provided with a proper threat. Epigram ii is bracketed between the aphorisms about selfish daughters and a nasty son, all of whom treat their parents contemptuously. This context underscores the grim selfishness of the forces listed in the epigram.

obedience: This is written as an anomalous *lîqqăhat* in the major MT manuscripts. We should vocalize *lᵉyiqqᵉhat-* as in Ehrfurtensis p.m.; cf. Baer *1880*: 52 (where, however, its originality is doubtful). This agrees with Gen 49:10, *yiqqᵉhat-*. Lit., "the obedience of." This is clearly the sense of the word in the latter verse, the only other occurrence. On the basis of an Arabic cognate, Winton Thomas (1941) emends to *lhqt* and derives it from an otherwise unknown *lᵉhîqāh* or *lᵉhāqāh*, from an otherwise unattested Heb *l-h-q* "white (of hair)." Though emendation to *zqnt* "old age" (Toy, BHS) makes sense, LXX's *gēras* "old age" is uncertain evidence because it was probably influenced by Prov 23:22b.

Epigram iii. Four Wondrous Ways—and One More

30:18 Three things there are too wondrous for me,
four I cannot comprehend:
19 the way of the eagle in the sky,
the way of a snake on a rock,
the way of a ship in the heart of the sea,
and the way of a man with a maid.
20 Such is the way of an adulterous woman.
She eats and wipes her mouth,
and says: "I have done no wrong."

This epigram should be interpreted first without v 20, which is a later addition written in a different spirit from the original list-proverb. (The person who added it may, however, be considered the author of 30:18–20 in its present form.) The wondrousness of the first three phenomena constitutes a premise from which the fourth is deduced by analogy (cf. Saʿadia). The fourth item, "the way of a man with a maid," is the epigram's culmination, and v 20 stands beyond that. Cohesiveness is enhanced by the fourfold repetition of *derek* "way."

The four wondrous things are clearly itemized, but it is left to the reader to discover what makes them amazing. The numerical part of the epigram (vv 18–19) may be an enigma of the sort mentioned in the Prologue (1:6). The quality shared by the first three ways, let alone the fourth and fifth, is disputed. Explanations include the following:

(1) *Mysteriousness of destinations*. An observer cannot determine where the

eagle, snake, and ship are heading, but they do have their destinations. Likewise it is a marvel that the course of the relationship of man and woman makes them one (Murphy). However, it is not particularly difficult to see where a snake is heading, or even a boat, unless at a distance. Also, the fact that they have destinations is not wondrous. Moreover, the "way" of a man's behavior with a maid does not necessarily "make them one."

(2) *Mystery of birth.* It is a wonder that sexual intercourse produces a new life (Ehrlich). But the other images describe a quality of the movement itself, not its outcome. And the mystery of birth lies not in the relations between the sexes but in the formation of the fetus in the womb (Ps 139:14–16 and esp. Qoh 11:5).

(3) *Mystery of sexual attraction.* It is remarkable that a man and a woman are mutually attracted. Clifford, strangely, believes that this attraction was "especially notable in ancient Near Eastern society, where boys and girls were raised separately." Or, the first three "ways" are suggestive of the "mystery of sexuality" (McKane). But sexual attraction is so conspicuous (even outside the ancient Near East!) as to seem natural and self-evident, not mysterious. In any case, the first three ways are not examples of attraction and are poor analogies to mutual attraction.

(4) *Sublimity.* The first three ways are elegant and graceful movements; compare the interest in excellent gaits in Epigram vi (30:29–31). Likewise, love is beautiful, a joy to behold. Toy understands the "ways" to be things that excite the admiration. (And indeed, a snake can be remarkably quick.) Van Leeuwen says that the poem "sings implicit praise to God for the glories of creation, especially for sexual love."

This is the way I have often read the passage—as a lyrical and romantic evocation of the wonder of love. But perhaps this common denominator is too subjective, residing in the individual reader's feelings about the phenomena. Is a snake's slithering really sublime? In any case, the image shows no trace of hymnic exultation in God's creation.

(5) *Lack of a trace.* The very earliest interpreters and the great majority of later ones, medieval and modern, follow this interpretation. The four "ways" or movements do not leave a trace and one does not know where they went (Rashi, Riyqam). The earliest interpreter of 30:18–19, namely, the editor who added v 20 (see below), understood vv 18–19 to allude to tracelessness. The adulteress wipes away the evidence (though not the moral stain) of her sexual transgression. Another early interpreter was the author of the Wisdom of Solomon. Elaborating on vv 18–20, he describes human transience by the images of a shadow, a quick messenger, a ship, a flying bird, and an arrow (Wis 5:9–12).

If tracelessness is the point of the analogies, the "way of a man with a maid" must mean that a man can have sex with an unmarried girl and leave no one the wiser (assuming that she does not become pregnant). This observation cannot be a celebration of sexuality, for tracelessness is irrelevant to conjugal sex. Anyway, marital intercourse would be expressed as *derek ʾiš bᵉʾišto*, "the way of a man with his wife."

What, then, would be the purpose of observing that sex does not leave tracks?

Saʿadia believes that it is to condemn fornication. However, the other "ways" do not have bad effects and an admonitory tone is absent. If the point is that having sex does not leave evidence of the deed, the author of the numerical epigram—without v 20—is actually chuckling in a conniving tone at the man who seduces a girl and gets off the hook. In this case, the passage was originally a ribald ditty. Though the first three images seem rather lofty for that purpose, the incongruity of the beautiful and the bawdy could be meant as humorous. The original poem was not wisdom until the author-editor appropriated it for a moralistic purpose by adding v 20. As for what he did with it, see below on v 20.

30:19d. *way of a man*: This is usually understood as a euphemism for sexual intercourse (Saʿadia, Riyqam, and most); see interpretation 5 (above). It is not an allusion to courtship and love, which do leave a "trace"—marriage.

maid [*ʿalmah*]: An *ʿalmah* is a young woman, married or not. However, the epigram speaks of an unmarried one. The terms *geber* ("man") and *ʿalmah* ("maid") are not equivalent in status. A *geber* is a mature, robust man, whereas *ʿalmah* is closer to "girl." The scope of *ʿalmah* includes young women but also younger girls, such as Moses's unmarried sister (Exod 2:8). In Cant 6:8, the "countless" *ʿălamot* are on a rank lower than the royal concubines and queens. (Concubinage was a contracted, legal status.) The *ʿălamot* in Cant 6:8 are the young servant girls living in the palace. Though an *ʿalmah* could be of a higher status than theirs, the term has a tone of condescension when used of women beyond adolescence. The translation, "the way of a man with a maid" is suggestive of this asymmetry.

with a maid [*b^eʿalmah*]: The preposition *b^e*- is ambiguous. It is usually the equivalent of English "in" or "into" in a spatial sense, or "by," "with" in an instrumental sense. In v 19ac, the preposition means "in." If it means "in" or "into" in v 19d (hence, "the way of a man in [or "into"!] a maid"), then "in a maid" is a transparent allusion to sexual intercourse, one that is ribald, if not lewd, in its physiological specificity. Then, in addition to tracelessness, the shared quality of the "ways" would be smoothness and slipperiness. Somewhat more delicately, this preposition can indicate accompaniment and be translated "with," as in Gen 32:11; Num 20:20; Josh 22:8; and Judg 11:34. This use of *b^e*- usually occurs with verbs of movement. It would imply that the man is doing something accompanied by the girl. In either case, the phrasing does not describe the activity from the standpoint of mutuality, which would call for the preposition *ʿim* "with."

Despite the possible ambiguity, it is very likely that the man's deed in Prov 30:19d is sex with a girl, a maidservant perhaps, rather than courtship. This act would not be adultery (which means violating another man's marriage), but it would be licentious and "wondrous" only facetiously, perhaps in the sense of "surprising." (*Nipla'ot* refers to amazingly *bad* deeds in Dan 8:24 and 11:36.) Non-adulterous licentiousness behavior is little discussed in Wisdom Literature. Ben Sira says, "Give not yourself to a woman to have her trample on your dignity" (9:2; see Skehan and Di Lella, p. 218). Ben Sira warns against adultery but also against intercourse with prostitutes, virgins, and singers (9:1–9), who are examples of unmarried women with whom a man might have sex. The rabbis forbade this as *z^enut* "fornication." Rabban Gamaliel warned that amassing slave-girls increases *zimmah* "lewdness"; see the Comment on Prov 29:3. Such licentiousness is not considered nearly as heinous as adultery. Comparable behavior by or with a married woman would be adultery.

30:20. *the way of an adulterous woman*: This verse stands outside the series of four ways and departs from its pattern of syntax (Haran 1972: 261–62). The verse is certainly an addition to the original epigram and is thus the first interpretation of v 19.

The author of v 20 must understand the fourth "way" to be fornication because he *compares* to it the "way" of the adulteress. Unlike the "way" in v 19, the "way" in v 20 is not the specific act of intercourse but the entirety of the adulteress's behavior: having sex, then denying her deed. Her behavior is made all the worse by her smugness and impudence. Like the earlier ways, this one leaves no visible traces. She enjoys the sex, thinking that she can wipe away her sin as if brushing crumbs off her face. The author does not tell us that she cannot escape the consequences, but lets the piggishness of the behavior speak for itself.

eats: Eating and drinking are allusions to sexual pleasures in Cant 5:1 and Prov 5:19. Further, as Clifford notes, "mouth" is sometimes a euphemism for vagina in rabbinic usage (*b. Sanh.* 100a; *b. Menaḥ.* 98a; *b. Ketub.* 65.13–23). One cannot be certain about hidden meanings in matters of sexual allusion, but given the unmistakable meaning of "eats" in v 20, the phrase "wipes her mouth" at least allows one to suspect that something vulgar is intended. This would be a deliberately crude jibe aimed at the adulteress. The tone recalls Ezekiel's rhetorical obscenity in Ezek 16:25; 23:8, 20, and Ben Sira's use of "quiver" as a deliberately crude term for vagina (Sir 26:12).

As a metaphor, the adulteress's wiping crumbs off her face exposes the way she trivializes her offense and blithely denies wrongdoing. This calls to mind the hypocrisy of the man who robs his parents and says, "No wrong was done" (Prov 28:24).

Epigram iv. Four Things That Shake the Earth

30:21 Under three things the earth quakes,
under four it cannot stand:
22 under a slave, when he becomes king,
and a scoundrel, when he has his fill of bread;
23 under a hateful woman, when she gains mastery,[a]
and a maidservant, when she disinherits her mistress.

[a] *tibʿāl* (MT *tibbāʿēl*).

Four things, the author believes, violate the right order so severely that the earth itself shudders in revulsion or dismay. The violation might be very localized—as in the cases of the scoundrel, the hateful woman, and the maidservant—but the offense is actually to the world order as a whole, and the earth itself reacts. Perhaps we are to understand this reaction as simply "emotional," a vivid way of saying that the offense is shocking, but perhaps we are to think in terms of an earthshaking event, with disastrous consequences spreading far and wide. The fourth case, that of the maidservant, is probably meant to be the most shocking, even though it at first seems to be the most private and limited disruption.

The events described belong to the "world-turned-upside-down" topos described by Van Leeuwen 1986b and discussed in the Comment on 19:10. Van Leeuwen believes that Epigram iv inculcates a royalist hierarchical ethic. But though such an ethic certainly existed, it could, contrary to Van Leeuwen, motivate only v 22a, and even that line is not inculcating a royalist ethic so much as assuming it. If, as suggested below, the "scoundrel" is a wayward slave, the epigram as a whole is really a warning to keep order in one's household.

The sages were socially conservative. They approved of the existing order and were committed to its preservation, demanding only that it be maintained with justice and that people (especially the king) treat others fairly and help the unfortunate. As Van Leeuwen observes (1986b: 603), Epigram iv is concerned not with types of individuals but with inverted social relations. Taken as a whole, the inversions describe significant social disturbance.

McKane and Toy think that the epigram is humorous and hyperbolic. After all, a scoundrel who has his fill of food does not really endanger society. What the author finds offensive, according to McKane, is the arrogance and insufferability of the people who rise to higher station. But, granted that the earth's shaking is certainly an hyperbole, the dismay expressed is quite serious. When the "world-turned-upside-down" topos is used humorously, it pokes fun at the higher orders, which is not the case here. Sometimes the reversals are an occasion for exultation, as when they are thought to demonstrate God's power (as in 1 Sam 2:4–8). But in the present epigram, the social dislocations are a grave matter, at least to the author, for the disinheriting of an older wife is no joke. Deuteronomic law forbids it (Deut 21:15–17). When a slave becomes king, the disruption is felt right down the social ladder. When a scoundrel is sated, public morale is undermined. In a well-ordered society, satisfaction rightly belongs to the diligent (Prov 20:13; 28:19). That the satiety of the scoundrel was not taken lightly is shown by the complaint in the Egyptian "prophecy" of Neferti, which describes the land in chaos. Among other things, Neferti declares:

> I will show you the master in mourning, the outsider content.
> He who does nothing fills for himself,
> while he who does act is empty.
>
> * * *
>
> I will show you the land in distress.
> The weak has become the possessor of an arm,
> one who was greeted now gives the greeting (first).
>
> * * *
>
> I show you the undermost uppermost,
>
> * * *
>
> The wretched will make wealth,
> The great [will rob] (merely) to exist.

It is the poor who will eat bread,
the slaves who will be exalted.
(selected from §§X–XIII [cf. AEL 1.142–43])

It is not that a beggar getting rich is inherently *bad*. Rather, it is distressing because it is a symptom of social upheaval.

30:21. *the earth quakes* [*rag*ᵉ*zah*]: The verb means both "to quake" and "to be angry." It designates a variety of emotions, including anger (e.g., Gen 45:24), agitation (2 Sam 7:10; 19:1), and, most often, fear (Exod 15:14; Deut 2:25). The earth and its mountains shake when God is angry (1 Sam 14:15; 2 Sam 22:8; Isa 5:25), as do the heavens themselves (Isa 13:13).

According to Saʿadia (sim. Ramaq, Hameʾiri), *ʾereṣ* ("earth," "land") here refers to its inhabitants. Examples of this usage are Gen 11:1; 1 Kgs 2:2; Ps 33:8; and Qoh 1:4. "The inhabitants of the earth" are said to "shake" (*rgz*) in Joel 2:1aβ, while the *earth* is said to "shake" in Joel 2:10a. In the present verse, the "quaking"—whether of the physical earth or humanity—is metaphoric and hyperbolic, since people do not literally shake when the social order is violated. They can, however, shudder.

cannot stand: Lit., "cannot bear / hold up under." This has the same connotations of disgust and intolerability as the English idiom "can't stand" something, but it can also be construed as being unable to bear up under a physical weight. This suggests, hyperbolically, that the earth could collapse under these violations of order.

30:22. *a slave* [*ʿebed*]: Even if a slave is clever, he is believed to be unfit by nature and position to rule over others. As Prov 19:10 says, "Luxury is unsuitable for a dolt. How much the more so for a slave to rule over princes!" The sages' attitude toward slaves is described in the Comment on 19:10. Qohelet, however unconventional in other regards, shares the conservatism of the other sages about social position and is distressed to see "slaves on horses and princes walking on the ground like slaves" (10:7b).

when he becomes king [*ki yimlok*]: In this and parallel phrases, "when" can be translated "if." The verb *mlk* means to become king or to rule *as* king (*melek*). It is nowhere used of holding authority of a lower rank. (A different verb, *mšl*, is used in Prov 19:10a, which speaks of a slave "ruling" over princes.) It is unclear which cases, if any, the author has in mind in the present verse. It does not speak of an official or courtier of high rank becoming king, which could happen through a coup d'état. Though even the highest royal officials could be called *ʿabdey hammelek* "servants [or "slaves"] of the king" (e.g., 1 Sam 22:17; 2 Sam 15:15; 1 Kgs 1:47), the word *ʿebed* "slave," without further specification, does not refer to them.

What, then, is meant by a slave becoming king? Three possibilities come to mind:

(1) A slave becoming king may be mentioned as the extreme case of disruption of social hierarchy and is placed first to epitomize the category of which these events are examples and to show their absurdity and offensiveness.

(2) A slave may become the power behind the throne and act as king. This

could happen when a strong-willed and cunning slave serves a weak ruler. If so, "king" is meant ironically.

(3) "Becomes king" may be hyperbolic and facetious, a way of making a slave's holding *any* power look offensive. The LXX understands this to mean that the slave deposes his master; see the Textual Note. A slave may be said to be playing the king if he comes into a position of authority or simply is allowed to lord it over others in the household. Joseph's brothers express their contempt of his dreams by asking, "Will you really be king [*mlk*] over us? Will you really rule [*mšl*] over us?" (Gen 37:8). The brothers are not using "be king" literally, because their tribe cannot be a kingdom, and indeed, when the dream comes to pass, Joseph does *not* rule as king. The brothers exaggerate Joseph's fantasies to mock them as preposterous.

scoundrel: On the *nabal* see the Comment on 17:7. Standing parallel to "slave," "scoundrel" here may allude to a particular kind of *nabal*, namely, a disobedient slave. Such a one should be punished by deprivation of food, his only wage (compare Prov 19:10a). Note how Neferti too (above) juxtaposes the eating of bread with slaves being exalted.

30:23. *hateful* [*śᵉnuʾah* (fem.)]: Or "hated." JPSV: "loathsome." Gen 29:32–33 and Deut 21:15–17 speak of two wives of one man, one of them beloved, the other "hated." Translations often tone this down to "unloved" (JPSV in Genesis and Deuteronomy; NRSV here). It is hard to determine the intensity of the emotion intended, but *śnʾ* usually refers to real hatred, and that sense is applicable in the above-mentioned passages. The word indicates that Jacob felt real hostility toward Leah, who was imposed on him by a ruse. This makes her story all the more poignant. In Deut 21:15–17, the law is probably stating the extreme case: Even if a man downright *hates* his first wife, he must not deprive her sons of their due.

Though "hate" can be used in legal documents as a term for divorce, divorce is not relevant to the passages cited above or to the present one. There would be nothing disturbing in the remarriage of a divorced woman. The law forbids only a woman's remarriage to a former husband after having married another (Deut 24:1–4).

gains mastery [*tibʿāl*]: MT's *tibbāʿēl* (passive) is usually translated "get married." The passive does have that sense in the Bible (e.g., Gen 20:3; Deut 22:22; Isa 62:4), and the active can mean "to marry" (e.g., Deut 24:1; Isa 26:13; 62:5). In Rabbinic Hebrew, *bʿl* means "have intercourse." But what is so bad about a "hateful" (or "hated") woman being married or having intercourse, except to the man who marries her? Many commentators think that this refers to an unattractive woman finding a husband, but what would anyone care about how another man's wife looked? The crisis is rather when an obnoxious woman gains authority in her household.

Saʿadia glosses *tibbāʿēl* as "gain authority," "have power over" (Arabic *raʾusat*). The verb in the N-stem (as in MT) would not have this sense, but with a change of vocalization to *tibʿāl* (G-stem), it would mean "gain authority," "rule" (Van Leeuwen 1986b: 602, ref. van der Ploeg 1952: 103). The verb *b-ʿ-l* (G-stem) means "to rule" in Isa 26:13; Jer 3:14; and 31:32, though, as DCH (2.237) says, this meaning cannot always be fully distinguished from the word's other sense—"marry," "take as sexual partner." This ambiguity may be at play in the present verse: The hateful woman plays the husband's role and lords it over the household.[383] There is a strong parallel in the Babylonian "Counsels of Wisdom":

> You must not make a slave-girl important in your house,
> She must not rule your bedroom like a wife.
>
> * * *
>
> Let your people have this to tell you:
> "The household that a slave-girl rules, she will break up."
>
> (ll. 66–67, 70–71; trans. BTM 329)

"Rule(s)" in this passage is Akkadian *i-be-el,* the exact counterpart of Hebrew *tibʿal.* By this reading, what the sage in Proverbs finds so grating is the thought of a hated woman, presumably disliked for her faults, taking control of a household. Rather, the beloved, virtuous woman should be *baʿălat habbayit* "mistress of the household" (to use a phrase from 1 Kgs 17:17). The way that a worthy woman rules her household—alongside her husband, though subject to him—is described in Prov 31:10–31.

disinherits [*tiyraš*] *her mistress*: This maidservant is the counterpart of the slave mentioned in v 22a. *Tiyraš* does not only mean that the maid "succeeds" (NRSV) or "supplants" (JPSV) her mistress. The verb *yaraš* means to dispossess someone, usurp another's inheritance (*yᵉruššah*). This violates a wife's marital rights, specifically her right to the portion of her husband's estate that her sons should receive. This offense is committed against the woman, not the man. This is a rare instance in the Bible in which gain or loss is assessed according to the woman's interests. The right situation is described by Ben Sira (22:4a), who inverts the present verse: "An intelligent woman [lit., "daughter"] will inherent from her husband."

According to Deut 21:15–17, a man was obliged to give his firstborn two shares. The firstborn takes the first share (the *reʾšit*), then all sons, including the firstborn, divide the remainder by lot (DNF). The Deuteronomic law refers to the case when there are only two sons, so the firstborn gets two shares and the other receives one share. The law does not forbid the reallocation of an inheritance in all circumstances, but rather prohibits favoritism based on a man's feelings toward his wives (Westbrook *1991*: 20). An example of reallocation that would not violate Deuteronomy's law is Jacob's depriving Reuben of the right of primogeniture because of a sexual offense (Gen 35:22; 49:3–4; 1 Chr 5:1).

The rights of slave-wives are not defined in Pentateuchal law, but they too could expect a certain share of the estate. Sarah is worried that the son of her slave-girl will share her own son's inheritance (Gen 21:10). Jephthah's half-brothers banish him, the son of a prostitute, lest he share in the inheritance (Judg 11:2). The rights of the sons of slave-wives are not specified in the Law and would have depended

[383] The ambiguity also occurs in Jer 3:14 because the verb is used in an extended metaphor of God marrying/ruling Israel.

on prior contractual agreement and the husband's goodwill. In a document from Nuzi, a man assigns his elder son a double portion and says that the younger son shall take "according to his share." After detailing the property to be allocated, he says, "Of the [sons of the] slave-girls, each one shall take according to his share" (Westbrook *1991*: 19).

Favoritism toward a lower-ranking wife or concubine is the disturbance envisaged in Prov 30:23b. A man might take a fancy to a slave-girl and take her sexually and perhaps marry her. This he was allowed to do, but it would be wrong for him to then displace his first wife from her rightful claim to his wealth.

The same ethic is held by the Egyptian Djefai-hapi, who boasts in his autobiography: "I hav[e] done what people love and gods praise; I have judged between two to their contentment, . . . [I did not let] a servant woman be valued above her mistress" (trans. Lichtheim 1992: 38).

C. Fontaine observes that this text and others, including those quoted above, attribute to slave-women a certain wisdom: the awareness of their inferior status and the "innate intelligence and the drive to improve their lot—sure signs of a pragmatic wisdom, even if one which operates at the end of the social continuum of status!" (*2002*: 50). Since slave-women were sexually accessible to their masters in any case, if one succeeded in displacing her mistress, she must have been employing cunning beyond sexual allures to gain her goals. The same action that so shocks the author of this epigram, the slave-woman's displacing her mistress, reveals the slave-woman, who stands at the very bottom of the social hierarchy, as an *agent*, a person capable of actively pursuing her own designs. *Of course* the sage's world shudders.

Epigram v. Four Creatures Small but Wise

30:24 Four things there are, among the smallest on earth,
yet they are wise and skilled:
25 The ants are a people not strong,
but they ready their bread in the summer.
26 The badgers are a people not numerous,
but they make their home in the rock.
27 The locusts have no king,
but they all go forth in file.
28 The spider can be caught[a] in the hands,
but it is in the palaces of kings.

---

[a] *tittāpēś* (MT *t[e]tappēś*).

Though these four creatures are small and seem to be weak, they overcome their vulnerability by cunning: the ants by preparing their provisions in advance of need; the badgers by living in the inaccessible crevices of cliffs; the locusts by attacking in disciplined formations; the spider by living in palaces.

This listing is not simply descriptive—"a bit of natural history" (Toy). It gives little zoological information. Rather, like Prov 6:6–11 and LXX 6:8a–c, this epigram offers a set of animal exemplars for human behavior, though it does not explicitly draw the moral. Its purpose is to praise wisdom. It also shows that looks can be deceptive and that a small body can hold much wisdom. On the use of nature analogies, see Vol. I, 218.

30:24. *wise and skilled* [*ḥăkamim m*ᵉ*ḥukkamim*]: Lit., "wise (things) that are taught [or "erudite"]." Saʿadia (elaborated by Naḥmias) explains this phrase to mean "stamped with the wisdom of nature." Or, we might say, "instructed by instinct." How much the more so, Saʿadia concludes, should humans, who can learn by the intellect, do what is wise!

*ḥăkāmîm m*ᵉ*ḥukkāmîm*: *Ḥ-k-m* in the D-stem means "teach" in Pss 105:22; 119:98; Job 35:11; and Sir 6:37 (and often in RH, Syriac, and Jewish Aramaic). The Dp-stem (used here) means "skilled" or "learned." A snake charmer, whose competence is a learned skill, is called *m*ᵉ*ḥukkām* in Ps 58:6. Some, following the LXX, emend the second word, unnecessarily, to *mēḥăkāmîm* and translate as a superlative, "wisest of the wise" (e.g., McKane, HALOT 314a). However, the article would be expected in the second word if it were a superlative. The proposed emendation seems to be prompted by the overly literalistic assumption that animals cannot be taught; but see Hos 10:11.

30:25. Prov 6:8 uses the same language in observing that ants store up food for the winter. Prov 30:25b ≈ 6:8a.

30:26. Ps 104, surveying God's provision for all his creatures, observes that "rocks are a shelter for badgers" (v 18b).

30:27. Though leaderless (like the ant in 6:7), locusts seem to march in a military formation. An invasion of locusts is described as a military invasion in Joel 2:1–11, where they are called "a mighty people, arranged for war" (v 5).

in file [*ḥoṣeṣ*]: Lit., "dividing" (intransitive). They organize themselves by separating into formations that seem like military marching columns, as described in Joel 2:8.

30:28. *spider* [*ś*ᵉ*mamit*]: The identity of this creature is uncertain.

*ś*ᵉ*māmît*: This is usually translated "gecko," based on LXX *kalabōtēs* and Vul *stilio*. Other identifications are the ape (thus Ramaq, on the grounds that the animal in question can grasp with its hands), the swallow (Saʿadia), and the spider (Ralbag). The last is supported by RH *smmyt*, which means "spider" in *b. Šabb.* 16b and *Midr. Ps.* (Buber) 18:5 (and parallels). These passages use a different spelling and are not directly based on this verse.

be caught [*tittāpēś*]: MT's *t*ᵉ*tappēś* (D-stem) means "you can grasp" or "she can grasp," but *t-p-ś* D is not used elsewhere in BH. In RH, *tippēs* (D) means "climbs," but this is probably based on an interpretation of this verse (*Gen. Rab.* §66). We should point the verb as an N-stem (BHS).

in the palaces of kings [lit., "king"]: Rather than being an act of prudent self-preservation like the other examples, this behavior exemplifies either cleverness (the spider's ability to go wherever it wants) or the benefit its cleverness brings it (living in luxury). In line with the latter, Naḥmias deduces from the analogy that, even if one is lowly, if he works hard and intelligently, he can rise to high rank. Tur-Sinai (p. 53) explains that the spider lives in its web *as if it were* a royal palace. Tending against this intriguing idea, though not decisively, is the fact that "palaces" is in the plural, whereas the singular would probably be used in reference to the spider's own web.

Epigram vi. Four Creatures with a Stately Gait

30:29 Three things there are that are excellent of stride,
four excellent of walk.
30 The lion is mightiest of beasts,
and he retreats from nothing.
31 The cock (girded) of loins or the he-goat,
and the king, whom none can withstand[a].

---

[a] *ʾal-qôm* (MT Oc *ʾalqûm*, Or *ʾal-qûm*).

These four creatures walk in an excellent fashion. The quality of their stride, which is not explicit in the Hebrew phrase, is almost always understood to be aesthetic: they are "stately of stride" and "carry themselves well" (JPSV; sim. most). Saʿadia identifies the definitive trait not as "the beauty of the walk" but as "the honesty of their behavior and their success." Judging from the statement about the lion, however, the creatures' excellence lies in their pride and confidence. The lion walks proudly and fearlessly. This is true of the rooster (if that is what the *zarzir* is) and the he-goat, both of whom strut about and clash with other males, and it is true of the king as well. The king is the climax of the list and its true topic. His will cannot be resisted (Prov 16:10, 14; 19:12; 20:2, 8; 24:21). Unfortunately, 30:31 is obscure, so all interpretations of the epigram are tentative.

30:29. *excellent of stride . . . excellent of walk*: Lit., "that make (their) stride good . . . that make (their) walk good."

30:30. *retreats from nothing*: This phrase signifies fearlessness, as in Job 39:22. Lion and king are associated in Prov 19:12 and 20:2 and elsewhere.

30:31. *The cock* [*zarzir motnayim*]: The identity of this animal ("the *zarzir* of loins") is something of a guess. The ancient versions identify it as the rooster. The rooster (the modern *Gallus domesticus*, at least) has a white body with reddish legs, and his coloring sets off his flanks as though they were girded for battle. The Rabbis understood the *zarzir* to be a fighting cock: "It is the way of the world that one seeks to aid his *zarzir*, and another his *zarzir*, to obtain victory" (*y. Roš Haš.* §3; see also *Midr. Lam.* 5:1). The identification is still problematic, however, because another source assigns the *zarzir* to the same genus as the raven, which is unclean (*Gen. Rab.* §65), whereas the domesticated rooster is clean. Other identifications are the greyhound (LXX^{V}; Riyqam), the eagle (Saʿadia), and the warhorse (Gesenius).

zarzîr motnayim: In a thorough survey of the older explanations of this phrase, Delitzsch observes that *motnayim* is not a descriptive attribute but part of the proper name of the animal, lit., the "*zarzîr* of loins." Delitzsch accepts the identification with the greyhound. Syr *zarzîrāʾ* and Arab *zurzūr* mean "sparrow," but the sparrow is neither stately of walk nor aggressive. For *mtnym ʾw* Plöger proposes reading *mitnaśśēʾ* "wenn er [der Hahn] sich erhebt (?)"; sim. Clifford.

or [*ʾo*] *the he-goat*: The conjunction *ʾo*—"or" instead of "and"—is peculiar, unless "he-goat" is meant to define the *zarzir motnayim*. In that case, there are only three items in the list. In rare cases, the listing in a graded numerical saying corresponds to the first number (e.g., Ps 62:12; see Haran 1972: 253–56).

the king, whom none can withstand: Lit. (perhaps), "the king—let there not be standing with him!" That is, let no one dare to stand with (= against) him in strife or competition. This is the best-available explanation of a text that is almost certainly corrupt. Rashi: "No one stands with him." Ramaq: "No one arises to fight with him." Vulgate: "a king who cannot be resisted." *B. Sanh.* 82b identifies "a king with whom one cannot stand" as God.

ʾal-qôm: MT *ʾlqwm* should be divided as *ʾal-qûm* with Orientalis (thus in several MSS K-R; cf. Vul), but vocalized *ʾal-qôm* (inf. abs.). Syntactically, *ʾal* + *qôm* (inf. abs.) is equivalent to *ʾal* + noun, which means "let there not be X" (2 Sam 1:21; Isa 62:6; Ps 83:2; cf. Prov 31:4). The negative jussive here has asseverative force. (For the syntagm *ʾal* + noun in this sense, see GBH §114h.). The jussive attached to the final noun in the series gives it a dramatic flourish. As in the present verse, *qûm* + *ʿim* means "stand up against" in Ps 94:16, lit., "Who will stand for me against [*yāqûm lî ʿim*] evildoers? Who will stand for me against [*yityaṣṣēb lî ʿim*] the doers of iniquity?"

Other proposals have been offered, all tentatively: (1)Translating *ʾlqwm* as "the summons," based on Arabic *âlqawm* "the summons," that is, the call to arms, the *Heerbann* (Delitzsch). (2) Emending to either (a) *qm ʾl ʿmw* "he stood before his people" (McKane), or (b) *ʾl qdm ʿmw* "to the front of his people" (Murphy), or (c) *ûmelek lōʾ qāmû ʿimmô* "et le roi auprès de qui personne ne se dresse" ("and the king, next to whom no one can stand," i.e., resist) (Barucq).

Epigram vii. Churning Up Quarrels

30:32 If in arrogance you have acted vilely,
or if you have schemed, put your hand on your mouth!
33 For the churning of milk produces curds,
and the churning of the nose produces blood,
and the churning of anger produces strife.

If you have behaved like a scoundrel or have sneaky intentions, shut your mouth and say no more, before you get a bloody nose! Arrogance leads to strife (Prov 13:10; 17:19; 29:8). The scoundrel crafts trouble and foments conflict (6:14), and "the lips of the dolt come into strife, and his mouth calls for blows" (18:6).

As surely as churning milk produces curds, and churning the nose makes it bleed, so does "churning" anger (by persisting in insolence, pressing one's demands, nursing old grudges, or the like) incite conflict. In other words, "The start of strife is (like) releasing water, so before a quarrel breaks out, leave off!" (17:14).

The words *ʾap* ("nose" and "anger") and *ʾappayim* ("anger" and "nostrils") play on each other (see below), and the wordplay connects "blood" with "strife." This calls to mind fistfights and bloody noses.

In form, v 33 is a sorites or chain-syllogism. Clifford observes that the syntax resembles that of 6:1–3: If you have done such and such, then do such and such. Even closer is the Syriac Ahiqar:

My son, do not remain in the house of those who quarrel;
because from a word there comes a quarrel,

and from a quarrel vexation is stirred up,
and from vexation comes murder. (S_1 8)

Lichtheim (1983: 16) observes that Anchsheshonq 22.21–25 is dependent on this passage in Ahiqar. From this we may deduce that (1) though the Syriac version is much later, it goes back (via the Greek) to an Aramaic version available also to the author of Anchsheshonq; (2) that version differed from the Elephantine Ahiqar; and (3) the above quoted passage is not simply a rewriting of Prov 30:32–33 but has its own antiquity. See also the Comment on 22:3 and the quotation from the Arabic Ahiqar there.

30:32. *acted vilely* [*nabalta*]: That is, acted like a *nabal*, on whom see Prov 17:7. Arrogance (lit., "exalting oneself") provokes quarrels; see 22:10.

put your hand on your mouth!: Lit., "hand to mouth!"; in other words, Shut up! (Judg 18:19).

30:33. *churning* [*miṣ*, an infinitive absolute of *m-y-ṣ*]: Thus Held *1985*. The "churning" of the nose would be a mauling in a fistfight. The word can also mean "squeezing" or "pressing" (Judg 6:38). In Prov 30:33b this would suggest emotional pressure on an already angry man.

nose [*'ap*], *anger* [*'appayim*]: *'ap* means both "nose" and "anger." The dual *'appayim* by itself means "anger" only here and in Dan 11:20. The wordplay is double: Churning the *'ap* (nose/anger) produces blood, just as "churning" the *'appayim* (anger/nostrils) produces a quarrel, and so the antagonism cycles on. There is a further pun in that *ḥem'āh* "curds" sounds like *ḥēmāh* "wrath" (Clifford).

PART VIC: 31:1–9

THE TEACHING OF LEMUEL'S MOTHER

31:1 The words of Lemuel, king of Massa,
whom his mother instructed:
2 No, my son,
no, son of my womb,
no, son of my vows—
3 Do not give your strength to women,
nor your ways to the destroyers[a] of kings.
4 Not for kings, Lemuel,
not for kings is the drinking of wine,
nor[b] for governors beer.
5 Lest he drink and forget the statute,
and alter the verdict of any of the poor.
6 Give beer to him who is perishing,
and wine to the bitter of soul,
7 that he may drink and forget his poverty,
and think no more of his toil.

8 **Open your mouth for the dumb,**
for the judgment of all who are about to expire.
9 **Open your mouth, give righteous judgment,**
give justice to the poor and needy.

---

[a] *lᵉmōḥôt* (MT *lamḥôt*). [b] *ʾî* (MT qeré *ʾēy*; ketiv *ʾw*).

This poem is a royal instruction, like the Egyptian books Djedefhar, Amenemhet, and Merikare, and, perhaps, the Babylonian "Advice to a Prince" (BTM 760–62). (The audience of the latter, however, is not specified.)

This is the only ancient Near Eastern Wisdom text attributed to a woman, though Proverbs elsewhere credits the substance of a teaching to the mother as well as the father (1:8; 6:20; 31:26; and probably 23:22), as do some Egyptian instructions. (See "Mothers as Teachers," Vol. I, 82–83.) To the references there, we can add the intriguing reference to the teachings, written and oral, of the Egyptian woman Renpet-nefret, quoted below in Part VId; see below "Genre and Purpose."

Both Parts VIc and Vd (31:10–31) refer to a wise mother. The present unit is spoken by a wise woman and warns against (bad?) women; the next praises a good one. This one is the teaching of a woman; the next speaks of a woman opening "her mouth in wisdom" and praises her "teaching of kindness" (31:26). These associations probably were one reason for the juxtaposition of the "Woman of Strength" and the present unit.

Structure. M. Lichtenstein (1982) and V. Hurowitz (*2001b*) try to establish the unity of the entire chapter 31 on the basis of certain thematic and verbal chiasms running through the two units. Hurowitz affirms and extends Lichtenstein's claims.

Hurowitz (p. 216) sees three superimposed structures in chapter 31:

I. Thematic	A Mother rebukes son	A′ Sons praise mother	
	B Women C Wine // C′ Wine B′ Women		
	A 1–2		A′ 28–29
	B 3a + 3b C 4 + 5 // C′ 6–9	B′ 10–19	+ 20–31
II. Chiasm 31	2———9	xxxxxx	// 20–31
III. Chiasm Woman of Valor	xxxxxx	10–19	// 20–31

The chapter, he says, is given cohesion by "a partially interlocking and partially overlapping pair of chiastic word chains," namely, vv 1–9 // 20–31 and 10–19 // 20–31 (p. 215). The pattern is even more intricate, since *within* vv 10–31 there is an envelope structure: the description of the woman in vv 12–27 is framed by vv 11 + 28–31, which speak of or address other people (p. 212). *In addition,* and without regard to the envelope structure, the unit consisting of vv 10–19 is chiastically paired with vv 20–31 at the same time it is chiastically paired with vv 1–9. (Several verses do not come into play; see ibid., p. 215.)

In my view, the pattern is too intricate to be absorbed by the reader and to be rhetorically effective. The intricacies of the overlapping and clashing designs as well as the severe imbalances in a supposedly symmetrical structure (Section A, with one verse, is matched by A′, with 22 verses) obscure whatever rhetorical impact the design might have.

Language. The passage has some apparent Aramaisms: *bar* "son" (v 2—3x) and the plural *-yn* in *mlkyn* "kings" (v 3), though vocalized according to Hebrew morphology (*mᵉlākîn*) rather than Aramaic (*malkîn*). These forms may, however, be only ostensibly Aramaic. Plurals in *-yn* are also used in Moabite, as is *br* "son." Given that Lemuel is from Massa, in a region not distant from Moab, the apparent Aramaisms in this text may be characteristic of a dialect close to that of the Deir-ʿAlla and Mesha inscriptions. S. Kaufman (*1988*: 54) observes the affinities of Prov 31:1–9 as well as the Balaam oracles in Numbers with the dialect of Deir-ʿAlla. That dialect, according to J. Huehnergard (*1991*: esp. 292), is a Northwest Semitic dialect that is neither Aramaic or Canaanite, but derives its features from the common ancestral stock. "Aramaisms" in the present discussion should be understood to refer to "Aramaic-like" features.

31:1. *The words of Lemuel*: These are Lemuel's words in the sense that he had received them from his mother and then spoke them in his own teaching. This is similar to the usage in *Pirqey ʾAbot* 4:24: "Samuel the Younger used to say . . ." Then follows a citation of his favorite saying, Prov 24:17–18.

Lemuel: This king is otherwise unknown. Traditional commentators identified Lemuel with Solomon.

lᵉmûʾēl [v 1], *lᵉmôʾēl* [v 4]: Jirku (*1954*: 151) explains the name as meaning "Lim is God," after a deity *possibly* known in Mari personal names, for example, Zimri-Lim. The older explanation, that Lemuel means "to God" (Rashi, Hameʾiri, etc.), is more likely. The expected vocalization would be *lᵉmôʾēl* (v 4), which means "belonging to [*lᵉmô*] God" or (originally) "belonging to El." This is identical in structure and meaning to the name Lael (Num 3:24).

Massa: A North Arabian people (Gen 25:14 and 1 Chr 1:30). See the Comment on 30:1b.

instructed [*yissᵉrattu*]: This verb means "teach *musar*," "give disciplinary instruction."

The MT, by placing the major disjunctive on "king," would have us translate, "The words of Lemuel, king. An oracle [*maśśaʾ*] which his mother taught him." The syntagm implied by the accents—*lmwʾl mlk*—runs counter to Hebrew usage. "Lemuel, king," that is, "King Lemuel," would require either *lᵉmûʾēl hammelek* or *hammelek lᵉmûʾēl*. (Ugaritic does allow for "PN *mlk*"; e.g., *nqmd.mlk* "King Niqmaddu." Aramaic would have *lmwʾl mlkʾ*, which would be Hebraized as *lmwʾl hmlk*.) Also problematic is that the MT segmentation implies a Heb idiom *yissēr maśśāʾ* "to instruct an oracle," whereas elsewhere *yissēr* takes the recipient of the instruction as its dir. obj. The antecedent of *ʾăšer* must be Lemuel, not "words" or "oracle."

F. Deist supports the translation, "The words of Lemuel, the king of Massa, whose mother instructed him" (1978: 3). The teaching is supposedly *Lemuel's* words to his son, and the phrase "whose mother instructed him" describes Lemuel, not the teaching. The phrase "son of my womb [*biṭnî*]" (v 2), by this interpretation, is spoken by Lemuel and means "my own son"; compare the use of *beṭen* to designate the male's source of reproduction in Deut 28:53; Ps 132:11; and Mic 6:7. But what would be the point of adding the biographical detail that Lemuel's mother instructed him, then not citing her teachings? Furthermore, Lemuel's son is not mentioned.

31:2. *No . . . no . . . no . . .* : Hebrew *mah* basically and usually means "what?," but translating "What, my son?" would make it sound as if Lemuel just said something that his mother didn't quite catch. *Mah* occasionally functions as a negative (GBH §144*h*). A rhetorical question such as "What is our portion?" is equivalent to a negative, "We have no portion"; compare 1 Kgs 12:16 (*mah // loʾ*) and 2 Sam 20:1 (*ʾeyn // loʾ*). See also Job 16:6 (*loʾ // mah*) and Cant 8:4.

In the present verse, the repeated *mah* is proleptic, held in suspense and completed only in v 3. This heightens the intensity of the admonition. (In v 3, a different negative particle is used, *ʾal.*) The intensity of the repeated proleptic negatives, together with the exceptional focus on filiation—"my son" three times—suggests that Lemuel's mother is doing more than offering advice in the abstract. Other sages address the son in formulaic fashion with no particular urgency. The tone of urgency here gives the impression that Lemuel has already done wrong and his mother is imploring him to cease. A reproachful note is heard also in the verb *yisser* "instruct" (v 1), which connotes discipline, rebuke, and even punishment.

Saʿadia says that Solomon's mother (Bat Sheba) is "complaining" against him. Rashi, retelling a midrash found in various forms (*b. San* 70b, *Num. Rab.* 10.14, *Mid. Prov.*, and elsewhere), explains that these words are an oracle from God chastising Solomon for disobedience. At the time when Solomon married Pharaoh's daughter, which was also the day of the dedication of the Temple, he celebrated all night and slept late the next day—with the keys to the Temple under his pillow! Then his mother came and castigated him. (According to one version, she had him bound to a post for a whipping.) Thereupon he confessed his folly in the words of Prov 30:2. Such anecdotes are a way of fleshing out the attitudes and relationships that the text conveys to the commentator.

mah: Toy thinks that this is elliptical for "What shall I say to you?," but this expansion is arbitrary. McKane and Plöger (ref. E. Ben Yehuda) equate *mah* with Arabic *ma* "listen"; but that is otherwise unknown in Hebrew. Clifford explains *mah* here as elliptical for *mah lᵉkā* "What is it with you?," implying a rebuke. He compares Isa 3:15: "What is it with you that you crush my people . . . ?" But the additional *lākem* is crucial to that idiom, because that is what points to the offending individuals.

my son, son of my womb, son of my vows: Lemuel's mother conveys just how precious he is to her and how close she feels to him. He came from her body, and he came in response to her vows. This fact, as well as the plural of "vows," implies that the conception did not come easily and that his birth was a special gift from God. (Compare Hannah's vow in 1 Sam 1:11.) Now, it seems, he is going astray. Saʿadia sees a reverse progression in the vocatives: from the living son she raised, back to the mother's pregnancy, back to her vows before he was conceived. She thereby reminds him of the toil and pain she has borne on his behalf, pressuring him to give her the attention she deserves.

bar biṭnî: The idiom "son of my womb" is in this case literally applicable, but its point is to emphasize Lemuel's closeness to his mother. Ahiqar (139 [1.1.139]) addresses his adopted son as "son of my womb" when he wants to emphasize the young man's closeness to him (and hence the gravity of his treachery).

31:3. *strength* [*ḥayil*]: This can refer to strength of any sort, including sexual vigor and wealth.

your ways [*dᵉrakeyka*]: "Way" (sg. and pl.) here, as often, means behavior (cf. Jer 10:2; Prov 29:27; 30:20, and elsewhere; see also "Paths through Life" in Vol. I, 128–31). The kind of behavior in question can be sexual. This is clear in Jer 3:13bα, "And you scattered your ways to strangers, under every leafy tree";

cf. Prov 30:19d and Gen 19:31. "Your ways" here can be a euphemism for coitus (Ehrlich) or, more likely, sexual virility, parallel to "your strength." This makes excellent sense in a warning against improper involvement with women.

dᵉrākeykā ["your ways"]: This is commonly understood to mean "dominion" or the like, on the basis of Ugaritic *drkt* "dominion," where it parallels *mlk* "reign" (CAT 1.2 iv 10; 1.14 i 42; 1.16 vi 38) and *ksth* "his throne" (CAT 1.2 iv 13). By something of a semantic stretch, Heb *drk* is supposed to mean "strength" (Murphy) or "vigor" (JPSV; Clifford). None of the verses adduced for this sense in the HB (Jer 3:13; Hos 10:13; Ps 138:5 [HALOT 232b]) are unambiguous, and the plural argues against that use in the present verse. (HALOT simply emends to sg.) Two suggested emendations are *yrkyk* "your loins" (McKane, BHS; see Sir 47:19, though that uses a different word) and *dwdyk* "lovemaking" (Plöger, ref. Dyserinck). Both readings are meaningful, but change is unnecessary.

the destroyers [*lᵉmoḥot*, fem. pl.] *of kings*: This phrase restricts the parallel, "women," to a certain type of woman. The clause does not mean that all women are king-destroyers ("women, who destroy kings"), but warns against women of the sort who destroy kings ("women who destroy kings").

those who destroy [*lᵉmōḥôt*]: As revocalized, the word means "to those [fem.] who destroy kings" (thus Delitzsch, Toy, BHS, and many). MT's enigmatic *lamḥôt* may be intended as an H inf. from *m-ḥ-h*, with elision of the *h* (Riyqam), but the root is not used elsewhere in the H-stem. Ehrlich emends to Aram *lᵉlaḥănôt* "to the concubines of" (Dan 5:2, 3, 23), but the graphic difference is considerable. Lipiński (1973) associates this word with Akkadian *maḫḫūtu/muḫḫūtu* "female ecstatic." But, besides the fact that the word is not used in West Semitic languages, a warning against prophetesses would be out of place in an admonition against dissolution.

kings [*mᵉlākîn*]: Ibn Janaḥ (*Sefer Hashorashim*), Riyqam, and some others take this as an Aramaism for "advice," but "to smite advice" is not meaningful.

31:4. Lemuel's mother implores him to shun wine and beer. Prov 31:4 is formulated as an absolute prohibition, though absolute abstinence is probably not intended. Though drunkenness is condemned in Proverbs and elsewhere (see the Comment on 23:29–35), drinking wine and beer is not. They were a staple of diet and were used at festive meals, which were called *mištaʾim* (= RH *mištaʾot*], lit., "drinking-occasions." Certainly royal banquets included wine.

Egyptian school letters, purportedly written by father to schoolboy son and chastising him for neglecting his studies, warned against alcohol and sexual dissoluteness. For example: "Beer makes (one) cease being a man. . . . If only you knew that wine is an abomination, you would renounce pomegranate and not set the beer-jug in your heart. You would forget wine" (LEM 47.7, 12–13). The father goes on to describe the youth sprawling drunk in the dirt in a whorehouse. A similar letter declares: "Beer undoes a man" (LEM 88.6–8). It is immoderation in drink that is condemned.

ʾal: The negative jussive particle can negate a noun and is equivalent to *ʾal yᵉhî* X "let there not be X" (2 Sam 1:21; Isa 62:6; Ps 83:2). On the irregular inf. const. *šᵉtô* (like *qᵉnōh* in Prov 16:16a) see GKC §75*n*.

nor: The negative comes from vocalizing the consonants of the qeré *ʾy* as *ʾî*. The ketiv is *ʾw* ("or"), which is impossible in the middle of the clause. The qeré is *ʾēy* ("where?"), which does not make good sense. Hameʾiri understands "where is beer?" as a question that should *not* be asked by rulers; sim.

Delitzsch. Tsumura (1978) argues that *ʾy* should be vocalized *ʾay* and construed as a vetitive particle, as in Akkadian. Carrying the force of *šᵉtô* into the second line, he translates: "for rulers (let there be) no (drinking of) strong drink." But the Heb evidence for this usage is nil. Winton Thomas (1962) emends to *rᵉʾô*, supposedly a by-form of *rᵉwô* "drink deeply." G. R. Driver (1951: 194–95) emends to *ʾawwô*, a D inf. from *ʾ-w-h* "desire," or, alternatively, *ʾēw*, an Aramaizing noun like *rēaʿ* and *gēw*. This noun, however, is not attested. We should vocalize *ʾî*. This particle negates nouns in 1 Sam 4:21 (in a name); Job 22:30; Lachish Ost. 2.6 (*ʾy dbr* = "no thing"); and also in Phoenician. Radaq explains the present occurrence of *ʾy* as a negative (*Sefer Hashorashim*, *ʾê*). Prov 31:4b thus means, lit., "and for governors (let there be) not-beer," that is, "no beer."

31:5. The legendary Sumerian sage Shuruppak admonishes his son, "When you are drunk, do not judge!" (Shuruppak l. 131; Alster 1974 ad loc.).

he drink, etc.: The verbs in v 5 are singular, referring to any individual among the persons mentioned in v 4.

and forget the statute [*wᵉyiškaḥ mᵉḥuqqaq*]: S. Paul (1979: 235) explains *mᵉḥuqqaq* as "that which is written," referring to the record of the verdict. Elsewhere in the Hebrew Bible, however, *ḥqq* in a legal context designates legislation and law. The worry in this verse is that the ruler, in his capacity as judge, may forget the law and render a faulty verdict. The next line indicates a different consequence of drunkenness.

alter the verdict [*wiyšanneh din*]: This phrase is unique in the Hebrew Bible but has an exact Akkadian equivalent: *dīnam enû / šunnû*, meaning "to revoke, alter, change a verdict" (Paul 1979: 232–35). The offense envisioned is prohibited in Codex Hammurapi §5: "If a judge renders a verdict, gives a decision, deposits a sealed tablet, but later alters his verdict, they shall prove that judge of having altered the verdict he has given" (trans. Paul, p. 233). If found guilty, the judge is consequently severely fined and dismissed from his position.

31:6–7. Whereas a ruler should avoid alcohol so that he *not* forget the law, the poor should be given wine *so that* they forget their misery. Alcohol is here commended as an anodyne to dull the pain of him who is embittered and declining to death. Such a one does not have royal responsibilities that require alertness. Though the speaker demands that her son execute justice, she seems to assume that poverty and misery are inalterable facts of life, for she does not demand that he fight them as a social malady but only that he alleviate the pain they cause individuals.

Give: Unlike the other imperatives, this one is in the plural, suggesting that v 6 is a traditional saying that Lemuel's mother quotes.

beer, wine: Wine is elsewhere praised as making the heart happy: "wine, which cheers the heart of man" (Ps 104:15a; sim. Judg 9:13a; Qoh 10:19a; Sir 31:36 [34:28]). The Hellenistic Egyptian book of Phibis recognizes the medicinal value of wine: "(God) created remedies to end illness, wine to end affliction" (32.12; trans. AEL 3.210). 1 Esd 3:18–24 describes wine's *strength* (not necessarily its virtue). Its main power is causing forgetfulness, for better *and* worse. Among other things, "It changes every mind to cheer and happiness, and it does not remember any grief or debt" (v 20). But it also leads the mind astray and causes quarreling (vv 18, 22). (Parallels noted by Crenshaw 1988: 17–18.)

31:8–9. Do not open your mouth for drinking wine (implied in vv 4–5). Open it instead on behalf of the helpless and wretched! Since other kinds of physical handicaps are not mentioned, "dumb" stands for all who lack an effective voice in obtaining justice: the widow, the orphan, the alien resident, and the poor, who are deprived of political and social power. Saʿadia identifies the dumb man more narrowly as a defendant who does not understand his own arguments. He observes that in capital cases, at least, the judge must help him present his case.

who are about to expire [*bᵉney ḥălop*]: Lit., "sons of passing away." This could mean all mortals (see the use of *ḥlp* in Ps 90:5–6; Job 9:26), in which case the phrase would be extending the range of the king's beneficiaries from the dumb to everyone. But since Prov 31:9 continues to focus on the poor, the phrase is best understood as equivalent to *ʾobed* "him who is perishing" (v 6a). These are people on the verge of death, whether from starvation or from persecution. Compare the phrase *bᵉney mawet*, lit., "sons of death," which means those who are in immediate danger of death (1 Sam 20:31; 26:16; 2 Sam 12:5).

who are about to expire [*bᵉnê ḥălôp*]: Toy emends to *bᵉnê ḥŏlî* "(sons of) illness," treating the final *peh* as a dittog. But the MT construction is clear (inf. const. as genitive; GKC §114*b*).

give righteous judgment: On *špṭ* "judge," "give justice to," see the Comment on 29:14.

give justice [*din*]: Verse 9 defines "open your mouth for" (v 8) as to speak on their behalf in court, to ensure that they receive justice.

THE MESSAGE OF LEMUEL'S MOTHER

Lemuel's mother presses him to avoid (or stop) dissipating his strength on wine and women (vv 3–5). Instead, he should give wine to the poor to ease their pain (vv 6–7). As king, he must ensure justice for the poor (vv 8–9). More precisely, she urges him to avoid dissipation *so that* he can rule justly. This recalls the way that Prov 1:3 does not demand the virtues of righteousness, justice, and rectitude, but instead *promises* them as a reward for wisdom. For a profile of the king's duties in terms similar to this poem, see Ps 72:1–4. Justice was the duty of the king throughout the ancient Near East (Weinfeld 1995: 45–56). For an overview of issues and a different interpretation of this poem see Crenshaw 1988.

PART VID: PROVERBS 31:10–31

THE WOMAN OF STRENGTH

31:10 A woman of strength, who can find?
Her price is greater than rubies.
11 Her husband's heart trusts in her,
and he does not lack for gain.

12 She repays him with good, not evil
all the days of her life.
13 She seeks out wool and flax,
and she works with willing hands.
14 Like merchant ships
she brings her bread from afar.
15 She rises while it is still night,
and gives food to her household,
and a portion to her maids.
16 She plans a field and buys it,
from the fruit of her hands she plants a vineyard.
17 She girds her loins with power,
and gives strength to her arms.
18 She realizes that her wares are good.
Her lamp does not go out at night.
19 She stretches out her hands to the spindle,
and her palms grasp the spinning-rod.
20 She opens her palm to the poor,
and stretches out her hands to the needy.
21 She does not fear for her household because of snow,
for all her household are dressed in scarlet.
22 She makes herself coverings;
linen and purple is her raiment.
23 Her husband is known in the gates,
when he sits with the elders of the land.
24 She makes fine linen and vends it,
and sells loincloths to the trader.
25 Strength and majesty are her raiment,
and she laughs at future days.
26 She opens her mouth in wisdom,
and the teaching of kindness is on her tongue.
27 She looks to the ways of her household,
and eats not the bread of idleness.
28 Her sons arise and laud her;
her husband (arises and) praises her:
29 "Many daughters have done noble things,
but you have surpassed them all."
30 Comeliness is deceit and beauty a vapor,
but a woman who fears the Lord—*she* will be praised.
31 Give her of the fruit of her hands,
and let her deeds praise her in the gates.

The book of Proverbs is devoted to cultivating wise *men*. Throughout it addresses men's concerns (such as avoiding promiscuous women), and the wise people it describes are almost all men. Now it concludes by describing a wise woman, but this too is a man's concern. The poem praises her capabilities in bringing income into the home, caring for her household, showing charity to the poor, speaking wisdom and kindness, and living in fear of God.

She is a proud and splendid lady, mistress of a prosperous manor in the vicinity of a city, in charge of many of her household's commercial activities. Contrary to a common modern stereotype of ancient women, this one has considerable independence in interacting with outsiders and conducting her business, and she can even purchase real estate. She serves her home, but her home is her base of operations in communal life (W. Brown 1996: 48). She brings her husband prestige as he sits in the city gates, participating in the commercial, personal, and civic business that went on there.

The poem has no strict comprehensive structure, but it does cohere. First of all, it is structured as an acrostic, with each couplet starting with a letter of the Hebrew alphabet in sequence. Saʿadia suggests that the acrostic is meant as a memory aid "for those who have to use it often," though it is unclear why this poem would require memorization, especially since the acrostic would work only for a literate audience. The alphabet connotes totality, since it encompasses all possible words (DNF).

The poem also has a degree of organization by perspective: "[T]he poem moves from a view of the woman as being the center and source of activity concerned for others to another view which regards her as the center and object of praise of others" (T. McCreesh 1985: 36). We may add that the poem begins with a declaration of her value to others. There is a logical flow from her value to her achievements to the praise these bring her. The words *ḥayil* (translated "strength" in v 10 and "noble things" in v 29) and *baʿlahh* ("her husband"; vv 11, 28) occur in adjacent verses at the beginning of the poem and again in two couplets near the end of the poem (vv 28, 29). They do not form a precise inclusio, because vv 28b and 29a are not at the poem's end (which is definitively marked by the final letter of the acrostic). Still, the words do point back to the beginning of the poem and have somewhat of a bracketing effect.

Is there further structuring, such as proposed by Lichtenstein (1982) and Hurowitz (*2001b*)? (See the introduction to Prov 31:1–9.) McCreesh asks, "Was the poet looking for the kind of order that we find lacking?" (1985: 35). But perhaps "we"—contemporary scholars, that is—are expecting a kind of order that is indeed lacking. C. Yoder aptly compares the poem to an impressionistic painting. "Viewed up close, the individual brush strokes seem scattered and haphazard, but from only a step or two away, dots and splatters merge to become the cumulative portrait of a woman" (*2000*: 75–76).

Discussion of the poem's setting and teachings follows the Comments. For a survey of the history of interpretation from late antiquity on, see Wolters *2001*: 59–154. The following notes will interact especially with C. R. Yoder's comprehensive study of this unit, *Wisdom as a Woman of Substance, 2000* (henceforth "Yoder").

In the LXX, 31:10–31 follows 29:27.

31:10. *who can find?*: Similar rhetorical questions in Prov 30:4 call for the answer "No one!" (see the Comment there), and that is the expected response here. This response is a hyperbole, an exclamation of awe at the cherished woman's worth. It does not mean that such a woman does not exist (as Qohelet 7:28 asserts) or even that she is a statistical rarity—one in a thousand, say (as he concedes for men in the same verse). Nor does "a trustworthy man, who can find?" (Prov 20:6b) deny the existence of such a one. If the present verse were saying that a woman like this is extraordinarily rare, its effect would only be to discourage young men from seeking one. Such a woman may not be easy to come by (in the author's view), but the main implication of "rare" is that she is *precious*.

Hausmann (1992: 262) insists that the rhetorical question is a strict denial of possibility: No man can find such a woman, nor can any woman come to resemble her. Hence she cannot be a "concrete" (i.e., real) woman. But this construes the rhetorical question too rigidly. If the point were that no human can be a woman of strength (despite Prov 12:4a), the poem would merely be a put-down of real women and "[the poet's] word would be pointless" (Saʿadia). Anyway, someone *did* find her (vv 11, 23, 28). It does not help to say that she is "a symbolic representation of personified wisdom" (Hausmann, ibid.; see "Modern Allegorical Interpretations" after the Comments). In that case, the rhetorical question, construed strictly, would mean (contrary to 3:13 and 8:35) that wisdom can *not* be found, a claim that would render the book of Proverbs useless.

strength [*ḥayil*]: This is commonly translated "valor," and the poem is usually called "the Woman of Valor." But the qualities listed here do not include courage of the sort usually called valorous. *Ḥayil* means strength, whether in wealth, physical power, military might, practical competencies, or character; see the Comment on 12:4. The last two strengths are praised here, but others also come into the portrait. Terms with military connotations are used—*šalal* ("gain" but usually "booty"; v 11b) and "girds her loins with power" (v 17a). There are also implications of physical strength in the statement that she "gives strength to her arms" (v 17b) and certainly in her indefatigable energy—note especially the length of her work day (vv 15a, 18b). Even wealth is relevant, not because she brings it to the marriage as a dowry but because she produces material goods and shares them. Her primary strength is in character, because even her practical competencies are not simply technical skills but manifestations of her focus, selflessness, and determination.

Her price [*mikrahh*]: She is precious beyond compare. If this makes her sound like a commodity, it should be noted that a wife did have a price, namely, the *mohar* "bride-price," paid to the bride's father or the woman herself upon betrothal. But is that what is intended here?

Yoder understands "price" as the actual bride-price (pp. 51–58; 77–78). The "Woman of Substance" (as Yoder renders *ʾešet ḥayil*) is "*expensive to attain* (*mṣʾ*)" (pp. 77–78; emphasis in original). Yoder illustrates these marriage negotiations from marriage contracts of Persian-period Elephantine. The groom would agree to pay a *mohar*, while the bride would bring a dowry with her. If she were of "high price," her dowry would be sizable. Such a bride was thus a good investment because her husband could draw on this sum, though legally it remained her property and would have to be restored to her upon divorce or given to her sons in inheritance.

It must be noted, however, that the *mohar* was not (in the extant sources) burdensome, and to say that a Woman of Strength was *literally* more expensive than rubies would have been a meaningless exaggeration. The *mohar* was in effect a short-term investment, since it was typically added to the dowry, to which the husband had access. The *mohar* was, as Yoder says, a legal formality (p. 49, n. 50).

The bride-prices at Elephantine were typically added to the bride's dowry. They ran from zero for a slave-woman (whose dowry was 22 shekels), to five shekels for an older widow (whose dowry was 60½ shekels), to ten shekels for a virgin freewoman (whose dowry was 68⅛ shekels); see Yoder, p. 49. By way of comparison, a wool garment cost between seven and twelve shekels, and an average-sized house could be bought for thirteen shekels (Yoder, p. 49, n. 48).

While Yoder illustrates these arrangements from Achaemenid period Elephantine documents, the basic procedures probably pertained in Israel and Judea as well, and not only in Achaemenid times. In fact, traditional Jewish marriage contracts have maintained the same basic components throughout the centuries, with the groom promising the woman a sum of money, called a *kᵉtûbbāh* (rather than a *mōhar*). Until recently (and even now, in some communities), a woman would bring a dowry, subject to conditions similar to those evidenced in the Elephantine contracts.

Westbrook too frames the issue as one of economics, but he identifies the woman's "price" not as the bride-price but as the dowry (*1991*: 147). The poem teaches that an industrious wife is worth *more*, in mercenary terms, than one with a big dowry (ibid.). However, although the poet would certainly agree with this proposition, he does not draw this comparison. A *meker* is a "price," the cost to the purchaser. In the case of marriage this could only be the *mohar*, the "bride-price," not the dowry.

The "price," then, in Prov 31:10 is indeed a bride-price, but a figurative one. The poet can hardly be saying that an expensive wife is hard to find, or that the price of a costly bride is greater than rubies. If a particular bride is expensive (which would mean that she comes from a wealthy family), that would not make her precious in the values that the poem promotes. There is no virtue in costing a lot. The point is rather that the Woman of Strength is truly priceless: Money cannot buy her; she is off the scale of monetary value. This does not mean that she is impossible to obtain—after all, she *is* married—but it is not money that gets her. What gets her is presumably good judgment, which is what the poem tries to inculcate in the male reader. Likewise of wisdom it is said, "Beaten gold cannot be paid for it, nor silver weighed out as its price" (Job 28:15). According to Job 28, no precious stones or metals can equal wisdom's value. It must be attained by other means, namely, by the fear of the Lord and avoidance of sin (v 28). Just as "wisdom is better than rubies; no valuables can match it" (Prov 8:11; sim. 3:15)—and only a fool would imagine he could *purchase* it (17:16)—so is the wise woman beyond monetary value. Yet both she and wisdom *are* obtainable.

greater than [*raḥoq mi-*]: Lit., "more distant," thus harder to attain and more valuable.

31:11. *trusts in her*: It is *because* her husband trusts her and allows her to go about her business freely that he does not lack for gain. But his trust need not be restricted to practical matters, for her virtues go beyond the economic (vv 12, 20, 25, 26, 27a, 30b). The next verse says that he can rely on her to treat him well in all regards. The importance of trust in Prov 31:10–31 and elsewhere is discussed below in "The Value of the Woman of Strength," after the Comments on this poem.

In Prov 31:11a, the assonance of /b/, /l/, and consonantal /h/ (transcribed "hh") is striking: ***baṭaḥ bahh leb baʿlahh.***

gain [*šalal*]: *Šalal* usually means booty taken in war or theft. Here it is used in an extended sense to mean "a great find"—"booty" in quotation marks, as it were (sim. Ps 119:162: "I rejoice at your word like one who finds great *šalal*"). In Prov 31:11, *šalal* is used to indicate that the woman's husband gains wealth without working for it. His own earnings would not be called *šalal*. (This is not to say that he does *not* work. If he were not diligent, he would not be wise and hence would not be worthy of the reward of such a wife. But his efforts are not what the poem is speaking about.) At the same time, the word is used so often to mean "booty" that martial overtones cling to it, which "suggests the woman is like a warrior bringing home booty from her victories" (Van Leeuwen).

31:12. *She repays him* [*gᵉmalathu*] *with good*: She requites his trust well. This must refer not only to her financial contributions but to the entirety of her life with him, because the poem describes many virtues beyond the financial. The verb *gml* means to treat another in response to that person's past actions. This treatment may be good or bad, and it is not necessarily deserved or appropriate (see Joel 4:4; 1 Sam 24:18). Hence *gml* is not exactly "recompense," but a response to a prior deed, in this case, her husband's choosing her as wife.

31:13. Not only does she do the weaving, she actively seeks the necessary materials and gives herself to the task with zest.

with willing hands [*bᵉḥepeṣ kappeyha*]: Lit., "with the willingness of her hands." *Ḥepeṣ* also means "delight," and we could translate, "with the delight of her hands." Ramaq infers that "It is as if her hands desired to work." This is the opposite of 21:25a, "for [the sluggard's] hands refuse to work."

Ḥēpeṣ can also mean "matter" or "business," whatever one wants to do. This allows Yoder to translate, "the business of her hands," but for that, *ḥēpeṣ* would have to be a direct object (*wattaʿaś ḥēpeṣ*), as in 1 Kgs 5:22, 23; Isa 58:13, rather than a prepositional phrase (*wattaʿaś bᵉḥēpeṣ*), as here.

31:14. *Like merchant ships she brings*: Lit., "She is like merchant ships. She brings her food from afar." Her activities outside the household are again in view.

The verse does not imply that she is herself engaged in international trade. The comparison is not between the woman and a ship (as the plural "ships" shows), but rather between the distance from which she brings provisions and the extent of the trade of merchant ships. Hence I translate, "Like merchant ships she brings . . ." While most of the food for her family would be produced on its estate, she may purchase some nonperishables from foreign traders (such as the "Canaanite" mentioned in v 24).

bread: For consistency, I translate *leḥem* as "bread," but, like the English word, it often refers to food in general. It is clearly not baked bread in Prov 27:27. Here too it refers to other foodstuffs, for actual bread would not travel well.

31:15. *food* [*ṭerep*]: In eighteen of its twenty-two occurrences, *ṭerep* means "prey" or, figuratively, robbed or plundered goods (e.g., Gen 49:9; Ezek 22:25). It is used in the extended sense of "food" here and in Mal 3:10; Ps 111:5; Job 24:5. Also, the denominative *hiṭrip* means "give food" (with *ḥoq* "portion" as its object) in Prov 30:8. Still, the word's predominant meaning, "prey," "plunder," gives it overtones of aggression and pugnacity, as if to hint that the Woman of Strength is something of a lioness in providing for her young. *Šalal* "gain," "booty," is used with similar connotations in 31:11b.

Prov 27:23–27, addressed to men, commends animal husbandry as providing goat's milk for "the food of your household, and provisions for your maidservants" (v 27). Both that passage and this regard provision of food to the household (i.e., the family) and (even) the maidservants as basic duties of a householder. Here, the wife carries it into action.

portion [*ḥoq*]: Since *ḥoq* usually means "law," this verse is usually understood as referring to the orders the mistress gives her maidservants. However, to "give a *ḥoq*" is not used of individuals giving verbal orders. *Ḥoq* means "portion" in 30:8; see the Comment there. Malbim explains *ḥoq* as "a fixed allocation" (*ḥoq qiṣbah*); sim. Delitzsch, Van Leeuwen, Yoder (p. 86). Malbim draws a distinction between the woman's servants, who receive a fixed portion, and her family ("household"), who receive food without a fixed limit.[384]

her maids: A multiplicity of maidservants (slaves or hirelings) indicates wealth.

31:16. *plans* [*zam^{e}mah*]: She deliberates the purchase of a field, then carries it out. *Z-m-m* (verb and noun) refers to private thoughts (see Vol. I, 34). The implication is that she independently initiates the undertaking and sees it through. She is able to make plans, an ability much esteemed in Proverbs (2:11; 5:2; 12:15; 20:5; etc.).

buys it: The verb *lqḥ* (usually "take" or "acquire") often means "buy" in Rabbinic Hebrew, but the usage goes back to Late Biblical Hebrew (Neh 5:2).

from the fruit of her hands: She does not necessarily perform the physical labor herself, other than the spinning. Rather, she uses her earnings to buy a field and have it planted; thus Ramaq, who compares "And Solomon built the Temple" (1 Kgs 6:14), meaning that he "caused it to be built by his wisdom." She is diligent, a quality often praised in men (Prov 10:4; 12:24; 13:4; 21:5; and elsewhere).

31:17. *girds her loins . . . gives strength*: She demonstrates physical strength by vast stamina. She *makes* herself strong, "even if it was not in her nature to work so hard" (thus Hame'iri, referring to her innate physical strength). Girding the loins, that is, tucking in one's tunic into a belt in preparation for battle, can connote preparation for strenuous activity. Indeed, both the phrases in this verse have con-

[384] Malbim's approach is to insist on distinctions between parallel lines, at least in nuance if not in substance. Sometimes his distinctions are forced, but his basic sensitivity to differences of nuance in synonymous parallelism was effectively supported by J. Kugel (1981: esp. 287–92). The distinction Malbim draws here seems to the point.

notations of military readiness suggestive of the woman's intensity and tenacity in pursuit of her goals. M. T. Novick (forthcoming) argues that "*watt*ᵉ'*ammeṣ* (translated above as "gives strength) to her arms" means that she tucks in her sleeves so that they will not encumber her in her work. It seems to me that both senses are in play: She prepares her garments for work and (psychologically) makes her arms ready for her task.

31:18. *She realizes* [*ṭaʿămah*]: Lit., "tastes." She *knows* that her wares are good. She is not a dull-minded workhorse. She can savor her achievements.

Her lamp does not go out at night: This is a hyperbole meaning that she works well into the night. The chore most feasible during the early hours of darkness would be spinning, mentioned in the next verse.

31:19. *hands, palms*: Strictly speaking, *yad* ("hand") includes both the forearm and hand, while *kap* ("palm") is the hand below the wrist, as the earliest forms of the letters *yod* and *kaph* show (DNF).

spindle [*kiyšor*], *spinning-rod* [*pelek*]: The *kiyšor* was the large "grasped spindle" held in both hands (note the plural in v 19a) and rotated to double or re-spin single-ply yarn (Wolters 1994). The *pelek*, commonly understood as the spindle-whorl (the weight on the spindle that allowed it to spin) was, according to Wolters, the generic term for spindle.

The spinning of textiles was a time-consuming chore. It could be delegated to servants, female or male. This task, unlike the others mentioned in this poem, was not held in particular respect, as 2 Sam 3:29 shows. The fact that this well-to-do woman performs it is evidence of special industriousness.

31:20. Lichtenstein (1982: 207) observes that the key words of vv 19 and 20 form a chiasm:

ydyh šlḥh	"stretches out her hands"	(19a)
kpyh	"her palms"	(19b)
kph	"her palm"	(20a)
ydyh šlḥh	"stretches out her hands"	(20b)

Because of the order of the Hebrew alphabet, v 19 starts with the letter *yod*, the equivalent of *yad*, which means "hand," and v 20 starts with the letter *kaph*, which means "palm" or "hand." This accidental semantic link makes vv 19 and 20 into a quatrain showing industry and charity as two aspects of the woman's handiwork. Hame'iri connects the verses in two ways: Even when the Woman of Strength is busy in her tasks, she finds time to aid the poor. And, though she invests much labor in her products, she does not begrudge giving them to the needy. Malbim laces the verses together thus: "Her hands, which she stretches out to the spindle, she stretches forth to the impoverished, and her palms, which grasp the whorl, she opens to the poor."

opens [*par*ᵉ*śah*] *her palm, stretches out* [*šill*ᵉ*ḥah*] *her hands*: She gives charitable aid to the poor. Contrary to Yoder (p. 89), the woman of this poem is most certainly not extending her hands to the poor in order to lend them money at high interest. Would she do this to the *poor*, in violation both of common decency and the ethic formulated in different law codes (Exod 22:24; Lev 25:36–37; Deut 23:20)? If she were after a profit, she would earn more by lending to the rich.

31:21–22. She makes fine textiles and clothes her family in luxurious scarlet cloth, makes bed coverings, and crafts elegant garments for her own use.

scarlet [*šanim*]: Like "purple" in v 22, scarlet was an expensive cloth worn by the rich (2 Sam 1:24; Isa 1:18; Jer 4:30). Some commentators wonder how scarlet would keep the family warm. Some (such as Gemser, Barucq), cued by the translation "two-ply" in the LXX and Vulgate, vocalize the word as *šᵉnayim* and understand it to mean "double." However, *šᵉnayim* means "two," not "double." The MT is correct. It is not the scarlet dye that provides warmth, but the clothing itself. So sumptuously does she provide for her family that even clothes meant for warmth are luxurious. For the winter, the scarlet garments would probably be lined with wool.

She makes herself coverings, etc.: This is the only mention of her taking care of herself, and it is important. The Woman of Strength is devoted to others but does not neglect herself. To do so in a family of such affluence would be demonstrative self-sacrifice. She is a woman of substance and public stature, and she has a sense of her own dignity.

coverings [*marbaddim*]: These are elegant coverings used for beds, as in Prov 7:16 and Ugaritic CAT 4.385.9–10 (// *mškbt* "bed"). Possibly they could also be used as wraps.

31:23. *known in the gates*: Civic, personal, and judicial business was conducted in the gates by the city elders; see the Comment on 1:21. Her husband is certainly not "lounging" or "reduced to hanging out with the crowd at the gates," as Murphy puts it. First of all, it is not said that this is *all* he does. Much remains for him to do in the way of business and agriculture. It says that *when* he sits in the gates, he is known and respected. The commercial, public, and judicial activities that took place in the gates were vital to the life of the community. Lady Wisdom herself frequents the city gates (1:21; 8:3).

Why is the husband of the exemplary woman "known" there? Rashi says that it is because of his fine clothes. But though the poet includes the making of fineries among her achievements, he would not regard the wearing of fineries as a source of special honor (see Prov 31:30a). Rather, her husband's prestige comes from his wife, for "The woman of strength is her husband's diadem" (12:4a). Maybe it is the reflected glory of her achievements (Yoder, p. 89). It does not come from her beauty (of which we are not told), but from her virtues and achievements, which the poem details.

31:24. She even produces surplus clothing, which she sells.

fine linen: This is probably linen worn as outer wrappings (Judg 14:12, 13; Isa 3:23). Isa 3:23 indicates that it was a luxury item.

trader: Lit., "Canaanite." This is synonymous with Phoenicians, the great maritime traders who worked the entire Mediterranean basin. Phoenicians (specifically Tyrians) sold their wares in Jerusalem (Neh 13:16), and in the Persian empire they were assigned the administration of the Carmel and Sharon coastal regions. Yoder (p. 79) says that in the Persian period, "Canaanite" came to mean "trader"

(Zech 14:21; Job 40:30). But the evidence is too limited to determine that this was not the case earlier.

31:25. *Strength and majesty are her raiment*: Job uses a similar metaphor: "I put on righteousness and it clothed me" (29:14a; sim. Ps 93:1). The Woman of Strength wears fine attire as befits her status (Prov 31:22), but her true beauty comes from her spiritual strengths, manifest to all like elegant raiment. Clothing, literal and metaphorical, also provides protection.

laughs: Her confidence shows that she has prepared well for the future. "Laughing" has a similar significance in Eliphaz's assurance to Job, "You will laugh at robbery and starvation, and not fear the beasts of the land" (5:22)—not because these concerns are to be taken lightly, but because one whom God favors will be safe from them.

at future days [*l*ᵉ*yom ʾaḥăron*]: This refers either to the future generally or to her old age—"when she will not be able to labor" (Ramaq). In either case, she has readied herself for the future and can "laugh" at it with aplomb.

31:26. *opens her mouth*: She speaks wisdom and kindness. She may do this in all her dealings or, more particularly, when teaching her children—"commanding them to treat the poor kindly," Riyqam says, as indicated by the next line.

the teaching of kindness [*torat ḥesed*]: In this construct phrase, "kindness" can modify "teaching" adjectivally (= a kindly teaching) or it can be its implicit object (= a teaching that instills kindness). The latter recalls Lemuel's mother's teaching of compassion in Prov 31:6–9 (Van Leeuwen).

In the LXX, the order of vv 25 and 26 (the letters *ʿayin* and *peh*) is reversed. See the Textual Note.

31:27. *looks to the ways of her household*: She oversees their behavior.

ṣôpiyyāh hălîkôt bêtāhh: Wolters (1985) argues that *ṣôpiyyāh* ("looks to") is a pun on Greek *sophia* "wisdom." The similar sounds, he believes, "can hardly be coincidental" (p. 582). He notes that this is the only participle among the verbs describing the woman's actions, and it has an unusual form. These peculiarities supposedly show that the Hebrew word was chosen for the sake of a double entendre. But Wolters's arguments are weak. The "unusual" form, with the retention of the original radical *yod*, is attested elsewhere (GKC §75*v*), including in Prov 7:11; and the lone use of a participle (which Wolters explains as "hymnic" on p. 580) is not evidence for a Greek pun. Wolters translates the hidden meaning as "The ways of her house are *sophia*, wisdom" (p. 582). But this makes poor sense, for the "ways of her house" are what the *members* of the household do, and it is not these actions but the woman herself who, according to Wolters (p. 532), "embodies wisdom."

ways: Lit., "goings," that is, what they do, their behavior (cf. Ps 68:25).

bread of idleness: The bread of idleness is idleness itself, in whose false pleasures a lazy person would indulge. Similarly, Wisdom's bread is wisdom itself (Prov 9:5). However, the "bread of deceit" in 20:17 is profit gained by deceit, and in 23:3 it is actual bread. But "the bread of idleness" is not bread gained through idleness, because idleness bears no profits.

31:28. *(arises and)*: The verb "arises" in the first line applies also to her husband's action in the second.

31:29. *"Many daughters . . ."*: These are the words of her husband and children.

daughters [*banot*]: This is invariably translated "women" (RSV, NRSV, JPSV, etc.). But *bat* (pl. *banot*) is used either in reference to female children and young women prior to marriage or to females of any age in phrases of filiation ("daughter of so-and-so"). Since the woman in question is mature, *banot* here does indeed allude to filiation, namely, her relation to her father's house. The implication is that she went forth from there and brought credit to it.

rabbôt bānôt: See the Comment on Prov 19:21.

have done noble things [*ʿaśu ḥayil*]: *Ḥayil* here echoes *ḥayil* in v 10, where it was rendered "strength." To translate this clause as "Many women may make money" (Yoder, p. 90) both slights the breadth of the estimable woman's activities and imputes to the poem a coarseness absent elsewhere—as if the poet considered making money the height of feminine virtue. Here (as in Num 24:18; Ruth 4:11; 1 Sam 14:48; Ps 60:14; etc.), *ʿaśah ḥayil* means "do valiantly," "do great things," or the like.

31:30. *Comeliness is deceit and beauty a vapor*: Appearances are untrustworthy and transitory. Ramaq suggests that this statement continues her husband's and children's words. But the pronouncement would be pompous and patronizing if her husband said it and impudent if her children did. Rather, this verse returns to the poet's voice and is a moralistic (not feminist!) warning against valuing women according to their looks.

But not valuing women by their looks is different from not valuing looks. Good looks are appreciated in the Bible, both in men (e.g., Gen 39:6b; 1 Sam 16:18aβ; Cant 1:16) and in women (e.g., 1 Kgs 20:3; Prov 5:19; Esth 2:7b; Ps 45:12; Cant 1:15; Sir 26:17–18; 36[33]:27); see the Comment on Prov 11:22. Beauty is one piece of God-given good fortune among many—like wealth or strength. But such blessings are fragile and can fail (1 Kgs 1:6; Ezek 16:15).

We may ask whether the present verse opposes the usual appreciation of beauty by condemning beauty as *bad*. "Deceit" and "vapor" are, after all, strong negatives. Still, this seems unlikely because the poem has not said enough about female beauty to prepare the way for a radical revision of attitude. Also, a puritanical repudiation of feminine beauty would not accord with the poem's approval of attractive clothing (v 22). Instead, the present verse says that beauty, whatever its worth, is potentially delusive and certainly transitory. A beautiful woman may enjoy admiration and compliments for the moment, but the one who will *really* be praised is she who fears the Lord.

who fears the Lord: Fear of the Lord is the crowning virtue of the Woman of Strength, just as it is wisdom's starting point (Prov 1:7; 9:10) and high point (2:5). Contrary to some commentators, this is not the first mention of religious virtue in the poem and for that (feeble!) reason suspect of being a later addition (see the Textual Note). Wisdom and kindness (Prov 31:20, 26) *are* religious virtues. Moreover, the prudence and industry for which the woman is praised throughout the poem constitute wisdom and thus, in Proverbs' view, are tantamount to fear of the Lord.

yirʾat-: This form would normally be a construct noun meaning "fear of," but that does not fit here. Without a *b-* before *yirʾat*, the sentence cannot mean "It is for her fear of the Lord that a woman is to be praised" (JPSV; sim. Clifford). (On the doubtful category of the accusative of cause, see GBH §126k.) Certainly a preposition would be necessary with a passive/reflexive verb. Rather, *yirʾat* is a contracted form of the fem. const. ptcp. equivalent to *yᵉrēʾat* "fearer of"; cf. *yirʾê YHWH*, Ps 15:4 etc.

31:31. *Give her of the fruit of her hands* [*tᵉnu lahh mippᵉri yadeyha*]: The poet, speaking to the male readers, urges them to render to such a woman "of the fruit of her hands," that is, *some* of what she earns.

Give [*tᵉnû*]: This line is often thought to be a call to give her praise, and it is true that the parallel line has that sense. But "give" is not used of honoring someone unless the dir. obj. is "honor" or the like, as in "Give to the Lord the honor due his name" (Ps 96:7, using the synonym *hābê* [adduced by Ramaq]; sim. Ps 115:1; Prov 26:8; cf. Ps 68:35; Mal 2:2).Yoder (p. 83) translates: "Ascribe to her the fruit of her hands," citing Ps 28:4a, which she translates, tendentiously: "Ascribe to them [*ten-lāhem*] [sc. the wicked] according to their work." But *ntn* there does not mean "give them credit for" but rather "give," "repay," synonymous with *hāšēb gᵉmûlām lāhem*, lit., "return their retribution to them" (Ps 28:4b), that is, give them what they deserve. This is the meaning of Prov 31:31a as well. In any case, "according to" would require the prep. *k-*, not *m-*.

Wolters (1988: 454), Murphy, Clifford, and others vocalize *tannû*, from *t-n-h* "sing," "extol," as in Judg 5:11; 11:40; cf. Ps 8:2; thus JPSV: "Extol her for the fruit of her hand." Actually, *tinnāh* means "repeat," "rehearse," "recount." It is an Aramaism cognate to Heb *šnh*. But neither "recount to her from the fruit of her hands" nor "sing to her from the fruit of her hands" makes good sense. The verse envisions two kinds of recognition: material and verbal.

THE WOMAN OF STRENGTH: CONTEXT AND CONTENT

1. Date of Composition

Prov 31:10–31 has been dated anywhere from the premonarchic period (E. Lyons 1987: 238) to the second century B.C.E. (M. Waegeman 1992: 101), not on very strong grounds. Most commentators avoid putting a date on a text that is detached from any particular historical setting. The only sustained effort to date the text is Yoder's, who assigns the poem to the Persian period (pp. 15–39). It should be noted that the major turning point in the Hebrew language was not the first wave of return from exile in 535 B.C.E. (yielding LBH^1, which is very close to CBH) but rather the second, with Nehemiah, in the early to mid-fifth century (yielding LBH^2). The language of this poem is compatible with the former, as Yoder says, but the evidence does not allow a firm determination.

Yoder combines data from Prov 1–9 and 31:10–31 in arguing for a postexilic dating for both. This distorts the evidence. The two passages are not a single text written by one author. (She calls the supposed author of both "the sage" in the singular, thereby begging the question.) The two units differ from each other in form, in the types of women described, and in the kind of wisdom ascribed to women (in the case of Prov 1–9, Lady Wisdom). The evidence therefore is not additive.

Among the lexical items that Yoder lists as evidence for the postexilic dating of the two units, only three appear in the present one: (1) *Pᵉnînîm* "rubies" (or "corals") in Prov 31:10 (also 3:15 [qeré]; 8:11; 20:15; Job 28:18; and Lam 4:7, all of which are postexilic). It may, however, be accidental that no earlier text mentions rubies—if that is what the word means. The name Peninnah in 1 Sam 1:2, which is certainly early, is based on this word. (2) *Meker* "purchase price" in Prov 31:10 (also Neh 13:16; Sir 42:5; and Num 20:19, whose dating is in dispute). In any case, the root is common in early texts and the formation is a natural one. (3) *Kᵉnaʿănî* "Canaanite" in the sense of "merchant" in Prov 31:24 (also Zech 14:21; see Yoder p. 79). But we do not know how early it gained this sense. We can add two more possibly LBH (not distinctively LBH^2) features: (4) *Lāqaḥ* in the sense of "buy" in Prov 31:16 (also Neh 5:2 and often in RH; noted by Ehrlich). (5) The placement of the adjective before the noun in *rabbôt bānôt* in Prov 31:29 (also 7:26 and 19:21; see the Comment on the latter). But Aramaisms such as item 5 are problematic evidence for dating in Proverbs; see "Linguistic Indicators of Dating" (III.C) in the Introduction to Vol. II. An item of counterevidence is *šēš* "linen" (31:22), an Egyptianism replaced by *bûṣ* after the exile (Hurvitz 1968).

2. *Social Setting*

Yoder (pp. 39–91) provides a thoroughgoing account of the scope of women's activities using documentary evidence from the Persian period. The evidence helps illustrate the background of the present unit, though the types of activities described here were not necessarily restricted to that period, nor were practices in Elephantine, deep in southern Egypt, necessarily in use in the Levant.

Prov 31:10–31 was, according to Yoder, written by and for "affluent and moderately wealthy members of an urban commercial class" (p. 103). This is correct, except that the divide between urban and rural should not be overemphasized, for a landowner with holdings near a city would participate in the city life. The Woman of Strength buys fields and plants vineyards (v 16), but she also has dealings with merchants and traders (v 24), who would be situated in cities, and her husband plays a role in city affairs (v 23). Moreover, her family enjoys an opulence that bespeaks proximity to an urban setting (vv 21–22).

On the basis of the evidence from the Achaemenid period, Yoder concludes that

> "Woman's work" in the Achaemenid economy was varied. Among their responsibilities as managers of the household, women manufactured textiles, traded in the marketplaces, and might own or supervise slaves. Women also made and received deliveries, managed properties, and were parties to the purchase and sale of slaves and land. As workers in the royal economy, non-royal women engaged in a wide range of skilled and unskilled professions in numbers equivalent to or greater than men; women also worked at varying ranks and degrees of specialization. Moreover, women with sufficient amounts of capital might get into the credit business, making loans of cash and other goods at favorable interest rates.
>
> Finally, royal women and women of high rank were often property owners and estate owners. (Yoder, p. 71)

This picture contradicts the modern stereotype of women in ancient, male-dominated societies being severely restricted in the scope of their economic activity and personal independence. This is not to say that they had economic or social equality, but they were not confined to childbearing and drudge work in the home. To be sure, Ps 128:3a idealizes the wife who is secluded at home: "Your wife will be like a fruitful vine in the depths of your house." Still, the picture of women we get in the Bible does not suggest confinement. The original readers of the poem would not have found it outlandish for a woman to deal with merchants, buy land, plant vineyards, and so on.

The socioeconomic background of the Woman of Strength is illuminated by the picture Yoder assembles of upper-class women in the Achaemenid period. She does not show, however, that this situation pertains *only* in the Achaemenid period. Her conclusion of a Persian-period dating is biased by the fact that her survey is based on corpora of texts *from* that period (listed in Yoder, pp. 40–41). An examination of texts from earlier and later times would be needed to exclude alternative settings, such as the Hellenistic period. The state of woman's scope of action and rights in economic matters in the urban centers of the Greco-Roman world as pictured by S. Pomeroy (*1975*: 125–39) is not unlike the one suggested by Prov 10:10–31. According to Pomeroy, "The less-restricted movement of queens in spheres of activity formerly reserved for men set a style that was emulated by some wealthy and aristocratic women. The legal and economic responsibilities of women increased, but political gains were more illusory" (ibid., p. 125). In response, R. van Bremen (*1993*) emphasizes that Hellenistic women did not gain meaningful legal emancipation from male control, yet women of the urban elite were able to take on liturgies and offices and become public benefactors (pp. 207; 223–42 passim). These pictures are not contradictory, and both pertained to a degree in postexilic Judea. The evidence does not as yet exclude the Hellenistic period.

Another problem with using data from Achaemenid Elephantine to reconstruct the background setting of Prov 31:10–31 is that we do not know if women like the one in this poem were allowed as great a scope in economic activity as were those in Elephantine. The Woman of Strength buys and sells, but those activities were never denied to women in ancient Israel, or, to my knowledge, in the ancient Near East. More striking is her purchase of a field, an activity we do not read of women performing in earlier Israelite law and literature. Even in this regard, however, she might be acting as her husband's agent, not as property owner (thus Westbrook *1991*: 80).[385]

Yoder (p. 105) identifies the author and audience as members of the *golah*, the community of Jews whose forebears had returned to Judea from Babylonian exile. But nothing warrants this identification to the exclusion of others. She believes that the use of female figures, the metaphor of marriage, and the motif of the woman "stranger" "resonate with the ideological campaign against exogamous

---

[385] In Ruth 4:9, Boaz is said to buy/acquire (*qnh*) the property in question "from the hand of Naomi." However, the property is by legal fiction possessed by the deceased males, Elimelech, Chilion, and Mahlon. Thus Naomi is acting in the capacity of an agent in the transaction. (In Ruth 4:5, we should read *ʾēt* [dir. obj. marker] *rût* for *mēʾēt rût* "from Ruth" [as in 4:9], for Ruth is being "acquired" [v 10], not doing the selling.)

marriages" waged by Ezra and Nehemiah (Ezr 9:2–5; Neh 6:18–19; 13:23–31). But there is no such resonance. If the authors of Parts I and VId were really disturbed by intermarriage, as Ezra and Nehemiah were, they could have said so, as the authors of Ezra and Nehemiah did. And if the Strange Woman and Woman of Strength passages were polemical, they would have been clear about the woman's foreignness. The Strange Woman is not a foreigner (see Vol. I, 134–35, 139–40), and she is already married (Prov 2:17; 6:26–35; 7:19–20).

The context for the Woman of Strength's economic activities has been further clarified by B. Lang (*2004*). He compares the responsibilities of the woman described in this poem to those advised in Xenophon's *Oeconomicus*, from early fourth-century B.C.E. Athens. This is a tract on management of the landed estate, telling a man how to instruct his wife in household economy. She is to receive food and see to its storage and oversee its preparation, which would be carried out mainly by the slaves (sim. Prov 31:14–15). She is responsible for textile production, from spinning to clothing manufacture (cf. Prov 31:21–22). The well-off Athenian wife is involved more in planning and overseeing the work of slaves than in doing the work herself. The Woman of Strength is involved in both; see vv 15, 16, 27. In the Athenian household, and, it seems, the Israelite, the man's primary sphere is outside the house, in agriculture (cf. Prov 27:23–27) and public affairs (31:23). The woman's domain is the household, in which she exercises considerable independence. The woman contributes to the profitability and growth of the estate (cf. Prov 31:11, 16), but her husband is the owner. Lang (p. 203) contrasts the woman's purchase of land in Prov 31:16 with the Athenian woman's inability to own land, but he recognizes that women's rights to land ownership in Israel were ambiguous. Finally, the *Oeconomicus*, like Prov 31:30, assures the bride that "it is not because of youthful grace that beautiful and good things increase for human beings, but rather because of the virtues of the latter" (viii 42–43; Lang, p. 207). The affinities to Prov 31:10–31 are deep and respond to comparable social and economic realities.

3. *Genre and Purpose*

Since there is nothing quite like the poem of the Woman of Strength elsewhere, it is difficult to determine its genre. Several classifications are possible. We should look for a category that is not so broad as to be useless ("poetry") or so narrow as to have only a couple of known members ("poems in praise of capable women"). The purpose of the poem will be an expression of its genre.

A. Wolters (1988) classes Prov 31:10–31 as a hymn and sees in it features of heroic poetry, which celebrates the deeds of heroes in battle. But, contrary to Wolters, "hymn" is properly used of songs in praise of God, whose deeds are of a unique sort. Moreover, the present poem lacks the characteristic "hymnic participles," except for one in 31:27 (whose uniqueness Wolters believes important; see the Comment). There is nothing to be gained from stretching the concept of hymn beyond its usual use. Wolters is right that some of the imagery has heroic or martial overtones, but it is still distant from heroic poetry, which eulogizes the exploits of a warrior.

Prov 31:10–31 is best classified as an *encomium*. The encomium, best known from Greco-Roman lyric and rhetoric, is a declamation of lofty praise for a person or a type of person. A. Schmitt surveys Greek and Jewish encomia and includes Prov 31:10–31 among the latter (2003: 360, n. 7).

An example of the Greek encomium is Theocritus's Idyll XVI, which praises a wise man's generosity, especially to guests and, above all, to poets. It includes these lines:

> Riches give the wise man pleasure
> not in this, but in being indulgent
> to himself and perhaps to some poet.
> He provides for many of his kinsmen
> and for many others, and is always
> sacrificing on the gods' altars.
> And he never treats strangers badly,
> but uses them kindly at his table
> and sends them graciously home again
> when they are ready to go. (trans. B. Mills 1963: 61–61)

Another encomium on a woman, like Theocritus's from Hellenistic Egypt but written in Egyptian, is an inscription in the tomb of Petosiris in praise of his wife Renpet-nefret. The virtues ascribed to this woman recall the Woman of Strength:

> His wife, his beloved:
> mistress of grace,
> sweet in love,
> expert with her mouth,
> sweet in speech,
> excellent in counsel in her writings.
> Whatever passes over her lips
> surpasses the work of truth.
> An excellent wife,
> great of praise in her city,
> who stretches forth her hand to everyone,
> who speaks good things,
> and repeats what is loved.
> Who does what everyone loves,
> upon whose lips no bad thing passes,
> greatly beloved by all:
> Renpet-nefret. (trans. Fox 1985b: 350)

V. Hurowitz (2005) compares the present poem to a Babylonian text called "Woman Large of Head." This is a physiognomic text coordinating certain physical features of a woman with her character or the kind of life she may expect. While underscoring the differences between the two texts, Hurowitz notes that both are advisory, indicating features their respective societies considered desirable in a wife. Both speak of the woman's success and prosperity, good cheer, and soft-spokenness, and both marginalize the importance of physical beauty.

In the Bible, the encomium is found in psalms that praise the righteous man, as in the examples cited below. The righteous man, like the Woman of Strength, is a type, not an individual. One kind of encomium is the macarism or beatitude (see the discussion in Vol. I, 161). Macarisms too have didactic intent, for they depict an ideal to be emulated and tell of the blessings such a one enjoys. Ps 112 is a macarism on the God-fearer. Ps 128 praises the good fortune of the God-fearing man, who will enjoy the fruits of his labors and have a fertile wife and sturdy sons, among other blessings. (One can imagine him as the husband of the Woman of Strength.) Another example, which like Prov 31:10–31 uses the third rather than the second person, is Ps 1:1–3:

Happy is the man
who walks not in the counsel of the wicked,
nor stands in the path of sinners,
nor sits in the company of the impudent.
Rather, he delights in the law of the Lord,
and on his law meditates day and night.
He shall be like a tree planted beside streams of water,
that yields its fruit in its season,
whose foliage does not wither,
and all that he does prospers.

There are differences (as there always are among members of a category). Prov 31:10–31 does not begin with *ʾašrey* but with a different exclamation, "Who can find?" Whereas a macarism lists the benefits a certain behavior has for the fortunate person, Prov 31:10–31 primarily proclaims the value of the praiseworthy behavior for *others* and only secondarily for the object of the praise. When it does the latter, the poem uses the word *way^{e}ʾašš^{e}ruha*, "and they laud her" or "declare her happy" (v 28), which is the verbal cognate of *ʾašrey*.

Other encomia are not macarisms. Ps 15 begins with questions in a form that recalls Prov 31:10: "O Lord, who will sojourn in your tents? Who will dwell in your holy mountain?" (Ps 15:1). The psalm's purpose is clearly didactic, to define an ideal type as an object of emulation. Sir 38:34b–39:11 is a grand encomium on the student of the Torah. It surveys the variety of things he does and concludes by promising that he will be praised in the *qahal* ("assembly" or simply "public")—compare Prov 31:28–31—and remembered after his death. The last sentence uses the verb *ʾšr*: "If he endures, he will be declared happier [*y^{e}ʾuššar*] than a thousand (others), and when he comes to an end, (his) name will suffice" (39:11). Ben Sira's long and lavish praise of the ancestors (44:1–50:24) is also an encomium, but unlike the others it describes historical personages, culminating in Ben Sira's contemporary, Simon the High Priest (50:1–21). Other examples are 1 Macc 3:3–9 (Judah Maccabee) and 1 Macc 14:4–15 (Simon Maccabee). Rather different are words of praise or blessing *to* a person, as the encomia to Judith in Jdt 13:18–20; 14:7; and 15:9–10.

The ostensive audience of Prov 31:10–31 is not explicitly indicated within the poem. (The poem lacks, e.g., a vocative like "my son.") But the editor has determined the audience by attaching the poem to a book that defines its audience as uneducated boys and young men (1:4). The poem itself implies a male readership, for it speaks of the benefit that *they* would derive from such a woman. (This is also the case in 12:4.) In 31:31, the author implicitly addresses men—the husband and future husbands mentioned in 31:28—and calls upon them to extol and reward such women in their lives.

The poem can work in various ways. When read by a young man, it teaches him to choose a wife not for her beauty but for her practical and moral strengths. These are what will really benefit him. When heard by young women, the poem would hold up to them a standard of excellence. The striking parallels to Xenophon's *Oeconomicus* (see above, (2) "Social Setting") enhance the likelihood that Prov 31:10–31, though speaking about the woman in the third person, is also an instruction for girls and young women, teaching them how to succeed in the domestic life and win prosperity and esteem. When recited to a wife and mother (as in contemporary Jewish practice), it expresses gratitude for her achievements and contributions to the family.

4. *Figurative and Historical Identifications of the Woman of Strength*

Commentators agree that, at least on the surface, an actual human woman is being described. Some, however, add a further, allegorical, level of meaning and consider that as conveying the poem's most significant message. Malbim (commenting on 31:10) remarks approvingly: "The commentators have already agreed that this text holds a figure and trope [*mašal um^{e}liṣah*]." A considerable variety of figurative decodings have been offered by traditional and modern interpreters.

a. Traditional Jewish Interpretations

Prov 31:10–31 was a rich resource for allegorical and "historical" readings in the midrash and medieval commentaries. The Woman of Strength (the entire description or components thereof) has been identified with the following:

The Torah. A presupposition of traditional Jewish exegesis is that wisdom means Torah, hence if this woman is wisdom, she must be Torah itself. Statements in *Midrash Proverbs* identify various items in the poem with Torah. For example, commenting on "Like merchant ships she brings her bread from afar" (Prov 31:14), Simon ben Halafta explains that bread means Torah (citing Prov 9:5) and that one must "exile himself" to Torah. However, the midrash does not simply equate the Woman of Strength with Torah. A later compilation, *Yalquṭ Shimoni*, further identifies components of the poem with Torah, and Rashi, followed by Naḥmias, develops it systematically.

The Shekinah. The Kabbalists sang this poem in honor of the Shekinah on arriving home for the Sabbath meal (Scholem *1965*: 142). Later, this practice continued in honor of the mother of the home and is still in use.

Matter. Ralbag identifies the Woman of Strength with the material body (*ḥomer*), which "serves the intellect [*śekel*] completely in such a way that (the intellect) can attain its perfection." In other words, the "husband" is the intellect and the "wife" is the body, which supplies the intellect's needs.

The Soul. Alsheikh reverses Ralbag's decoding. The woman is the soul, and the soul's "husband" is the body. The body "weds" the soul to beget "sons," that is, good deeds. Alsheikh traces in detail how the soul supplies spiritual needs and comforts to the physical self and every night ascends to heaven, to return the next day. Mezudat David, in an allegorical interpretation that he appends to his literal one, identifies the woman more specifically as *hannepeš hammaśkelet* "the "intelligent soul."

The Material ("Hylic") Soul (*hnpš hhywlnyt*). According to Malbim, the woman is the hylic or material, soul, which is to be distinguished from "the soul which emanates [*hn'ṣlt*] from the eternal heights." (Alsheikh [see above] is referring to the latter soul.) Her "husband" is the intellect, who rules her by reason.

A Historical (Biblical) Woman. Yalquṭ Shimoni (ad loc.) assembles midrashic comments that identify the Woman of Strength with Sarah. For example:

> "Woman of Strength": This is Sarah, as it is written, "See, I know that you are a woman of beautiful looks" [Gen 12:11b]. "The heart of her husband trusts in her": [It is as Abraham said to Sarai], "so that it may go well with me on your account." [Gen 12:13b]

Memories of other women are evoked as well. "Strength and majesty are her raiment" (v 25a) was associated with Elisheba daughter of Amminadab (Exod 6:23),[386] and "She opens her mouth in wisdom" (v 26a) brought to mind the wise woman who spoke with Joab (2 Sam 14:2). These and similar associations were not meant to be exclusive identifications but to point to women who exemplify the qualities described in this poem.

Mezudat David (before offering the allegorical interpretation summarized above) historicizes the Woman of Strength as Solomon's mother Bath Sheba, whom he assumes is speaking in Prov 31:1–9. "After quoting her admonitions, Solomon proceeded to praise the Woman of Strength in her honor, that she might be remembered" (at 31:10).

A Historical Man or Type of Actual Man. In some decodings, the Woman of Strength represents men. Some homilies found in *Midrash Proverbs* apply certain verses to a wise man, simply ignoring the gender. For example, using Prov 31:15, Simon ben Halafta explains that whenever a wise student sits and busies himself

---

[386] Elisheba had four "joys" that were like glorious raiments: Her husband was a priest, her brother saved her (priestly) descendents from idolatry with Ahab, and she numbered David and Solomon among her descendents.

with Torah at night, God draws over him the thread of mercy during the day, as it is said, "By day the Lord will command [his mercy], and at night his song is with me, a prayer to the God of my life" (Ps 42:9). What is more, God brings forth food for him every day, as it is said, "She [!] gives food to her house" (Prov 31:15b). "House" is understood as the House of Study.

Midrash Proverbs further explains the "comeliness" (or "grace") that is "deceitful" (v 30a) as belonging to Noah and Adam (*Midr. Prov.*). *Yalqut Shimoni* (§964) applies the line, "You have surpassed them all" (v 30b), to Moses.

Saʿadia systematically parses the Woman of Strength as a figure of the wise man. In his introduction to this unit, he explains that the plain meaning of the poem is clear: It describes the good woman. On the allegorical level (the *nimšal*), however, it refers to "every wise and excellent (man)." There is, he explains, a hierarchy of three components in every man: the body, the soul, and the intellect. Since the body is what is perceptible to the senses, Solomon describes the physical virtues and allows the virtues of the higher levels to be inferred from them. He chose woman as the symbol of the body "for the honor of men, in order to associate with them the (higher) perfections [Arabic *maṣāliḥ*] of the soul and the intellect." Saʿadia proceeds to explicate the poem in terms of the wise *man's* virtues. For example:

> "All the days of her life" (31:12b): He who busies himself with earning money must attend to sound management all the days of his life, as it is said, "that you may learn (to fear the Lord all the days)" (Deut 14:23b). Likewise the righteous man must tend to his righteousness all his life, as it is said, "These are the ordinances and the laws which you shall carefully keep (in the land which the Lord the God of your fathers gives you to inherit, all the days that you live on the land)." (Deut 12:1)

It is notable that these commentators did not feel the qualities of the Woman of Strength to be so gender-specific that they were inapplicable to men.

b. Traditional Christian Interpretations

The Church Fathers and medieval Christian interpreters identified the Woman of Strength as the soul (*psychē*) (Origen), mind (*nous*) (Didymus of Alexandria), wisdom (Hilary of Poitiers), the Virgin Mary (Andrew of Crete), and, most influentially, the Church (Augustine) (Wolters *2001*: 67–79). Medieval Christians consistently understood the Woman of Strength to be a figure of the Church (ibid., pp. 81–99). For a survey of Christian interpretation up to modern times, see Wolters *2001*: 59–154.

c. Modern Allegorical Interpretations

The ancient allegorical identification of the woman as wisdom has again become prominent, possibly predominant, as Wolters (*2001*: 152) says. The Woman of Strength is regarded as a personification of wisdom, like the figure who speaks in Interludes A, D, and E, and, more allusively, B. The allegorical reading is not meant to displace the surface description of an excellent woman but coexist with it on a higher plane of significance.

According to T. McCreesh, Lady Wisdom in Prov 9:4–6 is depicted as "the young marriageable woman seeking lovers who would accept the gifts and life she could offer" (1985: 46). As for 31:10–31, McCreesh says, "Now that time of courtship, or learning, is over. In chapter 31, Wisdom is a faithful wife and a skilled mistress of her household, finally settled down with her own" (ibid.).

McCreesh's reading is open to a number of objections: Lady Wisdom is far from young (8:22!). She has built her own house (9:1), which few girls do. Nor do they (or, at least, should they) have a party and invite in a bunch of fools (9:4–5). Moreover, Wisdom *never* "settles down," but is ever going about searching for adherents. When she finds them, she does not simply provide for them but, by giving them ingenuity, prudence, and industry, helps them provide for *themselves*. If one presses the marriage analogy, Lady Wisdom would be polyandrous. However, marriage does not come into the picture of Lady Wisdom. Her status is that of a teacher with pupils and a noble woman with protégés.

G. Hausmann too believes that on a "higher plane" (*Metaebene*), the woman of Prov 31:10–31 symbolizes wisdom in a way that harks back to chapter 8 (1992, passim). No actual woman, Hausmann asserts, could fit the extravagant description, and 31:10, as Hausmann construes it, insists that no one *can* find such a one, meaning that she is beyond human attainment. Moreover, Hausmann argues, women in Proverbs are praised only in the form of personified wisdom—except (she concedes) for 12:4; 18:22; 19:14, and, indirectly, sayings in which woman is mentioned in her role as mother. It would therefore be very surprising to have a passage at the end of the book that praises the positive behavior of a woman, "und damit zum ganzen sonstigen Reden kontär liegt" ("and which thereby runs contrary to all the other sayings") (p. 264).

But the exceptions to the negative portrayal of women noted by Hausmann, to which we can add 5:18–19; 11:16; and 14:1, are not a trivial batch, especially since Proverbs makes only a few mentions of women altogether. In fact, Proverbs says nothing bad about women as such, but only about foolish, bad, and unpleasant women, just as it says nothing bad about men as such, but only about foolish, bad, unpleasant men. The present poem's positive view of woman—that is, a certain *type* of woman—is fully in harmony with the rest of the book.

There are undoubtedly similarities between the Woman of Strength and wisdom, and between her and wise women, and between her and personified Wisdom, as the following comparison shows:

Virtue	*Woman of Strength*	*Lady Wisdom*	*Wisdom*	*Wise women*
is more precious than rubies	31:10	8:11	3:15	
produces profit (*saḥar*)	31:18		3:14	
brings wealth	31:11	8:18, 21	3:14	
is mistress of a household	31:15, 21, 27	8:34; 9:1		cf. 14:1

makes her household thrive	31:15, 21, 27			cf. 14:1
has maidservants	31:15	9:3		
provides food	31:14	9:5		
produces fruit	31:16, 31	8:19		
speaks teachings	31:26	8:6–9[387]		
has honor	31:25, 28–31	8:18	3:16	11:16
possesses strength	31:17, 25	8:14		

This does not mean that the Woman of Strength and wisdom), or Lady Wisdom, are the same person, but only that they have the qualities of wisdom described in Prov 1–9 *and elsewhere in Proverbs as well*.

There is also a crucial distinction: The Woman of Strength is hard to find (31:10), whereas Lady Wisdom is available to all who seek her (8:17, 35), and in fact she takes the initiative to seek *them* (1:20–21, 24; 8:1–6; 9:3–5). (It is otherwise in Job 28, but that chapter is denying the accessibility of a different kind of wisdom.) Wisdom itself is an infinite pleroma that is not depleted however many men take of it for themselves.

Prov 31:10–31 has often been allegorized, and this has been productive for homiletics. But allegorical readings can be performed on any text, and even on inanimate objects ("sermons in stones"). A genuine allegory, a text written to be understood as one, operates on two levels, the surface reading and a figurative sense. (The latter has been called both "higher" and "deeper" on grounds that the reader must work to reach it—as if the literal sense were unproblematic.) In real allegory, something must disturb the surface reading and reveal its inadequacy, so as to cue the reader to shift to a different level of interpretation. For example, in Jotham's fable (Judg 9:8–15), it is immediately evident that Jotham is not *really* speaking about trees because trees don't talk. Moreover, Jotham, like many allegorists, also identifies his figures plainly (Judg 9:16–20). Compare how Ezekiel identifies the two adulterous sisters in 23:4, 33. In the personification Interludes, a number of rather obvious clues show us that the figure called "Wisdom" in 1:20–33; 8:1–36; and 9:1–6 + 11 is not a wise human: She is ubiquitous. She calls to fools everywhere (1:22, 24; 8:5; 9:4), which would be a risky thing for a human woman to do. She will be at hand whenever fools suffer their downfall (1:26–27). She was at God's side before and during creation (8:22–31). These are not subtle hints, and there is no reason to expect special subtlety in 31:10–31.

What is it that is supposed to signal a higher level of reading in Prov 31:10–31? For Hausmann (1992), it is the implausibility of the woman's huge and variegated workload, which goes beyond what can plausibly be borne by a "concrete" woman, even an "ideal" one (p. 265). This is disputable. First, the Woman of Strength *is* an ideal, and ideals can do what mortals cannot. Second, the scope of her activities is *not* incredible. She is very talented and she works hard at many tasks, but none beyond the range of the feasible. We could as well say that "taken as a whole," the wise man of Proverbs is impossible as a portrayal of a "concrete

[387] Though sometimes harshly: 1:23; contrast 31:26.

man." Hausmann also sees a fissure in the literal surface in the question "who can find?" (v 10a), which she reads as meaning that such a woman truly can *not* be found. But this reading is too mechanical. "Who can find?" does not mean that she does not exist or is beyond anyone's reach; see the Comment on 31:10. And if that is what it meant, the verse would be claiming that wisdom, contrary to 8:35, cannot be found.

For McCreesh (1985: 27–28), the clue to allegory is the one-sidedness of the description of this woman, with its focus on her activities to the exclusion of her husband's. Now it is true that the focus is on the woman, but that is because the poem is about *her*, not her husband or family. Ps 136 recounts the achievements of Yahweh alone, but he is nevertheless a god and not a symbol of the divine. Another of McCreesh's objections to a literal reading uses a religious criterion. "Is it possible," he asks rhetorically, "that only such a role-model as this has been canonized for all time?" (p. 27). In other words, could the portrayal of a human role model alone be significant enough for a canonical text? The answer is supposed to be no, but why not? Role models are what the book of Proverbs is about. More fundamentally, McCreesh's puzzlement retrojects the process of canonization into authorship, as if the authors and editors of Proverbs knew they were writing for the Bible. He presumes that something grand, sublime, and *religious* must be intended in every patch of the crazy quilt that grew into the sacred compilation of later centuries. This assumption has driven the allegorical interpretation of the Song of Songs for two thousand years. Ordinary human sexual love, it is assumed, cannot be the whole story; there must be something *more* to it. Similar reasoning makes the Strange Woman of Prov 7 into something other, more abstract, than an ordinary, pathetically ordinary, human adulteress. She must be made to represent heresy, or Greek philosophy, or woman as the "radical Other," a process I describe in Vol. I, 254–62.

The Woman of Strength is in any case a poor fit for a figurative role. Who would her sons be? If they are, say, Wisdom's disciples, who is her husband? Yahweh? To be sure, Yahweh was at one time assigned a consort, namely, the goddess Asherah. But Proverbs presumes a strict monotheism, and the Woman of Strength is hardly an Asherah figure, whose main role is fertility.[388] And how could Wisdom, in the figurative role of Yahweh's wife, be thought to support him? Also, as noted, a Woman of Strength may be hard to find, but wisdom is always available to those who sincerely desire it.

The Woman of Strength is not a figure for wisdom. While Lady Wisdom per-

---

[388] It has been suggested that the memory of Asherah may underlie the figures of both Wisdom and Folly; see Vol. I, 335, n. 209. J. Hadley (1997) argues that "the apparent apotheosis of Lady Wisdom in the biblical literature is not a legitimization of the worship of 'established' goddesses, but rather is a literary compensation for the eradication of the worship of these goddesses" (p. 396), in particular, Asherah, Astarte, and the "Queen of Heaven" (p. 393). Still, the figure of Wisdom is devoid of any attributes distinctively associated with the goddesses, especially Asherah, though there is a pale and indirect association in the metaphor of the "tree of life" in Prov 3:18. Fontaine (2002) sees "a legacy of divine females lurking behind the composition of the cosmic figures in Proverbs 1–9" (p. 149). The only goddess I see back there is the Hellenistic Isis (see Vol. I, 336–38 of this commentary), for whom Lady Wisdom is a substitute without becoming herself a goddess.

sonifies wisdom, the Woman of Strength *typifies* it, and both have their negative counterparts:

Abstraction	*Type*	*Personification*
folly and evil	Strange Woman	Lady Folly
wisdom and virtue	Woman of Strength	Lady Wisdom

The Woman of Strength has her negative counterpart in the Strange Woman, also a type figure.[389] The Strange Woman and the Woman of Strength both own expensive coverings, including *marbaddim* "coverings" (Prov 7:16a; 31:22a); for the former these adorn the couch of fornication, for the latter, the conjugal bed. The Strange Woman is dressed "in harlot's garb" (7:10), while the Woman of Strength is arrayed in "strength and majesty" (31:25) as well as fine (actual) garments (31:22). The former sneers at her husband and deceives him (7:19–20), the latter gives hers every reason to trust her fully (31:11–12). Both go out and about in their affairs, but the former is seeking to betray her marriage (2:17; 6:29–35; 7:11–12), the latter to provide for her family (31:13–14, 16). Both excel in powerful speech, the one in seduction (5:3; 6:24; 7:13–20)—ironically called "her instruction" in 7:21—the other in teaching wisdom and kindness (31:26). The illicit consort of the former suffers public disgrace (5:14; 6:33); the rightful mate of the latter basks in public esteem (31:23). The former has physical beauty and misuses it (6:25); the latter may have beauty—the young wife of 5:19 may become a Woman of Strength, and the mature Woman of Strength is certainly elegant (31:22b)—but she does not need it (31:30). The Strange Woman and Woman of Strength are polar opposites, but both belong on the map of humanity.

Both type-figures are humans and their humanness should not be blurred by turning them into allegories of something supposedly more important. Even *adding* an allegorical level to the literal blurs their profiles without contributing new insights. If the Woman of Strength is a trope for Torah or wisdom, all that the poem can say are things already assumed to be true of Torah and wisdom. The true allegories are Lady Folly (9:13–18), who embodies stupidity and wickedness, and Lady Wisdom, who typifies wisdom and virtue.

5. The Woman of Strength as a Type-Figure

"Who could possibly achieve in many lifetimes what she achieves in these verses?" (R. E. Murphy, *Proverbs*, p. 245)

"All this she must possess," added Darcy, "and to all this she must yet add something more substantial, in the improvement of her mind by extensive reading."

"I am no longer surprised at your knowing *only* six accomplished women. I rather wonder now at your knowing *any*."

[389] The Strange Woman appears in Prov 2:16–19; 5:1–23; 6:20–35; 7:1–27; 22:14; and (as emended) 23:27. See Vol. I, 134–41; 252–62.

> "Are you so severe upon your own sex, as to doubt the possibility of all this?"
> "*I* never saw such a woman. *I* never saw such capacity, and taste, and application, and elegance, as you describe united." (Mr. Darcy and Elizabeth Bennet, arguing in *Pride and Prejudice*, chapter 8)

I do not share Murphy's skepticism about the human feasibility of the Woman of Strength's achievements or Elizabeth's doubts about the possibility of an "accomplished woman," even by Mr Darcy's rigorous standards.

The picture of the Woman of Strength is realistic insofar as it describes a real type of woman, albeit impressive and rare. But perhaps not all that rare: certainly more than the half-a-dozen that Mr. Darcy would concede. We would slight human women to assume otherwise. Indeed, there are a great many women whose activities equal the ones described in Prov 30:10–31 in scope and variety. Glückel of Hameln, a Jewish widow in seventeenth-century Germany, ran her own factory, traded goods far and near, and raised fourteen children and oversaw *their* affairs, all in dangerous and turbulent times. She wrote her memoirs in the 1690s with no self-dramatization and certainly no self-pity. She was doing what she had to do and savoring her success. And the typical American farm wife in the nineteenth century, and often even today, would need a broad array of skills in handicraft, agriculture, poultry farming, and commerce, as well as home economics and child-rearing, and she would work from before dawn to after dark, at least in the winter. There were undoubtedly not a few who did this while remaining generous and God-fearing. As for the woman in Prov 31:10–31, she does not do all these things every day. Some activities, such as buying fields, planting vineyards, and dealing with traders, would be occasional tasks. She also has a staff of maids to help her. What she does is impressive but doable.

The Woman of Strength is not a particular woman, but an ideal. (Ideal, i.e., from the author's perspective, not shared by all modern readers.) She is a paragon of feminine virtues, practical and ethical. She is the counterpart of the wise man portrayed throughout Proverbs and serves the same paradigmatic role.

The Woman of Strength does not signify the entirety of womanhood, any more than the Strange Woman does (as a widespread view, which I dispute in Vol. I, 258–62, would have it). Nothing indicates that either is a trope for some other entity, foolish or wise, evil or righteous. An actual woman of strength is quite valuable and important enough to justify a poem in her praise.

6. *Feminist Readings*

It is somewhat surprising to see just how much independence and economic importance the poem ascribes to a woman in a patriarchal society. Feminists have recognized these welcome qualities while criticizing the poem for its patriarchal perspective. Here are some claims and my comments:

The woman's achievements are "no mean accomplishment, and such a woman undoubtedly would be strong and self-confident" (Carmody 1988: 73). Nevertheless, "much of her status seems auxiliary" (ibid.), for "[t]he text implies that her diligence supports her husband's more public affairs, her care enables her children to live well, perhaps even to be spoiled" (ibid.). Thus, "Even at its moment of high praise, the Bible reflects a man's world" (ibid.). (True. But it *was* a man's world, as feminists have trenchantly argued.)

The Woman of Strength "is viewed from the perspective of what she provides for her husband and children. It is her fulfillment of the roles in the home assigned to her by society that causes her to be praised in the very gates of the city where Woman Wisdom first raised her cry" (Fontaine *1992*: 152). (True, but it should be remembered that the woman is a beneficiary as well, and that the children are *hers* too. And of course she is praised in accordance with the values of her society. What other ones would be relevant?)

"Woman Wisdom is the most valuable of all a young man's possessions (4:7). Both are compared favorably to other expensive items (cf. 3:14–15; 8:11; 31:10b)" (Yoder, p. 109). (True, except that the cost of each is not really at issue.)[390]

"The husband is truly the *spectator* here, the fifth wheel of the cart, an admirer who does not seem to realize that these are the traits of a slave-woman that he delineates, not of a woman whose partner he should be" (Maillot *1989*: 110). Maillot wonders if there may be some irony in this portrait: "In actuality the power, with the work, has changed hands" (ibid.). Moreover, "This woman exists only in working for others" (ibid.).[391] Nevertheless, she retains one trait of humanity: she gives to the poor (ibid.). (It is true that her portrait does describe—mostly but not entirely—her work for others, but this is the work of a "woman of substance" [as *ʾēšet ḥayil* can be translated] and in no way would be viewed as slave-like. In any case, there is no sign that the power has "changed hands," nor is power at issue.)

And so on. But what if, as A. Brenner conjectures (1993: 127–30), the poem is written or spoken by a woman, an "F voice" (which does not necessarily mean a female author; see above, Vol. I, 256)? A mother (who, in Brenner's view, "is Wisdom the bountiful") is presumed to be instructing her daughter and "can thus empower her textual 'daughter' in a way unimaginable by the (M) world outside the realm of women's culture" (p. 129). This woman "lives to advance male interests and male well-being," yet "[i]n so doing . . . she ultimately subverts the male order by becoming its focal point and essential requisite" (ibid.). Hence "the final victory and perhaps revenge—so whispers the secondary muted voice—is the woman's, for she is the actual controller of the family" (ibid.) But it seems that the victory is not quite final because "the price for this implicit victory is explicit complicity with the system. . . . Thus is male dominance preserved while being overcome" (ibid.). (Now it's clear.)

Whether the Woman of Strength suits a reader's values—social, ideological, or religious—depends on what these are as much as on the portrait itself. If caring for one's family is a primary value, a poem dedicated to appreciating the effort and

---

[390] It should be noted that 4:7 speaks about wisdom, not personified Wisdom.

[391] "Le mari est vraiment ici le *spectateur,* cinquième roue de la charrette, admirateur qui ne semble pas s'apercevoir que ce sont les traits d'une femme-esclave qu'il dessine, et non pas d'une femme doit il doit être le partenaire. . . . En fait de pouvoir, avec le travail, a changé de mains. [C]ette femme n'existe qu'en travaillant pour les autres" (Maillot *1989*: 110).

zeal a woman invests in this massive duty is less troubling than, say, a poem extolling a woman for aggrandizing her own property would be. (One wonders what kind of feminist critique *that* poem would provoke.) We must also note that the same virtues are praised in men throughout the book of Proverbs, including the crucial ones of wise speech, kindness, industry, and fear of God.

A more trenchant feminist critique might observe the asymmetry in the sages' perspectives on men's and women's earnings. The Woman of Strength is praised for her success in business and home crafts, whereas a man would not be. Proverbs often commends diligence in men and promises that it will bring rewards (e.g., 10:4b; 12:24a; 13:4b; 21:5a), but what is esteemed is the diligence itself, not the prosperity it brings. That is because a man's success, though undoubtedly helping his family, is viewed as accruing to his own benefit. Whatever he earns is his. In contrast, for a woman to bring in wealth is praiseworthy because this is seen as a selfless endeavor, performed, as it were, for her husband's benefit. She is like an employee in a firm owned by her husband. As a valued and high-level employee, who may even serve as operations manager, she is appreciated for her contributions to the success of the firm, and she too will prosper as the business thrives and even be granted some of the profits as a bonus (31:31). But it is not her own business. If it were, all her efforts might be viewed as "hastening to get rich" (28:20b).

Be that as it may, it must be granted that women are taken with full gravity in this book, and especially in this poem:

> Proverbs contains a loud psalm to woman—divine, thus terrible—and what is refused is the "rehearsed response," as if we knew how to read her. The adulteress is portrayed as a demon as glidingly powerful as any girl of Avignon. On the other hand, the "Good Wife," charitable, working, and loving, is a finale, radiant as a fundamental eulogy—I still recall the effect of the rabbinic recitation at my grandmother's funeral. Woman is the key to our seemingly opaque allegory. (D. Shapiro 1987: 318)

7. The Woman of Strength in the Canonical Book of Proverbs

In *Wisdom and the Feminine in the Book of Proverbs* (1985), C. Camp argues that Prov 31:10–31 plays a crucial role in the canonical shape of the book of Proverbs. Collected proverbs present a problem, because proverbial sayings have their primary function in performance, that is, in actual use (Fontaine 1982, chap. III and passim; Camp, pp. 180–82). When they are gathered and written down, they become decontextualized and lack external reference. In the written text, they must be recontextualized, and thereby they gain the status of a literary work. This is achieved, Camp says, through the "bracketing" of the proverb collections (Prov 10–30, in her view) by woman figures in Prov 1–9 and Prov 31. Prov 1–9 introduces personified Wisdom, and Prov 31 comprises poems by and about women (Camp, p. 186). Or, more narrowly, the proverb collections are bracketed by the poems on personified Wisdom and the woman of worth (p. 182). This bracketing provides an "interpretive framework" for the body of the book (chaps. 10–30) and reorients it "from its original function as a schoolboy lesson-book to its later function as part of a canon of religious literature" (ibid.).

Camp builds her argument on the presence of female imagery and a variety of other correlations between Parts I and VIcd (1985: 188–98). Most of these have been adduced by advocates of the allegorization of the Woman of Strength and are summarized above in "Modern Allegorical Interpretations." Whybray too finds "unmistakable" affinities between chapters 1–9 and 31:10–31: (1) the prominence given women in the two units; (2) the fact that these female figures are active and "dominant"; (3) the presentation of Wisdom (8:14) and the Woman of Strength as teachers; (4) the theme-word "find," which has wisdom as its object five times in chapters 1–9 (1:28; 3:13; 4:22; 8:17, 35) and the worthy woman as its object in 31:10 (Whybray 1994: 161–62).

There are indeed affinities between Parts I and VId (less so in VIc), but these units were not composed for the purpose of bracketing the middle of the book. An author who wished to do that would have made the echoes more specific and not so diffuse. (Nine chapters is a rather thick opening "bracket.") Much more likely, Part I resonates in VId because both speak about women, both actual and figurative. There is nothing surprising in these affinities, because the author of Part VId undoubtedly knew the earlier chapters and assimilated their language, imagery, and ideas.

Though Camp pushes the correlations between the two units too far, her approach is valuable for moving our attention from authorship to editorship. Even if Part VId was not written as a conclusion to the book, it was used for that purpose. We may thus ask what *editorial* role it has in this position.

Part I was certainly written as a hermeneutical guide to the proverb collections. In Essay 4 (esp. Vol. I, 357–59), I give my view (not identical to Camp's) of how this guide would have us read and "recontextualize" the sayings of the proverb collections: We should regard them as precipitates of the unitary and transcendental wisdom that pervades all creation. They speak with the voice of countless sages (represented by Solomon), but at the same time with the single voice of Wisdom itself, who is God's first creation and his joyous intimate. Through these sayings, whether elegant or homely, profound or banal, and through other wise words of sages past and present, we—even the simple among us—can draw near to God and hear *his* wisdom and *his* instruction, also called his *torah*.

What role does the ending of the book of Proverbs play in this recontextualization? It is fair to surmise that the primary reason the poem was appended was to say something about wise women in a book that usually neglects them. The scribe who added the poem might reasonably have concluded the book with a grand encomium on the wise *man*, summarizing all that has been said about him so far. Instead, he chose to have the culmination be an encomium on the wise woman, in which there resonates all that is said about wise women and Lady Wisdom elsewhere. But she does not personify wisdom; she *instantiates* it.

Camp conjectures that in the postexilic period (when the book was edited, whatever the dating of its components), special importance was ascribed to family and thus to women. The nation was no longer defined by kingship but by the home, whose character and identity were in turn defined by women (Camp, p. 264). A renewed emphasis (such as supposedly existed in premonarchic times) was placed on the realm of everyday life. Female imagery coalesced into a viable religious symbol in an era without a king (p. 282).

I do not think that the emphasis on the home is a development of postexilic times, because the deeds of Lady Wisdom and wise human women in earlier times were not performed by the king, nor was the family then less significant as a constituent of society. But even without the proposed historical setting, and quite apart from the possible "bracketing" of the central chapters, the feminine does serve the role Camp assigns it. The editors of the *book* of Proverbs (as distinct from the various collections) chose the feminine to convey the principle bridging the transcendent and the mundane realms. The imagery does not *legitimize* female authority (as Camp, p. 4, would have it) so much as underscore female significance, in heaven as on earth, as provider and mediator of wisdom. Ben Sira, crabby and sexist though he was, read Proverbs this way and let it shape his thought when he made wisdom a woman (Sir 24). Wisdom, in the form of Torah (Sir 24:23), dwells in Israel (v 8) and cares for its people (vv 16–22), granting them her fruits (v 19) and satisfying their spiritual hunger (v 21). She too is a Woman of Strength.

8. The Value of the Woman of Strength

However the Woman of Strength may fare when judged by modern criteria, the fact is that she excels in the very qualities most important to the sages themselves, the authors and collectors of the book of Proverbs. For them, she is not just an ideal woman, she is an ideal person. By reminding us that the most important features of the wise man characterize the woman too, the whole book of Proverbs, despite its male orientation, is made to apply to women as well.

As seen in the previous chart (in "Modern Allegorical Interpretations") and in the references in the Comments on Prov 31:10–31, the Woman of Strength shares the most important traits of wisdom and the wise: strength, preciousness, diligence, skill, generosity, self-confidence, and wise teachings. For these reasons, she is secure in herself and earns praise from others. And all this culminates in her fear of God. The poem does not so much form an end-bracket to the book as a culmination and recapitulation, drawing together in the woman figure the virtues it teaches throughout.

Little space is given to her husband's feelings toward her. One thing notably unmentioned is love. Perhaps this marriage grew out of romantic love, such as is exalted in the Song of Songs, and perhaps not, but that is not what the present poem is about. It is not about the one-on-one relationship so much as the marital union in the service of economic, familial, and social goals. It is not about the wife as lover (a role zestily described in Prov 5:15–20) but about the wife as partner, parent, and provider. A relationship such as described in Prov 31:10–31 may evolve in an arranged marriage as well as an amorous one, and perhaps this is part of the hidden message to a young man looking for beauty and passion.

Her husband's feelings are encapsulated in one word, *bṭḥ*, "trusts" or "has confidence," in v 11: "Her husband's heart trusts in her." In Proverbs, trust is both a virtue and a reward. As a virtue, it is the way one should feel toward God: a reliance on his will and his plans (3:5; 16:20; 28:25; 29:25). It is essentially the same as *fear* of God, though it may sound like its opposite. As a reward, the feeling of trust or confidence the virtuous person enjoys flows naturally out of moral and religious virtues—obedience to wisdom (1:33; 3:23–25), integrity (10:9), righteousness (28:1), and trust in God (3:26). The confidence that the husband here places in his wife is a both a joy—a wonderful support in facing life—and a virtue in their relationship, and it is rewarded by "gain" (31:11) and "good" (v 12), just as trust in Yahweh is repaid with confidence (3:26; 28:1) and prosperity (28:25).

Indeed, *confidence*—true, justified confidence, not the fool's smugness or the cynic's smirking complacency—is the state of soul that Proverbs seeks to achieve throughout, the condition that wisdom is conducive to and required for. In life we walk through a landscape fraught with perils and uncertainties, traps and pitfalls (Prov 24:11), but wisdom brings us through securely. "He who obeys me," promises Lady Wisdom, "shall dwell in safety [*betaḥ*], secure [*šaʾănan*] from fear of harm" (1:33). The material reward that wisdom grants is not necessarily great wealth, but a sufficiency to provide for needs and comforts. The righteous man's "house"—that is, his family, present and future—stands firm (12:7).

The Woman of Strength inspires this highly prized state of soul. All that she does for her household affords her husband the financial stability and social stature that a responsible husband desires for himself, his children—and his wife.

ESSAYS

INTRODUCTION TO ESSAYS 5–8

◆

Despite its indisputable diversity of origins and multiplicity of authors, Proverbs has one constant focal point, and that is *wisdom*. The subsequent essays will explore some of the implications and consequences of this central idea. These essays are sequential to Essays 3 and 4 in Vol. I, 346–59. Those essays actually discuss a *later* stage in the book's growth than the chapters studied in Vol. II. They will be referenced and summarized as necessary.

Essay 5. The Growth of Wisdom. Wisdom is the capacity of the human mind to determine the right course of behavior and to apply this knowledge in achieving a successful life. But different periods understood this capacity differently.

Essay 6. Ethics. The foundational axiom of Proverbs' ethics is the "Socratic" principle that virtue is knowledge.

Essay 7. Revelation. Wisdom is not communicated by divine revelation. Some thinkers insisted on the necessity of revealed Torah, and for that reason wisdom became progressively identified with, then subordinated to, Torah.

Essay 8. Knowledge. The epistemology underlying Wisdom thought—the unverbalized "philosophy" of knowledge that allows sages to produce and recognize knowledge—is not empiricism but a *coherency theory* of truth.

Words for Wisdom. A variety of practical synonyms are used for "wisdom" and (the virtually indistinguishable) "knowledge." The most important wisdom-words are *ḥokmah* ("wisdom"), *binah* ("understanding"), *tᵉbunah* ("good sense"), *daʿat* ("knowledge"), and sometimes *śekel* ("discretion," "good sense"). The concept of wisdom can also be deduced from verses that use the corresponding adjectives and participles, namely, *ḥakam* ("wise"), *nabon* ("astute"), *mebin* ("discerning"), and *maśkil* ("discreet," "perceptive").[392] These words have their own nuances and syntactic constraints, and various scholars have drawn distinctions among them; see Vol. I, 28–38 and N. Shupak 1993: 31–53. For one thing, *daʿat* and *binah* are nouns derived from transitive verbs and can have objective suffixes, while *ḥokmah* is related to an intransitive verb and cannot. But in practice, especially in the Wisdom books, the wisdom-words are pragmatic synonyms, conveying basically the same ideas and labeling the same phenomenon. (Thus also J. Hausmann 1995: 34.)

Though the terms have different focuses, which I earlier tried to identify, their

---

[392] The Hebrew words are not as discrete as the English glosses might suggest. Also, a few other words, such as *tušiyyah*, *taḥbulot*, *mezimmot*, and *ʿormah*, belong to the semantic field of wisdom or at least overlap part of it. These, however, designate narrower aspects of the faculty in question, and in any case they do not change the conclusions offered here.

range is overlapping and the terms are never mutually exclusive. So far as I can determine, there is little that the sages would say about *ḥokmah* that they would not believe true of *daʿat, binah, śekel*, or *tᵉbunah*. Moreover, when wisdom is personified, it has several names: *ḥokmot* (1:20), *ḥokmah* (8:1a), *tᵉbunah* (8:1b), and *binah* (8:14). Thus the wisdom-words form a lexical group that as a whole conveys the concept of wisdom.

There is a motive to this heaping up of synonyms beyond just variety. As von Rad recognized, "Der Text scheint durch die Kumulierung vieler Begriffe etwas Umfassenderes, Grösseres anzuvisieren, das mit einem der verwendeten Begriffe unzureichend umschrieben wäre" ("By amassing a number of terms the text seems to aim at something greater and more comprehensive, something that would not be adequately expressed by just one of the terms") (1970: 26).

ESSAY 5. THE GROWTH OF WISDOM

I. STAGES IN PROVERBS

The concept of wisdom in Proverbs grew in stages. Awareness of the particular character of the concept of wisdom in each stage can help us recognize the diversity of ideas of wisdom within Proverbs and recover something of the dynamism of Wisdom thought. Wisdom is not only a genre of literature, it is a *process*, a dialectic in which thinkers of different times meditated on ideas they had learned from their predecessors and shaped them in new ways. In this dialectic, the new concepts did not displace the old ones, but rather extended and enriched them. The stages in the development of the wisdom-concept in Proverbs are as follows:

Stage 1 appears in Prov 10–29 (Parts II–V), the "old collections"
Stage 2 appears in Prov 1–9 (Part I), the ten Lectures and the Prologue[393]
Stage 3 appears in Prov 1–9 (Part I), the five Interludes[394]

Agur (30:1–9; Part VIa) differs from the rest of the book in his understanding of wisdom and will be discussed in "Agur's Teaching" after the Comments on 30:1–9 and also in "Agur" (III.C) in Essay 7.[395]

The other components of Part VI—VIb, Epigrams and Aphorisms (30:10–33); VIc, The Teaching of Lemuel's Mother (31:1–9); and VId, The Woman of Strength (31:10–31)—are not relevant to the development of the concept discussed in this essay.

Chapters 10–29 are themselves composite, holding four collections (Parts II–V), but since no conceptual distinctions can be discerned among these collections with respect to the nature of wisdom, I treat them as a compositional unit—a single "stage"—for the present purpose.

Both Hebrew *ḥokmah* (and its synonyms) and English "wisdom" are ambiguous. Both refer to two distinct phenomena:

(1) Wisdom as a set of teachings. In a generic sense, everything taught in Proverbs is wisdom, because all of its teachings are considered wise and wisdom is promised to him who learns them (Prov 1:2–7).

(2) Wisdom as a *faculty*, a power of the mind used in achieving one's goals. A

---

393 See Essay 3; Vol. I, 347–51.

394 See Essay 4; Vol. I, 352–59.

395 The relative dating of the components of Prov 30 and 31 is very uncertain. The author of Prov 31:10–31 was certainly aware of ideas of wisdom expressed in chapters 10–29, and the author of Agur, or at least the person who appended it to the book, was responding to the claims of wisdom put forth in the rest of the book. See the Commentary on Prov 30:1–9 and 31:10–31.

faculty may be innate or learned. In Proverbs wisdom is considered the latter. As a type of expertise, the wisdom faculty includes both abilities and knowledge.

The second use of wisdom is in focus in this essay, which seeks to draw the contours of the concept rather than just redescribe the book's teachings. Only some of the proverbs written or collected for the book of Proverbs mention wisdom and the wise. My assumption is that these proverbs had something special to say, and the concept of wisdom must be deduced from them.

The words designating the wisdom faculty are examined from a semantic perspective in "Words for Wisdom," Vol. I, 29–38; see further "The Wisdom Words" in Vol. II, Introduction to Essays 5–8. These words are *ḥokmah* ("wisdom"), *binah* ("understanding"), *tᵉbunah* ("good sense"), *daʿat* ("knowledge"), and sometimes *śekel* ("discretion," "good sense"), as well as the corresponding adjectives and person-nouns ("wise man," etc.).

This essay seeks to trace the history of a concept rather than to date particular proverbs or teachings. We cannot deduce the relative dating of the concepts from the *nature* of the concepts, for that would assume what remains to be proved, namely, that the idea of wisdom evolved in a certain developmental course. Rather, I regard the *concept* of wisdom in Stage 1 as older than the concepts in Stages 2 and 3 because, in my view, the collections in chapters 10–29 (Stage 1) are older than the Lectures (Stage 2), which are older than the Interludes (Stage 3). I seek to trace this development in Essay 1 (Vol. I, 322–30) and in "Dating" in the Introduction to Vol. II (III). My dating of the Parts of the book is based on literary considerations rather than on the nature of the concepts described in the present essay.

My thesis is distinct from McKane's theory that all the proverbs that offer practical advice for successful living belong to the "old wisdom" while those with an ethical or religious message belong to a later, "Yahwistic," redaction (1970: 10–22). (See "Religious Proverbs" [I.C] in the Introduction to Vol. II.) Since both practical and religious teachings are present in foreign and ancient wisdom, most notably in Ahiqar and Amenemope, there is no reason to doubt that religious teachings were present in Israelite Wisdom from the start. Some of the proverbs that mention religious and moral virtues in Prov 10–29 may be as old as those that speak of practical wisdom.

Like McKane, G. von Rad (1956) sees an evolution in wisdom. Early wisdom, which supposedly arose in the Solomonic court, was practical insight founded on experience. The later wisdom was theological and engaged in reflection about God and the mysteries of creation. It is represented in Prov 8, Job 28, and Sir 24. Though von Rad's dating of these passages is feasible, the teachings of Wisdom included religious concerns even prior to the emergence of Israelite Wisdom, and these would not have disappeared. It is true that some postexilic sages developed a reflective theological perspective, represented clearly in Prov 8 and culminating in the Wisdom of Solomon. However, this never displaced the pragmatic concerns.

II. STAGE 1: THE OLDER COLLECTIONS (PROVERBS 10–29)

Wisdom in chapters 10–29 is a practical, prudential faculty. It consists of the knowledge and skills that enable a man to succeed and thrive, to define worthy goals and attain them.[396] (If his goals are not worthy, he is not, in Proverbs' view, wise.)[397] Moreover, this faculty is always a *disposition*: an inclination to *do* what serves one's goals. This concept of wisdom is closest to the one found in the rest of the Bible outside of Wisdom Literature. Wisdom in its oldest and broadest sense is the expertise that allows one to assess a situation and choose effective means to carry out one's intentions. This expertise can be applied to a vast range of activities. Most significantly, outside Proverbs, wisdom is not an inherently ethical power, for it can be put to ethically neutral or even negative uses; see esp. Vol. I, 32–34.

A. Attributes of the Wise

Only certain traits are expressly called wise. These can be grouped into a few categories:

(1) *Receptivity to wisdom.* This is the most prominent attribute of the wise in Stage 1. The wise man is ready and eager to listen to words of wisdom and to take correction (Prov 10:8; 12:15b; 13:10b; 15:14a; 17:10; 20:5; etc.). A keen attentiveness to wisdom is his defining characteristic (12:15; 13:1; 15:31, 32; 23:19; 25:12). He "seeks" (*bqš*) wisdom (15:14; 18:15) and absorbs it (21:11b), even when it comes in the form of rebukes and chastisement (13:1; 15:31; 19:25b; 25:12b). Indeed, to love knowledge means to love correction, *musar* (12:1). Note that even the wise man may be in need of reprimand; he is not necessarily flawless. He is, however, able, even eager, to absorb criticism and correct his ways; see esp. 25:12 and 19:25b: "Rebuke an astute person and he will gain knowledge." Wisdom is not necessarily an invariable or indelible quality; what is permanent is the ability and readiness to learn (cf. Hausmann 1995: 14).

Achieving wisdom requires focus and zeal, but it is not an arduous task, for, as Prov 17:24a says, "Wisdom is before the face of the perceptive man," that is, he sees it right before his eyes, without searching for it "in the ends of the earth," as 17:24b puts it (see also 14:6b; 18:15a). Pursuit of wisdom is not burdensome for the discerning, because wisdom is as sweet as honey (24:13–14), and it is a pleasure and joy to the wise (10:23).

(2) *Verbal skills.* The power of speech is exalted with great frequency in sayings about the wise. In short, "On the lips of the discerning man wisdom is found" (10:13a). The wise man knows how to adapt his words to the needs of circumstances and to shape them effectively, especially when speaking words of counsel,

[396] R. N. Whybray characterizes Israelite Wisdom thus: "[The Israelite's] reasoning was not in principle opposed to his faith, but it was used, at first at least, in relation to aspects of life concerning which his specifically religious teaching gave him no information or guidance. The knowledge thus acquired, which the Israelite called 'wisdom', was essentially practical: the attempt to understand the nature of things was dictated not so much by intellectual curiosity as by man's practical need to control his environment sufficiently to be able to survive and flourish; and 'wisdom' covered a wide range of such useful information, from skill in using tools to a knowledge of the art of personal relationships. It also included the skillful use of language such as is displayed in the making of proverbs, riddles, etc." (1965b: 115). In my view, this applies only to Stage 1 in Proverbs.

[397] See Essay 6, esp. "Principle 2: No One Does Wrong Willingly" (II.B).

criticism, and instruction (15:2a, 7a; 16:21, 23; 18:4; 20:15). He knows how to calm angry spirits (12:18; 29:8), something that can be done only through speech, and also how to heal and cheer somber souls (12:18b). The wisdom of speech includes the good sense to be silent, as circumstances demand. The wise man is restrained and reserved in speech (10:19; 12:23a; 17:27, 28b), even in the face of insult and offense (11:12b). He is able to express his wisdom or to hide it, all as the moment requires (10:14a; 14:33a; cf. 12:23a).

(3) *Emotional composure.* The wise man is calm (17:27), patient (14:29a; 19:11), and modest (11:2; 15:33b).

(4) *Forethought and preparedness.* The wise man is diligent and tends to his material solvency. This is the meaning of "building a house" (24:3a; cf. v 4) and is said also of the wise woman (14:1).

(5) *Cunning.* In Proverbs, but not elsewhere, *ʿormah*, "cunning, shrewdness," is a virtue. It consists in shrewdness or prudence, not wiliness and certainly not deviousness. Cunning is an aspect of wisdom in Proverbs because the book will not concede that the cognitive power it esteems can be other than virtuous or produce anything but the good.[398] The purpose of the statement, "Every shrewd man acts thoughtfully" (lit., "in knowledge") (13:16a), is to encourage people to embrace knowledge, that is, wisdom, in the rich way that Proverbs understands this concept. Wisdom is a unity.[399] The message to the young man is: If you want to be a sharp guy—and who doesn't?—you must act in wisdom (cf. 12:23a; 14:18b; 15:5b).

(6) *Avoidance of conflicts.* "The wise man fears and turns away from trouble [*raʿ*], while the dolt confidently butts in" (14:16). The antithesis shows that *raʿ* here means "trouble," rather than acts of evil, and refers to quarrels.

(7) *Honesty.* In the words of 15:21, "Folly [*ʾiwwelet*] is pleasure to the mindless, while the sensible [*tᵉbunah*] man walks straight." *Tᵉbunah* generally emphasizes the pragmatic, applied aspect of wisdom, operating in the realm of action rather than intellectual perspicuity (see Vol. I, 37–38). Hence this saying teaches the *usefulness* of honesty. It is noteworthy that, although the proverbs in chapters 10–29 have much to say about honesty and ethical virtues, these qualities are only rarely associated explicitly with wisdom or the wise.

(8) *Justice.* "The wise king scatters the wicked and rolls a wheel over them" (Prov 20:26). This is said of the king, not the private man. Enforcing justice is part of the king's professional responsibility, and the knowledge to execute it is for him practical wisdom. For the private man, pursuit of justice belongs to the realm of righteousness, not *ḥokmah*.

These *and no more* are the essential traits ascribed to wisdom in Stage 1. Other virtues would most probably have been thought wise, but they seem not to have been what came to mind when the early sages spoke about wisdom.

---

[398] There is one development in this regard. In chaps. 10–29, *mezimmah* is regarded with suspicion (12:2; 14:17; 24:8), whereas in chaps. 1–9 it is viewed positively (2:11; 5:2; 8:12) and is akin to circumspection or discretion, not scheming.

[399] See Essay 6 (II.C), "All Virtues Are One."

B. The Rewards of Wisdom

The rewards of wisdom promised in the older collections are many and varied, but they can be grouped into a few categories:

(1) Wealth and material success (Prov 14:24; 17:2; 21:20a).

(2) Protection and deliverance from dangers (Prov 14:3b; 28:26b).

(3) Life (Prov 15:24; 16:22a; contrast 21:16).

(4) An *ʾaḥărit* ("end," "future") and a *tiqwah* ("hope") (Prov 24:14). Both refer to a good future in life, and perhaps beyond, in the form of posterity. See the Comment on 19:20.

(5) Strength (in overcoming obstacles, achieving success) (Prov 21:22; 24:5; cf. #1). A wise man, even if enslaved, will rule over a fool, even if he is free (Prov 11:29).

(6) Effectiveness in speech (Prov 15:2, 7 [see Commentary]; 16:23).

(7) Favor and praise (Prov 12:8; 13:15).

(8) Joy to one's parents (Prov 10:1; 15:20; 23:15, 24–25; 27:11). This frequently promised reward is reckoned a benefit to the son himself, as shown by the way it is adduced as an incentive for him to seek wisdom.

These benefits are all practical and worldly. The emotional rewards (## 7 and 8) are given by and to people. Among the profits of wisdom there is—in Stage 1—no mention of spiritual benefits or favor in God's eyes. Nor is God the direct source of wisdom's benefits. Wisdom brings its own rewards.

This set of rewards has an almost mirror opposite in what fools suffer. The following unhappy consequences of folly are stated explicitly (sometimes in the wider context) or implied by contrast with the wise in the parallel line:

(1) Financial loss and impoverishment (Prov 12:11; 14:1; 17:18; 24:30–34).

(2) Harm, including disaster (Prov 10:14; 18:7) and beatings (10:13; 18:6).

(3) Death (Prov 10:21).

(4) Lack of hope for a future or posterity (Prov 11:19).

(5) (Weakness: implied in 11:29).

(6) Ineffective or even self-destructive speech (Prov 10:13; 12:23; 13:16; 15:2; 26:9).

(7) Disgrace and hostility (Prov 18:13; 24:9).

(8) Grief to one's parents (Prov 10:1; 15:29; 17:21, 25; 19:13).

C. The Nature of Wisdom

This survey has shown wisdom in Stage 1 to be a pragmatic, worldly faculty, with no inherently religious motivation or goal.[400] It also lacks a tight association with ethics, although the sages of Proverbs 10–29 certainly demanded moral virtues and assumed that nothing immoral could be wise. At this stage, the cognitive powers called wisdom operate in the realm of daily life, and their rewards are their natural products.

[400] This is observed by Hausmann 1995: 35.

This wisdom is subtle, flexible, and adaptive. The choices facing the wise are not usually binary decisions, matters of yes or no, good or bad. The wise man knows how to adjust his responses to the demands of diverse situations and conditions, many of them amorphous and unclear. He must analyze and evaluate the circumstances, the people, and the times, and find exactly the right response. Sometimes he hides his wisdom; sometimes he reveals it in public. Sometimes he soothes tempers; sometimes he scolds and chastises. He knows how to say the right things at the right time, and also when to be silent. He must furthermore be flexible in his own self-image, otherwise he could not take correction and grow. The pragmatic wisdom of Stage 1 thus operates in a wide and varied realm vis-à-vis innumerable possibilities.

D. Wisdom and Righteousness

To clarify the distinctiveness of wisdom, it helps to compare what is said about righteousness. The words *ṣaddiq* and *ḥakam* are, as K. Heim has argued (*2001*: 77–108), not synonymous but *co-referential*; that is, they have different meanings but designate the same persons, by and large. Some things are said about both types, but the overlap is not complete. Relevant here are the traits of the righteous that are not ascribed to the wise in Prov 10–29. An incisive definition of "righteousness" is provided by S. M. Lyu:

> Righteousness is the all-encompassing quality of human or divine character *in toto* above and beyond specific behaviors, which actualizes as rectitude in moral choices and fairness and benevolence in social transactions. A righteous person embodies righteousness as the internalized and pervasive character trait, cultivates the desire to be righteous, and finds pleasure when that desire is met. (*2005*: 20)

Whereas the wise man is strongly receptive to learning and correction, nothing is said about a *ṣaddiq* ("righteous man") learning more. He is a static type, and it is never suggested that he may require warning or correction. This is why, although the reader is often urged to get wisdom, he is never told to seek righteousness or to *become* righteous. One either is or is not a *ṣaddiq*. Proverbs' characterization of the righteous man's behavior is meant as a paradigm for emulation. Perhaps by following the righteous man's example, one can be, or show oneself to be, righteous, but no sayings deal with this development itself. Wisdom, however, like any practical skill, is a work in progress.

In the bundle of associations attached to wisdom, only a very minor role is assigned to traits and demands that are specifically religious, ethical, or humanitarian. Little is said about the wise man's honesty. Rather, in commending honesty, words with moral valence such as *ṣaddiq*, *tam* ("honest"), and *yašar* ("upright") are usually used. The wise man is not called generous or compassionate. These traits are associated particularly with the righteous, or, more precisely, with the man whose worthiness in context is his righteousness, not his wisdom. God's activity and his relationship to individuals are scarcely mentioned in sayings about the wise, nor is there reference to God's favor and love, his protection, his rewards, or his attention to prayers. It is not said that the wise man's reward comes from God. All these things *are* said of the righteous and upright, and frequently so.[401] It is not that these things are untrue of the wise man. It is just that they are not what the concept of wisdom, in its early sense, is *about*.[402]

Only one saying in Stage 1 pictures Yahweh as actively aiding the wise: "The eyes of the Lord guard knowledge, while he confounds the words of the treacherous" (Prov 22:12). The parallelism shows that "knowledge" refers to *words* of knowledge. The saying teaches that God watches over the words and counsels of the wise man to ensure that they achieve their goals. Even here, God's role is not exactly to *execute* recompense and give the wise man his due reward so much as to *guard* the dependability of the nexus between deed and consequence. This is how K. Koch (1972) described God's role in the "Tat-Ergehen Zusammenhang" ("deed-consequence nexus"),[403] and it is accurate with regard to the workings of wisdom according to Proverbs, though not always in contexts that do not speak of wisdom. God need not intervene to ensure recompense for wisdom because this faculty, by its very nature, is a prudential skill that prevents harm to its possessor and secures his goals. A mental faculty would not be wisdom if it did not secure a benefit. (As I understand the terms, sacrificing oneself for a greater cause could be deemed "righteous" but not "wise.")

Only one saying in Stage 1, Prov 15:33, associates wisdom with a religious trait: *Yir'at YHWH musar ḥokmah, w^e^lipney kabod ʿănawah*, "What wisdom teaches is the fear of the Lord, and before honor comes humility." *Musar ḥokmah* is the lesson that wisdom teaches, just as *musar 'ab* "the father's teaching" (4:1; 15:5), is the lesson that the father teaches. In other words, wisdom teaches one to fear Yahweh. The reason is given in the second line, which declares that humility "comes before" honor—priority implying causality. The fear of Yahweh is a form of humility, because it is founded on the awareness that God controls human lives. (The causality goes the other direction as well: "The reward of humility is fear of the Lord, wealth and honor and life"; 22:4.) The point of 15:33 is that it is *ḥakam*—wise, prudent, smart—to fear God and be humble, and it pays off with a practical benefit, namely, honor. The verse is evaluating the fear of God by a utilitarian measure rather than evaluating wisdom by a religious one. In any case, this saying is unique in Prov 10–29 and does not undermine the fundamental

[401] The following topics of an ethical-religious nature appear with reference to the righteous: generosity and compassion (e.g., 12:10; 21:26b; 29:7); God's relation to individuals (e.g., 10:3a, 24b; 18:10); God's favor and love (e.g., 15:9b; 11:20b; 21:3; cf. 12:2 [*ṭob*]; 12:22 ["those who act faithfully"]); God's protection (18:10); divine rewards (e.g., 10:3a, 24); God's attention to prayers (15:29b).

[402] R. B. Y. Scott observes that in only one or two verses in chaps. 10–15 (10:31; 11:9) is the righteous man associated with wisdom, and only once is he contrasted with the fool (10:21) (1972: 153). The wise man is never contrasted with the wicked. But Scott errs in concluding from this that the wise/foolish and righteous/wicked antitheses "present alternative ways of life and divide men into two classes accordingly, each with its appropriate destiny" (ibid.). Wisdom and righteousness are manifest largely in the same behaviors, but viewed from different perspectives.

[403] See the discussion of this theory and responses to it in Vol. I, 91–92.

secularity of the concept of wisdom in this stage. (By "secular" I mean that the passage or quality in question is not placed in explicit relation to God.) But the verse does constitute a bridge to the next stage, in which wisdom becomes a distinctly religious quality.

III. STAGE 2: THE PROLOGUE AND LECTURES

Proverbs 1–9 was prefixed to the old collections as an introduction to the book. This introduction is composed of two compositional layers: the ten Lectures and the Prologue (Stage 2 in the development of the concept of wisdom) and the five Interludes that were inserted among the Lectures at various times (Stage 3). These developments are discussed in Vol. I, 44–45 and 322–29. The following remarks summarize and develop the observations in Essays 2 and 3 (Vol. I, 346–59).

Whereas in discussing Stage 1, I adduced as evidence only the sayings that mention wisdom, in discussing Stage 2, the cohesiveness of each Lecture and of the Lectures as a unified cycle (see Vol. I, 324–26) allows us to base the description of wisdom on the entirety of each Lecture, when this is designated "wisdom." This is the case in Lectures II, V, VI, VIII, and X. The other Lectures, which use different terms for the teachings ("words," "instruction," "discipline," and "precepts") can provide supportive illustrations.

In the Lectures, together with the Prologue (1:1–7), wisdom is religious at its very foundations. Whereas Prov 15:33a declares that it is wise to fear God (see above, "Wisdom and Righteousness" [II.D]), the Lectures identify fear of Yahweh as the foundation and aim of wisdom, and not just one of several principles that wisdom promotes. To be sure, Yahweh is not mentioned with great frequency in the Lectures. (He is mentioned most often in Lecture III, whose central topic is piety [3:5, 7, 9, 11, 12].) Nevertheless, God's role in wisdom is pivotal and programmatic in this stratum. Wisdom both begins with fear of Yahweh (1:7) and leads to this essential virtue (2:5). Wisdom is a gift of God rather than the direct outcome of the striving (2:6).[404] Conversely, wisdom resides not only in human actions, but also in one's attitude toward God, which is a combination of fear of God and trust in God (Prov 1:7; 3:5).[405]

The practical content of wisdom in the Lectures is encapsulated in Prov 4:23a: "Above all else, guard your heart," that is, control your thoughts, desires, and feelings. Such wisdom serves as *protection*—not against direct attacks, but against the

[404] Frydrych says: "[T]he relationship between wisdom and *fear of Yahweh* is portrayed here as reciprocal, each one being the source and consequence of the other; wisdom promotes piety and piety promotes wisdom. Thus *fear of Yahweh* is not only the beginning of proverbial wisdom, it is also its end; it is the one phrase that the sages choose to summarize their entire undertaking" (2002: 171). This is true of the book in its present form, including Stage 2. The fear of Yahweh did not have this significance in Stage 1.

[405] Steiert's discussion of these concepts (1990: 91) is insightful, but one may doubt his assertion that the equation of fear of Yahweh with avoidance of evil is peculiar to Proverbs (except insofar as Yahweh is naturally the divinity in the Hebrew book). Amenemope's teachings in §§7, 8, 18, and 22 express basically the same attitude toward God, who is usually unnamed.

danger of seduction. The Lectures do not offer a multiplicity of counsels about how to succeed in life. They warn against surrendering to temptations (I, II, VIII, IX, and X) and demand that a person keep to the right path (VI, VII). They extol piety (III) and laud wisdom (II, V), for these virtues help one shun the titillations of evil (V). Only Lecture IV makes specific ethical demands, prohibiting four types of mistreatment of others (3:27–31). Taken as a whole, the message of the Lectures is simple and consistent: Avoid evil. Wisdom is the power that will help you do this.

In Stage 2, wisdom has become a moral virtue, almost identical with righteousness.[406] It is a form of moral character—the disposition and will to stay on the right path. It is still a cognitive power, a form of knowledge that one learns and strives for. Yet no special wit, learning, or even experience is required to attain it. Even the *peti*, the simple lad devoid of ingenuity and experience, is able to become wise, on the condition that he determine to make basic moral distinctions. Achieving this requires not only cognitive knowledge of what is right but also *desiring* it, even *loving* it (4:6; 7:4).

Though this wisdom is qualitatively simple, it is not easy to attain. Desire-driven wisdom is so difficult to attain that human effort does not bring it about so much as prepare the ground for its reception: When one strives for wisdom (2:1–5), God grants it (2:6).[407] The Lectures describe wisdom as a goal demanding long and intensive effort, requiring also divine favor for its achievement (2:6). The difficulty arises from the fact that wisdom is, in this view, moral character, which is achieved only with effort. Indeed, the effort itself is crucial to the shaping of character. See Essay 3, esp. Vol. I, 347–48.

The rewards promised for wisdom in the Lectures are of vital importance:

(1) *Guidance and understanding* (2:9–10; 6:22a). According to 2:9–10, achieving wisdom will give you *understanding* of the right path.

(2) *Protection against temptations* (2:7–8, 11, 12, 16; 6:24; 7:5).

(3) *Fear of Yahweh* (2:5).

(4) *Favor* in the eyes of God and man (3:4, 32 ["intimacy"]), in other words, *honor* (3:35).

(5) *Security and confidence* (3:6, 23–26, 33 [blessing of habitation]; 4:6; 6:22bc).

(6) *Health and well-being* (3:2, 8; 4:22b).

(7) *Life* (3:2, 16, 18, 22; 4:4, 13, 22a; 7:2a).

These rewards fall into two groups. The first, ##1–3, comprises ethical-religious virtues. Wisdom gives one the conscience, the enlightenment, and the guidance that will help him avoid temptation. Thus, one of the rewards of wisdom is wisdom. The second, ##4–7, comprises the personal benefits that flow from wisdom

[406] The difference is that wisdom in this conception is still a prudential faculty—the avoidance of evil for the sake of preventing harm to oneself—whereas full-fledged righteousness demands the proactive pursuit of justice and the right state of affairs, including the rectification of wrongs, for the sake of others as well as oneself.

[407] Compare Sir 6:37: If you meditate on God's Law, "he will inform your mind and grant you the wisdom you desire." The study of Torah lays the groundwork for God's gift.

and virtue: honor, well-being, and long life. There is no further attention to the particulars of the rewards. This array of promises overlaps with the rewards offered in Stage 1 but lacks some of the utilitarian benefits promised there: wealth and material success (though in 3:10 this is promised as a reward for sacral donations); strength; efficacious speech; joy to one's parents (even though the speaker is the father himself!); and a "future" or "hope." The absence of the first four of these utilitarian benefits is significant. The moral wisdom of Stage 2 provides physical and social well-being but does not guarantee material gains or tactical powers, at least not explicitly. An exception is in the Prologue, 1:5, which says that the book provides *taḥbulot*, "strategy" or "guidance," to the advanced student, the man who is already *nabon*, "astute." The Prologue has chapters 10–29 as well as the Lectures in view.[408] In the Lectures proper, this kind of astuteness is not promised.

In Stage 2, Proverbs teaches that wisdom—the smartness that according to the later chapters makes for success in practical matters, the savvy that is nigh to shrewdness (8:12)—is also the faculty that governs moral virtue.

What is new in the Lectures is not the teaching of moral virtue—this had a strong presence in Stage 1 and, for that matter, in Wisdom Literature from earliest times—but rather the *intellectualization* of moral virtue: It is now associated with a set of concepts that earlier designated cognitive powers. In Essay 6, "Ethics," this view of wisdom will be compared to the Socratic doctrine that virtue is knowledge, and that he who knows the good will do it.

IV. STAGE 3: THE INTERLUDES[409]

In Stage 3, wisdom is still the faculty possessed by humans, now with both practical and ethical-religious powers, but at the same time it also transcends the human mind and permeates all space and all time. Stage 3 comes to expression in the Interludes that describe and praise wisdom: A, B, E, and, most clearly and strikingly, D. These poems were probably not composed as a unit, but they express a new and fairly unified concept of wisdom. (Interlude C is not relevant to this issue.)

Interlude B (3:13–20) continues the exaltation of wisdom found already in Stage 1. It speaks of wisdom's value in lofty terms, culminating in the statement that Yahweh used it in creation. This statement is not a deep innovation because God's wisdom is still the practical skill that can be employed in all actions, including craftsmanship. Yahweh's wisdom is just a greater instance of the same faculty that man has, and the fact that God used wisdom in creating the world (3:19–20) is also, in context, the reason man too should gain and employ it. Still, Interlude B places wisdom in special proximity to God, and this idea is developed and escalated in Interlude D.

The Interludes that show Wisdom personified as a woman (A [1:20–33], D [8:1–35], and E [9:1–18]) introduce a new concept of wisdom. Wisdom, as represented

[408] The Prologue was probably composed prior to the Interludes; see Vol. I, 325–26.

[409] This section is based on Vol. I, 326–29, 352–56 in this Commentary.

by the trope of Lady Wisdom, exists as a *universal*, similar to a Platonic *idea*. Lady Wisdom represents the transcendent universal of wisdom. Wisdom is still a property of individual human minds, but it also transcends them. The transcendent wisdom exists before and beyond human wisdom but is also manifest in it. Every wise word and deed is an imperfect actualization or reflection of this eternal and immutable principle.

Wisdom, embodied in Lady Wisdom, is the wisest of court counselors (8:14). She is the source of righteous rule and just laws (8:15–16). She grants wealth to the upright (8:21). She is the fount of life (8:35; cf. 3:2, 18, 22; 4:23; also in the old collections: 13:14; 16:22). Through her mediation one can find favor with God (8:35), as if she were the most influential of officials in his court—a vizier, as it were. She speaks righteous and honest words (8:8–9), and if one harkens to her and keeps her ways—*her* ways—he will find good fortune (v 32). Like a prophet, Wisdom castigates the sinful and declares their doom (1:20–33). Her words and ways are undoubtedly a mirror of the divine will, but it is they, and not a direct revelation, that will guide man in the way of life. This transcendent, nearly divine, wisdom radiates something of her glory onto human wisdom and infuses it with powers that the individual mind, however talented, would lack on its own.

ESSAY 6. ETHICS

◆

I. THE PRIMARY AXIOM

Though the book of Proverbs evolved in a complex process of authorship and editing, the result was a document with a considerable degree of cohesion. It shows consistency in style and thought, and its components are in harmony. This is because the book grew organically, with later authors and editors aware of and responding to the earlier ones and unfolding the potentials they saw in the texts of their predecessors. This unity allows us to discuss various topics in the book as a whole. The ethical ideas to be described in this essay are the contribution mainly of chapters 1–9, which postdate the older collections, in chapters 10–29, but they are latent in the latter. In the book's present form, its major components work together to convey meanings perhaps not envisioned or sensed clearly by the early authors.

The feature that distinguishes the book of Proverbs from non-Israelite Wisdom is its concern for wisdom as such. Foreign Wisdom offers wise teachings, but says little *about* wisdom. Egyptian instructions speak about wisdom from time to time, but usually with reference to the ancient teachings. Mesopotamian Wisdom rarely mentions it. The book of Ahiqar, Syrian in origin, gives it more attention but does not make wisdom its focus.[410] Proverbs, however, dwells on wisdom constantly. This focus is closely bound to its ethics.

The following features, central to the construction of Proverbs' ideas of wisdom and ethics, are rare or entirely absent in foreign Wisdom Literature and elsewhere in the Bible, outside of texts of clear sapiential character (Job, Qohelet, Pss 37 and 111):

(1) The identification of wisdom with righteousness.
(2) The direct praise of wisdom.
(3) The identification of wisdom with piety.
(4) The demand to love and seek wisdom

For a more detailed comparison of Proverbs with other Wisdom (prior to it), see Fox 1997c.

The primary axiom of Proverbs' ethics is that *the exercise of the human mind is the necessary and sufficient condition of right and successful behavior in all reaches of life: practical, ethical, and religious.* This is the central axiom of Socratic ethics as well.

[410] Wisdom is praised in Ahiqar 94b–95 (1.12.97), cited in Vol. I, 332–33. On Ahiqar's background and relation to Proverbs, see "Ahiqar and Proverbs," after the Commentary on Prov 22:17–24:22.

II. THE ETHICS OF PROVERBS AND THE SOCRATIC PRINCIPLES[411]

Throughout my study of Proverbs, I have been impressed by the *Socratic* quality of its epistemology and ethics.[412] The affinity between Proverbs and Socrates is not due to influence but to the fact that the sages of Proverbs and Socrates were thinking in similar ways about the same issues.[413] Both seek to answer the question (as phrased by Qohelet): "What is good for man to do under the heavens?" (Qoh 2:3).[414] Both Socrates and the sages had a practical goal: to teach young men how to lead the good and fortunate life. Their methods in achieving this goal were radically different.

Socratic ethics rests on three great principles. The first two are called the "ethical paradoxes." They are paradoxical not because they are irrational or self-contradictory, but because they run contrary to *doxa*, the common opinion. The third principle also, it seems to me, is a paradox in this sense, though it is not usually enumerated among the standard ones. The three principles are (1) virtue is knowledge; (2) no one does wrong willingly; and (3) all virtues are one.

A. Principle 1: Virtue Is Knowledge

Socrates teaches that knowledge of the good is both a necessary and a sufficient condition to being good and doing the good (see especially *Apology* 30b, 41d; *Protagoras* 352c–355e). He calls "virtue" (*aretē*) both "knowledge" (*epistēmē*) (*Meno*

---

[411] The dialogues most relevant to this discussion are *Euthydemus*, *Laches*, *Meno*, and *Protagoras*. This idea is developed mainly in the *Protagoras*, especially in 352a–360d. The following remarks on Socratic ethics draw especially on Gulley *1968*: 75–109 and integrate observations by Prior *1991*; Santas *1979*: 183–217; Saunders *1987*: 13–36; and Coby *1987* (a commentary on the *Protagoras*). Since I am using Socrates' central ideas as a heuristic model, I have tried to base their description on concepts that are explicit, or nearly so, in the dialogues and accord with widely accepted interpretations.

I set aside the question of whether and to what degree these ideas are Plato's creations rather than Socrates', except to note that the most relevant sources are the earlier dialogues, which are generally considered as best representing Socrates' own thinking. Moreover, some of the principles in question are ascribed to Socrates by Xenophon as well as Plato.

Translations of classical sources are referenced in the Bibliography by the names of the ancient authors.

[412] I have earlier compared the status of the wisdom as represented by Lady Wisdom to a Platonic "idea" or Universal (see Vol. I, 355–56), and I use Socratic ethics, as construed by Hannah Arendt, as an aid in interpreting 16:2; see the Comment. Socratic thought is also central to the description of Proverbs' epistemology in Essay 8.

[413] With regard to the personification of wisdom, I raised, but left open, the possibility of a loosely Platonic background for the concept of Wisdom as a universal or *idea* (see Vol. I, 355–56). But the dating of Prov 8 is uncertain and the connection cannot be proved, and the Platonic concept must remain an analogy.

[414] As Zimmerli (1933: 178) recognized, this question, to which the entirety of Proverbs offers an answer, is explicitly posed only by Qohelet, for it is he who undertakes to scrutinize and re-evaluate the value of wisdom.

87d) and "wisdom" (*sophia*) (*Meno* 88d).[415] In Aristotle's formulation of Socratic ethics, "All virtues are forms of knowledge, so that knowing justice and being just must go together" (*Eudemian Ethics* 1.216b, cf. *Nicomachaean Ethics* 1144b). I will refer to this principle, even when speaking about Proverbs, as the "Socratic equation" because it was Socrates who formulated it and made it central in ethical thought. This principle also entails the converse, that vice is ignorance.

To probe the nature of ethical knowledge, Socrates uses the analogy of professional skills. Just as a man must attain the knowledge of a craft in order to practice it successfully, so must he know the good in order to do it. To be sure, in the case of professional skills, carpentry for example, one might have knowledge but choose not to apply it. But moral knowledge is different. As knowledge of the good, moral knowledge is the understanding of what constitutes *eudaimonia*—"happiness" or (better) "well-being"—which is the universally desired end. And to know the good is to *desire* it (*Prot.* 352d).

Desire, Socrates believes, is directly consequent on a calculation of benefits. Socrates assumes a "strict correspondence between intensity of desire and the rational assessment of consequences" (Coby 1987: 109). The identification of knowledge with virtue thus effectively intellectualizes desire.[416]

But knowing what is really good is no simple matter. The magnitudes of long-term goods, like the size of objects seen from afar, are not evident to all. Therefore correct moral decisions require a *metrētikē technē*, a "metric art," which can overcome the distortions of perspective:

> If then our well-being depended upon this, doing and choosing large things, avoiding and not doing the small ones, what would we see as our salvation in life? Would it be the art of measurement or the power of appearance? While the power of appearance often makes us wander all over the place in confusion, often changing our minds about the same things and regretting our actions and choices with respect to things large and small, the art of measurement, in contrast, would make the appearances lose their power by showing us the truth, would give us peace of mind firmly rooted in the truth and soul and would save our life. (*Prot.* 356de)

Philosophy, as Socrates describes it, is a *technē*, a skill or art. In fact, *sophia*, the term Socrates uses to designate moral wisdom, was earlier used also for expertise in the crafts.[417]

In Proverbs, the Socratic equation is a deep but unarticulated premise. Though not formulated theoretically, it comes to expression in several ways:

Mixing of sayings on wisdom and sayings on righteousness. Like *sophia*, *ḥokmah* basically refers to skill or expertise; see Vol. I, 32–34. In Proverbs the domain of

---

[415] A better translation of *aretē* than the conventional "virtue" may be "excellence" (Saunders 1987: 26). In ordinary Greek usage, *aretē* is "excellence *in* or *for* something" (ibid.).

[416] See esp. Gulley 1968: 83–91.

[417] *Encyclopedia of Philosophy* 7.483.

the expertise is the art of living right, with regard to both moral behavior and practical matters.

In the old collections (Parts II–V; chapters 10–29), sayings on wisdom—a pragmatic faculty—are interspersed with ones on moral virtue (both designated by various names).[418] This is an editorial choice, for the editors could have kept the themes distinct. Within individual sayings, the concept of wisdom is rarely implicated in matters of moral virtue.[419] At the earliest stage, the Socratic equation does not apply to individual sayings on wisdom taken in themselves.[420] The Socratic equation was introduced into Proverbs in the process of editing. The editors thoroughly interspersed the sayings on wisdom with ones on righteousness. The reader of Proverbs naturally assumes that all the qualities and behaviors ascribed to the righteous are wise, and that the deeds of the wise, when moral factors are at play, are all righteous and honest.

According to McKane, the sayings about righteousness and piety in these chapters are later additions intended to reinterpret the old wisdom and bring the book closer to "Yahwistic piety."[421] While I do not think it can be shown that such sayings were written or collected later than the others, their presence does have the effect ascribed to them: extending the ideal of the wise man to embrace the virtues of righteousness and fear of God.

Conflation of wisdom and righteousness. In the Lectures and Interludes of chapters 1–9, wisdom and moral virtue are bound as cause and effect. The Exordia of the Lectures insist that hearkening to wisdom guarantees that one will walk the path of righteousness. For example, according to Lecture IX, the father's teaching will stay with you "to guard you from another man's wife, from the smooth talk of the alien" (6:24). Learning wisdom (in the form of the father's words) will bring favor, security, *and* the prime religious virtue of trust in God (3:26a).

The conflation of wisdom and moral virtue is explicit in Lecture II. Seeking wisdom (2:1–4) will bring one to fear of Yahweh and knowledge of Yahweh (v 5) because it is he who gives wisdom (v 6). He stores up resourcefulness for the righteous (v 7) so that they may keep the ways of justice (v 8). Once wisdom has entered your heart (v 10a) and (synonymously) knowledge has become delightful to your soul (v 10b), *then* "you'll perceive righteousness, justice, and equity—every good course" (v 9). Then wisdom (including "shrewdness" and "good sense") will toughen your resistance to evil temptations (2:11–12, 16). The causal link is clear and constant: Wisdom (taught by the father and gained with God's help) leads to and guarantees righteousness.

The Prologue (Prov 1:1–7) explains how to read the book that lies ahead. The book is for use

---

[418] Wisdom: *ḥokmah, binah, tebunah, śekel,* and *daʿat.* See "Words for Wisdom," Vol. I, 29–38. Moral virtue: *ṣedeq* "righteousness," *yošer* "honesty," *tom* "innocence," and sometimes *ṭob* "good," as well as words from the same roots referring to types of person and deeds.

[419] Wisdom and righteousness are compared in Essay 5 (I.D), "Wisdom and Righteousness."

[420] See Essay 5 (I.C), "The Nature of Wisdom."

[421] See "Religious Proverbs" in the Introduction to Vol. II (II.C.); see also the index entries on Yahwistic piety.

(2) in learning wisdom and discipline,
in understanding words of understanding,
(3) in absorbing the discipline of insight:
righteousness, justice, and rectitude.

The goals of learning wisdom and gaining righteousness are inseparable. The order of these achievements may be sequential, with the capacities in vv 2–3a providing the foundation of the virtues in v 3b. The triad of "righteousness, justice, and rectitude" is defined appositionally as "the discipline of insight" [*musar haśkel*]." Similarly, in 4:11 the teaching is called both "wisdom's way" and "routes of rectitude."

Though Proverbs constantly demands that the reader become wise, it never calls on him to be or become righteous. It only details what the righteous do and describes what righteousness is. It seems that one does not aim for righteousness directly but rather seeks wisdom, which can then be applied in emulating the righteous and choosing the righteous path. Wisdom means knowing the good, and this is tantamount to doing it.

Praise of wisdom. The book of Proverbs is a paean to wisdom. Praise of wisdom is almost unique to Proverbs and its heirs.[422] Wisdom and its benefits are extolled in numerous passages, such as "Discretion [or: perceptiveness] is a fount of life for its possessor" (Prov 16:22a); "for wisdom is better than rubies; no valuables can match it" (8:11); and often (see Essay 5 [II.A] "Attributes of the Wise" and [II.B] "The Rewards of Wisdom"). In the Ten Lectures, the Exordia typically laud wisdom's benefits. Interlude B (3:13–20) eulogizes wisdom at length, as does Lady Wisdom herself in Interlude D (8:1–36). Other proverbs simply promise benefits for wisdom; for example, 19:8: "He who acquires a mind loves himself, and he who keeps good sense will surely find good fortune." Such praise is an attempt to guide people in the "art of metrics," to inform them that their true profit lies in the engagement of the mind.

Wisdom as piety. The book of Proverbs in its present form makes wisdom a prime religious virtue. Wisdom is founded on the fear of Yahweh, an attitude compounded of knowledge, love, humility, and appropriate trepidation—in brief, piety (see Vol. I, 69–71). The Prologue culminates in the principle, "The fear of the Lord is the beginning of knowledge" (1:7a). This is not a necessary or even predictable assertion. By the presuppositions usual in the Bible, one might be

[422] Wisdom is not directly praised in the Bible prior to Proverbs. After Proverbs, Job 28 praises wisdom insofar as it takes the form of piety and moral behavior, and Qohelet occasionally endorses wisdom as practical good sense. Elsewhere various behaviors are commended as wise. It is assumed that wisdom, like wealth, is desirable and desired, but no one isolates wisdom as an object of praise in itself.

When the Egyptian sages praise wisdom or knowledge, they are usually referring to specific teachings or the scribal skills. Wisdom in a general sense is praised in Ptahhotep ll. 524–45 (AEL 1.73), Merikare §IX 5–6 (AEL 1.99); and Amenemope §30 AEL 2.162 (quoted in the Comment on 22:20). Mesopotamian Wisdom Literature scarcely mentions wisdom. Ahiqar praises it warmly in 94b–95 (1.12.97; cited in Vol. I, 332–33). See "Ahiqar and Proverbs," after the Commentary on Prov 22:17–24:22.

clever and erudite yet lack fear of God and other religious attitudes (see, e.g., Jer 8:9; 9:22; 18:18; Isa 47:10; Job 5:13). Conversely, a humble, simple person, even one devoid of cleverness, might fear God and trust him wholeheartedly.[423] Only Proverbs insists on the mutual implication of wisdom and piety. Prov 1:7 does not say that "fear of the Lord" suffices, but rather that it is the first step to wisdom.

The fear of God is not itself the Socratic art of metrics—*that* is wisdom. Rather, it is the attitude that motivates the acquisition of this art. Even before a child learns how to gauge what is truly best, if he fears God, this mind-set will prompt him to consider the consequences of his actions beyond the immediate gratifications.

Wisdom as obligation. The sages of Proverbs require the reader to seek and acquire wisdom. This demand is a direct reflection of the great ethical-religious weight they assign to wisdom. Several proverbs exhort the reader to *get* or *receive* wisdom (4:5, 7; 8:5–10, 33; 18:15; 23:23), to *understand* or *know* it (8:5; 24:14), to *call* to it (2:3), and to *seek* it (2:4; 18:15b). The demand to seek wisdom is a religious as well as prudential demand, because wisdom engenders fear of God (2:5).

The obligation to get wisdom is an imperative not only of fear but also of love (12:1; 29:3). One should love wisdom as a sister (7:4—possibly alluding to a lover) or matron (8:17). Wisdom and mankind are drawn together by a sort of eros; see Vol. I, 275–76; 294–95; 339. Put figuratively, people are obliged to answer the summons of Lady Wisdom (1:20–33; 9:4–5; cf. 7:4).

Wisdom and desire. Wisdom, especially in chapters 1–9 has (as argued in Essay 3, in Vol. I, 347–48) a strong affective component, namely the desire to do the right thing; hence: "Doing justice is a pleasure to a righteous man" (21:15a). The virtuous man not only does what is right, he delights in it and desires it: "The righteous desire what is good" (11:23a). The idea that wisdom is moral character, the configuration of soul that makes one naturally want to know and do what is right, is developed in the Lectures; see Vol. I, 347–48. This idea is encapsulated in 2:10: When you gain wisdom, you will know the right (v 9), "for wisdom will have entered your heart, knowledge become delightful to your soul."[424]

The "better than" sayings of Proverbs are precise examples of instruction in the "art of metrics" that is required for the attainment of wisdom. "Good" ("better") in these sayings means "beneficial." A saying like Prov 15:16, "Better a little [A] with the fear of the Lord [B], than a great storehouse [A′] with turmoil in it [B′]," is molded on the template $A + B > A' + B'$ and teaches how to calculate relative values. This template and the subtlety of its deep structure are discussed in the excursus after 15:17.

---

[423] The "simple" in Pss 19:8; 116:6; and 119:130 are also *innocent*, insofar as they are open to God's Torah and trust in it. The Torah then makes them wise.

[424] I earlier translated Prov 2:10a as "for wisdom will enter your heart" (Vol. I, 106). This is satisfactory, but, for present purposes, a rendering in the future perfect more precisely reflects the causal relationship: "Wisdom *will have entered* your heart" (v 10a) is the reason that you will "perceive righteousness, etc." (v 9).

B. Principle 2: No One Does Wrong Willingly

The most disputed of Socrates' paradoxes is the assertion that no one does wrong willingly, that is, chooses to do something while knowing that it is wrong (*Meno* 77cd). The premises of this principle are that (a) willingness requires full knowledge of the consequences of a deed (as well as the freedom to choose it); (b) wrong action is always harmful to the agent; and (c) no one desires his own harm. Therefore no one willingly does what he knows to be wrong. Socrates asks Protagoras: "[O]r does it seem to you that knowledge is a fine thing capable of ruling a person, and if someone were to know what is good and bad, then he would not be forced by anything to act otherwise than knowledge dictates, and intelligence would be sufficient to save a person?" (*Prot.* 352b). The affirmative is Socrates' own view. A person who does evil must lack the art of metrics and be unable to weigh the apparent magnitude of an immediate pleasure against the far greater pain that awaits him who seizes pleasure wrongfully or foolishly. He does the wrong because he imagines that it is good.

Proverbs does not state this principle, but it is implicit in its assumption that folly is tantamount to sin—not just that sin is foolish, but that folly causes sin. Three kinds of ignorance are conducive to sin:

Naïveté. The *peti*, or naïf, is easily seduced into different kinds of temptations because he does not assess consequences. The naïf who accepts the invitation to Folly's banquet heeds only the immediate gratification, ignoring the deadly price he will pay farther down the road (9:18). Until he gains wisdom, he is vulnerable to all temptation.

The type of wisdom the *peti* particularly lacks is *ʿormah*, "cunning" or "shrewdness," which includes alertness to dangers and traps. The Prologue promises that the book will provide this (1:4). Chastisement, which communicates wisdom, can help the *peti* gain cunning (15:5), as can observing the punishment of others (19:25a). But the *peti* is not merely unaware of dangers; he is drawn to them. He *loves* his callowness (1:22a). Wisdom pedagogy, with its constant promises, warnings, and chastisements, is intended to change this predilection and push him toward wisdom.

The notion that naïveté or simplicity is akin to virtue is foreign to Proverbs. Though the cause of simplicity may merely be immaturity, until the *peti* changes he can be grouped with cynics (*leṣim*) and dolts (*kᵉsilim*) (1:22) because his ignorance unmended will lead to folly of the worst sort: *ʾiwwelet*, perverse folly (14:18). Nothing will protect him—contrary to a psalmist's belief that "the Lord protects the simple [*petaʾyim*]" (Ps 116:6). But once the *peti* knows the good—*really* knows it—he is no longer "simple" and he will choose the right path. No further barriers to virtue are envisioned.

Obtuseness. The *kᵉsil*, the "dolt" or "stupid" person, being smug and indifferent about knowledge, is one step away from sin, if not already there. This is also true of the brutish *baʿar* and the mindless *ḥăsar-leb* (lit., "lacking of heart"). Such fools go astray not so much out of malign desires as from a refusal to engage their minds and judge consequences. Fools enjoy folly, for "Folly is pleasure to the mindless" (15:21a). From 13:19—"A desire fulfilled is sweet to the soul. What dolts loathe is turning away from evil"—we are to conclude that dolts *desire* evil; that is, the objects of their desire are bad—morally evil and injurious to themselves. In 6:32—"An adulterer lacks sense; a self-destroyer—he's the one who does this [that is, commits adultery]"—the author does not blame sin on lust (which, after all, can be gratified wisely; see 5:15–20) but rather on *ignorance*, the lack of "sense" or "mind."

The fool is given to immoderation. While not in itself a sin, it is impelled by ignorance and pushes one into corruption: "He who loves pleasure (becomes) a needy man; the lover of wine and oil will not grow rich" (21:17). This assumes that if the indulgent man knew that the unhappiness of long-term poverty outweighs the happiness afforded by short-term pleasures, he would not indulge in the latter. He would not "love" them. The benefits of pleasures appear deceptively great when near at hand, and one needs the art of metrics to put them in perspective.

Moral perversion. For the perversely foolish man (the *ʾĕwil*), and the wicked man (*rašaʿ*) and synonyms), to whom he is virtually identical, sin is a symptom and consequence of ignorance, a blindness to what is really good. His is a willed ignorance, because he chooses not to know the good. He despises his father's instruction (Prov 15:5a). Indeed, the teaching that the *ʾĕwil* imparts is itself folly (16:22b), for that is what counts as "wisdom" in his eyes. His folly is therefore indelible (27:22). He is so profoundly ignorant that he reverses good and evil and fails to identify his own advantage and harm: "The way of the fool is right in his own eyes" (12:15a). Similarly of the evildoer it is said: "Doing justice is a pleasure to the righteous man, but a ruin to evildoers" (21:15). That is, evildoers regard righteous behavior as disastrous to themselves. "The wicked man does not have knowledge" (29:7b); his wickedness makes him want the wrong things. The wicked man "needs" evildoing and can get no rest without it (4:16–17). He does not know that its consequence is his own disaster (4:19).

This idea has a precedent in Ptahhotep. The fool is he who does not, or can not, *hear*, that is, absorb and obey the teaching. Therefore he confuses good and evil and can only do what is wrong (ll. 575–84 [cf. AEL 1.74]; quoted in Vol. I, 117–18).

Fools and knaves of various sorts fail because they are blind to the further consequences of their deeds. This is the problem with the man who grasps for wealth. "The greedy man rushes after wealth" (28:22a). He has his eye on quick gain and is blind to the poverty to which his straining will bring him (28:22b); see the Comments on 10:22 and 28:20. Wisdom requires perceiving the *ʾaḥărit* "end" or "future" of a deed (5:1–5, 11; 14:12; 20:21; 23:32).

The knowledge of what is evil and the awareness that evil invariably harms its agent are enough to keep the wise from surrender to impulse. If someone does what is wrong, he must be on some level *ignorant*, that is, foolish, for all ignorance is folly.

Aristotle criticized Socrates for failing to recognize that there exist people who know what is good yet do not desire to do it. Aristotle called their condition *akrasia*, weakness of will (*Nicomachean Ethics* VII; 1145b25–28). A modern approach might explain wrongdoing in terms of drives, impulses, neuroses, and various psychological pathologies. With a celerity that is often mistaken for dogmatism, the sages of Proverbs, like Socrates, believed that ignorance alone is the problem and wisdom alone the solution. But they were aware of obstacles to learning, namely, callowness, smugness, cynicism, and moral perversion.

Proverbs assumes and asserts that wise man's wisdom will keep him from the major failings, though he may still make mistakes. Certainly he knows that the major sins are wrong and harmful; that is what the youth is taught in the Lectures. But even a wise man may lapse in some regard, because human wisdom is not absolute knowledge. It is knowledge to a high degree of competence along with (most important) an eagerness to gain more. (This eagerness is lifelong. The Prologue promises to help the mature wise man *increase* wisdom; 1:5.) If a wise man errs, it is because he did not know what was good in a particular situation. Then reproof and advice—in other words, the correction of ignorance—will set him aright. See Essay 5 (II.A), "Attributes of the Wise."

C. *Principle 3: All Virtues Are One*[425]

For Socrates, there is only one good; hence knowledge of the good is a unity. And since all virtues are applications of this knowledge, all virtue is one. This is a holistic concept of virtue. There is a single entity that makes a man wise, courageous, temperate, and just—namely, the knowledge of good and evil. We might say that knowledge is a *system* rather than an agglomeration of data, and therefore the virtues to which it corresponds (according to Principle 1) must likewise constitute a single system.

The third principle is well summarized by Xenophon, quoting Socrates:

> [Socrates] said that Justice and every other form of Virtue is Wisdom. "For just actions and all forms of virtuous activity are beautiful and good. He who knows the beautiful and good will never choose anything else, he who is ignorant of them cannot do them, and even if he tries, will fail. Hence the wise do what is beautiful and good, the unwise cannot and fail if they try. Therefore since just actions and all other forms of beautiful and good activity are virtuous actions, it is clear that Justice and every other form of Virtue is Wisdom." (*Memorabilia* 3.9.5)

This statement could as well describe the mind-set of Proverbs, for in it wisdom subsumes and generates all virtues, practical and moral. This axiom comes to fruition in chapters 1–9, in the Lectures and the Wisdom Interludes (A, D, and E), where wisdom is made to encompass all moral and religious virtue; see on Stages

[425] The argument is developed in the *Protagoras* and refined in the *Laches*; see esp. *Prot.* 329d, 349b. The present summary is based on Gulley 1968: 151–64. Penner (1992*a*: 161–84) argues that "virtue is one" is meant strictly, that there is a single entity to which all the virtue-words refer. In this sense, the principle does not apply to Proverbs.

2 and 3 in Essay 5 (III, IV). In the older collections, it is only the moral and religious virtues that are said to elicit God's favor. In the Lectures, "the favor and high regard of God and man alike" is a reward for learning and obeying the teachings of Wisdom (3:4). Wisdom will bring security *and* trust in God (3:26a). There is no suggestion of any moral or religious virtues not governed by wisdom, or of different kinds of knowledge for different virtues. It is Proverbs' fundamental—and radical—claim that one wisdom embraces them all. Seeking wisdom (2:1–4) will lead to fear of the Lord (v 7) and "*every* good course" (v 9).

Though the moral virtues are not all precisely equated in Proverbs, in the book's present form they are bundled together in a way not paralleled elsewhere in the Bible, not even in the older sayings in Prov 10–29. In Prov 1–9, it is asserted that all virtues are learned in the same way, by means of the same wisdom, just as all are possessed by Lady Wisdom. There is only one path to life, the path of virtue and wisdom. There is no notion of righteousness without wisdom, or wisdom without generosity, or generosity without honesty.

III. THE USE OF THE MIND

Socrates puts extraordinary faith in the power of the mind. Socrates, according to Gulley, "assumes that the dominant influence of the intellect is sufficient to convert the whole character to a pattern which excludes acting against knowledge" (*1968*: 153). Hence "[t]he intellect has supremacy over all else in determining moral behavior" (ibid., p. 162). Likewise, the sages of Proverbs intellectualized virtue by making it a species of knowledge. Virtue is an act of cognition.

The attainment of wisdom (= knowledge, understanding) inevitably produces the right desires, and these protect one from dangers and lead to happiness:

> Get wisdom, get understanding,
> do not forget, do not stray
> from the words of my mouth.
> Don't desert her—then she'll keep you,
> love her and she'll guard you. (4:5–6)
>
> I guide you in wisdom's way,
> lead you in routes of rectitude.
> In walking, your stride won't be hobbled,
> and if you run you will not trip.
> Hold fast to discipline, don't let go,
> guard it, for it is your life. (4:11–13)

"Discipline"—*musar,* a term for wisdom—is something that the youth must incorporate and take with him through life, for it is wisdom, and wisdom *is* life. Wisdom is the art of metrics, which Socrates calls "our *sōtēria*—'salvation' or 'well-being'—in life" (*Prot.* 356de).

Knowledge is a sufficient condition for virtue because it is seamlessly joined to desire; to know the good is to desire it, and to desire it is (in the absence of external constraints) to do it. The upshot of this principle is an extraordinary assertion of individual responsibility. Each person constantly faces moral choices, with only wisdom to guide him. But wisdom is universally available (1:20–29; 8:1–4; 9:4–6); it is directly before the eyes of the one who looks carefully (17:24), and if one lacks wisdom, it is because he has chosen to spurn it (1:7b, 22, 29), to desire evil (21:10), and to love mindlessness (1:22). Sin is folly, and folly is ignorance, and ignorance is no excuse. It is itself a moral failing, the root of all failure.

Why does Proverbs consistently identify virtue with knowledge? There is no definite answer, because this principle is a deep axiom whose roots are not explored. The following considerations are offered as reasonable surmises about the motives of the sages in making this identification.

First, the engagement of the mind elevates the moral stature of a good deed. Although doing the right thing is in itself a worthy course of behavior, doing the good in active awareness of its goodness, having attained this awareness through thought and study, is dynamic and interactive. Gaining wisdom requires receptivity to the wisdom of others, which must be heard, absorbed, and applied. That is why there is great emphasis on the process of attaining wisdom, not only on its outcome. This happens especially in the Exordia to the Lectures and is articulated most clearly in the programmatic Lecture II; see Vol. I, 131–34. Wisdom is never static. The wise man must always be increasing his knowledge (Prov 1:5).

Second, the teachings of wisdom are encapsulated principles of behavior that must constantly be unpacked and applied to new situations, and this requires wisdom, not only the wish to do the right thing. There can never be enough maxims to fit all circumstances. Rather, the maxims constitute "paradigms" (Frydrych 2002: 19–23), for they compress and represent complex rules of behavior in a simple and memorable. To be sure, law too must be constantly interpreted and reapplied, but this task belonged to judges and, later, scholars of the Law, not to everyone.

Third, the editors of Proverbs exalted the human intellect for social reasons. The social matrix of Wisdom Literature was the royal court (see "Social Setting" in the Introduction to Vol. II (III.B.). The self-image of the officials and scribes in the royal service was that of men who worked by their wits (Jer 9:22). They were called "wise" not because "wise" was a professional designation but because they worked, or claimed to work, by their intellect and learning. Those among them who authored and assembled the book of Proverbs naturally underscored the centrality and viability of wisdom in the moral realm. The same expertise and shrewdness on which they prided themselves (to Jeremiah's chagrin; see Jer 9:22a) was, they felt, applicable to securing moral knowledge and action. (Jeremiah did not agree. He distinguished "wisdom" from "understanding and knowing me" [v 23], a distinction the sages of Proverbs would have thought meaningless.)

In sum, the principle that human knowledge is a sufficient precondition for virtue allows Proverbs to provide a comprehensive guide to individual behavior without recourse to divine Torah or other communication. Fear of Yahweh and trust in him are sufficient to motivate the search for wisdom and the avoidance of sin. The wisdom one gains from one's parents and other teachers and applies to particular situations by one's own faculties is all that is needed for attaining the good and blessed life—*eudaimonia*, as Socrates calls it. But, as I argue in the next essay, this principle met with some resistance and engendered new ways of thinking about the sources of moral knowledge.

Essay 7. Revelation

◆

I. The Autonomy of Wisdom

Proverbs' exaltation of wisdom is audacious and unparalleled in other books of the Bible. Proverbs treats wisdom as a sufficient source of practical success, ethical knowledge, social harmony, and piety. The book gives the impression that the guidance needed for leading a good and happy life is available from wisdom. Yet for Proverbs (as for all Wisdom Literature prior to Ben Sira), wisdom is human in its particulars and in its workings.[426] To be sure, the outcome of one's efforts depends on God's blessing, and this requires his favor. But what God loves and hates is fully knowable through wisdom, and his favor goes to those who deserve it.[427] The sages certainly realized that much remains unknown, particularly the outcome of human plans, for unexpected outcomes are due to God's mysterious designs.[428] But there is no mystery about what is right and wrong, wise and foolish, and no suggestion that if one follows wisdom's commands only, one would be in any way deficient in moral compass or personal blessing. Wisdom offers itself as a complete and self-contained moral system.

Proverbs shows no interest in Yahweh's revealed Torah. In the Interludes, especially D (Prov 8), Wisdom is exalted to the point that her near-divine origin and the authority she gains from her antiquity and proximity to God leave little room for a significant role for revelation. Wisdom's status is the reason men should listen to her (v 32a). Should one listen to Wisdom *and* to the Torah of Moses? Proverbs certainly does not say no, but affirmation of Torah is not part of its message.

There are, of course, laws, customs, and cultic regulations not specified in Proverbs, and the authors show an awareness of their existence. Sacrifices are valued (Prov 3:9–10 and 15:8) and must have been performed according to priestly regulations. Major crimes are assumed to be prohibited, though the prohibitions are not usually explicit.[429] We hear of law courts, but are not told which laws they

---

[426] Though divine origin is ascribed to wisdom (in the sense of knowledge of all the arts) in Mesopotamian literature, in didactic Wisdom Literature it is scarcely mentioned. One exception is Shuruppak l. 278, "for the gift of wisdom [is like] the stars (of heaven)" (trans. Alster 1974: 41). This refers to wisdom as a faculty, not the contents of the teaching. Ahiqar 94b–95 (1.12.97) says that wisdom comes from the gods; see Vol. I, 332–33 in this Commentary and n. 410 on p. 934. In a late stage of biblical literature, in the second part of Daniel (early second c. B.C.E.), when Daniel asks God for *binah* ("understanding") to explain his dreams (Dan 8:15), this *binah* comes in the form of the explanation itself (9:22), not in the form of the faculty of understanding.

[427] While Proverbs has no doubts about whom God loves and whom he loathes, Qohelet explicitly rejects the possibility of this knowledge (Qoh 9:1).

[428] See the introduction to the Commentary on 16:1–9.

[429] When murderers are mentioned in 29:10 and 28:17 (uncertain), the focus is not on the crime but on how other people relate to the murderer. The prohibition is assumed. Murder and robbery are

enforce. Most likely they are the king's laws, since social order depends on the king, and he is the guarantor of human justice (20:8, 26; 25:5; 29:4, 14). Though the king, and even his desires, are controlled by God (21:1), it is his own *wisdom* that guides him in administering law and justice.

Nor does Proverbs show much interest in prophetic revelation, but only vaguely recognizes its social utility in 29:18. This is strange in a culture that considered itself blessed with a plenitude of revelations, except in times of visionary drought (1 Sam 3:1). Throughout the Bible, God speaks often and freely in narratives, visions, dreams, and prophecies. Oracles are available through priestly mediation. The law is, in all Pentateuchal sources, given by divine utterance in the archetypal act of prophetic revelation at Sinai-Horeb. Later, in Dan 8–12, even dream interpretations—not just the ability to interpret dreams but the interpretations themselves—come from God, communicated by angels. Proverbs pays virtually no attention to these media. Rather, it treats the powers of the human mind as adequate to the attainment of all sorts of knowledge. This is a feature of the book in all its stages, except for Agur (30:1–9), who stands apart and will be discussed as a response to the book of Proverbs later in this essay.

II. PROVERBS' VIEW OF REVELATION

What need, indeed what *room*, is there for revealed Torah in all this? Would Proverbs be any different if the Pentateuch in whole or in part did not exist when Proverbs was being composed?

The apparent absence of revealed Torah in Proverbs has been an object of concern for scholars and theologians. (This issue should be kept distinct from the question of whether the book is "religious" or "secular." It is both.) The following are some notable points of view on the issue of divine communication in Proverbs.

A. Yahweh's Torah in Proverbs

F. Steiert (1990) argues that Proverbs in its entirety holds to Yahwistic Covenant theology, with all its distinguishing beliefs: monotheism, divine transcendence, absence of magic, the structure of ethics, divine revelation, and more. Wisdom itself, he argues, is manifest as a form of revelation most clearly in Prov 1–9, where the communication operates on two planes: from father-teacher to pupil and from God to man (p. 240). The father-teacher represents Yahweh, as is shown by the fact that much of the vocabulary of teaching in Prov 1–9 is used also of Yahweh's and Moses's teaching of Israel in Deuteronomy. Moreover, the fullness of blessings promised to the wise in Prov 1–9, represented by the complex concept of "life," alludes to divine blessing (p. 241).

---

warned against in 1:8–19, but the motivation given is that it is imprudent in the extreme. Likewise, adultery is alluded to in 22:14 and (as emended) 23:27, again as a danger to the adulterer. These warnings are not laws or legal prohibitions.

This approach can claim the antiquity of midrash, for the rabbis usually identify "my *torah*" and "my words" in Proverbs as God's.[430] But this is far from the intention of the author, because the father who speaks in Prov 1–9 is a man with a wife and a father of his own. The didactic language in Deuteronomy naturally has its source in didactic wisdom, and not the other way around; see below, "Deuteronomy" (III.A).[431]

Steiert is arguing against the view that Wisdom Literature is theologically out of place in the Old Testament. An extreme expression of that view was put forward by H. D. Preuss, who observes that "Wisdom does not speak of the patriarchs, Covenant, Promise and Fulfillment, Moses, Exodus, Divine Law, Israel as Covenant People; nor of David and the Davidic Covenant; nor of history and eschatology" (*1970*: 414), absences that Preuss considers theologically invalid. He also faults Wisdom Literature for being based on the idea of order ("Ordnungsdenken"), whose center is the concept of the deed-consequence nexus (see Vol. I, 91–92 in this Commentary) rather than Yahweh's active intervention in the events of life and history (Preuss, pp. 396–400; 415). Wisdom, Preuss believes, "thereby stands outside all that is specific to the Old Testament" (p. 414). He concludes that Wisdom Literature is not well integrated in the Christian Canon and can be deleterious in preaching (pp. 414–17). Other scholars respond to Proverbs' apparent deficiencies by appealing to allusions, intertextuality, and allegory in order to uncover the expected beliefs.

Whether the lacks that Preuss observes are theological and homiletic flaws is a matter of personal religious judgment. But viewing the issue from a canonical viewpoint, I cannot help wondering why one would expect every book in the Bible to have everything. A canon (whether one means the Hebrew Bible or the Old Testament + New Testament) is more than the sum of its parts. In it, the parts work together to create and convey religious ideas in a new synthesis that would have been foreign to the original authors. In any case, the issue of revelation is separate from the question of specifically Israelite beliefs in Proverbs. A revelation could be an individual visionary experience or communication with no national or covenantal concerns (e.g., Ps 73; see v 17).

B. Wisdom as Mediated Revelation

Lady Wisdom in Prov 8 is often regarded as the mediator or bearer of God's word or will.[432] Most influentially, G. von Rad called Wisdom an "Offenbarungsträger," a "revelation bearer," who has inserted herself into the dialogue between Yahweh and Israel (1970: 213). This voice is the "Selbstoffenbarung der Schöpfung"—the "self-revelation of creation"—which now speaks to Israel alongside and (as von Rad recognized) in tension with the other means of revelation, namely cult, prophecy, and (in von Rad's view) narrative history (p. 213). As the voice of creation, Wisdom reveals both Yahweh's order and the ineluctable mystery of his creation. In other words, the order seen in the natural world itself has meaning, and it "speaks" this meaning to the human mind, using forms of speech and making promises that we would expect from a god.

---

[430] Such readings are gathered in *Midrash Proverbs*; see Visotzky 1990, 1992. This was not the dominant approach among the medieval *peshat* commentators, who usually understand "wisdom" and *torah* as human faculties and teachings.

[431] I review Steiert's book in Fox 1992.

[432] Interpretations of Prov 8 and the nature of personified Wisdom are discussed in Vol. I, 293–95, 353–56 of the present commentary.

Von Rad's description of the function of personified wisdom nicely synthesizes revelation and intellect. In Interludes A, D, and E, Wisdom is no longer just an object of search but herself takes the initiative and turns to men, indeed, *pursues* them. There is, however, no implication that her words are a message from God. Moreover, it is *not* the created world or the world-order speaking. Wisdom is carefully distinguished from the rest of creation by preceding it and by existing at Yahweh's side while he—not she—created the world. And in the proverbs themselves, no "order" communicates with man, except in the very attenuated sense that looking at the world can teach anyone things; see Vol. I, 352–53 and Fox 1995.

C. *Wisdom as Indirect Revelation*

Frydrych (2002: 61) calls Wisdom a bearer of *indirect* revelation. The revelation is indirect insofar as "it does not revolve around dreams, visions and auditions, but rather, it is implied that God uses the normal intellectual processes to indirectly speak to those who revere him" (ibid.). This description is accurate, though it is not what is usually meant by "revelation," which is the communication of God's word to man, and the term is probably best avoided. In any case, not even indirect revelation comes into the purview of the old collections in Prov 10–29. "Vision," that is, prophecy, is mentioned once in Prov 29:18, and there the vision in question is not the source of sapiential teaching.

D. *Wisdom Is Not Revelation*

As I understand it, Lady Wisdom speaks wisdom—her own, not God's. Nowhere does she "bear" revelation. She is not a prophet or messenger transmitting God's message, although she does have certain features of a prophet (Vol. I, 104–105; 333–34) and an angel (Vol. I, 334).

The relation of God to Wisdom in Prov 8:22–31 resembles that of a man raising a child to be wise, in order to make her intellectually and morally fit to teach others. She will become, as it were, an *'ešet ḥayil*, a Woman of Strength, providing her children's material needs and speaking instruction. This is why Lady Wisdom recounts the time of her youth, when she was "growing up" or "being raised" (*'amon*) by God himself (8:30–31a). Just as a son taught by a wise father can himself teach wisdom, not merely repeating his father's words but also unfolding the principles of wisdom in his own words, so can Lady Wisdom, the daughter-like ward of Yahweh, give new expression to the most ancient and exalted of truths.[433] It is not said that God imparts to her certain teachings. What is relevant here is

[433] Compare the statement in Merikare: "Truth [*m*ꜥꜣ*t*] comes to him [the wise man] fully brewed, by the sayings of the ancestors. Imitate your fathers and ancestors [or "ancients"]" (IX; l. 34). (AEL 1.99 translates, "Justice comes to him distilled, / Shaped in the sayings of the ancestors. Copy your fathers, your ancestors.") Egyptian *m*ꜥꜣ*t* means both "truth" and "justice."

not a verbal communication but Wisdom's preeminent status as God's ward. This qualifies her to treat humans as *her* wards and instruct them.

In Interlude D, God creates (personified) Wisdom and sends her into the world to help humans make their way through its dangers and potentials. To use the terms favored in the ongoing scholarly discussion of Prov 8, Wisdom is an intermediary but not a revelation bearer. Since Wisdom did not receive a specific message from God, her role is better described as an alternative to revelation.

The teaching of Proverbs is, to use the term favored by Zimmerli, "anthropological" and even (to use a term he finds inadequate) "anthropocentric" (1933: 178). The background question of Wisdom Literature is formulated by Qohelet: "What is good for man?" (Qoh 1:3; Zimmerli, ibid.). The answer is to be discovered by human resources. This is what Wisdom Literature is all about.

To the view that Wisdom Literature is secular and "eudaimonistic" or "utilitarian," terms used dismissively, C. Rylaarsdam, in his influential *Revelation in Jewish Wisdom Literature* (1946), responded that although Proverbs, like Wisdom thought generally, was indeed "humanistic" and devoid of revelation, it was also religious from the start. With regard to Prov 10–29 he says:

> The earliest strata of Proverbs are "secular" in the sense that they apply what they have discovered about life to all human situations. The earliest sages are "humanists" because they seek wisdom as natural men, unaided by special divine initiative. But they are also "religious," for they are conscious of living as creatures in an order of creation whose controlling intelligence is their Judge. Their manner of obtaining wisdom differs from that of the prophets. Since there is no divine initiative supplementing creation, there is no word of God beyond that given by human reason; and the deliverances of reason are not called the "word" of God. (1946: 72)

This is accurate. Proverbs is infused with religious aspiration and feeling. It constantly, and at all stages, speaks of Yahweh, his oversight of justice, his care for humanity, his demand for righteousness, his loves and his hates. The book of Proverbs can be judged as simply "secular"[434] only if judged by extraneous standards, such as fealty to Yahweh's revealed Torah, a belief in immortality, and a concern for national history. However, it is not at all evident that Proverbs fails to meet some other criteria of religiosity, such as a concern for divine grace, "great affective devotion and enthusiasm for the divine," and "deep personal experience of religious truth" (the last two criteria in Rylaarsdam 1946: 68). Even so, verbal revelation is not part of Proverbs' religious system.

---

[434] In Essay 5 (II), "Stage 1," I argue that the *faculty* of wisdom is perceived as secular and pragmatic in the book's early stages, but the *book* even then had religious concerns.

III. TORAH AND WISDOM

The absence of divine revelation in Proverbs has been treated as a major problem by scholars and theologians, but is it really noteworthy? If Proverbs is read as a document of ancient Near Eastern literature, the absence is to be expected. Divine revelation is not mentioned anywhere in didactic Wisdom prior to Ben Sira. Oracles are occasionally mentioned in Egyptian Wisdom, but the contents of the teachings are in no way derived from them. There is, moreover, no reason to expect reference to Israelite law or history in Proverbs. They just do not come into its purview.

However, when Proverbs is read as a book of Israelite literature and as a document in the Hebrew canon, Proverbs' treatment of wisdom as autonomous and self-sufficient is noteworthy, and some ancient authors noted it. The rest of this essay deals with some of their responses to it. These responses are not polemical, as if *attacking* an opposing view, but they do assign wisdom a lesser status relative to revealed Torah. Ben Sira was the first to identify wisdom with Torah, thus removing any tension between them and obviating the need to negotiate their relative status.

A. Deuteronomy

The earliest major components of the book of Proverbs, namely, Parts II–IV in Prov 10–29, are the products of the eighth and seventh centuries B.C.E., though many of their components were certainly older. (See "The Growth of the Book of Proverbs" in the Introduction to Vol. II [III.A].) The book of Deuteronomy, too, was coming into shape during the seventh century, with the core of Deuteronomic law being promulgated in 622 or 621 B.C.E.[435]

Deuteronomy shows clear signs of Wisdom influence. Its authors knew the early collections of Proverbs or something much like them. M. Weinfeld (1972: 244–74) argues that Deuteronomy arose from a distinct ideological-professional group, the scribes of the royal court, whom he sometimes calls "Wisdom circles." A. Rofé, while agreeing that Wisdom left its impression on Deuteronomy, assigned the book to "those who maintained traditional priestly teachings" and who "came under the influence of the Wisdom circle and infused their own traditions with its content and forms" (*2002b*: 222–27, at 224). Wisdom influence on Deuteronomy is clear, but the differences between the books are no less pronounced.

A large number of Deuteronomistic features show an affiliation with Wisdom. M. Weinfeld (1972: 244–74) adduces the following, among others:

---

[435]The present essay premises the classic and still widely accepted theory that the core laws of Deuteronomy formed the document promulgated in the time of Josiah (2 Kgs 22–23), in 622–621 B.C.E. Strong arguments for this view are offered from different perspectives by A. Rofé (*2002b*: 4–9) and M. Weinfeld (1972: 244-81; *1991*: 6–9, 16–19). Expansion of the book continued after its promulgation.

(1) In Deuteronomy, Moses appoints leaders with the *intellectual* qualities that Wisdom literature prizes: wisdom, astuteness, and knowledge (Deut 1:13, 15).

(2) The phrase *hikkîr pānîm bammišpāṭ*, "to favor persons in judgment" (Deut 1:17; 16:19), appears elsewhere only in Proverbs (24:23; 28:21).

(3) Wisdom for the Deuteronomist is the knowledge of proper behavior and morality, not just cunning or pragmatic talent, or even the possession of extraordinary knowledge.

(4) The prohibition on displacing ancient landmarks in Deut 19:14 (cf. Deut 27:17) is based on Prov 22:28 and 23:10. (In this case, the direction of influence from Proverbs to Deuteronomy is indisputable, since the prohibition is known to derive from Amenemope; see the Comment on Prov 23:10–11.)

(5) The condemnation of deceptive weights in Prov 11:1 and 20:23 (cf. 20:10) is reused in Deut 25:13–16 (see the Comment on Prov 20:10).

(6) Deut 23:16 is dependent on Prov 30:10 and Deut 16:20 on Prov 21:21. (Contrary to Weinfeld, in the case of Prov 30:6 and Deut 4:2 the direction of influence is from Deuteronomy to Proverbs; see the Comment on Prov 30:6.)

While Weinfeld convincingly shows the relation of Deuteronomy to Wisdom, his conclusion that the social setting of Deuteronomy is in "Wisdom circles" in the royal court is problematic. A. Rofé (*2002b*: 222–27) raises some telling objections to this conclusion:

(1) The concept of "Wisdom circles" is poorly defined. As Weinfeld uses it, it seems that anything associated with the royal court falls under the aegis of wisdom.

(2) The presence of a concept in both Deuteronomy and Wisdom Literature—"abomination," for example—does not prove its origin in the latter.

(3) Deuteronomy has inherited literature that has no relationship to Jerusalem or the king ship.

(4) There is no sign that the men of the court had an influence where we would most expect it, in the "constitutional" chapters of Deuteronomy (17–21). The authors have not even assigned themselves a role in the administration of the state. (According to Deut 1:13–17, the judiciary is to be composed of "wise men," but this is a personal trait, not a professional status.)

In support of Rofé's reservations, I would add that the ideological divide between Deuteronomy and Prov 10–29 is widened by their treatment of the king. Proverbs promotes a royalist ideology; see the introduction to the Commentary on Prov 16:10–15. The king is virtually God's viceroy, to be feared and obeyed almost like God himself (Prov 24:21) and to be held in awe above other men (16:15; 19:12; 20:8; 25:3). In Deuteronomy, the perspective on kingship is quite different. The people appoint the king (Deut 17:15a), and God allows this begrudgingly, as a concession to the people's unworthy wishes (17:14b). The benefits the king may bring to the people is of little interest to the Deuteronomist, who devotes most of the short passage on kingship (Deut 17:14–20) to circumscribing the king's freedom of action. He is prohibited from amassing horses, wives, and wealth, and from sending people back to Egypt. The king's judicial role is eliminated. Throughout the ancient Near East, the administration of justice was the king's primary responsibility. Deuteronomy, however, deliberately and methodically *ousts* the king from this role and shifts the judicial forum to the Temple (Deut 17:8–13); see B. Levinson *1997*: 138–43. The only positive duty laid on the king is to read a copy of the Torah continually. This is to teach him the law and (consequently) to prevent him from exalting himself above his brothers (Deut 17:18–19). The reading of Prov 10–29 would hardly have that effect!

The fact that the book with Deuteronomic prescriptions was found, or claimed to have been found, in the Temple and sent by the high priest to the king (2 Kgs 22:8) supports Rofé's theory that the book was shaped and preserved there. It was not meant specifically for priestly use, but it does serve the goals of the Jerusalem priesthood.

In spite of the influence of Wisdom thought and language on Deuteronomy, the latter has little to say about wisdom itself. Even when Deuteronomy does gives wisdom some prominence and affirm its value, it effectively *subordinates* it to Torah: "You shall observe [these laws] diligently, for *this* will be your wisdom and understanding in the eyes of the nations who, when they hear all these statutes, will say, 'Surely this great nation is a wise and discerning people!' " (Deut 4:6). Rather than identifying wisdom with Torah, Deuteronomy sets Torah above wisdom and makes wisdom one of its benefits. The point is that Israel needs no wisdom besides *this* Torah—the instruction in *this* book—to make it wise, and wise in a way that foreigners will grasp and appreciate. Israel's Torah is sui generis, because it is Yahweh's own teaching, but the face it presents to the outside is wisdom, such as is known to all the nations. This verse shows that the Deuteronomist was aware of a way of thinking that knew about foreign wisdom and sought to emulate it—which is exactly what Proverbs does, as is most evident in Prov 22:17–24:22. The Deuteronomist would convince his countrymen that all the wisdom they need is to be found in revealed Torah, by which he means the one contained in Deuteronomy itself.[436]

A fundamental divergence between the attitudes of Deuteronomy and Proverbs is revealed in Deut 16:19: "You shall not pervert justice; you shall not show partiality; and you shall not take a bribe, for a bribe blinds the eyes of the wise and distorts the words of the righteous." The notions of the wise being morally blinded and the righteous being corrupt in speech would be oxymora in Proverbs. For Proverbs, only fools could be morally obtuse, and righteousness is inherently immutable.

While Proverbs marginalizes Law (making only a few references to the judiciary and the royal obligation to enforce justice), Deuteronomy places wisdom on a lower rung than Law. For Deuteronomy, the Law provides the obedient with the very blessings that wisdom promises its adherents: long life, security, and prosperity. Deuteronomy leaves little role for the independent operation of human wisdom so important in Proverbs. The role of wisdom is marginalized even in matters of government. Instead of having wise counselors speaking in the king's ear, Deuteronomy has the king reading the Law and learning its precepts. The Law is the royal advisor, a role Wisdom has in Prov 8:14–16. In Deuteronomy, wisdom is required in matters of judgment and administration, for applying the specifics of the Law, but not for discovering God's will.

The profile of the anonymous sages of early Wisdom becomes better defined when seen through Deuteronomic eyes. The Deuteronomist speaks much the same language as the sages of Proverbs while saying different things. For the sages, Yahwism was fully expressed by their confidence that God's will was easily accessible through human wisdom. For the Deuteronomists, Yahweh's will is known through *torah*, which no longer means simply "instruction," but rather *the* Torah, which for the Deuteronomist is Deuteronomy itself.[437]

---

[436] As D. Carr says, what makes Deuteronomy unique is its "totalizing claim": "This is not an instruction to be set alongside others. This is not just another collection of proverbs or didactic narrative. Rather, the book constantly presents itself as a yet earlier and more foundational Mosaic Torah. *This* is the Torah that Israelites are to recite all day and night. There is no room for another" (2005: 141–42).

[437] The word *torah*, without the article, appears in Deuteronomy only in Deut 33:4, the Blessing of Moses, which is not the Deuteronomist's work.

B. Psalm 119

The massive Psalm 119 is virtually a book in itself, one affiliated with several genres.[438] Most prominently, it is a Torah-psalm, along with Psalms 1 and 9B (i.e., 9:8–14). Its primary purpose is to exalt Torah above all else besides God and to pray for illumination in and through Torah. Psalm 119 has also been designated a "portrait of a confessor" + "portrait of the godless" (Gerstenberger *2001*: 315). It is affiliated—to a degree—with Wisdom, and it may be classed as a Wisdom Psalm insofar as it draws on the characteristic vocabulary of Wisdom.[439] But its ideas differ sharply from Proverbs'.

The linguistic affiliations of Ps 119 with Wisdom have been identified by A. Hurvitz (1991: 100–119). The following locutions are unique to Ps 119 and the Wisdom books of Proverbs, Job and Ben Sira:

(1) *'hb* ["love"] + "wisdom" or + *tôrāh* (or synonyms): Ps 119:47, 48, 97, 113, 119, 127; Prov 4:6; 8:17, 21; 12:1; 29:3. With other synonyms for love: Ps 119:20, 31, 40, 131.

(2) *yr'* ["fear"] + words for law (*mišpāṭ* "judgment," *miṣwāh* "precept"): Ps 119:120; Prov 13:13.

(3) *mᵉlammēd* ["teacher"]: Ps 119:99; Prov 5:13.

(4) *nēr* ["lamp"] // *'ôr* ["light"] + *tôrāh*, (or synonyms): Ps 119:105; Prov 6:23. (As a parallel pair, *nēr* // *'ôr* occurs only in these two verses.)

(5) *'ôzᵉbê tôrāh* ["those who abandon the Law/instruction"]: Ps 119:53; Prov 28:4; cf. 4:6.

(6) *'ānāh/hēšîb ḥôrᵉpî* ["respond to him who insults me"]: Ps 119:42; Prov 27:11.

(7) *ṣpn* ["store away"] + "word" (of the father's or God's teaching): Ps 119:11; Prov 2:1 (see Commentary); 7:1.

(8) *šgh mn* ["go astray from"]: Ps 119:10, 21, 118; Prov 19:27.

(9) *š'š'* ["take pleasure in"] + words for wisdom and commandments, including *tôrāh*: Ps 119:16, 24, 47, 70, 77, 92, 143, 174; Prov 8:30, 31 (see the Commentary). (Whereas the word is natural in Prov 8, which shows Wisdom as a child playing before her father, it is not the obvious choice to designate the speaker's feelings in Ps 119. In that context, the word itself is a playful usage and could be translated "have fun.")

(10) *tûgāh* ["misery"]: Ps 119:28; Prov 10:1; 14:13.

Proverbs resonates in Ps 119 in numerous ways besides the unique lexical correspondences; see Deissler *1955* passim (see "Weisheit" in his index) and A. Robert *1939*.

Psalm 119 borrows from all the major components of Proverbs, including the Interludes, the latest major component of Part I (see Vol. I, 326–29) and thus the latest in the book of Proverbs, apart from the appendices. The psalm also draws on other biblical texts (particularly Deuteronomy and Jeremiah) and in that sense is "anthological" (Deissler *1955*: 19–31).[440] Ideologically, Ps 119 is rooted in Deuteronomy. Deuteronomy is the only Pentateuchal document that requires people to meditate on Torah, remember it, and teach it (Deut 4:39; 6:6, 7; 17:19; 30:14), activities that together constitute the central concern of the psalm. Though the psalmist probably knew of the entire Pentateuch, he is taking his ideas of To-

[438] A text can belong to (or overlap with) a variety of genres. A genre is a set with a number of criterial traits. A text belongs to a genre to the degree that it shares these features. It is a leap to deduce a text's social setting from its genre (or one of its genres) alone, as Deissler does in locating this psalm in a postexilic "wisdom school" (*1955*: 118). We have no knowledge of such a school.

[439] On the Wisdom Psalms see Vol. II, xv.

[440] D. N. Freedman (*1999*) argues that Ps 119 is a carefully crafted and well-structured poem.

rah and study from Deuteronomy because that book is most relevant to his purposes.[441]

With its distinctive Wisdom locutions, listed above, Psalm 119 approaches Wisdom Literature, then veers away. This does not indicate an *opposition* to Wisdom; it is, rather, the choice of a different path. The psalm employs some of the distinctive vocabulary and concepts of Wisdom Literature in the praise of revealed Torah and the wonders of its study.

Among all the synonyms for teaching and knowledge used in Ps 119, a notable set of words is missing—the wisdom-words: *ḥokmah* and *ḥakam*; *binah*, *tᵉbunah*, and *nabon*; *śekel* and *maśkil*. *Daʿat*—almost as frequent in Proverbs as *ḥokmah*—appears only once (Ps 119:66). Verbal forms from these roots do appear, but they are not frequent and are used differently from Proverbs.[442] The nouns and adjectives, which characteristically designate the qualities that Proverbs seeks to inculcate and the type of person it wishes to form, are absent, even though the enlightenment the psalmist desires could easily have been designated by any of the wisdom words.

The psalmist does reapply some of Proverbs' locutions to Torah. In 119:105 he says: "Your word is a lamp to my foot and light to my path." This is based on Prov 6:23a, "For the precept [*miṣwah*] is a lamp and the teaching [*torah*] a light." Although "precept" and "teaching" in the latter verse are clearly the parental instructions (see 6:20), the psalmist could naturally have construed these words in accordance with his own orientation. Yet he never does this with any of the wisdom-words. In light of the psalm's numerous and distinctive borrowings from Proverbs, the avoidance of Proverbs' key terms for wisdom and the wise seems intended to distance the poem from Wisdom ideology in favor of a Torah-centered doctrine.

Psalm 119 formulates an unusual concept of education. The boast in v 99a, "I have become more astute than all my teachers," seems like a deliberate twist on the sinner's confession in Prov 5:13b, "I did not give my ear to my teachers." The psalmist's brash assertion, "I have become more perceptive than the elders, because I have kept your ordinances" (v 100), sounds like a rebuff to Proverbs' as-

---

[441] This is emphasized by K. Koch (1958: 186–87), who ascribes the psalm to postexilic "Deuteronomic circles." All we actually know is that the author was influenced by deuteronomistic sources.

J. Levenson argues that the *torah* in question lacks a consistent identity. It includes biblical books, but also immediate revelations and sapiential motifs (1987: 567). It is true that the psalmist's Torah extends beyond the Pentateuch. However, since the psalm is a pastiche of paraphrased biblical verses, the author is very much oriented to *books*, and it would be puzzling if he did not relate to the Pentateuch as one. And, as M. Greenberg observes, the psalmist speaks of *God's* commandments, precepts, etc. (1995: 24–25). Moreover, some of the words for laws—*ḥuqqim*, *ʿedot*, and *mišpaṭim*—when said to be God's, refer only to regulations commanded in the Pentateuch. As in rabbinic usage, "Torah" refers first of all to the Pentateuch, then to the entirety of learning believed to radiate from it.

[442] The verb *hebin* means "to understand" in Proverbs but "to give understanding" in Ps 119 (vv 27, 34, 73, etc.). The root *ḥ-k-m* is used in Ps 119, but only in the D-stem (v 98), where it means "make clever" (so as to outwit one's enemies). In Proverbs, with one exception (the Dp in 30:24) only the G-stem is used, meaning "become wise" (13x; e.g., 6:6; 8:33). The verb *hiśkil*, "become astute," is used in Ps 119:99 and several times in Proverbs.

sumption that wisdom comes from the father and other elders. The psalmist's real teacher, as he often declares, is God (vv 26, 34, 64, 66, 99, 102, 171), and the Torah is—though the psalmist would not put it this way—God's Wisdom book, meant for teaching the devout the way that Proverbs teaches the naïve (Prov 1:4). When the psalmist asks, "How can a youth [*naʿar*] make his way pure?" (Ps 119:9a), he has himself in mind, as seen in the fact that his focus throughout is his own moral enlightenment.

The idea that enlightenment is a gift consequent on study is not foreign to Proverbs (2:5–6; see Vol. I, 132), but, for the most part, the sages assume that the student's mental efforts will take him incrementally toward wisdom. In Ps 119, knowledge of Torah comes not as the direct outcome of study and attentiveness but as God's gracious gift. The psalmist repeatedly implores God to *give* him understanding (vv 27, 34, 73, 125, 130, 144, 169). The psalmist *yearns* to understand God's word (v 82a). He *prays* for enlightenment and God grants it (vv 10, 34, 73, 144, 169). This grant is an act of kindness or grace (vv 82b, 124, 135), a quality emphasized by the verb *ḥnn* "grant graciously" (or even "gratuitously") in v 29. Also, enlightenment may be the reward for a religious virtue, such as giving "the freewill offerings of the mouth" (v 108), that is, words of prayer and praise of God (Deissler 1955: 207–208). *Keeping* the Torah's commandments is what makes a man astute and pure (v 100; cf. 104–105). When the psalmist is threatened, he looks to God's ordinances—not to his own wisdom, and not even directly to God himself—as the prime source of security (v 95; cf. v 155).

In Proverbs, being a *mebin*—a perceptive person—is a predisposition that allows one to gain wisdom (Prov 8:9; 17:10, 24; 28:7). In Prov 28:7, being a "perceptive son" is a precondition of keeping *torah* in the sense of instruction. But understanding is also *demanded*, even of the simple, as in Prov 8:5. In Ps 119, *studying* Torah or *seeking* God—the verb *drš* is used of both actions—is an act of fealty that can be expected to bring rewards from God rather than yield its own practical benefits (vv 10, 45, 94, 155).

What Interlude D says about the joy of wisdom (Prov 8:30–31; see Vol. I, 294), Ps 119 says about the joy of Torah, and even more emphatically (vv 14, 16, 24, 29, 47, 77, 92, 103, 111, 143, 162, 174). It would be a short step to link joy in Torah to joy in wisdom, but the psalmist does not take it. Enlightenment comes from God's Torah alone. The entire human duty and hope is to meditate on Torah and keep its ordinances.

C. *Agur (Proverbs 30:1–9)*[443]

Though now joined to the book of Proverbs, Agur's oracle is really a reaction to it. The poem may have been written earlier or composed for this purpose. In either case, it was appended as a cautionary response to the exaltation of wisdom that characterizes the rest of the book. The date of the poem is uncertain, but Agur is aware of Deuteronomy (Prov 30:6).

---

[443] See "Agur's Teaching" after the Comments on Prov 30:1–9.

Agur disclaims having wisdom, which he calls "human understanding" (Prov 30:2), in favor of a higher knowledge—"God's words," that is, written Torah (see the Comment on 30:6). Along with this knowledge comes a keen awareness of human ignorance and a sense of utter dependency on God's will. Agur prays to be kept far from temptation, lest he find himself pressured to sin (vv 7–9). In his view, God himself now must do what the sages (of Prov 1–9, at least) considered to be fully in the power of human wisdom: to harden a man against temptation.

For Agur, fear of God—which is the attitude he expresses in Prov 30:8–9 though he does not use the term—is not so much the beginning of wisdom as its replacement. The wisdom he speaks of in v 2 is of lesser value. The editor who added Agur's poem sought to rectify the lack of concern for divine revelation in the book of Proverbs that had reached him.

D. Ben Sira

In most of Ben Sira, as in Proverbs, wisdom means practical good sense coupled with moral and religious virtue. It is a human faculty, possessed by the individual mind and transmitted from person to person. But in Sir 24, wisdom emerges as a transcendent force, personified as a woman who tells her story and praises herself.

Lady Wisdom delivers her speech in two dimensions at once. She addresses "her people" (Sir 24:1), which must mean Israel, among whom she has come to dwell, and she also speaks "in the assembly of the Most High" (24:2), as an angelic being in God's council.[444] Thus she is still in heaven (v 4), even though she has ventured out into the world (v 6).[445] She issued from God's mouth and covered the earth like a mist (v 3); in other words, Wisdom is a hypostasis of God's *ruaḥ*, his breath or spirit (cf. Prov 2:6b). She dwells in the vault of heaven but governs the seas and land, ruling over every nation (Sir 24:3–6).[446] She wandered in the world like Israel in the desert, and she too found no rest until she reached Zion,

[444] Thus J. J. Collins 1997: 50. J. Rogers (*2001*) argues that wisdom is personified not as a woman but as an angel in Sir 24. Rogers's arguments for wisdom's angelic status are persuasive, but wisdom is figured by a number of tropes that are not mutually exclusive. The feminine gender of Wisdom, in both Hebrew and Greek, virtually forces the image of a female figure on the personification. The situation is much the same in the case of Lady Wisdom in Prov 8. I discuss the relevance of her gender in Vol. I, 339–40.

[445] This contradiction seems to reveal a reflection, or perhaps a disagreement, on wisdom's localization. In Prov 8, Wisdom dwelt with God as a child, but it is not said that she abandoned him, and it is unlikely that she loses her heavenly status even as she travels the inhabited world to address humans. This is sorted out in 1 Enoch 42:1–2: At first, Wisdom settled in the heavens, then went out to dwell with humans, then returned to dwell permanently among the angels. This idea has its precedent in Ps 119:89, "O Lord, your Word is forever stationed [*niṣṣab*] in heaven." God himself, especially in deuteronomistic sources, is said to dwell both in heaven and in Jerusalem (e.g., 1 Kgs 8:27–29).

[446] Wisdom tells her story in the past tense. The Greek uses aorist verbs. These probably reflect suffix-conjugation verbs in the Hebrew base-text, which is not extant here. But the events she describes are actually timeless. As Sir 1:1 explains, Wisdom proceeded from God but remains with God forever.

where she took up her residence (vv 7–11). She is verdant like a tree (vv 12–22)—an image taken from Prov 3:18—and her fruits are sweet (Sir 24:17, 20)—an image derived from Prov 24:13–14.

There is an important difference between this poem and its model, Prov 8. Whereas in Proverbs Lady Wisdom is consistently a human-like (but supernatural) female, in Ben Sira she is figured in various ways. The inconsistency in figuration shows that Ben Sira's description of wisdom is driven not by a particular image or myth but by the idea he seeks to convey.[447] This is a complex and rather paradoxical idea that required depiction from various perspectives. Wisdom and Torah are at once universal and local, general and specific.

The first twenty-two verses of Sir 24 could stand alone, as a poem in praise of wisdom. Then, in vv 23–29 there is a shift, as Ben Sira steps back from Wisdom's self-description and, in his own voice, ascribes wisdom's qualities to Torah: "All this," Sira says of the qualities he has ascribed to wisdom in 24:1–22, "(is true of) the book of the covenant of God Most High, the law Moses commanded us as an inheritance for the congregations of Jacob" (24:23).

The relation between wisdom and Torah in Ben Sira is not one of strict equation. Wisdom is available to the nations who have not received Torah (see Vol. I, 358). She ruled over the nations from the start (Sir 24:6), and presumably did not lose her universality when she chose Zion as her home. Torah is the core of wisdom, the sublime form of wisdom given to Israel, and it is itself *full* of wisdom (Sir 24:25). Possibly Torah is reconceived as a power of enlightenment available to some degree to the nations who are not aware of wisdom as Torah. It seems that Ben Sira has not worked through the nature of the wisdom-Torah identification precisely. However that may be, this new conception overrides Agur's distinction between having wisdom and knowing God's word (Prov 30:3, 5). For Ben Sira, to know the latter is certainly to have the former.

The Torah that Ben Sira links to wisdom includes the Pentateuch but also extends far beyond it. Wisdom/Torah existed before the revelation at Sinai. It is not confined to a document or even to verbal content, though the written Pentateuch is its finest distillate. Torah, Ben Sira believes, generates or *radiates* all wisdom (24:32), including his own teachings, whether religious exhortations, ethical precepts, or mundane guidance like banqueting etiquette. The human mind is not the great source of truths but their conduit. The wise man taps into the boundless waters of Torah and *channels* them to other gardens (Sir 24:30–31). But the results are not just reinterpretations and applications of Scripture. One studies Torah and is shaped intellectually and spiritually so that he is himself able to produce wisdom.

The identification of Torah with wisdom is present but not fully developed in Ben Sira. Rather than being well integrated into his teachings or distributed throughout them, it is concentrated in one passage, chapter 24, especially vv 23–29. To be sure, components of the identification are adumbrated earlier in Sira and echoed later. At the very start Ben Sira says that wisdom—without mention

[447] The Hellenistic Isis aretalogies have made an impression on this chapter; see Vol. I, 336.

of Torah—was created before all things; it is eternal; and it was poured out on all creation (1:1–9). If one meditates on the Torah of God, God will grant him wisdom (6:37). Studying the Torah brings one to wisdom (15:1). Wisdom is subsumed under piety and Torah: "The entirety of wisdom is fear of the Lord; the entirety of wisdom is the fulfillment of the Torah" (19:20). (Ben Sira means that these things are the essence of wisdom, not that there is no more to be said.) Obedience to the commandments is identified with fear of the Lord (23:27). Still, this adumbration does not amount to a deliberate identification of wisdom with Torah such as emerges in chapter 24. The identification becomes prominent again in 39:1–11, the description of the scribe of the Law. The identification of wisdom and Torah is something Ben Sira is thinking through and trying to convey by a profusion of images.

Though Ben Sira declares that his own wisdom is a mere rivulet (24:30), his modesty is deceptive. He has in fact exalted his wisdom. His rivulet received the waters of the Torah itself and soon grew into a great river, then a sea (24:31). Not only in his exposition of the Law, but in his own teachings, the sage gives utterance to the divine spirit (to use the metaphor in Sir 24:3) and thus "pours out instruction like prophecy" (Sir 24:33). In 51:23–26, Ben Sira alludes to Deut 4:6–7 and 30:14 to conflate his wisdom with Torah itself.[448]

In his portrayal of the learned scribe (39:1–11), Ben Sira describes the process whereby the study of Torah issues in specific wisdom teachings (such as Ben Sira's own). The man who would devote himself to study of the Torah

(1b) will contemplate the wisdom of all the ancients
and busy himself with the prophecies,
(2) listening carefully to the conversation of prominent men
and entering into the complexities of parables,
(3) examining the secrets of proverbs,
and exploring the enigmas of parables. (39:1b–3)

The Torah scholar's field of study extends to the entirety of Scripture and beyond. In fact, "the wisdom of all the ancients" (v 1b) probably includes foreign, particularly Greek, literature (see Skehan and Di Lella 1987: 46–50). This accumulated learning enables the scribe to serve in lofty offices. *Then* he prays to God, *and if God wants*, the scribe will be filled with the spirit of understanding (Sir 39:6a; sim. 51:19b).[449] He will be qualified to teach his wisdom to others and will gain renown (39:6b–11; cf. 51:25). Again, in a motif we have seen in several texts, the study of wisdom prepares the ground for the divine gift of wisdom.

Ben Sira's own wisdom is very much in the mold of the older teachings. Despite his attention to Torah and his citations and paraphrases of numerous Pentateuchal verses, he does not use his wisdom for exposition of Pentateuchal law. Nor

[448] See G. Sheppard 1973: 171.

[449] The Wisdom of Solomon makes this point at length. Solomon asks God for wisdom because no one can gain it on his own (8:21). Then Solomon declaims a long prayer for wisdom (chap. 9).

does he cite Torah as a warrant for his advice, even with regard to actions commanded in the Torah, such as honoring one's parents (Sir 3:2). In the "Praise of the Fathers" (chaps. 44–50), he does adapt the Pentateuchal narrative, but his advice, which constitutes most of the book, does not claim to rest on Torah. For Ben Sira, wisdom is for all practical purposes a different face of Torah, the one that turns toward individual ethics and good sense. As J. T. Sanders observes, Ben Sira

> could not imagine, could not conceive that [the Torah's] morality could be other than his traditional sapiential morality. In his work we see one way in which the Mosaic Torah, representing a competing approach to religion and life, could be received by the wisdom tradition. Ben Sira neutralizes the opposition of the Torah by absorbing much of it; yet he maintains the sapiential tradition. (*2001*: 125)

Ben Sira does not explore the implications of this identification. For him it is a means of heightening the status of wisdom and firming up its religious legitimacy. Nevertheless, he has achieved the synthesis of revelation and wisdom that became axiomatic in Rabbinic Judaism. Though the book of Ben Sira was known to later Judaism, we cannot know if this idea came to the rabbis from him. Still, the identification of wisdom and Torah is already premised in the earliest rabbinic sources, and there is no alternative precedent in extant texts besides Ben Sira. In any case, he was the first to present the idea clearly, and it subsequently became central to the ideology of rabbinism, which harnessed human intellect to the exposition of Torah.

E. The Wisdom of Solomon

The Wisdom of Solomon, dating from the first century B.C.E. or first century C.E., is clearly indebted to Ben Sira for its idea of wisdom. It also drew on Greek philosophical traditions. Though the Wisdom of Solomon does have canonical status in some branches of Christianity, it had no impact on the development of rabbinic Judaism. But the book calls for mention because it takes wisdom to a height found nowhere else. Wisdom becomes a near-divinity, the means through which God conducts history. Even more, Wisdom *herself* conducts history. In Egypt, for example, "She saved the holy people and blameless race from a nation of oppressors. She entered the soul of the servant of the Lord, and with signs and wonders stood up to fearsome kings" (Wis 10:15–16). Indeed, she sits next to God's throne (9:5).[450]

In this book, wisdom is the Logos as described by Philo, or something very close to it, though it is not so designated. Wisdom is called God's own spirit (Wis 1:7), that is, the divine mind, through which he performs his works (D. Winston 1979: 38). J. J. Collins describes wisdom thus: "In the cosmic analogy, Wisdom is the

[450] A *paredros*, "one who sits next to the throne," can be "the assessor or coadjutor" of a king or magistrate (LSJ 1332b).

mind or spirit of the universe. In effect, Wisdom embodies the Stoic concept of the Pneuma or Logos, but subordinates it to a transcendent God, who is affirmed as its source" (1997: 200).

Torah is not equated with wisdom. Rather, it is encompassed by it; it is wisdom's highest manifestation. Concerned with wisdom's universality, the author in effect elevates wisdom above the Law (Sanders *2001*: 128). Torah is *wisdom's* laws (Wis 6:18), the expression of wisdom's will. But as a manifestation of the divine mind, Torah has a universal force, and through Israel "the imperishable light of the Law was to be given to the world" (Winston 1979: 38, citing Wis 18:4).

F. The Rabbis

In a parable often quoted in Jewish commentaries and homiletics, *Gen. Rab.* 1.2 reappropriates biblical references to wisdom to describe Torah. Commenting on Prov 8:30a, "And I was with him as an *ʾamon*," the midrash explains:

> *ʾAmon* means *ʾomman*, "artisan." The Torah says, "I was God's tool of artisanry." It is the ordinary practice that when a mortal king builds a palace he does not build it from his own mind [*middaʿat ʿaṣmo*] but from the mind of an artisan. And the artisan does not build it from his own mind, but uses records and writing tablets, so as to know where to place rooms, where to place wickets. Thus did God look into the Torah and create the world. And the Torah said, "*Bᵉreʾšit* ["in"—or "*by*"—"the beginning"] God created . . ." Now *reʾšit* means Torah, as it is written, "The Lord created me [Wisdom] as the *reʾšit* of his way" (Prov 8:22).[451]

For the rabbis, it is a given that *ḥokmah* "wisdom" is Torah. Hence, when Wisdom in Prov 8:22 says that God made her *reʾšit*, that means that God made Torah *reʾšit*. Since *bᵉ*- can mean "by" as well as "in," when Gen 1:1 says that God created the world *bᵉrešit*, it means that God created the world *by* Torah.

The midrash's own explanation of the allegory does not fit the allegory precisely. In the allegory, a king engages an artisan (*ʾomman*), who looks in the blueprints, which are a "tool of artistry. The Torah first says that she was God's *ʾamon* = *ʾomman* "artisan," then that she was God's "tool of artistry." But in the explication, it is God who looks in the blueprints, which are the Torah. The artisan has disappeared.

It seems that the allegory originally had a meaning that does not fit the use to which it is put, with some straining, in the midrash. The allegory lends itself most naturally to a different set of equations: king = God; artisan = demiurge; blueprints = Torah. The notion of a demiurge, a divine intermediary or associate who created the material world, was prevalent in Gnosticism. This notion is mentioned—and strongly repudiated—shortly afterwards, in *Gen. Rab.* 1.3. The

---

[451] I translate Proverbs here according to the understanding assumed in the midrash. Compare my translation and interpretation in the Commentary on Prov 8.

latter midrash rejects the possibility that God had an "associate" (*šutap*) in the work of creation.[452]

As the allegory is explained in *Gen. Rab.* 1.2, Torah is not the artisan but the blueprint or inscribed plan of the universe, which God created before the work of creation and then used in creation. (Prov 8:22 is again the proof text.) Torah perceived as a "world order," one that God designed and consulted in constructing the world. By reading the Torah as his notebook to call to mind his own designs, God made himself the first student of Torah. Later, at Sinai, he gave Israel his notebooks, so to speak. Now they, as students of Torah, can replicate in miniature the process of divine thought and follow God's creative example in an extraordinary act of *imitatio dei*.

At this point, wisdom is entirely submerged in Torah and has no independent function, while Torah is elevated to a universal power that precedes and transcends its own words. The words of the Pentateuch are the first and highest manifestation or realization of Torah, but not its entirety. "Torah" is an entity that "reads" Torah and "speaks" Torah—an entity that embraces the entirety of written and oral Torah and all study of Torah.

This recalls Wisdom in Prov 8. She is the being that existed before particular words of wisdom were composed, but they too are her words, and she will go on speaking them for as long as wisdom is taught, in the same way that Torah speaks in the words of every Torah scholar.

[452] The "two powers in heaven" heresy was a target of rabbinic polemic. It probably labeled a variety of apocalyptic, Christian, and gnostic heresies. Particularly precarious to the rabbinic position were creation passages in which God speaks in the plural, esp. Gen 1:27; 11:7. The Talmud, in *b. San.* 38b, brings these passages together to refute any implication of divine plurality. See A. Segal *2002*: 121–34 and passim. Sophia had a creative role in gnostic thought, which may be a reason that the rabbis virtually secreted wisdom behind Torah.

ESSAY 8. KNOWLEDGE

◆

Although knowledge (also called "wisdom" and "understanding"[453]) is at the center of Proverbs' concern, little is said about how knowledge is created, where it comes from, and how truth-claims are verified.[454] Still, there must have been an implicit epistemology—ideas about what knowledge is and what its sources are. Some propositions were considered true and others false, and the authors of Proverbs believed that they had the means for distinguishing them. That is, they had an epistemology, albeit unreflective and unsystematic. The present essay tries to describe its main lines.

I. EMPIRICISM?

Before addressing the question of what Wisdom epistemology is, it is important to determine what it is *not*. Contrary to the scholarly consensus, it is not empiricism, the philosophical principle that all knowledge ultimately derives from sensory experience. Scholars have considered Wisdom to be empirical because the sayings are largely about daily life and thus presumably based on the experiences of daily life, and because they seem to reflect *Erlebnisweisheit*, the wisdom of experience. Moreover, since the sages never invoke divine revelation or a tradition claiming to derive from it, it might seem that only observation was available as the source of knowledge. Wisdom empiricism is understood to mean that the sages gained and validated their knowledge by looking at the world, observing what was beneficial and harmful, and casting their observations in the form of proverbs and epigrams.

Some sayings do seem to be based on experience. Assertions like "Hatred stirs up conflict, while love covers up all transgressions" (Prov 10:12) seem like commonsense observations of people dealing with each other. The teachings about the danger of the king's wrath and the prudence of appeasing it (14:35; 16:14; 19:12; 20:2) sound like something a royal official could have learned firsthand, the hard way. The warning against providing surety (6:1–5; 11:15; 17:18; 20:16; 22:26; 27:13) is probably a lesson of experience, because it teaches a strictly prudential, not moral, principle. Still, empiricism is not the epistemological foundation of

[453] These are for all practical purposes synonymous in Proverbs; see "The Wisdom Words" in the Introduction to Essays 5–8.

[454] This issue must be distinguished from the question of how knowledge is learned and transmitted. Frydrych includes "Collective Experience" in his chapter on the epistemology of Proverbs (2002: 52–82, at 57). But this collective experience belongs to pedagogy or cultural transmission and is quite a different issue from epistemology. Every epistemological system, including empiricism, recognizes that knowledge is transmitted collectively. Once a proverb was accepted as valid and included in a collection, it could be conveyed as knowledge and accepted uncritically.

wisdom. The experiences from which some teachings derive belong to the authors' biographies, to a stage before epistemological standards decide just what is true.

Experience, as G. von Rad (1970) emphasizes, is not an immediate source of wisdom. Experiences themselves are created. To be sure, experiential knowledge ("Erfahrungswissen") is constructed from experiences, "But experiences without presuppositions do not exist. Man creates the experiences which he expects and for which he is prepared on the basis of the conception he has formed of the world around him."[455] Experience does not translate directly into wisdom. An observation must meet some other test first. Consider the saying in Ezek 18:2 (called a *mašal*, like the sayings in Proverbs): "The fathers have eaten sour grapes, and the children's teeth stand on edge." This conforms to the experience of the people who are using it, namely, the Jerusalemites who are still reeling from the disaster of 597 B.C.E. Moreover it conforms to the observable fact that some—or much—parental behavior harms the children, sometimes disastrously. Yet it is doubtful that this proverb would have qualified as wisdom by Proverbs' standards. Proverbs insists on individual responsibility for one's fate, and the idea of punishment transferred between generations is contrary to the sapiential view of individual retribution.[456] In distinction, Prov 10:12 (cited above) is wise not so much because it is empirically based as because it warns against a social evil and affirms the accepted virtues of love and concord.

In any case, empiricism is irrelevant to most of Proverbs. It is inconceivable that proverbs such as the following were extracted from experiential data:

> The Lord will not let a righteous man starve,
> but he rebuffs the desire of evildoers. (10:3)
>
> No trouble shall befall the righteous man,
> but the wicked are filled with evil. (12:21)
>
> When the Lord favors a man's ways,
> even his enemies make peace with him. (16:7)

To claim that these dicta describe an observed reality is simply to affirm the sages' beliefs. They are statements of faith, not abstractions from experiential data.

Many proverbs are assertions of consequences that do not even hint at an experiential basis:

> Do not say, "I will repay (evil) with harm";
> wait for the Lord, and he will give you victory. (20:22)

[455] "Aber voraussetzungslose Erfahrungen gibt es ja nicht. Der Mensch macht weithin die Erfahrunge, die er erwartet und auf die er auf Grund der Vorstellungen, die er sich von seiner Umwelt gemacht hat, gerüstet ist" (G. von Rad 1970: 13).

[456] Sons may benefit from their father's righteousness (Prov 13:22; 14:26; 20:7), but this is reckoned as *the father's* reward. Job's friends believe in transferred punishment (e.g., Job 5:3–5; 17:5; 20:10; 21:19; 27:14), but they differ from the sages of Proverbs in profound ways.

This is good ethics, but it could not have been inferred from multiple observations of people who eschewed revenge and were some time later rewarded with God-given victory.

> He who curses his father or his mother—
> his lamp will be extinguished in deep darkness. (20:20)

It must be extraordinarily rare to see someone curse his parents, and, even if that happens, the results would not be actually seen, especially if they occur "in deep darkness," which alludes to death.

Even in mundane matters, and even when the assertions are reasonable, the empirical base of most proverbs must be, at best, ambiguous.

> Have you seen a man adept in his work?
> He will stand before kings.
> He will not stand before the lowly. (22:29)

This is likely something that courtiers often saw, or believed they saw. Still, it is improbable that the author of the saying came to this conclusion by following the career paths of numerous diligent men. Unless government has changed radically—and there is much testimony to the contrary (Isa 1:3–25, e.g.)—not all appointments were so judicious, nor was every aspirant for a position who was held back undeserving. The sages filtered their experiences and perceptions through expectations of what diligence and skill *should* bring.

The passages in which experience, or the claim of experience, is most important are those that report the speaker's observation. The scene with the Strange Woman in Prov 7 is often thought to manifest sapiential empiricism at its purest, because it recounts an event that the speaker himself has putatively witnessed. He claims to have watched a silly boy being sexually enticed and led away by a woman. But that is all that he observes. The punishment is beyond the vignette and foretold, not reported. The speaker is certain that this woman will be the death of the man, because

> Many a victim she's laid low;
> numerous are those she has slain!
> Her house is the way to Sheol,
> descending to the chambers of Death. (7:26–27)

The sage does not say that he has seen this; he does not have to. It is something that *will* happen, that *must* happen. None of the sages of Proverbs musters observations, whether his own or his predecessors', to support the principle of retributionary balance. That would be weak support, for human observation is flawed and often blind to the workings of God's wisdom.

T. Frydrych, in support of the empirical interpretation, says that the threat that the fool will pay with his life (7:23c) is based on past observation. "The father's claim that *she has caused the fall of many* (v 26) indicates clearly that the whole paradigm relies on reocurring [*sic*] experience, so that even if some prior knowledge is used here in evaluating the story, it is based on observation of the same type" (Frydrych *2002*: 54). But this is not clear at all. Just because the speaker claims that something happened does not mean that he *saw* it happen. In fact, he does not even make this claim. It is not feasible for the sage to have observed this recurring "experience." Could he have spied on numerous adulteresses in his city, then followed the lives of the men they seduced and discovered that they were eventually killed as a direct result of the seduction? For the author of Prov 7 it is a given that adultery kills, and he is only looking for ways to bring this home to the reader.

When the speaker in Prov 6:6–11 sends the sluggard to the ant, he is using the creature as a teaching device to illustrate diligence. It is unwarranted to assume (as does Frydrych, *2002*: 56) that the author has studied ants for several seasons and knows the reward they earn. All that he could have seen was ants bringing bits of food to the anthill. He "knows" the result because he presumes that hard work yields profit. The sage does not even claim to have gone to the ant. He just sends the loafer to see for himself. There the loafer will only see an exemplar: a creature that (the author wrongly assumes) stores up food in harvest. Similar rhetorical devices are applied in Ahiqar 105a [1.1.89] and 112 [1.1.160]. What is at work here is analogy, not entomology.

Another passage that reports an observation is the anecdote of the lazy man's field and vineyard in Prov 24:30–34.[457] According to R. Clifford, "Verse 32 provides a glimpse of the learning process in Proverbs: one sees, stores what one sees in his heart, and draws a conclusion" (1999: 218). There is indeed an observational component here. The sage saw the vineyard of a man he knew was lazy (that is the way he is defined in v 30), noted its run-down condition, and "took a lesson." But his observation does not ground his actual conclusion, which is that *a bit more sleep* (not necessarily a lifestyle of sloth) brings on poverty. What happens in v 32 is not inference of a conclusion but the taking of a lesson. As always in the Bible, to "take a lesson" (*laqaḥ musar*) means to take something (usually an admonition or a punishment) to heart, to take it seriously and apply it. The anecdote does not report the discovery of knowledge but an experience that reinforces a known principle. The observation is an occasion for reflection, not inference, and the anecdote is a testimonial to an axiomatic belief.[458]

Saʿadia, commenting on Prov 24:30–34, explains precisely the function of such anecdotes: "It is not entirely necessary that the wise man passed by the field of the sluggard and saw it sprouting weeds and nettles. Rather, he knew this (event) conceptually and shaped it into a *mašal*, as if it were a report, because learning

[457] Actually, as M. Haran shows (1972: 243–44), the depiction focuses on the vineyard. The field is mentioned only for the sake of the parallelism.

[458] J. L. Crenshaw, who regards the standard Wisdom epistemology as empirical, notes that in Prov 7:6–27 and 24:30–34 the speaker interposes his subjective consciousness between his experience and the reader, a phenomenon he compares to Qohelet's empiricism (*1998a*: 206). There is, however, a significant difference: In the passages in Proverbs, the subjective observer testifies to the teaching, whereas in Qohelet the observer *probes* the phenomena. Moreover, in Qohelet, consciousness is reflexive and serves to test subjectivity itself, for the speaker is scrutinizing his own reactions and his own experience of wisdom; see Fox *1999*: 71–83. Crenshaw *1998a* also examines Qohelet's subjectivity.

a lesson comes from whatever penetrates deeper (into the heart of the listener)." Saʿadia mentions similar exemplary narratives in Qoh 9:14–15 and Prov 7:1–27. He explains that "these things, which wisdom conveys in *mᵉšalim*, make a person (feel) as if he saw them and fully prepare him for obedience."[459] In other words, such anecdotes belong to pedagogy, not epistemology.

The only sage who did embrace what may fairly be called empiricism is Qohelet, for he seeks to achieve new knowledge by means of observation.[460] He reports that he resolved to explore the world by wisdom, to "see"[461] all that occurs on earth. From the database he gathered he would discover—"see"—what is good for man (Qoh 1:13). But he was quickly frustrated, "For in much wisdom there is much irritation, and whosoever increases knowledge increases pain" (1:18).

Theodicy may use claims of personal experience. The sufferers insist that they have experienced the failure of divine justice on their own flesh, while its defenders insist that they have always witnessed its triumph. Eliphaz does the latter: "(It is) as I have seen: Those who plot iniquity and those who sow wrong harvest it. At the breath of God they perish, and at the blast of his anger they die off" (Job 4:8–9). Eliphaz musters his observations in order to underscore what he believes to be obvious, what *must* be true.[462] It is when old truths are being challenged that individual experience becomes most important, almost as a last resort. It may serve either to probe the givens or to confirm them. Neither happens in Proverbs.

The sages of Proverbs undoubtedly saw many things that provided ingredients for wisdom, but this is not the decisive factor in what counts for them as true. In the following deliberation, I seek to describe an epistemology that encompasses all passages in Proverbs, both those that grew out of observation and those that are expressions of prior principles and attitudes.[463]

II. COHERENCE THEORY

While the book of Proverbs is far from systematic, it is not a haphazard bunch of adages propounding opinions on this or that topic. It grew by a long process of composition and collection, in which the editors wrote and gathered proverbs that served their goals. In this way the book achieved a fair degree of ideological unity.

[459] Introduction to Saʿadia's commentary; 15–16 in Qapaḥ's edition.

[460] I examine Qohelet's epistemology in *1998*: 225–38 and *1999*: 71–83. I argue that Qohelet is empirical in the way he defines his quest, not necessarily in his practice. His claim to have derived his conclusions from his independent observations—and these alone—is the most radical proposition in the book.

[461] The verb *rʾh* in the G-stem basically means "see" but also refers to nonvisual experiences. It is the most natural way to speak about observing "empirical" data. A comparison of frequencies (occurrences per total number of verses) of *rʾh* G is revealing. Qohelet: 45 of 222 verses = .20; Proverbs: 11 of 915 = .012; rest of the Bible: 1022 of 22,066 = .046. Qohelet has a vastly greater interest in perception (visual and mental) than the rest of the Bible and certainly than Proverbs.

[462] Other examples are Ps 37:25, 35–36; see Fox *1999*: 77–85.

[463] Agur's Oracle (Prov 30:1–9) is a response to Proverbs' non-revelatory epistemology. Agur is a case apart and is not included in references to Proverbs in this essay.

The author of the Prologue (Prov 1:1–7), certainly, understood Proverbs as a single book with unified goals.

Whenever there are claims to knowledge, as there most emphatically are in Proverbs, there are ideas about what constitutes it. There must be an underlying system of assumptions about knowledge for the book to hold together. This system—Proverbs' background epistemology—is best described as a *coherence theory of truth*. As J. O. Young defines it, "A coherence theory of truth holds that the truth of any (true) proposition consists in its coherence with some specified set of propositions" (*2001*). According to one version of this theory: "The coherence relation is some form of entailment. Entailment can be understood here as strict logical entailment, or entailment in some looser sense. According to this version, a proposition coheres with a set of propositions if and only if it is entailed by members of the set" (Young *2001*).

Socratic epistemology, as H. Benson describes it, is a form of coherence theory. Benson's description is closely applicable to Proverbs:

> Socrates understood knowledge as a kind of *dunamis*, that is to say, a power, capacity, or ability for doing a particular thing. . . . According to this theory, knowledge, wisdom, and expertise (*epistēmē, sophia, technē*) are one and the same. They are a power or capacity (*dunamis*) to make judgments resulting in an interrelated coherent system of true cognitive states involving a particular object or subject matter. The latter cognitive states, when coherently interrelated and resulting from judgments occasioned by such knowledge, are knowledge states. . . . Knowledge is both the power or capacity that occasions an interrelated coherent system of true cognitive states and one of those cognitive states. (Benson *2000*: 220)

The philosophical terms used here, including "epistemology," "empiricism," and "coherence theory," are applicable to biblical systems of thought only by analogy to the modern philosophical concepts for which the terminology was devised. The application of modern labels to ancient thought is valid heuristically insofar as the basic definitions of the philosophical systems can help organize and encapsulate the ancient ideas. Rarely, however, will the subtleties and ramifications of the philosophical ideas, as developed by their modern advocates, apply precisely to the ancient concepts.

The propositions, stated and assumed, of the sayings and epigrams in Proverbs receive their validation by virtue of consistency with the integrated system of assumptions that inform the book (and the earlier Wisdom from which it emerged). The propositions of sapiential knowledge (or the propositions on which sapiential advice is founded) are considered valid insofar as they are concordant with each other and are supported by common principles. To the degree that actual experiences contributed to the knowledge-store of Wisdom, they themselves were shaped and interpreted by assumptions that were already considered wise and (synonymously) true.

It must be stressed that the "new knowledge" in Wisdom thought is not radically innovative, in the way that a scientific theory can be. Wisdom was given in essence at the start, at least according to Prov 8, and only in details and formulations can further knowledge be drawn forth, expanded, and refined (see Vol. I, 355–56). It is immediately clear that a coherence theory of truth is more amenable to this static concept of knowledge than empiricism would be. In empiricism, an individual may see radically new things, and these may be discontinuous with previous knowledge.

If coherence theory is accepted as a valid characterization of the implicit epistemology of Proverbs, we may still wonder where the axioms came from in the first place. The answer to this important question lies not in epistemology but in the realm of historical anthropology and related disciplines, which attempt to account for the innumerable assumptions and attitudes that are embedded in a society or cultural group and transmitted for generations. One society may admire assertiveness and initiative; another may esteem reserve and submersion of the individual in the collectivity. Each group assumes that its style is the way of wisdom. But the origin of each assumption lies outside epistemology, which is the study of the nature and validation of knowledge.

One immediate indicator of the coherence principle at work in Proverbs is the system of templates active in the formation of its sayings in a way unparalleled elsewhere in Wisdom Literature. A template is a recurrent pattern of syntax or wording that serves as a framework for constructing new couplets; see "Templates" in the Introduction to Vol. II (II.C.1). Examples are the "better than" template and lines that are matched with different parallels to form new proverbial couplets.[464] The reuse of lines and patterns as the basis for new sayings is not just an artistic convenience. It is a means of incorporating accepted truths in new proverbs and thereby integrating the latter into the existing system of knowledge. The network of correspondences that these templates create is vividly graphed by D. Snell (1993: 42–48), who lists the verses of Proverbs and draws lines between the "duplicates," as he calls them. The dense and random web of crisscrossing lines thus formed reveals the numerous and intricate relationships among proverbs, and this is itself suggestive of conceptual cohesiveness.

The relevance of these relationships to epistemology can be explained in the terms that T. Perry uses to define what he calls quadripartite structures, which are most clearly exemplified in the "better than" proverbs.

> Quadripartities constitute a class of proverbial expressions in which the primary motive seems to be neither aesthetic nor even valuational but experimental, as if the wisdom of experience could be explored, perhaps even generated, from the systematic exploration of all virtualities of a given structure. It is thus necessary to qualify Cervantes' suggestion that proverbs are

[464] For example, Prov 12:14a; 13:2a; and 18:20a are close variants and can be considered a single line or "template." To this template are paired three very different lines, and three different couplets are produced, all with the same premise.

> "short sentences drawn from long experience." Rather, at least in one important sense they are drawn from wisdom's own structures. In such experiments, where the goal is to discover rather than teach, the contribution of the author seems to lie especially in the skillful use and elaboration upon a comprehensive formula, and such conventional frames are to be considered, in Abraham's (1983, 20) felicitous phrase, as "meaning-producing structures." These are figures of thought rather than of speech, less literary structures than logical ones, less forms of expression than ways of thinking. (Perry 1993: 95)

The following discussion explores how new wisdom is "drawn from wisdom's own structures." It does not catalogue the axioms that constitute the truth-grid into which new knowledge must be fit; the system is too vast and complex for that. We can, however, trace a single path to see how one idea flows into another in accordance with a framework of assumptions. There is no prime axiom from which all ideas are spun out; the system itself is primary. But, I suggest, an ideal of harmony is central to the system, and a sense for what is harmonious—the moral equivalent of a musical ear—is important in both the formation of a wise man and the validation of new wisdom.

To enter the web of assumptions we can begin with a pair of proverbs in the "better than" template:

> Better to dwell on the corner of a roof,
> than with a contentious woman in a house with other people.
> (Prov 21:9 = 25:24)
>
> Better to dwell in a desert land,
> than with a contentious and angry woman. (21:19)

If living with a contentious woman is high on the scale of misery, then it is worse than other unpleasant ways of living, and the harshness of the latter miseries can serve to gauge the severity of the former. Instances of severe but lesser miseries—in this case living in the desert and living on the corner of a roof—are easily plugged into the template.

How does the author of a proverb like this "know" that living with a contentious woman ranks high among nasty experiences? Whether an author's "life-experience" underlay the evaluation is indeterminable. Maybe he had a bad marriage, but maybe not. He need only place situations on a scale of values accepted by others. In any case, various experiences can give rise to the same maxims. A man with a pleasant wife can invert his experience and declare how hard it must be to live with a cantankerous one. (In fact, the sayings about cranky wives may be read as oblique appreciation for amiable ones.)

What made the contentious-wife sayings sound to the sages like wisdom (rather than like wisecracks or grousing) was that the collective enterprise that shaped the book of Proverbs repeatedly warns about the baleful effects of contentiousness.

The large number of verses on this topic—thirty-one in all[465]—shows just how important this issue was to the sages. They knew that disharmony in marriage was grievous because they knew that harmony was precious.

From the ideal of harmony among persons, numerous interconnecting and mutually validating proverbs could be drawn. Advice is reckoned wise if it is felt to promote the vision of a concordant society, with appropriate and agreeable relations on all levels, ranging from the immediate family (husband-wife; father-son; brother-brother), to the residential unit (master-slave, mistress-maid), to the village and city, to the whole kingdom, to God's realm (God-humans). Indeed, harmony *within* the individual is essential as well. This is called *šalwah* "security," "composure" (1:32; 17:1) and *šalom* "peace," "well-being" (3:2, 17; 12:20). Every proverb that promotes harmony at any level is reckoned *true*.

The human guarantor of the harmonious society is the king. Subjects owe the king allegiance in the form of fear and obedience (24:21). The king is duty-bound to maintain the social order (29:4). He should do so graciously (20:28; 31:8). When he must use harsh means (20:26), which are temporary "discords," he does so to restore the harmony of justice. He must create cohesion and stability beneath him by justice (16:12; 29:14; 31:9), by showing favor to worthy people (14:35; 16:13), and by treating underlings and the poor graciously (20:28; 31:6–9). The social order is a hierarchy, one justified, according to Wisdom, not by nobility of birth or wealth but by the concord and stability it creates and guards (29:4). Fathers over sons, masters over slaves, princes over commoners, kings over subjects, and God over all. Any violation of this order is not only dangerous but *ugly*. A slave lording it over princes is "unsuitable" or "unlovely" (19:10). A slave coming to rule makes the very earth shudder (30:22), as do dislocations in private affairs, such as in marital and household relationships (30:23). The ideal that frames the social principles, though not often labeled thus, is *šalom*, peace in the sense of wholeness, with the parts of the whole intermeshing effectively and supportively.

Wisdom also promotes harmony between God and humanity. Little is said about God's demands. More central in Proverbs are his attitudes: his loves and his hates, his favor and his disgust. People must cultivate good relations with God, just as a courtier must please the king. The wise man seeks and receives "the favor and high regard of God and man alike" (3:4).

Numerous proverbs offer moral direction by defining the polarities of divine attitudes.[466] For example:

> The Lord loathes deceitful scales,
> while he favors an undiminished weight. (11:1)
>
> The Lord loathes the plans of the evil man,
> but pleasant words are pure. (15:26)

[465] These are Prov 3:30; 6:14, 19; 13:10; 15:18; 16:28; 17:1, 14, 19; 18:6, 18, 19; 19:13; 20:3; 21:9, 19; 22:10; 23:29; 25:24; 26:17, 20, 21, 22, 23, 24, 26; 27:15; 28:24, 25; 29:22; 30:33.

[466] What Yahweh loathes (*tʿb*): Prov 3:32; 6:16-19; 11:1, 20; 12:22; 13:19; 15:8, 9, 26; 16:5, 12; 17:15; 20:10, 23; 21:27; 26:25; 28:9. What he favors (*rṣh*): 8:35; 11:1, 20; 12:2, 22; 14:9; 15:8; 18:22; 19:12.

The practical consequences of God's feelings are easily inferred and sometimes stated, as in 16:5—"The Lord loathes every haughty-hearted man; hand to hand, he will not go unpunished"—but that is not the only consideration. Utilitarian concerns alone would not explain the emphasis on God's likes and dislikes or the scarcity of explicit references to reward and punishment in the "loathing-favor" series. This series in effect demands sensitivity to God's *feelings*, not just his commands and prohibitions. When God looks at the world, he should see a harmony in society and in every person's deeds and soul. When he does not, he will through salvation or retribution set things aright.

Harmony is the rule and the ideal also in matters of justice, though here I would use the metaphor of balance, for balance is harmony between two parts, in this case deed and consequence.

Justice is understood to mean that God repays people in accordance with their deeds or—putting the same idea neutrally—that people are repaid according to their deeds.[467] The desideratum is balance: good deeds balanced by good results (for the doer and others), bad deeds by bad results (mainly for the doer), with divine correctives remedying any imbalance. Sayings can easily be constructed on this principle.

> He who is kind to the lowly lends to the Lord,
> and he will pay him the recompense of his hands. (19:17)
>
> He who digs a pit will fall in it,
> and he who rolls a stone—it will come back on him. (26:27)
>
> The righteousness of the upright will save them,
> while the treacherous will be trapped by deceit. (11:6)
>
> The righteous man is extricated from trouble,
> and the wicked comes into his place. (11:8)

And so on. The book is full of polar proverbs contrasting in binary fashion the fates of the righteous and the wicked. These proverbs are all expressions of the same axiom and all mutually validating.

To the modern ear, the long strings of righteous-wicked antitheses in Prov 10–15 may sound mechanical, if not tedious. But the back-and-forth, tick-tock quality of these series gives voice to the belief in the moral balance whereby God runs the world. The "tick" and the "tock" really say the same thing, count off the same pace, but the "tock" is necessary to complete the pair and tells us that things

[467] L. Boström (1990: 134–40) argues convincingly against drawing a dichotomy between sayings that assign the retribution explicitly to Yahweh ("God-sayings") and those that formulate the results impersonally. The God-sayings are not necessarily late additions to secular Wisdom, and the impersonal ones are not expressions of a concept of a mechanistic world-order. Rather, even in the earlier sentence literature, "[T]he anthropocentric material already had a complementary relationship to the theological approach to reality" (p. 140). I would call these different kinds of sayings alternative formulations of a reality rather than different "approaches" to it.

are right with the world. The ideal of moral balance must have been aesthetically pleasing to the sages, and these proverbs give it literary form.

The way of wisdom it is not only righteous and rewarding; it is also beautiful: straight, pleasant, smooth, and shining "like the glow of dawn" (4:18a). Wisdom will "place a graceful garland on your head; grant you a splendid diadem" (4:9); and "give . . . grace to your neck" (3:22b). The very first exordium or call to attention in Prov 1–9 describes the teaching as "a graceful garland for your head and a necklace for your throat" (1:9). This verse introduces a unit, namely, 1:9–19, whose lesson is a distinctly ethical admonition: Avoid the temptation to get mixed up in crimes or you'll die. This blunt demand with its grim warning is wisdom, and therefore it too is lovely and graceful.

The mind-set of Wisdom, as G. E. Bryce notes, identifies the good with the beautiful (1979: 151). (This is true also of Socrates, for whom the two kinds of good, both called *kalos*, were inseparable.) Bryce is on the mark when he says, "Right is extended to include the realm of aesthetics, and goodness is manifested by its pleasantness. The good is that which contributes to harmony and order in human relationships and thereby fosters a life-style in accord with the best standards of social etiquette" (1979: 151–52). Bryce cites Prov 17:7 and 22:18, which use "not fitting" and "pleasant" to judge morally tainted and virtuous actions, respectively, rather than employing terms of moral evaluation, such as "wicked" or "upright." He also adduces 23:1–11, which treats matters of etiquette alongside ethical behavior—and with the same gravity.

To be wise, one must acquire a sense of harmony, a sensitivity to what is fitting and right, in all realms of attitude and behavior. This may be called a moral aesthetic. "A righteous man tottering before a wicked one" (25:26b), is, of course, unjust, but it is also, to the moral aesthetic, repulsive, like "a muddied spring and a polluted well" (25:26a). The moral aesthetic is active even when no sin or crime is involved. There is no law forbidding arrogance, yet God loathes it, and it will not go unpunished (16:5). Arrogance is repugnant to the moral aesthetic, which prizes the right measure in all regards. An arrogant man's self-esteem is out of line with his actual status, which for all mortals is very modest. Likewise it is foolish to boast of the morrow, meaning to feel smug about one's ability to achieve success, because doing so is to ignore the limits of human knowledge (27:1). An excess of ambition is overweening and unseemly, for it violates the equilibrium between reasonable investment and respectable gain (see the Comment on 10:22). But laziness too is arrogant. The sluggard thinks himself wise (26:16). He is, it may be said, "boasting of the morrow," for he imagines that he can gain his needs without a commensurate investment of effort. (Thus he holds to his desires without putting out effort to satisfy them [13:4; 21:25]). Laziness is not only self-destructive, it is ludicrous (26:13–16), hence ugly.

Certain things just do not belong together, and joining them offends the sages' sensibilities. "Excessive speech is not fitting for a scoundrel; how much the less so false speech for a noble!," according to Prov 17:7. The main point is in the second line, which declares that falsity does not *befit* the noble. Much worse could be said of dishonesty, but here the issue is viewed from an aesthetic perspective.

It is likewise unsuitable for fools to receive honor (26:1) or even pleasure (19:10). Though it is not exactly *unjust* for a slave to become king or for a maidservant to disinherit her mistress, such things are *unseemly*, out of kilter (30:22, 23; sim. 19:10), and the earth's shuddering (30:21) suggests that bad consequences will ensue.

The principle of balance is nicely encapsulated in Prov 16:11: "A just balance and scales are the Lord's. All the weights of the purse are his work." If Yahwism were iconic, Yahweh could be pictured like the Egyptian Thoth, judging everyone by his balance-scales. This is the essence of God's justice and his demands in Proverbs, and it is fully sufficient. No promises to the forefathers, no covenantal ties, demands, or rewards, not even divine laws, come into the picture. They are not rejected; they are simply *unnecessary* in Proverbs' system.

But what about the sayings that seem to concede violations of the right order without including assurance of rectification? What coherence could they claim with the axioms of Proverbs' truth system?

> A muddied spring and a polluted well:
> a righteous man tottering before a wicked one. (25:26)
>
> The rich man's wealth is his fortified city;
> the poverty of the poor is their ruin. (10:15)
>
> The great man devours the tillage of the poor,
> and some people are swept away without justice. (13:23)
>
> A poor man is hated even by his fellow,
> while the friends of the rich are many. (14:20)

Similarly 18:23; 22:7; 28:3; 30:11–14; and more. See further R. Van Leeuwen, 1992: 25–36.

First of all, these "anomaly-proverbs" are inherently no more heretical or ideologically disruptive than any mention of the wicked. After all, the wicked must have succeeded in doing *something* bad to those who did not deserve it or they wouldn't be reckoned wicked. Even theologically unproblematic sayings such as 28:6—"Better a poor man who goes in his innocence than a man of crooked ways who is rich"—concede the obvious, that wealth is not proportionate to righteousness. Still, the anomaly-proverbs do shift the focus from the agent of the injustice to the facts of the injustice and thereby sharpen the question of how there can be violations of God's order.

The answer is that, even in the face of these anomalies, the principle of justice is still not defeated, because it is axiomatic and inviolable, and any violation must be illusory or temporary: "For the righteous man may fall seven times, but he will rise, while the wicked will stumble in evil" (24:16). Recompense must come, even if it waits till death: "For there shall be no future for the evil man; the light of the wicked will go out" (24:20); that is, the wicked will die and leave no offspring. As Van Leeuwen says, the sages' global, confident insistence on eventual justice is an assertion of faith—"belief in something that experience does not verify" (1992: 34), and as such it can withstand problematic facts.

Taken each one by itself, the anomaly-proverbs do not cohere with the axioms of Wisdom. Originally they may have been independent sayings expressing bitterness or cynicism, like Ezek 12:22 and 18:2. At that stage they were *not* wisdom, at least not by the standards of Wisdom Literature. But once incorporated into Proverbs, they were put to a different use and are now to be read in the light of the rest of the book, and, sometimes, reinterpreted within their immediate context. This happens in Prov 14:20, "A poor man is hated even by his fellow, while the friends of the rich are many," which receives an immediate corrective in v 21, "He who despises his fellow sins, while he who is kind to the poor—how fortunate is he!" Similarly 22:7 is controlled by 22:8.[468] Sometimes the remedy is built into the verse, as in 28:6: "Better a poor man who goes in his innocence than a man of crooked ways who is rich." Here the "better than" template lets us know that, on some level, justice is being done or will be done.

Most fundamentally, the anomaly-proverbs, when read in the context provided by the other proverbs, describe a stage before the eventual rectification, whose inevitability is asserted repeatedly.The moral order—which is the way that deeds are rewarded and punished, whether by divine intervention or the natural course of events—prevails and the violations are, in the larger picture, nullified. Moreover, the anomaly-proverbs convey an ethical teaching because they describe social evils that must be counteracted by human justice and mercy.

The book of Proverbs focuses on the normal, indeed, *sees* little but the normal. It sees an orderly world, without deep disruptions. Wisdom's coherence system sifts out some realities that would be obtrusive in the orderly world it posits. It offers no advice about dealing with disaster or famine, invasion or plague. Such events are held in store as punishments, and the righteous may be confident of deliverance. The wise will have the advantage in crisis, but Wisdom Literature does not say what they should do to meet it. Disruptions are local and specific. A large-scale disaster is a "day of wrath" (11:4), which has the restorative purpose of sorting out deserts. More diffuse is the damage caused by a wicked ruler (28:15), but then the disruption is an extension of his individual wickedness. There are times when the wicked have the upper hand, but these are temporary disruptions and are mentioned to warn against wickedness and to emphasize the certainty of the triumph of the righteous (28:12; 29:16).

The sages of Wisdom recognized coherence not by logical testing but by their sense for what fits the system—what I have called moral aesthetics. Sensitivity to moral aesthetics is the quality I have elsewhere called *moral character* and described as "a configuration of soul" (Vol. I, 348). This configuration is wisdom

[468] The process of reinterpretation by contextual pressure has been noted by several scholars. H. Washington (1994b: 191–202) discusses its workings in proverbs on wealth and poverty. Sayings that "describe objectively the situation of the poor without ethical evaluation" (ibid., p. 183) are, in context, employed in judgments of social ethics (pp. 171–202). See also Hermisson 1968:182; Whybray 1979 (summarized in "Religious Proverbs" (I.C) in the Introduction to Vol. II); and Van Leeuwen 1992: 31–33.

itself. It is what the sages of Proverbs teach their disciples, not by pounding in doctrines, or not by that alone, but in the way that an artist conveys an ineffable sense of color, proportion, and shape to his apprentice: by pointing to what he himself sees. In fact, wisdom *is* an art, not a science, and the sages of Wisdom are artists—*ḥăkāmîm*, as artists are called in Exod 36:4. The sages are artists painting a world whose realities often lie beneath the visible surface. We can sum up this art by applying Socrates' words, as cited by Xenophon: "For just actions and all forms of virtuous activity are beautiful and good. . . . Therefore since just actions and all other forms of beautiful and good activity are virtuous actions, it is clear that Justice and every other form of Virtue is Wisdom" (*Memorabilia* 3.9.5; trans. E. C. Marchant *1923*).

In Essay 3, "What Is Wisdom?," I wrote that "[w]isdom has an attitudinal or emotional as well as an intellectual component" (Vol. I, 348). But, to be more precise: These are not just *components*. They are, in Wisdom epistemology, one and the same thing, only seen from different angles. Using Socrates' holistic model of ethical epistemology, in which knowledge (or wisdom), desire for the good, and love of beauty are all one,[469] I would say that wisdom is by nature cognitive *and* emotional *and* aesthetic. No one can be wise who desires the good but does not engage his mind in absorbing and understanding it. No one can be wise who knows what is good but does not desire it. No one can be wise who knows what is good but does not feel its beauty and love it. Only together and inseparably can all these acts of mind and heart be wisdom.

This wisdom is something that humans can have only imperfectly. In the view of the sages of Wisdom Literature—and the rest of the Bible—God alone has it all, in perfect fusion. The quintessence of his wisdom came at the moment when he crafted an elegant, well-ordered world, looked at it, and judged it "very good," in Gen 1:31. We can see this moment of primal and paradigmatic wisdom in Prov 3:19 as well:

YHWH bᵉḥokmah yasad 'areṣ	By wisdom the Lord founded the earth,
konen šamayim bitbunah	established the heavens by skill.

[469] See Benson *2000*: 220, quoted earlier.

TEXTUAL NOTES

USING THE TEXTUAL TRADITIONS

◆

This introduction expands and develops the remarks in Vol. I, 360–66. The Textual Notes here and in Volume I include the following kinds of material:

(1) Variants.
(2) Possible variants that are best explained on other grounds.
(3) Interesting interpretations of the text implied in a translation.
(4) Pluses and minuses of stich length and more.

I am preparing a critical edition of Proverbs for the Oxford Hebrew Bible, which will include comments on the major versions and will enter more fully into the textual issues.

I. QUMRAN

The critical edition of the Qumran fragments has appeared in *Qumran Cave 4* (DJD XVI) 181–86 = Ulrich *2000*. Ulrich notes the following variants:

4QProv[a]
  1:32a. *mwškt* for MT *mšwbt*
4QProv[b]
  14:34. *wḥsr* for MT *wḥsd*
  15:19. *swllh* for MT *sllh*
  15:28. MT's *yhgh* is omitted.

II. THE VERSIONS: FURTHER REMARKS (SEE VOL. I, 361–66)

In "LXX-Proverbs as a Text-Critical Resource" (= Fox *2005a*), I propose several considerations that can help retroversions in the LXX-Prov, despite its sometimes paraphrastic translation and its numerous pluses that have no basis in the MT. The Syriac and, less often, the Vulgate witness to variants.

The Syriac is an occasional source of variants, though its text is closely aligned with the MT. When it agrees with the LXX, we cannot usually determine whether this is due to the LXX's influence or to a shared Hebrew variant. The Syriac serves as evidence for variants only when it is distinctly independent of the LXX, either by witnessing to a different variant or by implying the same variant while diverging from the LXX's treatment of it.

In my view, it is clear that the Syriac translator is using the LXX in tandem with his Hebrew text. This technique is evident in Prov 10:1, 4, 10, 13, 14, 19; 11:15, 16, 24, 31; 12:4, 17, 23, 25, 27; 14:22, 23; 16:10; 17:4, 10, 12; 18:3, 19; 19:7, 18, 25; 20:5, 30; 21:10, 22:10, 15; 23:28, 34; 24:34; 25:1, 26, 26:1, 2, 3, 18; 27:16; and 28:21; see the Textual Notes. These are cases when Syr agrees with LXX in an unexpected and even strange way. For example, in 16:10, LXX translates *mʿl* "rebel," "violate" as *planēthę̄* "stray." Syriac has *nṭʿʾ* "stray." Since this rendering is unique and not required by context, Syr must be dependent on the Greek. In 14:22, Syr = MT in v 22ab, then follows the LXX strictly in v 22cd, where no corresponding Heb was available. In 15:15, where MT has "a perpetual feast," LXX has a more cautious "is always at rest," which Syr follows. In 10:14, Syr translates MT's *py ʾwyl* "mouth of the fool"—hardly an obscure phrase—as "a hasty mouth," which can only come from LXX narrow rendering, *stoma de propetous* "mouth of the reckless." In 12:23, Syr *kwrsyʾ* "throne" for MT's *ksh* "covers" must derive from LXX's strange *thronos*. In 23:34, Syr translates ʾyš mgn as "a runner," following LXX's "good runner [*dromeus*]," not its own translation of the word in 6:11. To these examples we can add Syr's occasional rendering of Septuagintal pluses, namely, in 9:12a–c; 9:18a–d; 11:16γδ; 13:13a; 14:22γδ; 25:20a; 27:21a. Of these, only 11:16γδ shows signs of a Heb source text. J. Joosten (1995: 63–72) calls translations that fuse the LXX and the Hebrew "patchworks." For further discussion and examples of LXX influence on Syr, see M. Weitzman 1999: 70–83.

The Vulgate's text-critical value is complicated by the fact that it is a revision of the Vetus Latina, using hexaplaric materials, the Septuagint, and a Hebrew text. The situation is further complicated by Jerome's use of interpretations probably derived from the rabbis, on which see Gordon 1930. Occasionally, however, the Vulgate does attest to a Hebrew variant, perhaps by way of hexaplaric sources. An example of the Vulgate witnessing to a minor variant is Prov 23:10. The Vulgate is adduced occasionally for its interpretation or for independent support of a variant, usually in implied vocalization.

The Targum has very almost no text-critical value. It either reflects the Syriac, of which it is a rewriting, or the MT, to which it constantly adjusts. The present Notes mention the Targum only sporadically, when it offers an interesting interpretation or aligns itself with another version on a difficult issue.

It must be emphasized that the variants reflected in the versions are not necessarily preferable to the MT. They are not even all grammatically correct or meaningful. Some were simple scribal errors in the translators' Hebrew texts. The choice between variants belongs to the Commentary, where only viable variants will be weighed.

References to textual scholarship prior to the mid-nineteenth century are usually based on Baumgartner, Pinkuss, and Lagarde. These sources are commonly cited as "ref." For example, "Capellus, ref. Lag." means "Capellus, as referred to by Lagarde." Jäger's seminal *Observationes* (1788), which is cited directly ("Jäg."), proposes many valuable retroversions and emendations. It is sometimes unclear, however, whether Jäger is affirming an emendation or just retroverting the LXX.

Since the appearance of the first volume of this commentary, d'Hamonville's *La Bible d'Alexandrie: Les Proverbes* ("BA") has appeared. It provides an elegant translation of the LXX (often better than the original) and an appreciation of the version's literary features, as well as annotations on its hapax legomena, its numerous classicisms in language and thought, and its treatment by the Church Fathers. D'Hamonville points out the LXX's frequent creation of anaphoras, wordplays, and tighter antitheses, and shows the version's Stoic reverberations. (This does not change my assessment [p. 361] of the LXX as a "fairly faithful" translation of *a* Hebrew original. It is usually faithful to the sense, as it understands it, and very often to the wording.)

Variants in Kennicott and Rossi ("K-R") are noted sporadically, as examples of the kinds of variants that can arise in Hebrew transmission. On the limited value of these variants, see Tov 1992: 36–39. Manuscript B^{19} ("Leningradensis") is the base text used here. The variants in the Aleppo Codex are in matters of vocalization and accents and do not bear on the meaning.

TEXTUAL NOTES

◆

10:1. In v $1a^{\alpha}$, LXX, followed by Syr and some Vul MSS, omits *mšly šlmh* "proverbs of Solomon." A new ascription to Solomon at this point might imply that 1:1 does not apply to the entire book. Since LXX obscures the other headers except for the Solomonic ascription in 25:1, and since MT would have had no reason to add a title to a completed collection (unlike in Psalms, where distinct compositional units are evident), we may assume that the header was present and that LXX has removed it, for reasons evident in its treatment of 24:23; 30:1; and 31:1; see the Textual Notes.

Syr's omission of $10{:}1a^{\alpha}$ shows that it is sometimes willing to follow LXX in omitting MT words even when these are clear and not theologically problematic. Syr does not follow LXX's programmatic omission of ascriptions. Tg maintains the header.

10:3. For MT's *hwt*, LXX has *zōēn* "life," reflecting *ḥyt*, from *ḥayyāh* "life." Heb *ḥayyāh* can also mean "appetite" (Job 33:20; 38:39), which is the sense it would have had in LXX's source text: To "push away" or "rebuff" (*yhdp*) the appetite means to prevent its satisfaction. This provides a better antithesis to 3^{α}.

Several Heb MSS have *bôgᵉdîm* "traitors" for *rᵉšāʿîm* "wicked men." This is due to the influence of 11:6 (BHS), but the motive for the transfer is unclear.

Variant: *wḥyt* (MT *wᵉhawwat*).

10:4. LXX: "$^{\alpha}$ Poverty humbles [*tapeinoi*] a man, $^{\beta}$ but the hands of the vigorous [*cheires de andreiōn*] make rich." LXX makes Heb *rʾš* [read as *rēʾš* "poverty"] the subject. LXX's "humbles a man" paraphrases MT's *ʿśh kp rmyh* by associating *kp* with *k-p-p*/*k-p-h* "subdue," "force." In 19:15, *npš rmyh* is rendered *psychē aergou* "the idle man" and is parallel to *androgynaion* "effeminate." The choice of *andreiōn* for Heb *ḥrwṣym* introduces a moral factor, but subtly, since the Gk word embraces a broad range of pragmatic and moral virtues. Syr ≈ LXX.

10:4a. LXX: "$^{\alpha}$ An educated [*pepaideumenos*] son will be wise, $^{\beta}$ and will use [*chrēsetai*] the fool as a servant [*diakonǭ*]." V $4a^{\beta}$ resembles 11:29b. The couplet is Gk in origin, since the Heb would have used *ʿebed* for "servant" in this context, but *ʿebed* is never rendered by Gk *diakonos*.

10:5. LXX: "$^{\alpha}$ A thoughtful son is saved [*diesōthē*] from heat [*apo kaumatos*], $^{\beta}$ but a lawless son becomes wind-blasted [*anemophthoros*] in (the) harvest." Gk *diasozein* "save," "preserve through a danger," is loosely related semantically to the rare *ʾgr* "gather" (which is translated differently elsewhere). "Heat" paraphrases *qayiṣ* "summer" (cf. LXX 25:13). The source-text may have had *mqyṣ* ("from heat"). "Wind-blasted" represents *ndp* (*niddap*) "blown away" (as in Isa 19:7) or *nrdp* "pursued" (though that correspondence is not found elsewhere) for MT *nrdm* "drowses off." The blasted ears of corn in Pharaoh's dream are called *anemophthoroi* (Gen 41:6, 7, etc.).

Variant: *ndp* (*niddāp*) (MT *nirdām*).

10:6. LXX: "α The blessing of the Lord [*eulogia kyriou*] is upon the head of (the) righteous [sg.], β and untimely grief [*penthos aōron*] will cover the mouth of the wicked." "The blessing of the Lord" is taken from v 22 to emphasize God's role in retribution (Dick 1990: 27–28). LXX assumes that 10:6b alludes to the evildoers' future punishment rather than to their deeds and interprets *ḥamas* accordingly.

10:7. LXX: "α The memory of the righteous [pl.] is with praises [*meta egkōmiōn*], β but the name of the impious [sg.] is extinguished [*sbennutai*]." The praise in question is the funeral eulogy (BA). Gk *sbennutai* = *ydʿk* (thus Syr), for MT's *yirqāb* "rots." This shows the influence of 13:9b and 24:20b. Syr *ndʿk* "will be extinguished" = LXX.

10:8. LXX: α = MT; "β but he who is unguarded with (his) lips, being crooked, will stumble [*ho de astegos cheilesin skoliazōn hyposkelisthēsetai*]." *Astegos* is, lit., "unroofed," "exposed"; GELS: "unguarded." In 26:28, Gk *stoma astegon* corresponds to MT *peh ḥālāq* "slippery mouth," meaning seductive and deceitful. In 10:8, the LXX is trying to be more precise about what kind of fool is in question, as in 10:14β. LXX 10:8 seems to be influenced by mention of *ʿqš śptyw* "one stubborn in his lips" in 19:1, even though that verse is lacking in the LXX. Or perhaps *mʿqš* intruded from the next verse. Gk *skoliazōn* is a gloss on the unexpected *astegos* (Toy). Vul: "but the fool is beaten (*caeditur*) with the lips" (sim. in v 10). The versions show uncertainty about the meaning of the rare *ylbṭ*.

10:10. LXX: "α He who signals with (his) eyes with deceit causes sorrows to men, β but he who reproves openly makes peace" (α *ho enneuōn ophthalmois meta dolou synagei andrasi lupas*, β *ho de elegchōn meta parrēsias eirēnopoiei*). LXX makes *qoreṣ* ("squints," "winks") into a more obviously pernicious act. The antithesis in the second line shows that the deceitful eye signals are thought to be false signs of friendship. (Ben Sira [27:22–23] also interprets the gesture in this way.) Gk *andrasi* is to make it clear that harm to others rather than oneself is the issue here. (Possibly it is added for the rhythm; thus BA.) There is a good chance that a different Heb underlies LXX 10β. Possible retroversions are: *wmwkyḥ ʿl pnym yšlym* (Gemser); *wtwkḥt mglh* [*mᵉgullāh*] *šlwm* "and open reproof (makes) peace" (Ehrlich, cf. 27:5); *wmwkyḥ yʿśh šlwm* (Clifford; cf. Isa 27:5). Better Hebrew would be: *wᵉhammôkîaḥ yaʿăśeh* [or *ʿōśeh*] *šālôm*. (Note that Gk *parrēsia* is added exegetically in 1:20 and 13:5.)

Syr: "(a) He who hints with his eyes in deceit causes pain, (b) and he who reproves openly makes peace" [(a) *drmz bʿynwhy*pl *bnklʾ yhb kʾbʾ*, (b) *wdmks glyʾyt ʿbd šlmʾ*]. Syr (a) = MT. In (b), Syr ≈ LXX. Tg = MT in 10b, but using *slyp* "distorted" for *ʾwyl*, whereas it used *syklʾ* "fool" in 8b.

Variant: *wᵉhammôkîaḥ yaʿăśeh šālôm* (MT *weʾĔwîl śᵉpātayim yillābēt*).

10:11. LXX: "α A fount of life is in the hand of the righteous man, β but destruction covers the mouth of the impious." Gk *en cheiri* "in the hand" (MT *wpy-* "and the mouth") is an inner-Gk error for *en cheilei* "in the lip," a synonym variant for "mouth" (Grabe, ref. Lag.). LXX again interprets *ḥms* as punishment, this time translating it as *apōleia* "destruction" (≠ LXX 10:6).

Syr 11b reflects *pny* "faces" for *py* "mouth." The former reading would fit well in both vv 6b and 11b. Tg (b): "and the mouth of the wicked is covered with robbery."

Variant: *pny* (MT *pî*).

10:13. LXX: "α The one who brings forth wisdom from (his) lips [om. α B] β smites (the) senseless man with a rod" (α *hos ek cheileōn prospherei sophian*, β *rhabdǭ tuptei andra akardion*). The syntax is rearranged, but no variants are indicated. MT's *nābôn* "discerning man" is implied but not represented, and *tmṣ'* (N in MT) is associated with *môṣî'* "bring forth," perhaps by analogy with Aram *'amṭē'* "to bring." The verb "smite" is deduced from context. LXX more tightly connects the lines of the couplet by making the speaker of wisdom the one who smites the fool.

Syr is directly dependent on the LXX for the sense, even while reflecting MT's word order. Tg = MT.

10:15. LXX: α ≈ MT; "β but poverty is the disaster of the weak [pl.] [*asthenōn* [23 336 613]; *asebōn* "wicked" [ASB]]." By the majority reading, *asebōn*, LXX moralizes the severe observation in 15b, but *asthenōn* "weak" is supported by the third c. Antinoe Pap.; cf. 21:13; 2 Sam 13:4 (Grabe, ref. Lagarde; Zuntz 1956: 161).

10:17. LXX: "α Education guards the right ways of life, β but the unchastised education goes astray" (α *hodous dikaias zōēs phylassei paideia*, β *paideia de anexelegktos planatai*). LXX construes *mwsr* as the subject in 17α and repeats it in 17β, making *paideia* the topic of the couplet. The phrase (*mwsr*) *'wzb twkḥt* was then taken to mean, "education which leaves-off [i.e., neglects to provide] chastisement." (Gk *anexelegktos* here [but not in 25:3] means "unchastised" or "without chastisement"; cf. *exelegchein* for *hôkîaḥ* in 24:9; Mic 4:3; Isa 2:4. GELS: "incapable of disproof *or* criticism"; BA: "sans examen.") LXX adds *dikaias* for moral emphasis. This may be later in the LXX transmission since it is omitted in [ASc, Ant]. Sym, Theod, and SyrH witness to *šwmry* (pl.) in 17b. A significant LXX variant is [Ant] *hodos zoēs phy*[*lassei akakous*] (without repetition of *paideia*): "The way of life guards the innocent"; cf. 13:6α. Zuntz (1956: 161–62) argues for the validity of this reading.

10:18. LXX: "α Righteous lips [*cheilē dikaia*] conceal hatred, β but they who bring forth slanders are very foolish [*aphronestatoi*]." The MT has *śiptê šāqer*, "deceitful lips." It seems that the translator did not understand why it is wrong to conceal hatred and so reversed the sense of the stich by substituting "righteous lips" for "deceitful lips." Praise for concealment is found in 10:12b; 11:13b; 17:9a—and the very next verse.

10:19. LXX: "α By many words you will not escape sin [*ek polylogias ouk ekpheuxę̄* (*ouk ekpheuxetai* [A]) *hamartian*], β but, being sparing of lips, you will be intelligent." LXX probably represents *tḥdl* rather than *yḥdl*. Since the 2nd per. is incongruous here, it is unlikely to be a deliberate translational choice. For possible *y-t* confusions see Kennedy 1928: 81–82.

Syr *l' mtpṣ' 'wl'* "the sinner [*'awālā'*] shall not escape." Syr *l' mtpṣ'* = LXX[A] *ouk ekpheuxetai*.

Variant: *tḥdl* (MT *yeḥdal*).

10:20. LXX *pepyrōmenos* ("burnt," "purged") understands *nibḥar* as "assayed" (used of metallurgy), as in Aramaic. This is the meaning of *bḥr* in Isa 48:10 and Sir 4:17. Syr has a puzzling *mrtʾ* "bile," "bitterness,"for MT's *kmʿṭ*, a word which is translated elsewhere as *qlyl* or *zʿwrʾ*.

10:21. LXX: "α The lips of (the) righteous [pl.] understand lofty things [*epistatai hypsēla*], β but the fools die in neediness." Instead of MT's *yrʿw* "will shepherd," Gk has *epistatai* = Heb *ydʿw*, understood as *yēdeʿû* or *yādeʿû* (Lagarde). A better vocalization would be *yōdîʿû* "inform." The latter is supported by Vul *erudiunt* "instruct." C. Gordon (1930: 392), however, thinks Vul is based on the rabbinic understanding of Torah as *the* food par excellence, an interpretation maintained by Radaq. A simpler explanation is that both LXX and Jerome represent *ydʿw*. Since Heb *rab* is consistently translated *polys* or *megas* (exceptions only in 28:2 and 29:22), *hypsēla* probably represents *rmym* "lofty things" (Lagarde). In 21β *en endeią̄* = Heb *beḥōser* "in lack." Gk does not represent *lēb* "heart," and it was probably lacking in its source text. Possibly it was incorrectly copied into the next line.

Syr: "(a) The lips of the righteous (man) are very conciliatory [*mrḥmnyn*pl]"; (b) = MT. Syr's "conciliatory" associates Heb *yrʿw* with Aram *rʿy* "be willing," "favor" (Baum.). Tg *rʿyyn* "shepherd" (ptcp.).

Variants: *ydʿw* (*yōdîʿû*) (MT *yirʿû*); *rmym* (MT *rabbîm*); omission of *lēb*.

10:22. LXX: "α The blessing of the Lord is on the head of the righteous [sg.]. β It makes rich, γ and misery is not added to it in the heart." LXX adds *epi kephalēn dikaiou* "upon the head of the righteous" (from 10:6), lest one think that *anyone's* wealth evidences God's favor; see Giese 1992a: 417. The superfluous "in the heart" was likely displaced in the Heb of the source text from v 21b.

The LXX does not denigrate wealth as such or deny that wisdom has material rewards, but it does emphasize, often by adding words, that wealth is valued only when accompanied by righteousness and wisdom. This is a matter of emphasis, not a fundamental departure from the Hebrew. There is nothing specifically Stoic in the LXX's ideas of wisdom and wealth (Giese, ibid.).

Variant: (end of verse) + *lb*.

10:23. LXX: "α In laughter [*en gelōti*] a fool does evils, β but wisdom engenders discernment for a man." The source text in α had (a clearly erroneous) *bśḥwq* (= some Heb MSS) for MT's *kiśḥôq*. (Syr *kd gḥk* = *bśḥwk*.) LXX may have read *ksyl* "fool" instead of MT's *liksîl* "to a fool," though, to be sure, prepositions are often treated flexibly in LXX-Prov. Consequent upon these differences, the syntax was treated loosely. The article with *sophia* suggests that this is Wisdom personified (BA). The verse shows that "wisdom" (*sophia*) is prior to and engenders *phronēsis*, which is practical discernment or discretion.

Variant: *bśḥwq* (MT *kiśḥôq*).

10:24. LXX: "α A wicked (man) is carried about [*peripheretai*] in destruction, β but the desire of the righteous (man) is acceptable [*dektē*]." (BA: "est entraîné.") It is difficult to associate 24α with the MT or to reconstruct a different source text. In Gk *dektē* "acceptable" paraphrases *ytn* understood as *yuttān*, on the assumption that what is "granted" by God is "acceptable" to him.

After 24α, LXXA adds *douleusei de aphrōn phronimǭ*, borrowed from 11:29β, and after 24$^{\beta}$ it adds *kardia de asebous ekleipsei*, borrowed from 10:20$^{\beta}$. Two new couplets result:

> The wicked man wanders about [*peripheretai*] in destruction,
> and the fool will serve the prudent.
> The desire of the righteous is acceptable,
> but the intelligence [lit., "heart"] of the impious will cease.

This illustrates how a proverbial text can continue to develop and even produce new sayings, whether in translation or in Hebrew.

Syr: "(a) The sinner is dragged away to destruction, (b) but hope [*sbr'*] is given [*mtyhb*] to the righteous" (sim. Tg.). Syr is influenced by LXX in (a). In (b), Syr vocalizes *yuttān* (pass.) for *yittēn*. Sim. Vul *dabitur* "shall be given." Weitzman (1999: 224) observes that Syr-Prov several times introduces the theme of *hope* where it is not literally present in the Heb: 2:7; 8:21; 10:24; 11:3; 13:12; sim. Ps 10:17. Contrary to Weitzman (ibid.), in 10:24 and 13:12 the translator is not "misreading" *t'wh* "desire" as *twqh*, but is choosing a morally unambiguous word. Likewise in 8:21, the translator prefers "hope" to "wealth" as a translation of *yeš* to avoid excessive enthusiasm for material goods.

10:25. LXX: "$^{\alpha}$ When a storm passes, (the) wicked (man) disappears, $^{\beta}$ but the righteous man, turning aside, is saved forever" (*dikaios de ekklinas sǭzetai eis ton aiōna*). "Turning aside" = *yswr* (*yāsûr*) for MT *yswd* "foundation." LXX adds "is saved" to specify the benefit that the righteous man receives from "turning aside." (Gk *sōzein* never represents *y^{e}sôd* or other forms of *y-s-d* elsewhere.)

Variant: *yswr* (MT *y^{e}sôd*).

10:26. LXX: "$^{\alpha}$ As sour grapes are noxious [*blaberon*] to the teeth and smoke to the eyes, $^{\beta}$ so is lawlessness to those who practice it [*houtōs paranomia tois chrōmenois autēn*]." LXX moralizes MT by substituting "lawlessness" for "laziness" and having the unworthy person (fool or lawbreaker), rather than someone else (the sender), suffer the consequences of the bad behavior. The LXX is too paraphrastic to justify emendations in either the Gk (such as *oxos* "vinegar," for *omphax* "unripe grape"; Baum.) or the Heb (*'wl* for *'ṣl*; Baum.). Syr moralizes, like the LXX: "(b) thus does evil harm those who do it."

10:29. LXX: "$^{\alpha}$ Fear of the Lord is the fortress of the pious (man) [*hosiou*], $^{\beta}$ but (it is) destruction for those who work evil." LXX^{AB} have *phobos kyriou* for MT's *derek YHWH* "way of the Lord." (The hexaplaric reading is *hodos kyriou*.) Dick (1990: 37) says that *phobos kyriou* is the translator's interpretation of the unusual *derek YHWH*, perhaps influenced by v 27. BA observes that by repeating this phrase, LXX gives 27–29 a certain cohesiveness. In $^{\beta}$ the LXX must mean that evildoers *regard* the fear of the Lord as destructive. LXX implicitly vocalizes *lattām* for MT's *lattōm*.

10:31. LXX renders *ynwb* "yields fruit" as *apostazei* "drips" and *tahpukot* "perversity" as *adikou* "unjust man," taking it as an abstract-for-concrete trope.

10:32. LXX: $^{\alpha}$ *apostazei* "drips" for MT *yd'wn* "know." Although *apostazein* = *n-w-b* in v 31 and *n-ṭ-p* "drip" in 5:3 and Cant 4:11, here it probably represents *yb*ʿ*wn* (*yabbî*ʿ*ûn*), indicating a *d-b* interchange (on which see LSF §131). In ᵝ, Heb *thpkwt* is parsed as a verb, *apostrephetai* "is turned back."

Some Heb MSS read *yir*ʿ*ûn* "shepherd," as in v 21a, though "goodwill" is not appropriate as the dir. obj. of that verb.

Variants: *yb*ʿ*wn* (MT *yabbî*ʿ*ûn*) and *yir*ʿ*ûn* (MT *yedᵉ*ʿ*ûn*).

11:1. LXX ≈ MT, but explains Heb *šlmh* "complete" as *dikaion* "just" ≈ Syr.

11:2. LXX: "ᵅ Wherever arrogance enters, there too (enters) disgrace, ᵝ but the mouth of the humble [pl.] utters [or "meditates"; *meletą̄*] wisdom Gk *melatan* usually renders *hgh*, whose second sense, "utter," would fit well here as the antithesis of arrogance. This seems to indicate a variant source text, namely *wpy ṣnw*ʿ*ym yhgh ḥkmh* "and the mouth of the modest utters wisdom."

Variants: *wpy ṣnw*ʿ*ym yhgh* (MT *w'et ṣᵉnû*ʿ*îm*)

11:3. LXXᴬ: "ᵅ When the righteous man dies he leaves behind regret, ᵝ but the destruction of the wicked is speedy and joyous" (ᵅ *apothanōn dikaios elipen metamelon*, ᵝ *procheiros de ginetai kai epichartos asebōn apōleia*). OG read *bmt* [i.e., *bᵉmōt*] for MT's *tummat* and loosely associated MT's *tnḥm* ("guides them") with *n-ḥ-m* "regret." LXXBS adjust to MT. OG lacked 3ᵝ (MT 3b). It was supplied in expanded form from MT 11:10b (Jäg.).

Syr constructs a different proverb with little connection to either the MT or the LXX: "(a) The hope of the righteous shall be built up, (b) but the pride of the wicked will be torn down" [(a) *sbr' dtryṣ*'ᵖˡ *ntbn'*, (b) *wrmwt' w*ʿ*wl*'ᵖˡ *tstḥp*]. Tg is corrupt and difficult. Healey (1991: 29) translates, "The integrity of the upright leads them, but robbers *are exiled* and *crushed*."

Variant: omission of 11:3b.

Ketiv *wšdm*, qeré *yᵉšoddēm*.

11:4. Missing in OG; supplied in ᴮˢ. There is no reason to doubt the originality of MT v 4. If the OG of this verse ended in *apōleia* (as does the sentence supplied in the SyrH), the loss could be due to parablepsis from *apōleia* at the end of v 3 to the same word at the end of v 4 (DNF). Vul *autem liberabit* "saves them" = *tṣylm* (dittog.).

11:6. LXX: ᵅ = MT; "ᵝ but transgressors will stumble in their destruction [*tę̄ de apōleią̄ autōn*; var(s). *asebeia* ˢᶜ; *abouleia* ᴬ]." "And their destruction" = *wbhwtm* for MT's impossible *wbhwt* "and in the disaster of."

Syr *b*ʿ*w*ʿ*lhwn* "in their wickedness" = *bhwtm* (= LXX); sim. Tg *bšylwmyhwn* "in their retributions"; and Vul *in insidiis suis* "in their snares." The likely reading is *wbhwtm* (*ûbᵉhawwātām*) "in their disaster," but *wbhwt* "in disasters" is possible.

Variant: *wbhwtm* (*ûbᵉhawwātām*) (MT *ûbᵉhawwat-*)

11:7. LXX: "ᵅ When a just man dies, hope is not lost, ᵝ but the pride [*kauchēma*] of the wicked [pl.] perishes." The translator associates Heb *'wnym* (actually "strength") with *'āwen*, "wickedness." (6Q30 4 [*r*]*š*ʿ = MT.) By negating the opposite of the MT in 7ᵅ, LXX creates antithetical parallelism. Orlinksy (1958: 231–38) discusses the frequent use of this device in LXX-Job. Klein *1976*, writing on Tg Onqelos, calls this "converse translation" (cf. R. Gordon *1999*). Gk *kauchēma* = Heb *thlt* (*tᵉhillat-*) "praise of," "glory of," for MT's *t(w)ḥlt*. By means of the converse translation, LXX creates an allusion to the afterlife. Since MT's *twḥlt* "hope" would have reinforced that move, the translator would have used it if he had it. Hence Gk *kauchēma* certainly represents a Hebrew variant, namely, *wthlt* "and the glory of."

Syr: "(b) and the hope of the wicked [*dbyš*^{ʾpl}] perishes." Syr parses *ʾwnym* (actually "strength") as a pl. of *ʾāwen* "wickedness." A similar parsing occurs in Ps 94:23 and Job 21:19.

Variant: *thlt* (MT *tôḥelet*).

11:8. LXX: "from (the) hunt" (*ek thēras*) = *mṣdh* (*miṣṣēdāh*), for MT's *mṣrh* "from trouble." LXX associates *mṣdh* with *ṣ-w-d* "hunt," though *ṣêdāh* means "provisions" and is consistently translated *episitismos* elsewhere. LXX interprets *wybʾ* as *paradidotai* "is delivered" (≈ Vul *tradetur*), alluding to direct divine punishment.

6Q30 skips from v 7 to v 10b. This may be parablepsis due to the repetition of *ʾbd*, or it may have resulted from thematic clustering of verses that deal with the wicked (Eshel 2003: 545).

Variant: *mṣdh* (MT *miṣṣārāh*).

11:9. LXX: "$^{\alpha}$ In the mouth of (the) wicked [pl.] there is a trap [*pagis*] for (their) countrymen, $^{\beta}$ but the knowledge of (the) just [pl.] is successful [*eudos*]." LXX's *pagis* = *šḥt* "pit," "pitfall," though this equivalence is unique. Gk *euodos* = *yṣlḥw* (*yaṣlîḥû*) (Lag.); cf. Num 14:41. (MT's *nḥlṣ* was translated correctly in v 8.) These two copying errors led to adjustments in syntax. Gk *politais* for *rēaʿ* (11:12; 24:28; Jer 29[36]:23; 31[38]:34). The next verse makes the *polis* the setting.

Syr ≈ MT, except that *ntʿšnwn* "be strengthened" is probably based on *yṣlḥw*, independently of the LXX.

Variants: *šḥt* (MT *yašḥit*); *yṣlḥw* (MT *yēḥālēṣû*).

11:10. LXX: "$^{\alpha}$ By the good deeds of (the) just [pl.], the city is put aright" (*en agathois dikaiōn katōrthōsen polis*). V 10b, missing from OG, is supplied in ^{B*S*}. MT's *tʿlṣ* "rejoices" is translated loosely, as *katōrthōsen*, in order to sharpen the antithesis with LXX 11$^{\beta}$, which was originally contiguous to 10$^{\alpha}$; see below. In view of the antithesis with the "mouths" (a destructive power) of the wicked, the *agathoi* "goodnesses" of the just in 10$^{\alpha}$ must be the good things they do for others rather than their own prosperity. An expanded form of 10b appears in LXX 11:3$^{\beta}$.

11:11. LXX: "but by the mouths of the ungodly it is torn down" (*stomasin de asebōn kateskaphē*). MT's 11a is missing. It is supplied in ^{B*S*} from Theod. The loss of 10b–11a was probably due to homeoarcton from *qryh* to *qrt*. The translator shaped the remaining 10a + 11b into a nice couplet:

By the good deeds of the just, the city is set aright,
but by the mouths of the ungodly it is torn down.

Variant: omission of vv 10b–11a.

11:12. LXX ≈ MT. *Politas* "citizens" for Heb *rʿhw* "his fellow"; see 9$^{\alpha}$. Toy observes that "a political interpretation is natural in a city like Alexandria." Cf. 24:28.

11:13. LXX: "$^{\alpha}$ A forked-tongued man reveals counsels [*boulas*] in (the) assembly [*en synedriǭ*]." LXX brings out two meanings of Heb *swd*, namely, *boulas* and *synedriǭ*. The latter was added under the influence of LXX 26:26 and the context of 11:9–13, namely, civic life.

11:14. LXX has "(will fall) like leaves" (*hōsper phylla*) for MT's *ʿm* "a people," apparently reading *kʿlh* (*keʿāleh*). This may be a contamination by association with v 28 (*ypl wkʿlh*), despite the distance (Jäg.). In 14$^{\beta}$, *ywʿṣ* "counselor" is rendered *boulȩ̄* "counsel" for better parallelism. Vul: *gubernator* "helmsman" hence "leader" for Heb *tḥblwt* (≠ Vul 1:5; 20:18).

Variant: *kʿlh* (MT *ʿām*).

11:15. LXX: "$^{\alpha}$ A bad man does harm whenever he consorts with a just man, $^{\beta}$ and he hates the sound of safety" ($^{\alpha}$ *ponēros kakopoiei hotan symmeichȩ̄ dikaiǭ*, $^{\beta}$ *misei de ēchon asphaleias*). LXX's source text had *zk* (lit., "pure") for MT's *zār* and a different word division. LXX relates *tqʿy* to *tēqaʿ* "blowing," "sounding" (of horn), which is translated by *ēchos* in Ps 150:3. These errors led the translator to misconstrue several words, reading the verse as if it were vocalized *raʿ yārēaʿ kî ʿārēb zāk, weśōnēʾ tēqaʿ mibtāḥ*, lit., "a bad man does harm when he goes surety for a pure man, and he hates the sounding of safety." Heb *ʿrb* "goes surety for" was probably understood as "associates with." Theod translates *tqʿym* as *pagideuthēnai* "to be trapped," deriving it from *tqʿ* "be stuck (in)."

Variants: *zk* (MT *zār*); *tqʿy mbtḥ* (MT *tōqeʿîm bôṭēaḥ*).

11:16. LXX: "$^{\alpha}$ A gracious woman arouses [*egeirei*] honor for a man, $^{\beta}$ but a woman who hates righteous things is a seat of dishonor. $^{\gamma}$ Slothful (men) become lacking of wealth, $^{\delta}$ but the vigorous are supported by wealth." Gk *egeirei* should be corrected to *ereidei* "supports." This is confirmed by Syr, which follows LXX here. In 16$^{\alpha}$ *andri* is explanatory: This woman elicits honor for her husband, not only herself. V 16$^{\beta}$ is lacking in the MT, but the content and wording have affinities with the translation elsewhere and the stich is OG; see Tov 1990: 46. Line 16$^{\gamma}$ is related to MT only by the word "wealth." Its wording is based on 6:6, 11a. Line16$^{\delta}$ follows MT, except that MT's unsatisfactory *ʿryṣym* ("tyrants," "violent") is rendered *andreioi* "virtuous," "vigorous." Gk *andreios* = *ḥrwṣ* in 10:4 and 13:4. The *ḥ-ʿ* interchange may be explained as an auditory error, but it is also possible that the LXX is eliminating the moral awkwardness of MT, which (in LXX's understanding of *tmk*) would mean, "the violent are supported by wealth."

With the expansion, the Gk forms two distinct couplets, 16$^{\alpha\beta}$ and 16$^{\gamma\delta}$. Compare the way that LXX^{A} creates two couplets in 10:24 by inserting two lines. The OG source text can be retroverted to $^{\alpha}$ *ʾšt ḥn ttmk kbwd*, / $^{\beta}$ *wksʾ qlwn śnʾt ṣdq*. / $^{\gamma}$ *ʿṣl ywrš*, / $^{\delta}$ *wʿryṣym ytmkw ʿšr*. The first couplet, on two contrary kinds of women, was inspired by Prov 31, esp v 23. The second couplet contrasts the lazy man with the vigorous or virtuous one.

Syr: "(a) A merciful woman upholds honor for a man, (b) but a woman who hates truth is a throne of disgrace. (c) Lazy men are needy even in their wealth, (d) and the powerful uphold [*msmkyn*] knowledge" [(a) *ʾnttʾ mrḥmntʾ msmkʾ tšbwḥtʾ lgbrʾ* (b) *kwrsyʾ dyn dṣʿrʾ ʾnttʾ snyt šrrʾ* (c) *ḥbnnʾ*^{pl} *ʾp bʿwtrhwn hwyn ṣrykyn*^{pl} (d) *wʿšynʾ*^{pl} ydʿtʾ]. Syr 16ab = LXX16$^{\alpha\beta}$ (if emended to *ereidei*). Syr *šrrʾ* "truth" (used only here in Proverbs), and Gk *dikaia* "just," both represent Heb *mšpṭ*. Syr 16c is close to Gk 16$^{\gamma}$ but phrases the proverb in a more interesting way. In 16d, Syr *ʿšynʾ*^{pl} =

MT *ʿryṣym*, but for Heb *ʿšr* "wealth" Syr substitutes a moralizing *ydʿtʾ* "knowledge."

Syr stays close to the LXX throughout the verse and maintains its expansion in (b)–(c), but it does not simply translate the Gk. In 16(c), Syr shows an independent rendering of the same Hebrew source-text as the LXX. Also, the roughness of 16d suggests that the Syr was following a Heb text. These considerations make it likely that Syr's source-text had an expanded text of 11:16 similar to LXX's. A plausible retroversion would be: (a) *ʾšt ḥn ttmk kbwd lʾyš*, (b) *wksʾ qlwn ʾšh śnʾt mšpṭ*, (c) *wʿṣlwt gm bʿšr yḥsrw*, (d) *wʿryṣym ytmkw ʿšr* [possibly *dʿt*] ("A gracious woman holds honor for (her) husband, but she who hates justice is a throne of disgrace"). Tg works from MT but smoothes it out: "A kind woman shares in honor, but the powerful run after wealth."

Variants: *ḥrwᵉym* (?) (MT *ʿărîṣîm*). Expanded verse.

11:19. LXX: "$^{\alpha}$ A righteous son [*huios dikaios*] is born for life [*gennatai eis zōēn*], $^{\beta}$ but the wicked (man's) pursuit is to death" = Heb *bn ṣdqh lḥyym wmrdp* [*wᵉmirdap*] *rʿh lmwt* [*lammāwet*]. Variants are *bn* (= one Heb MS) and possibly *lmwt*. Syr "a son of righteousness" = LXX.

Variants: *bn* (MT *kēn*); *lmwt* (?) (MT *lᵉmôtô*).

11:20. LXX: "$^{\alpha}$ Twisted paths [*diestrammenai hodoi*] are an abomination to the Lord, $^{\beta}$ but favored by him are all who are innocent in their ways." "Twisted paths" (for MT's *ʿqšy lb* "twisted of heart") creates a stricter antithesis to the second stich. LXX adds *pantes* "all" in 20$^{\beta}$. According to Thackeray (1912: 52), *en tais hodois autōn* at the end of the verse is a hexaplaric gloss and omitted by several MSS. This is uncertain, since the change in 20$^{\alpha}$ seems to presuppose this phrase.

11:21. LXX: "$^{\alpha}$ He who strikes [*embalōn*] (his) hands to (another's) hand unjustly shall not be unpunished, $^{\beta}$ but he who sows righteousness shall receive a faithful reward." LXX's *adikōs* "unjustly" corresponds to *rʿ*, though the word order is violated; see the Textual Note on 15:26. The translator has in mind clasping hands to seal an agreement, as in 16:5. However, *emballein* is not used for this idiom in verses where the meaning of this gesture is clear (6:1; 11:15; 17:18; 22:26). LXX 11:21$^{\beta}$ = MT 11:18b, though LXX 11:18 diverges from MT 11:18.

Syr: "(a) "He who stretches out his hand against his fellow will not be held innocent of evil"—an interpretion of the idiom *yd lyd* "hand to hand."

11:22. LXX: "$^{\alpha}$ As a ring [*enōtion*] in the snout of a pig, $^{\beta}$ thus is beauty to a malevolent [*kakophroni*] woman." OG omits "gold" (restored in ABS*), perhaps because "ring" was enough to make the point. OG makes the comparison (ring// beauty) explicit and emphasizes the woman's immorality rather than her stupidity. (Gk *kakophrōn* = *gdl ḥmh* "great of wrath" in 19:19.) Cognates to *kakrophōn* mean "(be) malevolent," "evil-minded" in *T. Abr.* A 14:11 and *Sib. Or.* 4.171.

Syr: "(a) Like an ornament of gold in the nose of a sow, thus is a beautiful woman stinking of sense [*sryt tʿmʾ*]." The rendering "stinking" for Heb *srt* (lit., "who departs from") was motivated by homeophony. Hyun *2000*: 71–77 claims that phonic resemblance was a guiding principle in word choice in Syr-Prov.The role of homeophony in the LXX has been extensively discussed; see esp. Tov *1979*, with references, but see also the doubts of Barr *1985*. In any case, for the ancient translator, homeophony (which has a major role in midrash) was closer to a grammatical principle than an aesthetic one. In this case, the translator associated Heb *srt* (from *s-w-r* "turn aside") with Syr *sr*ʾ "stink."

11:23. LXX's *apoleitai* "will perish" parses *ʿbrh* (MT *ʿebrah* "wrath") as *ʿābārāh* "pass away," perhaps correctly; sim. hexaplaric (Allos) *apolutai, aperchetai.*

11:24. LXX: "α There are those who, sowing their own (property) make abundance, β and there are also those who gather (yet) lack." A loose rendering of a paradoxical and difficult saying, introducing agricultural imagery. Heb *mpzr* "scatter" is understood to mean the (purposeful) scattering of seed. Heb *ḥwśk* "hold back" is understood to mean "gather"; *myšr* is ignored.

Syr: "(a) There is one who sows and brings in much, (b) and there is one who gathers what is not his and it is little to him." (a) ≈ LXX. Syr (b) is influenced by a Gk text that had *ta allotria* after *synagontes* (Sc MSS) (Pink. 108). This moralizing addition reverses the point of the MT.

Vul similarly translates 24b: *alii rapiunt non sua et semper in egestate sunt*, "Others take away what is not their own and are always in want."

11:25. LXX: "α Every sincere/simple soul is blessed, β but a hot-tempered man is not graceful" (α *psychē eulogoumenē pasa haplē,* β *anēr de thymōdēs ouk euschēmōn*). (Or, "Every sincere (person) is a blessed soul.") Except for "blessed soul," this is distant from the MT, scarcely even interpreting it. Gk *haplē* "simple," "honest" accords with the late Hellenistic emphasis on simplicity as an ethical virtue (Dick 1990: 24).

Syr: "(b) and the curser will also be cursed" (*wlyṭʾ twb nttlyṭ*)—associating Heb *ywrʾ* with *ʾ-r-r* "curse." Tg[L]: *wmn dmʾlyp ʾwp hwʾ ylyp* "and he who teaches will also learn." Tg associates *mrwh* and *ywrʾ* with *y-r-h* (H) "teach"; see the Note on 5:19. Both associate Heb *mrwh* "give drink" with similar-looking didactic notions.

11:26. LXX: "α May he who withholds grain leave it [*hypolipoito auton*] to the gentiles, β but a blessing is upon the head of him who shares." For MT's *yiqqᵉbuhû*, LXX has *hypoleipein*. This probably represents *yšbqhw* (for *yšbqnw*) "he will leave it," which would be an Aramaism, clearly erroneous. LXX and Syr understood *q-b-b* as "curse" in 24:24. Because of the error in this verse, Heb *lʾwm* "nation" was parsed as *l-* "to" + *ʾôm* "people(s)."

Syr: "(a) He who withholds produce in distress shall abandon it to his enemies [*dklʾ ʿbwrʾ bʾwlṣnʾ nšbqywhy lbʿldbbwhy*[pl]]." Syr diverges from the LXX in (a) and offers independent evidence for *yšbqnw*. Syr's "in distress," that is, famine, specifies the circumstance in which withholding grain would be cursed. Tg stays close to Syr.

Variant: *yšbqwhw* (MT *yiqqᵉbuhû*).

11:27. LXX's *tektainomenos* "he who devises (good)" = *ḥrš*, a metathesis of MT's *šḥr* "seeks." De Waard (1993: 250) believes that this metathesis was a translation technique rather than a scribal error. This change, he argues, was motivated by the uniqueness of *šḥr* in the G-stem and the familiarity of the locution *ḥrš* "devise" + words for good or evil. But this would be a weak motivation. D-stem verbs frequently have a ptcp. in the G ptcp. form (e.g., *qôwēh, dôbēr*). Moreover, the translator would have no reason to think that *šḥr* is a D-stem. And, if unfamiliarity were a problem, a copyist could have been influenced to use the more familiar word just as easily as a translator could have been. Other proposed examples are at Prov 24:21; 29:9; and 30:10. Though exegetical metathesis is possible, it is almost impossible to distinguish from graphic metathesis. In practice, it is always adduced to protect the MT.

Variant: *ḥrš* (MT *šōḥēr*).

11:28. LXX: "β but the one who assists the righteous [pl.]—he shall spring up [*ho de antilambanomenos dikaiōn houtos anatelei*]." Though the correspondence would be unique, it is hard to see how Gk *antilambanomenos* could arise except as a rendering of Heb *mʿlh* "raise up" (understood as implying assistance), where MT has *kʿlh* ("like foliage") (Jäg.).

Variant: *mʿlh* (MT *keʿāleh*).

11:29. LXX: "α He who is not in concord [*ho mē symperipheromenos*] with his own house will inherit wind" ≈ MT. "He who is not in concord" is a converse translation of *ʿwkr* ("he who troubles"). Gk *symperipheresthai* refers to conjugal amity in Sir 25:1.

Syr: "(a) He who builds his house deceitfully will leave groans to his children. (b) He who does not remain tranquil in his house will apportion to his children winds. (c) And the fool will be slave to the wise." MT's *ynḥl rwḥ* is construed as *yanḥîl ruaḥ*, "bequeathes the wind," with "wind" taken as an allusion to groaning. The doublet in (b) seems to be influenced by the LXX but diverges from it. See Joosten 1995: 66–67.

11:30. LXX: "α From the fruit of righteousness the tree of life grows, β but the souls of transgressors are untimely removed." LXX's source-text, with the implied vocalization, read: *mippᵉrî ṣedeq ʿēṣ ḥayyîm, wᵉluqqaḥ napšôt ḥāmās*. Translated literally, this would be "From the fruit of righteousness is a tree of life, but the lives of the lawless are taken away." The source-text's *ḥms* "lawlessness" is construed as a metonymy for lawless *people*. Consonantal variants, both erroneous, are *mpry* and *ḥms*. Lag. retroverts *aōroi* to *nšp* (lit., "evening"), an equivalence found in Ps 119[118]:147. In that case, *nšp* is an erroneous near-dittog. of *npšwt*. More likely, however, *aōroi* was added for the sake of the logic: Since *everyone* is ultimately "removed," "untimely" was added to clarify why being "removed" was a special punishment. Syr ≈ LXX, without *aōroi*.

Variants: *mpry* (MT *pᵉrî*); *ḥms* (MT *ḥākām*).

11:31. LXX: "α But if the righteous man barely be saved, β where shall the wicked and sinner appear?" (Quoted in 1 Pet 4:18.) Once the translator understood *yšlm* as "be saved" (by association with *šālēm* "be whole" and *šālôm* "peace," "welfare"), he added "scarcely" in the first line so as to maintain an *a fortiori* structure. The verse assumes that all human beings, even the righteous, are flawed, and so they are at best *barely* saved. Gk *molis* maintains the rhetorical structure of the Heb *a fortiori*; see Barr 1975.

Syr: "(a) If the righteous (man) scarcely lives, where will the wicked-and-sinner be found?" = LXX, even in the treatment of "wicked and sinner" as sg.

12:2. LXX: "α Better is the one who finds favor with the Lord, β but the lawless man will be passed over in silence." Apparently the translator began a comparative sentence before realizing that it would not work but did not go back to revise it. Instead he added a stich unrelated to the MT. The resulting Gk is not very meaningful, but may be understood as comparing the person in 2^{α} to the one in 1^{β}.

12:3. LXX: "$^{\alpha}$ A man will not be established by a wicked man [*ex anomou*], $^{\beta}$ but the roots of the just [pl.] will not be removed [*ouk exarthēsontai*]." Gk *ex anomou* = *bᵉrāšāʿ*. It might reflect *mršʿ*, but the preposition *b-* is rendered by Gk *ek* six times in LXX-Prov (out of the 195 times that *b-* is represented by a Gk preposition). Especially when the prep. *b-* means "by" it can be translated *ek*. In $^{\beta}$, "be removed"—a converse translation—is intended to improve the logic, since a root does not "totter," as MT's *yimmōṭ* would have it.

12:4. LXX: "$^{\beta}$ but as a worm in wood so does an evildoing woman destroy (her) husband." "Worm" is a sort of metonymy for *rāqāb* "rot"—agent for effect. In $^{\beta}$, the source text probably had *bʿṣ ymyt*, lit., "in wood kills," and the translator supplied a dir. obj. ("her husband") from the preceding sentence.

Syr: "(b) but like a boring-worm and a worm in wood [*blṭytʾ wtwlʿʾ bqysʾ*]" supports LXX, but is expansive.

Variant: *bʿṣ ymyt* (MT *bᵉʿaṣmôtāyw*).

12:5. LXX: "$^{\alpha}$ Calculations of the righteous [pl.] are judgments [*krimata*], $^{\beta}$ but the wicked maneuver [*kybernōsin*] deceits." LXX is based on MT, but restructures the syntax. Syr ≈ MT, but has *hwpkhwn* "perversities" for MT's *tḥblwt* "stratagems." Syr uses "perversities" to specify the moral quality of the evildoers' "stratagems."

12:6. LXX ≈ MT, but translates *ʾrb dm* ("an ambush for blood") more abstractly as *dolioi* "deceits." This rendering ties the present verse to the preceding (*logismoi-logoi* and *dolous-dolioi*) (BA). (Some Gk MSS add *eis haima* "for blood," which is inappropriate after *dolioi*.)

12:8. LXX: "$^{\alpha}$ The mouth of the intelligent man is praised by a man, $^{\beta}$ but the lazy-hearted [*nōthrokardios*] is mocked." The *lamed* of *lpy* ("according to") was taken as a dir. obj. marker + "mouth" (thus Syr). Heb *nʿwh lb* "perverted of heart" is translated as *nōthrokardios* "lazy-hearted," that is, stupid.

12:9. LXX: "$^{\alpha}$ Better a man in disgrace serving himself [*douleuōn heautǭ*], $^{\beta}$ than one who wraps himself in honor [*ē timēn heautǭ perititheis*] but lacks bread." Heb *wʿbd lw* is understood as *wʿōbēd lô*. The translator was probably puzzled with the notion that having a slave would outweigh disgrace, whereas he could accept self-sufficiency as an important value.

Syr: "(a) Better a poor man [*msknʾ*] who serves himself [*dmšmš npšh*] (b) than one who boasts [*mštbhr*] but is in need of bread." Syr 9(a) shares the interpretation of the LXX but proceeds directly from the Heb. Vul translates similarly, "Better is a pauper who provides for himself than he who is famous [or "pretentious"—*gloriosus*] and lacks bread."

12:10. LXX explains *ywdʿ* "knows" as *oiktirei* "has compassion," strengthening the contrast with 10^{β}. Syr has "their mercies are withheld [*ʾḥydyn*]," which avoids the oxymoron of "mercies" being cruel.

12:11. Syr (a): "He who works on the land [*dplḥ bʾrʿʾ*] will be satisfied with bread." By substituting "the land" for "his land," Syr treats the verse as praising agriculture rather than industriousness in general. Thus too in 28:19.

12:11a. LXX: "α He who takes pleasure in diversions [or "banquets"] of wine β will leave behind disgrace [as a legacy] in his own fortresses" (α *hos estin hēdys en oinōn diatribais* β *en tois heautou ochyrōmasin kataleipsei atimian*). This couplet, present also in Vul, is a translation of a variant form of Heb v 12. It continues the theme of "pursuing vanities" from v 11. LXX's *oinōn* represents *ḥmr* (*ḥemer*) "wine," a corrupt doublet of *ḥmd*. The latter word, understood as *ḥōmēd*, is translated expansively as *hos estin hēdys*, Gk *kataleipsei* ≈ *ytr* (i.e., *yōtîr*), as it is often. Compare *wytr* // *wytn* in Ps 18:33 // 2 Sam 22:33. "In his own fortresses" renders *mṣwd* (with variation of number, common in the LXX). In the MT, this means "net," but the translator construes it as equivalent to *mṣwdh* "fortress." From a disturbed Hebrew text, the translator creates a more or less meaningful proverb that envisions a king (who alone would possess fortresses) who pursues frivolities; cf. Qoh 10:16–19.

Variants: *ḥmr* (MT [v 12] *ḥemed*); *ytr* (MT *yittēn*); some dislocation.

12:12. LXX: "α The desires of the wicked [pl.] are bad, β but the roots of the pious [pl.] are in fortresses [*en ochyrōmasin*]." "Fortresses" corresponds to a displaced *mṣwd*, again equated with *m^{e}ṣûdāh*. The awkwardness of roots growing in fortresses (which would be no more secure than roots growing elsewhere) indicates that the translator is constrained by his source text.

Syr: "The evildoer desires to do [*lmʿbd*] evil, but the root of the righteous flourishes [*nšwḥ*]. Syr *nšwḥ* "flourishes" is a contextual guess for MT's difficult *ytn* "give" (sc. root). Tg's *ntqyym* "endures" associates *ytn* with *ʾytn* "enduring" (Hitzig). This is probably the original text (see the Comment), but the Tg is uncertain evidence for it.

Variant: *ʾêtān* (MT *yittēn*).

12:13. LXX: "α Through sin of the lips, the sinner falls in traps [*empiptei eis pagidas hamartōlos*], β but the righteous [sg.] escapes from them [*ex autōn*]." LXX parses *mwqš* as a passive, that is, *mûqāš*. Gk *ex autōn* refers to the traps. This is a way of identifying the "trouble" in question rather than a corruption of *ek anagkōn* "from tribulation," as Baum. suggests. Syr *mtthd* "is seized" = *mûqāš*.

12:13a. "α He who gives gentle looks [*ho blepōn leia*] will receive mercy, β but he who meets [*synantōn*] (men) in the gates will afflict souls." *Ho blepōn leia* "Que a l'air doux" (BA). *Synantōn* implies seeking a quarrel (BA). The addition draws a contrast between mild and litigious men and gives an example of "sin of the lips" and its opposite (v 13).

12:14. LXX: "α From the fruits of the mouth, the soul [*psychē*] of a man will be filled with good things, β and the recompense of his lips [*cheileōn autou*] will be given to him." The added "soul" clarifies *what* will be "filled." LXX has *cheileōn* "lips" for MT's *ydy* "hands of." This may be an inner-Gk corruption of *cheirōn*, induced by the mention of "mouth." (MSS$^{23, 157}$ and SyrH have the latter, but that is presumably a correction.) LXX's proverb has greater unity than the MT's and represents a less predictable statement, but MT too is meaningful.

Syr: "(a) A good man will be satisfied from the fruit of his mouth, (b) and every man will be recompensed according to the work of his hands." Syr overrides the Hebrew syntax (the verb intervenes) and paraphrases for the sake of moral emphasis.

Variant: *śpty* (MT *y*^e*dê-*).

Ketiv *yšwb*, qeré *yāšîb*.

12:16. LXX: "^α A fool declares [*exaggellei*] his anger on the same day, ^β but the shrewd man covers his own disgrace [*tēn heautou atimian*]." Gk *exaggellei* understands *ywdʿ* as *yôdîaʿ* (lit., "makes known"), where MT has *yiwwādaʿ* "becomes known." LXX "*his own* disgrace" (sim. Sym) correctly clarifies whose disgrace is being covered up. Syr *mwdʿ* = *yôdîaʿ* = LXX; sim. Theod *gnōrisei*, Sym *dēlōsei*.

Vocalization variant: *yôdîaʿ* (MT *yiwwādēaʿ*).

12:18. LXX: "^α There are those who wound with a sword when they speak." V 8^α is a reasonable expansion of MT's comparison. Theod *pepoithōs* = *bwṭḥ* "trusts" = Vul (*pungitur*), Theod (*pepoithōs*), some MSS.

Variant: *bwṭḥ* (MT *bôṭeh*).

12:19. LXX: "^α True lips give honest testimony [lit., "make testimony straight"], ^β but a hasty witness has an unjust tongue." LXX reads *tkwn* (MT *tikkōn*) as *tākîn* (H) and *lʿd* as *l*^e*ʿēd* (as in 29:14), and associates *ʾrgyʿ* with *regaʿ* "moment." By introducing the theme of *witnessing*, LXX links this verse with 17 and encourages us to read 18 as a comment on true and false testimony. Syr *msrhbʾ* "hasty witness" shows the influence of LXX.

12:21. LXX: "^α No injustice will please [*aresei*] the righteous person, ^β but the impious [pl.] will be filled with evils." LXX's "will please" reads *ynʾh* for MT's *yʾnh* ("happen"). This is unlikely to be either an exegetical metathesis (for the concept see de Waard 1993) or an exegetical association with *nāʾeh*, since *yʾnh* would have given an acceptable sense. LXX describes conduct, the MT consequences.

Syr: "(a) Something that is dishonest is not good [*špyr*] to a righteous man." Syr *špyr* = *ynʾh*. This translation is quite different from the LXX and is thus independent evidence for the variant.

Variant: *ynʾh* (MT *y*^e*ʾunneh*).

12:23. LXX: "^α The intelligent (man) is a throne [*thronos*] of knowledge, ^β but the heart of the foolish [pl.] will meet with curses [*synantēsetai arais*]." LXX (1) construes *ksh* as *kissēh* = *kissēʾ* "throne"; (2) construes MT *yqrʾ* "calls" as *yqrh* "meets," "happens"; and (3) reads *ʾwlt* "folly" as *ʾālōt* "curses." Change (1) is surprising, since the same word was translated, correctly, as *kryptei*, in 12:16. As for (3), LXX would have recognized the frequent *ʾwlt* "folly" and so must have had *ʾlwt* or ʾlwt in the source text. *ʾlwt* = *arai* in Deut 29:20. These differences have no ideological motivation and are consequential on the trivial error of *ʾlwt* instead of *ʾwlt*.

Syr's *kwrsyʾ* "throne" = LXX; *qrʾ lbyštʾ* "calls out evil" = MT.

Variant: *ʾlwt* (MT *ʾiwwelet*).

12:24. LXX: "^α The hand of the chosen [*eklektos*; sg.] will readily rule, ^β but the deceitful will be for plunder [*pronomē*]." The renderings *eklektos* for *ḥrwṣym* ("diligent") and *pronomē* for *mas* ("forced labor") are unique. The former is based on an etymological association with *ḥārûṣ* "choice gold" (Baum.) but also has a theological motivation, for it is the *elect* who one day "will rule." This is a theme of NT eschatology and elevates this verse from a practical to a theological statement (D. A. Teeter, personal communication). *Eucherōs* is added for emphasis and wordplay with *cheir.*

12:25. LXX: "$^{\alpha}$ A frightening word disturbs the heart of a just man [*phoberos kardian tarassei andros dikaiou*], $^{\beta}$ but a good report makes him happy [*euphrainei auton*]." V 25$^{\alpha}$ is a loose paraphrase of the obscure Heb, using the antithesis to clarify *dʾbh blb.* Syr ≈ LXX, but omits "just."

12:26. LXX: "$^{\alpha}$ A just arbiter will be his own friend, $^{\beta}$ but the decisions of the wicked are unreasonable. $^{\gamma}$ Evils will pursue sinners, $^{\delta}$ and the way of the wicked will lead them astray" ($^{\alpha}$ *epignōmōn dikaios heautou philos estai,* $^{\beta}$ *hai de gnōmai tōn asebōn anepieikeis,* $^{\gamma}$ *hamartanontas katadiōxetai kaka* $^{\delta}$ *hē de hodos tōn asebōn planēsei autous*). Alternatively: "$^{\alpha}$ A just man will be the judge of his own friend" (reading *philou,* with Baum.). Stichoi $^{\alpha\delta}$ are OG. V 26$^{\alpha}$ corresponds loosely to the MT. V 26$^{\beta}$ (supplied with an asterisk for an obelus in SyrH) is absent in ^{BSV} and is later. 26$^{\gamma}$ is taken from 13:21a. 26$^{\delta}$ = MT 26b.

Vul: "(a) He who overlooks a loss for the sake of a friend is just" (*qui neglegit damnum propter amicum iustus est*), understanding *ytr* (and having *ywtr* in his source-text) as *y*^{e}*wattēr* "concede," "overlook a loss," a rabbinic usage.

12:27. LXX: "$^{\alpha}$ A deceitful man will not come upon [*epiteuxetai*] game, $^{\beta}$ but a pure man (will come upon [or "is"]) an honorable possession [*ktēma de timion*]." LXX guesses at the meaning of an obscure sentence. (Saʿadia too understands *yaḥărōk* as "meet.") Vul: "The deceitful man will not come upon [*inveniet*] a profit [*lucrum*], but the substance of a man will be precious gold."

Syr: "(a) Game shall not happen upon a deceitful man, (b) but an eminent man is a precious possession." A guess, independent of LXX.

12:28. LXX: "$^{\beta}$ but the ways of the malicious [*mnēsikakōn*] (lead) to death." LXX's *mnēsikakōn* ("malicious" or "grudge-bearers") for MT's *n*^{e}*tîbāh* is a guess motivated by the need to supply a word indicating a bad quality in 28$^{\beta}$. Perles (1895: 87) retroverts to *ntʿb* or *ntʿbym* "despicable," but *t-ʿ-b* is never rendered by *mnēsikakōn* or cognates. Jäg. retroverts *mnēsikakōn* "malicious" to *m*^{e}*rîbāh* "strife. Gk *eis* = Heb *ʾel* "to," for MT's *ʾal* "not." Vul b: "but a detour [*devium*] leads to death." Syr: "(b) and the way of angry people is to death [*wʾwrḥʾ dʾktnʾ*^{pl} *lmwtʾ*]" = LXX; sim. Tg.

LXX, Syr, Tg, and, independently, Vul, all understand the last two words as *ʾel mwt* "to death." None follow MT's *ʾal māwet* "not death."

13:1. LXX: "$^{\alpha}$ A clever [*panourgos*] son is obedient [*hypēkoos*] to (his) father, $^{\beta}$ but a disobedient son is in destruction [*huios de anēkoos en apōleią*]." (LXX^{A*}, interestingly, has *mētri* "to (his) mother" for "to (his) father.") Heb *mwsr* is perhaps understood as a passive of *y-s-r*: "is [successfully] chastised," hence "is obedient." In $^{\beta}$, *anēkoos* = *lʾ šmʿ*, construed as a relative clause, and *en apōleią* = *gwʿh*, associated with *g-w-h* "dying" (in Num 20:3, *en tę̄ apōleią* = *bgwʿ*).

Overall, the LXX gives this chapter a heightened spiritual quality (see v 11$^{\gamma}$) suggestive of a Stoic attitude.

Syr: "(a) A wise son obeys [*mštmʿ*] his father" ≈ MT. "(b) but a bad son, who does not accept reproof, will perish" ≈ LXX.

Variants: *gʿwh* (MT *gᵉʿārāh*).

13:2. LXX: "The good man shall eat from the fruits of righteousness [*dikaiosynēs*], but the souls of transgressors untimely [*aōroi*] perish." By substituting "righteousness" for "mouth," LXX avoids the implication that even the unworthy will enjoy the fruit of his speech. LXX avoids a truism in ᵝ by treating *ḥms* "lawlessness" as the violence done *to* transgressors.

13:4. LXX: "ᵅ Every sluggard is in longing [*en epithymiais*], ᵝ but the hands of the virtuous [pl.] are in care [*en epimeleią*]." LXX introduces a strict antithesis. *Epimeleia* may mean "à l'enterprise" (BA), but the antithesis suggests that it more likely refers to the benefits of God's care. *Epimeleia* = *dšn* (lit., "fattened") in 28:25; cf. 3:8, 22a. Gk *cheires* "hands" (for MT's *npš* "soul," "appetite") is probably induced by recollection of the phrase *yad ḥārûṣîm* in 10:4 (where Gk also uses the pl.) and 12:24.

13:5. LXX understands *yb'š* (*yab'îš*) as *yēbōš* "be ashamed" (*aischynetai*) and interprets *yḥpyr* "and be abashed" as *ouch hexei parrēsian* "and not speak boldly," in other words, is shamed into silence.

13:6. LXX (OG) lacks. Supplied in ᴬ with asterisk: "ᵅ Righteousness guards (the) innocent [*akakous*; pl.], ᵝ and sin makes the wicked worthless [*phaulos*]," understanding *ršʿh* ("wickedness") as a metonymy for a wicked person; sim. Vul.

Syr: "(b) and sin will destroy [*twbdywhy*] the sinner," guessing at the meaning of *tslp*. Syr does not turn to the LXX for help here, apparently lacking it in its Gk text.

4QProvᵇ has 13:6b–9b (fragmentary) = MT.

Variant: omission of v 6.

13:7. LXX: "ᵅ There are those who enrich themselves [*ploutizontes heautous*] while having nothing, ᵝ and there are those who bring themselves low [*tapeinountes*] in much wealth." LXX understands the verbs as referring to actual wealth and poverty rather than to pretense. Vul understands the latter and adds *quasi* to both stichoi.

13:8. LXX: ᵅ = MT; "ᵝ but a lowly man cannot endure a threat" (*ptōchos de ouch hyphistatai apeilēn*). (BA's "n'est point soumis à la menace" would require the dative, according to LSJ.) This is an attempt to make sense of the illogical MT ("a poor man does not hear/obey a rebuke").

13:9. LXX: For the obscure metaphor of the light of the righteous rejoicing (as *yśmḥ* was understood to mean), LXX has a serviceable *dia pantos* "forever."

13:9a. LXX: "ᵅ The deceitful souls wander in sins, ᵝ but the righteous have compassion and show mercy." This is a new proverb composed of two lines that seem unrelated to each other. It was put here because of its connection to v 9. Since the light of the wicked goes out (9ᵝ), they wander in the darkness of sin (9aᵅ). 9aᵝ ≈ Prov 21:26ᵝ; cf. LXX-Ps 112[111]:5a. Compare LXX-Prov 13:11ᵞ.

13:10. LXX: "ᵅ An evil man [*kakos*] does evils [*kaka*] with insolence, ᵝ but those who are their own judges [*hoi de heautōn epignōmones*] are wise." LXX probably understands *rq* as *rēq* (lit., "empty man") and moralizes it as *kakos*, to clarify the nature of the blemish. (Other additions of *kakos* are 1:18, 28; 6:11a; 14:25; 16:28; 17:12; 18:3; 21:26; 27:21a; 28:20; 30:11–14. This belongs to the moralizing tendency described by Dick 1990: 21–26.) *Hoi de heautōn epignōmones* paraphrases MT's *nwʿṣym* "those who take counsel," understood as reflexive. LXX's phrase recalls the Delphic oracle quoted by Plato, though it uses different wording (Gerleman 1956: 29–30). Aq, Sym, Theod do not represent *rq*. Syr ≈ LXX.

13:11. LXX: "$^{\alpha}$ Property gathered hastily with illegality [*hyparchis epispoudazomenē meta anomias*] dwindles, $^{\beta}$ but he who gathers for himself with piety will be increased. $^{\gamma}$ The righteous man has mercy and lends." The moralizing in 11^{α} and 11^{β} is clearly the work of the translator, who wants us to understand that the fault in question is illegality, not hard work as such, and that increase of wealth requires piety as well as hard work. See Giese 1992a: 418; 1993a: 112. Likewise, many medieval commentators understood *hebel* in this verse as delusion and deceit. Since Gk's *epispoudazomenē* does not reinforce this moralizing, it probably represents a variant, namely, *mbhl* (*m^{e}bōhāl*); this is supported by Vul *festinata* "got in haste" and Sym and Quinta *hyperspoudazomenē* "to take exceedingly great pains" (LSJ 1868b). In Prov 20:21 (LXX 20:9b), *mbhlt* (*m^{e}bōhelet*) is represented by *epispoudazomenē*. *Meta anomias* = *mhbl* (*mēhebel*; see Sir 49:2). The Gk had a conflation: *mbhl mhbl*. The latter word alone is witnessed in Syr (*mn ʿwlʾ*).

Stich $^{\gamma}$, like LXX $13{:}9a^{\beta}$, of which it is a variant, is based on Pss 37[36]:21b and 112[111]:5a. The addition explains what gathering "with piety" means and further tempers the praise of "gathering" in $^{\beta}$, lest it be misread as affirming greed. Compare LXX $17{:}5^{\gamma}$.

Syr: "Possession which (comes) from iniquity" ≈ MT; cf. LXX. Heb *ʿl yd* is interpreted as "gathered in righteousness" ≈ LXX.

Variant: *m^{e}bōhāl* (MT *mēhebel*).

13:12. LXX: "$^{\alpha}$ Better is he who begins to help with heart $^{\beta}$ than him who promises and leads (others) to hope, $^{\gamma}$ for a good desire is a tree of life." LXX is distant from the MT, with lines $^{\alpha}$ and $^{\beta}$ rendering components of Heb 12a expansively and without regard to syntax. What sent LXX off track was probably having *tḥlh* or *tḥlt* "begin(ning)" at the start of the verse. Then *mḥlh* (actually "makes ill") was loosely represented by *eis elpida* "to hope." The awkwardness in 12^{α}, with its superfluous "begins" and "with heart," indicates that the LXX is struggling with a difficult Heb text rather than composing freely. Gk's "to help" is hard to explain, but *mšk ḥsd* is translated *antilēptōr* "helper" in Ps 109[108]:12.

The LXX means that actually helping someone wholeheartedly is better than raising false hopes. The former alone is an *epithymia agathē*, a "good desire" or "good intention." This is indeed "interpretive" and moralizing, arising from a hesitation to give a blanket endorsement to the fulfillment of desire, but the change probably occurred in Heb transmission. Sym, Theod, and Quinta = LXX (according to SyrH), and they would be unlikely to reinterpret the phrase thus. The versions had *ṭwbh* for *bʾh*.

Syr: "(a) Better is the man who begins to help (b) than him who depends on hope. (c) And the tree of life brings hope." Syr may be dependent on LXX in (a), but its different treatment of 12b suggests that it is seeing a Hebrew variant, which cannot be reconstructed. The Syr also shows that "a desire fulfilled" was problematic for the ancient translators and, probably, scribes.

Variants: *tḥlt* (MT *tôḥelet*); *ṭwbh* (MT *bāʾāh*).

13:13a. LXX: "$^{\alpha}$ For a deceitful son, there shall be nothing good, $^{\beta}$ but for a wise servant, affairs will be successful [*euodoi esontai praxeis*], $^{\gamma}$ and his way will prosper [*kateuthynēsetai*]." 13a$^{\alpha\beta}$ seems to be inspired by 17:2, though the phraseology differs. In its present place "the deceitful son" adumbrates "he who scorns a word" in 13$^{\alpha}$, and "a wise servant" echoes the phrase, "he who fears a command." The superfluous $^{\gamma}$ reinforces the latter part of $^{\beta}$.

Syr: "(a) To the deceitful man, there will be nothing good, (b) but the wise man, whose deeds are honest [*dtryṣn*^{pl} *ʿbydth*^{pl}]—his way too will rise to the top." Syr basically follows LXX but interprets $^{\beta}$ as describing a moral quality

13:14. LXX: "$^{\alpha}$ The law [*nomos*] of the wise (man) is a fountain of life, $^{\beta}$ but the mindless man will die by a snare [*ho de anous hypo pagidos thaneitai*]." LXX represents a variant text in $^{\beta}$, namely, *ûkᵉsîl mimmōqēš yāmût* (Baum.), a corruption of MT's *lswr mmqšy mwt*. The MT is easy to understand, and there is no ideological motivation for the difference. Though 14$^{\beta}$ creates an antithesis, it is a very loose one and certainly not the motive for all these differences from MT (contrary to Gerleman 1956: 20).

Syr's *lʾylyn dsṭyn* ("to those who turn aside") reads MT's consonantal text, *lswrmmqšy*, as *lassûrîm mimmōqšê-* = 14:27.

Variant: *wksyl mmqš ymwt* (MT *lāsûr mimmōqᵉšê māwet*).

13:15. LXX: "$^{\alpha}$ Good sense [*synesis*] gives (one) favor, $^{\beta}$ and knowing (the) law [*gnōnai nomon*] is (the part of) a good intellect. $^{\gamma}$ But the ways of scorners are in destruction [*en apōleią*]." LXX 15$^{\beta}$ is taken from—or is the source of—LXX 9:10$^{\alpha}$. V 15$^{\gamma}$ is close enough to the MT to indicate that it is based on a text that had *ʾydm* "their destruction." In both places it is an insertion teaching that knowledge of law is the best part of wisdom.

M. Dick (1990: 26, 41) identifies "law" in 15$^{\beta}$ as sapiential teaching, while Cook (2002*a*: 280–88) explains it as the Law of Moses. Dick says that as a group, references to *nomos* would tend to make one think of the Law of Moses, but LXX-Prov uses language that leaves this vague, so that "law" could be understood as communal law rather than specifically the Law of Moses (1990: 40, 42). Still, the mention of "law" with no indication of source (such as "the wise") does seem to allude to the Law of Moses. See the Note on 6:23. This is clearer when *nomos* has the article. Other cases without the article are 6:23; 9:10; 28:7, 9. With the article: 28:4 (2x); 29:18.

It is noteworthy how rarely and allusively the Law of Moses is introduced into LXX-Prov, even though its centrality was undoubtedly a given for the translators. Moreover, some of the allusions to the Law are in secondary strata. The identification of Law and Wisdom is not a major goal of the OG translator, who was largely content to adhere to the older concepts of wisdom.

Variant: *ʾydm* (MT *ʾêtân*).

13:17. LXX: "$^{\alpha}$ A rash king [*basileus thrasys*] falls into evils, $^{\beta}$ but a faithful [*pistos* ^{S*}; *sophos* "wise" ^{ABSc}] messenger will save him [*rhysetai auton*]." "King" =

mlk for *ml'k*. The poorly attested *pistos* (S*, *103*, *253*) looks like a correction of an original *sophos*. LXX's "saves him" is an attempt to bring logic and cohesion into the verse. Since the king is being saved by the wise messenger, he is presumed to be merely "rash" and not actually "evil," as MT's *rāšāʿ* has it.

Variant: *mlk* (MT *mal'āk*).

13:19. LXX: "α The desires of the pious [*epithumiai eusebōn*] please the soul, β but the works of the impious are far from knowledge [*makran apo gnōseōs*]." This is a moralizing interpretation, to make it clear that only pious desires are sweet (sim. Syr *rgt' y'yt'* "proper desire"). Nevertheless, we can retrovert Gk *apo gnōseōs* to *mdʿ* (understood as *middēaʿ*) for *mrʿ* (Lag.); this forced the substitution of "works" for "abomination" and the addition of "far from." Syr *rgt' y'yt'* "proper desire" represents *mrʿ*, as in MT, but Syr understood it as *rēaʿ* "thought," "desire," then modified it by *y'yt'* for propriety's sake.

Variant *mdʿ* (MT *mērāʿ*).

13:20. LXX: α *ho symporeuomenos* "he who goes about with" = qeré. β *gnōsthēsetai* "will be known" = *yiwwādēaʿ*.

Variants: *yiwwādēaʿ* (MT *yērôaʿ*).

Ketiv *hlwk*, qeré *hōlēk*; ketiv *wḥkm*, qeré *yeḥkām*.

13:22. LXX: "α The good man will have sons of sons as his heritage [*klēronomēsei*]." MT's *yanḥîl* was understood as intransitive, or (more likely) the source-text lacked the m.l. *yod* of *yanḥîl*. The LXX's promise is less material than in the MT but is the same as in Ps 127[126]:3. Syr = MT.

13:23. LXX: "α The righteous [pl.] will spend many years in wealth, β but the unjust [pl.] will perish suddenly." V 23α has no contact with the MT. It takes the word "wealth" from v 22. V 23β paraphrases *rb* "great(ly)" as "suddenly" and takes *bl' mšpṭ* as a noun phrase, "he who is in unjustice" = unjust (people). The LXX expresses confidence in recompense where the MT recognizes the existence of inequities.

Vul: *multi cibi in novalibus patrum, et alii congregantur absque iudicio* ("Much food is in the tillage of fathers, but for others it is gathered without judgment"). This continues the theme of inheritance from v 22 and understands *nsph* as *n'sph* "gathered," as in *Gen. Rab.* 49:15 (57b) (C. Gordon 1930: 390).

Syr: "(a) Those for whom no house is provided, lose wealth for many years, (b) and men perish entirely." This continues the theme of v 22, by speaking of the impoverishment of the sons of sinners. Given Syr's distance from the LXX along with the absence of LXX's moralizing tack, it is possible that a different Hebrew source-text lay behind both in 24a, and that it included "years" and "wealth."

Tg^Z has *rb' 'kyl 'rʿ lmskn' w'yt gbr' mtngyd bl' dyn'* ("The important man devours the land of the poor man, and there is a man who is swept away unjustly"). On this understanding of the consonantal text, see the Commentary.

13:25. LXX: "α The righteous, when eating, fills his soul, β but the souls [*psychai*] of the wicked are lacking." LXX makes satisfaction the result, not the goal, of "eating." By using *psychai* (lit., "souls") for *bṭn* "belly" in β, LXX makes the punishment psychological and tightens the antithesis.

14:1. The versions construe *ḥkmwt nšym* variously. LXX: *sophai gynaikes* "wise women"; Vul *sapiens mulier* "wise woman"; Syr: *ʾnttʾ ḥkymtʾ* "wise woman"; Tg^{Z}: *ḥkymtʾ bnšyʾ* "the wisest among women."

14:2. LXX translates Heb *bwzhw* "despises him" as *atimasthēsetai* "will be despised," which reduces the apparent banality of the sentence.

14:5. 4QProv^{b} has 14:5–10 (fragmentary) = MT.

14:6. LXX: "$^{\alpha}$ (If) you [sg.] seek wisdom with [*para*; i.e., near] the wicked, you will not find (it), $^{\beta}$ but knowledge is readily (available) with sensible people." Since it is unclear why an impudent man would seek wisdom, the translator departs from MT's syntax for the sake of logic.

14:7. LXX: "$^{\alpha}$ Everything is against [*enantia*] a foolish man, $^{\beta}$ but wise lips are weapons of knowledge [*hopla de aisthēseōs*]." LXX reads *kl* "everything" for MT's *lk* "go" and *wkly dʿt* for *wbl ydʿt* (Jäg.). LXX's variants are graphic errors: metathesis, *b-k* interchange, and different word division. De Waard (1993: 250) believes that these changes were deliberate attempts to deal with interpretive problems and to create antithesis and alliteration. But the MT is not very difficult, and there is no reason to ascribe the differences to a complex interpretive process in which the translator somehow mimics common scribal errors in order to produce a rather fuzzy antithesis with no theological gain.

Variants: *kl* (MT *lēk*); *wkly dʿt* (MT *ûbal yādatā*).

14:9. LXX: "$^{\alpha}$ The houses of transgressors [^{A} "fools"] will require purification, $^{\beta}$ but the houses of the righteous are acceptable" ($^{\alpha}$ *oikiai paranomōn* [*aphrōn* ^{A}] *opheilēsousin katharismon*, $^{\beta}$ *oikiai de dikaiōn dektai*). The LXX offers partial help in reconstructing the text of this obscure verse. The source-text had *ʾhlym* ("tents" = houses) for MT's *ʾwlym* "fools." (Heb *ʾhl* "tent" is translated *oikos* 15x; e.g., Gen 7:1; 9:27; Job 15:34.) Then the problematic *ʾšm* "guilt" was rephrased as "requiring purification." Where MT has *wbyn* "and among," the LXX saw *wbyt* "and the house of." (In the source-text, *byt* was an Aramaism, as in Prov 8:2.) These considerations allow for the following retroversion: *ʾohŏlê lēṣîm ʾāšām, ûbêt y^{e}šārîm rāṣôn*. This is still difficult, and we should probably emend the first word of the restroversion to *bʾhly* and translate: "In the tents of mockers is guilt [i.e., the guilty], but the houses of the upright are favor [i.e., favored]." (Heb *rāṣôn* can mean "what is desired," "object of favor," as in 11:20; 12:22; 15:8; etc.) BA notes the cultic terminology resonances of *katharismon* and *dektai*. Syr is mainly dependent on LXX here.

Variants: *ʾhly* (MT *ʾŽwîlîm*); *lyṣym* (MT *yālîṣ*); *wbyt* and *wbny* (MT *ûbên*).

14:10. LXX: "$^{\alpha}$ (As for) the knowledgeable [*aisthētikē*] heart of a man—his soul is sad, $^{\beta}$ but when it [he?] rejoices, it is not mingled with arrogance." Or: "$^{\alpha}$ (If) the heart of a man is knowledgeable, his soul is sad, $^{\beta}$ but when it [he?] rejoices, it is not mingled with arrogance." (Since *aisthēsis* most often translates *dʿt* "knowledge," *aisthētikē* [used only here and in 14:30] should be translated "knowledgeable" rather than "sensible," that is, sensitive [BA].) (The latter meaning would give the verse a Stoic cast.) The idea of 10$^{\alpha}$ is similar to Qoh 7:4. LXX read *zēd* "arrogant," which it then had to treat as an abstract. See 14:30.

Syr: "(a) The knowledgeable heart is anxious for itself [*lbʾ ydwʿtnʾ krywtʾ hw lnpšh*], (b) and no stranger mingles in its joy." 10(a) is based on LXX, (b) on

MT. Syr suggests that the wise man keeps his emotions, good and bad, to himself.

Variant: *zd* (MT *zār*).

14:12. 4QProv[b] has 14:12–13 (fragmentary) = MT.

14:13. LXX: "[α] Pain does not mingle in pleasures, [β] but in the end, happiness [*teleutaia de chara*] comes to sorrow." LXX imports some of the phraseology of v 10 and reverses the meaning of MT 13a. If the motive was to introduce a positive attitude, it is puzzling that the same was not done to 13[β]; as it is, the verse remains pessimistic. LXX's version means that while one is happy (or, enjoying pleasures), he does not feel grief, but ultimately his joy becomes sorrow. OG *teleutaia de chara* represents the same problematic word division as MT. Syr's *wḥrtʾ dḥdwth* "the end of *its* happiness" is not evidence for *wʾḥryt hśmḥh* either, though that division is certainly correct.

14:14. LXX: [β] "from his devisings" (*apo de tōn dianoēmatōn*) = *wmmʿlyw*. Syr "from his own fear" (*mn dḥltʾ dnpšh*). In other words, he will enjoy the benefits of his fear of God (sim. Tg). Syr is trying to extract out the meaning of Heb *mʿlyw*, lit., "from upon himself" (= MT).

Variant: *wmmʿlyw* (*ûmimmaʿălāyw*) (MT *umēʿālāyw*).

14:15. LXX: "[β] but a clever man comes to a change of heart" (*panourgos de erchetai eis metanoian*) ≠ MT. The reason for the difference is unclear.

14:16. LXX: "[α] A wise man, being afraid, turns away from evil [or "misfortune"—*kakou*], [β] but the fool, trusting in himself, associates [*meignytai*] with a wicked man [or "wickedness"]." "Associates" probably reflects an understanding of *mtʿbr* as equivalent to *mtʿrb* (lit., "mix in," "interfere"). (Heb *mtʿbrw* is translated *paroxynōn* in 20:2.) LXX rearranges the syntax in 16[β] and expands the sentence to provide a logical sequence: trusting, then associating.

Syr: "but the fool mixes in confidently" (*wsklʾ mtḥlṭ bh tkylʾyt*) ≈ LXX; sim. Tg. Heb *mtʿbr wbwtḥ* is correctly taken as a hendiadys. It is hard to know if LXX and Syr are construing *mtʿbr* as a by-form of *mtʿrb* (as it may indeed be) or have the latter in their text.

14:17. LXX: "[α] He who is quickly angered acts carelessly, [β] but the intelligent man bears much [*polla hypopherei*]." "Bears" = *yśʾ* (*yiśśāʾ*) for MT's *yśnʾ*. Consequently Heb *ʾyš mzmwt*, "a man of shrewdness," was interpreted positively. Gk *polla hypopherei* implies that the intelligent man can or will put up with much irritation.

Tg: "He whose spirit is sick [*kryʾ*] is reckoned a fool, and he is hated [*snyʾ* Tg[Z]] by the man whose temper is patient [*dʾrykʾ trʿytyh*, lit., "whose thoughts are long"]." This is an independent but strained interpretation of MT, playing on *kryʾ* and its anagram and homeophone *ʾrykʾ*.

Variant: *yśʾ* (MT *yiśśānēʾ*).

14:18. LXX: "[α] Fools will divide up [*meriountai*] evil [*kakian*], [β] but the clever will take hold of [*kratēsousin*] knowledge" ≈ MT, but with greater moral sharpness. The *ptʾym* are "fools" (*aphrones*), not merely *nēpioi* or *akakoi* (see the Note on 1:4), and their punishment is not merely to receive folly (which would be tautological, since in LXX they are already *aphrones*), but to "divide up *kakia*," that is, receive a portion in misfortune. The background image of "dividing up" and "taking hold of" is of dividing profits or spoil.

14:19. LXX: "$^{\alpha}$ (The) wicked [pl.] will trip [*olisthēsousin*] before (the) good [pl.], $^{\beta}$ and (the) wicked will serve [*therapeusousin*] at the doors [*thyra*] of the righteous [pl.]." MT's phrase "before the gates of the righteous" is construed on the basis of the Gk idiom *tas thyras tinos therapeuein* "to serve at the gates of someone"; see LSJ 793a, II.2 (D. A. Teeter, personal communication).

14:21. LXX: "$^{\alpha}$ He who despises the wretched [pl.] [*penētas*] sins." "The wretched [pl.]" interprets MT's *lrʿhw* "neighbor" narrowly, in the light of 20$^{\alpha}$ and the parallel *ʿnyym* "poor" (ketiv).

Ketiv *ʿnyym*, qeré *ʿănāwîm*.

14:22. LXX: "$^{\alpha}$ Those who go astray devise evils, $^{\beta}$ while good people devise mercy and faithfulness [*eleos kai alētheia*]. $^{\gamma}$ The devisers of evil do not understand mercy and faithfulness, $^{\delta}$ while compassions and loyalties [*eleēmosynai kai pisteis*] are with those who devise good [lit. "good devisers]." Stichoi 22$^{\gamma\delta}$ have the obelus in SyrH and are presumably OG. BA observes that the expression *eleēmosynai kai pisteis* (pl.) in 22$^{\delta}$ is typical of LXX-Prov, while *eleos kai alētheia* is systematically used for *ḥesed weʾĕmet* in LXX-Psalms and the "Others." Gk *tektainousi* = *ḥršw* (verb), for MT *ḥršy*. Gk's reading forces a loose rendering of *ytʿw* as a ptcp. Heb *ḥršw* was read in $^{\beta}$ as well, which required identifying *ṭwb* "good" as the subj. Stichoi $^{\beta}$ and $^{\delta}$ are partial doublets of the Heb, sharing *ḥsd wʾmt*. The underlying (erroneous) reading of 22$^{\gamma\delta}$ is *lwʾ* [or *hlwʾ*] *ydʿw ḥršy rʿ ḥsd wʾmt ḥršy ṭwb*.

Syr: "(a) The wicked forget that they do evil, (b) but the merciful and righteous do all good things. (c) Those who do evil do not understand mercy and faithfulness, (d) but compassion and faithfulness are with those who do good." Syr too has a double rendering, probably made by the first translator of Syr (Joosten 1995: 71). Heb *ytʿw* "go astray" was translated (wrongly) by the similar sounding Syr *ṭʿyn* "forget," and the subject and predicate in 22a were inverted, a mistake possible only when reading the Heb. Syr translates LXX $^{\gamma\delta}$ exactly, lacking a corresponding couplet in the Heb. This process shows how Syr wishes to preserve the substance of the LXX while recognizing the Heb as its authority. Tg ≈ MT.

Variants: *ḥršw* (twice) (MT *ḥōršê-*); *ydʿw* (MT *yitʿû*).

14:23. LXX: "$^{\alpha}$ For [*en*, lit., "in"] everyone who takes care [*merimnōnti*] there is a profit, $^{\beta}$ but the comfortable and indifferent will be in need." Heb *ʿṣb* "toil" is rather awkwardly construed as a metonymy for people who toil carefully. V 23$^{\beta}$ is a reasonable paraphase of the MT, reading "word of the lips" as a metonymy for those who merely talk and don't take action.

Syr: "(a) In all about which you are anxious, there is one profitable thing. (b) And the one who is poor in his dwelling [or "life"] will be comfortable and happy. (c) The Lord heals all pain, (d) but by the utterance of the lips of evildoers he will damage." S has a double translation of this verse. V 23(a)(b) is derived from G, v 23(c)(d) from MT. On the intricate relations between the Syr and the LXX in this verse, see Joosten 1995: 67–68. By inverting "sweet" and "poor," the translator has provided a theological explanation for the absence of pain. In (a), Syr read *yhwh* (understood as "the Lord") for *yhyh* "will be" and possibly *kl* for *bkl* (ibid.).

Variants: *kl* (MT *b*ᵉ*kōl*); *yhwh* (MT *yihyeh*).

14:24. LXX: "α The crown of the wise [pl.] is clever [*panourgos*], β but the pastime [*diatribē*] of fools is evil [*kakē*]." *Panourgos* ("clever" or "a clever man") reflects Heb *ʿrmh*, construed by LXX as *ʿărûmāh* (fem. adj.) but probably originally intended as *ʿormah*. Some assume that the LXX read *ʿrmm* "their cleverness," but *ʿrmh* is supported by the parallel *ʾwlt* and the syntax in the similarly structured 16:31 and 17:6, in which the predicate is an indefinite noun. In 24β, *diatribē* and *kakē* eliminate MT's tautology ("The folly of dolts is folly") by interpreting the first *ʾwlt* as a type of behavior and the second as the moral quality of folly, namely evil.

Variant: *ʿrmh* (MT *ʿošrām*).

14:27. LXX: "The command [*prostagma*] of the Lord is a fount of life. β It makes (one) turn away [*poiei de ekklinein*] from the trap of death." *Prostagma* is probably influenced by Heb of 13:14, though in that verse *twrt* is translated *nomos*. There is no graphic explanation in Heb or an ideological motive to explain the change. The LXX and MT are variant proverbs. In α, LXX read *lsyr*, parsing it as *lāsîr* (an H-stem with elision of the *h*-) "to cause to turn away."

Syr: (b) *lʾylyn dsṭyn* "to those who turn aside"; see 13:14.

Variants: *twrt* (MT *yrʾt*); *lsyr* (= *lāsîr*) (MT *lāsûr*).

14:28. LXX = MT, but *ʿm* "people" is understood as *ethnei*, "nations," presumably those subjugated to the king in question. Gk *dynastou* = *rwzn*, correctly, for MT's *rāzôn* "hunger." It is impossible to tell if this interprets *rzwn* or reflects *rwzn* (*rôzen*).

14:29. LXX: "α A man of patient temper is great in good sense [*makrothymos anēr polys en phronēsei*], β but an impatient one [*oligopsychos*] is exceedingly foolish." In 29β, "exceedingly foolish" is a contextual guess at a difficult *mrym ʾwlt* ≠ 3:35. Gk *oligopsychos* (and cognates) includes a range of undesirable emotions, including faintheartedness (e.g., Isa 35:4; Sir 4:9), despondency and distress (e.g., Ps 55[54]:6; Jdt 7:19; Isa 25:5), and impatience (as here and probably Exod 6:9, where it translates Heb *qōṣer ruaḥ*). These are not distinct meanings, but rather a bundle of emotions that tend to go together.

14:30. LXX: "α The man of gentle temper [*prauthymos*] is a healer of (the) heart, β but a knowledgeable heart [*kardia aisthētikē*] is a rot of bones." *Prauthymos* is added to echo *macrothymos* and reinforce the Stoic tone (BA). LXX α continues the praise of patience from 29a, ignoring *ḥyy bśrym* and construing *lb* "heart" as the dir. obj. of *mrpʾ* "heals," taken as an H or D ptcp. 30β seems at odds with Proverbs' view of wisdom, but 14:10 expresses a similar attitude. (Gk *aisthēsis* translates words for knowledge and wisdom and is always a virtue.)

4QProvᵇ contains Prov 14:31–15:31.

14:31. LXX translates *ḥrp* euphemistically as "angers" (*paroxynei*) (as in 17:5). (LXX 27:22 shows that the translator knew that *ḥrp* means "insult.") Heb *ʿšq* is translated narrowly as *sykophantein* (sim. Ps 119[118]:122; Prov 28:3, 16; etc.), whose classical meaning is "to slander, accuse."

14:32. LXX: "β He who trusts in his own piety [*tȩ̄ eautou hosiotēti*] is righteous." LXX's "in his own piety" = *btmw* (*b*ᵉ*tummô*); Jäg., Lag., etc. The restored Hebrew of 13$^{\beta}$ would be better translated as "but the righteous trusts in his innocence." The MT (= 4QProv^{b}, Aq, Sym, Theod, Vul, and Tg) resulted from a metathesis and, subsequently, received a vowel letter. If the LXX had seen MT's reading, it would have had no reason to avoid it. The afterlife is affirmed in LXX 11:7a.

The fact that 4Q103 Prov^{b} agrees with the MT does not, contrary to J. de Waard (*1998*: 93), "reinforce the thesis that the reading in LXX is due to a kind of *ʾal tiqrā* treatment." It shows only that the reading arose sometime before the mid-first century C.E.—as we knew in any case from Aq, Sym, and Theod.

Syr: (b) *wdtkyl dlyt lh ḥṭhʾ*^{pl} ("He who is confident that he has no sins"). This witnesses to *btmw* independently of the LXX, as does the doublet in Syr 14:35(c). Tg: (b) *wdtkyl dmʾyt ṣdyqʾ hwʾ*—an awkward clause that perhaps is to be understood as "he who has trust, who is dying, is righteous," that is, one who has faith even when he is dying is righteous.

Variant: *btmw* (*b^{e}tummô*) (MT *b^{e}môtô*).

14:33. LXX: "$^{\alpha}$ In the good heart of a man is wisdom, $^{\beta}$ but in the heart of fools it is not perceived" ($^{\alpha}$ *en kardią agathę andros* [+ *anapausetai* ^{Sc}] *sophia*, $^{\beta}$ *en de kardią aphronōn ou diaginōsketai*). (^{Sc} adds "will rest.") Gk *agathę* = *nkwn*, as in Job 42:8 $^{A\,(Theod)}$. In 33$^{\beta}$ a negative is supplied to ease an apparent paradox. This is found in Theod and Aq. While LXX might supply a negative for the sake of logic or moralization (as in 3:32; 5:5, 16; etc.), Theod and Aq would not. The negative was inserted within the Heb transmission for the sake of "logic," for the notion of wisdom being known among fools seemed on the face of it outlandish. Other examples of an added negative in the LXX (not necessarily the translator's doing) are 1:17, 24; 3:32; 5:5, 16; 18:9; and 25:27.

Syr *dkʾnʾ*^{pl} "of the honest [pl.]" reflects Heb *nkwn* = LXX. Syr has a negative in 33b = LXX.

Variant: + *lʾ* [before *twdʿ*] (MT lacks).

14:34. LXX: "$^{\beta}$ but sins reduce tribes" (*elassonousi de phylas hamartiai*). LXX's "reduces" = *wḥsr* (*w^{e}ḥissēr*); sim. Syr *mzʿryn*. Ulrich *2000*: 185 sees this reading in 4QProv^{b}, but the *reš* is damaged and *wḥsd* = MT is quite possible. Neither the verb *ḥissēr* nor the noun *ḥeser* fits the sentence as well as MT's *w^{e}ḥesed* "disgrace."

Variant: *wḥsr* (MT *w^{e}ḥesed*).

14:35. LXX: "$^{\alpha}$ The intelligent [*phronomous*] servant is favored by (the) king, $^{\beta}$ and by his own adaptability [*eustrophią*] he removes disgrace. $^{\gamma}$ Anger also destroys the intelligent [*orgē apollysin kai phronimous*]" (14:35$^{\gamma}$/15:1$^{\alpha}$ [= MT 14:35b] continues in 15:1$^{\beta}$). LXX 14:35 and 15:1 form a unit teaching political opportunism (BA). The hapax means "the ability to adapt," "to change one's view" (BA). It is uncertain what motivates *eustrophią*; Jäg. retroverts to *ʿrmtw* "his cleverness." The latter, clearly wrong in context, would have forced the LXX to treat the rest of 35b loosely.

4QProv^{b} has *wʿb tw*, with a space where the *reš* should be. It is likely that the *reš* was damaged or has faded. De Waard (*1998*: 93) considers this a deliberate writing that is the basis for LXX's *eustrophią*, with *ʿbtw* parsed as a form of *ʿbt* "twist." But it is a semantic jump from "twisting" (as in a rope) to *eustrophia*. It is no argument against the reading *wʿrmtw* to observe that *ʿormāh* does not have a suffix elsewhere (ibid.), since the variant was an error. One might note that the nonexistent *ʿbt* "twisting" does not take a suffix elsewhere either.

Variant: *wbʿrmtw* (MT *w*^{e}*ʿebrātô*).

15:1. LXX: "$^{\alpha}$ [In 14:35b], $^{\beta}$ but a submissive answer turns aside wrath, $^{\gamma}$ and a painful word stirs up anger [pl.]." By changing the notion of softness or gentleness (Heb *rak*) into submissiveness, LXX continues the situation of 14:35, in which a royal official placates the king.

B. Ber. 17a quotes this verse using *mšyb* for *yšyb*.

15:4. LXX: "$^{\alpha}$ The healing of the tongue is a tree of life, $^{\beta}$ and he who guards [*syntērōn*] it will be filled with spirit [var(s). *piotētos* ^{S*} "fatness"; *tōn karpōn autēs* "its fruit" ^{Sc}]." According to Jäg. and Baum., LXX read *śbʿ* or *yśbʿ* "be sated" instead of *šbr* "breaking" and *pls* instead of *slp*. The first retroversion is plausible, the *ʿayin* having been lost in the dittog. of *br*. But Heb *pls* would not have been translated "guards." Elsewhere, LXX *slp* (noun and verb) is translated by words indicating causing harm or degradation. The phrase "filled with spirit" is unparalleled in the HB and the LXX but prominent in the NT (Luke 1:15, 41; Acts 2:4; 4:8, etc.).

Vul = MT but translates *wslp bh* as *quae inmoderata est* "that which is immoderate"—a unique understanding of *slp*. This too seems to associate 4b with the theme of *eating*. There is thus evidence for a variant line persisting quite late, but it is impossible to retrovert it.

Syr: "(b) and he who eats of its fruits will be sated from it" (*wdʾkl mn pʾrwhy*^{pl} *nsbʿ mnh*). Syr combines reminiscences of various verses: MT 18:20b, *wtbwʾt śptyw yśbʿ* ("and will be sated with the produce of his lips"); MT 18:21b, *wʾwhbyh yʾkl pryh* ("and those who love it [sc. the tongue] will eat [sg.] its fruit"); LXX's "be filled"—or possibly *yśbʿ* in Syr's own source text. Perhaps Syr had *tōn karpōn autēs* (= LXX^{Sc}) in its Gk text, and this was what sparked these associations.

Variants: *yśbʿ* (MT *šeber*); *wšmr* (MT *wslp*).

15:5. LXX has *entolas* "commandments" for *twkḥt* "reproof." "Keeping the commandments" is the usual expression.

15:6. LXX "$^{\alpha}$ In abundant righteousness there is much strength, $^{\beta}$ but the wicked [pl.] will perish entirely, uprooted [*holorrizoi olountai*] from the earth. $^{\gamma}$ There is much strength for the houses of the righteous, $^{\delta}$ but the fruits of sinners perish." Stichoi $^{\alpha\beta}$ have the obelus in SyrH and are OG. They cannot be fully related to the MT. LXX *en pleonazousę̄ dikaiosynę̄* = *brbt ṣdyq* (*birbōt ṣaddîq*), for MT's *byt ṣdyq* "in the house of the righteous." In fact, *brbt* could more easily be a permutation of *bbyt* (*yod* to *reš*, with metathesis). Heb *bbyt* "in the house" is probably the correct reading, though the versional evidence is ambiguous. Gk "uprooted" associates *nʿkrt* with *nʿqrt*. V6$^{\gamma\delta}$ are represented in Vul.

15:7. LXX: "The lips of the wise [pl.] are bound to [or "by"] knowledge [*dedetai aisthēsei*], $^{\beta}$ but the hearts of fools are not secure [*ouk asphaleis*]." In 7$^{\alpha}$, *yzrw* "disperse" is parsed as a passive of *ʾzr* "gird on." In 7$^{\beta}$, Heb *kn* is associated with *k-w-n* "make/be firm." Sym *phylassousi* identifies *yzrw* with *yṣrw* (*n-ṣ-r*).

15:8. Cov. Damascus 11.20–21 quotes this verse as *zbḥ ršʿym twʿbh wtplt ṣdqm* [var. *ṣdqym*, 4Q271] *kmnḥt rṣwn*. This, as often in the Qumran citations, is a reworking of a biblical sentence, not a variant text.

4QProv^{b} has 15:1–8 (fragmentary) = MT. 4Q271 has 15:8, reading *tʿbh* for MT's *tʿbt yhwh*. The fuller phrase is probably a harmonization with the usual usage, though a bare *tʿbh* "abomination" is possible.

Variants: *tʿbh* (MT *tôʿăbat* YHWH).

15:10. LXX: "$^{\alpha}$ The education of the innocent <guilty> man is known by those who pass by [*paideia akakou gnōrizetai hypo tōn pariontōn*], $^{\beta}$ and those who hate reproofs will perish shamefully [*aischrōs*]." Gk *akakou* is an error for *kakou*, a straightforward translation of Heb *rʿ* (Jäg.). Gk *tōn pariontōn* = *lʿwbr ʾrḥ* ("he who passes on the way," with number variance). LXX 10$^{\alpha}$ says that the discipline of the evildoer will be public and visible; sim. 10:9. Gk *gnōrizetai* and *aischrōs* are added for clarification and emphasis.

Variant: *lʿbr* [*l^{e}ʿōbēr*] (MT *l^{e}ʿōzēb*).

15:12. LXX: "$^{\beta}$ and will not associate with [*homilēsei meta*] wise men." LXX *homilēsei meta* = *ylk ʾt*, "go with," for MT *ylk ʾl* "go to." Syr = Gk.

Variant: *ʾt* (MT *ʾel*).

15:13. LXX: "$^{\alpha}$ When the heart is happy, the face flourishes, $^{\beta}$ "but when it [the heart] is in sadness, it [the face] is sorrowful [*skythrōpazei*]." The LXX aligns 13$^{\beta}$ better with 13$^{\alpha}$ by replacing "spirit" with "face." The subj. of *skythrōpazei* is *prosōpon* "face"; compare how *skythrōpos* modifies *prosopon* in Gen 40:7; Dan^{Theod} 1:10; and Sir 25:23.

15:14. "$^{\alpha}$ The straight [*orthē*] heart seeks knowledge, $^{\beta}$ but the mouth of the uneducated [*apaideutōn*] will know evils [*gnōsetai kaka*]." Variants are "straight" = *nkwn* (Jäg.) for *nbwn* and *gnōsetai* = *ydʿ* or an ungrammatical *ydʿh*. For *apaideutōn*, LXX^{S*} has *asebōn* "wicked." This variant continues the tendency, begun in OG (e.g., 10:26), to render words for ignorance and folly by words for immorality. LXX's "but the mouth" agrees with qeré *wpy*.

Ketiv *wpny*, qeré *ûpî*.

Variants: *nkwn* (MT *nābôn*); *ydʿ* (MT *yirʿeh*).

15:15. LXX: "$^{\alpha}$ All the time, the eyes of the evil people expect evil, $^{\beta}$ but the good are always at rest." Lag. retroverts 15$^{\alpha}$ to an awkward *kl ywm ʿyny rʿym rʿt* [*rōʿōt*] *rʿh*. But Heb *rʿh* "shepherd," "seek," is never rendered by *prosdechesthai*. Minimally, the LXX had *ʿyny* "the eyes of" instead of *ʿny* "poor man" and took liberties to make sense of the rest of the verse. Whether deliberately or not, LXX presents a moral antithesis—*kakōn*/*agathoi*—for MT's morally neutral "poor"/"cheerful." LXX construes "feast" metaphorically as repose, lest the line be read as encouraging hedonism.

Variant: *ʿyny* (MT *ʿānî*).

15:16. LXX: "$^{\beta}$ than great treasuries with lack of fear [*meta aphobias*]." LXX creates a more exact antithesis to "fear of the Lord" and gives *mhwmh* "turmoil" a religious sense.

Variant: *yrʾt* (MT *b^{e}yirʾat*).

15:17. LXX: "$^{\alpha}$ Better a feast of vegetables for (the sake of) love and favor [*pros philian kai charin*] $^{\beta}$ than a meal of oxen with hostility." ("A feast" is *xenismos*, i.e., entertainment of a guest.) Gk *pros philian* "for love" (i.e., for the purpose of friendship) is an attempt to clarify MT's *wʾhbh šm*, lit. "and love is there," for it may have been unclear how love can literally be *in* the provisions. Gk *philian kai charin* is a double translation elaborating the concept of *ʾhbh* "love." Other examples of double translations, cited by Jäg. 115, are *authadēs kai alazōn* for Heb *yhyr* (21:24); *sophia kai ennoia* for Heb *ḥkmh* (24:7); *ouk apostrephetai oude kataptēssei* for Heb *wlʾ yšwb* (30:30); *kratos kai ischys* for Heb *ḥsn* (Prov 27:24); *kriseis kai machai* for Heb *ryb* (30:33); also 17:9, 15, 18; 21:19, 26; 22:13; 23:21, 29, 31; 29:25; 30:30.

Syr's *wḥwbʾ dšmʾ* "and love of name/reputation" = *wʾhbt šm* [*šēm*] (Pink.)

Variant: *wʾhbt* (MT *w*[e]*ʾahăbāh*).

15:18. LXX: "[α] A hot-tempered man prepares conflicts, [β] but a patient man calms even one in the offing [*kai tēn mellousan*]." The last phrase underscores the power of patience: It prevents quarrels from even arising.

15:18a. "[α] A patient man extinguishes contentions, [β] but the impious one stirs (them) up (even) more." V 18a has the obelus in SyrH (Fritsch 1953: 174). This, however, may be wrong. Given its differences from the MT, LXX 18 is probably not hexaplaric. On the other hand, v 18a shows signs of being based on the Gk form of 28:2. Note also the unhebraic word order in 18a[α] and the adverbial use of *mallon*, which in translated verses in Proverbs is only a comparative particle. V 18 is probably the OG and v 18a a later addition, composed and placed here by association with v 18. Paronomasia of *makrothymos* with *thymōdēs* helps join the two couplets (BA). LXX 18a is interesting not so much as a "pertinent religious interpretation" (Cook *2000*: 174)—the religious enhancement is too slight to be the motive—as it is as an example of the ongoing emergence of proverbs within the Greek scribal tradition.

15:19. 4QProv[b] has much of 15:19–31, with different readings in vv 19 and 28. For MT's *sllh* (*s*[e]*lûlāh*), 4QProv[b] has *swllh*, presumably to be read as *sull*[e]*lāh* "is smoothed," "leveled," a true Gp. As the more archaic form, the latter is probably what was originally intended by the consonants *sllh*, rather than MT's G pass. ptcp. (*s*[e]*lûlāh*), especially since the long *û* of that form is regularly written with a *waw*, unless (as in Gen 31:39) it has a possessive suffix.

Variant: *swllh* (MT *s*[e]*lûlāh*).

15:21. LXX: "[α] The paths of the mindless [sg.] lack sense [pl.] [*anoētou triboi endeeis phrenōn*]." The translator, perhaps thinking it absurd that folly could be a joy to anyone, substitutes a more predictable statement about the mindless. Syr resolves the same difficulty differently: "A man who is foolish lacks sense."

15:22. LXX: "[α] Those who do not respect assemblies [*synhedria*] put off plans [*hypertithentai logismous*], [β] but counsel abides in the hearts of those who take counsel." Gk *hypertithenai* (only here for *p-r-r* H "confound," "violate") means "put off, defer" (GELS) and also "to omit" (LSJ). "In the hearts" ≈ *b*[e]*lēb* (Baum.); thus too in LXX 24:6. The LXX creates a wordplay on *boulē*. Apparently LXX is saying that if people fail to respect deliberations in the assembly, their own plans will fail, whereas those who confer with others gain wise counsel and thus will succeed.

LXX has changed the verse from a recommendation to have many advisors (probably with reference to the royal court) into an affirmation of public councils or assemblies, such as existed in the Hellenistic period in various forms—for example, the *gerousia* in Palestine and Alexandria and the Lesser *synhedria* in Palestine; see the Textual Note on Prov 31:23.

Variant: *wblb* (*ûb*^{e}*lēb*) (MT *ûb*^{e}*rōb*).

15:23. LXX: "$^{\alpha}$ The bad man will surely not obey it [sc. counsel, v 22], $^{\beta}$ nor will he say anything that is timely or good for the commonweal" ($^{\alpha}$ *ou mē hypakousę̄ ho kakos autę̄,* $^{\beta}$ *oude mē eipę̄ kairion ti kai kalon tō̧ koinō̧*). This is a new proverb loosely based on the MT. It continues the thought of v 22. V 23$^{\alpha}$ is paraphrastic: A man (obviously of a bad sort) enjoys answering back. This is equivalent to saying that he does not listen to counsel or obey it. In $^{\beta}$, *wdbr* is understood as *w*^{e}*dibbēr,* with the neg. carried forward from $^{\alpha}$. *Kairion ti* = *bʿtw mh*; *kalon* = *ṭwb*; and the notion of *tō̧ koinō̧* is based on *synedria* in 22$^{\alpha}$. It is a new proverb, composed in Gk. Stich $^{\beta}$ in particular is unhebraic in syntax and word use.

15:24. LXX: "$^{\alpha}$ The thoughts [*dianoēmata*] of an intelligent man are ways of life, $^{\beta}$ so that by inclining away from Hades, he might be preserved [$^{\beta}$ *hina ekklinas ek tou hą̄dou sōthę̄*]." LXX's "thoughts" seems to correspond to a form of Heb *lmʿlh.* MT's up/down imagery is eliminated. It is hard to find an exegetical or textual motivation for these differences. Baum. points to *maʿălah rûḥăkem,* "what your spirit brings up" (LXX *ta diaboulia tou pneumatos hymōn*; Ezr 11:5), but recognizes the difference between the passages.

15:26. LXX: "$^{\beta}$ but the sayings of the pure are august [*hagnōn de rhēseis semnai*]"—as if reading *wnʿm ʾmry ṭhwrym,* but perhaps just overriding the word order, as in 11:21; 15:33; 16:15, 24; 17:12; 19:7$^{\alpha}$; 31:1; and elsewhere. (*Semnos* = *nʿm* only here.)

15:27. LXX: "$^{\alpha}$ The gift-taker [*dōrolēmptēs*] destroys himself, $^{\beta}$ but he who hates the taking of gifts is saved." LXX (correctly) understands *bytw* "his house" as equivalent to one's possessions, hence "himself," and construes *bwṣʿ bṣʿ* ("he who takes unjust gains") narrowly (and probably correctly) as bribe-taking, in the light of the B-line. Syr ≈ LXX.

15:27a–16:9. The LXX verse-sequence differs from the MT.

Using the Hebrew numbering, with Rahlfs' numbering in brackets, the LXX's sequence is:

LXX	*MT*	*LXX*	*MT*
[15:27]	15:27	[lacking]	16:1
[15:27a]	16:6	[16:2]	≈ 16:4
[15:28]	15:28	[lacking]	16:3
[15:28a]	16:7	[lacking]	16:4
[15:29]	15:29	[16:5]	16:5
[15:29a]	16:8	[lacking]	(16:6)
[15:29b]	16:9	[16:7]	(≠ MT 16:7)
[15:30]	15:30	[16:8]	(≠ 16:8)
[lacking]	15:31	[16:9]	≈ 16:4
[15:32]	15:32	[16:10 ff.]	= MT
[15:33]	15:33		

The shared core is MT 15:27–30, 32, 33; 16:4–9. The LXX maintained the sequence of MT 16:6–9 while interlacing the verses in 15:27–30. See Tov 1990: 50. Both the LXX and MT must descend from a different original. The verses lacking in one or the other of the versions are probably later additions, since there is no reason, deliberate or mechanical, for their omission.

There is a certain logic in LXX's arrangement that could only have originated in Gk. LXX 15:28, 28a, 29, 29a, 29b are linked by the root *dikai-*. This clustering depends on the presence of *dektai* in 28a and *dikaia* in 29b, which appear to originate with the translator. Moreover, the paronomasia between *pistesin* in 27a and *pisteis* in 28 clearly originates with the Gk translator (D. A. Teeter, personal communication).

BA (pp. 45–47), however, proposes that the MT represents an editorial reworking that created a block of "Yahwistic" sayings (15:33–16:9), while the LXX has more of a "theistic" series, using *theos*. In the LXX, this section has an unusually large number of cases in which the LXX has *theos* for MT's YHWH (12 out of 35). Elsewhere, the LXX equivalence is *kyrios* = YHWH, *theos* = *ʾlhym*, with few exceptions. The problem with this theory is that YHWH is used throughout Proverbs, with six exceptions, and this pattern is reflected overall in the LXX. We would have to presume that the Yahwistic redactors did their work everywhere *except in 15:33–16:9* before the LXX source-text diverged from the proto-MT. The theory also does not account for other disruptions in the section.

In the comments on this section, the MT order and numbering will be followed. Hexaplaric restorations will not be discussed.

15:27a. See MT 16:6.

15:28. LXX: "$^{\alpha}$ The hearts of the righteous [pl.] meditate faithfulness [*meletōsin pisteis*], $^{\beta}$ but the mouth of the wicked [pl.] answers [*apokrinetai*] evils." Gk *pisteis* for *lʿnwt* ("to answer") and *apokrinetai* for *ybyʿ* "pour forth" are loose translations that improve the "logic": The object of righteous people's meditation is more naturally a virtue such as faithfulness rather than "answering." *Pisteis* is influenced by *pisteis* in v 27a. Baum. says that *pisteis* associates *lʿnwt* with *lʿnwh* "humility," but *pistis* nowhere else renders words for humility.

4QProv[b] lacks *yhgh* for unclear reasons.

15:29a. See MT 16:8.

15:29b. See MT 16:9.

15:30. LXX: "$^{\alpha}$ The eye that beholds [*theōrōn*] good things [*kala*] makes the heart rejoice, $^{\beta}$ and a good saying [*phēmē*] fattens the bones." Gk *theōrōn* = *mrʾh* "vision" for MT *mʾwr* "light" and treats it as a verb. The translator added *kala* for logical clarity, because not everything the eye sees is pleasing. The adjustment would make sense only in response to *mrʾh* in the source text.

Variant: *mrʾh* (MT *māʾôr*).

15:31. LXX lacks.

15:32. LXX $^{\alpha}$ ≈ MT; "$^{\beta}$ but he who keeps [*tērōn*] reproofs loves his soul." LXX's "loves his soul" (i.e., his life) is a converse translation of MT 32a. It is based on 19:8 *qwnh lb ʾhb npšw*, though MT 15:32a is clear and unobjectionable. LXX is thus associating two passages with the same expressions and interpreting them in the light of each other. Perhaps the translator borrowed *ʾhb npšw* from 19:8 for the sake of antithesis (D. A. Teeter, personal communication). Or the variation may be the work of a Heb scribe, who produced the LXX source-text *or* the MT of v 32a in order to create a variant proverb, as happens often *within* MT Proverbs. Whether LXX's *šwmr* (as in 13:18) or MT's *šwmʿ* (as in 15:31) was the original, the versions now represent legitimate variant proverbs.

Variant: *šwmr* (MT *šômēaʿ*).

15:33. LXX: "$^{\alpha}$ Fear of God is education and [*kai*] wisdom, $^{\beta}$ and the beginning of honor is to respond [*apokrithēsetai*] to it." The *kai* in 33$^{\alpha}$ keeps "education" and "wisdom" distinct, as they are in MT 1:2, 7; and 23:23. V 33$^{\beta}$ has the asterisk in SyrH because of its displacement. The differences from MT were provoked by the misreading of *ʿnwh* as *ʿānûhā* "answer it" (sc. Lady Wisdom's summons; cf. 1:20; 8:1). This form was then translated as an inf. Compare the treatment of *ʿnwh* in 18:12. LXX^{ASs} and some minuscules add (with minor variants): $^{\gamma}$ *prosporeutai de tapeinois doxa* "and honor goes before the humble one." Lag. retroverts this to *wlpny ʿnwym kbwd*. LXX ignores word order on several occasions; see the Note on 15:26.

Syr: "(a) The fear of the Lord is the teaching [var. "fount"] of life, (b) and the glory of the humble goes before him" ((a) *dḥlth dmryʾ ywlpnʾ* [var. *mbwʿʾ*] *hy dḥyʾ*^{pl}, (b) *wtšbwḥth dmkykʾ ʾzlʾ qdmwhy*). "Teaching of life" or "fount of life" (the latter very likely the original) is influenced by 14:27a. Also, *ywlpnʾ* and *mbwʿʾ dḥyʾ*^{pl} are conjoined in 16:21–22. Stich (b) looks like a rephrasing of Gk 33$^{\gamma}$; see above. Tg: "(b) and whoever is honored, let him be humble" (^{Z} *wmn dmtyyqr yhwy ʿnwn*). This interprets "before" as priority in importance rather than time.

16:1. OG (LXX^{B}) lacks. SyrH adds Sir 3:18 here.

16:2. LXX: "All the works of the humble are visible to God, but the wicked perish in the evil day." This is a variant proverb, only loosely related to the MT. Vul ≈ LXX. LXX v 2$^{\beta}$, which is hardly related to v 2$^{\alpha}$, is lacking in LXX^{B}.

16:3. LXX lacks.

16:5. LXX: "$^{\alpha}$ Impure with God is everyone haughty of heart. $^{\beta}$ He who sets hands to hand unjustly will not be held innocent." See Textual Note on 11:21.

16:7. LXX (at 15:28a): "$^{\alpha}$ The ways of the just [pl.] are acceptable to the Lord. $^{\beta}$ Through them even enemies become friends." This is a paraphrase, possibly motivated by reading *nrṣwt* "acceptable" for MT's *brṣwt* (Baum.).

At this point, LXX has a different proverb: "$^{\alpha}$ The beginning of the good way (is) to do righteous deeds. (These are) more acceptable to God than offering sacrifices." Stich $^{\beta}$ ≈ MT 21:3b.

16:8. LXX (at Gk 15:29a) ≈ MT. The LXX has a different proverb at 16:8: "$^{\alpha}$ He who seeks the Lord will find knowledge with righteousness, $^{\beta}$ and those who seek him uprightly will find peace."

16:9. LXX (at 15:29b): "$^{\alpha}$ Let the heart of a man plan [*logizesthō*] righteous things [*dikaia*], $^{\beta}$ so that his steps may be made straight by God." LXX makes the proverb into a moral instruction by construing the first verb as jussive and substituting "righteous things" for "his way." At 16:9, LXX has MT 16:4.

16:11. LXX: "$^{\alpha}$ The weight of (the) balance is righteousness before the Lord, [β] and his works are honest weight-stones" ([α] *rhopē zygou dikaiosynē para kyriou,* [β] *ta de erga autou stathmia dikaią̄*). Possibly v 11[α] should be translated "Righteousness is the weight of the balance-scale." The LXX seems to be saying that a true balance-weight is considered as righteousness in God's eyes, and that he is the creator of *honest* weights, not of *all* of them. V 11[α] may reflect *pls m'znym mšpṭ*.

16:15. LXX: "[α] The son of the king is in the light of life [*en phōti zōēs huios basileōs*], [β] and those who are acceptable to him are like the late rain." There was no translational or ideological need for the translator to violate the word order and to add the royal son to the picture. The source-text must have had *bn* for MT's *pny*. It also appears that the translator was willing to treat *b'wr* and *ḥyym* as a bound construction though they are not adjacent. On the existence of the broken construct chain in Hebrew, see D. N. Freedman *1972b*; relevant examples are Hos 6:9; 8:2; and 14:3. It is uncertain that the LXX translators recognized (or imposed) the construction, since the MT word order is overridden in other circumstances too (see the Note on 15:26).

Variant: *bn* (MT *pᵉnê*).

16:16. LXX: "[α] Nests [*nossiai*] of wisdom are preferable [*hairetōterai*] to gold, [β] and nests [*nossiai*] of understanding are preferable to silver." Heb *qnwt* was misread (or interpreted) as *qinnôt* "nests," though it was rendered correctly elsewhere. LXX had *qnwt* in its source text in 16a too, a normalization of the rare inf. cst. *qᵉnōh*. The exclamatory *mh* is missing. It may be a dittog. in MT, but it must be noted that a similar *mh* is not reflected in LXX 30:13 either, so it may have been omitted for the sake of the Gk syntax. Gk *hairetōterai* = *nbḥr* (MT *ṭôb*), as in 22:1. Vul's *quia* may be a way of treating MT's exclamatory *mh*.

16:17. LXX "[α] The ways of life turn away from evils, [β] and the ways of righteousness are length of life. [γ] He who receives instruction will be in good (fortune), [δ] and he who keeps reproof will become wise. [ε] He who keeps his ways guards his own soul, [ζ] and the one who loves his life will restrain his mouth." V 17[α] ≈ MT 17a. V 17[ε] ≈ MT 17b. In 17[ε] the dir. objects *npšw* and *drkw* are switched because it is more logical to say that a behavior (watching one's way) has a reward (preserving one's life) than the other way around. A scribe (Heb or Gk) has split the couplet and inserted the other stichoi, making three couplets.

16:19. Syr: (a) "Better is one humble of spirit and humble of eyes." "Humble of eyes" (*mkyk ʿyn'*[pl]) = *ʿynym*, by metathesis for *ʿnyym* (ketiv). "Humble" is repeated out of necessity.

Ketiv *ʿnyym*, qeré *ʿănāwîm*.

Variant: *ʿynym*.

16:21. LXX: "[α] (People) call the wise and intelligent base, [β] but those who are sweet in word shall hear more" ([α] *tous sophous kai synetous phaulous kalousin,* [β] *hoi de glykeis en logǭ pleiona akousontai*). "Wise and intelligent" is a double rendering of *ḥkm lb* (see the Note on 15:17). LXX's strange sentence presupposes *nbl* "knave" (Gk *phaulous*) for MT's *nbwn*. (Confusion between *lamed* and *nun* is not frequent, but see Kennedy *1928*: 89; cf. 20:13.) LXX *akousontai* understands *lqḥ* as "taking in," that is, hearing.

Variant: *nbl* (MT *nābôn*).

16:22. LXX: "$^{\alpha}$ Cognition [*ennoia*] is a spring of life to (its) possessors [*tois kektēmenois*], $^{\beta}$ but the education of fools is bad [*kakē*]." LXX eliminates the tautology of MT ("the education of fools is folly") by changing "folly" to "bad," meaning that it is worthless; there is no point in even trying. The source-text apparently had *lbʿlyw* "for its possessor(s)" for *bʿlyw* "its possessor(s)," a dittog. of initial *l*. Either variant is possible.

Syr: "(b) and discipline/punishment of fools is contempt [*šyṭwtʾ*]."

Variant: *lbʿlyw* (MT *bᵉʿālāyw*).

16:23. LXX: "$^{\alpha}$ The heart of the wise man will understand [*noēsei*] the things that come from his own mouth [*ta apo tou idiou stomatos*], and will carry intelligence [*phoresei epignōmosynēn*] on (his) lips." The wise man understands what he is saying rather than babbling mindlessly. Stich $^{\beta}$ uses unique equivalances for *ysyp* and *lqḥ*.

16:24. LXX: "$^{\alpha}$ Beautiful words are honeycombs [*kēria melitos*], $^{\beta}$ and their sweetness is a healing of the soul [*glykasma de autōn iasis psychēs*]." The last phrase overrides MT's word order and treats *lnpš mrpʾ* as if it were *wmtqw lnpš* [or *lnpšw*] *mrpʾ* (Baum.); see the Note on 15:26. MT's *ʿṣm* "bone" was left without function and was not translated.

Variants: *mtqw* (MT *mātôq*); *mrpʾ* (MT *ûmarpēʾ*).

16:25. LXX: "$^{\alpha}$ There are ways that seem to be [*dokousai einai*] straight to a man. $^{\beta}$ Their ends, however, look into the depths of Hades [*blepei eis pythmena hᾳdou*]." LXX interprets this verse as in 14:12, q.v.

Syr *wšbylyh*^{pl} "their paths" for MT's *wʾḥryth*; see the Note on 14:12, where Syr uses a different wording.

16:26. LXX: "$^{\alpha}$ A man of [lit., "in"] toils toils for himself $^{\beta}$ and pushes away his destruction [*apoleian*]. $^{\gamma}$ The perverse one, however, bears destruction on his own mouth." LXX understands *npš* as "person," "man." In 26$^{\beta}$ and $^{\gamma}$, "his destruction" = *pydw* (Lag.). Gk had *pydw* in its source text in 26$^{\beta}$, and $^{\gamma}$ is a moralizing elaboration that shows awareness of both *pyhw* and *pydw*. LXX avoids the implication that toil is forced or harmful.

Syr: "(a) A person who causes suffering—he has sufferings, (b) and from his own mouth destruction comes upon him." Syr places an unusual construction on Heb *ʿml* and *ʿmlh* to avoid giving the impression that someone who works hard harms himself. The verse becomes a maxim on self-wrought retribution.

Variants: *pydw* (MT *pîhû*).

16:27. For MT *ṣrbt* "scorching," LXX has *thēsaurizei* "stores up" = *ṣābār* (Jäg.) or *ṣōbēr*. The Gk is structured like MT 26b.

Ketib *śptyw*; qeré *śᵉpātô*.

Variant: *ṣbr* (MT *ṣārābet*).

16:28. LXX: "$^{\alpha}$ A perverse man spreads evils [*kaka*] about, $^{\beta}$ and kindles a torch of deceit by evil deeds [or "for evil people" (*kakois*)] and separates friends." *Kaka* = *mdwn* "strife," sim. to 13:10 (*ryb*) and 18:6 (*zdwn*). The word-choice emphasizes the scope of the damage. In $^{\beta}$, *lamptēra* treats the first two letters of *nrgn* as *nēr*. The continuation, *dolou pyrseuei kakois*, has no connection with the MT but develops the fire imagery implicit in "torch." Vul translates *ʾlwp* as *principes* "princes."

Syr (a) = MT; (b) "and a worthless man [*sryq'*] persecutes [*rdp*] friends." "Persecutes" = *mrdp*, for *mpryd*.

Variant: *mrdp* (MT *maprîd*).

16:30. LXX: "α Fixing his eyes, he plans crooked things. β He marks out with his lips all the evils. γ This one is a furnace of evil." The LXX pictures the lawless man as staring while he cogitates his schemes. "All the evils" = *kl hrʿh*, for MT's *klh rʿh* "completes evil." LXX handles similar phraseology quite differently in 6:13–14.

Variant: *kl hrʿh* (MT *killah rāʿāh*).

16:32. LXX = MT, but using "anger" instead of "spirit" for greater specificity. BA speaks of the "Stoic spirit" of this verse, reminding us that some Stoic qualities are native to Hebrew (and other) Wisdom, and when they appear in the LXX they should not be too quickly ascribed to external influences.

16:33. LXX: "α Everything comes into the bosom for the unjust [pl.], β and from the Lord are all just things." So as not to give credibility to lot-casting (which was a common way of inquiring of foreign gods), the translator transforms the verse into a new proverb. See the Note on 18:18.

17:1. LXX: "α Better a morsel with pleasure in peace [*meth' hēdonēs en eirēnę̄*] β than a house full [*plērēs*; B lacks] of many good things and unrighteous sacrifices with contention." An expansive translation, showing the influence of 16:8 (*meta adikias*). The translation in effect fills out the "better than" template described in the excursus after 15:17.

17:2. For MT's *bn mbyš* "a disappointing son," LXX uses "foolish masters" (*despotōn aphronōn*). This creates an antithetical pair "servant"/"masters" and heightens the assertion: Not only will this servant rule the foolish son, he will rule over his own master (Giese 1992b: 408).

17:3. LXX: "α As silver and gold are tested in a furnace, β so are hearts chosen [*eklektai*] by the Lord." For MT's *bōḥen* "tests," LXX has *eklektai* "chosen," which probably reflects *bḥr* in the source text, where it would have been an Aramaism meaning "test" (used in Prov 10:20; Sir 4:27; Isa 48:10). LXX misread it as standard Hebrew *bḥr* "to choose." This is not certain, however, since *'bn bḥn* is translated *lithon polytelē eklekton* in Isa 28:16, which ascribes the sense of "chosen" to *bḥn*. As it often does, the LXX supplies coordinating adverbs; for example, 21:1; 25:14, 16, 19, 20; 26:14.

17:4. LXX: In 4β "a righteous man does not hearken" is a converse translation of MT's "deceit [= deceitful man] hearkens," creating an antithesis, as often; see the Note on 11:7. LXX transposes "tongue" and "lip(s)."

17:5. LXX adds a third line, 5γ: "But he who shows compassion will receive mercy." The line is added to enhance the teaching of compassion as well as to create an antithesis to 5α.

17:6a. LXX: "α To the faithful person (belongs) the entire world of possessions, β but to the unfaithful one, not a penny." An independent saying, whose syntax indicates Gk origin. Most MSS add this to v 4, but LXX[B] appends it to v 6. The wealth in question is spiritual; see the Commentary.

17:7. LXX: "α Trustworthy lips [*cheilē pista*] do not befit [*ouch harmosei*] a fool, nor deceitful lips the righteous (man)." Since MT's *śpt ytr* "excessive speech" (lit., "lip") is not difficult, it is likely that LXX read *yōšer* (BHS), though *pistos* is not used elsewhere for *yšr*. While "trustworthy lips" provides an antithesis to the parallel phrase, it does not make good sense, for a fool would not have trustworthy lips, and if he did, they *would* befit him, like everybody else. Gk *ouch harmosei* here means "do not naturally accompany," hence "do not befit."

17:8. LXX: "$^{\alpha}$ Instruction [*hē paideia*] is a reward of grace for those who use (it), $^{\beta}$ and wherever it turns, it succeeds." Or: $^{\beta}$ and wherever he turns he succeeds," with the implicit subject being *one* who uses instruction, despite the shift of number. In either case, LXX steers away from MT's praise of bribes.

Syr avoids praise of bribes by translating: "(a) A stone of loves [*k'p' drḥm*$^{\text{c'pl}}$] is beautiful in the eyes of whomever it belongs to, (b) and wherever it [fem.] turns, it is intelligence [*swkl' hy*]."

17:9. LXX's *misei* "hates" misconstrues *šnh* as *śn'*. *Philous kai oikeious* "friends and kin" is a double translation of *'lwp* "friend."

17:10. LXX: "$^{\alpha}$ A threat breaks the heart of a prudent (man), $^{\beta}$ but a fool, (even when) beaten, does not perceive." Heb *tḥt* is understood as a causative H (*tāḥēt*), as if from *ḥ–t–t*. Heb *g'r* is rendered *apeilē* in 13:8; Isa 50:2; 54:9. "Does not perceive" (or "take notice") is a guess for *m'h* "hundred," which became obscure once *tḥt* was assumed to be causative.

17:11. LXX: "$^{\alpha}$ Every bad man stirs up conflicts [*antilogias*], $^{\beta}$ and the Lord will send out a merciless angel against him." LXX takes *mry* "rebellion" as the dir. obj. in 11$^{\alpha}$ and clarifies 11$^{\beta}$ by introducing "the Lord" as the subject of *yšlḥ*, understood as G, *yišlaḥ*.

17:12. LXX: "$^{\alpha}$ Cares will befall an intelligent man, $^{\beta}$ but fools are preoccupied with evils" ($^{\alpha}$ *empeseitai merimna andri noēmoni*, $^{\beta}$ *hoi de aphrones dialogiountai kaka*). Jäg. retroverts 12$^{\alpha}$ to *pgwš d'bh b'yš śkl*. Strangely, in 28:15 *db* is associated with Aram *d'b'* "wolf," while here it is associated with Heb *d'bh* "worry." Perhaps *d'b'* was already in the source-text here, possibly as an exegetical replacement for MT's *db*. This variant forced a strained translation of the rest of the line and produced an idea contrary to the usual assumptions of the book (though LXX 17:10 does concede the occasional vulnerability of the wise). (Gk *andri noēmi* may simply be ignoring the Heb word order; see the Note on 16:15.) Given these uncertainties, further retroversion is not feasible. The point of the saying in the LXX is that the intelligent man is not immune to worries, but a fool preoccupies himself with wickedness and thus puts himself into the sphere of evil. Thus *w'l ksyl* was understood as elliptical for "and (cares fall) upon [*'el*] a fool."

Variant: *d'bh* (MT *dōb*).

17:13. LXX, Syr = qeré.

Ketiv *tmyš*, qeré *tāmûš*.

17:14. LXX: "$^{\alpha}$ Righteous rule gives authority to words, $^{\beta}$ but sedition and strife precede poverty." LXX is a guess at a difficult verse. It connects to the MT only in miscellaneous words. LXX's *logois* = *mlym* "words" for MT's *mym* "water." In spite of the confusion, the validity of this reading is supported by the idiom in Ps 22:8b (Jäg). LXX's source text should have been translated, "$^{\alpha}$ Releasing words starts a quarrel." See the Comment. Syr reads *dmym* "blood" for *mym* (distorted dittog. of the *reš* of *pwṭr*).

Variants: *mlym*; *dmym* (MT *mayim*).

17:15. LXX: "$^{\alpha}$ He who judges the unjust just and the just unjust $^{\beta}$ is impure and disgusting [*akathartos kai bdeluktos*] to God." $^{\beta}$ has a double translation of *twʿbt* "abomination," perhaps for the sake of quantitative balance (Gerleman 1956: 25). Gk *theǭ* for YHWH. LXX speaks of one person in $^{\alpha}$, hence ignores *šnyhm* "both of them."

17:16. LXX: "$^{\alpha}$ Why do valuables belong to a fool [*hina ti hypērxen chrēmata aphroni ktēsasthai*], $^{\beta}$ since a mindless (man) will not be able to acquire wisdom?" Paraphrastic, with the break after *lqnwt*. Syr: "(a) Why has property [*qnynʾ*] come to the fool." LXX and Syr (sim. Vul.) think of the money (Heb *mḥyr*) as wealth that the fool has received—probably inherited—rather than as a payment for tuition.

17:16a. LXX: "$^{\alpha}$ He who raises high [*hypsēlon poiei*] his own house seeks disaster [*syntribēn*], $^{\beta}$ and he who turns aside from learning will fall into evils." LXX 17:16a$^{\alpha}$ ≈ MT 17:19b. "His house" rather than the latter's "his door" (*pitḥô*) gives a clearer image of haughtiness. 16a$^{\beta}$ represents (and paraphrases) a few words dislocated from v 20a, namely *wʿqš lb ypl brʿ*.

17:17. LXX: "$^{\alpha}$ For every occasion [*kairon*], you should have [*hyparchetō soi*] a friend, $^{\beta}$ and let (your) brothers be useful in tribulations [*anagkais*], $^{\gamma}$ because for this were they born." LXX turns MT's statement into counsel but is to the point. Stichs 17$^{\beta\gamma}$ explain MT 17b expansively.

17:18. LXX: "$^{\alpha}$ A foolish man applauds and takes pleasure in himself, $^{\beta}$ and like one giving surety he gives surety for his." Heb *twqʿ kp* "strikes the hand" is translated twice in $^{\alpha}$ and is understood as an expression of joy, as in Ps 47[46]:2, where *tqʿw kp* is rendered *krotēsate cheiras* ("you shall clap hands"). The strained translation in $^{\beta}$ results from the assumption that the guarantor is offering surety *for* his friend, as in LXX 6:1. Syr ≈ MT.

17:19–21. LXX shapes these verses into three couplets, whose pairing is marked by the particle *de* (BA): 19–20$^{\alpha}$, 20$^{\beta}$–21$^{\alpha}$, and 21$^{\beta}$–21$^{\gamma}$. MT 19b is after LXX 17:16.

17:19. LXX: "A sin-lover [*philamartēmōn*] enjoys [*chairei*] conflicts" (continues in v 20). MT 17:19b: see 17:16a.

17:20. LXX: "$^{\alpha}$ and the hard-hearted man does not meet up with good [pl.]. $^{\beta}$ A man changeable in tongue [*anēr eumetabolos glōssę̄*] will fall into evils." LXX makes *nhpk blšwnw* (lit., "he who turns about on his tongue") into a broader category. See the Note on 17:16a$^{\beta}$. Syr: "(a) He whose heart is oppressed [*ʿšyq*] does not find good." Syr *ʿšyq* = *ʿšq*, understood as *ʿāšûq*. Syr's awkward reading arose by a metathesis that was certainly not exegetical.

Variant: *ʿšq* (MT *ʿiqqēš*).

17:21. LXX: "$^{\alpha}$ and the heart of the fool is a grief to its begetter. $^{\beta}$ A father does not rejoice over an uneducated son, $^{\gamma}$ but a prudent son makes his mother rejoice." Stich $^{\alpha}$ continues the preceding verse. *Kardia de aphronos* = *yld lb* (Jäg.). Stich $^{\gamma}$, added for the sake of antithesis (Baum.), is based on, and reverses, 10:1bc. Vul: *natus est stultus in ignominiam suam* "the fool is born [i.e., *yullād*] to his (own) disgrace."

Variant: *yld lb* (MT yōlēd).

17:22. LXX: "$^{\alpha}$ A happy heart puts (one) in good health [*euektein poiei*], $^{\beta}$ but the bones of a sorrowful man dry up." Free but accurate. Vul translates the obscure *ghh* as *aetatem* "age." Sym has *hēlikian*, "age" or (as here) "stature" (*gōbahh*). Syr understands Heb *ghh* as *gwšmʾ* "body," probably by association (correctly?) with Heb *g*^{e}*wiyyāh* "body."

17:23. LXX: "$^{\alpha}$ The ways of him who unjustly takes gifts in the bosom do not prosper, $^{\beta}$ and a wicked man perverts the ways of righteousness." Though the verse is translated freely, we can retrovert *en kolpǭ* to *bḥyq*. Heb *ršʿ* "evildoer" was first understood as *rešaʿ*, used adverbially, then used as the subject of 24^{β}. LXX construes *lhṭwt* as a participle and adds *asebēs* "wicked" for the sense. According to Fritsch (1953: 180), the clause *adikōs ou kateuodountai hodoi* is OG, whereas *ekklinei hodous dikaiosynēs,* though unmarked, is a hexaplaric addition based on Sym's *ekklinein hodous.*

Variant: *bḥyq* (MT *mēḥêq*).

17:24. LXX: "$^{\alpha}$ The intelligent countenance of a wise man [*prosōpon syneton andros sophou* ^{AB}], $^{\beta}$ but the eyes of the fool are on [*ep'*] the ends of the earth." In $^{\alpha}$, we should read *prosōpon synetou andros sophon* ($^{103, 147, 253}$), "The countenance of the intelligent man is wise" (Lag.).

Syr: "(b) but the eyes of the fool are in the depths [*bʿwmqyh*^{pl}] of the earth." Syr's "in the depths" (for MT's *bqṣh* "in the end") alludes to the underworld and hints that this is the fool's (early) destination.

Many MSS K-R normalize *ʾāreṣ* as *hāʾāreṣ.*

17:26. LXX: "$^{\beta}$ nor is it pious to scheme against righteous princes" (*oude hosion epibouleuein dynastais dikaiois*). It is hard to relate 26^{β} to the MT except for the (discontinuous) words *ndybym* "princes" and *yšr* "righteousness." See the Note on 16:15. LXX makes loyalty to princes a religious duty.

17:27. LXX: In $^{\alpha}$ "harsh" is added to explain what kind of words should be curbed. Syr *dngyrʾ rwḥh* "whose spirit is patient" = MT ketiv *qr rwḥ*.

Ketiv *wqr*, qeré *y*^{e}*qar.*

17:28. LXX: "$^{\alpha}$ Wisdom will be reckoned to the unintelligent (man) who consults wisdom, $^{\beta}$ and whoever makes himself mute [*eneon*] will be thought to be prudent." The translator understood *mḥryš* ("be silent") in the extended sense of "be quiet and pay attention," as in Isa 41:1. Heb *ḥkm* is translated twice, by *sophian* and *sophia*, perhaps representing a dittog *ḥkm ḥkmh*. The message is that the ignorant and dull can and should consult wisdom, that is, the wise.

Variant: *ḥkm ḥkmh* (MT *ḥākām*).

18:1. LXX: "$^{\alpha}$ A man who wishes to separate himself from friends seeks pretexts [*prophaseis*] $^{\beta}$ and at all times he will be disgraced [*eponeidistos*]." Gk *prophaseis* = *ltʾnh* (*l*^{e}*tōʾănāh*) (Cappellus, ref. Lag.).

Syr: "(a) And in silence he thinks about desire (b) and mocks good instruction." Syr continues 17:28a, which describes the fool who is able to keep silent. He is merely preoccupied with his cravings and lusts [*rnʾ brgtʾ*]; see 18:2b. Syr *mmyq* "mocks" translates *ytglʿ*, as in 20:3. Sim. Tg *mṣṭdy* "is ridiculed," here and in 20:3.

Variants: *ltʾnh* (MT *l*^{e}*taʾăwāh*).

18:2. LXX: "α He who lacks good sense [pl.] has no use for wisdom, β because he is instead led by folly." LXX 2β is based on the idea that the fool inevitably reveals his heart, that is, displays its folly (12:23).

Syr: "The fool does not desire wisdom, because his heart thinks about folly [*mṭl drn' lbh bšṭywt'*]." This continues the theme of the silent fool, despite a clear Heb text to the contrary.

18:3. LXX: "α When a wicked man comes to the depth of evils [*eis bathos kakōn*] he shows scorn, β and dishonor and disgrace come upon him." "To the depth of evils" paraphrases *b'gm* (*bᵉ'āgām*), lit., "in a pool" (Jäg.), instead of MT's *b' gm* "enters too," which would have been easy to translate. The translator was influenced by "deep waters" in the next verse.

Variant *b'gm* (MT *bā' gām-*).

18:4. For MT's "fountain of wisdom" LXX has "a fountain of life" (*pēgē zōēs*). It is impossible to determine if the latter was in the Hebrew source-text, and, if so, whether it was the original form or an adaptation to the more common *mᵉqôr ḥayyîm* (10:11; 13:14; 14:27). These differences could have arisen in the course of translation or in the Heb transmission. Several Heb MSS have *ḥayyîm*, which almost certainly is an adjustment, probably accidental, to the expected idiom.

18:6. LXX: "α The lips of a fool lead him to evils, β and his rash mouth calls to death [or "summons death")" (α *cheilē aphronos agousin auton eis kaka*, β *to de stoma autou to thrasu thanaton epikaleitai*). Gk vocalizes *yābî'û* (MT *yābō'û*) or perhaps represents *yby'w*. In β, *to thrasu thanaton* represents *hhmhlmwt* (i.e., *hāhōmeh lammāwet*). Heb *hmwyh* is translated *thraseia* in 9:13. This is a scrambling of MT's consonants, *lmhlmwt* (*lᵉmahălumôt*). The first three letters of *lmhlmwt* were lost by parablepsis, due to their similarity with the following *lm*.

Syr: "The lips of the fool enter into litigation [*bdyn'*], (b) and his mouth brings him to death [*mmṭ' lh lmwt'*]." Syr is independent of LXX in this verse. Hence Syr's *lmwt'* is an independent witness to a Heb variant, *lmwt*, which must have arisen by parablepsis in *lm*[*hlm*]*wt*, skipping over *hlm* because of the repeated *lm*.

Variants: *hhmh lmwt* (MT *lᵉmahălumôt*); *lmwt* (MT *lᵉmahălumôt*).

18:8. LXX: "α Fear casts lazy people down, β and the souls of effeminate (men) [*androgynōn*] will starve." This is a reworking of MT 19:15. The translation there, however, is quite different. Vul translates *nrgn* as *bilinguis* "two-tongued."

18:9. LXX: "α He who does not heal [*iōmenos*] himself by his labors β is the brother of the one who harms himself [*lymainomenou eauton*]." Since LXX could easily have understood *mtrph* as "slack off," its natural sense in this context, the source text probably had *mtrp'* (= some Heb MSS). This reading forced the addition of the negative and created a rather awkward statement.

Variant: *mtrp'* (MT *mitrappeh*).

18:11. LXX: "α The property of a rich man is a strong city, β and its honor gives much shade." LXX must have read *wkbwdh* (*ûkᵉbôdāhh*) for MT's *wkḥwmh* ("and like a wall") (Hitzig) because *ḥwmh* presents no problem. In 11β, LXX's "shadow" associates MT's *wbmśkytw* with *ś-k-k* "to cover over." Sim. Vul *circumdans eum* "surrounding him."

Syr: "(a) Glory and wealth is the city of his strength, (b) and within a strong wall is his dwelling." Syr v 11 continues the description of the rewards of the righteous man and avoids praise of wealth, which seemed devoid of a moral component.

18:14. LXX: "[α] A sensible servant eases a man's anger, [β] but who will bear a discouraged [*oligopsychon*] man?" Heb *mḥlhw* is associated with *y-ḥ-l* "implore" and understood as one who treats others in an obsequious and dutiful manner (Jäg.). The LXX here teaches a rather subtle lesson: Although it is prudent to appease one's master's anger, lack of confidence just irritates people.

18:15. Syr: *tqnʾ* "steady" = Heb *nkwn* for the similar-looking *nbwn*.

Variant: *nkwn* (MT *nābôn*).

18:17. LXX: "[α] A righteous man is his own opponent at the start of the plea [*prōtologią̄*], [β] but when the litigant responds, he [the latter] is refuted." *Prōtologia* is the prosecutor's right to speak first (GELS). Gk *epiballein* here means "respond to an accusation," and *elegchein* has its classical sense of "refute," "disprove" (BA). Using technical judicial terminology, the verse says that the righteous man can effectively plead his own case and rebut accusations. Righteousness endows a man with rhetorical powers.

Ketiv *ybʾ*, qeré *ûbāʾ*.

18:18. LXX: "[α] A silent man [*sigēros* [ABS*, MSS]; var. "the lot" *klēros* [ScV, MSS]] stops [*pauei*] conflicts"; [β] = MT. Contrary to Rahlfs, it is *klēros* "lot" that is the correction (SyrH *psʾ*), while *sigērōs* is OG. The latter is motivated by a hesitation to praise lot-casting; sim. 16:33.

18:19. LXX: "[α] A brother helped by a brother is like a fortified and lofty city, [β] and is as strong as a well-founded palace." This is something of a guess at an obscure verse. Nevertheless, *boēthoumenos* can be plausibly retroverted to *nwšʿ* (lit., "is saved," i.e., "helped") and *hōs polis* to *kqryt*. Gk *boēthein* renders *y-š-ʿ* (H) in, for example, Deut 22:7, 27; 28:29, 31; Josh 10:6; and most significantly (N) in Prov 28:18.

The frequent ketiv-qeré pair *mdwnym-midyānîm* occurs in 18:19; 21:19; 23:29; 25:24; 26:21; and 27:15. Prov 6:14 and 19 have a related variant pair: ketiv *mdnym*, qeré *midyānîm*. In the plural, this pair is a peculiarity of Proverbs. (The singular occurs in 2 Sam 21:20.) This pair is too frequent to be explained as scribal error in either direction, but its cause and significance have not been accounted for. It would seem to reflect the merging of two textual traditions.

Ketiv *wmdwnym*, qeré *ûmidyānîm*.

Variants: *nwšʿ* (MT *nipšāʿ*); *kqryt* (MT *miqqiryat*); *wmrwmym* (MT *wmdwnym*, ketiv).

18:20. LXX's "and from the fruits" for MT's *t*^{e}*bûʾat* "the produce of" (his lips) was influenced by the phrase "the fruit of the mouth" (*pry py-*) in 20a as well as 12:14a and 13:2a.

18:21. LXX: "and those who seize it" (*hoi de kratountes autēs*) = *wʾḥzyh* (*w*^{eʾ}*ōḥăzeyhā*) (Jäg.).

Variant: *wʾḥzyh* (MT *w*^{eʾ}*ōhăbeyhā*).

18:22. LXX: "[α] He who has found a good wife [*gynaika agathēn*] has found favor [pl.] [*charitas*] [β] and has received cheerfulness [*hilarotēta*] from God." LXX makes it clear that only a good woman (for MT's "a woman"/"wife") is intended;

likewise Vul and a Heb MS add "good," as do quotations in *b. Ber.* 8a; *b. Yeb.* 63b; *Mid. Shoḥer Ṭov* 151ab. Hexaplaric "others" have *chrēstēn* "good," "useful." Syr: *ʾnttʾ ṭbtʾ "good* wife" in (a) = LXX; likewise Tg. The diversity of these sources suggests that *ṭwbh* "good" was supplied in some Heb MSS. The medieval commentators also emphasize this point.

18:22a. LXX: "α He who expels a good wife expels happiness [lit., "the good"; pl.], β but he who retains an adulteress is foolish and wicked." LXX 22aα is a variant translation of MT 22a, also with *ṭwbh* "good" (wife). The Gk vocalizes *mōṣîʾ* ("expel") twice. LXX 22aβ is a later addition (see below, on Syr) that supplies an antithesis to 22aα. Vul has 22aαβ.

Syr has only: "And he who expels a good wife expels good from his house." If Syr were dependent on the LXX here, it would have copied the entire added verse. Since it does not copy LXX's 22aβ, it probably had the equivalent of LXX 22aα in its source text (perhaps without "from his house"). This variant had either *mwṣyʾ* (*y-ṣ-ʾ* H, ptcp.) or *mwṣʾ* parsed as *y-ṣ-ʾ* H, ptcp.

Variant: *mwṣ(y)ʾ ʾšh ṭwbh mwṣyʾ ṭwb* [additional line].

18:23. OG lacks.

18:24. OG lacks. Syr: "(a) There are [*ʾyt*] those who are friends." Syr construes *ʾyš* as "there is," in accordance with the sebirin (see the Comment).

Sebirin *yēš* for *ʾyš*.

19:1. LXX lacks. In v 1b, where MT has "than a man of crooked lips who is foolish," some Vul MSS read *quam diues torquens labia* [var. + *sua*] *insipiens*. This is independent of Syr, but it is unclear whether Jerome took it from another Hebrew MS or from MT 28:6b.

Syr: "(b) more than a rich man whose ways are twisted." Syr (b) = Heb *mʿqš drkyw whwʾ ʿšyr* = MT 28:6b, but with *drkyw* instead of *drkym*, as the MT has there. Since the MT is easily translatable and ideologically unexceptionable, it is likely that Syr had a different source-text, with *ʿšyr* and *drkyw*.

Variants: variant line in 1b (≈ 28:6b); *drkyw* (MT *śᵉpātāyw*); *ʿšyr* (MT *kᵉsîl*).

19:2. LXX lacks.

19:6. LXX: "α Many serve the faces of kings [var. "king"], β but every bad man becomes a reproach to (another) man." Similar phraseology occurs in 29:26α, where *therapeusousin* = *mbqšym*, lit. "seek." LXX has "kings" for MT's *ndyb* "noble." As in 25:15; 28:16; and 29:12, the translation elevates the status of a high-ranking person (*qāṣîn, nādîb, môšēl*) to royalty so as to underscore the seriousness of the advice. In 6β, *oneidos* = *mdwn* for MT's *mtn* (GELS) and *kakos* construes *hrʿ* as *hārāʿ*.

Variant: *mdwn* (MT *mattān*).

19:7. LXX: "α Everyone who hates a poor brother β will also be far from friendship. γ Good understanding will come near those who know it, δ and a sensible man will find it. ϵ He who does much evil fully accomplishes evil, ζ and he who gives provocation (by) words will not be saved" (α *pas hos adelphon ptōchon misei* β *kai philias makran estai* γ *ennoia agathē tois eidosin autēn eggiei* δ *anēr de phronimos heurēsei autēn* ϵ *ho polla kakopoiōn telesiourgei kakian* ζ *hos de erethizei logous* [*logois* Complut. MSS] *ou sōthēsetai*).

The first couplet, $7^{\alpha\beta}$, converts a cynical assertion into a moral lesson, partly by ignoring the word order and treating the morphology loosely.

The second couplet, $7^{\gamma\delta}$, is an independent proverb absent from the MT. It can be retroverted to $^{\gamma}$ *śkl ṭwb lywdʿyw,* $^{\delta}$ *wʾyš tbwnh ymṣʾnw* ("$^{\gamma}$ There will be good regard for those who know it, $^{\delta}$ and the man of good sense will attain it").

The third couplet, $7^{\epsilon\zeta}$, probably had a Heb source. The idiom *telesiourgei kakian* = *klh rʿh* (see 1 Sam 20:7–9; 25:17). It is impossible to retrovert the rest of the sentence, which is unfortunate because MT 7c is an isolated fragment (*mrdp ʾmrym lʾ hmh*) and LXX $7^{\epsilon\zeta}$ might hold within it the lost mate of MT 7c. Stich 7^{ζ} is related to the enigmatic MT 7c only by *logois* = *ʾmrym*.

Ketiv (7c) *lʾ*, qeré *lô*.

Variants: Two additional couplets.

19:12. LXX: "$^{\alpha}$ The threat of a king is like a bite of a lion."

19:13. LXX: "$^{\alpha}$ A foolish son is a disgrace [*aischynē*] to his father, $^{\beta}$ and vows [*euchai*] (paid) from a harlot's wages are not sacred." The verse looks like a cautionary response to 7:14, in which the woman says, "I have peace offerings. Today I pay my vows [*euchas*]." LXX's *aischynē* "disgrace" for *hwt* "disaster" is probably influenced by knowledge of what a foolish son is said to do in 19:26 and 29:15. LXX $19{:}13^{\beta}$—or its Heb source-text—substitutes a teaching based on Deut 23:18–19 for the MT, perhaps to make a statement of greater moral weight (contrast 27:15). The association with Deuteronomy may have been cued by a textual variant in the Heb of v 13b, perhaps *ndr* "vow" for *ṭrd* and/or *mndny* "from the gifts" (see Ezek 16:33) for *mdyny* "quarrels" (D. A. Teeter, personal communication). LXX^{A}, continuing the ancient practice of combining monostichs into new proverbs, adds after 13^{α}, *kai odunę tę tekousē autou* "and misery to his mother," from $17{:}25^{\beta}$.

19:14. LXX: "$^{\alpha}$ Fathers bequeath a house and possession(s) to sons, $^{\beta}$ but by God a woman is matched [or "betrothed"] to a man [*harmozetai gynē andri*]." A midrash says that God has been arranging marriages ever since creation (Ber. Rab §68). The translation of *mśklt* as "matched" may be playing on *ś-k-l* "cross," hence "interleave."

19:15. LXX: "$^{\alpha}$ Timidity [*deilia*] seizes the effeminate (man) [*androgynaion*], $^{\beta}$ and the soul of the lazy [*aergou*] will starve." Heb *trdmh* (actually "deep sleep") is understood to mean fear also in LXX Gen 15:12 and Prov 18:8. The lazy man is called "effeminate" just as the diligent one is called *andreios*, that is, possessing the manly virtues (10:4; 13:4; etc.). BA sees an affiliation between 19:14–15 and Plato's *Symposium* 189de, which speaks of man, woman, and androgynous as the three primordial human types.

19:16. LXX, Syr ≈ MT (qeré).

Ketiv *ywmt*, qeré *yāmût*.

19:17. Syr "(a) He who joins himself [vocalizing as *m^{e}luwweh*] to the Lord has compassion for the poor."

19:18. LXX: "$^{\beta}$ and do not lift up your soul to arrogance [*hybrin*]." LXX vocalizes *hemyātô* for MT's *hămîtô* "to his death" Cf. *hybristikon* = *hmh* in 20:1.

19:19. LXX: "$^{\alpha}$ A malicious man will be severely punished, $^{\beta}$ and if he is pestilent [*loimeuētai*] he will also add [*prosthēsei*] (punishment) to his soul." *Loimeuētai* =

ylyṣ, for MT *tṣyl* (Lag.) or possibly *tlyṣ*, which is ungrammatical but closer to the MT. Compare how LXX treats *twsp* in 19b as 3rd per. masc. sg.; sim. 19:25, etc. Syr *mʿlʾ* "sin" (MT *tṣyl*) = *tlyṣ*, but may be influenced by LXX.

Ketiv *grl*, qeré *gᵉdol*.

Variant: *ylyṣ* or *tlyṣ* (MT *taṣṣîl*).

19:20. LXX: "ᵅ Hear, son, the instruction of your father" = *šmʿ bny mwsr ʾbyk*, taken from 1:8a, either in the Heb source text or in the Gk.

Syr (b) *bʾwrḥtk*ᵖˡ "in your ways" = *bʾḥrytyk*

Variant: *bʾḥrytyk* (MT *bʾḥrytk*)

19:21. LXX ᵝ + *eis ton aiōna* "for ever," as in Ps 33[32]:11.

19:22. LXX: "ᵅ Kindness is fruit for a man. ᵝ And better a righteous poor man than a rich liar" (ᵅ *karpos andri eleēmosynē*, ᵝ *kreissōn de ptōchos dikaios ē plousios pseustēs*). Gk *karpos* = *tbwʾh*, lit., "produce"; cf. LXX 10:16 and 15:6. The added *dikaios* "righteous" makes it clear that only the *honest* poor man is superior to the liar. The added "rich" makes the contrast more specific and less banal. Syr ≈ LXX.

Variant: *tbwʾt* (MT *taʾăwat-*).

19:23. LXX: "ᵅ The fear of the Lord is for the life of a man, ᵝ but the unfearing [*aphobos*] will dwell in places where knowledge [*gnōsis*] does not visit." Heb *śbʿ* "sated" is understood to mean overconfident, hence *aphobos* "fearless." Alternatively, "fearless" may imply lacking fear of the Lord. "Places where knowledge does not visit" are spiritual wastelands, such as are mentioned in LXX 9:12c. *Gnosis* = *dʿ* (*dēaʿ*).

Variant: *dʿ* (MT *rāʿ*).

19:24. LXX: "ᵅ He who hides (his) hands in his bosom [*kolpon*] unjustly [*adikos*] ᵝ certainly cannot bring them forth to (his) mouth." The translator misunderstood *ṣlḥt* ("dish") as "bosom" (as in 26:15ᵅ, q.v.), making this verse into a warning against taking bribes. (Rashi mentions this interpretation of *ṣlḥt*.) Consequently, MT's *ʿṣl* "sluggard" was replaced by *adikos*, to make the deed a moral issue. Alternatively, "hides his hands in his bosom" means to be stingy, like the idiom *kolpǭ cheiras echein* "to keep one's hand in one's pocket" (LSJ 974, *kolpos* II; suggested by D. A. Teeter, personal communication, comparing 11:24b).

Syr: "(a) A sluggard who hides his hands in his bosom (b) does not even bring them near to his mouth." Syr combines MT and LXX. The image in M and Syr is of a man hugging himself in inactivity, as in Qoh 4:5.

19:25. LXX: "ᵅ When a pest is beaten, a fool becomes more clever, ᵝ and if you [sg.] chastise a sensible man, he understands knowledge."

Syr: "(a) When a fool is beaten, the wise man takes warning [*ḥkymʾ mzdhr*], (b) and if you rebuke a wise man, he understands knowledge." Syr follows the syntax of LXX but translates *pty* ("callow") as *ḥkymʾ* "wise man," because it is more "logical" for a wise man than a naïf to learn a lesson. This is a good example of the subtle and flexible way in which the translator draws upon his two sources.

19:27. LXX: "ᵅ A son who ceases to keep the instruction of (his) father ᵝ will think about bad words" (ᵅ *huios apoleipomenos phylaxai paideian patros* ᵝ *meletēsei* *rhēseis kakas*). The LXX is trying to make sense of a difficult text, and it is hard to know what variants he was working with. Possible variants are *lšmr* for *lšmʿ* (*ʿ-r* confusion in the archaic script); *lšnwt* ("repeat," hence "study," as in RH) for *lšgwt*; *rʿt* (*rāʿōt*) for *dʿt*; and perhaps *bʾmry* for *mʾmry*. Vul supplies the negative *nec* in 27b.

Syr: "(a) Cease my son, and hear instruction, (b) and you will not forget words of knowledge." Syr is straining to make the text meaningful. Sim. Tg.

Variants: *lšmr* (MT *lišmōaʿ*); *lšnwt* (MT *lišgôt*); *rʿt* (MT *dāʿat*).

19:28. LXX: "α He who gives surety for a foolish child dishonors what is just [*ho egguōmenos paida aphrona kathybrizei dikaiōma*], β and the mouth of the wicked [pl.] swallows down judgments [*kriseis*]." MT's *ʿd blyʿl* became *ʿrbbnblyʿl* (Lag.) (i.e., *ʿōrēb ben beliyyaʿa*). This was a mechanical process, not an interpretive one. There would be no ethical or religious motive to convert a condemnation of a dishonest witness, however obscure the Hebrew, into a strange warning against giving surety—specifically for a foolish child—and also to condemn this not as foolish leniency but as a dishonor to justice. The very awkwardness of this advice indicates that the translator was pressured into it by his text. The translator would have had no problem rendering the MT form of 28b literally.

Syr: "(a) A wicked witness strengthens [*mʿšn*] litigation [*dynʾ*], (b) and the mouth of the evildoer swallows [*mṭbʿ lh*]"—that is, the litigation. Syr (b) ≈ LXX.

For MT's *yeballaʿ*, some conjecture *yabbîaʿ* "pours forth" for *yeballaʿ*. Tg's *mpyq* "brings forth" might seem to support this, but elsewhere Tg uses *habbēaʿ* for Heb *hibbîaʿ*.

Variants: *ʿrb bn blyʿl* (MT *ʿēd beliyyaʿal*.

19:29. LXX: "α Blows are readied for the licentious [*akolastois*]." LXX associates this verse with the following context by using *akalastos* for *lēṣîm*.

Syr: "(a) Pains are readied for those who strengthen litigation [*mʿšnyn dynʾ*] and blows for the foolish nation." Syr's *kʾbʾ*pl "pains" interprets *špṭym* as punishments, influenced by LXX. Syr *lʿmʾ* represents Heb *lgwy* (*legôy*) "for a (foolish) nation" (near-dittog. *w-y*). The same happens in LXX 26:3. *Num. Rab.* 13:6 (103a) applies this verse to foreigners, perhaps being aware of this variant and using it interpretively.

Variants: *šbṭym* (MT *šepāṭîm*); *lgwy* (MT *legēw*).

20:4. LXX: "α The sluggard when reproached [*oneidizomenos*] is not ashamed [*ouk aischynetai*], β just like the one who borrows grain in the harvest." This presupposes the vocalizations *meḥōrāp* "disgraced" and *yeḥĕrāš*, lit., "be silent." LXX *ho danizomenos* = *wšʾl* (qeré), with the *waw* understood as comparative. "Grain" (instead of MT's *wʾyn* "and there is nothing") was motivated by the new context. LXX turns a practical comment into a psychological observation. The sluggard is as brazen as one who has the nerve to borrow grain in the harvest when he had failed to plant it himself. Vul *propter frigus* "because of the cold" = *mēḥōrep*. Syr reads the qeré and includes the first word of v 5, *mym* "water."

Ketiv *yšʾl*, qeré *wešāʾal*.

20:5. LXX = MT. Syr (*mym* with preceding): "(a) A word is deep in the heart of the king." "King" for MT's *ʾyš* is influenced by 25:3. Syr *mltʾ* is based on *logos* (in place of *boulē*) found in LXX[109 147; 157 297]. This is proof that the Syr is aware of and partly dependent on the LXX.

20:6. LXX: "$^{\alpha}$ A man is great, and a merciful man is precious [*mega anthrōpos kai timion anēr*] $^{\beta}$ and it is (hard) work to find a faithful man." Gk$^{\alpha}$ = *rb (rāb) ʾdm wyqr ʾyš ḥsd*. All the differences are due to common mechanical errors. Vul *misericordes vocantur* "are called merciful" = *yqrʾ ʾyš ḥsd*, independently of LXX. Syr (a) *gbrʾ*^{pl} *mrḥmnʾ*^{pl} ("merciful men") supports *ḥsd* (understood as abstract-for-concrete) independently of LXX.

Variant: *wyqr* (MT *yiqrāʾ*); *ḥsd* (MT *ḥasdô*).

20:8. LXX: "$^{\alpha}$ When a righteous king sits on the throne, $^{\beta}$ no evil can stand [*enantioutai*] before his eyes." LXX adds a moralizing *dikaios* and omits *dyn*, though possibly deriving the notion of *dikaios* from it. In $^{\beta}$, LXX indicates the *effect* of "scattering," understanding the verb as passive, *m*^{e}*zōrāh* for MT *m*^{e}*zāreh*; sim. Syr *wmtbdrn*^{pl} "are scattered."

LXX 20:9a, 9b, 9c = MT 20:20, 21, 22, q.v.

20:10. LXX: "$^{\alpha}$ A big and a small stone, and a double measure, $^{\beta}$ both [*kai amphotera*] are unclean before the Lord . . ." (continues in 11$^{\alpha}$). Though SyrH identifies *kai amphotera* (MT *gm šnyhm*) as hexaplaric (Fritsch 1953: 177), the Heb is loosely represented in LXX 11$^{\alpha}$.

20:11. LXX: (continuing 10) "$^{\alpha}$ and he who does [*ho poiōn*; var. *hoi poiountes auta* ("they who do") LXX[23]] these things will become entangled in his [their] practices. $^{\beta}$ A youth (who goes) with a pious man—his way is straight." "He who does" or "they who do" = *gm ʿśyhm* (*ʿōśêhem*), a distortion of MT's *gm šnyhm* at the end of 10b (Jäg., Lag.). This phrase has an obelus in SyrH and is OG. *Sympodisthēsetai* "entangled," "hindered," might represent *ytlkd* (Jäg.), though the equivalence is not otherwise attested. V 11$^{\beta}$ has only vague contacts with MT 11b.

Variant: *gm ʿśyhm* (MT [10b] *gam š*^{e}*nêhem*).

20:13. LXX: "$^{\alpha}$ Do not love to babble [*katalalein*], so that you not be removed [*exarthę̄s*]." LXX's "babble" parses *šnh* (MT *šēnāh* "sleep") as some form of *šnh* "to repeat." (The Heb has this sense in 17:9, but the LXX does not recognize it there. Sim. Sir 44:15, and compare Sir 19:7, which seems to be based on the present verse.) Gk does not necessarily translate *tgrš* for MT's *twrš* (Baum.). Elsewhere *exairein* represents *y-r-š* several times (e.g., Judg 1:20, 21; 1 Kgs 13:24).

20:14–19 are lacking in OG. The absence has not been explained. They are supplied in many MSS from Theod. LXX has an equivalent of MT vv 20–22 after 20:9.

20:14. LXX lacks. Syr misconstrues *rʿ* as *rēaʿ* "friend" (twice).

20:15. LXX lacks.

20:16. LXX lacks. Syr = ketiv.

Ketiv *nkrym*, qeré *nokriyyāh*.

20:17. LXX lacks.

20:18. LXX lacks. Syr ≈ MT, but *mtʿbd* ("is done") = *tʿśh* (*tēʿāśeh*)—a haplog. of *taw*—for MT's *ʿăśēh* (impv.). In 24:6, where MT has *taʿăśeh l*^{e}*kā*, Syr also translates *mtʿbd* = *tēʿāśeh*.

Variant: *tʿśh* (MT *ʿśh*).

20:19. LXX lacks.

Syr: "(a) He who reveals a secret is a slanderer [*ʾklqrṣʾ*], (b) and he who is faithful in his spirit hides a word. (c) And with him whose lips are rash, do not mix [*wʿm mn dmwrhbn*^pl *spwth*^pl *lʾ tthlṭ*]." Syr inserts 11:13b between 19a and 19b to complement 20:19a. Syr v 19(b) is, however, omitted in some ninth- to twelfth-century Syr MSS and may well be a later addition.

20:20. LXX: "^β and the pupils of his eyes will see darkness." Heb *ʾyšwn* "darkness" (ketiv) was associated with *ʾîšôn*, "pupil" (of the eye).

Ketiv *bʾyšwn*, qeré *beʾĕšûn*.

20:21. LXX (at 20:9b) and Syr follow the qeré.

Ketiv *mbḥlt*, qeré *m*^e*bōhelet*.

20:22. LXX (at 20:9c).

20:24. Syr *dntqn* = *ykyn* for MT's *ybyn*. Syr agrees with several Heb MSS K-R.

Variant: *ykyn* (MT *yābîn*).

20:25. LXX: "^α It is a snare to a man to hastily sanctify [*tachu . . . hagiasai*] something of his own (property), ^β for after vowing comes repentance [*metanoein ginetai*]." LXX construes *ylʿ* and *lbqr* by context. Vul b: *post vota retractare* "and after vows to retract." C. Gordon (1930: 390–91) associates this translation with a rabbinic interpretation. Aq *katapietai* understands *ylʿ* as "swallow" (≈ *l-ʿ-ʿ*, cf. Ob 16; Sir 34:17). This understands the snare as the unauthorized consumption of sanctified food. Syr: "(a) It is a snare to a man that he vows to the sanctuary (b) and after he has vowed, his soul regrets it [*twyʾ lh npšh*]."

20:29. LXX uses *sophia* to translate *kḥm* "their strength," as a way of explaining the kind of strength that is truly a young man's glory: his wisdom. See the principle in LXX 24:5^α.

20:30. LXX: "^α Black eyes and fractures happen to evil (people), ^β and blows to the chambers of the belly." LXX construes *ḥbrwt pṣʿ* as two items and guesses at the obscure *tmryq*/*tmrwq*. Sym *aposmēxei kakian* "will wipe off evil," deriving *tmryq*/*tmrwq* from *m-r-q* "rub," etc. Sim. Vul: *absterget* "wipes away." Syr ≈ LXX.

Ketiv *tmryq*, qeré *tamrûq*.

21:2. LXX: "^β but the Lord guides [*kateuthynei*] hearts (aright)." Heb *tkn* is associated with *k-w-n*, which is often translated by *kateuthynein*, for example, 4:26.

21:3. LXX: "^β is preferable to the Lord than sacrifices of blood [*ē thysiōn haima*]." "Than sacrifices of blood" = *mzbḥ(y) dm*. The last word is a near-dittog. of *rwm* (v 4) (Kaminka 1931–1932: 175).

Variant: *dm* (MT lacks).

21:4. LXX: "^α An arrogant [lit., "high-minded"] man is insolent-hearted in (his) arrogance [*megalophrōn epʾ hybrei thrasykardios*]." The awkwardness in 4^α reflects *wrhb rḥb lb* (dittog.) or a double translation of *rḥb lb*. *Lamptēr* = *nēr* (written thus in some Heb MSS).

Variants: *rḥb* (MT *ûr*^e*ḥab-*); *nēr* (MT *nir*).

21:5. LXX lacks. Syr avoids the appearance of praising laziness by translating "one who hurries" as *byš'* "the wicked." Vul interprets *'ṣ* ("hurries") as *piger* ("sluggish"), assuming a contrast with *ḥrwṣ* "diligent" and perhaps sharing Syr's motivation.

21:6. LXX: "$^{\alpha}$ He who earns [*energōn* "works"] treasures by a deceitful tongue, $^{\beta}$ pursues vanities on snares of death [*mataia diōkei epi pagidas thanatou*]." LXX 6$^{\beta}$ reflects *hbl rdp bmqšy mwt* (*hebel rōdēp bᵉmōqᵉšê' māwet*) (cf. BHS).

Vul: "(b) is vain and will stumble [Heb *ndp*] on the snares of death" (*vanus est et inpingetur ad laqueos mortis*). *Ad laqueos* supports *mwqšy*, as do a few Heb MSS, and, interestingly, Rashi—exegetically if not textually. Rashi says, "These things [mentioned in 6a] are snares of death for him [*mwqšy mwt hm lw*]."

Variants: *hbl* (MT *hebel*); *rdp* (MT *niddāp*); *bmwqšy* (MT *mᵉbaqšê*).

21:7. LXX's "lodges [*epixenōthēsetai*]" derives *ygwrm* from *g-w-r* "to sojourn."

21:8. LXX: "$^{\alpha}$ God sends crooked ways to crooked (men) [*skolious*], $^{\beta}$ for pure and straight are his works." V 8$^{\alpha}$ is an attempt to paraphrase an obscure sentence. Gk *tous skolious* corresponds to *wzr*, perhaps read *zr*.

Syr: (a) *nwkry'* "alien" probably represents *zr* for *wzr* (near-dittog. *r-w*, as in 2 MSS K-R) = LXX.

Variant: *zr* (MT *wāzār*).

21:9. LXX: "$^{\alpha}$ It is better to dwell in a corner in open air [*hypaithrou*], $^{\beta}$ than in plastered (rooms) [*kekoniamenois*] with injustice and in a common house [*oikǭ koinǭ*]." Dwelling in "plastered (rooms)" indicates living in a well-built, dry house. It seems that Heb *'št mdwnym* is here interpreted as a metaphor for wickedness; compare the metaphorical treatment of the "Strange Woman" (Vol. I, 376). The same proverb is translated literally in 25:24.

21:10. LXX: "The soul of the impious [sg.] shall not receive mercy by any men." LXX omits *'wth rʿ* "desires evil," apparently a parablepsis from *ršʿ* to *rʿ*; = Syr.

Variants: lack of *'twh rʿ*; *yḥz* (MT *yuḥan*).

21:11. LXX $^{\alpha}$ = MT; "$^{\beta}$ when a wise man understands [*syniōn de sophos*]" = *wbhśkyl ḥkm* (haplog. of *lamed*).

Variant: *ḥkm* (MT *lᵉḥākām*).

21:12. LXX: "$^{\alpha}$ A righteous man understands the hearts [*kardias*] of the impious [pl.] $^{\beta}$ and despises [*phaulizei*] the impious [pl.] in evils." That is, he holds them in contempt when they fall into misfortune. Compare Lady Wisdom's behavior in 1:26–27. "Hearts" = *lbwt*. Gk *phaulizein* = Heb *slp* D also in 22:12.

Variant: *lbwt* (MT *lᵉbêt*).

21:14. LXX: "$^{\alpha}$ A secret gift turns away [*anatrepei*] wrath [pl.], $^{\beta}$ but he who refrains from gifts stirs up strong anger [$^{\beta}$ *dōrōn de ho pheidomenos thymon egeirei ischyron*]." The LXX rewrites the second line to create antithetical parallelism and, more important, to change the verse from praise of bribes to praise of gifts, perhaps charitable ones. To be sure, *šōḥad* is translated *dorōn* in 6:35, where a pay-off rather than a simple gift is meant, but in 17:8, praise of bribes is avoided by rendering the word as *paideia*.

Sym *sbesei*, Tg *mdʿk'*, and Vul *extinguet* "extinguish" seem to represent *ykbh*, but these later versions are unlikely to maintain common variants independently of the major witnesses. (Syr, with *mprq'*, is not the source of Tg in this case.) It is likely that the three versions are independently assimilating the hapax *ykph* to the expected *ykbh* "extinguish," under the influence of 26:20. Still, even if this evidence is ambiguous, the reading *ykbh* (*b-p* graphic confusion) may be original.

21:15. LXX: "β and a pious man is unclean among evildoers [*hosios de akathartos para kakourgois*]." Verse 15β is distant from the MT. The Hebrew sentence is clear and was translated accurately in 10:29β. It is hard to explain *akathartos* for MT's *mḥth*, either as a translator's choice or as a Heb variant in the source text.

21:17. LXX: "α A poor man loves merriment, β loving wine and oil in abundance [*eis plouton*, lit., "for wealth"]." The LXX misses the point of the proverb. *Eis plouton* = *lʿšr*, for MT's *lʾ yʿšyr*. Some Gk MSS read *ou ploutēsei*, which Baum. and Lag. prefer, but SyrH ascribes the latter (*lʾ nʿtr*) to Aq, Sym, and Theod.

Vul translates *śmḥh* as *epulas* "feasts," a correct interpretation in line with the rabbinic understanding of *śmḥh* as feasting; see C. Gordon 1930: 393.

Variant: *lʿšr* (MT *lōʾ yaʿăšîr*).

21:18. LXX lacks 18β. This leaves 18α isolated, so the omission is probably accidental.

21:19. LXX: "β than with a quarrelsome and talkative and irascible woman [*ē meta gynaikos maxēimou kai glōssōdous kai orgilou*]." *Machimou kai glōssōdous* is an expansive translation of *mdynym* "quarrels," giving a clearer picture of the woman's failings. (Note that *mdyn* = *antilogia* in 18:18.) Heb *wkʿs* is treated as an adj., indicating that the anger is a personality trait and not anger she *causes*.

Ketiv *mdwnym*, qeré *midyānîm*.

21:20. LXX: "α A desirable treasure will rest on the mouth [*anapausetain epi stomatos*] of the wise man, β but foolish men will drink it down." *Anapausetai* = *yškn* (*yiškōn*) for *wšmn* (Jäg.). The letter *mem* can easily become *kap-waw* by the detachment of the left arm (Baum.), and the reverse fusion is equally possible. Gk *epi stomatos* = *bpy* or an ungrammatical *bph*, the latter being closer graphically to Heb *bnwh*. A *nun-waw* ligature can resemble a *peh*. The resulting sentence means that the wise man has a "treasury" of wise things to say. This makes sense, but stich β is then difficult because it affirms that the fool will absorb the wise man's wisdom. The lack of coordination and logic in the couplet must have resulted from textual constraints rather than from free literary production. The correct text can be reconstructed by combining the Gk and the MT: *ʾwṣr nḥmd yškwn bnwh ḥkm, wksyl ʾdm yblʿnw* "A delightful treasure dwells in the habitation of the wise, but a foolish man devours it"—that is, his own treasure, improvidently.

Variants: *yškn* (MT *wāšemen*); *bph* (MT *binwēh*).

21:21. LXX *hodos* "way" = *drk*, for MT's *rdp* (metathesis + *k-p* graphic confusion, before the use of final letters). LXX lacks *ṣdqh*, which in MT looks like an accidental repetition from the first stich (Baum.).

Variant: *drk* (MT *rōdēp*); absence of *ṣᵉdāqāh* in 21b.

21:22. LXX: "β and brought down the fortress upon which the impious [pl.] relied [*ephʾ hō̧ epepoitheisan hoi asebeis*]." LXX's addition of "the impious" introduces a moralizing note.

21:26. LXX: "α The impious man [*asebēs*] desires bad things [*epithumei . . . epithumias kakas*—lit., "desires bad desires"] the entire day, β but the righteous man has mercy and shows compassion unsparingly [*eleą̄ kai oiktirei apheidōs*]." LXX adds "the impious man" to change the subject from the sluggard (otherwise supplied from v 25) to the wicked man, and moreover adds *kakas* "bad" (desires). By moralizing the first line, the LXX creates a clear antithesis to the second. On the difficulties of the MT, see the Commentary. In [β], *eleą̄ kai oiktirei* is a double translation of *yḥn*, where MT has *ytn* "gives."

Variant: *yḥn* (MT *yittēn*).

21:27. For "abomination" LXX has "abomination to the Lord [*kyriǭ*]" (= 15:8), for the sake of greater specificity.

21:28. LXX uses *phylassomenos* "cautiously" for Heb *lnṣḥ*, "forever" or "victoriously." Lag. (following Capellus) retroverts this to *lnṣr* "to keep." However, *lnṣḥ* may have been difficult in this context, provoking ad hoc renderings. Syr too has an unexpected rendering of *lnṣḥ*: *tryṣʾyt* "truthfully," which heightens the moralism of the attentive man's reward. Vul b: *vir oboediens loquitur victoriam*, "an obedient man shall speak of victory"; cf. Aq, Sym, Theod: *eis nikos poreusetai* "will go to victory."

21:29. LXX *syniei* "understands" = the qeré; *tas hodous autou* "his ways" = the ketiv. Aq, Sym *hetoimasei* = ketiv *ykyn*. Syr *mtqn* "fixes" = ketiv and *ʾwrḥtʾ*[pl] "ways" = ketiv. On *ykyn/ybyn* interchanges and the difficulty in deciding between the variants, see the Comment on 14:8.

Ketiv *ykyn*, qeré *yābîn*; ketiv *drkyw*, qeré *darkô*.

21:30. LXX: "[α] There is no wisdom, there is no valor [*andreia*], [β] there is no counsel to the impious (man) [*pros ton asebē*]." The last phrase is difficult. Gk *pros* + accusative can mean "against," and BA translates, "il n'y a pas de conseil à opposer à l'impie!" This would mean that no counsel can (successfully) oppose the ungodly, a peculiar sentiment. More likely *pros* indicates "toward": No counsel comes to the wicked when they most need it. Syr has *ʾyk dmryʾ* "like the Lord's," correctly understanding *lngd* YHWH as "vis-à-vis," hence, "in comparison with."

22:1. LXX adds *kalon* "a *good* name," for moral clarity; cf. Tg *šmʾ ṭbʾ*.

22:3. LXX: "[α] When a clever man sees the bad man being punished strongly [*timōroumenon krataiōs*], he takes instruction [*autos paideusetai*], [β] but when the fools pass by they are penalized [*ezēmiōthēsan*]." The same proverb is handled quite differently in 27:12. There, *rʿh* is understood as "evils," from which the clever man *does* hide. Here it is understood as "bad punishment" (of another), from which hiding would be unnecessary. The LXX adds a moral lesson similar to that of 19:25 and 21:11. Apparently LXX had *wystr* (the ketiv) and associated it with *y-s-r* "to discipline," "instruct."

Ketiv *wystr*, qeré *wᵉnistār*.

22:4. LXX: "[α] The offspring of wisdom [*genea sophia*] is the fear of the Lord." Heb *ʿqb* = "consequence" or "reward," hence *genea* "offspring," "generation." By changing *ʿnwh* "humility" to *sophia*, the translator—or a Hebrew scribe—associates this verse with Wisdom's promises in 8:18 and 35.

22:6. LXX lacks. Vul: "It is a proverb [*proverbium est*]: A young man according to his way, and even when he is old, he will not depart from it." *Proverbium est* for Heb *ḥnk* is puzzling. The verse seems to say that a young man does as he is inclined to do, and he persists in this for the rest of his life.

22:7. LXX: "$^{\alpha}$ (The) rich [pl.] will rule (the) poor, $^{\beta}$ and servants will lend to their own masters [*kai oiketai idiois despotais daniousin*]." Mistaking *ʿbd* as the subj. of *lwh* "borrow(er)," LXX identified the *ʾyš mlwh* ("the man who lends") as the master, on the assumption that the two types are opposites, as they are in line 7^{α}. In this way, LXX shapes the verse into a "world turned upside down" saying, on which see the Comment on 30:21–23.

Syr: "(a) As for the rich man, the poor man will rule over him [*ʿtyrʾ nštlṭ bh msknʾ*], (b) and the slave will lend to him who lent to him." Syr turns the Heb into a promise of the eventual domination of the poor over the rich. This is an eschatological expectation. Compare the ethic of Syr 28:6 and the way that Syr understands Ps 37:11 to mean that "the *poor* [*msknʾ*^{pl}] will inherit the earth"; sim. Luke 6:20.

22:8. LXX: "$^{\alpha}$ He who sows worthlessness will harvest evils, $^{\beta}$ and the rod will end his works [*plēgēn de ergōn autou syntelesei*]." Gk *plēgēn* "blow" can correspond to "rod" (Prov 29:15; Isa 30:31; thus Carmignac 1980: 34, who translates "celui qui a semé l'injustice moissonnera l'inanité, et le bâton terminera ses oeuvres"). *Ergōn* = *ʿbdtw*, understood as *ʿăbōdōtāyw*. *Syntelesei* = *y*^{e}*kalleh* (MT *yikleh*).

Ketiv *yqṣwr*, qeré *yiqṣor*.

Variant: *ʿbdtw* (MT *ʿebrātô*).

22:8a. LXX: "$^{\alpha}$ God will bless a cheerful and gift-giving man, $^{\beta}$ and he will make an end to the vanities of his works" ($^{\alpha}$*andra hilaron kai dotēn eulogei ho theos*, $^{\beta}$ *mataiotēta de ergōn autou syntelesei*). There is considerable confusion in LXX vv 8–9. Like LXX v 8, LXX $8a^{\beta}$ read *ʿbdtw*. LXX 8^{β}, $8a^{\beta} \approx$ MT 8b, while LXX $8a^{\alpha}$, $9^{\alpha} \approx$ MT 9a. Carmignac 1980: 36 says that the identical endings in the Heb text represented by 8^{β} and $8a^{\beta}$ occasioned a parablepsis, with the result that MT lacks v $8a^{\beta}$. He emends to *ʾyš rwṣh wnwtn ybrk ʾlhym*. However, *rwṣh* does not mean "genereux," as Carmignac translates it. I suggest that *andros hilaron* = *ḥwnn* (*ḥōnēn*) "he who is kind," used in Prov 14:31; 19:17; 28:8, though this word is translated *eleōn* there. Note the phrase *ḥwnn wnwtn*, "is generous and gives," in Ps 37:23a. The lost line in MT (Gk $8a^{\alpha}$) read *ḥwnn wnwtn ybrk ʾlhym* and is to be translated "God will bless him who is kind and gives" (or "who graciously gives"). LXX $8a^{\beta}$ makes no sense coupled with LXX $8a^{\alpha}$, and it is unlikely to mean "et il suppléera à la faiblesse de ses oeuvres" ("and he will compensate for the weakness of his works"), as Carmignac (1980: 40) translates it. LXX $8a^{\beta}$ looks like a distorted dittog. of MT v 8b.

Variant: *ḥwnn wnwtn ybrk ʾlhym* (MT lacks).

22:9. "$^{\alpha}$ He who has mercy on a poor (man) [*ptōchon*], he (too) will be supported [*diatraphēsetai*], $^{\beta}$ for he gave of his bread to the poor." Stich 9^{α} is a paraphrase of MT 9a. The LXX explains how the kind man will be blessed, namely, by being supported financially. LXX $8a^{\alpha} \approx$ MT 9a; see above. Gk *ptōchon* "poor" = Heb *ʿny* "poor man" for *ʿyn* "eye" (Giese 1993a: 114).

Variant: *ʿny* (MT *ʿayin*).

22:9a. LXX: "$^{\alpha}$ He who gives gifts secures victory and honor, $^{\beta}$ but he takes away the life of (their) possessors"; or: "^{β} but they [sc., the gifts] take away the life of (their) possessors" (^{α} *nikēn kai timēn peripoieitai ho dōra dous*, ^{β} *tēn mentoi psychēn aphaireitai tōn kektēmenōn*). Sim. Vul. 22:9a^{α} is associated with the "gift giving" man of 22:8a^{α}. V 9a^{β} recalls LXX 1:19^{β}. The two lines of LXX 22:9a are not just fragments (contrary to Baum. and Lag.) but constitute a new couplet. The unhebraic syntax of 9a^{β}, with the verb inside the genitive phrase, suggests that the couplet was composed in Gk, not Heb. The couplet says that although gifts (bribes) bring victory (in court, perhaps) and honor (i.e., prestige), they destroy their recipients. LXX 9a^{β} recalls MT (not LXX) 15:27b.

22:10. LXX: "^{α} Expel a pest [*loimon*] from the assembly [*ek synedriou*], and conflict will leave with him, ^{β} for when he sits in the assembly, he dishonors everybody." The notion of assembly is inferred from *dyn* in MT 10b, which the translator understands as referring to a setting of judgment. LXX's "he dishonors all" turns *qlwn* into a verb. On the "assembly," see the Note on 31:23.

22:11. LXX: "^{α} The Lord loves the pious [pl.] of heart, ^{β} and all the blameless are favored by him. ^{γ} The king shepherds with his lips." In ^{α}, LXX adds "the Lord." V 11^{β} corresponds in part to Heb 11a (*ṭhwr lb ḥn*), but is largely derived from 11:20^{β}. V 11^{β} overlaps with ^{α}, rendering *ṭhwr lb ḥn* again, but loosely, without *kyrios*. 11^{γ} = *biśᵉpātāyw rōʿēh hmlk*.

Syr "(a) God loves him who is pure in his heart, (b) and he shows mercy to the lips of the friends of the king." Syr (a) adds "God" (≈ LXX; sim.Tg). For MT's *rʿhw mlk* Syr reflects either *rʿy hmlk* (Pink.) or *rʿh mlk*, treated as a pl., as often. Given the difficulty the translator had with the syntax, retroversions are shaky. Nevertheless, LXX and Syr agree on *rʿh hmlk*.

Ketiv *ṭhwr*, qeré *ṭᵉhor*.

Variant: *bśptyw rʿh hmlk* (MT *śᵉpātāyw rēʿēhû melek*).

22:12. LXX: "^{β} but the transgressor despises words [*logous phaulizei*]," that is, words of the Lord. The forced construction in ^{β} could come about only if the translator read *dbrym* for *dbry* (near-dittog. of *m* with *b*).

Variant: *dbrym* (MT *dibrê-*).

22:13. LXX: "^{α} The sluggard makes excuses [*prophasizetai*] and says, ^{β} 'A lion in the streets and murderers [*phoneutai*] in the plazas!' " LXX adds "makes excuses," unnecessarily explaining the sluggard's intent. LXX reads *rṣḥ* (*rōṣēaḥ*) for *ʾrṣḥ*, the *ʾaleph* being lost through haplog. with the *taw*, which is very similar in the archaic script. Since the translator was alert to the fact that the sluggard is making excuses and inventing pretexts, he would have had no reason to avoid the 1st per. of *ʾrṣḥ*, had it been in his text. This is evidence that the predecessor of LXX's source-text diverged from the proto-MT quite early, when the ancestral text was in the archaic script.

Syr: "(a) The sluggard says, when he is sent out [*mʾ dmštd*], 'A lion is in the street, (b) behold a killer in the streets!' " Syr adds an explanatory clause, "when he is sent out." This is taken from Syr 26:13, where it is based on an error. This shows that the translator knows what is ahead of him in the book and is not just translating sequentially. Syr *qṭlʾ* ≈ LXX "murderers."

Variant: *rṣḥ* (MT *ʾērāṣēaḥ*).

22:14. LXX: "[α] The mouth of the transgressor [*paranomou*] is a deep pit, and he who is hated by the Lord will fall into it." This interprets MT *zrwt* as "strange" or "strange woman" = "transgressor" (*paranomou* is masc. or fem.). Compare 23:33.

Syr *nwkryt'* "the foreign woman" (sg. = LXX), for Heb *zrwt*.

Ketiv *ypwl*, qeré *yippol*.

22:14a. "[α] There are evil ways [*hodoi kakai*] before a man, and (yet) he does not like to turn away from them. [β] But it is necessary to turn away from a crooked and evil way." A rather banal moralizing elaboration of the Hebrew of v 14. Heb *zarot* is understood as "strange things" = evil ways.

22:16. LXX: "[α] He who lays false charges [*sykophantōn*] against the wretched increases his own troubles [*poiei ta heautou kaka* ([BS] lacks *kaka*)], [β] and gives to the rich unto lack [*ep' elassoni*]." In other words, he who oppresses the poor will end up losing his own wealth to the rich and himself lacking all. In the [BS] reading that lacks the moralizing *kaka*, the sentence expresses indignation: "He who lays false charges against the wretched increases his own (property). He gives to a rich man at the expense of a lowlier one" (cf. BA).

Syr adds *byšt'* = Gk *kaka*.

22:17. LXX: "[α] To the words of the wise direct your ear [β] and hear my word, and set your heart, [γ] so that you may know that they are beautiful" ([α] *Logois sophōn paraballe son ous,* [β] *kai akoue emon logon tēn de sēn kardian epistēson,* [γ] *hina gnǭs hoti kaloi eisin*). It is more likely that LXX had *dbry ḥkmym* before *hṭ 'znk* in its source text than that the phrases were transposed translation. In 17[γ], the translator read *ldʿt* or construed MT's *ldʿty* as *lādaʿat* and took *ky nʿym* from 18. The source-text read: (17) *dbry ḥkmym / hṭ 'znk wšmʿ dbry / wlbk tšyt ldʿt* / (18) *ky nʿym*. This should be translated: (17) "The words of the wise. / Incline your ear and hear my words, / and set your heart on knowledge. (18) For it is pleasant . . ."

A. Luc (2000: 253) argues that LXX 17[αβ] is not part of a section title and that the *logois sophōn* is part of a poetic line: "To the words of the wise direct your ear," which represents *dbry ḥkmym hṭ 'znk*, "to the words of the wise direct your ear." But while it is true that the LXX, in accordance with its consistent obscuring of all non-Solomonic ascriptions, does not intend the words to represent a title, the underlying Hebrew does. Heb *hṭ 'znk* requires an ind. obj. and cannot govern *dbry ḥkmym* directly. The Heb must be construed differently from the LXX's interpretation. Vocalized, the original would read: *dibrê ḥăkāmîm haṭ 'ozn*^{e}*kā ûš*^{e}*maʿ d*^{e}*bārāy*.

Variants: *dbry ḥkmym hṭ 'znk wšmʿ dbry* (MT *haṭ 'ozn*^{e}*kā ûš*^{e}*maʿ dibrê ḥăkāmîm*); *ldʿt* (MT *l*^{e}*daʿtî*).

22:18. LXX: "[α] And if you put them into your heart, [β] they will together gladden [*euphranousin*] you on your lips. . . ." LXX substitutes the expected "heart" for "belly." *Euphranousin = yrnw* for MT's *yknw* ("they are established"), though the variant does not fit the context well (Wm. Tooman, private communication).

Variant: *yrnw* (MT *yikkōnû*).

22:19. LXX: "[α] so that your hope may be in the Lord, [β] and so that he may let you know his way [*gnōrisę̄ soi tēn hodon autou*]." LXX[B] has *tēn hodon sou* "your way." V 19[β] is a loose rephrasing of the difficult MT 19b. *'p 'th* is joined to 20. (Syr does not represent these two words.) For 19b, Aq and Sym have *gnōstēn epoiēsa soi zōēn* ("I have made you know life"), which must represent *ḥyym* for *hywm*. It is not clear how they handled the next two words.

Variant: *ḥyym* (MT *hayyôm*).

22:20. LXX: "$^{\alpha}$ And as for you—write these for yourself thrice [*trissōs*], $^{\beta}$ for counsel and knowledge $^{\gamma}$ on the tablet of your heart." The loose treatment of the syntax of 20a resulted from the assumptions that *ʾp ʾth* "even you" (from MT 19) is the subject of the sentence, and that *šlyšym* (qeré), or perhaps *šlwšym*, means "three-fold," "thrice" (sim. Syr). LXX added 20$^{\gamma}$, borrowed from 7:3b, to clarify what the command to write refers to.

Ketiv *šlšwm*, qeré *šālîšîm*.

22:21. LXX: "$^{\alpha}$ I will teach you a true word and good knowledge, $^{\beta}$ to understand how to answer (with) true words to those who confront [*proballomenois*] you." This is an expansive treatment of the MT. Gk *proballein* is used only here for *šlḥ*. (GELS defines the middle as "to confront somebody with a problem, to question." For the latter see Judg 14:12.) The translation pictures the reader as the one *to whom* a message is being sent rather than as the messenger, probably because it was not clear to the translator why a messenger would "answer" those who sent him on an errand. Vul $^{\beta}$ *respondere ex his illi qui misit te*, "to respond from these (words) to them that sent you." Vul lacks *ʾmt*.

Syr: "(b) [MT 21a] and tranquility [*wšlyʾ*] and words of truth." Syr *šlyʾ* = *šqṭ* "quiet" for MT's *qšṭ* (Pink.). It is hard to know whether *šqṭ* was in the source-text or was an effort to make sense of Heb *qšṭ*, which, though an Aramaism, has the form of *qwštʾ* in Syriac.

22:23. LXX: "$^{\alpha}$ For the Lord will judge [*krinei*] his [the poor man's] case, $^{\beta}$ and you will rescue your soul unharmed." LXX guesses at the rare verb *qbʿ* ("rob"). LXX must mean that if you obey the admonition in 22, you will be safe. It seems to be influenced by Ezek 3:19, 21, which could explain the awkward 2nd person in 23$^{\beta}$.

22:25. LXX, Syr "ways" = qeré.

Ketiv *ʾrḥtw*, qeré *ʾorḥōtāyw*.

22:26. LXX: "Do not give yourself as surety, being diffident toward others [*aischynomenos prosōpon*, lit. "feeling awe/shame toward face"]." LXX $^{\alpha}$ interprets the gesture of clasping hands. For *mśʾwt*, LXX had *mśʾt* (a m.l. difference), which it understood as *miśś*^{e}*ʾēt*, lit., "from lifting up," sc. *pānîm* "face." The idiom appears without *pānîm* in Gen 4:7, where the LXX understands it differently.

Syr ≈ LXX, using *bdbht ʾnt mn prṣwpʾ*^{pl}, lit., "because you are ashamed of faces," that is, diffident.

Variant: *mśʾt*/*mšʾt* (MT *maššāʾôt*).

22:27. LXX and Syr ≈ MT but omit *lmh* "why." It is impossible to determine whether this was missing in LXX's Heb source due to haplog. or was omitted in translation because of the difficulty of fitting *lmh* into the Gk syntax.

22:29. "$^{\alpha}$ It is necessary for a man who is observant [*oratikon*] and keen in his works $^{\beta}$ to attend on kings $^{\gamma}$ and not attend on sluggish men." The LXX uses the hapax *oratikon* "observant," "perceptive," deriving the notion of seeing from *ḥzyt* (actually, "have you seen?"), but the LXX overrides MT's morphology and syntax. (Heb *ḥzyt* is translated correctly in 29:20.) LXX explains *ḥšwkym* (lit., "dark, obscure," a hapax) as the opposite of "observant" and "keen" in 29[α].

23:2. LXX: "[α] And lay your hand on what is placed before you, [v 1], [β] knowing that it is right for you to prepare such things." Perhaps puzzled as to why one would put a knife to his throat, the literal-minded translator composed a proverb with slight relation to the MT.

Syr (continuing v 1): "(a) so that you *not* place a knife in your mouth, (b) if [you] [*'nt* for *'yt*], are a man of appetite." Like LXX, Syr misunderstands the metaphor of placing a knife to one's throat. Syr's "placing a knife in your mouth" may signify either endangering oneself or eating a piece of meat by skewering it on a knife.

23:3. LXX: "[γ] for these belong to a false life [*zōēs pseudous*]." Heb *whwʾ lḥyy kzbym* (Baum.). The final *mem* of *lḥm* had split into two *yods*. (See LSF §§132e–f for similar phenomena, such as *m* becoming *yw*.)

Variant: *lḥyy* (MT *lḥm*).

Ketiv: *tt'w*, qeré *titāyw*.

23:4. LXX: "[α] (If) you are poor, do not measure yourself [*parekteinou*; lit., "stretch yourself out"] to a rich man, [β] but in your mind, refrain." Rather than allowing the impression that one should refrain from working hard, the LXX composes a very different proverb. This one warns not against striving for wealth but against dissatisfaction with one's given station in life. If one is poor, one should not compare himself to the rich, for that would breed envy. The theme of envy serves to link the verse better to vv 2–3, 5. Heb *lhʿšyr* is understood as "to the rich man," with an unassimilated article. See the Note on 28:20.

Syr: "(a) Do not approach a rich man, (b) but in your wisdom, depart [*'tprq*] from him." MT *tygʿ* was construed as *taggîaʿ*, from *n-g-ʿ*. This led to a contextual rendering of *ḥdl*. Syr 23:4 speaks about the rich man, as in LXX (and Tg), rather than wealth.

23:5. LXX: "[α] If you place your eye on him, he in no way appears [*oudamou phaneitai*], [γ] for he has made for himself wings like an eagle's, [δ] and returns to the house of his superior [*tou proestēkotos autou*]." "His superior" is God. "Heaven" here is not an epithet of God, as in the rabbinic usage, but God's dwelling place. LXX continues the theme of the rich man (v 4), producing a strange image.

Syr: "(a) If you fix your eye on him, he is not visible to you, (b) for he makes wings like an eagle and flies to the sky." Syr combines MT and LXX, still speaking about the rich man and his unreliability but ending with *wprḥ lšmyʾ* "and flies to heaven"; sim. Tg.

LXX and Syr agree with the qeré *hătāʿîp*. They also read *w*^{eʿ}*āp* (correctly) or have *wyʿp* and interpret it thus.

Ketiv *htʿwp*, qeré *hătāʿîp*; ketiv *wʿyp*, qeré *yāʿûp*.

Variant: *w*^{eʿ}*āp* (MT ketiv *wʿyp*, qeré *yāʿûp*).

23:6. Ketiv *tt'w*, qeré *titʾāyw*.

23:7. LXX: "[α] For just as if someone swallowed down a hair [*tricha*], [β] thus he eats and drinks." LXX merges 7c (*wlbw bl ʿmk*) with 8a, ignoring *y'mr lk*. "Hair" = *śēʿār* (MT *šāʿar*).

LXX uses part of 7b in 8[α], where Gk *mēde pros se eisagagēs auton* ("And do not bring him to you") can be retroverted to *wlhblw* (*ûlᵉhôbîlô*) *ʿmk*, lit., "and to bring him with you"—a distortion of MT's *wlbw bl ʿmk*. These are not usual correspondences, but Heb *h-l-k* Hp is translated by *eisagein* (pass.) in Ezek 40:24, and Heb *y-b-l* Hp is translated by *agein* (pass.) in Isa 53:7 and Jer 11:19.

Vul: "For after the manner of a diviner or soothsayer, he estimates that of which he is ignorant" (*quoniam in similitudinem arioli et coniectoris aestimat quod ignorat*). *Aestimat* = *šōʿēr*, from *šāʿar* "to estimate," "calculate."

Syr understands *š/śʿr* as "a bristle." Tg, understanding *šāʿar* as "gate," takes its own approach to the verse: "Because as a gate is high, thus is he [the rich man] high [i.e., haughty] in his soul [*mṭwl dʾyk trʿʾ rmʾ, hkn hwʾ rm bnpšyh*] (Tg[L]). 'Eat and drink,' he says to you, but his heart is deceitful [*nkyl*] toward you."

Variant: *wlhblw* (MT *wᵉlibbô bāl*).

23:8. LXX (continuing MT 7[β]): "[α] And do not bring him to you and eat your morsel with him. [β] For he will vomit it up and spoil [*kai lymaneitai*] your lovely words." See the note on v 7. The LXX continues the description of the envious man. LXX understands *wšḥt* as *wᵉšiḥēt* "and spoil" (MT *wᵉšiḥattā*). V 8[α] uses part of 7b, q.v.

23:10.. Vul has *parvulorum* "children" = *ʿûlîm*, for MT's *ʿôlām*. The reading *ʿûlîm* is presumed in *m. Peʾah* 5:6, though there it is interpreted as *ʿôlîm* "those who ascend." It also seems to be presumed in *y. Sota* 4:4. Since Vul does not reflect LXX's "orphans" here, and since Jerome recognized *ʿôlām* as "ancient" in the doublet 22:28, he probably had *ʿwlym* in his Heb text in 23:10. This variant probably arose under the influence of "orphans" in the second stich.

Variant: *ʿwlym* (MT *ʿôlām*).

23:18. LXX: "[α] For if you keep them [*ean gar tērēsēs auta*], you will have offspring [*ekgona*]." Something is missing in MT after *ʾm yš*. LXX apparently had *tšmrm* ("keep them," sc. "my words") or *tšmrnh* ("keep it," sc. "fear of God"). To be sure, LXX might have had the lacuna and felt constrained to supply a verb.

Variant: *tšmrm* or *tšmrnw* (MT lacks).

23:19. LXX: "[β] and make the reflections of your heart straight" (*kai kateuthyne ennoias sēs kardias*). LXX associates *wʾšr* "and go straight"with *y-š-r* "straight." Heb *bdrk* [*bᵉderek*] *lbk* "in the way of your heart" is understood as the *thoughts* of your heart.

Syr: "(b) and my thought will rejoice in your heart [*wtdwṣ trʿyty blbk*]." Syr associates *ʾšr* with the homonym *ʾaššēr* "declare happy" (as in 4:14) and must treat the rest of the stich flexibly. Hence retroversion to *wʾšr drky blbk* is not justified (Baum., Pink.).

23:20. LXX: "[β] and do not spend much time at feasts or with purchases [*agorasmois*] of meat [*kreon*]." LXX *kreōn* and *agorasmois* reflect a near-dittog., *bśr šbr* (*šeber*), "food," as in Gen 42:19 (D. A. Teeter, personal communication).

Variant: + *šbr*.

23:21. LXX translates *zll* (usually "glutton") as "whoremonger" (*pornokopos*), only here. The translator is extending the warning against drunkenness and gluttony to other types of dissoluteness. (This is probably correct; see the Comment.)

23:22. LXX: "$^\alpha$ Hear, my son, etc.," adding *huie*, as in 9:12; 24:1; and 27:27, thus assimilating to v 15 and 19.

23:23. LXX lacks. See Comment.

23:24. LXX: "$^\alpha$ A righteous father raises (his son) well [*kalōs ektrephei*]." LXX reads *gdl ygdl*. (For *d/y* interchange, see the qeré-ketiv *mlbw/mlbd* in 1 Kgs 12:33; cf. Kennedy 1928: 53–54.) Heb (qeré) *wywld* (vocalized in the ketiv as *yôlēd*) was implicitly vocalized as *w*e*yēled* or *w*e*yūlad* (Gp ptcp.).

Syr: "(a) The father of a righteous man will rejoice and be glad [*nrwz wndwṣ*], (b) and he will beget a wise (son), (c) and his father will take pleasure in him [*wnwld ḥkym' wnḥd' bh 'bwhy*]." The subj. of (b) seems to be the righteous man, who is also the "father" in (c). A wise son makes his father happy and is himself rewarded by begetting a wise son. This is a possible reading of the Heb, if read as follows: *gyl ygyl 'by ṣdyq, wywld ḥkm wyśmḥ bw*. This follows the qere in *gyl ygyl* and *wywld* but the ketiv in *wyśmḥ*. Without *wyśmḥ* Syr's understanding would not arise.

Ketiv *gwl*, qeré *gîl*; ketiv *ygwl*, qeré *yāgîl*; ketiv *ywld*, qeré *w*e*yôlēd*; ketiv *wyśmḥ*, qeré *yiśmaḥ*.

Variant: *gdl ygdl* (MT ketiv: *gwl / ygwl*).

23:26. LXX, Syr = qeré. Sym *thelēsatōsan* "let them delight" = ketiv.

Ketiv *trṣnh*; qeré *tiṣṣōrnāh*.

23:27.. LXX: "$^\alpha$ For a strange house is a pierced jar, $^\beta$ and a narrow well is strange" ($^\alpha$ *pithos gar tetrēmenos estin allotrios oikos*, $^\beta$ *kai phrear stenon allotrion*). Stich $^\alpha$ is scarcely related to the MT, though the Heb is clear and not contrary to the translator's ideas. (Contrast LXX 22:14.) Gerleman (1956: 33) says that the LXX refers to a household whose members behave as strangers and take no interest in their common interest.

"A pierced jar" is a Gk mythological motif. The Danaides were condemned to draw water with a pierced jar, an image used more broadly to indicate futility and wastefulness (BA 105). Esp. relevant here is Aristotle's statement: "The master of a house who is unable to conserve his property is what is called a pierced jar [*pithos tetrēmenos*]" (*Econ*. 1.6; 1344 B 25). LXX 23:27 seems to echo that very statement. A "strange house" wastes its possessions. Compare "and he who consorts with harlots loses money" (MT 29:3b). Despite the paraphrastic character of this verse, *allotrios* in 27$^\alpha$ can be retroverted to *zrh* "strange," for MT's *zwnh*.

Variant: *zrh* (MT *zônāh*).

23:28. LXX: "$^\alpha$ For this [i.e., house (v 27$^\alpha$)] will suddenly be destroyed [*apoleitai*], $^\beta$ and every transgressor will be cut off [*analōthēsetai*]." *Apoleitai* = *t'bd* for *t'rb* (Jäg.). Gk's *analōthēsetai* associates *twsp* with *s-w-p* or *s-p-h* (cf. 13:23$^\beta$).

Syr (continuing 27): "(a) And quickly she destroys [*wmn šly' mwbd'*], (b) and many men increase [*msgyn*] sin." Syr's *mwbd'* reflects *t'bd* (D or H), independently of LXX, which uses the passive and presumes a different subj. Syr understands *twsp* as *tôsîp* "cause to increase" and adjusts the syntax accordingly, taking *bwgdym* as abstract, "treachery," hence "sin." Tg (b): "and captures naïve sons" (*wṣ'd' bny' šbry*).

Variant: *t'bd* (MT *te'Žrōb*).

23:29. LXX: "$^\alpha$ To whom is woe? To whom tumult [*thorybos*]? To whom conflict [*krisis*]? [β] To whom unpleasantness and gossip [*aēdiai kai leschai*]? [γ] To whom wounds in vain? [δ] Whose eyes are dim [*peleioi*]?" *Krisis* = the qeré, *mdynym*, associated with *dyn* "judgment"; cf. 28:25. Gk *aēdiai kai leschai* is a double translation of *wśyḥ*, which means both "complaints" and "talk." Heb *ḥkllwt* is translated *peleioi* "pale" in [B*S*A], but *palidnoi* "livid" in other MSS. Syr *mqn'n*[pl] "dim," "livid" could correspond to either.

Vul *cuius patri vae* ("whose father has woe?") divides *'bwy* into *'ab 'wy*. Sim. *Num. Rab.* 10:6 (88b): *zh 'b 'wy*, "This one is the father of woe"; cf. *Yal. Shimoni* ad loc. (C. Gordon 1930: 390).

Ketiv *mdwnym*; qeré *midyānîm*.

23:31. LXX: "[α] Do not get drunk [*methuskesthe*] on wine, but converse with righteous men, [β] and converse in (public) walks [*en peripatois*]. [γ] For if you set your eyes to the bowls and the cups, [δ] later you will walk about more naked than a pestle [*gymnoteros hyperou*]." Some of the words and roots of the MT are discernible behind the translation, but they do not appear in MT's order and are scarcely related to MT's syntax. Baum. says that the translator is deliberately playing with the text in midrashic fashion. Gk *methuskesthe* associates *tr'* with *riwwāh* "slake thirst." V 31[β] alludes to speaking of God's commandments when walking in the way (Deut 6:7; 11:19) and possibly to peripatetic philosophical conversations (BA). "More naked than a pestle" is a Gk commonplace; see BA, p. 104.

Syr: "(a) Do not fix [*tṣd*] your eye on wine, whose eye is reddish [*zrg'*] in the cup [*bks'*], (b) but meditate on righteousness." Syr 31(a) is a very loose and erroneous rendering of MT 31ab. Since *myšrym* elsewhere means "rectitude," the translator probably thought he was staying close to the original.

Ketiv *bkys*, qeré *bakkôs*.

23:32. LXX: "[α] In the end, he is stretched out [*ekteinetai*] as one bitten by a snake; [β] the venom is dispersed through him as if he were bitten by a horned viper." Gk has lost track of the subject of the first verb, *ekteinetai*. This verb reflects *yškb* "lie down" for MT *yšk* "bite." *Yiškb* could arise by near-dittog. of *yšk*: *yškyškb*. In 32[β], Heb *yprś/š* (MT *yaprîš*) is first translated "dispersed" (understood as *yippārēš*?).

Variant: *yšk yškb* (MT *yšk*).

23:33. LXX: "[α] When [*hotan*] your eyes see a strange woman [*allotrian*], [β] your mouth [*stoma*] will then speak crooked things." Heb *zrwt* ("strange things") is treated as a sg. (as in 22:14). The fem. indicates that it is construed as "strange woman" (sim. Syr). Instead of MT's *lbk* "your heart," LXX has "your mouth," as the logical organ of speech. LXX says that if you are drunk, you will speak sinful things with a strange woman, that is, agree to her blandishments. In 23:21, LXX interpreted *zll* "gluttony" as whoremongering.

23:34. LXX: "[β] and as a pilot in great waves." This omits the repeated *kškb* "as one who lies down" and construes *ḥbl* as *ḥôbēl* "sailor," "pilot" (sim. Syr). Having misidentified the subject (actually "one who reclines"), the translator treats *brʾš* freely. Vul: "(b) and as a pilot fast asleep, when the rudder is lost" (*et quasi sopitus gubernator amisso clavo*).

24:1. LXX prefixes *huie* "my son"; see the Note on 23:22.

Ketiv *tt'w*, qeré *tit'āyw*.

24:2. For MT's *šōd* "destruction," LXX has *pseudē* "deceit" and Syr uses *byšt'* "evil." Both are using broad terms to explicate a metaphor. (The translators may have wondered how one can "speak destruction.") On LXX-Prov's predilection for words from *pseud-* and *alēth-*, see Dick 1990: 23.

24:5. LXX: "α Better a wise man than a strong one [*ischyrou*], β and a man who has good sense than a great field [*geōrgiou megalou*]." LXX reads *mʿz* or *mʿwz* (understood as "strong") for MT *bʿz* (*m/b* similarity) and derives the comparative idea from the *m-*. It is hard to see what could lie behind "than a field" other than a textual difference, namely, *m'rṣ* (lit., "from a land") for *m'mṣ*. *M-r* confusion could occur if the left arm of the *mem* were lost. *Geōrgios* does not correspond to *'ereṣ* elsewhere, but "a great field" would be a reasonable paraphrase of a faulty text, namely, *m'rṣ kḥ*. According to the Hexapla, the "Others" read: *hyper krataion ischui* "above one strong in strength" = *mē'ammîṣ kōaḥ*.

Syr: "(b) and a man of knowledge than a mighty man [*mn gnbr ḥyl'*]." Syr implicitly vocalizes *m'mṣ kḥ* as *mē'ammîṣ kōaḥ* (assimilating to the phrase in Job 9:4 and Isa 40:26), but possibly it had *m'myṣ kḥ*.

Variants: *mʿz* (MT *baʿôz*); *m'rṣ* (MT *me'ammēṣ*).

24:6. LXX: "β and help is with the heart [*meta kardias*] of a counselor." "With the heart" = *blb* for *brb*, a change abetted by the assumption that the heart is the locus of counsels. The same happens in LXX 15:22.

Syr uses *mtʿbd* = *tēʿāśeh* for MT's *taʿăśeh* and ignores *lk*; cf. 20:18.

Variant: *blb* (MT *bᵉrōb*).

LXX 24:7–10 is a cohesive unit, and the textual issues in each verse involve the others. The verses are divided and associated differently from the MT; see the remarks after v 10. The variants suggested in the following Notes seem to be the likely explanation for the divergence from the MT, but it is possible that the LXX is simply a strong rewriting of the MT.

24:7. LXX: "α Wisdom and good understanding are in the gates of the wise. β The wise do not turn away from the mouth of the Lord [*ek stomatos kyriou*]" (continues in 8α). Faced with a verse that seemed to say that "wisdom is corals" for the fool—as if he could appreciate it!—the translator substituted a more expected sentiment, only loosely related to the Heb. Gk *ek stomatos kyriou* probably reflects *py yhw* for MT's *pyhw*. Perles (1895: 17) says that the LXX saw *py-h* as an abbreviation of *py haššēm*, but the abbreviation *heh* and the epithet "the Name" were not in use yet.

Syr: "(a) Wisdom throws the fool down [*ḥkmt' rmy' lskl'*]." Syr *rāmyā'* for Heb *r'mwt* is a clever homeophonic translation. Tg *mtrʿm* "is rebellious, agitated," also homeophonic.

Variant: *py yhw* (MT *pîhû*).

24:8. LXX: (continuing 7β) "α but instead, they deliberate in assemblies [*synhedriois*]. β The ignoramus—death comes upon him [*apaideutois synantą̄ thanatos*]" (continues in 9α). MT's *bʿl mzmwt yqr'w* supplied the letters of *bʿr mwt yqr'w* (*baʿar māwet yiqrā'ô*, i.e., *yiqrā'ennû*), "The ignoramus—death comes upon [*q-r-h*] him." Though *apaideutos* does not translate *baʿar* elsewhere, this is the best explanation of *apaideutos* where the Heb has *bʿl* "possessor." The letters *zm* were lost by parablepsis due to the repeated *m*: *m[zm]wt*.

Variant: *bʿr mwt yqrʾw* (MT *baʿal mᵉzimmôt yiqrāʾ û*).

24:9. LXX: (continuing 8b) "$^{\alpha}$ and the fool dies by sins, $^{\beta}$ and impurity will be a blemish for the pestilent" (continues in 10$^{\alpha}$). This is a loose (mis)reading of the MT, except that LXX's source text had *wmt* (*w-z* graphic confusion). The problem facing the translator was that the verse seems to say that sin is an abomination to the *lēṣ*, whereas such a man would be expected to *like* it. The hapax and neologism *emmolynthēsetai* presumably corresponds to *htrpyt* (properly, "you slack off") in v 10a.

Syr: "(a) And the thoughts of the fool [*dsklʾ*] are sin, (b) and a man's impurity is evil [*byštʾ*]." Syr is largely a guess. It is interesting that the Syr does not always turn to LXX when in difficulties. TgL: "(b) and scoffing is an abomination to a wise man [*ḥkymʾ*]." Syr and Tg make adjustments for the same reason as the LXX.

Variant: *wmt* (MT *zimmat*).

24:10. LXX: (continuing 9$^{\beta}$) "$^{\alpha}$ in the evil day and in the day of affliction, $^{\beta}$ until he comes to an end [*heōs an eklipę̄*]." V 10$^{\alpha}$ has a double translation of *bywm ṣrh*. LXX 10$^{\beta}$ represents *ʿd kḥdh* "until he is destroyed," for *ṣr kḥkh*. The change was occasioned by graphic similarity of *ʿ-ṣ* [LSAT §108] and *k-d*. Gk *ekleipein* = *kḥd* in Zech 11:9, 16.

Syr: "and evildoers—evil takes them in the day of tribulation." A guess, distant from the MT.

Variants: *ʿd* (MT *ṣar*); *kḥdkh* (MT *kōḥăkāh*).

In LXX 24:7–10 the translator, working with a difficult text and a few variants, shaped a coherent epigram contrasting the wise (7$^{\alpha}$–8$^{\alpha}$) and the foolish (8$^{\beta}$–10$^{\beta}$):

7$^{\alpha}$ Wisdom and good understanding are in the gates of the wise.
$^{\beta}$ The wise do not turn away from the mouth of the Lord,
8$^{\alpha}$ but, instead, they deliberate in assemblies.
$^{\beta}$ The ignoramus—death comes upon him,
9$^{\alpha}$ and the fool dies by sins,
$^{\beta}$ and impurity will be a blemish for the pestilent,
10$^{\alpha}$ in the evil day and in the day of affliction,
$^{\beta}$ until he comes to an end.

24:11. LXX: "$^{\beta}$ and redeem [*ekpriou*] those who are being killed. Do not forbear [*mē pheisę̄*]!" *Ekpriasthai* means "buy off," "rachète" (BA). It was added as a parallel to *rhysai*, "those who are being killed" ≈ *wmṭym lhrg*. Gk *mē* = *ʾl*, a normalization of the negative *ʾim*; see below.

Syr: "(b) and do not refrain from redeeming [*lmzbn*] those who are seized for death." Paraphrastic.

Several Midrashim (*Lev. Rab.* 10:4; *Pesiq. Rab.* 33; *S. Eli. Zut.* 22) cite this verse using *ʾl tḥśwk* = LXX, Syr.

Variant: *ʾl* (MT *ʾim*).

24:12. LXX: "$^{\alpha}$ If you [sg.] say, 'I did not know this one [*touton*],' $^{\beta}$ know that [*ginōske hoti*] the Lord knows the hearts of all, $^{\gamma}$ and he who formed breath for all, he knows all [*kai ho plasas pnoēn pasin autos oiden panta*]—$^{\delta}$ (he) who will repay to each according to his works." $^{\alpha}$ Gk makes *lʾ ydʿnw* "we did not know" agree with the sg. of *ki tʾmr* "if you [sg.]." LXX's *ginōske* ≈ *tbn* or *tbyn* (*tābîn*) for MT's *tōkēn* "he who weighs." LXX's "and he who formed" associates *wnwṣr* (actually, "and he who keeps") with *yṣr* "form." In 12$^{\beta}$ and $^{\gamma}$, "all" is added for generality, making the verse into a statement of God's omniscience (cf. BA; cf. Acts 1:24). Vul modifies the rationalization: "If you say, 'I am not strong enough' " (*si dixeris vires non suppetunt*). After *touton*, LXX[23, 106, SyrH] add *kai autos me ou ginōskei*, "and he does not know me," a variant that must rest on Heb *ydʿny*, since it is not an assimilation to MT.

Variants: *ydʿny* (MT *yādaʿnû*); *tb(y)n* (MT *tōkēn*).

24:14. LXX explains *yš ʾḥryt*, "there is an end" (which could sound threatening), as *kalē hē teleutē sou* "your [sg.] end (will be) good," which is indeed the sense of the phrase.

24:15. LXX: "$^{\alpha}$ Do not bring [*mē prosagagęs*] an impious man into the pasturage of the righteous [pl.], $^{\beta}$ nor be misled by the feeding of the belly [*mēde apatēthęs chortasią koilias*]." "Do not bring" = *tbʾ* (*tābēʾ*) for MT's *ʾl tʾrb* (*prosagein* = *bwʾ* H in Lev 19:21; Num 6:12; 1 Sam 1:25). However, the correct vocalization would be *tābōʾ* "come." The MT was produced by near-dittog. of *b*, producing *tʾbr*, then metathesis to *tʾrb*. LXX $^{\beta}$ ≠ MT, but the underlying text cannot be recovered.

Variant: *tbʾ* (MT *teʾĕrōb*).

24:16. H. G. von Matius (1998: 16–20) observes a possible variant to v 16b in *b. San*. 7a. Whereas the MT has *wršʿym ykšlw brhʿ* ("and the wicked will stumble in [or "into"] evil"), the Amorai Samuel cites this line as *wršʿ ypwl bʾḥt*, "doch ein Frevler fällt über (oder: Durch) eine einzige Sache" ("but a wicked man falls over [or: through] a single thing." Von Matius argues that this is a textual variant, and not a reworking of the MT. Still, the citation's difference from MT is considerable and its attestation is slim. Rather than a written variant, Samuel's citation seems to be a mnemonic conflation of 24:16a with *b. San*. 7a.

24:17. LXX *ho echthros sou* "your enemy" = qeré. (The ketiv probably intends the plural, though the Masorah says that the *yod* is superfluous.) In $^{\beta}$, MT's *ʾl ygl lbk* "let your heart not rejoice" is translated *mē epairou*, "do not exalt yourself" = *ygdl* (*yagdēl*). The same set of variants appears in 23:24. Syr too follows the qeré.

Ketiv *ʾybyk*, qeré *ʾôyibkā*.

24:19. LXX *mē chaire* "do not rejoice" = *ʾl tḥd* (*tiḥadd*) (Lag.); cf. Jer 31[38]:13.

Variant: *tḥd* (MT *tithar*).

24:20. LXX *egkona* "offspring" for *ʾḥryt* "end," as in 23:18.

24:21–22e. Together with vv 21 and 22, five additional verses in the LXX (vv 22a–22e) form a prose epigram on the power and responsibilities of the king and the danger of his wrath. Attempts have been made to reconstruct a Heb source-text. There is some indication of a Hebrew basis in the pleonastic construction in v 22a, but the evidence is not definitive. BA notes that in the LXX, the unit break comes after v 20, and the scribe of LXX^{B} has placed a large dash here, apparently to mark a break he saw. Syr lacks the additional verses. The epigram in its entirety, translated somewhat freely, reads:

(24:21) Fear God, O son, and the king, and do not disobey either of them. (22) For suddenly they will punish the wicked, and who knows the punishments either may bring? (22a) A son who keeps the command will be free from destruction, and when he receives (a command), he truly absorbs it. (22b) Let no tongue speak falsehood to the king, nor let any falsehood go forth from *his* tongue. (22c) For the tongue of a king is a sword, not flesh, and whoever is delivered (to its power) will be shattered. (22d) For should his anger be provoked, he destroys men with sinews, (22e) and the bones of men he gnaws up. Like a flame he burns them up, so that even young eagles cannot eat them.

This essay recalls a long proverb-poem in the Aramaic Ahiqar, quoted in the Comment on 24:22. Since Ahiqar was popular in the Hellenistic period and known in Greek, there is a good chance that Ahiqar's influence on the LXX here was direct.

24:21. LXX: "$^{\alpha}$ Fear God, O son, and the king, $^{\beta}$ and do not disobey [*apeithēsęs*] either of them [*kai mētheterǫ*]." *Mētheterǫ* = *wʿm šnyhm*, for MT's *ʿm šwnym* "with dissenters" (meaning uncertain). "Do not disobey" probably reflects *ttʿbr*, associated with *ʿbr ʿl* "transgress." De Waard considers LXX's "do not disobey" a case of exegetical metathesis (1993: 25), but it could render *ttʿbr* in the source text. Vul translates *šwnym* as *detractoribus* "detractors."

Syr: "(a) Fear, my son, the Lord, and rule [*wʾmlk*], (b) and do not mix with fools [*wʿm šṭy*^{ʾpl} *lʾ tthlṭ*]." Syr *wʾmlk* = *ûmᵉlōk*, where MT vocalizes *wāmelek*. The imperative apparently shows Solomon speaking to his son, telling him to reign as a consequence of fearing God. Syr *šṭy*^{ʾpl} associates Heb *šwnym* with Syr *šnʾ*, one of whose meanings is "go mad" (Pink.); sim. Tg.

B. Soṭa 22b and *Num. Rab.* 15.14 (116a) read *wʿm* "and with" for *ʿm* "with." The rabbis probably introduced the natural syntax into their recollection of the verse.

Variants: *ttʿbr* (MT *titʿārāb*); *šnyhm* (MT *šônîm*).

24:22. LXX: "$^{\alpha}$ For suddenly they [sc. God and king] will punish the wicked, $^{\beta}$ and who knows the punishments of either [*tas de timōrias amphoterōn*]?" In the MT, it is unclear whether v 22 describes the punishment suffered *by* the *šwnym* "dissenters" (?) or the disaster they cause. LXX assumes the former and recasts the verse in the active voice. The verse then clearly describes the actions of the two powers and gives them an explicit moral motivation. This recasting suits the message of the following verses as well.

Syr: "(b) and the end [*swpʾ*] of their years [*dšnyhwn*^{pl}] who knows?" That is, one does not how fools (*šṭy*^{ʾpl}) will end up. Syr derives Heb *šnyhm* from *šānāh* "year."

24:22a. LXX: "$^{\alpha}$ A son who keeps a word is free from destruction [*apōleias ektos estai*], $^{\beta}$ and receiving it, he received it [*dechomenos de edexato auton*]." BA: $^{\beta}$ "en la recevant, il l'a vraiment reçue" ("in receiving it, he has truly received it"). The repetition in 22a$^{\beta}$ probably represents an inf. abs. construction, *wᵉqabbēl qibbᵉlô*. By itself, 22a inculcates the importance of obedience to the father's teaching. In context, it tells the son to obey the king's command.

24:22b. LXX: "Let no falsehood from the tongue be said to a king, nor any falsehood proceed from *his* tongue." On the special emphasis given to truth and falsehood in LXX-Prov, see Dick 1990: 23.

24:22c. LXX: "For the tongue of a king is a sword and not flesh, and whoever is delivered (to it) will be shattered." Ahiqar says, "The king's word is soft, but it is sharper and stronger than a double-edged sword" (100b [1.1.85]; passage quoted in Comment on 24:14).

24:22d. LXX: "For if his anger is provoked, he consumes [*analiskei*] men with sinews [*neuroi*]." In 2 Mac 7:1, sinews or cords (*neura*, pl.) are an instrument of torture.

24:22e. LXX: "$^{\alpha}$ And the bones of men he gnaws up [*katatrōgei*]. $^{\beta}$ Like a flame he burns them up, $^{\gamma}$ so that they are inedible (even) for young eagles." The wording of the threat in 22e$^{\gamma}$ resembles 30:17.

LXX continues with 30:1–14, then 24:23–34.

24:23. LXX: "$^{\alpha}$ These things I say to you, wise men, to make (them) known [*tauta de legō hymin tois sophois epiginōskein*]. $^{\beta}$ To respect a face in judgment is not good." Heb *lḥkmym* (probably meaning "of" or "by" the wise) is understood as "*to* the wise," and the verse becomes an exhortation directed to them. In this way, and consistent with the translator's procedure in 30:1 and 31:1, the LXX avoids ascription of authorship to anyone but Solomon. Heb *hkr* is rendered twice: $^{\alpha}$ *epiginōskein* (a frequent correspondence) and $^{\beta}$ *aideisthai prosōpon*. Jäg. says that *tauta de* in 24:23$^{\alpha}$ corresponds to *tade* in 30:1$^{\gamma}$, which in LXX begins the immediately preceding unit.

Vul corresponds to the MT but construes it similarly to LXX: *haec quoque sapientibus*, "These are also to the wise."

Syr: "(a) These things I say to the wise" (*hlyn lḥkym*^{ʾpl} *ʾmr ʾnʾ*) ≈ LXX. (b) ≈ MT.

24:26. LXX (continuing 25): "and they will kiss lips that answer (with) good words [*logous agathous* ^{BS}; *sophous* ^{ACSc}; *orthous* ^{V}]." The subject of "kiss" is an indefinite "they." The translation is a strained construal of the difficult Heb syntax.

Syr: "and they will kiss the lips of those who reprove [*dmksnyn*^{pl}]." The implied subject of "kiss" is indefinite. Syr's "those who reprove" associates *nkḥym* "honest" with the homeophonic *môkîḥîm* "reprovers." This is the way Syr construes *n*^{e}*kōḥāh* in Amos 3:10 and *n*^{e}*kōḥôt* in Isa 30:10. Tg^{Z}: "And (people) will kiss the lips of those who answer (with) honest words [*mly tryṣtʾ*]."

24:27. LXX: "$^{\alpha}$ Make ready your [sg.] works for the departure [*exodon*], $^{\beta}$ and make preparations for the field. $^{\gamma}$ And come after me [*kai poreuou katopisthen mou*], $^{\delta}$ and you shall build up your house." LXX read *lk ʾḥry* "go after me" (near-dittog. *w/y* with next word) for MT's *lk wʾḥr* "to you, and after." The change led to other deviations from the MT. Gerleman (1956: 29) reads this verse as a reminder of death. To be sure, this idea might make sense for an Egyptian, who would hope to depart for the paradise in the "Field of Reeds" and live in his "Eternal House," but it is impossible that Alexandrian Jews accepted this foreign belief.

Variant: *lk ʾḥry* (MT *lāk ʾaḥar*).

24:28. LXX translates *rʿk* as *son politēn* "your fellow citizen"; see 11:12.

24:29. LXX: $^{\alpha}$ = MT; "$^{\beta}$ I will repay him with the harm he has done me" (*teisomai de auton ha me ēdikēsen*). This reformulation of the MT contradicts the law of talion even more strongly than does the MT (BA). The addition of "the harm" leaves no doubt that "what he has done to me" refers to an inimical act.

Syr connects this verse to the preceding by a *waw*—"(a) And do not say, etc."—thereby making it an admonition against using false testimony to get revenge.

24:30–34. In 24:30–34, LXX has composed an epigram that draws imagery and phraseology from the MT but uses them very differently, so much so that there is no point in trying to connect the LXX in detail to the Hebrew. In vv 30–32, the lazy, foolish man is *compared* to a field. Then in 33, the sluggard announces his intention to be lazy, or perhaps the sage speaks the words as a hypothetical thought, what one *might* think. Then, in v 34, the sage follows up with a warning against such behavior. Syr, Vul, and Tg ≈ MT.

24:30. LXX: "A foolish man is like a field [*hōsper geōrgion*], and like a vineyard is the man who lacks sense."

24:31. LXX: "If you leave it alone, it will go to waste and run entirely to weeds and be abandoned. And the walls of stones are demolished." In other words, one must constantly "tend" to the idler—that is, scold him.

24:32. LXX: "Later I reconsidered, looking to (him), so as to take a lesson."

24:33. LXX: " 'I snooze a little, I sleep a while, I clasp my bosom with (my) hands.' " The sluggard speaks. In 6:10, LXX used the 2nd per.

Syr sets the verse in the 2nd sg., "If you snooze a little, etc.," as in 6:10–11, where it was influenced by the LXX. Tg also uses the 2nd sg.

24:34. LXX: "[α] If you do this, your poverty will arrive advancing, [β] and your neediness (arrive) like a good runner [*agathos dromeus*]." See the Textual Note on 6:11. In 24:34 and 6:11, the fast runner is called "good" (rather than "fast") even though he is the analogy for a misfortune. This calls to mind Plato's *Hippias Minor* 373c–e, in which "goodness" is defined as the skill or potential (*dunamis*) for achieving goals relevant to a particular activity; an example is the *agathos dromeus*. Unlike LXX 6:11, the additional verse in LXX 6:11a misses the point entirely, showing that that the latter is a later extension of v 11.

Syr: "Poverty will come to you and need will advance upon you [*wtdrkk*], (b) like a runner [*gbrʾ ṭblrʾ*]." Syr shows the influence of LXX without conforming to it entirely. Syr diverges from its own translation of the doublet in 6:11, where it uses *kšyrʾ* for Heb *mgn*.

LXX continues with 30:15–31:9, followed by 25:1ff.

25:1. LXX: "[α] These are the miscellaneous teachings of Solomon [β] which the friends of Ezekias king of Judah copied out" ([α] *hautai hai paideiai* [*paroimiai* [ASc, MSS]] *salōmōntos hai adiakritoi* [β] *has exegrapsanto hoi philoi Ezekiou tou basileōs tēs ioudaias*). BA understands this verse as summarizing the preceding section (LXX 30:15–31:9). The *adiakritoi*, a hapax in LXX, has nothing corresponding in the MT. Some glosses are "mixed" (GELS); "qui ne sont pas triées" ("which are not selected [or "sorted"]") (BA); "undistinguishable," "mixed," "not discriminated" (LSJ); and "profound" (Syr). In Jas 3:17 *adiakritos* is a virtue; there it describes the wisdom from above and means something like "impartial," "without prejudice." Vul leaves it out.

Syr: "(a) These too are the profound [*ʿmyqʾ*[pl]] proverbs of Solomon, (b) which the friends [*rḥmʾ*[pl]] of Hezekiah king of Judah wrote [*ktbw*].” *Adiakritoi* is understood to mean “inscrutable,” hence profound. Syr *rḥmʾ* is used of “friend” [*rᵉʿēh*, *rēah*] of the king, that is, royal confidant, in 1 Kgs 4:5; 2 Sam 15:37; 16:16.

25:2. LXX: “α The glory of God hides a word, β but the glory of a king honors [*timą̄*] matters [*pragmata* S].” “Honors” = *hqr* (*hōqar*), for MT *ḥqr*; sim. in 25:27.

Variant: *hqr* (MT *ḥăqōr*).

25:3. LXX: “α The sky is high, and the earth is deep, β but the heart of a king is irrefutable [or “beyond criticism”; *anexelegktos*].” *Anexelegktos* can mean “unfathomable” (BA: “insondable”) or “unchastised,” as in Prov 10:17. In 18:17, *ḥqr* is translated *elegchetai* “refuted.”

25:4. LXX: “α Smite [*typte*] the drossy [*adokimon*] silver, β and the pure shall be entirely purified [*kai katharisthēsetai katharon hapan*].” LXX α alludes to beating fools. The next verse too (using *kteinein* “kill”) shows that the translator thinks that *hgw* (actually “remove”) has to do with smiting, perhaps by association with *hakkŽ*. Gk *hapan* = Heb *klw* (*kullô*), for MT’s *kly* “vessel.”

Variants: *klw* (MT *kelî*).

25:5. LXX renders *hgw* here as *kteine* “kill” (cf. v 1), showing deliberate variation in translation equivalents.

25:7c–8b. Vul reads 7c–8b as a unit, with attention to the MT: “ (7c) The things your eyes have seen (8) do not bring forth [*ne proferas* = *tōṣēʾ*] hastily in a quarrel, lest you are subsequently unable to make amends, having dishonored your friend.”

25:9 (MT 9b) LXX: “Withdraw backwards, do not show contempt [*anachōrei eis ta opisō, mē kataphronei*],” (continues in 10α). MT 9a is omitted presumably because it seems to advocate conflict, contrary to v 8. Gk *anachōrei eis ta opisō* = Heb *wswr ʾḥr* (*wᵉsûr ʾaḥar*), for MT’s *wswd ʾḥr* “the secret of another.” MT’s *ʾl tgl* (“do not reveal”) was understood as *ʾal tāgîl* “do not rejoice,” that is, maliciously, hence “show contempt.”

Variants: *wswr* (MT *wᵉsôd*).

25:10. LXX (continuing 9): “α so that your friend not insult you, β and your [sg.] quarrel and hatred persist [lit., “not cease”] γ but be with you like death.” LXX is loosely related to the MT. 10γ is part of an expansion that continues in 10a.

25:10a. LXX: “α Graciousness and love make (one) free [*eleutheroi*]. β Guard them for yourself, so that you do not become disgraceful. γ But guard your ways peacefully.” A concluding summary of 7γ–10.

25:11. LXX: “An apple of gold in a necklace of sardius stone: thus it is to say a word [*houtōs eipein logon*].” The difficult *ʿl ʾpnyw* is skipped. Gk *eipein logon* implicitly vocalizes the Heb as *dabbēr dābār.*

25:14. LXX: “α As the wind and clouds and rains are very conspicuous [*epiphanestatoi*], β so are those who boast over a false gift.” LXX understands MT’s *nśyʾym* as “lifted up,” hence *epiphanestatoi* “evident,” “conspicuous.” LXX’s proverb derides the insincere gift-givers for their ostentation (BA).

25:15. LXX: “α In patience there is success [*euodia*] for kings”; β ≈ MT. “Success” relates *ypth* to “wide” (cf. 24:28). In Gen 9:27—*yapt ʾŽlōhîm lᵉyepet* (“May God give spaciousness to Japheth”)—*p-t-h* has a meaning close to *euodia* “success." LXX's *basileusin*, "for kings," renders MT's *qṣyn* "officer"; see the Note on 19:6. The LXX instructs kings on how to succeed, whereas the MT tells courtiers how to influence officials.

25:19. LXX: "$^{\alpha}$ The tooth of an evil man and the foot of a transgressor [*pous paranomou*] $^{\beta}$ will perish [*oleitai*] in an evil day." LXX lacks *mwʿdt mbṭḥ* and consequently reads *rgl bwgd* as a bound phrase, *pous paranomou*. The LXX misses the point of the verse and, as often, substitutes an expected message: the certainty of retribution. Syr too understands Heb *rʿh* as "bad man" (*dbyšʾ* = *kakou*). See the Note on 25:14.

25:20. LXX: "$^{\alpha}$ As vinegar is unpleasant [or "useless"] to a wound, $^{\beta}$ so does suffering that befalls the body grieve the heart." LXX does not represent the first clause of MT 20: *mʿdh bgd bywm qrh*, "One who removes a garment on a cold day." These words might be a distorted dittog. of the end of 19b (Hitzig). The matter is complicated, however, by the fact that LXX 20a is aware at least of *bgd* "garment." The rest of 20 is treated very freely, with *bšrym* understood as *bśrym* "flesh" (the pl. occurs in 14:30). Syr ≈ MT.

25:20a. LXX: "$^{\alpha}$ As a moth (does) to a garment and a worm to wood, $^{\beta}$ so does a man's suffering harm (his) heart." Sim. Vul. This proverb was placed here (or composed) because of its thematic associations with 20 ("garment" and "grieves the heart"). LXX 20a$^{\beta}$ is a rephrasing of part of 20$^{\beta}$ or possibly of a variant Heb proverb. BHS suggests that the source-text read *kss bbgd wrqb lʿṣ kn twgt ʾyš mklh lbw*, "Like a moth in a garment and rot to wood, thus the misery of a man makes his heart waste away."

25:21. LXX and Syr omit "bread" and "water" as superfluous.

25:23. LXX: "$^{\alpha}$ The north wind stirs up clouds [*exegeirei nephē*], $^{\beta}$ and a brazen [*prosopōn anaides*] face provokes [*erethizei*] (the) tongue." In 23$^{\alpha}$, as in 25:14 and 26:1, the LXX treats meteorological phenomena differently than the MT (BA). The unique correspondences *anaides* for *nzʿmym* and *erethizei* for *str* arise from the assumptions that the metaphor in 23$^{\alpha}$ refers to provocation and that the "face" is what is being compared to the wind. LXX reorganizes the syntax in 23$^{\beta}$.

Vul: "The north wind scatters rain [*dissipat pluvias*], as a sad face does to a slanderous tongue [*linguam detrahentem*]." Compare *b. Taʿan.* 7b: "Rain is withheld only because of those who speak with an evil tongue," citing this verse (C. Gordon 1930: 402).

Syr: "(a) Just as the north wind is pregnant with [*bṭnʾ*] rain, (b) so are an angry [lit., "bad"] face and a hidden tongue [*ʾpʾpl byštʾ*^{pl} *wlšnʾ mṭšyʾ*]." Syr (sim. Tg) restructures the comparison. Syr *bṭnʾ* conveys the etymological sense of Heb *tḥwll* "gives birth to." The Syr proverb says that an angry face and a tongue that gossips behind people's backs cause provocation—though "provocation" or the like is left unstated.

25:24. LXX = MT. Contrast the freer treatment of the near-doublets in 21:9 and 19. Syr translates Heb *byt ḥbr* as *wbbytʾ dplgwtʾ*^{pl} "and in a house of factions"—a guess at an unsual phrase, which was ignored in 21:9.

Ketiv *mdwnym*, qeré *midyānîm*.

25:25. LXX: "$^{\alpha}$ As [*hōsper*] cold water is pleasant [*prosēnes*] to the thirsting soul, [β] thus [*houtōs*] is good news from a far land." LXX phrases the juxtaposition as an explicit comparison by adding *hōsper . . . houtōs* (so also Syr); likewise in 25:26 and 26:3, thereby (as BA observes) creating a cohesive series of six comparisons: 25:25, 26, 28; 26:1, 2, 3.

Syr ≈ MT. In 25:25, 26, 28; 26:1, 2, 3, Syr follows the syntax of LXX, but chooses its own way of dealing with the Hebrew; for example, 25:25 adds *dʾtʾ* "that comes," not in LXX or MT.

25:26. LXX: "[α] Just as if someone were to block up a spring and spoil the exit of water, [β] thus is it improper [*akosmon*] for a righteous person to fall before the impious [pl.]." LXX puts 26[a] into the active voice and defines the situation as a matter of propriety or aesthetics. This is not far from MT Proverbs' own moral aesthetics; see Essay 8 (II), "Coherence Theory."

25:27. LXX: "[β] But it is necessary to honor esteemed words [*timan de chrē logous endoxous*]." Gk *timan de* = *whqr* (*w*[e]*hôqēr*) (Jäg.), as in LXX 27:2. The Heb inf. would account for *chrē*. In 27[β] LXX represents *whqr dbr mkbd* (*w*[e]*hōqēr dābār m*[e]*kubbād*). However, this Hebrew would be better translated "and being sparing of a word is honorable." The differences between this reading and the consonants of the MT are common graphic mutations (*h-ḥ, b-k, r-d* confusions, *d-b* metathesis, different word division). Van Leeuwen suggests that the LXX confused the common *ḥqr* with the rare *hqr*, vocalized *kbdm* as *k*[e]*bēdîm* (supposedly meaning "difficulties") and added *logous* "words" for explication (1986a: 106–107). This explanation, however, is too intricate. LXX's *timan* resulted from the extremely common *ḥ*/*h* confusion, not a misunderstanding of a common word.

Vul: "Just as it is not good for one to eat much honey, so shall he who is an examiner of majesty [*maiestatis*] be crushed [*opprimitur*] by glory." Heb *kbdm* is taken as "majesty," while *kbwd* is related to *kābēd* "heavy." This recalls the sentiments of Sir 3:21–23.

Syr: "(a) It is not good to eat much honey, (b) nor to examine glorious [or "complimentary"] words [*mlʾ*[pl] *mšbḥtʾ*[pl]]." The added negative in the second line, though accepted by some modern commentators as original (see the Comment), is an attempt to make sense of an obscure line.

Variants: *whqr dbr mkbd* (MT *w*[e]*ḥēqer k*[e]*bōdām kābôd*).

25:28. LXX's "without counsel" (*ou meta boulēs*)" = *ʾyn mʿṣh* (*ʾên mōʿēṣāh*) for MT's *ʾyn mʿṣr* (Jäg.).

Variant: *mʿṣh* (MT *maʿṣār*).

26:1. LXX: "[α] Like dew [*drosos*] in harvest [*amētǭ*] and like rain in summer [*therei*], [β] so is there no honor for a fool." The LXX substitutes *drosos* "dew" for Heb *šlg* "snow." The LXX compares a fool's honor to things that do not exist, whereas the MT compares it to things that are inappropriate and useless. The MT could not use dew in this way because dew *does* fall in summer in Palestine. The LXX adjusts the meteorological phenomena to the Egyptian climate; cf. 25:14, 23.

26:2. LXX: "[α] As birds fly, and (also) sparrows, [β] so does a vain curse come upon no one [*oudeni*]." Gk *oudeni* reflects the ketiv. Vul *in quempiam superveniet*, "shall come upon himself" = qeré.

Syr: "go astray [*phy*ʾ]" ≈ ketiv.

Ketiv *l*ʾ, qeré *lô*.

26:3. LXX: "$^{\alpha}$ A whip for a horse, a goad [*kentron*] for an ass: $^{\beta}$ so too a rod for a lawless nation [*ethnei paranomǭ*]." By using "goad" for Heb *meteg* ("bridle"), the LXX tightens the analogy among the three figures: horse, ass, fool (BA). *Ethnei* represents *lgwy* (*l*^{e}*gôy*) for MT's *lgw* (also Sym, Quinta; cf. Syr 19:29). Because of this change, "lawless" was used instead of "fools" because the former is typical of wicked nations.

Variant: *lgwy* (MT *l*^{e}*gēw*).

26:4. LXX: "$^{\alpha}$ Do not answer a fool in accordance with [*pros*] his folly, $^{\beta}$ so that you not become like him."

26:5. LXX: "$^{\alpha}$ Rather [*alla*], answer the fool because of his folly [*kata tēn aphrosynēn*], $^{\beta}$ so that he not appear wise to himself." The distinction between *pros* in 4 and *kata* in 5 is an attempt to resolve the contradiction: (4) You should not answer the fool in a way that *resembles* his folly, but rather (5) respond *because of* his folly, that is, rebuke his nonsense. BA: "(4) à proportion de . . . (4) en raison de."

Syr: "(a) But speak with a fool according to your wisdom [ʾ*yk ḥkymwtk*], (b) lest he think in his soul that he is wise." Syr (sim. Tg) boldly reverses the meaning of the MT in order to avoid the contradiction with v 4.

26:6. LXX: "$^{\beta}$ He who sends a word by a foolish messenger, $^{\alpha}$ drinks shame [*oneidos pietai* ^{A}] from his own feet [*ek tōn heautou podōn* $^{\text{SyH, 106, etc.}}$]." The text is Rahlfs; it conveys an image suggestive of drinking one's own urine. However, *podōn* is hexaplaric and *pietai* too looks like an adjustment to MT. We should perhaps read, "$^{\alpha}$ makes (for himself) [*poieitai* $^{\text{BS, MSS}}$] shame from his own ways [*hodōn* $^{\text{BSA, MSS}}$]." This explains the metaphor in 6a and vocalizes *miqṣēh* (lit., "from the ends of" [his feet]) for MT's *m*^{e}*qaṣṣeh* "cuts off."

Syr: "(a) From under his feet [*mn tḥyt rglh*] he drinks iniquity—(b) he who sends a word by means of a fool." In Syr the image suggests drinking water from a mud puddle.

26:7. LXX: "$^{\alpha}$ Remove walking from legs [*aphelou poreian skelōn*] $^{\beta}$ and transgression [*paranomian* $^{\text{BSA, Swete}}$; *paroimian* "a parable" $^{\text{SyH, 3 MSS}}$] from the mouth of fools." V 7$^{\alpha}$ is an attempt to explain the metaphor of legs hanging down from a cripple. With the reading *paranomian*, the proverb means that crime is as natural to the mouth of fools as walking is to the legs (BA). *Paroimian* (followed by Rahlfs) is hexaplaric. The translator probably chose *paranomian* out of a hesitation to credit the fool with the ability to use a proverb at all.

Syr: "(a) If you can give walking to a cripple [ʾ*n ttl hlkt*ʾ *lḥgyr*ʾ], (b) you can receive a word [*mlt*ʾ] from the mouth of the fool." This is a paraphrase suggesting the impossibility of learning something from a fool. Rather than conceding that fools can use proverbs at all (see above on LXX and 26:9), Syr uses *mlt*ʾ "word," which can be any utterance. It is not necessary to emend *mlt*ʾ to *mšl*ʾ (Pink.).

26:8. Vul: "Like him who throws a stone into the heap of Mercury" (*sicut qui mittit lapidem in acervum Mercurii*)—that is, before his idol. This corresponds to *Yal. Sh.* (ad loc.), cf. *b Ḥullin* 133a: "Hama bar Hanina said that one who benefits a person whom he does not know is like one who throws a stone to Mercury" (C. Gordon 1930: 388). This alludes to the Greco-Roman custom of placing votive stones alongside roads in honor of Hermes/Mercury, the patron of roads and travel (Delitzsch).

Variant: *kṣrr* (MT *kiṣrôr*).

26:9. LXX: "$^{\alpha}$ Thorns grow [*phyontai*] in ["by"?] [*en*] the hand [*cheiri*] of the drunkard, $^{\beta}$ and bondage [*douleia*] in ["by"?] [*en*] the hand of the fools." The point of comparison is either that thorns and bondage are cultivated and produced *by* these types, or that these misfortunes grown *in* them and afflict them. The notion of "bondage" comes from parsing Hebrew *mšl* ("proverb" in the MT) as a passive verb, "being ruled." Since *māšāl* was obviously well known to the translator, this must be a deliberate homiletical twist.

Syr has "folly" (*wšṭywt'*) rather than "proverb" (sim. Tg). The translator was apparently puzzled that a proverb should be in the fool's mouth and so substituted something more logical; cf. 26:7.

26:10. LXX: "$^{\alpha}$ All the flesh of fools is greatly battered, $^{\beta}$ because their fury is shattered" ($^{\alpha}$ *polla cheimazetai pasa sarx aphronōn*, $^{\beta}$ *syntribetai gar hē ekstasis autōn*). *Cheimazetai* (= MT *mḥwll*, understood as passive) means "driven by a storm," hence "be afflicted" (cf. MT Isa 53:5). The meaning of *ekstasis* in this context is unclear, but since it translates some form of *ʿbrh* "wrath" (*ʿebrātô* or *ʿebrātām*), it probably is to be understood as "being outside oneself with rage." LXX seems to mean that fools are punished when their anger is destroyed. The translator read this verse as, approximately, *rab mᵉḥolāl kol bᵉśar kᵉsîl, wᵉšubbar ʿebrātām* (treating the number of the last suffix loosely). Sym: "He who muzzles [*phrassōn*] a fool muzzles up [*emphrassei*] his anger," relating *śwkr* to *skr* "dam up." Sim. Theod. Vul: *iudicium determinat causas et qui inponit stulto silentium iras mitigat* ("Judgment decides cases, and he who puts a fool to silence soothes anger") (≈ Sym, Theod). This looks like a guess, except that it understands *rb* as *rîb* and parses *wśkr* both times as *wᵉsōkēr*, lit., "he who stops up"; cf. Rashi; C. Gordon 1930: 404.

Syr: "(a) The flesh of the fool suffers [*ḥ'š*] greatly, (b) and the drunkard crosses the sea [*ʿbr ym'*]." (a) = *rb mḥwll ksyl* ≈ LXX. (b) = *wᵉšikkōr ʿōbēr yām*. The first *wškr* in the MT is not represented. The translator perhaps read—or at least treated the verse as if he read—*rb mḥll bśr ksyl, wškr ʿbr ym* (*rab mᵉḥōlāl bᵉśār kᵉsîl, wᵉšikkōr ʿōbēr yām*). See the Comment.

Variants: *bśr* (MT *wᵉśōkēr*); *wšbr, wškr* (MT *wᵉśōkēr*); *ʿbr ym* (MT *ʿōbᵉrîm*).

26:11. LXX adds an explicatory *kai misētos genētai* "and becomes hateful" in 11$^{\alpha}$. LXX has a double translation of *b'wltw* "in his folly" as *kakią* "evil" and *hamartian* "sin." This strongly emphasizes the moral corruption of the fool's behavior.

Syr: "(b) Thus is a fool who acts stupid in his folly [*dšṭ' bsklwth*]." Heb *šwnh* is associated with Syr *šanyā'* "madman"; see 24:21.

26:11a. LXX: "$^{\alpha}$ There is a shame that brings on sin, and $^{\beta}$ there is a shame that is honor and grace." This is a later insertion quoting Sir 4:21. In Sir 4:20–21 and 41:14–22, Ben Sira distinguishes worthy shame (including shame for one's sins, humility before men of high degree, and modesty before women) and unworthy shame (such as embarrassment about the Law [i.e., about being publicly Jewish], diffidence in commercial dealings, and more); see Skehan and Di Lella 1987: 480–83). This insertion comments on 26:11, indicating that one *should* be ashamed of his own folly so as to avoid repeating it, and on v 12, implying that a proper "shame" (i.e., humility, the opposite of being wise in one's own eyes) can bring honor. Forti (2007: 252–56) says that the ideational deviation between the MT and the LXX of 26:11 reflects an interpretive process in the spirit of Ben Sira's exhortations, in particular the heightened concern for sin and the respresentation of the fool as a sinner and its linkage with shame.

26:12. LXX *eidon* "I saw" = *rʾyty*, for MT *rʾyt* "have you seen?" (near-dittog. with *ʾyš*).

Variant: *rʾyty* (MT *rāʾîtā*).

26:13. LXX: "[α] A sluggard says when he is sent [*apostellomenos*] to the street, [β] 'A lion in the streets, [γ] and murderers in the plazas!' " *Apostellomenos* = *šlḥ* (as if pointing *šālûaḥ*) for MT *šḥl* "lion." "Murderers" is supplied to make sense of 13[β]. Most MSS have a third stich ([γ]) that is copied from 22:13[β], which is itself influenced by the present verse.

Syr: "(a) The sluggard says when he is sent [*mʾ dmštdr*]." Syr probably borrows *apostellomenos* from the LXX, but then translates *šḥl* as "lion." Syr lacks LXX stich [γ]. This verse affected the rendering of 22:13, q.v.

26:15. LXX: "[α] The sluggard, hiding his hand in (his) bosom." The versions did not understand *ṣalaḥat* as "plate," but translated it here and at 19:24 as "bosom" (LXX, Syr) or "armpit" (Aq, Sym, Theod, Vul, Tg). The resulting image is one of inactivity; see 24:33 LXX; cf. 6:10 and Qoh 4:5.

26:16. LXX: "[β] than the one who brings back a report in satisfaction [*plēsmonę̄*]." LXX construes MT's *mšbʿh* ("than seven") as *miśśobʿāh*, lit., "from satisfaction" (= "satisfactorily"? Or "when he is satisfied" [BA]?). Heb *ṭʿm* is given the sense of Aram *ṭᵉʿēm* "report" (Baum.).

26:17. LXX: "Like one who grabs the tail [kerkou] of a dog, thus is he who puts himself forward [proestōs] in a conflict of another." LXX speaks of grabbing the tail of a dog, perhaps because the tail is easier to grasp than the ears. LXX's *ho proestōs* "one who stands up for" (GELS) or "one who makes himself the mouthpiece" (GELS) could correspond to either *mtʿbr* (MT) or *mtʿrb*. The notion of becoming a spokesman in litigation is more specific than interfering in another's quarrel.

26:18. LXX: "[α] As the healers hurl [*proballousin*] words at men, [β] and he who encounters the word first will stumble . . . " (continues in 19) ([α] *hōsper hoi iōmenoi proballousin logous eis anthrōpous,* [β] *ho de apantēsas tǭ logǭ prōtos hyposkelisthēsetai*). BA: "Comme les guérisseurs donnent aux gens de belles paroles—et celui qui s'y prête va rechuter le premier" ("Just as healers give fine words to people—and he who yields to it is going to relapse first"). This is a cynical remark about physicians. LXX, which is itself obscure, is unrelated to the Heb and does not provide a meaningful analogy to v 19.

26:19. LXX (continuing 18): "[α] thus are all who lie in wait [*enedreuontes*] for their friends—[β] when they are discovered [*hotan de phōrathōsin* [A]; *orathōsin* "are seen" [BS*, MSS] = Syr], $^{\gamma}$ they say, 'I acted in jest.' " With the exception of this verse and 2 Sam 3:27, *enedreuein* always translates *ʾrb* "to ambush." LXX adds "and when they are discovered" to make a logical connection between the crime ($^{\alpha}$) and the excuse ($^{\gamma}$).

26:20. LXX: "$^{\alpha}$ By much wood [pl.], fire flourishes, $^{\beta}$ and where there is no dissenter (?) [*dithymos* [B]; *oxythymos* "quick tempered" [ASc]], conflict quiets down." LXX 20$^{\alpha}$ is a converse translation that creates an antithesis within the verse but disturbs the analogy.

26:21. LXX ≈ MT, but *eschara* "hearth" is a synecdoche for Heb *pḥm* "coals." Gk *loidoros* = *mdwnym*, ketiv.

Ketiv *mdwnym*, qeré *midyānîm*.

26:22. LXX: "The words of knaves [*kerkōpōn*] are soft [*malakoi*], but they strike [*typtousin*] the chambers of the innards [*splagchnōn*]." The hapax *kerkōps* actually means "monkey-man," "ape" (LSJ), hence "knaves" (LSJ), "tellers of false tales" (GELS), "malins singes" ("mischievous apes"; BA), or the like. "Soft" is a contextual guess at the obscure *mtlhmym*. Vul translates *nirgan* as *susurronis* "murmurer." Heb *nrgn* was translated differently in Vul 26:20.

26:23. LXX: "$^{\alpha}$ Silver given with deceit should be considered [*hēgēteon*] as a potsherd. $^{\beta}$ Smooth [var. "deceitful"] lips hide a grieving heart [*cheilē leia* (*dolia* [S, MSS]) *kardian kalyptei lypēran*]." The translation of the Heb is loose, but it is likely that Gk *leia* = *ḥlqym* "smooth" for MT's *dlqym* "burning" (Jäg.). V 23$^{\beta}$ belongs with 24$^{\alpha}$.

Variant: *ḥlqym* (MT *dōl^{e}qîm*).

26:24. LXX (continuing 23$^{\beta}$): "$^{\alpha}$ An enemy, weeping, promises all things by (his) lips [*cheilesin panta epineuei apoklaiomenos echthros*], $^{\beta}$ but in the heart he devises deceits." This continues the theme of "lips" from 23$^{\beta}$. Heb *ynkr* (MT N-stem) is taken as an active (D, as in Job 21:29 and 34:19) and is translated *epineuein* "to give recognition by nodding," hence "to promise" (not used elsewhere in translating a Heb text). "All things" and "weeping" are added, to enhance the drama, a quality continued in 25$^{\alpha}$ ("in a *great* voice").

Syr translates MT's unusual *yšyt mrmh* (lit., "sets deceits") as *kmyn kmʾnʾ* "an ambush is concealed," producing a more concrete image.

Ketiv *bśptw*, qeré *biśpātāyw*.

26:25. LXX and Syr treat Heb *yḥnn qwlw* ("beseeches [by] his voice," that is, "speaks graciously") differently. LXX has speaking *loudly*, Syr has speaking *quietly*, lit., "makes his voice low." Vul is closer to the Syr: *quando submiserit vocem suam*, "when he lowers his voice." Apparently "his voice" by itself seemed superfluous, so the versions elaborated.

26:26. LXX: "$^{\alpha}$ He who hides [*ho kryptōn*] hostility contrives deceit [*synistēsin dolon*], $^{\beta}$ but, being well known, he reveals his sins in assemblies [*synhedriois*]." LXX draws together themes from the preceding three verses: enmity (24$^{\alpha}$, 25$^{\alpha}$), deceit (23$^{\alpha}$, 24$^{\beta}$), and uncovering/covering (23$^{\beta}$) (BA). LXX renders MT *tksh* as a ptcp., but it is uncertain whether it is reading *mksh* or adapting to context. LXX adds *eugnōstos* "well known" to explain why the secret will be exposed.

26:27. After "He who digs a pit," LXX adds *tǭ plēsion* "for (his) neighbor" to make it clear that the saying does not apply to digging legitimate holes.

26:28. LXX: "α A deceitful tongue hates truth [*alētheian*], β and an unguarded [*astegon*] mouth causes disorders [*akatastasias*]." For MT's difficult *dkyw* ("those it afflicts" [?], "those crushed by it" [?; JPSV]), LXX has *alētheian* "truth," perhaps by association with Aram *dkʾ* "pure" (Baum.); sim. Syr *qwštʾ*, Vul *veritatem* "truth."

27:1. For MT *ywm* "day" in 1b, LXX has *hē epiousa* "the morrow," in accordance with *maḥar* "morrow" in 1a. See the Note on 3:28.

27:2. LXX: "α Let (your) neighbor [*ho pelas*] praise you and not your mouth, a stranger [*allotrios*] and not your lips." The use of the Septuagintal hapax *pelas* "neighbor" for *zr* "stranger" shows a correct understanding of the Heb word in this context, which means another person, someone not properly belonging to a situation. See Vol. I, 139. In this case it is equivalent to *reaʿ* "fellow."

27:4. LXX: "α Anger is merciless and wrath is swift [*oxeia*], β but jealousy bears [*hyphistatai*] no one." This is an example of the way the LXX can translate "freely" and modify the syntax considerably while conveying the sense of the Hebrew. The rhetorical question in β is reformulated as a negative indicative. (For the phenomenon see Orlinksy 1958: 244–46.) Then the clause is reformulated from the standpoint of "jealousy." Gk *oxeos* means not only "sharp" but also "swift," and is used to translate *mhyr* (22:29) and *ql* (Am 2:15). "Swift" is its sense here, where it explains the metaphorical "torrent."

27:6. LXX: "α More trustworthy are wounds from a friend β than willing kisses of an enemy [*ē hekousia philēmata echthrou*]." LXX introduces a moral lesson by formulating the verse as a comparison and translating *nʿtr* as *hekousia*, a unique etymologizing translation: *neʿtar* means to agree to an entreaty, hence to show willingness. LXX probably shaped the proverb as a comparative parallelism in imitation of vv 3–5 (Cook *1999b*: 143).

27:7. LXX explains *tbws* ("trample") as *empaizei* "mock," by association with the similar-sounding Heb *tbwz* "mock."

27:8. LXX: "α As when a bird flies down [*katapetasthę̄*] from its own nest, β thus a man is enslaved [*douloutai*] when he migrates [*apoxenōthę̄*] from his own places." Whereas the MT suggests the loneliness of a wanderer, the LXX makes the point of comparison enslavement and migration from one's *own* places. We may hear in this the Alexandrian Jew's feelings of alienation.

27:9. LXX: "α By myrrh and wines and incense the heart is pleased, β but by misfortunes a soul is rent [*katarrēgnytai de hypo symptōmatōn psychē*]." The first stich adds "wines" to fill out the picture of merrymaking. The second stich reflects *wmtqrʿh mʿṣbt npš* (Jäg.) for MT's *wmtq rʿhw mʿṣt npš*. The variant involves the loss of *bet*, probably by near-haplog with the similar-looking *t-* and the later addition of a *waw* to *rʿh*, which was thought to mean "friend," hence "his friend."

Variant: *wmtqrʿh mʿṣbt* (MT *ûmeteq rēʿēhû mēʿăṣat-*).

27:10. The qeré and the ketiv are synonym-variants.

Ketiv *wrʿh*; qeré *wᵉrēaʿ*.

27:11. LXX: "α Be wise, my son, so that my heart may rejoice; β and deflect [impv.] from yourself [var. "me"] disgraceful words [*kai apostrepson apo sou* (ABS,

[MSS]; *mou* [CV, MSS]) *eponeidistous logous*].” LXX understands *ḥrpy dbr* as “disgraces of words,” hence “disgraceful words.”

27:13. LXX: “[α] Take away his garment, for an arrogant man has passed by [*parēlthen gar hybristēs*], [β] who damages [*lymainetai*] what does not belong to him.” It is unlikely that the translator is availing himself of “remarkable freedom” in rendering a text identical to the MT (Cook *1999b*: 145). Why would he use this freedom to produce such an obscure proverb? In Prov 6:1; 17:18; and 22:26, the translator conveyed the warning against surety and recognized the relevant words. In 11:15, textual differences and a lexical misunderstanding obscured this theme. In the present verse, slight textual differences obscured this theme: *ʿbr* “passed by” for *ʿrb* (“take in pledge”) and *zd* (*zēd*) “arrogant” for *zr* (“stranger”). (The graphic similarity of *daleth* and *resh* supports this retroversion, though elsewhere *hybristēs* renders *rām* [Prov 6:17] and *gēʾ*/*gēʾeh* [Prov 16:19; Isa 2:12; 16:6; Job 40:6].) Once the verse was detached from the theme of surety, it was natural to construe *ḥblhw* as if from *ḥ-b-l* D “damage” rather than G “seize his pledge.”

Variants: *ʿbr* (MT *ʿārab*); *zd* (MT *zār*).

27:15. Ketiv *mdwnym*, qeré *midyānîm*.

27:16. LXX: “[α] The north wind is a hard wind, [β] but it is called ‘Favorable’ by name [*onomati de epidexios kaleitai*].” 16[α] is a guess at an obscure text. 16[β] can be retroverted to *wšmw ymyny yqrʾ*, lit., “its name is called ‘right’ ” (Jäg.). The right hand is *dexios* and, in Gk, connotes good fortune. It is strange to have the north wind called “right,” since the right side is the south in the Palestinian (and Greek) orientation. Lag. refers to Plutarch *Isis* 32, “The Egyptians think the dawn to be the face of the world, northward to be the right, and southward to be the left.” For the earlier Egyptians, at least, the west (*imnty*) was on the right. Aq, Sym, and the “others” also bring out the concept of north here: *kekrummenos boreas anemos* “the north wind is hidden”; but this does not represent a different consonantal Heb.

Syr: “(a) A northern wind is hard, (b) and it is called by the name of ‘right (hand).’ ” Syr depends on the LXX for the gist of the verse, but it also pays attention to its Heb source-text, as shown by *dymynʾ* “the right” for Heb *ymynw*.

Variants: *wšmw* (MT *w^{e}šemen*); *ymyny* (MT *y^{e}mînô*).

27:17. LXX: “[α] Iron sharpens [*oxynei*] iron, [β] but a man provokes [*paroxynei*] the face of (his) companion.” *Oxynei* and *paroxynei* vocalize *yḥd* (twice) as *y^{e}ḥad*, a shortened impf. from *ḥ-d-d* D “sharpen” (MT has *yāḥad, yaḥad* “together”). The translator plays on words by translating the second occurrence of *yḥd* as *paryxenei* “provokes.” Syr ≈ LXX.

27:19. LXX: “[α] Just as faces are not similar to (other) faces, [β] so too are the hearts [var. “minds”] of men not (similar to each other)” ([α] *hōsper ouch homoia prosōpa prosōpois*, [β] *houtōs oude hai kardiai* [[A, MSS]; var. *dianoiai* [BS*]; + *homoiai* [S*]] *tōn anthrōpōn*). (The variant *dianoiai*, more distant from the MT, is probably original.) LXX read *kmw* “like” for *kmym* “like water” and then supplied *ouch homoia* “not similar,” thereby reversing the meaning of the Heb. Other retroversions have been suggested that preserve the negative (e.g., *kʾyn dwmym*; see Baum.), but they are distant from the MT. Syr follows LXX.

Vul interprets the analogy in an unusual way: "Just as the faces of them that look (in the water) shine in it, so the hearts of men are revealed to the prudent" (*quomodo in aquis resplendent vultus prospicientium sic corda hominum manifesta sunt prudentibus*). This accords with *Mid. Prov.*, *Yal.* (C. Gordon 1930: 395).

Variant: *kmw* (MT *k^e mayim*).

27:20. Some Heb MSS have the qeré as *waʾăbaddôn* (BHS).

Ketiv *wʾbdh*, qeré *waʾăbaddô*.

27:20a. LXX: "α An abomination to the Lord is he who stares [*stērizōn ophthalmon*; lit. "fixes the eye"], β and the uninstructed (are) intemperate of tongue." The addition is based on 6:13 and 16:30 and inserted here because of the mention of the eye in v 20. Not in Syr or Vul.

27:21. LXX α ("Burning is a test for silver and gold") is close to the consonantal MT but does not represent *wkwr* ("and a furnace"), perhaps combining it with *mṣrp*.

Syr: "(a) A smelter assays silver and a furnace gold. (b) But a man by the mouth of those who esteem him [*mi pwmʾ dmḥšbnwhy*^pl]." Syr ≈ MT but adds a verb, (a smelter) "tests [*bqʾ*]." Syr, as well as LXX, VulMSS, and Tg have the pl. "those who esteem/praise." Since the disparate witnesses agree, they are probably reading *mhllyw* (*mahăl^e lāyw*) (thus one MS in K-R).

Variant: *mhllyw* (MT *mahălālô*).

27:21a. LXX: "α The heart of a wicked man seeks evils, β but the upright heart seeks knowledge" (α *kardia anomou ekzētei kaka*, β *kardia de eythēs ekzētei gnōsin*). V 21aβ ≈ MT 18:15. LXX 27:21a reflects, approximately, α *lb ršʿym mbqš rʿ*, β *wlb yšrym mbqš dʿt*. Vul ≈ LXX; Syr = LXX.

Variant: + *lb ršʿym mbqš rʿ*, *wlb yšrym mbqš dʿt*.

27:22. LXX: "α If you whip a fool, disgracing (him) in the midst of the assembly [*en mesǭ synedriou atimazōn*], β you will surely not remove [*ou mē perielę̄s*] his folly." LXX introduces an interesting interpretation of the mortar-in-pestle metaphor: disgracing a fool in public is an ineffective corrective for folly. V 22β is closer to MT, but "you will not remove" = *tāsîr* H-stem (MT *tswr* G-stem).

Syr: "(a) If you beat a fool in the midst of the assembly, (b) you will surely not benefit him [*mdm lʾ mwtr ʾnt lh*] (c) nor remove his folly." Syr follows LXX but adds 22(b) to further explain the consequence of (a). Tg^Z: "If you beat a fool in a mortar [*bmktš*] in the midst of the assembly and with a pestle [*ʾwrdk*?], you will not remove his folly from him." Tg works from Syr but supplements it from the MT.

Variant: *tsyr* (MT *tāsûr*).

27:23. LXX: "α You [sg.] should know well [*gnōstōs epignōsę̄*] the souls [*psychas*] of your flock, and set your heart to your herds." "Souls" is taken from 12:10. LXX 27:23–24 and 25–26α are formulated as two sentences. In 25–26α in particular, the LXX diverges from the Heb sharply to convey a new message, though the Heb is fairly clear.

Syr: "(a) When you are a shepherd [*mʾ drʿʾ ʾnt*]." Syr prefixes a stich to give context to the following epigram.

27:24. LXX: "α For power and strength do not belong to a man forever, β nor does [*oude*] he transmit [*paradidōsin*] them from generation to generation." Heb *ḥsn* "strength" or (as here) "wealth" is translated twice: *kratos kai ischys*. 24$^{\beta}$ adjusts the meaning of *nzr* to the idea expressed in 24$^{\alpha}$ (sim. Tg *šlm*).

Syr: "(a) For power [*'wḥdn'*] is not forever, (b) nor does (one) generation transmit (it) to (another) generation [*w'pl' mšlm dr' ldr'*]." Syr works from the MT, but relies on LXX for the meaning of *nzr*.

Ketiv *dwr*, qeré *wādôr*.

27:25. LXX: "$^{\alpha}$ Cultivate [*epimelou*] vegetation in the field and you will cut [*kereis*] grass. $^{\beta}$ And gather mountain-herbage [*chorton oreinon*] . . ." (continues in 26$^{\alpha}$). LXX uses MT's nouns, but changes the tenor of the first two verbs—and the verse.

27:26. LXX (continuing 25): "$^{\alpha}$ so that you may have sheep for clothing. $^{\beta}$ Honor the field so that you may have lambs." LXX $^{\beta}$ fills out (and misconstrues) an elliptical Hebrew.

27:27. LXX: "$^{\alpha}$ My son, from me you have powerful words [*rhēseis ischyras*] for your life $^{\beta}$ and for the life of your servants [*therapontōn* (masc.)]." LXX uses most of the words of the Heb (ignoring *llḥm bytk*) while shifting the import of the promise from the material to the spiritual realm. LXX thereby suggests that in retrospect 23–26 can be read as an allegory for cultivation of the teachings. BA says that the rendering of *ḥlb* "milk" as *rhēseis* "words" is based on a traditional rabbinic metaphor, but he cites NT passages (1 Cor 3:2; Heb 5:12–13; 1 Pet 2:2) in which milk signifies elementary teachings.

28:2. LXX: "$^{\alpha}$ By the transgression of the impious [pl.], contentions are stirred up, $^{\beta}$ but a clever man will extinguish them" ($^{\alpha}$ *di' hamartias asebōn kriseis egeirontai*, $^{\beta}$ *anēr de panourgos katasbesei autas*). Compare 15:18. The LXX translates a few MT words loosely or with different vocalization (*kriseis* = *rîbîm*). The only variant indicated is *katasbesei autas* = *yd'kwn* or *yd'kn* (*yid'ākûn*), translated with change of voice, where MT has *yd' kn*. The LXX departs entirely from the well-known meanings of *'rṣ* and *śryh*. MT *y'ryk* "is patient" is ignored or implied by "extinguishes them" (Baum.).

Vul translates 2b expansively: "and for a man's wisdom and the knowledge of what is said, the life of the prince shall be prolonged." The idea of the last clause is drawn from 28:16.

Syr: "(b) but righteous men who know honesty will live long." Based on MT.

Variant *yd'kwn* (MT *yōdēa' kēn*).

28:3. LXX: "$^{\alpha}$ A vigorous man [*andreios*] by impieties falsely accuses the lowly [pl.]. $^{\beta}$ As a violent and unprofitable rain . . ." (continues in 4). LXX 3$^{\alpha}$ is an isolated monostich. It represents Heb *gibbōr rāšā' 'ōšēq dallîm* (Lag.), with the ' of *rš'* a dittog. from the next word. It is strange to see the cardinal virtue of *andreia* connected with wrongdoing. The use of the word was probably triggered by reading *gbr* as *gibbôr*. MT's *w'yn lḥm*, "there is no bread," is explained as *anōphelēs* "unprofitable," that is, a rain that does not produce grain.

Variant: *rš' 'šq* (MT *rāš* w^{e}*'ōšēq*).

28:4. LXX (continuing 3$^{\beta}$): "$^{\alpha}$ so do those who abandon the Law praise wickedness [*asebeian*]. $^{\beta}$ But those who love the Law surround themselves with a wall."

"Surround themselves with a wall" = *ytgdrw bm* (Jäg) or *bh* "thereby" (implied in the verb). This resulted from a *d-r* dittog. (Gk *teichos* = *gādēr* in Isa 5:5.)

The LXX alludes to the Law (of Moses) in vv 4 (twice) and (probably) 7, 9, 10. The use of the article in 4 indicates clearly the Law of Moses, but that is the likely intention in the other verses as well. Johann Cook (*2002a*: *282*) compares the image in LXX 28:4$^{\beta}$ to *Ep. Aristeas* 139: "When therefore our lawgiver, equipped by God for insight into all things, had surveyed each particular, he fenced us about with impregnable palisades and with walls of iron, to the end that we should mingle in no way with any of the other nations, remaining pure in body and in spirit, emancipated from vain opinions, revering the one and mighty God above the whole of creation" (quoted in *1999c*: 459, from Hadas *1973*: 157). Israel is surrounded by the wall of Torah to keep it from mingling with foreign nations.

Syr: "(a) Those who abandon the law [*nmwsʾ*] praise themselves for wickedness [*mštbḥyn bʿwlʾ*], (b) but those who keep the law strengthen themselves [*mʿšnyn npšhwn*]." Syr *nmwsʾ* need not mean the Law of Moses, since the word has conformed itself to Heb *twrh* and can mean "teaching," as in 1:8; 6:20; 13:14; and often. "Praise themselves for wickedness" is an explanation of MT's "praise wickedness" (*rāšāʿ*, understood as *rešaʿ*). "Strengthen themselves" represents (and demetaphorizes) LXX's *periballousin heautois teichos*, whether or not Syr had *ytgdrw* in its source text. Tg: "(b) but those who keep the Law argue with them that they might repent."

Variants: *ytgdrw* (MT *yitgārû*).

28:6. LXX: "$^{\alpha}$ Better a lowly man who walks in truth $^{\beta}$ than a deceitful rich man [*plousiou pseudous*]." LXX condenses the second stich in dependence on 19:22$^{\beta}$ and turns the proverb into a monostich.

Syr: "A poor man goes about in honesty [*mskn*ʾ *mhlk btmymwtʾ*] and a rich man makes his ways crooked." Having already used Heb *ṭwb* with v 5, Syr is left with two clauses that, intentionally or not, idealize the poor; see the Note on 22:7. "His ways" is an assimilation to 10:9. The versions do not reflect MT's dual *d*^{e}*rākayim*.

28:8. Ketiv *wbtrbyt*, qeré *w*^{e}*tarbît*.

28:10. LXX: "$^{\alpha}$ He who misleads the honest into a bad way—$^{\beta}$ he will fall into corruption. " This is interpreting *bšḥwtw* as *b*^{e}*šiḥutô*. The LXX has an additional couplet: "$^{\gamma}$ The lawless will pass through good things [or "goodness"] $^{\delta}$ but not enter into them [or "it"]" ($^{\gamma}$ *hoi de anomoi dieleusontai agatha* $^{\delta}$ *kai ouk eiseleusontai eis auta*). It is hard to relate 10$^{\gamma}$ to MT 10c. V 10$^{\delta}$ is an explanatory complement. Before $^{\gamma}$ some MSS have *hoi de amōmoi dielountai agatha* "the innocent will share in good" = MT 28:10c.

28:12. LXX: "$^{\alpha}$ By the help [or "salvation"—*boētheian*] of (the) righteous [pl.], honor becomes great [*pollē ginetai doxa*], $^{\beta}$ but in the places of (the) wicked [pl.], men are captured [*haliskontai*]." "In the places of" does not necessarily represent *bmqm* or *bmqwm* (Lag. and many) for MT *bqwm*, since *bqwm* is translated the same way in 28:28. Heb *bqwm* may have been interpreted as "places" because it was unclear why the wicked could "arise." LXX's "are captured" = *yittāpēś*. "By the help of" for *bʿlṣ* is puzzling. Retroversions to *baʿăzōr* (Baum.) or, less likely, *b*^{e}*haṣṣēl* (de Waard 1993: 255–56, Ps 70[69]:1) are graphically distant.

Variant: *ytpś* (MT *y*ᵉ*ḥuppaś*).

28:13. LXX: "ᵝ but he who declares rebukes will be loved" (*ho de exēgoumenos elegchous agapēthēsetai*). Gk *elegchos* elsewhere in Proverbs corresponds to *twkḥt* "rebuke." The LXX seems to praise *rebukers,* not penitents. "Will be loved" treats *yrḥm* as an Aramaism.

28:14. LXX: "ᵅ Happy is the man who fears [*kataptēssei*] always out of respectfulness [*di' eulabeian*]." *Eulabeia* is the virtue of discretion and respect, which the Stoics considered an acceptable emotion, while fear (*phobos*) was not; see Dick 1990: 25, and cf. BA. *Kataptēssein,* though literally "cower," signifies a good type of fear in 29:9ᵝ.

28:15. LXX has *lykos* "wolf" for *db* "bear," by association with Aram *di'bā'* "wolf." (He does not translate *db* as "bear" in 17:12 either, though the word is not rare.) LXX *ptōchos* = *rš* (haplog.). (The opposite happens in LXX 28:3: *rš* to *ršʿ*.)

Variant: *rš* (MT *rāšāʿ*).

28:16. LXX: "ᵅ A king [*basileus*] lacking revenues [*prosodōn*] is a great oppressor, ᵝ but he who hates injustice will live a long time." Gk *basileus* ≈ *ngyd*; see the Note on 19:6. The *waw* of *wrb* is not represented; so too in Syr and Vul (*w-r* near-dittog.). *Prosodōn* "public revenues" = *tbw'wt* "produce," for MT *tbwnwt* "understanding" (metathesis, prior to insertion of the m.l. *w*). MT has *rb tbw'wt* in 16:8. LXX and Syr follow the qeré. "Oppressor" is *sykophantēs,* which is "false accuser." But *sykophantēs*/*sykophantein* in Proverbs (14:31; 22:16; 28:3, 16), and usually elsewhere, translates forms of *ʿ-š-q* and seems to refer to oppressive practices more generally.

Syr: "(a) A ruler who lacks sense—many are his injuries [*sgy'yn*ᵖˡ *twkwhy*ᵖˡ], (b) and one who hates deceit [*nkl'*] will lengthen his days." Syr, perhaps puzzled by the fact that the MT says nothing *about* the foolish prince, interprets Heb *mʿšqwt* as the misfortunes that *he* will suffer.

Ketiv *śn'y,* qeré *śōnē'*.

Variants: *rb* (MT *w*ᵉ*rab*); *tbw'wt* (MT *t*ᵉ*bûnôt*).

28:17. LXX: "ᵅ He who provides bail for a man charged with murder ᵝ will be a fugitive and not (live) in security." LXX 17 is a paraphrastic rendering induced by reading, approximately, *ʿrbw ns* (*ʿōrbô nās*) (cf. Lag.), a graphic distortion of *ʿd bwr ynws.*

Variant: *ʿrbw ns* (MT *ʿad bôr yānûs*).

28:17a. "ᵅ Educate (your) son and he will love you ᵝ and give an ornament to your soul. ᵞ You should not obey [var. "he will not obey"] a lawless nation." LXX 28:17aᵅᵝ ≈ MT 29:17ab, where the LXX is closer to the Heb (*anapausei se* for *wynyḥk* "give you rest"). 17aᵞ is loosely related to MT 29:18a, indicating that the original placement of 28:17a was at 29:17. The reason for the transfer is unclear.

28:18. LXX: "ᵝ . . . will become entangled [*emplakēsetai*]." This is an interpretive translation of *ypwl b'ḥt,* lit., "will fall in one" (= MT), with the latter word understood as "together," like Aram *kḥd'*, RH *k'ḥd.*

Syr has *bgwmṣ'* = *bšḥt* for MT's *b'ḥt*. If Syr had *b'ḥt*, it would probably have tried to render it with the help of the LXX or used *b*ᵉ*'aḥdā'* "together." Note that *šin* and *'aleph* could be confused in the palaeo-Hebrew script.

Variant: *bšḥt* (MT *b^{e}ʾeḥāt*).

28:20. LXX: "[β] but the evil man [*ho de kakos*] will not go unpunished." The translator is hesitant to threaten punishment for the man who strives for wealth, because this is not prohibited. Compare how the LXX avoids disparaging the striving for wealth in 23:4. (Two proverbs that warn against haste and overwork are omitted, namely, 19:2; 21:5.)

Syr: "(b) and the bad man in his iniquity will not be forgiven [*wbyšʾ bʿwlh lʾ ntḥsʾ*]." Syr elaborates LXX's *ho kakos* by adding "in his iniquity." Syr allows that a bad man *can* be forgiven if he repents, but not if he is *in his iniquity.* Tg: *drhyṭ bʿwlʾ dnʿtr,* "and he who hurries in iniquity to become rich," fusing Syr and MT.

28:21. LXX: "[α] He who does not respect [*aischynetai prosōpa*, lit., "feel awe/shame toward the faces of"] the righteous [pl.] is not good. [β] Such a one will deliver [or "sell"—*apodōsetai*] a man for a bit of bread." LXX rewrites the verse radically. It seems to say that the righteous should not be sold into debt slavery.

28:22. LXX: "[α] An envious [*baskanos*] man hurries to get rich, [β] and he does not know that a merciful man will rule over him [*hoti eleēmōn kratēsei autou*]." "Merciful man" = *ḥsd* (*ḥesed*), interpreted as an abstract-for-concrete trope. Because the mean-spirited man is too fixated on pursuing wealth to give alms (cf. BA), the merciful one will rule over him. This is the message of 28:27 as well.

Most MSS have *nibŏhāl* (Aleppo, Leningradensis [BHS]; recognized by Radaq [*Sefer Hašorašim*] and preferred by Minḥat Shay). A minority reading is *nibăhāl* (Codex Yaman and others, recognized by Hameʾiri).

Variant: *ḥsd* (MT *ḥeser*).

28:23. LXX: "[α] He who rebukes the ways [*hodous*] of a man [β] will have favor more than the flatterer [*glōssocharitountos*]." Gk *hodous* = *ʾrḥwt* (*w-y* confusion and near-dittog. *ḥ-t*). De Waard argues that *ʾrḥwt* was not in LXX's source-text because "the expression is rather unnatural and unknown in Hebrew" (1993: 256). Therefore, he concludes, it is an exegetical metathesis for the sake of assonance. One might wonder why, if the expression were so awkward, a *translator* would have created it. "Ways" is indeed unnatural, at least within the MT text, but so is MT's *ʾaḥăray.* More fundamentally, we must recognize that the LXX source-text could have had erroneous, "unnatural," and "unknown" readings.

Syr: "(a) He who reproves a man finds friends (b) more than him who divides by his tongue [*dmplg blšnh*]." Syr understands Heb *ʾdm ʾḥry* as if it were *ʾādām ʾāḥēr* "another man," which is equivalent to "a man," or he has this in his Hebrew. He then interprets *ḥn* "favor" as a metonymy for "friends." Heb *mmḥlyq lšwn* is translated "etymologically"; cf. Syr-Prov 29:5.

Variant: *ʾrḥwt* (MT *ʾaḥăray*).

28:25. LXX: "[α] An insatiable [var. "unfaithful"] man judges rashly [*aplēstos anēr* [A] (*apistos* [BS]) *krinei eikę̄*], [β] but he who trusts in the Lord will be attentive [*en epimeleią̄ estai*]." "Judges rashly" construes *mdwn* as if it were *dyn* "judgment"; cf. 23:29. Gk *en pepimeleią̄* translates *ydšn* in 13:4 too. This may have a more edifying tone than "made fat."

28:26. LXX has "in an arrogant [or "bold"] heart" (*thraseią̄ kardią̄*) for MT's *blbw* "in his heart." Because "heart" is often equivalent to wisdom (e.g., 15:32), the translator assumes that the warning must concern a bad type of heart.

28:28. LXX: "ᵅ In the places [*en topois*] of the wicked [pl.], (the) righteous groan [*stenousi*]." On *en topois* for *bqwm*, see 28:12. The groaning of the righteous (as in 29:2 and Ezek 9:4) replaces the unbefitting notion of them hiding. (The clever man does hide in 27:12, but there it is to avoid a quarrel.) The connection with 29:2 is strengthened by the phrase *brbwt ṣdyqym* in both verses.

29:1. LXX: "ᵅ Better [*kreissōn*] a man who reproves than a stiff-necked man. ᵝ When he is suddenly burnt up [*phlegomenou autou*] there is no remedy." LXX derives the notion of "better than" by construing *mqšh* as *miqqᵉšeh* "than the stiff of (neck)" (≠ MT *maqšeh*). In ᵝ, "when he is burnt up" = *yiśśārēp* for MT's *yšbr* ("is broken") (*b-p* similarity and metathesis). The fate of the wicked created by this variant matches texts like Isa 66:24; Dan 12, etc. The verse has the appearance of a theological *Tendenz*, but that does not mean that it was imposed on the Hebrew text.

Syr explains the problematic *ʾyš twkḥwt* ("a man of reproofs")—see the Comment—as *gbrʾ dlʾ mqbl mksnwtʾ* "the man who does not accept reproof." Possibly Syr reflects *wmqšh*.

Variant: *yśrp* (MT *yiššābēr*).

29:2. LXX: *egkōmiazomenōn* = *bbrkwt* (Jäg.), or, better, *bbrkt*, treated as inf. abs. Heb *ʿm* is translated *laoi* in ᵅ, *andres* in ᵝ.

Some Heb MSS have *ršʿym*, perhaps to parallel *ṣdyqym*; thus LXX *asebōn*, Syr *dʿwlʾ*ᵖˡ.

Variants: *bbrkt* (MT *birbôt*); *ršʿym* (MT *rāšāʿ*).

29:3. LXX, Syr = MT. LXX translates *rʿh* ("he who consorts with") as *poimainei* "shepherds," Syr as *drʿʾ b-* "grazes upon." Tg: *dmtḥbr* ᴸ *ʿm bznywtʾ* "who associates with prostitution"; cf. 28:7. Note the striking alliteration in LXX ᵝ: *hos de poimainei pornas apolei plouton*.

29:4. LXX: ᵝ *paranomos* "transgressor," either reading *ʾyš trmyt* "deceit" (Jäg.) or construing *ʾyš trwmwt* (MT) in that sense.

Syr: "(b) and a wicked man makes it [sc. the land] needy" (*wgbrʾ ʿwlʾ mḥsr lh*). Syr ≈ Gk but reflects *yḥsrnh*, a *h-ḥ* error and *s/r* transposition.

Variant: *yḥsrnh* (MT *yehersennāh*).

29:5. LXX: "ᵅ He who who prepares [*paraskeuazetai*] a net before the face of his friend—ᵝ he throws it about his own feet." The translator assumed that *ršt* belonged to the first clause and so found it necessary to give *mḥlyq* a vague translation ("prepares") that could take "net" as its dir. obj.

29:6. LXX: "ᵅ For a sinning man there is a great [*megalē*] trap." It is hard to see a motivation for LXX's *megalē* other than a reading *rb* for *rʿ* "evil" (Jäg.), though the letters *ʿ* and *b* are not similar. Both *bpšʿ ʾyš* and *r(b) mwqš* are translated contrary to Heb syntax.

Syr "is trapped" (*mttṣyd*) construes *mwqš* as a Hp, *mûqāš*; cf. 12:13a.

Variant: *rb* (MT *rāʿ*).

29:7. LXX: "ᵅ The righteous man knows how to judge (on behalf of) the poor [pl.], ᵝ but the impious does not understand knowledge; ᵞ the lowly man does not have an understanding mind [*kai ptōchǭ ouch hyparchei nous epignōmōn*]." Stichoi 7$^{\beta}$ and $^{\gamma}$ are forms of MT 7b, with 7$^{\beta}$ apparently an adjustment to MT. The statement in 7$^{\gamma}$ (which recalls *Pirqe 'Avot* 2:5) apparently is based on reading *rš* instead of *rš'*. BA translates *nous epignōmōn* more narrowly, as "l'esprit d'arbitrage" ("the spirit of arbitration").

Variant: *rš* (MT *rāšāʿ*).

29:9. LXX: "$^{\alpha}$ A wise man judges nations [*krinei ethnē*], but a worthless man, being angry, mocks and does not fear [*ou kataptēssei*]." Baum. retroverts *krinei ethnē* to *yišpōt 'ōm* "will judge a people," but the graphic difference is great. Also, *'ōm* is not a word, though a scribe may have mistakenly created it as a back-formation from *'ummîm*. De Waard suggests that *l'wm* is an exegetical metathesis of *'wyl* (1993: 257). The latter, however, lacks a *mem* and *'wyl* is already represented by *phaulos*. Most likely, the source text had *ʿm* "with," a synonym variant of *'t* "with," but the translator construed it as *ʿam* "people." Otherwise the verse is translated freely, with *nḥt* derived from *ḥ-t-t* "fear."

Variant: *ʿm* (MT *'et*).

29:10. For "men of blood" LXX has *andres haimatōn metochoi*, "Men who take part (in crimes of) blood," with the added *metochoi* based on *metechontes* in 1:18.

Syr: "(b) but the righteous love him [*rḥmyn*^{pl} *lh*]." Syr uses the parallelism to make sense of MT's puzzling *wyšrym ybqšw npšw*, "and the upright seek [the innocent man's] life." Tg: "Men who spill blood hate innocence [*tmymwt'*], but the upright seek it."

29:11. LXX: "$^{\beta}$ but the wise man reserves (it) in part [*tamieuetai kata meros*]." BA translates the last phrase as "la dispense à mesure" ("dispenses it by measure") in accordance with the classical usage (*tamieuesthai* = "to be treasurer"), but the word means "hold in store" in 4 Macc 12:12. LXX is reading *yḥśknh* "hold it back" (Lag.), and *kata meros* corresponds loosely to *b'ḥwr*. Vul: "$^{\beta}$ but the wise man defers and reserves [his thought] until later" (*sapiens differt et reservat in posterum*). This seems to attest to the same variant as the LXX, because it shows independence in the handling of *b'ḥwr*.

Variants: *yḥśknh*, *yḥšbnh* (?) (MT *y^{e}šabb^{e}ḥennāh*).

29:12. LXX: Heb *mšl* (*mōšēl*) "governor" is uniquely translated *basileōs* "king"; see the Note on 19:6.

29:13. LXX: "$^{\alpha}$ When creditor and debtor have a meeting with each other, $^{\beta}$ the Lord has them both under observation" (trans. McKane). LXX's "creditor" and "debtor" are a narrower interpretation of *rš* "poor man" and *'yš tkkym* "oppressor" (in reverse order). This makes for a stronger antithesis and a closer association between the two men who meet. They not only represent types, they interact in a particular way. (Lag. suggests that LXX associates *'yš tkkym* with Gk *tokos* "usury.") The Heb *m'yr ʿyny-* is understood as God making *his* eyes "shine on," that is, look upon, the two. This formulation provides a warning pertinent to the situation envisioned: If, in such an encounter, the lender may wish to pressure the debtor, he should remember that God is overseeing them both. Vul: *pauper et creditor* "a poor man and a creditor," combining MT and LXX.

29:14. LXX *eis martyrion* "for a witness" vocalizes *lʿd* as *lāʿēd* (MT *lāʿad* "forever"); sim. 12:9. Syr omits *dlym* "the poor," thereby broadening the statement to include all royal judgments.

29:15. For MT's *ʾmw* "his mother," LXX has *goneis autou* "his parents," since logically both of them must feel the shame.

29:16. LXX "become fearful [*kataphoboi ginontai*]" confuses *yrʾw* "see" with the homograph *yîrāʾû* "fear."

29:17. This verse appears also in LXX 28:17a$^{\alpha\beta}$.

29:18. LXX: "$^{\alpha}$ For a lawless nation there is no interpreter [*exēgētēs*], $^{\beta}$ but he who keeps the Law is most fortunate." Rather than implying the necessity of prophecy (MT *ḥzwn* "vision"), which was no longer sanctioned, the LXX declares *interpreters* to be indispensable to the social order. GELS alternatively relates *exēgētēs* (one of whose meanings is "leader, "guide" [LSJ]) to Aram *ḥazzān* "superintendent, guide." BA notes that the dream-interpreters in Gen 41:8, 24 are called *exēgētai* (cf. Judg^{B} 7:13), but in this context, the *exēgētai* are interpreters of the Law. LXX 29:18$^{\alpha}$ ≈ LXX 28:17a$^{\gamma}$. Vul maintains *prophetia* "prophecy."

Syr: "(a) By the multiplicity of evildoers [*dʿwlʾ*^{pl}] a people is broken [*mttrʿ*]." Syr apparently shares LXX's scruple about calling "vision" necessary, but it solves the problem differently.

29:19. LXX: "$^{\alpha}$ By words a stubborn slave will not be instructed." LXX adds "stubborn" to avoid the implication that *no* slaves will accept verbal rebuke.

Syr: "(b) for he knows that he is not beaten [*dlʾ blʿ*]," implicitly vocalizing *mʿnh* as *m*^{eʿ}*unneh*, lit., "tortured" (Pink.).

29:21. LXX: "$^{\alpha}$ He who lives luxuriously [*kataspatalą̄*] from childhood will be a servant, $^{\beta}$ and will in the end be miserable about himself [*odynēthēsetai eph' heautǭ*]." The differences from MT follow from LXX's assumption that *mpnq* is passive. The last phrase is a contextual guess for the obscure *mnwn*. Vul interprets it as *contumacem* "obstinate."

29:22. LXX: "$^{\alpha}$ A hot-tempered man digs up [*oryssei* $^{AS, MSS}$; *egeirei* "stirs up" ^{B}] conflict, $^{\beta}$ and an angry man digs out [*exōryxen*] sins." In $^{\beta}$, *exōryxen* is used for the sake of paronomasia with *oryssei*. The wordplay would not have come about, however, unless the source text had *ykrh* "digs up" in v 22a.

Variant: *ykrh* (MT *y*^{e}*gāreh*).

29:23. LXX: $^{\alpha}$ = MT; "$^{\beta}$ but the Lord supports the humble-minded [pl.] [*tapeinophronas*] with honor." The LXX assumes that *tāmak* means "support" (see the Note on 4:4) and so supplies an appropriate subject, the Lord.

29:24. LXX: "$^{\alpha}$ He who shares with a thief hates his own soul. $^{\beta}$ If, hearing a vow being put forth, they not make a report [*ean de horkou protethentos akousantes mē anaggeilōsin*] . . ." (continues in v 25). Vv 24–25 form a quatrain on the dangers of becoming involved with a thief. The pl. *anaggeilōsin* (MT sg.) must refer to unmentioned witnesses.

Syr: "(b) and they decree oaths for him but he does not confess [*wpsqyn ʿlwhy mwmtʾ*^{pl} *wlʾ mwdʾ*]." The translator has a different legal procedure in mind, namely, that the suspect is forced to swear to his innocence but chooses to perjure himself.

29:25. LXX (continuing 24$^{\beta}$): "$^{\alpha}$ fearing and reverencing men, they will be overthrown [var. "have been overthrown"]. $^{\beta}$ He who has trust in the Lord shall be happy. $^{\gamma}$ Impiety will make a man stumble, $^{\delta}$ but he who trusts in the Master will be saved." There is some confusion in the hexaplaric markings (see Fritsch 1953: 179), but $25^{\gamma\delta}$ is clearly a corrective doublet of the freer $25^{\alpha\beta}$. Line 25^{α} has a double translation of *ḥrdt ʾdm*.

After 29:27, LXX continues with 31:10–31.

30:1. LXX: "$^{\alpha}$ Fear my words, son, $^{\beta}$ and receiving them, repent. $^{\gamma}$ These things says the man to those who have faith in God, and I cease" ($^{\alpha}$ *tous emous logous huie phobēthēti,* $^{\beta}$ *kai dexamenos autous metanoei.* $^{\gamma}$ *tade legei ho anēr tois pisteuousin theǭ kai pauomai*). This radical paraphrase eliminates any attribution of authorship other than to Solomon. Given the liberties it takes, retroversions are shaky, though *wqḥ* or *wqḥm* ("take," "take them"; impv.) for *yqh* (Jakeh) seems likely, as does the omission of one occurrence of *lʾytyʾl*.

LXX interprets the verse as if reading $^{\alpha}$ *dᵉbāray, bᵉnî, tāgûr,* $^{\beta}$ *wᵉqāḥēm wᵉhinnāśēʾ.* $^{\gamma}$ *nᵉʾum haggeber lô ʾîtay ʾēl, wāʾēkel.* In $^{\beta}$, *metanoei* "repent" associates *hmśʾ* with *n-ś-ʾ*, which sometimes means "forgive" or, in the passive, "forgiven" (e.g., Isa 33:24; Ps 32:1) and thus implies its antecedent, repentance. The phrase *tois pisteuousin theǭ* probably construes *lʾytyʾl* as "to whom there is God" (cf. Vul, Syr), which is paraphrased as "those who have faith in God." The letters *ʾyty* were read as biblical Aramaic *ʾîtay* "there is."

LXX $30:1^{\beta}$ recalls $24:22a^{\beta}$ *dexamenos echos dechomenos de edexato auton* (lit., "and receiving it, he received it") (BA). Indeed, LXX 30:1 recalls the entirety of LXX 24:22a (an additional verse in the LXX). Without the presence of LXX 24:22b–e, which is an independent unit, 24:22a would have directly preceded 30:1. (See the Note on 24:22a.) The two verses go well together in the LXX:

(24:22a) $^{\alpha}$ A son who keeps a word is free from destruction,
$^{\beta}$ and receiving it, he has (really) received it.
(30:1) $^{\alpha}$ Fear my words, son,
$^{\beta}$ and receiving them, repent.

What is more, $30:1^{\gamma\delta}$ has no necessary relationship to $30:1^{\alpha\beta}$. On the contrary, $30:1^{\gamma\delta}$ would be a natural start to the unit in the LXX.

Vul: "(a) The words of the Collector son of Vomiter [*Congregantis filii Vomentis*]. (b) The vision that the man spoke, with whom is God, (c) and who, as he was strengthened by God, while tarrying with him, said." Using midrashic techniques, Vul construes MT v 1ab as if it read, (a) *dibrê ʾôgēr ben yāqeh* (b) *hammaśśāʾ nāʾam haggeber lô ʾîtay ʾel.* (The name *yqh* is understood as if it were *maqqîʾ*, and *nʾm* is treated like RH *nāʾam* "spoke.") Stich 1(c), however, can hardly be correlated to MT's *lʾytyʾl wʾkl. Num. Rab.* 10:4 (88a) (sim. *Tanḥ. Waʾeraʾ* 8 [73a]) explains that Solomon was called *yqh* because "he disgorged" (*hiqqîʾ*) the words of Torah like a bowl. That same midrash also says that Solomon used to say, *ʾyty ʾl* [*ʾittî ʾēl*] "God is with me."

Syr: "(a) The words of Agur son of Yqy, who received a prophecy, (b) and he prevailed and said to Ithliel." Syr understands *hmśʾ* as "prophecy" (which it can mean), *n'm* as "said" (as in RH; = Vul), and *hgbr* as *(ha)ggōbēr* "prevailed." Heb *w'kl* is not reflected, unless *w'tmṣy ḥyl'* is a displaced rendering of *w'kl* (understood as *wayyûkāl*). The form of the son's name in Syr, *'ytly'l*, means *'yt-ly-'yl* "I have God." (By sound, but not by spelling, *'yl* is a Hebraism. It is used in Syriac; see Brockelmann 115a.) Neither Syr nor LXX represents the second *l'yty'l*, which is probably a dittography. Both the LXX and the Syr are highly "interpretive" here, but one must ask why they would ignore rather than interpret the second occurrence if they had it.

Variant: *yqḥ* (MT *yāqeh*); absence of *l'yty'l*.

30:2. LXX: "$^{\alpha}$ For I am the most foolish of all men, $^{\beta}$ and intelligence [*phronēsis*] of men is not in me."

Syr: "(a) Because my mind is lacking"—omitting the seemingly superfluous *m'yš* "than (any) man"; (b) = MT.

30:3. LXX: "$^{\alpha}$ God taught me wisdom, $^{\beta}$ and I know knowledge of the holy ones [*gnōsin hagiōn*]." The translator takes it as a given that the speaker—Solomon no less!—*did* know wisdom, and since he did not have merely *human* wisdom (2b), the wisdom he does have must be from God himself (3a). For the translator, the converse of "I did not learn wisdom" (MT 2a) is "*God* taught me wisdom."

Syr: "(a) and I did not know [*yd't*] wisdom (b) and I did not learn [w*l' ylpt*] the knowledge of the holy beings [or "saints"—*qdyš*^{pl}]." Syr continues the negative into the second stich, denying that the speaker has knowledge, human or angelic.

30:4. LXX $^{\beta}$ has *en kolpǭ* "in the bosom" for MT *bḥpnyw* "in the hollow of his hands." Jäg. retroverts this to *ḥṣnw* "his bosom," but LXX's "his bosom"—that is, in the opening of his robe—is influenced by "in his garment" in 4c. V 4$^{\delta}$ has *ekratēsen* "mastered" for Heb *hqym* "established." Because God and only God set up the ends of the earth, *hēqîm* demands the answer "God." But since a human *could have* mastered the entire earth, using *ekratēsen* allows for the answer, "No one." In 4ϵ, *tois teknois autou* "his children" reads *bnw* as *bānāyw*. LXX ^{BS} = OG lacks the phrase *hina gnǭs* (lit., "that you may know"), corresponding to *ky td'*. Though Rahlfs includes it, it is probably secondary in the Gk.

Syr prefixes *'mr ly*. If the verb is a perfect, the clause means "He [God] said to me." If it is an imperative, the clause means "Tell me!" In the latter case, God challenges Agur in the same way he challenged Job (38:5a). Then the Syriac follows the MT, ending *'n yd' 'nt* "*if* you know." By either translation, vv 5–7 are an oracle spoken by God.

Variant: absence of *ky td'*.

30:7. LXX: "$^{\beta}$ Do not remove favor [*charin*] before I die." The added *charin* refers to God's grace.

30:8. LXX: "$^{\alpha}$ A vain word and deceit [*mataion logon kai pseudē*]," restructuring the MT phrase. $^{\beta}$ = MT. "$^{\gamma}$ but prescribe for me what is necessary and sufficient [pl.] [*syntaxon de moi ta deonta kai ta autarkē*]," a paraphrase.

Syr ≈ MT. Heb *lḥm ḥwqy*, "my daily bread," is translated *'wmr' msty* "a sufficient living for me," probably based on LXX.

30:9. LXX: "$^{\beta}$ Who sees me [*tis me horą̄*]?" = *my yḥzh* (with the obj. inferred), for MT's *my yhwh*—a *w-z* graphic error. (Sim. Isa 2:2 *emphanes* = *yḥzh* for *yhwh*.)

It is possible that MT's *my yhwh* "who is Yahweh" is the secondary reading, influenced by Exod 5:2.

Variant: *yḥzh* (MT *yhwh*).

30:10. LXX: "$^{\alpha}$ Do not deliver [*mē paradǭs*] a slave to the hands of (his) master, $^{\beta}$ lest he curse you and you be annihilated [*aphanisthę̄s*]." De Waard suggests that LXX is an exegetical metathesis that treats MT's *tlšn* as if it were *tšlm* because of what he believes to be a "tendency toward intensification and radicalization" (1993: 258). In fact, the LXX is influenced by the command in LXX-Deut 23:16, which uses *paradōseis* for *tsgyr* "turn over to." *Aphanisthę̄s* associates *wʾšmt* ("and you be guilty") with *w*^{e}*šammōtā* "and you will be destroyed," because the consequence of a malediction is not guilt but punishment.

Ketiv *ʾdnw*, qeré *ʾădōnāyw*.

30:11. By using *ekgonon kakon* "bad offspring" rather than "generation," LXX condemns individuals, as is usual in Prov, and not an entire generation. LXX adds "bad" to clarify what kind of offspring does these things.

30:12. LXX: "$^{\alpha}$ A bad offspring judges himself righteous $^{\beta}$ and did not wash off his exit [*exodon*]." The translator read *mṣʾtw* and understood it as *miṣṣēʾtô* "from his going out," which is probably a euphemism. Whether or not he was aware of the vocalization *miṣṣōʾātô* "his excrement" as in MT, *exodon autou* is a euphemism for "his anus"; cf. LSJ 596a.II.3.

30:14. LXX: "$^{\delta}$ and their wretched [pl.] from men." The suffix "their" lacks an antecedent and is awkward. It is not a natural translational addition. "Their wretched" represents *wʾbywnm*, a defective writing of *wʾbywnym*, with the *–m* construed as a 3rd pers. masc. pl. suffix.

Variant: *wʾbynm* (MT *w*^{e}*ʾebyônîm*).

The LXX continues with 24:23–34.

30:15. LXX: "$^{\alpha}$ To the leech there were three daughters, truly beloved. $^{\beta}$ And these three did not satisfy her, $^{\gamma}$ and the fourth was not satisfied, so as to say 'Enough!' " LXX takes v 15 as a single saying and rewrites it as a prose parable. Gk $^{\alpha}$ *agapēsei agapōmenai* represents a Heb inf. abs. construction, which was suggested to the translator by the repetition of *hb*. Possibly LXX had *ḥb ḥb* (from *ḥbb*) (Lag.), but given the free treatment of this passage, it could as well be associating *hb* with *ʾhb*, "love." MT's "two" was made into "three" to fuse 15a with the number series in 15b. LXX translates *ʾrbʿ* ("four") as an ordinal, *hē tetartē* "the fourth," as in 18, 21 and 29 (sim. Vul). Whereas MT speaks of "three or four" items, LXX, construing the numbers more precisely, reads the series as an X + 1 numerical saying, in which the last item stands apart from the others.

Syr has "three beloved [*ḥbybn*^{pl}] daughters," as in LXX. For Syr *ḥbybn*^{pl} Tg has *mhbhbn* "greedy," a clever play on Heb (and Aram) *hab hab* "give give."

30:16. LXX: "$^{\alpha}$ Hades and the love [*erōs*] of a woman and Tartarus, and the earth, which is not filled with water [*ouk empiplamenē hydatos*], $^{\beta}$ and water [*kai hydōr*] and fire do not say, 'It is enough.' " LXX makes the four insatiables into six. Gk *erōs* appears elsewhere in the LXX only in Prov 7:18, where, too, it means sexual passion. LXX departs considerably from the MT's *ʿṣr rḥm* ("the closing of the womb") to introduce a moral warning against lustful women. It associates *rḥm* with Aram *rḥm* "love," cf. 28:13 and LXX Judg A 5:30. The second "water" has no exegetical function and is in a different syntactic position from the first. Hence it is not a double translation but a dittog. in the source text. "Sheol," on the other hand, is given a double translation, Hades and Tartarus.

Syr: ≈ MT, but *wʾḥdt rḥmyh*^{pl}, "and the shutting up of her wombs," must refer to *Sheol's* (fem.) "wombs." This recalls the metaphor of the earth as the mother of all; see Ps 139:13 with 15; Job 1:20; Sir 40; 4 Ezra 5:48. Tg^{L}: *wʾḥdt rḥmy* "barrenness."

Variant: *mym mym* (MT once).

30:17. The Heb crux *yqht* is translated "old age" in the LXX (*gēras*) and Syr (*sybwtʾ*). Vul renders it "childbearing" (*partum*). These are all guesses.

The major MT MSS have the anomalous vocalization *liyqqăhat* (preferred by Ben Naphtali). The minority reading is *l^{e}yiqq^{e}hat* (Cod. Erfurt 1). See Baer-Delitzsch *1880*: 52. The second form conforms to Tiberian practice.

30:18. LXX: "and there are three [*tria de estin*] . . . and the fourth [*to tetarton*]." See the Note on 30:15. Syr ≈ MT, but *wdʾrb*^{ʿpl} "and the fourth" ≈ LXX.

Ketiv *wʾrbʿ*, qeré *w^{e}ʾarbāʿāh*.

30:19. LXX translates *bʿlmh* ("with a maid") as "in youth," probably for propriety's sake. Sim. Vul, Syr *bʿlymwth* "in his youth," Tg *bʿwlmtʾ* "in youth."

30:20. LXX: "$^{\gamma}$ and says that she has not done anything improper [*atopon*]." Gk demetaphorizes 20b. Syr: "and says, 'I didn't do anything [*mdm lʾ ʿbdt*].' " Syr makes the woman more disingenuous.

30:21. LXX: "three . . . fourth," as in 30:15.

30:23. LXX: "$^{\alpha}$ And (the earth shakes) if a maidservant casts out [*ekbalę̄*] her own mistress, $^{\beta}$ and if a hateful [*misētē*] woman happens to get [*tychę̄*] a good man." The LXX reverses the order of the lines, perhaps to tighten the parallelism between *oiketēs* in 22 and *oiketis* in 23 (BA). For the LXX, a slave coming to rule (22$^{\alpha}$) means deposing [*ekballein*] his master, like a slave-woman displacing her mistress. *Ekbalę̄* understands *tyrš* (*twrš*?) as *tōrîš* (as in Exod 34:24) or understands the G-stem to mean this. Alternatively, *ekbalę̄* may represent *tgrš* (K. Reynolds, personal communication).

30:24. LXX: *sophōtera tōn sophōn* "wisest of the wise" vocalizes *ḥăkāmîm mēḥăkāmîm*. Sim. Syr *ḥkymn*^{pl} *mn ḥkym*^{ʾpl}.

30:28. LXX has the lizard dwelling "in fortresses" (*ochyrōmasin*), continuing the martial imagery from v 27 (BA).

30:29. LXX ≈ MT, but using "fourth"; see 30:15.

30:30. LXX structures the epigram in 30–31 as a series of nouns + rel. clauses (with rel. pronouns or ptcps.). It is rhythmic and has alliterations and classical usages; see BA.

30:31. LXX: "$^{\alpha}$ And a cock, who walks about boldly among hens [*thēleiais*] $^{\beta}$ and a he-goat, who leads the herd, $^{\gamma}$ and a king, who delivers a harangue among nations [*dēmēgorōn en ethnei*]." The translator pictures creatures who proudly lead their kind. He apparently construed the last phrase as if it were *ûmelek qām ʾel ʿammô*, lit., "and a king standing to [over] his people." The Greeks viewed the cock as a "proud and pugnacious bird" (Gerleman 1956: 31).

Vul "[γ] and a king who cannot be resisted [*nec est rex qui resistat ei*]" construes Hebrew as *melek ʾal qām ʿimmô*, equating *ʾal* with *lōʾ*.

Oc. *ʾalqûm*. Or. *ʾal-qûm*; cf. Vul.

30:32. LXX: "[α] If you give yourself to pleasure, [β] and stretch out your hand in conflict, you will be disgraced." This corresponds only to a few unconnected words in the Hebrew. The LXX introduces the theme of conflict, which is continued in 33.

31:1. LXX: "[α] My words have been spoken by God. [β] An oracle of (the) king which his mother taught him" ([α] *hoi emoi logoi eirēntai hypo theou.* [β] *basileōs chrēmatismos hon epaideusen hē mētēr autou*). In order to avoid ascribing this section to a sage other than Solomon, the LXX implicitly vocalizes the first two words as *d^{e}bāray l^{e}mô ʾēl*, understanding *l^{e}mô* as "by," where the MT has *dibrê l^{e}mûʾēl*. The word order of *mlk mśʾ* is reversed; see the Textual Note on 15:26. As in 30:1, the LXX has Solomon claiming a divine source for his wisdom. Vul ≈ MT, with *visio* "prophecy" for *mśʾ*. There are great differences in the way the name is handled in the translations: Aq *Lammoun*; Sym *Iamoul*; Theod *Rebuēl*; Vul *Lamuhel*.

Syr: "(a) The words of Muel the king (and) prophet, (b) which his mother taught him and said to him" [(a) *mlwhy*[pl] *dmwʾyl mlkʾ nbyʾ* (b) *drdth ʾmh wʾmrt lh*]. Syr understands the first *l-* of *lmwʾl* as "to." For *mśʾ* "burden," which could be understood as "prophecy," Syr has *nbyʾ* "prophet." Tg has a double translation for *mśʾ*: *mrdwtʾ wnbywtʾ* "instruction and prophecy," to express two meanings of *maśśāʾ*.

31:2. LXX: "[α] What, child, will you keep? What? The words of God. [β] (O my) firstborn, I speak to you, (my) son. [γ] What, child of my womb? What, child of my vows?" ([α] *ti teknon tērēseis? ti? rhēseis theou.* [β] *prōtogenes soi legō huie.* [γ] *ti teknon emēs koilias?* [δ] *ti teknon emōn euchōn?*). In 2[α], the translator fills out and answers the rhetorical question *mh bry* ("What, my son?") with an idea entirely absent from the MT. The son must keep *God's* words, which, as v 1 says, the mother is now teaching her son. We have here the bold notion of the mother as Torah mediator and teacher. The entirety of [β] is an expansion in the translation. Vul ≈ MT, but rendering Aram *bry* as *dilecte* "beloved," associating it with *b-r-r* "to purify," "choose." This same etymology is used in *Lev. Rab.* 12:8 (19a) (C. Gordon 1930: 411).

31:3. LXX: "[α] Do not give your wealth to women, [β] nor your mind and life to regret" (*kai ton son noun kai bion eis hysteroboulian*). 3[β] is loosely related to the Heb. GELS glosses the hapax *hysteroboulia* as "deliberation after the facts, remorse, wisdom after the events, hindsight." Theod gives the Heb a similar sense: *eis metameleian* "to repentance," "remorse." MT's *mlkyn* (which has an Aramaic ending) was, not unnaturally, associated with Aram *milkāʾ* "counsel."

31:4. LXX: "[α] Do all things with counsel [*boulēs*]. [β] Drink wine with counsel [*meta boulēs oinopotei*]. [γ] The princes are hot-tempered [*thymōdeis*]—[δ] let them not drink wine." LXX [αβ] replaces MT 4a with a precept relevant to context, probably in order to avoid mentioning Lemuel. Heb *mlkym* is twice construed as Aram *milkāʾ* "counsel." LXX 4[γδ] gets the gist of the Heb 4bc. Gk *mē* reflects the qeré, the negative particle *ʾy*.

Vul supplies a different reason for kings to abstain from wine: "Give not to kings, O Lamuel, give not wine to kings, because there is no secret [*quia nullum secretum*] where drunkenness reigns." This interprets *rwznym* as *rāzîm* "secrets," as does *b. San.* 70b (C. Gordon 1930: 391).

Syr (sim. Tg): "Beware [*tzdhr*] of kings, Muel, of kings who drink [*dštyn*] wine, and of rulers who drink beer." Syr maintains "Muel" from v 1, though the preposition *l-* cannot be functional here. For MT's *štw*, Syr's source text may have had *šty* (*šōtê*). Syr's verb "drink" in (b) indicates that it understood *'w* (ketiv) as "or" (though English translation requires "and").

Ketiv *'w*, qeré *'ê*.

31:5. LXX: "Wisdom" is substituted for *mḥqq*, whose usual meaning is "lawmaker," which is difficult as a dir. obj. of "forget."

31:6. Syr: "(a) Beer is given [*mtyhb*] to mourners [*l'byl*^{pl}], (b) and wine to those bitter of soul." The passive verb makes the verse into a description of a common practice rather than a command to give strong drink to the poor.

31:8. LXX: "$^{\alpha}$ Open your mouth with the word of God [*logǭ theou*] $^{\beta}$ and judge all soundly [*hygiōs*]." The king pronounces God's teachings and judgments; see v 1. Gk *logǭ theou* treats *l'lm* as *lē'lîm*, understood as *lē'lōhîm*. "Soundly" seems to be a guess at *bnyḥlwp*, read as one word (Baum.).

Syr: "(a) Open your mouth in a word of truth [*bmlt' dqwšt'*], (b) and judge all wicked sons [*bny*^{pl} *'wl*^{pl}]." The translation of the hapax *ḥlwp* as "wicked" was motivated by logic, for the wicked are what one naturally judges. Tg^{L}: "Open your mouth to those who do not pervert judgment [*lhlyn dl' mstw dyn'*]." The versions try independently to make sense of *l'lm*, though there is no apparent difficulty with its meaning "for the dumb." TgZ corrects to *bny ḥlwp'* "mortals."

After 31:9, LXX continues with 25:1–29:27. Hence Prov 31:10 follows upon 29:27, which speaks of the mutual loathing between the righteous and the unrighteous man. Cook (CSP 312–15) believes that these chapters were rearranged by the translator for thematic and literary purposes. Prov 31:1–9 was moved so that 29:27, which mentions the "unjust man," would be next to 31:10, which speaks of the "virtuous woman," thus creating a contrast of the sort that the translator is fond of. Also, he wanted 31:1–9, which deals with kingship, to be followed by 25:1–8, which is likewise about kingship. However, the gains would be rather small for such a major dislocation, and *adikos* and *andreios* are not elsewhere in antithesis. If the move was deliberate, it could as well have been made by a Hebrew scribe.

31:10. LXX: "$^{\alpha}$ A valorous woman [*gynaika andreian*] who will find? $^{\beta}$ Such a one [*hē toiautē*] is more valuable than precious stones."

31:11. LXX "$^{\alpha}$ The heart of her husband finds courage [*tharsei*] in her. $^{\beta}$ Such a one [fem.] does not lack good booty [$^{\beta}$ *hē toiautē kalōn skylōn ouk aporēsei*]." The use of *tharsei* implies that not only does her husband trust her and rely on her, but he gets courage and confidence. She gains booty via her husband. Heb *šll* "booty," often toned down in modern translations (e.g., "good thing"; JPSV), maintains its military connotations in Gk *skylōn*, though a cautionary "good" is added. Moreover, by making the woman the subject in $^{\beta}$, contrary to the grammar, LXX imbues her with even greater connotations of power. This reinforces the nuance of valor in *andreia* (10) as well.

31:13. "Weaving wool and flax, she made something useful [*euchrēston*] by her hands." LXX restates *dršh* "seeks" by *mēruomenē* "weaving," to conform to the expected picture of weaving.

At this point, LXX starts to use mostly aorist forms mixed with present tense ones in a way that does not allow for distinction. The aor. here does not really indicate past tense (see 25[β]), but it also does not function as an atemporal gnomic aorist. The translator is cued by the morphology of the Hebrew, and translates perfect verbs and most *waw*-conversives as aorist. Still, the result is that vv 10–12 are cast as a summary of her value, while 13–31 tend to describe things she has done to establish it.

31:16. Ketiv *nṭʿ*, qeré *nāṭᵉʿāh*.

31:17. LXX ends + *eis ergon* "for work," to make it clear that she is girding loins and "strengthening her hands" for work, not war.

31:18. The ketiv, to be vocalized *ballêl*, is the older and rarer form and is probably the original.

Ketiv *blyl*, qeré *ballaylāh*.

31:19. LXX translates *kyšwr* (actually "spindle") as *ta sympheronta* "things that are useful," deriving the word from *k-š-r* "be useful" or "successful." Other etymological renderings are Aq, Sym, Theod *andreią̧* (see Qoh 2:21b; 4:4b; 10:10b, with forms of *k-š-r* "be successful"); Syr *bkšyrwtʾ* "in skill"; Vul *ad fortia* "to strong things."

31:22. LXX: "[α] She made for her husband a two-ply mantle [*dissas chlaionas*]." LXX understands *šnym* (from v 21) as *šᵉnayim* "two"; sim. Vul (*duplicibus*, in 21), for MT *šānîm* "scarlet." LXX treats *lh* ("herself") as Aram *lēh* "for him," then expands it into "her husband." The translator is deliberately emphasizing that the woman serves her husband's needs, reinforcing the added "her husband" in 21.

31:23. LXX: "[α] Her husband is notable [*peribleptos*] in the gates [β] when he sits in council [*en synedrią̄*] with the elders who dwell [*katoikōn*] in the land." LXX enhances the husband's status—he is *peribleptos*, "notable," "looked at from all sides." His sitting in the gates, LXX explains, is not for leisure but to serve in the city assembly. *Synhedrion* is added or introduced artificially here and in 11:13; 15:22; 22:10 (2x); 24:8; 27:22. The local assembly was clearly an important part of the communal life of the translator. This is not the Sanhedrin in Jerusalem (contrary to Cook *1999b*: 151). The advice is pertinent to all readers, or at least "the elders who dwell in the land" (31:23b), not only the (traditionally) 71 men in the Sanhedrin. Moreover, the plural is used in 15:22 and 24:8. In 31:23 the assembly is said to meet in the city gate, though this may be a carryover from the Hebrew and not a reflection of contemporary practice. Possibly these are local assemblies such as are called *synhedria* in Mark 13:9 = Matt 10:17, which had judicial authority in Palestine. But the assemblies may be informal gatherings of elders to discuss communal affairs, conduct business, and adjudicate conflicts.

31:25. LXX [26]: "[β] and she rejoiced [aor.] in the last days," that is, at the end of her life. Perhaps MT's "she laughs at the latter day" sounded overconfident.

In the LXX, the *ʿayin* verse (LXX 26 = MT 25) follows the *peh* verse (LXX 25 = MT 26). This is the order in Lam 2, 3, 4, and Ps 10 and in some ancient epigraphic abecedaries (from ʿIzbet Zarta, Kuntillet ʿAjrud, and Tel Zayit (see Tappy et al. 2006: 26). This it represents an alternate, more ancient alphabetical order. It must have been present in LXX's source text, since there would have been as no motive for switching the verses in translation. Since the MT's order is the usual one and is standard in postexilic usage, it is likely that the reversal has taken place in the MT. But the MT's order has the literary advantage of keeping the lines regarding clothing together.

31:26. LXX [25]: "ᵅ She opened her mouth attentively [*prosechontōs*] and lawfully [*ennomōs*], ᵝ and she controlled her tongue [*kai taxin esteilato tę̄ glōssę̄ autēs*; lit., "set an order to her tongue"]." LXX 25ᵝ is loosely related to MT 26b. Heb *twrh* "instruction," "law," receives a double translation: *ennomōs* and *taxin esteilato*. There is considerable variation in the LXX manuscript tradition; see Lag. MT 26 is also translated in 31:28 and 3:16a, but differently.

Variant: different placement of v 26.

31:27. LXX: "ᵅ The ways of her household are covered, ᵝ and she has not eaten lazy food" (ᵅ *stegnai diatribai oikōn autēs*, ᵝ *sita de oknēra ouk ephagen*). If *diatribai* means "way of life, practices," then "covered" must be a metaphor for "careful" (GELS). If it means "place of habitation, haunts" (GELS), as in Lev 13:46, then "covered" can be understood literally: "Ils sont bien couverts, les séjours de sa maison" ("The dwelling places of her house are well covered"; BA). LXX takes the second meaning of Heb *ṣ-p-h*—"to cover," "overlay," instead of "watch." On the pl. of *oikōn*, see the Note on 7:8.

Syr: "(a) The ways of her house are revealed [*wglyn*^pl^ *ʾwrḥtʾ*^pl^ *dbyth*]," understanding *ṣwpyh* (MT *ṣôpiyyāh*) as *ṣᵉpûyāh*, lit., "is seen."

31:28. LXX: "ᵅ [MT 26a] She opens her mouth to the wise [*sophois* ^BS*^; var. *sophōs* ^A^] in accordance with the Law. ᵝ And her kindness [MT 28a] brought up her children, and they grew rich. ᵞ [MT 28b] And her husband praised her." LXX 31:28 is a blend of MT 31:26 and 28 that probably arose in part in a Hebrew text. The changes were caused by (1) duplication and displacement of MT 26 (present in LXX in a different form); (2) a mistaken construal of *qmw* as a causal; and (3) a confusion of *wyʾšrwh* with the root *ʿ-š-r*, due to the weakening of the gutturals in the first century B.C.E. The rendering of *wtwrt* "and the law of" by the hapax *nomothesmōs* is probably the translator's work.

In 28ᵅ, the variant *sophois*, read by LXX^BS^, seems to be original, while *sophōs* "wisely," which Rahlfs prefers, looks like an adjustment to MT. Whichever is OG, when read with *sophois* the verse gives the interesting picture of a woman instructing wise men in God's word. The woman is a teacher of Torah also in LXX 31:2.

Variant: *wayyaʿšîrû* (MT *wayyᵉʾaššᵉrûhā*).

31:29. LXX: "ᵅ Many daughters have acquired wealth [*ektēsanto plouton*]; ᵝ many have done mighty deeds [*dynata*], ᵞ but you have surpassed and exceeded all [*hyperkeisai kai hyperēras pasas*]." Stichoi ᵅᵝ are doublets bringing out the two meanings of *ḥyl*, "wealth" and "power." LXX mentioned wealth in 28 also. LXX assumes that women can amass wealth. *Hyperkeisai* and *hyperēras* are also doublets.

Syr: "(a) And many of her daughters [*dbnth*^pl^] have acquired wealth [*qny*^pl^ *ʿwtrʾ*],

but you have surpassed [ʿ*brty*] them all." Syr "her daughters" (≠ MT, LXX) corresponds to "her sons" in 28 and suggests that the woman's own daughters follow in her enterprising footsteps. Syr interprets *ʿśw ḥyl* as "acquired wealth" = LXX.

31:30. LXX: "$^{\alpha}$ Desires for favor are deceitful and the beauty of woman is vain. $^{\beta}$ For it is the intelligent woman [*gynē synetē*] that is praised. $^{\gamma}$ Let her praise the fear of the Lord." In 30$^{\alpha}$, "of woman" serves to indicate that not all beauty, but only a woman's, is to be thus denigrated. Heb *ḥn* "favor" is given an unusual meaning, conveyed by the hapax *areskeia*, because *ḥēn* in the sense of *charis*, as it is translated almost everywhere, is a reward for wisdom and virtue (3:4, 22; 13:15, etc.). Stichoi $^{\beta}$ and $^{\gamma}$ are doublets, neither one an adjustment to MT.

In 30$^{\beta}$, *gynē synetē* may represent *ʾiššāh maśkelet* (Rofé *2002a*: 144–55), but not the anomalous *ʾšt bynh* or *ʾšh nbwnh*, as Toy suggests. Gk *synetos* and *syneinai* often translate forms of *ś-k-l*, which means "be intelligent" but also "succeed." It should be noted, however, that *ʾšh mśklt* is treated quite differently in LXX 19:14. LXX 31:30$^{\beta}$ could equally well be a converse translation of 30$^{\alpha}$, and 30$^{\gamma}$ be an addition approximating the MT—but in an erroneous form, with *thll* for *tthll*. Rofé (*2001*: 388–89) argues that a scribe replaced *yrʾt YHWH* with *ʾšh mśklt* in order to give the woman the quality of piety, otherwise unmentioned in the poem; sim. Toy. But the motive that Rofé and Toy ascribe to this later copyist could equally well have influenced the author. Also, the translator could have concluded from 1:7 and 9:10, where *bînāh* is defined as *yirʾat YHWH*, that an "intelligent woman" is one who fears God (D. A. Teeter, personal communication). The double translation would show this equation.

Schroer believes that the LXX is deliberately devaluing women by declaring that it is the intelligent or sensible woman, rather than the God-fearing one, who is praiseworthy (*1991*: 161). This makes no sense, because fear of God would in any age be the most valued virtue in women as in men, and no one would hesitate to say that a God-fearing woman will be praised. Schroer also believes that stich $^{\gamma}$ counteracts the exaltation of woman by having her praise the Lord rather than being praised herself (ibid.)—as if giving praise to God were less esteemed than receiving it oneself.

Variant: *thll* (MT *tithallāl*).

31:31. LXX: "$^{\alpha}$ Give her from the fruits of her lips [*cheileōn* $^{\text{ABS, MSS}}$; *cheirōn* "hands" $^{\text{SyrH, Complut, Rahlfs}}$]; $^{\beta}$ and let her husband praise her in the gates." Rahlfs accepts the hexaplaric *cheirōn*, but, as BA observes, "fruit of the lips" is equivalent to *pᵉrî peh* "fruit of the mouth," an established usage (12:14; 13:2; 18:20). Also, this reading ties in nicely with LXX v 30: The woman praises God and should be rewarded for this verbal virtue. The idea of her *husband* praising her in the gates was inspired by v 23, perhaps because this is more logical than her *works* doing the praising. "Gates" in both verses provides a linkage.

Translation of the Book of Proverbs

PART I. THE LECTURES AND INTERLUDES

Prologue

1:1 The proverbs of Solomon the son of David, king of Israel,
1:2 (for use)
in learning wisdom and discipline,
in understanding words of understanding,
1:3 in absorbing the discipline of insight:
righteousness, justice, and rectitude,
1:4 in giving the callow cunning,
to the young—knowledge of shrewdness.
1:5 Let the wise man listen and enhance his instruction,
the astute man gain guidance,
1:6 in understanding proverbs and epigrams,
the words of the wise and their enigmas.
1:7 The fear of the Lord is the beginning of knowledge;
Fools despise wisdom and correction.

Lecture I

1:8 Listen, my son, to your father's instruction;
neglect not your mother's teaching,
1:9 for they are a graceful garland for your head,
and a necklace for your throat.
1:10 My son,
if criminals lure you,
don't give in.
1:11 If they say,
"Come with us, let's lurk for blood,
waylay the innocent man without cause.
1:12 Let us swallow them alive, just as Sheol does,
(swallow) the blameless ones, like those who go down to the Pit.
1:13 Treasure of all sorts we'll seize,
our houses cram with loot.
1:14 Throw in your lot with us,
we'll all share one purse"—
1:15 my son, don't go in the way with them;
don't step upon their path,
1:16 for their feet run to harm;
they rush to shed blood.
1:17 For "No bird is caught in a net
set out before his eyes."
1:18 Yet *they* lie in wait—for their very own blood,
set an ambush—for their very own lives.

1:19 This is what happens to everyone who grasps ill-gotten gain:
it robs him who holds it of life.

Interlude A

1:20 Wisdom cries aloud in the streets,
in the plazas gives forth her voice.
1:21 At the bustling crossroads she calls out,
where the gates open into the city,
there she has her say:
1:22 "How long, callow ones,
will you love being callow?
(you) impudent ones treasure scorn?
and (you) dolts hate knowledge?
1:23 Turn back toward my reproof!
See, I pour out to you my spirit,
make you know my words:
1:24 'Since you spurned me when I called,
took no heed when I stretched forth my hand,
1:25 brushed aside all my advice,
accepted not my reproof,
1:26 I, for my part, will laugh at your downfall,
mock when your worst fear arrives,
1:27 when your worst fear arrives like a storm,
and your downfall comes nigh like a gale,
when trouble and torment come upon you.'
1:28 Then they'll call me, but I won't answer,
they will seek me but find me not,
1:29 because they spurned knowledge,
and did not choose the fear of the Lord,
1:30 did not accept my advice,
but despised all my reproof.
1:31 So they shall eat of the fruit of their way,
from their own devices be stuffed full.
1:32 For the waywardness of the callow will kill them,
and the dolts' complacency will destroy them.
1:33 But he who obeys me shall dwell in safety,
secure from fear of harm."

Lecture II

2:1 My son,
if you take in my words,
store up my precepts within you,

2:2 making your ear attend to wisdom,
directing your heart to good sense;
2:3 if you call out to understanding,
cry aloud to good sense;
2:4 if you seek it like silver,
delve for it like treasure;
2:5 then you'll understand the fear of the Lord;
and knowledge of God you will find.
2:6 For the Lord grants wisdom,
at his behest come knowledge and good sense.
2:7 For the upright he stores up resourcefulness—
a shield for those who go with integrity.
2:8 to guard the paths of justice,
protecting the way of his faithful.
2:9 Then you'll perceive righteousness, justice, and equity—
every good course,
2:10 for wisdom will enter your heart,
knowledge become delightful to your soul.
2:11 Shrewdness will watch over you,
good sense protect you,
2:12 to save you from the way of the evildoer,
from the man who speaks distortions,
2:13 who abandons the paths of rectitude,
to walk in the ways of darkness,
2:14 who delights in doing evil,
rejoices in evil duplicity,
2:15 whose paths are crooked,
and who is devious in all his tracks,
2:16 to save you (also) from a strange woman—
an alien who speaks smooth words,
2:17 who abandons the mate of her youth,
ignores the covenant of her God.
2:18 For her path descends to death,
her tracks go down to the ghosts.
2:19 Of her visitors none return,
or regain the paths to life.
2:20 So shall you go where good men walk,
and keep to the paths of the righteous,
2:21 for the upright will abide on the earth,
the blameless remain therein;
2:22 but the wicked shall be cut off from the earth,
traitors torn away from it.

Lecture III

3:1 My son, forget not my teaching;
let your heart retain my precepts,
3:2 for length of days and years of life
and peace they'll add to you.
3:3 <Let kindness and constancy not forsake you!>
Tie them about your neck,
inscribe them on the tablet of your heart,
3:4 and you'll gain the favor and high regard
of God and man alike.
3:5 Trust in the Lord with all your heart
and rely not on your own understanding.
3:6 In all that you do, hold him in mind,
and *he* will keep your path smooth.
3:7 Do not reckon yourself wise,
but fear the Lord and shun evil,
3:8 and there will be health to your flesh
and vigor to your bones.
3:9 Honor the Lord from your wealth,
with the firstfruits of all your produce,
3:10 and your barns will overflow with abundance,
your vats burst with new wine.
3:11 Do not, my son, reject the Lord's discipline,
nor despise his chastisement,
3:12 For the one whom the Lord loves—him he reproves,
as a father does to a favored son.

Interlude B

3:13 Happy the man who has found wisdom,
the man who obtains good sense!
3:14 For better her profit than the profit of silver,
her yield than that of fine gold.
3:15 More precious is she than rubies;
no valuables can match her.
3:16 Long life is in her right hand,
in her left—wealth and honor.
3:17 Her ways are pleasant ways,
and all her paths are peace.
3:18 A tree of life is she for those who grasp her;
and those who hold her are deemed fortunate.
3:19 By wisdom the Lord founded the earth,
established the heavens by skill.
3:20 By his knowledge the waters of the abyss gush forth,
and the skies drip down dew.

Lecture IV

3:21 My son, let not (my words) escape your eyes;
  retain competence and shrewdness.
3:22 They'll give vitality to your throat,
  grace to your neck.
3:23 Then you'll go your way securely
  and never stub your toe.
3:24 When you sit down you'll have no fear,
  when you recline, your sleep will be sweet.
3:25 You will not fear the sudden terror,
  the calamity of the wicked, when it comes,
3:26 for the Lord will be your trust,
  and keep your foot from the snare.
3:27 Don't deny a benefit to the one to whom it is due,
  when you have the ability to do it.
3:28 Don't say to your fellow,
  "Go away and come back,
and tomorrow I'll give it to you,"
  when you have it all along.
3:29 Don't devise harm against another person,
  when he dwells in trust with you.
3:30 Don't quarrel with a man without reason,
  if he has done you no wrong.
3:31 Don't envy the lawless man,
  and don't choose any of his ways,
3:32 for the Lord loathes the crooked man
  but with the honest he is intimate.
3:33 The Lord's curse is in the house of the wicked,
  but he blesses the abode of the righteous.
3:34 As for the scornful—them he scorns,
  but upon the humble he bestows favor.
3:35 The wise inherit honor,
  while dolts gain only contempt.

Lecture V

4:1 Hear O sons a father's instruction,
  listen to learn understanding!
4:2 For I give you a good lesson;
  forsake not my teaching.
4:3 For when I was a child with my father,
  a tender darling before my mother,
4:4   he gave me instruction and said to me:
"Let your heart hold my words;
  keep my precepts and live.

4:5 Get wisdom, get understanding,
do not forget, do not stray
from the words of my mouth.
4:6 Don't desert her—then she'll keep you,
love her and she'll guard you.
4:7 The first step to wisdom is: get wisdom!
With all you possess, get understanding.
4:8 Cherish her and she'll exalt you,
she'll bring you honor if you embrace her.
4:9 She'll place a graceful garland on your head;
grant you a splendid diadem."

Lecture VI

4:10 Attend, my son, and take my words,
that the years of your life may increase.
4:11 I guide you in wisdom's way,
lead you in routes of rectitude.
4:12 In walking, your stride won't be hobbled,
and if you run you will not trip.
4:13 Hold fast to discipline, don't let go,
guard it, for it is your life.
4:14 Enter not on the way of the wicked,
nor tread on the path of evildoers.
4:15 Shun it, pass not upon it;
veer away from it, then pass on.
4:16 For they cannot sleep unless they've done harm;
they're robbed of sleep if they've made no one stumble,
4:17 for they feed on the food of evil,
drink the wine of lawlessness.
4:18 But the way of the righteous is like the glow of dawn,
shining ever brighter till the day sets in.
4:19 The way of the wicked is as the murk:
they know not on what they may stumble.

Lecture VII

4:20 Attend, my son, to my words,
incline your ear to my sayings:
4:21 Don't let them slip from your sight;
keep them within your heart,
4:22 for to those who find them they give life—
healing to their whole body.
4:23 Above all else, guard your heart,
for it is the source of life.

4:24 Remove from yourself crookedness of mouth,
and banish from you deceit of lips.
4:25 Keep your eyes looking forward,
your gaze straight ahead.
4:26 Make level the path you travel,
and you'll walk steady wherever you go.
4:27 Swerve neither to right nor left;
Keep your feet from evil.

Lecture VIII

5:1 My son, attend to my wisdom,
give ear to my good sense,
5:2 so that you may keep shrewdness
b and your lips guard knowledge,
c {to keep you from the strange woman,
from the alien who speaks smooth words.}
5:3 For the strange woman's lips drip honey;
her palate is smoother than oil.
5:4 But her after-effect is as bitter as wormwood,
sharp as a two-edged sword.
5:5 Down to Death-Land go her feet;
she holds fast to Sheol's path.
5:6 She refuses to go straight in the path of life;
her courses wander but she knows it not.
5:7 So now, my sons, listen to me;
depart not from the words of my mouth:
5:8 Distance yourself from her,
approach not the door of her house,
5:9 lest you yield your vigor to others,
and your years to a ruthless man;
5:10 lest strangers sate themselves with your strength,
and your toil end up in an alien's house;
5:11 and in the end you groan,
as your body and flesh waste away,
5:12 and you say:
"How I hated discipline,
and my heart did scorn reproof!
5:13 And I heeded not my teachers' voice,
nor to my instructors gave ear.
5:14 Quickly I fell into all sorts of trouble,
within the assembly and congregation."
5:15 Drink water from your own cistern,
liquids from your well,

5:16 lest your springs disperse outward,
through the plazas, as channels of water.
5:17 Let them be yours alone,
no strangers joining with you.
5:18 Let your fount be blessed,
take pleasure in the wife of your youth:
5:19 a loving doe, a graceful gazelle—
let her lovemaking ever slake your thirst,
lose yourself always in her love.
5:20 Why lose yourself, my son, with a stranger,
or embrace an alien's bosom?
5:21 For a man's ways are before the Lord,
and he assesses all his paths.
5:22 His (the evildoer's) iniquities will trap him,
in the cords of his sin he'll be seized.
5:23 He will die for lack of discipline,
and be lost in the greatness of his folly.

Interlude C

6:1 My son, if you've provided surety to your neighbor,
shaken hands for a stranger,
6:2 (if) you have ensnared yourself by your own words,
trapped yourself by your own words,
6:3 do this, then, my son, and save yourself
(for you have fallen into your neighbor's hands):
Go and grovel, and badger your neighbor.
6:4 Allow your eyes no sleep,
your eyelids no snoozing.
6:5 Escape like a gazelle from a hunter,
like a bird from the fowler's hand.
6:6 Go to the ant, you loafer!
Observe its ways, and wise up.
6:7 It has no leader,
no chief, no ruler,
6:8 yet it prepares its bread in the summer,
stores up its food at harvest.
6:9 How long will you lie there, loafer?
When will you get up from your sleep?
6:10 A bit more sleep, a bit more snoozing,
a bit more lying with folded arms,
6:11 and penury will come upon you like a vagabond,
and poverty like a man of arms.
6:12 It's a worthless man, a man of iniquity,
who goes about with crooked mouth;

6:13 who squints his eyes,
shuffles his foot,
points his finger;
6:14 with perversity in his heart,
he crafts trouble,
constantly foments strife.
6:15 That's why his ruin will come abruptly,
he'll be shattered all at once, beyond cure.
6:16 Six things there are that the Lord hates,
seven his soul does loathe:
6:17 arrogant eyes, a lying tongue,
hands that spill innocent blood,
6:18 a heart that crafts wicked plans,
feet that hasten to run evil.
6:19 a lying witness who breathes out deceits,
and a fomenter of strife among brothers.

Lecture IX

6:20 Keep, my son, your father's precepts,
forsake not your mother's teaching.
6:21 Bind them always upon your heart,
tie them about your throat,
6:23 For the precept is a lamp and the teaching a light,
and disciplinary reproof is the way to life.
6:22 When you walk about it will guide you,
when you lie down it will watch over you,
when you wake up it will converse with you,
6:24 to guard you from another man's wife,
from the smooth talk of the alien.
6:25 Don't desire her beauty in your heart,
or let her take you in with her glances.
6:26 For a whore costs but a loaf of bread,
but a married woman hunts for a precious life.
6:27 Can a man scoop up fire in his lap
without his clothes getting burnt?
6:28 Can a man walk on glowing embers
without his feet getting scorched?
6:29 So too with him who approaches another man's wife:
none who touches her goes unpunished.
6:30 People don't despise a thief
if he steals to fill his belly when starving.
6:31 Still, if caught, he'll repay sevenfold—
even surrendering all the wealth of his house.

6:32 An adulterer lacks sense;
a self-destroyer—he's the one who does this.
6:33 Wounds and insult are all he gains,
and his disgrace will not be expunged.
6:34 For jealousy enrages a man;
he'll not relent in the day of vengeance.
6:35 He'll accept no ransom, however large,
nor be appeased, however big your bribe.

Lecture X

7:1 My son, keep my words,
store my precepts within you.
7:2 Keep my precepts and live,
my teaching, as the pupil of your eye.
7:3 Bind them on your fingers,
inscribe them on the tablet of your heart.
7:4 Say to wisdom, "You are my sister,"
and call understanding "friend"—
7:5 that she may guard you from a strange woman,
an alien who speaks smooth words.
7:6 For once, through the window of my house,
through my lattice, I was gazing down,
7:7 when I saw among the callow, spied among the youngsters,
a lad devoid of sense,
7:8 passing down the street, by her corner,
toward her house he strode,
7:9 at dusk, when evening was falling,
in the dark of night and gloom.
7:10 And now: a woman comes toward him,
in harlot's garb, her intent hidden.
7:11 Rowdy and defiant is she,
her feet stay not at home,
7:12 now in the street, now in the plazas,
in ambush at every corner.
7:13 She seized him and kissed him,
and with brazen face she said:
7:14 "I had to make well-being offerings:
today I paid my vows.
7:15 That's why I have come out to you,
to seek you eagerly—and I found you!
7:16 I've decked my bed with covers,
dyed drapes of Egyptian linen.
7:17 I've sprinkled my bed with myrrh,
with aloes and cinnamon.

7:18 Come, let's slake our thirst on love till dawn
take our delight in lovemaking!
7:19 For the man's not at home,
he's gone on a journey afar.
7:20 A purse of money he took in his hand;
he'll not return till mid-month."
7:21 She enticed him with her soft "instruction,"
misled him with her smooth speech.
7:22 Impulsively he followed her—
like an ox going to slaughter,
like a stag bounding to bonds,
7:23b like a bird rushing to a trap:
7:23c He wasn't aware that he'll pay with his life—
7:23a till an arrow split his liver.
7:24 So now, my sons, listen to me,
give heed to the words of my mouth.
7:25 Let not your heart veer to her ways,
stray not upon her paths.
7:26 For many a victim she's laid low,
numerous are those she has slain!
7:27 Her house is the way to Sheol,
descending to the chambers of Death.

Interlude D

8:1 Listen! isn't it Wisdom calling,
Good Sense raising her voice?
8:2 Atop the heights near the road,
at the crossroads, she takes her stand;
8:3 near the gates at the city entrance,
at the portals she cries aloud:
8:4 "To you, O men, I call,
my voice is to mankind.
8:5 Learn cunning, you who are callow,
and you dolts—put some sense in your heart!
8:6 Pay heed, for I have candid things to say,
the opening of my lips is rectitude,
8:7 for it is truth that my mouth declares,
and my lips loathe wickedness.
8:8 All the words of my mouth are in righteousness,
not one is contorted or warped.
8:9 The discerning man sees that they're all honest,
The knowledgeable know they are straight.
8:10 Take correction, not silver,
and knowledge rather than choice gold,

8:11 for wisdom is better than rubies;
no valuables can match it.
8:12 I am Wisdom. I inhabit cunning;
knowledge of shrewdness I find.
8:13a <The fear of the Lord means hating evil.>
8:13b Pride and arrogance and wicked behavior,
8:13c and duplicitous speech do I hate.
8:14 Mine are counsel and competence,
I am Understanding, power is mine.
8:15 By me kings reign,
and governors decree righteous laws.
8:16 By me princes rule,
so too nobles, all the judges of the earth.
8:17 I love those who love me,
and those who seek me find me.
8:18 Wealth and honor are with me,
enduring riches and righteousness.
8:19 <Better my fruit than finest gold,
my yield than choice silver.>
8:20 I walk in the way of righteousness,
within the paths of justice,
8:21 to grant wealth to those who love me,
their storehouses to fill.
8:22 The Lord created me at the beginning of his way,
at the start of his works of old.
8:23 In primeval days I was formed,
at the start, at the world's origin.
8:24 When there were yet no deeps I was born,
when there were yet no springs, sources of water.
8:25 Before the mountains were set down,
before the hills I was born,
8:26 ere he made the earth and the ground,
the land's first lumps of soil.
8:27 When he established the heavens, there was I,
when he inscribed a circle on the face of the deep,
8:28 when he secured the clouds on high,
when he strengthened the founts of the deep,
8:29 when he marked the bounds of the sea,
that the waters transgress not his command,
when he firmed up the foundations of the earth.
8:30 And I was near him, growing up,
and I was his delight day by day,
frolicking before him at all times.
8:31 frolicking in his habitable world.
And *my* delight is in mankind.

8:32 And now, my sons, listen to me.
Happy are they who keep to my ways!
8:33 Heed correction and become wise;
brush it not aside.
8:34 Happy is the man who listens to me,
keeping vigil at my doors day by day,
watching the posts of my portals!
8:35 For he who finds me finds life,
and obtains favor from the Lord.
8:36 But he who offends against me harms himself;
all those who hate me love death."

Interlude E[470]

9:1 Wisdom has built her house,
set up her pillars seven,
9:2 slaughtered her cattle,
mixed her wine,
set her table.
9:3 Having sent forth her maids, she cries
at the tops of the city heights:
9:4 "Whoever is callow—let him come over here!
Whoever is senseless—to him I'll say:
9:5 'Come, dine on my food;
drink of the wine I have mixed.
9:6 Abandon callowness and live;
walk in the path of understanding,
9:7 <He who chastises an impudent man receives insult,
he who reproves an evildoer gets hurt.
9:8 Don't reprove an impudent man lest he hate you;
9:9 Give (reproof) to the wise, and he'll grow even wiser.
Instruct the righteous man and he'll enhance his learning.>
9:10 <Wisdom begins with the fear of the Lord,
and understanding—with the knowledge of the Holy One.>
9:11 For through me your days will increase,
and years be added to your life.' "
9:12 <If you grow wise, you benefit yourself,
but if you are impudent, you bear it alone>
9:13 The foolish woman is boisterous—
callowness itself! She knows nothing at all.
9:14 She sits at the door of her house,
on a chair at the city heights,

[470] Suggested order of reading in Interlude E: 9:1–6 + 11; 9:13–18 (The Two Banquets); 9:7–10 (An insertion: Advice to the Adviser); 9:12 (An insertion: Wisdom's Value); see Vol. I, 306–307, 317.

9:15 calling to those who pass by,
who are going straight ahead.
9:16 "Whoever is callow, let him come over here!
Whoever is senseless—to him I'll say:
9:17 'Stolen water is sweet,
secret food a delight.' "
9:18 But he knows not that ghosts are there,
that her guests are in the depths of Sheol.

PART II. PROVERBS OF SOLOMON

10:1a Proverbs of Solomon
A wise son makes his father rejoice,
while a stupid son is his mother's misery.
10:2 Treasures of wickedness will not avail,
but righteousness saves from death.
10:3 The Lord will not let a righteous man starve,
but he rebuffs the desire of evildoers.
10:4 The hand of the deceitful causes poverty,
while the hand of the diligent brings wealth.
10:5 He who builds his stores in the summer is an astute son;
he who drowses off at harvest is a disgraceful son.
10:6 Blessings for the head of the righteous man!
But the mouth of the wicked covers up lawlessness.
10:7 The memory of the righteous is for a blessing,
while the name of evildoers will rot.
10:8 The wise of heart takes in precepts,
while one foolish of lips will be cast aside.
10:9 He who goes in innocence goes in confidence,
while he who makes his ways crooked will be found out.
10:10 He who winks his eye causes grief,
and the one with foolish lips will be cast aside.
10:11 The mouth of the righteous is a fount of life,
while the mouth of the wicked covers up lawlessness.
10:12 Hatred stirs up conflict,
while love covers up all offenses.
10:13 On the lips of the discerning man wisdom is found—
and a rod for the back of the senseless.
10:14 Wise men store up knowledge,
and the mouth of the fool, imminent ruin.
10:15 The rich man's wealth is his fortified city;
the poverty of the poor is their ruin.
10:16 The wage of the righteous man leads to life;
the produce of the wicked to sin.

10:17 He who obeys an admonition is a path to life,
while he who ignores reproof leads (others) astray.
10:18 Deceitful lips cover up hatred,
while the slanderer is a dolt.
10:19 In a multitude of words offense will not be absent,
while he who restrains his lips is astute.
10:20 The tongue of the righteous man is choice silver;
the heart of the wicked is but a trifle.
10:21 The lips of the righteous man shepherd many,
while fools die because of senselessness.
10:22 The Lord's blessing is what makes one rich,
and striving adds nothing more thereto.
10:23 Committing vice is like an amusement to a dolt,
but wisdom (is thus) to the man of good sense.
10:24 What the wicked man dreads—that will come upon him,
but (the Lord) will grant what the righteous desire
10:25 When the gale has passed, the wicked man is no more,
while the righteous man is an enduring foundation.
10:26 Like vinegar to the teeth and smoke to the eyes,
so is the sluggard to his senders.
10:27 The fear of the Lord increases one's days,
while the years of the wicked are cut short.
10:28 The expectation of the righteous is joy,
while the hope of the wicked will perish.
10:29 The way of the Lord is a stronghold for the innocent,
but a ruin for those who commit iniquity.
10:30 The righteous man will never totter,
while the wicked will not abide in the earth.
10:31 The mouth of the righteous man produces wisdom,
while the perverse tongue is cut off.
10:32 The lips of the righteous express favor,
and the mouth of the wicked—perversities.
11:1 The Lord loathes deceitful scales,
while he favors an undiminished weight.
11:2 When the arrogant come then insult comes (too),
while wisdom is with the modest.
11:3. The innocence of the upright guides them,
while the corruption of the treacherous destroys them.
11:4 Wealth will not avail in the day of wrath,
while righteousness saves from death.
11:5 The innocent man's righteousness makes his way straight,
while the wicked man falls in his wickedness.
11:6 The righteousness of the upright will save them,
while the treacherous will be trapped by deceit.

11:7 When the wicked man dies, hope perishes,
and the expectation of strength perishes.
11:8 The righteous man is extricated from trouble,
and the wicked comes into his place.
11:9 By (his) mouth the impious man harms his fellow,
but the righteous are extricated by knowledge.
11:10 When it goes well with the righteous, the city rejoices,
and when the wicked perish, there is jubilation.
11:11 By the blessing of the upright, a city is exalted,
but it is ruined by the mouth of the wicked.
11:12 The senseless man insults his fellow,
while the man of good sense keeps silent.
11:13 The slanderer reveals secrets,
while the man of loyal spirit covers up a matter.
11:14 Without strategy a people will fall,
while there is victory in a multitude of counselors.
11:15 "He shall be severely harmed, because he has given surety for a stranger!"
But he who hates agreements will feel secure.
11:16 A gracious woman holds honor,
and diligent men hold wealth.
11:17 A kind man rewards himself,
while the cruel one troubles his flesh.
11:18 The wicked man produces a deceitful wage,
while he who sows righteousness has a reliable reward.
11:19 So does righteousness go to life,
and he who pursues evil (goes) to death.
11:20 The Lord loathes the crooked of heart,
while he favors those whose way is innocent.
11:21 Hand to hand: the evil man will not go unpunished,
while the descendants of the righteous will escape.
11:22 A gold ring in a pig's snout:
a beautiful woman lacking good sense.
11:23 The righteous desire what is good.
What the wicked can hope for is wrath.
11:24 There is one who scatters yet gets more,
and one who saves out of honesty yet ends up in need.
11:25 A generous person will be sated;
he who gives drink—his own thirst will be slaked.
11:26 He who withholds grain—the nation will curse him,
while there will be blessing for the head of a distributor.
11:27 One who pursues the good seeks good will,
but as for him who pursues evil—it will come upon him.
11:28 He who trusts in his wealth—he will fall,
while the righteous will flourish like foliage.

11:29 He who troubles his house will inherit the wind,
and the fool will be slave to the wise of heart.
11:30 The fruit of the righteous is a tree of life,
and the wise man captivates souls.
11:31 Since the righteous man receives what he deserves on the earth,
how much the more so do the wicked man and the sinner!
12:1 He who loves discipline loves knowledge,
while he who hates reproof is an ignoramus.
12:2 The good man will receive favor from the Lord,
but he will condemn the scheming man.
12:3 No one is established by wickedness,
but the root of the righteous does not totter.
12:4 The woman of strength is her husband's diadem,
while the disgraceful one is like a rot in his bones.
12:5 The plans of the righteous are just;
the stratagems of the wicked are deceitful.
12:6 The words of the wicked are a murderous ambush,
but the mouth of the upright will save them.
12:7 Overturn the wicked and they are no more,
but the house of the righteous will stand.
12:8 A man is praised according to his good sense,
while he who is perverse of heart becomes an object of scorn.
12:9 Better a lowly man who has produce
than one who glorifies himself and lacks bread.
12:10 The righteous man understands what his beast desires,
while the "mercies" of the wicked are cruel.
12:11 He who works his land will be sated with bread,
while he who pursues trifles lacks sense.
12:12 The wicked man covets a snare for the wicked,
but the root of the righteous is secure.
12:13 In the transgression of the lips there is an evil snare,
but the righteous man escapes the trouble.
12:14 From the fruit of his mouth, a man will be sated with good things,
and the recompense of a man's hands will return to him.
12:15 The fool's way is right in his own eyes,
while the wise man listens to counsel.
12:16 The fool makes his anger known at once,
while the shrewd man covers up an insult.
12:17 The faithful witness speaks the truth,
and the lying witness—deceit.
12:18 There is one whose speech is like a sword's stabs,
but the tongue of the wise is a balm.
12:19 Honest lips will be established forever,
while the deceitful tongue is for but a moment.

12:20 Deceit is in the hearts of those who devise evil,
while those who plan peace have joy.
12:21 No trouble shall befall the righteous man,
but the wicked are filled with evil.
12:22 The Lord loathes deceitful lips,
while he favors those who act faithfully.
12:23 The shrewd man covers up knowledge,
while the heart of dolts cries out folly.
12:24 The hand of the diligent will rule,
while the slack will be put to forced labor.
12:25 Worry in a man's heart brings him low,
while a good word cheers him up.
12:26 The righteous man is released from misfortune,
while the way of the wicked leads them astray.
12:27 The slacker will not roast his game,
but the wealth of the honorable man is pure gold.
12:28 In the path of righteousness there is life,
while the way of [wickedness] leads to death.
13:1 A wise son—a father's discipline,
while an impudent one does not heed a rebuke.
13:2 From the fruit of his mouth a man will eat good things,
and the gullet of the treacherous, lawlessness.
13:3 He who watches his mouth guards his life.
He who opens wide his lips—disaster is his.
13:4 It hungers but has nothing: the appetite of the sluggard;
but the appetite of the diligent will be sated.
13:5 The righteous man hates a deceitful word,
while the wicked man will be ashamed and disgraced.
13:6 Righteousness will guard him whose way is innocent,
while wickedness will ruin the sinner.
13:7 There is one who pretends to be rich and has nothing,
and one who pretends to be poor and has great wealth.
13:8 The ransom of a man's life is his wealth,
but the poor man does not heed a rebuke.
13:9 The light of the righteous will shine,
while the lamp of the wicked will go out.
13:10 A shallow man causes strife by arrogance,
while wisdom is with those who take counsel.
13:11 Wealth got in a rush will dwindle,
but he who gathers carefully gains increase.
13:12 A drawn-out hope sickens the heart,
but a desire fulfilled is a tree of life.
13:13 He who despises a word will be harmed,
while he who fears a precept will be well.

13:14 The teaching of a wise man is a fount of life
for avoiding deadly snares.
13:15 Good sense bestows favor,
but the way of the treacherous is their destruction.
13:16 Every shrewd man acts thoughtfully,
while the dolt spews out folly.
13:17 A wicked messenger will fall into evil,
but a trustworthy envoy brings healing.
13:18 Poverty and disgrace: he who casts off discipline.
But he who heeds a rebuke will be honored.
13:19 A desire fulfilled is sweet to the soul.
What dolts loathe is turning away from evil.
13:20 He who goes with the wise becomes wise,
but he who consorts with dolts will be harmed.
13:21 Evil will pursue sinners,
while (the Lord) will repay the righteous with good.
13:22 A good man will pass on an inheritance to his sons' sons,
while the wealth of the sinner is stored away for the righteous man.
13:23 The great man devours the tillage of the poor,
and some people are swept away without justice.
13:24 He who spares the rod hates his son,
while he who loves him disciplines him zealously.
13:25 The righteous man eats till his appetite is sated,
while the belly of the wicked is empty.
14:1 Wisdom builds her house,
while folly tears hers down with her own hands.
14:2 He who walks in his rectitude fears the Lord,
while he whose ways are twisted despises him.
14:3 In the mouth of the fool is a rod of pride,
but the lips of the wise will guard them.
14:4 In the absence of oxen, the stall is bare,
while by the bull's strength there is much produce.
14:5 A trustworthy witness does not deceive,
while a lying witness breathes out deceits.
14:6 The insolent man seeks wisdom but cannot find it,
while knowledge comes easy to the sensible one.
14:7 Go before a dolt,
and you will not know knowledgeable lips.
14:8 The shrewd man's wisdom consists in considering his way,
while the folly of dolts is deceit.
14:9 In the tents of the impudent there is guilt,
but among the upright there is favor.
14:10 The heart knows its own bitterness,
and no one else shares in its happiness.

14:11 The house of the wicked will be destroyed,
while the tent of the righteous will flourish.
14:12 There is a way that is straight before a man
but that turns out to be the way to death.
14:13 Even in merriment a heart may hurt,
and the outcome of pleasure is sadness.
14:14 The man of devious heart will be sated from his ways,
and the good man (will be sated) from his deeds.
14:15 The callow man believes everything,
while the shrewd one watches his step.
14:16 The wise man fears and turns away from trouble,
while the dolt confidently butts in.
14:17 The short-tempered man commits folly,
and the scheming man is hated.
14:18 The callow inherit folly,
while the shrewd are crowned with knowledge.
14:19 Evil men bow before good ones,
and the wicked (bow) at the gates of the righteous.
14:20 A poor man is hated even by his fellow,
while the friends of the rich are many.
14:21 He who despises his fellow sins,
while he who is kind to the poor—how fortunate is he!
14:22 Surely the devisers of evil will go astray,
while the devisers of good are kindness and fidelity itself.
14:23 In all striving there is profit,
but mere talk just leads to neediness.
14:24 The diadem of the wise is their wealth;
the garland of dolts is folly.
14:25 A faithful witness saves lives,
while a deceiver breathes out lies.
14:26 In the fear of the Lord there is a mighty stronghold,
and for his sons there will be a shelter.
14:27 The fear of the Lord is a fount of life,
for avoiding deadly snares.
14:28 A king's majesty lies in a multitude of people,
while a governor's disaster lies in a lack of a nation.
14:29 The patient man has much good sense,
while the short-tempered one gains folly.
14:30 A gentle heart is the life of the body,
while jealousy is a rot in the bones.
14:31 He who oppresses the poor insults his maker,
while he who is kind to the needy honors him.
14:32 The wicked man will be shoved down in his wickedness,
while the righteous man trusts in his innocence.

14:33 Wisdom rests in the heart of the sensible man,
but in the midst of dolts it makes itself known.
14:34 Righteousness exalts a nation,
while sin is the disgrace of peoples.
14:35 The king favors an astute servant,
while his wrath is directed toward the disappointing one.
15:1 A soft reply turns away wrath,
while an irritating word provokes anger.
15:2 The tongue of the wise adorns knowledge,
while the mouth of dolts pours out folly.
15:3 The eyes of the Lord are everywhere,
observing the wicked and the good.
15:4 The tongue's balm is a tree of life,
while any distortion in it breaks the spirit.
15:5. A fool despises his father's discipline,
while he who accepts reproof becomes shrewd.
15:6 In the house of the righteous there is much wealth,
but the produce of the wicked is troubled.
15:7 The lips of the wise disperse knowledge,
not so the heart of dolts.
15:8 The Lord loathes the sacrifice of the wicked,
while he favors the prayer of the upright.
15:9 The Lord loathes the way of the wicked,
but the pursuer of righteousness he loves.
15:10 Harsh discipline for him who abandons the way:
He who hates reproof shall die.
15:11 Sheol and Abaddon are before the Lord:
All the more so human hearts!
15:12 The impudent man does not like being rebuked.
He will not go to the wise.
15:13 A happy heart brightens the face,
while by the heart's sadness the spirit grows ill.
15:14 The heart of the astute man seeks knowledge,
while the mouth of dolts feeds on folly.
15:15 All the days of the poor man are bad,
but he whose heart is cheerful (has) an ongoing feast.
15:16 Better a little with the fear of the Lord,
than a great storehouse with turmoil in it.
15:17 Better are provisions of greens where there is love
than a fattened ox where there is hatred.
15:18 The heated man provokes strife,
while the patient one quiets conflicts.
15:19 The sluggard's path is like a hedge of thorns,
while the way of the upright is smoothed down.

15:20 The wise son makes his father rejoice,
while the dolt despises his mother.
15:21 Folly is pleasure to the mindless,
while the sensible man walks straight.
15:22 Plans are thwarted by lack of counsel,
while by a multitude of advisors they succeed.
15:23 A man gets pleasure from his mouth's response,
and a word in its time—how good it is!
15:24 The way of life is upward for the astute man,
that he may turn away from Sheol below.
15:25 The Lord will rip away the house of the arrogant
and secure the boundary of the widow.
15:26 The Lord loathes the plans of the evil man,
but pleasant words are pure.
15:27 He who grasps ill-gotten gain troubles his house,
while he who hates gifts will live.
15:28 The heart of the righteous man reflects before responding,
while the mouth of the wicked pours out evils.
15:29 The Lord is far from the wicked,
but he hears the prayer of the righteous.
15:30 The sight of the eyes makes the heart glad;
a good report fattens the bones.
15:31 The ear that listens to the reproof of life
dwells among the wise.
15:32 He who casts off discipline despises himself,
while he who hears reproof acquires a mind.
15:33 What wisdom teaches is the fear of the Lord,
and before honor comes humility.
16:1 The dispositions of the heart belong to a man,
but the answer of the tongue is from the Lord.
16:2 The ways of a man are all pure in his own eyes,
but the Lord examines spirits.
16:3 Entrust your deeds to the Lord,
and your plans will succeed.
16:4 The Lord made everything for its purpose—
even the evildoer for the day of evil.
16:5 The Lord loathes every haughty-hearted man;
hand to hand, he will not go unpunished.
16:6 Through kindness and constancy, iniquity will receive atonement,
but by the fear of the Lord evil is avoided.
16:7 When the Lord favors a man's ways,
even his enemies make peace with him.
16:8 Better a little with righteousness
than great produce without justice.

16:9 A man's heart plans his way,
but it is the Lord who makes his step secure.
16:10 There is divination on the king's lips.
In judgment no one can defy what he says.
16:11 A just balance and scales are the Lord's.
All the weights of the purse are his work.
16:12 Kings loathe the doing of evil,
for the throne is established by righteousness.
16:13 Kings favor righteous lips,
and they love the word of the upright.
16:14 The wrath of kings is a deadly messenger,
but a wise man can assuage it.
16:15 In the light of the king's face there is life,
and his favor is like the cloud of the spring rain.
16:16 How much better to gain wisdom than fine gold!
And gaining understanding is preferable to silver.
16:17 The high road of the upright is the avoidance of evil.
He who watches his way guards his life.
16:18 Pride comes before a fall,
and before stumbling—haughtiness of spirit.
16:19 Better to be humble of spirit and to be with the lowly
than to divide booty with the proud.
16:20 He who is astute in a matter will gain a benefit,
and he who trusts in the Lord—how fortunate is he!
16:21 The wise of heart is called astute.
and he whose speech is pleasing increases instruction.
16:22 Discretion is a fount of life for its possessor,
while the "education" of fools is folly.
16:23 The wise man's heart instructs his mouth,
and it enhances instruction on his lips.
16:24 Pleasant words are honeycomb—
sweet to the taste and healing to the bones.
16:25 There is a way that is straight before a man,
but which turns out to be the way to death.
16:26 The appetite of the toiler toils for him,
because his mouth forces it on him.
16:27 The worthless man mines evil,
and on his lips there is a scorching fire.
16:28 The perverse man foments strife,
and the slanderer separates friends.
16:29 The lawless man entices his fellow
and leads him in a path not good.
16:30 He squints his eyes to plan perversities,
winces his lips, while planning evil.

16:31 Gray hair is a splendid diadem.
It is found on the way of righteousness.
16:32 Better the patient man than the mighty one,
and he who controls his temper than he who captures a city.
16:33 The lot is cast into the bosom,
and whatever it decides is from the Lord.
17:1 Better a dry piece of bread with tranquility in it,
than a house full of contentious sacrifices.
17:2 An astute slave will rule over a disappointing son
and divide an inheritance among brothers.
17:3 A smelter for silver and a furnace for gold—
and the tester of hearts is the Lord.
17:4 An evildoer pays attention to iniquitous lips,
a liar listens to a deceitful tongue.
17:5 He who mocks the poor insults his maker.
He who takes joy in (another's) disaster will not go unpunished.
17:6 The diadem of the aged is sons of sons,
and the splendor of sons is their fathers.
17:7 Excessive speech is not fitting for a scoundrel;
how much the less so false speech for a noble!
17:8 A bribe is a beautiful jewel in its possessor's eyes:
Wherever he turns he succeeds.
17:9 He who seeks love covers up an offense,
while he who repeats a matter alienates a friend.
17:10 A rebuke comes down harder on a perceptive person
than a hundred blows on a dolt.
17:11 A rebel seeks only evil,
and a cruel messenger will be sent against him.
17:12 Better to come upon a bear bereft of her young
than a dolt in his folly!
17:13 He who returns evil for good—
evil will not depart from his house.
17:14 The start of strife is (like) releasing water,
so before a quarrel breaks out, leave off!
17:15 He who exonerates the guilty and he who condemns the innocent—
the Lord loathes them both.
17:16 What's the point of a payment in a dolt's hand
to buy wisdom, when he lacks a mind?
17:17 A friend loves at all times,
and a brother is born for sorrow.
17:18 A senseless man clasps hands,
giving surety to his acquaintance.
17:19 He who loves an offense loves strife,
and he who makes his door high seeks a fall.

17:20 He whose heart is crooked will not attain good,
and he who is perverse of tongue will fall into evil.
17:21 He who begets a dolt gets grief,
and the father of a scoundrel knows no joy.
17:22 A cheerful heart improves the body,
and an ill spirit dries up the bones.
17:23 The wicked man takes a bribe from the bosom
to pervert the ways of justice.
17:24 Wisdom is before the face of the perceptive man,
while the eyes of the dolt are in the ends of the earth.
17:25 A stupid son is an irritation to his father
and an embitterment for his mother.
17:26 Also, punishing the righteous man is not good—
smiting noble people for honesty.
17:27 The knowledgeable man restrains his words,
and the is sensible man is calm.
17:28 Even a fool who keeps silent is reckoned wise;
he who keeps his lips closed—astute.
18:1 The misfit seeks pretexts;
he attacks all competence.
18:2 The dolt does not desire good sense,
but only to reveal his heart.
18:3 When the wicked man enters, contempt enters too,
and with insult (comes) reproach.
18:4 The words of a man's mouth are deep waters,
a flowing stream, a fount of wisdom.
18:5 It is not good to be partial to the guilty,
to subvert the innocent in judgment.
18:6 The lips of the dolt come into strife,
and his mouth calls for blows.
18:7 The dolt's mouth is his ruination,
and his lips are his mortal snare.
18:8 The words of the slanderer are like delicacies,
and they descend to the chambers of the belly.
18:9 He who is slack in his work—
he too is brother to a vandal.
18:10 The name of the Lord is a fortified tower,
into which the righteous can run and be safe.
18:11 A rich man's wealth is his fortified city
and like a lofty wall—in his imagination.
18:12 Before a man falls his heart grows haughty,
but humility precedes honor.
18:13 As for him who replies before listening—
this is folly for him, and disgrace!

18:14 A man's spirit can sustain him in sickness,
but an ill spirit—who can bear it?
18:15 The heart of the astute man gets knowledge,
and the ear of the wise seeks knowledge.
18:16 A man's gift clears his way
and leads him before the great.
18:17 The first (to speak) in his lawsuit is "right,"
until the other person comes and sees through him.
18:18 The lot stops quarrels
and separates litigants.
18:19 A offended brother is like a fortified city,
and quarrels are like the bar of a palace.
18:20 A man's belly will be sated by the fruits of his mouth;
he will be sated by the produce of his lips.
18:21 Life and death are held by the tongue,
and those who love it will eat its fruit.
18:22 He who has found a wife has found something good
and received favor from the Lord.
18:23 The poor man speaks entreaties,
and the rich one answers with harsh words.
18:24 There are companions for socializing with,
and (then) there is a friend who cleaves closer than a brother.
19:1 Better a poor man who walks in his innocence
than a man of crooked lips who is rich.
19:2 Without knowledge, desire is not good,
and he who hurries with his feet sins.
19:3 A man's folly corrupts his way,
but his heart rages against the Lord.
19:4 Wealth adds many friends,
but the poor man is separated from his fellows.
19:5 A lying witness will not go unpunished,
and he who testifies deceitfully will not escape.
19:6 Many make entreaties to the noble,
and everyone is a friend to the gift-giver.
19:7 All the poor man's brothers hate him.
How much the more so do his friends distance themselves from him!

* * *

19:8 He who acquires a mind loves himself,
and he who keeps good sense will surely find good fortune.
19:9 A lying witness will not go unpunished,
and he who testifies deceitfully will perish.
19:10 Luxury is unsuitable for a dolt.
How much the more so for a slave to rule over princes!
19:11 A man's insight makes him patient,
and overlooking an offense is his splendor.

19:12 Like a lion's growl is the king's wrath,
while his favor is like dew on the grass.
19:13 A stupid son is his father's ruin,
and a woman's bickering is an irksome dripping.
19:14 A house and wealth are an inheritance from fathers,
but an astute wife comes from the Lord.
19:15 Sloth brings on a stupor,
and the deceitful man will starve.
19:16 He who guards a precept guards his life,
while he who despises a word will die.
19:17 He who is kind to the lowly lends to the Lord,
and he will pay him the recompense of his hands.
19:18 Discipline your son, for there is hope,
and do not desire to kill him.
19:19 The hot-tempered man bears (his) punishment,
for if you save him, you will have to do so again.
19:20 Hear counsel and receive discipline,
that you may become wise in the future.
19:21 Many designs are in a man's heart,
but it is Lord's plan that comes to pass.
19:22 A man's kindness is his fruit,
and better a poor man than a deceitful man.
19:23 The fear of the Lord (leads) to life,
and he (who fears the Lord) will dwell content, unafflicted by evil.
19:24 The sluggard hides his hand in the bowl,
and he won't even bring it back to his mouth.
19:25 Strike a scoffer and the callow will gain shrewdness,
but rebuke an astute person and he will gain knowledge.
19:26 He who robs his father and drives away his mother
is a shameful and disgraceful son.
19:27 Cease, my son, to listen to instruction,
to stray from words of knowledge!
19:28 A corrupt witness mocks justice,
and the mouth of the wicked swallows iniquity.
19:29 Rods are readied for the impudent,
and blows for the back of dolts.
20:1 Wine is a mocker and beer is rowdy,
and no one who goes astray in them will become wise.
20:2 The king is as fearsome as a lion's growl;
the man who provokes his anger harms himself.
20:3 It is to a man's honor to avoid conflict,
while every fool has tantrums.
20:4 After the rainy season the sluggard does not plow.
Then in the harvest he inquires and there is nothing.

20:5 The counsel in a man's heart is deep waters,
and a sensible man will draw it up.
20:6 Many a one is called a kind man,
but a trustworthy man, who can find?
20:7 The righteous man goes about in his innocence.
Happy are his children after him!
20:8 A king sits on the throne of judgment
and scatters all evil with his eyes.
20:9 Who can say, "I have made my heart pure,
I am cleansed from my sins."
20:10 Disparate stones and disparate measures:
the Lord loathes them both.
20:11 Even by a child's actions it is known
whether his behavior is pure and upright.
20:12 An ear that hears and an eye that sees—
the Lord made them both.
20:13 Do not love sleep lest you become impoverished.
Open your eyes and have your full of bread.
20:14 "Bad bad!" the buyer says,
but when he goes away, then he boasts.
20:15 There are gold and much rubies,
but knowledgeable lips are a precious ornament.
20:16 "Take his garment, because he has given surety for a stranger!"
And seize it, (because he has given surety) for aliens."
20:17 The bread of deceit is sweet to a man,
but later it fills his mouth with gravel.
20:18 Plans succeed by counsel,
so wage war by strategy.
20:19 The slanderer reveals secrets,
so do not associate with a big-mouth.
20:20 He who curses his father or his mother—
his lamp will be extinguished in deep darkness.
20:21 An inheritance gained in a rush at first—
its outcome will not be blessed.
20:22 Do not say, 'I will repay (evil) with harm.'
Wait for the Lord, and he will give you victory.
20:23 The Lord loathes disparate weights,
and deceitful scales are not good.
20:24 A man's steps are from the Lord,
and a human—how can he understand where he is going?
20:25 It is a snare to a man to blurt out "Holy!,"
and after making vows to reconsider.
20:26 The wise king scatters the wicked
and rolls a wheel over them.

20:27 The life-breath of man is the lamp of the Lord.
He examines all the chambers of the belly.
20:28 Kindness and fidelity guard the king,
and he supports his throne by kindness.
20:29 The splendor of young men is their strength,
and the grandeur of old men is white hair.
20:30 Severe bruises scour the mind,
and they smite the chambers of the belly.
21:1 The king's heart is like channels of water in the hand of the Lord:
he directs it wherever he wishes.
21:2 A man's every way is straight in his eyes,
but the Lord examines hearts.
21:3 Doing righteousness and justice
is more valued by the Lord than sacrifice.
21:4 Haughtiness of eyes and arrogance of heart:
the lamp of the wicked is sin.
21:5 The plans of the diligent surely lead to a surplus,
but everyone who hastens is surely headed for want.
21:6 He who gains treasures by a deceitful tongue
is a driven vapor who seeks death.
21:7 The violence of the wicked will drag them away,
because they refuse to do justice.
21:8 A man's behavior may be tortuous,
(even) while his deeds are pure and upright.
21:9 Better to dwell on the corner of a roof
than with a contentious woman in a house with other people.
21:10 The soul of the wicked man desires what is bad;
he will find no forgiveness in the eyes of others.
21:11 When a scoffer is punished the callow person will gain wisdom,
and when a wise person is taught he gains knowledge.
21:12 The righteous one observes the house of the wicked,
confounding the wicked into evil.
21:13 He who blocks his ear from hearing the cry of the lowly—
he too will call out and will not be answered.
21:14 A gift in secret assuages anger,
and a bribe in the bosom—strong wrath.
21:15 Doing justice is a pleasure to a righteous man,
but a ruin to evildoers.
21:16 A man who strays from the way of insight
will repose in the community of the ghosts.
21:17 He who loves pleasure (becomes) a needy man;
the lover of wine and oil will not grow rich.
21:18 The wicked man is ransom for the righteous one,
and the treacherous man is substituted for the upright.

21:19 Better to dwell in a desert land
than with a contentious and angry woman.
21:20 A delightful treasure dwells in the habitation of the wise,
but a stupid man swallows it up.
21:21 He who pursues righteousness and kindness
will find life and honor.
21:22 A wise man went up against the city of warriors
and brought down its strong fortifications.
21:23 He who guards his mouth and his tongue
guards himself from troubles.
21:24 The arrogant, insolent man—*leṣ* is his name;
he acts in the rage of arrogance.
21:25 The sluggard's desires kill him,
because his hands refuse to work.
21:26 He feels desire constantly,
but the righteous man gives without stinting.
21:27 The sacrifice of the wicked is loathsome.
All the more so when he offers it with some scheme in mind.
21:28 The deceitful witness will perish,
but the man who listens will speak victoriously.
21:29 The wicked man puts on a bold face,
but the upright understands where he is going.
21:30 There is no wisdom or understanding
or counsel before the Lord.
21:31 The horse is ready for the day of battle,
but victory belongs to the Lord.
22:1 A name is preferable to great wealth,
and good favor to silver and gold.
22:2 The rich man and the poor man meet:
the Lord is maker of both.
22:3 The shrewd man sees trouble and hides,
while the callow pass and are punished.
22:4 The reward of humility is fear of the Lord,
wealth and honor and life.
22:5 Thorns and snares are in the path of the crooked man.
He who guards his life will keep far from them.
22:6 Train a youth according to his way,
and even when he grows old he will not depart from it.
22:7 The rich man rules over the poor,
and the borrower is slave to the lender.
22:8 He who sows wickedness will harvest evil,
and the rod of his wrath will fail.
22:9 As for the generous man, he will be blessed,
because he has given of his bread to the lowly.

22:10 Banish the impudent and conflict will depart,
and disputes and insult will cease.
22:11 He who loves purity of heart,
whose speech is gracious—
the king is his companion.
22:12 The eyes of the Lord guard knowledge,
while he confounds the words of the treacherous.
22:13 The sluggard says, "There is a lion in the street,
among the plazas I will be murdered!"
22:14 The mouth of strange women is a deep pit.
It is the man cursed by the Lord who falls into it.
22:15 Folly is bound to the heart of a child.
The rod of discipline will remove it from him.
22:16 There is one who oppresses a poor man yet he ends up giving him more.
There is one who gives to a rich man yet he ends up in need.

PART III. WORDS OF THE WISE

Part IIIa. The Amenemope Collection

22:17 Words of the wise.
Incline your ear and hear my words,
and direct your heart to my knowledge;
22:18 for it will be pleasant if you keep them in your belly,
that they may all be secure on your lips.
22:19 In order that your trust may be in the Lord,
I have taught them to you, even you, today.
22:20 Have I not written for you thirty (maxims)
in deliberation and knowledge?—
22:21 to teach you the truest of words,
to give answer to those who send you.
22:22 Do not rob a lowly man because he is lowly,
and do not oppress the poor man at the gate.
22:23 For the Lord will strive on their behalf,
and will steal away the life of those who steal from them.
22:24 Do not consort with an ill-tempered man,
and do not go with a hot-head.
22:25 lest you learn his ways
and get yourself snared.
22:26 Do not be among those who shake hands,
among those who guarantee loans,
22:27 lest—if you don't have the wherewithal to pay—
they take your bedding from beneath you.

22:28 Do not encroach on the ancient boundary,
which your ancestors made.
22:29 Have you seen a man adept in his work?
He will stand before kings.
He will not stand before the lowly.
23:1 When you sit to dine with an official,
look carefully at what is before you,
23:2 and put a knife to your throat,
if you are a voracious man.
23:3 Do not desire his delicacies,
for they are deceitful bread.
23:4 Don't strain to get rich.
Leave off your staring!
23:5 If you but let your eye fly on it, it is no more.
for it will surely make itself wings like an eagle's
and fly off to the sky.
23:6 Do not eat the bread of the stingy man,
nor desire his delicacies.
23:7 For like one who calculates in his mind, thus is he:
"Eat and drink" he says to you,
but his heart is not with you.
23:8 You eat your morsel, you vomit it up,
and ruin your fine words.
23:9 Do not speak in the ears of a dolt,
for he will despise the insight of your words.
23:10 Do not encroach on the ancient boundary,
nor enter the fields of orphans,
23:11 for their redeemer is strong.
He will contend with you on their behalf.

Part IIIb. Words of the Wise, Continued

23:12 Bring your heart to discipline
and your ear to words of knowledge.
23:13 Do not withhold discipline from a youth,
for if you smite him with a rod he will not die.
23:14 If you smite him with a rod,
you will save his life from Sheol.
23:15 My son, if your heart becomes wise,
my heart too will rejoice,
23:16 and my kidneys will exult
when your lips speak rectitude.
23:17 Let not your heart envy sinners,
but rather the fear of the Lord every day.

23:18 for if you {maintain it}, there is a future,
and your hope will not be cut off.
23:19 Listen, my son, and become wise,
and go straight in the way of your heart.
23:20 Do not be among the wine-bibbers,
among those who gorge on meat,
23:21 for he who imbibes and gorges himself will be impoverished,
and sleep will clothe one in rags.
23:22 Listen to your father, who begot you,
and be not contemptuous when your mother grows old.
23:23 <Get truth and do not sell it:
wisdom and discipline and understanding.>
23:24 The father of a righteous (son) will greatly rejoice,
and he who begets a wise (son) will rejoice in him.
23:25 Let your father and mother rejoice,
and she who bore you exult!
23:26 Give your heart to me, my son,
and let your eyes keep my ways,
23:27 for the strange woman is a deep pit,
the alien woman a narrow well.
23:28 She also lurks like a bandit,
and eliminates traitors among men.
23:29 Who (cries) "Woe!"? Who cries "Alas!"?
Who has quarrels? Who has complaints?
Who has wounds without cause?
Who has bloodshot eyes?
23:30 Those who tarry late over wine,
who come to inspect mixed wine.
23:31 Don't look at wine when it glows red,
when it gives its gleam in the cup,
flowing down smoothly.
23:32 In the end it bites like a serpent,
and spews (venom) like a viper.
23:33 Your eyes will see strange things,
and your heart speak perversities.
23:34 And you will be like one who lies (in bed) in the heart of the sea,
or like one who lies in the rigging.
23:35 "They beat me but I felt no hurt,
battered me but I was unaware.
When will I wake up?
I'll go and look for more."
24:1 Do not envy evil men,
nor desire to be with them.
24:2 For their heart meditates destruction,
and their lips speak deceit.

24:3 By wisdom a house is built,
and by good sense it is established;
24:4 and by knowledge rooms are filled
with all sorts of wealth, precious and pleasant.
24:5 Stronger a wise man than a mighty one,
and a man of knowledge than one great in power.
24:6 For you should make war by strategy,
and victory comes through many counselors.
24:7 Wisdom is beyond the fool's reach:
In the gate he cannot open his mouth.
24:8 He who plans to do evil—
he will be called a schemer.
24:9 Foolish scheming is sin itself,
and people loathe the scoffer.
24:10 If you are lax in the day of distress,
your strength will be constrained.
24:11 Save those who are being taken away to death,
and those who are tottering on (the brink of) slaughter, do not stint (in helping),
24:12 For if you say, "We did not know this,"
will not he who examines hearts perceive,
will not the guardian of your soul know,
and repay a man in accordance with his deed?
24:13 Eat honey, my son, because it is good,
and honeycomb (because it is) sweet to your palate.
24:14 So should you learn wisdom for yourself.
If you find it, there is a future,
and your hope will not be cut off.
24:15 Do not enter the habitation of the righteous—
don't plunder the field of his pasturing!
24:16 Though the righteous man may fall seven times, he will rise,
while the wicked will stumble in evil.
24:17 When your enemy falls, do not rejoice,
and when he stumbles, don't let your heart exult,
24:18 lest the Lord see and be displeased,
and turn his wrath away from him.
24:19 Be not vexed at evildoers
and don't envy the wicked,
24:20 for there shall be no future for the evil man;
the light of the wicked will go out.
24:21 Fear the Lord, my son, and the king.
Do not anger either of them.
24:22 For suddenly catastrophe will go forth from them;
and who can understand the disaster either can cause?

PART IV. MORE WORDS OF THE WISE

24:23 These too are of the wise.
Showing partiality in judgment is not good.
24:24 He who says to the guilty, "You are innocent"—
peoples will curse him and nations revile him.
24:25 But with those who rebuke it shall go well,
upon them shall come a blessing of good.
24:26b He who answers with honest words
24:26a kisses the lips.
24:27 Prepare your work in the soil,
and ready it in the field.
Afterwards build your house.
24:28 Do not be a gratuitous witness against another person,
nor open your lips wide.
24:29 Do not say, "As he did to me so I will do to him,
I will repay the man according to what he did."
24:30 I passed by the field of a lazy man,
and by the vineyard of a senseless person,
24:31 and I saw that it was overgrown with weeds,
the ground was covered with nettles,
and its stone wall was destroyed.
24:32 And I looked and took note,
I saw and drew a lesson:
24:33 A bit more sleep, a bit more snoozing,
a bit more lying with folded arms,
24:34 and penury will come upon you like a vagabond,
and poverty like a man of arms.

PART V. THE HEZEKIAN COLLECTION

25:1 These too are proverbs of Solomon,
which the men of Hezekiah king of Judah transcribed.
25:2 It is to God's honor to conceal a matter,
and to the honor of kings to examine a matter.
25:3 The heavens for height and the earth for depth,
and the heart of kings for being unsearchable.
25:4 Remove dross from silver,
and a vessel comes forth for the smith.
25:5 Remove the wicked from before the king,
and his throne will be established in righteousness.
25:6 Do not exalt yourself before the king,
and do not stand in the place of the great.

25:7 For better that he say, "Come up here,"
than that he degrade you before a nobleman
whom your eyes have seen.
25:8 Do not go out to quarrel hastily,
for what will you do afterwards,
when your neighbor insults you?
25:9 Have your quarrel with your neighbor,
but do not reveal another's secret.
25:10 lest one who hears revile you,
and your bad reputation never end.
25:11 Apples of gold in engravings of silver:
a word spoken in the right way.
25:12 A ring of gold and an ornament of fine gold:
a wise man giving a rebuke to a listening ear.
25:13 Like the chill of snow on a harvest day
is a reliable envoy to his senders:
He refreshes the soul of his masters.
25:14 Clouds with wind and no rain:
a man who boasts of a gift that disappoints.
25:15 By patience an official can be beguiled,
and a soft tongue breaks a bone.
25:16 If you find honey, eat just enough,
lest you become satiated with it and vomit it up.
25:17 Go but rarely to your neighbor's house,
lest he become satiated with you and hate you.
25:18 A club and a sword and a sharpened arrow:
a man who testifies falsely against his neighbor.
25:19 A broken tooth and a shaky foot:
a treacherous refuge in a day of trouble.
25:20a ⟨One who removes a garment on a cold day.⟩
25:20bc Vinegar on natron:
one who sings songs to a sad heart.
25:21 If your enemy hungers,
feed him bread,
and if he is thirsty,
give him water to drink.
25:22 For you will heap coals on his head,
and the Lord will reward you.
25:23 The north wind produces rain,
and a secretive tongue, an angry face.
25:24 Better to dwell on the corner of a roof
than with a contentious woman in a house with other
people.
25:25 Cold water to a thirsty soul:
good news from a distant land.

25:26 A muddied spring and a polluted well:
a righteous man tottering before a wicked one.
25:27 Eating honey too much is not good,
and being sparing in speech is honorable.
25:28 A breached city without a wall:
a man whose spirit lacks restraint.
26:1 Like snow in summer and a downpour in harvest,
so honor is not suitable to a dolt.
26:2 As a sparrow for wandering and a swallow for flying,
so a gratuitous curse will not alight.
26:3 A whip for a horse and a bridle for an ass—
and a rod for the back of dolts.
26:4 Don't answer a dolt according to his folly,
lest you become just like him.
26:5 Answer a dolt according to his folly,
lest he be wise in his own eyes.
26:6 One who cuts off his legs and drinks violence:
he who sends word by means of a dolt.
26:7 Legs dangle from a cripple,
and a proverb in the mouth of dolts.
26:8 Like one who binds a stone in a sling,
so is he who gives honor to a dolt.
26:9 A thorn coming into the hand of a drunk:
a proverb in the mouth of dolt.
26:10 The flesh of the fool is greatly wounded,
and the drunkard crosses the sea.
26:11 Like a dog returning to his vomit,
so is a dolt repeating his folly.
26:12 Have you seen a man wise in his own eyes?
There is more hope for a dolt than him.
26:13 The sluggard says, "There is a young lion in the street,
a lion in the plazas."
26:14 The door turns on its hinge,
and the sluggard on his bed.
26:15 The sluggard hides his hand in the bowl,
too weary to bring it back to his mouth.
26:16 The sluggard is wiser in his own eyes
than seven men who can respond intelligently.
26:17 One who seizes the ears of a passing dog:
he who interferes in a conflict not his own.
26:18 Like a reckless man shooting deadly darts and arrows,
26:19 so is the man who cheats his fellow and says,
"Look, I was just joking."
26:20 When there's no wood, the fire dies out,
and when there's no slanderer, contention is hushed.

26:21 Charcoal for embers and wood for fire:
and a contentious man for kindling strife.
26:22 The words of the slanderer are like delicacies,
and they descend to the chambers of the belly.
26:23 Adulterated silver glazed on earthenware:
smooth lips and an evil heart.
26:24 An enemy disguises himself in his speech,
while he sets deceit within him.
26:25 When he makes his voice pleasant, do not believe him,
for seven abominations are in his heart.
26:26 He who covers up his hatred by deceit:
his evil will be exposed in public.
26:27 He who digs a pit will fall in it,
and he who rolls a stone—it will come back on him
26:28 A deceptive tongue hates those it afflicts,
and a smooth mouth gives a shove.
27:1 Do not boast of the morrow,
for you know not what a day may bring forth.
27:2 Let a stranger praise you, and not your own mouth,
an alien, and not your own lips.
27:3 The weight of stone and the burden of sand—
the fool's anger is heavier than either.
27:4 The cruelty of fury and a torrent of anger—
but who can stand before jealousy?
27:5 Better open rebuke than hidden love.
27:6 Faithful are wounds by a friend,
and profuse the kisses of an enemy.
27:7 A sated appetite scorns (even) the honeycomb,
but to a hungry appetite, everything bitter is sweet.
27:8 As a bird wandering from its nest,
so is he who wanders from his place.
27:9 Oil and incense please the heart,
and the sweet advice of a friend (pleases the heart) more than the soul's counsel.
27:10ab Do not ignore your friend or your father's friend,
and go not into your brother's house on the day of your disaster.
27:10c Better a nearby neighbor than a distant brother.
27:11 Be wise, my son, and make my heart rejoice,
that I may reply to him who insults me.
27:12 The shrewd man, seeing trouble, hides;
callow men, passing, are punished.
27:13 "Take his garment, for he has given surety for a stranger!
And seize it, (because he has given surety) for aliens."

27:14 He who greets his neighbor in a loud voice
early in the morning—
it will be reckoned to him as a curse.
27:15 An irksome dripping on a rainy day
and a contentious woman are alike.
27:16 He who hides her hides the wind,
and he is called, "Right."
27:17 Iron joins to iron,
and a man joins with the face of his fellow.
27:18 He who tends a fig tree will eat its fruit,
and who keeps his master will be honored.
27:19 As in water, a face to a face,
so a man's heart to a man.
27:20 Sheol and Abaddon are not satisfied,
and the eyes of man are not satisfied.
27:21 A smelter for silver and a furnace for gold,
and a man (is tested) by the mouth of him who
praises him.
27:22 Even if you crush the fool in a mortar
with a pestle amidst the groats
his folly will not leave him.
27:23 Know well the appearance of your sheep;
give thought to the herds.
27:24 For wealth is not forever,
nor does a crown endure generation after generation.
27:25 (When) grass disappears and verdure appears,
and the grasses of the hills are gathered,
27:26 (there will be) sheep for your clothing
and goats—the price of a field;
27:27 and enough goat's milk for your food,
the food of your household,
and provisions for your maidservants.
28:1 The wicked flee with no one pursuing,
while the righteous are as confident as a lion.
28:2 For the transgression of a land, its princes are many,
but through an understanding man honesty endures.
28:3 A man who is poor and oppresses the lowly:
a torrential rain without bread.
28:4 Those who ignore the teaching praise the wicked man,
but those who keep the teaching contend with them.
28:5 Evil men do not understand what is just,
but those who seek the Lord understand everything.
28:6 Better a poor man who goes in his innocence
than a man of crooked ways who is rich.

28:7 The perceptive son keeps the teaching,
while he who consorts with gluttons shames his father.
28:8 He who amasses his wealth by interest and usury—
is (actually) gathering it for him who is kind to the lowly.
28:9 He who turns a deaf ear to the teaching,
even his prayer is loathsome.
28:10 As for him who misleads the upright into a bad path—
he will fall into his own pit,
but the righteous will inherit goodness.
28:11 A rich man is wise in his own eyes,
but a perceptive pauper can see through him.
28:12 When the righteous exult, great is the splendor,
but when the wicked arise, men are sought.
28:13 He who covers up his offenses will not prosper,
while he who confesses and leaves off them will receive mercy.
28:14 Happy is the man who fears continually,
while he who hardens his heart will fall into evil.
28:15 A growling lion and a ravenous bear:
a wicked ruler over a wretched people—
27:16a a prince devoid of good sense and abounding in oppression.
28:16b He who hates ill-gotten gain will live long.
28:17 A man who oppresses by bloodshed,
will flee to a pit.
Let no one hold him!
28:18 He who goes in innocence will be kept safe,
while the man of crooked ways will fall in a pit.
28:19 He who works his land will be sated with bread,
while he who pursues trifles will be sated with poverty.
28:20 The faithful man has many blessings,
but he who hastens to get rich will not go unpunished.
28:21 Showing partiality is not good,
but a man may transgress for a piece of bread.
28:22 The greedy man rushes after wealth,
unaware that penury will come upon him.
28:23 He who reproves another
will find more favor than a flatterer.
28:24 He who robs his father and mother
and says "No wrong was done"—
he is companion to a vandal.
28:25 The greedy man provokes conflict,
but he who trusts in the Lord will prosper.
28:26 He who trusts in his own heart—he is a dolt;
while he who goes in wisdom—he will escape.

28:27 He who gives to the poor will not go needy,
while he who turns his eyes aside will be much cursed.
28:28 When the wicked arise, men hide,
and when they perish, the righteous increase.
29:1 A man often rebuked, who stiffens his neck
will suddenly be broken, beyond remedy.
29:2 When the righteous increase, the people rejoice,
but when the wicked man rules, the people groan.
29:3 A man who loves wisdom makes his father rejoice,
but he who consorts with harlots loses money.
29:4 By justice a king gives stability to the land,
while a deceitful man destroys it.
29:5 A man who flatters his fellow
spreads a net for his feet.
29:6 In the transgression of an evil man there is a snare,
and the righteous will rejoice and be glad.
29:7 The righteous man knows the rights of the lowly;
the wicked man does not have knowledge.
29:8 Impudent men inflame a city,
while the wise assuage anger.
29:9 A wise man disputes with a foolish one,
and he is angry and laughs and there is no calm.
29:10 Men of blood hate the innocent man,
while the upright seek his life.
29:11 A dolt lets all his emotions out,
while a wise man quiets them down.
29:12 An official who heeds a lying word—
all his servants are wicked.
29:13 A poor man and an oppressive man meet:
It is the Lord who gives light to the eyes of both.
29:14 A king who judges the poor faithfully—
his throne will be established forever.
29:15 The rod of rebuke gives wisdom,
while a youth let loose disgraces his mother.
29:16 When the wicked increase, transgression increases,
but the righteous will see their downfall.
29:17 Discipline your son and he will bring you comfort,
and give delight to your soul.
29:18 When there is no vision, the nation is disorderly,
but he who keeps the teaching, how happy he is!
29:19 A slave will not take discipline by words (alone),
for if he understands, there will (still) be no response.
29:20 Have you seen a man hasty in his words?
There is more hope for a dolt than him.

29:21 He who pampers his slave from youth—
he will be a misery afterwards.
29:22 The angry man provokes strife,
and the heated one is full of offenses.
29:23 A man's pride will cast him down,
but he whose spirit is humble will hold honor.
29:24 He who divides (spoil) with a thief hates himself.
When he hears the curse he will not testify.
29:25 The fear of man sets a snare,
but he who trusts in the Lord will be safe.
29:26 Many make entreaties of an official,
but a man's judgment comes from the Lord.
29:27 The righteous loathe the iniquitous man,
while the wicked loathe him whose way is straight.

PART VI. FOUR APPENDICES

Part VIa. The Words of Agur

30:1 The words of Agur the son of Yaqeh,
the pronouncement, the oracle of the man:
I am weary, God,
I am weary, God, and have wasted away,
30:2 for I am the most ignorant of men,
and have not human understanding.
30:3 I have not learned wisdom
or have knowledge of the Holy One.
30:4 Who has ascended to the heavens and come down?
Who has gathered the wind in his lap?
Who has wrapped the waters in his garment?
Who has set up all the ends of the earth?
What is his name and what is the name of his son?—
For you know.
30:5 All of God's words are pure;
he is a shield to those who trust in him.
30:6 Add not to his words,
lest he chastise you and you be proved false.
30:7 Two things I ask of you;
do not deny me them before I die:
30:8 Falsehood and deceit keep far from me.
Give me neither poverty nor wealth,
but grant me my apportioned bread,
30:9 lest I become sated and renounce (you),
and I say, "Who is Yahweh?,"
and lest I become poor and steal,
and misuse the name of my God.

Part VIb. Epigrams and Aphorisms

30:10 Do not denounce a slave to his master,
lest he curse you and you be held guilty.
30:11 A generation that curses its father,
and does not bless its mother.
30:12 A generation that is pure in its own eyes
and is not cleansed of its filth.
30:13 A generation of arrogant eyes,
and whose eyelids are haughty.
30:14 A generation whose teeth are swords,
and its molars knives—
to devour the poor from off the earth,
and the indigent from among men.
30:15a The leech has two daughters: "Give!" "Give!"
30:15b Three things there are that are insatiable,
four that do not say "Enough!":
30:16 Sheol, and barrenness,
the earth, which is not sated with water,
and fire, which does not say "Enough!"
30:17 An eye that mocks the father
and disdains to obey the mother—
the ravens of the creek will gouge it out,
and the young of the eagle will devour it.
30:18 Three things there are too wondrous for me,
four I cannot comprehend:
30:19 the way of the eagle in the sky,
the way of a snake on a rock,
the way of a ship in the heart of the sea,
and the way of a man with a maid.
30:20 Such is the way of an adulterous woman.
She eats and wipes her mouth,
and says: "I have done no wrong."
30:21 Under three things the earth quakes,
under four it cannot stand:
30:22 under a slave, when he becomes king;
and a scoundrel, when he has his fill of bread;
30:23 under a hateful woman, when she gains mastery,
and a maidservant, when she disinherits her mistress.
30:24 Four things there are, among the smallest on earth,
yet they are wise and skilled:
30:25 The ants are a people not strong,
but they ready their bread in the summer.
30:26 The badgers are a people not numerous,
but they make their home in the rock.

30:27 The locusts have no king,
but they all go forth in file.
30:28 The spider can be caught in the hands,
but it is in the palaces of kings.
30:29 Three things there are that are excellent of stride,
four excellent of walk.
30:30 The lion is mightiest of beasts,
and he retreats from nothing.
30:31 The cock (girded) of loins or the he-goat,
and the king, whom none can withstand.
30:32 If in arrogance you have acted vilely,
or if you have schemed, put your hand on your mouth!
30:33 For the churning of milk produces curds,
and the churning of the nose produces blood,
and the churning of anger produces strife.

Part VIc. The Teaching of Lemuel's Mother

31:1 The words of Lemuel, king of Massa,
whom his mother instructed:
31:2 No, my son,
no, son of my womb,
no, son of my vows—
31:3 Do not give your strength to women,
nor your ways to the destroyers of kings.
31:4 Not for kings, Lemuel,
not for kings is the drinking of wine,
nor for governors beer.
31:5 Lest he drink and forget the statute,
and alter the verdict of any of the poor.
31:6 Give beer to him who is perishing,
and wine to the bitter of soul,
31:7 that he may drink and forget his poverty,
and think no more of his toil.
31:8 Open your mouth for the dumb,
for the judgment of all who are about to expire.
31:9 Open your mouth, give righteous judgment,
give justice to the poor and needy.

Part VId. The Woman of Strength

31:10 A woman of strength, who can find?
Her price is greater than rubies.
31:11 Her husband's heart trusts in her,
and he does not lack for gain.

31:12 She repays him with good, not evil
all the days of her life.
31:13 She seeks out wool and flax,
and she works with willing hands
31:14 Like merchant ships
she brings her bread from afar.
31:15 She rises while it is still night,
and gives food to her household,
and a portion to her maids.
31:16 She plans a field and buys it,
from the fruit of her hands she plants a vineyard.
31:17 She girds her loins with power,
and gives strength to her arms
31:18 She realizes that her wares are good.
Her lamp does not go out at night.
31:19 She stretches out her hands to the spindle,
and her palms grasp the spinning-rod.
31:20 She opens her palms to the poor,
and stretches out her hands to the needy.
31:21 She does not fear for her household because of snow,
for all her household are dressed in scarlet.
31:22 She makes herself coverings;
linen and purple is her raiment.
31:23 Her husband is known in the gates,
when he sits with the elders of the land.
31:24 She makes fine linen and vends it,
and sells loincloths to the trader.
31:25 Strength and majesty are her raiment,
and she laughs at future days.
31:26 She opens her mouth in wisdom,
and the teaching of kindness is on her tongue.
31:27 She looks to the ways of her household,
and eats not the bread of idleness.
31:28 Her sons arise and laud her;
her husband (arises and) praises her:
31:29 "Many daughters have done noble things,
but you have surpassed them all."
31:30 Comeliness is deceit and beauty a vapor,
but a woman who fears the Lord—will be praised.
31:31 Give her of the fruit of her hands,
and let her deeds praise her in the gates.

BIBLIOGRAPHY FOR VOLUMES I AND II

◆

Works marked by an asterisk are referenced by name of author only, ad. loc. unless otherwise indicated. Works listed only in the bibliography in volume II are distinguished by italicization of dates.

I. PRIMARY SOURCES, FOREIGN

A. Egyptian Wisdom and Related Texts

See Vol. I, 19–24. The major sources of Egyptian Wisdom literature and their places of publication are listed below. Eclectic texts are usually referenced by the section numbering (in capital roman numerals) in the KÄT (Kleine Ägyptische Texte) editions.

Amenemḥet I: Pap. Millingen; Pap. Sallier I, II, et al. Volten 1945; Helck 1969. AEL 1.135–39, AW 169–77.

Amenemḥet Priest of Amon (tomb autobiography): Helck, *Urk. 18. Dyn.*, nos. 1408–1411. AW 389–91.

Amenemope: Pap. BM 10474 et al. Lange 1925. AEL 2.146–63, AW 234–56.

Amennakhte: Various ostraca (only the introduction and two maxims remain). Posener 1955 and COHL III, no. 1596; Beckenrath, *Studien zur altägyptischen Kultur* 1983 (numbering accd. to Posener's edition). See also Bickel and Mathieu 1993: 33–35. AW 231–33.

Anchsheshonq: Pap. BM 10508. Glanville 1955. LEWL 70–92; quoted from AEL 3.159–84; also AW 257–91.

Anii: Quack 1994. Five papyri, one writing tablet, and some nine ostraca. Unless otherwise noted, references are to Pap. Boulaq IV ("B" in Quack's edition[471]). Text, transl., commentary: Quack 1994. AEL 2.135–46, AW 196–217.

Brooklyn Wisdom Papyrus: Pap. Brooklyn 47.218.135. Jasnow 1992.

Pap. Chester Beatty IV: HPBM, pls. 37–44. A miscellany of Wisdom texts. AW 218–30.

Djedefḥar (or Ḥardjedef): New Kingdom ostraca and wooden tablet of Late Period. Brunner-Traut 1940; Posener 1952, 1966. Helck 1984. AEL 1.58–59, AW 101–103.

Duachety (or Chety; first part commonly called the "Satire of the Trades"): Pap. Amherst (18th dyn.), Pap. Sallier II (19th dyn.), Pap. Anastasi VII (19th dyn.), Pap. Chester Beatty XIX (19th dyn.), plus wooden tablets and scores of ostraca. Brunner 1944; Helck 1970a. AEL 1.184–92, AW 155–68.

"Eloquent Peasant": (Middle Kingdom) Four incomplete papyri. AEL 1.169–84, AW 358–67.

Ḥori (O. Gardiner 2, rco.): Fischer-Elfert 1986: 1–4. Bickel and Mathieu 1993: 49–50.

Kagemeni: Pap. Prisse 1–2. Text: K. Sethe, *Lesestücke* 42–43; Gardiner 1946; AEL 1.59–61, AW 133–36.

Kemit ("The Compilation"): Writing board and many ostraca. Posener 1951, pls. 1–21; Barta 1978. LAE 15–16; AW 368–69.

Louvre Demotic Papyrus 2414: LEWL 94–95. AW 292–94.

"Loyalist Teaching": Collated from the stele of Seḥetibre (which incorporates a partial version of the instruction) and numerous fragmentary copies; see G. Posener,

[471] Note that Quack's cols. 14–23 = Suys's cols. 1–10. Suys numeration is commonly used in translations. His transcription is faulty and outdated, and translations based on it must be regarded with caution.

L'Enseignment loyaliste (1976). (Original version from the time of Sesostris I.) References according to Posener's edition. AEL 1.125–29 (partial), AW 178–84.

"A Man to His Son": Text: Helck 1984. AW 185–93.

Menena (or Menna), a letter including proverbs and instructions: Oriental Inst. Ost. 12074. Gugliemi 1983; J. L. Foster 1984. AW 399–402.

Merikare: Pap. Leningrad 116A, Pap. Moscow 4658, Pap. Carlsberg 6; ostraca. Volten 1945; Helck 1977; COHL 18: pls. 2–21. AEL 1.97–109, AW 137–54.

O. Petrie 11 ("Instruction According to Old Writings"): HO LXXXVIII vso. (title) + I rto. LEWL 7, AW 215–17.

Phibis ("Demotic Wisdom Book"): Pap. Insinger; Pap. Carlesberg: Volten 1941 (partial). LEWL 197–234; AW 295–349. Quoted from AEL 3.184–217.

Ptaḥḥotep: Pap. Prisse. Žába 1956. AEL 1.61–80, AW 104–32.

Ramesseum Papyri I and II: J. W. B. Barns, *Five Ramesseum Papyri* (1956), I: pll. 1–6, pp. 1–10; II: pll. 7–9, pp. 11–14. AW 178–84 (partial).

"Satirical Letter": Pap. Anastasi I. Gardiner 1911. Selections in AW 396–402.

B. Mesopotamian Wisdom

See Vol. I, 23. (For a comprehensive translation of Mesopotamian literature, see B. Foster, *Before the Muses* [BTM], 1993.)

"Counsels of Wisdom": Babylonian. Translation in BTM 328–31. Text BWL, 27–29.

Shubeʾawilum: Latter part of second millenium. Text Dietrich 1991; text and translation Nougayrol et al. 1968. Translation BTM 1.332–35.

Shuruppak (Suruppak): Three Sumerian versions, dating from ca. 2500 B.C.E. to ca. 1800 B.C.E. (texts and translation in Alster 1974) and a fragment of an Akkadian translation, ca. 1100 B.C.E. Text and translation in Alster 1974: 33–51.

C. Syrian Wisdom

See Vol. I, 23.

Aḥiqar: Aramaic; 7th c. in origin; widely translated and revised. Aramaic: Lindenberger 1983 and Porten and Yardeni 1993 (TAD). Syriac and other versions in Coneybeare et al. 1913. (References are by Lindenberger's numbering in parentheses. In Vol. II this is followed by TAD's numbering in brackets; for example, (100a–102 [1.1.84–86]).

II. TRADITIONAL JEWISH EXEGESIS

Midrashim, Medieval Commentaries, and Some Later Commentaries in the Traditional Mode. Printed texts are listed, with reference to the most accessible edition or editions. Midrash Rabba and Tanḥuma are cited according to the Vilna editions.

Alsheikh

Moshe ben Ḥayyim Alsheikh (1508–1601, Safed). *Rav Peninim*. Vilna: the Widow and Brothers Rom. (Abridged trans.: E. Munk, Jerusalem, 1991).

Baḥyeh
Baḥyeh ben Asher (13th c., Saragosa). (Through chap. 15). Collated by Y. Heine. Jerusalem, 1950.
Benjamin ben Judah
Benjamin ben Judah (1285–1330, Rome). Ed. H. Berger. Pressburg: Alkalay, 1901.
Elijah, Gaon of Vilna
Tana' debey Eliyahu. Prague: Scholl, 1814.
"Frankfort"
Anonymous Frankfort Manuscript (ms. dated 1340, commentary 11th–13th c.; France or Provence). Ed. Georg Kantorowsky, *Ein anonymer hebräischer Commentar zu den Proverbien*. Breslau: Fleischmann, 1907.
Gavishon
Abraham ben Jacob Gavishon (1520–578, Algeria). *ʿOmer Hašikḥah*. Jerusalem: Kedem, n.d.
Gerundi, Sheshet
Sheshet ben Isaac Gerundi (13th–14th c., Gerona and Palestine). Ed. Karl Koch, Erlangen: Vollrath, 1893 (repr. Jerusalem: Hasekhel, 1992).
Gerundi, Yonah
Yonah ben Abraham Gerundi (1200–1263, Spain). Commentary to Proverbs, etc. Ed. Y. Gloskinus. Spring Valley, N.Y.: Feldheim, 1993.
Hameʾiri
R. Menachem ben Shelomo Hameʾiri (1249–1316? Provence and Toledo). Ed. Menachem Mendel Meshi-Zahav. Otzar Haposqim. Jerusalem, 1969.
Ibn Janaḥ
Yonah Abu al-Walid Marwan ibn Janaḥ (first half of 11th c., Spain). *Peruš Lekitvey Haqodeš*. Tel Aviv, 1926, 1936. See also Ibn Janaḥ's *Sefer Hariqmah*, below.
Ibn Yaḥyah
Yosef ben David ibn Yaḥyah (1494–1534, Italy). Bologna, 1539; also in the *Qᵉhilat Yaʿaqov* Bible (Amsterdam 1724–1727).
Immanuel of Rome
Immanuel ben Solomon (1260–ca. 1330, Rome). Naples, 1487. Repr. with intro. by David Goldstein, Jerusalem: Magnes, 1981.
Isaiah di Trani
Isaiah ben Mali di Trani (13th c., Italy). Commentary. Ed. A. J. Würtheimer. Jerusalem: Ketav Yad vaSefer, 1978.
Isaac ben Arama
Isaac Arama (1420–1494, Spain). *Yad Avshalom*. Ed. I. Freimann. Leipzig: 1858/1859.
Jephet ben Ali
Jephet ben Ali Halevi (Karaite) (Second half of 10th c., Basra and Jerusalem). *Der Commentar des Karäers Jephet ben ʿAli Halevi zu den Proverbien*. Ed. Israel Günzig. Krakau: J. Fischer, 1898.
Kaspi
Yosef ibn Kaspi (1279–1340, Spain). *Ḥaṣoṣᵉrot Kesef* ("Trumpets of Silver"), in *ʿAsarah Kley Kesef* ("Ten Instruments of Silver"). Ed. Isaac Last. Pressburg: Alkalay, 1903 (repr. Jerusalem 1969–1970).
Malbim
Meir Loeb ben Yechiel Michael (1809–1879, Poland). *Musar Haḥokmah* (Com-

mentary on Proverbs) in *'Otzar Haperushim*, Vol. X. [Vilna: The Widow and Brothers Rom, 1923].

Mezudat David

David Altschuler (18th c., Galicia). Rabbinic Bible.

Midrash Proverbs (ca. 9th c.)

Ed. B. Visotzky. New York: Jewish Theological Seminary, 1990.

Midrash Shoḥer Tov

Jerusalem: Midrash Publishers, n.d.

Naḥmias

Yosef ben Yosef ibn Naḥmias (first half of 14th c., Toledo). Ed. A. L. Bamberger. Berlin: Itschkowsky, 1911 (repr. Israel, 1969[?]).

Pinto

Josia ben Joseph Pinto Commentary on Proverbs. Amsterdam: Isaac Timpelo, 1729.

Pseudo-Ibn Ezra

A Commentary on the Book of Proverbs Attributed to Abraham Ibn Ezra [Opp. Add. 8°.48, Oxford Bod. no. 2487]. Ed. S. R. Driver. Oxford: Clarendon, 1880.

Radaq

R. David Qimḥi (1160–1235?, Spain). Ed. Talmage 1990. See also Qimḥi, *Sefer Hashorashim*, below.

Ralbag

R. Levi ben Gershon (Gersonides) (1288–1344, France). Rabbinic Bible.

Ramaq

R. Moses Qimḥi (d. 1190, Spain). See Talmage 1990. [A flawed edition appears in the Rabbinic Bible, where it is incorrectly ascribed to Abraham Ibn Ezra.]

Rashi

Solomon ben Isaac (1040–1105, Troyes). Rabbinic Bible.

Riyqam

R. Yoseph Qimḥi (ca. 1105–1170, Spain). See Talmage 1990.

Saʿadia

Saʿadia Gaon (882–942, Egypt, Palestine, Babylonia). Commentary translated into Hebrew from Judeo-Arabic and edited by Yosef Qafiḥ. Jerusalem, 1975–1976 (?). (cf. Jonas Bondi, *Das Spruchbuch nach Saadja*. Halle, 1988).

Shadal

Samuel David Luzzatto (1800–1865, Italy). See Luzzatto 1876.

Yalqut Machiri

Machir bar Abba Mari, Hamachiri (14th c., southern France). *Yalqut Hamachiri*. Ed. Yehuda Shapira. Berlin: Itzkowsky (repr. Jerusalem, 1964). Ed. Eliezer Grünhut. Jerusalem, 1902 (1964).

Yalqut Shimoni

Midrash anthology, 17th c. Mosad HaRav Kuk, 1960. n.p.

Zeraḥiah ben Shealtiel

Zeraḥiah ben Isaac ben Shealtiel Ḥen (13th c., Barcelona). *Imrey Daʿat*. Ed. I. Schwartz. Vienna: Hafferburg & Mann, 1871.

III. MODERN SCHOLARSHIP

Abrahams, Israel

1948 *Hebrew Ethical Wills*. 2 vols. Philadelphia: Jewish Publication Society.

Abrahams, Roger D.

1983 "Open and Closed Forms in Moral Tales." Pp. 19–33 in *Studies in Aggadah and Jewish Folklore*. Ed. I. Ben-Ami and Joseph Dan. Jerusalem: Magnes.

Ackroyd, Peter R.

1968 The Meaning of Hebrew *dwr* Considered." *JSS* 13: 3–10.

Ahlström, Gösta W.

1979 "The House of Wisdom [Prv 9,1]." *Svensk Exegetisk Arsbok* 44: 74–76.

Albright, William Foxwell

1919–20 "The Goddess of Life and Wisdom." *ASJL* 36: 258–94.

1945 "A New Hebrew Word for 'Glaze' in Proverbs 26: 23." *BASOR* 98: 24–25.

1955 "Some Canaanite-Phoenician Sources of Hebrew Wisdom." Pp. 1–15 in *Wisdom in Israel and in the Ancient Near East*. Ed. M. Noth and D. Winton Thomas. VTSup 3. Leiden: Brill.

1982a "The Hapax *ḥarak* in Proverbs 12,27." *Bib* 63: 60–62.

1982b "Philological Observations on Five Biblical Texts (Prv 14,35)." *Bib* 63: 370–89.

Aletti, J. N.

1976 "Proverbes 8,22–31. Etude de structure." *Bib* 57: 25–37.

1977 "Séduction et parole en Proverbes I–IX." *VT* 27: 129–44.

Allegro, John M.

1964 "The Wiles of the Wicked Woman." *PEQ* 96: 53–55.

Alster, Bendt

1974 *The Instructions of Suruppak*. Copenhagen Studies in Assyriology 2. Copenhagen: Akademisk.

1975a "Paradoxical Proverbs and Satire in Sumerian Literature." *JCS* 27: 201–27.

1975b *Studies in Sumerian Proverbs*. Studies in Assyriology 3. Copenhagen: Akademisk.

Alt, Albrecht

1951E Weisheit Salomos." *TZ* 76: 139–44 [ET in SAIW 102–12].

1955 "Zur literarische Analyse der Weisheit des Amenemope." Pp. 16–25 in *Wisdom in Israel and in the Ancient Near East*. Ed. M. Noth and D. Winton Thomas. VTSup 3. Leiden: Brill.

Altenmüller, Hartwig

1983 "Bemerkungen zu Kapitel 13 der Lehre des Amenemope." Pp. 1–17 in *Fontes atque pontes*. Ed. H. Brunner. Bamberg: Manfred Görg.

Alter, Robert

1985 *The Art of Biblical Poetry*. New York: Basic Books.

Anat, M. A.

1969 "Von der Form zur Bedeutung im Buch Mischle." *Beth Mikra* 39/4: 77–86.

Anbar (Bernstein), M.

1972 "Proverbes 11,21; 16,5: *yd lyd* 'sur le champ.' " *Bib* 53: 537–38.

Anderson, Bruce W.

1967 "Human and Divine Wisdom in Proverbs: Readings in Biblical Morality." Pp. 55–60 in *Understanding the Old Testament*. Englewood Cliffs, N.J.: Prentice Hall.

Anderson, Gary A.
1991 *A Time to Mourn, A Time to Dance*. University Park: Pennsylvania State University Press.
Andrew, M. E.
1978 "Variety of Expression in Proverbs XXIII 29–35." *VT* 28: 120–30.
Anthes, Rudolf
1977 "Zur Echtheit der Lehre des Amenemhet." *FAL* 42–54.
Arambarri, Jess
1990 *Der Wortstamm 'Hören' im Alten Testament*. Stuttgarter Biblische Beiträge 20. Stuttgart: Katholisches Bibelwerk.
Arendt, Hannah
1978 *The Life of the Mind*. San Diego: Harcourt Brace Jovanovich (original 1974).
Aristotle. See Rackham, H.
Arzt, Paul Josef
1993 "Braucht es den erhobenen Zeigefinger?" *Protokolle zur Bibel* 2: 77–87.
Assmann, Jan
1975 *Ägyptische Hymnen und Gebete*. Zurich: Artemis. [= ÄHG]
1979 "Weisheit, Loyalismus und Frömmigkeit." SAL 12–70.
1985 "Die Entdeckung der Vergangenheit: Innovation und Restauration in der ägyptischen Literaturgeschichte." Pp. 484–99 in *Epochenschwellen und Epochenstrukturen im Diskurs der Literatur- und Sprachhistorie*. Ed. H. U. Gumbrecht and U. Link-Herr. Frankfurt am Main: Suhrkamp.
1989 "State and Religion in the New Kingdom." Pp. 56–88 in *Religion and Philosophy in Ancient Egypt*. Ed. W. K. Simpson. YES 3. New Haven, Conn.: Yale University Press.
1990 *Maʿat: Gerechtigkeit und Unsterblichkeit im alten Ägypten*. Munich: Beck.
1996 "Die Wende der Weisheit im alten Ägypten." Pp. 20–38 in *Weisheit ausserhalb der kanonischen Weisheitsschriften*. Ed. Bernd Janowski. Gütersloh: Chr. Kaiser.
Assmann, Jan, Erika Feucht, and Reinhard Grieshammer, eds.
1977 *Fragen an die altägyptische Literatur*. Wiesbaden: Reichert. [= FAL]
Audet, Jean-Paul
1962 "Origines comparées de la double tradition de la loi et de la sagesse dans le Proche-Orient ancien." *Int. Congress of Orientalists* (Moscow) 1: 352–57.
Auffret, Pierre
1980 "Note sur la structure littéraire de Proverbes 22,8–9 selon la restitution proposée par J. Carmignac." *Folia Orientalia* 21: 43–46.
Augustin, Matthias
1983 *Der schöne Mensch im Alten Testament und im hellenistischen Judentum*. Frankfurt am Main: Lang.
Avishur, Yitzhaq
1975 "Phoenician Topoi in Proverbs 3" [Hebrew]. *Shnaton* 1: 13–25.
Backhaus, F. J.
1993 "Qoheleth und Sirach." *BN* 69: 32–55.
Badawy, Alexander
1961 "Two passages from ancient Egyptian literary texts reinterpreted." ZÄS 86: 144–45.
Baer, Seligmann, with preface and annotations by Franz Delitzsch
1880 *Liber Proverbiorum*. Leipzig: Tauchnitz.

Barbiero, G.
1982 "Il testo massoretico di Prov 3,34." *Bib* 63: 370–89.
Barker, Kenneth L.
1989 "Proverbs 23: 7—'To Think' or 'To Serve Food'?" *JANES* 19: 3–8.
Barley, Nigel
1972 "A Structural Approach to the Proverb and the Maxim." *Proverbium* 20: 737–50.
1974 "The Proverb and Related Problems of Genre Definition." *Proverbium* 23: 880–84.
Barns, John W. B.
1956 *Five Ramesseum Papyri*. Oxford: Griffith Inst., Oxford University Press.
Barns, John W. B., and H. Zilliacus
1967 *The Antinoopolis Papyri*. Part III. London: Egypt Exploration Society.
Barr, James
1974 "*Erizō* and *ereidō* in the Septuagint: A Note Principally on Gen. XLIX.6." *JSS* 19: 198–215.
1975 "Ba'areṣ—*Molis*: Prov. XI.31, I Pet. IV.18." *JSS* 20: 149–64.
1979 " 'If the Righteous Scarcely be Saved' (A Note on Prov. 11:31)." Pp. 5–17 in *Studies in the Bible and the Hebrew Language* (FS Meir Wallenstein). Ed. Chaim Rabin et al. Jerusalem: M. Wallenstein.
1981 "A New Look at Kethibh-Qere." *OTS* 21: 19–37.
1985 "Doubts About Homoeophony in the Septuagint." *Textus* 12: 1–77.
Barré, Michael L.
1981 " 'Fear of God' and the World View of Wisdom." *BTB* 11: 41–43.
Barta, Winfried
1978 "Das Schulbuch Kemit." *ZÄS* 105: 6–14.
Barucq, André
*1964 *Le Livre des Proverbes*. Paris: Gabalda.
1976 "Dieu chez les sages d'Israël." BETL 41: 169–89.
Bauckmann, E. G.
1960 "Die Proverbien und die Sprüche des Jesus Sirach." ZAW 72: 33–63.
Bauer, Hans, and Pontus Leander
1922 *Historische Grammatik der Hebräischen Sprache des ATs*. Bd. I (repr. 1962. Hildesheim: Georg Olms). [= B-L]
Bauer, Jean Baptiste
1958 "Encore une fois Proverbes VIII 22." *VT* 8: 91–92.
Baumann, Gerlinde
1996 *Die Weisheitsgestalt in Proverbien 1–9*. FAT 16. Tübingen: Mohr-Siebeck.
Baumgartner, Antoine J.
*1890 *Etude critique sur l'état du texte du Livre des Proverbes d'après les principales traductions anciennes*. Leipzig: Drugulin.
Baumgartner, Walter
1933 *Israelitische und altorientalische Weisheit*. Tübingen: Mohr.
Baumgartner, Walter, and Johann Jakob Stamm
1967–90 *Hebräisches und Aramäisches Lexikon*. 4 vols. Leiden: Brill. [HALAT]
Beardslee, William A.
1980 "Plutarch's Use of Proverbial Forms of Speech." *Semeia* 17: 101–11.
Beaucamp, Evode
1982 "Sagesse et salut dans l'Ancien Testament." *LTP* 18: 239–44.

Bechtel, Lyn M.
1991 "Shame as a Sanction of Social Control in Biblical Israel." *JSOT* 49: 47–76.

Beckenrath, Jürgen von
1983 "Ostrakon München ÄS 396." *Studien zur altägyptischen Kultur* 10: 63–69.

Becker, Joachim
1965 *Gottesfurcht im Alten Testament*. Rome: Pontifical Biblical Institute.

Beckman, Gary
1986 "Proverbs and Proverbial Allusions in Hittite." *JNES* 45: 19–30.

Beentjes, Pancratius C.
1997 *The Book of Ben Sira in Hebrew*. Leiden: Brill.

Ben Sira
1973 *Sefer Ben Sira* [Heb]: Text, Concordance, and an Analysis of Vocabulary. A publication of The Historical Dictionary of the Hebrew Language. Jerusalem: Academy of the Hebrew Language.

Bendavid, Abba
1967 *Lešon Miqra' Ulešhon Hakhamim* [*The Language of the Bible and the Language of the Rabbis*]. Tel Aviv: Devir.

Benson, Hugh H.
2000 *Socratic Wisdom: The Model of Knowledge in Plato's Early Dialogues*. New York: Oxford University Press.

Bentzen, Aage
1957 *Introduction to the Old Testament*. Copenhagen: Gad.

Berger, Klaus
1989 *Die Weisheitsschrift aus der Kairoer Geniza*. TANZ 1. Tübingen: Francke.
1991 "Die Bedeutung der wiederentdeckten Weisheitsschrift aus der Kairoer Geniza für das Alte Testament." ZAW 103: 113–21.

Berger, P. R.
1987 "Zum Huren bereit bis hin zu einem Rundlaib Brot: Prov 6,26." ZAW 99: 98–106.

Bergey, Ronald
1983 "The Book of Esther—Its Place in the Linguistic Milieu of Post-Exilic Biblical Hebrew Prose." Ph.D. Diss., Dropsie College, Philadelphia.

Bergman, Jan
1968 *Ich bin Isis*. Uppsala: Universitet.
1979 "Gedanken zum Thema 'Lehre—Testament—Grab—Name." SAL 74–103.

Bergmeier, Roland
1981 "Weisheit-Dike-Lichtjungfrau." *JSJ* 12: 75–86.

Berlin, Adele
1985 *The Dynamics of Biblical Parallelism*. Bloomington: Indiana University Press.
1989 "Lexical Cohesion and Biblical Interpretation." *HS* 30: 29–40.
2005 "The Wisdom of Creation in Psalm 104." SWA 71–83.

Berndt, Rainer
1994 "Skizze zur Auslegungsgeschichte der Bücher *Prouerbia und Ecclesiastes* in der abendländlischen Kirche." *Sacris Erudiri* 34: 5–32.

Bertram, Georg
1936 "Die religiöse Umdeutung altorientalischer Lebensweisheit in der griechischen Übersetzung des ATs." ZAW 54: 153–67.

1953 "Die religiöse Umdeutung altorientalischer Lebensweisheit in der griechischen Übersetzung des ATs." ZAW 12: 153–67.
1969 "Weisheit und Lehre in der Septuaginta." ZDMG Sup. I: 302–19.

Bible d'Alexandrie (BA). See Hamonville.

Bickel, Susanne, and Bernard Mathieu
1993 "L'écrivain Amennakht et son enseignement." *BIFAO* 93: 31–51.

Bickell, Georg
1891 "Kritische Bearbeitung der Proverbien." *Wiener Zeitschrift für die Kunde des Morgenlandes* 5: 79–102.

Bien, Günther
1988 "Ueber den Begriff der Weisheit in der antiken Philosophie." *Studia Philosophica* 47: 33–51.

Bitzer, Lloyd
1959 "Aristotle's Enthymeme Revisited." *Quarterly Journal of Speech* 45: 399–409.

Bjørndalen, Anders Jørgen
1970 " 'Form' und 'Inhalt' des Motivierenden Mahnspruches." ZAW 82: 347–61.

Blanshard, Brand
1967 "Wisdom." *Encyclopedia of Philosophy* 8.322–24. New York: Macmillan.

Blenkinsopp, Joseph
1983 *Wisdom and Law in the Old Testament*. Oxford: Oxford University Press.
1991 "The Social Context of the Outsider Woman." *Bib* 72: 457–72.

Blocher, Henri
1977 "The Fear of the Lord as the 'Principle' of Wisdom." *TynBul* 28: 3–28.

Bloomfield, Morton
1984 "The Tradition and Style of Wisdom Literature." Pp. 19–30 in *Biblical Patterns in Modern Literature*. Ed. D. H. Hirsch and N. Aschkenasy. Chico, Calif.: Scholars Press.

Blumenthal, Elke
1980 "Die Lehre für König Merikare." ZÄS 107: 5–41.
2003 "Die Rolle des Königs in der ägyptischen und biblischen Weisheit." Pp. 1–36 in in *Weisheit in Israel*. Altes Testament und Moderne 12. Ed. David J. A. Clines et al. Münster: Lit.

Bonnard, P. E.
1979 "De la Sagesse personnifiée dans l'Ancien Testament à la Sagesse en personne dans le Nouveau." Pp. 117–49 in *La Sagesse de l'Ancien Testament*. Ed. M. Gilbert. Leuven: Leuven University.

Bonora, Antonio
1987 "La via dell'amore in Pr 30,18–20." *RivB* 35: 51–55.

Borowski, Oded
1987 *Agriculture in Iron Age Israel*. Winona Lake, Ind.: Eisenbrauns.

Boström, Gustav
1928 *Paronomasi i den äldre hebreiska maschallitteraturen*. Lund: Ohlssons boktryckeri.
*1935 *Proverbiastudien: Die Weisheit und das fremde Weib in Sprüche 1–9*. Lund: Gleerup.

Boström, Lennart
1990 *The God of the Sages*. Stockholm: Almqvist & Wiksell.

Botterweck, G. Johannes, and Helmer Ringgren, eds.

1970ff. *Theologisches Wörterbuch zum Alten Testament*. Stuttgart: W. Kohlhammer. [= TWAT]
1974ff. *Theological Dictionary of the Old Testament*. Grand Rapids, Mich.: Eerdmans. [= TDOT]

Bratcher, Robert G.
1983 "A Translator's Note on Proverbs 11,30." *BT* 34: 337–38.

Brekelmans, C.
1979 "Wisdom Influence in Deuteronomy." Pp. 28–38 in *Sagesse de l'Ancien Testament*. Ed. M. Gilbert. Leuven: Leuven University.

Bremen, Riet van
1993 "Women and Wealth." Pp. 223–42 in *Images of Women in Antiquity*. Ed. A. Cameron and A. Kuhrt. Detroit: Wayne State University.

Brenner, Athalya
1993 "Proverbs 1–9: An F Voice?" Pp. 113–30 in *On Gendering Texts*. Ed. A. Brenner and F. van Dijk-Hemmes. Leiden: Brill.

Brenner, Athalya, and F. van Dijk-Hemmes
1993 *On Gendering Texts*. Leiden: Brill.

Brichto, Herbert C.
1963 *The Problem of "Curse" in the Hebrew Bible*. SBLMS 13. Philadelphia: Scholars Press.

Brockelmann, Karl
**1928* *Lexicon Syriacum*. Halle an der Saale: Max Niemeyer (repr. 1995, Georg Olms).

Brongers, H. A.
1965 "Bemerkungen zum Gebrauch des adverbielen *Wᵉʿattāh* im Alten Testament." *VT* 15: 289–99.
1977 "Miscellanea Exegetica" [part III: *tušiyya*]. Pp. 30–49 in *Übersetzung und Deutung* (FS Alexander R. Hulst). Ed. A. R. Hulst. Nijkerk: Callenbach.

Bronzick, Nahum
2001 *LeNigud beyn Haʿeṣel ubeyn Yešarim bᵉMišley 15, 19*" ("The Antithesis between *ʿṣl* and *yšrym* in Prov 15:19" [Hebrew]). *Beit Mikra* 46: 171–76.

Brown, John P.
1981 "Proverbs-Book, Gold-Economy, Alphabet." *JBL* 100: 169–91.

Brown, William P.
1996 *Character in Crisis*. Grand Rapids, Mich: Eerdmans.
2002 "The Pedagogy of Proverbs 10:1–31:9." Pp. 150–82 in *Character and Scripture*. Ed. W. P. Brown. Grand Rapids, Mich.: Eerdmans.
2004 "The Didactic Power of Metaphor in the Aphoristic Sayings of Proverbs." *JSOT* 29: 133–54.
2005 " 'Come O Children . . . I will Teach You the Fear of the Lord' (Psalm 34:12): Comparing Psalms and Proverbs." SWA 85–102.
2005a "The Law and the Sages: A Reexamination of *tôrâ* in the Book of Proverbs." Pp. 251–90 in *Constituting the Community: The Polities of Ancient Israel in Honor of S. Dean McBride, Jr.* Ed. John T. Strong and Steven S. Tuell. Winona Lake, Ind.: Eisenbrauns.

Brueggemann, Walter
1972 *In Man We Trust*. Richmond: John Knox Press.
1977 "A Neglected Sapiential Word Pair." ZAW 89: 234–58.

1990 "The Social Significance of Solomon as a Patron of Wisdom." SIANE 117–32.

Brunner, Hellmut

1944 *Die Lehre des Cheti, Sohnes des Duauf.* Ägyptologische Forschungen, XIII. Glückstadt: J. J. Augustin.

1954 "Das hörende Herz." *TLZ* 79: 697–700. [= 1988b: 3–5]

1955 "Die Lehre vom Königserbe im frühen Mittleren Reich." AS 4–11.

1956 "Das Herz als Sitz des Lebensgeheimnisses." *AfO* 17: 140–41. [= 1988b: 6–7]

1957 *Altägyptische Erziehung.* Wiesbaden: Harrassowitz.

1958 "Gerechtigkeit als Fundament des Thrones." *VT* 8: 426–28.

1961 "Ptahhotep bei den koptischen Mönchen." *ZÄS* 86: 145–47.

1963 "Der freie Wille Gottes in der ägyptischen Weisheit." SPOA. Pp. 103–20. [= 1988b: 85–102]

1966 "Die 'Weisen', ihre 'Lehren' und 'Prophezeiungen' in altägyptischer Sicht." *ZÄS* 93: 29–35. [= 1988b: 59–65]

1978 "Zur Datierung der 'Lehre eines Mannes an seinen Sohn." *JEA* 64: 142–43.

1979 "Zitate aus Lebenslehren." SAL 105–71.

1981 "L'éducation en ancienne Egypte." Pp. 65–86 in *Histoire Mondiale de l'éducation.* Ed. G. Mialaret and J. Vial. Paris: Presses Universitaires.

1984 "Zentralbegriffe ägyptischer und israelitischer Weisheitslehren." *Saeculum* 35: 185–99.

1988a *Altägyptische Weisheit.* Zurich: Artemis. [= AW]

1988b *Das hörende Herz.* (Kleine Schriften zur Religions- und Geistesgeschichte Ägyptens). Ed. W. Röllig. OBO 80. Göttingen: Vandenhoeck & Ruprecht.

1991 "Die menschliche Willensfreiheit und ihre Grenzen in ägyptischen Lebenslehren." Pp. 32–46 in *Biblische und ausserbiblische Spruchweisheit.* Ed. H.-J. Klimkeit. Wiesbaden: Harrassowitz.

Brunner-Traut, Emma

1940 "Die Weisheitslehre des Djedef-Hor." *ZÄS* 76: 3–9.

1979 "Weiterleben der ägyptischen Lebenslehren in den koptischen Apophthegmata am Beispiel des Schweigens." SAL 173–216.

Bryce, Glendon E.

1972 "Another Wisdom-'Book' in Proverbs." *JBL* 91: 145–57.

1975 "Omen-Wisdom in Ancient Israel." *JBL* 94: 19–37.

1978 "The Structural Analysis of Didactic Texts." Pp. 107–21 in *Biblical and Near Eastern Studies.* Ed. Gary A. Tuttle. Grand Rapids, Mich.: Eerdmans.

1979 *A Legacy of Wisdom.* Lewisburg, Penn.: Bucknell University Press.

Buccellati, Giorgio

1981 "Wisdom and Not: The Case of Mesopotamia." *JAOS* 101: 35–47.

Buchanan, George Wesley

1965 "Midrashim pré-Tannaites." *RB* 72: 227–39.

Buchberger, Hannes

1989–90 "Zum Ausländer in der altägyptischen Literature—eine Kritik."WO 20–21: 5–34.

Budge, E. A. Wallace

1923 *Facsimiles of Egyptian Hieratic Papyri in the British Museum, Second Series.* London: British Museum.

Buhl, Frants

1914 "Die Bedeutung des Stammes *lûṣ* oder *lîṣ*." Pp. 81–86 in *Studien zur semi-*

tischen Philologie und Religionsgeschichte (FS Julius Wellhausen). BZAW 29. Giessen: Töpelmann.

Bühlmann, Walter
1976 *Vom rechten Reden und Schweigen: Studien zu Proverbien 10–31*. OBO 12. Freiburg: Universitätsverlag.

Burden, J. J.
1990 "The Wisdom of Many." *OT Essays* 3: 341–59.

Burkard, Günter
1977 *Textkritische Untersuchungen zu ägyptischen Weisheitslehren des alten und mittleren Reiches*. ÄA 34. Wiesbaden: Harrassowitz.

Burnett, Joel S.
2001 *A Reassessment of Biblical Elohim*. SBLDS 183. Atlanta: Scholars Press.

Caminos, Ricardo
1954 *Late-Egyptian Miscellanies*. London: Oxford University Press. [= CLEM]

Camp, Claudia
1985 *Wisdom and the Feminine in the Book of Proverbs*. Sheffield: Almond.
1987 "Woman Wisdom as Root Metaphor: A Theological Consideration." Pp. 45–76 in *The Listening Heart*. Ed. K. Hoglund et al. Sheffield: Sheffield Academic Press.
1988 "Wise and Strange: An Interpretation of the Female Imagery in Proverbs in Light of the Trickster Mythology." *Sem* 42: 14–36.
1991 "What's So Strange about the Strange Woman." Pp. 17–31 in *The Bible and the Politics of Exegesis* (FS N. Gottwald). Ed. D. Jobling et al. Cleveland: Pilgrim.
2005 "Becoming Canon: Women, Texts, and Scribes in Proverbs and Sirach." SWA 371–407.

Camp, Claudia, and Carole Fontaine
1990 "The Words of the Wise and Their Riddles." Pp. 127–59 in *Text and Tradition*. Ed. Susan Niditch. Atlanta: Scholars Press.

Canney, Maurice A.
1923–24 "The Hebrew *Meliṣ*." *AJSL* 40: 135–37.

Caquot, André
1978 "Israelite Perceptions of Wisdom and Strength in the Light of the Ras Shamra Texts." IW 25–33.
1979 "Deux proverbes Salomoniens." *Revue d'Histoire et de Philosophie Religieuses* 59: 577–81.

Carasik, Michael
1994 "Who Were the 'Men of Hezekiah' (Proverbs XXV 1)?" *VT* 44: 289–300.
2000 "The Limits of Omniscience." *JBL* 119: 221–32.

Carmignac, Jean
1980 "Critique textuelle de Proverbes 22,8–9." *Folia Orientalia* 21: 33–41.

Carmody, Denise. L.
1988 *Biblical Women: Contemporary Reflections on Scriptural Texts*. New York: Crossroads.

Carr, David M.
2005 *Writing on the Tablet of the Heart*. Oxford: Oxford University Press.

Caspari, W.
1928 "Über den biblischen Begriff der Torheit." *Neue Kirchliche Zeitschrift* 39: 668–95.

Cassuto, M. D. (Umberto)
1974 *The Book of Exodus* [Hebrew]. Jerusalem: Magnes.
Cathcart, Kevin J.
1970 "Proverbs 30,4 and Ugaritic *ḤPN*, 'Garment.' " *CBQ* 32: 418–20.
Causse, A.
1938 "La Sagesse et la propaganda juive à l'époque perse et hellénistique." Pp. 148–54 in *Werden und Wesen des Alten Testament*. BZAW 60. Berlin: Töpelmann.
Cazelles, Henri
1959 "L'Enfantement de la Sagesse en Prov., VIII." BETL 12: 511–15.
1963 "Les débuts de la sagesse en Israel." *SPOA* Pp. 27–40.
1979 "Les nouvelles études sur Sumer (Alster) et Mari (Marzal) nous aident-elles à situer les origines de la sagesse israélite?" BETL 51: 17–27.
1995 "Aḥiqar, *Ummân* and *Amun*, and Biblical Wisdom Texts." Pp. 45–55 in *Solving Riddles and Untying Knots, Essays in Honor of Jonas Greenfield*. Ed. Z. Zevit, S. Gitin, and M. Sokoloff. Winona Lake, Ind.: Eisenbrauns.
Černý, Jaroslav
1939 *Late Ramesside Letters*. Bibliotheca Aegyptiaca IX. Brussels: Fondation égyptologique Reine Elisabeth.
1978 *Papyrus hiératiques de Deir el-Médineh*. FIFAO 8,22.
Černý, Jaroslav, and Alan H. Gardiner
1957 *Hieratic Ostraca*. Oxford: Griffith Inst., Oxford University Press. [= HO]
Chabas, F.
1872 "*Hébraeo-Aegyptiaca*." Trans. Soc. Biblical Archaeology *1: 173–82*.
Chajes, Hirsch Perez
1899 *Proverbia-Studien zu der sog. Salomonischen Sammlung, C. X–XXII, 16*. Berlin: Schwetschke.
Cholin, Marc
2001 "*Structure de Proverbes 31,10–31*." RB *108: 331–48*.
Christianson, Otto H.
1951 "The Scholia of Bar Hebraeus to Proverbs and Job." PhD Diss., University of Chicago.
Claasen, W. T.
1983 "Speaker-oriented Functions of *kî* in Biblical Hebrew." *JNSL* 11: 29–46.
Clements, Ronald E.
1988 "Solomon and the Origins of Wisdom in Israel." Pp. 32–35 in *Perspectives on the Hebrew Bible* (FS W. J. Harrelson). Ed. J. L. Crenshaw. Macon, Ga.: Mercer University Press.
1993 "The Good Neighbor in the Book of Proverbs." Pp. 209–28 in *Of Prophets' Visions and the Wisdom of Sages*. (FS R. N. Whybray). Ed. Heather A. McKay and David J. A. Clines. JSOTSup 162. Sheffield: JSOT Press.
1996 "The Concept of Abomination in the Book of Proverbs." Pp. 211–25 in *Texts, Temples, and Traditions: A Tribute to Menahem Haran*. Ed. M. V. Fox et al. Winona Lake, Ind.: Eisenbrauns.
Clifford, Richard J.
1975 "Proverbs IX: A Suggested Ugaritic Parallel." *VT* 25: 298–306.
1993 "Woman Wisdom in the Book of Proverbs." Pp. 61–72 in *Biblische Theologie und gesellschaftlicher Wandel* (FS N. Lohfink). Ed. G. Baraulik, W. Gross, and S. McEvenue. Freiburg: Herder.

1997 "Observations on the Text and Versions of Proverbs." Pp. 62–77 in *Wisdom, You Are My Sister* (FS R. E. Murphy). Ed. M. L. Barré (CBQMS 29). Washington, D.C.: Catholic Biblical Association.
*1999 *Proverbs* (OTL). Louisville, Ky.: Westminster/John Knox.
2002 "The God Who Makes People Wise." Pp. 57–74 in *The Forgotten God: Perspectives in Biblical Theology* (FS Paul J. Achtemeier). Ed. A. Andrew Das, Frank J. Matera, and Leander E. Keck; Louisville, Ky.: Westminster/John Knox.
2004 "Your Attention Please! Heeding the Proverbs." JSOT *29: 155–63.*
2007 *Wisdom Literature in Mesopotamia and Israel.* Ed. R. J. Clifford, Atlanta: Society of Biblical Literature.

Clines, David J. A
1993ff. *The Dictionary of Classical Hebrew.* Sheffield: Sheffield Academic Press. [= DCH]

Clines, David J. A., Hermann Lichtenberger, and Hans-Peter Müller, eds.
2003 *Weisheit in Israel.* Altes Testament und Moderne 12. Münster: Lit.

Coby, Patrick
1987 *Socrates and the Sophistic Enlightenment.* Lewisburg, Penn.: Bucknell University Press.

Cody, Aelred
1980 "Notes on Proverbs 22,21 and 22,23b." *Bib* 61: 418–26.

Cohen, Amoz
1979 "Wer einen Feigenbaum pflegt, wird seine Frucht essen (Spr 27,18)." *Beth Mikra* 80: 81–82.

Cohen, Chaim
1996 "The Meaning of *ṣalmawet* ["darkness]" Pp. 287–309 in *Texts, Temples, and Traditions: A Tribute to Menahem Haran.* Ed. M. V. Fox et al. Winona Lake, Ind.: Eisenbrauns.
1997 "Two Misunderstood Verses in the Book of Proverbs." *Shnaton* 11: 139–52.

Cohen, Jeffrey M.
1982 "An Unrecognized Connotation of *nšq peh.*" *Bib* 32: 416–24.

Collins, John J.
1977 "Cosmos and Salvation: Jewish Wisdom and Apocalyptic in the Hellenistic Age." *HR* 17: 121–42.
1980 "Proverbial Wisdom and the Yahwist Vision." *Semeia* 17: 1–17.
1997 *Jewish Wisdom in the Hellenistic Age.* Louisville, Ky.: Westminster/John Knox.
1997a "Wisdom Reconsidered, in Light of the Scrolls." *DSD* 4: 265–81.

Coneybeare, Frederick C., J. R. Harris, and A. S. Lewis
1913 *The Story of Aḥikar.* Cambridge: Cambridge University Press.

Conrad, Joachim
1967 "Die Innere Gliederung der Proverbien: zur Frage nach der Systematisierung des Spruchgutes in den älteren Teilsammlungen." ZAW 79: 67–76.

Conzelmann, Hans
1964 "Die Mutter der Weisheit." Pp. 225–34 in *Zeit und Geschichte* (FS Rudolph Bultmann). Ed. Erich Dinkler. Tübingen: Mohr.

Cook, Johann
1987 "Hellenistic Influence on the Book of Proverbs (Septuagint)?" *BIOSCS* 20: 30–42.

1991a "Hellenistic Influence in the Septuagint Book of Proverbs." VII Cong. of the IOSCS (1989). SCS 31. 341–53.

1991b "Reflections on the Role of Wisdom in Creation with Special Reference to the Intertestamental Period." *Acta Academica* 23: 47–66.

1993 "The Dating of Septuagint Proverbs." *ETL* 69: 383–99.

1994a "Are the Syriac and Greek Versions of the *ʾiššah zarah* (Prov 1 to 9) Identical?" *Textus* 14: 117–32.

1994b "A Comparison of Proverbs and Jeremiah in the Septuagint." *JNSL* 20: 49–58.

1994c "*ʾIššah Zara* (Proverbs 1–9 Septuagint): A Metaphor for Foreign Wisdom?" ZAW 106: 458–75.

1996 "Exodus 38 and Proverbs 31." BETL 126: 537–49.

1997 *The Septuagint of Proverbs: Jewish or Hellenistic Proverbs?* VTSup 69. Leiden: Brill. [= CSP]

1998a "The Ideological Stance of the Greek Translator of Proverbs." Pp. 479–91 in *IX Congress of the International Organization for Septuagint and Cognate Studies*. Ed. B. A. Taylor. Atlanta: Scholars Press.

1998b "Septuagint Proverbs and Canonization." Pp. 79–91 in *Canonization and Decanonization*. Ed. A. van der Kooij and K. van der Toorn. Leiden: Brill.

1999a "Apocalyptic Terminology in the Septuagint of Proverbs." *JNSL* 25: 251–61.

1999b "Contextual Exegetical Interpretations in the Septuagint of Proverbs." *JNSL* 25: 119–52.

1999c "The Law of Moses in Septuagint Proverbs." *VT* 49: 448–61.

2000 "Textual Problems in the Septuagint Version of Proverbs." *JNSL* 26: 171–76.

2001 "Ideology and Translation Technique: Two Sides of the Same Coin?" Pp. 195–216 in *Helsinki Perspectives on the Translation Technique of the Septuagint*. Ed. R. Sollamo and S. Sipilä. Göttingen: Vandenhoeck & Ruprecht.

2002a "The Law of Moses as a Fence and a Fountain." Pp. 280–88 in *Sense and Sensitivity . . . in Memory of Robert Carroll*. Ed. A. G. Hunter and P. R. Davies. JSOTSup 348. London/New York: Sheffield Academic Press.

2002b "The Translator(s) of the Septuagint of Proverbs." *TC* 7 (http://rosetta.reltech.org/TC/vol07/Cook2002.html).

2003 "The Greek of Proverbs—Evidence of a Recensionally Deviating Hebrew Text?" Pp. 605–18 in *Emanuel: Studies in Hebrew Bible, Septuagint and Dead Sea Scrolls in Honor of Emanuel Tov*. Ed. S. M. Paul et al. Leiden: Brill.

2004 "The Theory and Practice of Textual Criticism." *OTE* 17: 531–43.

2005 "The Text-Critical Value of the Septuagint of Proverbs." SWA 407–20.

Cook, John A.

2005 "Genericity, Tense, and Verbal Patterns in the Sentence Literature of Proverbs." SWA 117–34.

Cooper, Alan

1987 "On Reading the Bible Critically or Otherwise." Pp. 61–79 in *The Future of Biblical Studies: The Hebrew Scriptures*. Ed. R. E. Friedman and H. G. M. Williamson. Atlanta: Scholars Press.

Cooper, John M.

1997 *Plato: Compete Works*. Ed. J. M. Cooper, with various translators. Indianapolis/Cambridge: Hackett.

Corley, Jeremy

2005 "An Intertextual Study of Proverbs and Ben Sira." Pp. 155–182 in *Intertextual Studies in Ben Sira and Tobit* (FS Alexander Di Lella). Ed. Jeremy Corley and Vincent Skemp. CBQMS 38. Washington, D.C.: Catholic Biblical Association.

Cornelius, Izak

1994 "The Visual Representation of the World in the Ancient Near East and the Hebrew Bible." *JNSL* 20: 193–218.

Cosser, William

1953–54 "The Meaning of 'Life' (*Hayyim*) in Proverbs, Job, and Ecclesiastes." *Glasgow University Oriental Society Transactions* 15: 48–53.

Couroyer, Bernard

1949 "Le Chemin de vie en Egypte et en Israël." *RB* 56: 412–32.

1961 "Amenemopé, I, 9; III, 13: Egypte ou Israël." *RB* 68: 394–400.

1963 "L'origine égyptienne de la sagesse d'Amenemopé." *RB* 70: 214–21.

1983 "La Tablette du coeur." *RB* 90: 416–34.

1987 "Le 'Dieu des Sages' en Egypte, I." *RB* 94: 574–603.

Couturier, Guy

1962 "Sagesse Babylonienne et sagesse Israélite." *Sciences ecclésiastiques* 14: 293–309.

1980 "La Vie familiale comme source de la sagesse et de la loi." *Science et Esprit* 32: 177–92.

Cowley, A. E.

1923 *Aramaic Papyri of the Fifth Century B.C.* (repr. 1923). Osnabrück: O. Zeller.

1929 "Two Aramaic Ostraca." *JRAS* 61: 107–11.

Cox, Dermot

1977 "Ṣedaqa and Mišpaṭ." *Studium Biblicum* 27: 33–50.

1982a "Fear or Conscience?: *Yir'at YHWH* in Proverbs 1–9." *Studia Hierosolymitana* 3: 83–90.

1982b *Proverbs*. Wilmington: Michael Glazier.

Crenshaw, James L.

1969 "Method in Determining Wisdom Influence upon 'Historical' Literature." *JBL* 88: 129–42 (repr. SAIW 481–94).

1970 "Popular Questioning of the Justice of God in Ancient Israel." ZAW 82: 380–95 (repr. SAIW 289–304).

1974 "Wisdom." Pp. 225–64 in *Old Testament Form Criticism*. Ed. John H. Hayes. San Antonio, Tex.: Trinity University Press.

1976 *Studies in Ancient Israelite Wisdom* (selected, with a prolegomenon by James L. Crenshaw). New York: KTAV. [= SAIW]

1977 "In Search of Divine Presence." *Review and Expositor* 74: 353–369.

1980 "Impossible Questions, Sayings, and Tasks." *Semeia* 17: 19–34.

1981a "Wisdom and Authority: Sapiential Rhetoric and Its Warrants." Pp. 10–29 in *Congress Volume: Vienna, 1980*. VTSup 32. Ed. J. A. Emerton. Leiden: Brill.

1981b *Old Testament Wisdom*. Atlanta: John Knox.

1983 *Theodicy in the Old Testament*. Philadelphia: Fortress.

1984 "A Mother's Instruction to her Son (Proverbs 31: 1–9)." Pp. 9–22 in *Perspectives on the Hebrew Bible* (FS Walter J. Harrelson). Ed. J. L. Crenshaw. Macon, Ga.: Mercer University Press.

1985 "Education in Ancient Israel." *JBL* 104: 601–15.
1987 "The Acquisition of Knowledge in Israelite Wisdom Literature." *Word and World* 7: 245–52.
1988 "A Mother's Instruction to her Son (Proverbs 31:1–9)." Pp. 9–22 in *Perspectives in the Hebrew Bible.* (FS W. J. Harrelson). Ed. J. L. Crenshaw. Macon, Ga.: Mercer University Press.
1989a "Clanging Symbols." Pp. 51–64 in *Justice and the Holy* (FS Walter Harrelson). Ed. D. A. Knight and P. J. Paris. Atlanta: Scholars Press.
1989b "Poverty and Punishment in the Book of Proverbs." *Quarterly Review* 9: 30–43.
1992 "Prohibitions in Proverbs and Qoheleth." Pp. 115–24 in *Priests, Proverbs and Scribes.* Ed. E. Ulrich et al. (FS J. Blenkinsopp). JSOTSup 149. Sheffield: Sheffield Press.
1993 "The Concept of God in Old Testament Wisdom." Pp. 1–18 in *In Search of Wisdom.* Ed. L. Perdue et al. (Essays in Memory of John G. Gammie). Louisville, Ky.: Westminster/John Knox.
1995 *Urgent Advice and Probing Questions.* Macon, Ga.: Mercer University Press.
1998 *Education in Ancient Israel.* New York: Doubleday.
1998a "Qoheleth's Understanding of Intellectual Inquiry." BETL 136: 206–24.
2000 "Wisdom Psalms?" *CRBS* 8: 9–17.
2005 "A Proverb in the Mouth of a Fool." SWA 103–16.

Crepaldi, Maria Grazia
1982 "Il tempo nei libri sapienziali." *Studia Patavina* 29: 25–47.

Crook, M. B.
1954 "The Marriageable Maiden of Prov 31,10–31." *JNES* 13: 137–40.

Cross, Frank M., and David Noel Freedman
1953 "A Royal Psalm of Thanksgiving." *JBL* 72: 15–34.

Crossan, J. D., ed.
1980 "Gnomic Wisdom." *Semeia* 17. Chico, Calif.: Scholars Press.

Dahood, Mitchell
1960 "Immortality in Proverbs 12,28." *Biblica* 41: 176–81.
1963 *Proverbs and Northwest Semitic Philology.* Rome: Pontifical Biblical Institute.
1965 "Hebrew-Ugaritic Lexicography III." *Bib* 46: 311–32.
1968 "The Phoenician Contribution to Biblical Wisdom Literature." Pp. 123–48 in *The Role of the Phoenicians in the Interaction of Mediterranean Civilizations.* Ed. W. A. Ward. Beirut: American University.
1973 "Honey that Drips: Notes on Proverbs 5,2–3." *Bib* 54: 65–66.
1982a "The Hapax *ḥarak* in Proverbs 12,27." *Bib* 63: 60–62.
1982b "Philological Observations on Five Biblical Texts." *Biblica* 63: 370–89.

Dalley, Stephanie
1989 *Myths from Mesopotamia.* Oxford: Oxford University Press.

Dathe, J. A.
1764 *De ratione consensus versionis Chaldaicae et Syriacae Proverbiorum Salomonis.* Leipzig.

Daube, David
1964 *The Sudden in Scripture.* Leiden: Brill.
1985 "A Quartet of Beasties in the Book of Proverbs [30,24]." *JTS* 36: 380–86.

Davies, E. W.
1980 "The Meaning of *Qesem* in Prv 16,10." *Bib* 61: 555–56.
Davies, Graham
1995 "Were There Schools in Ancient Israel?" WAI 199–211.
Davies, Philip R.
2002 "The 'False Pen of the Scribes': Intellectuals Then and Now." Pp. 117–26 in *Sense and Sensitivity: Essays on Reading the Bible in Memory of Robert Carroll*. JSOTSup 348. London/New York: Sheffield Academic Press.
Day, John
1995a "Foreign Semitic Influence on the Wisdom of Israel and its Appropriation in the Book of Proverbs." WAI 55–70.
Day, John, Robert Gordon, and H. G. M. Williamson
1995 *Wisdom in Ancient Israel: Essays in Honour of J. A. Emerton*. Cambridge: Cambridge University Press. [= WAI]
De Rossi, G. B.
1784 *Variae lectiones Veteris Testamenti librorum*. Vols. I–IV (repr. 1969). Amsterdam: Philo.
De Vries, Simon J.
1978 "Observations on Quantitative and Qualitative Time in Wisdom and Apocalyptic." IW 263–76.
Deissler, Alfons
1955 *Psalm 119 (118) und seine Theologie*. Münchner Theologische Studien I,11. Munich: Zink.
Deist, Ferdinand
1978 "Prov 31: 1. A Case of Constant Mistranslation." *JNSL* 6: 1–3.
Delitzsch, Franz
*1873 *Biblical Commentary on the Proverbs of Solomon*. ET James Martin. Repr. 1983. Grand Rapids, Mich.: Eerdmans.
Delitzsch, Friedrich
1920 *Die Lese- und Schreibfehler im AT*. Berlin/Leipzig. [= LSF]
Dell, Katherine J.
2006 *The Book of Proverbs in Social and Theological Context*. Cambridge: Cambridge University Press.
Derousseaux, Louis
1970 *La Crainte de Dieu dans l'Ancien Testament*. Paris: Cerf.
Deutsch, Hermann
1885 *Die Sprüche Salomo's nach der Auffassung im Talmud und Midrasch*. Berlin: Mampe.
Devettere, Raymond J.
2002 *Introduction to Virtue Ethics: Insights of the Ancient Greeks*. Washington, D.C.: Georgetown University Press.
Dhorme, Edouard
[1967] *A Commentary on the Book of Job*. ET Harold Kznight. Nashville: Thomas Nelson.
Dick, Michael B.
1990 "The Ethics of the Old Greek Book of Proverbs." *Studia Philonica Annual* 2: 20–50.
Dietrich, M.
1991 "Der Dialog zwischen šupe'ameli und seinem 'Vater.' " *UF* 23: 33–74.

Dietrich, Manfried, and Oswald Loretz
1976 "Die angebliche Ug. He. Parallele SPSG // SPS(J)G(JM)." *UF* 8: 37–40.
1993 "Proverb Collection of Šupê-amēli from Ugarit, Emar and Bogazköy." Pp. 52–62 in *Verse in Ancient Near Eastern Prose.* Ed. J. C. de Moor and W. G. E. Watson. AOAT 42. Neukirchen-Vluyn: Butzon and Bercker.
1995 *The Cuneiform Alphabetic Texts from Ugarit, Ras Ibn Hani and Other Places.* (KTU, 2nd ed.). Münster: Ugarit-Verlag. [= KTU]

Dietrich, M., O. Loretz, and J. Sanmartín
1976 *Die keilalphabetischen Texte aus Ugarit.* Teil 1, Transkription. AOAT 24. Neukirchen-Vluyn: Neukirchener Verlag. [= KTU]

Díez Merino, Luis
1984 *Targum de Proverbios.* Madrid: Consejo Superior de Investigaciones Cientificas.

Di Lella, Alexander A.
1979 *Proverbs: The Old Testament in Syriac According to the Peshitta Version.* 2.5. Leiden: Brill.
1993 "The Meaning of Wisdom in Ben Sira." Pp. 133–48 in *In Search of Wisdom.* Ed. L. Perdue et al. (Essays in Memory of John G. Gammie). Louisville, Ky.: Westminster/John Knox.

Di Lella, Alexander A., and Patrick Skehan
*1987 *The Wisdom of Ben Sira.* AYB 39. New York: Doubleday (repr. New Haven: Yale University Press).

Doll, Peter
1985 *Menschenschöpfung und Weltschöpfung in der alttestamentlichen Weisheit.* Stuttgarter Bibel-Studien 117. Stuttgart: Katholisches Bibelwerk.

Domeris, W. R.
1996 "Shame and Honour in Proverbs: Wise Women and Foolish Men." *OTE* 8: 86–102.

Donald, Trevor
1963 "The Semantic Field of 'Folly' in Proverbs, Job, Psalms, and Ecclesiastes." *VT* 13: 285–92.
1964 "The Semantic Field of Rich and Poor in the Wisdom Literature of Hebrew and Accadian." *Oriens Antiquus* 3: 27–41.

Donner, H., and W. Röllig
1962 *Kanaanäische und Aramäische Inschriften.* Vols. I–III. Wiesbaden: Harrassowitz. [= KAI]

Dorsey, David A.
1991 *The Roads and Highways of Ancient Israel.* Baltimore: Johns Hopkins.

Drioton, Emil
1959 "Le Livre des Proverbes et la sagesse d'Aménémope." In *Sacra Pagina: Miscellenea Biblica Congressus internationalis Catholici de Re Biblica,* Vol. I. Ed. J. Coppens, A. Descamps, E. Massaux (Bibliotheca ephemeridum theologicum Lovaniensium 12 and 13). Gembloux: Duculot.

Driver, G. R.
1932a "Problems in 'Proverbs.' " ZAW 50: 141–48.
1932b "Studies in the Vocabulary of the Old Testament." *JTS* 33: 38–47; 34: 375–85.
1934 "Hebrew Notes." ZAW 52: 51–56.
1940 "Hebrew Notes on Prophets and Proverbs." *JTS* 41: 162–75.

1947 "Hebrew Roots and Words." *WO* 1: 406–15.
1947a "Misreadings in the Old Testament." *WO* 1 (1947–52): 234–38.
1950 "Hebrew Notes." *VT* 1: 241–50.
1951 "Problems in the Hebrew Text of Proverbs." *Bib* 32: 173–97.
1954 "Problems and Solutions." *VT* 4: 223–45.
1967 "Playing on Words." Pp. 1.121–29 in *Papers of the Fourth World Congress of Jewish Studies*. Jerusalem.

Driver, S. R.
1880 *A Commentary on the Book of Proverbs Attributed to Abraham Ibn Ezra*. Oxford: Clarendon. [= "Pseudo-Ibn Ezra"]

Drubbel, Adrien
1936a "Le Conflit entre la sagesse profane et la sagesse religieuse." *Bib* 17: 45–70.
1936b *Les livres sapientiaux d'Isräel dans leurs sources pré-exiliques*. Rome: Pie X.

Duesberg, Hilaire
1938 *Les Scribes inspirés*. Paris: de Brouwer.

Duhaime, Jean-L.
1980 "Perception de Dieu et comportement moral chez les sages d'Israël." *Science et Esprit* 32: 193–97.

Dunsmore, Marion Hiller
1925 "An Egyptian Contribution to the Book of Proverbs." *JR* 5: 300–308.

Dürr, Lorenz
1932 *Das Erziehungswesen im Alten Testament und im antiken Orient*. MVAG 36,2. Leipzig: Hinrichs.

Eaton, John
1989 *The Contemplative Face of Old Testament Wisdom*. Philadelphia: Trinity.

Ebeling, Erich, and Bruno Meissner, eds.
1932ff. *Reallexikon der Assyriologie*. Berlin: de Gruyter. [= RA]

Ehrlich, Arnold B.
*1908–14 *Randglossen zur hebräischen Bibel*. Hildesheim: Georg Olms (repr. 1968; unless otherwise specified, references are to the notes on Proverbs, vol. 6, 1913, ad loc.).

Eissfeldt, Otto
1913 *Der Maschal im Alten Testament*. BZAW 24. Giessen: Töpelmann.

Elioni, M.
1977 *Meḥqarim BeQohelet UveMishley*. Jerusalem: Society for Biblical Study.

Emerton, John A.
1964 "A Note on Proverbs xii.26." ZAW 76: 191–93.
1965 " 'Spring and Torrent' in Psalm LXXIV 15." Pp. 122–33 in *Congress Volume. Geneva, 1965*. VTSup 15. Ed. G. W. Anderson. Leiden: Brill.
1968 "A Note on the Hebrew Text of Proverbs i. 22–3." *JTS* 19: 609–14.
1969 "Notes on Some Passages in the Book of Proverbs" (Prv. 14,31; 19,16; 24,21; 26,9; 28,12). *JTS* 20: 202–20.
1979 "A Note on Proverbs 2,18." *JTS* 30: 153–58.
1984 "The Meaning of Proverbs 13,2." *JTS* 35: 91–95.
1988 "The Interpretation of Proverbs 21,28." ZAW 100: 161–70.
1991 "A Further Consideration of D. W. Thomas's Theories about *Yādaʿ*." *VT* 46: 144–63.
2001 "The Teaching of Amenemope and Proverbs XXII 17–XXIV 22: Reflections on a Long-Standing Problem." *VT* 51: 431–65.

Encyclopedia Miqra'it
1965–88 *Encyclopedia Miqra'it* [Hebrew]. Jerusalem: Bialik.
Encyclopedia of Philosophy
1967 *Encyclopedia of Philosophy*. Volumes 1–8. Ed. Paul Edwards. New York: Macmillan.
Englund, Gertie
1987 "The Treatment of Opposites in Temple Thinking and Wisdom Literature." Pp. 77–88 in *The Religion of the Ancient Egyptians. Cognitive Structures and Popular Expressions*. Ed. G. Englund. Uppsala: Acta Universitatis Upsaliensis.
Erman, Adolf
1924a "Eine ägyptische Quelle der 'Spruch Salomos.' " *SPAW* (phil-hist. Kl. 15): 86–93.
1924b "Das Weisheitsbuch des Amen-em-ope." *OLZ* 27: cols. 241–52.
Eshel, Hanan
2003 "6Q30, a Cursive *šin*, and Proverbs 11." *JBL* 122: 544–46.
Eshel, Hanan, and Esti Eshel
1987 *L^e^mishneh Hahora'ah šel Hamillah Delet BeMishley* ["The Ambiguity of the Word *delet* in Proverbs" (Hebrew)]. *Megadim* 3: 52–54.
Estelle, Bryan
2004 "Proverbs and Ahiqar Revisited." *The Biblical Historian* 1: 1–19.
Estes, Daniel J.
1997 *Hear, My Son: Teaching and Learning in Proverbs 1–9*. Grand Rapids, Mich.: Eerdmans.
Faulkner, Raymond O.
1955 "Ptaḥḥotpe and the Disputants." AS 81–84.
Fecht, Georg
1958 *Der Habgierge und die Maat in der Lehre des Ptahhotep (5.und 19. Maxime)*. ADAIK I. Glückstadt-Hamburg-N.V.: Augustin.
Fensham, F. C.
1971 "The Change of Situation of a Person in Ancient Near Eastern and Biblical Literature." *Annali dell'Instituto Orientale di Napoli* 21: 155–64.
Fichtner, Johannes
1933 *Die altorientalische Weisheit in ihrer israelitisch-jüdischen Ausprägung*. BZAW 62. Giessen: Töpelmann.
1949 "Jesaja unter den Weisen," *TLZ* 74: 75–80.
1955 "Der Begriff des 'Nächsten' im Alten Testament." *Wort und Dienst* 4: 23–52.
1965 *Gottes Weisheit*. Arbeiten zur Theologie 2. Reihe, 3. Stuttgart: Calwer.
Firchow, Otto
1955 *Ägyptologische Studien*. Ed. Otto Firchow. Deutsche Akad. d. Wiss. Institut für Orientforschung. Berlin. Akademie Verlag. [= AS]
Fischer, Irmtraud, Ursula Rapp, and Johannes Schiller, eds.
2003 *Auf den Spuren der schriftgelehrten Weisen* (FS Johannes Marböck). BZAW 331. Berlin: de Gruyter.
Fischer, Stefan
2001 "Egyptian Personal Piety and Israel's Wisdom Literature." *Acta Theologica* 21: 1–24.
Fischer-Elfert, Hans-Werner
1983 *Die satirische Streitschrift des Papyrus Anastasi I*. KÄT. Wiesbaden: Harrassowitz.

1984 " 'Ich bin das Schiff—du bist das Ruder.' " HO I.3, 3; COHL 1254–56.
1986 *Literarische Ostraka der Ramessidenzeit in Übersetzung*. KÄT. Wiesbaden: Harrassowitz.
1997 *Lesefunde im literarischen Steinbruch von Deir el-Medineh*. KÄT 12. Wiesbaden: Harrassowitz.

Fishbane, Michael
1974 "Accusations of Adultery." *HUCA* 45: 25–45.
1985 *Biblical Interpretation in Ancient Israel*. Oxford: Clarendon.
1992 "The Well of Living Water: a Biblical Motif and its Ancient Transformations." Pp. 3–16 in *Sha'arei Talmon* (FS S. Talmon). Ed. M. Fishbane and E. Tov. Winona Lake, Ind.: Eisenbrauns.

Fontaine, Carole
1982 *Traditional Sayings in the Old Testament*. Sheffield: Almond.
1985 "Proverb Performance in the Hebrew Bible." *JSOT* 32: 87–103.
1990 "The Sage in Family and Tribe." SIANE 155–64.
1992 "Proverbs" in *The Women's Bible Commentary*. Ed. C. A. Newsom and S. H. Ringe. Louisville, Ky.: Westminster/John Knox.
1993 "Wisdom in Proverbs." Pp. 99–114 in *In Search of Wisdom* (FS J. G. Gammie). Ed. L. Perdue et al. Louisville, Ky.: Westminster/John Knox.
2002 *Smooth Words: Women, Proverbs and Performance in Biblical Wisdom*. JSOTSup 356. Sheffield: Sheffield Academic Press.
2004 "The Proof of the Pudding: Proverbs and Gender in the Performance Arena." *JSOT* 29: 179–204.
2005 "Visual Metaphors and Proverbs 5:15–20: Some Archaeological Reflections on Gendered Iconography." SWA 185–202.

Forti, Tova
1996 "Animal Images in the Didactic Rhetoric of the Book of Proverbs." *Bib* 77: 48–63.
2006 "Bee's Honey—From Realia to Metaphor in Biblical Wisdom Literature." *VT* 56: 327–341.
2007 "Conceptual Stratification in LXX Prov 26,11: Toward Identifying the Tradents Behind the Aphorism." ZAW 119: 241–58.
2008 *Animal Imagery in the Book of Proverbs. VTSup* 118. Leiden: Brill.

Foster, Benjamin R.
1993 *Before the Muses*. Bethesda, Md.: CDL. [= BTM]
1994 "Wisdom and the Gods in Ancient Mesopotamia" (*Or* [ser. 2] 43: 344–65).

Foster, John L.
1977 *Thought Couplets and Clause Sequences in a Literary Text: The Maxims of Ptah-Hotep*. Toronto: The Society of the Study of Egyptian Antiquities.
1984 "Oriental Institute Ostracon 12074: 'Menna's Lament' or 'Letter to a Wayward Son.' " *Journal of the Society for the Study of Egyptian Antiquities* 14: 88–99.
1986 "Texts of the Egyptian Composition 'The Instruction of a Man for His Son' in the Oriental Institute Museum." *JNES* 45: 197–211.

Fox, Michael V.
1968 "Aspects of the Religion of the Book of Proverbs." *HUCA* 39: 55–69.
1973 "Jeremiah 2: 2 and the 'Desert Ideal.' " *CBQ* 35: 441–50.
1980 "Two Decades of Research in Egyptian Wisdom Literature." ZÄS 107: 120–35.

1981 "Job 38 and God's Rhetoric." *Semeia* 19:53–61.

1983 "Ancient Egyptian Rhetoric." *Rhetorica* 1: 9–22.

1985a "LXX Proverbs 3: 28 and Ancient Egyptian Wisdom." *HAR* 8: 63–69.

1985b *The Song of Songs and the Ancient Egyptian Love Songs*. Madison: University of Wisconsin Press.

1986 "Egyptian Onomastica and Biblical Wisdom." *VT* 36: 302–10.

1989 *Qohelet and his Contradictions*. JSOTSup 71. Sheffield: Almond.

1992 Review of *Die Weisheit Israels—ein Fremdkörper im Alten Testament?* by F.-J. Steiert. *JBL* 111: 134–37.

1993a Review of *Wurzeln der Weisheit* by C. Westermann. *JBL* 111: 529–32.

1993c "Wisdom in Qohelet." Pp. 115–32 in *In Search of Wisdom*. Ed. L. Perdue et al. (Essays in Memory of John G. Gammie). Louisville, Ky.: Westminster/John Knox.

1993d "Words for Wisdom." *ZAH* 6: 149–69.

1994 "The Pedagogy of Proverbs 2." *JBL* 113: 233–43.

1995 "World Order and Maʿat: A Crooked Parallel." *JANES* 23: 37–48.

1995a "Twice-Told Proverbs and the Composition of the Book of Proverbs." (Review of D. Snell, *Twice-Told Proverbs*, 1993). CRBR 8:147–54.

1996a "*ʾAmon* Again." *JBL* 115: 699–702.

1996b "The Social Location of the Book of Proverbs." Pp. 227–39 in *Texts, Temples, and Traditions: A Tribute to Menahem Haran*. Ed. M. V. Fox et al. Winona Lake, Ind.: Eisenbrauns.

1996c "The Strange Woman in Septuagint Proverbs." *JNSL* 22: 31–34.

1997a "Ideas of Wisdom in Proverbs 1–9." *JBL* 116: 613–33.

1997b "Who Can Learn? A Dispute in Ancient Pedagogy." Pp. 62–77 in *Wisdom, You Are My Sister* (FS R. E. Murphy). Ed. M. L. Barré. CBQMS 29. Washington. D.C.: Catholic Biblical Association.

1997c "What the Book of Proverbs Is About." *Congress Volume*, VTSup 66: 153–67.

1997d "Words for Folly." *ZAH* 10: 1–12.

1998 "The Inner Structure of Qohelet's Thought." BETL 136: 225–38.

1999 *A Time to Tear Down and A Time to Build Up: A Rereading of Ecclesiastes*. Grand Rapids, Mich.: Eerdmans.

2003a "Like Grapes of Gold Set in Silver: An Interpretation of Proverbial Clusters in Prov. 10:1–22:16" (Review of K. M. Heim, *Like Grapes of Gold Set in Silver*, 2001). *HS* 44: 267–72.

2003b "Wisdom and the Self-Presentation of Wisdom Literature." Pp. 153–72 in *Reading from Right to Left: Essays on the Hebrew Bible in honour of David J. A. Clines*. Ed. J. Cheryl Exum and H. G. M. Williamson. JSOTSup 480. Sheffield: Sheffield Academic Press.

2004a *Ecclesiastes*: A Commentary. Philadelphia: Jewish Publication Society.

2004b *Essays on the Art of the Aphorism*. Ed. M. V. Fox. *JSOT* 29.

2004c "The Rhetoric of Disjointed Proverbs." *JSOT* 29: 165–77

2005a "LXX-Proverbs as a Text-Critical Resource." *Textus* 22: 95–128.

2005b "Job the Pious." *ZAW* 117: 351–66.

2007a "The Epistemology of the Book of Proverbs." *JBL* 126: 669–84.

2007b "Ethics and Wisdom in the Book of Proverbs." *HS* 48: 75–88.

2007c Review of Dell, *The Book of Proverbs in Social and Theological Context* [= Dell *2006*]. *CBQ* 70: 109–10.

2008 "Concepts of Wisdom in the Book of Proverbs." Pp. 381–398 in *Birkat Shalom: Studies . . . Presented to Shalom M. Paul*. Ed. by C. Cohen et al. Winona Lake, Ind.: Eisenbrauns.

Fraine, J. de

1967 "*Margemah* (Prov 26, 8)." Pp. 1.131–35 in *Papers of the Fourth World Congress of Jewish Studies*. Jerusalem: World Union of Jewish Studies.

Frankenberg, W.

1892 *Proverbien*. HKAT. Göttingen: Vandenhoeck & Ruprecht.

1895 "Über Abfassungs-Ort und -Zeit, sowie Art und Inhalt von Prov. I–IX." ZAW 15: 104–32.

Franklyn, Paul

1983 "The Sayings of Agur in Proverbs 30: Piety or Scepticism?" ZAW 95: 238–51.

Franzmann, Majella

1991 "The Wheel in Proverbs XX 26 and the Ode of Solomon XXIII 11–16." *VT* 41: 121–22.

Freedman, David Noel

1972a "Acrostics and Metrics in Hebrew Poetry." *HTR* 65: 367–92.

1972b "The Broken Construct Chain." *Bib* 53: 534–36.

1992 *Anchor Yale Bible Dictionary*. 7 vols. New York: Doubleday, repr. New Haven: Yale University Press [= AYBD]

1997 "Proverbs 2 and 31: A Study in Structural Complementarity." Pp. 47–55 in *Tehilla le-Moshe* (FS Moshe Greenberg). Ed. M. Cogan et al. Winona Lake, Ind.: Eisenbrauns.

1999 *Psalm 119: The Exaltation of Torah*. Winona Lake, Ind.: Eisenbrauns.

Freuling, Georg

2004 *"Wer eine Grube gräbt—": der Tun-Ergehen-Zusammenhang und sein Wandel in der alttestamentlichen Weisheitsliteratur*. Neukirchen-Vluyn: Neukirchener Verlag.

Friedländer, Moriz

1904 *Griechische Philosophie im Alten Testament*. Berlin: Reimer.

Frisch, Amos

1999 *Yegiaʿ Keppeykha* [*The Bible's View of Labor* (Hebrew)]. Hakibbutz Hameʾuchad, Tel Aviv: Heilal Ben-Haim's Library—Basic Books in Jewish Studies.

Fritsch, Charles T.

1953 "The Treatment of the Hexaplaric Signs in the Syro-Hexaplar of Proverbs." *JBL* 72: 169–81.

Frydrych, Tomas

2002 *Living under the Sun: Examination of Proverbs and Qoheleth*. VTSup 90. Leiden: Brill.

Frymer-Kensky, Tikva

1992 *In the Wake of the Goddesses*. New York: Free Press.

Gaboriau, F.

1968 "Enquête sur la signification biblique de connaître." *Angelicum* 45: 3–43.

Gammie, John G.

1974 "Spatial and Ethical Dualism in Jewish Wisdom and Apocalytic Literature." *JBL* 93: 356–85.

1987 "The Septuagint of Job: Its Poetic Style and the Relationship to the Septuagint of Proverbs." *CBQ* 49: 14–31.

1990 "Paranetic Literature: Toward the Morphology of a Secondary Genre." *Semeia* 50: 41–75.

Gammie, John G., W. A. Brueggemann, W. L. Humphreys, and J. M. Ward, eds.

1978 *Israelite Wisdom: Theological and Literary Essays in Honor of Samuel Terrien*. New York: Union Theological Seminary. [= IW]

Gammie, John G., and Leo G. Perdue, eds.

1990 *The Sage in Israel and the Ancient Near East*. Winona Lake, Ind.: Eisenbrauns. [= SIANE]

Garbini, Giovanni

1984 "Proverbi per un anno. Il libro dei *Proverbi* e il calendario." *Henoch* 6: 139–46.

Garca Martnez, Florentino

1994 *The Dead Sea Scrolls Translated*. Leiden: Brill. [= DSST]

Gardiner, Alan H.

1911 *Egyptian Hieratic Texts*. Series I: Literary Texts of the New Kingdom. Leipzig: Hinrichs.

1937 *Late-Egyptian Miscellanies*. BibAeg VII. Brussels: La Fondation Egyptologique. [= LEM]

1946 "The Instruction Addressed to Kagemni and His Brethren." *JEA* 32: 71–74.

1947 *Ancient Egyptian Onomastica*. London: Oxford University Press.

Garr, W. Randall

2004 "Hēn." *RB* 111: 321–44.

Garrett, Duane A.

1990 "Votive Prostitution Again: A Comparison of Proverbs 7: 13–14 and 21: 28–29." *JBL* 109: 681–82.

1993 *Proverbs, Ecclesiastes, Song of Songs*. NAC, Vol.14. Nashville: Broadman.

Gaspar, Joseph W.

1947 *Social Ideas in the Wisdom Literature of the Old Testament*. Washington, D.C.: Catholic University of America.

Gasser, Johann Conrad

1904 *Die Bedeutung der Sprüche Jesu ben Sira für die Datierung des althebräischen Spruchbuches*. Gütersloh: Bertelsmann.

Gaster, Theodor H.

1954 "Proverbs [viii 30]." *VT* 4: 77–78.

Geiger, Abraham

1857 *Urschrift und Übersetzung der Bibel*. Second ed. Frankfort am Main: Madda, 1928.

Gemser, Berend

1953 "The Importance of Motive Clauses in Old Testament Law." Pp. 50–66 in *Congress Volume: Copenhagen, 1953*. VTSup 1. Ed. G. W. Anderson. Leiden: Brill.

1960 "The Instructions of 'Onchsheshonqy and Biblical Wisdom Literature." Pp. 102–28 in *Congress Volume: Oxford, 1959*. VTSup 7. Ed. G. W. Anderson (repr. SAIW 134–60).

*1963 *Sprüche Salomos*. HAT I.16, 2nd ed. Tübingen: Mohr.

1968 "The Spiritual Structure of Biblical Aphoristic Wisdom." Pp. 138–49 in *Adhuc Loquitor*. Ed. A. Van Selms and A. S. Van der Woude. Leiden: Brill (repr. SAIW 208–19).

Genug, John Franklin

1911 "Meaning and Usage of the Term *tušiyyah*." *JBL* 30: 114–22.

Geradon, Bernard de
1974 *Le Coeur, la langue, les mains*. Paris: Desclée De Brouwer.
Gerleman, Gillis
1950 "The Septuagint Proverbs as a Hellenistic Document." *OTS* 8: 15–27.
*1956 *Studies in the Septuagint. III: Proverbs*. Lund: Gleerup.
Gerstenberger, Erhard
1965 *Wesen und Herkunft des "apodiktischen Rechts."* WMANT 20. Neukirchen-Vluyn: Neukirchener Verlag.
1969 "Zur alttestamentlichen Weisheit." *Verkundigung und Forschung* 14: 28–44.
2001 *Psalms (Part 2) and Lamentations*. FOTL XV. Grand Rapids, Mich.: Eerdmans.
Gese, Hartmut
1958 *Lehre und Wirklichkeit in der alten Weisheit*. Tübingen: Mohr.
1984 "Wisdom Literature in the Persian Period." Pp. 189–218 in *The Cambridge History of Judaism*, Vol.1. Ed. W.D. Davies and L. Finkelstein. Cambridge: Cambridge University Press.
Gewalt, Dietfried
1985 " 'Öffne deinen Mund für den Stummen'—zu Proverbia 31,8." *Dielheimer Blätter zum Alten Testament* 21: 133–38.
Gibson, J. C. L.
1978 *Canaanite Myths and Legends*. Edinburgh: T. & T. Clark.
Giese, Ronald L., Jr.
1990 "Wisdom and Wealth in the Septuagint of Proverbs." Ph.D. diss., University of Wisconsin–Madison.
1992a "Quantifying Wealth in the Septuagint of Proverbs." *JBL* 111: 409–25.
1992b "Strength through Wisdom and the Bee in LXX-Prov 6,8^{a-c}." *Bib* 73: 404–11.
1993a "Compassion for the Lowly in Septuagint Proverbs." *JSP* 11: 109–17.
1993b "Dualism in the LXX of Prov 2: 17." *JETS* 36: 289–95.
Gilbert, Maurice
1974 "L'éloge de la Sagesse (*Siracide* 24)." *RTL* 5: 326–48.
1979a "Avant-propos." BETL 51: 7–13.
1979b "Le discours de la Sagesse en Proverbs, 8. Structure et cohérence." BETL 51: 202–18.
1979c *La Sagesse de l'Ancien Testament*. Ed. M. Gilbert. Leuven: Leuven University.
1980 "La Sagesse personnifiée dans les textes de l'Ancien Testament." *Cahiers Evangile* 32: 5–36.
1991 "Le Discours menaçant de Sagesse en Proverbes 1,20–33." Pp. 90–119 in *Storia e tradizioni di Israele*. Brescia: Paideia.
1995 "Qu'en est-il de la Sagesse?" Pp. 19–60 in *La Sagesse Biblique*. Lectio Divina 160. Paris: Cerf.
Ginsberg, H. L.
1945 "The North-Canaanite Myth of Anath and Aqhat." *BASOR* 98: 15–23.
Gitay, Yehoshua
2001 "Rhetoric and Logic of Wisdom in the Book of Proverbs." *JNSL* 27: 45–56.
Glanville, Stephen R. K.
1955 *The Instructions of 'Onchsheshongy*. Catalogue of Demotic Papyri in the British Museum, Vol. II. London: British Museum.

Glazier-McDonald, Beth
1987 *Malachi*. SBLDS 98. Atlanta: Scholars Press.
Glück, J. J.
1964 "Proverbs XXX 15a." *VT* 14: 367–70.
1977 "The Figure of 'Inversion' in the Book of Proverbs." *Semitics* 5: 24–31.
Glückel of Hameln
1977 *The Memoirs of Glückel of Hameln*. Trans. M. Lowenthal. New York: Schocken.
Glueck, Nelson
1927 *Das Wort ḥesed im alttestamentlichen Sprachgebrauche*. Giessen: Töpelmann. [ET: A. Gottschalk; Cincinnati: Hebrew Union College, 1967.]
Godbey, Allen H.
1922–23 "The Hebrew *Mašal*." *AJSL* 39: 89–108.
Godlovitch, S.
1981 "On Wisdom." *Canadian Journal of Philosophy* 11: 137–55.
Goedicke, H.
1967 "Die Lehre eines Mannes für seinen Sohn." *ZÄS* 94: 62–71.
Goldingay, J. E.
1977 "Proverbs V and IX." *RB* 84: 80–93.
1994 "The Arrangement of Sayings in Proverbs 10–15." *JSOT* 61: 75–83.
Golka, Friedemann W.
1983 "Die israelitische Weisheitsschule oder 'der Kaisers neue Kleider.' " *VT* 33: 257–70.
1986 "Die Königs- und hofsprüche und der Ursprung der israelitischen Weisheit." *VT* 36: 13–36.
1989 "Die Flecken des Leoparden." Pp. 149–65 in *Schöpfung und Befreiung* (FS C. Westermann). Ed. R. Alberz et al. Stuttgart: Calwer.
1993 *The Leopard's Spots: Biblical and African Wisdom in Proverbs*. Edinburgh: T. & T. Clark.
Gordis, Robert
1943 "The Social Background of Wisdom Literature." *HUCA* 18: 77–118.
Gordon, Cyrus H.
1930 "Rabbinic Exegesis in the Vulgate of Proverbs." *JBL* 49: 384–416.
Gordon, R. P.
1999 " 'Converse Translation' in the Targums and Beyond." *JSP* 19: 3–21.
Goshen-Gottstein, I. M.
1957 "The History of the Bible-Text and Comparative Semitics." *VT* 7: 195–201.
1963 "Theory and Practice of Text Criticism." *Textus* 3: 130–58.
Gottlieb, Isaac B.
1990 "Pirqe Abot and Biblical Wisdom." *VT* 40: 152–64.
Graetz, Heinrich
1884 "Exegetische Studien zu den Salomonischen Sprüchen." *Monatschrift für die Wissenschaft des Judentums* 33: 145–447.
Greenberg, Moshe
1977 "The Use of the Ancient Versions for Interpreting the Hebrew Text." Pp. 131–47 in *Congress Volume: Göttingen, 1976*. VTSup 29. Ed. J. A. Emerton. Leiden: Brill.
1995 "Three Conceptions of Torah in Hebrew Scriptures." Pp. 11–24 in *Studies in the Bible and Jewish Thought*. Philadelphia: Jewish Publication Society.

[Originally published in *Festschrift für Rolf Rendtorff, zum 65* Neukirchen-Vluyn: Neukirchener, 1990].

1996 "Noisy and Yearning: The Semantics of *šqq* and its Congeners." Pp. 339–44 in *Texts, Temples, and Traditions: A Tribute to Menahem Haran*. Ed. M. V. Fox et al. Winona Lake, Ind.: Eisenbrauns.

Greenfield, Jonas C.

1958 "Lexicographical Notes I." *HUCA* 29: 203–28.

1959 "Lexicographical Notes II." *HUCA* 30: 141–51.

1971 "The Background and Parallel to a Proverb of Ahiqar." Pp. 49–59 in *Hommages à André Dupont-Sommer*. Paris: Adrien-Maisonneuve.

1978 "The Dialects of Early Aramaic." *JNES* 37: 93–99.

1985 "The Seven Pillars of Wisdom (Prov 9:1). A Mistranslation." *JQR* 76: 13–20.

1995 "The Wisdom of Ahiqar." WAI 43–52.

Greenspahn, Frederick E.

1989 "Why Prophecy Ceased." *JBL* 108: 37–49.

1994 "A Mesopotamian Proverb and its Biblical Reverberations." *JAOS* 114: 33–38.

Gressmann, Hugo

1924 "Die neugefundene Lehre des Amen-em-ope und die vorexilische Spruchdichtung Israels." *ZAW* 42: 272–94.

1927 *Israels Spruchweisheit im Zusammenhang der Weltliteratur*. Berlin: Karl Curtius.

Grimm, Karl J.

1901 "The Meaning and Etymology of the Word *tušiyyah* in the OT." *JAOS* 22: 35–44.

Grollenberg, Luc

1952 "A Propos de Prov., VII, 6 et XVII, 27." *RB* 59: 40–43.

Grossberg, Daniel

1994 "Two Kinds of Sexual Relationships in the Hebrew Bible." *HS* 35: 7–25.

Gruber, Mayer I.

1980 *Aspects of Nonverbal Communication in the Ancient Near East*. 2 vols. Rome: Biblical Institute Press.

1986 "Hebrew *q^e dešah* and Her Canaanite and Akkadian Cognates." *UF* 18: 133–48.

Grumach, Irene. See Shirun-Grumach

Gugliemi, Waltraud

1983 "Eine 'Lehre' für einen reiselustigen Sohn (Ostrakon Oriental Institute 12074)." *WO* 14: 149–66.

Gulley, Norman

1962 *Plato's Theory of Knowledge*. London: Methuen.

1968 *The Philosophy of Socrates*. London: Macmillan.

Gunn, Battiscombe

1926 "Some Middle-Egyptian Proverbs." *JEA* 12: 282–84.

Gunneweg, Antonius H. J.

1992 "Weisheit, Prophetie und Kanonformel. Erwägungen zu Proverbia 30,1–9." Pp. 253–60 in *Alttestamentliche Glaube und Biblische Theologie* (FS H. D. Preuss). Ed. J. Hausmann and H.-J. Zobel. Stuttgart: Kohlhammer.

Habel, Norman C.

1972 "The Symbolism of Wisdom in Proverbs 1–9." *Int* 26: 131–57.

Hadas, Moses

1973 *Aristeas to Philocrates (Letter of Aristeas)*. New York: KTAV.

Hadley, Judith

1995 "Wisdom and the Goddess. WAI 234–43.

1997 "From Goddess to Literary Construct: The Transformation of Asherah into Hokmah." Pp. 360–99 in *A Feminist Companion to Reading the Bible*. Ed. A. Brenner and C. Fontaine. Sheffield: Sheffield Academic Press.

Halbe, Jörn

1979 " 'Altorientalisches Weltordnungsdenken' und alttestamentliche Theologie." *ZTK* 76: 381–418.

Halperin, David J.

1981 "*The Book of Remedies* [cited in bBer 10b, Pes 56a], the Canonization of the Solomonic Writings, and the Riddle of Pseudo-Eusebius." *JQR* 72: 269–92.

Hamonville, David-Marc d', with E. Dumouchet

2000 *La Bible d'Alexandrie*. Vol. 17, Les Proverbes. Paris: Cerf. [= BA]

Haran, Menachem

1972 "The Graded Numerical Sequence and the Phenomenon of 'Automatism' in Biblical Poetry." Pp. 238–67 in *Congress Volume: Uppsala, 1971*. VTSup 22. Ed. G. W. Anderson. Leiden: Brill.

1985 "Das Böcklein in der Milch seiner Muter und das säugende Muttertier." *TZ* 41: 135–59.

1988 "On the Diffusion of Literacy and Schools in Ancient Israel." Pp. 81–95 in *Congress Volume: Jerusalem, 1986*. VTSup 40. Ed. J. A. Emerton. Leiden: Brill.

1996 *Ha'asuphah Hamiqra'it* ["The Biblical Collection"; Hebrew]. Jerusalem: Mosad Bialik.

Harrington, Daniel J.

1996 *Wisdom Texts from Qumran*. London and New York: Routledge.

Harris, Scott L.

1995 *Proverbs 1–9: A Study of Inner-Biblical Interpretation*. SBLDS. Atlanta: Scholars Press.

Hartman, Louis F., and Alexander A. Di Lella

1978 *The Book of Daniel*. AYB 23. Garden City, N.Y.: Doubleday (repr. New Haven: Yale University Press).

Hasan-Rokem, Galit

1990 "And God Created the Proverb." Pp. 107–20 in *Text and Tradition*. SBL Semeia Studies. Ed. Susan Niditch. Atlanta: Scholars Press.

Hatch, Edwin

1889 *Essays in Biblical Greek*. Oxford: Clarendon.

Haupt, Paul

1926 "Mistranslated Lines in Proverbs." *JBL* 45: 350–57.

Hausmann, Jutta

1991? "Studien zum Menschenbild der älteren Weisheit." Habilitationschrift Augustana-Hochschule (unpub.). Neuendettelsau. n.d.

1992 "Beobachtungen zu Spr 31,10–31." Pp. 261–66 in *Alttestamentliche Glaube und Biblische Theologie* (FS H. D. Preuss). Ed. J. Hausmann and H.-J. Zobel. Stuttgart: Kohlhammer.

1995 *Studien zum Menschenbild der älteren Weisheit (Spr. 10ff.)* FAT 7. Tübingen: Mohr-Siebeck.

1996 " 'Weisheit' im Kontext alttestamentlicher Theologie: Stand und Perspektiven gegenwärtiger Forschung." Pp. 9–19 in *Weisheit ausserhalb der kanonischen Weisheitsschriften*. Ed. Bernd Janowski. Gütersloh: Chr. Kaiser.

Hausmann, Jutta, and Hans-Jürgen Zotta, eds.

1992 *Alttestamentlicher Glaube und biblische Theologie* (FS H. D. Preuss). Ed. J. Hausmann and H.-J. Zobel. Stuttgart: Kohlhammer.

Hayes, W.

1948 "A Much Copied Letter of the Early Middle Kingdom." *JNES* 7: 1–10.

Healey, John F.

*1991 *The Targum of Proverbs*. The Aramaic Bible, XV. Collegeville, Minn.: Michael Glazier.

Heidenheim, M.

*1865 ff. "Zur Textkritik der Proverbien." *Deutsche Vierteljarschrift* 2 (1865) 395–414 (Prov 1–3); 3 (1867) 51–60 (Prov 4–7); 327–46 (Prov 8–9); 445–60 (Prov 10–14); 468–87 (Prov 15–31).

Heijerman, Mieke

1994 "Who Would Blame Her? The 'Strange' Woman of Proverbs 7." Pp. 21–31 in *Reflections on Theology and Gender*. Ed. F. van Dijk-Hemmes and A. Brenner. Kampen: Kok Pharos.

Heim, Knut M.

2001 *Like Grapes of Gold Set in Silver*. BZAW 273. Berlin: de Gruyter.

2008 "A Closer Look at the Pig in Proverbs XI 22." *VT* 58:13–27.

Heinisch, Paul

1933 *Die persönliche Weisheit des Alten Testaments in religionsgeschichtlicher Beleuchtung*. Münster-in-Weisf.: Aschendorff.

Helck, Wolfgang

1956 *Urkunden der 18. Dynastie*. (Transl. 1961). Leipzig.

1969 *Der Text der "Lehre Amenemhets I. für seinen Sohn."* KÄT. Wiesbaden: Harrassowitz.

1970a *Die Lehre des Dw'-Ḥtjj*. 2 vols. KÄT. Wiesbaden: Harrassowitz.

1970b *Die Prophezeiung des Nfr.tj*. KÄT. Wiesbaden: Harrassowitz.

1977 *Die Lehre für König Merikare*. KÄT. Wiesbaden: Harrassowitz.

1984 *Die Lehre des Djedefhor und Die Lehre eines Vaters an Seinen Sohn*. KÄT. Wiesbaden: Harrassowitz.

Helck, Wolfgang, Eberhard Otto, et al.

1972–92 *Lexikon der Ägyptologie*. Wiesbaden: Harrossowitz. [= LÄ]

Held, Moshe

1985 "Marginal Notes to the Biblical Lexicon." Pp. 97–103 in *Biblical and Related Studies Presented to Samuel Iwry*. Ed. A. Kort and S. Morschauser. Winona Lake, Ind.: Eisenbrauns.

Hempel, Johannes

1929 [Remarks on Cowley, "Two Aramaic Ostraca" (1929)], ZAW 47: 150–51.

1936 *Gott und Mensch im Alten Testament*. Chap. 1: "Die Furcht vor Jahve," pp. 4–33. BWANT 38. Stuttgart.

Hengel, Martin

1974 *Judaism and Hellenism* (ET J. Bowden). Philadelphia: Fortress.

Herbert, A. S.

1954 "The Parable (*Māšāl*) in the Old Testament." *Scottish Journal of Theology* 7: 180–96.

Herdner, Andrée
1963 *Corpus des tablettes en cunéiformes alphabétiques découvertes à Ras Shamra-Ugarit de 1929 à 1939*. Paris: Geuthner.

Hermisson, Hans-Jürgen
1968 *Studien zur israelitischen Spruchweisheit*. WMANT 28. Neukirchen: Neukirchener Verlag.
1971 "Weisheit und Geschichte." Pp. 136–54 in *Probleme biblischer Theologie* (FS Gerhard von Rad). Ed. H. W. Wolff. Munich: Chr. Kaiser.
1978 "Observations on the Creation Theology in Wisdom." IW 43–57.
1990 "Zur 'feministischen' Exegese des ATs." *EpD/Evangelische Information* 52a/90: 3–7.

Hesselgrave, Charles Everett
1910 *The Hebrew Personification of Wisdom; Its Origin, Development and Influence*. New York: Stechert.

Hildebrandt, Ted
1988a "Proverbs 22: 6a: Train Up a Child?" *Grace Theological Journal* 9: 3–19.
1988b "Proverbial Pairs: Compositional Units in Proverbs 10–29." *JBL* 107: 207–24.
1990 "Proverbial Strings: Cohesion in Proverbs 10." *Grace Theological Journal* 11: 171–85.
1992 "Motivation and Antithetic Parallelism in Proverbs 10–15." *JETS* 35: 433–44.

Hillers, Delbert
1964 *Treaty-Curses and the OT Prophets*. BO 16. Rome: Pontifical Biblical Institute.

Hitzig, F.
*1858 *Die Sprüche Salomons*. Leipzig: Weidmann.

Ho, Ahuva
1991 *Ṣedeq and Ṣedaqah in the Hebrew Bible*. New York: Peter Lang.

Höffken, Peter
1985 "Das Ego des Weisen." *TZ* 41: 121–34.

Hoglund, Kenneth G., E. F. Huwiler, J. T. Glass, and R. W. Lee
1987a *The Listening Heart* (FS Roland E. Murphy). JSOTSup 58. Sheffield.
1987b "The Fool and the Wise in Dialogue." Pp. 161–80 in *The Listening Heart* (Hoglund et al., 1987a).
1987c "Murphy's Axiom: Every Gnomic Saying Needs a Balancing Corrective." Pp. 1–13 in *The Listening Heart* (Hoglund et al., 1987a).

Holladay, William
1958 *The Root šubh in the Old Testament*. Leiden: Brill.

Holmstedt, Robert D.
2002 "The Relative Clause in Biblical Hebrew: A Linguistic Analysis." Ph. D. Diss., University of Wisconsin–Madison.
2005 "Word Order in the Book of Proverbs." SWA 135–54.

Hornung, Erik
1979 "Lehren über das Jenseits?" SAL 217–24.
1982 *Conceptions of God in Ancient Egypt*. Ithaca, New York: Cornell University Press.

Hornung, Erik, and Othmar Keel, eds.
1979 *Studien zu altägyptischen Lebenslehren*. OBO 28. Freiburg. [= SAL]

Houston, Walter J.

2003 “The Role of the Poor in Proverbs.” Pp. 229–40 in *Reading from Right to Left: Essays on the Hebrew Bible in Honour of David J. A. Clines*. Ed. J. Cheryl Exum and H. G. M. Williamson. JSOTSup 480. Sheffield: Sheffield Academic Press.

Hubbard, David A.

1966 “The Wisdom Movement and Israel’s Covenant Faith.” *TynBul* 17: 18.

Hudal, Alois

1914 *Die religiösen und sittlichen Ideen des Spruchbuches*. Rome: Pontifical Biblical Institute.

Huehnergard, John

1991 “Remarks on the Classification of the Northwest Semitic Languages.” Pp. 282–93 in *The Balaam Text from Deir ʿAlla Re-evaluated*. Ed. J. Hoftijzer and G. van der Kooij. Leiden: Brill.

Hugenberger, Gordon P.

1993 *Marriage as a Covenant*. VTSup 52. Leiden: Brill.

Humbert, Paul

1929 *Recherches sur les sources égyptiennes de la littérature sapientiale d’Israël*. Neuchâtel.

1937 “La ‘Femme étrangère’ du Livre des Proverbes.” *Revue des études sémitiques* 4: 49–64.

1939 “Les adjectifs ‘Zâr’ et ‘Nokrî’ et la ‘Femme Etrangère’ des proverbes bibliques.” *Mélanges Syriens*, 1.259–66.

1950 “ ‘Qānāʾ en Hêbreu biblique.” Pp. in 259–67 in *FS Alfred Bertholet*. Tübingen: Mohr.

1960 “Le substantif *tôʿēbā* et le verbe *tʿb* dans l’AT.” ZAW 72: 217–37.

Hurowitz, Victor A.

2000a “An Often Overlooked Alphabetic Acrostic in Proverbs 24:1–22.” *RB* 107: 526–40.

2000b “Two Terms for Wealth in Proverbs VIII in Light of Akkadian.” *VT* 50: 252–57.

2001a “Proverbs 29:22–27: Another Unnoticed Alphabetic Acrostic.” *JSOT* 92: 121–25.

2001b “The Seventh Pillar—Reconsidering the Literary Structure and Unity of Proverbs 31.” ZAW 113: 209–18.

2001c “Thirty (?) Counsels of Knowledge: Structural and Exegetical Remarks on ‘The Words of the Wise’ (Prov 22:14–24:22) [Hebrew].” Pp. 146–60 in *Teshurah Li-Shmuel* (FS Shemuel Ahituv). Ed. Daniel Sivan et. al. Jerusalem: Mosad Bialik; Beer Sheva: Ben Gurion University.

2004 “Paradise Regained—Proverbs 3:13–20 Reconsidered.” Pp. 49–62 in *Sefer Moshe (Moshe Weinfeld Jubilee Volume)*. Ed. Chaim Cohen, Avi Hurvitz, and Shalom Paul. Winona Lake, Ind.: Eisenbrauns.

2005 “The Woman of Valor and a Woman Large of Head: Matchmaking in the Ancient Near East.” SWA 221–34.

Hurvitz, Avi

1967 “The Usage of *šš* and *bwṣ* in the Bible and its Implications for the Date of P.” *HTR* 20: 117–21.

1968 “The Chronological Significance of ‘Aramaisms’ in Biblical Hebrew.” *IEJ* 18: 234–40.

1972 "Diachronic Chiasm in Biblical Hebrew" [Hebrew]. Pp. 248–55 in *The Bible and the History of Israel* (FS J. Levor). Ed. B. Uffenheimer. Tel Aviv: Tel Aviv Students Organization.

1986 *ʿIyyunim Bilšono šel Sefer Mišley: L*[e]*šimmušo šel Mivneh Hasmikhut baʿal* X ["Studies in the Language of the Book of Proverbs: Concerning the use of the Construct Pattern *baʿal* X" ([Hebrew)]. *Tarbiz* 55: 1–17.

1988 "Wisdom Vocabulary in the Hebrew Psalter: A Contribution to the Study of the 'Wisdom Psalms.' " *VT* 38: 41–51.

1991 *Š*[e]*qiʿey Ḥokmah Besefer T*[e]*hillim* [*Wisdom Language in Biblical Psalmody* (Hebrew)]. Jerusalem: Magnes.

1992 "*Ṣaddiq* = 'wise' in Biblical Hebrew and the Wisdom Connections of Ps 37." Pp. 109–13 in *Goldene Äpfel in silbernen Schalen: Collected Communications to the XIIIth Congress of the International Organization for the Study of the Old Testament*. Ed. Klaus-Dietrich Schunck and Matthias Augustin. Frankfurt am Main: Lang.

Hyun, Changhak

2000 "A Study of the Translation Technique of Peshitta Proverbs." Ph. D. Diss., University of Wisconsin–Madison.

Ibn Janaḥ, Jonah

[1965] *Sefer Hariqmah*. 2 vols. Ed. M. Wilensky (first ed. 1929). Jerusalem: Academy for the Hebrew Language.

[1969] *Sefer Hashorashim*. Trans. Judah ibn Tibon; ed. B. Z. Bacher (1896). Amsterdam: Philo.

Imschoot, Paul van

1938 "Sagesse et Esprit dans l'A.T." *RB* 47: 23–49.

Irwin, William A.

1961 "Where Shall Wisdom Be Found?" *JBL* 80: 133–42.

1984 "The Metaphor in Prov 11,30." *Bib* 65: 97–100.

Israeli, Shlomit.

1990 "Chapter Four of the Wisdom Book of *Amenemope*." Pp. 464–83 in *Studies in Egyptology Presented to Miriam Lichtheim*. Ed. Sarah Israelit-Groll. Jerusalem: Magnes.

Iwry, Samuel

1966 "*whnmṣ'*—a striking variant reading in 1QIsa[a]." *Textus* 5: 34–43.

Jacob, Edmond

1971 "Sagesse et alphabet. A propos de Proverbes 31:10–31." *Homages à André Dupont-Sommer*. Paris.

1978 "Wisdom and Religion in Sirach." IW 247–60.

Jacobson, Arland D.

1990 "Proverbs and Social Control." Pp. 75–88 in *Gnosticism & the Early Christian World*. Ed. James E Goehring et al. Sonoma, Calif.: Polebridge.

Jäger, Johannes G.

1788 *Observationes in Proverbium Salomonis versionem alexandrinam*. Meldorf: Boie. [= Jäg.]

Jakobson, Roman

1979 "Notes on the Makeup of a Proverb." *Linguistic and Literary Studies* 4: 83–85.

Jamieson-Drake, David

1991 *Scribes and Schools in Monarchic Judah*. JSOTSup 109. Sheffield: Almond.

Janowski, Bernd, ed.
1996 *Weisheit ausserhalb der kanonischen Weisheitsschriften*. Gütersloh: Chr. Kaiser.
Jasnow, Richard
1982 "An Unrecognized Parallel in Two Demotic Wisdom Texts." *Enchoria* 11: 59–61.
1992 *A Late Period Hieratic Wisdom Text (p. Brooklyn 47.218.135)*. SAOC 52. Chicago: Oriental Institute.
Jastrow, Marcus
1950 *A Dictionary of the Targumim* [etc.]. New York: Pardes.
Jenkins, R. Geoffrey
1987 "The text of P. Antinoopolis 8/210." Pp. 65–77 in *VI Congress of the International Organization for Septuagint and Cognate Studies*. Ed. Claude Cox. SBLSCS 23. Atlanta: Scholars Press.
Jenks, Alan W.
1985 "Theological Presuppositions of Israel's Wisdom Literature." *Horizons in Biblical Theology* 7: 43–75.
Jenni, Ernst
1999 "Epistemische Modalitäten im Proverbienbuch." Pp. 107–17 in *Mythos im Alten Testament und seiner Umwelt* (FS H.-P. Müller). Ed. A. Lange et al. Berlin: de Gruyter.
Jepsen, Alfred
1965 "*Ṣedeq* und *Ṣᵉdaqah* im Alten Testament." Pp. 78–89 in *Gottes Wort und Gottes Land* (FS H.-W. Hertzberg). Ed. H. G. Reventloh. Göttingen: Vandenhoeck & Ruprecht.
Jequier, G.
1911 *Les Papyrus Prisse et ses Variants*. Paris: Geuthner.
Jirku, Anton
1954 "Das n. pr. Lemu'el (Prov 31:1) und der Gott Lim." ZAW 66: 151.
Johnson, A. R.
1955 *Mašal*. Pp. 162–69 in *Wisdom in Israel and in the Ancient Near East*. VTSup 3. Ed. M. Noth and D. Winton Thomas. Leiden: Brill.
Jones, Scott C.
2003 "Wisdom's Pedagogy: A Comparison of Proverbs vii and 4Q184." *VT* 43: 65–80.
Joosten, Jan
1995 "Doublet Translations in Peshitta Proverbs." Pp. 63–72 in *The Peshitta as a Translation*. Ed. P. B. Dirksen and A. van der Kooij. Leiden: Brill.
Joüon, Paul, and Takamitsu Muraoka
1991 *A Grammar of Biblical Hebrew*. Rome: Pontifical Biblical Inst. [= GBH]
Kaiser, Walter C.
1978 "Wisdom Theology and the Centre of Old Testament Theology." *EvQ* 50: 132–46.
Kalugila, Leonidas
1980 *The Wise King*. Lund: Gleerup.
Kaminka, A.
1931–32 "Septuaginta und Targum zu Proverbia." *HUCA* 8–9: 169–91.
Kaspi, Yosef ibn
*[1903] *Ḥaṣoṣᵉrot Kesef* in *'Aśarah Kᵉley Kesef*. Ed. Isaac Last. Pressburg: Alkalay.

Kaufman, Stephen A.

1988 "The Classification of the North West Semitic Dialects of the Biblical Period and Some Implications Thereof." Pp. 41–57 in *Proceedings of the Ninth World Congress of Jewish Studies, Panel Sessions, Hebrew and Aramaic Languages*. Ed. Moshe Bar-Asher. Jerusalem: Magnes.

Kaufmann, Yehezkel

1960 *The Religion of Israel*. Trans. and ed. M. Greenberg. Chicago: University of Chicago.

Kautzsch, Emil

1910 *Die Sprüche*. HSAT II. Tübingen: Mohr.

Kayatz, Christa

1966 *Studien zu Proverbien 1–9*. WMANT 22. Neukirchen-Vluyn: Neukirchener Verlag.

Kedar-Kopfstein, Benjamin

1977 "Semantic Aspects of the Pattern *qôṭēl*." *HAR* 1: 155–76.

Keel, Othmar

1971 "Eine Diskussion um die Bedeutung polarer Begriffspaare in den Lebenslehren." SAL 225–34.

1974 "Die Weisheit 'spielt' vor Gott." *Freiburger Zeitschrift für Philosophie und Theologie* 21: 1–66.

Kellenberger, Edgar

1982 *Ḥäsäd wäʾämät als Ausdruck einer Glaubenserfahrung*. ATANT 69. Zürich: Theologischer Verlag.

Keller, Carl A.

1977 "Zum sogenannten Vergeltungsglauben im Proverbienbuch." Pp. 223–38 in *Beiträge zur atl. Theologie* (FS W. Zimmerli). Ed. Herbert Donner, Robert Hanhart, and Rudolf Smend. Göttingen: Vandenhoeck & Ruprecht.

Kennedy, James

1928 *An Aid to the Textual Amendment of the Old Testament*. Ed. N. Levison. Edinburgh: T. & T. Clark.

Kennicott

**1776–80* *Vetus Testamentum hebraicum cum variis lectionibus*. Oxford: Clarendon.

Kevin, Robert O.

1930 "The Wisdom of Amen-em-apt and its Possible Dependence upon the Hebrew Book of Proverbs." *JSOR* 14: 115–57.

Kim, Seenam

2007 *The Coherence of the Collections in the Book of Proverbs*. Eugene, Ore.: Pickwick.

Kister, Menahem

2004 "Wisdom Literature and its Relation to Other Genres: From Ben Sira to *Mysteries*." Pp. 13–47 in *Sapiential Perspectives: Wisdom Literature in Light of the Dead Sea Scrolls*. Ed. by John J. Collins, Gregory E. Sterling, and Ruth A. Clements. Leiden: Brill.

Kitchen, Kenneth A.

1969 "Studies in Egyptian Wisdom Literature—I: The Instruction of a Man for His Son." *OrAnt* 8: 189–208.

1977–78 "Proverbs and Wisdom Books of the Ancient Near East." *TynBul* 28: 69–114.

1979 "The Basic Literary Forms and Formulations of Ancient Instructional Writings in Egypt and Western Asia." SAL 235–82.

1988 "Egypt and Israel During the First Millenium." Pp. 106–25 in *Congress Volume: Jerusalem, 1986*. VTSup 40. Ed. by J. A. Emerton. Leiden: Brill.

Klein, Michael L.

1976 "Converse Translation: A Targumic Technique." *Bib* 57: 515–37.

Kleinig, John W.

1983 "The Banquet of Wisdom—An Exegetical Study of Proverbs 9: 1–12." *Lutheran Theological Journal* 17: 24–28.

Klopfenstein, Martin

1964 *Die Lüge nach dem Alten Testament* (AThANT 62). Zurich: Gotthelf.

1991 "Auferstehung der Göttin in der spätisraelistischen Weisheit von Prov 1–9?" Pp. 531–42 in *Ein Gott allein?* Ed. W. Dietrich and M. A. Klopfenstein (OBO 139). Göttingen: Vandenhoeck & Ruprecht.

Kloppenborg, John S.

1982 "Isis and Sophia in the Book of Wisdom." *HTR* 75: 57–84.

Knox, Wilfred L.

1937 "The Divine Wisdom." *JTS* 38: 230–37.

Koch, Klaus

1958 "Psalm 119 (118) und seine Theologie" [Review of Deissler 1955]. *TLZ* 83: 186–87.

1972 "Gibt es ein Vergeltungsdogma im Alten Testament?" Pp. 130–80 in *Um das Prinzip der Vergeltung in Religion und Recht des Alten Testaments*. Ed. K. Koch. Darmstadt (first published in *ZTK* 52 [1955] 1–42; ET in Crenshaw 1983, 57–87).

Koehler, Ludwig, Walter Baumgartner, and Johann Jakob Stamm

1994ff. *Hebrew and Aramaic Lexicon of the Old Testament*. Trans. M. E. J. Richardson. Leiden: Brill. [= HALOT; trans. of HALAT]

König, Eduard

1897 *Lehrgebäude der hebräischen Sprache*. II.2 (Syntax). Leipzig: Hinrichs.

Kopf, Lothar

1959 "Arabische Etymologien und Parallelen zum Bibelwörterbuch." *VT* 9: 247–87.

Körbert, R.

1982 "Zu Prov 23,1–2." *Bib* 63: 264–65.

Kottsieper, Ingo

1990 *Die Sprache der Aḥiqarsprüche*. BZAW 194 Berlin: de Gruyter.

1996 "Die alttestamentliche Weisheit im Licht aramäischer Weisheitstraditionen." Pp. 128–62 in *Weisheit ausserhalb der kanonischen Weisheitsschriften*. Ed. Bernd Janowski. Gütersloh: Chr. Kaiser.

2002 "Alttestamentliche Weisheit: Proverbia und Kohelet." *TRu* 67: (I) 1–34; (II) 201–37.

2008 "The Aramaic Tradition: Ahikar." Pp. 109–24 in *Scribes, Sages, and Seers: The Sage in the Eastern Mediterranean World*. Ed. Leo Perdue. Göttingen: Vandenhoeck & Ruprecht.

Kovacs, Brian W.

1974 "Is There a Class-Ethic in Proverbs?" Pp. 171–89 in *Essays in OT Ethics*. Ed. J. L. Crenshaw and James Willis. New York: KTAV.

Kramer, Samuel N.

1955 "A Man and His God." Pp. 170–82 in *Wisdom in Israel and in the Ancient Near East*. VTSup 3. Ed. M. Noth and D. Winton Thomas. Leiden: Brill.

Krantz, Eva S.
1996 " 'A Man Not Supported by God': On Some Crucial Words in Proverbs XXX 1." *VT* 46: 548–53.
Kraus, Hans-Joachim
1951 *Die Verkündigung der Weisheit*. Neukirchen: Kreis Mohrs.
Krispenz, Jutta
1989 *Spruchkompositionen im Buch Proverbia*. Frankfurt am Main: Peter Lang.
Kruger, Paul A.
1987 "Promiscuity or Marriage Fidelity? A Note on Prov. 5:15–18." *JNSL* 13: 61–68.
Krüger, Thomas
2000 "Ambiguity and Wordplay in Proverbs XI." *VT* 52: 545–48.
2003 "Erkenntnisbindung im Weisheitspruch." Pp. 53–66 in *Weisheit in Israel*. Altes Testament und Moderne 12. Ed. David J. A. Clines et al. Münster: Lit.
Kselman, John S.
2000 "Ambiguity and Wordplay in Proverbs XI." *VT* 52: 545–47.
Küchler, Max
1966 *Frühjüdische Weisheitstraditionen*. OBO 26. Fribourg: Universitätsverlag.
1992 "Gott und seine Weisheit in der Septuaginta. (Ijob 28; Spr 8)." Pp. 118–43 in *Monotheismus und Christologie*. Ed. H.-J. Klauck. Freiburg: Herder.
Kugel, James L.
1981 *The Idea of Biblical Poetry*. New Haven: Yale University Press.
1997 "Wisdom and the Anthological Temper." *Prooftexts* 17: 9–32.
Kuhn, Gottfried
1931 *Beiträge zur Erklärung des Salomonischen Spruchbuches*. BWANT 57. Stuttgart: W. Kohlhammer.
Kuhrt, Amélie
1995 *The Ancient Near East*. 2 vols. London: Routledge.
Kuntz, J. Kenneth
2003 "Reclaiming Biblical Wisdom Psalms: A Response to Crenshaw." *CBR* 1: 145–54.
2004 "Affirming Less as More: Scholarly Engagements with Aphoristic Rhetoric." *JSOT* 29: 205–42.
Lagarde, Paul de
*1863 *Anmerkungen zur griechischen Übersetzung der Proverbien*. Leipzig: Brockhaus. [= Lag.]
1873 *Hagiographa Chaldaice*. Leipzig: Teubneri. [= Tg^L]
Lambert, W. G.
1960 *Babylonian Wisdom Literature*. Oxford: Clarendon. [= BWL]
1995 "Some New Babylonian Wisdom Literature." WAI 30–42.
Lanczkowski, Günter
1955 "Reden und Schweigen im ägyptischen Verständnis." AS 186–96.
Landes, George M.
1956 "The Fountain at Jazer." *BASOR* 144: 30–37.
1978 "Jonah: A *Māšāl*?" IW 137–58.
Lang, Bernhard
1972 *Die weisheitliche Lehrrede*. SBT 54. Stuttgart: KBW.
1979 "Schule und Unterricht im alten Israel." BETL 51: 186–201.
1981 "Vorläufer von Speiseeis in Bibel und Orient. Eine Untersuchung von Spr 25,13." AOAT 212: 219–32.

1983 "Die sieben Säulen der Weisheit (Sprüche IX 1) im Licht israelitischer Architektur." *VT* 33: 488–91.

1986 *Wisdom and the Book of Proverbs*. New York: Pilgrim.

1995 "Figure ancienne, figure nouvelle de la sagesse en Pr 1 à 9." Pp. 61–97 in *La Sagesse Biblique*. Lectio Divina 160. Paris: Cerf.

2004 "Women's Work, Household and Property in Two Mediterranean Societies: A Comparative Essay on Proverbs XXXI 10–31." *VT* 54: 188–207.

Lange, Hans O.

1925 *Das Weisheitsbuch des Amenemope*. Copenhagen: A. F. Host.

LaPointe, Roger

1970 "Foi et vérifiabilité dans le langage sapiential de rétribution." *Bib* 51: 349–67.

Lebram, J. C.

1965 "Nachbiblische Weisheitstraditionen." *VT* 15: 167–237.

Leclant, Jean

1963 "Documents nouveaux et points de vue récents sur les sagesses de l'Egypte ancienne." SPOA 4–26.

Leiden Peshitta, Proverbs. See Di Lella

Lelière, A., and Maillot, A.

1996 *Commentaire des Proverbes*. Paris: Cerf.

Lemaire, André

1981 *Les écoles et la formation de la Bible dans l'ancien Israel*. Fribourg: Editions Universitaires.

1984 "Sagesse et écoles." *VT* 34: 270–81.

1990 "The Sage in School and Temple." SIANE 165–81.

Levenson, Jon D.

1987 "The Sources of Torah: Psalm 119 and the Modes of Revelation in Second Temple Judaism." Pp. 559–784 in *Ancient Israelite Religion* (FS F. M. Cross). Ed. P. D. Miller, Jr., P. D. Hanson, and S. D. McBride. Philadelphia: Fortress.

Lévêque, Jean

1974 "Le Contrepoint théologique apporté par la réflexion sapientielle." BETL 33: 183–202.

1983 "Sagesses de l'Egypte ancienne." *Cahiers Evangile Sup*. 46.

1985 *Les motivations de l'acte moral dans le livre des "Proverbes."* Pp. 105–21 in *Ethique, Religion et Foi*. Ed. J. Doré et al. Paris: Beauchesne.

Levin, Yael

1985–86 "The 'Valiant Woman' in Jewish Liturgy." *Beth Miqra* 31: 339–47.

Levinson, Bernard

1997 *Deuteronomy and the Hermeneutics of Legal Innovation*. New York/Oxford: Oxford University Press.

Lewis, Theodore J.

1989 *Cults of the Dead in Ancient Israel and Ugarit*. Atlanta: Scholars Press.

1996 "Toward a Literary Translation of the Rapi'uma Texts." Pp. 115–49 in *Ugarit, Religion and Culture* (FS John Gibson). Ugaritisch-Biblische Literature 12. Ed. N. Wyatt, W. G. E. Watson, and J. B. Lloyd. Münster: Ugarit-Verlag.

Lichtenstein, Murray H.

1973 "The Poetry of Poetic Justice." *JANES* 5: 255–65.

1982 "Chiasm and Symmetry in Proverbs 31." *CBQ* 44: 202–11.

Lichtheim, Miriam

1973–80 *Ancient Egyptian Literature*. Vols. 1–3. Berkeley: University of California. [= AEL]

1979 "Observations on Papyrus Insinger." SAL 283–305.

1983 *Late Egyptian Wisdom Literature in the International Context*. OBO 52. Freiburg: Universitätslag. [= LEWL]

1992 *Maat in Egyptian Autobiographies and Related Studies*. OBO 120. Göttingen: Vandenhoeck & Ruprecht.

1997 *Moral Values in Ancient Egypt*. OBO 155. Göttingen: Vandenhoeck & Ruprecht.

Liddell, H. G., R. Scott, and H. S. Jones.

1996 *A Greek-English Lexicon*. 9th ed. with revised supplement. Oxford: Clarendon. [= LSJ]

Lindenberger, James M.

1983 *The Aramaic Proverbs of Ahiqar* (Johns Hopkins Near Eastern Studies). Baltimore: Johns Hopkins.

1994 *Ancient Aramaic and Hebrew Letters*. Atlanta, Ga.: Scholars Press.

Lipiński, Edward

1967 "Peninna, Iti'el et l'Athlète." *VT* 17 (1967) 68–75.

1968 "Macarismes et Psaumes de congratulation." *RB* 75: 321–67.

1973 "Les 'voyantes des rois' en Prov. XXXI 3." *VT* 23: 246.

Lipscomb, W. Lowndes, with James Sanders

1978 "Wisdom at Qumran." IW 277–85.

Loader, J. A.

1999 "Wisdom by (the) People for (the) People." ZAW 111: 211–33.

Loewenstamm, Samuel E.

1987 "Remarks on Proverbs XVII 12 and XX 27." *VT* 37: 221–24.

Loprieno, Antonio

1980 "Amenemope ed i Proverbii: Un Problema di Comparazione Lessicale." *Vicino Oriente* 3: 47–76.

Loretz, Oswald

1974 "ʾjš Mgn in Proverbia 6,11 und 24,34." *UF* 6: 476–77.

1985 "Ein kanaanäisches Fragment in Proverbia 9, 1–3a.5." *Studi Epigrafici e Linguistici* 2: 127–31.

Lowe, A. D.

1980 "Some Correct Renderings in Ancient Biblical Versions." Pp. 24–38 in *Oriental Studies Presented to B. J. Isserlin*. Ed. R. Y. Ebied and M. J. L. Young. Leiden: Brill.

Luc, Alex

2000 "The Title and Structure of Proverbs." ZAW 112: 252–55.

Lust, J., E. Eynikel, and K. Hauspie

1996 *A Greek-English Lexicon of the Septuagint*. Stuttgart: Deutsche Bibelgesellschaft. [= GELS]

Luzzatto, Samuel David (Shadal)

*1876 *Comments of Shadal on Prophets and Writings* [Hebrew]. Lemberg: Budweiser.

Lyons, Ellen L.

1987 "A Note on Proverbs 31.10–31." Pp. 237–45 in *The Listening Heart*. Ed. K. Hoglund et al. Sheffield: Sheffield Academic Press.

Lyu, Sun Myung

2005 "The Concept of Righteousness in the Book of Proverbs." Ph. D. Dissertation, University of Wisconsin–Madison.

Maag, V.

1965 "*Bᵉlijaʿal* im AT." *TZ* 21: 287–99.

MacDonald, John

1976 "The Status and Role of the Naʿar in Israelite Society." *JNES* 35: 147–70.

Mack, Burton L.

1970 "Wisdom Myth and Myth-ology." *Int* 24: 46–60.

1973 *Logos und Sophia*. SUNT 10. Göttingen: Vandenhoeck & Ruprecht.

1985 *Wisdom and the Hebrew Epic*. Chicago: University of Chicago.

Magass, Walter

1985 "Die Rezeptionsgeschichte der Proverbien." *Linguistica Biblica* 57: 61–80.

Maier, Christl

1995 *Die "fremde Frau" in Proverbien 1–9*. Göttingen: Vandenhoeck & Ruprecht.

Maillot, A.

1989 *Eve, ma Mère*. Paris: Letouzey et Ané.

Maire, Thierry

1995 "Proverbes XXII 17ss.: Enseignement à Shalishom?" *VT* 45: 227–38.

Malbim (Meir Loeb b. Yechiel Michael)

*1923 *Musar Haḥokmah* (Comm. on Proverbs). Vilna: Rom.

1982 *Malbim on Mishley*. Trans. Charles Wengrov. Jerusalem: Feldheim.

Malchow, Bruce V.

1985 "A Manual for Future Monarchs." *CBQ* 47: 238–45.

Malul, Meir

1997 "*Kappî* (Ex 33,22) and *bᵉḥopnāyw* (Prov 30,4): Hand or Skirt?" ZAW 109: 356–68.

Mandry, Stephen A.

1972 *There Is No God!: A Study of the Fool in the Old Testament*. Rome: Catholic Book Agency.

Marchant, E. C., trans.

[*1923*] *Xenophon . . . with an English Translation*. Loeb Classic Library. London: W. Heinemann; New York: G. P. Putnam's Sons.

Marcus, Ralph

1943 "The Tree of Life in Proverbs." *JBL* 62: 117–20.

1950–51 "On Biblical Hypostases of Wisdom." *HUCA* 25: 157–71.

Margalith, Othniel

1976 *'Arbaʿ Pᵉsuqim Bᵉsefer Mišley* ["Four Verses in Proverbs." (Hebrew)]. *Beth Mikra* 67: 517–23.

Martin, Tony Michael

1981 "Sages and Scribes." *SBT* 11: 93–94.

Matius, Hans-Georg von

1998 "Eine bisher nicht beachtete hebräische Textvariante zu Proverbia 24,16 aus dem Babylonische Talmud." *BN* 92: 16–20.

Maybaum, S.

1871 "Über die Sprache des Targum zu den Sprüchen und dessen Verhältnis zum Syrer." *Archiv für wiss. Erforschung des AT* 2: 66–93.

McAlpine, Thomas H.

1987 *Sleep, Divine and Human, in the OT*. JSOTSup 38. Sheffield: JSOT Press.

McCreesh, Thomas P.
1985 "Wisdom as Wife: Proverbs 31:10–31." *RB* 92: 25–46.
1991 *Biblical Sound and Sense: Poetic Sound Patterns in Proverbs 10–29.* JSOTS 128. Sheffield: Sheffield Academic Press.
McDowell, Andrea
2000 "Teachers and Students at Deir el-Medinah." Pp. 217–33 in *Deir el-Medinah in the Third Millennium AD.* Ed. R. J. Demarée and A. Egbert. Leiden: Nederlands Instituut voor het Nabije Oosten.
McKane, William
1965 *Prophets and Wise Men.* Naperville, Ill.: Allenson.
*1970 *Proverbs.* OTL. London: SCM.
1979 "Functions of Language and Objectives of Discourse according to Proverbs 10–30." BETL 51: 166–85.
McKinlay, Judith E.
1996 *Gendering Wisdom the Host.* JSOTSup 216. Sheffield: JSOT Press.
Meier, Samuel A.
1988 *The Messenger in the Ancient Semitic World.* HSM 44. Atlanta: Scholars Press.
1991 "Women and Communication in the Ancient Near East." *JAOS* 111: 540–47.
Meinhold, Arndt
1987 "Gott und Mensch in Proverbien III." *VT* 37: 468–77.
*1991 *Die Sprüche.* Zürcher Bibelkommentare 16 (2 vols). Zürich: Theologischer Verlag.
1992 "Der Umgang mit dem Feind nach Spr 25,21f. als Masstab für das Menschsein." Pp. 244–52 in *Alttestamentliche Glaube und Biblische Theologie* (FS H. D. Preuss). Ed. J. Hausmann and H.-J. Zobel. Stuttgart: Kohlhammer.
Melammed, Ezra Z.
1972 *Targum Mishley. Bar Ilan* 9: 18–91.
Metzger, Bruce M.
1972 "Literary Forgeries and Canonical Pseudepigrapha." *JBL* 91: 3–24.
Meyers, Carol L.
1974 *The Tabernacle Menorah: A Synthetic Study of a Symbol from the Biblical Cult.* ASORDS 2. Missoula, Mont.: Scholars Press.
Mezzacasa, Giacomo
*1913 *Il libro dei Proverbi di Salomone: Studie critico sulle aggiunte Greco-Alessandrine.* Rome: Pontifical Biblical Inst. [= Mezz.]
Michel, Dieter
1992 "Proverbia 2—ein Dokument der Geschichte der Weisheit." Pp. 233–43 in *Alttestamentlicher Glaube und Biblische Theologie* (FS H. D. Preuss). Ed. J. Hausmann and H.-J. Zobel. Stuttgart: Kohlhammer.
Mieder, Wolfgang
1974 "The Essence of Literary Proverb Studies." *Proverbium* 23: 888–94.
1993 *Proverbs Are Never Out of Season.* New York: Oxford University Press.
Mieder, Wolfgang, ed.
1994 *Wise Words: Essays on the Proverb.* New York: Garland.
Mieder, Wolfgang, S. A. Kingsbury, and K. B. Harder, eds.
1992 *A Dictionary of American Proverbs.* New York: Oxford University Press.
Milgrom, Jacob
*1991 *Leviticus 1–16.* AYB 3. New York: Doubleday (repr. New Haven: Yale University Press).

2000 *Leviticus 17–22*. AYB 3A. New York: Doubleday (repr. New Haven: Yale University Press).
2001 *Leviticus 23–27*. AYB 3B. New York: Doubleday (repr. New Haven: Yale University Press).

Miller, Cynthia L.
2003 "A Linguistic Approach to Ellipsis in Biblical Poetry." *Bulletin of Biblical Research* 13: 251–70.
2005 "Ellipsis Involving Negation in Biblical Poetry." SWA 37–52.

Miller, Patrick D.
1970 "Apotropaic Imagery in Proverbs 6,20–22." *JNES* 29: 129–30.
1982 *Sin and Judgment in the Prophets*. SBLMS 27. Chico, Calif.: Scholars Press.

Mills, Barriss, trans.
1963 *The Idylls of Theocritos*. West Lafayette, Ind.: Purdue University Press.

Minsker, Frank
1940 "Syriacisms in the Targum to the Book of Proverbs." Rabbinic Thesis. Hebrew Union College, Cincinnati.

Mitchell, Christopher
1987 *The Meaning of BRK "To Bless" in the OT*. SBLDS 95. Atlanta: Scholars Press.

Moffatt, James
*1954 A *New Translation of the Bible*. New York: Harper & Row (orig. 1922).

Montet, Pierre
1963 "Les fruits défendus et la confession des péchés." SPOA 53–62.

Moore, Rick D.
1994 "A Home for the Alien: Worldly Wisdom and Covenantal Confession in Proverbs 30,1–9." ZAW 106: 96–107.

Moran, William L.
1963 "The Ancient Near Eastern Background of the Love of God in Deuteronomy." *CBQ* 25: 77–87.

Morenz, Ludwig D.
1996 *Beiträge zur Schriftlichkeitskultur im Mittleren Reich und in der 2. Zwischenzeit*. Ägypten und Altes Testament. Wiesbaden: Harrassowitz.

Morenz, Siegfried
1953 "Feurige Kohlen auf dem Haupt." *TLZ* 78: 187–92.
1959 "Ein weitere Spur der Weisheit Amenopes in der Bibel." ZÄW 84: 79–80.
1963 "Aegyptologische Beiträge zur Erforschung der Weisheitsliteratur Israels." SPOA 63–72.

Morgan, Donn F.
1981 *Wisdom in the Old Testament Traditions*. Oxford: Blackwell.

Moss, Alan J.
1993 "Wisdom, the Wife, as Beloved, Home-Builder, and Teaching Mother." Ph.D. Diss., University of Queensland.

Mowinckel, Sigmund
1955 "Psalms and Wisdom." Pp. 205–24 in *Wisdom in Israel and in the Ancient Near East*. VTSup 3. Ed. M. Noth and D. Winton Thomas. Leiden: Brill.

Mühll, Peter von der
1976 "Das griechische Symposion." Pp. 483–505 in *Ausgewählte kleine Schriften*. Ed. B. Wyss. Basel: Reinhardt (orig. 1957).

Müller, August, and Emil Kautzsch
*1901 *The Book of Proverbs: A Critical Edition of the Hebrew Text*. Leipzig: Hinrichs.

Müller, Hans-Peter
1970 "Der Begriff 'Rätsel' im Alten Testament." *VT* 20: 465–89.
1977 "Die weisheitliche Lehrerzählung im Alten Testament und seiner Umwelt." *WO* 9: 77–98.

Muraoka, Takamitsu
1977 "Status Constructus of Adjectives in Biblical Hebrew." *VT* 27: 375–80.

Murphy, Roland E.
1962 "The Concept of Wisdom Literature." Pp. 46–54 in *The Bible in Current Catholic Thought*. Ed. John L. McKenzie. New York: Herder & Herder.
1969 "Form Criticism and Wisdom Literature." *CBQ* 31: 475–83.
1977 "What and Where Is Wisdom?" *Currents in Theology and Mission* 4: 283–87.
1978 "Wisdom—Theses and Hypotheses." IW 35–41.
1981a "The Faces of Wisdom in the Book of Proverbs." *Mélanges . . . Cazelles*. AOAT 212: 337–45.
1981b "Hebrew Wisdom." *JAOS* 101: 21–34.
1981c *Wisdom Literature* (Forms of the Old Testament Literature, XIII). Grand Rapids, Mich.: Eerdmans.
1984 "The Theological Contributions of Israel's Wisdom Literature." *Listening* 19: 30–40.
1985 "Wisdom and Creation." *JBL* 104: 3–11.
1986 "Wisdom's Song: Proverbs 1: 20–33." *CBQ* 48: 456–460.
1987 "Proverbs 22: 1–9." *Int* 41: 398–402.
1988 "Wisdom and Eros in Proverbs 1–9." *CBQ* 50: 600–603.
1990 *The Tree of Life*. New York: Doubleday.
1993 "Recent Research on Proverbs and Qoheleth." *Currents in Research: Biblical Studies* 1: 119–40.
1995 "The Personification of Wisdom" WAI 222–34.
*1998 *Proverbs* (WBC). Dallas, Tex.: Word Books.
2000 "Wisdom and Yahwism Revisited." Pp. 191–200 in *Shall Not the Judge of All the Earth Do What Is Right* (FS James L. Crenshaw). Ed. David Penchansky and Paul L. Redditt. Winona Lake, Ind.: Eisenbrauns.
2001 "Can the Book of Proverbs Be a Player in 'Biblical Theology?' " *Biblical Theology Bulletin* 31: 4–9.

Murray, Oswyn
1983 "The Greek Symposion in History." Pp. 257–72 in *Tria Corda* (FS A. Momigliano). Ed. E. Gabba. Como: New Press.

Naḥmias, Joseph ben Joseph
*[1912] *Commentary on Proverbs* [Hebrew]. Ed. Moshe Bamberger. Berlin: Itskowski.

Navarro Peiro, Angeles
1976 *Biblia babilónica: Proverbios*. Madrid: Consejo Superior de Investigaciones Cientficas.

Nebe, Gerhard Wilhelm
1972 "Lexikalische Bemerkungen zu *'wšwn* 'Fundament, Tiefe' in 4 Q 184, Prov 7,9 und 20,20." *RevQ* 8: 97–103.

Nel, Philip Johannes
1977 "The Concept 'Father' in the Wisdom Literature of the Ancient Near East." *JNSL* 5: 53–66.
1978 "A Proposed Method for Determining the Context of Wisdom Admonitions." *JNSL* 6: 33–39.
1981a "Authority in the Wisdom Admonitions." *ZAW* 93: 418–27.
1981b "The Genres of Wisdom Literature." *JNSL* 9: 129–42.
1982 *The Structure and Ethos of the Wisdom Admonitions in Proverbs*. BZAW 158. Berlin: Töpelmann.
1998 "Juxtaposition and Logic in the Wisdom Saying." *JNSL* 24: 115–27.
2000 "Righteousness from the Perspective of the Wisdom Literature of the Old Testament." *OTE* 13: 309–28.

Neuberg, Frank J.
1950 "An Unrecognized Meaning of Hebrew *Dôr*." *JNES* 9: 215–17.

Newsom, Carol A.
1989 "Woman and the Discourse of Patriarchal Wisdom: A Study of Proverbs 1–9." Pp. 142–60 in *Gender and Difference*. Ed. Peggy L. Day. Minneapolis: Fortress.
1992 "Proverbs." Pp. 145–52 in *The Women's Bible Commentary*. Ed. C. A. Newsom and S. H. Ringe. Louisville, Ky.: Westminster/John Knox.

Niccacci, Alviero
1979 "Proverbi 22,17–23,11." *Studium Biblicum Franciscanum* 29: 42–72.
1983 "Aspetti della religiositá egizia e biblica." *Terra Santa* 59: 188–92.
1984 "La teologia sapienziale nel quadro dell' Antico Testamento a proposito di alcuni studi recenti." *Studium Biblicum Franciscanum* 34: 7–14.
1990 *The Syntax of the Verb in Classical Hebrew Prose*. JSOTSup 86. Sheffield.

Niditch, Susan
1976 "A Test Case for Formal Variants in Proverbs." *JTS* 27: 192–94.

Nilsson, Martin P.
1955 *Die hellenistische Schule*. Munich: Beck.

Nir, Rafael
1995 *Hapitgam K^{e}text Za'ir* ["The Proverb as a Mini-Text" (Hebrew)]. *Hadassah Kantor Jubilee Book*. Ed. O. Schwarzwald and Y. Schlesinger. Ramat Gan: Bar Ilan.

Nöldeke, Theodor
1871 "Das Targum zu den Spruchen von der Peschita abhängig." *Archiv für wiss. Erforschung des ATs*, 2.1: 246–49.

Nordheim, Eckhard von
1985 *Die Lehre der Alten*. Vol. 2. Leiden: Brill.

Norrick, Neal R.
1985 "How Proverbs Mean: Semantic Studies in English Proverbs." *Trends in Linguistics* 27: 1–213.

North, F. S.
1965 "The Four Insatiables." *VT* 15: 281–82.

Noth, Martin, and D. Winton Thomas, eds.
1955 *Wisdom in Israel and in the Ancient Near East*. VTSup 3. Leiden: Brill.

Nougayrol, Jean
1963 "Les Sagesses babyloniennes: Etudes récentes et textes inédits." SPOA 41–51.

Nougayrol, Jean, Charles Virolleaud, and Emmanuel Laroche
1968 [Wisdom of Shube'awelum]. R.S. 22.439. *Ugaritica* 5: 273–97.
Novick, Tzvi
forthcoming "She Binds her Arms: Rereading Proverbs 31:17." *JBL 2009.*
Ockinga, Boyo
1994 *Die Gottebenbildlichkeit im alten Ägypten und im Alten Testament.* ÄAT 7. Wiesbaden: Harrassowitz.
Oesterley, W. O. E.
1927a "The Teaching of Amen-em-opet and the Old Testament." ZAW 45: 9–24.
1927b *The Wisdom of Egypt and the Old Testament.* London: Society for Promoting Christian Knowledge.
*1929 *The Book of Proverbs.* Westminster Commentaries. London: Methuen.
Olivier, J. P. J.
1975 "Schools and Wisdom Literature." *JNSL* 4: 49–60.
Orlinsky, Harry
1958 "Studies in the Septuagint of the Book of Job: Chapter II." *HUCA* 29: 229–71.
Otto, Eckart
1999 "Woher weiss der Mensch um Gut und Böse." Pp. 207–31 in *Recht und Ethos im AT—Gestalt und Wirkung* (FS Horst Seebass). Ed. S. Beyrle, G. Mayer, and H. Strauss. Neukirchen: Neukirchener.
Otzen, Benedict
1975 "Old Testament Wisdom Literature and Dualistic Thinking in Late Judaism." Pp. 146–57 in *Congress Volume: Edinburgh, 1974.* VTSup 28. Ed. G. W. Anderson. Leiden: Brill.
Owens, Robert J., Jr.
1998 "The Relationship Between the Targum and Peshitta Texts of the Book of Proverbs." *Targum Studies* 2: 105–207.
Oxford Book of Aphorisms
1983 *The Oxford Book of Aphorisms.* Ed. John Gross. Oxford: Oxford University Press.
Oyen, Hendrik van
1967 *Ethik des Alten Testaments.* Gütersloh: Gerd Mohn.
Paran, Meir
1978 *Ḥudo šel Hadegem Qal-Vaḥomer B^{e}sefer Mišley.* ["The Point of the A Fortiori Pattern in Proverbs" (Hebrew)]. *Beth Miqra* 73: 221–23.
Pardee, Dennis
1982 *Handbook of Ancient Hebrew Letters.* Chico, Calif.: Scholars Press. [= HAHL]
1988 *Ugaritic and Hebrew Poetic Parallelism, A Trial Cut (ʿnt I and Proverbs 2).* VTSup 39. Leiden: Brill.
Parker, Simon B., ed.
1997 *Ugaritic Narrative Poetry.* SBLWANS 9. Atlanta: Scholars Press.
Parkinson, R. B.
1997 *The Tale of Sinuhe and Other Ancient Egyptian Poems.* Oxford and New York: Clarendon. [= TS]
2002 *Poetry and Culture in Middle Kingdom Egypt.* London and New York: Continuum.

Passoni dell'Acqua, Anna
1982 "L'elemento intermedio nella versione greca di alcuni testi sapienziali e del libro Salmi." *RivB* 30: 79–90.
1984 "La Sapienza e in genere l'elemento intermediario tra Dio e il creato nelle versioni greche dell'Antico Testamento." *Ephemenides Litugicae* 98: 97–147.

Paul, Shalom
1979 "Unrecognized Biblical Legal Idioms." *RB* 86: 231–39.

Pedersen, Johannes
1955 "Wisdom and Immorality." Pp. 238–46 in *Wisdom in Israel and in the Ancient Near East*. Ed. Martin Noth and D. Winton Thomas. VTSup 3. Leiden: Brill.

Peels, Hendrick
1994 "Passion or Justice? The Interpretation of *b*[e]*yôm nāqām* in Proverbs vi 34." *VT* 44: 270–74.

Peet, T. Eric
1923 *The Rhind Mathematical Papyrus*. Liverpool: Liverpool University Press.

Peles, M.
1981 "Proverbia, nach ihren Themen geordnet." ZAW 93: 324.

Pemberton, Glenn D.
2005 "The Rhetoric of the Father in Proverbs 1–9." *JSOT* 30: 63–82.

Penchansky, David, and Paul L. Redditt, eds.
2000 *Shall Not the Judge of All the Earth Do What is Right?* (FS James L. Crenshaw). Winona Lake, Ind.: Eisenbrauns.

Penner, Terry
1992 "Socrates and the Early Dialogues." Pp. 121–69 in *The Cambridge Companion to Plato*. Ed. Richard Kraut. Cambridge: Cambridge University Press.
1992a "The Unity of Virtue." Pp. 162–84 in *Essays on the Philosophy of Socrates*. Ed. H. H. Benson. New York: Oxford University Press.

Perdue, Leo G.
1977 *Wisdom and Cult*. SBLDS 30. Missoula, Mont.: Scholars Press.
1981 "Limnality as a Social Setting for Wisdom Instructions." ZAW 93: 114–26.
1994 *Wisdom and Creation*. Nashville: Abingdon.
2000 "Revelation and the Problem of the Hidden God in Second Temple Wisdom Literature." Pp. 201–22 in *Shall Not the Judge of All the Earth Do What Is Right?* Ed. David Penchansky and Paul L. Redditt. Winona Lake, Ind.: Eisenbrauns.
2009 *Scribes, Sages, and Seers in Israel and the Ancient Near East*. Ed. by L. G. Perdue. FRLANT 219. Göttingen: Vandenhoeck & Ruprecht.

Perdue, Leo G., Bernard B. Scott, and William J. Wiseman, eds.
1993 *In Search of Wisdom: Essays in Memory of John G. Gammie*. Louisville, Ky: Westminster/John Knox.

Perles, Felix
1895 *Analekten zur Textkritik des Alten Testaments*. Munich: Theodor Ackermann.
1905–6 "The Fourteenth Edition of Gesenius-Buhl's Dictionary." *JQR* 18: 383–94.
1922 *Analekten zur Textkritik des Alten Testaments*. Neue Folge. Leipzig: Gustav Engel.

Perlitt, Lothar
1976 "Der Vater im Alten Testament." Pp. 50–101 in *Das Vaterbild in Mythos und Geschichte.* Ed by H. Tellenbach. Stuttgart: Kohlhammer.

Perry, Theodore A.
1993 *Dialogues with Kohelet.* University Park: Pennsylvania State University Press.
1993a *Wisdom Literature and the Structure of Proverbs.* University Park: Pennsylvania State University Press.

Peshitta. See Di Lella 1979

Peterson, Bengt Julius
1966 "A new fragment of *The Wisdom of Amenemope.*" *JEA* 52: 120–28.
1974 "A Note on the Wisdom of Amenemope 3. 9–4. 10." *Studia Aegyptiaca* 1: 323–27.

Pfeifer, Gerhard
1967 *Ursprung und Wesen der Hypostasenvorstellungen im Judentum.* Arbeiten zur Theologie, I. Reihe, Heft 31. Stuttgart: Calwer.

Pfeiffer, Robert H.
1926 "Edomitic Wisdom." ZAW 44: 13–25.
1933 "Wisdom and Vision in the Old Testament." ZAW 58: 93–101.

Piankoff, Alexandre
1930 *Le "Coeur" dans les textes égyptiens.* Paris: Geuthner.

Pinkuss, Hermann
*1894 "Die syrische Übersetzung der Proverbien." ZAW 14: 65–141, 161–222. [= Pink.]

Pirot, Jean
1950 "Le 'Mâšâl' dans l'Ancien Testament." *Recherches des Sciences Religieuses* 37: 565–80.

Plath, Siegfried
1963 *Furcht Gottes.* Arbeiten zur Theologie, II. Reihe, Bd. 2. Stuttgart: Calwer.

Plato. See Cooper, John

Pleins, J. David
1987 "Poverty in the Social World of the Wise." *JSOT* 37: 61–78.

Ploeg, J. van der
1952 *Spreuken uit de grondtekst vertaald en uigeledg.* Roermond: Romen.
1953 "Prov. XXV 23." *VT* 3: 189–92.

Plöger, Otto
1964 "Besprechung von U. Sklandy, *Die Ältesten Spruchsammlungen in Israel.*" *Gnomon* 36: 297–300.
1965 "Wahre die richtige Mitte; solch Mass ist in allem das Beste!" Pp. 159–173 in *Gottes Wort und Gottes Land.* Ed. H. G. Reventlow. Göttingen: Vandenhoeck & Ruprecht.
1971 "Zur Auslegung der Sentenzensammlung des Proverbienbuches." Pp. 402–16 in *Probleme Biblischer Theologie* (FS G. von Rad). Ed. Hans Walter Wolff. Munich: Chr. Kaiser.
*1984 *Sprüche Salomos (Proverbia).* *BKAT* XVII.

Polaćek, Adalbert
1969 "Gesellschaftliche und juristische Aspekte in altägyptischen Weisheitslehren." *Aegyptus* 49: 14–34.

Polk, Timothy

1983 "Paradigms, Parables, and *M^ešālîm*: On Reading the *Māšāl* in Scripture." *CBQ* 45: 564–83.

Polzin, Robert

1976 *Late Biblical Hebrew: Toward an Historical Typology of Biblical Hebrew Prose*. Missoula, Mont.: Scholars Press.

Pomeroy, Sarah B.

1975 *Goddesses, Whores, Wives, and Slaves: Women in Classical Antiquity*. New York: Schocken.

Porten, Bezalel, and Ada Yardeni

1993 *Literature, Accounts, Lists*. Vol. 3 of *Textbook of Aramaic Documents from Ancient Egypt. Lists*. Jerusalem: Hebrew University. [= TAD]

Posener, Georges

1938– *Catalogue des ostraca hiératiques littéraires de Deir el Médineh*. Cairo. Vols. 1 (1938; FIFAO I), 2 (1951; FIFAO XVIII = OHDM), 3.3 (1977–80) (FIFAO XX). [= COHL; reference by ostracon number]

1951 *Ostraca hiératiques littéraires de Deir el Médineh* (FIFAO XVIII). Cairo. [= OHDM]

1955 "L'Exorde de l'instruction éducative d'Amennakhte." *Rd*E 61–72.

1963a "Aménémopé 21,13 et bj3j.t au sens d"oracle.' " ZÄS 90: 98–102.

1963b "Sur une Sagesse égyptienne de basse époque (Papyrus Brooklyn no. 47.218.135)." SPOA 153–56.

1966 "Quatre tablettes scolaires de basse époque (Aménémopé et Hardjédef)." *RE* 18: 45–65.

1973a "Le chapitre IV d'Aménémopé." ZÄS 99: 129–35.

1973b "Une nouvelle tablette d'Aménémopé." *RE* 25: 251–52.

1976 *L'Enseignement loyaliste: Sagesse égyptienne du Moyen Empire*. Geneva: Librairie Droz.

1979 "L'Enseignement d'un homme à son fils." SAL 308–16.

1981 "Sur le monothéisme dans l'ancienne Egypte." *Mélanges . . . Cazelles*. AOAT 212: 347–51.

Postel, Henry J.

1976b "The Form and Function of the Motive Clause in Proverbs 10–29." Ph.D. Diss., University of Iowa.

Pottgieter, J. H.

2002 "The (Poetic) Rhetoric of Wisdom in Proverbs 3:1–12." *HTS* 58: 1357–74.

Preuss, Horst Dietrich

1970 "Erwägungen zum theologischen Ort alttestamentlicher Weisheitsliteratur." *EvT* 30: 417.

1972 "Das Gottesbild der älteren Weisheit Israels." Pp. 117–45 in *Studies in the Religion of Ancient Israel*. VTSup 23. Ed. G. W. Anderson. Leiden: Brill.

Prijs, Leo

1948 *Jüdische Tradition in der Septuaginta*. Leiden: Brill.

Prinsloo, G. T. M.

2002 "Reading Proverbs 3:1–12 in its Social and Ideological Context." *HTS* 58: 1375–1400.

Prior, William J.

1991 *Virtue and Knowledge*. London: Routledge.

Puech, Emile

1988 "Les Ecoles dans l'Israël préexilique: données epigraphiques." Pp. 189–203 in *Congress Volume: Jerusalem, 1986*. VTSup 40. Ed. J. A. Emerton. Leiden: Brill.

1991 "4Q525 et les Péricopes des Béatitudes en Ben Sira et Matthieu." *RB* 98: 80–106.

Qimḥi, David

[1847] *Sefer Hashorashim*. Ed. J. H. R. Biesenthal and F. Lebrecht. Berlin: Berthge, 1847 (repr. Jerusalem 1967).

Quack, Joachim Friedrich

1994 *Die Lehren des Ani*. OBO 141. Göttingen: Vandenhoeck & Ruprecht.

Rabin, Chaim

1948 "*Mᵉʿaṭ ḥibbuq yadayim liškab*. (Proverbs vi, 10; xxv, 33)." *JJS* 1: 197–98.

Rackham, H., trans.

1981 *Aristotle in 23 Volumes*, Vol. 20. Cambridge, Mass: Harvard University Press; London: Heinemann.

Rad, Gerhard von

1956 "Die ältere Weisheit Israels." *Kerygma und Dogma* 2: 54–72.

1970 *Weisheit in Israel*. Neukirchen-Vluyn: Neukirchener Verlag. [ET *Wisdom in Israel*; James D. Martin. London: SCM, 1972.]

Ramaroson, Léonard

1970 " 'Charbons ardents': 'sur la tête' ou 'pour le feu'? (Pr 25,22a–Rm 12,20 b)." *Bib* 51: 230–34.

Rankin, Oliver Shaw

1936 *Israel's Wisdom Literature*. New York: Schocken.

Ranston, Harry

1930 *The Old Testament Wisdom Books and Their Teaching*. London: Epworth.

Ray, John D.

1995 "Egyptian Wisdom Literature. WAI 17–29.

Redford, Donald B.

1992 *Egypt, Canaan, and Israel in Ancient Times*. Princeton: Princeton University Press.

2001 *Oxford Encyclopedia of Ancient Egypt*. 3 vols. Edited by D. B. Ray. Oxford: Oxford University Press. [= OEAE]

Reider, Joseph

1957 *The Book of Wisdom*. New York: Harper.

1966 *An Index to Aquila*. VTSup 12. Ed. Nigel Turner. Leiden: Brill.

Reitzenstein, Richard

1904 *Poimandres*. Darmstadt: Wissenschaftliche Buchgesellschaft (repr. 1966).

Rendtorff, Rolf

1977 "Geschichtliches und weisheitliches Denken im Alten Testament." Pp. 344–53 in *Beiträge zur at. Theologie* (FS W. Zimmerli). Ed. Herbert Donner, Robert Hanhart, and Rudolf Smend. Göttingen: Vandenhoeck & Ruprecht.

Renfroe, F.

1989 "The Effect of Redaction on the Structure of Prov 1,1–6." ZAW 101: 291–93.

Revell, Ernest J.

1989 "The System of the Verb in Standard Biblical Prose." *HUCA* 60: 1–37.

Rice, Eugene, Jr.,

1958 *The Renaissance Idea of Wisdom*. Cambridge, Mass.: Harvard University Press.

Richardson, H. N.
1955 "Some Notes on *lyṣ* and Its Derivatives." *VT* 5: 163–79.
Richter, Hans-Friedemann
2001 "Hielt Agur sich für den Dümmsten aller Menschen?" ZAW 113: 419–21.
Richter, Wolfgang
1966 *Recht und Ethos*. SANT XV. München: Kösel.
Rinaldi, G.
1982 "Nota: *Maktêš* (Prov 27,22)." *Bibbia e Oriente* 24/133: 174.
Ringgren, Helmer
1947 *Word and Wisdom: Studies in the Hypostatization of Divine Qualities and Functions in the Ancient Near East*. Lund: Ohlsson.
*1962 *Sprüche*. ATD 16. Göttingen: Vandenhoeck & Ruprecht.
Robert, André
1934 "Les Attaches Littéraires Bibliques de Prov. I–IX." *RB* 43: 42–68, 172–204, 374–84.
1939 "Le Psaume cxix et les sapientiaux." *RB* 48: 20.
1940 "Le Yahwisme de Prov 10,1–22,16; 25–29." Pp. 163–82 in *Mémorial Lagrange*. Paris: Gabalda.
Roberts, Colin H.
1950 *The Antinoopolis Papyri*. Part I. London: Egypt Exploration Society.
Rofé, Alexander
1978 "The Angel in Qohelet 5:5 in the Light of a Sapiential Disputation Formula." *Eretz Israel* 14: 105–109.
2001 "*ʾEšet ḥayil, gunē synetē*, and the Editing of the Book of Proverbs" (Hebrew). Pp. 382–90 in *Teshura Lišmuel* (FS S. Ahituv). Jerusalem: Ben Gurion University and Mosad Bialik.
2002a "The Valiant Woman, *gunē sunetē*, and the Redaction of the Book of Proverbs." Pp. 144–55 in *Vergegenwärtigung des Alten Testaments*. Ed. Ch. Bultmann, W. Dietrich, and Ch. Levin. Göttingen: Vandenhoeck & Ruprecht.
2002b *Deuteronomy: Issues and Interpretation*. London: T. & T. Clark.
Rogers, Jessie
2001 "Wisdom—Woman or Angel in Sirach 24?" *JNSL* 27: 45–56.
Römheld, Diethard
1989 *Wege der Weisheit*. BZAW 184. Berlin: de Gruyter.
Roth, Martha T.
1987 "Age at Marriage and the Household: A Study of Neo-Babylonian and Neo-Assyrian Forms." *Comparative Studies in Society and History* 29: 715–39.
Roth, Wolfgang M. W.
1960 "NBL." *VT* 10: 394–409.
1965 *Numerical Sayings in the OT*. VTSup 13. Leiden: Brill.
Rottenberg, Meir
1980 "Recent Exegesis of the Proverbs of Solomon." *Beth Mikra* 82: 263–71.
1983 *Hapitgamim šebesefer Mišley*. Tel Aviv: Reshafim.
Rudman, Dominic
2001 *Determinism in the Book of Ecclesiastes*. JSOTSup 316. Sheffield: Sheffield Academic Press.
Ruffle, John
1977 "The Teaching of Amenemope and Its Connection to the Book of Proverbs." *TynBul* 28: 29–68.

Rüger, Hans Peter
1959 "Vier Aquila-Glossen in einem hebräischen Proverbien-Fragment aus der Kairo-Geniza." *ZNW* 50: 275–77.
1977 "Amon—Pflegekind. Zur Auslegungsgeschichte von Prv. 8: 30a." Pp. 154–63 in *Übersetzung und Deutung* (FS A. R. Hulst). Nijkerk: Callenbach.
1981 "Die gestaffelten Zahlensprüche des ATs und aram. Achikar 92." *VT* 31: 229–34.
1991 *Die Weisheitsschrift aus der Kairoer Geniza*. WUNT 53. Tübingen: Mohr.

Ruhl, Charles
1989 *On Monosemy*. Albany: State University of New York Press.

Rylaarsdam, J. Coert
1946 *Revelation in Jewish Wisdom Literature*. Chicago: University of Chicago Press.

Saʿadia ben Yosef Gaon
[1976] *Commentary on Proverbs*. Trans. to Hebrew from Judeo-Arabic and ed. by Yosef ben David Qafiḥ. Jerusalem: Hava'ad Lehotza'at Sifrey Rasag.
[*1969*] *Ha'egron*. Ed. N. Allony. Jerusalem: Academy of the Hebrew Language.

Saebø, Magne
1986 "From Collection to Book." Proceedings of the Ninth World Congress of Jewish Studies, Division A, Jerusalem: World Union of Jewish Studies.

Sagesses du Proche-orient ancien
1963 Paris: Presses Universitaires. [= SPOA]

Sakenfield, Katherine D.
1978 *The Meaning of Ḥesed in the Hebrew Bible*. HSS 17. Missoula, Mont.: Scholars Press.

Salisbury, Murray
1994 "Hebrew Proverbs and How to Translate Them." Pp. 434–61 in *Biblical Hebrew and Discourse Linguistics*. Ed. Robert D. Bergen. Dallas, Tex.: Summer Inst. of Linguistics (Eisenbrauns).

Sandelin, K.-G.
1986 *Wisdom as Nourisher*. Abo: Academiae Aboensis.

Sander-Hanson, C. E.
1956 *Die Texte der Metternichstele*. Analecta Äegyptiaca 7. Copenhägen: Munksgaard.

Sanders, Jack T.
2001 "When Sacred Canopies Collide. The Reception of the Torah of Moses in the Wisdom Literature of the Second-Temple Period." *JSJ* 32: 121–36.

Sanders, James A.
1967 *The Dead Sea Psalms Scroll*. Ithaca, N. Y.: Cornell.

Sandoval, Timothy J.
2005 *The Discourse of Wealth and Poverty in the Book of Proverbs*. Leiden: Brill.
2006 "Revisiting the Prologue of Proverbs." *JBL* 126: 455–73.

Santas, Gerasimos X.
1979 *Socrates: Philosophy in Plato's Early Dialogues*. London: Routledge & Kegan Paul.

Sauer, Georg
1963 *Die Sprüche Agurs*. BWANT 4. Stuttgart: Kohlhammer.

Saunders, Trevor J.
1987 *Plato: Early Socratic Dialogues*. New York: Viking Penguin.

Savignac, Jean de
1954 "Note sur le sens du verset VIII 22 des Proverbes." *VT* 4: 429–432.
Scharff, Alexander
1941–42 "Die Lehre für Kagemni." *ZÄS* 77: 13–21.
Schechter, Solomon and C. Taylor
1899 *The Wisdom of Ben Sira*. Cambridge: Cambridge University Press.
Schencke, Wilhelm
1913 *Die Chokma (Sophia) in der jüdischen Hypostasenspekulation*. Kristiania: Jacob Dybwad.
Scherer, Andreas
1999 *Das weise Wort und seine Wirkung: Eine Untersuchung zur Komposition und Redaktion von Proverbia 10,1–22,16*. WMANT 83. Neukirchen: Neukirchener Verlag.
2003 " 'Frau Weisheit' und die 'fremde Frau': Personifikation und Symbolfigur in den Sprüchen Salomos." *Biblische Notizen* 119–120: 35–41.
Schipper, Berndt U.
1999 *Israel und Ägypten in der Königzeit*. OBO 170. Göttingen: Vandenhoeck & Ruprecht.
Schmid, Hans Heinrich
1966 *Wesen und Geschichte der Weisheit*. BZAW 101. Berlin: Töpelmann.
1968 *Gerechtigkeit als Weltordnung*. BHT 40. Tübingen.
1988 "Alttestamentliche Weisheit und ihre Rationalität." *Studia Philosophica* 47: 11–31.
Schmidt, Johann
1936 *Studien zur Stilistik der alttestamentlichen Spruchliteratur*. Alttestamentliche Abhandlungen 13,3; Münster: Aschendorff.
Schmidt, Werner H.
1992 "Wie kann der Mensch seinin Weg verstehen." Pp. 287–97 in *Alttestamentliche Glaube und Biblische Theologie* (FS H. D. Preuss). Ed. J. Hausmann and H.-J. Zobel. Stuttgart: Kohlhammer.
Schmitt, Armin
2003 "Enkomien in griechischer Literatur." Pp. 359–81 in *Auf den Spuren der schriftgelehrten Weisen* (FS Johannes Marböck). Ed. Irmtrad Fischer et al. Berlin: de Gruyter.
Schnabel, Eckhard J.
1985 *Law and Wisdom from Ben Sira to Paul*. WUNT 2. Reihe. Tübingen: Mohr.
Schneider, Heinrich
1961 "Die 'Töchter des Blutegels in Spr 30,15." Pp. 257–64 in *Lex Tua Veritas* (FS Hubert Junker). Ed. Heinrich Gross and Franz Mussner. Trier: Paulinus.
1962 *Die Sprüche Salomos*. Herder Bibelkommentar. Freiburg: Herder.
Scholem, Gershom
1965 *On the Kabbalah and Its Symbolism*. Trans. R. Manheim. London: Routledge and Kegan Paul.
Schroer, Silvia
1991 "Die göttliche Weisheit und der nachexilische Monotheismus." Pp. 151–82 in *Der eine Gott und die Göttin*. Ed. M.-T. Wacker and E. Zenger. QD 135. Freiburg: Herder.
1996 *Die Weisheit hat ihr Haus gebaut*. Mainz: Grünwald.

Scoralick, Ruth

1995 *Einzelspruch und Sammlung: Komposition im Buch der Sprichwörter Kapitel 10–15*. BZAW 232. Berlin: de Gruyter.

Scott, Charles T.

1976 "On Defining the Riddle: The Problem of a Structural Unit." Pp. 77–90 in *Folklore Genres*. Ed. Dan Ben-Amos. Austin: University of Texas.

Scott, Melville

*1927 *Textual Discoveries in Proverbs, Psalms, and Isaiah*. New York: Macmillan.

Scott, R. B. Y.

1955 "Solomon and the Beginnings of Wisdom in Israel." Pp. 262–79 in *Wisdom in Israel and in the Ancient Near East*. VTSup 3. Ed. M. Noth and D. Winton Thomas. Leiden: Brill.

1960 "Wisdom in Creation: The *'Amon* of Proverbs VIII 30." *VT* 10: 213–23.

*1965 *Proverbs, Ecclesiastes*. AYB 18. New York (repr. New Haven: Yale University Press).

1970 "The Study of Wisdom Literature." *Int* 24: 21–45.

1972 "Wise and Foolish, Righteous and Wicked" [Prv 10–29]. Pp. 146–65 in *Studies in the Religion of Ancient Israel*. VTSup 23. Ed. G. W. Anderson. Leiden: Brill.

Seeligmann, I. L.

1953 "Voraussetzungen der Midraschexegese." Pp. 150–81 in *Congress Volume: Copenhagen, 1953*. VTSup 1. Ed. G. W. Anderson. Leiden: Brill.

Segal, Alan F.

2002 *Two Powers in Heaven*. Leiden: Brill.

Segal, Moshe Zvi

1958 *Sefer Ben Sira Hašalem* [*The Complete Book of Ben Sira*]. Jerusalem: Bialik.

Segert, Stanislav

1987 " 'Live coals heaped on the head.' " Pp. 159–64 in *Love and Death in the Ancient Near East: Essays in Honor of M. H. Pope*. Ed. J. H. Marks and R. M. Good. Guilford, Conn.: Four Quarters.

Seitel, Peter

1976 "Proverbs: A Social Use of Metaphor." Pp. 125–43 in *Folklore Genres*. Ed. Dan Ben-Amos. Austin: University of Texas.

Seow, Choon Leong

1997 *Ecclesiastes*. AYB 18C. Garden City, N.Y.: Doubleday (repr. New Haven: Yale University Press).

Sethe, Kurt

1959 *Ägyptische Lesestücke*. Darmstadt: Wissenschaftliche Buchgesellschaft.

Shachter, Jacob

1963 *Sefer Mišley Basifrut Hatalmudit* [*The Book of Proverbs in Talmudic Literature*] (includes his commentary, "Words of Jacob.") Jerusalem, pub. by author.

Shapiro, David

1987 "Proverbs." Pp. 313–30 in *Congregation*. Ed. David Rosenberg. New York: Harcourt Brace Jovanovich.

Sheppard, Gerald T.

1973 "Wisdom and Torah: The Interpretation of Deuteronomy Underlying Sirach

24:23." Pp. 166–76 in *Biblical and Near Eastern Studies* (FS W. S. La Sor). Ed. G. A Tuttle. Grand Rapids, Mich.: Eerdmans.

1980 *Wisdom as a Hermeneutical Construct*. BZAW 151. Berlin: de Gruyter.

Shirun-Grumach, Irene

1972 *Untersuchungen zur Lebenslehre des Amenope*. Münchner Ägyptologische Studien 23. Munich: Deutscher Kunstverlag.

1979 "Bemerkungen zu Rhythmus, Form und Inhalt in der Weisheit." SAL 317–51.

Shupak, Nili

1984–85 "Matbeᵉot lašon verišumim miṣri'im baḥokhmah hamiqra'it" ("Egyptian Idioms and Impressions in Biblical Wisdom") [Hebrew]. *Tarbiz* 54: 475–84.

1987 "The 'Sitz im Leben' of the Book of Proverbs in the Light of a Comparison of Biblical and Egyptian Wisdom Literature." *RB* 94: 98–119.

1993 *Where Can Wisdom Be Found?* OBO 130. Göttingen: Vandenhoeck & Ruprecht.

1999 "The Father's Instruction to the Son in Ancient Egypt" [Hebrew]. Pp. 13–21 in *Hinukh Vehistoria*. Ed. R. Feldhay. Jerusalem: Merkaz Zalman Shazar.

1999a *Proverbs* [Hebrew]. *Olam Hatanakh*. Tel Aviv: Divrey Hayamim.

2005 "The Instruction of Amenemope and Proverbs 22:17–24:22 from the Perspective of Contemporary Research." SWA 203–20.

Simpson, D. C.

1926 "The Hebrew Book of Proverbs and the Teaching of Amenophis." *JEA* 12. 232–39.

Sjöberg, Ake W.

1976 "The Old Babylonian Eduba." Pp. 159–79 in *Sumerological Studies in Honor of T. Jacobsen*. Ed. St. J. Lieberman. Chicago: University of Chicago Press.

Skehan, Patrick W.

1946 "Proverbs 5: 15–19 and 6: 20–24." *CBQ* 8: 290–97. [Revised in Skehan 1971: 1–8]

1947 "The Seven Columns of Wisdom's House in Proverbs 1–9." *CBQ* 9: 190–98.

1948 "A Single Editor for the Whole Book of Proverbs. *CBQ* 10: 115–30.

1967 "Wisdom's house." *CBQ* 29: 162–80.

1971 *Studies in Israelite Poetry and Wisdom*. CBQMS 1. Washington, D.C.: Catholic Biblical Association.

1971a "A Single Editor for the Whole Book of Proverbs. Pp. 15–26 in Skehan, *Studies* (1971). [Revision of article in *CBQ* 10 [1948] 115–30.]

1971b "Wisdom's house." Pp. 27–45 in Skehan, *Studies* (1971). [Revision of Skehan 1967 (*CBQ* 29: 162–80).]

1979 "Structures in Poems on Wisdom: Proverbs 8 and Sirach 24." *CBQ* 41: 365–79.

Skehan, Patrick, and Alexander A. Di Lella

*1987 *The Wisdom of Ben Sira*. AYB 39. New York: Doubleday (repr. New Haven: Yale University Press).

Skladny, Udo

1962 *Die ältesten Spruchsammlungen in Israel*. Göttingen: Vandenhoeck & Ruprecht.

Slater, William J.

1991 *Dining in a Classical Context*. Ed. W. J. Slater. Ann Arbor: University of Michigan Press.

Smalley, Beryl

1986 *Medieval Exegesis of Wisdom Literature*. Ed. Roland E. Murphy. Atlanta: Scholars Press.

Smend, Rudolph

1995 "The Interpretation of Wisdom in Nineteenth Century Scholarship." WAI 257–68.

Smith, Mark S.

2001 *The Origins of Biblical Monotheism*. Oxford: Oxford University Press.

Snaith, Norman

1967 "Biblical Quotations in the Hebrew of Ecclesiasticus." *JTS* 18: 1–12.

Sneed, Mark

1995 "Wisdom and Class: A Review and Critique." *JAAR* 62: 651–71.

1996 "The Class Culture of Proverbs: Eliminating Stereotypes." *JSOT* 10: 296–308.

Snell, Daniel C.

1983 " 'Taking Souls' in Proverbs XI 30." *VT* 33: 362–65.

1987 "Notes on Love and Death in Proverbs." Pp. 165–68 in *Love and Death in the Ancient Near East: Essays in Honor of M. H. Pope*. Ed. J. H. Marks and R. M. Good. Guilford, Conn.: Four Quarters.

1989 "The Wheel in Proverbs XX 26." *VT* 39: 503–507.

1991 "The Most Obscure Verse in Proverbs: Proverbs XXVI 10." *VT* 41: 353–55.

1993 *Twice-Told Proverbs and the Composition of the Book of Proverbs*. Winona Lake, Ind.: Eisenbrauns.

1998 "The Relation Between the Targum and the Peshiṭta of Proverbs." ZAW 110: 72–74.

Snijders, L. A.

1954 "The Meaning of *zar* in the OT." *OTS* 10: 1–154.

Socrates. See Plato

Soden, Wolfram von

1990 "Kränkung, nicht Schläge in Sprüche 20,30." ZAW 102: 120–21.

Sommers, C. F.

1989 *Vice and Virtue in Everyday Life*. San Diego: Harcourt, Brace, and Jovanovich.

Sperber, Alexander

1966 *A Historical Grammar of Biblical Hebrew*. Leiden: Brill.

Spiegel, Joachim

1935 *Die Präambel des Amenemope und die Zielsetzung der ägyptischen Weisheitsliteratur*. Glückstadt: J. J. Augustin.

Stadelmann, Luis I. J.

1970 *The Hebrew Conception of the World*. Rome: Pontifical Biblical Institute.

Steiert, Franz-Josef

1990 *Die Weisheit Israels—ein Fremdkörper im Alten Testament?* Freiburg: Herder.

Steiner, Richard C.

2000 "Does the Biblical Hebrew Conjunction *w*- Have Many Meanings?" *JBL* 119: 249–67.

Steinmann, Andrew E.
2001 "Three Things . . . Four Things . . . Seven Things: The Coherence of Proverbs 30:1–33 and the Unity of Proverbs 30." *HS* 42: 59–66.
Story, Solfrid
1993 "On Proverbs and Riddles." *SJOT* 7: 270–84.
Støry, Cullen I. K.
1945 "The Book of Proverbs and Northwest Semitic Literature." *JBL* 64: 319–37.
Suter, David Winston
1981 "*Māšāl* in the Similitudes of Enoch." *JBL* 100: 193–212.
Suys, Emil
1934 "La théologie d'Aménémopé." *Miscellania Biblica* 2: 1–36.
1935 *La Sagesse d'Ani*. Rome: Pontifical Biblical Institute.
Swete, Henry Barclay
1907 *The Old Testament in Greek*. Cambridge: Cambridge University Press.
Talmage, Frank (Ephraim)
1990 *Perušim Lᵉsefer Mišley Lᵉveyt Qimḥi* [*Commentaries on the Book of Proverbs by Joseph Kimḥi, Moses Kimḥi, and David Kimḥi* (Hebrew)]. Jerusalem: Magnes.
Talmon, Shemaryahu
1960 "Double Readings in the Massoretic Text." *Textus* 1: 144–84.
1981 "The Ancient Hebrew Alphabet and Biblical Text Criticism." Pp. 497–530 in *Mélanges Dominique Barthélemy*. Ed. P. Casetti, O. Keel, and A. Schenken. OBO 38. Göttingen: Vandenhoeck & Ruprecht.
2003 "*The Signification of ʾḥryt and ʾḥryt hymym* in the Hebrew Bible." Pp. 795–810 in *Emanuel* (F.S. Emanuel Tov). Ed. S. Paul, R. A. Kraft, L. H. Schiffman, and W. W. Fields. VTSup 94. Leiden: Brill.
Tate, Marvin E.
1990 *Psalms 51–100*. WBC 20. Dallas, Tex.: Word.
Tavares, Ricardo
2007 *Eine königliche Weisheitslehre?* OBO 234. Fribourg: Vandenhoeck & Ruprecht.
Taylor, Archer
1987 "The Study of Proverbs." *Proverbium* 1: 1–10.
Thackeray, H. St. J.
1912 "The Poetry of the Greek Book of Proverbs." *JTS* 13: 46–66.
Theocritus. See Mills, Barriss
Thomas, D. Winton
1934 "The Root *š-n-h* = [Arabic] *sny* in Hebrew." ZAW 52: 237.
1935 "The Root *šnh* = [Arabic] *sny* in Hebrew." ZAW 2–3: 207–208.
1937a "Notes on Some Passages in the Book of Proverbs." *JTS* 38: 400–403.
1937b "The Root *šnh* = [Arab.] *sny* in Hebrew, II." ZAW 55: 174–6.
1941 "A Note on *lyqht* in Proverbs xxx. 17." *JTS* 42: 154–55.
1953 "A Note on *bl ydʿh* in Prov 9: 13." *JTS* 4: 23–24.
1955 "Textual and Philological Notes on Some Passages in the Book of Proverbs." Pp. 280–92 in *Wisdom in Israel and in the Ancient Near East*. VTSup 3. Ed. M. Noth and D. Winton Thomas. Leiden: Brill.
1962 "*ʾw* in Proverbs XXXI 4." *VT* 12: 499–500.
1963a "*Blyʿl* in the Old Testament." Pp. 11–19 in *Biblical and Patristic Studies in Memory of R.P. Casey*. Ed. J. N. Birdsall and R. W. Thomson. Freiburg: Herder.

1963b "A Note on *daʿat* in Proverbs XXII. 12." *JTS* 14: 93–94.
1964a "Additional Notes on the Root *ydʿ* in Hebrew." *JTS* 15: 54–57.
1964b "The Meaning of *ḥataʾt* in Proverbs X. 16." *JTS* 15: 295–96.
1965 "Notes on some Passages in the Book of Proverbs." *VT* 15: 271–79.

Thompson, John Mark
1974 *The Form and Function of Proverbs in Ancient Israel*. The Hague: Mouton.

Tigay, Jeffrey H.
1996 *Deuteronomy*. The JPS Torah Commentary. Philadelphia: Jewish Publication Society.

Toeg, Aryeh
1974 "*Bammidbar 15: 22–31—Midraš Halakah*" ["A Halakhic Midrash in Num 15: 22–31" (Hebrew]). *Tarbiz* 43: 1–20.

Toorn, Karel van der
1989 "Female Prostitution in Payment of Vows in Ancient Israel." *JBL* 108: 193–205.

Torrey, Charles C.
1954 "Proverbs, Chapter 30." *JBL* 73: 93–96.

Tov, Emanuel
1979 "Loan-words, Homophony, and Transliteration in the Septuagint." *Bib* 60: 216–36.
1990 "Recensional Differences Between the Masoretic Text and the Septuagint of Proverbs." Pp. 43–56 in *Of Scribes and Schools*. Ed. H. W. Attridge, J. J. Collins, and T. H. Tobin. Lanham, Md.: University Press of America.
1992 *Textual Criticism of the Hebrew Bible*. Minneapolis: Fortress.
2003 "The Nature of the Large-Scale Differences Between the LXX and MT, S, T, V, Compared with Similar Evidence in Other Sources." Pp. 121–43 in *The Earliest Text of the Hebrew Bible*. Ed. Adrian Schenker. LXXCS 52. Leiden: Brill.

Towner, W. Sibley
1973 *The Rabbinic 'Enumeration of Scriptural Examples.'* Leiden: Brill.
1995 "Proverbs and Its Successors." Pp. 157–75 in *Old Testament Interpretation*. Ed. J. L. Mays, D. L. Petersen, and K. H. Richards. Nashville: Abingdon.

Toy, Crawford H.
*1899 *The Book of Proverbs*. ICC. Edinburgh: T. & T. Clark (repr. 1959).

Trible, Phyllis
1975 "Wisdom Builds a Poem: The Architecture of Proverbs 1: 20–33." *JBL* 94: 509–18.

Troxel, Ronald L., Kelvin G. Friebel, and Dennis R. Magary
2005 *Seeking Out the Wisdom of the Ancients. Essays Offered to Honor Michael V. Fox on the Occasion of His Sixty-Fifth Birthday*. Winona Lake, Ind.: Eisenbrauns. [= SWA]

Tsumura, David
1978 "The Vetitive Particle *ʾy* and the Poetic Structure of Proverbs 31: 4." *Annual of the Japanese Biblical Institute* 4: 23–31.

Tur-Sinai, Naphtali Herz [= Harry Torczyner]
1924 "The Riddle in the Bible." *HUCA* 1: 125–49.
*1947 *Mišley Šᵉlomoh*. Tel Aviv: Yavneh.
1967 *Pᵉšuṭo šel Miqraʾ* [*The Plain Meaning of the Bible* (Hebrew)] 4.1. Jerusalem: Kiryat Sefer.

Ulrich, Eugene C., Jr.

2000 *Qumran Cave 4. XI: Psalms to Chronicles.* DJD XVI, pp. 180–86. Ed. E. Ulrich et al. Oxford: Clarendon.

Ulrich, Eugene, et al., ed.

1992 *Priests, Prophets, and Scribes* (FS J. Blenkinsopp). JSOTSup 149. Sheffield: Sheffield Academic Press.

Van Leeuwen, Raymond C.

1986a "Proverbs XXV 27 Once Again." *VT* 36: 105–14.

1986b "Proverbs 30: 21–23 and the Biblical World Upside Down." *JBL* 105: 599–610.

1986c "A Technical Metallurgical Use of *yṣ'*." ZAW 98: 112–13.

1988 *Context and Meaning in Proverbs 25–27.* SBLDS 96. Atlanta: Scholars Press.

1990a "Limnality and Worldview in Proverbs 1–9." *Semeia* 50: 111–44.

1990b "The Sage in the Prophetic Literature." SIANE 295–306.

1992 "Wealth and Poverty: System and Contradiction in Proverbs." *HS* 33: 25–36.

*1997 *Proverbs*. New Interpreter's Bible, Vol. V. Nashville: Abingdon.

1997a "The Background to Proverbs 30:4aα." Pp. 102–21 in *Wisdom, You Are My Sister* (FS R. E. Murphy). Ed. M. L. Barré (CBQMS 29). Washington: Catholic Biblical Association.

1997b "Scribal Wisdom and a Biblical Proverb at Qumran." *DSD* 4: 255–64.

Vattioni, F.

1967a "La casa della saggezza (Prov. 9,1; 14,1)." *Augustinianum* 7: 349–51.

1967b "La 'straniera' nel libro dei Proverbi." *Augustinianum* 7: 352–57.

1969a "Note sul libro dei Proverbi." *Augustinianum* 9: 124–33.

1969b "Note sul libro dei Proverbi II." *Augustinianum* 9: 531–36.

1972 "Studi sul Libro de Proverbi." *Augustinianum* 12: 121–68.

Vawter, Bruce

1972 "Intimations of Immortality and the OT." *JBL* 91: 158–71.

1980 "Prov 8: 22: Wisdom and Creation." *JBL* 99: 205–16.

1986 "Yahweh: Lord of the Heavens and the Earth." *CBQ* 48: 461–67.

Vergote, Jozef

1963 "La notion de Dieu dans les livres de sagesse égyptiens." SPOA 159–190.

Vílchez-Líndez, José

1995 "Panorama des recherches actuelles sur la sagesse dans l'Ancien Testament." Pp. 129–37 in *La Sagesse Biblique.* Lectio Divina 160. Paris: Cerf.

Vischer, Wilhelm

1975 "L'Hymne de la sagesse dans les Proverbs de Salomon 8,22–31." *Etudes Théologiques et Religieuses* 50: 175–94.

Visotzky, Baruch (Barton)

1990 *Midrash Mishle.* New York: Jewish Theological Seminary.

1991 *Reading the Book.* New York: Doubleday.

1992 *The Midrash on Proverbs.* New Haven, Conn.: Yale University Press.

Volten, Aksel

1937 *Studien zum Weisheitsbuch des Anii.* Kopenhagen: Levin & Munksgaard.

1941 *Das Demotische Weisheitsbuch.* Analecta Ägytiaca II. Copenhagen: Munksgaard.

1945 *Zwei altägyptische politische Schriften*. Analecta Ägyptiaca IV. Copenhagen: Munksgaard.
1963 "Der Begriff der Maat in den Ägyptischen Weisheitstexten." SPOA 73–102.

Volz, Paul
1921 *Hiob und Weisheit*. SAT 3,2. Göttingen: Vandenhoeck & Ruprecht.

Vries, Simon J. de
1978 "Observations on Quantitative and Qualitative Time in Wisdom and Apocalyptic." IW 263–76.

Waard, Jan de
1993 "Metathesis as a Translation Technique?" Pp. 249–60 in *Traducere Navem* (FS K. Reiss). *Studia Translatologica* A, 3. Tampere: Tampereen.
1998 "4QProv and Textual Criticism." *Textus* 19: 87–96.
2001 "Some Unusual Translation Techniques Employed by the Greek Translator(s) of Proverbs." Pp. 185–93 in *Helsinki Perspectives on the Translation Technique of the Septuagint*. Ed. R. Sollamo and S. Sipilä. Göttingen: Vandenhoeck & Ruprecht.

Waegeman, Maryse
1992 "The Perfect Wife of Proverbs 31: 10–31." Pp. 101–107 in *Goldene Äpfel in silbernen Schalen*. Edited by Klaus-Dietrich Schunk and Matthias Augustin. Frankfurt am Main: Lang.

Wagner, Max
1966 *Die Lexikalischen und grammatikalischen Aramaismen im alttestamentlichen Hebräisch*. BZAW 96. Berlin: Töpelmann.

Waldman, Nahum M.
1976 "A Note on Excessive Speech and Falsehood." *JQR* 67 (1976–77): 142–45.

Walle, Baudouin van de
1963 "Problèmes relatifs aux méthodes d'enseignement dans l'Egypte ancienne." SPOA 191–207.

Wallis, G.
1960 "Zu den Spruchsammlungen Prov 10: 1–22,16 und 25–29." *TLZ* 85: 147/8.

Waltke, Bruce K.
1979a "The Book of Proverbs and Ancient Wisdom Literature." *BS* 136: 221–38.
1979b "The Book of Proverbs and Old Testament Theology." *BS* 136: 302–17.
**2004* *The Book of Proverbs: Chapters 1–15*. NICOT. Grand Rapids, Mich.: Eerdmans.
**2005* *The Book of Proverbs: Chapters 15–31*. NICOT. Grand Rapids, Mich.: Eerdmans.

Waltke, Bruce K., and M. O'Connor
1990 *An Introduction to Biblical Hebrew Syntax*. Winona Lake, Ind.: Eisenbrauns.

Washington, Harold C.
1994a "The Strange Woman of Proverbs 1–9 and Post-Exilic Judean Society." Pp. 217–42 in *Second Temple Studies* 2. Ed. T. C.Eskenazi and K. H. Richards. Sheffield: JSOT Press.
1994b *Wealth and Poverty in the Instruction of Amenemope and the Hebrew Proverbs*. SBLDS 142. Atlanta: Scholars Press

Watson, Wilfred G. E.
1984 *Classical Hebrew Poetry*. JSOTSup 26. Sheffield: Sheffield Academic Press.

Weeks, Stuart
1994 *Early Israelite Wisdom*. Oxford: Clarendon.
2006 "The Context and Meaning of Proverbs 8:30a." *JBL* 125: 433–42.
Wehmeier, Gerhard
1970 *Der Segen im AT*. Basel: F. Reinhardt.
Wehrle, Josef
1993 *Sprichwort und Weisheit: Studien zur Syntax und Semantik der Tob . . . min-Sprüche im Buch der Sprichwörter*. St. Ottilien: EOS.
Weiden, W. A. van der
1970a *Le Livre des Proverbes*. BibOr 23. Rome: Pontifical Biblical Institute.
1970b "Prov. XIV 32b, 'Mais le juste a confiance quand il meurt.' " *VT* 20: 339–50.
Weigl, Michael
2001 "Compositional Strategies in the Aramaic Sayings of Ahiqar: Columns 6–8." Pp. 22–82 in *The World of the Aramaeans*, Vol. III. Ed. P. M. M. Daviau, J. W. Wevers, and M. Weigl. JSOTSup 326. Sheffield: Sheffield Academic Press.
Weinberg, Joel P.
1972 "Demographische Notizen zur Geschichte der nachexilischen Gemeinde in Juda." *KLIO* 54 (45–58).
1976 "Die Agrarverhaltnässe in der Bürger-Tempel-Gemeinde der Achämenidenzeit. Pp. 473–86 in *Wirtschaft und Gesellschaft im alten Vorderasien*. Ed. J. Harmatta and G. Komoróczy. Budapest: Akad. Kiadö.
Weinfeld, Moshe
1972 *Deuteronomy and the Deuteronomic School*. Oxford: Clarendon.
1982 *L^egilguleyha šel Miš'alah B^eYisra'el Uva'ammim* ["Concerning the Transformations of a Wish in Israel and the Nations (Proverbs 3: 4)" (Hebrew)]. *Eretz Israel* 16: 93–99.
1991 *Deuteronomy 1–11*. AYB 5. New York: Doubleday (repr. New Haven: Yale University Press).
1995 *Social Justice in Ancient Israel and in the Ancient Near East*. Jerusalem: Magnes.
Weingreen, Jacob
1973 "Rabbinic-type commentary in the LXX version of Proverbs." Pp. 407–15 in *Proceedings of the Sixth World Congress of Jewish Studies*. Jerusalem: World Organization for Jewish Studies.
Weitemeyer, Mogens
1956 "Archive and Library Technique in Ancient Mesopotamia." *Libri* 6: 217–38.
Weitzman, Michael P.
1994 "Peshitta, Septuagint, and Targum." Pp. 51–84 in *VI Symposium Syriacum*. Ed. René Lavenant. *Orientalia Christiana Analecta* 247. Rome: Pontifical Biblical Institute.
1999 *The Syriac Version of the Old Testament*. Cambridge: Cambridge University.
Wente, E. F.
1967 *Late Ramesside Letters*. SAOC 33. Chicago: Oriental Institute. [= LRL]
1990 *Letters from Ancient Egypt*. SBL-WAW 1. Ed. E. S. Meltzer. Atlanta: Scholars Press. [= LAE]
Westbrook, Raymond
1988 *Studies in Biblical and Cuneiform Law*. CRB 26. Paris: Gabalda.
1991 *Property and the Family in Biblical Law*. JSOTSup 113. Sheffield: Sheffield Academic Press.

Westermann, Claus

1956 *Sprüche, Prediger, Hohelied*. Stuttgart: Quell.

1974 "Weisheit im Sprichwort." *Theologische Bücherei* 55: 149–61.

1984 *Vergleiche und Gleichnisse im Alten und Neuen Testament*. Calwer Theologische Monographien 14. Stuttgart: Calwer.

1990 *Wurzeln der Weisheit*. Göttingen: Vandenhoeck & Ruprecht. [ET: J. D. Charles, *The Roots of Wisdom*. Louisville, Ky.: Westminster/John Knox, 1995]

1991 *Forschungsgeschichte zur Weisheitsliteratur 1950–1990*. Stuttgart: Calwer.

Whedbee, J. William

1971 *Isaiah and Wisdom*. Nashville: Abingdon.

Whybray, R. N.

1965a "Proverbs VIII 22–31 and Its Supposed Prototypes." *VT* 15: 47–56 (repr. SAIW 390–400).

1965b *Wisdom in Proverbs*. SBT 41. London: SCM Press.

1966 "Some Literary Problems in Proverbs I–IX." *VT* 16: 482–96.

1972 *The Book of Proverbs*. CBC. Cambridge: Cambridge University Press.

1974 *The Intellectual Tradition in the OT*. BZAW 135. Berlin: de Gruyter.

1978 "Slippery Words. IV. Wisdom." *ExpTim* 89: 359–62.

1979 "Yahweh-sayings and Their Context in Proverbs 10: 1–22, 16." BETL 51: 153–65.

1982 "Prophecy and Wisdom." Pp. 181–96 in *Israel's Prophetic Tradition*. Ed. Peter Ackroyd. Cambridge: Cambridge University Press.

1989 "The Social World of the Wisdom Writers." Pp. 227–50 in *The World of Ancient Israel*. Ed. R. E. Clements. Cambridge: Cambridge University Press.

1990 *Wealth and Poverty in the Book of Proverbs*. JSOTSup 99. Sheffield: Sheffield Academic Press.

1992 "Thoughts on the Composition of Proverbs 10–29." Pp. 102–14 in *Priests, Proverbs and Scribes*. Ed. N. E. Ulrich et al. Sheffield: Sheffield Academic Press.

1994 *The Composition of the Book of Proverbs*. JSOTSup 168. Sheffield: Sheffield Academic Press.

1995 *The Book of Proverbs: A Survey of Modern Study*. History of Biblical Interpretation 1. Leiden: Brill.

1996 "City Life in Proverbs 1–9." Pp. 243–50 in *"Jedes Ding hat seine Zeit . . . "*: (FS D. Michel). Ed. A. A. Diesel et al. BZAW 241. Berlin: de Gruyter.

Wildeboer, D. G.

*1897 *Die Sprüche*. KHAT XV. Freiburg: Mohr.

Williams, James G.

1980 "The Power of Form: A Study of Biblical Proverbs." *Semeia* 17: 35–58.

1981 *Those Who Ponder Proverbs*. Sheffield: Almond.

Williams, Ronald J.

1961 "The Alleged Semitic Original of the 'Wisdom of Amenemope.' " *JEA* 47: 102–103.

1972 "Scribal Training in Ancient Egypt." *JAOS* 72: 214–21.

1981 "The Sages of Ancient Egypt in the Light of Recent Scholarship." *JAOS* 101: 1–20.

Wilson, Frederick M.

1987 "Sacred and Profane? The Yahwistic Redaction of Proverbs Reconsidered."

Pp. 313–34 in *The Listening Heart*. Ed. K. Hoglund et al. Sheffield: Sheffield Academic Press.

Winston, David
*1979 *The Wisdom of Solomon*. AYB 43. Garden City, N.Y.: Doubleday (repr. New Haven: Yale University Press).

Wittenberg, G. H.
1987 "The Situational Context of Statements Concerning Poverty and Wealth in the Book of Proverbs." *Scriptura* 21: 1–23.

Wolf, Philip
1897 "The Septuagintal Rendering of Hebrew Synonyms in the Book of Proverbs." Rabbinic Thesis, Hebrew Union College, Cincinnati.

Wolff, Hans Walter
1937 *Das Zitat im Prophetenspruch*. EvTh Beiheft 4. München: Kaiser.
1955 "Erkenntnis Gottes im Alten Testament." *EvTh* 15: 426–31.

Wolters, Al
1985 "*Ṣôpiyyâ* (Prov 31: 27) as Hymnic Participle and Play on *Sophia*." *JBL* 104: 577–87.
1988 "Proverbs XXXI 10–31 as Heroic Hymn: A Form-critical Analysis." *VT* 38: 446–457.
1994 "The Meaning of *Kišôr* (Proverbs 31: 19)." *HUCA* 65: 91–104.
2001 *The Song of the Valiant Woman*. Waynesboro, Ga.: Paternoster. [Includes reprints of Wolters 1985, 1988, 1994]

Woude, A. S. van der
1995 "Wisdom at Qumran." WAI 244–56.

Würthwein, Ernst
1960 *Die Weisheit Ägyptens und das Alte Testament*. Marburg: Elwert.

Xenophon. See Marchant, E. C.

Yankah, Kwesi
1989 *Proverb in the Context of Akan Rhetoric*. Bern: Lang.
1994 "Do Proverbs Contradict?" Pp. 127–42 in *Wise Words*. Ed. W. Müller. New York: Garland.

Yardeni, Ada
1991 *The Book of Hebrew Script*. Jerusalem: Carta.

Yaron, R.
1985 "The Climactic Tricolon." *JJS* 37: 153–59.

Yee, Gale A.
1982 "An Analysis of Prov 8,22–31 According to Style and Structure." ZAW 94: 58–66.
1989 " 'I Have Perfumed My Bed with Myrrh': The Foreign Woman (*ʾiššâ zārâ*) in Proverbs 1–9." *JSOT* 43: 53–68.
1992 "The Theology of Creation in Proverbs 8: 22–31." Pp. 85–96 in *Creation on the Biblical Traditions*. Ed. Richard J. Clifford and John J. Collins. CBQMS 24. Washington, D.C.: Catholic Biblical Association.

Yoder, Christine Roy
*2000 *Wisdom as a Woman of Substance: A Socioeconomic Reading of Proverbs 1–9 and 31:10–31*. BZAW 304. Berlin: de Gruyter.
2003 "The Woman of Substance (*ʾēšet ḥayil*): A Socioeconomic Reading of Proverbs 31:10–31." *JBL* 122: 427–47.

2005 "Forming 'Fearers of Yahweh': Repetition and Contradiction as Pedagogy in Proverbs." SWA 167–84.

Yonah, Shamir

2005 "Exegetical and Stylistic Analysis of a Number of Aphorisms in the Book of Proverbs: Mitigation of Monotony in Repetitions in Parallel Texts." SWA 155–66.

2008 "The Influence of Legal Style on the Style of Aphorism." Pp. 411–22 in *Shalom Paul Jubilee Volume*. Ed. B. Schwartz, V. Hurowitz, et al. Winona Lake, Ind.: Eisenbrauns.

Young, Gordon D.

1972 "Utu and Justice: A New Sumerian Proverb." *JCS* 24: 132.

Young, James O.

2001 "The Coherence Theory of Truth." *The Stanford Encyclopedia of Philosophy (Summer 2001 Edition)*. Ed. Edward N. Zalta. URL = http://plato. stanford. edu/archives/sum2001/entries/truth-coherence.

Žába, Zbynek

1956 *Les Maximes de Ptahhotep*. Prague: Editions de l'Académie Tchécoslovaque des Sciences.

Zauzich, Karl-Theodor

1976 "Demotische Fragmente zum Ahiqar-Roman." Pp. 180–85 in *Folia Rara* (FS W. Voight). VOHD, sup. 19. Ed. H. Franke et al. Wiesbaden: Harrassowitz.

Zer-Kavod, Mordecai

1975 *Ḥidot Besefer Mišley* [*Riddles in the Book of Proverbs* (Hebrew)]. *Beth Mikra* 64: 7–11.

Zer-Kavod, Mordecai, and Yehudah Keel

1983 *Sefer Mišley* [*The Book of Proverbs* (Hebrew)]. Jerusalem: Mosad HaRav Kook.

Zevit, Ziony

1990 "Roman Jakobson, Psycholinguistics, and Biblical Poetry." *JBL* 109: 385–401.

2001 *The Religions of Ancient Israel*. London: Continuum.

Zimmerli, Walther

1933 "Zur Struktur der alttestamentlichen Weisheit." ZAW 51: 177–204 (ET in SAIW 175–207).

*1962 *Sprüche*. ATD 16. Göttingen: Vandenhoeck & Ruprecht.

1963 "Ort und Grenze der Weisheit im Rahmen der alttestamentlichen Theologie." SPOA 121–38 (ET in SAIW 314–26).

1979, 1983 *Ezekiel*, vols. 1–2. Hermeneia. Philadelphia: Fortress.

Zohary, Menahem

1987 *M[e]qorot Rashi* [*Rashi's Sources* (Hebrew)]. Jerusalem: Kanah.

1990 *The Absolute Infinitive and Its Uses in the Hebrew Language* [Hebrew]. Jerusalem: Carmel.

Zuntz, G.

1956 "Der Antinoe Papyrus der Proverbia und das Prophetologion." ZAW 68: 124–84.

General Index

◆

This index is both a thematic key to the proverbs and a topical index to the two volumes of this commentary. It includes some familiar proverbial phrases the reader may wish to locate. This index does not catalogue all occurrences of a word or an idea, nor does it attempt to catch all the permutations or applications of a particular theme. It will, however, guide the reader to Comments that have a relatively expansive treatment of the theme.

Discussions of themes and issues in the body of the commentary are referenced by chapter and verse. Discussions elsewhere are cited by the first page of the treatment (pages 1–474 = Vol. I; pages 475–1182 = Vol. II). Where a topic receives special attention, the citation is in **boldface.**

Abaddon 15:11, 27:20; *see also* Sheol, underworld
abominations *see* loathsome
adage 14
add not to God's words 30:6
admonition 14; *see also* instruction; rebukes, chastisement; teaching
adultery **139**; 2:16–17, 5:3–14, 6:24–35, 7:5–27, 22:14, **23:28**, 30:20; *see also* Strange Woman
advice *see* advisors; counsel
advisors 11:14, 12:20, 13:10, 15:22, 24:6; *see also* counsel
agriculture 3:10, 24:27,30–34, 27:18,23–27, 28:19
Agur 861, **956**; **30:1**
Ahiqar **767**; *see also entry in* Index of Ancient Near Eastern Sources
Akan proverbs 485
alcohol *see* beer and wine
allegory, allegorical readings **254**, 907
ambush 1:11–12, 12:6; *see also* hunting
Amenemope 753; *see also entry in* Index of Ancient Near Eastern Sources
  ideology 765
  lines from Amenemope reworked into Proverbs 757 (table)
  translation and transmission 763
amulets *see* ornaments (teaching as)
analogy 19
angel? 17:11
anger 1039; 6:34–35, 12:16, 14:17,29, 15:1,18, 16:32, 19:11,19, 20:2, 21:14, 22:8,24, 24:18, 27:3,4, 29:8,11,22, 30:33
  of the king 14:35, 16:14, 19:12, 20:2, 24:21–22
animal husbandry 12:10, 14:4, 27:23–27
animals 12:10, 30:24–31
"anomaly proverbs" *see* proverbs: "anomaly proverbs"
Antinoe Papyrus Vol. I xvii
ants 6:6, 30:25
aphorism 14, 862
apothegm 14
appetite 6:30, 10:3, 12:10, 13:4,19,25, 16:26, 19:2, 21:10,26, 23:1–3,6, 27:7
"apple of the eye" 7:2
apples of gold 25:11
Aramaisms 504
Aristotle
  Eudemian Ethics 936
  Nicomachaean Ethics 936, 941
arrogance *see* pride
assembly (LXX) 1066
associative thinking 480
audience 92; *see also* listener and reader
author and speaker 11, **73**
avoiding trouble 4:27, 13:14, 14:16,27, 22:3, 27:12

barrenness 30:16
"a bear bereft of its young" 17:12
beating *see* corporal punishment
beauty 6:25, 11:22
  transience of 31:30
bee 397
beer and wine 3:9, 20:1, 21:17, **23:30–35**, 31:4–7
Belial, "son of" or "man of" *see* worthless man
belly, store of words or thoughts 18:8,20, 20:27,30, 22:18, 26:22

INDEX OF AUTHORS

Lang, B. 97, 322, 334, 902
Levinson, B. 952, 955
Lichtheim, M. 17
Lyu, S. M. 928

Mack, B. 342, 352
Maier, C. 48, 134
Maillot, A. 913
Maimonides 241
Malbim 100, 160, 255, 655, 665, 702, 786, 806, 854
Malchow, B. 815, 817
McCreesh, T. 486, 890, 908, 910
McKane, W. 55, 61, 68, 113, 128, 177, 182, 231, 267, 273, 292, 304, 482, 510, 709, 823, 827, 874, 924, 937
McKinlay, J. 257, 335
Meinhold, A. 48, 126, 170, 173, 254, 322, 770
Michel, D. 127
Mieder, W. 484, 491
Milgrom, J. 846
Miller, P. D., Jr. 91
Morenz, S. 787, 789
Murphy, R. E. 546, 647, 651, 820, 822, 912

Naḥmias 55, 91, 173, 560, 649, 723, 812, 824, 848
Newsom, C. 94, 119, 257, 338

Oesterley, O. E. 754
Oyen, H. van 131

Pardee, D. 126
Penner 942
Perdue, L. 304, 348, 591
Perry, T. 62, 597, 969
Plöger, O. 98, 123, 564, 626, 662, 780, 843, 844
Polk, T. 55
Pomeroy, S. 901
Preuss, H. D. 948

Rad, G. von 69, 150, 353, 922, 924, 948, 964
Radaq 56, 100, 138, 150, 181, 182
Ramaq 55, 156, 479
Rashi 59, 124, 186, 209, 254
Riyqam 100
Robert, A. 104
Rofé, A. 951, 952
Rogers, J. 957
Römheld, D. 483, 722, 746, 765
Roth, W. 863
Ruffle, J. 755
Rüger, H. P. 26
Rylaarsdam, C. 950

Saʿadia 82, 121, 132, 143, 149, 156, 209, 233, 234, 495, 627, 630, 650, 663, 669, 697, 885, 907, 966
Sanders, J. T. 960
Sandoval, T. 512
Schipper, B. 763
Scoralick, R. 481, 488
Scott, R. B. Y. 56, 482, 929
Sheppard, G. 959
Shirun-Grumach, I. 755
Shupak, N. 28, 37, 921
Skehan, P. 126, 292, 322, 481, 777
Skladny, U. 817
Snell, D. 487, 509, 969
Snijders, L. 212
Steiert, F. 948, 930, 947
Steiner, R. Vol. II xviii
Suter, D. W. 55

Tavares, R. 818
Toorn, K. van der 138
Toy, C. H. 80, 127, 180, 270, 874
Trible, P. 104
Tur-Sinai, N. H. 65, 66, 193, 789, 796

Van Leeuwen, R. 92, 129, 481, 499, 547, 576, 776, 789, 816, 851, 874, 974, 975

Washington, H. 135, 503, 519, 742, 975
Weeks, S. 479, 483
Weinfeld, M. 79, 951
Weitzman, M. 366
Westbrook, R. 235, 892
Westermann, C. 6, 9, 27, 131
Whybray, R. N. 7, 9, 17, 127, 292, 322, 481, 483, 755, 816, 915, 925, 975
Williams, J. G. 15, 561, 621
Wilson, F. M. 483
Wolters, A. 899

Yee, G. 292
Yoder, C. R. 487, 898, 900, 901
Yonah, S. 489
Young, J. O. 968

Zer-Kavod, M. 66
Zimmerli, W. 108, 935, 950

INDEX OF SELECTED ARTICLES

◆

Articles are indexed by Proverbs citation.

INDEX OF SCRIPTURAL AND POSTBIBLICAL JEWISH SOURCES

◆

The indicator "tr" precedes each page number with a translation, or partial translation, of the passage cited. Where a passage receives special attention, the citation is in **boldface.**

POSTBIBLICAL JEWISH SOURCES

INDEX OF ANCIENT NEAR EASTERN SOURCES

For source details and referencing systems, see the introduction to the Bibliography. The indicator "tr" precedes each page with a translation, or partial translation, of the passage cited. Where a passage receives special attention, the citation is in **boldface.**

EGYPTIAN

MESOPOTAMIAN

PHOENICIAN AND UGARITIC

Index of Hebrew and Aramaic Words

◆

Entries are alphabetized in Hebrew consonantal order. Additional words are discussed in the Commentary at their first occurrence.

ʾĕwil, ʾiwwelet 40, 205, 572
ʾaḥărit 927
ʾetun 247
ʾallup 120
ʾamon 285
ʾereṣ 123
ʾišon 239
ʾašrey 161
ʾiššah zarah 134; see also *zar*
ʾiššim 268

byn 30
biynah 30, 723
beyt ʾab 83
beyt ʾem 83
beyt midraš 7
b^{e}liyyaʿal 219
baʿar 39
beṣaʿ 90
beṭaḥ, boṭeaḥ 103, 148, 536

dodim 203
dam naqi 85
daʿat 31, 68

hebin 268
hod 194
heḥĕliq 119, 241
hamah 244
homiyyot 97
hăsar leb 39
haśkel 59

zimmah 525, 691
zar 139

ḥidah 54, 64
ḥayyim 143
ḥokmah 32, 59, 113
ḥakam 32, 928
ḥokmot 96, 97
ḥălalim 251
ḥesed 144, 587
ḥuṣot 283
ḥaruṣ 513

yodeaʿ 31
yoʿeṣ 32
yapiaḥ 49, 582
yašar, yošer 117, 577
yeter 627

kabod 157
koaḥ 195
k^{e}silut, k^{e}sil 41, 511, 630
koper 563

leb 109
l^{e}zut 187
leṣ, laṣon 42, 609
leqaḥ 63, 619

mebin 30, 37
mebiš 513
m^{e}humah 595
m^{e}zimmah 34, 546, 926
m^{e}zorah 88
meyšarim 60
m^{e}liṣah 63, 64
mum 307
musar 34, 59, 592, 943, 966
miṣwah, miṣwot 108
m^{e}romim 265
maśkil 36
mašbir 9
mašal 54, 485
mošel 503
m^{e}šubah 103
mišpaṭ 60, 686
mašḥit 235

nabal 627
nabon 30, 37
n^{e}gidim 269
nogah 182
nagaʿ 235
nikbad 283
nokri 139
nissakti 281
naʿar 61, 62
nepeš 163, 232, 511, 561
naṣar 142
n^{e}šamah 676

slp 532
soreret 244

ʿebrah 690
ʿedah 199
ʿkr 538
ʿănaqim 83
ʿanaš 696
ʿeṣeb, ʿăṣabeyka 195, 523
ʿeṣah 32, 108
ʿarab 212
ʿormah 35, 590
ʿet 600
ʿateq 277

pwṣ 201
palles 187
paʿam 245
pisqaʾot 47
peti, p^{e}taʾim, p^{e}tayyut 42, 61, 98

ṣedeq 60
ṣapan 114

qᵉdošim 308
qanah 279, 280

rʾh 967
roʾš 284
reʾšit 67, 280
rab 570
ruaḥ 100
rak 173
rᵉmiyyah 512
reaʿ 165
rʿh 522, 594
rpʾ 584, 590
rᵉpaʾim 122

ṣaddiq 928
śḥ 229
śᵉḥoq 577
śekel 36, 147; see also *haśkel*
śimḥah 577, 600

šagah 203, 205
šḥr 247
šit 243
šakaḥ 142
šaʿăšuʿim 287

tᵉbunah 37
tahpukot 117
taḥbulot 37, 63
tᵉhillah 68
tokaḥat 99
toʿebah 166, 167
tušiyyah 38, 114, 163